W9-BVK-497

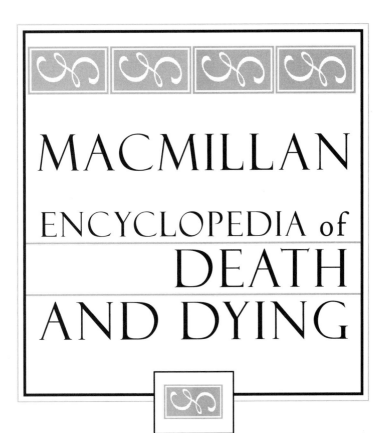

# MACMILLAN
## ENCYCLOPEDIA of
# DEATH
# AND DYING

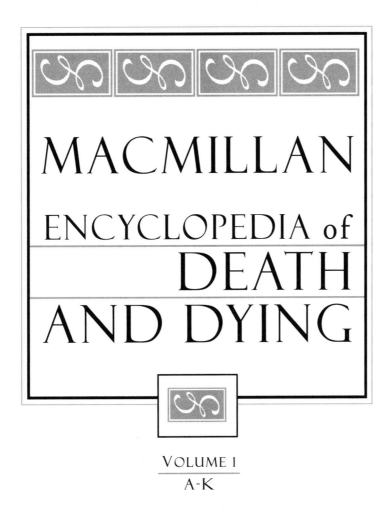

# MACMILLAN

## ENCYCLOPEDIA of
## DEATH
## AND DYING

VOLUME 1

A-K

ROBERT KASTENBAUM

Editor in Chief

**MACMILLAN
REFERENCE
USA™**

**THOMSON**

™

**GALE**

New York • Detroit • San Diego • San Francisco • Cleveland • New Haven, Conn. • Waterville, Maine • London • Munich

**Macmillan Encyclopedia of Death and Dying**
Robert Kastenbaum

© 2003 by Macmillan Reference USA.
Macmillan Reference USA is an imprint of
The Gale Group, Inc., a division of
Thomson Learning, Inc.

Macmillan Reference USA™ and
Thomson Learning™ are trademarks used
herein under license.

*For more information, contact*
Macmillan Reference USA
300 Park Avenue South, 9th Floor
New York, NY 10010
Or you can visit our Internet site at
http://www.gale.com

While every effort has been made to ensure
the reliability of the information presented in
this publication, The Gale Group, Inc. does not
guarantee the accuracy of the data contained
herein. The Gale Group, Inc. accepts to payment for listing; and inclusion in the publication of any organization, agency, institution,
publication, service, or individual does not
imply endorsement of the editors or publisher.
Errors brought to the attention of the publisher and verified to the satisfaction of the
publisher will be corrected in future editions.

**LIBRARY OF CONGRESS CATALOGING-IN-PUBLICATION DATA**

Macmillan encyclopedia of death and dying / edited by Robert Kastenbaum.
    p. cm.
        Includes bibliographical references and index.
        ISBN 0-02-865689-X (set : alk. paper) — ISBN 0-02-865690-3 (v. 1 :
alk. paper) — ISBN 0-02-865691-1 (v. 2 : alk. paper)
        1.  Thanatology. 2.  Death—Cross-cultural studies.
        I. Kastenbaum, Robert.

   HQ1073 .M33 2002
   306.9—dc21
   2002005809

Printed in the United States of America
10 9 8 7 6 5 4 3 2 1

# CONTENTS

MACMILLAN ENCYCLOPEDIA of DEATH AND DYING
1

# Editorial and Production Staff

Joseph Clements
*Production Editor*

Shawn Beall
*Project Editor*

Christine Slovey
Nicole Watkins
*Editorial Support*

William Kaufman
Gina Misiroglu
Dave Salamie
*Copy Editors*

Beth Fhaner
Ann Weller
*Proofreaders*

Cynthia Crippen
AEIOU, Inc.
*Indexer*

Tracey Rowens
*Art Director*

Argosy
*Compositor*


MACMILLAN REFERENCE USA

Elizabeth Des Chenes
*Managing Editor*

Jill Lectka
*Associate Publisher*

# PREFACE

The *Macmillan Encyclopedia of Death and Dying* is a contribution to the understanding of life. Scientists and poets have long recognized that life and death are so intimately entwined that knowledge of one requires knowledge of the other. The Old Testament observes that "all flesh is as grass." Religions have addressed the question of how one should live with the awareness of inevitable death. Often the answer has been based upon the vision of a life beyond death. Societies have developed systems of belief and practice to help their people cope with the prospect of death and the sorrow of grief. Children are often puzzled by the curious fact that flowers fade and animals stop moving. This incipient realization of mortality eventually becomes a significant part of the adult's worldview in which hope contests with fear, and faith with doubt.

The twenty-first century has inherited an anxiety closet from the past, a closet packed with collective memories of unsettling encounters with death. This history of darkness concealed threats from predators and enemies; child-bearing women and their young children would suddenly pale and die; terrible plagues would periodically ravage the population; the dead themselves were sources of terror when resentful of the living; contact with corpses was perilous but had to be managed with diligence, lest the departing spirit be offended; the spirit world often intervened in everyday life; gods, demi-gods and aggrieved or truculent ancestors had to be pacified by gifts, ceremonies, and conformity to their wishes; animal and human sacrifices were deaths intended to protect the lives of the community by preventing catastrophes or assuring good crops. Everyday life was permeated by rituals intended to distract or bribe the spiritual forces who controlled life and death. Fairly common were such customs as making sure not to speak ill of the dead and protecting home and person with magic charms.

Particular diseases have also left their lingering marks. Tuberculosis, for example, horrified several generations as young men and women experienced a long period of suffering and emaciation before death. The scourge of the industrial era did much to increase fears of dying slowly and in great distress. Syphillis produced its share of unnerving images as gross disfiguration and a descent into dementia afflicted many victims near the end of their lives. All of these past encounters and more have bequeathed anxieties that still influence attitudes toward death today.

The past, however, offers more than an anxiety closet. There was also comfort, wisdom, and the foundation for measures that greatly improved the chances of enjoying a long, healthful life, and to palliate the final passage. The achievements of public health innovations and basic biomedical research are fulfilling dreams that motivated the inquisitive minds of early healers. The hospice care programs that provide comfort and pain relief to terminally ill people build upon the model demonstrated by devoted caregivers more than 2,000 years ago. The peer support groups that console grieving people were prefigured by communal gatherings around the survivors in many villages. Religious images and philosophical thought have helped people to explore the meanings and mysteries of death.

The *Macmillan Encyclopedia of Death and Dying* draws extensively from the past, but is most concerned with understanding the present and the future. The very definition of death has come into question. The ethics of assisted death and euthanasia have become the concern of judges and legislators as well as physicians and clergy. Questions about ongoing changes in society are raised by the facts that accidents, homicide, and suicide are the leading causes of death among youth, and that the suicide rate rises so precipitously for aging men. Continuing violence in many parts of the world suggests that genocide and other forms of mass killing cannot only be of historical concern. Other death-related issues have yet to receive the systematic attention they deserve. For example, widowhood in third world nations is a prime example of suffering and oppression in the wake of death, and, on a different front, advances in the relief of pain too often are not used in end-of-life medical management.

Each of these issues are addressed in this two-volume set as part of a more comprehensive exploration of the place of death in contemporary life. The coverage of the topics is broad and multidisciplinary because death threads through society in so many different ways. Attention is given to basic facts such as life expectancy and the changing causes of death. Many of the entries describe the experiences of terminally ill people and the types of care available while others focus on the situation of those who grieve and mourn. How people have attempted to understand the nature and meaning of death is examined from anthropological, historical, psychological, religious, and sociological perspectives. The appendix, which complements the substantive entries, can be found near the end of the second volume. It provides information on numerous organizations that are active in education, research, services, or advocacy on death-related topics.

The contributors are expert scholars and care providers from a variety of disciplines. Many have made landmark contributions to research and practice, and all have responded to the challenge of presenting accurate, up-to-date, and well-balanced expositions of their topics. As editor in chief, I am much indebted to the distinguished contributors for giving their expertise and time so generously. Contributing mightily to the success of this project were associate editors Jim Crissman, Mike Kearl, and Brian Mishara, each also providing many illuminating articles of their own. Macmillan has published reference books of the highest quality on many topics; the high standards that have distinguished their publications have assured the quality of this project as well. The editor appreciates the opportunity to have worked with Macmillan's Shawn Beall, Joe Clements, Elly Dickason, Brian Kinsey, and Jill Lectka.

ROBERT KASTENBAUM

# LIST OF ARTICLES

# LIST OF CONTRIBUTORS

SHELLEY R. ADLER
Department of Anthropology, History, and Social Medicine, University of California, San Francisco
*Sudden Unexpected Nocturnal Death Syndrome*

ASIF AGHA
Department of Anthropology, University of Pennsylvania
*Tibetan Book of the Dead*

ALLAN ANDERSON
Graduate Institute for Theology and Religion, University of Birmingham, United Kingdom
*African Religions*

JAMES AUSTIN
George Washington University
*Capital Punishment*

JEFFREY P. BAKER
Center for the Study of Medical Ethics and Humanities, Duke University
*Bioethics*

CHRIS BALE
Befrienders International, London
*Befriending*

MICHEL RENE BARNES
*Augustine*
*Catholicism*

JULIA BARTEL
Hospice of the Western Reserve
*Symptoms and Symptom Management*

KIMBERLY A. BEACH
Benedictine University
*Assassination*
*Children, Murder of*

NANCY L. BECKERMAN
*Informed Consent*

JOAN BEDER
Wurzweiler School of Social Work, Yeshiva University
*Animal Companions*
*Grief: Anticipatory*

ROBERT A. BENDIKSEN
Center for Death Education and Bioethics, University of Wisconsin, La Crosse
*Technology and Death*

PETER BERTA
Institute of Ethnology, Hungarian Academy of Sciences, Budapest, Hungary
*Afterlife in Cross-Cultural Perspective*
*Anthropological Perspective*
*Omens*

SANDRA L. BERTMAN
University of Massachusetts Medical School
*Visual Arts*

RUSSELL L. BLAYLOCK
Advanced Nutrition Concepts, Jackson, MS
*Nutrition and Exercise*

RICHARD BONNEY
Centre for the History of Religious and Political Pluralism, University of Leicester
*Buddhism*
*Jainism*
*Sikhism*
*Taylor, Jeremy*

JEAN-YVES BOUCHER
Center for Research and Intervention on Suicide and Euthanasia, University of Quebec, Montreal
*Camus, Albert*
*Charon and the River Styx*
*Hindenburg*
*Lazarus*
*Phoenix, The*

GLENNA BRADSHAW
St. Jude Children's Research Hospital
*Children and Their Rights in Life and Death Situations*

JAMES BRANDMAN
Division of Hematology/Oncology, Northwestern University Medical School
*Cancer*

DANA G. CABLE
Hood College
*Internet*
*Support Groups*

SILVIA SARA CANETTO
Colorado State University, Fort Collins
*Suicide Influences and Factors: Gender*

MARTIN CARVER
University of York
*Sutton Hoo*

MICHAEL S. CASERTA
Gerontology Center, University of Utah
*Widowers*

JOHN P. CHARLOT
Department of Religion,
University of Hawai'i
*Polynesian Religions*

JAMES C. CHATTERS
Foster Wheeler Environmental, Inc.,
Seattle, WA
*Kennewick Man*

KEITH CHENG
Oregon Health and Science University
*Suicide Influences and Factors: Rock
Music*

SANDRA BURKHALTER CHMELIR
Benedictine University
*Mass Killers*
*Serial Killers*

DAVID CLARK
University of Sheffield, United Kingdom
*Brompton's Cocktail*
*Hospice in Historical Perspective*
*Saunders, Cicely*

MICHAEL S. CLARK
Argosy University
*Missing in Action*

ARYEH COHEN
University of Judaism
*Judaism*

WILLIAM COONEY
Briar Cliff University
*Epicurus*
*Heidegger, Martin*
*Mind-Body Problem*
*Philosophy, Western*
*Plato*
*Plotinus*

INGE B. CORLESS
MGH Institute of Health Professions,
Boston, MA
*Hospice around the World*

CHARLES A. CORR
Southern Illinois University,
Edwardsville
*Children*
*Kübler-Ross, Elisabeth*
*Organ Donation and
Transplantation*
*Stage Theory*
*Sudden Infant Death Syndrome*

DONNA M. CORR
Southern Illinois University,
Edwardsville
*Children*
*Kübler-Ross, Elisabeth*
*Organ Donation and
Transplantation*
*Stage Theory*
*Sudden Infant Death Syndrome*

GERRY R. COX
University of Wisconsin, La Crosse
*Technology and Death*

JAMES K. CRISSMAN
Benedictine University
*Assassination*
*Children, Murder of*
*Epitaphs*
*Exhumation*
*Folk Music*
*Homicide, Definitions and
Classifications of*
*Homicide, Epidemiology of*
*Mass Killers*
*Notifications of Death*
*Spiritualism Movement*

MARY A. CRISSMAN
Little Friends, Inc., Naperville, IL
*Notifications of Death*

MARC S. DAIGLE
University of Quebec
*Suicide Types: Murder-Suicide*

DAVID S. DANAHER
Department of Slavic Languages,
University of Wisconsin, Madison
*Ivan Ilych*

GLEN W. DAVIDSON
Southern Illinois University School
of Medicine
*Human Remains*

DOUGLAS J. DAVIES
University of Durham, England
*Cremation*
*Gennep, Arnold van*
*Hertz, Robert*
*Jesus*
*Rites of Passage*

DIEGO DE LEO
Australian Institute for Suicide Research,
Griffith University, Mt. Gravatt,
Queensland
*Suicide over the Life Span:
The Elderly*

JOHN DEFRAIN
University of Nebraska, Lincoln
*Abortion*
*Miscarriage*

TOM D. DILLEHAY
Department of Anthropology,
University of Kentucky, Lexington
*Incan Religion*

KENNETH J. DOKA
Department of Gerontology, The
College of New Rochelle *and* Hospice
Foundation of America
*Death System*
*Grief: Acute*
*Grief: Disenfranchised*
*Grief: Gender*

DONALD F. DUCLOW
Gwynedd-Mercy College
*Ars Moriendi*
*Memento Mori*
*Virgin Mary, The*

JERRY D. DURHAM
University of Missouri, St. Louis
*AIDS*

JAMES W. ELLOR
National-Louis University
*Frankl, Viktor*
*Sartre, Jean-Paul*
*Thou Shalt Not Kill*

RICHARD K. EMMERSON
Medieval Academy of America,
Cambridge, MA
*Apocalypse*

NORMAN L. FARBEROW
University of Southern California
*Grief: Suicide*
*Suicide Basics: History*

HERMAN FEIFEL
University of Southern California
School of Medicine
*Psychology*

STEPHEN C. FEINSTEIN
University of Minnesota, Minneapolis
*Genocide*

BETTY R. FERRELL
City of Hope National Medical Center
*Nursing Education*

KATHLEEN GALLAGHER
Ontario Institute for Studies in Education
of the University of Toronto
*Theater and Drama*

GENEVIÈVE GARNEAU
Centre for Research and Intervention on
Suicide and Euthanasia, University of
Quebec, Montreal
*Voodoo*
*Zombies*

ELLEN M. GEE
Simon Fraser University, Vancouver,
British Columbia
*Causes of Death*
*Demographics and Statistics*
*Gender and Death*
*Life Expectancy*
*Malthus, Thomas*
*Mortality, Childbirth*
*Mortality, Infant*
*Population Growth*

SHMUEL GLICK
Jewish Theological Seminary of
America, NY *and* Schechter Institute of
Jewish Studies, Jerusalem
*Kaddish*

OGDEN GOELET JR.
Department of Middle Eastern Studies,
New York University
*Egyptian Book of the Dead*
*Pyramids*

LAURENCE R. GOLDMAN
University of Queensland
*Cannibalism*

ROBERT D. GOLDNEY
The Adelaide Clinic, Gilberton,
South Australia
*Suicide Influences and Factors:*
*Biology and Genetics*

ROGER GRAINGER
Greenwich School of Theology, United
Kingdom *and* Potchefstroom University,
South Africa
*Wake*

LESLIE A. GROUT
Hudson Valley Community College
*Replacement Children*

HAMZA YUSUF HANSON
Zaytuna Institute, Hayward, CA
*Islam*

DESLEY HARVEY
School of Population Health,
University of Queensland, Australia
*Suicide Influences and Factors:*
*Indigenous Populations*

NARELLE L. HAWORTH
Monash University, Australia
*Injury Mortality*
*Safety Regulations*

BERT HAYSLIP JR.
University of North Texas
*Communication with the Dying*

PAMELA S. HINDS
St. Jude Children's Research Hospital
*Children and Their Rights in Life*
*and Death Situations*

CHARLES A. HITE
Biomedical Ethics, Carilion Health
System, Roanoke, VA
*Do Not Resuscitate*

VALERIE M. HOPE
Department of Classical Studies, Open
University, United Kingdom
*Tombs*

SARAH J. HORTON
Macalester College
*Shinto*

JANIE HOULE
Center for Research and Intervention on
Suicide and Euthanasia, University of
Quebec, Montreal
*Suicide Types: Suicide Pacts*

DONNA E. HOWARD
Department of Public and Community
Health, University of Maryland, College
Park
*Hunger Strikes*

ERNEST HUNTER
*Suicide Influences and Factors:*
*Indigenous Populations*

ANN C. HURLEY
Brigham and Women's Hospital,
Boston, MA
*Hospice, Alzheimer Patients and*

JAMES F. IACCINO
Benedictine University
*Horror Movies*

KENNETH V. ISERSON
University of Arizona College
of Medicine
*Autopsy*
*Death Certificate*
*Life Support System*
*Persistent Vegetative State*
*Resuscitation*
*Rigor Mortis and Other Postmortem*
*Changes*

CHRISTIAN JOCHIM
Comparative Religious Studies, San Jose
State University
*Chinese Beliefs*

ARUN KALYANASUNDARAM
University of Maryland, College Park
*Hunger Strikes*

BEATRICE KASTENBAUM
College of Nursing, Arizona State
University
*Hospice Option*
*Pain and Pain Management*

ROBERT KASTENBAUM
Arizona State University
*Anxiety and Fear*
*Black Death*
*Children and Adolescents'*
*Understanding of Death*
*Communication with the Dead*
*Cryonic Suspension*
*Danse Macabre*
*Death Instinct*
*Definitions of Death*
*Dying, Process of*
*Freud, Sigmund*
*Ghosts*
*Good Death, The*
*Grief: Overview*
*Immortality*
*Kevorkian, Jack*
*Last Words*
*Moment of Death*
*Mummification*
*Sacrifice*
*Saints, Preserved*
*Schopenhauer, Arthur*
*Seven Deadly Sins*
*Socrates*
*Suicide Types: Physician-Assisted*
*Suicide*
*Terrorist Attacks on America*
*Thanatology*
*Thanatomimesis*
*Triangle Shirtwaist Company Fire*
*Vampires*

JEFFREY KAUFFMAN
Bryn Mawr College
*Kierkegaard, Søren*

WILLIAM KAUFMAN
*Titanic*

MICHAEL C. KEARL
Trinity University
*Celebrity Deaths*
*Cemeteries, Military*
*Elvis Sightings*
*Extinction*
*Immortality, Symbolic*
*Metaphors and Euphemisms*
*Nuclear Destruction*
*Sex and Death, Connection of*
*Social Functions of Death*
*Thrill-Seeking*
*War*

ALLAN KELLEHEAR
Faculty of Health Sciences, La Trobe
University, Australia
*How Death Came into the World*
*Near-Death Experiences*

DENNIS KLASS
Webster University
*Grief and Mourning in Cross-*
  *Cultural Perspective*

TERRY F. KLEEMAN
University of Colorado, Boulder
*Taoism*

KENNETH P. KRAMER
San Jose State University
*Hinduism*

GARY M. LADERMAN
Emory University
*Brown, John*
*Civil War, U.S.*
*Funeral Industry*
*Washington, George*

KENNETH LAFAVE
Music and Dance Critic, *Arizona
Republic*
*Mahler, Gustav*
*Music, Classical*
*Operatic Death*

ELIZABETH P. LAMERS
The Lamers Medical Group, Malibu, CA
*Literature for Children*

WILLIAM M. LAMERS JR.
Hospice Foundation of America
*Cruzan, Nancy*
*Forensic Medicine*
*Hippocratic Oath*
*Quinlan, Karen Ann*
*Sin Eater*

JOHN M. LAST
Professor Emeritus, University of Ottawa
*Public Health*

VICKI LENS
Wurzweiler School of Social Work,
Yeshiva University
*Advance Directives*
*End-of-Life Issues*
*Living Will*
*Natural Death Acts*

DAVID LESTER
Richard Stockton College of New Jersey
*Suicide Types: Theories of Suicide*

MARCIA LEVETOWN
Pain and Palliative Care Educator,
Houston, TX
*Children, Caring for When Life-*
  *Threatened or Dying*

DANIEL LEVITON
University of Maryland, College Park
*Death Squads*
*Famine*

JONATHAN F. LEWIS
Benedictine University
*Cadaver Experiences*
*Durkheim, Émile*
*Revolutionaries and "Death for the*
  *Cause!"*
*Terrorism*

HELENA ZNANIECKA LOPATA
Loyola University, Chicago
*Widows*

RICHARD S. MACHALEK
Department of Sociology, University of
Wyoming
*Hunting*

MUI HING JUNE MAK
*Confucius*
*Qin Shih Huang's Tomb*

ISABELLE MARCOUX
Center for Research and Intervention on
Suicide and Euthanasia, University of
Quebec, Montreal
*Death Mask*
*Necromancy*
*Orpheus*
*Osiris*
*Suicide Types: Suicide Pacts*

SAPNA REDDY MAREPALLY
University of Maryland, College Park
*Death Squads*

ROBERT L. MARRONE
*deceased,* California State University,
Sacramento
*Spiritual Crisis*

ALFRED R. MARTIN
Benedictine University
*Brain Death*
*Cell Death*
*Darwin, Charles*
*Exhumation*

NICOLAS S. MARTIN
American Iatrogenic Association,
Houston, TX
*Iatrogenic Illness*

ROBERT MASSON
Marquette University
*Rahner, Karl*

POLLY MAZANEC
Hospice of the Western Reserve
*Symptoms and Symptom*
  *Management*

MARSHA MCGEE
University of Louisiana, Monroe
*Sympathy Cards*

JACQUELINE M. MCGRATH
College of Nursing,
Arizona State University
*Neonatal Intensive Care Unit*

J. A. MCGUCKIN
Union Theological Seminary
*Hell*
*Purgatory*

FARHANG MEHR
Boston University
*Zoroastrianism*

JASON D. MILLER
University of Arizona
*Organized Crime*

BRIAN L. MISHARA
Centre for Research and Intervention on
Suicide and Euthanasia, University of
Quebec, Montreal
*Autopsy, Psychological*
*Euthanasia*
*Firearms*
*Suicide*
*Suicide Basics: Prevention*
*Suicide Basics: Warning Signs and*
  *Predictions*
*Suicide Influences and Factors:*
  *Physical Illness*

BRIAN L. MISHARA (CONTINUED)
*Suicide over the Life Span:*
   *Adolescents and Youths*
*Suicide over the Life Span: Children*
*Suicide Types: Indirect Suicide*
*Suicide Types: Rational Suicide*

DAVID WENDELL MOLLER
Wishard Health Services,
Indiana University
   *Taboos and Social Stigma*

DIANNE R. MORAN
Department of Psychology,
Benedictine University
   *Infanticide*

ROBIN D. MOREMEN
Northern Illinois University
   *Gender Discrimination after Death*

BRENDA C. MORRIS
College of Nursing, Arizona State
University
   *Cardiovascular Disease*

RICHARD MORRIS
Arizona State University West
   *Burial Grounds*
   *Gravestones and Other Markers*
   *Lawn Garden Cemeteries*
   *Lincoln in the National Memory*

JOHN MORTON
La Trobe University,
Melbourne, Australia
   *Australian Aboriginal Religion*

MICHAEL NEILL
University of Auckland, New Zealand
   *Shakespeare, William*

PATRICE K. NICHOLAS
MGH Institute of Health Professions,
Boston, MA
   *Hospice around the World*

KENNETH D. NORDIN
Benedictine University
   *Ghost Dance*
   *Native American Religion*

LINDA L. OAKES
St. Jude Children's Research Hospital
   *Children and Their Rights in Life*
   *and Death Situations*

RANDOLPH OCHSMANN
University of Mainz, Germany
   *Bonsen, F. Z.*
   *Necrophilia*
   *Ontological Confrontation*

MARGARET OWEN
Empowering Widows in Development,
Widows for Peace and Reconstruction,
*and* Girton College, United Kingdom
   *Widows in Third World Nations*

JENNIFER PARKIN
Benedictine University
   *Homicide, Epidemiology of*

FREDERICK S. PAXTON
Connecticut College
   *Ariès, Philippe*
   *Christian Death Rites, History of*
   *Theodosian Code*

MARTIN PERNICK
Department of History,
University of Michigan
   *Black Stork*

MICHELE PRITCHARD
St. Jude Children's Research Hospital
   *Children and Their Rights in Life*
   *and Death Situations*

LAURA PROUD
Independent Media Consultant
   *Suicide Influences and Factors: Rock*
   *Music*

GERALD F. PYLE
University of North Carolina, Charlotte
   *Influenza*

THERESE A. RANDO
Institute for the Study and Treatment of
Loss, Warwick, RI
   *Bereavement, Vicarious*
   *Mourning*

LILLIAN M. RANGE
University of Southern Mississippi
   *Grief: Traumatic*

EVA REIMERS
Department of Thematic Studies,
Linköping University, Sweden
   *Cemeteries and Cemetery Reform*

PAMELA ROBERTS
California State University, Long Beach
   *Memorialization, Spontaneous*
   *Memorial, Virtual*
   *Vietnam Veterans Memorial*

BRONNA D. ROMANOFF
The Sage Colleges
   *Replacement Children*

F. ARTURO ROSALES
Department of History,
Arizona State University
   *Days of the Dead*

BRUCE RUMBOLD
Faculty of Health Sciences, La Trobe
University, Australia
   *Protestantism*

MARK A. RUNCO
University of Hawaii, Hilo *and*
California State University, Fullerton
   *Sexton, Anne*

JEFFREY BURTON RUSSELL
University of California, Santa Barbara
   *Heaven*

BARBARA RYAN
Widener University
   *Lopata, Helena Z.*

DANIELLE SAINT-LAURENT
National Public Health Institute
of Quebec
   *Suicide Basics: Epidemiology*

CICELY SAUNDERS
St. Christopher's Hospice, London
   *Lessons from the Dying*

GERHARD SCHMIED
Johannes Gutenberg University,
Mainz, Germany
   *Cemeteries, War*

ANDREW J. SCHOPP
University of Tennessee, Martin
   *Literature for Adults*

HENK SCHUT
Department of Psychology, Utrecht
University, Netherlands
   *Grief: Theories*

REIKO SCHWAB
Old Dominion University
   *Grief: Child's Death*
   *Grief: Family*

VANDA SCOTT
   *Varah, Chad*

MOSHE SHARON
Hebrew University of Jerusalem
   *Bahá'í Faith*

G. M. SIFAKIS
Department of Classics,
New York University
   *Greek Tragedy*

PHYLLIS R. SILVERMAN
Department of Psychiatry,
Massachusetts General Hospital,
Harvard Medical School
*Continuing Bonds*

SAM SILVERMAN
*Buried Alive*
*Catacombs*
*Charnel Houses*
*Dead Ghetto*

LACEY BALDWIN SMITH
Northwestern University
*Martyrs*

TRACY L. SMITH
University of Maryland,
Baltimore County
*Emergency Medical Technicians*

REINER SÖRRIES
Arbeitsgemeinschaft Friedhof und
Denkmal (Study Group for Cemeteries
and Memorials), Erlangen, Germany
*Museums of Death*

STEVEN STACK
Center for Suicide Research,
Wayne State University
*Suicide Influences and Factors:*
*Media Effects*

CHERYL B. STEWART
Benedictine University
*Cult Deaths*
*Heaven's Gate*
*Jonestown*
*Waco*

DENNIS D. STEWART
University of Minnesota, Morris
*Cult Deaths*
*Heaven's Gate*
*Jonestown*
*Waco*

STEPHEN STRACK
U.S. Department of Veterans Affairs,
Los Angeles
*Feifel, Herman*
*Psychology*

MARGARET STROEBE
Department of Psychology, Utrecht
University, Netherlands
*Grief: Theories*

WOLFGANG STROEBE
Department of Psychology, Utrecht
University, Netherlands
*Grief: Theories*

JEREMY SUGARMAN
Center for the Study of Medical Ethics
and Humanities, Duke University
*Bioethics*

MAARE E. TAMM
Department of Health Sciences,
Luleå University of Technology,
Boden, Sweden
*Personifications of Death*

KARL A. TAUBE
Department of Anthropology,
University of California, Riverside
*Aztec Religion*
*Maya Religion*

ADRIAN TOMER
Shippensburg University
*Becker, Ernest*
*Life Events*
*Terror Management Theory*

MICHEL TOUSIGNANT
University of Quebec, Montreal
*Suicide Influences and Factors:*
*Alcohol and Drug Use*
*Suicide Influences and Factors:*
*Culture*
*Suicide Influences and Factors:*
*Mental Illness*

JIM B. TUCKER
Department of Psychiatric Medicine,
University of Virginia Health System,
Charlottesville, VA
*Reincarnation*

LADISLAV VOLICER
Hospice, Alzheimer Patients and

ROGER N. WALSH
University of California, Irvine
*Shamanism*

JOHNETTA M. WARD
University of Notre Dame
*Epitaphs*
*Organized Crime*
*Weber, Max*

RETHA M. WARNICKE
Arizona State University
*Funeral Orations and Sermons*

VINCENT WARREN
Bibliothéque de la Danse de L'École
supérieure de danse de Québec
*Dance*

HANNELORE WASS
University of Florida
*Children and Media Violence*
*Death Education*

JOHN D. WEAVER
Eye of the Storm, Nazareth, PA
*Disasters*

GREGORY PAUL WEGNER
University of Wisconsin, La Crosse
*Holocaust*

MATT WEINBERG
Clinical Consultation Services,
Bryn Mawr, PA
*Right-to-Die Movement*

CATHERINE WEINBERGER-
THOMAS
Centre d'Etudes de l'Inde es de l'Asie
du Sud, Paris
*Widow-Burning*

GREGORY L. WEISS
Roanoke College
*Do Not Resuscitate*

THOMAS B. WEST
Franciscan School of Theology,
University of California, Berkeley
*Deathbed Visions and Escorts*
*Dehumanization*
*Empathy and Compassion*

JENNIFER WESTWOOD
The Folklore Society, London
*Gilgamesh*
*Gods and Goddesses of Life and*
*Death*
*Kronos*
*Soul Birds*

ALLISON K. WILSON
Benedictine University
*Drowning*
*Exposure to the Elements*

SHERYL SCHEIBLE WOLF
School of Law,
University of New Mexico
*Wills and Inheritance*

BEN WOLFE
St. Mary's/Duluth Clinic Health System's
Grief Support Center, Duluth, MN
*Grief Counseling and Therapy*

JOHN WOLFFE
*Royalty, British*

TARA S. WOOD
Arizona State University
*Funeral Orations and Sermons*

FRANK M. YATSU
Houston Medical School,
University of Texas
*Stroke*

# ABORTION

Abortion is one of the most emotional and divisive moral issues of twenty-first-century American life. Consensus has not been reached on the numerous questions that swirl around the subject, including whether or not a woman has the right to choose a legal abortion, and under what conditions; the role of parents if she is not legally an adult; and the roles of the state and religion having veto power. In addition, the questions of when life begins and at what point it should be protected remain controversial.

Strictly defined, abortion is the expulsion or removal of an embryo or fetus from the uterus before it has developed sufficiently to survive outside the mother (before viability). As commonly used, the term *abortion* refers only to artificially induced expulsions caused by mechanical means or drugs. Spontaneous abortions occurring naturally and not artificially induced are commonly referred to as miscarriages.

Women choose to have abortions for a variety of reasons: They have had all the children they wish to have; want to delay the next birth; believe they are too young or too poor to raise a child; are estranged or on uneasy terms with their sexual partner; or they do not want a child while they are in school or working.

**Artificially Induced Abortion around the World**

Unplanned and unwanted pregnancies are common, and this fact fuels the controversy in every region of the world. Globally, more than one in four women who become pregnant have an abortion or an unwanted birth. In the developed countries of the world, including those in North America and Western Europe, where average desired family size is small, an estimated 49 percent of the 28 million pregnancies each year are unplanned and 36 percent of the total pregnancies end in abortion. In the developing countries, including parts of Eastern Europe, the Middle East, and Africa, where desirable family sizes are larger, an estimated 36 percent of the 182 million pregnancies each year are unplanned and 20 percent end in abortion.

Women worldwide commonly initiate sexual intercourse by age twenty, whether they are married or unmarried. In the developed countries, 77 percent have had intercourse by age twenty. This compares to 83 percent in sub-Saharan Africa and 56 percent in Latin America and the Caribbean. Couples in many countries have more children than they would like, or have a child at a time when they do not want one. The average woman in Kenya has six children, while the desired family size is four; the average Bangladeshi woman has four children but desires three.

From a global perspective, 46 million women have abortions each year; 78 percent of these live in developing countries and 22 percent live in developed countries. About 11 percent of all the women who have abortions live in Africa, 58 percent in Asia, 9 percent in Latin America and the Caribbean; 17 percent live in Europe, and the remaining 5 percent live elsewhere in the developed world.

Of the 46 million women who have abortions each year in the world, 26 million women have abortions legally and 20 million have abortions in countries where abortion is restricted or prohibited by law. For every 1,000 women of childbearing age in the world, each year 35 are estimated to have an induced abortion. The abortion rate for women in developed regions is 39 abortions per 1,000 women per year; in the developing regions the rate is 34 per 1,000 per year. Rates in Western Europe, the United States, and Canada are 10 to 23 per year.

## Methods of Abortion

About 90 percent of abortions in the United States are performed in the first twelve weeks of the pregnancy. The type of procedure used for an abortion generally depends upon how many weeks the woman has been pregnant.

*Medical induction.* The drug mifepristone combined with misoprostol has been used widely in Europe for early abortions, and is now used routinely in the United States. Mifepristone blocks uterine absorption of the hormone progesterone, causing the uterine lining and any fertilized egg to shed. Combined with misoprostol two days later, which increases contractions of the uterus and helps expel the embryo, this method has fewer health risks than surgical abortion and is effective 95 percent of the time. Researchers in Europe report few serious medical problems associated with this method. Some of the side effects include cramping, abdominal pain, and bleeding like that of a heavy menstrual cycle.

Both pro-choice activists and pro-life activists see mifepristone with misoprostol as an important development in the abortion controversy. If abortion can be induced simply, safely, effectively, and privately, the nature of the controversy surrounding abortion will change dramatically. Clinics that perform abortions are regularly picketed by antiabortion protesters in the United States, making the experience of obtaining a legal abortion difficult for many women. If use of this method spreads in spite of opposition from antiabortion groups, abortion will become an almost invisible, personal, and relatively private act.

*Vacuum aspiration.* Also called vacuum suction or vacuum curettage, vacuum aspiration is an abortion method performed during the first trimester of pregnancy, up to twelve weeks from the beginning of the last menstrual period. It is the most common abortion procedure used during the first trimester in the United States, requiring a local or general anesthetic. The procedure takes about ten to fifteen minutes, although the woman stays in the doctor's office or hospital for a few hours afterward. Preparation for the procedure is similar to preparing for a pelvic examination. An instrument is then inserted into the vagina to dilate the opening to the cervix. The end of a nonflexible tube connected to a suction apparatus is inserted through the cervix into the uterus and the contents of the uterus, including fetal tissue, are then sucked out. Vacuum aspiration is simple and complications are rare and usually minor.

*Dilation and curettage or dilation and evacuation.* Dilation and curettage (D and C) is similar to vacuum aspiration but must be performed in a hospital under general anesthetic. It is performed between eight and twenty weeks after the last menstrual period. By the beginning of the second trimester of pregnancy, the uterus has enlarged and its walls have thinned. Its contents cannot be as easily removed by suction, and therefore the D and C procedure is used. The cervix is dilated and a sharp metal loop attached to the end of a long handle (the curette) is inserted into the uterus and used to scrape out the uterine contents. Dilation and evacuation (D and E) is a related procedure used between thirteen and sixteen weeks after the last menstrual period. D and E is similar to both D and C and vacuum aspiration, but is a bit more complicated and requires the use of forceps and suction.

*Induced labor.* For abortions later in the pregnancy (sixteen to twenty-four weeks), procedures are employed to render the fetus nonviable and induce delivery through the vagina. Only 1 percent of abortions in the United States are performed by inducing labor and a miscarriage. Because the woman experiences uterine contractions for several hours and then expels a lifeless fetus, these procedures are more physically uncomfortable and often more emotionally upsetting. The two most common procedures used in this period are prostaglandin-induced and saline-induced abortions. Prostaglandins can be injected directly into the amniotic sac through the abdominal well, injected intravenously into the woman, or inserted into the vagina as a suppository. They stimulate uterine contractions that lead to delivery. Saline (salt) solution can also be injected into the amniotic fluid and has a similar effect. Late-term abortions, also called partial-birth abortions by some, stir considerable controversy in the United States.

*Hysterotomy.* This extremely rare procedure, also performed from sixteen to twenty-four weeks after the woman's last menstrual period, is limited to cases in which a woman's uterus is so malformed that a D and E would be dangerous. In essence, a cesarean delivery is performed and the fetus is removed.

*Methotrexate and Misoprostol.* Because of social and political pressure from antiabortion activists, the number of obstetricians, gynecologists, and hospitals performing abortions in the United States has been steadily dropping, but this trend could change as doctors adopt a nonsurgical alternative using prescription drugs already marketed for other purposes. A combination of the drug methotrexate, which is toxic to the embryo, with misoprostol, which causes uterine contractions that expel the dead embryo, has been shown to be effective in inducing abortions at home.

## The Abortion Issue in the United States

In 1973 the U.S. Supreme Court overturned by a 7–2 vote laws that had made abortion a criminal act. Since that decision by century's end approximately 21 million American women have chosen to have 35 million abortions. Researchers estimate that 49 percent of pregnancies among American women are unintended, and half of these are terminated by abortion. Forty-three percent of women in the United States will have at least one abortion by the time they reach the end of the childbearing period of life, age forty-five. Fifty-eight percent of the women who had abortions in 1995 had used a contraceptive method during the month they became pregnant.

Induced abortion rates vary considerably by age. Figure 1 shows the proportion of pregnancies ending in live births, induced abortion, and fetal loss compared to the age of the woman. Induced abortion rates also differ considerably by race and Hispanic origin. About 16 percent of pregnancies among non-Hispanic white women end in abortion (1 in 6); 22 percent of pregnancies among Hispanic women (1 in 5); and 38 percent of pregnancies among non-Hispanic black women (2 in 5).

**FIGURE 1**

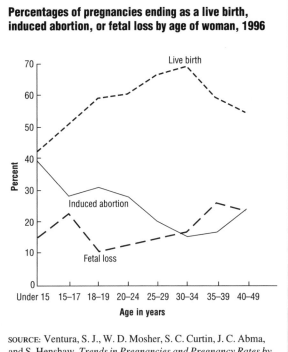

**Percentages of pregnancies ending as a live birth, induced abortion, or fetal loss by age of woman, 1996**

SOURCE: Ventura, S. J., W. D. Mosher, S. C. Curtin, J. C. Abma, and S. Henshaw. *Trends in Pregnancies and Pregnancy Rates by Outcome: Estimates for the United States, 1976–96.* Washington, DC: U.S. Department of Health and Human Services, 2000.

On average, women in the United States give at least three reasons for choosing an abortion: three-fourths say that having a baby would interfere with work, school, or other responsibilities; approximately two-thirds say that they cannot afford to have a child; and half say that they do not want to be a single parent or are having problems with their husband or partner. Support for abortion varies considerably by social class, with support consistently increasing by income and education.

For more than two centuries in early U.S. history (from the 1600s to the early 1900s), abortion was not a crime if it was performed before quickening (fetal movement, which begins at approximately twenty weeks). An antiabortion movement began in the early 1800s, led by physicians who argued against the validity of the concept of quickening and who opposed the performing of abortions by untrained people, which threatened physician control of medical services. The abortion controversy attracted minimal attention until the mid-1800s when newspapers began advertising abortion preparations. Opponents of these medicines argued that women used them as birth control measures and that women could also hide extramarital affairs through their use. The medicines were seen by some as evidence that immorality and corruption threatened America. By the early 1900s, virtually all states (at the urging of male politicians; women could not vote at the time) had passed antiabortion laws.

In the landmark 1973 case *Roe* v. *Wade,* the U.S. Supreme Court made abortion legal by denying the states the right to regulate early abortions. The court conceptualized pregnancy in three parts (trimesters) and gave pregnant women more options in regard to abortion in the first trimester (three months) than in the second or third trimester. The court ruled that during the first trimester the abortion decision must be left to the judgment of the woman and her physician. During the second trimester, the right to abortion remained but a state could regulate certain factors in an effort to protect the health of the woman, such as the type of facility in which an abortion could be performed. During the third trimester, the period of pregnancy in which the fetus is viable outside the uterus, a state could regulate and even ban all abortions except in situations in which they were necessary to preserve the mother's life or health.

The controversy over abortion in the United States did not end with the Supreme Court's decision, but rather has intensified. Repeated campaigns have been waged to overturn the decision and to ban abortion altogether. Although the high court has continued to uphold the *Roe* decision, support for abortion rights has decreased with the appointment of several conservative judges.

A *New York Times*/CBS News Poll taken twenty-five years after *Roe* v. *Wade* found that the majority of the American public still supports legalized abortion but says it should be harder to get and less readily chosen. Some observers call this a "permit-but-discourage" attitude. Overall, 32 percent of the random sample of 1,101 Americans in the poll said abortion should be generally available and legal; 45 percent said it should be available but more difficult to obtain; and 22 percent said it should not be permitted.

## Physical and Emotional Aspects of Abortion

The chance of dying as a result of a legal abortion in the United States is far lower than the chance of dying during childbirth. Before the nine-week point in pregnancy, a woman has a one in 500,000

**TABLE 1**

**Abortion risks**

|  | Risk of Death In Any Given Year |
|---|---|
| Legal abortion | |
| Before 9 weeks | 1 in 500,000 |
| 9–12 weeks | 1 in 67,000 |
| 13–16 weeks | 1 in 23,000 |
| After 16 weeks | 1 in 8,700 |
| Illegal abortion | 1 in 3,000 |
| Pregnancy and childbirth | 1 in 14,300 |

SOURCE: Carlson, Karen J., Stephanie A. Eisenstat, and Terra Ziporyn. *The Harvard Guide to Women's Health.* Cambridge, MA: Harvard University Press, 1996.

chance of dying as a result of an abortion. This compares to a one in 14,300 chance of dying as a result of pregnancy and childbirth (see Table 1). Infection is a possibility after an abortion, but long-term complications such as subsequent infertility, spontaneous second abortions, premature delivery, and low birthweight babies are not likely.

Some women experience feelings of guilt after an abortion, while others feel great relief that they are no longer pregnant. Still other women are ambivalent: They are happy to not be pregnant, but sad about the abortion. Some of these emotional highs and lows may be related to hormonal adjustments and may cease after the woman's hormone levels return to normal. The intensity of feelings associated with an abortion usually diminish as time passes, though some women may experience anger, frustration, and guilt for many years.

Those experiencing severe, negative psychological reactions to abortion are rare, according to research findings reviewed by a panel commissioned by the American Psychological Association. The panel wrote, "the question is not simply whether abortion has some harmful psychological effects, but whether those effects are demonstrably worse than the psychological consequences of unwanted childbirth." Women experiencing distress could find comfort in talking with loved ones, sensitive and trusted friends, and professional counselors experienced in working with abortion issues.

*See also:* BIOETHICS; BLACK STORK; CHILDREN, MURDER OF; INFANTICIDE; MORTALITY, CHILDBIRTH; MORTALITY, INFANT

***Bibliography***

Adler, Nancy E., et al. "Psychological Factors in Abortion: A Review." *American Psychologist* 47 (October 1992):1194–1204.

Alan Guttmacher Institute. *Sharing Responsibility: Women, Society and Abortion Worldwide.* New York: Author, 1999a.

Alan Guttmacher Institute. *Induced Abortion Worldwide.* New York: Author, 1999b.

Alan Guttmacher Institute. *Into a New World: Young Women's Sexual and Reproductive Lives.* New York: Author, 1998.

Alan Guttmacher Institute. *Hopes and Realities: Closing the Gap between Women's Aspirations and Their Reproductive Experiences.* New York: Author, 1995.

Boston Women's Health Book Collective. *Our Bodies, Ourselves for the New Century: A Book By and For Women.* New York: Touchstone/Simon & Schuster, 1998.

Brody, J. E. "Abortion Method Using Two Drugs Gains in a Study." *New York Times,* 31 August 1995, A1.

Francoeur, Robert T., ed. *International Encyclopedia of Sexuality.* New York: Continuum, 1997.

Goldberg, C., and J. Elder. "Poll Finds Support for Legal, Rare Abortions." *Lincoln Journal Star,* 16 January 1998, 1.

Hausknecht, Richard U. "Methotrexate and Misoprostol to Terminate Early Pregnancy." *New England Journal of Medicine* 333, no. 9 (1995):537.

Hyde, Janet Shibley, and John D. DeLamater. *Understanding Human Sexuality,* 7th edition. Boston: McGraw-Hill, 2000.

Insel, Paul M., and Walton T. Roth. *Core Concepts in Health,* 8th edition. Mountain View, CA: Mayfield, 2000.

Kelly, Gary F. *Sexuality Today: The Human Perspective,* 7th edition. Boston: McGraw-Hill, 2001.

Landers, S. "Koop Will Not Release Abortion Effects Report." *American Psychological Association Monitor* (March 1989):1.

Olson, David H., and John DeFrain. *Marriage and the Family: Diversity and Strengths,* 3rd edition. Mountain View, CA: Mayfield, 2000.

Strong, Bryan, Christine DeVault, and Barbara Werner Sayad. *Human Sexuality: Diversity in Contemporary America,* 3rd edition. Mountain View, CA: Mayfield, 1999.

Winikoff, Beverly, and Suzanne Wymelenberg. *The Whole Truth about Contraception.* Washington, DC: National Academy of Sciences, 1997.

***Internet Resources***

Alan Guttmacher Institute. "Abortion in Context: United States and Worldwide." In the Alan Guttmacher Institute [web site]. Available from www.agi-usa-org/pubs/ib_0599.htm

Alan Guttmacher Institute. "Induced Abortion." In the Alan Guttmacher Institute [web site]. Available from www.agi-usa-org/pubs/fb_induced_abortion.html

National Opinion Research Center (NORC). "General Social Surveys." In the NORC [web site]. Available from www.norc.org/projects/gensoc.asp

JOHN DeFRAIN

# ACCIDENTS

*See* CAUSES OF DEATH; INJURY MORTALITY.

# ADVANCE DIRECTIVES

An advance directive is a statement that declares what kind of lifesaving medical treatment a patient wants after he or she has become incompetent or unable to communicate to medical personnel. Advance directives, which are recognized in every state, are a response to the increasing ability of physicians since the 1950s to delay death through an array of medical technology, such as respirators, feeding tubes, and artificial hydration. This ability to prolong life has led to the need for doctors, patients, and patients' families to make decisions as to whether such technology should be used, especially in those situations when the patient is either near death, comatose, or severely and chronically ill.

Advance directives are an outgrowth of the doctrine of "informed consent." This doctrine, established by the courts, holds that patients, and not their physicians, are responsible for making the final decision about what medical care they want after being provided with complete and accurate medical information. It represents a shift from an earlier more paternalistic model of the doctor-patient relationship in which the physician made most medical decisions. The doctrine is based on the principles of autonomy and self-determination, which recognize the right of individuals to control their own bodies. An advance directive is a way of recognizing this right prospectively by providing instructions in advance on what the patient would want after he or she is no longer able to communicate his or her decision.

**Types of Advance Directives**

There are two forms of advance directives: living wills and health care powers of attorney. A living will, so named because it takes effect while the person is still alive, is a written statement expressing whether or not a person wants to accept life-sustaining medical treatment and under what conditions. For example, a living will may state that a person wants a ventilator, but not a feeding tube, in the event of an irreversible or terminal illness. Many states also have Do Not Resuscitate laws, a narrowly tailored type of living will, that allows patients to indicate that they do not want cardiopulmonary resuscitation if they suffer cardiac arrest. These laws also protect health providers from civil or criminal liability when honoring advance directives.

A health care power of attorney, also known as a durable power of attorney or a proxy, provides for someone else, usually a family member or close friend, to make decisions for the patient when he or she is unable. It is broader than a living will because it includes all medical decisions, not just those pertaining to life-sustaining medical treatment. It does not require that the person be terminally ill or in a vegetative state before it is triggered. However, unlike a living will, a proxy may not contain specific instructions on a patient's willingness to accept certain life-sustaining treatment. Instead it is left up to the appointed family member or close friend to determine what the patient would want, based on what the patient has said in the past or the patient's overall life philosophy. For this reason, it is helpful to combine living wills and a power of attorney in one document. Every state has laws that provide for living wills, health care proxies, or both. These laws are commonly referred to as Natural Death Acts.

Advance directives do not have to be in writing and can include oral statements made to family, friends, and doctors before the patient became unable to make a decision regarding his or her medical care. Most states require that evidence concerning these statements be clear and convincing. In other words, they should not be "casual remarks" but "solemn pronouncements" that specifically indicate what type of life-sustaining treatments the patient wants, and under what conditions. Because such statements are open to interpretation, and past remarks may not be indicative of what a patient presently wants, oral advance directives are often not effective.

If a patient has failed to execute a living will or health care proxy, many states provide for the designation of a surrogate decision maker (usually a family member). However, the situations when a surrogate may be appointed are limited. Depending upon the state, it may only apply when the individual has a terminal illness or is permanently unconscious, or to certain types of treatment, such as cardiopulmonary resuscitation. The surrogate must consider the wishes of the patient, if known, and his or her religious views, values, and morals.

Advance directives may not apply in an emergency situation, especially those that occur outside of a hospital. Emergency medical services (EMS) personnel are generally required to keep patients alive. Some states allow EMS personnel not to resuscitate patients who are certified as terminal and have an identifier, such as a bracelet.

Although the law encourages people to complete advance directives, most do not. It is estimated that only between 10 to 20 percent of the population have advance directives. There are several reasons for this. Young people think that they do not need one, even though the most well-known cases involving the right to die—Karen Ann Quinlan and Nancy Cruzan—involved young women in their twenties in persistent vegetative states. For old and young alike, bringing up the issue with potential surrogates, such as family and friends, can be uncomfortable and upsetting. Some individuals, especially those from traditionally disenfranchised populations such as the poor and minority groups, may fear that an advance directive would be used to limit other types of medical care.

Another primary reason why advance directives are not completed is that oftentimes patients wait for their physicians to broach the subject, rather than initiating it themselves. In a 1991 Harvard study four hundred outpatients of thirty primary care physicians and 102 members of the general public were interviewed to determine the perceived barriers to executing an advance directive. The most frequently cited reason for not completing an advance directive was the failure of physicians to ask about it. There are several reasons why physicians often do not initiate such discussions, including a belief that such directives are unnecessary (especially for younger patients) and lack of specific knowledge on how to draft one. Also, insurance companies do not reimburse physicians for their time spent discussing advance directives.

## Limitations of Advance Directives

Even when advance directives are completed, they may not be complied with. One reason is that they may not be available when needed. In a self-administered questionnaire distributed to 200 outpatients in 1993, half of the patients who had executed an advance directive kept the only copy locked in a safe-deposit box. Hospitals may also fail to include a copy of the patient's advance directive in his or her chart. Physicians may be unaware of a patient's advance directive even when the document is placed in the patient's chart.

Another obstacle to the implementation of advance directives is that the documents themselves may contain ambiguities or terms open to interpretation, making it difficult to apply. For example, some living wills may simply state that the patient does not want heroic medical measures to be undertaken if the condition is terminal. But the term "heroic measures" can mean different things to different people. Artificial nutrition and hydration may be considered heroic to some, but not to others. Other living wills (and some state laws) require that a patient be terminally ill before it is activated. But physicians may disagree over the definition of *terminally ill*; for some it means imminent death and for others it means an irreversible condition that will ultimately result in death. And even a clearly written advance directive may no longer represent a patient's wishes as death becomes imminent.

Health care proxies also have limitations. They often contain no guidance for the appointed person on the patient's views toward life-sustaining medical interventions. Decisions may therefore be based on what the proxy wants and not the patient. Because the proxy is usually a relative or close friend, this person's strong connections to the patient, and own feelings and beliefs, may influence the decisions made. This is especially true when it comes to withholding certain controversial treatments, such as a feeding tube. Figuring out what the patient would want can also be difficult. Past statements may not be indicative of present desires because a grave illness can alter views held when healthy.

Even when a patient's preference is clear, as expressed by the surrogate or within the document itself, physicians may not always comply with the patient's wishes. One of the largest studies of clinical practices at the end of life, the Study to Understand Prognoses and Preferences for Outcomes and Risks of Treatment (the Support study) involved 4,805 patients in advanced stages of serious illnesses in five teaching hospitals located throughout the United States. The study found that physicians often ignore advance directives. This was true even where, as in the Support study, efforts were made to improve physician-patient communication on end-of-life decisions. The reasons are several, including unclear advance directives and pressure exerted by family members to ignore directives. Physicians may also fear that they may be sued for withholding life supports, although no such lawsuits have ever been successful.

Advance directives also pose a direct challenge to a physician's medical judgment. While the paternalistic model of the physician-patient relationship has been supplanted by one based on shared decision making and informed consent, remnants of the old model still remain. Physicians who see their primary goal as saving lives may also be less willing to yield to the patient's judgment, especially when it is difficult to predict with certainty whether life supports will enhance the patient's life or render dying more painful.

## Improving Advance Directives

Attempts to address some of the deficiencies in advance directives have taken several tracks. One approach is to make advance directives more practical and easier to interpret and apply. One suggestion is to include specific medical scenarios and more detailed treatments (although too much specificity can leave out the present scenario). Partnership for Caring, an advocacy group located in Washington D.C., suggests including whether or not artificial nutrition and hydration should be provided being that these types of treatment often create disagreements. Another suggestion is to include a values history, a detailed rendition of the patient's religious, spiritual, and moral beliefs, which can provide guidance and clarification of the reasons for not choosing life supports. Still another approach recommended by the American Medical Association is the inclusion of general treatment goals, for example "restoring the ability to communicate," that can be used to assess the appropriateness of a given intervention.

Other approaches to increase compliance with advance directives have focused on the behavior of physicians. The medical profession has been criticized for not adequately preparing physicians for dealing with death. Professional medical groups, such as the American Medical Association, have become more involved in preparing physicians by issuing guidelines and reports. A more extreme approach is advocated by some who have proposed imposing sanctions, either professional disciplinary action or penalties and fines, for ignoring an advance directive. Although some state laws provide for such sanctions, they are rarely if ever applied. Legal actions to recover monetary damages from the physician or health care provider for ignoring advance directives have also been initiated.

Other approaches include making the public and medical providers more aware of advance directives, and making them more accessible. A 1990 federal law, the Patient Self-Determination Act, requires hospitals, health maintenance organizations, and others that participate in Medicaid or Medicare to tell patients their rights under state laws to make end-of-life medical decisions. It also requires that advance directives be maintained in patients' charts. An important public education component of the law requires health care providers to educate their staff and the public about advance directives. Several states have tried more experimental approaches, including allowing advance directives to be displayed on driver's licenses and identification cards.

Advance directives are a relatively new phenomenon in medical care, with the first laws providing for them passed in the latter part of the twentieth century. Although there is widespread public support, that support is often more theoretical than practical. Changes in medical practices,

the public's awareness, and the documents themselves have been proposed in order to encourage their use.

*See also:* BIOETHICS; CRUZAN, NANCY; END-OF-LIFE ISSUES; INFORMED CONSENT; LIVING WILL; NATURAL DEATH ACTS; QUINLAN, KAREN ANN

## Bibliography

Cantor, Norman L. "Advance Directive Instruments for End-of-Life and Health Care Decision Making." *Psychology, Public Policy and Law* 4 (1998):629–652.

Danis, Marion, Leslie I. Southerland, Joanne M. Garrett, Janet L. Smith, Frank Hielema, C. Glenn Pickard, David M. Egner, and Donald L. Patrick. "A Prospective Study of Advance Directives for Life-Sustaining Care." *New England Journal of Medicine* 324 (1991):882–888.

Emanuel, Linda L., Michael J. Barry, John D. Stoeckle, Lucy M. Ettelson, and Ezekiel J. Emanual. "Advance Directives for Medical Care—A Case for Greater Use." New England Journal of Medicine 324 (1991):889–895.

Furrow, Barry R., Thomas L. Greaney, Sandra H. Johnson, Timothy Stoltzfus Jost, and Robert L. Schwartz. *Health Law.* St. Paul, MN: West Publishing Company, 1995.

Koch, Tom. "Life Quality vs. the Quality of Life: Assumptions Underlying Prospective Quality of Life Instruments in Health Care Planning." *Social Sciences and Medicine* 51 (2000):419–427.

Lens, Vicki, and Daniel Pollack. "Advance Directives: Legal Remedies and Psychosocial Interventions." *Death Studies* 24 (2000):377–399.

LoBuono, Charlotte. "A Detailed Examination of Advance Directives." *Patient Care* 34 (2000):92–108.

Loewy, Erich H. "Ethical Considerations in Executing and Implementing Advance Directives." *Archives of Internal Medicine* 158 (1998):321–324.

Rich, Ben A. "Advance Directives: The Next Generation." *The Journal of Legal Medicine* 19 (1998):1–31.

Sabatino, Charles P. "Ten Legal Myths about Advance Directives." *Clearinghouse Review* 28 (October 1994):653–656.

Sass, Hans-Martin, Robert M. Veatch, and Rihito Kimura, eds. *Advance Directives and Surrogate Decision Making in Health Care: United States, Germany, and Japan.* Baltimore: Johns Hopkins University Press, 1998.

Silveira, Maria J., Albert DiPiero, Martha S. Gerrity, and Chris Feudtner. "Patients' Knowledge of Options at

the End of Life: Ignorance in the Face of Death."
*Journal of the American Medical Association* 284
(2000):2483–2488.

Teno, Joan, et al. "Advance Directives for Seriously Ill
Hospitalized Patients: Effectiveness with the Patient
Self-Determination Act and the Support Intervention."
*Journal of the American Geriatrics Society* 45
(1995):500–507.

VICKI LENS

# AFRICAN RELIGIONS

In the religions of Africa, life does not end with death, but continues in another realm. The concepts of "life" and "death" are not mutually exclusive concepts, and there are no clear dividing lines between them. Human existence is a dynamic process involving the increase or decrease of "power" or "life force," of "living" and "dying," and there are different levels of life and death. Many African languages express the fact that things are not going well, such as when there is sickness, in the words "we are living a little," meaning that the level of life is very low. The African religions scholar Placide Tempels describes every misfortune that Africans encounter as "a diminution of vital force." Illness and death result from some outside agent, a person, thing, or circumstance that weakens people because the agent contains a greater life force. Death does not alter or end the life or the personality of an individual, but only causes a change in its conditions. This is expressed in the concept of "ancestors," people who have died but who continue to "live" in the community and communicate with their families.

This entry traces those ideas that are, or have been, approximately similar across sub-Saharan Africa. The concepts described within in many cases have been altered in the twentieth century through the widespread influence of Christianity or Islam, and some of the customs relating to burials are disappearing. Nevertheless, many religious concepts and practices continue to persist.

## The African Concept of Death

Death, although a dreaded event, is perceived as the beginning of a person's deeper relationship with all of creation, the complementing of life and the beginning of the communication between the visible and the invisible worlds. The goal of life is to become an ancestor after death. This is why every person who dies must be given a "correct" funeral, supported by a number of religious ceremonies. If this is not done, the dead person may become a wandering ghost, unable to "live" properly after death and therefore a danger to those who remain alive. It might be argued that "proper" death rites are more a guarantee of protection for the living than to secure a safe passage for the dying. There is ambivalence about attitudes to the recent dead, which fluctuate between love and respect on the one hand and dread and despair on the other, particularly because it is believed that the dead have power over the living.

Many African peoples have a custom of removing a dead body through a hole in the wall of a house, and not through the door. The reason for this seems to be that this will make it difficult (or even impossible) for the dead person to remember the way back to the living, as the hole in the wall is immediately closed. Sometimes the corpse is removed feet first, symbolically pointing away from the former place of residence. A zigzag path may be taken to the burial site, or thorns strewn along the way, or a barrier erected at the grave itself because the dead are also believed to strengthen the living. Many other peoples take special pains to ensure that the dead are easily able to return to their homes, and some people are even buried under or next to their homes.

Many people believe that death is the loss of a soul, or souls. Although there is recognition of the difference between the physical person that is buried and the nonphysical person who lives on, this must not be confused with a Western dualism that separates "physical" from "spiritual." When a person dies, there is not some "part" of that person that lives on—it is the whole person who continues to live in the spirit world, receiving a new body identical to the earthly body, but with enhanced powers to move about as an ancestor. The death of children is regarded as a particularly grievous evil event, and many peoples give special names to their children to try to ward off the reoccurrence of untimely death.

There are many different ideas about the "place" the departed go to, a "land" which in most cases seems to be a replica of this world. For some it is under the earth, in groves, near or in the homes of earthly families, or on the other side of a deep river. In most cases it is an extension of what is known at present, although for some peoples it is a much better place without pain or hunger. The Kenyan scholar John Mbiti writes that a belief in the continuation of life after death for African peoples "does not constitute a hope for a future and better life. To live here and now is the most important concern of African religious activities and beliefs. . . . Even life in the hereafter is conceived in materialistic and physical terms. There is neither paradise to be hoped for nor hell to be feared in the hereafter" (Mbiti 1969, pp. 4–5).

## The African Concept of the Afterlife

Nearly all African peoples have a belief in a singular supreme being, the creator of the earth. Although the dead are believed to be somehow nearer to the supreme being than the living, the original state of bliss in the distant past expressed in creation myths is not restored in the afterlife. The separation between the supreme being and humankind remains unavoidable and natural in the place of the departed, even though the dead are able to rest there and be safe. Most African peoples believe that rewards and punishments come to people in this life and not in the hereafter. In the land of the departed, what happens there happens automatically, irrespective of a person's earthly behavior, provided the correct burial rites have been observed. But if a person is a wizard, a murderer, a thief, one who has broken the community code or taboos, or one who has had an unnatural death or an improper burial, then such a person may be doomed to punishment in the afterlife as a wandering ghost, and may be beaten and expelled by the ancestors or subjected to a period of torture according to the seriousness of their misdeeds, much like the Catholic concept of purgatory. Among many African peoples is the widespread belief that witches and sorcerers are not admitted to the spirit world, and therefore they are refused proper burial—sometimes their bodies are subjected to actions that would make such burial impossible, such as burning, chopping up, and feeding them to hyenas. Among the Africans, to be cut off from the community of the ancestors in death is the nearest equivalent of hell.

The concept of reincarnation is found among many peoples. Reincarnation refers to the soul of a dead person being reborn in the body of another. There is a close relationship between birth and death. African beliefs in reincarnation differ from those of major Asian religions (especially Hinduism) in a number of important ways. Hinduism is "world-renouncing," conceiving of a cycle of rebirth in a world of suffering and illusion from which people wish to escape—only by great effort—and there is a system of rewards and punishments whereby one is reborn into a higher or lower station in life (from whence the caste system arose). These ideas that view reincarnation as something to be feared and avoided are completely lacking in African religions. Instead, Africans are "world-affirming," and welcome reincarnation. The world is a light, warm, and living place to which the dead are only too glad to return from the darkness and coldness of the grave. The dead return to their communities, except for those unfortunate ones previously mentioned, and there are no limits set to the number of possible reincarnations—an ancestor may be reincarnated in more than one person at a time. Some African myths say that the number of souls and bodies is limited. It is important for Africans to discover which ancestor is reborn in a child, for this is a reason for deep thankfulness. The destiny of a community is fulfilled through both successive and simultaneous multiple reincarnations.

Transmigration (also called metempsychosis) denotes the changing of a person into an animal. The most common form of this idea relates to a witch or sorcerer who is believed to be able to transform into an animal in order to perform evil deeds. Africans also believe that people may inhabit particular animals after death, especially snakes, which are treated with great respect. Some African rulers reappear as lions. Some peoples believe that the dead will reappear in the form of the totem animal of that ethnic group, and these totems are fearsome (such as lions, leopards, or crocodiles). They symbolize the terrible punishments the dead can inflict if the moral values of the community are not upheld.

## Burial and Mourning Customs

Death in African religions is one of the last transitional stages of life requiring passage rites, and this too takes a long time to complete. The deceased must be "detached" from the living and make as smooth a transition to the next life as possible

*In the village of Eshowe in the KwaZulu-Natal Province in South Africa, a Zulu Isangoma (diviner), with a puff adder in his mouth, practices soothsaying, or predicting, with snakes. It is impossible to generalize about concepts in African religions because they are ethno-religions, being determined by each ethnic group in the continent.*
GALLO IMAGES/CORBIS

protecting ancestor. The "home bringing" rite is a common African ceremony. Only when a deceased person's surviving relatives have gone, and there is no one left to remember him or her, can the person be said to have really "died." At that point the deceased passes into the "graveyard" of time, losing individuality and becoming one of the unknown multitude of immortals.

Many African burial rites begin with the sending away of the departed with a request that they do not bring trouble to the living, and they end with a plea for the strengthening of life on the earth and all that favors it. According to the Tanzanian theologian Laurenti Magesa, funeral rites simultaneously mourn for the dead and celebrate life in all its abundance. Funerals are a time for the community to be in solidarity and to regain its identity. In some communities this may include dancing and merriment for all but the immediate family, thus limiting or even denying the destructive powers of death and providing the deceased with "light feet" for the journey to the other world.

Ancient customs are adapted in many South African urban funerals. When someone has died in a house, all the windows are smeared with ash, all pictures in the house turned around and all mirrors and televisions and any other reflective objects covered. The beds are removed from the deceased's room, and the bereaved women sit on the floor, usually on a mattress. During the time preceding the funeral—usually from seven to thirteen days—visits are paid by people in the community to comfort the bereaved family. In the case of Christians, consolatory services are held at the bereaved home. The day before the funeral the corpse is brought home before sunset and placed in the bedroom. A night vigil then takes place, often lasting until the morning. The night vigil is a time for pastoral care, to comfort and encourage the bereaved. A ritual killing is sometimes made for the ancestors, as it is believed that blood must be shed at this time to avoid further misfortune. Some peoples use the hide of the slaughtered beast to cover the corpse or place it on top of the coffin as a "blanket" for the deceased. Traditionally, the funeral takes place in the early morning (often before sunrise) and not late in the afternoon, as it is believed that sorcerers move around in the afternoons looking for corpses to use for their evil purposes. Because sorcerers are asleep in the early morning, this is a good time to bury the dead.

because the journey to the world of the dead has many interruptions. If the correct funeral rites are not observed, the deceased may come back to trouble the living relatives. Usually an animal is killed in ritual, although this also serves the practical purpose of providing food for the many guests. Personal belongings are often buried with the deceased to assist in the journey. Various other rituals follow the funeral itself. Some kill an ox at the burial to accompany the deceased. Others kill another animal some time after the funeral (three months to two years and even longer is the period observed). The Nguni in southern Africa call the slaying of the ox "the returning ox," because the beast accompanies the deceased back home to his or her family and enables the deceased to act as a

In some communities children and unmarried adults are not allowed to attend the funeral. During the burial itself the immediate family of the deceased is expected to stay together on one side of the grave at a designated place. They are forbidden from speaking or taking any vocal part in the funeral. It is customary to place the deceased's personal property, including eating utensils, walking sticks, blankets, and other useful items, in the grave. After the funeral the people are invited to the deceased's home for the funeral meal. Many people follow a cleansing ritual at the gate of the house, where everyone must wash off the dust of the graveyard before entering the house. Sometimes pieces of cut aloe are placed in the water, and this water is believed to remove bad luck. Churches that use "holy water" sprinkle people to cleanse them from impurity at this time.

In southern Africa the period of strict mourning usually continues for at least a week after the funeral. During this time the bereaved stay at home and do not socialize or have sexual contact. Some wear black clothes or black cloths fastened to their clothes, and shave their hair (including facial hair) from the day after the funeral. Because life is concentrated in the hair, shaving the hair symbolizes death, and its growing again indicates the strengthening of life. People in physical contact with a corpse are often regarded as unclean. The things belonging to the deceased should not be used at this time, such as the eating utensils or the chairs the deceased used. Blankets and anything else in contact with the deceased are all washed. The clothes of the deceased are wrapped up in a bundle and put away for a year or until the extended period of mourning has ended, after which they are distributed to family members or destroyed by burning. After a certain period of time the house and the family must be cleansed from bad luck, from uncleanness and "darkness." The bereaved family members are washed and a ritual killing takes place. The time of the cleansing is usually seven days after the funeral, but some observe a month or even longer. Traditionally, a widow had to remain in mourning for a year after her husband's death and the children of a deceased parent were in mourning for three months.

A practice that seems to be disappearing in African urban areas is the home-bringing ritual, although it is still observed in some parts of Africa. A month or two after the funeral the grieving family slaughters a beast and then goes to the graveyard. They speak to the ancestors to allow the deceased to return home to rest. It is believed that at the graves the spirits are hovering on the earth and are restless until they are brought home—an extremely dangerous situation for the family. The family members take some of the earth covering the grave and put it in a bottle. They proceed home with the assurance that the deceased relative is accompanying them to look after the family as an ancestor. Some Christian churches have a night vigil at the home after the home-bringing. The theologian Marthinus Daneel describes the ceremony in some Zimbabwean churches, where the living believers escort the spirit of the deceased relative to heaven through their prayers, after which a mediating role can be attained. The emphasis is on the transformation of the traditional rite, while providing for the consolation of the bereaved family. This example shows how these churches try to eliminate an old practice without neglecting the traditionally conceived need that it has served.

These burial and mourning customs suggest that many practices still prevailing in African Christian funerals are vestiges of the ancestor cult, especially the ritual killings and the home-bringing rites. Because a funeral is preeminently a community affair in which the church is but one of many players, the church does not always determine the form of the funeral. Some of the indigenous rites have indeed been transformed and given Christian meanings, to which both Christians and those with traditional orientation can relate. Sometimes there are signs of confrontation and the changing and discontinuance of old customs to such an extent that they are no longer recognizable in that context.

African funerals are community affairs in which the whole community feels the grief of the bereaved and shares in it. The purpose of the activities preceding the funeral is to comfort, encourage, and heal those who are hurting. Thereafter, the churches see to it that the bereaved make the transition back to normal life as smoothly and as quickly as possible. This transition during the mourning period is sometimes accompanied by cleansing rituals by which the bereaved are assured of their acceptance and protection by God. Because the dominance of Christianity and Islam in Africa has resulted in the rejection of certain mourning customs, the funeral becomes an opportunity to declare faith.

See also: AFTERLIFE IN CROSS-CULTURAL PERSPECTIVE; BUDDHISM; CHINESE BELIEFS; HINDUISM; IMMORTALITY; ISLAM; MIND-BODY PROBLEM; PHILOSOPHY, WESTERN

### Bibliography

Anderson, Allan. *Zion and Pentecost: The Spirituality and Experience of Pentecostal and Zionist/ Apostolic Churches in South Africa*. Tshwane: University of South Africa Press, 2000.

Berglund, Axel-Ivar. *Zulu Thought Patterns and Symbolism*. London: Hurst, 1976.

Blakely, Thomas, et al., eds. *Religion in Africa*. London: James Currey, 1994.

Bosch, David J. *The Traditional Religions of Africa*. Study Guide MSR203. Tshwane: University of South Africa, 1975.

Daneel, Marthinus L. *Old and New in Southern Shona Independent Churches*, Vol. 2: *Church Growth*. The Hague: Moulton, 1974.

Idowu, E. Bolaji. *African Traditional Religions*. London: SCM Press, 1973.

Magesa, Laurenti. *African Religion: The Moral Traditions of Abundant Life*. New York: Orbis, 1997.

Mbiti, John S. *African Religions and Philosophy*. London: Heinemann, 1969.

Parrinder, Geoffrey. *African Traditional Religion*. London: Sheldon, 1962.

Sawyerr, Harry. *The Practice of Presence*. Grand Rapids, MI: Eerdmans, 1996.

Taylor, John V. *The Primal Vision: Christian Presence Amidst African Religions*. London: SCM Press, 1963.

Tempels, Placide. *Bantu Philosophy*. Paris: Présence Africaine, 1959.

Thorpe, S. A. *Primal Religions Worldwide*. Pretoria: University of South Africa Press, 1992.

ALLAN ANDERSON

# AFTERLIFE IN CROSS-CULTURAL PERSPECTIVE

The fear of death and the belief in life after death are universal phenomena. Social scientists have long been interested in the questions of how the similarities and the differences in the views of afterlife and the social reactions to death of different cultures be explained, and the systematic order that can be found in these similarities and differences. This entry attempts to shed light on a few anthropological, sociological aspects of the organization and distribution of these ideas in connection with the afterlife.

## Death As Empirical Taboo and the Consequent Ambivalence

Human consciousness cannot access one's own death as an inner experience. In other words, death is an ineluctable personal experience, which remains outside of an individual's self-reflection throughout his or her entire life.

However, during their lives humans might be witnesses to several deaths, for the quest of the survivors after the substance of death follows the same Baumanian "cognitive scheme" as when they think about the substance of their own mortality. "Whenever we 'imagine' ourselves as dead, we are irremovably present in the picture as those who do the imagining: our living consciousness looks at our dead bodies" (Bauman 1992, p. 15) or, in the case of someone else's death, the agonizing body of "the other."

Therefore, when speaking about the cognitive ambivalence of death, this entry refers to the simultaneous presence of (1) the feeling of uncertainty emerging from the above-mentioned empirical taboo character of death, and (2) the knowledge of its ineluctability. This constellation normally constitutes a powerful source of anxiety.

It is obvious that a number of other situations can also lead to anxieties that, at first sight, are very similar to the one emerging from the cognitive ambivalence of death. However, while such experiences can often be avoided, and while people normally have preceding experiences about their nature, by projecting these people might decrease their anxiety. The exceptionally dramatic character of the cognitive ambivalence of death emerges both from its harsh ineluctability, and from the fact that people have to completely renounce any preceding knowledge offered by self-reflection.

## The Concept of Death As a Social Product

In order to locate the problem of death in the social construction of reality in a more or less reassuring way, and thus effectively abate the anxiety emerging from the cognitive ambivalence of death, every culture is bound to attribute to it some meaning.

This meaning, accessible and perceivable by human individuals, involves constructing a unique concept of death and afterlife. Naturally, there is great difference in the intensity of the necessity of meaning attribution to death between different cultures. The construction of a death concept (partially) alleviates the empirical taboo of death, and makes it meaningful. This "slice" of knowledge as an ideology, as a "symbolic superstructure" settles on the physiological process of death, covering, reconceptualizing, and substituting it with its own meanings (Bloch 1982, p. 227).

*The necessity of anthropomorphizing.* It can hardly be argued that more or less the whole process of the construction of knowledge on the nature of death is permeated by the epistemological imperative of anthropomorphizing. The essence of this mechanism, necessarily resulting from death as an empirical taboo, is that individuals essentially perceive death and afterlife on the pattern of their life in this world, by the projection of their anthropomorphic categories and relations.

The significance of anthropomorphizing was emphasized at the beginning of the twentieth century by a number of scholars. As Robert Hertz claims, "Once the individual has surmounted death, he will not simply return to the life he has left . . . He is reunited with those who, like himself and those before him, have left this world and gone to the ancestors. He enters this mythical society of souls which each society constructs in its own image" (Hertz 1960, p. 79). Arnold van Gennep argues, "The most widespread idea is that of a world analogous to ours, but more pleasant, and of a society organized in the same way as it is here" (van Gennep 1960, p. 152).

Anthropomorphizing the ideas concerning the other world, in other words "their secularization," is present in all religious teachings with greater or less intensity. It can also be found in systems of folk beliefs that are not in close connection to churches or religious scholars. It is an obviously anthropomorphic feature of the Hungarian peasant system of folk beliefs that is far from being independent from Christian thinking. According to the members of the Hungarian peasant communities, for example, the surviving substance generally crosses a bridge over a river or a sea in order to reach the other world. Before crossing, the soul has to pay a toll. It is also an anthropomorphic

image from the same cultural sphere that on the night of the vigil the departing soul may be fed with the steam of the food placed on the windowsill of the death house, and can be clad by clothes handed down to the needy as charity. Anthropomorphic explanation is attributed to the widespread practice of placing the favorite belongings of the deceased in the tomb. These items are usually placed by the body because the deceased is supposed to be in need of them in the afterlife.

*The need to rationalize the death concept.* In most cases images concerning the other world take an institutionalized form, that is their definition, canonization, and spreading is considerably influenced by certain social institutions—generally by a church or an authorized religious scholar.

While constructing the reality enwrapping death, the assertions of these social institutions draw their legitimacy from two basic sources. The first is the anthropomorphic character of their death concept, namely that this concept promises the fulfillment of the people's natural desire for a more or less unbroken continuation of existence, which almost equals to an entire withdrawal of death as a metamorphose. The second is the worldly influence these social institutions, comprising mostly the control of the process and social spaces of socialization, which lays at the basis of the normative efficiency of these social institutions, and which thus endows the beliefs distributed by them with the appearance of reality and legitimacy.

A key duty of those constructing the death concept is, therefore, to create a feeling of probability and validity of this slice of knowledge, and to provide the continuous maintenance of the same. This can be fulfilled on the one hand by the reproduction of the normative competence laying at the basis of the legitimacy, and on the other hand by the "rationalization" or "harmonization" of the death concept—that is, by the assimilation of its elements to (1) the extension and certain metamorphoses of the normative competence; (2) the biological dimension of death; and (3) other significant social and cultural changes.

The necessity of the harmonization of some of the changes of normative competence with the death concept is well exemplified by the twentieth-century eschatological, ceremonial, and moral Christian sanctions against suicides. In the background of this change can be found both the decomposition of the (at least European) hegemony of Christian readings of reality, the pluralization of religiosity at the end of the millennium, and the exacerbation of the "open market competition" for the faithful, as well as the modification of the social judgement or representation on the "self-determination of life" (Berger 1967, pp. 138–143).

On the other hand, the social institution responsible for constructing and controlling death concepts can never lose sight of the biological aspect of life, which obviously sets limits to their reality-constructing activity: They are bound to continuously maintain the fragile harmony between the physiological dimension of mortality and the ideology "based on it," and to eliminate the discomposing elements (Bloch and Parry 1982, p. 42). The same concept is emphasized by Robert Hertz based on Melanesian observations:

> . . . the dead rise again and take up the thread of their interrupted life. But in real life one just has to accept irrevocable fact. However strong their desire, men dare not hope for themselves 'a death like that of the moon or the sun, which plunge into the darkness of Hades, to rise again in the morning, endowed with new strength.' The funeral rites cannot entirely nullify the work of death: Those who have been struck by it will return to life, but it will be in another world or as other species. (Hertz 1960, p. 74)

The aforementioned thoughts on the harmonizing of the physiological dimensions of death and the death concept can be clarified by a concrete element of custom taken from the European peasant culture. It is a well-known phenomenon in most cultures that the survivors strive to "blur" the difference between the conditions of the living and the dead, thus trying to alleviate the dramatic nature of death. It is the most practically and easily done if they endow the corpse with a number of features that only belong to the living. However, the psychological process induced by death obviously restrains these attempts. The custom of feeding the returning soul, which was present in a part of the European peasant cultures until the end of the twentieth century, provides a great example. The majority of the scholarship discussing this concept is about symbolic forms of eating/feeding

(that is, the returning soul feeds on the steam of food; the food saved for the dead during the feast or given to a beggar appear on the deceased person's table in the afterlife). Texts only occasionally mention that the dead person takes the food as the living would do. If the returning soul was supposed to eat in the same manner as the living, it would have to be endowed with features whose reality is mostly and obviously negated by experience (according to most reports the prepared food remains untouched), thus they would surely evoke suspect concerning the validity and probability of the beliefs. The soul must be fed in a primarily symbolic way because the worldly concept of eating needs to be adjusted to the physiological changes induced by death as well, so that it would also seem real and authentic for the living.

Finally, the social institution controlling the maintenance of the death concept has to harmonize its notions about the substance of death continuously with other significant slices of reality as well, namely, with some changes of society and culture. Consider the debates on reanimation and euthanasia in the second half of the twentieth century. These debates constrained the Christian pastoral power to create its own standpoints, and to partly rewrite some details of the Christian concept of death such as other-worldly punishments of the suicides.

These examples demonstrate that the complete freedom of the attribution of meaning in the construction of death concept is a mere illusion. This freedom is significantly limited by the fact that these beliefs are social products; in other words, that the factors indispensable to the successful social process of reality construction—to make a belief a solid and valid reading of the reality for the "newcomers in socialization"—are generally fairly limited.

*See also:* BUDDHISM; CHINESE BELIEFS; DEATH SYSTEM; GENNEP, ARNOLD VAN; HINDUISM; IMMORTALITY; MIND-BODY PROBLEM; NEAR-DEATH EXPERIENCES; SOCIAL FUNCTIONS OF DEATH; PHILOSOPHY, WESTERN

### Bibliography

Bauman, Zygmunt. *Mortality, Immortality and Other Life Strategies.* Cambridge, England: Polity Press, 1992.

Berger, Peter L. *The Sacred Canopy. Elements of a Sociological Theory of Religion.* New York: Doubleday, 1967.

Bloch, Maurice. "Death, Women, and Power." In Maurice Bloch and Jonathan Parry eds., *Death and the Regeneration of Life*. Cambridge: Cambridge University Press, 1982.

Bloch, Maurice, and Jonathan Parry. "Introduction." *Death and the Regeneration of Life*. Cambridge: Cambridge University Press, 1982.

Gennep, Arnold van. *The Rites of Passage*. Chicago: University of Chicago Press, 1960.

Hertz, Robert. "A Contribution to the Study of the Collective Representation of Death." In Rodney and Claudia Needham trans., *Death and the Right Hand*. New York: Free Press, 1960.

PETER BERTA

# AIDS

In June 1981 scientists published the first report of a mysterious and fatal illness that initially appeared to affect only homosexual men. Subsequent early reports speculated that this illness resulted from homosexual men's sexual activity and, possibly, recreational drug use. In the months that followed, however, this same illness was diagnosed in newborns, children, men, and women, a pattern strongly suggesting a blood-borne infection as the cause of the observed illness. The illness was initially identified by several terms (e.g., "gay bowel syndrome," "lymphadenopathy virus (LAV)," and AIDS-associated retrovirus (ARV), but by 1982 this disease came to be known as acquired immune deficiency syndrome (AIDS) because of the impact of the infectious agent, human immunodeficiency virus (HIV), on an infected person's immune system. Since about 1995 the term *HIV disease* has been used to describe the condition of HIV-infected persons from the point of early infection through the development of AIDS.

Over the next two decades AIDS became one of the leading causes of death in the United States and in other parts of the world, particularly in persons younger than forty-five years of age. Since the 1990s in the United States AIDS has come to be viewed as an "equal opportunity" disease, because it affects persons of all colors, class, and sexual orientation. Despite the evolution of major treatment advances for HIV infection and AIDS, HIV disease has been the cause of death for about 450,000 persons living in the United States since the onset of the epidemic. In addition, an estimated 800,000 to 900,000 Americans are infected with the virus that causes AIDS—and perhaps as many as 300,000 are unaware of their infection. Better treatments for HIV infection have resulted in a reduction in the number of deaths from AIDS and an increase in the number of persons living with HIV infection.

The cause of AIDS was identified in 1983 by the French researcher Luc Montagnier as a type of virus known as a "retrovirus." This newly identified retrovirus was eventually called "human immunodeficiency virus," or HIV. Scientists have established HIV as the cause of AIDS, even though a small group of individuals have questioned the link between HIV and AIDS. An HIV-infected person who meets specific diagnostic criteria (i.e., has one or more of the twenty-five AIDS-defining conditions indicative of severe immunosuppression and/or a seriously compromised immune system) is said to have AIDS, the end stage of a continuous pathogenic process. Multiple factors influence the health and functioning of HIV-infected persons. For example, some persons who meet the diagnostic criteria for AIDS may feel well and function normally, while other HIV-infected persons who do not meet the diagnostic criteria for AIDS may not feel well and have reduced functioning in one or more areas of their lives.

While drugs are now available to treat HIV infection or specific HIV-related conditions, these treatments are expensive and unobtainable to most of the world's infected individuals, the vast majority of whom live in poor, developing nations. Thus the most important and effective treatment for HIV disease is prevention of infection. Preventive measures are challenging because sexual and drug use behaviors are difficult to change; certain cultural beliefs that influence the potential acquisition of infection are not easily modified; many persons at highest risk lack access to risk-reduction education; and many persons (especially the young) deny their vulnerability to infection and engage in behaviors that place them at risk of infection.

An individual may be infected with HIV for ten years or more without symptoms of infection. During this period, however, the immune system of the untreated person deteriorates, increasing his or her risk of acquiring "opportunistic" infections and developing certain malignancies. While HIV disease is still considered a fatal condition, the development in the 1990s of antiretroviral drugs and other drugs to treat opportunistic infections lead many infected individuals to hope that they can manage their disease for an extended period of time. Unfortunately, the view that HIV disease is a "chronic" and "manageable" condition (as opposed to the reality that it is a fatal condition) may lead persons to engage in behaviors that place them at risk of infection. In the United States, for example, epidemiologists have noted an upswing in the number of HIV infections in young homosexual men who, these experts believe, engage in risky behaviors because HIV disease has become less threatening to them. These individuals are one generation removed from the homosexual men of the 1980s who saw dozens of their friends, coworkers, and neighbors die from AIDS and thus may not have experienced the pain and grief of the epidemic's first wave.

## Origin of HIV

The origin of the human immunodeficiency virus has interested scientists since the onset of the epidemic because tracing its history may provide clues about its effects on other animal hosts and on disease treatment and control. While HIV infection was first identified in homosexual men in the United States, scientists have learned from studies of stored blood samples that the infection was present in human hosts years—and perhaps decades—before 1981. However, because the number of infected individuals was small and the virus was undetectable prior to 1981, a pattern of disease went unrecognized. HIV disease may have been widespread, but unrecognized, in Africa before 1981.

While a number of theories, including controversial conspiracy theories, have been proposed to explain the origin of HIV and AIDS, strong scientific evidence supports the view that HIV represents a cross-species (zoonosis) infection evolving from a simian (chimpanzee) virus in Southwest Africa between 1915 and 1941. How this cross-species shift occurred is unclear and a topic of considerable debate. Such an infectious agent, while harmless in its natural host, can be highly lethal to its new host.

## Epidemiology of HIV Disease

Because HIV has spread to every country of the world, it is considered a pandemic. By the end of 2001 an estimated 65 million persons worldwide had been infected with HIV and of these, 25 million had died. An estimated 14,000 persons worldwide are infected every day. Most (95%) of the world's new AIDS cases are in underdeveloped countries. About 70 percent of HIV-infected persons live in sub-Saharan Africa. Globally 1 in 100 people are infected with HIV. The effects of HIV disease on the development of the world have been devastating. Millions of children in developing nations are infected and orphaned. The economies of some developing nations are in danger of collapse; and some nations risk political instability because of the epidemic.

Over the past decade an estimated 40,000 persons living in the United States have become infected with HIV every year, a figure that has remained relatively stable. Between 1981 and 2000 more than 774,000 cases of AIDS were reported to the Centers for Disease Control and Prevention (CDC). Of these cases, more than 82 percent were among males thirteen years and older, while more than 16 percent were among females thirteen years and older. Less than 2 percent of AIDS cases were among children younger than thirteen years of age. More than 430,000 persons living in the United States had died from AIDS by the end of 1999. The annual number of deaths among persons with AIDS has been decreasing because of early diagnosis and improved treatments for opportunistic infections and HIV infection.

The epidemiologic patterns of HIV disease have changed significantly since the onset of the epidemic. In 1985, for example, 65 percent of new AIDS cases were detected among men who have sex with other men (MSM). Since 1998 only about 42 percent of new AIDS cases have been detected among MSM, although the rate of new infections in this group remains high. Increasing numbers of new AIDS cases are attributed to heterosexual contact (but still only about 11 percent of the cumulative AIDS cases) and among injection drug users (about 25 percent of cumulative AIDS cases). In 2002 women, who are primarily infected through heterosexual contact or injection drug use, account for about 30 percent of all new HIV infections, a dramatic shift in the United States since 1981. In developing parts of the world men and women are infected in equal numbers.

In the United States new HIV infections and AIDS disproportionately affect minority populations and the poor. Over half (54%) of new HIV infections occur among African Americans, who represent less than 15 percent of the population. Hispanics are disproportionately affected as well. African-American women account for 64 percent (Hispanic women, 18%) of new HIV infections among women. African-American men account for about half of new HIV infections among men, with about equal numbers (18%) of new infections in white and Hispanic men. HIV infections in infants have been dramatically reduced because of the use of antiretroviral drugs by HIV-infected women who are pregnant.

**HIV Disease: The Basics**

There are two major types of human immunodeficiency virus: HIV-1 and HIV-2. HIV-1 is associated with most HIV infections worldwide except in West Africa, where HIV-2 is prevalent. Both types of viruses may be detected through available testing procedures. HIV is a retrovirus and member of a family of viruses known as lentiviruses, or "slow" viruses. These viruses typically have a long interval between initial infection and the onset of serious symptoms. Lentiviruses frequently infect cells of the immune system. Like all viruses, HIV can replicate only inside cells, taking over the cell's machinery to reproduce. HIV, once inside a cell, uses an enzyme called reverse transcriptase to convert ribonucleic acid (RNA) into deoxyribonucleic acid (DNA), which is incorporated into the host cell's genes. The steps in HIV replication include: (1) attachment and entry; (2) reverse transcription and DNA synthesis; (3) transport to nucleus; (4) integration; (5) viral transcription; (6) viral protein synthesis; (7) assembly and budding of virus; (8) release of virus; and (9) maturation. In addition to rapid replication, HIV reverse transcriptase enzyme makes many mistakes while making DNA copies from HIV RNA, resulting in multiple variants of HIV in an individual. These variants may escape destruction by antibodies or killer T cells during replication.

The immune system is complex, with many types of defenses against infections. Some parts of this system have key coordinating roles in mobilizing these defenses. One such key is the CD4+ T-lymphocyte (also known as CD4+T cell and T-helper cell), a type of lymphocyte that produces chemical "messengers." These messengers strengthen the body's immune response to infectious organisms. The cell most markedly influenced by HIV infection is the CD4+T-lymphocyte. Over time HIV destroys these CD4+T cells, thus impairing the immune response of people with HIV disease and making them more susceptible to secondary infections and some types of malignant tumors.

If HIV infection progresses untreated, the HIV-infected person's number of CD4+T-lymphocytes declines. Therefore, early in the course of HIV disease the risk for developing opportunistic infections is low because the CD4+T-lymphocytes may be nearly normal or at least adequate to provide protection against pathogenic organisms; however, in untreated individuals the risk of infection increases as the number of CD4+ cells falls. The rate of decline of CD4+T lymphocyte numbers is an important predictor of HIV-disease progression. People with high levels of HIV in their bloodstream are more likely to develop new AIDS-related symptoms or die than individuals with lower levels of virus. Thus early detection and treatment of HIV infection and routine use of blood tests to measure viral load are critical in treating HIV infection. HIV may also directly infect other body cells (e.g., those of the brain and gastrointestinal tract), resulting in a range of clinical conditions. When cells at these sites are infected with HIV, such problems as dementia and diarrhea may result; thus even if HIV-infected persons do not develop an opportunistic infection or malignancy, they may experience a spectrum of other clinical problems that require medical treatment or interfere with their quality of life.

**How Is HIV Spread?**

The major known ways by which HIV infection is spread are: (1) intimate sexual contact with an HIV-infected person; (2) exposure to contaminated blood or blood products either by direct inoculation, sharing of drug apparatus, transfusion, or other method; and (3) passage of the virus from an infected mother to her fetus or newborn in utero, during labor and delivery, or in the early newborn (including through breast-feeding). Some health care workers have become occupationally infected with HIV, but these numbers are small in light of the millions of contacts between health care workers and persons with HIV infection. Most occupationally acquired HIV infections in such workers have occurred when established "universal precautions" have not been followed.

HIV-infected blood, semen, vaginal fluid, breast milk, and other bodily fluids containing blood have been proven to have the potential to transmit HIV. While HIV has been isolated from other cells and tissues, the importance of these bodily fluids in transmission is not entirely clear. Health care workers may come into contact with other bodily fluids that can potentially transmit HIV. While HIV has been transmitted between members in a household setting, such transmission is extremely rare. There are no reports of HIV being transmitted by insects; by nonsexual bodily contact (e.g., handshaking); through closed mouth or social kissing; or by contact with saliva, tears, or sweat. One cannot be HIV-infected by donating blood. Transfusion of blood products can pose a risk of infection, but the risk is low in the United States, where all such products are carefully tested.

Several factors (called "cofactors") may play a role in the acquisition of HIV infection, influence its transmission, affect development of clinical signs and symptoms, and influence disease progression. Cofactors that have been mentioned in scientific literature include anal receptive sex resulting in repeated exposure to absorbed semen; coexistence of other infections (e.g., syphilis, hepatitis B); injection and recreational drug use; use of immunosupressant drugs (e.g., cocaine, alcohol, or amyl/butyl nitrites); douching or enemas before sexual intercourse; malnutrition; stress; age at time of seroconversion; genetic susceptibility; multiple sexual partners; and presence of genital ulcers.

**Preventing HIV Infection**

HIV infection is almost 100 percent preventable. HIV infection may be prevented by adhering to the following measures:

- engaging in one-partner sex where both participants are HIV-negative and are maintaining a sexual relationship that only involves those two participants;

- using latex or polyurethane condoms properly every time during sexual intercourse, including oral sex;

- not sharing needles and syringes used to inject drugs or for tattooing or body piercing;

- not sharing razors or toothbrushes;

- being tested for HIV if one is pregnant or considering pregnancy;

- prohibiting oneself from breast-feeding if HIV-positive; and

- calling the CDC National AIDS Hotline at 1-800-342-AIDS (2437) for more information about AIDS prevention and treatment (or by contacting www.cdc.gov/hiv to access the CDC Division of HIV/AIDS for information).

**What Happens after Infection with HIV?**

Following infection with HIV the virus infects a large number of CD4+ cells, replicating and spreading widely, and producing an increase in viral burden in blood. During this acute stage of infection, which usually occurs within the first few weeks after contact with the virus, viral particles spread throughout the body, seeding various organs, particularly the lymphoid organs (lymph nodes, spleen, tonsils, and adenoids). In addition, the number of CD4+ T cells in the bloodstream decreases by 20 to 40 percent. Infected persons may also lose HIV-specific CD4+ T cell responses that normally slow the replication of viruses in this early stage. Within a month of exposure to HIV the infected individual's immune system fights back with killer T cells (CD8+ T cells) and B-cell antibodies that reduce HIV levels, allowing for a rebound of CD4+ T cells to 80 to 90 percent of their original level. The HIV-infected person may then remain free of HIV-related symptoms for years while HIV continues to replicate in the lymphoid organs seeded during the acute phase of infection. Also at this point many infected persons experience an illness (called "primary" or "acute" infection) that mimics mononucleosis or flu and usually lasts two to three weeks.

In untreated HIV-infected persons, the length of time for progression to disease varies widely. Most (80 to 90 percent) HIV-infected persons develop AIDS within ten years of initial infection; another 5 to 10 percent of infected persons progress to AIDS within two to three years of HIV infection; about 5 percent are generally asymptomatic for seven to ten years following infection and have no decline in CD4+T lymphocyte counts. Efforts have been made to understand those factors that affect disease progression, including viral characteristics and genetic factors. Scientists are also keenly interested in those individuals who have repeated exposures to HIV (and may have been acutely infected at some point) but show no clinical evidence of chronic HIV infection.

**Testing and Counseling**

Testing for HIV infection has complex social, ethical, legal, and health implications. HIV testing is done for several reasons: to identify HIV-infected persons who may benefit from early medical intervention; to identify HIV-negative persons who may benefit from risk reduction counseling; to provide for epidemiological monitoring; to engage in public health planning. Individuals who seek HIV testing expect that test results will remain confidential, although this cannot be entirely guaranteed. Anonymous testing is widely available and provides an additional measure of confidentiality.

HIV testing has been recommended for those who consider themselves at risk of HIV disease, including:

- women of childbearing age at risk of infection;

- persons attending clinics for sexually transmitted disease and drug abuse;

- spouses and sex- or needle-sharing partners of injection drug users;

- women seeking family planning services;

- persons with tuberculosis;

- individuals who received blood products between 1977 and mid-1995; and

- others, such as individuals with symptoms of HIV-related conditions; sexually active adolescents; victims of sexual assault; and inmates in correctional facilities.

Detection of HIV antibodies is the most common approach to determine the presence of HIV infection, although other testing approaches can detect the virus itself. Testing for HIV infection is usually accomplished through standard or rapid

detection (results are obtained in five to thirty minutes) of anti-HIV antibodies in blood and saliva. The most common types of antibody test for HIV serodiagnosis include the enzyme-linked immunosorbent assay (ELISA), the Western blot, immunofluorescence, radioimmuno-precipitation, and hemagglutination. These tests do not directly measure the presence of the virus but rather the antibodies formed to the various viral proteins. One home testing kit—the Home Access HIV-1 Test System—is approved by the U.S. Food and Drug Administration. Oral and urine-based tests are available for rapid screening in medical offices but are typically followed up by one or more tests for confirmation. Most tests used to detect HIV infection are highly reliable in determining the presence of HIV infection, but false-positive and false-negative results have been documented by Niel Constantine and other health care professionals.

Testing for HIV infection should always include pre- and posttest counseling. Guidelines for such testing have been published by the CDC. Pretest counseling should include information about the test and test results, HIV infection, and AIDS; performance of a risk assessment and provision of information about risk and risk reduction behaviors associated with the transmission of HIV; discussion about the consequences (i.e., medical care, pregnancy, employment, insurance) of a positive or negative result for the person being tested and for others (family, sexual partner(s), friends); and discussion about the need for appropriate follow-up in the event of positive test results. Post–test counseling is dependent upon test results, but generally includes provision of test results, emotional support, education, and, when appropriate, referral for medical or other forms of assistance.

**Clinical Manifestations of HIV Disease**

The clinical manifestations of HIV vary greatly among individuals and depend upon individual factors and the effectiveness of medical intervention, among other factors. Primary infection may also offer the first opportunity to initiate antiretroviral therapy, although all experts do not agree that such therapy should be initiated at this stage of the infection. The symptom-free period of time following primary infection has been extended in many infected persons by the introduction of highly active antiretroviral therapy (HAART). Many HIV-infected persons, especially those who do not

*Patchwork of the 1996 AIDS Memorial Quilt covers the grass of the Mall in Washington, D.C. Since the onset of the epidemic, HIV, the virus that causes AIDS, has caused the death of an estimated 450,000 people living in the United States.* PAUL MARGOLIES

receive antiretroviral therapy, those who respond poorly to such therapy, and those who experience adverse reactions to these drugs, will develop one or more opportunistic conditions, malignancies, or other conditions over the course of their disease.

## Opportunistic Infections

Prior to the HIV epidemic, many opportunistic infections (OIs) seen in HIV-infected persons were not commonly encountered in the health care community. Many of the organisms responsible for these OIs are everywhere (ubiquitous) in the environment and cause little or no disease in persons with competent immune systems. However, in those who are immunocompromised, these organisms can cause serious and life-threatening disease. Since the introduction of HAART the incidence of HIV-related opportunistic infections and malignancies has been declining. The epidemiological patterns of at least some of these opportunistic diseases vary by region and country. Ideally,

treatment of OIs is aimed at prevention of infections, treatment of active infections, and prevention or recurrences. Over the course of the HIV epidemic several new drugs and treatment approaches aimed at OIs have been introduced or refined. Guidelines have also been developed concerning the prevention of exposure to opportunistic pathogens.

Opportunistic infections affecting HIV-infected persons fall into four major categories:

1. Parasitic/Protozoa infections—cryptosporidiosis, toxoplasmosis, isosporiasis, and microsporidiosis.

2. Fungal infections—pneumocystosis, cryptococcus, candidiasis (thrush), histoplasmosis, and coccidioidomycosis.

3. Bacterial infections—*mycobacterium avium* complex (MAC), *mycobacterium tuberculosis* (TB), and salmanellosis.

4. Viral infections—cytomegalovirus, herpes simplex types 1 and 2, and varicella-zoster virus (shingles), cytomegalovirus, and hepatitis.

Parasitic infections can cause significant illness and death among HIV-infected persons. Fungal diseases may vary widely among persons with HIV disease because many are commonly found in certain parts of the world and less common in others. Bacterial infections are also seen as important causes of illness and death in HIV-infected persons. Viral infections are common in this population and are often difficult to treat because of the limited number of antiviral drugs that are available. Persons with HIV disease often suffer from recurrences of viral infections. Those whose immune systems are severely compromised may have multiple infections simultaneously.

Two categories of malignancies that are often seen in persons with HIV disease are Kaposi's sarcoma (KS) and HIV-associated lymphomas. Prior to the HIV epidemic KS was rarely seen in the United States. Since the mid-1990s, researchers have also suggested an association between cervical and anal cancers. When cancers develop in a person with HIV disease these conditions tend to be aggressive and resistant to treatment.

In addition to the opportunistic infections and malignancies, persons with HIV disease may experience Wasting syndrome and changes in mental functioning. Wasting syndrome is a weight loss of at least 10 percent in the presence of diarrhea or chronic weakness and documented fever for at least thirty days that is not attributable to a concurrent condition other than HIV infection. Multiple factors are known to cause this weight loss and muscle wasting, including loss of appetite, decreased oral intake, and nausea and vomiting. Wasting is associated with rapid decline in overall health, increased risk of hospitalization, development of opportunistic infection, decreased quality of life, and decreased survival. Interventions include management of infections, oral nutritional supplements, use of appetite stimulants, management of diarrhea and fluid loss, and exercise.

AIDS dementia complex (ADC) is a complication of late HIV infection and the most common cause of neurological dysfunction in adults with HIV disease. Its cause is believed to be direct infection of the central nervous system by HIV. This condition can impair the intellect and alter motor performance and behavior. Early symptoms include difficulty in concentration, slowness in thinking and response, memory impairment, social withdrawal, apathy, personality changes, gait changes, difficulty with motor movements, and poor balance and coordination. As ADC advances, the affected person's cognitive functioning and motor skills worsen. Affected persons may enter a vegetative state requiring total care and environmental control. Treatment focuses on supportive care measures and aggressive use of HAART.

Finally, persons with HIV disease frequently experience mental disorders, especially anxiety and depression. These are typically treated by standard drug therapy and psychotherapy. Persons with HIV disease are also at greater risk of social isolation, which can have a negative impact on their mental and physical health.

## Management of HIV Disease

Better understanding of HIV pathogenesis, better ways to measure HIV in the blood, and improved drug treatments have greatly improved the outlook for HIV-infected persons. Medical management focuses on the diagnosis, prevention, and treatment of HIV infection and related opportunistic infections and malignancies. HIV-infected persons who seek care from such providers should expect to receive compassionate and expert care in such settings. Management of HIV disease includes:

- early detection of HIV infection;
- early and regular expert medical evaluation of clinical status;
- education to prevent further spread of HIV infection and to maintain a healthy lifestyle;
- administration of antiretroviral drugs;
- provision of drugs to prevent the emergence of specific opportunistic infections;
- provision of emotional/social support;
- medical management of HIV-related symptoms;
- early diagnosis and appropriate management of OIs and malignancies; and
- referral to medical specialists when indicated.

The mainstay of medical treatment for HIV-infected persons is the use of antiretroviral drugs. Goals of antiretroviral therapy are to prolong life and improve quality of life; to suppress virus below limit of detection for as long as possible; to optimize and extend usefulness of available therapies; and to minimize drug toxicity and manage side effects.

Two major classes of antiretroviral drugs are available for use in the treatment of HIV infection—reverse transcriptase inhibitors (RTIs) and protease inhibitors (PIs). These drugs act by inhibiting viral replication. RTIs interfere with reverse transcriptase, an enzyme essential in transcribing RNA into DNA in the HIV replication cycle. Protease inhibitor drugs work by inhibiting the HIV protease enzyme, thus preventing cleavage and release of mature, infectious viral particles. Dozens of other drugs that may become available in the next few years to treat HIV infection are under development and testing. Because of the high costs of these drugs, individuals needing assistance may gain access to HIV-related medications through the AIDS Drug Assistance Program (ADAP) and national pharmaceutical industry patient assistance/expanded access programs.

Panels of HIV disease experts have released guidelines for the use of antiretroviral agents in infected persons. The guidelines, which are revised periodically to reflect rapidly evolving knowledge relative to treatment, are widely available on the

Internet. These guidelines have greatly assisted practitioners to provide a higher standard of care for persons living with HIV disease.

Viral load tests and CD4+ T-cell counts are used to guide antiretroviral drug treatment, which is usually initiated when the CD4+ T-cell count falls below 500 and/or there is evidence of symptomatic disease (e.g., AIDS, thrush, unexplained fever). Some clinicians recommend antiretroviral drug treatment to asymptomatic HIV-infected persons.

Because HIV replicates and mutates rapidly, drug-resistance is a challenge, forcing clinicians to alter drug regimens when these instances occur. Inadequate treatment, poor adherence, and interruptions in treatment increase drug resistance. This resistance can be delayed by the use of combination regimens to achieve CD4+T-cell counts below the level of detection. Careful adherence to prescribed HAART regimens is crucial in treatment and many interventions have been tried to improve patient adherence. Because some HIV-infected persons are taking multiple doses of multiple drugs daily, adherence challenges patients and clinicians alike. Once antiretroviral therapy has been initiated patients remain on this therapy continuously, although intermittent drug treatment is being studied. Because persons living with HIV disease may take numerous drugs simultaneously, the potential for drug interactions and adverse reactions is high. These persons typically have a higher incidence of adverse reactions to commonly used drugs than do non-HIV-infected patients.

In the United States HIV/AIDS is an epidemic primarily affecting men who have sex with men and ethnic/racial minorities. Homophobia, poverty, homelessness, racism, lack of education, and lack of access to health care greatly influence testing, treatment, and prevention strategies. While an effective vaccine is crucial to the prevention of HIV, efforts to develop such a vaccine have been unsuccessful to date; therefore, current and future prevention efforts, including behavior modification interventions, must be aimed at ethnic minorities, men who have sex with men, and other high-risk populations. Finally, a safe, effective antiviral product that women can use during sexual intercourse would greatly reduce their risk of infection.

*See also:* CAUSES OF DEATH; PAIN AND PAIN MANAGEMENT; SUICIDE INFLUENCES AND FACTORS: PHYSICAL ILLNESS; SYMPTOMS AND SYMPTOM MANAGEMENT

*Bibliography*

Adinolfi, Anthony J. "Symptom Management in HIV/AIDS." In Jerry Durham and Felissa Lashley eds., *The Person with HIV/AIDS: Nursing Perspectives.* New York: Springer, 2000.

Berger, Barbara, and Vida M. Vizgirda. "Preventing HIV Infection." In Jerry Durham and Felissa Lashley eds., *The Person with HIV/AIDS: Nursing Perspectives.* New York: Springer, 2000.

Centers for Disease Control and Prevention. *HIV/AIDS Surveillance Supplemental Report, 2000.* Rockville, MD: Author, 2001.

Centers for Disease Control and Prevention. "HIV/AIDS—United States, 1981–2000." *Morbidity and Mortality Weekly Report* 50 (2001):430–434.

Cohen, Philip T., and Mitchell H. Katz. "Long-Term Primary Care Management of HIV Disease." In Philip T. Cohen, Merle A. Sande, and Paul Volberding, et al. eds, *The AIDS Knowledge Base: A Textbook on HIV Disease from the University of California, San Francisco and San Francisco General Hospital.* New York: Lippincott Williams & Wilkins, 1999.

Coleman, Rebecca, and Christopher Holtzer. "HIV-Related Drug Information." In Philip T. Cohen, Merle A. Sande, and Paul Volberding, et al. eds., *The AIDS Knowledge Base: A Textbook on HIV Disease from the University of California, San Francisco and San Francisco General Hospital.* New York: Lippincott Williams & Wilkins, 1999.

Corless, Inge. "HIV/AIDS." In Felissa Lashley and Jerry Durham eds., *Emerging Infectious Diseases.* New York: Springer, 2002.

Deeks, Steven, and Paul Volberding. "Antiretroviral Therapy for HIV Disease." In Philip T. Cohen, Merle A. Sande, and Paul Volberding, et al. eds., *The AIDS Knowledge Base: A Textbook on HIV Disease from the University of California, San Francisco and San Francisco General Hospital.* New York: Lippincott Williams & Wilkins, 1999.

Erlen, Judith A., and Mary P. Mellors. "Adherence to Combination Therapy in Persons Living with HIV: Balancing the Hardships and the Blessings." *Journal of the Association of Nurses in AIDS Care* 10, no. 4 (1999):75–84.

Ferri, Richard. "Testing and Counseling." In Jerry Durham and Felissa Lashley eds., *The Person with HIV/AIDS: Nursing Perspectives.* New York: Springer, 2000.

Horton, Richard. "New Data Challenge OPV Theory of AIDS Origin." *Lancet* 356 (2000):1005.

Kahn, James O., and Bruce D. Walker. "Primary HIV Infection: Guides to Diagnosis, Treatment, and Management." In Philip T. Cohen, Merle A. Sande, and Paul Volberding, et al. eds., *The AIDS Knowledge Base: A Textbook on HIV Disease from the University of California, San Francisco and San Francisco General Hospital.* New York: Lippincott Williams & Wilkins, 1999.

Lamptey, Peter R. "Reducing Heterosexual Transmission of HIV in Poor Countries." *British Medical Journal* 324 (2002):207–211.

Lashley, Felissa. "The Clinical Spectrum of HIV Infection and Its Treatment." In Jerry Durham and Felissa Lashley eds., *The Person with HIV/AIDS: Nursing Perspectives.* New York: Springer, 2000.

Lashley, Felissa. "The Etiology, Epidemiology, Transmission, and Natural History of HIV Infection and AIDS." In Jerry Durham and Felissa Lashley eds., *The Person with HIV/AIDS: Nursing Perspectives.* New York: Springer, 2000.

Osmond, Dennis H. "Classification, Staging, and Surveillance of HIV Disease." In P. T. Cohen, Merle A. Sande, and Paul Volberding, et al. eds, *The AIDS Knowledge Base: A Textbook on HIV Disease from the University of California, San Francisco and San Francisco General Hospital.* New York: Lippincott Williams & Wilkins, 1999.

Wightman, Susan, and Michael Klebert. "The Medical Treatment of HIV Disease." In Jerry Durham and Felissa Lashley eds., *The Person with HIV/AIDS: Nursing Perspectives.* New York: Springer, 2000.

Young, John. "The Replication Cycle of HIV-1." In Philip T. Cohen, Merle A. Sande, Paul Volberding, et al. eds, *The AIDS Knowledge Base: A Textbook on HIV Disease from the University of California, San Francisco and San Francisco General Hospital.* New York: Lippincott Williams & Wilkins, 1999.

Zeller, Janice, and Barbara Swanson. "The Pathogenesis of HIV Infection." In Jerry Durham and Felissa Lashley eds., *The Person with HIV/AIDS: Nursing Perspectives.* New York: Springer, 2000.

*Internet Resources*

Centers for Disease Control and Prevention (CDC). "Basic Statistics." In the CDC [web site]. Available from www.cdc.gov/hiv/stats.htm#cumaids.

Centers for Disease Control and Prevention (CDC). "Recommendations to Help Patients Avoid Exposure to Opportunistic Pathogens." In the CDC [web site]. Available from www.cdc.gov/epo/mmwr/preview/mmwrhtml/rr4810a2.htm.

Centers for Disease Control and Prevention (CDC). "Revised Guidelines for HIV Counseling, Testing, and Referral." In the CDC [web site]. Available from www.cdc.gov/hiv/ctr/default.htm.

Constantine, Niel. "HIV Antibody Assays." In the InSite Knowledge Base [web site]. Available from http://hivinsite.ucsf.edu/InSite.jsp?page=kb-02-02-01#S6.1.2X.

Department of Health and Human Services. "Guidelines for the Use of Antiretroviral Agents in HIV-Infected Adults and Adolescents." In the HIV/AIDS Treatment Information Service [web site]. Available from www.hivatis.org/trtgdlns.html.

UNAIDS. "AIDS Epidemic Update—December 2001." In the UNAIDS [web site]. Available from www.unaids.org/epidemic_update/report_dec01/index.html.

United States Census Bureau. "HIV/AIDS Surveillance." In the U.S. Census Bureau [web site]. Available from www.census.gov/ipc/www/hivaidsn.html.

JERRY D. DURHAM

# ANIMAL COMPANIONS

There are more than 353 million animal companions in the United States. More than 61 percent of households own a pet; 39 percent have dogs as pets; and 32 percent have cats. In addition to dogs and cats, other animals considered animal companions—that is, pets—are birds, fish, rabbits, hamsters, and reptiles. Every year, millions of pets die from natural causes or injury, or are euthanized. Because many people form deep and significant emotional attachments to their pets, at any given time the number of people suffering from grief in relation to the loss of a pet is quite high. Pet loss has been shown to potentially have a serious impact on an owner's physical and emotional wellbeing. Part of what accounts for the profoundness of the human reaction can best be explained through a discussion of the bond between animal and human.

Factors contributing to the formation of bonds between people and their pets include companionship, social support, and the need for attachment. Pets often become active members of a household, participating in diverse activities with the owners. Indeed, according to the grief expert

Therese Rando, pets have some outstanding qualities as a partner in a relationship. "They are loyal, uncritical, nonjudgmental, relatively undemanding, and usually always there. Many of them are delighted merely to give and receive affection and companionship. They can be intuitive, caring and engaging, often drawing us out of ourselves" (Rando 1988, p. 59). Understandably, therefore, when the bond between pet and owner is broken, a grief response results.

Grief is defined as "the complex emotional, mental, social, and physical response to the death of a loved one" (Kastenbaum 1998, p. 343). Rando adds that grief is a process of reactions to the experience of loss: It has a beginning and an end. "Research and clinical evidence reveal that in many cases the loss of a pet is as profound and far-reaching as the loss of a human family member" (Rando 1988, p. 60), with grief, sometimes protracted and crippling, as an outcome. However, there is generally little social recognition of this form of loss. Despite the fact that the resolution of the grief often surpasses the length of time seen with human losses, the easy accessibility and replacement of the lost animal often provokes hidden grief reactions. Grief may also be hidden because of the owner's reluctance and shame over feeling so intensely over a nonhuman attachment. People who have lost a pet may repress their feelings, rationalize or minimize their loss, or use denial as a way to cope. The intensity and stages of grieving depend on various factors, including the age of the owner, the level and duration of the attachment between pet and owner, the owner's life situation, and the circumstances surrounding the loss.

In 1998 social worker JoAnn Jarolmen studied pet loss and grief, comparing the reactions of 106 children, 57 adolescents, and 270 adults who had lost pets within a twelve-month period. In her study, the scores for grief for the children were significantly higher than for the adults. The fact that children grieved more than adults over the loss of a pet was surprising being that children seem more distractible and are used to the interchangeability of objects. The grief score was higher for the entire sample of the one-to-four-month group—after death—than the five-to-eight-month group. Similarly, in 1994 John Archer and George Winchester studied eighty-eight participants who had lost a pet, and found that 25 percent showed signs of depression, anger, and anxiety a year after

the loss. Grief was more pronounced among those living alone, owners who experienced a sudden death, and those who were strongly attached to their pets. Pet owners who are elderly may suffer especially profound grief responses because the presence of a companion animal can make the difference between some form of companionship and loneliness.

Within a family, the loss of a pet can have a significant impact. Pets frequently function as interacting members of the family; hence, the absence of the pet will affect the behavior patterns of the family members with the potential for a shift in roles.

Grief from pet loss is not confined to owners. For veterinarians, the option of euthanasia places the doctor in the position of being able to end the lives, legally and humanely, of animals they once saved. As the veterinarian injects the drugs that end the suffering of the animal, he or she is involved in the planned death of a creature, perhaps one dearly loved by the owner(s). In the presence of death and grief, the veterinarian is often placed in a highly stressful situation.

For people with disabilities, the loss of a pet takes on another dimension because the animal not only provides companionship but is relied on to assist its owner with a level of independence and functioning. For this population, the necessity to replace the animal is paramount to maintain a level of functioning; the grief over the loss may become secondary. Counseling may be important to help the owner remember the unique qualities of the deceased animal as he or she works to train a new one.

When to replace the animal is often a dilemma. Quickly replacing a pet is rarely helpful and does not accelerate the grieving process. The loss of a pet is significant and immediate replacement tends to negate the healing aspects of grief.

Counseling for grieving pet owners should be considered when individuals experience a prolonged period of grief with attendant depression, when it is the first experience of death (usually for young children), and when a family seems to be struggling to realign itself after the loss. The focus of counseling is to help clients cope with the loss through discussion of their feelings, fostering of remembrances, and support of positive coping mechanisms.

*See also:* GRIEF: OVERVIEW; HUNTING

## Bibliography

Archer, John. *The Nature of Grief*. London: Routledge, 1999.

Archer, John, and George Winchester. "Bereavement Following the Loss of a Pet." *British Journal of Psychology* 85 (1994):259–271.

Association for Pet Product Manufacturers of America. *Annual Survey of Pet Products and Owners*. Greenwich, CT: Author, 2000–2001.

Jarolmen, JoAnn. "A Comparison of the Grief Reaction of Children and Adults: Focusing on Pet Loss and Bereavement." *Omega: The Journal of Death and Dying* 37, no. 2 (1998):133–150.

Kastenbaum, Robert. *Death, Society and Human Experience*, 6th edition. Boston: Allyn & Bacon, 1998.

Lagoni, Laurel, Carolyn Butler, and Suzanne Hetts. *The Human-Animal Bond and Grief*. Philadelphia: W.B. Saunders, 1994.

Quackenbush, John E. *When Your Pet Dies: How to Cope with Your Feelings*. New York: Simon & Schuster, 1985.

Rando, Therese A. *How to Go On Living When Someone You Love Dies*. New York: Bantam Books, 1988.

Rando, Therese A. *Grief, Dying, and Death*. Champaign, IL: Research Press, 1984.

Rynearson, E. K. "Humans and Pets and Attachment." *British Journal of Psychiatry* 133 (1978):550–555.

Sharkin, Bruce, and Audrey S. Barhrick. "Pet Loss: Implications for Counselors." *Journal of Counseling and Development* 68 (1990):306–308.

Weisman, Avery S. "Bereavement and Companion Animals." *Omega: The Journal of Death and Dying* 22, no. 4 (1991):241–248.

JOAN BEDER

# ANTHROPOLOGICAL PERSPECTIVE

It is rather hard, if not impossible, to answer the question of how long anthropology has existed. Should social scientists consider anthropology the detailed descriptions appearing in the work of ancient and medieval historians—which deal with the culture of certain ethnic groups, such as their death rites, eating habits, and dressing customs—just as they consider the fieldwork reports based on long-term participating observations published in the twenty-first century? Although it is not easy to find the unambiguous answer to this question, it is obvious that no work in history of science can lack a starting point, which helps its readers pin down and comprehend its argumentation. During the mid-1800s anthropology first appeared as a "new" independent discipline in the fast-changing realm of social sciences.

## The Evolutionist Perspective

Searching the origins of society and religion, writing the "history of their evolution," seemed to be the most popular topic of nineteenth-century anthropology. Death and the belief in the soul and the spirits play important roles in the evolutionist-intellectual theories of origin written by Edward Burnett Tylor in 1871 and other scholars of the nineteenth century.

Tylor assumed that in the background of the appearance of the soul beliefs, there may be such extraordinary and incomprehensible experiences as dreams and visions encountered in various states of altered consciousness, and the salient differences between the features of living and dead bodies. In his view, "the ancient savage philosophers" were only able to explain these strange, worrying experiences by considering humans to be a dual unity consisting of not only a body but of an entity that is able to separate from the body and continue its existence after death (Tylor 1972, p. 11). Tylor argues that this concept of spirit was later extended to animals, plants, and objects, and it developed into "the belief in spiritual beings" that possess supernatural power (polytheism) (ibid., p. 10). Eventually it led to monotheism. Tylor, who considered "the belief in spiritual beings," which he called animism, the closest definition and starting point of the concept of religion, argues that religion and notion of death were brought into being by human worries concerning death.

Tylor's theory was attacked primarily because he did not attribute the origin of religion to the interference of supernatural powers but rather to the activity of human logic. He was also criticized on the grounds that a part of his concept was highly speculative and unhistorical: He basically intended to reconstruct the evolution of religion from contemporary ethnographic data and through the deduction of his own hypotheses. Although most of these critiques were correct, Tylor can only partly be grouped among the "armchair anthropologists" of his time.

Two other individuals—Johann Jakob Bachofen and James G. Frazer—are also acknowledged as pioneers during this early period of anthropology. Bachofen prepared a valuable analysis of the few motives of wall paintings of a Roman columbarium in 1859 such as black-and-white painted mystery eggs. He was among the first authors to point out that the symbolism of fertility and rebirth is closely connected with death rites. Based on his monumental collection of ethnographic data from several cultures, Frazer, in the early twentieth century and again in the 1930s, intended to prove that the fear of the corpse and the belief in the soul and life after death is a universal phenomenon.

## The French Sociology School

The perspective of the authors of the French sociology school differed considerably from the primarily psychology-oriented, individual-focused views of these evolutionist-intellectual anthropologists. Émile Durkheim and his followers (including Robert Hertz and Marcell Mauss) studied human behavior in a "sociological framework," and focused their attention primarily on the question of societal solidarity, on the study of the social impact of rites, and on the various ties connecting individuals to society. In other words, they investigated the mechanisms by which societies sustain and reproduce themselves.

In his monumental work *The Elementary Forms of the Religious Life* (1915), Durkheim argues that the most important function of death rites and religion in general is to reaffirm societal bonds and the social structure itself. In his view, a society needs religion (totem as a sacral object in this case) to represent itself in it, and it serves to help society to reproduce itself. In his other work of the same subject (*Suicide: A Study in Sociology,* 1952) Durkheim studies the social and cultural determination of a phenomenon that is considered primarily psychological.

However, it was undoubtedly the 1907 work of Durkheim's disciple, Robert Hertz, that has had the most significant impact on contemporary anthropological research concerning death. Hertz primarily built his theory on Indonesian data, and focused his attention on the custom of the secondary burial.

Hertz discovered exciting parallels among (1) the condition of the dead body, (2) the fate of the departing soul, and (3) the taboos and restricting measures concerning the survivors owning to their ritual pollution. In his view, where the custom of the secondary burial is practiced, the moment of death can be considered the starting point for these three phenomena: the corpse becomes unanimated and the process of decomposition starts; the taboos concerning survivors become effective; and the soul starts its existence in the intermediary realm between the world of the living and the deceased ancestors. (In this liminal state of being the soul is considered to be homeless and malignant.) This intermediary period ends with the rite of the secondary burial, which involves the exhumation of the corpse and its burial in a new, permanent tomb. This rite also removes the taboos of the survivors, thus cleansing them from the pollution caused by the occurrence of the death. The same rite signals, or performs the soul's initiation to the realm of the ancestors, by it the soul takes its permanent status in the other world.

Hertz argues that the most important function of these death rites is to promote the reorganization of the social order and the restoration of faith in the permanent existence of the society, which had been challenged by the death of the individual. In addition to these functions, they serve the confirmation of solidarity among the survivors.

The utmost merit of Hertz's work is undoubtedly the novelty of his theoretical presuppositions. Like Durkheim, he concentrated on the social aspects of death and not on its biological or psychological sides. Hertz was among the first to point out how human death thoughts and rituals are primarily social products, integrated parts of the society's construction of reality that reflect the sociocultural context (religion, social structure). According to Hertz, the deceased enters the mythic world of souls "which each society constructs in its own image" (Hertz 1960, p. 79).

Hertz emphasized that social and emotional reactions following death are also culturally determined, and called attention to numerous social variables that might considerably influence the intensity of these reactions in different cultures (i.e., the deceased person's gender, age, social status, and relation to power).

In one and the same society the emotion aroused by death varies extremely in intensity according to the social status of the deceased, and may even in certain cases be entirely lacking. At the death of a chief, or of a man of high rank, a true panic sweeps over the group . . . On the contrary, the death of a stranger, a slave, or a child will go almost unnoticed; it will arouse no emotion, occasion no ritual. *(Hertz 1960, p. 76)*

From the commentaries on Hertz's work, only one critical remark needs mentioned, which calls attention to the problem of exceptions and the dangers of the overgeneralization of the model of secondary burials.

## Arnold van Gennep and the Model of the *Rites of Passage*

In his book *The Rites of Passage* (1960), Arnold van Gennep places the primary focus on rites, in which individuals—generally with the proceeding of time—step from one social position/status to another. (Such events are birth, various initiations, marriage, and death.) The author considers these "border-crossings" crisis situations.

Van Gennep claims that these rites accompanying transitions generally consist of three structural elements: rites of separation—preparing the dying person, giving the last rite; rites of transition—for example, the final burial of the corpse in the cemetery or the group of rites that serve to keep the haunting souls away; and the rites of incorporation—a mass said for the salvation of the deceased person's soul. In the case of a death event, the individual leaves a preliminary state (living) by these rites and through a liminal phase in which the deceased usually is in a temporary state of existence between the world of the living and the dead), and reaches a post-liminary state (dead).

Van Gennep argues that these rites socially validate such social/biological changes as birth, marriage, and death. They also canalize the accompanying emotional reactions into culturally elaborated frames, thus placing them under partial social control, consequently making these critical situations more predictable. His theory served as a starting point and pivot of several further rite studies (including the liminality theory of Victor Turner in 1969), inspired the study of the rites' symbolic

meanings, and promoted research that investigated the ways of an individual's social integration.

## The British Functionalist School

While the evolutionist-intellectual anthropologists were interested in finding the reason of the origin of religion and the followers of the French sociology school concentrated on the social determination of attitudes concerning death, members of the British functionalist school were concerned with the relation of death rites and the accompanying emotional reactions. They focused their attention on the question of the social loss caused by death (such as the redistribution of status and rights).

The two most significant authors of this school had opposing views of the relationship between religion/rites and the fear of death. Bronislaw Malinowski considered the anxiety caused by the rationally uncontrollable happenings as the basic motivation for the emergence of religious faith. He suggested that religion was not born of speculation and illusion,

but rather out of the real tragedies of human life, out of the conflict between human plans and realities. . . . The existence of strong personal attachments and the fact of death, which of all human events is the most upsetting and disorganizing to man's calculations, are perhaps the main sources of religious belief. *(Malinowski 1972, p. 71)*

In his view the most significant function of religion is to ease the anxiety accompanying the numerous crises of a life span, particularly the issue of death.

However, according to Arnold Radcliffe-Brown in the case of certain rites, "It would be easy to maintain . . . that they give men fears and anxieties from which they would otherwise be free—the fear of black magic or of spirits, fear of God, of the devil, of Hell" (Radcliffe Brown 1972, p. 81). It was George C. Homans in 1941 who succeeded in bringing these two competing theories into a synthesis, claiming that they are not exclusive but complementary alternatives.

## From the 1960s to Present

There has been continual interest in the anthropological study of death, marked by the series of books and collections of studies published. Among these works, scholars note the 1982 collection of studies edited by Maurice Bloch and Jonathan Parry that intends to provide a comprehensive coverage of one single area: It studies how the ideas of fertility and rebirth are represented in the death rites of various cultures. The equally valuable book *Celebrations of Death: The Anthropology of Mortuary Ritual* (1991) by Richard Huntington and Peter Metcalf, which relies extensively on the authors' field experience, discusses the most important questions of death culture research (emotional reaction to death; symbolic associations of death, etc.) by presenting both the corresponding established theories and their critiques.

*See also:* AFTERLIFE IN CROSS-CULTURAL PERSPECTIVE; CANNIBALISM; DURKHEIM, ÉMILE; GENNEP, ARNOLD VAN; HERTZ, ROBERT; HUMAN REMAINS; OMENS; RITES OF PASSAGE; SACRIFICE; VOODOO

### *Bibliography*

Bachofen, Johann Jakob. "An Essay on Ancient Mortuary Symbolism." In Ralph Manheim trans., *Myth, Religion, and Mother Right*. London: Routledge & Kegan Paul, 1967.

Bloch, Maurice, and Jonathan Parry, eds. *Death and the Regeneration of Life*. Cambridge: Cambridge University Press, 1982.

Durkheim, Émile. *Suicide: A Study in Sociology*. London: Routledge & Kegan Paul, 1952

Durkheim, Émile. *The Elementary Forms of the Religious Life*. London: George Allen & Unwin, 1915.

Frazer, James George. *The Belief in Immortality and the Worship of the Dead*. 3 vols. London: Dawsons, 1968.

Frazer, James George. *The Fear of the Dead in Primitive Religion*. 3 vols. New York: Arno Press, 1977.

Gennep, Arnold van. *The Rites of Passage,* translated by Monika B. Vizedom and Gabrielle L. Caffee. Chicago: Chicago University Press, 1960.

Hertz, Robert. "A Contribution to the Study of the Collective Representation of Death." *Death and the Right Hand,* translated by Rodney and Claudia Needham. Glencoe, IL: Free Press, 1960.

Homans, George C. "Anxiety and Ritual: The Theories of Malinowski and Radcliffe-Brown." *American Anthropologist* XLIII (1941):164–172.

Huntington, Richard, and Peter Metcalf. *Celebrations of Death: The Anthropology of Mortuary Ritual,* 2nd edition. Cambridge: Cambridge University Press, 1991.

Malinowski, Bronislaw. "The Role of Magic and Religion." In William A. Lessa and Evon Z. Vogt eds., *Reader in Comparative Religion: An Anthropological Approach*. New York: Harper and Row, 1972.

Malinowski, Bronislaw. *Magic, Science, and Religion*. London: Faber and West, 1948.

Metcalf, Peter. "Meaning and Materialism: The Ritual Economy of Death." *MAN* 16 (1981):563–578.

Radcliffe-Brown, Arnold. "Taboo." In William A. Lessa and Evon Z. Vogt eds., *Reader in Comparative Religion: An Anthropological Approach*. New York: Harper and Row, 1972.

Turner, Victor. *The Ritual Process*. Chicago: Aldine, 1969.

Tylor, Edward Burnett. "Animism." In William A. Lessa and Evon Z. Vogt eds., *Reader in Comparative Religion: An Anthropological Approach*. New York: Harper and Row, 1972.

Tylor, Edward Burnett. *Primitive Culture*. London: John Murray, 1903.

PETER BERTA

# ANXIETY AND FEAR

A generalized expectation of danger occurs during the stressful condition known as anxiety. The anxious person experiences a state of heightened tension that Walter Cannon described in 1927 as readiness for "fight or flight." If the threat passes or is overcome, the person (or animal) returns to normal functioning. Anxiety has therefore served its purpose in alerting the person to a possible danger. Unfortunately, sometimes the alarm keeps ringing; the individual continues to behave as though in constant danger. Such prolonged stress can disrupt the person's life, distort relationships, and even produce life-threatening physical changes. Is the prospect of death the alarm that never stops ringing? Is death anxiety the source of people's most profound uneasiness? Or is death anxiety a situational or abnormal reaction that occurs when coping skills are overwhelmed?

There are numerous examples of things that people fear—cemeteries, flying, public speaking, being in a crowd, being alone, being buried alive, among others. Unlike anxiety, a fear is associated with a more specific threat. A fear is therefore less likely to disrupt a person's everyday life, and one can either learn to avoid the uncomfortable situations or learn how to relax and master them. Fears that are unreasonable and out of proportion to the actual danger are called phobias. Many fears and phobias seem to have little or nothing to do with death, but some do, such as fear of flying or of being buried alive.

## Theories of Death Anxiety and Fear

Two influential theories dominated thinking about death anxiety and fear until the late twentieth century. Sigmund Freud (1856–1939) had the first say. The founder of psychoanalysis recognized that people sometimes did express fears of death. Nevertheless, thanatophobia, as he called it, was merely a disguise for a deeper source of concern. It was not death that people feared because:

> Our own death is indeed quite unimaginable, and whenever we make the attempt to imagine it we . . . really survive as spectators. . . . At bottom nobody believes in his own death, or to put the same thing in a different way, in the unconscious every one of us is convinced of his own immortality. *(Freud 1953, pp. 304–305)*

The unconscious does not deal with the passage of time nor with negations. That one's life could and would end just does not compute. Furthermore, whatever one fears cannot be death because one has never died. People who express death-related fears, then, actually are trying to deal with unresolved childhood conflicts that they cannot bring themselves to acknowledge and discuss openly.

Freud's reduction of death concern to a neurotic cover-up did not receive a strong challenge until Ernest Becker's 1973 book, *The Denial of Death*. Becker's existential view turned death anxiety theory on its head. Not only is death anxiety real, but it is people's most profound source of concern. This anxiety is so intense that it generates many if not all of the specific fears and phobias people experience in everyday life. Fears of being alone or in a confined space, for example, are fears whose connections with death anxiety are relatively easy to trace, but so are the needs for bright lights and noise. It is more comfortable, more in keeping with one's self-image, to transform the underlying anxiety into a variety of smaller aversions.

According to Becker, much of people's daily behavior consists of attempts to deny death and thereby keep their basic anxiety under control. People would have a difficult time controlling their anxiety, though, if alarming realities continued to intrude and if they were exposed to brutal reminders of their vulnerability. Becker also suggested that this is where society plays its role. No function of society is more crucial than its strengthening of individual defenses against death anxiety. Becker's analysis of society convinced him that many beliefs and practices are in the service of death denial, that is, reducing the experience of anxiety. Funeral homes with their flowers and homilies, and the medical system with its evasions, are only among the more obvious societal elements that join with individuals to maintain the fiction that there is nothing to fear.

Ritualistic behavior on the part of both individuals and social institutions generally has the underlying purpose of channeling and finding employment for what otherwise would surface as disorganizing death anxiety. Schizophrenics suffer as they do because their fragile defenses fail to protect them against the terror of annihilation. "Normal" people in a "normal" society function more competently in everyday life because they have succeeded at least temporarily in denying death.

Other approaches to understanding death anxiety and fear were introduced in the late twentieth century. Terror management theory is based on studies finding that people who felt better about themselves also reported having less death-related anxiety. These data immediately suggested possibilities for preventing or reducing disturbingly high levels of death anxiety: Help people to develop strong self-esteem and they are less likely to be disabled by death anxiety. If self-esteem serves as a buffer against anxiety, might not society also be serving this function just as Becker had suggested? People seem to derive protection against death anxiety from worldview faith as well as from their own self-esteem. "Worldview faith" can be understood as religious belief or some other conviction that human life is meaningful, as well as general confidence that society is just and caring.

Another fresh approach, regret theory, was proposed in 1996 by Adrian Tomer and Grafton Eliason. Regret theory focuses on the way in which people evaluate the quality or worth of their lives. The prospect of death is likely to make people more anxious if they feel that they have not and cannot accomplish something good in life. People might torment themselves with regrets over past failures and missed opportunities or with thoughts of future accomplishments and experiences that will not be possible. Regret theory (similar in some respects to Robert Butler's life review approach) also has implications for anxiety reduction. People can reconsider their memories and expectations, for example, and also discover how to live more fully in the present moment.

Robert Kastenbaum suggests that people might not need a special theory for death anxiety and fear. Instead, they can make use of mainstream research in the field of life span development. Anxiety may have roots in people's physical being, but it is through personal experiences and social encounters that they learn what might harm them and, therefore, what they should fear. These fears also bear the marks of sociohistorical circumstances. For example, fear of the dead was salient in many preliterate societies throughout the world, while fear of being buried alive became widespread in nineteenth-century Europe and America. In modern times many people express the somewhat related fear of being sustained in a persistent vegetative state between life and death. Death-related fears, then, develop within particular social contexts and particular individual experiences. People do not have to rely upon the untested and perhaps untestable opposing views of Freud and Becker—that they are either incapable of experiencing death anxiety, or that death anxiety is the source of all fears. It is more useful to observe how their fears as well as their joys and enthusiasms are influenced by the interaction between cognitive development and social learning experiences. In this way people will be in a better position to help the next generation learn to identify actual threats to their lives while not overreacting to all possible alarms all the time.

**Death Anxiety Studies**

There have been many empirical studies of death anxiety, but many questions also remain because of methodological limitations and the difficulties inherent in this subject. Nevertheless, a critical review of the literature does reveal some interesting patterns:

- Most people report that they have a low to moderate level of death-related anxiety.

- Women tend to report somewhat higher levels of death-related anxiety.

- There is no consistent increase in death anxiety with advancing adult age. If anything, older people in general seem to have less death anxiety.

- People with mental and emotional disorders tend to have a higher level of death anxiety than the general population.

- Death anxiety can spike temporarily to a higher level for people who have been exposed to traumatic situations.

*Religion.* The relationship between death anxiety and religious belief seems to be too complex to provide a simple pattern of findings. Death-related teachings differ, and believers may take different messages from the same basic doctrine. Historical studies also suggest that religious faith and practices seem to have sometimes reduced and sometimes increased death anxiety.

*Health.* The findings already mentioned come mostly from studies in which respondents in relatively good health reported on their own fears. Other studies and observations, though, give occasion for further reflection. There is evidence to suggest that people may be experiencing more anxiety than they are able to report. Even people who respond calmly to death-related words or images show agitation in breathing, heart rate, and reaction time, among other measures. Researchers Herman Feifel and B. Allen Branscomb therefore concluded in 1973 that everybody, in one way or another, is afraid of death. Presumably, people may have enough self-control to resist death-related anxiety on a conscious level but not necessarily to quell their underlying feelings of threat.

*Gender.* The gender differences also require a second look. Although women tend to report higher levels of death-related anxiety, it is also women who provide most of the professional and volunteer services to terminally ill people and their families, and, again, it is mostly women who enroll in death education courses. Women are more open to death-related thoughts and feelings, and men are somewhat more concerned about keeping these thoughts and feelings in check. The relatively higher level of reported death anxiety among women perhaps contributes to empathy with dying and grieving people and the desire to help them cope with their ordeals.

*Age.* The relationship between age and death anxiety is also rather complex. Adolescents may at the same time harbor a sense of immortality and experience a sense of vulnerability and incipient terror, but also enjoy transforming death-related anxiety into risky death-defying activities. What people fear most about death often changes with age. Young adults are often mostly concerned about dying too soon—before they have had the chance to do and experience all they have hoped for in life. Adult parents are often more likely to worry about the effect of their possible deaths upon other family members. Elderly adults often express concern about living "too long" and therefore becoming a burden on others and useless to themselves. Furthermore, the fear of dying alone or among strangers is often more intense than the fear of life coming to an end. Knowing a person's general level of anxiety, then, does not necessarily identify what it is that most disturbs a person about the prospect of death.

*Anxiety levels.* The fact that most people report themselves as having a low to moderate level of death anxiety does not offer support for either Freud's psychoanalytic or Becker's existential theory. Respondents do not seem to be in the grips of intense anxiety, but neither do they deny having any death-related fears. Kastenbaum's *Edge theory* offers a different way of looking at this finding. According to the theory, most people do not have a need to go through life either denying the reality of death or in a high state of alarm. Either of these extremes would actually interfere with one's ability both to enjoy life and cope with the possibility of danger. The everyday baseline of low to moderate anxiety keeps people alert enough to scan for potential threats to their own lives or the lives of other people. At the perceived moment of danger, people feel themselves to be on the edge between life and death, an instant away from catastrophe. The anxiety surge is part of a person's emergency response and takes priority over whatever else the person may have been doing. People are therefore not "in denial" when, in safe circumstances, they report themselves to have a low level of death anxiety. The anxiety switches on when their vigilance tells them that a life is on the edge of annihilation.

## Anxiety and Comfort Near the End of Life

What of anxiety when people are nearing the end of their lives, when death is no longer a distant prospect? The emergence of hospice programs and the palliative care movement is stimulating increased attention to the emotional, social, and spiritual needs of dying people. Signs of anxiety are more likely to be recognized and measures taken to help the patient feel at ease. These signs include trembling, restlessness, sweating, rapid heartbeat, difficulty sleeping, and irritability. Health care professionals can reduce the anxiety of terminally ill people by providing accurate and reassuring information using relaxation techniques, and making use of anxiolytics or antidepressants.

Reducing the anxiety of terminally ill people requires more than technical expertise on the part of physicians and nurses. They must also face the challenge of coping with their own anxieties so that their interactions with patients and family provide comfort rather than another source of stress. Family and friends can help to relieve anxiety (including their own) by communicating well with the terminally ill person.

*See also:* BECKER, ERNEST; BURIED ALIVE; CADAVER EXPERIENCES; DYING, PROCESS OF; FEIFEL, HERMAN; FREUD, SIGMUND; TERROR MANAGEMENT THEORY

### *Bibliography*

Becker, Ernest. *The Denial of Death.* New York: Free Press, 1973.

Bondeson, Jan. *Buried Alive.* New York: Norton, 2001.

Butler, Robert N. "Successful Aging and the Role of Life Review." *Journal of the American Geriatric Society* 27 (1974):529–534.

Cannon, Walter B. *Bodily Changes in Pain, Hunger, Fear, and Rage.* New York: Appleton-Century-Crofts, 1927.

Chandler, Emily. "Spirituality." In Inge B. Corless and Zelda Foster eds., *The Hospice Heritage: Celebrating Our Future.* New York: Haworth Press, 1999.

Choron, Jacques. *Modern Man and Mortality.* New York: Macmillan, 1964.

Chung, Man, Catherine Chung, and Yvette Easthope. "Traumatic Stress and Death Anxiety among Community Residents Exposed to an Aircraft Crash." *Death Studies* 24 (2000):689–704.

Feifel, Herman, and B. Allen Branscomb. "Who's Afraid of Death?" *Journal of Abnormal Psychology* 81 (1973):282–288.

Freud, Sigmund. "Thoughts for the Times on War and Death." *The Standard Edition of the Complete Psychological Works of Sigmund Freud,* Vol. 4. London: Hogarth Press, 1953.

Greyson, Bruce. "Reduced Death Threat in Near-Death Experiences." In Robert A. Neimeyer ed., *Death Anxiety Handbook.* Washington, DC: Taylor & Francis, 1994.

Hamama-Raz, Yaira, Zahava Solomon, and Avrahm Ohry. "Fear of Personal Death among Physicians." *Omega: The Journal of Death and Dying* 41 (2000):139–150.

Jalland, Pat. *Death in the Victorian Family.* Oxford: Oxford University Press, 1996.

Kastenbaum, Robert. "Death-Related Anxiety." In Larry Michelson and L. Michael Ascher eds., *Anxiety and Stress Disorders.* New York: Guilford Press, 1987.

Kastenbaum, Robert. *The Psychology of Death,* 3rd edition. New York: Springer, 2000.

Page, Andrew C. "Fear and Phobias." In David Levinson, James J. Ponzetti Jr., and Peter F. Jorgenson eds., *Encyclopedia of Human Emotions.* New York: Macmillan, 1999.

Pontillo, Kathleen A. "The Role of Critical Care Nurses in Providing and Managing End-of-Life Care." In J. Randall Curtis and Gordon D. Rubenfeld eds., *Managing Death in the Intensive Care Unit.* Oxford: Oxford University Press, 2001.

Selye, Hans. *The Stress of Life.* New York: McGraw-Hill, 1978.

Tomer, Adrian. "Death Anxiety in Adult Life: Theoretical Perspectives." In Robert A. Neimeyer ed., *Death Anxiety Handbook.* Washington, DC: Taylor & Francis, 1994.

Tomer, Adrian, and Grafton Eliason. "Toward a Comprehensive Model of Death Anxiety." *Death Studies* 20 (1996):343–366.

ROBERT KASTENBAUM

# APOCALYPSE

The word *apocalypse* has many meanings. In religious usage, it identifies the last book of the Christian Bible, the Revelation of John; a genre of ancient Judeo-Christian visionary literature; or doomsday, the destruction of the world at the end of time prophesied by the Apocalypse. In more popular usage, it identifies any catastrophic or violent event, such as the Vietnam War (e.g., the movie *Apocalypse Now*). Apocalypticism is the religious belief system that interprets human history from its origins to the present as signs of the imminent end of the world. It is one feature of Christian eschatology, the branch of theology dealing with the state of the soul after death, purgatory, hell, and heaven.

The adjective *apocalyptic* also has many meanings, from attitudes characteristic of apocalypticism (e.g., the world is so evil it will soon be destroyed), to features of literary apocalypses (e.g., the seven-headed dragon of Apoc. 12), to cultural references to apocalyptic expectations (e.g., the movie *Armageddon*), to exaggerated fears of a crisis (e.g., the apocalyptic reaction to the Y2K "bug").

Apocalypticism is a feature of all three monotheistic religions. The Book of Daniel describes the Hebrew prophet's vision of the end, and messianism has regularly flared up in Jewish diaspora communities, as when Sabbatai Sevi (1626–1676) predicted the end of the world. In the twentieth century apocalypticism influenced responses to the Holocaust and supported religious Zionism. In Islam, the resurrection, day of judgment, and salvation are apocalyptic features of orthodox belief as evident in the Koran, and apocalypticism influenced expectations of an Islamic messiah in Sunni belief, Iranian Shi'ism, and the Bahá'í faith. Apocalypticism, however, is most common in Christianity, probably because of the continuing influence of the biblical Apocalypse, which has informed not only the eschatology of Christianity but also its art, literature, and worship. Its rich, otherworldly symbolism and prophecies of the end of time are well-known and include the Four Horsemen, Lamb of God, Whore of Babylon, Mark of the Beast (666), Armageddon, Last Judgment, and New Jerusalem.

Apocalyptic belief has been associated with heretical and extremist movements throughout history. For example, the Fraticelli, Franciscan dissidents of the fourteenth century, accused Pope John XXII of being the Antichrist; Thomas Müntzer, an apocalyptic preacher, was a leader in the German Peasants' War of 1525; the American Millerites left crops unplanted, expecting Christ to return in 1844; and David Koresh, leader of the Branch Davidians before the conflagration that destroyed their Waco compound in 1993, claimed to be the Lamb of the Apocalypse. Nevertheless, there is nothing necessarily unorthodox or radical about apocalypticism, which the theologian Ernst Kaseman has called "the mother of all Christian theology" (1969, p. 40). The sermons of Jesus (e.g., Matt. 24) and the theology of Paul are filled with apocalyptic prophecies, and Peter identified Pentecost—the traditional foundation of the Christian church—as a sign of the end of time (Acts 2). Furthermore, the creed followed by many Christian faiths promises the return of Christ in majesty to judge the living and the dead, and many Protestant denominations, such as Baptists and Adventists, have strong apocalyptic roots that support a conservative theology.

The expectation that Antichrist will appear in the last days to deceive and persecute the faithful is based on apocalyptic interpretations, and during the Middle Ages and Renaissance this belief informed drama, poetry, manuscript illustrations, and paintings, from the twelfth-century Latin *Play of Antichrist* to Luca Signorelli's compelling fresco at Orvietto Cathedral (1498). The twentieth century, with its numerous wars and social upheavals, has thinly disguised the figure of Antichrist and integrated other apocalyptic images into its literature (e.g., William Butler Yeats's poem "The Second Coming") and popular culture (e.g., the movie *The Omen*). Apocalyptic notions also pervade religious polemic; during the debates of the Reformation, for example, Protestants and Catholics identified each other as Antichrists, a term still used by some fundamentalists attacking the papacy.

Another expectation derived from the Apocalypse is the millennium, the thousand-year period of peace and justice during which the Dragon is imprisoned in the abyss before the end of time. More generally, the term *millennium* refers to any idealized period in the future. Communism, for example, has been described as a millenarian movement because of its promise of a classless society; like the Russian Revolution of 1917, millenarian movements have often been associated with violence of the sort that occurred during the Brazilian slave revolts in the 1580s. The Center for Millennium Studies at Boston University maintains a database of contemporary millenarian movements.

These social movements indicate the tremendous influence of the Apocalypse and the ways in which religious apocalypticism has been secularized. Secular apocalypticism is manifest in popular appropriations of physics that, in one way or another, predict the extermination of life, with references to entropy and the infinite expansion of the universe until it fizzles into nothingness or recoils into a primal contraction. It is also evident in environmentalist forecasts of the extinction of species and the greenhouse effect, in predictions of famine and hunger arising from the exponential increase in world population, and in responses to the devastations of the worldwide AIDS epidemic. Modern secular apocalypticism was particularly strong during the cold war in predictions of nuclear destruction, as evident in Ronald Reagan's references to Armageddon in the 1980s and popular culture (e.g., the movie *Dr. Strangelove* and the ABC television film *The Day After*).

Although the term *apocalypse* brings to mind images of destruction and violence, and although the sociologist Michael Barkun has linked millennarian hopes to various forms of disaster, the biblical Apocalypse includes many promises of peace and assurances of rewards for the faithful, including a millennium ushered in by Jesus—a far cry from dire predictions of bloody revolution and disaster. For Christians, the apocalypse need not be negative, because the New Jerusalem follows the destruction of an evil world, and life in heaven follows death. In an increasingly secular world, however, the apocalypse summons lurid visions of individual or mass death.

*See also:* AIDS; EXTINCTION; NUCLEAR DESTRUCTION

### Bibliography

AHR Forum. "Millenniums." *American Historical Review* 104 (1999):1512–1628.

Barkun, Michael. *Disaster and the Millennium*. New Haven: Yale University Press, 1974.

Emmerson, Richard K., and Bernard McGinn, eds. *The Apocalypse in the Middle Ages*. Ithaca, NY: Cornell University Press, 1992.

Funk, Robert W., ed. "Apocalypticism." Special issue of *Journal for Theology and the Church* 6 (1969).

McGinn, Bernard, John J. Collins, and Stephen J. Stein, eds. *The Encyclopedia of Apocalypticism*. New York: Continuum, 1998.

O'Leary, Stephen D. *Arguing the Apocalypse: A Theory of Millennial Rhetoric.* New York: Oxford University Press, 1994.

Patrides, C. A., and Joseph Wittreich, eds. *The Apocalypse in English Renaissance Thought and Literature: Patterns, Antecedents, and Repercussions.* Ithaca, NY: Cornell University Press, 1984.

Strozier, Charles B., and Michael Flynn. *The Year 2000: Essays on the End.* New York: New York University Press, 1997.

RICHARD K. EMMERSON

# APPARITIONS

*See* GHOSTS.

# APPROPRIATE DEATH

*See* GOOD DEATH, THE.

# ARIÈS, PHILIPPE

Philippe Ariès (1914–1984) did not let a career at a French institute for tropical plant research prevent him from almost single-handedly establishing attitudes toward death as a field of historical study. After publishing a number of prize-winning books in France, Ariès came to international attention with the publication of his study of attitudes toward children, *Centuries of Childhood* (1962). In 1973 Johns Hopkins University invited him to America to lecture on "history, political culture, and national consciousness." Ariès readily accepted the invitation, but his ongoing research into collective mentalities had led him to conclude that death too has a history—and that was the subject he wished to address.

The lectures delivered at Johns Hopkins, published as *Western Attitudes toward Death* in 1974, presented an initial sketch of Ariès's findings. Surveying evidence from the Middle Ages to the present, Ariès had discovered a fundamental shift in attitude. Where death had once been familiar and

"tamed" (*la mort apprivoisée*) it was now strange, untamed, and "forbidden" (*la mort interdite*). Medieval people accepted death as a part of life—expected, foreseen, and more or less controlled through ritual. At home or on the battlefield, they met death with resignation, but also with the hope of a long and peaceful sleep before a collective judgment. Simple rural folk maintained such attitudes until the early twentieth century. But for most people, Ariès argued, death has become wild and uncontrollable.

The change in Western European society occurred in identifiable stages. During the later Middle Ages, religious and secular elites progressively abandoned acceptance of the fact that "we all die" (*nous mourons tous*) to concentrate on their own deaths, developing an attitude Ariès dubbed *la mort de soi* ("the death of the self") or *la mort de moi* ("my death"). Anxious about the state of their souls and increasingly attached to the things their labor and ingenuity had won, they represented death as a contest in which the fate of the soul hung in the balance.

The rise of modern science led some to challenge belief in divine judgment, in heaven and hell, and in the necessity of dying in the presence of the clergy. Attention shifted to the intimate realm of the family, to *la mort de toi* ("thy death"), the death of a loved one. Emphasis fell on the emotional pain of separation and on keeping the dead alive in memory. In the nineteenth century, some people regarded death and even the dead as beautiful. With each new attitude, Western Europeans distanced themselves from the old ways. Finally, drained of meaning by modern science and medicine, death retreated from both public and familial experience. The dying met their end in hospitals, and the living disposed of their remains with little or no ceremony.

Ariès was particularly interested in presenting his findings in America because he noted a slightly different attitude there. While modern Americans gave no more attention to the dying than Europeans, they lavished attention on the dead. The embalmed corpse, a rarity in Europe but increasingly common in America after the U.S. Civil War, became the centerpiece of the American way of death. Although embalming attempted, in a sense, to deny death, it also kept the dead present. Thus Ariès was not surprised that signs of a reaction to "forbidden death" were appearing in the United States. He ended his lectures with the possibility that death might once more be infused with meaning and accepted as a natural part of life.

In 1977 Ariès published his definitive statement on the subject, *L'Homme devant la mort,* which appeared in English as *The Hour of Our Death* several years later. Besides its length and mass of detail, the book's chief departure from Ariès' earlier work was the inclusion of a fifth attitude, which emerged in the seventeenth and eighteenth centuries. Ariès dubbed this attitude *la mort proche et longue,* or "death near and far." As death became less familiar, its similarities to sex came to the fore, and some people found themselves as much attracted to as repelled by cadavers, public executions, and the presence of the dead. The appearance of the psychoanalytic notions of *eros* and *thanatos* at this point in Ariès's schema illuminate the deeply psychological nature of his approach, most clearly articulated in the conclusion to *The Hour of Our Death.* This aspect of his thinking generated criticism from historians who see the causes of change, even in collective attitudes, in more objective measures, but most have accepted his reading of the modern period. There are problems with the notion of "tamed death," however, which Ariès regarded as universal and primordial. Subsequent research has shown how peculiar the "tamed death" of the European Middle Ages was, and how great a role Christianity played in its construction. Nevertheless, his work has become a touchstone for nearly all research in the field and his contributions to death studies, and to history, are universally admired.

*See also:* ARS MORIENDI; CHRISTIAN DEATH RITES, HISTORY OF; GOOD DEATH, THE; MEMENTO MORI

### Bibliography

Ariès, Philippe. *Images of Man and Death,* translated by Janet Lloyd. Cambridge, MA: Harvard University Press, 1985.

Ariès, Philippe. *The Hour of Our Death,* translated by Helen Weaver. New York: Alfred A. Knopf, 1981.

Ariès, Philippe. *Western Attitudes toward Death: From the Middle Ages to the Present,* translated by Patricia M. Ranum. Baltimore: Johns Hopkins University Press, 1974.

Ariès, Philippe. *Centuries of Childhood: A Social History of Family Life,* translated by Robert Baldick. New York: Alfred A. Knopf, 1962.

McManners, John. "Death and the French Historians." In Joachim Whaley ed., *Mirrors of Mortality: Studies in the Social History of Death.* London: Europa, 1981.

Paxton, Frederick S. *Liturgy and Anthropology: A Monastic Death Ritual of the Eleventh Century.* Missoula, MT: St. Dunstan's, 1993.

FREDERICK S. PAXTON

# ARS MORIENDI

The *Ars Moriendi,* or "art of dying," is a body of Christian literature that provided practical guidance for the dying and those attending them. These manuals informed the dying about what to expect, and prescribed prayers, actions, and attitudes that would lead to a "good death" and salvation. The first such works appeared in Europe during the early fifteenth century, and they initiated a remarkably flexible genre of Christian writing that lasted well into the eighteenth century.

## Fifteenth-Century Beginnings

By 1400 the Christian tradition had well-established beliefs and practices concerning death, dying, and the afterlife. The Ars Moriendi packaged many of these into a new, concise format. In particular, it expanded the rite for priests visiting the sick into a manual for both clergy and laypeople. Disease, war, and changes in theology and Church policies formed the background for this new work. The Black Death had devastated Europe in the previous century, and its recurrences along with other diseases continued to cut life short. Wars and violence added to the death toll. The Hundred Years' War (1337–1453) between France and England was the era's largest conflict, but its violence and political instability mirrored many local conflicts. The fragility of life under these conditions coincided with a theological shift noted by the historian Philippe Ariès whereas the early Middle Ages emphasized humanity's collective judgment at the end of time, by the fifteenth century attention focused on individual judgment immediately after death. One's own death and judgment thus became urgent issues that required preparation.

To meet this need, the Ars Moriendi emerged as part of the Church authorities' program for educating priests and laypeople. In the fourteenth century catechisms began to appear, and handbooks were drafted to prepare priests for parish work, including ministry to the dying. The Council of Constance (1414–1418) provided the occasion for the Ars Moriendi's composition. Jean Gerson, chancellor of the University of Paris, brought to the council his brief essay, *De arte moriendi.* This work became the basis for the anonymous *Ars Moriendi* treatise that soon appeared, perhaps at the council itself. From Constance, the established networks of the Dominicans and Franciscans assured that the new work spread quickly throughout Europe.

The Ars Moriendi survives in two different versions. The first is a longer treatise of six chapters that prescribes rites and prayers to be used at the time of death. The second is a brief, illustrated book that shows the dying person's struggle with temptations before attaining a good death. As Mary Catharine O'Connor argued in her book *The Arts of Dying Well,* the longer treatise was composed earlier and the shorter version is an abridgment that adapts and illustrates the treatise's second chapter. Yet O'Connor also noted the brief version's artistic originality. For while many deathbed images predate the Ars Moriendi, never before had deathbed scenes been linked into a series "with a sort of story, or at least connected action, running through them" (O'Connor 1966, p. 116). The longer Latin treatise and its many translations survive in manuscripts and printed editions throughout Europe. The illustrated version circulated mainly as "block books," where pictures and text were printed from carved blocks of wood; Harry W. Rylands (1881) and Florence Bayard reproduced two of these editions.

An English translation of the longer treatise appeared around 1450 under the title *The Book of the Craft of Dying.* The first chapter praises the deaths of good Christians and repentant sinners who die "gladly and wilfully" in God (Comper 1977, p. 7). Because the best preparation for a good death is a good life, Christians should "live in such wise . . . that they may die safely, every hour, when God will" (Comper 1977, p. 9). Yet the treatise focuses on dying and assumes that deathbed repentance can yield salvation.

The second chapter is the treatise's longest and most original section. It confronts the dying with five temptations and their corresponding "inspirations" or remedies: (1) temptation against faith versus reaffirmation of faith; (2) temptation to despair versus hope for forgiveness; (3) temptation to impatience versus charity and patience; (4) temptation to vainglory or complacency versus humility and recollection of sins; and (5) temptation to avarice or attachment to family and property versus detachment. This scheme accounts for ten of the eleven illustrations in the block book *Ars Moriendi,* where five scenes depict demons tempting the dying man and five others portray angels offering their inspirations.

Of special importance are the second and fourth temptations, which test the dying person's sense of guilt and self-worth with two sharply contrasting states: an awareness of one's sins that places one beyond redemption and a confidence in one's merits that sees no need for forgiveness. Both despair and complacent self-confidence can be damning because they rule out repentance. For this reason the corresponding remedies encourage the dying to acknowledge their sins in hope because all sins can be forgiven through contrition and Christ's saving death.

As Ariès notes, throughout all five temptations, the Ars Moriendi emphasizes the active role of the dying in freely deciding their destinies. For only their free consent to the demonic temptations or angelic inspirations determines whether they are saved or damned.

The third chapter of the longer treatise prescribes "interrogations" or questions that lead the dying to reaffirm their faith, to repent their sins, and to commit themselves fully to Christ's passion and death. The fourth chapter asks the dying to imitate Christ's actions on the cross and provides prayers for "a clear end" and the "everlasting bliss that is the reward of holy dying" (Comper 1977, p. 31). In the fifth chapter the emphasis shifts to those who assist the dying, including family and friends. They are to follow the earlier prescriptions, present the dying with images of the crucifix and saints, and encourage them to repent, receive the sacraments, and draw up a testament disposing of their possessions. In the process, the attendants are

*The Devil with a hooking staff and Death himself with a soldier's pike are attempting to snare the soul of this dying man. The threatened soul, pictured as a tiny person, prays for help as an Angel offers protection. Ars Moriendi depictions such as this manuscript illustration from fourteenth century England warned believers that they must live the good life or face hideous punishment after death.* DOVER PUBLICATIONS, INC.

to consider and prepare for their own deaths. In the sixth chapter the dying can no longer speak on their own behalf, and the attendants are instructed to recite a series of prayers as they "commend the spirit of our brother" into God's hands.

The illustrated Ars Moriendi concludes with a triumphant image of the good death. The dying man is at the center of a crowded scene. A priest helps him hold a candle in his right hand as he breathes his last. An angel receives his soul in the form of a naked child, while the demons below vent their frustration at losing this battle. A crucifixion scene appears to the side, with Mary, John, and other saints. This idealized portrait thus completes the "art of dying well."

**The Later Tradition**

The two original versions of the Ars Moriendi initiated a long tradition of Christian works on preparation for death. This tradition was wide enough to

accommodate not only Roman Catholic writers but also Renaissance humanists and Protestant reformers—all of whom adapted the Ars Moriendi to their specific historical circumstances. Yet nearly all of these authors agreed on one basic change: They placed the "art of dying" within a broader "art of living," which itself required a consistent *memento mori,* or awareness of and preparation for one's own death.

The Ars Moriendi tradition remained strong within the Roman Catholic communities. In his 1995 book *From Madrid to Purgatory,* Carlos M. N. Eire documented the tradition's influence in Spain where the Ars Moriendi shaped published accounts of the deaths of St. Teresa of Avila (1582) and King Philip II (1598). In his 1976 study of 236 Ars Moriendi publications in France, Daniel Roche found that their production peaked in the 1670s and declined during the period from 1750 to 1799. He also noted the Jesuits' leading role in writing

Catholic Ars Moriendi texts, with sixty authors in France alone.

Perhaps the era's most enduring Catholic text was composed in Italy by Robert Bellarmine, the prolific Jesuit author and cardinal of the church. In 1619 Bellarmine wrote his last work, *The Art of Dying Well*. The first of its two books describes how to live well as the essential preparation for a good death. It discusses Christian virtues, Gospel texts, and prayers, and comments at length on the seven sacraments as integral to Christian living and dying. The second book, *The Art of Dying Well As Death Draws Near,* recommends meditating on death, judgment, hell, and heaven, and discusses the sacraments of penance, Eucharist, and extreme unction or the anointing of the sick with oil. Bellarmine then presents the familiar deathbed temptations and ways to counter them and console the dying, and gives examples of those who die well and those who do not. Throughout, Bellarmine reflects a continuing fear of dying suddenly and unprepared. Hence he focuses on living well and meditating on death as leading to salvation even if one dies unexpectedly. To highlight the benefits of dying consciously and well prepared, he claims that prisoners facing execution are "fortunate"; knowing they will die, they can confess their sins, receive the Eucharist, and pray with their minds more alert and unclouded by illness. These prisoners thus enjoy a privileged opportunity to die well.

In 1534 the Christian humanist Erasmus of Rotterdam wrote a treatise that appeared in English in 1538 as *Preparation to Death*. He urges his readers to live rightly as the best preparation for death. He also seeks a balance between warning and comforting the dying so that they will be neither flattered into arrogant self-confidence nor driven to despair; repentance is necessary, and forgiveness is always available through Christ. Erasmus dramatizes the deathbed scene in a dialogue between the Devil and the dying Man. The Devil offers temptations to which the Man replies clearly and confidently; having mastered the arts of living and dying, the Man is well prepared for this confrontation. While recognizing the importance of sacramental confession and communion, Erasmus says not to worry if a priest cannot be present; the dying may confess directly to God who gives salvation without the sacraments if "faith and a glad will be present" (Atkinson 1992, p. 56).

The Ars Moriendi tradition in England has been especially well documented. It includes translations of Roman Catholic works by Petrus Luccensis and the Jesuit Gaspar Loarte; Thomas Lupset's humanistic *Way of Dying Well;* and Thomas Becon's Calvinist *The Sick Man's Salve*. But one literary masterpiece stands out, which is Jeremy Taylor's *The Rule and Exercises of Holy Dying*.

When Taylor published *Holy Dying* in 1651, he described it as "the first entire body of directions for sick and dying people" (Taylor 1977, p. xiii) to be published in the Church of England. This Anglican focus allowed Taylor to reject some elements of the Roman Catholic Ars Moriendi and to retain others. For example, he ridicules deathbed repentance but affirms traditional practices for dying well; by themselves the protocols of dying are "not enough to pass us into paradise," but if "done foolishly, [they are] enough to send us to hell" (Taylor 1977, p. 43). For Taylor the good death completes a good life, but even the best Christian requires the prescribed prayers, penance, and Eucharist at the hour of death. And *Holy Dying* elegantly lays out a program for living and dying well. Its first two chapters remind readers of their mortality and urge them to live in light of this awareness. In the third chapter, Taylor describes two temptations of the sick and dying: impatience and the fear of death itself. Chapter four leads the dying through exercises of patience and repentance as they await their "clergy-guides," whose ministry is described in chapter five. This bare summary misses both the richness of Taylor's prose and the caring, pastoral tone that led Nancy Lee Beaty, author of *The Craft of Dying,* to consider *Holy Dying,* the "artistic climax" of the English Ars Moriendi tradition (Beaty 1970, p. 197).

Susan Karant-Nunn, in her 1997 book *The Reformation of Ritual,* documented the persistence of the Ars Moriendi tradition in the "Lutheran Art of Dying" in Germany during the late sixteenth century. Although the Reformers eliminated devotion to the saints and the sacraments of penance and anointing with oil, Lutheran pastors continued to instruct the dying and to urge them to repent, confess, and receive the Eucharist. Martin Moller's *Manual on Preparing for Death* (1593) gives detailed directions for this revised art of dying.

Karant-Nunn's analysis can be extended into the eighteenth century. In 1728 Johann Friedrich

Starck [or Stark], a Pietist clergyman in the German Lutheran church, treated dying at length in his *Tägliches Hand-Buch in guten und bösen Tagen.* Frequently reprinted into the twentieth century, the *Hand-Book* became one of the most widely circulated prayer books in Germany. It also thrived among German-speaking Americans, with ten editions in Pennsylvania between 1812 and 1829, and an 1855 English translation, *Daily Hand-Book for Days of Rejoicing and of Sorrow.*

The book contains four major sections: prayers and hymns for the healthy, the afflicted, the sick, and the dying. As the fourth section seeks "a calm, gentle, rational and blissful end," it adapts core themes from the Ars Moriendi tradition: the dying must consider God's judgment, forgive others and seek forgiveness, take leave of family and friends, commend themselves to God, and "resolve to die in Jesus Christ." While demons no longer appear at the deathbed, the temptation to despair remains as the dying person's sins present themselves to "frighten, condemn, and accuse." The familiar remedy of contrition and forgiveness through Christ's passion comforts the dying. Starck offers a rich compendium of "verses, texts and prayers" for bystanders to use in comforting the dying, and for the dying themselves. A confident, even joyful, approach to death dominates these prayers, as the dying person prays, "Lord Jesus, I die for thee, I live for thee, dead and living I am thine. Who dies thus, dies well."

## Ars Moriendi in the Twenty-First Century

Starck's *Hand-Book* suggests what became of the Ars Moriendi tradition. It did not simply disappear. Rather, its assimilation to Christian "arts of living" eventually led to decreasing emphasis on the deathbed, and with it the decline of a distinct genre devoted to the hour of death. The art of dying then found a place within more broadly conceived prayer books and ritual manuals, where it remains today (e.g., the "Ministration in Time of Death" in the Episcopal Church's *Book of Common Prayer*). The Ars Moriendi has thus returned to its origins. Having emerged from late medieval prayer and liturgy, it faded back into the matrix of Christian prayer and practice in the late seventeenth and eighteenth centuries.

The Ars Moriendi suggests useful questions for twenty-first century approaches to dying. During its long run, the Ars Moriendi ritualized the pain and grief of dying into the conventional and manageable forms of Christian belief, prayer, and practice. In what ways do current clinical and religious practices ritualize dying? Do these practices place dying persons at the center of attention, or do they marginalize and isolate them? What beliefs and commitments guide current approaches to dying? Although the Ars Moriendi's convictions about death and afterlife are no longer universally shared, might they still speak to believers within Christian churches and their pastoral care programs? What about the views and expectations of those who are committed to other religious traditions or are wholly secular? In light of America's diversity, is it possible—or desirable—to construct one image of the good death and what it might mean to die well? Or might it be preferable to mark out images of several good deaths and to develop new "arts of dying" informed by these? Hospice and palliative care may provide the most appropriate context for engaging these questions. And the Ars Moriendi tradition offers a valuable historical analogue and framework for posing them.

*See also:* ARIÈS, PHILIPPE; BLACK DEATH; CHRISTIAN DEATH RITES, HISTORY OF; GOOD DEATH, THE; MEMENTO MORI; TAYLOR, JEREMY; VISUAL ARTS

### *Bibliography*

Ariès, Philippe. *The Hour of Our Death,* translated by Helen Weaver. New York: Knopf, 1981.

Atkinson, David William. *The English Ars Moriendi.* New York: Peter Lang, 1992.

Beaty, Nancy Lee. *The Craft of Dying: A Study in the Literary Tradition of the Ars Moriendi in England.* New Haven, CT: Yale University Press, 1970.

Bellarmine, Robert. "The Art of Dying Well." In *Spiritual Writings,* translated and edited by John Patrick Donnelly and Roland J. Teske. New York: Paulist Press, 1989.

Comper, Frances M. M. *The Book of the Craft of Dying and Other Early English Tracts concerning Death.* New York: Arno Press, 1977.

Duclow, Donald F. "Dying Well: The *Ars Moriendi* and the Dormition of the Virgin." In Edelgard E. DuBruck and Barbara Gusick eds., *Death and Dying in the Middle Ages.* New York: Peter Lang, 1999.

Duffy, Eamon. *The Stripping of the Altars: Traditional Religion in England, c. 1400–c. 1580.* New Haven, CT: Yale University Press, 1992.

Eire, Carlos M. N. *From Madrid to Purgatory: The Art and Craft of Dying in Sixteenth-Century Spain*. Cambridge: Cambridge University Press, 1995.

Karant-Nunn, Susan C. *The Reformation of Ritual: An Interpretation of Early Modern Germany*. London: Routledge, 1997.

O'Connor, Mary Catharine. *The Arts of Dying Well: The Development of the Ars Moriendi*. New York: AMS Press, 1966.

Rylands, Harry W. *The Ars Moriendi (Editio Princeps, circa 1450): A Reproduction of the Copy in the British Museum*. London: Holbein Society, 1881.

Starck [Stark], Johann Friedrich. *Daily Hand-Book for Days of Rejoicing and of Sorrow*. Philadelphia: I. Kohler, 1855.

Taylor, Jeremy. *The Rule and Exercises of Holy Dying*. New York: Arno Press, 1977.

DONALD F. DUCLOW

# ASSASSINATION

The term *assassin* comes from the Arabic word *hashashin,* the collective word given to the followers of Hasan-e Sabbah, the head of a secret Persian sect of Ismailities in the eleventh century who would intoxicate themselves with hashish before murdering opponents. The word has since come to refer to the premeditated surprise murder of a prominent individual for political ends.

An assassination may be perpetrated by an individual or a group. The act of a lone assassin generally involves jealousy, mental disorder, or a political grudge. The assassination performed by more than one person is usually the result of a social movement or a group plot. Both forms of assassination can have far-reaching consequences.

**Major Assassinations in World History**

One of the earliest political assassinations in recorded history occurred in Rome on March 15, 44 B.C.E. when members of the Roman aristocracy (led by Gaius Cassius and Marcus Brutus), fearing the power of Julius Caesar, stabbed him to death in the Senate house. Caesar had failed to heed warnings to "Beware the Ides of March," and paid the ultimate price (McConnell 1970).

An assassination is usually performed quickly and involves careful planning. The "Thuggee" cult (from which the word *thug* is derived), which operated in India for several centuries until the British eliminated it in the mid-nineteenth century, consisted of professional killers who committed ritual stranglings of travelers, not for economic or political reasons, but as a sacrifice to the goddess Kali. One thug named Buhram claimed to have strangled 931 people during his forty years as a Thuggee.

The eighteenth and nineteenth centuries saw a plethora of assassinations throughout the Western world. Among the most noteworthy were the murders of Jean-Paul Marat and Spencer Perceval. For his role in the French Revolution, Marat was assassinated in his residence with a knife wielded by Charlotte Corday, a twenty-four-year-old French woman, on July 13, 1793. It is uncertain whether she committed the act for patriotic reasons of her own or whether she was acting on orders. On May 11, 1812, John Bellingham entered the lobby of the House of Commons and assassinated the British prime minister, Spencer Perceval, because he refused to heed Bellingham's demand for redress against tsarist Russia.

The victim of the most momentous political assassination of the early twentieth century was the Archduke Franz Ferdinand, heir to the Austro-Hungarian Empire of the Hapsburgs, slain during a parade in Sarajevo on June 28, 1914. The assassination helped trigger World War I. The world was shocked once again on October 9, 1934, when King Alexander I, who had assumed a dictatorial role in Yugoslavia in the 1920s in an effort to end quarreling between the Serbs and Croats, was murdered by a professional assassin hired by Croat conspirators led by Ante Pavelich.

Russia experienced two major assassinations in the early twentieth century. Having allegedly saved the life of the son of Tsar Nicholas, Grigori Rasputin (the "Mad Monk") gained favor with the Tsarina and, through careful manipulation, became the virtual leader of Russia. However, his byzantine court intrigues, coupled with pro-German activities, led to his assassination on December 29, 1916, by Prince Youssoupoff, husband of the tsar's niece. Ramon Mercader, an agent of the Soviet dictator Joseph Stalin, assassinated Leon Trotsky, who had co-led the Russian Revolution in 1917, in Mexico on August 21, 1940.

On January 30, 1948, India suffered the loss of Mahatma Gandhi, murdered by Nathuram Godse, a religious fanatic who feared the consequences of the partition that created Pakistan in 1947. The South Vietnamese leader Ngo Dinh Diem was killed on November 2, 1963, by a Vietnamese tank corps major (whose name was never released) because of his submission to the tyrannical rule of his brother, Ngo Dinh Nhu.

## Assassinations in U.S. History

The United States experienced a number of major losses to assassins in the twentieth century. Huey Long, an icon in Louisiana politics, was assassinated on September 8, 1935, in the corridor of the capitol building by Carl Weiss, a medical doctor in Baton Rouge and son-in-law of one of Long's many political enemies. Mark David Chapman shot John Lennon, one of the most politically active rock stars of his generation, on December 8, 1980. Attempts were made on other noteworthy men such as George Wallace (May 15, 1972, in Laurel, Maryland) and civil rights leader James Meredith (June 1966 during a march from Memphis, Tennessee to Jackson, Mississippi).

The 1960s was an era of unrest in the United States. Civil rights, women's rights, the war in Vietnam, the student movement, and the ecology controversy were major issues. Malcolm X, who advocated black nationalism and armed self-defense as a means of fighting the oppression of African Americans, was murdered on February 21, 1965, by Talmadge Hayer, Norman Butler, and Thomas Johnson, alleged agents of Malcolm's rival Elijah Muhammud of the Nation of Islam. Martin Luther King Jr. was killed on April 4, 1968, in Memphis, Tennessee by James Earl Ray, who later retracted his confession and claimed to be a dupe in an elaborate conspiracy. Robert F. Kennedy, then representing New York State in the U.S. Senate, was shot by a Palestinian, Sirhan Sirhan, on June 5, 1968, in Los Angeles, shortly after winning the California presidential primary.

## Attempted Assassinations of U.S. Presidents

The first attempt to assassinate a sitting president of the United States occurred on January 30, 1835, when Richard Lawrence, an English immigrant, tried to kill President Andrew Jackson on a street in Washington, D.C. Lawrence believed that he was heir to the throne of England and that Jackson stood in his way. He approached the president with

a derringer and pulled the trigger at point-blank range. When nothing happened, Lawrence reached in his pocket and pulled out another derringer, which also misfired. Lawrence was tried, judged insane, and sentenced to a mental institution for the rest of his life.

On February 15, 1933, while riding in an open car through the streets of Miami, Florida, with Chicago's mayor, Anton Cermak, President Franklin D. Roosevelt nearly lost his life to Giuseppe (Joseph) Zangara, an unemployed New Jersey mill worker who had traveled to Florida seeking employment. Caught up in the throes of the depression and unable to find work, he blamed capitalism and the president. The assassin fired several shots at the presidential vehicle and fatally wounded Cermak and a young woman in the crowd; Roosevelt was not injured. Zangara was executed in the electric chair, remaining unrepentant to the end.

While the White House was being renovated in 1950, and Harry Truman and his wife were residing in the poorly protected Blair House nearby, two Puerto Rican nationalists—Oscar Collazo and Grisello Torresola—plotted Truman's death, believing "that the assassination of President Truman might lead to an American Revolution that would provide the Nationalists with an opportunity to lead Puerto Rico to independence" (Smith 2000, p. 3). On November 1, 1950, the two killers attempted to enter the Blair House and kill the president. Truman was not harmed, but in the gun battle that took place, one security guard was fatally shot and two were injured. Torresola was also killed. Collazo, although wounded, survived to be tried, and he was sentenced to death. Not wishing to make him a martyr, Truman commuted his sentence to life in prison. During his presidency in 1979, Jimmy Carter ordered the release of Collazo, and he died in Puerto Rico in 1994.

While President Ronald Reagan was leaving the Washington Hilton in Washington, D.C., on March 30, 1981, he was seriously injured by a .22-caliber bullet fired by twenty-five-year-old John W. Hinckley Jr. After watching the movie *Taxi Driver,* Hinckley was impressed by Robert DeNiro's role as a man who tries to assassinate a senator. Hinckley also became infatuated with Jodie Foster, a young actress in the film, and decided that the way to

*Malcolm X, who fought against the oppression of African Americans, on a stretcher after being shot and killed by assassins on February 21, 1965.* CORBIS

impress her was to kill the president. Reagan survived major surgery to repair a collapsed lung, and Hinckley was sentenced to a psychiatric facility.

President Gerald Ford survived two attempts on his life. On September 5, 1975, while in Sacramento, California, Ford was nearly killed by Lynette "Squeaky" Fromme, a devoted follower of the cult leader Charles Manson. Fromme believed that killing Ford would bring attention to the plight of the California redwood trees and other causes she supported. Fromme was three to four feet from the President and about to fire a .45-caliber handgun when she was thwarted by Secret Service agents. Seventeen days later, in San Francisco, Sara Jane Moore, a civil rights activist, attempted to take the president's life. Moore was a member of a radical group and believed she could prove her allegiance by killing the president. Both women were sentenced to life imprisonment.

Theodore Roosevelt was the only former president to face an assassination attempt. In 1912,

after serving two terms as president, Roosevelt decided to seek a third term at the head of the Bull Moose Party. The idea of a third-term president was disturbing to many because no president theretofore had ever served more than two consecutive terms. A German immigrant, John Shrank, decided that the only way to settle the issue was to kill Roosevelt. On October 14, 1912, at a political rally, Shrank fired a bullet that went through fifty pages of speech notes, a glasses case made of steel, and Roosevelt's chest, penetrating a lung. Covered with blood, Roosevelt completed his speech before being treated. Shrank was adjudicated as mentally ill and spent the rest of his life in a mental institution.

## Assassinations of U.S. Presidents

The first president to be assassinated was Abraham Lincoln on April 14, 1865. Believing that he could avenge the loss of the South in the U.S. Civil War, the actor John Wilkes Booth entered the President's box at the Ford Theater in Washington, D.C., where Lincoln had gone with friends and family to see a play. Booth fired a bullet into the back of the President's head and then leaped from the stage shouting, "sic semper tyrannis!" and "The South is avenged!" Despite fracturing his shinbone, he successfully escaped. Twelve days later, Booth was trapped in a Virginia barn and killed when he refused to surrender. The coconspirators in the murder were hanged.

James A. Garfield was shot once in the arm and once in the back on July 1, 1881, in a Baltimore and Potomac train station on his way to deliver a speech in Massachusetts. Charles Guiteau, the assassin, had supported the president's candidacy and erroneously believed that he had earned a political appointment in Garfield's administration. When he was rejected, the killer blamed the president. Garfield survived for seventy-nine days before succumbing to his wound. Guiteau was hanged on June 30, 1882, at the District of Columbia jail.

In September 1901 President William McKinley traveled to the Pan-American Exposition in Buffalo, New York, to give a speech on American economic prosperity. While greeting an assembled crowd on September 6, he encountered twenty-eight-year-old Leon Czolgosz, a laborer and self-professed anarchist. The assassin approached McKinley with a handkerchief wrapped around his wrist, and when the President reached to shake his hand, Czolgosz produced a .32-caliber pistol and fired two shots into the chief executive's abdomen. McKinley died eight days later from gangrene that developed because of inadequate medical treatment. Czolgosz was executed, exclaiming that he was "not sorry" (Nash 1973, p. 143).

On November 22, 1963, while traveling in a motorcade through the streets of Dallas, Texas, John F. Kennedy became the fourth U.S. president to be assassinated. Lee Harvey Oswald, a communist malcontent, was accused of the crime and all evidence pointed to his guilt. However, before he could be adjudicated, Jack Ruby, a Texas nightclub owner, killed Oswald. Oswald's motivation for killing Kennedy has never been fully determined: "The only conclusion reached was that he acted alone and for vague political reasons" (Nash 1973, p. 430). Conspiracy theories concerning the murder have not been substantiated.

*See also:* DEATH SYSTEM; HOMICIDE, DEFINITIONS AND CLASSIFICATIONS OF; HOMICIDE, EPIDEMIOLOGY OF; REVOLUTIONARIES AND "DEATH FOR THE CAUSE!"; TERRORISM

## Bibliography

Bak, Richard. *The Day Lincoln was Shot: An Illustrated Chronicle.* Dallas, TX: Taylor, 1998.

Barkan, Steven E. *Criminology: A Sociological Understanding.* Upper Saddle River, NJ: Prentice Hall, 2001.

Bruce, George. *The Stranglers: The Cult of Thuggee and Its Overthrow in British India.* New York: Harcourt, Brace & World, 1968.

Bresler, Fenton. *Who Killed John Lennon?* New York: St. Martin's Press, 1998.

Cavendish, Marshall. *Assassinations: The Murders That Changed History.* London: Marshall Cavendish, 1975.

Gardner, Joseph L. *Departing Glory: Theodore Roosevelt as Ex-President.* New York: Charles Scribner's Sons, 1973.

Lesberg, Sandy. *Assassination in Our Time.* New York: Peebles Press International, 1976.

McConnell, Brian. *The History of Assassination.* Nashville: Aurora, 1970.

McKinley, James. *Assassinations in America.* New York: Harper and Row, 1977.

Nash, Jay Robert. *Bloodletters and Badmen.* New York: M. Evans and Co., 1973.

Remini, Robert V. *Andrew Jackson and the Course of American Democracy, 1833–1845.* New York: Harper & Row, 1984.

Roy, Parama. "Discovering India, Imagining Thuggee." *The Yale Journal of Criticism* 9 (1996):121–143.

Strober, Deborah H., and Gergald S. Strober. *Reagan: The Man and His Presidency.* New York: Houghton Mifflin, 1998.

### Internet Resources

"The Assassination of Huey Long." In the Louisiana Almanac [web site]. Available from http://louisianahistory.ourfamily.com/assassination.html.

Smith, Elbert B. "Shoot Out on Pennsylvania Avenue." In the HistoryNet at About.com [web site]. Available from www.historynet.com/AmericanHistory/articles/1998/06982_text.htm.

JAMES K. CRISSMAN
KIMBERLY A. BEACH

# AUGUSTINE

For over 1,600 years, the works of Augustine of Hippo (354–430 C.E.), the great Christian theologian and teacher, have strongly influenced religious, philosophical, and psychological thought. His ideas of mortality were informed by various belief systems, such as the early Christian view that death is punishment for original sin and the Platonic notion of the immaterial and immortal essence of the soul.

This instinct is the basis for morality, as the rational self strives to preserve its rational nature and not to become irrational or inorganic in nature. Augustine takes from Greco-Roman culture, particularly from the Stoics, the notion that every living thing has an "instinct" for self-preservation. From the books of the Pentateuch, Augustine receives a juridical account of the origin and character of death: Death is a punishment (Gen. 3:19). In his epistles to early Christian communities, the apostle Paul (an ex-rabbi) makes a juridical understanding of death central to the Christian faith (2 Cor. 1:9); these letters become increasingly important for Augustine's understanding of the significance of death.

Augustine's evaluation of death undergoes a profound change after he encounters the theology of Pelagius. In his earlier writings, such as *On the Nature of the Good,* Augustine regards death as good because it is natural: Death is the ordered succession of living entities, each coming and going the way the sound of a word comes and goes; if the sound remained forever, nothing could be said. But in Pelagius's theology, Augustine encounters a radical statement of the "naturalness" of death: Even if there had never been any sin, Pelagius says, there would still be death. Such an understanding of death is very rare in early Christianity, and Augustine eventually stands with the mass of early Christian tradition by insisting upon the exegetically derived (from the Pentateuch) judgment that death is a punishment that diminishes the original "all life" condition of human nature. It is a distinctive and consistent feature of Augustine's theology of death that it is developed and articulated almost exclusively through the opening chapters of the Book of Genesis.

The fact of death has ambivalent significance. On the one hand, death is an undeniable reality, universally appearing in all living organisms: Life inevitably ceases, however primitive or rational that life may be. On the other hand, just as inevitably and as universally, death demands denial: Consciousness rejects the devolution from organic to inorganic.

*See also:* CATHOLICISM; CHRISTIAN DEATH RITES, HISTORY OF; PHILOSOPHY, WESTERN

MICHEL RENE BARNES

# AUSTRALIAN ABORIGINAL RELIGION

Notwithstanding the diversity of Australian Aboriginal beliefs, all such peoples have had similar concerns and questions about death: What should be done with the body? What happens to the soul? How should people deal with any disrupted social relationships? And how does life itself go on in the face of death? All of these concerns pertain to a cosmological framework known in English as "The Dreaming" or "The Dreamtime," a variable mythological concept that different groups have combined in various ways with Christianity.

There are many different myths telling of the origins and consequences of death throughout Aboriginal Australia and versions of the biblical story of the Garden of Eden must now be counted among them. Even some of the very early accounts of classical Aboriginal religion probably unwittingly described mythologies that had incorporated Christian themes.

There are many traditional methods of dealing with corpses, including burial, cremation, exposure on tree platforms, interment inside a tree or hollow log, mummification, and cannibalism (although evidence for the latter is hotly disputed). Some funeral rites incorporate more than one type of disposal. The rites are designed to mark stages in the separation of body and spirit.

Aboriginal people believe in multiple human souls, which fall into two broad categories: one is comparable to the Western ego—a self-created, autonomous agency that accompanies the body and constitutes the person's identity; and another that comes from "The Dreaming" and/or from God. The latter emerges from ancestral totemic

*An Aborigine from the Tiwi tribe in Bathurst, New South Wales, Australia, stands beside painted funeral totems. Phases of funerary rites are often explicitly devoted to symbolic acts that send ancestral spirits back to their places of origin where they assume responsibility for the wellbeing of the world they have left behind.* CHARLES AND JOSETTE LENARS/CORBIS

sites in the environment, and its power enters people to animate them at various stages of their lives.

At death, the two types of soul have different trajectories and fates. The egoic soul initially becomes a dangerous ghost that remains near the deceased's body and property. It eventually passes into nonexistence, either by dissolution or by travel to a distant place of no consequence for the living. Its absence is often marked by destruction or abandonment of the deceased's property and a long-term ban on the use of the deceased person's name by the living. Ancestral souls, however, are eternal. They return to the environment and to the sites and ritual paraphernalia associated with specific totemic beings and/or with God.

The funerary rites that enact these transitions are often called (in English translation) "sorry business." They occur in Aboriginal camps and houses, as well as in Christian churches because the varied funerary practices of the past have been almost exclusively displaced by Christian burial. However, the underlying themes of the classical cosmology persist in many areas. The smoking, (a process in which smoke, usually from burning leaves, is allowed to waft over the deceased's property) stylized wailing, and self-inflicted violence are three common components of sorry business, forming part of a broader complex of social-psychological adjustment to loss that also includes anger and suspicion of the intentions of persons who might have caused the death. People may be held responsible for untimely deaths even if the suspected means of dispatch was not violence but accident or sorcery. The forms of justice meted out to such suspects include banishment, corporal punishment, and death (even though the latter is now banned by Australian law).

*See also:* HOW DEATH CAME INTO THE WORLD; SUICIDE
INFLUENCES AND FACTORS: INDIGENOUS POPULATIONS

## Bibliography

Berndt, Ronald M., and Catherine H. Berndt. *The World of the First Australians: Aboriginal Traditional Life: Past and Present.* Canberra: Aboriginal Studies Press, 1988.

Elkin, A. P. *The Australian Aborigines: How to Understand Them,* 4th edition. Sydney: Angus & Robertson, 1970.

Maddock, Kenneth. *The Australian Aborigines: A Portrait of Their Society.* Ringwood: Penguin, 1972.

Swain, Tony. *A Place for Strangers: Towards a History of Australian Aboriginal Being.* Cambridge: Cambridge University Press, 1993.

JOHN MORTON

# AUTOPSY

Autopsies, also known as necropsies or post-mortem examinations, are performed by anatomic pathologists who dissect corpses to determine the cause of death and to add to medical knowledge. "Autopsy," from the Greek *autopsia,* means seeing with one's own eyes.

Greek physicians performed autopsies as early as the fifth century B.C.E.; Egyptian physicians used them to teach anatomy between 350 and 200 B.C.E.; and doctors with the Roman legions autopsied dead barbarian soldiers. In 1533 the New World's first autopsy supposedly determined whether Siamese twins had one soul or two. In 1662 the Hartford, Connecticut, General Court ordered an autopsy to see if a child had died from witchcraft (she died of upper airway obstruction). Into the early twentieth century, many physicians performed autopsies on their own patients, often at the decedent's residence.

In the twenty-first century, pathologists perform nearly all autopsies. After at least four years of pathology training (residency), anatomic pathologists spend an additional one to two years becoming forensic pathologists. These specialists are experts in medicolegal autopsies, criminal investigation, judicial testimony, toxicology, and other forensic sciences.

While autopsies are performed primarily to determine the cause of death, they also ensure quality control in medical practice, help confirm the presence of new diseases, educate physicians, and investigate criminal activity. Modern medicine does not ensure that physicians always make correct diagnoses. More than one-third of autopsied patients has discrepancies between their clinical and autopsy diagnoses that may have adversely affected their survival. By identifying treatment errors, autopsies also helped clinicians develop the methods in use today to treat trauma patients. Society also benefits from autopsies; for example, between 1950 and 1983 alone, autopsies helped discover or clarify eighty-seven diseases or groups of diseases.

## Who Gets Autopsied?

Whether or not people are autopsied depends on the circumstances surrounding their deaths, where they die, their next of kin, and, in some cases, their advance directives or insurance policies. For many reasons, pathologists in the United States now autopsy fewer than 12 percent of nonmedicolegal deaths. Less than 1 percent of those who die in nursing homes, for example, are autopsied.

Medical examiners perform medicolegal, or forensic, autopsies. The 1954 Model Post-Mortem Examination Act, adopted in most U.S. jurisdictions, recommends forensic examination of all deaths that (1) are violent; (2) are sudden and unexpected; (3) occur under suspicious circumstances; (4) are employment related; (5) occur in persons whose bodies will be cremated, dissected, buried at sea, or otherwise unavailable for later examination; (6) occur in prison or to psychiatric inmates; or (7) constitute a threat to public health. Many also include deaths within twenty-four hours of general anesthesia or deaths in which a physician has not seen the patient in the past twenty-four hours. They can order autopsies even when deaths from violence are delayed many years after the event.

Not all deaths that fall under a medical examiner's jurisdiction are autopsied because they generally work within a tight budget. Approximately 20 percent of all deaths fall under the medical examiner/coroner's purview, but the percentage that undergoes medicolegal autopsy varies greatly by location.

In the United States, medical examiners autopsy about 59 percent of all blunt and penetrating trauma deaths, with homicide victims and trauma deaths in metropolitan areas autopsied most often. Some states may honor religious objections to medicolegal autopsies, although officials will always conduct an autopsy if they feel it is in the public interest. In 1999 the European Community adopted a comprehensive set of medicolegal autopsy rules that generally parallel those in the United States.

## Autopsy Permission

While medical examiner cases do not require consent, survivors, usually next of kin, must give their permission before pathologists perform a nonmedicolegal autopsy. A decedent's advance directive may help the survivors decide. Survivors may sue for damages based on their mental anguish for autopsies that were performed without legal approval or that were more extensive than authorized; monetary awards have been relatively small.

Autopsy permission forms usually include options for "complete postmortem examination," "complete postmortem examination—return all organs" (this does not include microscopic slides, fluid samples, or paraffin blocks, which pathologists are required to keep), "omit head," "heart and lungs only," "chest and abdomen only," "chest only," "abdomen only," and "head only." Limitations on autopsies may diminish their value.

U.S. military authorities determine whether to autopsy active duty military personnel. Some insurance policies may give insurance companies the right to demand an autopsy, and Workman's Compensation boards and the Veterans Administration may require autopsies before survivors receive death benefits.

Consent is not required for autopsies in some countries, but families may object to nonforensic autopsies. When individuals die in a foreign country, an autopsy may be requested or required upon the body's return to their home country (even if it has already been autopsied) to clarify insurance claims or to investigate criminal activity.

College-educated young adults are most likely to approve autopsies on their relatives. Contrary to popular wisdom, the type of funeral rite (burial vs. cremation) a person will have does not affect the rate of autopsy permission, at least in the United States. Although most people would permit an autopsy on themselves, the next of kin or surrogate often refuses permission based on seven erroneous beliefs:

1. Medical diagnosis is excellent and diagnostic machines almost infallible; an autopsy is unnecessary.

2. If the physician could not save the patient, he or she has no business seeking clues after that failure.

3. The patient has suffered enough.

4. Body mutilation occurs.

5. An autopsy takes a long time and delays final arrangements.

6. Autopsy results are not well communicated.

7. An autopsy will result in an incomplete body, and so life in the hereafter cannot take place.

Increasingly, however, survivors contract with private companies or university pathology departments to do autopsies on their loved ones because they either could not get one done (e.g., many hospital pathology departments have stopped doing them) or they do not accept the results of the first examination.

Religious views about autopsies generally parallel attitudes about organ or tissue donation. They vary not only among religions, but also sometimes within religious sects and among co-religionists in different countries. The Bahá'í faith, most nonfundamentalist Protestants, Catholics, Buddhists, and Sikhs permit autopsies. Jews permit them only to save another life, such as to exonerate an accused murderer. Muslims, Shintos, the Greek Orthodox Church, and Zoroastrians forbid autopsies except those required by law. Rastafarians and Hindus find autopsies extremely distasteful.

## Autopsy Technique

Complete autopsies have four steps, including inspecting the body's exterior; examining the internal organs' position and appearance; dissecting and examining the internal organs; and the laboratory analysis of tissue, fluids, and other specimens. In medicolegal cases, an investigative team trained in criminal detection first goes to the death scene to glean clues from the position and state of the body, physical evidence, and the body's surroundings. They also photograph the body, the evidence, and the scene for possible use in court.

The first step in the autopsy is to examine the corpse's exterior. Pathologists carefully examine clothing still on the body, including the effects of penetrating objects and the presence of blood or body fluid stains, evidence most useful in medicolegal cases. They use metric measurements (centimeters, grams) for the autopsy records and the U.S. system of weights and measurements for any related legal documents. Disrobing the body, they carefully examine it for identifying marks and characteristics and signs of injury or violence. They scrape the corpse's nails, test the hands for gunpowder, and collect any paint, glass, or tire marks for future identification. The pathologist also tries to determine the number, entry, and exit sites of gunshot wounds. Radiographs are frequently taken.

In the second step, pathologists open the thoracoabdominal (chest-belly) cavity. The incision, generally Y-shaped, begins at each shoulder or armpit area and runs beneath the breasts to the bottom of the breastbone. The incisions join and proceed down the middle of the abdomen to the pubis, just above the genitals. The front part of the ribs and breastbone are then removed in one piece, exposing most of the organs. Pathologists then examine the organs' relationships to each other. They often examine the brain at this stage. To expose the brain, they part the hair and make an incision behind the ears and across the base of the scalp. The front part of the scalp is then pulled over the face and the back part over the nape of the neck, exposing the skull. They open the skull using a special high-speed oscillating saw. After the skull cap is separated from the rest of the skull with a chisel, the pathologist examines the covering of the brain (meninges) and the inside of the skull for signs of infection, swelling, injury, or deterioration.

For cosmetic reasons, pathologists normally do not disturb the skin of the face, arms, hands, and the area above the nipples. For autopsies performed in the United States, pathologists rarely remove the large neck vessels. However, medical examiners must examine areas with specific injuries, such as the larynx, in possible strangulation cases. In suspected rape-murders, they may remove reproductive organs for additional tests.

In the third step, pathologists remove the body's organs for further examination and dissection. Normally, pathologists remove organs from the chest and belly either sequentially or *en bloc* (in

one piece, or "together"). Using the en bloc procedure allows them to release bodies to the mortician within thirty minutes after beginning the autopsy; the organs can be stored in the refrigerator and examined at a later time. Otherwise, the entire surgical part of an autopsy normally takes between one and three hours. During the en bloc procedure, major vessels at the base of the neck are tied and the esophagus and trachea are severed just above the thyroid cartilage (Adam's apple). Pathologists pinch off the aorta above the diaphragm and cut it and the inferior vena cava, removing the heart and lungs together. They then remove the spleen and the small and large intestines. The liver, pancreas, stomach, and esophagus are removed as a unit, followed by the kidneys, ureters, bladder, abdominal aorta, and, finally, the testes. Pathologists take small muscle, nerve, and fibrous tissue samples for microscopic examination. Examining and weighing the organs, they open them to check for internal pathology. They remove tissue fragments anywhere they see abnormalities, as well as representative pieces from at least the left ventricle of the heart, lungs, kidneys, and liver.

Pathologists remove the brain from the skull by cutting the nerves to the eyes, the major blood vessels to the brain, the fibrous attachment to the skull, the spinal cord, and several other nerves and connections. After gently lifting the brain out of the skull and checking it again for external abnormalities, they usually suspend it by a thread in a two-gallon pail filled with 10 percent formalin. This "fixes" it, firming the tissue so that it can be properly examined ten to fourteen days later. (Bone is rarely removed during an autopsy unless there is suspected to be injury or disease affecting it.) Pathologists then sew closed any large incisions.

Step four, the most time consuming, consists of examining minute tissue and fluid specimens under the microscope and by chemical analysis. Medical examiners routinely test for drugs and poisons (toxicology screens) in the spinal fluid, eye fluid (vitreous humor), blood, bile, stomach contents, hair, skin, urine, and, in decomposing bodies, fluid from blisters. Pathologists commonly test infants with congenital defects, miscarried fetuses, and stillborns for chromosomal abnormalities, and fetuses and infants, as well as their placenta and umbilical cords, for malformations suggesting congenital abnormalities.

After an autopsy, pathologists usually put the major organs into plastic bags and store them in body cavities unless they have written permission to keep them. Medical examiners must keep any organs or tissues needed for evidence in a legal case. Medical devices, such as pacemakers, are discarded. They routinely keep small pieces of organs (about the size of a crouton) for subsequent microscopic and chemical analysis. National standards require that "wet tissue" from autopsies be held for six months after issuing a final autopsy report, tissue in paraffin blocks (from which microscope slides are made) must be kept for five years, and the slides themselves along with the autopsy reports must be retained for twenty years.

After completing the autopsy, pathologists try, when possible, to determine both a "cause of death" and the contributing factors. The most common misconception about medicolegal investigations is that they always determine the time of death. The final autopsy report may not be available for many weeks. The next of kin signing a routine autopsy authorization need only request a copy of the report. In medical examiners' cases, if they do not suspect suspicious circumstances surrounding the death, next of kin need to request the report in writing. When the autopsy results may be introduced into court as evidence, a lawyer may need to request the report.

Forensic pathologists also perform autopsies on decomposing bodies or on partial remains to identify the deceased and, if possible, to determine the cause and time of death. Pathologists usually exhume bodies to (1) investigate the cause or manner of death; (2) collect evidence; (3) determine the cause of an accident or the presence of disease; (4) gather evidence to assess malpractice; (5) compare the body with another person thought to be deceased; (6) identify hastily buried war and accident victims; (7) settle accidental death or liability claims; or (8) search for lost objects. In some instances, they must first determine whether remains are, in fact, human and whether they represent a "new" discovery or simply the disinterment of previously known remains. This becomes particularly difficult when the corpse has been severely mutilated or intentionally misidentified to confuse investigators.

*See also:* AUTOPSY, PSYCHOLOGICAL; BURIED ALIVE; CADAVER EXPERIENCES; CRYONIC SUSPENSION

## Bibliography

Anderson, Robert E., and Rolla B. Hill. "The Current Status of the Autopsy in Academic Medical Centers in the United States." *American Journal of Clinical Pathology* 92, Suppl. 1 (1989):S31–S37.

Brinkmann, Bernard. "Harmonization of Medico-Legal Autopsy Rules." *International Journal of Legal Medicine* 113, no. 1 (1999):1–14.

Eckert, William G., G. Steve Katchis, and Stuart James. "Disinterments—Their Value and Associated Problems." *American Journal of Forensic Medicine & Pathology* 11 (1990):9–16.

Heckerling, Paul S., and Melissa Johnson Williams. "Attitudes of Funeral Directors and Embalmers toward Autopsy." *Archives of Pathology and Laboratory Medicine* 116 (1992):1147–1151.

Hektoen, Ludvig. "Early Postmortem Examinations by Europeans in America." *Journal of the American Medical Association* 86, no. 8 (1926):576–577.

Hill, Robert B., and Rolla E. Anderson. "The Autopsy Crisis Reexamined: The Case for a National Autopsy Policy." *Milbank Quarterly* 69 (1991):51–78.

Iserson, Kenneth V. *Death to Dust: What Happens to Dead Bodies?* 2nd edition. Tucson, AZ: Galen Press, 2001.

Ludwig, Jurgen. *Current Methods of Autopsy Practice.* Philadelphia: W. B. Saunders, 1972.

Moore, G. William, and Grover M. Hutchins. "The Persistent Importance of Autopsies." *Mayo Clinic Proceedings* 75 (2000):557–558.

Pollack, Daniel A., Joann M. O'Neil, R. Gibson Parrish, Debra L. Combs, and Joseph L. Annest. "Temporal and Geographic Trends in the Autopsy Frequency of Blunt and Penetrating Trauma Deaths in the United States." *Journal of the American Medical Association* 269 (1993):1525–1531.

Roosen, John E., Frans A. Wilmer, Daniel C. Knockaert, and Herman Bobbaers. "Comparison of Premortem Clinical Diagnoses in Critically Ill Patients and Subsequent Autopsy Findings." *Mayo Clinic Proceedings* 75 (2000):562–567.

Start, Roger D., Aha Kumari Dube, Simon S. Cross, and James C. E. Underwood. "Does Funeral Preference Influence Clinical Necropsy Request Outcome?" *Medicine Science and the Law* 37, no. 4 (1997):337–340.

"Uniform Law Commissioners: Model Post-Mortem Examinations Act, 1954." In Debra L. Combs, R. Gibson Parrish, and Roy Ing eds., *Death Investigation in the United States and Canada, 1992.* Atlanta, GA: U.S. Department of Health and Human Services, 1992.

Wilke, Arthur S., and Fran French. "Attitudes toward Autopsy Refusal by Young Adults." *Psychological Reports* 67 (1990):81–91.

KENNETH V. ISERSON

# AUTOPSY, PSYCHOLOGICAL

The psychological autopsy is a procedure for investigating a person's death by reconstructing what the person thought, felt, and did preceding his or her death. This reconstruction is based upon information gathered from personal documents, police reports, medical and coroner's records, and face-to-face interviews with families, friends, and others who had contact with the person before the death.

The first psychological autopsy study was most likely Gregory Zilboorg's investigation of ninety-three consecutive suicides by police officers in New York City between 1934 and 1940. In 1958 the chief medical examiner of the Los Angeles Coroners Office asked a team of professionals from the Los Angeles Suicide Prevention Center to help in his investigations of equivocal cases where a cause of death was not immediately clear. From these investigations, the psychiatrist Edwin Shneidman coined the phrase "psychological autopsy" to describe the procedure he and his team of researchers developed during those investigations. The method involved talking in a tactful and systematic manner to key persons—a spouse, lover, parent, grown child, friend, colleague, physician, supervisor, and coworker—who knew the deceased. Their practice of investigating equivocal deaths in Los Angeles continued for almost thirty years and allowed for more accurate classification of equivocal deaths as well as contributing to experts' understanding of suicide.

In the 1970s and 1980s, researchers using the psychological autopsy method investigated risk factors for suicide. Psychological autopsies have confirmed that the vast majority of suicide victims could be diagnosed as having had a mental disorder, usually depression, manic depression, or alcohol or drug problems. Other studies focused upon the availability of firearms in the home of suicide completers, traumatic events in person's lives, and other psychological and social factors.

There are two major trends in the use of psychological autopsies: research investigation and clinical and legal use. Research investigations generally involve many people who died by suicide and comparing the results with another group, for example, accident victims, in order to see if some factors are important in discriminating between suicides and other deaths. Clinical and legal use of psychological autopsies involves investigations of a single death in order to clarify why or how a person died. These often involve descriptive interpretations of the death and may include information to help family and friends better understand why a tragic death occurred. They also may lead to suggesting means of preventing suicides, for example by suggesting improvements in hospital treatment or suicide prevention in jails.

Psychological autopsies have been conducted for literary interpretation of the deaths of famous people. Of note is Shneidman's analysis eighty-eight years later of the death of Malcolm Melville in 1867, the son of *Moby Dick* author Herman Melville. They also have been used in legal cases to settle estate questions concerning the nature of death; for example, the death of the billionaire Howard Hughes. Psychological autopsies have been used in criminal investigations of blame, including one case where a mother was found guilty of numerous abusive behaviors toward a child who had committed suicide.

There is no consensus on the exact procedure for conducting a psychological autopsy. However, psychological autopsy studies for research purposes often use complex methods to ensure that the information is reliable and valid. All psychological autopsies are based upon possibly biased recollections. Nevertheless, the psychological autopsy constitutes one of the main investigative tools for understanding suicide and the circumstances surrounding death.

*See also:* AUTOPSY; SUICIDE INFLUENCES AND FACTORS: ALCOHOL AND DRUG USE, MENTAL ILLNESS

## *Bibliography*

Friedman, P. "Suicide among Police: A Study of 93 Suicides among New York City Policemen, 1934–1940." In Edwin S. Shneidman ed., *Essays in Self-Destruction*. New York: Science House, 1967.

Jabobs, D., and M. E. Klein. "The Expanding Role of Psychological Autopsies." In Antoon A. Leenaars ed.,

*Suicidology: Essays in Honor of Edwin S. Shneidman.* Northvale, NJ: Aronson, 1993.

Litman, Robert, T. Curphey, and Edwin Shneidman. "Investigations of Equivocal Suicides." *Journal of the American Medical Association* 184, no. 12 (1963):924–929.

Shneidman, Edwin S. "Some Psychological Reflections on the Death of Malcom Melville." *Suicide and Life-Threatening Behavior* 6, no. 4 (1976):231–242.

BRIAN L. MISHARA

# AZTEC RELIGION

At the time of Spanish contact in the sixteenth century, the Aztec were the preeminent power in Mexico, and to the east controlled lands bordering the Maya region. Whereas the Maya were neither culturally nor politically unified as a single entity in the sixteenth century, the Aztec were an empire integrated by the state language of Nahuatl as well as a complex religious system. As the principal political force during the Spanish conquest, the Aztec were extensively studied at this time. Due to sixteenth-century manuscripts written both by the Aztec and Spanish clerics, a great deal is known of Aztec religious beliefs and ritual, including death rituals.

Probably the most discussed and vilified aspect of Aztec religion is human sacrifice, which is amply documented by archaeological excavations, pre-Hispanic art, and colonial accounts. To the Aztec, cosmic balance and therefore life would not be possible without offering sacrificial blood to forces of life and fertility, such as the sun, rain, and the earth. Thus in Aztec myth, the gods sacrificed themselves for the newly created sun to move on its path. The offering of children to the rain gods was considered a repayment for their bestowal of abundant water and crops. Aside from sacrificial offerings, death itself was also a means of feeding and balancing cosmic forces. Many pre-Hispanic scenes illustrate burial as an act of the feeding the earth, with the bundled dead in the open maw of the earth monster. Just as day became night, death was a natural and necessary fate for the living.

The sixteenth-century accounts written in Spanish and Nahuatl provide detailed descriptions of Aztec concepts of death and the afterlife. One of the most important accounts of Aztec mortuary rites and beliefs concerning the hereafter occurs in Book 3 of the *Florentine Codex,* an encyclopedic treatise of Aztec culture compiled by the Franciscan Fray Bernardino de Sahagún. According to this and other early accounts, the treatment of the body and the destiny of the soul in the afterlife depended in large part on one's social role and mode of death, in contrast to Western beliefs that personal behavior in life determines one's afterlife. People who eventually succumbed to illness and old age went to Mictlan, the dark underworld presided by the skeletal god of death, Mictlantecuhtli, and his consort Mictlancihuatl. In preparation for this journey, the corpse was dressed in paper vestments, wrapped and tied in a cloth bundle, and then cremated, along with a dog to serve as a guide through the underworld. The path to Mictlan traversed a landscape fraught with dangers, including fierce beasts, clashing mountains, and obsidian-bladed winds. Having passed these perils, the soul reached gloomy, soot-filled Mictlan, "the place of mystery, the place of the unfleshed, the place where there is arriving, the place with no smoke hole, the place with no fireplace" (Sahagún 1978, Book 3, p. 42). With no exits, Mictlan was a place of no return.

Aside from the dreary, hellish realm of Mictlan, there was the afterworld of Tlalocan, the paradise of Tlaloc, the god of rain and water. A region of eternal spring, abundance, and wealth, this place was for those who died by lightning, drowning, or were afflicted by particular diseases, such as pustules or gout. Rather than being cremated, these individuals were buried whole with images of the mountain gods, beings closely related to Tlaloc. Another source compiled by Sahagún, the *Primeros Memoriales,* contains a fascinating account of a noble woman who, after being accidentally buried alive, journeys to the netherworld paradise of Tlalocan to receive a gift and message from the rain god.

Book 3 of the *Florentine Codex* describes a celestial paradise. In sharp contrast to the victims of disease dwelling in Mictlan, this region was occupied by warriors and lords who died by sacrifice or combat in honor of the sun god Tonatiuh. The bodies of the slain heroes were burned in warrior bundles, with birds and butterflies symbolizing their fiery souls. These warrior souls followed the sun to

*A group of men in front of the Basilica of Our Lady of Guadalupe in Mexico perform an Aztec dance during the feast of the Virgin of Guadalupe on December 12, the most important religious holiday in Mexico. Here they reenact the preparation of a sacrifice, a recognition of the inextricable interdependence of life and death to the Aztec.* SERGIO DORANTES/ CORBIS

zenith in the sky, where they would then scatter to sip flowers in this celestial paradise. The setting western sun would then be greeted by female warriors, which were the souls of those women who died in childbirth. In Aztec thought, the pregnant woman was like a warrior who symbolically captured her child for the Aztec state in the painful and bloody battle of birth. Considered as female aspects of defeated heroic warriors, women dying in childbirth became fierce goddesses who carried the setting sun into the netherworld realm of Mictlan. In contrast to the afterworld realms of Mictlan and Tlalocan, the paradise of warriors did relate to how one behaved on earth, as this was the region for the valorous who both lived and died as heroes. This ethos of bravery and self-sacrifice was a powerful ideological means to ensure the commitment of warriors to the growth and well-being of the empire.

For the Aztec, yearly ceremonies pertaining to the dead were performed during two consecutive twenty-day months, the first month for children, and the second for adults, with special focus on the cult of the warrior souls. Although then occurring in the late summertime of August, many aspects of these ceremonies have continued in the fall Catholic celebrations of All Saints' Day and All Souls' Day. Along with the ritual offering of food for the visiting dead, marigolds frequently play a major part in the contemporary celebrations, a flower specifically related to the dead in Aztec ritual.

*See also:* AFTERLIFE IN CROSS-CULTURAL PERSPECTIVE; CANNIBALISM; INCAN RELIGION; MAYA RELIGION; SACRIFICE

### Bibliography

López Austin, Alfredo. *The Human Body and Ideology: Concepts of the Ancient Nahuas.* Salt Lake City: University of Utah Press, 1980.

Furst, Jill Leslie McKeever. *The Natural History of the Soul in Ancient Mexico.* New Haven, CT: Yale University Press, 1995.

Sahagún, Fray Bernardino de. *Primeros Memoriales,* translated by Thelma Sullivan. Norman: University of Oklahoma Press, 1997.

Sahagún, Fray Bernardino de. *Florentine Codex: General History of the Things of New Spain,* translated by Arthur J. O. Anderson and Charles E. Dibble. 13 vols. Santa Fe, NM: School of American Research, 1950–1982.

KARL A. TAUBE

# B

## BAHÁ'Í FAITH

Barely more than a hundred years old, the Bahá'í faith emerged from the region of what is now Iran and Iraq, preaching a vision of the unity of all religions and humankind. The Bahá'í's believe that the great founders of the major world religions were divine prophets who served as channels of grace between the unknowable god and humankind. They also believe that revelation is progressive. All the revelations are essentially the same, differing only by the degree of their compatibility with the state of the human race at the time of their appearance.

### Origins and Evolution of Bahá'í Faith

The Bahá'í faith is an offshoot of the Bábí religion, founded in 1844 by Mízrá 'Alí Mohammed of Shíráz, originally a Shí'ite Muslim, in present-day Iran. He declared himself a prophet with a new revelation, and spoke also about the future appearance, in exactly nineteen years, of a new prophet who would sweep away centuries of inherited superstition and injustice and inaugurate a golden age of peace and reconciliation among all humans of all religions, sects, and nationalities. Under his title of the "Báb" (Arabic for "gateway"), he propagated his universal doctrine throughout Persia, incurring the ire of the country's predominant Shí'ite Muslim religious establishment and their allies in the government. A massive campaign of official persecution over the next several years led to the death of thousands of Bábí followers and culminated in the execution of the Báb in 1850.

Mírzá Husayn 'Alí Núrí was among the Báb's most ardent and eloquent followers. Dubbing himself Bahá'u'lláh, he renounced his personal wealth and social position to devote himself to proselytizing the Bábí faith. While imprisoned in Tehran in 1852, Bahá'u'lláh experienced an epiphany, which he claimed divine appointment as the prophet announced by the Báb. At the end of the year he was released from prison and deported to present-day Iraq. Settling in Baghdad, he led a vigorous Bábí revival that prompted the Ottoman regime to relocate him to Constantinople, where the Bábí community embraced him as the prophet promised by the Báb and thereafter called themselves Bahá'í's in honor of their new leader.

Seeking to contain the influence of the growing new faith, the Ottomans exiled Bahá'u'lláh first to Adrianople in present-day Turkey and later to Acre in what is now Israel. Yet through the tenacity of his vision, he not only sustained his flock of followers but also managed a modest growth until his death in 1892, when the religion's leadership fell into the hands of his oldest son, 'Abdu'l-Bahá, who was succeeded by his own grandson Shoghi Effendi (d. 1951). Over the ensuing decades the faith won new adherents around the world, undergoing an especially rapid spurt of growth in the West. At the end of the twentieth century, the faith had approximately 6 million adherents worldwide.

The Bahá'í sacred scriptures consist of the formal writings and transcribed speeches of the Báb, Bahá'u'lláh, and 'Abalu'l-Bahá. There are no formally prescribed rituals and no priests or clerics. The only formalized prescriptive behavioral expectations of the faith are daily prayer; nineteen days of fasting; abstaining from all mind-altering agents, including alcohol; monogamous fidelity to one's spouse; and participation in the Nineteenth Day Feast that opens every month of the Bahá'í calendar, which divides the year into nineteen months, each nineteen days long, with four compensatory days added along the way. New Year's day is observed on the first day of spring.

## Bahá'í Beliefs on Death and Dying

The Bahá'í faith posits three layers of existence: the concealed secret of the Divine Oneness; the intermediary world of spiritual reality; and the world of physical realty ("the world of possibility"). It rejects the notion—common to Judaism, Christianity, and Islam—that life in this physical world is a mere preparation for an eternal life to come after death. The Bahá'í faith regards the whole idea of Heaven and Hell as allegorical rather than real. Bahá'ís believe that human life moves between the two interwoven poles of the physical and the spiritual. The only difference is that the world of physical existence has the dimension of temporality whereas the world of spiritual existence is eternal. Although one's physical life is not directly preparatory for a purely spiritual afterlife, the two are interrelated, the current course of life can influence its subsequent course. Death does not mean movement into another life, but continuation of this life. It is simply another category or stage of existence. The best that a person can do in this world, therefore, is to achieve spiritual growth, in both this and the coming life.

Death is regarded as the mere shedding of the physical frame while the indestructible soul lives on. Because the soul is the sum total of the personality and the physical body is pure matter with no real identity, the person, having left his material side behind, remains the same person, and he continues the life he conducted in the physical world. His heaven therefore is the continuation of the noble side of his earthly life, whereas hell would be the continuation of an ignoble life on earth. Freed from the bonds of earthly life, the soul is able to come nearer to God in the "Kingdom of Bahá." Hence the challenge of life in this world continues in the next, with the challenge eased because of the freedom from physical urges and imperatives.

Although death causes distress and pain to the friends and relatives of the deceased, it should be regarded as nothing more than a stage of life. Like birth, it comes on suddenly and opens a door to new and more abundant life. Death and birth follow each other in the movement from stage to stage and are symbolized some in other religions by the well-known ceremonies of the "rites of passage." In this way real physical death is also considered as a stage followed by birth into an invisible but no less real world.

Because the body is the temple of the soul, it must be treated with respect; therefore, cremation is forbidden in the Bahá'í faith, and the body must be laid to rest in the ground and pass through the natural process of decomposition. Moreover, the body must be treated with utmost care and cannot be removed a distance of more than an hour's journey from the place of death. The body must be wrapped in a shroud of silk or cotton and on its finger should be placed a ring bearing the inscription "I came forth from God and return unto Him, detached from all save Him, holding fast to His Name, the Merciful the Compassionate." The coffin should be made from crystal, stone, or hardwood, and a special prayer for the dead must be said before interment.

In its particular respect for the body of the dead, the Bahá'í faith shares the same values of Judaism and Islam, and was no doubt influenced by the attitude of Islam, its mother religion.

*See also:* ISLAM

### Bibliography

Buck, Christopher. *Symbol and Secret.* Los Angeles: Kalimát Press, 1995.

Cole, Juan Ricardo. *Modernity and the Millennium: The Genesis of the Bahá'í Faith in the Nineteenth-Century Middle East.* New York: Columbia University Press, 1998.

Hatcher, John S. *The Purpose of Physical Reality, The Kingdom of Names.* National Spiritual Assembly of the Bahá'ís of the United States. 1979.

Smith, Peter. *The Bábí and Bahá'í Religions: From Messianic Shí'ism to a World Religion.* Cambridge: Cambridge University Press, 1987.

MOSHE SHARON

# BECKER, ERNEST

The anthropologist Ernest Becker is well-known for his thesis that individuals are terrorized by the knowledge of their own mortality and thus seek to deny it in various ways. Correspondingly, according to Becker, a main function of a culture is to provide ways to engage successfully in death denial.

Becker was born on September 27, 1924, in Springfield, Massachusetts, to Jewish immigrants. His first publication, *Zen: A Rational Critique* (1961), was a version of his doctoral dissertation at Syracuse University, where he pursued graduate studies in cultural anthropology before becoming a writer and professor at Simon Fraser University in Vancouver, British Columbia, Canada. He authored nine books, with the last one, *Escape from Evil,* appearing after Becker's untimely death in March 1974. *Escape from Evil* is an application to the problem of evil of ideas Becker exposed in *The Denial of Death* (1973), a book for which he was awarded a Pulitzer Prize. Becker considered the two books to be an expression of his mature thinking.

*The Denial of Death* emerged out of Becker's previous attempts to create a unified "science of man" that he hoped would provide an understanding of the fundamental strivings of humans and the basis for the formulation of an ideal type of person—one who, being free from external constraints on freedom, might attain "comprehensive meaning" (Becker 1973). In the second edition of *The Birth and Death of Meaning* (1971) and, more elaborately, in *The Denial of Death* and *Escape from Evil,* Becker presents the more pessimistic view that the quest for meaning resides not outside but inside the individual. The threat to meaning is created by a person's awareness of his or her own mortality.

The change in Becker's view happened under the influence of the psychoanalyst Otto Rank, who viewed the fear of life and death as a fundamental human motivation. Becker used the idea of a "character armor" (taken from another psychoanalyst, Wilhelm Reich) as "the arming of personality so that it can maneuver in a threatening world" and enlarged it with the concept of the society as a symbolic hero system that allows the practice of "heroics" (Becker 1973). By fulfilling their role in such a society—"low heroics"—or by pursuing and realizing extraordinary accomplishments—"high heroics"—humans maintain a sense of self-esteem.

*The writings of the anthropologist Ernest Becker (1924–1974) inspired the formulation of a psychological theory of social motivation—Terror Management Theory—that is supported by extensive empirical work.* THE ERNEST BECKER FOUNDATION

In *The Denial of Death,* Becker presents examples of low and high heroics in the normal individual, the creator, and the mentally ill. For example, he portrays the schizophrenic as incapable of conforming to normal cultural standards and is thus incapable of death denial. To substantiate his thesis regarding the universality of the death terror, Becker employed arguments from biology, from psychoanalytic theory, and from existential philosophy, especially Kierkegaard. For example, Freud's Oedipus complex is reinterpreted to reflect the existential project of avoiding the implications of being a "body," and thus being mortal. The boy is attracted to his mother in an effort to become his own father, thereby attempting to transcend his mortality through an imagined self-sufficiency.

Notwithstanding his emphasis on death terror as a mainspring of human activity and as a foundation for human culture, Becker does not ignore the tendency of human beings to grow. This tendency has the form of merging with the cosmos (the Agape motive) or of development beyond the present self (the Eros motive). The psychoanalytic concept of transference, as identification with an external object, corresponds to the first motive. While life expansion forces coexist with the fear of death, it is the latter that imbues them with urgency. Transference, for example, reflects both fear of death and possibility for "creative transcendence." In both cases transference involves "distortion" or "illusion." The problem of an ideal life becomes the problem of the "best illusion," the one that allows maximum "freedom, dignity, and hope" (Becker 1973, p. 202). Only religion, with God as an object of transference, can satisfy these criteria. However, this is a religion that emphasizes an awareness of limits, introspection, and a confrontation with apparent meaninglessness.

Becker's academic career suffered enormously because of his intellectual courage and because of the skepticism of "tough-minded" social scientists toward his ideas. Becker's writings continue to influence psychotherapeutic, educational, and theoretical work, especially as regards the pervasiveness of the fear of death in governing individual and social behavior into the twenty-first century.

*See also:* Anxiety and Fear; Freud, Sigmund; Immortality, Symbolic; Sartre, Jean-Paul; Taboos and Social Stigma; Terror Management Theory

### *Bibliography*

Becker, Ernest. *Escape from Evil*. New York: Free Press, 1975.

Becker, Ernest. *The Denial of Death*. New York: Free Press, 1973.

Becker, Ernest. *The Birth and Death of Meaning*. New York: Free Press, 1971.

Becker, Ernest. *Angel in Armor*. New York: George Braziller, 1969.

Becker, Ernest. *Beyond Alienation*. New York: George Braziller, 1967.

Kagan, Michael A. *Educating Heroes*. Durango, CO: Hollowbrook, 1994.

Leifer, Ron. "Becker, Ernest." In David L. Sills ed., *The International Encyclopedia of the Social Sciences*, Vol. 18: *Biographical Supplement*. New York: Free Press, 1979.

Liechty, Daniel. *Transference & Transcendence*. Northvale, NJ: Jason Aronson, 1995.

### *Internet Resources*

Leifer, Ron. "The Legacy of Ernest Becker." *Psychnews International* 2, no. 4 (1997). Available from www.psychnews.net/2_4/index.htm.

ADRIAN TOMER

# BEFRIENDING

Befriending is a free, confidential, and nonjudgmental listening service offered by trained volunteers to help people who are lonely, despairing, and suicidal. Unlike some approaches to suicide prevention, befriending does not involve telling or advising a suicidal person what to do. Befriending respects the right of each person to make his or her own decisions, including the decision of whether to live or die. Befriending centers are nonpolitical and nonsectarian, and the volunteers do not seek to impose their own beliefs or opinions. Instead, they listen without judging, allowing suicidal people to talk about their fears and frustrations. It is common for callers to say that they have nobody else to whom they can turn, and simply talking through problems can begin to suggest solutions.

Befrienders are not paid professionals. They come from many different backgrounds and cultures, and range in age from eighteen to eighty. This diversity is central to the philosophy of the befriending movement, which recognizes the importance of professional psychiatric help but also believes that laypeople—carefully selected, trained, guided, and supported—provide a valuable service by simply listening.

The concept of befriending originated in England in 1953, when Reverend Chad Varah began a service in London. To meet the huge response, he organized laypeople to be with those waiting to see him, and soon noticed a wonderful interaction between the callers and the volunteers who listened to them with empathy and acceptance. He called what the volunteers were doing "befriending."

From that single center in London grew the Samaritans, which by 2001 had 203 centers across the United Kingdom and Northern Ireland. The concept also spread beyond Britain, and in 1966 Befrienders International was established to support befriending centers around the world. In 2001 this network spanned 361 centers in 41 countries. There were significant numbers of befriending centers in Brazil, Canada, India, New Zealand, Sri Lanka, the United Kingdom, and the United States. Two other organizations—the International Federation of Telephonic Emergency Services and LifeLine International—have networks of centers that provide similar services.

Befriending is provided in different ways. The most common form of contact is by telephone, but many people are befriended face to face. Some prefer to write down their feelings in a letter or an e-mail. One British center does not have a physical base but instead sends volunteers to major public events, such as shows and musical concerts, to offer face-to-face befriending to anyone who feels alone in the crowd. A number of centers have gone out to befriend people in the aftermath of earthquakes and other disasters. Many centers run outreach campaigns, working with children and young people, and promoting the concept of listening. The Internet provides an unprecedented opportunity to provide information about befriending to a global audience. As of the end of March 2002, the Befrienders International web site offers information in the first languages of half the world's population.

While the situations and processes of befriending can vary, the essence of the contact is always the same: an opportunity for suicidal people to talk through their deepest fears and to know that somebody is interested in them and is prepared to listen to them, without passing judgment or giving advice.

*See also:* SUICIDE BASICS: PREVENTION; VARAH, CHAD

CHRIS BALE

# BEREAVEMENT

*See* BEREAVEMENT, VICARIOUS; GRIEF: OVERVIEW.

# BEREAVEMENT, VICARIOUS

Vicarious bereavement is the state of having suffered a vicarious loss. A vicarious event is one that is experienced through imaginative or sympathetic participation in the experience of another person. Therefore, vicarious grief refers to grief stimulated by someone else's loss. It usually involves deaths of others not personally known by the mourner. Vicarious grief is genuine grief. It is differentiated from conventional grief insofar as it is sparked by another individual's loss, that person being the actual mourner, and it typically involves more psychological reactions than behavioral, social, or physical ones. Vicarious grief was first reported by the scholar and thanatology expert Robert Kastenbaum in 1987.

There are two types of vicarious bereavement. In Type 1, the losses to the vicarious mourner are exclusively vicarious, and are those that are mildly to moderately identified with as being experienced by the actual mourner. For instance, the vicarious mourner feels that this is what it must be like to be in the actual mourner's position.

In Type 2 vicarious bereavement, Type 1 vicarious losses occur, but there are also personal losses sustained by the vicarious mourner. These personal losses develop because: (a) the vicarious mourner has relatively intense reactions to the actual mourner's loss (e.g., the vicarious mourner feels so personally stunned and overwhelmed in response to the actual mourner's losing a loved one through a sudden death that he or she temporarily loses the ability to function normally); and/or (b) the vicarious mourner experiences personal assumptive world violations because of the loss. An assumptive world violation takes place whenever an element of an individual's assumptive world is rendered invalid by the death. The assumptive world is a person's mental set, derived from past personal experience, that contains all a person assumes, expects, and believes to be true about the self, the world, and everything and everyone in it.

Assumptive world violations occur in vicarious bereavement because the vicarious mourner has heightened identification with the actual mourner (e.g., the vicarious mourner so identifies with the actual mourner after that person's child dies that the vicarious mourner feels his or her own sense of parental control shattered, which invalidates one of the fundamental beliefs in the vicarious mourner's own assumptive world) and/or the vicarious mourner becomes personally traumatized by the circumstances under which the actual mourner's loved one dies (e.g., the vicarious mourner is so badly traumatized by the death of the actual mourner's loved one in a terrorist attack that the vicarious mourner experiences a shattering of his or her own personal security and safety in his or her own assumptive world). While Type 2 vicarious bereavement does stimulate actual personal losses within the vicarious mourner, technically making vicarious a misnomer, the term is retained because it focuses attention on the fact that bereavement can be stimulated by losses actually experienced by others.

Three sets of factors are especially influential in causing a person to experience vicarious bereavement, primarily because each factor increases the vicarious mourner's emotional participation in the loss and his or her personal experience of distress or traumatization because of it. These three sets of factors include: (a) the psychological processes of empathy, sympathy, and identification; (b) selected high-risk characteristics of the death—particularly suddenness, violence, preventability, and child loss; and (c) media coverage of the death that overexposes the person to graphic horrific images, distressing information, and/or distraught reactions of actual mourners.

Notable events prompting widespread vicarious grief include the September 11, 2001, terrorist attacks, the Oklahoma City bombing, the explosion of TWA Flight 800, and the Columbine school massacre. The phenomenon also explains in part the profound public reactions witnessed following the deaths of certain celebrities. For instance, the deaths of Princess Diana and John Kennedy Jr. appeared to catalyze unparalleled Type 2 vicarious bereavement, although in these cases other factors were present that further intensified that grief. These factors included what these individuals symbolized, what their deaths implied about the average person's vulnerability, and social contagion processes. Social contagion occurs when intense reactions became somewhat infectious to those who observed them and stimulated within these observers their own intense responses to the death.

Vicarious bereavement can provide valuable opportunities to rehearse future losses, challenge assumptive world elements, finish incomplete mourning from prior losses, and increase awareness of life's preciousness and fragility. On the other hand, it can be detrimental if the vicarious mourner becomes disenfranchised, propelled into complicated mourning, traumatized, bereavement overloaded, or injured from inaccurate imaginings or insufficient information. Many questions still remain about this experience and what influences it.

*See also:* GRIEF: DISENFRANCHISED, THEORIES, TRAUMATIC

## Bibliography

Kastenbaum, Robert. "Vicarious Grief." In Robert Kastenbaum and Beatrice Kastenbaum eds., *The Encyclopedia of Death*. Phoenix, AZ: The Oryx Press, 1989.

Kastenbaum, Robert. "Vicarious Grief: An Intergenerational Phenomenon?" *Death Studies* 11 (1987):447–453.

Rando, Therese A. "Vicarious Bereavement." In Stephen Strack ed., *Death and the Quest for Meaning: Essays in Honor of Herman Feifel*. Northvale, NJ: Jason Aronson, 1997.

THERESE A. RANDO

# BIOETHICS

Bioethics refers to the systematic study of the moral aspects of health care and the life sciences. Physicians have always made decisions with significant moral components in the context of medical practice guided by the Hippocratic obligation to help patients without causing harm. This traditional medical morality nonetheless became insufficient to address the ethical issues that arose as medical practice changed over the course of the twentieth century to include more care by medical specialists, extensive use of complex medical technologies, and a trend toward dying in the hospital rather than at home. A series of controversies involving research with human subjects and the allocation of scarce new technologies (e.g., kidney dialysis and organ transplantation) made clear that the wisdom of physicians and researchers was inadequate to ensure the appropriate treatment of patients and research subjects. In universities and hospitals, this widespread patients' rights movement galvanized the attention of a growing contingent of theologians, philosophers, and lawyers who came to identify themselves as medical ethicists or bioethicists.

A central task of bioethics has been the articulation of approaches to guide the moral aspects of medical decision making. Here, a core commitment has been to the empowerment of patients' meaningful participation in their own health care, which is typified by the now common practice of obtaining informed consent (the process in which a clinician gives a patient understandable information about a proposed procedure or intervention, including its risks, benefits, and alternatives, and then the patient makes a voluntary decision about whether to proceed with it). The ethical principle of "respect for autonomy" underpinning this approach distinguishes bioethics most sharply from earlier systems of medical ethics. Three other principles that are also influential include beneficence (doing good for the patient), nonmaleficence (not harming), and justice. These core principles lead to a set of rules such as those regarding truth-telling and confidentiality. Together, these principles and rules comprise a secular means of approaching ethical issues in medicine that is designed to be relevant in a pluralistic society. In practicality the great question in many situations is which principle takes precedence. This conflict is readily apparent in the two prominent bioethical discourses surrounding death and dying: withdrawal of support in the terminally ill and physician-assisted suicide.

## Withdrawal of Support in the Terminally Ill

The rise of mechanical ventilation and intensive care technology may be likened to a double-edged sword. While rescuing countless patients from acute illness, it has also made possible the preservation of bodily functions of patients following severe brain injury. The 1981 report of the President's Commission for the Study of Ethical Problems in Medicine and Biomedical and Behavioral Research, *Defining Death,* confirmed the appropriateness of the existing practice that allows withdrawal of life support from patients with absent brainstem functions as defined by the 1968 Harvard brain death criteria. Far more controversial have been those patients in irreversible coma who nonetheless still preserve brainstem reflexes, a condition designated as persistent vegetative state (PVS) that may continue many years with technological assistance. Perhaps the most famous such case was that of Karen Ann Quinlan, in which the New Jersey Supreme Court in 1976 recognized the right of the parents of a twenty-one-year-old woman with irreversible coma to discontinue her ventilator support over the objections of her physicians. The widely publicized decision opened the door for withdrawing such support legally, but still left open many ethical and practical questions.

Here the bioethicists stepped in. On one level, the Quinlan case confirmed their emerging role in the health care setting. Given the difficulty of ascertaining the patient's own wishes based upon the recollections of family and loved ones, the New Jersey Supreme Court recommended that hospitals develop ethics committees to guide such decisions when family and physicians are at odds. Ethicists thus gained a foothold in many hospitals. On a second level, discussions of discontinuing life support underlined the need for a more substantial framework to guide decision making. Many ethicists evoked the principle of autonomy to advocate advance directive—declarations such as living wills or the appointment of a durable power of attorney for health care—to minimize uncertainty regarding the patients' wishes should an event consign them to dependence upon invasive technology, making it impossible for them to participate in decision making about whether to continue the use of such technologies. Yet, less than 10 percent of Americans have completed such wills.

Following a series of legal cases the right to refuse life-sustaining therapies, including ventilator and feeding tube support from patients with irreversible coma, has been established. Nevertheless, in certain jurisdictions the process of refusing therapy may require clear evidence that this would indeed be in concert with the wishes of the patient.

## Physician-Assisted Suicide

In many ways, the movement in some parts of the United States and in the Netherlands promoting the legalization of physician-assisted suicide (PAS) carries the autonomy argument to its logical conclusion. Here, the patient with a terminal illness proceeds to take complete control of the dying process by choosing to end life before losing independence and dignity. During the 1990s, PAS gained widespread notoriety in the popular media thanks to the crusade of the Michigan pathologist Jack Kevorkian, who has openly participated in the suicides of over a hundred patients. Oregon legalized the practice in its 1997 Death with Dignity Act. Meanwhile, the Netherlands has legalized the practice of euthanasia (distinguished from PAS in that the physician directly administers the agent ending life) in 2000.

Bioethicists have generally condemned the approach to PAS represented by Kevorkian, but have been divided in opposing the practice under any circumstances. For many observers, Kevorkian's willingness to assist patients on demand devoid of any long-term doctor-patient relationship raises troubling questions about his patients' true prognoses, their other options, and the contribution of depression to their suffering. The physician Timothy Quill's decision to assist in the suicide of a forty-five-year-old woman described in an influential 1991 article has attracted much less condemnation. The woman "Diane" had been Quill's patient for eight years, and he wrote eloquently of how he had come to understand how her need for independence and control led her to refuse a cancer therapy with only a 25 percent success rate. For many ethicists the crucial question is whether PAS could be legalized yet regulated to assure the kinds of basic safeguards demonstrated by Quill's example, without placing vulnerable members of society at risk. In contrast, some ethicists have backed away from condoning any legalization of PAS as creating more potential for harm to the elderly than good—or perhaps marking a fateful step on a slippery slope leading to involuntary euthanasia.

However these issues are resolved, there is increasing recognition that a single-minded commitment to autonomy to the neglect of the other foundational principles of bioethics distorts how death and dying take place in reality. Whether they would allow PAS only rarely or not at all, most bioethicists would argue that a great challenge facing the care of the dying is the provision of palliative (or comfort) care for the terminally ill.

*See also:* ANTHROPOLOGICAL PERSPECTIVE; BLACK STORK; INFORMED CONSENT; PSYCHOLOGY; SUICIDE TYPES: PHYSICIAN-ASSISTED SUICIDE

### *Bibliography*

Beauchamp, Tom L., and James F. Childress. *Principles of Biomedical Ethics,* 4th edition. New York: Oxford University Press, 1994.

Buchanan, Allen E., and Dan W. Brock. *Deciding for Others: The Ethics of Surrogate Decision Making.* Cambridge: Cambridge University Press, 1990.

Filene, Peter G. *In the Arms of Others: A Cultural History of the Right-to-Die in America.* Chicago: Ivan R. Dee, 1998.

Fletcher, John C., et al., eds. *Introduction to Clinical Ethics,* 2nd edition. Frederick, MD: University Publishing Group, 1995.

Jonsen, Albert R. *The Birth of Bioethics.* New York: Oxford University Press, 1998.

President's Commission for the Study of Ethical Problems in Medicine and Biomedical and Behavioral Research. *Defining Death: A Report on the Medical, Legal and Ethical Issues in the Determination of Death.* Washington, DC: Author, 1981.

Quill T. E. "Death and Dignity: A Case of Individualized Decision Making." *New England Journal of Medicine* 324 (1991):691–694.

Rothman, David J. *Strangers at the Bedside: A History of How Law and Bioethics Transformed Medical Decision Making.* New York: Basic Books, 1991.

JEREMY SUGARMAN
JEFFREY P. BAKER

# BLACK DEATH

The Black Death pandemic of 1349 is considered to be one of the major events in world history, and it is still the subject of medical, historical, and sociological analysis. The evidence of the plague is found in the broad swath it cut across North Africa, Asia, and Europe, its terrifying symptoms, and its impact on society.

## History of the Disease

Ancient history includes vivid descriptions of epidemics that seized their victims suddenly and produced an agonizing death. One such episode occurred in Athens, Greece, in 430 B.C.E., and another occurred in Egypt, Persia, and Rome a century later. Some historians believe these lethal outbreaks were caused by the same disease responsible for the Black Death—the bubonic plague. Other historians, though, note some differences between the symptoms observed in the ancient episodes and those reported during the fourteenth century.

The growth of international trade and military invasions later provided the opportunity for diseases to spread rapidly from one population to another. Smallpox and measles came first, both causing high mortality within populations that had not previously been exposed. Bubonic plague arrived in force in the sixth century C.E., raging throughout most of Arabia, North Africa, Asia, and Europe. The death toll from what became known as "Justinian's Plague" was even greater than that of the previous epidemics. The powerful and still expanding Byzantine empire, centered in Constantinople (now Istanbul, Turkey), was so devastated that its political and military power sharply declined.

The plague did not entirely disappear but entered a long phase of withdrawal with occasional local outbreaks, especially in central Asia. When it did return it was with a furious rush that created widespread panic in populations already beset with both natural and human-made disasters. The fourteenth century suffered an entire catalog of catastrophes, including earthquakes, fires, floods, freezing weather, nauseating mists, and crop failures—all of which did not even seem to slow down the incessant warfare and banditry. Social order was weakened under the stress, and a hungry and exhausted population became more vulnerable to influenza and other opportunistic diseases.

It was within this already precarious situation that the plague once again crossed into Europe. There had been rumors about a deadly new epidemic sweeping through the Middle East, probably starting in 1338. The plague had taken hold among the Tartars of Asia Minor. Somebody had to be blamed—in this case, the Christian minority. (Later, as the plague devastated Europe, Jews were not only blamed but burned alive.) The Tartars chased Genoese merchants to their fortified town (now Feodosiya, Ukraine, then Kaffa) on the Crimean coast. The besieging army soon was ravaged by the plague and decided to leave. As a parting shot, the Tartars used catapults to hurl plague-infected corpses over the city walls. Some residents died almost immediately; the others dashed for their galleys (a type of oar-propelled ship) and fled, taking the disease with them. Sicily and then the rest of Italy were the earliest European victims of the plague. It would spread through almost all of Europe, wiping out entire villages and decimating towns and cities.

It is estimated that a third of the European population perished during the Black Death. The death toll may have been as high or even higher in Asia and North Africa, though less information is available about these regions. The world was quickly divided between the dead and their frequently exhausted and destitute mourners.

**The Disease and How It Spread**

As for the disease itself the bacterial agent is *Yersinia pestis*. It is considered to have permanent reservoirs in central Asia, Siberia, the Yunan region of China, and areas of Iran, Libya, the Arabian Peninsula, and East Africa. *Yersinia pestis* infects rodents, producing blood poisoning. Fleas that feed on the dying rodents carry the highly toxic bacteria to the next victim—perhaps a human. Among the first symptoms in humans were swollen and painful lymph glands of the armpit, neck, and groin. These swellings were known as *buboes,* from the Greek word for "groin." Buboes became dreaded as signals of impending death. Occasionally these hard knobs would spontaneously burst, pus would drain away and the victim might then recover if not totally exhausted or attacked by other infections. More often, however, the buboes were soon accompanied by high fever and agony. Sometimes the victim died within just a few hours; others became disoriented and either comatose or wildly delirious. Another symptom—perhaps even more certain than the buboes—was the appearance of postules, or dark points on various parts of the body. These splotches were most often called *lenticulae,* from the Italian word for "freckles."

Medical historians believe that the plague can spread in several ways but that it was the pneumonic or respiratory form that accounted for most of the deaths, being easily spread through coughing and sneezing. An interesting alternative was suggested in 1984 by the zoologist Graham Twigg, who had studied rat populations in more recent outbreaks of the plague in Asia. He doubts that the bubonic plague could have spread so rapidly in the fourteenth-century population; instead he nominates anthrax as the killer. Anthrax can be borne on the wind; it is known as a threat to sheep, goats, cattle, and pigs. Both plague and anthrax, then, are primarily found in animal populations, with humans becoming "accidental" victims under certain conditions. Whatever its specific cause or causes, the Black Death killed until it ran out of large numbers of vulnerable people. There have been subsequent plague epidemics, some also with high death tolls, and public health authorities continue to monitor possible new occurrences.

**Impact on Society**

Historians often divide European history into periods before and after the plague. There are several persuasive reasons for doing so. First, the population declined sharply—and then rebounded. Both the loss and the replenishment of the population had significant effects on all aspects of society, from agriculture to family structure to military adventuring.

Second, influential writers, such as the English clergyman Thomas Malthus (1766–1834), would propose that overpopulation produces its own remedy through epidemic, famine, and other means. Some areas of Europe might have been considered ripe for mass death because agricultural production had not kept up with population growth. The overpopulation theory has been criticized as inadequate to explain the catastrophic effects of the Black Death. Nevertheless, concerns about overpopulation in more recent times were foreshadowed by analyses of the plague years.

Third, feudalism—the political and social structure then prevalent in Europe—may have been the underlying cause of the mass mortality. A few people had everything; most people had very little. Those born into the lower classes had little opportunity for advancement. This situation perpetuated a large underclass of mostly illiterate people with limited skills, thereby also limiting technological and cultural progress. Furthermore, the feudal system was showing signs of collapsing from within in the years preceding the Black Death. In his 1995 book *The Black Death and the Transformation of the West,* David Herlihy explained:

> The basic unit of production was the small peasant farm, worked with an essentially stagnant technique. The only growth the system allowed was . . . the multiplication of farm units . . . subject to the law of diminishing returns. As cultivation

extended onto poorer soils, so the returns to the average family farm necessarily diminished. . . . As peasant income diminished, they paid lower and lower rents. . . . The lords took to robbery and pillage . . . and also hired themselves out as mercenaries . . . and pressured their overlords, notably the king, to wage wars against their neighbors. *(Herlihy 1995, p. 36)*

The almost continuous wars of the Middle Ages were attempts by hard-pressed nobles to snatch wealth from each other as well as grab whatever the peasants had left. The decline and crisis of the feudal system, then, probably did much to make people especially vulnerable to the plague, while the aftereffects of the plague would make feudal society even more of a losing proposition.

Fourth, loosely organized and short-lived challenges to authority arose from shifting coalitions of peasants and merchants. People laboring in the fields started to make demands, as though they too—not just the high and mighty—had "rights." Heads of state would remember and remain nervous for centuries to come.

Finally, the devastating and immediate impact of the Black Death prepared the way for a reconstruction of society. Deserted towns and vacant church and governmental positions had to be filled with new people. At first the demand was specific: more physicians, more clergy, and—of special urgency—more gravediggers were needed. The demand for new people to move into key positions throughout society opened the door for many who had been trapped in the ancient feudal system. It was also a rare opportunity for women to be accepted in positions of responsibility outside of the home (e.g., as witnesses in court proceedings). People who lacked "social connections" now could find more attractive employment; merit had started to challenge social class membership. These developments fell far short of equality and human rights as understood today, but they did result in significant and enduring social change.

**Long-term Influences of the Plague**

The plague years enabled European society to shake off the feudal system and make progress on many fronts. Death, however, had seized the center of the human imagination and would not readily ease its grip. The imagination had much to

*In this drawing, Saint Borromeo assists plague victims. In its most lethal periods, the ancient epidemic—whatever its cause—killed as many as four out of ten people in the areas affected.* BETTMANN/CORBIS

work on. Daily experience was saturated with dying, death, and grief. Religious belief and practice had given priority to helping the dying person leave this world in a state of grace and to providing a proper funeral with meaningful and comforting rituals. This tradition was overstressed by the reality of catastrophic death: too many people dying too quickly with too few available to comfort or even to bury them properly. Furthermore, the infectious nature of the disease and the often appalling condition of the corpses made it even more difficult to provide the services that even basic human decency required.

Fear of infection led many people to isolate themselves from others, thereby further contributing to social chaos and individual anxiety and depression. The fear for one's own life and the lives of loved ones was rational and perhaps useful under the circumstances. Rational fear, however, often became transformed into panic, and at times panic led to rage and the adoption of bizarre

practices. Some extremists became flagellants, whipping their bodies bloody as they marched from town to town, proclaiming that the plague was a well-deserved punishment from God. Others took the lead in persecuting strangers and minorities as well as those unfortunates who were perceived as witches. As though there was not enough death ready at hand, innocent people were slaughtered because somebody had to be blamed. Medieval medicine was not equal to the challenge of preventing or curing the plague, so there was a ready market for magic and superstition.

A personified Death became almost a palpable presence. It was almost a relief to picture death as a person instead of having to deal only with its horrifying work. Personified Death appeared as the leader in the Danse Macabre (the Dance of Death), and as "poster boy" for the Ars Moriendi (the art of dying) movement. (The now-familiar skull-and-crossbones image was highly popular, showing up, for example, on rings adorning the fingers of both prostitutes and ladies of high social standing.) Portraying Death as an animated skeleton was not entirely new; there are surviving images from ancient Pompeii as well. Depictions of Death as skeleton, corpse, or hooded figure, however, had their heyday during the plague years. This connection is not difficult to understand when one considers that social disorganization under the stress of the Black Death had severely damaged the shield that had protected the living from too many raw encounters with the dead.

Did another tradition also receive its impetus from the plague years? Throughout the post-Black Death years there have been people who identify themselves with death. The Nazi and skinhead movements provide ready examples. One way of trying to cope with overwhelming aggression is to identify with the aggressor, so perhaps this is one of the more subtle heritages of the Black Death. Furthermore, the fear that death is necessarily agonizing and horrifying may also owe much to the plague years and may have played a role in the denial of death and the social stigma attached to dying.

*See also:* ARS MORIENDI; CHRISTIAN DEATH RITES, HISTORY OF; DANSE MACABRE; DEATH SYSTEM; PERSONIFICATIONS OF DEATH; PUBLIC HEALTH

### *Bibliography*

Ariés, Phillipe. *The Hour of Our Death.* New York: Knopf, 1981.

Calvi, Giulia. *Histories of a Plague Year.* Berkeley: University of California Press, 1989.

Cohen, Samuel K., Jr. *The Cult of Remembrance and the Black Death in Six Central Italian Cities.* Baltimore, MD: Johns Hopkins University Press, 1997.

Geary, Patrick J. *Living with the Dead in the Middle Ages.* Ithaca, NY: Cornell University Press, 1994.

Gottfried, Robert S. *The Black Death.* New York: Free Press, 1983.

Herlihy, David. *The Black Death and the Transformation of the West.* Cambridge, MA: Harvard University Press, 1995.

Malthus, Thomas. *An Essay on the Principle of Population.* Hammondsworth: Penguin, 1970.

Platt, Colin. *King Death: The Black Death and Its Aftermath in Late-Medieval England.* Toronto: University of Toronto Press, 1997.

Tuchman, Barbara W. *A Distant Mirror.* New York: Knopf, 1978.

Twigg, Graham. *The Black Death: A Biological Reappraisal.* London: Batsford, 1983.

Zeigler, Philip. *The Black Death.* London: Collins, 1969.

ROBERT KASTENBAUM

# BLACK STORK

From 1915 to 1919, the prominent Chicago surgeon Harry Haiselden electrified the nation by allowing, or speeding, the deaths of at least six infants he diagnosed as physically or mentally impaired. To promote his campaign to eliminate those infants that he termed hereditarily "unfit," he displayed the dying babies and their mothers to journalists and wrote a book about them that was serialized for Hearst newspapers. His campaign made front-page news for weeks at a time.

He also starred in a film dramatization of his cases, an hour-long commercial melodrama titled *The Black Stork.* In the film a man suffering from an unnamed inherited disease ignores graphic warnings from his doctor, played by Haiselden, and marries his sweetheart. Their baby is born "defective" and needs immediate surgery to save its life, but the doctor refuses to operate. After witnessing a horrific vision, revealed by God, of the child's future of misery and crime, the mother agrees to withhold treatment, and the baby's soul leaps into the arms of a waiting Jesus. The film was shown around the country in several editions from 1916 to at least 1928, and perhaps as late as 1942.

Many prominent Americans rallied to Haiselden's support, from leaders of the powerful eugenics movement to Helen Keller, the celebrated blind and deaf advocate for people with disabilities. Newspapers and magazines published the responses of hundreds of people from widely varied backgrounds to Haiselden's campaign, more than half of whom were quoted as endorsing his actions. Groups disproportionately represented among these supporters included people under thirty-five years of age, public health workers, non-specialist physicians, lay women, socialists, and non-Catholic Democrats. However, advocates came from all walks of life, even a few Catholic clergymen.

## Euthanasia and Eugenics

These events are important for more than simply their novelty and drama; they constitute a unique record documenting the nearly forgotten fact that Americans once died because their doctors judged them genetically unfit, and that such practices won extensive public support. The events also recover a crucial, defining moment in the history of euthanasia and in the relation between euthanasia and eugenics.

Until late in the nineteenth century, the term *euthanasia* meant "efforts to ease the sufferings of the dying without hastening their death," but it soon came to include both passive withholding of life-prolonging treatment and active mercy killing. The term *eugenics* was first popularized by Charles Darwin's cousin Sir Francis Galton in the 1880s. Galton defined it as "the science of improving human heredity." To improve heredity, eugenicists pursued a diverse range of activities, including statistically sophisticated analyses of human pedigrees, "better-baby contests" modeled after rural livestock shows, compulsory sterilization of criminals and the retarded, and selective ethnic restrictions on immigration.

Beginning in the 1880s, a few supporters of each movement linked them by urging that active or passive euthanasia be employed to end both the individual sufferings and the future reproduction of those judged to have heritable defects. Yet prior to Haiselden's crusade such ideas rarely won public endorsement from the leaders of either movement. Most eugenic leaders, such as Charles Davenport, Irving Fisher, and Karl Pearson, explicitly distinguished their support for selective breeding from their professed opposition to the death of those already born with defects.

Yet when Haiselden moved the issue from theory to practice, these same leaders proclaimed him a eugenic pioneer. His attention-getting actions were a calculated effort to radicalize the leaders of both eugenics and euthanasia, a strategy anarchists at the time popularized as "propaganda of the dead." By gaining extensive media coverage of his dramatic acts, Haiselden was able to shift the boundary of what was included in mainstream eugenics and successfully prod the official movement leaders to publicly accept euthanasia as a legitimate method of improving heredity.

Haiselden's actions blurred the boundaries between active and passive methods of euthanasia. In his first public case, he refused to perform a potentially life-saving operation, but did not hasten death. In subsequent cases, however, he prescribed high doses of narcotics with the dual purposes of speeding and easing death. He also performed lethal surgical operations, and fatally restarted a previously treated umbilical hemorrhage.

Journalism and film enabled Haiselden to reshape the relation between eugenics and euthanasia, but, ironically, mass culture also contributed to the almost total erasure of his crusade from later memory. Haiselden's efforts to publicize his actions provoked more opposition than did the deaths of his patients. Three government investigations upheld Haiselden's right not to treat the infants, but the Chicago Medical Society expelled him for publicizing his actions. Even professional leaders who supported eugenic euthanasia often opposed discussing the issue in the lay media.

Promoters of the new mass media had their own reasons for repressing coverage of Haiselden's crusade. While his motion picture sought to make those he considered defective look repulsive, many viewers instead interpreted such scenes as making the film itself disgusting and upsetting. Even critics who lavishly praised his ideas found his graphic depictions of disease aesthetically unacceptable. Such responses were one important reason films about euthanasia and eugenics were often banned. *The Black Stork* helped provoke, and became one of the first casualties of, a movement to censor films for their aesthetic content. By the 1920s film censors went far beyond policing sexual morality to undertake a form of aesthetic censorship, much of it aimed at eliminating unpleasant medical topics from theaters.

Professional secrecy, combined with the growth of aesthetic censorship, drastically curtailed coverage of Haiselden's activities. In 1918 Haiselden's last reported euthanasia case received only a single column-inch in the *Chicago Tribune,* a paper that had supported him editorially and given front-page coverage to all of his previous cases. The media's preoccupation with novelty and impatience with complex issues clearly played a role in this change, as did Haiselden's death in 1919 from a brain hemorrhage at the age of forty-eight. But the sudden silence also reflected the conclusion by both medical and media leaders that eugenic euthanasia was unfit to discuss in public. The swiftness of Haiselden's rise and fall resulted from a complex struggle to shape the mass media's attitudes toward—and redefinitions of—eugenics and euthanasia.

Since 1919 the relationship between euthanasia and eugenics has been debated periodically. Although Haiselden's pioneering example was almost completely forgotten, each time it re-emerged it was treated as a novel issue, stripped of its historical context. In the United States and Great Britain, the debate begun by Haiselden over the relation between eugenics and euthanasia revived in the mid-1930s. At the same time, Germany launched the covert "T-4" program to kill people with hereditary diseases, a crucial early step in the Nazi quest for "racial hygiene." The techniques and justifications for killing Germans diagnosed with hereditary disease provided a model for the subsequent attempt to exterminate whole populations diagnosed as racially diseased.

## Postwar Developments

With the defeat of Nazism and the consequent postwar revulsion against genocide, public discussion of euthanasia and its relation to the treatment of impaired newborns was again repressed. In the early 1970s, the debate resurfaced when articles in two major American and British medical journals favorably reported cases of selective nontreatment. Nevertheless, it was not until the 1982 "Baby Doe" case in Indiana, followed by "Baby Jane Doe" in New York State a year later, that the subject once again aroused the degree of media attention occasioned by Haiselden's crusade. In response, the federal government tried to prevent hospitals from selectively withholding treatment, arguing such actions violated the 1973 ban on discrimination against people with disabilities. However, the Supreme Court held that antidiscrimination law could not compel treatment of an infant if the parents objected. Meanwhile, Congress defined withholding medically indicated treatment as a form of child neglect. That law favors treatment but allows for medical discretion by making an exception for

treatments a doctor considers futile or cruel. Conflicts still occur when doctors and parents disagree over whether treatments for specific infants with disabilities should be considered cruel or futile.

Understanding this history makes it possible to compare both the similarities and the differences between the past and the present. Concerns persist that voluntary euthanasia for the painfully ill will lead to involuntary killing of the unwanted. Such "slippery-slope" arguments claim that no clear lines can be drawn between the diseased and the outcast, the dying and the living, the voluntary and the coerced, the passive and the active, the intended and the inadvertent, the authorized and the unauthorized. Haiselden's example shows that these concerns are neither hypothetical nor limited to Nazi Germany. Americans died in the name of eugenics, often in cases where there were no absolute or completely objective boundaries between sound medical practice and murder. But that history does not mean that all forms of euthanasia are a prelude to genocide. Meaningful distinctions, such as those between the sick and the unwanted, are not logically impossible. However, they require sound ethical judgment and moral consensus, not solely technical expertise.

Haiselden's use of the mass media also provides intriguing parallels with the actions of Michigan pathologist Jack Kevorkian, who began publicly assisting the suicides of seriously ill adults in 1990. Both men depended on media coverage for their influence, and both were eventually marginalized as publicity hounds. But each showed that a single provocateur could stretch the boundaries of national debate on euthanasia by making formerly extreme positions seem more mainstream in comparison to their actions.

*See also:* ABORTION; CHILDREN, MURDER OF; EUTHANASIA; INFANTICIDE; KEVORKIAN, JACK; SUICIDE TYPES: PHYSICIAN-ASSISTED SUICIDE

### Bibliography

Burleigh, Michael. *Death and Deliverance: "Euthanasia" in Germany c. 1900–1945.* Cambridge: Cambridge University Press, 1994.

Fye, W. Bruce. "Active Euthanasia: An Historical Survey of Its Conceptual Origins and Introduction to Medical Thought." *Bulletin of the History of Medicine* 52 (1979):492–502.

Kevles, Daniel. *In the Name of Eugenics: Genetics and the Uses of Human Heredity*. Berkeley: University of California Press, 1985.

Pernick, Martin S. "Eugenic Euthanasia in Early-Twentieth-Century America and Medically Assisted Suicide Today." In Carl E. Schneider ed., *Law at the End of Life: The Supreme Court and Assisted Suicide*. Ann Arbor: University of Michigan Press, 2000.

Pernick, Martin S. *The Black Stork: Eugenics and the Death of "Defective" Babies in American Medicine and Motion Pictures since 1915*. New York: Oxford University Press, 1996.

Sluis, I. van der. "The Movement for Euthanasia, 1875–1975." *Janus* 66 (1979):131–172.

Weir, Robert F. *Selective Nontreatment of Handicapped Newborns: Moral Dilemmas in Neonatal Medicine*. New York: Oxford University Press, 1984.

MARTIN PERNICK

# BONSEN, F. Z.

Friedrich zur Bonsen (1856–1938) was a professor of psychology at the University of Muenster, Westphalia and author of *Between Life and Death: The Psychology of the Last Hour* (1927). In his book, Bonsen presents knowledge of his time about death and dying and his own reflections in a very emotive style. He is especially interested in presenting the transition from life to death and exploring the concept that dying is the biggest accomplishment of life. According to the work, the immense richness of the human soul will sometimes be revealed when death happens. Bonsen quotes a German bishop who, on his deathbed, asked his close friends to watch him carefully because they were about to witness one of the most interesting aspects of the world: transition into the afterlife.

In sixteen chapters, in a brief 173 pages, Bonsen wrote a compendium of a "Psychology of Death." His elaboration is based on books and articles in a variety of fields (philosophy, theology, folklore, history, and classical and popular literature), as well as local and national newspapers, and religious booklets.

For example, Bonsen observed no "fear of the soul" during the transition into the afterlife. Close to the end, there is a comforting well-being many dying patients never experienced before. Parallel to this increase in physical well-being is a strengthening of mental power. This idea was previously elaborated in 1836 by Gustav Theodor Fechner, and published *The Little Book of Life after Death* in 1904. During the final disintegration, supernormal abilities appear, and they enable the dying to have an overview over his or her entire life in one moment. The author presents cases where in the last moments of life even sanity came back to patients with longstanding mental illnesses.

Bonsen noticed a great calmness of the dying. With respect to religiosity, the author concludes that people will die the way they lived: Religious people will turn to religion, and nonreligious will not. However, there are cases in which nonreligious people, shattered by the power of the deathbed, became religious. This is not caused by fear, but rather a reversal to humankind's first and simple sentiments, which are religious in essence.

Very cautiously, Bonsen presents reports where people witnessed visions and hallucinations of dying persons. Explaining these phenomenon, he refers to physiological changes in the neurological system. Especially when people are dying of hunger and thirst, the impending death is mercifully, offering delusions. The author believes that in the moment of death, when the soul is separating from the body, the dead person might see everything and religious beliefs are promising; the soul might have a clear view on afterlife.

Most interesting are Bonsen's cases of near-death experiences, including drowning soldiers from World War I who were rescued and, without mentioning Albert Heim (1882), people who survived falls in wondrous ways. Heim was the first who collected and published reports of mountaineers who survived deep falls. The victims reported "panoramic views" and felt no pain as they hit the ground. Bonsen discusses favorably an explanation of near-death experiences that was forwarded by a person named Schlaikjer in a newspaper article published in 1915. "Panoramic view" is interpreted as an intervention of Mother Nature to protect humans from the terror of an impending death, an idea that was elaborated by the German psychiatrist Oskar Pfister in 1930.

*Friedrich zur Bonsen (1856–1938), in his influential work,* Between Life and Death: The Psychology of the Last Hour, *relied on his own personal experiences, but also collected information by talking to people about their death-related experiences.* MATTHIAS ZUR BONSEN

What kind of psychological processes accompany physical dying? Bonsen's best guess is based on an analogy with the experience of anesthesia, during which people report the feeling of plunging, falling, sinking, and floating. The author, therefore, describes the last moments in the following translation: "The consciousness of the dying is flickering and fleeing, and the soul is lost in confused illusions of sinking and floating in an infinity. The ear is filled with murmur and buzzing . . . until it dies out as the last of the senses" (p. 108).

Bonsen is often remembered as a pioneer of thanato-psychology, despite the fact that his observations and reflections never stimulated any research. At the very least, he is considered an early writer in the field of near-death experience that almost fifty years later was inaugurated by

Raymond A. Moody and his best-selling book *Life after Life* (1975).

*See also:* ARIÈS, PHILIPPE; NEAR-DEATH EXPERIENCES; THANATOLOGY

### Bibliography

Fechner, Gustav Theodor. *The Little Book of Life after Death,* edited by Robert J. Kastenbaum. North Stratford, NH: Ayer Company Publishers, 1977.

Moody, Raymond A. *Life after Life.* Atlanta, GA: Mockingbird Books, 1975.

RANDOLPH OCHSMANN

## BRAIN DEATH

The term *brain death* is defined as "irreversible unconsciousness with complete loss of brain function," including the brain stem, although the heartbeat may continue. Demonstration of brain death is the accepted criterion for establishing the fact and time of death. Factors in diagnosing brain death include irreversible cessation of brain function as demonstrated by fixed and dilated pupils, lack of eye movement, absence of respiratory reflexes (apnea), and unresponsiveness to painful stimuli. In addition, there should be evidence that the patient has experienced a disease or injury that could cause brain death. A final determination of brain death must involve demonstration of the total lack of electrical activity in the brain by two electroencephalographs (EEGs) taken twelve to twenty-four hours apart. Finally, the physician must rule out the possibilities of hypothermia or drug toxicities, the symptoms of which may mimic brain death. Some central nervous system functions such as spinal reflexes that can result in movement of the limbs or trunk may persist in brain death.

Until the late twentieth century, *death* was defined in terms of loss of heart and lung functions, both of which are easily observable criteria. However, with modern technology these functions can be maintained even when the brain is dead, although the patient's recovery is hopeless, sometimes resulting in undue financial and emotional stress to family members. French neurologists were the first to describe brain death in 1958. Patients with *coma depasse* were unresponsive to external stimuli and unable to maintain homeostasis. A Harvard Medical School committee proposed the definition used in this entry, which requires demonstration of total cessation of brain function. This definition is almost universally accepted.

Brain death is not medically or legally equivalent to severe vegetative state. In a severe vegetative state, the cerebral cortex, the center of cognitive functions including consciousness and intelligence, may be dead while the brain stem, which controls basic life support functions such as respiration, is still functioning. Death is equivalent to brain stem death. The brain stem, which is less sensitive to anoxia (loss of adequate oxygen) than the cerebrum, dies from cessation of circulation for periods exceeding three to four minutes or from intracranial catastrophe, such as a violent accident.

Difficulties with ethics and decision making may arise if it is not made clear to the family that brain stem death is equivalent to death. According to research conducted by Jacqueline Sullivan and colleagues in 1999 at Thomas Jefferson University Hospital, roughly one-third to one-half of physicians and nurses surveyed do not adequately explain to relatives that brain dead patients are, in fact, dead. Unless medical personnel provide family members with information that all cognitive and life support functions have irreversibly stopped, the family may harbor false hopes for the loved one's recovery. The heartbeat may continue or the patient may be on a respirator (often inaccurately called "life support") to maintain vital organs because brain dead individuals who were otherwise healthy are good candidates for organ donation. In these cases, it may be difficult to convince improperly informed family members to agree to organ donation.

*See also:* CELL DEATH; DEFINITIONS OF DEATH; LIFE SUPPORT SYSTEM; ORGAN DONATION AND TRANSPLANTATION; PERSISTENT VEGETATIVE STATE

### Bibliography

Ad Hoc Committee of the Harvard Medical School. "The Harvard Committee Criteria for Determination of Death." In *Opposing Viewpoint Sources, Death/Dying,* Vol. 1. St. Paul, MN: Greenhaven Press, 1984.

"Brain (Stem) Death." In John Walton, Jeremiah Barondess, and Stephen Lock eds., *The Oxford Medical Companion.* New York: Oxford University Press, 1994.

Plum, Fred. "Brain Death." In James B. Wyngaarden, Lloyd H. Smith Jr., and J. Claude Bennett eds., *Cecil Textbook of Medicine.* Philadelphia: W.B. Saunders, 1992.

Sullivan, Jacqueline, Debbie L. Seem, and Frank Chabalewski. "Determining Brain Death." *Critical Care Nurse* 19, no. 2 (1999):37–46.

ALFRED R. MARTIN

# BROMPTON'S COCKTAIL

In 1896 the English surgeon Herbert Snow showed that morphine and cocaine, when combined into an elixir, could give relief to patients with advanced cancer. About thirty years later a similar approach was used at London's Brompton Hospital as a cough sedative for patients with tuberculosis. In the early 1950s this formulation appeared in print for the first time, containing morphine hydrochloride, cocaine hydrochloride, alcohol, syrup, and chloroform water.

In her first publication, Cicely Saunders, the founder of the modern hospice movement, also referred to such a mixture, which included nepenthe, or liquor morphini hydrochloride, cocaine hydrochloride, tincture of cannabis, gin, syrup, and chloroform water; she was enthusiastic about its value to terminally ill patients. Over the next twenty years of writing and lecturing, Saunders did much to promote this mixture and other variants of the "Brompton Cocktail."

A survey of teaching and general hospitals in the United Kingdom showed the mixture and its variants to be in widespread use in 1972. Elisabeth Kübler-Ross, the psychiatrist and pioneer of end-of-life care, became one of its supporters, as did some of the pioneers of pain medicine and palliative care in Canada, including Ronald Melzack and Balfour Mount, who saw it as a powerful means of pain relief.

The Brompton Cocktail became popular in the United States, too, and at least one hospice produced a primer for its use which was distributed to both clinicians and patients. Indeed, as a leading pain researcher and hospice physician, Robert Twycross noted, there developed a "tendency to endow the Brompton Cocktail with almost mystical properties and to regard it as the panacea for terminal cancer pain" (1979, pp. 291–292).

The cocktail emerged as a key element in the newly developing hospice and palliative care approach. Then, quite suddenly, its credibility came into question. Two sets of research studies, published in the same year, raised doubts about its efficacy—those of Melzack and colleagues in Canada and Twycross and associates in the United Kingdom. Both groups addressed the relative efficacy of the constituent elements of the mixture. The Melzack study showed that pain relief equal to that of the cocktail was obtainable without the addition of cocaine or chloroform water and with lower levels of alcohol, and that there were no differences in side effects such as confusion, nausea, or drowsiness. Twycross's study found that morphine and diamorphine are equally effective when given in a solution by mouth and that the withdrawal of cocaine had no effect on the patient's alertness. Twycross concluded, "the Brompton Cocktail is no more than a traditional British way of administering oral morphine to cancer patients in pain" (1979, p. 298). Despite these critiques of the cocktail, its use persisted for some time; however, in the twenty-first century it does not have a role in modern hospice and palliative care.

*See also:* KÜBLER-ROSS, ELISABETH; PAIN AND PAIN MANAGEMENT; SAUNDERS, CICELY

### *Bibliography*

Davis, A. Jann. "Brompton's Cocktail: Making Goodbyes Possible." *American Journal of Nursing* (1978):610–612.

Melzack, Ronald, Belfour N. Mount, and J. M. Gordon. "The Brompton Mixture versus Morphine Solution Given Orally: Effects on Pain." *Canadian Medical Association Journal* 120 (1979):435–438.

Saunders, Cicely. "Dying of Cancer." *St. Thomas's Hospital Gazette* 56, no. 2 (1958):37–47.

Twycross, Robert. "The Brompton Cocktail." In John J. Bonica and Vittorio Ventafridda eds., *Advances in Pain Research and Therapy,* Vol. 2. New York: Raven Press, 1979.

DAVID CLARK

# BROWN, JOHN

The abolitionist crusader John Brown died on December 2, 1859, executed by the state of Virginia for charges relating to treason, murder, and promoting a slave insurrection. Although Brown's public execution took place before the start of the U.S. Civil War, his life and death anticipated the impending battle between the North and the South over the moral legitimacy of slavery in America, and served as a source of righteous inspiration for both sides immediately before and during the course of the war. Beyond that, Brown's death serves as a case study in the construction and power of martyrdom. Proslavery supporters reviled Brown, whose often bloody actions against the social institution fueled southern fears about northern aggression. Many supporters and fervent abolitionists, on the other hand, glorified Brown, whose sacrifice for a higher good transformed the unsuccessful businessman into a national martyr.

Born in Connecticut on May 9, 1800, Brown became involved in the abolitionist movement early in life. His father was a strict Calvinist who abhorred slavery as a particularly destructive sin against God. Brown himself witnessed the brutality of slavery when, as a twelve-year-old boy, he saw a young slave ferociously beaten with a shovel by his owner, an image that remained with Brown for the rest of his life. After the Illinois abolitionist publisher Elijah Lovejoy was murdered by a proslavery mob in 1837, Brown publicly declared his intention to find a way to end slavery in the United States.

In the midst of extreme economic hardships and failed business ventures, Brown moved with some of his sons to Kansas following the passage of the Kansas-Nebraska Act. This act, heavily supported by southern slave-holding states, allowed people in new territories to vote on the question of slavery. During the 1850s, Kansas was the scene of a number of horrific acts of violence from groups on both sides of the issue. Brown placed himself in the thick of these bloody conflicts and, with a group of other like-minded zealots, hacked five proslavery men to death with broadswords, an event that came to be known as the Pottawatomie Massacre.

In the summer of 1859, Brown led a small army of men, including his own sons, to Harper's

Ferry, Virginia, with a plan to invade the South and incite a slave rebellion. The group successfully raided the armory at Harper's Ferry but, after the arrival of Colonel Robert E. Lee and his troops, Brown's plans fell apart, and his men either escaped, died, or were captured by Lee's men in the ensuing battle. Brown himself was captured and stood trial in Virginia, where his fate was determined by an unsympathetic jury.

Brown, however, did not understand his failed invasion and impending death as a defeat for the abolitionist cause. Instead, he believed these events had crucial historical and religious significance, and that rather than signaling an end would be the beginning of the eventual elimination of slavery in America. Brown greatly admired stories about the prophets in the Bible, and came to believe that God, rather than a Virginia jury, had determined his fate. Convinced that his martyrdom could have more of an impact than any of his earlier schemes, Brown faced death with calm assurance and optimism that an abolitionist victory was secured with his imminent execution.

Brown was not the only one who understood the significant political implications of his execution in religious terms. Indeed, major northern abolitionists who would not countenance Brown's violent strategies to end slavery while alive, embraced the language of martyrdom after his death on the gallows. New England cultural figures like Ralph Waldo Emerson, Henry David Thoreau, and Lydia Maria Child, to name a few, identified Brown as the first true abolitionist martyr, serving as an iconic symbol of righteousness, redemption, and regeneration. Although others perished with him on the gallows, for many northerners John Brown was transformed into a hero who deserved to be included in the pantheon of great Americans and who died for the good of the United States.

Not everyone agreed with this assessment though. Immediately after his death, southern citizens and many in the North turned him into a demon rather than a hero, and wanted his corpse to suffer indignities reserved for the lowest criminals, including the suggestion that it be turned over to a medical school for dissection. The governor of Virginia decided to release the body of the deceased to Brown's wife, Mary, and allow it to be transported to the family farm in North Elba, New York. During the journey north, Brown's dead

*Abolitionist John Brown, being escorted from prison to his execution in Virginia, 1859. His death foreshadowed the approaching battle between the North and the South over the morality of slavery.* ARCHIVE PHOTOS, INC.

body aroused a great deal of interest. In Philadelphia, a large crowd of people from African-American abolitionist and proslavery communities turned out to meet the body upon its arrival in the city. The mayor, along with Mary Brown and her supporters, feared a riot might ensue, and decided to send an empty coffin to the local undertaker as a decoy so the container with Brown's body could make it to the wharf and continue its journey by boat to New York City.

Reaching its final destination, people came to see the coffin containing Brown's body, with some towns finding various ways to commemorate the martyr while the corpse passed through. On December 7, 1859, Brown's body arrived in North Elba, and was laid out in the front room of the house for visiting relatives, friends, and supporters to see before it vanished for good after the funeral the next day. After the corpse of John Brown had been placed in the ground at his home, the memory of his violent campaign to end slavery and the symbolism of his death in the state of Virginia continued to materialize in American imaginative and social landscapes. During the U.S. Civil War, for example, one of the most popular songs among Union forces urged soldiers to remember his body "a-mouldering in the grave"—in time, a song that would be transformed with new lyrics by Julia Ward Howe into "The Battle Hymn of the Republic." The cultural memory of John Brown's life after the war and into the twentieth century assumed a variety of forms, including Stephen Vincent Benét's famous Pulitzer Prize–winning poem, "John Brown's Body," and the establishment of schools bearing his name.

*See also:* CIVIL WAR, U.S.; LINCOLN IN THE NATIONAL MEMORY; MARTYRS

### *Bibliography*

Abels, Jules. *Man on Fire: John Brown and the Cause of Liberty.* New York: Macmillan, 1971.

Finkelman, Paul, ed. *His Soul Goes Marching On: Responses to John Brown and the Harper's Ferry Raid.* Charlottesville: University Press of Virginia, 1995.

Laderman, Gary. *The Sacred Remains: American Attitudes toward Death, 1799–1883.* New Haven, CT: Yale University Press, 1996.

Oates, Stephen B. *To Purge This Land with Blood: A Biography of John Brown.* New York: Harper and Row, 1970.

GARY M. LADERMAN

# BUDDHISM

"Decay is inherent in all compounded things, so continue in watchfulness." The last recorded words of Siddhartha Gautama (Gotama), the founder of Buddhism, might be taken to mean, "Work out your own salvation with diligence" (Bowker 1997, p. 169).

From its inception, Buddhism has stressed the importance of death because awareness of death is what prompted the Buddha to perceive the ultimate futility of worldly concerns and pleasures. According to traditional stories of the life of the Buddha, he first decided to leave his home and seek enlightenment after encountering the "four sights" (a sick person, an old person, a corpse, and someone who had renounced the world). The first three epitomized the sufferings to which ordinary beings were and are subject to, and the last indicates that one can transcend them through meditation and religious practice. The greatest problem of all is death, the final cessation of all one's hopes and dreams. A prince of the Shakya family in what is modern Nepal, Gautama became dissatisfied with palace life after witnessing suffering in the nearby city of Kapilavastu. At the age of 29, he renounced his former life, cut off his hair and started to wear the yellow robes of a religious mendicant. Buddhism, the faith he created through his teaching, thus originated in his heightened sense of suffering, and begins with the fundamental fact of suffering (*dukkha*) as the human predicament: "from the suffering, moreover, no one knows of any way of escape, even from decay and death. O, when shall a way of escape from this suffering be made known—from decay and from death?" (Hamilton, 1952, pp. 6–11).

## Origins of Buddhist Faith

The Buddhist faith originated in India in the sixth and fifth centuries B.C.E. with the enlightenment of Gotama (in Sanskrit, Gauatama), the historical founder of the faith (c. 566–486 B.C.E.). The teaching of Gotama Buddha, also known as Buddha Sakyamuni (that is, "the Wise One" or "Sage of the Sakya Clan") is summarized in the Four Noble Truths: the truth of suffering (existence is suffering); the truth of suffering's cause (suffering is caused by desire); the truth of stopping suffering (stop the cause of suffering (desire) and the suffering will cease to arise); and the truth of the way (the Eightfold Path leads to the release from desire and extinguishes suffering). In turn, the Eightfold Path requires right understanding, right thought, right speech, right action, right livelihood, right effort, right mindfulness, and right concentration. There is also a twelve-step chain of cause. This chain of conditions consists of (1) spiritual ignorance; (2) constructing activities; (3) consciousness; (4) mind-and-body; (5) the six sense-bases; (6) sensory stimulation; (7) feeling; (8) craving; (9) grasping; (10) existence; (11) birth; (12) aging, death, sorry, lamentation, pain, grief, and despair. This chain of cause or Doctrine of Dependent

Origination explains the dukka that one experiences in his or her life. Finally, there is the continuing process of reincarnation. "If, on the dissolution of the body, after death, instead of his reappearing in a happy destination, in the heavenly world, he comes to the human state, he is long-lived wherever he is reborn" (Nikaya 1993, p. 135). Disillusioned with the ascetic path, Gotama adhered to what he called "the middle way." He chose to sit beneath a Bo or Bodhi Tree (believed by scholars to now be situated at Bodhgaya, Bihar), concentrating on "seeing things as they really are" and passing through four stages of progressive insight (jhanas), which led to enlightenment (scholars believe this stage was achieved in c. 535 B.C.E.). The rest of his life was spent wandering in the area of the Ganges basin, gaining adherents and probably spending the rainy months in a community of followers, the beginnings of the Buddhist monastic establishment (vihara). The Buddha is said to have made no other claim for himself than that he was a teacher of transience or suffering (dukkha or duhkha), the first of his Four Noble Truths.

Two and a half centuries after the Buddha's death, a council of Buddhist monks collected his teachings and the oral traditions of the faith into written form, called the Tripitaka. This included a very large collection of commentaries and traditions; most are called Sutras (discourses). Some twelve centuries after the Buddha's death, the faith spread from India into Tibet and from the early seventh century C.E. onward, Buddhism became firmly entrenched in all aspects of Tibetan society.

The significance of the conversion of Tibet lies in the exceptionally rich early literature that survives: The original Sanskrit texts of the Sutra on "Passing from One Existence to Another" and the Sutra on "Death and the Transmigration of Souls" are no longer extant and are known only through their Tibetan versions. Buddhism spread also to central and southeast Asia, China, and from there into Korea (c. 350–668 C.E.) and Japan (c. 538 C.E.). Although there have been conversions to Buddhism in modern times, especially the mass conversion of dalits (or untouchables) following the leadership of Dr. Bhimrao R. Ambedkar, the dispersion of the centers of Buddhist learning led to a dwindling of the faith in most of India during the centuries of Islamic predominance.

## Buddhist Traditions

Buddhism has two (or in some interpretations, three) main divisions, or traditions: Mahayana and Hinayana. Those Buddhist adherents in Mongolia, Vietnam, China, Korea, and Japan follow Mahayana, the so-called Great Vehicle tradition, and those in Sri Lanka and southeast Asia, except Vietnam, where the Mahayan tradition was brought by Chinese settlers, follow Hinayana, also known as Theravada, the so-called Lesser Vehicle tradition. More controversial is whether Vajrayana (the "Diamond Vehicle" or Tantric tradition emanating from Mahayana, now dominant in Tibet and the Himalayas) constitutes a distinctive and separate tradition or not.

Mahayana emphasizes, among other things, the Sutras containing the developed teaching of the Buddha, and recognizes the Buddha-nature (Buddhata, or Buddha-potential) in all sentient beings (and not exclusively humans). Mahayana emphasizes the feeling of the suffering of others as one's own, which impels the soul to desire the liberation of all beings and to encourage adherence to the "enlightenment" (bodhisattva) path. A bodhisattva is defined as one who strives to gain the experience of things as they really are (as in the experience of Gautama under the tree, hence the name bodhi) and scorns nirvana "as he wishe(s) to help and succour his fellow-creatures in the world of sorrow, sin and impermanence" (Bowker 1997, p. 154). An early Buddhist, Candrakirti, calls nirvana "the cessation of every thought of non-existence and existence" (Stcherbatsky 1965, p.190).

In contrast, Hinayana or Theravada (the latter term meaning "teaching of the elders") emphasizes the aspect of personal discipleship and the attainment of the penultimate state of perfection (arhat). The followers of Mahayana view it as a more restricted interpretation of the tradition. There is also a basic disagreement on how many Buddhas can appear in each world cycle. In Theravada, there can only be one, the Buddha who has already appeared; hence only the penultimate state of perfection can be attained and Buddha-nature is not recognized. There are also other differences between the traditions, particularly with regard to the status of women (which is somewhat higher in the Mahayana tradition). Buddhism in its various manifestations is the world's fourth largest religion with about 362 million adherents in 2000,

*Buddhist Monks collect alms in Bangkok, Thailand. The Buddhist faith, which stresses the awareness of suffering and death, originated in sixth and fifth century B.C.E. India and then spread to Tibet, Asia, China, Korea, and Japan.* CORBIS

or about 6 percent of an estimated world population of 6 billion.

The Sutra on "Passing from One Existence to Another" relates that during the Buddha's stay in Rajagriha a king named Bimbisara questioned him on the transitory nature of action (*karma*) and how rebirth can be effected by thoughts and actions, which are by their very nature momentary and fleeting. For the Buddha, an individual's past thoughts and actions appear before the mind at the time of death in the same way that the previous night's dreams are recalled while awake; neither the dreams nor past karma have any solid and substantial reality in themselves, but both can, and do, produce real effects. An individual's past karma appears before the mind at the final moment of

death and causes the first moment of rebirth. This new life is a new sphere of consciousness in one of the six realms of rebirth (the worlds of the gods, demigods, humans, hungry ghosts, animals, and hell-beings) wherein the person experiences the fruits of his or her previous actions.

The discourse on "The Great Liberation through Hearing in the Bardo" is one of a series of instructions on six types of liberation: liberation through hearing, wearing, seeing, remembering, tasting, and touching. It is a supreme example of Tibetan esoteric teaching on how to assist in the "ejection of consciousness" after death if this liberation has not happened spontaneously. If the body is present, the guru or dharma-brother, that is, the fellow-disciple of the guru, should read the text of the Sutra close to his ear three or seven times. The first *bardo,* or intermediate state between life and death, is called "the luminosity of the essence of reality (*dharmata*)"; it is a direct perception of the sacredness and vividness of life (Fremantle and Trungpa 1975, p. 36). The work is thought to have been written by Padmasambhava, known by his followers as "precious teacher" (Guru Rinpoche), a great eighth-century Tantric master and founder of the Nyingma school. He is considered by Tibetans to be a second Buddha. He describes in detail the six bardos, or intermediate states, three of which comprise the period between death and rebirth and three which relate to this life: the bardo of birth; the bardo of dreams; the bardo of meditation, in which the distinction between subject and object disappears (*samadhi,* or meditation); the bardo of the moment before death; the bardo of the essence of reality (*dharmata*); and the bardo of becoming.

## The Tibetan *Book of the Dead*

The German Tibetologist and scholar of comparative religion Detlef Lauf regarded the Tibetan *Book of the Dead* (*Bar-do thos-grol* or *Bardo Thodrol,* or *Thötröl*) as an example of "yoga-practice" (Yogacara) or Vijnanavada idealism, "which proceed(s) from the premise that karmically laden awareness by far outlasts the earthly life span of the individual." This branch of Mahayana philosophy "places above all conceptualisation emptiness, suchness [sic], pure buddha-nature, or the crystal clear diamond nature of human awareness, which is of imageless intensity. . . . Therefore the Tibetan Book of the Dead can first proclaim the philosophical reality of the buddhas and their teachings, and after these have been grasped and penetrated, it can then say that these are only illusory images of one's own consciousness, for the pure world within needs no images of external form" (Lauf 1977, pp. 225–226).

Mind or pure awareness is, in Vijnanavada theory, "the indispensable basis and essence of reality and is therefore absolute. Because nothing is imaginable without mind, it is called the absolute, or all-pervading emptiness, or simply *nirvana*" (ibid., p. 221). Although appearing to be an instruction manual for the guidance of human awareness after death, Lauf argued that the *Bardo Thodrol* was in reality "primarily a book of life, for the knowledge

of the path through the bardo must be gained 'on this side' if it is to be put into practice 'on the other side'" (ibid., p. 228).

Lauf also generalized from the various Tibetan texts the duration of the bardo state: "It is generally accepted that the total time of the intermediate state between two successive earthly incarnations is forty-nine days. The various cycles of emanation of the deities divide this time into a rhythm that is always determined by the number seven. . . . From the fourth to the eleventh day there is the successive emanation of the forty-two peaceful bardo deities from out of the fivefold radiant light of the buddhas. From the twelfth until the nineteenth day the fifty-eight terrifying deities take shape out of the flames, and the journey through the [bardo and the experience of the worlds of hell] *Srid-pa'i bardo* lasts . . . twenty-one days in all. The last seven days are dedicated to the search for the place of rebirth which is supposed to take place on the eighth day . . ." (pp. 95–96).

Two modern approaches to the Tibetan *Book of the Dead* deserve mention. Based on lectures presented at his own Buddhist institute in Vermont, the charismatic Tibetan teacher Chögyam Trungpa (1939–1987) published his own edition of the work in 1975 with Francesca Fremantle. His highly individualized commentary to the translation certainly owes a debt to the psychoanalyst Carl Jung. In Chögyam Trungpa's view, the bardo experience is an active part of every human being's basic psychological makeup, and thus it is best described using the concepts of modern psychoanalysis, such as ego, the unconscious mind, neurosis, paranoia, and so on. This view was popularized in Trungpa's *Transcending Madness: The Experience of the Six Bardos* (1992).

A second approach is that of Robert Thurman, a professor at Columbia University, the first American to be ordained a Tibetan Buddhist monk and president of Tibet House in New York City, who sets out to produce an accessible version of the Tibetan text for those who might wish to read it at the bedside of their dying friend or relative. In this way, Thurman's Tibetan *Book of the Dead* is presented clearly as an "easy-to-read" guidebook for contemporary Americans. It is "easy for bereaved relatives to read and for lost souls to hear in the room where they anxiously hover about their corpses and wonder what has happened to them . . ." (Sambhava and Thurman 1994, p. xxi).

## Buddhism and Death and Dying

Robert Thurman's text leads to a consideration of the relationship of Buddhism to modern clinical medical ethics and attitudes to death and dying in particular as well as to the pastoral care of the terminally ill. The Swiss-born psychiatrist Elisabeth Kübler-Ross interviewed over 200 dying patients better to understand the psychological aspects of dying. She illustrates five stages that people go through when they know they are going to die. The stages include denial, anger, bargaining, depression, and acceptance. While a sequential order is implied, the manner is which a person comes to terms with impending death does not necessarily follow the order of the stages. Some of these phases are temporary; others will be with that person until death. The stages will exist at different times and can co-exist within each other. Denial and feelings of isolation are usually short lived. Isolation is related to the emotional support one receives. If a person feels alone and helpless he or she is more likely to isolate. During the anger stage, it is important to be very patient with the dying individual, who acts in apparent anger because of an inability to accept the reality of the diagnosis. Bargaining describes the period in which the ill person tries to bargain with doctors, family, clergy, or God to "buy more time."

When the denial, anger, and bargaining come to an end—and if the ill person continues to live—depression typically arises. Kübler-Ross talks about two forms of depression (reactive and preparatory). Reactive depression comes about from past losses, guilt, hopelessness, and shame. Preparatory depression is associated with impending loss. Most ill persons feel guilty for departing from family or friends, so require reassurance that life will change in the absence of the dead person but will nevertheless continue. The acceptance stage is a product of tiredness and numbness after the various preceding stages with their struggles. The model has been criticized and may not be applicable to the majority who die in old age, where a terminal diagnosis may be more acceptable to the individual. Many of the aged have experienced a gradual diminution of health and abilities that predates any knowledge of impending death. Such a diagnosis

may be better accepted by the elderly both because of gradual infirmity and because approaching death is not viewed as a "surprise," but rather as part of a long and total life experience. For all the caveats, there are important resonances between the Kübler-Ross model and the stages of liberation in the bardo experience described above.

Julia Ching writes that "the central Mahayan insight, that Nirvana is to be found in the *samsara,* that is, *in* this life and this world, has made the religion more acceptable to the Chinese and Japanese" (Ching 1989, p. 217). She questions the content of Buddhist belief in East Asia: ". . . it appears that many Chinese, Japanese, and Korean Buddhists are less than clear about their belief in the cycle of rebirth. Their accounts of samsara include the presupposition of a wandering *soul,* which is not in accord with strict Buddhist teaching, and they tend to perceive life in linear terms. Besides, they frequently equate Nirvana with the Pure Land [named after *Sukhavati,* a Sanskrit word representing an ideal Buddhist paradise this side of Nirvana, believed to be presided over by the Buddha Amitabha, the Buddha of infinite life and light], and the Buddhas with the bodhisattvas" (1989, p. 220).

Ch'an and Zen, the respective Chinese and Japanese transliterations of the Sankrit word for meditation (*dyhana*) are a distinctively East Asian development of the Mahayana tradition. Zen teaches that ultimate reality or emptiness (*sunya*), sometimes called "Buddha-nature," is, as described by Ching, "inexpressible in words or concepts and is apprehended only by direct intuition, outside of conscious thought. Such direct intuition requires discipline and training, but is also characterized by freedom and spontaneity" (Ching 1989, p. 211). Japanese Buddhism, she contends, "is so closely associated with the memory of the dead and the ancestral cult that the family shrines dedicated to the ancestors, and still occupying a place of honor in homes, are popularly called the Butsudan, literally 'the Buddhist altars.' . . . It has been the custom in modern Japan to have Shinto weddings . . . but to turn to Buddhism in times of bereavement and for funeral services" (Ching 1989, p. 219).

The tradition of death poems in Zen accounts for one way in which the Japanese regard Buddhism as a funerary religion. Minamoto Yorimasa

(1104–1180 C.E.), lamented that "Like a rotten log / half buried in the ground— / my life, which / has not flowered, comes / to this sad end" (Hoffman 1986, p. 48). Shiaku Nyûdo (d. 1333) justified an act of suicide with the words: "Holding forth this sword / I cut vacuity in twain; / In the midst of the great fire, / a stream of refreshing breeze!" (Suzuki 1959, p. 84). At what would be considered the relatively youthful age of fifty-four, Ota Dokan (1432–1486) clearly considered himself in decline already by the time of death: "Had I not known / that I was dead / already / I would have mourned / my loss of life" (Hoffman 1986, p. 52). For Ôuchi Yoshitaka (1507–1551) it was the extraordinary event that was significant: "Both the victor / and the vanquished are / but drops of dew, / but bolts of lightning—thus should we view the world" (1986, p. 53). The same image of dew, this time reinforced by dreams, was paramount for Toyotomi Hideyoshi (1536–1598): "My life / came like dew / disappears like dew. / All of Naniwa / is dream after dream" (Berry 1982, p. 235). Forty-nine years had passed as a dream for Uesugi Kenshin (1530–1578): "Even a life-long prosperity is but one cup of sake; /A life of forty-nine years is passed in a dream / I know not what life is, nor death. Year in year out—all but a dream. / Both Heaven and Hell are left behind; / I stand in the moonlit dawn, / Free from clouds of attachment" (Suzuki 1959, p. 82). The mists that cloud the mind were swept away at death for Hôjô Ujimasa (1538–1590): "Autumn wind of eve, / blow away the clouds that mass / over the moon's pure light / and the mists that cloud our mind, / do thou sweep away as well. / Now we disappear, / well, what must we think of it? / From the sky we came. / Now we may go back again. / That's at least one point of view" (Sadler 1978, pp. 160–161).

The death poems exemplify both the "eternal loneliness" that is found at the heart of Zen and the search for a new viewpoint, a new way of looking at life and things generally, or a version of enlightenment (*satori* in Japanese; *wu* in Chinese). Daisetz Suzuki writes: ". . . there is no Zen without satori, which is indeed the alpha and omega of Zen Buddhism"; it is defined as "an intuitive looking into the nature of things in contradistinction to the analytical or logical understanding of it." This can only be gained "through our once personally experiencing it" (1963, pp. 153, 154).

*See also:* CHINESE BELIEFS; HINDUISM; ISLAM; LAST WORDS; MOMENT OF DEATH

## Bibliography

Amore, Roy C., and Julia Ching. "The Buddhist Tradition." In Willard G. Oxtoby ed., *World Religions: Eastern Traditions*. Toronto: Oxford University Press, 1996.

Berry, Mary Elizabeth. *Hideyoshi*. Cambridge, MA: Harvard University Press, 1982.

Bowker, John. *The Oxford Dictionary of World Religions*. Oxford: Oxford University Press, 1997.

Ching, Julia. "Buddhism: A Foreign Religion in China. Chinese Perspectives." In Hans Küng and Julia Ching eds., *Christianity and Chinese Religions*. New York: Doubleday, 1989.

Dayal, Har. *The Bodhisattva Doctrine in Buddhist Sanskrit Literature*. 1932. Reprint, Delhi: Patna, Varanasi, 1975.

Fremantle, Francesca, and Chögyam Trungpa, trans. *The Tibetan Book of the Dead: The Great Liberation through Hearing in the Bardo*. Berkeley, CA: Shambhala, 1975.

Hughes, James J., and Damien Keown. "Buddhism and Medical Ethics: A Bibliographic Introduction." *Journal of Buddhist Ethics* 2 (1995).

Hoffman, Yoel, comp. *Japanese Death Poems*. Rutland, VT: C. E. Tuttle Col, 1986.

Kapleau, Philip, and Paterson Simons, eds. *The Wheel of Death: A Collection of Writings from Zen Buddhist and Other Sources on Death, Rebirth, Dying*. New York: Harper & Row, 1971.

Kübler-Ross, Elisabeth. *On Death and Dying*. New York: Macmillan, 1969.

Lauf, Detlef Ingo. *Secret Doctrines of the Tibetan Books of the Dead*, translated by Graham Parkes. Boston: Shambhala, 1977.

Sadler, A. L. *The Maker of Modern Japan: The Life of Tokugawa Ieyasu*. Rutland, VT: C. E. Tuttle, 1978.

Sambhava, Padma, comp. *The Tibetan Book of the Dead*, translated by Robert A. F. Thurman. London: Aquarian/Thorsons, 1994.

Shcherbatskoi, Fedor Ippolitovich. *The Conception of Buddhist Nirvana*. The Hague: Mouton, 1965.

Suzuki, Daisetz Teitaro. *The Essentials of Zen Buddhism: An Anthology of the Writings of Daisetz T. Suzuki*, edited by Bernard Phillips. London: Rider, 1963.

Suzuki, Daisetz Teitaro. *Zen and Japanese Culture*. New York: Pantheon Books, 1959.

RICHARD BONNEY

# BURIAL GROUNDS

Three kinds of gravescapes—that is, memorials and the landscapes containing them—have dominated the funerary scene in North America from colonial times to the present. The first, the graveyard, almost invariably is located in towns and cities, typically adjoined to a church and operated gratis or for a nominal fee by members of the congregation. The second, the rural cemetery, is usually situated at the outskirts of towns and cities and is generally owned and managed by its patrons. The third, the lawn cemetery, is typically located away from towns and cities and ordinarily is managed by professional superintendents and owned by private corporations. These locations are generalities; in the nineteenth century both the rural cemetery and the lawn cemetery began to be integrated into the towns and cities that grew up around them.

## The Graveyard

From the beginning of colonization and for many years thereafter, Euroamerican gravescapes in North America uniformly presented visitors with a powerful imperative: Remember death, for the time of judgment is at hand. The graveyard serves as a convenient place to dispose of the dead; however, its more significant purpose derives from its formal capacity to evoke or establish memory of death, which serves to remind the living of their own fragility and urgent need to prepare for death. Locating the dead among the living thus helps to ensure that the living will witness the gravescape's message regularly as a reminder "to manifest that this world is not their home" and "that heaven is a reality" (Morris 1997, p. 65). Devaluation of all things accentuating the temporal life is the starting point for a cultural logic that embraces the view that "the life of the body is no longer the real life, and the negation of this life is the beginning rather than the end" (Marcuse 1959, p. 68).

Inscriptions and iconography continually reinforce these imperatives by deemphasizing temporal life and emphasizing the necessity of attending to the demands of eternal judgment. Only rarely, for example, do the memorials indicative of this perspective provide viewers with information beyond the deceased's name, date of death, and date of birth. Icons reminiscent of death (for example, skulls, crossed bones, and the remarkably popular winged death's head) almost invariably appear at or near the center of the viewer's focus, while icons associated with life appear on the periphery. Popular mottos like *memento mori* ("remember death") and *fugit hora* ("time flies," or more literally "hours flee") provide viewers with explicit instruction.

Certain actions run contrary to the values that give this gravescape its meaning. For example, locating the dead away from the living, enclosing burial grounds with fences as if to separate the living from the dead, decorating and adorning the gravescape, or ordering the graveyard according to dictates of efficiency and structural linearity. The constant struggles to embrace and encourage others to embrace the view that life is nothing more than preparation for death demands constant attention if one seeks to merit eternal bliss and avoid eternal damnation. This view thus unceasingly insists upon a clear and distinct separation of "real life" (spiritual life, eternal life) from "illusory life" (physical life; the liminal, transitory existence one leads in the here and now). The formal unity of memorials in this gravescape both ensures its identity and energizes and sustains its rhetorical and cultural purpose.

Even from a distance the common size and shape of such memorials speak to visitors of their purpose. Although the graveyard provides ample space for variation, an overwhelming majority of the memorials belonging to this tradition are relatively modest structures (between one and five feet in height and width and between two and five inches thick), and most are variations of two shapes: single and triple arches. Single arch memorials are small, smoothed slabs with three squared sides and a convex or squared crown. Triple arch memorials are also small, smoothed slabs with three squared sides but feature smaller arches on either side of a single large arch, which gives the impression of a single panel with a convex crown

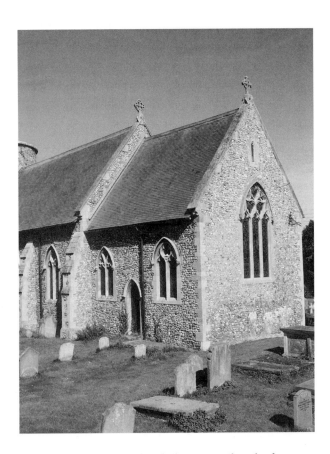

*This graveyard adjoined with the Saxon Church of Norfolk, England, is the type of traditional gravescape that dominated colonial North America.* CORBIS

conjoined on either side by similar but much narrower panels, or pilasters, with convex crowns. Together with location and general appearance, such minimal uniformity undoubtedly helped to ensure that visitors would not mistake the graveyard for a community pasture or a vacant lot.

## The Rural Cemetery

For citizens possessed of quite different sensibilities, the graveyard was a continual source of discontentment until the introduction of a cemeterial form more suited to their values. That form, which emerged on September 24, 1830, with the consecration of Boston's Mount Auburn Cemetery, signaled the emanation of a radically different kind of cemetery. Rather than a churchyard filled with graves, this new gravescape would be a place from which the living would be able to derive pleasure, emotional satisfaction, and instruction on how best to live life in harmony with art and nature.

Judging from the rapid emergence of rural cemeteries subsequent to the establishment of Mount Auburn, as well as Mount Auburn's immediate popularity, this new cemeterial form quickly lived up to its advocates' expectations. Within a matter of months travelers from near and far began to make "pilgrimages to the Athens of New England, solely to see the realization of their long cherished dream of a resting place for the dead, at once sacred from profanation, dear to the memory, and captivating to the imagination" (Downing 1974, p. 154). Part of the reason for Mount Auburn's immediate popularity was its novelty. Yet Mount Auburn remained remarkably popular throughout the nineteenth century and continues to attract a large number of visitors into the twenty-first century.

Moreover, within a few short years rural cemeteries had become the dominant gravescape, and seemingly every rural cemetery fostered one or more guidebooks, each of which provided prospective visitors with a detailed description of the cemetery and a walking tour designed to conduct visitors along the most informative and beautiful areas. "In their mid-century heyday, before the creation of public parks," as the scholar Blanche Linden-Ward has observed, "these green pastoral places also functioned as 'pleasure grounds' for the general public" (Linden-Ward 1989, p. 293). Mount Auburn "presented [and still presents] visitors with a programmed sequence of sensory experiences, primarily visual, intended to elicit specific emotions, especially the so-called pleasures of melancholy that particularly appealed to contemporary romantic sensibilities" (p. 295).

The owners of rural cemeteries played a significant role in the effort to capture the hearts and imaginations of visitors insofar as they sought to ensure that visitors would encounter nature's many splendors. They accomplished this not only by taking great care to select sites that would engender just such sentiments but also by purchasing and importing wide varieties of exotic shrubs, bushes, flowers, and trees. Both from within the gravescape and from a distance, rural cemeteries thus frequently appear to be lush, albeit carefully constructed, nature preserves.

Promoting a love of nature, however, was only a portion of what patrons sought to accomplish in their new gravescape. "The true secret of the attraction," America's preeminent nineteenth-century landscape architect Andrew Jackson Downing insisted, lies not only "in the natural beauty of the sites," but also "in the tasteful and harmonious embellishment of these sites by art." Thus, "a visit to one of these spots has the united charm of nature and art, the double wealth of rural and moral association. It awakens at the same moment, the feeling of human sympathy and the love of natural beauty, implanted in every heart" (Downing 1974, p. 155). To effect this union of nature and art, cemetery owners went to great lengths—and often enormous costs—to commission and obtain aesthetically appealing objects to adorn the cemetery and to set a standard for those wishing to erect memorials to their deceased friends and relatives.

In this way cemetery owners recommended by example that memorials were to be works of art. Even the smallest rural cemeteries suggested this much by creating, at the very least, elaborate entrance gates to greet visitors so that their cemeteries would help to create "a distinct resonance between the landscape design of the 'rural' cemetery and recurring themes in much of the literary and material culture of that era" (Linden-Ward 1989, p. 295).

## The Lawn Cemetery

The rural cemetery clearly satisfied the values and needs of many people; yet a significant segment of the population found this gravescape too ornate, too sentimental, too individualized, and too expensive. Even Andrew Jackson Downing, who had long been a proponent of the rural cemetery, publicly lamented that the natural beauty of the rural cemetery was severely diminished "by the most violent bad taste; we mean the hideous ironmongery, which [rural cemeteries] all more or less display. . . . Fantastic conceits and gimcracks in iron might be pardonable as adornments of the balustrade of a circus or a temple of Comus," he continued, "but how reasonable beings can tolerate them as inclosures to the quiet grave of a family, and in such scenes of sylvan beauty, is mountain high above our comprehension" (Downing 1974, p. 156).

Largely in response to these criticisms, in 1855 the owners of Cincinnati's Spring Grove Cemetery instructed their superintendent, Adolph Strauch, to remove many of the features included when John

Notman initially designed Spring Grove as a rural cemetery. In redesigning the cemetery, however, Strauch not only eliminated features typically associated with rural cemeteries, he also created a new cemeterial form that specifically reflected and articulated a very different set of needs and values.

In many ways what Strauch created and what lawn cemeteries have become is a matter of absence rather than of presence. The absence of raised mounds, ornate entrance gates, individualized gardens, iron fencing, vertical markers, works of art dedicated to specific patrons, freedom of expression in erecting and decorating individual or family plots, and cooperative ownership through patronage produces a space that disassociates itself not only from previous traditions but also from death itself. This is not to say that lawn cemeteries are devoid of ornamentation, as they often contain a variety of ornamental features. Nevertheless, as one early advocate remarked, lawn cemeteries seek to eliminate "all things that suggest death, sorrow, or pain" (Farrell 1980, p. 120).

Rather than a gravescape designed to remind the living of their need to prepare for death or a gravescape crafted into a sylvan scene calculated to allow mourners and others to deal with their loss homeopathically, the lawn cemetery provides visitors with an unimpeded view. Its primary characteristics include efficiency, centralized management, markers that are either flush with or depressed into the ground, and explicit rules and regulations.

Yet to patrons the lawn cemetery affords several distinct advantages. First, it provides visitors with an open vista, unobstructed by fences, memorials, and trees. Second, it allows cemetery superintendents to make the most efficient use of the land in the cemetery because available land is generally laid out in a grid so that no areas fail to come under a general plan. Third, by eliminating fences, hedges, trees, and other things associated with the rural cemetery and by requiring markers to be small enough to be level or nearly level with the ground, this gravescape does not appear to be a gravescape at all.

Although lawn cemeteries did not capture people's imaginations as the rural cemetery had in the mid–nineteenth century, they did rapidly increase in number. As of the twenty-first century they are considered among the most common kind of gravescape in the United States.

See also: CEMETERIES AND CEMETERY REFORM; CEMETERIES, WAR; FUNERAL INDUSTRY; LAWN GARDEN CEMETERIES

**Bibliography**

Downing, Andrew Jackson. "Public Cemeteries and Public Gardens." In George W. Curtis ed., *Rural Essays by Andrew Jackson Downing*. New York: Da Capo, 1974.

French, Stanley. "The Cemetery As Cultural Institution: The Establishment of Mount Auburn and the 'Rural Cemetery' Movement." In David E. Stannard ed., *Death in America*. Philadelphia: University of Pennsylvania Press, 1974.

Linden, Blanche M. G. "The Willow Tree and Urn Motif: Changing Ideas about Death and Nature." *Markers* 1 (1979–1980):149–155.

Linden-Ward, Blanche. "Strange but Genteel Pleasure Grounds: Tourist and Leisure Uses of Nineteenth Century Cemeteries." In Richard E. Meyer ed., *Cemeteries and Gravemarkers: Voices of American Culture*. Ann Arbor: University of Michigan Research Press, 1989.

Ludwig, Allan I. *Graven Images: New England Stonecarving and Its Images, 1650–1815*. Middletown, CT: Wesleyan University Press, 1966.

Marcuse, Herbert. "The Ideology of Death." In Herman Feifel ed., *The Meaning of Death*. New York: McGraw-Hill, 1959.

Morris, Richard. *Sinners, Lovers, and Heroes: An Essay on Memorializing in Three American Cultures*. Albany: SUNY Press, 1997.

Tashjian, Dickran, and Ann Tashjian. *Memorials for Children of Change: The Art of Early New England Stone Carving*. Middleton, CT: Wesleyan University Press, 1974.

RICHARD MORRIS

# BURIED ALIVE

"Buried alive"—the phrase itself frightens people with its thoughts of being enclosed in a narrow space with one's breathing air diminishing, helpless, and unable to escape. A 1985 Italian study of patients recovering from myocardial infarction, found that 50 percent of them suffered from phobias that included being buried alive. The fear of being buried alive is denoted by the word *taphephobia*. The state of the appearance of death while still alive has been denoted by the term *thanatomimesis*, although the phrase "apparent death" is used more frequently by medical professionals and those in the scientific community.

This fear of premature burial is not wholly without basis. On January 25 and 26, 2001, the *Boston Globe* reported the case of a woman found slumped lifelessly in her bathtub, with a suicide note and evidence of a drug overdose nearby. The police and the emergency medical technicians found no pulse, no sign of breathing, her skin was turgid, and her eyes were unresponsive. She was transported to a nearby funeral home, where the funeral director, on his way out, was startled to hear a faint sound, which he recognized as someone breathing. He quickly unzipped the body bag, held her mouth open to keep her air passages clear, and arranged for her removal to a hospital. Similarly, according to an 1815 volume of the *North American Review,* a Connecticut woman was nearly buried alive, but fortunately showed signs of life before the coffin was closed.

Cases of people thought dead and being disposed of are reported from ancient times. William Tebb and Vollum, in 1905, speak of Pliny the Elder (23–79 C.E.), who cites the case of a man placed upon a funeral pyre who revived after the fire had been lit, and who was then burnt alive, the fire having progressed too far to save him. Plutarch, Esclepiades the physician, and Plato give similar stories of men who returned to life prior to burial. Hugh Archibald Wyndham wrote a family history, published in 1939, which included the story of Florence Wyndham, who, after a year of marriage, was thought to be dead and buried in the family vault in 1559. The sexton, knowing there were three valuable rings on one of her fingers, went to the vault and began to cut the finger. Blood flowed, the body moved, and the sexton fled leaving his lantern behind. Florence returned to the house in her grave clothes, frightening the household who thought she was a ghost and shut the door against her.

A considerable number of similar premature burial stories have been reported. These burials occur when the individual gives the unmistakable appearance of being dead due to a trance state or a similar medical condition. Burial alive also occurs in natural disasters such as the earthquake in India in 2001, and in avalanches. In such cases the individual's thoughts turn to the hope of rescue.

According to Rodney Davies, author of *The Lazarus Syndrome: Burial Alive and Other Horrors of the Undead* (1998), the percentage of premature burials has been variously estimated as somewhere between 1 per 1,000 to as many as 1 or 2 percent of all total burials in the United States and Europe. The percentage increases in times of pestilence or war. Premature burials of Americans during World War II and during the Vietnam War has been estimated to have been as high as 4 percent (Davies 1998, p. 133).

Burial alive has sometimes been deliberate. In Rome, vestal virgins who had broken their vows of chastity were imprisoned in an underground chamber with a lighted candle, some bread, a little water mixed with milk, and left to die. In Edgar Allan Poe's story *The Cask of Amontillado* (1846), the narrator exacts revenge by luring his enemy to the wine cellar and then walling him in. Poe was obsessed with the theme of premature burial, which he used in many stories. William Shakespeare also used premature burial as a theme, the best known example occurring in *Romeo and Juliet* (1595). Juliet is given a potion that mimics death; Romeo, not knowing she is still alive, kills himself. Juliet, finding him dead, then kills herself. Shakespeare repeats this theme in *Henry IV, Part Two* (1598), and *Pericles, Prince of Tyre* (1607). A number of other authors, such as Bram Stoker, Gertrude Atherton, and Wilkie Collins have used variations of the buried alive theme.

Since the nineteenth century, the fear of being buried alive has resulted in the creation of devices that allow one to signal from the coffin. A 1983 U.S. patent (No. 4,367,461), describes an alarm system for coffins that is actuated by a movement of the body in the coffin. In the mid–nineteenth century in Munich, Germany, a building was set aside

in which bodies were kept for several days, with an attendant ready to rescue any who had been buried alive. The fingers of the body were fastened to a wire leading to a bell in the room of the attendant. Mark Twain visited this place in 1878 or 1879 and described it in a story which he included in chapter 31 in *Life on the Mississippi* (1883).

The deliberate invoking of a state mimicking death has been reported from India. Those adept in yoga are able to reduce their respiratory and pulse rates and then be buried for several days before being brought out alive.

*See also:* ANXIETY AND FEAR; CRYONIC SUSPENSION; DEFINITIONS OF DEATH; PERSISTENT VEGETATIVE STATE; WAKE

## Bibliography

Bondesen, Jan. *Buried Alive: The Terrifying History of Our Most Primal Fear.* New York: W. W. Norton , 2001.

Davies, Rodney. *The Lazarus Syndrome: Burial Alive and Other Horrors of the Undead.* New York: Barnes and Noble, 1998.

Kastenbaum, Robert, and Ruth Aisenberg. *The Psychology of Death.* New York: Springer, 1972.

"Obituaries." *The North American Review* 1 no. 1 (May 1815):141.

Tebb, William, and Edward Perry Vollum. *Premature Burial and How It May Be Prevented,* 2nd edition, edited by Walter R. Hadwen. London: Swan Sonnenschein, 1905.

Wyndham, Hugh Archibald. *A Family History 1410–1688: The Wyndhams of Norfolk and Somerset.* London: Oxford University Press, 1939.

Zotti, A. M., and G. Bertolotti. "Analisi delle reazioni fobiche in soggetti con infarto miocardico recente." (Analysis of phobic reactions in subjects with recent myocardial infarction.) *Medicina Psicosomatica* 30, no. 3 (1985):209–215.

SAM SILVERMAN

## CADAVER EXPERIENCES

Studies by sociologists have found that no experience has a more profound impact on medical school students than the first encounter with death, which typically occurs during the first-year course of gross anatomy. With its required dissection of human cadavers, the course seeks to impart a variety of explicit lessons, including the size, shape, and exact location of organs varies from one individual to another; organs vary in their "feel" and texture and are connected to other parts of the body in complex ways that textbook illustrations cannot effectively reproduce; and surgical instruments have specific purposes and must be handled properly to avoid injury to the patient or oneself. A less explicit, but no less important, result is overcoming the natural emotional repugnance at handling a cadaver.

First-year medical students report having the most difficulty dissecting those parts of the body with strong emotional associations, especially the hands, face, and genitals, as opposed to the arms, legs, and abdomen, which can more easily be bracketed as mere physical body parts. One common method of dealing with the emotional upset of cadaver dissection is the use of humor—students often circulate cadaver stories as a test of one another's proper emotional preparation through humor involving a dismembered corpse.

*Cadaver stories.* Cadaver stories (jokes involving anatomy-lab cadavers) have been studied by researchers interested in urban folklore.

Researchers have found that most of these stories are unlikely to be true and that they fall into five basic categories, all connected with the emotional socialization of medical students:

1. Stories describing the removal of cadaver parts outside of the lab to shock ordinary citizens (mailing body parts to friends or handing change to a toll collector with a severed hand are examples of this category).

2. Manipulation of the cadaver's sexual organs which shocks or offends another medical student.

3. The cadaver appearing to come to life at an unexpected time, supposedly frightening a novice student. One such story features a medical student taking the place of the cadaver under the sheet; at the right moment, the student twitches and then sits upright to the screams of the emotionally unprepared.

4. Stories featuring the cadaver as a food receptacle. Students may claim to have heard of a student in another lab who hid food in a corpse and later removed and ate it during class. Like the previous type of story, this category is supposed to test the queasiness of medical students who are expected to find the story amusing.

5. The realization that the medical student has finished dissecting a member of his or her own family (the head is the last part of the cadaver to be dissected and because it is so

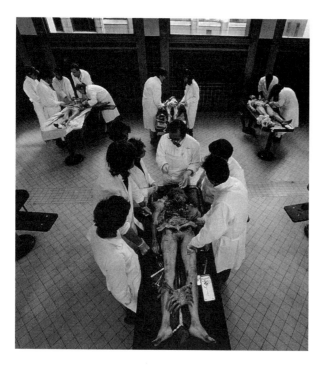

*The dissection of human cadavers in medical school imparts not only the lessons of gross anatomy, but lessons on dealing with death.* YANN ARTHUS-BERTRAND/CORBIS

emotionally charged, it is almost always kept covered until the end of the anatomy course).

Stories of this last kind have more credibility with medical students than those in the first four categories, which require conscious misbehavior on the part of some other medical student. In this cadaver story, a well-prepared medical student is still capable of being emotionally assaulted by the realization that she has spent the entire semester dissecting her own mother. Although such an event is highly unlikely, some physicians are obliged to operate on a friend or someone resembling a family member.

Taken together, cadaver stories reveal the common need for medical students to verbalize their discomfort with death and dead bodies. While the stories are about medical students or emotionally squeamish laypersons, the students reciting these legends are themselves skittish and use the stories as a type of emotional fortification.

*Dog labs.* A second stage in the emotional socialization of medical students is associated with so-called dog labs that, until recently, were found in many medical schools. In dog labs, medical students operate on anesthetized dogs supplied by local animal-control shelters. Unlike cadavers, these creatures are alive and must be kept alive during dissection. Overt learning outcomes include familiarity with anesthetics, care in working on a living creature that bleeds and needs to be kept breathing, and additional training in the use of surgical instruments. A less explicit outcome is another lesson in emotional socialization because the dogs are expected to die on the operating table. Anesthetized and thus incapable of feeling pain, the animals are given a fatal drug overdose. Recently, this practice has been eliminated from most medical schools, but for years it was considered a necessary step in preparing the student to work on living human patients.

*Witnessing an autopsy.* The third component in preparing future physicians for dealing with death involves attending and participating in an actual autopsy. Usually scheduled for the second year of medical school training, the autopsy moves students closer to what had very recently been a living human being. Unaffected by preservatives, the body's organs look and feel exactly as they would on the operating table, allowing students an opportunity to collect information even closer to the real thing. At this point, most students report that they have arrived at a new stage in emotional detachment from death. Shorn of the protective layer of cadaver stories, students use the scientific knowledge gained during their many chemistry and biology classes as a bulwark against emotional distress. Students report that cadaver dissection does not completely prepare them for the autopsy, and some experience difficulty remaining in the room during the procedure.

*Patients with terminal illnesses.* Having reached their third and fourth years of medical school, students begin to come into contact with actual patients. Some of these patients are terminally ill and represent a new challenge to emotional control and response to the prospect of death. None of the previous stages prepare students for interaction with a patient whose death is imminent. By this point in their education, some students report that they are troubled by their desensitization to the suffering and deaths of patients and fear that they will come to resemble the icy, hardened practitioners they have always despised. By the fourth year of medical school, however, most students report an overcoming of this feared detachment and an attainment of a proper emotional balance.

## Changes in Medical School

This sequence of stages in emotional socialization coincides with stages in the training of medical students. For many years, that training was fairly uniform among medical schools. Similarly, the sorts of students enrolling in medical school often shared certain characteristics: male, white, twenty-two to twenty-five years of age, middle- to upper-middle-class background, a thorough grounding in the hard sciences, and a high grade point average from a reputable undergraduate institution. By the end of the twentieth century, however, significant changes occurred in the training of medical students, who were increasingly likely to be female, non-white, and to have taken many non-science courses. These developments may mean that the model of emotional socialization for confronting death is changing. For example, many medical schools now routinely bring medical students into contact with patients during their first year. Although this usually involves taking medical histories or simply overcoming discomfort in speaking with strangers about their health problems, it may well affect the manner in which emotional detachment develops. Also, cadaver stories appear to be evolving. Initially, many stories featured female medical students as their target. Analysts interpreted this as a thinly veiled form of sexism. Recently, however, stories have appeared that feature pranks backfiring against male perpetrators. In another shift in gross anatomy labs, female students sometimes choose to work together in dissection of female cadavers, believing that male students do not show proper respect for female genitalia.

The studies summarized above describe the experience at institutions offering training in conventional allopathic medicine. Nontraditional medical training (e.g., homeopathy or chiropractic) may produce a very different set of reactions in the encounter with death. Likewise, the confrontation with death in medical schools in other countries varies with the unique cultural mores that have shaped the students.

*See also:* AUTOPSY; DEATH EDUCATION; NURSING
        EDUCATION

## Bibliography

Fox, Renee C. *The Sociology of Medicine: A Participant Observer's View*. Englewood Cliffs, NJ: Prentice Hall, 1989.

Furst, Lilian R. *Between Doctors and Patients: The Changing Balance of Power*. Charlottesville: University of Virginia Press, 1998.

Hafferty, Frederic W. "Cadaver Stories and the Emotional Socialization of Medical Students." *Journal of Health and Social Behavior* 29, no. 4 (1988):344–356.

Lantos, John. *Do We Still Need Doctors? A Physician's Personal Account of Practicing Medicine Today*. New York: Routledge, 1997.

Lawton, Julia. *The Dying Process: Patients' Experiences of Palliative Care*. London: Routledge, 2000.

Magee, Mike, and Michael D'Antonio. *The Best Medicine: Doctors, Patients, and the Covenant of Caring*. New York: St. Martin's Press, 1999.

Tauber, Alfred I. *Confessions of a Medicine Man: An Essay in Popular Philosophy*. Cambridge: MIT Press, 1999.

JONATHAN F. LEWIS

# CAMUS, ALBERT

Born in 1913, Albert Camus was a French philosopher, writer, and playwright of Algerian descent. Camus was confronted very early in his life by the contradictions that forged his conception of death. While celebrating the multiple splendours of life and the exuberance of nature, he was struck by an illness (tuberculosis) that had lasting effects throughout his life. This was the beginning of his conception of the absurdity of life, best summarized by the title character of his 1938 play *Caligula,* who said, "Men die, and they are not happy" (1.4).

Camus was an atheist, and the notions of divinity or life after death were evacuated from his philosophical conception. So, if one cannot find sense in dying, one must invest all of one's energies (despite the apparent absurdity of existence) into action: There is an obligation on humans to act—by revolting against things as they are, assuming their freedom, fighting for the values of justice, equality, and brotherhood. This, however, presupposes that one chooses to live; to Camus, as he writes at the very beginning of his essay on the absurd, *The Myth of Sisyphus,* "There is but one truly philosophical problem and that is suicide" (p. 11). This affirms the liberty that individuals have to dispose of their life as they wish. Camus is not, however, an apologist of suicide. He is a passionate advocate for the freedom of choice. In concluding *The Myth of Sisyphus,* Camus cannot help but ask the reader to "imagine Sisyphus happy." Camus was awarded the Nobel Prize for Literature in 1957. He died in a car accident in 1960.

*See also:* KIERKEGAARD, SØREN; PHILOSOPHY, WESTERN; SARTRE, JEAN-PAUL

### Bibliography

Camus, Albert. *The Myth of Sisyphus and Other Essays,* translated by Justin O'Brien. London: Hamish Hamilton, 1955.

Camus, Albert. *The Stranger.* New York: Random House, 1966.

Todd, Oliver. *Albert Camus: A Life,* translated by Benjamin Ivry. New York: Alfred A. Knopf, 1997.

JEAN-YVES BOUCHER

# CANCER

To many people, the word *cancer* is synonymous with death; however, that is not the reality. In industrialized countries cancer mortality rates have slowly and progressively declined between 1950 and 2000. In 2000 overall cure rates reached approximately 50 percent. Nevertheless, cancer remains the second leading cause of death in industrialized countries and a rapidly increasing cause of death in developing countries.

The scope of the problem in the United States is large. Some 1.2 million people were diagnosed with potentially fatal cancer in the year 2000. Of these, 59 percent were expected to live for at least five years (in some, the cancer may be continuously present for more than five years) with or without evidence of cancer. People of all ages, from birth to advanced age, can manifest cancer, making it the second-leading cause of death in the United States. In children cancer is unusual, but it has consistently been the leading cause of death from disease. As mortality rates from cardiovascular disease decline, the proportion of cancer deaths increases. It is anticipated that the mortality rate from cancer will surpass that from heart disease by the year 2050. Direct and indirect financial costs of cancer in the United States for the year 2000 were $178 billion.

Developing countries represented 80 percent of the world's approximately 6 billion people in the year 2000. In these countries, cancer has grown from a minor public health issue in the early 1990s to a rapidly expanding problem by the beginning of the twenty-first century. The emergence of a middle class, with attendant changes in lifestyle, increased longevity and exposure to potential carcinogens, and expectations of improved medical delivery systems have fueled the growing impact of cancer in the third world. The financial resources and socio-medical infrastructure needed to diagnose and treat, much less screen and prevent these cancers, are lacking in the developing world.

A controversial issue in the United States is whether there has been progress in the "War on Cancer" declared by Congress in 1971. Since then a large flow of tax dollars has been directed to basic and clinical research with the goal of eliminating cancer. Mortality rates from all forms of cancer have declined slightly from 1990 through 2000, but with large variations among different types of cancer. Optimistic explanations include significant improvements in treatment and prevention. More pessimistic analyses suggest that some of the more common cancers can be diagnosed earlier so that benchmark five-year mortality rates have diminished, but that the actual course of the disease is unaffected because treatments are not really more effective.

## Biology

Cancer is a disease whereby the genes regulating individual cell behavior and interactions with other cells malfunction. It is therefore a "genetic" disease, although not necessarily "inherited." Cancers clearly traced to inherited susceptibility are unusual, accounting for fewer than 10 percent of cases. Rather, the majority of cancers seem to result from complicated interactions between the environment and "normal" cells.

The routine operations of cell growth, division, cell-to-cell communication, and programmed cell death (apoptosis) are complex and must be tightly controlled to preserve the integrity of the organism. Chromosomes, which contain DNA molecules organized into genes, control these regulatory processes. Similar mechanisms are present in all animals and plants, are highly conserved through evolution, and so must provide significant survival benefit. The phenomenon of cancer is infrequent in wild animals and has only come to prominence in human beings since 1900. These statistics suggest that interactions of environmental agents with the genes result in fixed alterations that eventually manifest themselves as cancer. Public health measures have increased longevity so that the progressive, possibly inherent deterioration of regulatory functions accompanying aging allows less effective repair of chronic genetic damage.

Although no single cause has been or is likely to explain all of cancer, research has demonstrated that environmental factors predominate in the development of most cancer. Proven causes of DNA damage leading to malignant change include viruses, radiation, and chemicals. Viruses such as Epstein-Barr, HIV, and papilloma can contribute to cancer development (carcinogenesis). Both therapeutic and normal environmental exposure to radiation increase the risk of cancer. Multiple chemicals have been linked to cancer, of which the best examples are the constituents of tobacco. How these and other unknown environmental factors, particularly dietary and airborne, interact with human genes to cause irreversible, malignant transformation is the subject of intensive research.

Malignant cells can multiply and divide in the tissue of origin and can travel through the circulatory system and create secondary deposits (metastases) in vital organs. These capabilities underlie the phenomena of invasive lumps (tumors) and the potential for the dissemination of cancer. Most cancer cells, whether at the primary or secondary site, divide at about the same rate as their cells of origin. Malignant cells, however, do not typically undergo normal programmed cell death (apoptosis) and consequently accumulate. Most often, the cause of death in cancer is a poorly understood wasting process (cachexia).

**Prevention and Screening**

Prevention of cancer, or the reduction of risk for a person who has never experienced the disease, is a desirable goal. For those cancers resulting from known environmental exposures, such an approach has been most successful. Avoidance of tobacco products is no doubt the best proven means of preventing cancer. In industrialized countries, regulatory agencies monitor chemical and radiation exposure. Dietary habits are felt to influence the risk of developing certain cancers, but there is very little evidence that dietary manipulations lead to significant risk reduction.

Screening is the attempt to diagnose an established cancer as early as possible, usually before the onset of symptoms, in order to optimize the outcome. A screening technique is designed to simply, safely, and cheaply identify those patients who may have a certain type of cancer. If screening-test result is positive, further testing is always necessary to rule the diagnosis in or out. There is considerable controversy in this field. It cannot be assumed that early detection is always in the patient's best interest, and the overall financial costs in screening a population must be weighed against the actual benefits. Screening may be counterproductive under the following conditions:

1. Treatment is not more effective with early detection.

2. The patient will die of an unrelated condition before the diagnosed cancer could be troublesome or fatal.

3. The screening examination can be harmful.

4. The screening examination is falsely "negative" and thus falsely reassuring.

5. The treatment causes complications or death in a patient in whom the cancer itself would not have led to problems.

In spite of these limitations, there have been successes. Good evidence exists that not only early detection but also improved survival can be achieved in breast, cervical, and colorectal cancers. With minimal danger and cost, appropriate populations screened for these diseases benefit from reduced mortality. Prostate cancer, however, is more problematic. Measurement of prostate-specific antigen (PSA), a substance made by both normal prostate as well as malignant prostate cells, can identify a patient with prostate cancer before any other manifestations. But because of the relatively elderly population (often with unrelated potentially serious conditions) at risk, it has been difficult to prove that treatment confers a quantitative or qualitative benefit. Continued efforts will be made to create screening techniques that truly allow more effective treatment for cancers detected earlier.

## Diagnosis and Treatment

Once a malignancy is suspected, tests (usually imaging techniques, such as X rays, ultrasounds, nuclear medicine scans, CAT scans, and MRIs) are performed for confirmation. Ultimately a biopsy, or removal of a piece of tissue for microscopic examination, is necessary for determination of the presence and type of cancer. Staging tests reveal whether the disease has spread beyond its site of origin. Because of the inability of current techniques to detect microscopic deposits of cancer, a cancer may frequently appear to be localized but nevertheless exist elsewhere in the body below the threshold of clinical detection.

The diagnostic and staging process should permit the optimal clarification of the goals of treatment. Curative treatment intends permanent elimination of cancer, whereas palliative treatment intends to relieve symptoms and possibly prolong life. In every cancer situation there are known probabilities of cure. For example, a specific patient with "localized" breast cancer may have a 50–60 percent chance of cure based on predictive factors present at the time of diagnosis. Follow-up "negative" tests, however, do not yield the certainty that there is no cancer, whereas the documented presence of recurrent cancer has clear significance. Cancer, indeed, is the most curable of all chronic diseases, but only the uneventful passage of time allows a patient to become more confident of his or her status.

Surgery is the oldest and overall most effective cancer treatment, particularly when tumors appear to be localized and cure is the goal. It is a preferred modality for breast, prostate, skin, lung, colon, testicular, uterine, brain, stomach, pancreas, and thyroid tumors. The aims of cancer surgery include elimination of as much cancer as possible, preservation of organ function, and minimal risk and suffering for the patient. Occasionally surgery is intentionally palliative, particularly when other treatment modalities are added in an effort to improve symptoms.

Radiation therapy has been a mainstay of cancer treatment since the 1940s, when doctors first began to understand its potential benefits and short and long-term risks. Therapeutic ionizing radiation is generated by a linear accelerator and delivered externally to a well-defined area. It thus shares with surgery an advantage for localized tumors. The inherent differences in radiation sensitivity between malignant tissues and the surrounding normal tissues permits the exploitation of radiation for therapeutic benefit. When the cancerous tissue is less sensitive to radiation than the normal tissues, radiation can cause more harm than good. Radiation has been a useful primary treatment modality in tumors of the head and neck, lung, cervix, brain, pancreas, and prostate. For tumors that have metastasized to tissues such as bone and brain, radiation has been very useful for palliative purposes.

Systemic treatments, either by themselves or in concert with surgery and/or radiation, offer the most rational options for a disease, which so often has spread before diagnosis. The ideal treatment would be a substance that travels throughout the body, neutralizes every cancer cell, but causes no harm to any normal cell. Research has not yet yielded such a completely specific and nontoxic substance.

The 1950s saw the advent of anticancer drugs that came to be known as "chemotherapy." By the year 2001 approximately sixty chemotherapy drugs became commercially available. In general these drugs cause irreversible cell damage and death. They tend to be more destructive to rapidly dividing cells and so take their heaviest toll on relatively few malignancies as well as predictability on normal tissues (mucous membranes, hair follicles, and bone marrow). For some very sensitive disseminated cancers such as testicular, lymphomas, and leukemias, chemotherapy can be curative. For many others, such as advanced breast, ovarian, lung, colon cancers, chemotherapy may offer palliative benefits. Since the 1980s chemotherapy has played an important role in the multimodality treatment of localized breast, colon, lung, and bladder tumors. Except for curable and highly chemosensitive malignancies, chemotherapy kills at most 99.99999 percent of cells, but with a burden of trillions of cancer cells, millions of resistant cells remain. Even using high-dose chemotherapy, it appears that by the year 2001 chemotherapy may have reached a plateau of effectiveness.

Insights into the basic genetic, molecular, and regulatory abnormalities of malignant cells have opened up entirely new systemic approaches. "Natural" substances such as interferons and interleukins have therapeutically modulated cell proliferation and led to regression of some tumors. Antiangiogenesis agents interfere with the malignant cell's need for accessing new blood vessels. Chemicals designed to inhibit the inappropriate production of growth factors by malignant cells have been synthesized and show promise. Monoclonal antibodies aimed at proteins concentrated on the malignant cell's surface have achieved tumor shrinkage. By the year 2000 the thrust in basic cancer research had focused on manipulation of the fundamental processes that allow malignancies to grow and spread.

The Internet has allowed patients, families, and medical providers rapid access to information previously obtainable only through libraries or physicians. Such information, however, may be unfiltered, unsubstantiated, and misleading. Even when the information is correct, consumers may be unable to process it properly because of fears concerning their condition. All observers agree, however, that this form of communication will rapidly affect cancer research and treatment.

"Complementary" or "alternative" modalities have existed for many years and represent nonscientific means of attempting to cure or palliate cancer. The multitude of available products and techniques is enormous: herbal extracts, vitamins, magnetic therapies, acupuncture, synthetic chemicals, modified diets, and enemas. The vast majority of these have never been evaluated in a rigorously controlled scientific way that would allow more definitive and precise evaluation of their benefits and risks. Nevertheless, evidence has shown that as many as 50 percent of all cancer patients, irrespective of treatability by conventional methods, try at least one form of complementary medicine. Some proponents feel that these treatments should serve as adjuncts to conventional ones, while others feel that all conventional treatments are toxic and should be replaced by alternative ones. To investigate the potential of these approaches, the National Institutes of Health established the Institute of Alternative Medicine in 1996.

## End-of-Life Care

Because approximately 50 percent of cancer patients will die from their cancer, management of their dying takes on great importance. In the 1980s and 1990s multiple studies demonstrated that such basic concerns as pain and symptom control, respect for the right of the individual to forego life-prolonging measures, and spiritual distress have been mismanaged or ignored by many health care providers. In spite of the emergence of the modern hospice movement and improvements in techniques of symptom alleviation, most cancer patients die in hospitals or in nursing homes while receiving inadequate palliative care. The American Society of Clinical Oncology (ASCO) in 1998 mandated that part of fellowship training for oncologists include the basics of palliative care in order to rectify these problems.

*See also:* CAUSES OF DEATH; PAIN AND PAIN MANAGEMENT; SYMPTOMS AND SYMPTOM MANAGEMENT

### *Bibliography*

Ambinder, Edward P. "Oncology Informatics 2000." *Cancer Investigation* 19, supp. 1 (2001):30–33.

Burns, Edith A., and Elaine A. Leventhal. "Aging, Immunity, and Cancer," *Cancer Control* 7, no. 6 (2000):513–521.

Chu, Edward, and Vincent T. DeVita Jr. "Principles of Cancer Management: Chemotherapy." In Vincent DeVita, Jr., Samuel Hellman, and Steven A. Rosenberg eds., *Cancer: Principles and Practice of Oncology*, 6th edition. Philadelphia: Lippincott, Williams & Wilkins, 2001.

DeVita Jr., Vincent T. and Ghassan K. Abou-Alfa. "Therapeutic Implications of the New Biology." *The Cancer Journal* 6, supp. 2 (2000):S113–S121.

Groopman, Jerome. "The Thirty-Years War." *The New Yorker,* 4 June 2001, 52–63.

Hong, Waun Ki, Margaret R. Spitz, and Scott M. Lippman. "Cancer Chemoprevention in the 21st Century: Genetics, Risk Modeling, and Molecular Targets." *Journal of Clinical Oncology* 18, Nov. 1 supp. (2000):9s–18s.

Ishibe, Naoko, and Andrew Freedman. "Understanding the Interaction between Environmental Exposures and Molecular Events in Colorectal Carcinogenesis." *Cancer Investigation* 19, no. 5 (2000):524–539.

Lichter, Allen S. and Theodore S. Lawrence. "Recent Advances in Radiation Oncology." *New England Journal of Medicine* 332, no 6 (1995):371–379.

Plesnicar, Stojan, and Andrej Plesnicar. "Cancer: A Reality in the Emerging World." *Seminars in Oncology* 28, no. 2 (2000):210–216.

Rosenberg, Steven A. "Principles of Cancer Management: Surgical Oncology." In Vincent DeVita, Jr., Samuel Hellman, and Steven A. Rosenberg eds., *Cancer: Principles and Practice of Oncology*, 6th edition. Philadelphia: Lippincott, Williams & Wilkins, 2001.

Task Force on Cancer Care at the End of Life. "Cancer Care during the Last Phase of Life." *Journal of Clinical Oncology* 16, no. 5 (1998):1986–1996.

Walter, Louise C., and Kenneth E. Covinsky. "Cancer Screening in Elderly Patients." *Journal of the American Medical Association* 285, no. 21 (2001):2750–2778.

Wein, Simon. "Cancer, Unproven Therapies, and Magic," *Oncology* 14, no. 9 (2000):1345–1359.

*Internet Resources*

American Cancer Society. "Statistics." Available from www.cancer.org.

JAMES BRANDMAN

# CANNIBALISM

Cannibalism, or anthropophagy, is the ingestion of human flesh by humans. The idea of people eating parts of other people is something that has occurred wherever and whenever humans have formed societies. In traditional accounts cannibalism has emerged from peoples' history and cosmology, embedded in their myths and folklore. In all of these contexts, anthropophagy connotes moral turpitude.

The concept of cannibalism, its ethical encumbrances, and its cultural expression in history and myth are unquestionably universal. To be human is to think about the possibility of cannibalism. Anthropophagy is hard-wired into the architecture of human imagination. Cannibal giants, ogres, bogies, goblins, and other "frightening figures" populate the oral and literate traditions of most cultures, summoning images of grotesqueness, amorality, lawlessness, physical deformity, and exaggerated size. The Homeric tradition of the Greek Cyclops, the Scandinavian and Germanic folklore giants, or the Basque Tartaro find parallels in Asia, Africa, India, and Melanesia. In a fusion of the

historical and the fabled, these pancultural incidences of cannibal indicate a remarkable similarity in the way meanings are assigned to cannibalism across the world.

## Constructing History with Cannibals

Many cultural mythologies posit a prehistory that antedates the onset of acceptable mores, an epoch closed off from the beginnings of human settlement and social organization, when cannibalistic dynasties of giants prevailed. This common motif in cultural history indicates that cannibalism often symbolizes "others" that are less than fully human in some way. The imputation of anthropophagy draws a boundary between "us" and "them," the civilized and uncivilized, in a manner that depicts humans as emerging from a chaotic and bestial epoch dominated by a race of human-eating giants. These images of cannibal predecessors constitute a story that people tell themselves through myth to explain their past and present circumstances. So conventional are these patterns of thought across time and culture that we have come to understand cannibalism as the quintessential symbol of alterity, an entrenched metaphor of cultural xenophobia.

## Constructing Fiction with Cannibals

These themes of primordial anthropophagy serve other functions as well. Most oral traditions contain such folktales and fables that are passed down through the generations. One thinks here of the Western stories such as "Jack and the Beanstalk," "Hansel and Gretel," and early versions of "Little Red Riding Hood." These are not just dormant figures inhabiting the fairytale world, they convey for caretakers a vision of control and are frequently used—like the Western bogeyman or little green monster—to coerce, frighten, and cajole children into obedience. The threat of cannibalization provides an externalized and uncontrollable projection of parenthood capable of punishing misdeeds. In this sense, cannibal figures share certain characteristics with imaginary companions and fictions such as the Easter Bunny, Tooth Fairy, or Santa Claus, which, by contrast, project positive reward rather than negative punishment.

Cannibal representations are part of the universal stock of imaginative creations that foster obedience and conformity. Psychologists thus argue that anthropophagy is an archetype unaffected by cultural relativism and is, perhaps, a reflection of childhood psychodynamic processes. Flesh eating, from this perspective, may reflect child-engendered projections of parenthood and innate destruction fantasies.

Parallels between Western and non-Western fictional mediums illuminate the power cannibalism exerts on the human psyche. The commercial success of films such as *Silence of the Lambs, Manhunter,* and *The Cook, The Thief, His Wife, and Her Lover,* along with the extensive media coverage of cannibalistic criminals such as Jeffrey Dahmer, Gary Heidnik, and Albert Fish, speaks volumes about the public's fascination with cannibalism. Moviegoers' sympathetic cheering for Hannibal Lecter is a way of suspending disbelief, of inverting societal norms in the sanctuary of a movie theater. An alternative reality of moral turpitude is assumed as escapism, as if the audience is saying, "Do your best to scare me because I know it isn't really true." As a metaphor for abandonment, cannibalism scandalizes, titillates, and spellbinds.

In the context of folklore, cannibalism allows a rich re-imagining of the boundaries between the human and nonhuman, civilized and barbarian, male and female, the utopian and real. As such anthropophagy promotes not only social control but also teaches lessons about history, morality, and identity.

Cannibalism emerges in these discourses of imaginative literature and sacred history as an "otherworldly" phenomenon that is unfavorable to human survival and thus likely to command fear and respect—hence the prevalence of cannibalistic motifs in nursery rhymes. These profound pancultural similarities have led some analysts to argue that the term "cannibalism" should be reserved only for the fantasy, both European and native, of the flesh-eating "other" rather than the practice of flesh-eating.

## Constructing the Practice of Cannibalism

As soon as one starts to consider questions about which peoples have eaten human flesh, one finds controversy. The main issues are the colonial history of attributions of flesh-eating as a political form of domination; the problem of what is acceptable evidence in the context of scientific knowledge of the day; and the problems of interpreting oral, archaeological, and written evidence.

Although there is no accepted consensus on the various types of cannibalism encountered by researchers, the literature differentiates generally among a few types.

*Survival cannibalism.* This well-documented variant involves consumption of human flesh in emergency situations such as starvation. Some of the most famous cases are the 1846 Donner Party in the Sierra Nevada and the South American athletes stranded in the Andes in 1972, whose plight later became the subject of the film *Alive* (1993).

*Endocannibalism.* Endocannibalism is the consumption of human flesh from a member of one's own social group. The rationale for such behavior is usually that in consuming parts of the body, the person ingests the characteristics of the deceased; or through consumption there is a regeneration of life after death.

*Exocannibalism.* Exocannibalism is the consumption of flesh outside one's close social group—for example, eating one's enemy. It is usually associated with the perpetration of ultimate violence or again as a means of imbibing valued qualities of the victim. Reports of this practice suggest a high incidence of exocannibalism with headhunting and the display of skulls as war trophies. The majority of the controversies about the practice of cannibalism refer to endocannibalism and/or exocannibalism.

## Evidence in the Twenty-First Century

In the popular Western imagination, knowledge and understanding of cannibals were shaped by early explorers, missionaries, colonial officers, travelers, and others. The most commonly cited accounts are those about the South American Tupinamba Indians; the Caribbean Cariba (the word *cannibal* comes from, and is a corruption of, *carrib* and *Caliban*) of St. Vincent, St. Croix, and Martinique; and the South American Aztecs. These accounts were followed by numerous reported incidences of cannibalism in Africa, Polynesia, Australia, and Papua New Guinea. These often dubious attributions of cannibalism were a form of "othering"—denigrating other people and marking

*Similar to many tribes in Papua New Guinea, this group of Iwan warriors were once cannibals. While the tyranny of time often hampers these interpretive processes, the very act of attributing cannibalism to a society is now seen as a controversial political statement given modern sensitivities to indigenous peoples and cultures.* CHARLES AND JOSETTE LENARS/CORBIS

a boundary between the good "us" and the bad "them." The "primitive savage" was thus constructed as beyond the pale of civilization. As Alan Rumsey has noted, "Cannibalism has been most fully explored in its Western manifestations, as an aspect of the legitimating ideology of colonialism, missionization, and other forms of cultural imperialism" (1999, p. 105). Books that charted the travels of early explorers during the 1800s and early 1900s invariably carry titles with the term *cannibal*.

How reliable are these early accounts, and what kinds of evidence for cannibal practices do they contain or rely upon? One of the most famous commentators and critics, has concluded, "I have been unable to uncover adequate documentation of cannibalism as a custom in any form for any society. . . . The idea of the 'other' as cannibals, rather than the act, is the universal phenomenon" (Arens 1979, p. 139).

Many historical texts are compromised by Western prejudices, so that cannibalism emerges more as colonial myth and cultural myopia than as scientifically attested truth. The accounts do not stand the test of modern scholarly scrutiny. Most anthropologists, however, tend to reject the argument that unless one has photographic or first-hand evidence for a practice, one cannot infer its existence at some period. Anthropologists and archaeologists rely on a host of contextual clues, regional patterns, and material-culture evidence when drawing conclusions about past social practices. What the anthropologist gains by way of notoriety may be lost by heated dispute with ethnic descendants who find the attribution of past cannibalism demeaning because of the connotations of barbarism.

**The Main Disputes**

Among the principal academic disputes about evidence for cannibalistic practices, two in particular stand out. First, archaeologist Tim White has conducted an analysis of 800-year-old skeletal bone fragments from an Anasazi site at Mancos in south-west Colorado. William Arens has responded that White was seduced by the Holy Grail of cannibalism and failed to consider other explanations for the kind of perimortal bone trauma he encountered.

Second, Daniel Gajdusek found a fatal nervous disease known as *kuru* among a small population of the Fore people in Papua New Guinea. The disease is related to Creutzfeldt-Jacob, bovine spongiform encephalopathy (BSE), and Gertmann-Stausler-Scheinker syndrome. Working with anthropologists, Gajdusek claimed the disease was caught through the mortuary practice of eating the brains from dead people in Fore. Arens questioned the photographic evidence provided by Gadjusek and others. He suggested other forms of transmission by which the disease may have been contracted. The result is clashing scholarly perspectives on the historical occurrence of cannibalism.

## Social Explanations and Conditions for Cannibalism

The cross-cultural evidence for cannibalism among societies in Papua New Guinea, such as the Gimi, Hua, Daribi, and Bimin-Kuskusmin, suggests it is linked to the expression of cultural values about life, reproduction, and regeneration. Flesh is consumed as a form of life-generating food and as a symbolic means of reaffirming the meaning of existence. In other areas of Papua New Guinea, the same cultural themes are expressed through pig kills and exchanges. Cannibalism was a means of providing enduring continuity to group identity and of establishing the boundaries of the moral community. But it was equally a form of violence meted out to victims deemed amoral or evil, such as witches who brought death to other people.

A second line of research has suggested that this latter exocannibalism is an expression of hostility, violence, or domination toward a victim. In this interpretation, the perpetrator eats to inflict an ultimate indignity and thus an ultimate form of humiliation and domination. The archaeologist John Kantner, reviewing the evidence for reputed Anasazi cannibalism in the American Southwest, has concluded that with the gradual reduction in available resources and intensified competition, exocannibalism became a sociopolitical measure aimed at enforcing tribal inequities. However the evidence remains hotly disputed. Skeletal trauma is

indexed by bone markings made by tools or scrapers, disarticulations, breakage patterns, and "pot polish," blackened bone fragments suggesting abrasions caused by the boiling of bones. Such data indicate intentional and targeted defleshing of bones for the extraction of marrow. Such bone markings are quite different from mortuary bones found elsewhere in the region. Controversy surrounds these findings because other causes for the same bone markings have been proffered, including, second reburial of remains and external interference with bones by animals and natural hazards. Other scholars are therefore reluctant to impute cannibalism in the absence of any direct observation of it.

Other analysts, looking at the famous Aztec materials, have suggested that such large-scale cannibalism is related both to hunger and the appreciation of the nutritional value of flesh. In other words, cannibalism is a response to material conditions of existence such as protein depreciation and dwindling livestock. In Mesoamerica these predisposing conditions ensure that cannibalism is given a ritual rationale so that themes of renewal are manifested through flesh-eating. The evidence of perimortem mutilation is overwhelming; the inference from these data to cannibalism and its rationales remains, however, contestable and less compelling.

## Conclusion

From the available evidence, scholars have gleaned a seemingly reliable historical account of how cultures have constructed and used their concepts of cannibalism to provide a stereotype of the "other." Whatever technological advancements might yield in the way of more refined analysis of skeletal materials, proving that culture "X" or "Y" conducted cannibalism may not be quite the defining moment in human self-definition that some have thought it to be. The key insight is that in pancultural discourse and imaginative commerce, the human consumption of human flesh has served as a social narrative to enforce social control. Moreover, attributions of cannibalism remain a potent political tool wielded by those who pursue agendas of racial and ethnic domination.

The French philosopher Michel Montaigne long ago disabused society of the Western-centered notion that eating human flesh is somehow barbaric and exotic: "I consider it more barbarous to eat a man alive than eat him dead" (1958, p. 108). How one interprets cannibalism is thus always circumscribed and inflected by a culturally shaped morality.

For many researchers, then, the issue of whether cannibalism was ever a socially sanctioned practice is of secondary importance. Developments in experts' understanding of archaeological remains include the etiology and transmission of diseases like BSE, and interpretation of oral accounts and regional patterns that will likely point to some forms of cannibalism in some past cultures, even if such findings are tempered by contemporary cultural imperatives to avoid the appearance of stigmatization of the "other."

*See also:* AZTEC RELIGION; SACRIFICE

### Bibliography

Anglo M. *Man Eats Man*. London: Jupiter Books, 1979.

Arens, William. *The Man-Eating Myth: Anthropology and Anthropophagy*. New York: Oxford University Press, 1979.

Askenasy, Hans. *Cannibalism: From Sacrifice to Survival*. Amherst, NY: Prometheus, 1994.

Cortés, Hernando. *Five Letters 1519–1526*, translated by J. Bayard Morris. New York: W. W. Norton, 1962.

Davies, Nigel. *Human Sacrifice*. New York: William Morrow & Co., 1981.

Goldman, Laurence R. *Child's Play: Myth, Mimesis and Make-believe*. Oxford: Berg, 1998b.

Goldman, Laurence R., ed. *The Anthropology of Cannibalism*. Wesport, CT: Bergin & Garvey 1999.

Harris, Marvin. *Cannibals and Kings*. New York: Random House, 1977.

Hogg, G. *Cannibalism and Human Sacrifice*. London: Pan, 1962.

Montaigne, Michel de. *Essays*, translated by J. M. Cohen. Harmondsworth: Penguin, 1958.

Obeyesekere, G. "Review of the Anthropology of Cannibalism: (L. R. Goldman)." *American Ethnologist* 28, no. 1 (2001):238–240.

Pickering, M. "Cannibalism Quarrel." *New Scientist* 15 August 1992:11.

Rumsey, Alan. "The White Man As Cannibal in the New Guinea Highlands." In Laurence R. Goldman ed., *The Anthropology of Cannibalism*. Wesport, CT: Bergin & Garvey, 1999.

Sagan, Eli. *Cannibalism: Human Aggression and Cultural Form*. New York: Harper & Row, 1974.

Sahagón, Bernardino de. *Florentine Codex: General History of the Things of New Spain*, 13 vols., translated by Charles E. Dibble and Arthur O. Anderson. Santa Fe, NM: The School of American Research, 1950–1982.

Sanday, Peggy Reeves. *Divine Hunger: Cannibalism As a Cultural System*. Cambridge: Cambridge University Press, 1986.

Turner, Christy G., II, and Jacqueline A. Turner. *Man Corn: Cannibalism and Violence in the Prehistoric American Southwest*. Salt Lake City: University of Utah Press.

Tuzin, D., and Paula Brown, eds. *The Ethnography of Cannibalism*. Washington, DC: Society for Psychological Anthropology, 1983.

LAURENCE R. GOLDMAN

# CAPITAL PUNISHMENT

The death penalty, the most severe sanction or punishment a government entity can impose on an individual for a crime, has existed in some form throughout recorded history. The first known official codification of the death penalty was in eighteenth century B.C.E. in the Code of King Hammurabi of Babylon, where twenty-five crimes could result in the ultimate sanction by the state. From then until the twenty-first century the variants of capital punishment throughout the world have included crucifixion, drowning, beating to death, stoning, burning alive, impalement, hanging, firing squads, electrocution, and lethal injection. The death penalty has been abolished in Western Europe and Japan, but its persistence in the United States has incited heated debate over its efficacy and inherent justness.

## The Purposes and Effectiveness of Capital Punishment

The major rationalizations for capital punishment are retribution, deterrence, incapacitation, and rehabilitation. Obviously, the last bears no relation to the death penalty. Retribution, which argues that the state has the right to impose a level of pain and punishment equal to or greater than the pain suffered by the victim, seeks to justify the death penalty on principle rather than efficacy in reducing crime. The notion of deterrence does make this claim imply a utilitarian purpose. There are two forms of deterrence: general and specific. The latter focuses on the individual offender, who, it is claimed, is deterred from committing future crimes by punishing him/her for previous criminal activity. The former seeks to prevent such crimes from occurring in the first place. In the case of the death penalty, the well-publicized knowledge that the state punishes some crimes by death presumably deters potential criminals. Many criminologists argue that the goal of incapacitation—removing an offender from society—can be achieved equally effectively through a life sentence without the possibility of parole (LWOP).

The results of the more than 200 studies done on capital punishment are either inconclusive or adverse to the claim that it is an effective deterrent to murder. The typical research design compares murder rates in state that have and use the death penalty with (1) those that either have not used it, although the law permits its use and (2) states that have abolished it. In general, these studies tend to show no difference in homicide rates for comparable states that with and without capital punishment. Nor is there evidence that homicide rates decline or increase as states decide to reinstate or abolish the death penalty.

Why has the death penalty been an ineffective deterrent in the United States? First, capital punishment is applied with neither certainty nor swiftness, the two key characteristics of an effective deterrent. When the death penalty is imposed, it often takes many years for the sentence to be carried out, and in some cases the sentence is not upheld. In the United States in 1999, 271 prisoners were admitted to death row, while more than 15,000 murders were reported to police. In the same year, 88 persons had their sentences overturned.

The idea of deterrence presupposes rationality and premeditation on the part of the murderer. In most murders, such factors take a backseat to nonrational influences such as rage, alcohol or drug abuse, or psychological disorder, none of which are susceptible of deterrence by death sentence. For these reasons, the most persistent and persuasive arguments for the death penalty rely on notions of just retribution and revenge by the state on behalf of the citizenry.

Opponents of the death penalty point not only to its lack of deterrent effect but also raise other key arguments. First, from a moral perspective, the abolitionists believe state executions signal that violence is an acceptable means of resolving conflicts and thus actually contribute to a climate of increased violence. Second, opponents point to the unfair and discriminatory application of the death penalty, noting the disproportionate numbers of poor people and people of color on death row, many of them having lacked vigorous and effective legal counsel. Moreover, advances in DNA analysis have exonerated enough prisoners on death row to give pause to many lawmakers who point to the ever-present possibility that the state might, for lack of adequate probative or exculpatory evidence, take the life of an innocent person. This concern has led to several U.S. states to implement a moratorium on the death penalty until it can be shown to be applied fairly to all such cases.

**International Trends**

Comprehensive data on the use of the death penalty for all countries is difficult to collect and verify. Most of the data presented here come from two organizations opposed to capital punishment: Amnesty International and the Death Penalty Information Center. Yet the trend is clear; more and more countries are either abolishing or placing further restrictions and limitations on capital punishment.

As of 2001, 108 countries have abolished the death penalty in law or in practice, up from 62 in 1980. Of that 108, 75 have abolished it for all crimes while another thirteen have done so for "ordinary crimes." Another 20 have the authority to carry out this sanction but have not done so. Of those that have retained its use, the death penalty is used with regularity in the Islamic nations, in most of Asia, many parts of Africa, and the United States. The United States, Kyrgyzstan (the former Soviet republic), and Japan are believed to be the only other countries where the mentally retarded are put to death.

By far, the world's leader in the use of the death penalty is China. In 1998 China reported more than 1,000 executions, which represented two-thirds of all executions worldwide (see Table 1). The other leading counties were the Congo, the United States, Iran, and Egypt. These

**TABLE 1**

**Number of executions worldwide, 1998**

| Country | Number | Percent |
|---|---|---|
| China | 1,067 | 65.7% |
| Congo (DR) | 100 | 6.2% |
| USA | 68 | 4.2% |
| Iran | 66 | 4.1% |
| Egypt | 48 | 3.0% |
| Belarus | 33 | 2.0% |
| Taiwan | 32 | 2.0% |
| Saudi Arabia | 29 | 1.8% |
| Singapore | 28 | 1.7% |
| Sierra Leone | 24 | 1.5% |
| Rwanda | 24 | 1.5% |
| Vietnam | 18 | 1.1% |
| Yemen | 17 | 1.0% |
| Afghanistan | 10 | 0.6% |
| Jordan | 9 | 0.6% |
| Kuwait | 6 | 0.4% |
| Japan | 6 | 0.4% |
| Nigeria | 6 | 0.4% |
| Oman | 6 | 0.4% |
| Cuba | 5 | 0.3% |
| Kirgyzstan | 4 | 0.2% |
| Pakistan | 4 | 0.2% |
| Zimbabwe | 2 | 0.1% |
| Palestinian Authority | 2 | 0.1% |
| Lebanon | 2 | 0.1% |
| Bahamas | 2 | 0.1% |
| All others | 7 | 0.4% |
| **Total** | **1,625** | **100.0%** |

SOURCE: Death Penalty Information Center, Washington, DC. Available from www.deathpenaltyinfo.org.

**FIGURE 1**

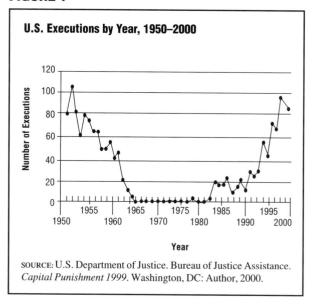

SOURCE: U.S. Department of Justice. Bureau of Justice Assistance. *Capital Punishment 1999*. Washington, DC: Author, 2000.

five countries accounted for more than 80 percent of all executions.

The use of executions in China is even greater than these numbers would suggest. According to Amnesty International, from 1990 to 2000, China has executed 19,446 people, which compares to the 563 the United States put to death over the same period. In 1996 alone, more than 4,000 persons were put to death by China as part of its "strike hard" campaign against crime. This policy results in mass application of the death penalty for persons convicted of both crimes of violence and property crimes. For example, on June 30, 2001, four tax cheats were executed for bilking the government out of nearly $10 million in tax rebates.

The divergence between the United States and Europe on this issue is quite striking. Prior to the 1970s, capital punishment was common in both the United States and Europe, while declining throughout the West after World War II. During the 1970s, however, the death penalty disappeared from Western Europe and it was repealed in Eastern Europe in the postcommunist regimes that

emerged beginning in the late 1980s. For example, from 1987 to 1992, East Germany, Czechoslovakia, Hungary, and Romania eradicated the death penalty, and all twelve of the Central European nations that retained the death penalty during the Soviet era have since abolished it. The Ukraine abolished its death penalty in 2000, and Russia suspended executions in mid-1999.

**U.S. Trends**

The death penalty has been a controversial part of the U.S. social and legal orders since the country's founding in the late eighteenth century. Initially persons were regularly put to death by the state for a wide array of criminal acts that included murder, witchcraft, and even adultery. And up until the 1830s, most executions were held in public. Public executions continued until 1936, when 20,000 citizens observed a public execution in Owensboro, Kentucky.

Prior to the 1960s, executions were relatively frequent in the United States, averaging about 100 per year during the early postwar period and slowly dwindling to fewer than ten per year in the mid-1960s. In 1967, executions were suspended by the U.S. Supreme Court in a series of landmark decisions that, among other things, found the application of the death penalty to be "arbitrary and capricious" and inhumane. Shortly thereafter, states reformed their death penalty statutes to meet the concerns of the Court. Subsequent Court rulings

**TABLE 2**

**Percent distribution of executions in the United States by region, five-year intervals**

| Year | Northeast | North Central | West | South | Total | |
|---|---|---|---|---|---|---|
| | % | % | % | % | # | % |
| 1950–1954 | 14 | 10 | 16 | 60 | 407 | 100% |
| 1955–1959 | 17 | 5 | 17 | 61 | 301 | 100% |
| 1960–1964 | 9 | 9 | 25 | 57 | 180 | 100% |
| 1980–1984 | — | 3 | — | 97 | 29 | 100% |
| 1985–1989 | — | 2 | 6 | 92 | 88 | 100% |
| 1990–1994 | — | 10 | 8 | 82 | 139 | 100% |
| 1995–1999 | 1 | 14 | 9 | 76 | 341 | 100% |

SOURCE: Death Penalty Information Center, Washington, DC. Available from www.deathpenaltyinfo.org; Zimring, Franklin E., and Gordon Hawkins. *Capital Punishment and the American Agenda.* Cambridge: Cambridge University Press, 1986.

in 1976—*Gregg* v. *Georgia, Proffit* v. *Florida,* and *Jurek* v. *Texas*—allowed the resumption of capital punishment. As shown in Figure 1, executions resumed shortly thereafter. By the late 1990s the totals were close to those of the early 1950s.

In 2001 there were approximately 3,500 prisoners under the sentence of death in the United States. Of this number, 55 percent were white and 43 percent were black. All have been convicted of murder; 2 percent received the death sentence as juveniles. Fifty women were on death row as of 2001. Fifteen states, along with the federal government, ban the execution of prisoners who are mentally retarded, but twenty-three do not. The most common form of execution is now lethal injection, which is used in thirty-four states.

## The Death Penalty by Geography

Although the federal courts have played a significant role in death penalty reforms, it is also true that until the 2001 execution of Timothy McVeigh, death sentences and executions since *Gregg* v. *Georgia* have been solely carried out by state courts. Moreover, there is considerable variation among the states in the use of the death penalty that seems to have little to do with crime rates.

As of 2000, thirty-eight states had death penalty statutes, although only twenty-nine actually executed prisoners; of those, only a handful account for most of the executions. According to the Bureau of Justice Statistics, as of 1999, there had been 4,457 persons executed since 1930. States that have conducted the most frequent number tend to be southern states, led by Texas (496) and Georgia (389).

Conversely, Michigan was the first state to abolish the death penalty for all crimes except treason, more than a century before France and England enacted such a reform. Seven states that provide a death sentence in their statutes have not conducted any executions for more than twenty-five years. South Dakota and New Hampshire have not had executions in more than half a century. New Jersey legislated a death penalty statute in 1980 but has not applied it thus far.

As shown in Table 2, the southern states have consistently and increasingly accounted for the vast majority of U.S. executions since the 1950s. In 2000 seventy-six of the eighty-five U.S. executions were in the South, even though that region accounts for about one-third of the population and about 40 percent of the American states that authorize a death penalty. Two-thirds of all American executions in 2000 were conducted in three of the thirty-eight states that authorize executions (Texas, Oklahoma, and Virginia).

## The Issue of Race and Class

A major topic revolving around the death penalty is the extent of racial and class bias in its implementation. As noted above, only very few persons convicted of murder actually receive the death penalty. This raises the important question of how decisions are reached by prosecutors to pursue punishment by death penalty. According to a recent U.S. Department of Justice study, in nearly 80 percent of the cases in which the prosecutor sought the death penalty, the defendant was a member of a minority group, and nearly 40 percent of the death penalty cases originate in nine of the states. Another study found that the race of the victim and the race of the offender were associated with death penalty sentences.

*See also:* DEATH SYSTEM; HOMICIDE, EPIDEMIOLOGY OF;

### Bibliography

Baldus, David, Charles Pulaski, and George Woodworth. "Comparative Review of Death Sentences: An Empirical Study of the Georgia Experience." *Journal of Criminal Law and Criminology* 74 (1983):661–685.

Bohm, Robert M. "Capital Punishment in Two Judicial Circuits in Georgia." *Law and Human Behavior* 18 (1994):335.

Clear, Todd R., and George F. Cole. *American Corrections,* 5th edition. Palo Alto, CA: Wadsworth, 2000.

U.S. Department of Justice. Bureau of Justice Assistance. *Capital Punishment 1999.* Washington, DC: U.S. Government Printing Office, 2000.

U.S. Department of Justice. Federal Bureau of Investigation. *Uniform Crime Reports, 1999.* Washington, DC: U.S. Department of Justice, 2000.

JAMES AUSTIN

---

# CARDIOVASCULAR DISEASE

The American Heart Association (AHA) uses the term cardiovascular disease (CVD) to describe various diseases that affect the heart and circulatory system. These diseases include coronary artery (heart) disease, hypertension, congestive heart failure, congenital cardiovascular defects, and cerebrovascular disease. CVD is a chronic disease. These diseases frequently progress as people age. This article limits discussion to the two most common forms of CVD—coronary artery disease and hypertension.

Cardiovascular disease is the leading cause of death in the United States, responsible for one death every 33 seconds or 2,600 deaths per day. In 1998 CVD claimed the lives of 949,619 Americans. The second leading cause of death, cancer, was responsible for 541,532 deaths. It is estimated that approximately 60.8 million individuals in the United States have one or more types of CVD. The most common form of cardiovascular disease is hypertension, which affects approximately 50 million Americans, or one in every four individuals. Hypertension is a significant risk factor for the

development of other types of CVD, including congestive heart failure and cerebrovascular accidents.

The second most prevalent form of CVD is coronary heart disease or coronary artery disease, which affects approximately 12.4 million individuals. Coronary heart disease includes both angina pectoris (chest pain) and myocardial infarction (heart attack). In 1998 the American Heart Association estimated that 7.3 million individuals had suffered a heart attack, and 6.4 million had experienced chest pain. The third most prevalent form of CVD is congestive heart failure, which affects 4.7 million Americans. Cerebrovascular accidents are the fourth most prevalent form of CVD, affecting 4.5 million individuals. Congenital cardiovascular defects affect 1 million Americans, comprising the fifth most prevalent form of CVD. In general, approximately one in five Americans will develop some form of cardiovascular disease in their lifetime.

## Risk Factors

Risk factors for CVD may be divided into three classifications: modifiable, nonmodifiable, and contributing factors.

*Modifiable factors.* Modifiable risk factors are those that an individual can change, including elevated serum cholesterol levels, a diet high in saturated fats, obesity, physical inactivity, hypertension, nicotine, and alcohol use. A serum cholesterol level greater than 200 mg/dl or a fasting triglyceride level more than 200 mg/dl is associated with an increased incidence of coronary artery disease. Obesity is associated with a higher incidence of mortality from CVD. Physical inactivity increases the risk for developing CVD as much as smoking or consuming a diet high in saturated fats and cholesterol.

The National Heart Lung and Blood Institute defines hypertension as a blood pressure greater than 140/90. Hypertension is a significant risk factor for the development of CVD and stroke. The AHA estimates that one in five deaths from cardiovascular disease are directly linked to cigarette smoking. Individuals who smoke are two to six times more likely to develop coronary artery disease than nonsmokers. However, individuals who quit smoking will reduce their risk to levels equivalent to those of a nonsmoker within three years.

*Nonmodifiable factors.* Nonmodifiable risk factors are those risk factors that an individual cannot

change, such as age, gender, ethnicity, and heredity. The incidence of CVD increases as people age.
However, 150,000 individuals die from it before 65
years of age. Males are more likely than females to
experience CVD, until the age of 65, when the incidence rate equalizes among genders. Young men
aged 35 to 44 years old are more than six times as
likely to die from CVD than their same-age female
counterparts. However, the death rates equalize
after 75 years of age. Furthermore, women may
experience different symptoms of CVD than those
experienced by men, thus causing women to be
underdiagnosed or diagnosed at a more advanced
stage of the disease.

Ethnicity also plays a role in the development
of CVD. Non-Hispanic black males have a higher
age-adjusted prevalence of CVD than Caucasian
or Mexican-American males. Black and Mexican-
American females have a higher age-adjusted prevalence of CVD than Caucasian females. Overall,
middle-aged Caucasian males have the highest
incidence of heart attacks.

Heredity may also play a role in the development of CVD. Individuals with a family history of
early heart disease are at a greater risk for the
development of elevated blood lipid levels, which
has been associated with the early development of
coronary artery disease. Additionally, most individuals who have experienced either chest pain or a
heart attack can identify a close family member
(father, mother, brother, or sister) who also had or
has CVD. It is expected that the role of genetics
and heredity will be more fully understood in the
future due to the advances associated with the
human genome project.

*Contributing factors.* Contributing factors are
those factors that may increase the risk for developing cardiovascular disease. Diabetes mellitus
and a stressful lifestyle are examples of contributing factors. Diabetics are more likely than the general population to experience CVD. Additionally,
they experience coronary artery disease at an earlier age than the nondiabetic individual. Two-thirds
of individuals with diabetes mellitus die from some
form of heart or blood vessel disease.

The role of stress in the development of coronary artery disease is not clearly understood. Historically it was believed that individuals with a type
A personality were at a greater risk for the development of CVD. However, the research findings

were mixed and did not clearly support this relationship. Stress may also increase the process of
atherogenesis (formation of plaque in arteries) due
to elevated lipid levels.

**Treatments**

Ischemic CVD, such as angina pectoris and myocardial infarction, are usually diagnosed based on
patient symptoms, electrocardiogram findings, and
cardiac enzyme results. Additionally, coronary
angiography may be performed to visualize the
coronary arteries and determine the exact location
and severity of any obstructions. Coronary artery
disease can be treated using medical treatments,
surgical treatments, or interventional cardiology.
The treatment goal for ischemic CVD is to restore
optimal flow of oxygenated blood to the heart.

Medical treatment for the patient with angina
includes risk factor modification, consumption of a
diet low in saturated fats and cholesterol, and
administration of pharmacological agents. Medications commonly used to treat chest pain or heart
attacks include drugs that decrease cholesterol levels, alter platelet aggregation, enhance the supply
of oxygenated blood to the heart, or decrease the
heart's need for oxygenated blood. Additionally,
the person experiencing an acute anginal attack or
a heart attack may also receive supplemental oxygen. Thrombolytic medications may be used to
treat a patient experiencing a attack, as they may
dissolve the blood clot, thus restoring blood flow
to the heart.

The blood flow to the heart may also be
restored surgically though the use of a common
procedure known as coronary artery bypass graft-
ing (CABG). This procedure bypasses the obstructed coronary artery or arteries, thus restoring
the flow of oxygenated blood to the heart. Women
have poorer surgical outcomes after coronary
bypass surgery than men. Specifically, women
have a higher relative risk of mortality associated
with CABG, longer intensive care unit stays, and
more postoperative complications than men.

Nonsurgical revascularization techniques, such
as percutaneous transluminal angioplasty, transmyocardial laser revascularization, or the placement
of stents in the coronary arteries, are techniques to
restore the flow of oxygenated blood to the heart.
Percutaneous transluminal angioplasty involves the

insertion of a balloon-tipped catheter into the coronary artery, and inflating the balloon at the location of the vessel obstruction. The balloon widens the blood vessel, restoring blood flow through the obstructed vessel. A wire mesh stent may be inserted into the coronary artery and placed at the location of the obstruction. The stent provides an artificial opening in the blood vessel, which helps to maintain the flow of oxygenated blood to the heart. Transmyocardial laser revascularization is a procedure that uses a laser to create channels in the heart to allow oxygenated blood to reach the heart, and is generally used when other techniques have failed.

Research into the efficacy of cardiac gene therapy is being studied to determine how to eliminate heart disease by replacing malfunctioning or missing genes with normal or modified genes. Gene therapy may be used to stimulate the growth of new blood vessels, prevent cell death, or enhance functioning of genes.

Hypertension is initially treated by behavioral and lifestyle modifications. If these modifications do not successfully manage the individual's hypertension, pharmacological agents are added. The lifestyle modifications recommended to control hypertension include diet, exercise, and weight reduction for the overweight individual. The recommended dietary modifications include increasing consumption of fruits, vegetables, low-fat dairy products, and other foods that are low in saturated fat, total fat, and cholesterol. Furthermore, the individual with hypertension is advised to decrease intake of foods high in fat, red meats, sweets, and sugared beverages. It is advisable for hypertensive individuals to decrease their intake of sodium to less than 1,500 mg/day. Not adding table salt to foods and avoiding obviously salty foods may accomplish this restriction. Doctors suggest that hypertensive individuals limit their consumption of alcohol to one to two drinks per day, and decrease or stop smoking. Smoking causes hardening of the arteries, which may increase blood pressure.

Various classes of pharmacological agents may be used to treat hypertension. They include drugs that relax the blood vessels, causing vasodilation, thus decreasing blood pressure, such as angiotensin converting enzyme inhibitors, calcium channel blockers, angiotensin antagonists, and vasodilators. Drugs such as alpha- and beta-blockers decrease nerve impulses to blood vessels, and decrease the heart rate, slowing blood flow through the arteries, resulting in a decreased blood pressure. Diuretics may also be used to manage hypertension. They work by flushing excess water and sodium from the body, causing a decrease in blood pressure.

## Reoccurrence

Coronary artery disease and hypertension are both chronic diseases that require lifelong treatment. Frequently, interventional cardiology techniques and surgical procedures produce palliative rather than curative results. For example, percutaneous transluminal angioplasty fails in six months in approximately 30 to 60 percent of the cases, resulting in restenosis of the blood vessel. Additionally, 50 percent of the grafts of patients who have undergone coronary artery bypass surgery reocclude within five years. Once this has occurred, the patient may be required to undergo additional procedures or surgery.

Individuals who have experienced a heart attack are at a significantly greater risk for future cardiovascular morbidity and mortality. The death rates for people after experiencing a heart attack are significantly higher than the general public. Twenty-five percent of males and 38 percent of females will die within one year of experiencing a heart attack. Additionally, morbidity from cardiovascular disease is higher in individuals who have previously experienced a heart attack. Two-thirds of all heart attack patients do not make a full recovery. CVD is progressive: Twenty-two percent of males and 46 percent of females who previously experienced a heart attack are disabled with heart failure within six years.

Hypertension increases the rate of atherosclerosis, resulting in common complications such as hypertensive heart disease, cerebrovascular disease, peripheral vascular disease, nephrosclerosis, and retinal damage. Uncontrolled hypertension is strongly correlated with the development of coronary artery disease, enlargement of the left ventricle, and heart failure. Additionally, hypertension is a major risk factor for the development of stroke and end stage renal disease.

*See also:* CAUSES OF DEATH; NUTRITION AND EXERCISE

## Bibliography

Agency for Health Care Policy and Research. "Unstable Angina: Diagnosis and Management." *Clinical Practice Guidelines,* Vol. 10. Rockville, MD: Author, 1994.

Casey, Kathy, Deborah Bedker, and Patricia Roussel-McElmeel. "Myocardial Infarction: Review of Clinical Trials and Treatment Strategies." *Critical Care Nurse* 18, no. 2 (1998):39–51.

Halm, Margo A., and Sue Penque. "Heart Disease in Women." *American Journal of Nursing* 99, no. 4 (1999):26–32.

Jensen, Louis, and Kathryn King. "Women and Heart Disease: The Issues." *Critical Care Nurse* 17, no. 2 (1997):45–52.

Levine, Barbara S. "Nursing Management: Hypertension." In Sharon Mantik Lewis, Margaret McLean Heitkemper, and Shannon Ruff Dirksen eds., *Medical-Surgical Nursing: Assessment and Management of Clinical Problems.* St. Louis, MO: Mosby, 2000.

Martinez, Linda Griego, and Mary Ann House-Fancher. "Coronary Artery Disease." In Sharon Mantik Lewis, Margaret McLean Heitkemper, and Shannon Ruff Dirksen eds., *Medical-Surgical Nursing: Assessment and Management of Clinical Problems.* St. Louis, MO: Mosby, 2000.

Metules, Terri J. "Cardiac Gene Therapy: The Future is Now." *RN* 64, no. 8 (2001):54–58.

## Internet Resources

American Heart Association. "Statistics Homepage." In the American Heart Association [web site]. Available www.americanheart.org

National Heart Lung and Blood Institute. "Statement from the National High Blood Pressure Education Program." In the National Heart Lung and Blood Institute [web site]. Available from www.nhlbi.nih.gov/health

BRENDA C. MORRIS

# CATACOMBS

Burial places for the dead come in a variety of forms. One ancient form is the catacomb, an underground city of the dead consisting of galleries or passages with side recesses for tombs. A related form is the ossuary, a Native American communal burial place or a depository (a vault, room, or urn) for the bones of the dead.

Catacombs originated in the Middle East approximately 6,000 years ago. These earliest examples were often secondary burials where the bones of the dead were placed in ossuary containers. Initially, the dead were buried within settlements, but with the progressive urbanization of the ensuing millennia, burials moved outside of the towns. From 3300 to 2300 B.C.E., several generations of one family were typically buried in a single cave, whether natural or artificial. Pastoral nomads also used caves that were entered through a vertical shaft. Multiple interments in caves continued over succeeding millennia, together with other forms of burial. There is evidence of the use of long subterranean channels and spacious chambers by about 1500 B.C.E. By the time of the Assyrian and Babylonian conquests of Israel and Judah, some burial caves were quite large and elaborate.

After the Roman conquest of Palestine, many Jews settled in Rome and adapted the burial customs of the Middle East to their new environment. In contrast to the Roman practice of cremation, the Jews buried their dead in catacombs they created for this purpose. Jewish catacombs can be recognized by inscriptions of the menorah, the seven-branched candlestick, on gravestones and lamps. Used only for burials, they are not as elaborate as the later multipurpose Christian catacombs.

Early Christians were regarded as a Jewish sect, and their dead were buried in catacombs modeled on those of the Jews. Early Christian martyrs buried in the catacombs became objects of veneration, so that the wish for burial near these martyrs ensured the continued use of the catacombs until the early fifth century C.E., when the Goths invaded. In the eighth and ninth centuries the remains of the martyrs were moved to churches, and the catacombs fell into disuse; by the twelfth century they were forgotten. Since their rediscovery in 1578, they have been the object of constant excavation, exploration, and research. Although the Roman catacombs are the best known, others have been found throughout Italy (in Naples, Chiusi, and Syracuse), in North Africa (in Alexandria and Susa), and in Asia Minor.

A vast literature describes and discusses the Roman catacombs. Because interment was forbidden within the boundaries of the city, these catacombs are all found outside the city. From the fourth century, consistent with the cult of martyrs,

*Loculi, shelves for remains, can be seen in the ancient catacombs of St. Sebastian in Rome.* ALINARI-ART REFERENCE/ART RESOURCE

the catacombs served not only as tombs but also for memorial services.

A first level of the catacombs is from thirty-three to forty-nine feet below the surface, with galleries ten to thirteen feet high; sometimes there are three or even four levels. Niches for the bodies line the passages. The walls and ceilings, made of plaster, are generally painted in the fresco manner—with watercolors before the plaster is dry. From about the fourth century C.E., shafts were dug from the galleries to the surface to provide light and air.

The inscriptions reflect the changing values of society. As conversions to Christianity became more common, nobler names appeared more frequently. With the gradual decline of slavery, there were fewer distinctions noted between slaves and freed men.

Catacombs, primarily a curiosity and tourist attraction in the twenty- and twenty-first centuries, are sparsely written about in fiction. However, one example by Arthur Conan Doyle, the creator of Sherlock Holmes, is "The New Catacomb," a story of two young colleagues, one extremely shy, the other a womanizer, both noted experts on catacombs. The womanizer has enticed a young woman away from an unknown fiancé, then abandoned her. The shy one tells the other of a new catacomb he has discovered, which will make him famous, and offers to show it to him. Deep in the labyrinth he leaves his colleague to die in the dark, informing him that it was his own fiancé who had been abandoned.

*See also:* BURIAL GROUNDS; CHARNEL HOUSES; CHRISTIAN DEATH RITES, HISTORY OF

## Bibliography

Avigad, Machman. "Beth Shearim." *Encyclopedia Judaica Yearbook.* Jerusalem: Keter Publishing House, 1972.

Doyle, Arthur Conan. "The New Catacomb." In *Tales of Terror and Mystery,* Harmondsworth: Penguin, 1979.

Mazar, Amihai. *Archaeology of the Land of the Bible: 10,000–586 B.C.E.* New York: Doubleday, 1990.

Murphy, F. X. "Catacombs." *New Catholic Encyclopedia,* Vol. 3. New York: McGraw-Hill, 1967.

Rabello, Alfredo Mordechai. "Catacombs." *Encyclopedia Judaica Yearbook.* Jerusalem: Keter Publishing House, 1972.

SAM SILVERMAN

# CATHOLICISM

In Roman Catholicism, death has been understood primarily in terms of an issue of justice. Having turned away from God, humans are deprived of the life-giving energy that they need and which is to be found solely in God. Death, then, is both a sign of and an effect of human estrangement from God. The radical character of this consequence mirrors the radical character of human (intended) dependence upon God for identity and existence. For some Catholic theologians in the past, death is the most symmetrical consequence of a desire for ontological independence, as death reveals the fundamental limitation of that very ontology. In the very early Church, Catholics were encouraged to reject any fear of death, as it seemed to express too great an attachment to the life of "this world." But by the end of the fourth century, fear of death was understood as an internal sign that something about the way things were—the cosmic order—was indeed wrong. As a pedagogic device, then, the fact of death should teach humility; fear of death is the beginning of a wise appreciation of human fragility. "Death" became an ascetic metaphor for selflessness and the end of pride.

If death is the greatest sign of human dislocation, it is the punishment for the act of will that produced the fundamental dislocation—sin. Traditional Catholic theology emphasized the just character of the punishment, in part to explain why the sentence of human mortality could not be simply overturned. Human explanation of the efficacy of the incarnation—God becoming human—and crucifixion has been that the unjust death of Jesus, the Son of God, ended the just claim death had upon humanity. In his resurrection, Jesus was thus the physician who dispensed the "medicine of immortality." The incarnation, crucifixion, and resurrection reveal something about God as well, namely that the old punishment was overturned "not through power," as St. Augustine put it, "but through humility."

As a community, Catholics live and die with the ambivalence typical of the modern world: A loved one's death is a great loss and an occasion of intense trauma, and must be acknowledged as such. Death is also a great transition for the deceased, who exchanges penalty for reward, replacing estrangement from God with fellowship. To deny grief is to deny what the experience of death teaches; to deny hope is to deny what the resurrection offers.

*See also:* CHRISTIAN DEATH RITES, HISTORY OF; HEAVEN; HELL; JESUS; PROTESTANTISM; PURGATORY

MICHEL RENE BARNES

# CAUSES OF DEATH

Data on the causes of death provide an important source of information on death. Such data are crucial for monitoring the reasons why people die and for targeting where, when, and how health resources should be expended. Causes of death can be categorized as proximate and non-proximate. Proximate (or immediate) causes of death are those that finally lead to death; for example, heart disease or cancer. Non-proximate causes of death are the factors that increase the likelihood of experiencing one of the proximate causes. For example, tobacco smoking is a non-proximate cause of death due to its link to lung cancer (a proximate cause). Non-proximate causes are the risk factors for dying from a particular proximate cause. Almost always the proximate causes of death are presented in discussions of death causation; this likely reflects the dominance of Western biomedicine in the conceptualization of cause of death.

The proximate causes of death are themselves further broadly categorized as: infectious and parasitic diseases (deaths of infants and maternal mortality are usually included in this category); chronic and degenerative diseases; and deaths due to injury (accidents, homicide, suicide). This distinction (and particularly the difference between infectious/parasitic diseases and chronic/degenerative diseases) figures prominently in later sections of this entry. The following commentary focuses upon proximate causes of death, unless specified otherwise.

## Measurement of Causes of Death

Deaths are classified using a standard coding system called the ICD (International Classification of Deaths), which has been organized and published by the World Health Organization since 1946. The ICD is revised periodically (approximately every ten years) to reflect changes in medical and epidemiological knowledge and in the light of diseases that are either new or of growing importance as takers-of-life, such as HIV/AIDS (human immunodeficiency virus/acquired immunodeficiency syndrome) and the cognitive dementias such as Alzheimer's disease. The tenth revision, which became effective in 1999, categorizes deaths into seventeen very broad categories. These are: (1) infectious and parasitic diseases; (2) neoplasms; (3) endocrine, nutritional, and metabolic diseases and immunity disorders; (4) diseases of the blood and blood-forming organs; (5) mental disorders; (6) diseases of the nervous system and sense organs; (7) diseases of the circulatory system; (8) diseases of the respiratory system; (9) diseases of the digestive system; (10) diseases of the genitourinary tract; (11) complications of pregnancy, childbearing, and the puerperium; (12) diseases of the skin and subcutaneous tissue; (13) diseases of the musculoskeletal system and connective tissue; (14) congenital anomalies; (15) certain conditions related to the perinatal period; (16) symptoms, signs, and ill-defined conditions; and (17) external causes, injury, and poisoning. These broad categories are similar to the ninth revision.

Within each category are several specific classes that are further divided into particular diseases, disease sites, or conditions. For example, circulatory diseases are further broken down into ischemic (coronary) heart disease and cerebrovascular diseases, among others, which are further divided into more detailed causes. External causes

are divided into accidents (further broken down by type), suicides (detailing several methods), and homicides. It is in the specificity of these subcategories that the ninth and tenth revisions differ most. While the ninth revision contains about 4,000 codes, the tenth revision contains nearly twice as many—approximately 8,000. Thus, users of the tenth revision are able to obtain much more finely tuned information.

## Measurement Limitations

In theory the ICD is a very useful tool in the analysis of trends and differentials in cause of death and in the assessment of progress in overcoming life-threatening diseases and conditions. In practice, however, the ICD contains a number of limitations. First, cross-national comparisons are affected by variations in data quality. These variations result from differences in the diagnostic skill and type of training of the certifying medical attendant or coroner, in the accuracy of the diagnosis recorded on the death certificate, and in the accurate coding of the information. At an even more fundamental level, the ICD is based on a number of assumptions (e.g., that medical personnel are present at or near a death, that deaths are recorded by medical personnel, that there are death certificates) that do not necessarily hold for less developed countries and/or in times of social and political upheaval, such as war. Thus, while ICD data are accurate for Western countries (and Eastern countries with a high level of economic development, such as Japan), they are not as accurate for less well developed countries. If countries do not have the infrastructure to systematically record causes of death (or even deaths), then no classification system will create high-quality data. Thus, cause of death data for less developed countries are "best estimates" only.

A second limitation is that ICD categories are based on a single cause of death. This is the "underlying" cause that is deemed by the medical examiner to have generated the sequelae leading to death. For populations in developed countries, in which most deaths occur in old age and in which multiple causes are often involved, a classification system based on a single cause of death can result in a distorted picture of mortality causation. At the same time, deaths due to HIV/AIDS may be underestimated since the disease lowers immunity and it may appear that the individual died from another infectious disease, such as pneumonia.

Third, trend analysis can be affected by changes over time in the ICD categories themselves. An apparent increase or decrease in a cause of death may be the result of a coding/classification change only. While changing categorization is necessary given advances in knowledge and transformation in disease patterns, a downside is that some distorted trends may emerge. Thus, any analyst of cause of death trends must be aware of ICD changes that could lead to findings that are merely artifacts of reclassification.

A fourth limitation is that a new cause of death may be uncategorized, which occurred in the case of HIV/AIDS. The ninth revision became effective in 1979, before medical professionals were aware of HIV/AIDS, and the tenth revision was not implemented until 1999 (the usual ten-year interval in revisions did not occur). In the interim, AIDS/HIV emerged as an important taker-of-life. In response to this epidemic, in the 1980s the United States began to include HIV/AIDS as a separate cause of death. However, this initiative was a national one, and as such included deaths to U.S. residents only. Given the crisis, in 1996 the United Nations, through UNAIDS, took on the task of globally monitoring the number of cases of the disease and deaths due to it. (In the 1980s, the World Health Organization attempted this, but the growing enormity of the undertaking led to the need for a larger, United Nations–coordinated effort.)

## Causes of Death in International Context

The more developed and less developed countries differ significantly in causes of death; hence a global summary of causes of death is not useful. As shown in Table 1, the distribution of causes of death is markedly different in the two areas of the world. In the developed countries, diseases of the circulatory system and cancer (both associated with advanced age) are the chief takers-of-life, accounting for approximately two-thirds of all deaths. In contrast, these diseases account for only one-third of deaths in the less developed world. Infectious and parasitic diseases—which often attack young people—are the major killers in the third world, making up 43 percent of deaths. Another important contrast lies in deaths associated with childbirth (both deaths to infants and to mothers), which make up 10 percent of deaths in less developed countries but only 1 percent in more developed countries. Overall, it can be concluded (keeping in mind that cause of death information for the non-Western world is plagued with data quality problems) that the chronic and degenerative diseases associated with old age predominate in the West, whereas the infectious and parasitic diseases (along with childbirth-related deaths) associated with much younger ages prevail in less developed countries.

## Epidemiologic Transition

The observation of this global dichotomy in causes of death led to the theory of epidemiologic transition—a three-stage model proposed in 1971 and based on the Western experience—that deals with changing mortality levels and causes of death. It is less a theory than it is a description of mortality decline and accompanying changes in causes of death as experienced in Western populations. Its basic premise is that a society or population goes through three mortality stages. The title of the first stage—The Age of Pestilence and Famine—is self-evident; this stage is characterized by high death rates that vacillate in response to epidemics, famines, and war. Epidemics and famines tend to go hand in hand, since malnourished people are particularly susceptible to infectious diseases. In the second stage, The Age of Receding Pandemics, death rates start to steadily decline and the proportion of deaths due to infectious diseases decreases as a result of the improved nutrition and sanitation and medical advances that accompany socioeconomic development. Eventually, the third stage is reached—The Age of Degenerative and (Hu)man-Made Diseases—in which death rates are low (life expectancy at birth is over seventy years) and the chief takers-of-life are chronic diseases associated with aging, such as cardiovascular disease and cancer. It is implicitly assumed that infectious and parasitic diseases become less and less important, and that causes of death in the less developed countries will eventually come to be like those in the West.

There is little doubt that the epidemiologic transition model generally holds for the Western case, at least for the time period from the agricultural revolution until the late twentieth century. Prior to the agricultural revolution, it is highly likely that malnutrition (starving to death) was a

**TABLE 1**

### Estimated number of deaths worldwide resulting from fifteen leading causes in 1998

| Rank | Males | Females | Both sexes |
|------|-------|---------|------------|
| 1 | Ischaemic heart disease 3,658,699 | Ischaemic heart disease 3,716,709 | Ischaemic heart disease 7,375,408 |
| 2 | Cerebrovascular disease 2,340,299 | Cerebrovascular disease 2,765,827 | Cerebrovascular disease 5,106,125 |
| 3 | Acute lower respiratory infections 1,753,220 | Acute lower respiratory infections 1,698,957 | Acute lower respiratory infections 3,452,178 |
| 4 | Chronic obstructive pulmonary disease 1,239,658 | HIV/AIDS 1,121,421 | HIV/AIDS 2,285,229 |
| 5 | HIV/AIDS 1,163,808 | Diarrhoeal disease 1,069,757 | Chronic obstructive pulmonary disease 2,249,252 |
| 6 | Diarrhoeal disease 1,149,275 | Perinatal conditions 1,034,002 | Diarrhoeal disease 2,219,032 |
| 7 | Perinatal conditions 1,120,998 | Chronic obstructive pulmonary disease 1,009,594 | Perinatal conditions 2,155,000 |
| 8 | Trachea/bronchus/ lung cancers 910,471 | Tuberculosis 604,674 | Tuberculosis 1,498,061 |
| 9 | Tuberculosis 893,387 | Malaria 537,882 | Trachea/bronchus /lung cancers 1,244,407 |
| 10 | Road-traffic injuries 854,939 | Measles 431,630 | Road traffic injuries 1,170,694 |
| 11 | Interpersonal violence 582,486 | Breast cancers 411,668 | Malaria 1,110,293 |
| 12 | Malaria 572,411 | Self-inflicted injuries 382,541 | Self-inflicted injuries 947,697 |
| 13 | Self-inflicted injuries 565,156 | Diabetes mellitus 343,021 | Measles 887,671 |
| 14 | Cirrhosis of the liver 533,724 | Trachea/bronchus /lung cancers 333,436 | Stomach cancers 822,069 |
| 15 | Stomach cancers 517,821 | Road traffic injuries 315,755 | Cirrhosis of the liver 774,563 |

SOURCE: Violence and Injury Prevention, World Health Organization. *Injury: A Leading Cause of the Global Burden of Disease,* edited by E. Krug. Geneva: World Health Organization, 1999.

three centuries. By the eve of the Industrial Revolution, the plague had virtually disappeared in Europe, as a result of changes in shipping, housing, and sanitary practices that affected the way that rats, fleas, and humans interacted. Other types of infectious diseases (such as cholera, influenza, smallpox, pneumonia) remained important killers, and were eventually conquered by improved nutrition, hygiene, and public health measures, and knowledge thereof. Medical advances played a small role, although the smallpox vaccine was important until well into the twentieth century. As we move into the twenty-first century, however, advances in bioterrorism (such as the post-September 11th anthrax assault in the U.S.) may lead to increasing deaths from infectious diseases).

The epidemiologic transition model applies less well to the developing world. Western mortality decline, and the changing configuration of causes of death associated with it, was fueled by socioeconomic development. In contrast, in third world countries, there is a much smaller relationship between morality and development. In the postwar decade of the 1950s, mortality declines in many third world countries were substantial. In those cold war years, the West (largely the United States) imported public health measures and death-reducing technologies to many less developed countries. As a result, deaths due to infectious diseases fell dramatically in the absence of any significant development.

However, probably the biggest challenge to epidemiologic transition theory comes from the emergence of new, and the reemergence of old, infectious diseases in the latter part of the twentieth century. This has led to debate about epidemiologic transition theory's end stage. Is the third stage the final one? A number of fourth states have been proposed by epidemiologists and demographers. The most popular is the Age of Delayed Degenerative Diseases, corresponding to declines in death rates due to cardiovascular disease experienced in Western countries through the 1970s and 1980s. This stage corresponds with the "compression of morbidity" hypothesis proposed by James Fries, stating that the future holds quick deaths due to degenerative diseases at very old ages. In other words, the typical death will be from a sudden heart attack at approximately age eighty-five, before which one was healthy and hearty. However, now a radically different fifth stage is being proposed in light of

more important killer than infectious diseases. Once agriculture predominated, the denser settlement pattern of humans as well as closer proximity to animals and animal waste contributed to the spread of infectious diseases. One of the most well-known examples of epidemic-caused loss of life in the West was the Black Death (the plague) that hit hardest in the middle of the fourteenth century but which continued to reoccur for more than increasing death rates due to viruses and bacteria. Indeed the anthropologist Ronald Barrett and his colleagues at Emory University view the trend of increasing mortality due to infectious disease as characterizing a new epidemiologic transition altogether. Others, such as Christopher Murray and Alan Lopez, taking both death and disability into account, argue that noncommunicable diseases will take on increasing importance in the "global burden of disease" (Murray and Lopez, 1996).

The emergence of new infectious and parasitic diseases (AIDS/HIV, Legionnaires' disease, Lyme disease), the reemergence of diseases (smallpox, malaria) that scientists thought had been conquered, and the evolution of antibiotic-resistant strains of bacteria have led to a reappraisal of the possible future role of microbes in mortality. While it does not seem likely that infectious and parasitic diseases will overtake degenerative and chronic diseases as killers, it is difficult to predict the relative importance of the two major categories of death causation in the future. Much appears to depend on how successful medical professionals will be in controlling HIV/AIDS, which is estimated to have taken anywhere between 1.9 million and 3.6 million lives worldwide in 1999 alone. (Given the depression of the immune system that comes with AIDS, it is possible that even the high estimate is low; some persons with AIDS might be counted as dying from another infectious disease to which they are vulnerable.)

## Proximate and Non-Proximate Causes of Death in the United States

Table 2 presents the five leading proximate and non-proximate causes of death in the United States. Of the proximate causes, the top four are the classic degenerative diseases associated with aging; the fifth cause is accidents. The non-proximate causes (the risk factors) provide a different lens through which to view death causation. The top three non-proximate causes include tobacco smoking, diets rich in sodium, cholesterol and fat in conjunction with sedentary lifestyles, and excessive alcohol drinking (which is, of course, implicated in accidental deaths as well as in degenerative conditions such as liver disease). The fourth non-proximate cause of death is microbial agents; that is, viruses and bacteria. While some proximate causes of death (such as HIV/AIDS and pneumonia) are directly linked to viruses/bacteria, research indicates that

**TABLE 2**

| Leading causes of death | |
| --- | --- |
| Five leading proximate causes of death in the United States, 1998 | Five leading non-proximate causes of death in the United States, 1990s |
| 1. Heart disease | 1. Tobacco |
| 2. Cancer | 2. Diet/activity patterns |
| 3. Stroke | 3. Alcohol |
| 4. Chronic obstructive pulmonary disease | 4. Microbial agents |
| 5. Accidents | 5. Toxic agents |

SOURCE: Adapted from National Center for Health Statistics. *Final Data for 1998: National Vital Statistics Report,* 48, no. 11. Hyattsville, MD: National Center for Health Statistics, 2000; McGinnis, J. M., and W. H. Foege. "Actual Causes of Death in the United States." *Journal of the American Medical Association* 270 (1993):2208.

some of the degenerative diseases, such as liver disease and cancers, have microbial causes. In fact, the classic dichotomy between infectious/parasitic diseases, on the one hand, and chronic/degenerative diseases, on the other hand, is being questioned by scientists. Microbes can both cause degenerative disease and increase peoples' susceptibility to them. Since this dichotomy is foundational to epidemiologic transition theory, health researchers are rethinking historical change in causes of death (both proximate and non-proximate).

All of the non-proximate causes of death listed in Table 2 are preventable through public health measures and education. However, this does not mean that all deaths can be prevented. While the researchers Michael McGinnis and William Foege estimate that 50 percent of deaths are due to preventable causes, eliminating these causes would not lower mortality by 50 percent. People are at multiple risk of death at all times, and eliminating one cause of death does not necessarily lower the risk of dying from some other cause. Nevertheless, it is true that healthy behaviors with regard to drinking, eating, smoking, and exercise increase the probability of living longer. However, individuals can only do so much; ultimately, public health measures are critical to mortality level and cause.

*See also:* AIDS; CARDIOVASCULAR DISEASE; MORTALITY, INFANT; LIFE EXPECTANCY; MORTALITY, CHILDBIRTH

## *Bibliography*

Barrett, Ronald, Christopher W. Kazawa, Thomas McDade, and George J. Armelagos. "Emerging and

Re-emerging Infectious Diseases: The Third Epidemiologic Transition." *Annual Review of Anthropology* 27 (1998):247–271.

Cipolla, Carlo M. *Fighting the Plague in Seventeenth-Century Italy.* Madison: University of Wisconsin Press, 1981.

Fries, J. F. "Aging, Natural Death, and the Compression of Morbidity." *New England Journal of Medicine* 303 (1980):130–135.

McGinnis, Michael J., and William H. Foege. "Actual Causes of Death in the United States." *Journal of the American Medical Association* 270 (1993):2207–2212.

McKeown, Thomas. *The Origins of Human Disease.* Oxford: Basil Blackwell, 1988.

McKeown, Thomas. *The Modern Rise of Population.* London: Edward Arnold, 1976.

McNeill, William H. *Plagues and People.* New York: Doubleday, 1976.

Murray, Christopher J. L., and Alan D. Lopez. *The Global Burden of Disease: A Comprehensive Assessment of Mortality and Disability from Diseases, Injuries, and Risk Factors in 1990 and Projected to 2020.* Boston: Harvard School of Public Health on Behalf of the World Health Organization and the World Bank, 1996.

Olshansky, S. Jay, and A. B. Ault. "The Fourth Stage of the Epidemiologic Transition: The Age of Delayed Degenerative Diseases." *Milbank Memorial Fund Quarterly* 64 (1986):355–391.

Olshansky, S. Jay, Bruce A. Carnes, Richard G. Rodgers, and Len Smith. "Infectious Diseases—New and Ancient Threats to World Health." *Population Bulletin* 52, no. 2 (1997):1–52.

Omran, A. R. "The Theory of Epidemiological Transition." *Milbank Memorial Fund Quarterly* 49 (1971):509–538.

UNAIDS. *Report of the Global HIV/AIDS Epidemic.* Geneva: UNAIDS, 2000.

Weeks, John R. *Population: An Introduction to Concepts and Issues.* Belmont, CA: Wadsworth, 1996.

Yaukey, David, and Douglas L. Anderton. *Demography: The Study of Human Population.* Prospect Heights, IL: Waveland, 2001.

*Internet Resources*

National Center for Health Statistics. *International Classification of Diseases—Tenth Revision (ICD-10).* In the Centers for Disease Control [web site]. Available from www.cdc.gov/nchs/about/major/dvs/icd10des.htm

ELLEN M. GEE

# CELEBRITY DEATHS

In 1999 nearly 100 people showed up at the Hollywood Forever Cemetery to visit the grave of the silent-screen heartthrob Rudolf Valentino on the seventy-third anniversary of his death. When the victim of acute peritonitis was buried at age thirty-one in 1926, 80,000 people showed up for the funeral. A pandemic of mass hysteria followed; dozens of women committed suicide.

In 1997 some 50,000 people gathered in Memphis to observe the twentieth anniversary of the death of Elvis Presley. The all-night candlelight vigil occurred during the same month that Britain's Lady Diana, Princess of Wales, died in a Paris automobile accident; her death engendered more column inches in Britain's largest newspapers than the most dramatic stages of World War II. Her funeral, broadcast to 180 countries, attracted history's largest television audience.

What accounts for the magnitude and emotional reactions to celebrity deaths? Does it involve some identification the public has with these individuals, or does the surfeit of mass-media attention create its own audience? Being unconsciously imitative, do we cry because mass mediums overwhelm us with images of weeping family and friends? Because grief involves some form of loss, it is necessary to begin with the connections individuals have with celebrities.

## On Celebrity

The essence of celebrity involves the focusing of public attention on select individuals. These recipients may be heroes who embody society's notion of goodness or villains who embody its notion of evil—for example, John Wilkes Booth, Adolf Hitler, or serial killer Ted Bundy. Or they may, like game show hosts or publicized socialites, be simply "well-known for [their] well-knowingness" (Boorstin 1962, p. 57). Such attention giving often does not end with death and, in fact, may even be enhanced, as evidenced by the post-mortem attention given to such rock stars as Buddy Holly and Ritchie Valens.

The rise of celebrities corresponds with the evolution of mass media and changes in public appetite for the stories of others. Leo Braudel has

*Graceland in Memphis, Tennessee, was the home of celebrity Elvis Presley for 20 years until his death in 1977. It is now one of the most popular tourist attractions in the United States, visited by thousands each year on the anniversary of Presley's death.* CORBIS

noted, "As each new medium of fame appears, the human image it conveys is intensified and the number of individuals celebrated expands" (1986, p. 4). The ubiquity of mass-media images creates familiarity with such persons, forming novel attachments and identifications between them and the general public.

The rise of celebrity also corresponds with a public increasingly devoid of total relationships with others, individuals' connectedness with others and the broader society dampened by the anonymity of urban life, reduced civic involvements, increasing rates of singlehood and living alone, and by the instrumental relationships demanded by the workplace and marketplace. Further amplifying appetites for celebrities' stories is the new personality type populating the social landscape, characterized by sociologist David Riesman as being "other-directed," relying on others to define one's own lifestyles and beliefs—particularly those publicly identified as living more interesting, glamorous, or important lives. Thus the public may know more about the celebrities' stories than they do of those of their neighbors and associates.

The grief over the death of a national leader can be understood in terms of feelings of loss of some father figure or of the symbol of a people. Broadly shared emotions produce a sense of community. Political regimes have long understood this and have capitalized on the power of state funerals as a mechanism by which to enhance social solidarities and to reaffirm the legitimacy of the power structure.

But the grief over celebrities like Valentino or James Dean (a screen idol of the early 1950s) is another matter. Here the sense of loss is more like that of a friend because these are not so much role models as reflections of who we are or who we want to be. These are individuals whom one has paid to see or who have been frequent televised "guests" in one's home.

People identify with their artists, whose gift, in part, is their ability to capture mass longings in art. Such individuals are generational totems, reflecting the identities and ideals of those who share their age. People grow old with them and project their own hopes and fears on to them. They imagine what they would do with virtually limitless resources if placed in similar circumstances. And when celebrities die so does a portion of their admirers; hence the appearance of the SuperNova card company, which markets thousands of celebrity condolence cards.

With the rise of celebrity tabloids, people are able to get even closer to the everyday lives of their favorite celebrities. There is an attraction to those whose private lives increasingly overlap with their public images, revealing ordinary human chinks in the armor of idolatry. And, in a curious twist of the economics of adulation, their mystique increases in proportion to the privacy they seek, as was the case with Charles Lindbergh, Greta Garbo, and Jackie Kennedy.

## Public Deaths in a Death-Denying Culture

In a society where, as Philippe Ariès observed, death is a cultural taboo and where most deaths occur hidden away in institutional settings, Americans' death knowledge is increasingly learned secondhand from the mass media. The styles in which celebrities die and grieve are matters of considerable interest. From the tabloids people learned of Jackie Kennedy's stoicism following the assassination of her first husband, and of her own efforts to die with dignity a quarter century later. With rapt attention they followed the death trajectories and good-byes of Michael Landon, Frank Sinatra, and Jimmy Stewart. Not only do the deaths of actors become "news," but so do the "deaths" of the characters they portray. On television, for instance, the demise of phased-out characters is a well-established tactic for enhancing ratings, such as Lt. Col. Henry Blake (McLean Stevenson) from *M.A.S.H.* or Bobby Ewing (Michael Duffy) from *Dallas*.

The more grisly the celebrities' demise, the more morbid the curiosities aroused, a syndrome that produces a lucrative market for death-scene mementos. When the body of the Lindbergh son was found two months after being kidnapped in 1932, reporters entered the morgue and broke into his casket to photograph the mangled remains. Prints were sold on the streets of New Jersey for five dollars each. A reported $5,000 was paid by the *National Enquirer* for the morgue photograph of John Lennon's corpse. In 1994 Post Mortem Arts was selling copies of Kurt Cobain's death certificate for twenty-five dollars. And in Los Angeles, during the 1990s, Graveline Tours transported curious fans in a classic hearse to view the places where stars were murdered, committed suicide, or were laid to rest.

In addition to their growing control over the traffic of death symbolizations, the media have

expanded the traditional ability of the arts to confer immortality on their creators and performers. Because of film, for instance, one can still see and listen to Thomas Edison and George Bernard Shaw, men who were teenagers during the U.S. Civil War. And as the power of celebrity is transferred in endorsements, so too can it transcend death. A great-great-great grandfather is remembered because he served with Ulysses S. Grant; the other great-great-greats who had no such associations are typically forgotten. This logic entered the decision of an Austrian novelty firm to approach Mick Jagger in 1988 for permission to market his cremated remains in million-dollar hourglasses.

A final cause of interest in celebrity deaths entails the perverse satisfaction in outliving such august personages, a feeling enhancing one's own illusions of personal immortality. The motivation for producing such books as *They Went That-A-Way: How the Famous, the Infamous, and the Great Died* clearly caters to such needs for identification rather than to any authentic personal grief.

## How the Timing of a Celebrity's Death Affects Grief and Immortality

In the death-denying United States there is a search for cultural scripts for the dying—guides to dying well. There is a fascination with the premature deaths of immortals (or their relations) fueled by Hollywood and the press. The degree of public mourning following the deaths of Lady Diana and John F. Kennedy Jr. led social observers to wonder if grief is an ever-present latent feeling just waiting to be exploited by the political elite, if people's lives are so empty that they engage in recreational grief, or whether empathic fusings of self with certain celebrities can be so great that the grief is as authentic as that experienced with the loss of a family member. Perhaps individuals are emotive puppets manipulated by the mass media and/or political elite, and people cry because they are shown other people crying for a celebrity.

In the case of JFK Jr. the grief was not for the man, whose accomplishments were quite modest when compared to his father and whose death was blamed on his own poor judgment, but rather for the young boy saluting the funeral cortege of his slain father. Public mourning was extensively orchestrated. The president authorized the use of a naval warship to conduct his burial at sea, even though Kennedy had never served in the military. Hours of prime television time were devoted to long-distance camera shots of grieving family members and of the vessel from which his ashes were scattered.

The untimeliness of a celebrity's demise cannot only provoke extreme adulation for the deceased but also enhance his or her prospects for cultural immortality. In sports and the performing arts, death comes disproportionately prematurely. From 1940 to the present, there have emerged about 300 entertainers whose names could be recognized easily by many people. Over thirty of them died early and tragic deaths—a proportion about three times that of famous politicians or sports celebrities. Writers have proved to be a suicide-prone lot, with notables such as Sylvia Plath, Anne Sexton, and Ernest Hemingway exemplifying research by the psychiatrist Kay Jaimison that shows that writers are ten to twenty times as likely as others to suffer manic depression or depressive illnesses.

The immortal cultural status of these celebrities who died prematurely is reflected by the fact that, like the Catholic Saints their memories are honored on their death days and not birthdays. Dying young, these celebrities remain frozen in time and never have to grow old like those who followed their lives. On the other hand, when death comes with forewarning, such as in old age or due to cancer, other machinery of celebrity canonization comes into play. Attention increases in a cultural deathwatch. Final performances hit paydirt as swan songs, even the mediocre ones, such as the concluding films of Gary Cooper and Steve McQueen. Lifetime achievement awards are given, and amends are made for past oversights. Henry Fonda had to wait until he was on his deathbed to receive an Oscar for his final role in *On Golden Pond*.

## Capitalizing on the Attraction to Deceased Celebrities

Celebrity death generates its own pattern of economics. Because the deceased celebrity will not create anymore performances or sign anymore autographs, whatever artifacts he or she leaves behind become more valuable. In the year following his death, Mickey Mantle's used bats, balls, and uniforms increased 25 to 100 percent in value.

There are, in addition, the unreleased and incomplete works that may have been left behind. Posthumous books and records have proved to be lucrative business; for example, the dozen years following the death of the novelist Vladimir Nabokov in 1977 saw the publication of ten of his previously unpublished manuscripts.

With new technologies, however, dead celebrities were put to work during the last decade of the twentieth century. Natalie Cole recorded a song with her long-dead father Nat; the deceased Frank Sinatra was nominated for a 2001 Grammy with Celine Dion, who performed a duet with his posthumously generated voice; and the surviving Beatles reunited with the voice of the late John Lennon to play "Free As a Bird" and "Real Love." Madison Avenue discovered that the dead make excellent spokespersons, because they never will embarrass the sponsor. In 1994 Babe Ruth was receiving 100 endorsement deals a year. Ruth, followed by James Dean, was the most popular client at Curtis Management Group, an Indianapolis firm that markets late "greats" on behalf of descendants (who, in some states, own the rights to their dead relatives' image for fifty years). Curtis's services triggered a trend of resurrected dead celebrities hawking products—through the 1990s Louis Armstrong sipped Diet Coke in television commercials, Groucho Marx danced with Paula Abdul, Fred Astaire pranced with a vacuum cleaner, and Janis Joplin peddled Mercedes Benzes.

In 2001 *Forbes* magazine published a ranking of the earnings of the images of dead celebrities. Heading the list was Elvis Presley, whose estate earned $35 million. He was followed by Charles Schulz ($20 million), John Lennon ($20 million), Theodor "Dr. Seuss" Geisel ($17 million), and Jimi Hendrix ($10 million).

Celebrities need not have to generate revenue in order to have their cultural immortality assured. In recent decades over two hundred halls of fame have been founded to preserve the memories of celebrities in sports, the arts, and entertainment. Concurrently, the U.S. Postal Service moved beyond the memorialization of dead presidents and founding fathers to issuing stamps with the images of such deceased celebrities as actresses Lucille Ball and Marilyn Monroe, football coaches Vince Lombardi and Bear Bryant, and musicians Louis Armstrong and Charlie Parker.

See also: ARS MORIENDI; ELVIS SIGHTINGS; GRIEF:
OVERVIEW; ROYALTY, BRITISH; SERIAL KILLERS;
TABOOS AND SOCIAL STIGMA

## Bibliography

Ariès, Philippe. *The Hour of Our Death*. New York: Alfred A. Knopf, 1981.

Bauman, Zygmunt. *Morality, Immortality, and Other Life Strategies*. Stanford, CA: Stanford University Press, 1992.

Boorstin, Daniel. *The Image, Or, What Happened to the American Dream*. New York: Atheneum, 1962.

Braudel, Leo. *The Frenzy of Renown: Fame and Its History*. New York: Oxford University Press, 1986.

Davis, Daphene. *Stars!* New York: Simon and Schuster, 1986.

"Fame: The Faustian Bargain." *The Economist*, 6 September 1997, 21–23.

Fong, Mei, and Debra Lau. "Earnings From the Crypt." *Forbes*, 28 February 2001.

Forbes, Malcolm. *They Went That-A-Way: How the Famous, the Infamous, and the Great Died*. New York: Simon & Schuster, 1989.

Giles, David. *Illusions of Immortality: A Psychology of Fame and Celebrity*. New York: Palgrave. 2000.

Jaimison, Kay. *Touched with Fire: Manic-Depressive Illness and the Artistic Temperament*. New York: Free Press, 1996.

Kearl, Michael. "Death in Popular Culture." In Edwin S. Shneidman and John B. Williamson eds., *Death: Current Perspectives*, 4th edition. Mountain View, CA: Mayfield Publishing, 1995.

Kearl, Michael, and Anoel Rinaldi. "The Political Uses of the Dead as Symbols in Contemporary Civil Religions." *Social Forces* 61 (1983):693–708.

Polunsky, Bob. "A Public Death Watch Fascinates Hollywood." *San Antonio Express-News*, 8 September 1985, 2–H.

Reisman, David. *The Lonely Crowd*. New Haven, CT: Yale University Press. 1950.

Sandomir, Richard. "Amid Memories and Profit, Mantle's Legend Lives On." *New York Times*, 22 August 1996, A1, B9.

MICHAEL C. KEARL

# CELL DEATH

Cell death is a vital and common occurrence. In humans, some 10 billion new cells may form and an equal number die in a single day. Biologists recognize two general categories of cell death, which include genetically programmed death and death resulting from external forces (necrosis).

Genetically programmed cell death is necessary for replacing cells that are old, worn, or damaged; for sculpting the embryo during development; and for ridding the body of diseased cells. Toward the end of the twentieth century biologists recognized several mechanisms by which cell death could occur. In apoptosis, the most common form of normal cell death, a series of enzyme-mediated events leads to cell dehydration, outward ballooning and rupture of the weakened cell membrane, shrinking and fragmentation of the nucleus, and dissolution of the cell. By a different mechanism some cells generate special enzymes that "cut" cellular components like scissors (known as autoschizis, or "self-cutting"). Damaged cells that will become necrotic may lose the ability to control water transport across the membrane, resulting in swelling from excess fluid intake and disruption of protein structure (oncosis).

Programmed cell death is an important component of embryonic development and eliminates cells that are no longer needed. These include, for example, the cells between what will become fingers, or cells making up the embryo's original fish-like circulatory system as adult blood vessels form. Coordinate processes are called "cell determination," which involves a cell line becoming progressively genetically restricted in its developmental potential. For example, a cell line might become limited to becoming a white blood cell, thus losing the ability to become a liver cell. Cell differentiation occurs when cells take on specific structure and functions that make them visibly different from other cells (e.g., becoming neurons as opposed to liver epithelium).

All life is immortal in the sense that every cell is descendent from a continuous lineage dating back to the first nucleated cells 1.5 billion years ago. Life has been propagated through a repeating process of gamete (egg and sperm) formation by meiotic cell division (which creates genetic diversity by blending maternal and paternal genes), fertilization, and the development of the fertilized egg into a new multicellular organism that produces new gametes.

Can individual cells or cell lines, however, become immortal? This may be possible. HeLa cells (tumor cells from a patient named Henrietta Lack) have been kept alive and dividing in tissue culture for research purposes since 1951. But normal cells have a limit to the number of times they can divide, which is approximately fifty cell divisions (known as the Hayflick limit). The key to cell immortality seems to be the tips of the chromosomes, or telomeres, that protect the ends from degradation or fusion. Telomeres consist of a repeating sequence of DNA nucleotides. They shorten with each replication so that after some fifty divisions replication is no longer possible. An enzyme called "telomerase" adds these sequences to the telomere and extends the Hayflick limit. However, this enzyme is not very abundant in normal cells. When the biologists Andrea G. Bodnar and colleagues introduced cloned telomerase genes into cells, the telomeres were lengthened and the Hayflick limit for the cells greatly extended, suggesting the potential for cellular immortality.

*See also:* BRAIN DEATH; DEFINITIONS OF DEATH

### *Bibliography*

Bodnar, Andrea G., et al. "Extension of Life Span by Introduction of Telomerase into Normal Human Cells." *Science* 279 (1998):349–352.

Darzynkiewics, Zbigniew, et al. "Cytometry in Cell Necrobiology: Analysis of Apoptosis and Accidental Cell Death (Necrosis)." *Cytometry* 27 (1997):1–20.

Raloff, Janet. "Coming to Terms with Death: Accurate Descriptions of a Cell's Demise May Offer Clues to Diseases and Treatments." *Science News* 159, no. 24 (2001):378–380.

ALFRED R. MARTIN

# CEMETERIES AND CEMETERY REFORM

When death strikes in society certain events and rituals must be undertaken. The decaying of the corpse and beliefs about death make the presence of the dead person among the living unacceptable. Throughout history almost all societies have employed different practices for disposing of and commemorating the dead. One such form is the cemetery.

The term *cemetery* derives from the Greek (*koimeterion*) and Latin (*coemeterium*) words for "sleeping place." The concept is closely related to *burial ground, graveyard, churchyard,* and *necropolis,* which is Greek for "city of the dead." The boundary between these designations is not clear-cut. A burial ground and a graveyard consist of one or several graves. The term *burial ground* is more often employed than the term *graveyard* to designate unplanned or nonconsecrated places for burial. A churchyard is a consecrated graveyard owned by the church and attached to church buildings. A necropolis is a large graveyard. In this entry cemetery is defined as a large area set apart for burial, which is not necessarily consecrated, and initially was situated on the outskirts of a municipality. In the following sections the focus will be on the development and function of cemeteries in the West, but will also touch on functions of other forms of burial places.

## Functions

The most evident function of all burial grounds is to provide a means for getting rid of a dead body. Although burial is the most common way it is not the sole option. Many Hindus, for example, cremate the body on a pyre and shed the ashes in the Ganges River.

Cemeteries have multifarious social- and personal-level functions. It is important to make a distinction between individual and societal functions of cemeteries. Besides disposing of bodies, communities commemorate the dead with the displaying and construction of identity that this entails. Yet another social function is to express basic cultural beliefs concerning death and the meaning of life. Throughout history burial grounds have also been places where people met for different sorts of social gatherings. The individual function primarily concerns commemoration. One way to assure oneself of symbolic immortality is to buy a sizeable grave plot and construct an impressive memorial. However, the dead do not bury themselves, and a grave is as much an index of the social status of the funeral organizers as of the deceased. For the bereaved, the cemetery is a place where the relationship between the dead and the bereaved is established and maintained. Consolation is taken from visits to the grave, and from planting around and decorating the plot. Cemeteries are sites where family and communal loyalties are linked and reaffirmed.

Cemeteries and graves dramatize the stratification orders of the living. The segregations of living are reaffirmed in death. In the United States there are often different cemeteries for different ethnic and religious groups and different social classes. Even when this is not the case, different sections of a cemetery can be designated to different categories of people. To deny someone a grave among others, or individuality at death, is a way for society to express repudiation. Another strategy, common in warfare or civil conflict, is to eliminate any reminder whatsoever of the deceased.

The location and organization of cemeteries, the way in which they are kept, and the inscriptions on, and shape and size of, grave markers reflect beliefs and notions about death and life and set the boundaries between the worlds of the living and the dead. For example, the original meaning of cemetery as a "sleeping place" reflects the notion of some kind of resurrection, and the diminishing frequency of crosses on grave markers reflects secularization. The emergence of inscriptions in Arabic and the symbolic use of a half moon reflect a growing presence and recognition of Muslims. Cemeteries are far more than space sectioned off and set aside for the burial of the dead: They are, as the scholar Richard E. Meyer has maintained, cultural texts to be read by anyone who takes the time to learn a bit of their language.

## From Parish Churchyards to Extramural Cemeteries

The most salient predecessor to the modern Western cemetery is the Roman cemetery, where each body was given an identifiable home in a separate grave. Excavations from fourth-century British cemeteries reveal extensive urban burial grounds, often on new sites outside the borders of town. The separation of the living from the dead, with the town boundary as the dividing line, was absolute. With the weakening of the Roman Empire, the organization of society in rural villages, and the Christian cult of martyrs, this practice gradually changed. When funerary chapels, baptisteries, and churches were constructed over the remains of martyrs, death moved into the center of the lives of the living. From approximately the tenth century the parish churchyard was the most common burial ground in all Christian countries. Except for the most honored members of the community, who had private burial grounds or vaults inside the church, and the most despised, who were buried outside the churchyard, the deceased were buried in collective burial pits surrounded by charnel houses. Due to an emerging individualism around the thirteenth century, the practice to bury in individual sepulchers with personalized tombstones became common custom.

The nineteenth century saw a development from churchyards to cemeteries. There were three major reasons for this change. First, urbanization led to overcrowded churchyards in the big cities. Second, the church became increasingly secularized. Besides being at risk of losing ideological and symbolic power over burial customs and death rituals, the churches wanted to sustain their significant income of burial fees. Lastly, many people believed that graveyards imposed health hazards. Together this led to an increase in establishment of cemeteries free from the control of the church and by the 1850s the monopoly of the churchyard was broken. In the United States, where immigrants to the New World did not have memories of numerous generations to maintain, or extreme class differences to exaggerate, people buried the dead in unattended graveyards or small churchyards in association with ethnic congregations. This procedure started to change in the 1830s with the creation of Mount Auburn near Boston, which initiated the aforementioned European kind of cemetery.

## Ethnic and Cultural Variations

It is common to equate home with the place where the ancestors are buried. This is salient at old rural churchyards where several generations are buried side by side, and in the not so uncommon practice of first generation immigrants to repatriate the remains of the dead. According to the scholar Lewis Mumford it is likely that it was the permanent location of graves that eventually made people settle in villages and towns.

People are stratified in death as they are in life. The location of burial is often based on ethnicity, religion, and social class. The size of the grave marker indicates the relative power of males over females, adults over children, and the rich over the poor. Inscriptions, epitaphs, and art reflect emotional bonds between family members and the degree of religious immanence in everyday life.

Ethnic difference in death can be expressed either through separate ethnic cemeteries, separate ethnic sections in cemeteries, or ethnic symbols inscribed on grave markers. These means of expressing ethnicity can also be regarded as three steps in the gradual enculturation of ethnic groups or reaffirmations of their ethnic identity despite enculturation. While ethnicity is not an essential trait, it is a possibility that can be actualized when individuals want to express membership and exclusion. One such situation is burial and cemeteries, where ethnicity often also becomes fused with religious identity.

It is possible to discern at least seven different ways different groups express their ethnic identity within an ethnic cemetery or an ethnic section of a cemetery:

1. The location of the grave.

2. The position of the grave; Muslims are buried on the side facing Mecca, and Orthodox Christians are buried in an eastward position.

3. The form and shape of the grave marker; Polish Romes in Sweden use large grave memorials in black marble.

4. Symbols on the grave marker, such as a flag, an orthodox cross, or a Muslim half moon.

5. The place of birth, which is clearly stated on the grave marker.

6. Epitaphs from the country of origin.

7. Inscriptions in a language or alphabet that differs from that of the majority.

Moreover, different nationalities employ different grave decorations and visit the grave at various occasions. Markers of ethnicity are by no means unambiguous. In cemeteries where different ethnic groups are buried next to each other the majority culture and minority cultures tend to incorporate practices from each other, thereby blurring the boundaries.

Although there are apparent similarities between cemeteries from the middle of the nineteenth century and forward, there are also differences between countries. These differences can be understood as cultural differences. For instance, the cemeteries in Sweden and France are usually well kept. In France cemeteries are in most cases surrounded by high walls, and are locked during the night. The same kind of high walls and locked gates can be found in Britain, but with less concern over the maintenance of the graves. This difference is partly a consequence of ideals concerning garden architecture; the British garden is less formal than the French garden.

**Graveyard Hazards to Community Health**

The view on the danger of the corpse spread in the eighteenth century from France to other nations. Immigration to industrializing towns and cities with high mortality rates resulted in overcrowded urban burial grounds, which rapidly degenerated into public health hazards. Corpses were buried in shallow graves and disinterred after a brief period, usually in a state of semi-decay, to make room for others. Scientific theory maintained that cemeteries threatened public health because of the emanations of air released from the dead. It was the cholera epidemics in the mid–nineteenth century that finally became decisive in closing down inner-city graveyards and establishing out-of-town cemeteries. Since the end of the nineteenth century, when the French scientist Louis Pasteur's discovery that microbes cause infection was accepted as doctrine, medical concern about cemeteries has concentrated on their effects on water supply.

Modern environmental laws circumscribe cemetery establishment and management of the twenty-first century. If bodies have not been subjected to preservative measures, and if they are buried at least three feet (one meter) above groundwater level, there is no risk for spread of infectious disease. However, groundwater can be contaminated from bodies injected with chemical preservatives, including formaldehyde, which is employed in embalming. Although sanitary reasons are brought forward as an argument for cremation, there is a growing awareness of the pollutants in crematory emissions, including high levels of dioxins and trace metals.

## Status

Burial laws vary between different countries. There are rules governing how close to a populated area a cemetery can be situated, how far down a corpse most be buried, how long a grave most be left untouched until it can be reused, and the size and form of tombstones.

In France, Sweden, and other countries where cemetery management is considered a public concern, and the cultural attitude has historically been marked by decorum for the dead, neglected burial grounds are a rare sight. Furthermore, unlike the United States and Britain, France and Sweden have laws regulating reuse of graves after a set time period (in Sweden it is twenty-five years). In Britain it is illegal to disturb human remains unless permission is secured from church authorities or the home office. Although graves are "leased" for a given period—usually up to 100 years—burial is essentially in perpetuity. This is also the case in the United States. Perpetual graves induce vast areas of cemeteries with unattended graves. In Britain there is a growing awareness of the problem of neglected cemeteries, which take up space and bring up the issue of how long a city should conserve old cemeteries. The British and the U.S. system induce a less regulated and more differentiated market. Environmental concerns, shortage of burial space in certain areas, and neglected cemeteries are likely to bring about cemetery reforms in these and other countries in the new future.

A clear trend in the Western world is increase in cremation at the expense of inhumation. Because urns and ashes require less space than coffins, and there is a growing preference of depersonalized gardens of remembrance instead of personalized graves, it is likely that cemeteries in the future will turn into forms of public parks or gardens. There is also a trend away from ethnic cemeteries, to more heterogeneous graveyards, reflecting the present multicultural society.

Countries that practice reuse of graves, and where cremation is common, have no shortage of burial space. However, countries that combine low rates of cremation with burials for perpetuity need to continually seek solutions regarding how to manage old neglected cemeteries and how to find

new burial space. It is likely that most of these countries will become more and more reluctant to allow burial in perpetuity, instead advocating for reuse of graves and cremation.

*See also:* BLACK DEATH; BURIAL GROUNDS; CEMETERIES, MILITARY; CHARNEL HOUSES; DEAD GHETTO; IMMORTALITY, SYMBOLIC

## *Bibliography*

Ariès, Philippe. *Western Attitudes toward Death.* Baltimore, MD: John Hopkins University Press, 1974.

Davies, Douglas J. *Death, Ritual and Belief.* London: Cassel, 1977.

Etlin, Richard A. *The Architecture of Death: The Transformation of the Cemetery in Eighteenth-Century Paris.* Cambridge: MIT Press, 1984.

Field, David, Jenny Hockey, and Neil Small, eds. *Death, Gender, and Ethnicity.* London: Routledge, 1997.

Houlbrooke, Ralph, ed. *Death, Ritual and Bereavement.* London: Routledge, 1996.

Iserson, Kenneth V. *Death to Dust: What Happens to Dead Bodies?* Tucson, AZ: Galen Press, Ltd., 1994.

Kearl, Michael C. *Endings: A Sociology of Death and Dying.* Oxford: Oxford University Press, 1989.

Kselman, Thomas A. *Death and the Afterlife in Modern France.* Princeton, NJ: Princeton University Press, 1993.

Meyer, Richard E. *Ethnicity and the American Cemetery.* Bowling Green, OH: Bowling Green State University Popular Press, 1993.

Mumford, Lewis. *The City in History: Its Origins, Its Transformations, and Its Prospects.* New York: Harcourt Brace Jovanovich, 1961.

Reimers, Eva. "Death and Identity: Graves and Funerals As Cultural Communication." *Mortality* 2 (1999):147–166.

Rugg, Julie. "A Few Remarks on Modern Sepulture: Current Trends and New Directions in Cemetery Research." *Mortality* 2 (1998):111–128.

EVA REIMERS

# CEMETERIES, MILITARY

After 174 years, twenty-eight American Revolutionary War soldiers were returned in aluminum coffins by Canada for burial in the United States in 1988. A dozen years later, the United States was annually spending $6 million to locate and retrieve the remains of fewer than 2,000 American MIAs from

*Military cemeteries, designated to honor men and women who served in national defense, are becoming overcrowded, forcing them to close.* COREL CORPORATION

Vietnam, Laos, and Cambodia. At the Tomb of the Unknown Soldier at Arlington Cemetery stand guards twenty-four hours a day, 365 days a year.

Across America and the world stretch the graves of approximately 1.1 million Americans killed in the line of military service. The federal government maintains 119 national cemeteries in the United States and twenty-four others in a dozen foreign countries, containing approximately 2.5 million gravesites. In addition, also restricted to those who served in the armed forces and their immediate families are sixty-seven state veterans' cemeteries. These homes for the dead are preserved by the nation for those who sacrificed their lives in its defense.

To understand such actions and expenditures one needs to consider the workings of civil religion, or the ways in which politics command the sacred and thereby divinely endow its causes. Evidence of civil religion is on U.S. currency ("In God We Trust") and within the Pledge of Allegiance (the phrase "under God" was added in 1954 in the

midst of the cold war). Memorial Day is the state holy day, and national cemeteries and memorials its sacred sites.

Political systems, like religion, confer immortality to their elect. And what more deserving recipients than those who sacrificed their lives for the state? In a highly individualistic culture such as the United States, the preservation of these individuals' unique identities is paramount in the immortality business, which explains in part the considerable lengths the military goes to recover and identify its fallen—and the ritual care given to those whose identities are unknown. The Department of Veterans Affairs furnishes at no charge a headstone or marker for the unmarked grave of any deceased U.S. Armed Forces veteran not dishonorably discharged. When in 1980 the Veterans Administration began removing 627 bodies of unknown Civil War soldiers in the Grafton National Cemetery in West Virginia from their individual grave sites to be placed in a mass grave (with an imposing headstone bearing the inscription "Now

We Are One") there was collective outrage from veterans and amateur historians. Despite the fact that space was badly needed, the right to individuated memorials was preserved.

To preserve the sanctity of these burial sites, the Veterans Administration runs a limited number of cemeteries, with one exception: the most sacred of sacred sites, Arlington National Cemetery. Administered by the Department of the Army, here across the Potomac from the national capitol lie the remains of more than 250,000 Americans. To preserve its purity occasional pollution rituals occur, as in late 1977 when the body of M. Larry Lawrence, the late ambassador to Switzerland and a fabricated World War II hero, was unceremoniously exhumed and removed.

With over 1,000 World War II veterans dying each day, and because the United States has been engaged in so many wars and "police actions," the problem faced by the National Cemetery Administration is lack of space. As of the beginning of 2001, thirty-one of the 119 national cemeteries are closed to new burials; only sixty of Arlington's 612 acres can hold new graves.

*See also:* BURIAL GROUNDS; CEMETERIES AND CEMETERY REFORM; CEMETERIES, WAR; CIVIL WAR, U.S.; FUNERAL INDUSTRY; IMMORTALITY, SYMBOLIC; TOMBS

### *Bibliography*

Douglas, Mary. *Purity and Danger: An Analysis of Concepts of Pollution and Taboo.* New York: Frederick A. Praeger, 1966.

Kearl, Michael, and Anoel Rinaldi. "The Political Uses of the Dead as Symbols in Contemporary Civil Religions." *Social Forces* 61 (1983):693–708.

*Internet Resources*

National Cemetery Administration. "Statistics and Facts." In the Department of Veterans Affairs [web site]. Available from www.cem.va.gov/facts.htm.

MICHAEL C. KEARL

# CEMETERIES, WAR

The question of what do with soliders killed in war has been a problem throughout recorded history, addressed in different ways by different cultures.

An extreme solution was eating the killed individual, an act often connected with the idea that the power of the victim would be added to that of the eaters. Or the deceased might be left on the ground until the corpse was decayed or devoured by animals, which would be considered a disgrace, especially to the losers of a fight or battle. More often than not, killed individuals would be buried.

Throughout history the dead, mainly the losers, were often deprived of their belongings. This was seen as part of the spoils of war. The winners often displayed a more honorable reaction to their own dead than to those of the losers. Another principle permitted the leaders to be appreciated in a special manner. One can find impressive monuments to the leaders, while ordinary fighters were buried anonymously. The so-called Drusus Stone, a huge monument in the town of Mainz, Germany, was erected for the Roman general Drusus, a brother of the emperor Tiberius, who was killed in 9 B.C.E. in a battle at the River Elbe.

## Burying the War Dead

Modern times saw the inauguration of the practice of burying soldiers who were killed in battle. This was done partly due to hygienic considerations common throughout the world—unburied corpses can soon create epidemics. The burial grounds are often found where the fights took place. However, there can also be "regular" cemeteries in which the bodies are buried side by side with the dead of the region or, more frequently, in war cemeteries dedicated exclusively to fallen soldiers.

Because of the huge numbers of casualties on both sides in the U.S. Civil War (more than 600,000 victims), the dead of both sides were often buried side by side, hence giving birth to the idea of posthumous reconciliation of the warring sides and respect for the sacrifice of the individual soldier, each of whom now had his own grave site, a contrast to earlier practices of mass military burials in which all soldiers achieved a rough equality in death, without all distinctions of rank, religion, and race erased by collective interment.

The uniformity of design of all U.S. war cemeteries was influential on the subsequent design of war cemeteries in other countries. Each nation selected its own special grave symbol. The French had a cross made of concrete with the victim's name and a rose; the British typically employed a stele.

The annual honoring of the American war dead occurs on Memorial Day, at the end of May. However, in some countries this day of remembrance has been expanded to the memory of all the war dead of all countries, as in Finland after World War II.

## German War Cemeteries

Although World War I primarily took place in Europe, many of the participating nations drafted men from their far-flung colonies. During World War I, 10 million people were killed, among them 2 million German soldiers. By 1928, 13,000 cemeteries had been completed in twenty-eight countries for these dead. World War I is also another example for the different attitudes toward losers and winners, as outlined above. The French government, for example, did not permit German officials to design their own war cemeteries.

Fifty-five million people were killed in World War II, among them 13.6 million soldiers of the Red Army and 4 million German soldiers. For those 1.8 million German soldiers who died beyond German borders, 667 cemeteries in forty-three countries were completed. Most of these were created in Western countries such as France, Italy, or Belgium. The task of properly burying all German soldiers of WWII has not yet been completed. With the lifting of the Iron Curtain in 1989, it was possible to lay out new cemeteries in former communist countries. In the 1990s a new cemetery was opened for 70,000 soldiers near St. Petersburg in Russia. The task of lying to rest all fallen German soldiers is expected to be completed by the end of 2010.

## Honoring the German War Dead

The body responsible for completing war cemeteries for passed German soldiers is an independent organization founded in 1926; its name is *Volksbund Deutsche Kriegsgräberfürsorge* (People's Community for the Care of German War Graves). It can be observed that the functions of this organization and of the cemeteries have changed since World War II. Its initial task was to bury the soldiers and to enable the families to visit the graves. Each year, between 700,000 and 800,000 persons visit the German war cemeteries. Originally, war cemeteries were established to honor those who gave their lives for their countries. The dead soldiers were declared heroes. The memorial day for killed soldiers was called *Heldengedenktag* (Heroes' Memorial Day) during the Third Reich in Germany. Such a name held strong connotations toward nationalism and chauvinism. After World War II the name for the memorial day was changed into *Volkstrauertag* (People's Mourning Day) and designated to be the Sunday two weeks before Advent. The new name signifies a change of attitudes. The idea of commemorating the deeds of proud heroes was abolished and has been replaced by the grief for killed fathers, brothers, and sons, which is the focus of memorial sermons.

In the case of Germany there is a special historical burden that required this change of attitudes. Not only had Germany lost World War II, but that war had been provoked by an authoritarian and terrorist regime. Thus, there is an ambiguity toward their soldiers who sacrificed their lives for their country. The Volkstrauertag remembrance sermons, held in many towns in the frame of a ceremony, are now not only for soldiers, but for *alle Opfer der Gewalt* ("all victims of violence")—as is now the official term. The victims include the refugees, the resistance fighters against Nazism and all those who died or were killed in the concentration camps. Thus, any glorification of war and Nazism is excluded.

There is another change in the purpose of war cemeteries, namely toward reconciliation and work for peace. The two slogans of the Volksbund *Arbeit für den Frieden* ("work for peace") and *Mahnung über den Gräberm* ("warning over the graves"), characterize its activities. The graves themselves, often many hundreds to a cemetery, point to the importance of peace. Different countries send participants to youth camps dedicated to this aim. These young people not only work in the cemeteries but they also learn to respect each other and permit new friendships to develop. Since 1953, 3,670 camps have been held involving 170,000 participants.

## Conclusion

An increasing number of the dead soldiers no longer have surviving family members. In just one generation there will be far fewer visitors going to the cemeteries. The dead have a right of eternal rest, so no war graves are levelled, which is a sensible principle in the light of the changing functions of war cemeteries. Visitors with no personal interest in the graves can still be impressed by the huge area of the cemetery and thereby be encouraged to contribute toward maintaining peace.

*See also:* CEMETERIES, MILITARY; MOURNING; WAR

### Bibliography

Walter, Tony. *The Eclipse of Eternity: A Sociology of the Afterlife.* New York: St. Martin's Press, 1996.

*Internet Resources*

"Introduction." *1949 Conventions and 1977 Protocols.* In the International Committee of the Red Cross [web site]. Available from www.icrc.org/ihl.

GERHARD SCHMIED

# CHANNELERS/MEDIUMS

*See* COMMUNICATION WITH THE DEAD.

# CHARNEL HOUSES

A *charnel house* is a building, chamber, or other area in which bodies or bones are deposited, also known as a mortuary chapel. Charnel houses arose as a result of the limited areas available for cemeteries. When cemetery usage had reached its limits, the bodies, by then only bones, would be dug up and deposited in the charnel house, thus making room for new burials. For example, at St. Catherine Monastery on Mount Sinai, where thousands of monks have lived and died over the centuries, the monks are buried in the small cemetery, later exhumed, and their bones placed in the crypt below the Chapel of St. Trifonio. The pile of skulls presents an imposing sight.

Charnel houses are fairly common. A Cornish (England) folktale tells of a wager in which a man offers to go into the parish charnel house and come out with a skull. As he picks one up a ghostly voice says, "That's mine." He drops it, and tries again a second and third time. Finally the man replies, "They can't all be yours," picks up another, and dashes out with it, winning the wager. His discomfited opponent then drops from the rafters. By speaking of the "parish" charnel house the story illustrates the widespread usage of such repositories.

Charnel houses can be found in many cultures and in many time periods, including the present. Late prehistoric peoples of Maryland saved the dead in charnel houses and periodically disposed of them in large mass graves. In Iroquoian and southeastern Algonquian Native American tribes corpses were first allowed to decompose and then placed in mortuaries, or charnel houses. They were then interred in an ossuary, a communal burial place for the bones, after a period of eight to twelve years (Blick 1994). In the Spitalfields section of London, a 1999 archaeological dig uncovered a medieval vaulted charnel house, used until the seventeenth century. The charnel house was beneath a chapel built between 1389 and 1391. In 1925 a memorial charnel house was built in Bukovik, Serbia (now the town of Arandjelovac) to contain the remains of several thousand soldiers, both Serbian and Austro-Hungarian, who died in nearby battles during World War I. In 1938 Italians completed a charnel house in Kobarid, Slovenia, to contain the remains of 1,014 Italian soldiers who also had been killed in World War I. Along the main staircase are niches with the remains of 1,748 unknown soldiers. Charnel houses still exist in the twenty-first century. A Korean manufacturer, for example, sells natural jade funeral urns and funeral caskets for use in charnel houses.

*See also:* BURIAL GROUNDS; CATACOMBS; CREMATION

### Bibliography

Hunt, Robert. *Popular Romances of the West of England.* 1865. Reprint, New York: B. Blom, 1968.

Stevens, Mark. "War Stories." *New York Magazine,* 22 February 1999.

*Internet Resources*

Blick, Jeffrey P. "The Quiyoughcohannock Ossuary Ritual and the Feast of the Dead." In the 6th Internet World Congress for Biomedical Sciences [web site]. Available from www.uclm.es/inabis2000/symposia/files/133/index.htm.

SAM SILVERMAN

# CHARON AND THE RIVER STYX

Charon, in Greek mythology, acts as the ferryman of the dead. Hermes (the messenger of the gods) brings to him the souls of the deceased, and he ferries them across the river Acheron to Hades (Hell). Only the dead who are properly buried or burned and who pay the *obolus* (silver coin) for their passage are accepted on his boat, which is why in ancient Greek burial rites the corpse always had an *obolus* placed under his tongue. A rather somber and severe character, Charon does not hesitate to throw out of his boat without pity the souls whose bodies received improper burial or cremation.

The Styx is only one of the five rivers of the underworld that separate Hades from the world of the living. These five rivers of Hell are Acheron (the river of woe), Cocytus (the river of lamentation), Phlegethon (the river of fire), Lethe (the river of forgetfulness), and finally, Styx. The word *styx* comes from the Greek word *stugein,* which means "hateful" and expresses the horror of death. The eighth century B.C.E. Greek poet Hesiod considered Styx to be the daughter of Oceanus and the mother or Emulation, Victory, Power, and Might. More recently, Styx has been identified with the stream called Mavronéri (Greek for "black water") in Arcadia, Greece. Ancient beliefs held that the Styx water was poisonous. According to a legend, Alexander the Great (356–323 B.C.E.), king of Macedonia and conqueror of much of Asia, was poisoned by Styx water.

The use of the figures of Charon and the River Styx is quite recurrent in Western literature. The most important occurrence is found in the Italian poet Dante's (1265–1321) *Divine Comedy,* in which Charon sees a living man (Dante's alter ego) journeying in the inferno and challenges him.

*See also:* GILGAMESH; GODS AND GODDESSES OF LIFE AND DEATH; HELL; ORPHEUS

### *Bibliography*

Cotterell, Arthur. *Classical Mythology: An Authoritative Reference to the Ancient Greek, Roman, Celtic and Norse Legends.* Lorenz Books, 2000.

Nardo, Don. *Greek and Roman Mythology.* Lucent Books, 1997.

JEAN-YVES BOUCHER

# CHILDREN

Most people in American society resist associating the words *children* and *death* in a single phrase. They do not wish to contemplate the possibility that children may encounter death-related events either in their own lives or in the lives of others. As a result, they try not to think about the actual realities implied by the phrase "children and death" and they attempt to shield children from contact with or knowledge of such realities.

Although this effort at "misguided protectionism" is usually well meant, it is unlikely in most instances to be either successful or helpful. To explain why this is true, this entry explores how death and death-related events impinge on the lives of children and what their significance is for such lives. In addition, this entry considers the elements of a constructive, proactive program that helps children in their interactions with death and death-related events.

## Children as Harbingers of the Future and Repositories of Hope

For many people in American society, children represent ongoing life and the promise of the future. In them, many hopes and ambitions are embodied. They foreshadow what is yet to come and act as a pledge of its surety. In a special way for females, they enter into life by emerging from their mothers' bodies. In addition, human children are vulnerable in special ways and for an unusually prolonged period of time. They call upon their adult caregivers to care for them. Their presence in adult lives is, more often than not, a source of pride and delight. As they grow and mature, children become their own persons and their parents' companions. In some cases, eventually they become caregivers of the adults who raised them. All these descriptions are true for one's natural children, as well as for those who are adopted or are foster children, and even when the latter are of a different ethnicity or culture.

## Children, Adolescents, and Normative Development

In the 1950s the psychoanalyst Erik Erikson proposed that there are four major eras (sometimes called "ages," "periods," or "stages") in the lives of children and an additional one for adolescents (see Table 1). His depiction of childhood has been highly influential to other developmental psychologists and scholars, although it is no longer universally accepted. Moreover, subsequent scholarship has sought to distinguish between three subperiods within adolescence. Still, a broad Eriksonian framework helps to draw attention to prominent aspects of physical, psychological, and social development in humans during childhood and adolescence, although it may not comment on spiritual development. Within limits, it can be useful as a general background for an overview of death in childhood and adolescence.

Erikson's model seeks to describe the normal and healthy development of an individual ego. It proposes that a predominant psychosocial issue or central conflict characterizes each era in human development. This is expressed as a struggle between a pair of alternative orientations, opposed tendencies, or attitudes toward life, the self, and other people. Successful resolution of each developmental struggle results in a leading virtue, a particular strength or quality of ego functioning. For Erikson, the task work in these developmental struggles is associated with normative life events, those that are expected to occur at a certain time, in a certain relationship to other life events, with predictability, and to most if not all of the members of a developmental group or cohort. This developmental framework is only roughly correlated with chronological age. Further, it might not apply at all or might only have limited relevance to individuals within different familial, cultural, and societal groups, and it might only apply uniformly to members of both genders when males and females are given equal options in life.

The importance of Erikson's work is the contrast between normative developmental events, however they may be described, and death-related events, primarily because most death-related events are nonnormative. They are unexpected or unforeseen events that occur atypically or unpredictably, with no apparent relationship to other life events, and to some but not all members of a developmental cohort. Still, nonnormative life events occur in a context of normative developmental events and each can influence the other in significant ways.

Both normative and nonnormative life events and transitions are life crises or turning points.

They present "dangerous opportunities" that offer occasions for growth and maturation if an individual copes with them effectively, but also the potential for psychological harm and distorted or unsatisfactory development if the coping response is inappropriate or inadequate. Accordingly, the way in which a child or adolescent resolves the issue that dominates a particular era in his or her development and thereby does or does not establish its corresponding ego quality or virtue is likely to be relatively persistent or enduring throughout his or her life.

With respect to adolescence, various scholars have offered a fine-tuned account that distinguishes between three developmental subperiods, along with their predominant issues and corresponding virtues:

- *Early adolescence*: separation (abandonment) versus reunion (safety); leading to a sense of emotional separation from dependency on parents
- *Middle adolescence*: independence or autonomy versus dependence; leading to a sense of competency, mastery, and control
- *Late adolescence*: closeness versus distance; leading to a sense of intimacy and commitment.

The Swiss developmental psychologist Jean Piaget looked at child development in a different way by focusing on processes involved in cognitive development during childhood. His work and later research on the development of death-related concepts in both childhood and adolescence is groundbreaking to the field of developmental psychology.

The various schemas all relay the fact that children and adolescents may encounter the deaths of others and even their own deaths. These and all other death-related events will be experienced within the ongoing processes of their own individual maturation. As the psychologist and gerontologist Robert Kastenbaum wrote in his article "Death and Development through the Life span": "Death is one of the central themes in human development throughout the life span. Death is not just our destination; it is a part of our 'getting there' as well" (Kastenbaum 1977, p. 43). Death-related events can affect human development during childhood and adolescence. Equally so, cognitive, psychological, biological, behavioral, social, and spiritual aspects

**TABLE 1**

| | | | |
|---|---|---|---|
| **Principal developmental eras during childhood and adolescence in the human life cycle** | | | |
| **Era** | **Approximate Age** | **Predominant Issue** | **Virtue** |
| Infancy | Birth through 12 to 18 months | Basic trust vs. mistrust | Hope |
| Toddlerhood | Infancy to 3 years of age | Autonomy vs. shame and doubt | Will or self-control |
| Early childhood, sometimes called "play age" or the "preschool period" | 3 to 6 years of age | Initiative vs. guilt | Purpose or direction |
| Middle childhood, sometimes called "school age" or the "latency period" | 6 years to puberty | Industry vs. inferiority | Competency |
| Adolescence | Puberty to about 21 or 22 years of age | Identity vs. role confusion | Fidelity |

Note: All chronological ages are approximate.

SOURCE: Adapted from Erikson, 1963, 1968.

of that development, along with life experiences and communications from the environment that surround children and adolescents, will all be influential in how they cope with intrusions into their lives by death. According to Kastenbaum, adults who help children and adolescents in this coping work need to be sensitive to the developmental context and the individual perspective of each child or adolescent in order to be successful.

## Encounters with Death during Childhood and Adolescence

"'The kingdom where nobody dies,' as Edna St. Vincent Millay once described childhood, is the fantasy of grown-ups" (Kastenbaum 1973, p. 37). In fact, children and adolescents do die, and all young people can be and are affected by the dying and deaths of others around them.

The most dangerous time for children themselves is prior to birth (where they face the implications of miscarriage, stillbirth, and spontaneous or elective abortion), at birth (with all its risks of perinatal death), immediately after birth (with the potential perils of neonatal death), and during the first year of life. The best data available are for infant mortality. Data from the National Center for Health Statistics indicated that a total of 27,953 infants died in the United States during

1999. This figure represents 7.1 infant deaths for every 1,000 live births, the lowest rate ever recorded for the United States.

More than twenty other countries with a population of at least 2.5 million have lower infant mortality rates than those in the United States. Moreover, it is also true that infant mortality rates in the United States are nearly 2.4 times higher for African Americans (8,832 deaths or 14.2 per 1,000 live births) than those for non-Hispanic Caucasian Americans (13,555 deaths or 5.8 per 1,000) and Hispanic Americans (4,416 deaths or 5.8 per 1,000).

Congenital malformations, disorders related to short gestation and low birth weight, sudden infant death syndrome (SIDS), and maternal complications of pregnancy caused just under one-half (49.6%) of all infant deaths in the United States in 1999. There was a decline from 1988 to 1999 of 53.4 percent in the rate of SIDS deaths (from 140.1 to 65.3 per 100,000 live births). However, SIDS still remains the leading cause of death for infants between one month and one year of age, accounting for 28 percent of all deaths during that period.

Overall data on deaths and death rates during childhood and adolescence in the United States in 1999 are provided in Table 2, along with more specific data by age, sex, race, and Hispanic origin. (Note that racial and cultural categories overlap in the data presented in this table; thus, totals for all races are not identical with the sum of each subordinate category.) From Table 2 one can see that the largest numbers of deaths take place in infancy or the first year of life in childhood and in middle to late adolescence. In every age, racial, and cultural category, more males die than females, especially during middle and late adolescence. And in every age and gender category, death rates for African-American children are notably higher than those for non-Hispanic Caucasian Americans and Hispanic Americans. Death rates among Native-American children are typically lower than those for African-American children, but higher than for children in other racial and cultural groups—with the exception of fifteen- to twenty-four-year-old Native-American females who have the highest death rate in their age group. Death rates for Asian Americans and Pacific Islanders are uniformly lower than those for all other racial and cultural groups.

The leading cause of death in all children from one year of age through adolescence is accidents.

**TABLE 2**

Deaths and death rates (per 100,000) in the specified population group by age, sex, race, and Hispanic origin, United States, 1999

**DEATHS**

| | Under 1 Year[a] | | | 1–4 Years | | | 5–14 Years | | | 15–24 Years | | |
|---|---|---|---|---|---|---|---|---|---|---|---|---|
| | Both Sexes | Males | Females | Both Sexes | Males | Females | Both Sexes | Males | Females | Both Sexes | Males | Females |
| All races | 27,953 | 15,656 | 12,297 | 5,250 | 2,976 | 2,274 | 7,595 | 4,492 | 3,103 | 30,664 | 22,419 | 8,245 |
| Non-Hispanic Caucasian Americans | 13,555 | 7,722 | 5,833 | 2,820 | 1,606 | 1,214 | 4,488 | 2,643 | 1,845 | 17,869 | 12,678 | 5,191 |
| African Americans[b] | 8,832 | 4,899 | 3,933 | 1,309 | 745 | 564 | 1,789 | 1,096 | 693 | 7,065 | 5,350 | 1,715 |
| Hispanic Americans[c] | 4,416 | 2,411 | 2,005 | 883 | 482 | 401 | 1,014 | 592 | 422 | 4,509 | 3,549 | 960 |
| Asian Americans & Pacific Islanders[b] | 708 | 375 | 333 | 167 | 97 | 70 | 207 | 112 | 95 | 699 | 467 | 232 |
| Native Americans[b] | 344 | 180 | 164 | 82 | 48 | 34 | 105 | 55 | 50 | 540 | 396 | 144 |

**DEATH RATES**

| | Under 1 Year[a] | | | 1–4 Years | | | 5–14 Years | | | 15–24 Years | | |
|---|---|---|---|---|---|---|---|---|---|---|---|---|
| | Both Sexes | Males | Females | Both Sexes | Males | Females | Both Sexes | Males | Females | Both Sexes | Males | Females |
| All races | 731.8 | 802.0 | 648.4 | 34.7 | 38.5 | 30.8 | 19.2 | 22.2 | 16.1 | 81.2 | 116.0 | 44.7 |
| Non-Hispanic Caucasian Americans | 572.7 | 636.8 | 505.4 | 29.7 | 33.0 | 26.2 | 17.5 | 20.1 | 14.8 | 71.4 | 98.7 | 42.6 |
| African Americans[b] | 1,552.8 | 1,694.6 | 1,406.2 | 58.8 | 65.9 | 51.4 | 28.7 | 34.6 | 22.6 | 123.1 | 185.7 | 60.0 |
| Hispanic Americans[c] | 612.0 | 655.3 | 567.0 | 32.2 | 34.4 | 29.8 | 16.9 | 19.4 | 14.4 | 82.4 | 125.0 | 36.5 |
| Asian Americans & Pacific Islanders[b] | 390.3 | 406.6 | 373.4 | 23.2 | 26.6 | 19.7 | 12.2 | 12.8 | 11.5 | 44.0 | 58.7 | 29.2 |
| Native Americans[b] | 808.6 | 839.5 | 777.3 | 51.4 | 59.4 | 43.1 | 22.4 | 23.1 | 21.7 | 125.9 | 183.5 | 67.5 |

[a] Death rates are based on population estimates; they differ from infant mortality rates, which are based on live births.

[b] Race and Hispanic origin are reported separately on death certificates. Data for persons of Hispanic origin are included in the data for each race group (unless otherwise specified), according to the decedent's reported race.

[c] Includes all persons of Hispanic origin of any race.

SOURCE: Adapted from Kochanek, Smith, and Anderson, 2001.

In children from one to four years of age, the second, third, and fourth leading causes of death are congenital malformations, cancer, and homicide. In children from five to fourteen years of age, the second, third, and fourth leading causes of death are cancer, homicide, and congenital malformations. In adolescents from fifteen to twenty-four years of age, the second and third leading causes of death are homicide and suicide, followed at some distance by cancer and heart disease.

Children encounter the deaths of others that are significant in their lives. Such deaths include those of grandparents or parents, siblings or peers, friends or neighbors, teachers and other school personnel, and pets or wild animals. Many adults undervalue the prevalence and importance of such deaths for children. However these experiences of childhood and adolescence can have immediate impact and long-term significance. Some prominent examples include the school shooting at

Columbine High School in Colorado in April 1999, the countless instances of fantasized deaths and violence that children witness on television at an early age, and the many children who are members of families in which someone has died or is dying of AIDS (acquired immunodeficiency syndrome).

## Children's Efforts to Understand Death

Children and adolescents are curious about the world around them. When death-related events intrude into their lives, they strive to understand them. Many factors affect such strivings, such as the intellectual capacities of the child, his or her life experiences, what society at large and adults around the child might say about the events, and the child's personality. Children's efforts to understand death may not always lead to thinking about death in the ways that adults do. It is incorrect to conclude from the way children respond to death that children have no concept of death or are never interested in the subject. To claim that "the child is so recently of the quick that there is little need in his spring-green world for an understanding of the dead" (Ross 1967, p. 250) is to be unfamiliar with the lives of children or to betray a personal difficulty in coping with death and a projection of those anxieties onto children. In reality children do try to make sense of death as they encounter it in their lives. According to Charles Corr, an educator who has written widely about issues related to children and death, such strivings should be aided by open communication and effective support from adults who love the child.

## Expressions of Death-Related Attitudes in Games, Stories, and Literature for Children

Play is the main work of a child's life, and many childhood games are related to death. For example, little boys often stage car crashes or other scenes of violent destruction that they can manipulate and observe from a safe psychic distance, while little girls sometimes act out the ritual of a funeral or compare the deep sleep of a doll to death. Adah Maurer described peek-a-boo as a game in which the entire world (except, of course, the participating child) suddenly vanishes (is whisked away from the child's life) only to reappear subsequently in an act of instantaneous resurrection or rebirth. There is also the song in which "the worms crawl in, the worms crawl out," the lullaby "Rock-a-Bye Baby" that sings about the bough breaking and the cradle falling, and the child's prayer, "Now I lay me down to sleep," which petitions for safekeeping against death and other hazards of the night.

Similarly, children's oral and written fairy tales offer many examples of death-related events. For example, Little Red Riding Hood and her grandmother are eaten by the wicked wolf in the original version of the story, not saved by a passing woodsman or hunter. The Big Bad Wolf in the "Three Little Pigs" died in a scalding pot of hot water when the wolf fell down the last chimney. And while Hansel and Gretel escaped being shut up in a hot oven, the wicked witch did not.

There is a very large body of literature for children and adolescents that offers stories with death-related themes or seeks to explain death to young readers. Books range from simple picture books about children who find and bury a dead bird in the woods to more detailed stories that relay experiences involving the death of a beloved grandparent or pet, parent, sibling, or peer.

## Children Who Are Coping with Life-Threatening Illnesses and Dying

Children with a life-threatening illness experience changes in their daily routines, acquire new information about their illnesses and themselves, and find themselves confronted with unexpected challenges. Many are anxious about those experiences, most need information that they can understand, and all need support as they make efforts to cope. In 1997 Michael Stevens, an Australian pediatric oncologist, suggested that the emotional needs of dying children include those of all children regardless of health, those that arise from the child's reaction to illness and admission to a hospital, and those that have to do with the child's concept of death. One twelve-year-old girl infected with HIV (human immunodeficiency virus) wrote: "Living with HIV and knowing that you can die from it is scary. . . . I think it is hardest in this order: Not knowing when this will happen. . . . Not knowing where it will happen. . . . Worrying about my family. . . . What will happen to my stuff and my room? . . . Thinking about what my friends will think" (Wiener, Best, and Pizzo 1994, p. 24).

## Children Who Are Coping with Loss and Grief

Three central issues likely to be prominent in the experiences of bereaved children are: Did I cause the death?; Is it going to happen to me?; and Who is going to take care of me? These issues of causality, vulnerability, and safety cry out for clear explanations and support. In response, in 1988 Sandra Fox identified four tasks that are central to productive mourning for children: (1) to understand and try to make sense out of what is happening or has happened; (2) to express emotional and other strong responses to the present or anticipated loss; (3) to commemorate the life that has been lost through some formal or informal remembrance; and (4) to learn how to go on with living and loving.

When confronted with a death-related event, adults often try to block children's efforts to acquire information, express their feelings, obtain support, and learn to cope with sadness and loss. According to Charles Corr, this strategy cannot be helpful to a child in the long run because its effect is to abandon a child and its major lesson is that the child should not bring difficult issues to such an adult. By contrast, emotionally sensitive adults anticipate that sooner or later children need to turn to someone for help with death and loss. On that basis, they can try to prepare themselves for such moments, strive to ensure that they are responding to a child's real needs, try to communicate clearly and effectively, and work cooperatively with children, other adults, and relevant resources in society. This leads to a proactive program of helping that involves three elements: education, communication, and validation.

Experts note a good way to begin is with education; for example, by teaching children about death and loss in relatively safe encounters and by exploiting "teachable moments" for the insights they can offer and the dialogue they can stimulate. Next, one can turn to effective communication by asking three questions:

1. What does a child need to know?

2. What does a child want to know?

3. What can a child understand?

Euphemisms and inconsistent or incomplete answers are not desirable because they easily lead to misunderstandings that may be more disturbing than the real facts. Honesty is dependable and encourages trust, the basis of all comforting relationships. So it is better to admit what you do not know than to make up explanations you really do not believe.

A third element of a proactive program is validation. Validation applies to children's questions, concepts, language, and feelings. It involves acknowledging these things in a nonjudgmental way and helping the child to name or articulate them so as to have power over them.

The advantages of a proactive program of education, communication, and validation can be seen in the examples of children who take part in funeral rituals and in support groups for the bereaved. Many adults in American society exclude children from funeral rituals, feeling that children might not be able to cope with such experiences and might be harmed by them. In fact, research has shown that taking part in funeral planning and funeral ritual in appropriate ways—not being forced to participate, being prepared ahead of time, given support during the event, and offered follow-up afterward—can help children with their grief work. Similarly, being given opportunities to interact and share experiences with others who are bereaved in the protected environment of a support group can help children and adolescents come to understand and learn to cope with death and grief.

## Adult Children

One other sense in which the term "children" can be and is used in connection with death-related experiences has to do with adults who remain the children of their older, living parents. As average life expectancy increases in American society, growing numbers of middle-aged and elderly adults are alive when their children become adults. Indeed, some of the oldest members of American society, including the so-called old-old who are more than eighty-five or even one hundred years of age, may find themselves with living children who are also elderly adults.

Death-related events are relevant to these population groups in many ways. Among these, two stand out. First, when an adult child dies that may constitute a particular tragedy for a surviving parent. For example, the adult child may have been the primary care provider for the parent in his or her home, the only person to visit that parent in a long-term care facility, the individual who took care of practical matters such as handling finances or filling out tax forms for the parent, or the sole survivor from among the parent's family members, peers, and offspring. In these and other situations, the death of an adult child may impact the surviving parent in myriad ways, invoking losses and challenges in forms that had not hitherto been faced.

Second, the death of a parent at an advanced age who is survived by an adult child has its own spectrum of ramifications. Deaths of family members (especially parents) from an earlier generation often exert a "generational push" on younger survivors. These younger survivors, especially adult children, are now no longer "protected" in their own minds by their perceptions of the "natural order" of things. Previously, death may have seemed to them to be less of a personal threat as long as their parents and other members of an older generation remained alive. Now the adult children themselves are the members of the "oldest" generation. These adult children may be relieved of care giving responsibilities and other burdens that they had borne when their parents were alive, but new and often highly personalized challenges frequently arise for these adult children in their new roles as bereaved survivors.

*See also:* CHILDREN AND ADOLESCENTS' UNDERSTANDING OF DEATH; CHILDREN AND MEDIA VIOLENCE; LITERATURE FOR CHILDREN; SUICIDE OVER THE LIFE SPAN: CHILDREN

### *Bibliography*

Balk, David E., and Charles A. Corr. "Adolescents, Developmental Tasks, and Encounters with Death and Bereavement." In *Handbook of Adolescent Death and Bereavement*. New York: Springer, 1996.

Blos, Peter. *The Adolescent Passage: Developmental Issues.* New York: International Universities Press, 1979.

Corr, Charles A. "Using Books to Help Children and Adolescents Cope with Death: Guidelines and Bibliography." In Kenneth J. Doka ed., *Living with Grief: Children, Adolescents, and Loss.* Washington, DC: Hospice Foundation of America, 2000.

Corr, Charles A. "What Do We Know About Grieving Children and Adolescents?" In Kenneth J. Doka ed., *Living with Grief: Children, Adolescents, and Loss.* Washington, DC: Hospice Foundation of America, 2000.

Corr, Charles A. "Children and Questions About Death." In Stephen Strack ed., *Death and the Quest for Meaning: Essays in Honor of Herman Feifel.* Northvale, NJ: Jason Aronson, 1996.

Corr, Charles A. "Children's Understandings of Death: Striving to Understand Death." In Kenneth J. Doka ed., *Children Mourning, Mourning Children.* Washington, DC: Hospice Foundation of America, 1995.

Corr, Charles A. "Children's Literature on Death." In Ann Armstrong-Dailey and Sarah Z. Goltzer eds., *Hospice Care for Children.* New York: Oxford University Press, 1993.

Erikson, Erik H. *Childhood and Society,* 2nd edition. New York: W. W. Norton, 1963.

Erikson, Erik H. *Identity: Youth and Crisis.* London: Faber & Faber, 1968.

Fleming, Stephen J., and Reba Adolph. "Helping Bereaved Adolescents: Needs and Responses." In Charles A. Corr and Joan N. McNeil eds., *Adolescence and Death.* New York: Springer, 1986.

Fox, Sandra S. *Good Grief: Helping Groups of Children When a Friend Dies.* Boston: New England Association for the Education of Young Children, 1988.

Kastenbaum, Robert. "Death and Development Through the Life Span." In Herman Feifel ed., *New Meanings of Death.* New York: McGraw-Hill, 1977.

Kastenbaum, Robert. "The Kingdom Where Nobody Dies." *Saturday Review* 56 (January 1973):33–38.

Kochanek, Kenneth D., Betty L. Smith, and Robert N. Anderson. "Deaths: Preliminary Data for 1999." *National Vital Statistics Reports* 49 (3). Hyattsville, MD: National Center for Health Statistics, 2001.

Metzgar, Margaret M., and Barbara C. Zick. "Building the Foundation: Preparation Before a Trauma." In Charles A. Corr and Donna M. Corr eds., *Handbook of Childhood Death and Bereavement.* New York: Springer, 1996.

Papalia, Diane E., S. W. Olds, and R. D. Feldman. *Human Development,* 8th edition. Boston: McGraw-Hill, 2000.

Papalia, Diane E., S. W. Olds, and R. D. Feldman. *A Child's World: Infancy through Adolescence,* 8th edition. Boston: McGraw-Hill, 1998.

Ross, Eulalie S. "Children's Books Relating to Death: A Discussion." In Earl A. Grollman ed., *Explaining Death to Children.* Boston: Beacon Press, 1967.

Silverman, Phyllis R., and J. William Worden. "Children's Understanding of Funeral Ritual." *Omega: The Journal of Death and Dying* 25 (1992):319–331.

Stevens, Michael M. "Psychological Adaptation of the Dying Child." In Derek Doyle, Geoffrey W. C. Hanks, and Neil MacDonald eds., *Oxford Textbook of Palliative Medicine.* New York: Oxford University Press, 1997.

Wiener, Lori S., Aprille Best, and Philip A. Pizzo comps., *Be a Friend: Children Who Live with HIV Speak.* Morton Grove, IL: Albert Whitman, 1994.

CHARLES A. CORR<br>DONNA M. CORR

# CHILDREN AND ADOLESCENTS' UNDERSTANDING OF DEATH

Parents often feel uneasy and unprepared in responding to their children's curiosity about death. Studies indicate that many parents felt they had not been guided to an understanding of death in their own childhood and as parents either had to improvise responses or rely on the same evasive techniques that had been used on them. It is useful, then, to give attention to the attitudes of adults before looking at the child's own interpretations of death.

## The Innocence of Childhood

Two contrasting developments occurred as a prosperous middle class arose during the Industrial Revolution, which began in the mid-eighteenth century. In the past children had been either economic assets or liabilities depending upon circumstances, but seldom the focus of sentiment. Now both children and childhood were becoming treasured features of the ideal family, itself a rather new idea. By Victorian times (the period of the reign of Britain's Queen Victoria, from 1837 to 1901), the family was viewed as a miniature replica of a virtuous society under the stern but loving auspices of God. Instead of being regarded primarily as subadults with limited functional value, children were to be cherished, even pampered. Frilly curtains, clever toys, and storybooks written especially for young eyes started to make their appearance. The idea of childhood innocence became attractive to families who had reached or were striving for middle-class success and respectability. Fathers and mothers had to meet obligations and cope with stress and loss in the real world, while it was considered that children should be spared all of that. It was believed that children cannot yet understand the temptations and perils of sex or the concept of mortality and loving parents should see to it that their children live in a world of innocence as long as possible.

Furthermore, Sigmund Freud suggested that in protecting their children from awareness of death, then, parents, in a sense, become that child and vicariously enjoy its imagined safety and comfort.

One of history's many cruel ironies was operating at the same time, however. Conditions generated by the Industrial Revolution made life miserable for the many children whose parents were impoverished, alcoholic, absent, or simply unlucky. The chimney sweep was one of the most visible examples. A city such as London had many chimneys that needed regular cleaning. Young boys tried to eke out a living by squeezing through the chimneys to perform this service. Many died of cancer; few reached a healthy adulthood. While mothers or fathers were reading storybooks to beloved children, other children were starving, suffering abuse, and seeing death at close range in the squalid alleys.

Children so exposed to suffering and death did not have the luxury of either real or imagined innocence; indeed, their chances for survival depended on awareness of the risks. Many children throughout the world are still exposed to death by lack of food, shelter, and health care or by violence. Whether or not children should be protected from thoughts of death, it is clear that some have no choice and consequently become keenly aware of mortality in general and their own vulnerability in particular.

## Children's Death-Related Thoughts and Experiences

Encounters with death are not limited to children who are in high-risk situations, nor to those who are emotionally disturbed. It is now well established that most children do have experiences that are related to death either directly or indirectly. Curiosity about death is part of the normal child's interest in learning more about the world. A goldfish that floats so oddly at the surface of the water is fascinating, but also disturbing. The child's inquiring mind wants to know more, but it also recognizes the implied threat: If a pretty little fish can die, then maybe this could happen to somebody else. The child's discovery of death is often accompanied by some level of anxiety but also by the elation of having opened a door to one of nature's secrets.

Child observation and research indicate that concepts of death develop through the interaction between cognitive maturation and personal experiences. Children do not begin with an adult understanding of death, but their active minds try to make sense of death-related phenomena within whatever intellectual capacities they have available to them at a particular time. Adah Maurer, in a 1966 article titled "Maturation of Concepts of Death," suggested that such explorations begin very early indeed. Having experienced frequent alternations between waking and sleeping, some three-year-olds are ready to experiment with these contrasting states:

> In the game of peek-a-boo, he replays in safe circumstances the alternate terror and delight, confirming his sense of self by risking and regaining complete consciousness. A light cloth spread over his face and body will elicit an immediate and forceful reaction. Short, sharp intakes of breath, and vigorous thrashing of arms and legs removes the erstwhile shroud to reveal widely staring eyes that scan the scene with frantic alertness until they lock glances with the smiling mother, whereupon he will wriggle and laugh with joy. . . . his aliveness additionally confirmed by the glad greeting implicit in the eye-to-eye oneness with another human. *(Maurer 1966, p. 36)*

A little later, disappearance-and-reappearance games become great fun. Dropping toys to the floor and having them returned by an obliging parent or sibling can be seen as an exploration of the mysteries of absence and loss. When is something gone for good, and when will it return? The toddler can take such experiments into her own hands—as in dropping a toy into the toilet, flushing, and announcing proudly, "All gone!" Blowing out birthday candles is another of many pleasurable activities that explore the riddle of being and nonbeing.

The evidence for children's exploration of death-related phenomena becomes clearer as language skills and more complex behavior patterns

*This popular image of the Kennedy family taken during John F. Kennedy's funeral shows John Jr. paying tribute to his father with a salute.* AP/WIDE WORLD PHOTOS

develop. Children's play has included death-themed games in many societies throughout the centuries. One of the most common games is tag and its numerous variations. The child who is "It" is licensed to chase and terrorize the others. The touch of "It" claims a victim. In some versions the victim must freeze until rescued by one of those still untouched by "It." The death-related implications are sometimes close to the surface, as in a Sicilian version in which a child plays dead and then springs up to catch one of the "mourners." One of the most elaborate forms was cultivated in the fourteenth century as children had to cope with the horrors of the Black Death, one of the most lethal epidemics in all of human history. "Ring-around-the-rosy . . . All fall down!" was performed as a slow circle dance in which one participant after another would drop to the earth. Far from being innocently oblivious to death, these children had discovered a way of both acknowledging death and making it conform to the rules of their own little game.

There are many confirmed reports of death awareness among young children. A professor of medicine, for example, often took his son for a stroll through a public garden. One day the sixteen-month-old saw the big foot of another passerby come down on a fuzzy caterpillar he had been admiring. The boy toddled over and stared at the crushed caterpillar. "No more!" he said. It would be difficult to improve on this succinct statement as a characterization of death. The anxiety part of his discovery of death soon showed up. He no longer wanted to visit the park and, when coaxed to do so, pointed to the falling leaves and blossoms and those that were soon to drop off. Less than two years into the world himself, he had already made some connections between life and death.

## Developing an Understanding of Death

Young children's understanding of death is sometimes immediate and startlingly on target, as in the fuzzy caterpillar example. This does not necessarily mean, however, that they have achieved a firm and reliable concept. The same child may also expect people to come home from the cemetery when they get hungry or tired of being dead. Children often try out a variety of interpretations as they apply their limited experience to the puzzling phenomena associated with death. Separation and fear of abandonment are usually at the core of their concern. The younger the child, the greater the dependence on others, and the more difficult it is for the child to distinguish between temporary and permanent absences. The young child does not have to possess an adult conception of death in order to feel vulnerable when a loved one is missing. Children are more attuned to the loss of particular people or animal companions than to the general concept of death.

A pioneering study by the Hungarian psychologist Maria Nagy, first published in 1948, found a relationship between age and the comprehension of death. Nagy described three stages (the ages are approximate, as individual differences can be noted):

- Stage 1 (ages three to five): Death is a faded continuation of life. The dead are less alive—similar to being very sleepy. The dead might or might not wake up after a while.

- Stage 2 (ages five to nine): Death is final. The dead stay dead. Some children at this level of mental development pictured death in the form of a person: usually a clown, shadowy death-man, or skeletal figure. There is the possibility of escaping from death if one is clever or lucky.

- Stage 3 (ages nine and thereafter): Death is not only final, but it is also inevitable, universal, and personal. Everybody dies, whether mouse or elephant, stranger or parent. No matter how good or clever or lucky, every boy and girl will eventually die, too.

Later research has confirmed that the child's comprehension of death develops along the general lines described by Nagy. Personifications of death have been noted less frequently, however, and the child's level of maturation has been identified as a better predictor of understanding than chronological age. Furthermore, the influence of life experiences has been given more attention. Children who are afflicted with a life-threatening condition, for example, often show a realistic and insightful understanding of death that might have been thought to be beyond their years.

## The Adolescent Transformation

Children are close observers of the world. Adolescents can do more than that. New vistas open as adolescents apply their enhanced cognitive abilities. In the terminology of influential developmentalist Jean Piaget, adolescents have "formal operations" at their command. They can think abstractly as well as concretely, and imagine circumstances beyond those that meet the eye. This new level of functioning provides many satisfactions: One can criticize the established order, take things apart mentally and put them back together in a different way, or indulge in lavish fantasies. The increased mental range, however, also brings the prospect of death into clearer view. The prospect of personal death becomes salient just when the world of future possibilities is opening up.

Adolescents have more than enough other things to deal with (e.g., developing sexual role identity, claiming adult privileges, achieving peer group acceptance), but they also need to come to terms somehow with their own mortality and the fear generated by this recognition. It is not unusual for the same adolescent to try several strategies that might be logically inconsistent with each other but that nevertheless seem worth the attempt. These strategies include:

Playing at Death: To overcome a feeling of vulnerability and powerlessness, some adolescents engage in risk-taking behavior to enjoy the thrilling relief of survival; dive into horror movies and other expressions of bizarre and violent death; indulge in computerized games whose object is to destroy targeted beings; and/or try to impersonate or take Death's side (e.g., black dress and pasty white face make-up worn by "goths").

Distancing and Transcendence: Some adolescents engross themselves in plans, causes, logical systems, and fantasies that serve the function of reducing their sense of vulnerability to real death within real life. Distancing also includes mentally splitting one's present self from the future self who will have to die. One thereby becomes "temporarily immortal" and invulnerable.

Inhibiting Personal Feelings: It is safer to act as though one were already nearly dead and therefore harmless. Death need not bother with a creature that seems to have so little life.

These are just a few examples of the many strategies by which adolescents and young adults may attempt to come to terms with their mortality. Years later, many of these people will have integrated the prospect of death more smoothly into their lives. Some will have done so by developing more effective defensive strategies to keep thoughts of death out of their everyday lives—until they become parents themselves and have to deal with the curiosity and anxiety of their own children.

*See also:* ANIMAL COMPANIONS; CHILDREN; DEATH SYSTEM; FREUD, SIGMUND

### Bibliography

Anthony, Sylvia. *The Discovery of Death in Childhood and After.* New York: Basic, 1972.

Bluebond-Langner, Myra. *In the Shadow of Illness.* Princeton, NJ: Princeton University Press, 1996.

Deveau, Ellen J., and David W. Adams, eds. *Beyond the Innocence of Childhood.* New York: Baywood, 1995.

Freud, Sigmund. "On Narcissism: An Introduction." In *The Standard Edition of the Complete Psychological Works of Sigmund Freud,* Vol. IV. London: Hogarth Press, 1953.

Maurer, Adah. "Maturation of Concepts of Death." *British Journal of Medicine and Psychology* 39 (1996):35–41.

Nagy, Maria. "The Child's View of Death." In Herman Feifel ed., *The Meaning of Death.* New York: McGraw-Hill, 1959.

Opie, Iona, and Peter Opie. *Children's Games in Street and Playground.* London: Oxford University Press, 1969.

Piaget, Jean. *The Child and Reality: Problems of Genetic Psychology.* New York: Grossman, 1973.

ROBERT KASTENBAUM

# CHILDREN AND MEDIA VIOLENCE

The impact of violent media on children and adolescents has been the subject of debate since the advent of mass media, and has involved a complex interplay of policies, politics, research, commercial interest, and public advocacy. The U.S. Congress and federal agencies, prodded by professional organizations and child advocacy groups, have claimed that violence in the entertainment media negatively affects children and have called for more self-regulation and social responsibility by the media industries. The industries, especially television, have responded by criticizing a number of studies on which the claims were based, disputing findings or their interpretations, and pointing to their First Amendment rights.

While the overall U.S. rate of individual homicide has been fairly consistent over the past decades, the rates of homicidal behavior in school-age children have risen sharply. Gun-related homicide among fifteen- to nineteen-year-olds has tripled since 1980. Several highly publicized murders in schools have alarmed the public and politicians.

Youth violence is a complex problem caused by the interaction of many factors, among them ineffective parenting (including inadequate or inappropriate patterns of communication, domestic violence, poor monitoring), drug use, poverty, racism, peer pressure, peer rejection, and violence in the culture. It is difficult to determine the impact of each of these factors because parents have been considered the most potent and prominent force in children's emotional and social development; the role of the media in this process has been underestimated.

The telecommunications media have become a pervasive feature of American family life and thus a powerful force in the child's socialization and cultural upbringing. As a result, symbolic violence is now recognized as a pressing social issue. The *Fifth Annual Survey of Media in the Home* (2000) shows that nearly all families have a television set and a VCR, and the majority have a computer and video game equipment. More than half of the children in the survey had a television set in their bedrooms. Children spend an average of four and a half hours per day looking at some form of video screen, half of this time being television.

Such extensive exposure underscores the question of the media's power to shape perceptions and attitudes. Death is not a topic parents like to discuss with their children. Because personal encounters with natural death are less frequent in the early twenty-first century than in previous eras, there are fewer counterbalances to media's violent death themes. In younger children, the distinctions between fantasy and reality are less clear, making them more susceptible to misunderstandings of death. Thus, what is at issue is the media's potential to adversely affect children's perceptions of reality. The high level of violence in entertainment media provides a model for understanding death and grief that is a gross distortion of the demographic facts, and a failure to portray adequately at least part of the pain and suffering a death causes surviving family members and friends. For the entertainment industry, whether in action drama or homicide/detective programs, violent death is a tool to drive tension and propel dramatic action. Pain, suffering, and funeral rituals do not contribute to this kind of plot.

**Violence in Television Programming**

Scholars have made extensive studies of both the extent of violence and the contexts in which it occurs. Since the 1967 television season, George Gerbner and his associates have analyzed prime-time programming and children's Saturday morning cartoons by network and number of violent acts per hour and have derived the "violence index" and what Gerbner calls the "cultivation effect."

In 1998 Barbara Wilson and her team sampled the entire television landscape (individual programs throughout the day and evening, including sitcoms, sports, and talk shows). They also performed content analyses of violent portrayals, building on factors identified in previous work by

George Comstock, who proposed that identifying the contexts in which violent acts occur may help to reveal the potential impact of depicted violence on the child viewer. The analysis of violent content is guided by questions such as:

- Is the aggressive behavior on the screen rewarded or punished?
- Is the violence gratuitous or justified? Does it have consequences?
- Does the child identify with the aggressor or the victim?
- Does the child see television violence as realistic?

Two key findings emerged: First, the amount of television violence has been consistently high over the years and has been rising. Nearly two-thirds of the programs contain violence, which is most prominent in action dramas and homicide/detective series. A third of violent programming contains at least nine violent interactions. Nearly one-half of the theatrical films shown on television depict acts of extreme violence (e.g., *The Gladiator* (Fox), *Marked for Death* (CBS), and *The Rookie* (ABC)), some of them containing more than forty scenes of violence.

The amount of violence in prime-time "family-oriented" programs has increased steadily over the years in violation of an agreement reached between network broadcasters and the Federal Communications Commission in the 1970s. Children are frequent viewers of prime-time and other programs designed for adults.

Violent incidents are highest in children's programming, with an average of twenty to twenty-five acts per hour. What mainly distinguishes children's cartoons from adult programs is that animated characters are repeatedly smashed, stabbed, run over, and pushed off high cliffs, but they do not stay dead for long. The portrayal of death as temporary and the characters as indestructible reinforces young viewers' immature understanding of death.

The second key finding is that the contexts in which most violence is presented also poses risks for the child viewers. Most violent incidents involve acts of aggression rather than threats: Perpetrators are frequently portrayed as attractive characters and heroes rather than as villains; perpetrators and victims are predominantly male; most violence is committed for personal gain or out of anger; and most violent acts do not have consequences—that is, they portray little or no pain and suffering by victims or survivors. In nearly three-fourths of the violent scenes, there is no punishment of the aggressor, no remorse or condemnation; some acts are even rewarded. In children's cartoons, humor is a predominant contextual feature.

There is a striking contrast in the depiction of death in the entertainment media: In prime-time action drama death is often glamorized, and in children's cartoons it is trivialized; depictions in both types of programs are a misrepresentation of real life and death.

## Effects on Children

Most studies are based on social learning theory, pioneered by psychologist Albert Bandura, particularly the principle of observational learning called "modeling." Models can be physical, involving real people, or symbolic, involving verbal, audio, or visual representations, or combinations of these. Modeling is recognized as one of the most powerful means of transmitting values, attitudes, and patterns of thought and behavior. According to modeling theory, television violence has negative effects on children, particularly when the perpetrators are attractive characters and are not punished, and when there is little pain and suffering by the victims.

Two distinct methodological approaches, correlational and experimental, have been employed. Correlational studies seek to determine whether exposure to television violence is indeed related to young viewers' behavior and attitudes and also tries to measure the strength of such relationships. However, a correlation between the two variables does not establish a cause-effect relationship. Violence in the media may lead a child viewer to aggressive behavior, but also an aggressive child may like to watch violent media.

The experimental method involves the manipulation of filmed or televised aggression shown to children. Most experimental studies are carried out in the laboratory. Children are randomly assigned to an experimental group that is shown aggressive videos and to a control group that is shown nonviolent programming, and then children are observed on the playground or in similar social settings to find out whether there are differences in the behavior between the two groups. The strength of experimental studies lies in their ability to attribute direct causality. Experimental studies can also be longitudinal, carried out in natural contexts or "the field." A widely known field experiment reported by Leslie Joy, Ann Kimball, and Merle Zabrack in 1986 involved children in three rural Canadian communities before and after the introduction of television in towns receiving either the government-owned channel (CBC), U.S. networks, or a combination. Children were studied in first and second grades and re-evaluated two years later.

The extensive research literature was reviewed in 1972 by the Surgeon General's Advisory Commission, in 1982 by the National Institute of Mental Health, and in 1993 by the American Psychological Association's Commission on Violence and Youth. Their reports and those of more recent investigations are consistent across time, methods, child populations, and funding sources. Key findings show the following:

1. There is a causal link between the viewing of televised violence and the subsequent aggressive behavior and attitudes in children who are frequent viewers of violent episodes, ranging from preschool to late adolescence. These children are more likely to model their behavior after aggressors in the programs than those who watch infrequently, particularly when the aggressors are depicted as attractive and get away without punishment, and when there is no apparent pain and suffering on the part of the victims. Children who have few positive role models in their lives are more vulnerable than those who do.

2. Aggressive behavior and attitudes are learned at young ages and can result in life-long violence unless there are interventions.

3. Violent behavior is a preventable problem. There is a wide availability of broad-based programs. Reduction in media violence and access to media violence are a component of these programs.

4. Frequent viewing of television violence leads to the belief that such violence is an accurate portrayal of real life, resulting in an exaggerated fear of violence from others. Fear stemming from watching scary media may be immediate and short-term but can also be enduring.

5. Prolonged viewing of filmed and televised violence can lead to emotional desensitization toward actual violence. Because young viewers tend to identify with the perpetrator and violent episodes seldom depict pain and suffering, there is a blunting of viewers' empathy for the victims and a reduced willingness and readiness to help.

Considering the finite amount of time in a child's day, frequent exposure to violent media content affects children's behaviors, attitudes, and perceptions while depriving them of opportunities for viewing equivalent amounts of prosocial behaviors as viable solutions to interpersonal problems.

## Government Policies to Benefit Child Viewers

Major policy battles over programming for children date back to the Communications Act of 1934 and to policies adopted in 1974 and 1990. Health professionals and private advocacy groups led the U.S. Congress to enact the Telecommunications Act of 1996, which mandates that parental guidelines and procedures be established by the industries for rating upcoming video programming; that parents be provided technological tools that allow them to block violent content ("V-chip"); and that regularly scheduled programming designed for children be developed. To gain license renewal, every broadcast station in the country is required to air a minimum of three hours per week of children's programming—this is known as the "three-hour rule."

Studies evaluating industry compliance with the Telecommunications Act show the following:

1. The broadcasting, cable, and program production industries have developed a rating system for children's and general programming, the "TV Parental Guidelines." It was found to be adequate for general classification but lacking in specific content categories that would guide parents. In addition, the "TV Parental Guidelines" are inadequately publicized.

2. V-chips have been installed in new televisions since 2000.

3. Commercial broadcasters appear to be complying with the three-hour rule. However, a fourth of the programs were found to be of questionable educational value, with most of them clustered around Saturday and weekday mornings; less than a tenth were during after-school hours and none during prime time, when children are most likely to watch television.

4. Children's programs sampled in this study contained less violence than those aired in the past.

## Feature Films, Home Videos, and Electronic Games

Experts agree the violence level found in feature films exceeds that on television. For years violent films have been among the top box-office draws in movie theaters across the country. Although the film industry rates films by age groups, local movie theaters often fail to adequately check ticket buyers' ages. Community standards for what is an acceptable level of violence have changed over the years. Many parents are more lenient or less concerned about possible negative influences. Parents can also be observed taking their preadolescent children and even young children to see feature films deemed unsuitable for children by the film industry's own ratings system. Home videos remain largely unrated. Studies have shown that parents are only slightly concerned that their children seek out extremely violent home videos.

Public health and advocacy groups are alarmed at the extent of violence in video games (among them Mortal Kombat, Lethal Enforcers, and Ground Zero Texas). Interactive media may have an even greater impact on children than the more passive media forms. According to a 2000 Federal Trade Commission Report, "Marketing Violent Entertainment to Children," the graphics in video games are approaching motion-picture quality, making them more realistic and exciting. Many parents are unfamiliar with the content of the video games that their children play in arcades or purchase and play at home.

## Television News

Television news has become a major source of information for children as well as adults; most children rank it as a more reliable source than teachers, parents, and peers. There is news coverage throughout the day and evening, with frequent repetitions and "breaking news." Because of the

*Sixty percent of the audience for interactive games, like this video hockey game, are children. The electronic gaming industry has voluntarily begun to rate its products, although rating labels and advisories are widely ignored by distributors and retailers.* CORBIS

capability for instant communication across the globe, an enormous number of events are potentially "newsworthy." Because most news programs are owned by the major conglomerates in the entertainment industry, an attendant blurring of news and entertainment values exists.

The major networks and cable companies are highly competitive. In all news programs there is a bias toward over-reporting dramatic events. Improved technologies for visual reconstruction or recreation of events make the portrayals more graphic. Depictions of violent actions and events are not balanced with representations of others that are positive and constructive. The merging of news and entertainment (e.g., the "docu-drama") may blur the distinction between fantasy and reality. Learning to distinguish between fantasy and reality is an important developmental task for the young child.

Media coverage of violent behavior in children seems particularly high, causing fears and alarm and unwittingly contributing to distorted perceptions in parents, children, and the public about the rates and incidence of youthful homicidal behaviors. Extensive attention to such behavior in the news tends to lead other young people to copy such acts.

**Suggestions for Parents**

While most scientists conclude that children learn aggressive attitudes and behavior from violent media content, they also agree that parents can be a powerful force in moderating, mediating, and reducing such influence.

*Talking about real deaths.* Parents can help their children deal with death as a natural and normal process by permitting them to share their thoughts and fears about death, answering questions honestly, and allowing children to participate in the care of ill and dying family members, in funerals and memorial services, and during the grieving process.

*Being informed.* Parents need to know the major risk factors associated with media violence. They should become familiar with the programs and video games that their children favor and with existing parental guidelines, ratings, and advisories. The Federal Communications Commission (FCC) publishes the "TV Parental Guidelines" on its web site at www.fcc.gov/vchip/#guidelines. Information on activating and programming the V-chip is available through the V-Chip Education web site at www.vchipeducation.org/pages/using.html. The National Institute on Media and the Family, an independent nonprofit organization, has developed a universal rating system that applies to video games, TV programs, and films, and can be found at www.mediaandthefamily.com.

*Setting limits.* A 2001 study by Thomas Robinson and colleagues shows that reducing children's television and video game use reduces aggressive behavior. The V-chip can be used to block out content that parents deem potentially harmful. In family discussion, parents may set up rules for extent, times, and types of media interaction by children.

*Mediation and intervention.* Mediation and intervention may be the most effective antidotes to media violence. Parents who watch television with their children can discern their children's preferences and level of understanding. This coparticipation provides an opportunity for parents to counteract violent messages in drama programs by pointing to their fictional nature. Watching the news with children enables parents to provide perspective and comfort, convey their values, and encourage their children to watch programs that demonstrate prosocial behavior. Family oriented activities away from the mass media can provide a healthy alternative to the violence-saturated airwaves and video games that increasingly dominate the consciousness of the youth of the United States.

*See also:* CHILDREN; GRIEF: FAMILY; HOMICIDE, EPIDEMIOLOGY OF; LITERATURE FOR CHILDREN

## *Bibliography*

American Psychological Association Commission on Violence and Youth. *Violence & Youth: Psychology's Response.* Washington, DC: American Psychological Association, 1993.

Bandura, Albert. *Social Foundations of Thought and Action: A Social Cognitive Theory.* Englewood Cliffs, NJ: Prentice-Hall, 1986.

Cantor, Joanne. "Ratings and Advisories for Television Programming, 3rd Year." *National Television Violence Study.* Thousand Oaks, CA: Sage Publications, 1998.

Cantor, Joanne, Kristen Harrison, and Amy Nathanson. "Ratings and Advisories for Television Programming, 2nd Year." *National Television Violence Study.* Thousand Oaks, CA: Sage Publications, 1998.

Comstock, George, and Hagj Paik. *Television and the American Child.* New York: Academic Press, 1991.

Donnerstein, Edward, Ronald Slaby, and Leonard Eron. "The Mass Media and Youth Violence." In John Murray, Eli Rubinstein, and George Comstock eds., *Violence and Youth: Psychology's Response,* Vol. 2. Washington, DC: American Psychological Association, 1994.

Gerbner, George, Larry Gross, Michael Morgan, and Nancy Signorielli. "Living with Television: The Dynamics of the Cultivation Process." In Bryant Jennings and Dolf Zillmann eds., *Perspectives on Media Effects.* Hillsdale, NJ: Lawrence Erlbaum, 1986.

Gerbner, George, Larry Gross, Michael Morgan, and Nancy Signorielli. "The 'Mainstreaming' of American Violence." *Journal of Communication* 30 (1980):10–29.

Grollman, Earl A. *Talking About Death: A Dialogue between Parent and Child,* 3rd edition. Boston: Beacon Press, 1990.

Harrison, Karin, and Joanne Cantor. "Tales from the Screen: Enduring Fright Reactions to Scary Media." *Media Psychology* 1, no. 2 (1999):97–116.

Joy, Leslie Anne, M. Kimball, and Merle L. Zabrack. "Television Exposure and Children's Aggressive Behavior." In Tannis M. Williams ed., *The Impact of Television: A Natural Experiment Involving Three Communities.* New York: Academic Press, 1986.

Kubey, R. W., and R. Larson. "The Use and Experience of the Video Media among Children and Young Adolescents." *Communication Research* 17 (1990):107–130.

Nathanson, Amy J., and Joanne Cantor. "Children's Fright Reactions to Television News." *Journal of Communication* 46, no. 4 (1996):139–152.

National Institute of Mental Health. *Television and Behavior: Ten Years of Scientific Progress and Implications for the Eighties,* Vol. 2: *Technical Reviews,* edited by

David Pearl, Lorraine Bouthilet, and Joyce Lazar. Rockville, MD: Department of Health and Human Services, 1982.

Surgeon General's Scientific Advisory Committee. *Television and Growing Up: The Impact of Televised Violence.* Washington, DC: U.S. Government Printing Office, 1972.

Wass, Hannelore. "Appetite for Destruction: Children and Violent Death in Popular Culture." In David W. Adams and Eleanor J. Deveau eds., *Beyond the Innocence of Childhood: Factors Influencing Children and Adolescents' Perceptions and Attitudes Toward Death.* Amityville, NY: Baywood, 1995.

Wass, Hannelore, and Charles A. Corr. *Helping Children Cope with Death: Guidelines and Resources,* 2nd edition. New York: Hemisphere Publishing, 1985.

Wilson, Barbara J., et al. "Violence in Television Programming Overall: University of California, Santa Barbara Study" In *National Television Violence Study.* Thousand Oaks, CA: Sage Publications, 1998.

Woodard, Emory H., and Natalia Gridina. *Media in the Home: The Fifth Annual Survey of Parents and Children.* Philadelphia: The Annenberg Public Policy Center of University of Pennsylvania, 2000.

*Internet Resources*

Federal Communications Commission. "TV Parental Guidelines." In the Federal Communications Commission [web site]. Available from www.fcc.gov/vchip/#guidelines.

Federal Trade Commission. "Marketing Violent Entertainment to Children: A Review of Self-Regulation and Industry Practices in the Motion Picture, Music Recording & Electronic Game Industries." In the Federal Trade Commission [web site]. Available from www.ftc.gov/opa/2000/09/youthviol.htm.

HANNELORE WASS

# CHILDREN AND THEIR RIGHTS IN LIFE AND DEATH SITUATIONS

In 2003 approximately 55,000 children and teenagers in the United States will die. Accidents and homicide cause the most deaths, and chronic illnesses such as cancer, heart disease, and congenital abnormalities are the next greatest cause. The loss of a child or adolescent is life-altering for the family, friends, community members, and health care providers, regardless of the cause of death. Most children and adolescents who have a terminal illness are capable of expressing their preferences about how they will die. These preferences have not always been solicited or honored by the adults involved in their care.

## Defining the End of Life in Pediatrics

The term *end-of-life care* for children and adolescents has a more global meaning than the commonly used terms *terminal care, hospice care,* and *palliative care.* Rather than defining a specific time period, "end-of-life care" denotes a transition in the primary goal of care from "curative" (in cases of disease) or "life sustaining" (in cases of trauma) to symptom management (the minimization or prevention of suffering) and on psychological and spiritual support for the dying child or adolescent and for the family. To provide this kind of care to fatally ill children and adolescents and to their family members, health care providers must focus on the individual patient's values and preferences in light of the family's values and preferences. *Hospice care* is considered to be end-of-life care, but it usually includes the expectation that the child's life will end in six months or less. *Palliative care* is defined variously among health care providers. Some characterize it as "a focus on symptom control and quality of life throughout a life-threatening illness, from diagnosis to cure or death." Others define it as "management of the symptoms of patients whose disease is active and far advanced and for whom cure is no longer an option." This entry uses the term *end-of-life care* in its broader sense.

## Historical Evolution of End-of-Life Care for Children and Adolescents

Today, as in the past, the values and preferences of children who are less than eighteen years of age have little or no legal standing in health care decision making. Some professionals doubt that children have the ability to adequately understand their health conditions and treatment options and therefore consider children to be legally incompetent to make such decisions. Instead, parents or guardians are designated to make treatment choices in the best interests of the minor child and to give consent for the child's medical treatment.

Since the 1980s clinicians and researchers have begun to challenge the assumption that children and adolescents cannot understand their serious medical conditions and their treatment options. Clinical anecdotes and case studies indicate that children as young as five years of age who have been chronically and seriously ill have a more mature understanding of illness and dying than their healthy peers. Still other case reports convey the ability of children and adolescents to make an informed choice between treatment options.

Researchers have documented children's preference to be informed about and involved in decisions regarding treatment, including decisions about their end-of-life care. Although there have been only a few studies about ill children's preferences for involvement in treatment decision making, a growing number of professional associations have published care guidelines and policy statements urging that parents and their children be included in such decision making. In fact, several Canadian provinces have approved legislative rulings supporting the involvement of adolescents in medical decision making. The American Academy of Pediatrics recommends that children be included in clinical decision making "to the extent of their capacity." At the federal level, the National Commission for Protection of Human Subjects of Biomedical and Behavioral Research identified the age of seven years as a reasonable minimum age at which assent of some type should be sought from a child for participation in a research protocol. According to the commission's findings, a child or adolescent at the end of life, as at other times, should be informed about the purpose of the research and given the option of dissent. In such cases, researchers should approach a child or adolescent about a study while the child is still able to give assent or to decline to participate. If this is not possible, a proxy (parent or guardian) must decide in the child's best interest.

Although parents or guardians generally retain the legal right to make final care decisions for their children, it is respectful of a child's dignity to engage the child in discussions about his or her wishes and goals. In one study, parents who were interviewed after the death of their child described finding comfort in the fact that they had made end-of-life treatment decisions that their child had preferred or that they felt certain their child would have preferred. In sum, children and adolescents

nearing the end of life benefit from age-appropriate explanations of their disease, treatment options, and prognosis, and from having their preferences about their care respected as much as possible.

## Talking about Dying with Children or Adolescents

One of the most difficult aspects of caring for seriously ill children or adolescents is acknowledging that survival is no longer possible. The family looks to health care providers for information about the likelihood of their child's survival. When it is medically clear that a child or adolescent will not survive, decisions must be made about what information to share with the parents or guardians and how and when to share that information. Typically, a team of professionals is involved in the child's care. Before approaching the family, members of the team first discuss the child's situation and reach a consensus about the certainty of the child's death. The team members then agree upon the words that will be used to explain this situation to the parents and the child, so that the same words can be used by all members of the team in their interactions with the family. Careful documentation in the child's medical record of team members' discussions with the patient and family, including the specific terms used, is important to ensure that all team members are equally well informed so that their care interactions with the child and family are consistent. Regrettably, a study by Devictor and colleagues of decision-making in French pediatric intensive care units reported in 2001 that although a specific team meeting had been convened in 80 percent of the 264 consecutive children's deaths to discuss whether to forgo life-sustaining treatment, the meeting and the decision had been documented in only 16 percent of the cases in the patient's medical record.

The greatest impediment to decision making at the end of life is the lingering uncertainty about the inevitability of a child's death. Such uncertainty, if it continues, does not allow time for a coordinated, thoughtful approach to helping the parents and, when possible, the child to prepare for the child's dying and death. Depending on the circumstances, such preparation may have to be done quickly or may be done gradually. The child's medical status, the parent's level of awareness, and the clinician's certainty of the child's prognosis are all factors in how much time will be available to prepare for the

**FIGURE 1**

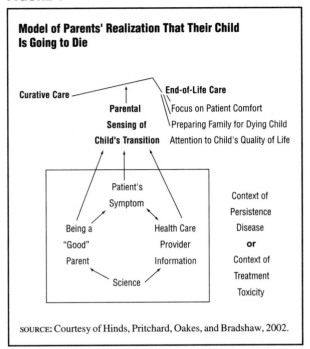

**Model of Parents' Realization That Their Child Is Going to Die**

Curative Care

End-of-Life Care
Focus on Patient Comfort
Preparing Family for Dying Child
Attention to Child's Quality of Life

Parental
Sensing of
Child's Transition

Patient's
Symptom

Context of
Persistence
Disease
**or**
Context of
Treatment
Toxicity

Being a
"Good"
Parent

Health Care
Provider
Information

Science

SOURCE: Courtesy of Hinds, Pritchard, Oakes, and Bradshaw, 2002.

child's dying. Figure 1 is a model that depicts the factors that influence efforts to prepare family members and the child who is dying of cancer. The factors that help parents to "sense" that their child is going to die include visible symptoms, such as physical changes and information obtained from trusted health care professionals. Parents are assisted in making end-of-life decisions for their child when they believe that they and the health care team have done all that is possible to save the child and that everything has been done well. Throughout the transition from curative care to end-of-life care, the partnership among patients, family members, and health care professionals must be continually facilitated to ensure that end-of-life care is optimal.

Although there is little research-based information about end-of-life decision making and family preparation, evidence-based guidelines for decision making are available. While some studies and clinical reports support the inclusion of adolescents in end-of-life discussions and decisions, there are no studies that examine the role of the younger child. Clinical reports do, however, support the idea that younger children are very much aware of their impending deaths, whether or not they are directly included in conversations about their prognosis and care.

Health care professionals uphold that continuous communication be maintained between the parents and the health care team about the status of the dying child. Parents may react to their child's terminal status in various ways, including denial. If parents appear to be in denial, it is important to ensure that they have been clearly told of their child's prognosis. In 2000 the researcher Joanne Wolfe and colleagues reported that some parents whose child had died of cancer realized after the death that they had perceived that their child was going to die significantly later than the health care team had known. Parents and other family members often vacillate between different emotional responses and seek opportunities to discuss and rediscuss their child's situation with the health care team.

Parents will often want to know when their child will die and exactly what will occur. Although it is difficult to predict when a child will die, useful information can be given about symptoms the child is likely to experience, such as breathing changes, decreasing appetite, and decreasing energy. Most importantly, parents will need to be assured that their child will be kept comfortable and that members of the health care team will be readily available to the child and the family.

Siblings may exhibit a variety of responses to the impending death of a brother or sister. These responses will be influenced by the sibling's age and developmental maturity, the length of time the dying child has been ill, and the extent to which the sibling has been involved in the patient's care. Siblings need to be told that it is not their fault that the brother or sister is dying. Siblings have indicated their need to be with the dying sibling and, if possible, to be involved in the sibling's daily care; if these are not possible, they need at least to be informed regularly about the status of their dying sibling.

**Keeping the Dying Child Comfortable: Symptom Management Strategies**

Children who have experienced suffering may fear pain, suffocation, or other symptoms even more than death itself. Anticipating and responding to these fears and preventing suffering is the core of end-of-life care. Families need assurance that their child will be kept as comfortable as possible, and clinicians need to feel empowered to provide care that is both competent and compassionate. As the illness progresses, treatment designed to minimize suffering should be given as intensively as curative treatments. If they are not, parents, clinicians, and other caregivers will long be haunted by memories of a difficult death.

The process of dying varies among children with chronic illness. Some children have relatively symptom-free periods, then experience acute exacerbation of symptoms and a gradual decline in activity and alertness. Other children remain fully alert until the final hours. Research specific to children dying of various illnesses has shown that most patients suffer "a lot" or "a great deal" from at least one symptom, such as pain, dyspnea, nausea, or fatigue, in their last month of life.

Although end-of-life care focuses on minimizing the patient's suffering rather than on prolonging life, certain supportive measures (such as red blood cell and platelet transfusions and nutritional support) are often continued longer in children than in adults with terminal illnesses. The hope, even the expectation, is that this support will improve the child's quality of life by preventing or minimizing adverse events such as bleeding. Careful discussion with the family is important to ensure that they understand that such interventions will at some point probably no longer be the best options. Discussions about the child's and family's definition of well-being, a "good" death, their religious and cultural beliefs, and their acceptance of the dying process help to clarify their preferences for or against specific palliative interventions. For example, one family may choose to continue blood product support to control their child's shortness of breath, whereas others may opt against this intervention to avoid causing the child the additional discomfort from trips to the clinic or hospital. Health care professionals should honor each family's choices about their child's care.

It is crucial that health care professionals fully appreciate the complexities of parental involvement in decisions about when to stop life-prolonging treatment. Parental involvement can sometimes result in the pursuit of aggressive treatment until death is imminent. In such cases, it becomes even more important that symptom management be central in the planning and delivery of the child's care. Conventional pharmacological and nonpharmacological methods of symptom control, or more invasive measures such as radiation for bone pain or thoracentesis for dyspnea, can improve the child's comfort and thus improve the child's and family's quality of life. As the focus of care shifts from that of cure to comfort, the child's team of caregivers should be aware of the family's and, when possible, the child's wishes regarding the extent of interventions.

Not all symptoms can be completely eliminated; suffering, however, can always be reduced. Suffering is most effectively reduced when parents and clinicians work together to identify and treat the child's symptoms and are in agreement about the goals of these efforts. Consultation by experts in palliative care and symptom management early in the course of the child's treatment is likely to increase the effectiveness of symptom control.

Accurate assessment of symptoms is crucial. Health care professionals suggest that caretakers ask the child directly, "What bothers you the most?" to assure that treatment directly addresses the child's needs. Successful management of a symptom may be confusing to the child and his parents, especially if the symptom disappears. It is important that they understand that although the suffering has been eliminated, the tumor or the illness has not.

Although it is not always research-based, valuable information is available about the pharmacological management of symptoms of the dying child. A general principle is to administer appropriate medications by the least invasive route; often, pharmacological interventions can be combined with practical cognitive, behavioral, physical, and supportive therapies.

*Pain.* A dying child can experience severe pain; vigilant monitoring of the child's condition and regular assessment of pain intensity is essential. When the child is able to describe the intensity of pain, the child's self-report is the preferred indicator. When a child is unable to indicate the intensity of the pain, someone who is very familiar with the child's behavior must be relied upon to estimate the pain. Observational scales, such as the FLACC, may be useful in determining the intensity of a child's pain (see Table 1).

Children in pain can find relief from orally administered analgesics given on a fixed schedule. Sustained-release (long-acting) medications can provide extended relief in some situations and can

**TABLE 1**

| FLACC Scale | | | |
|---|---|---|---|
| **Category** | **Scoring** | | |
| | **0** | **1** | **2** |
| Face | No particular expression or smile | Occasional grimace or frown, withdrawn, disinterested | Frequent to constant quivering chin, clenched jaw |
| Legs | Normal position or relaxed | Uneasy, restless, tense | Kicking or legs drawn up |
| Activity | Lying quietly, normal position, moves easily | Squirming, shifting back and forth, tense | Arched, rigid, or jerking |
| Crying | No crying (awake or asleep) | Moans or whimpers, occasional complaint | Crying steadily, screams or sobs, frequent complaints |
| Consolability | Content, relaxed | Reassured by occasional touching, hugging, or being talked to, distractible | Difficult to console or comfort |

Each of the five categories (F) Face; (L) Legs; (A) Activity; (C) Crying; (C) Consolability is scored from 0–2, resulting in a total score range of 0 to 10.
SOURCE Merkel, 1997.

be more convenient for patients and their families. Because the dose increments of commercially available analgesics are based on the needs of adults and long-acting medications cannot be subdivided, the smaller dose increments needed for children may constrain use of sustained-release formulations (see Table 2, which offers guidelines for determining initial dosages for children). The initial dosages for opioids are based on initial dosages for adults not previously treated with opioids. The appropriate dosage is the dosage that effectively relieves the pain. One review completed by Collins and colleagues in 1995 reported that terminally ill children required a range of 3.8 to 518 mg/kg/hr of morphine or its equivalent.

The appropriate treatment for pain depends on the type and source of the pain. Continuous clinical judgment is needed, especially when potentially interacting medications are given concurrently. If morphine is contraindicated or if the patient experiences unacceptable side effects, clinicians can use a conversion table (see Table 3) to calculate the equivalent dose of a different opioid. Approximately 50 to 75 percent of the morphine-equivalent dose should be used initially. It is usually not necessary to start at 100 percent of the equianalgesic dose to achieve adequate pain control. Constipation, sedation, and pruritus can occur as side effects of opioids. Table 2 lists medications

that can prevent or relieve these symptoms. The fear of addiction is a significant barrier to effective pain control, even in dying children. Family and patient fears should be actively addressed by the health care team.

*Dyspnea and excess secretions.* As the child's death approaches, respiratory symptoms may be distressing for both the child and the family. Anemia, generalized weakness, or tumor compression of the airways will further exacerbate respiratory symptoms. Air hunger is the extreme form of dyspnea, in which patients perceive that they cannot control their breathlessness. When a child becomes air hungry, the family may panic. Dyspnea must be treated as aggressively as pain, often with opioids. Although some medical practitioners believe that opioids should not be used to control air hunger at the end of life because they fear the opioids may cause respiratory depression, other medical professionals believe this is untrue and that the optimal dose of opioid is the dose that effectively relieves the dyspnea.

The management of dyspnea is the same in children and adults: positioning in an upright position, using a fan to circulate air, performing gentle oral-pharyngeal suctioning as needed, and supplementary oxygen for comfort. The child may have copious, thin, or thick secretions. Pharmacological options for managing respiratory symptoms are

**TABLE 2**

## Pharmacological approach to symptoms at the end-of-life of children

| Symptom | Medication | Route: Starting dose/schedule | Additional comments |
|---|---|---|---|
| Mild to moderate generalized pain | Acetaminophen (Tylenol) | PO: 10 to 15 mg/kg q 4 hrs<br>PR: 20 to 25 mg/kg q 4 hrs | Maximum 75 mg/kg/day or 4000 mg/day; limited anti-inflammatory effect |
| | Ibuprofin (Motrin) | PO: 5 to 10 mg/kg q 6 to 8 hrs | Maximum 40 mg/kg/dose or 3200 mg/day; may cause renal, gastrointestinal toxicity; interferes with platelet function |
| | Choline Mg Trisalicylate (Trilisate) | PO: 10 to 15 mg/kg q 8 to 12 hrs | Maximum 60 mg/kg/day or 3000 mg/day; may cause renal, gastrointestinal toxicity; less inhibition of platelet function than other NSAIDs |
| | Ketoralac (Toradol) | IV: 0.5 mg/kg q 6 hrs | Limit use to 48 to 72 hours |
| Mild to severe pain | Oxycodone | PO: initial dose of 0.1 to 0.2 mg/kg q 3 to 4 hrs (no maximum dose) | Available in a long-acting formulations (oxycontin) |
| | Morphine (for other opioids see conversion chart; usual dosages are converted to dose already established with the morphine) | All doses as initial doses (no maximum dose with triation)<br>PO/SL: 0.15 to 0.3 mg/kg q 2 to 4 hrs<br>IV/SC intermittent: 0.05 to 0.1 mg/kg q 2 to 4 hrs<br>IV continuous: *initial bolus* of 0.05 mg/kg *followed by an infusion* of 0.01 to 0.04 mg/kg/hr<br>IV PCA: 0.02 mg/kg with boluses of 0.02 mg/kg q 15 to 20 min. Titrate to desired effect | PO: available in several long-acting formulations (Oramorph; MS Contin) For severe acute pain, IV: 0.05 mg/kg boluses every 5 to 10 minutes until pain is controlled. Once controlled, begin continuous infusion and bolus as indicated on the left. |
| | Gabapentin (Neurontin) for neuropathic pain | PO: 5 mg/kg or 100 mg BID | Takes 3–5 days for effect; increase dose gradually to 3600 mg/day |
| | Amitriptyline (Elavil) for neuropathic pain | PO: 0.2 mg/kg/night | Takes 3–5 days for effect; increase by doubling dose every 3 to 5 days to a maximum of 1 mg/kg/dose; use with caution with cardiac conduction disorders |
| Bone pain | Prednisone | PO: 0.5 to 2 mg/kg/day for children > 1 year, 5 mg/day | Avoid during systemic or serious infection |
| Dyspnea | Morphine | PO: 0.1 to 0.3 mg/kg q 4 hrs<br>IV intermittent: 0.1 mg/kg q 2 to 4 hrs | |
| For secretions contributing to distress | Glycopyrrolate (Robinul) | PO: 40 to 100 mg/kg 3 to 4 times/day<br>IV: 4 to 10 mg/kg every 3 to 4 hrs | |
| Nausea | Promethazine (Phenergan) | IV or PO: 0.25 to 0.5 mg/kg q 4 to 6 hours | Maximum 25 mg/dose; may have extrapyramidal side effects |
| | Odansetron (Zofran) | IV: 0.15 mg/kg q 4 hrs<br>PO: 0.2 mg/kg q 4 hrs | Maximum 8 mg/dose |
| *If caused by increased intracranial pressure* | Lorazepam (Ativan) | PO/IV: 0.03 to 0.2 mg/kg q 4 to 6 hrs | IV: Titrate to a maximum 2 mg/dose |
| *If caused by anorexia* | Dexamethasone | IV/PO: 1 to 2 mg/kg initially; then 1 to 1.5 mg/kg/day divided q 6 hrs | Maximum dose of 16 mg/day |
| *If caused by reflux* | Metoclopramide (Reglan) | IV: 1 to 2 mg/kg q 2 to 4 hrs | Maximum 50 mg/dose; may cause paradoxical response; may have extrapyramidal side effects |
| Anxiety or seizures | Lorazepam (Ativan) | PO/IV: 0.03 to 0.2 mg/kg q 4 to 6 hrs | IV: Titrate to a maximum 2 mg/dose |
| | Midazolam (Versed) | IV/SC: 0.025 to 0.05 mg/kg q 2 to 4 hrs<br>PO: 0.5 to 0.75 mg/kg<br>PR: 0.3 to 1 mg/kg | Titrate to a maximum of 20 mg |
| Anxiety or seizures | Diazepam (Valium) | IV: 0.02 to 0.1 mg/kg q 6 to 8 hrs with maximum administration rate of 5 mg/kg<br>PR: use IV solution 0.2 mg/kg | Maximum dose of 10 mg |
| | Phenobarbital (for seizures) | For status epilepticus, IV: 10 to 20 mg/kg until seizure is resolved | Maintenance treatment IV/PO: 3 to 5 mg/kg/day q 12 hrs |
| | Phenytoin (Dilantin) for seizures | IV: 15 to 20 mg/kg as loading dose (maximum rate of 1 to 3 mg/kg/min or 25 mg/min | Maintenance treatment IV/PO: 5 to 10 mg/kg/day |

[CONTINUED]

**TABLE 2** [CONTINUED]

### Pharmacological approach to symptoms at the end-of-life of children [CONTINUED]

| Symptom | Medication | Route: Starting dose/schedule | Additional comments |
|---|---|---|---|
| For sedation related to opioids | Methylphenidate (Ritalin) | PO: 0.1 to 0.2 mg/kg in morning and early afternoon | Maximum dose of 0.5 mg/kg/day |
| | Dextroamphetamine | PO: 0.1 to 0.2 mg/kg in morning and early afternoon | Maximum dose of 0.5 mg/kg/day |
| **Pruritus** | Diphenhydramine (Benedryl) | PO/IV: 0.5 to 1 mg/kg q 6 hrs | Maximum dose of 50 mg/dose |
| Constipation | Senna (Senekot) | PO: 10 to 20 mg/kg/dose or 1 tablet BID | |
| | Bisacodyl | PO: 6–12 years, 1 table q day<br>> 12 years, 2 tablets q day | |
| | Docusate | PO divided into 4 doses:<br>< 3 years, 10–40 mg<br>3–6 years, 20–60 mg<br>6–12 years, 40–120 mg<br>> 12 years, 50–300 mg | Stool softener, not a laxative |
| | Pericolace | 1 capsule BID | Will help prevent opioid-related constipation if given for every 30 mg of oral morphine per 12-hour period |

PO = by mouth; SL = sublingual; PR = per rectum; IV = intravenous route; SC = subcutaneous route; PCA = patient controlled analgesia pump; q = every; NSAIDs = non-steroidal anti-inflammatory drugs

SOURCE: Adapted from McGrath, Patricia A., 1998; St. Jude Children's Research Hospital, 2001; Weisman, Steven J., 1998; World Health Organization, 1998; Yaster, M., E. Krane, R. Kaplan, C. Cote, and D. Lappe, 1997.

also outlined in Table 2. Anxiolytic agents are often needed to relieve the significant anxiety that can accompany dyspnea.

*Nausea.* Multiple effective options are available for the management of nausea and vomiting in dying children. Unrelieved nausea can make other symptoms worse, such as pain and anxiety (see Table 2).

*Anxiety and seizures.* Restlessness, agitation, and sleep disturbances may be caused by hypoxia and metabolic abnormalities related to renal and hepatic impairment. A supportive environment may be the most effective strategy to counter these symptoms. Cautious use of anxiolytics may also be helpful (see Table 2). Although dying children rarely have seizures, they are upsetting for the child and his caregivers. Strategies to manage seizures are listed in Table 2.

*Fatigue.* Dying children commonly experience fatigue, which can result from illness, anemia, or inadequate calorie intake. Fatigue may be lessened if care activities are grouped and completed during the same time period. The use of blood products to reduce fatigue should be carefully considered by the family and health care team.

**TABLE 3**

### Conversion of morphine dosage to dosage for non-morphine opioids

| Drug | Equianalgesic dose | |
|---|---|---|
| | IM/IV | PO |
| Morphine (mg) | 10 | 30 |
| Hydromorphone (mg) | 1.5 | 7.5 |
| Fentanyl (mg) | 0.1–0.2 | Not available |
| Oxycodone (mg) | Not available | 15–30 |

SOURCE: Adapted from Weisman, 1998; Yaster, 1997.

### Choosing a Hospice

Ensuring the availability of appropriate home care services for children who are dying has become more challenging in this era of managed care, with its decreasing length of hospital stays, declining reimbursement, and restricted provider networks. Health care providers and parents can call Hospice Link at 1-800-331-1620 to locate the nearest hospice. Callers should ask specific questions in order to choose the best agency to use for a child; for example, "Does your agency . . ."

- Have a state license? Is your agency certified or accredited?

- Take care of children? What percentage of patients are less than twelve years of age? From twelve to eighteen years?

- Have certified pediatric hospice nurses?

- Have a staff person on call twenty-four hours a day who is familiar with caring for dying children and their families?

- Require competency assessments of staff for caring for a child with _____ (specific disease of the child); certain health care equipment, etc.?

- Require a Do Not Resuscitate (DNR) order?

- Provide state-of-the art symptom management geared to children? Please describe.

- Not provide certain interventions such as parenteral nutrition or platelet transfusions?

- Commit to providing regular feedback from the referring agency/provider to promote continuity of care?

## Visiting the Web

The increasing number of web sites related to end-of-life care for children makes additional information available to both health care providers and families. Visiting a web site that describes a model hospice may be useful in selecting one that is within the family's geographic location (www. canuckplace.com/about/mission.html). Information about hospice standards of care can be found at www.hospicenet.org/ and www.americanhospice. org/ahfdb.htm (those associated with American Hospice Foundation).

*See also:* CHILDREN; CHILDREN AND ADOLESCENTS' UNDERSTANDING OF DEATH; CHILDREN, CARING FOR WHEN LIFE-THREATENED OR DYING; END-OF-LIFE ISSUES; INFORMED CONSENT

## *Bibliography*

American Academy of Pediatrics. Committee on Bioethics. "Guidelines on Foregoing Life-Sustaining Medical Treatment." *Pediatrics* 93, no. 3 (1994):532–536.

American Academy of Pediatrics. Committee on Bioethics. "Informed Consent, Parental Permission, and Assent in Pediatric Practice (RE9510)." *Pediatrics* 95, no. 2 (1995):314–317.

American Nurses Association, Task Force on the Nurse's Role in End-of-Life Decisions. *Compendium of Position Statements on the Nurse's Role in End-of-Life Decisions.* Washington, DC: Author, 1991.

Angst, D.B., and Janet A. Deatrick. "Involvement in Health Care Decision: Parents and Children with Chronic Illness." *Journal of Family Nursing* 2, no. 2 (1996): 174–194.

Awong, Linda. "Ethical Dilemmas: When an Adolescent Wants to Forgo Therapy." *American Journal of Nursing* 98, no. 7 (1998):67–68.

Buchanan, Allen, and Dan Brock. *Deciding for Others: The Ethics of Surrogate Decision Making.* Cambridge: Cambridge University Press, 1989.

Children's International Project on Palliative/Hospice Services (CHIPPS). *Compendium of Pediatric Palliative Care.* National Hospice and Palliative Care Organization, 2000.

Collins John J., Holcomb E. Grier, Hannah C. Kinney, and C. B. Berde. "Control of Severe Pain in Children with Terminal Malignancy." *Journal of Pediatrics* 126, no. 4 (1995):653–657.

Devictor, Denis, Duc Tinh Nguyen, and the Groupe Francophone de Reanimation et d'Urgences Pediatriques. "Forgoing Life-Sustaining Treatments: How the Decision Is Made in French Pediatric Intensive Care Units." *Critical Care Medicine* 29 no. 7 (2001):1356–1359.

Fraeger, G. "Palliative Care and Terminal Care of Children." *Child and Adolescent Psychiatric Clinics of North America* 6, no. 4 (1997):889–908.

Goldman, Ann. "Life Threatening Illness and Symptom Control in Children." In D. Doyle, G. Hanks, and N. MacDonald eds., *Oxford Textbook of Palliative Medicine,* 2nd edition. Oxford: Oxford University Press, 1998.

Goldman, Ann, and R. Burne. "Symptom Management." In Anne Goldman ed., *Care of the Dying Child.* Oxford: Oxford University Press, 1994.

Hanks, Geoffry, Derek Doyle, and Neil MacDonald. "Introduction." *Oxford Textbook of Palliative Medicine,* 2nd edition. New York: Oxford University Press, 1998.

Hinds, Pamela S., and J. Martin. "Hopefulness and the Self-Sustaining Process in Adolescents with Cancer." *Nursing Research* 37, no. 6 (1988):336–340.

Hinds, Pamela S., Linda Oakes, and Wayne Furman. "End-of-Life Decision-Making in Pediatric Oncology." In B. Ferrell and N. Coyle eds., *Oxford Textbook of Palliative Nursing Care.* New York: Oxford University Press, 2001.

James, Linda S., and Barbra Johnson. "The Needs of Pediatric Oncology Patients During the Palliative Care Phase." *Journal of Pediatric Oncology Nursing* 14, no. 2 (1997):83–95.

Kluge, Eike Henner. "Informed Consent By Children: The New Reality." *Canadian Medical Association Journal* 152, no. 9 (1995):1495–1497.

Levetown, Marcia. "Treatment of Symptoms Other Than Pain in Pediatric Palliative Care." In Russell Portenoy and Ednorda Bruera eds., *Topics in Palliative Care,* Vol. 3. New York: Oxford University Press, 1998.

Lewis Catherine, et al. "Patient, Parent, and Physician Perspectives on Pediatric Oncology Rounds." *Journal of Pediatrics* 112, no. 3 (1988):378–384.

Lindquist Ruth Ann, et al. "Determining AACN's Research Priorities for the 90's." *American Journal of Critical Care* 2 (1993):110–117.

Martinson, Idu M. "Caring for the Dying Child." *Nursing Clinics of North America* 14, no. 3 (1979):467–474.

McCabe, Mary A., et al. "Implications of the Patient Self-Determination Act: Guidelines for Involving Adolescents in Medical Decision-Making." *Journal of Adolescent Health* 19, no. 5 (1996):319–324.

McGrath, Patricia A. "Pain Control." In D. Doyle, G. Hanks, and N. MacDonald eds., *Oxford Textbook of Palliative Medicine,* 2nd edition. Oxford: Oxford University Press, 1998.

Merkel, Sandra, et al. "The FLACC: A Behavioral Scale for Scoring Postoperative Pain in Young Children." *Pediatric Nursing* 23, no. 3 (1997):293–297.

Nitschke, Ruprecht, et al. "Therapeutic Choices Made By Patients with End-Stage Cancer." *Journal of Pediatrics* 10, no. 3 (1982):471–476.

Ross, Lainie Friedman. "Health Care Decision Making by Children: Is It in Their Best Interest?" *Hastings Center Report* 27, no. 6 (1997):41–45.

Rushton, Cynthia, and M. Lynch. "Dealing with Advance Directives for Critically Ill Adolescents." *Critical Care Nurse* 12 (1992):31–37.

Sahler, Olle Jane, et al. "Medical Education about End-of-Life Care in the Pediatric Setting: Principles, Challenges, and Opportunities." *Pediatrics* 105, no. 3 (2000):575–584.

St. Jude Children's Research Hospital. *Guidelines for Pharmacological Pain Management.2001.*

Sumner, Lizabeth. "Pediatric Care: The Hospice Perspective." In B. Ferrell and N. Coyle eds., *Textbook of Palliative Nursing.* New York: Oxford University Press, 2001.

Vachon, Mary. "The Nurse's Role: The World of Palliative Care." In B. Ferrell and N. Coyle eds., *Textbook of Palliative Nursing.* New York: Oxford University Press, 2001.

Weir, Robert F., and C. Peters. "Affirming the Decision Adolescents Make about Life And Death." *Hastings Center Report* 27, no. 6 (1997):29–40.

Weisman, Steven. "Supportive Care in Children with Cancer." In A. Berger, R. Portenoy, and D. Weismann eds., *Principles and Practice of Supportive Oncology.* Philadelphia, PA: Lippincott-Raven, 1998.

Wolfe, Joanne, et al. "Symptoms and Suffering at the End of Life in Children with Cancer." *New England Journal of Medicine* 342, no. 5 (2000):326–333.

Wong, Donna, et al. *Whaley and Wong's Nursing Care of Infants and Children,* 6th edition. St. Louis, MO: Mosby, 1999.

World Health Organization. *Cancer Pain Relief and Palliative Care in Children.* Geneva: Author, 1998.

Yaster, Myron, et al. *Pediatric Pain Management and Sedation Handbook.* St. Louis, MO: Mosby, 1997.

*Internet Resources*

American Academy of Pediatrics. Committee on Bioethics and Committee on Hospital Care. "Policy Statement: Palliative Care for Children." In the American Academy of Pediatrics [web site]. Available from www.aap.org/policy/re0007.html.

PAMELA S. HINDS
GLENNA BRADSHAW
LINDA L. OAKES
MICHELE PRITCHARD

# CHILDREN, CARING FOR WHEN LIFE-THREATENED OR DYING

A child's terminal illness and/or death is an almost unspeakable and fortunately rare tragedy in the developed world; the death of a child is considered an affront to the natural order in these societies because parents are not supposed to outlive their children. However, the death of a child is a far more common experience in developing nations. The experience is colored by these relative frequencies. In nations with seemingly limitless resources for cure, the tragedy of a child's illness and death is often unwittingly compounded by well-meaning members of the family, the medical establishment, and the community, through lack of acknowledgement of the child's suffering; continued application of harmful and unhelpful therapies; and a lack of effective response to the human issues the child and family endure as they struggle to maintain dignity and normalcy. The repercussions of this approach are felt long after the death of the child. Increased knowledge of the circumstances of childhood death and helpful responses may prevent these problems and improve the quality of life for all concerned.

**Who Are the Children Who Die?**

Patterns of childhood death vary substantially among nations, related primarily to the level of education of the masses, availability of resources, and other public health issues. In developing countries, children often die in the first five years of life from diarrheal illnesses and pneumonia (the most common and most preventable causes, each accounting for 3 million childhood deaths worldwide per year) and other infectious diseases. AIDS (acquired immunodeficiency syndrome) is becoming epidemic in many countries, particularly in sub-Saharan Africa. Every day, 6,000 young people under age twenty-four are infected with HIV. Every day, 2,000 infants contract HIV through mother-to-child transmission. Every day, more than 6,000 children under age five are left orphans by AIDS. And every day, 1,600 children die of AIDS. Across the globe, children under eighteen make up approximately 10 percent of the 40 million people who are living with HIV. Prevention and treatment of AIDS and its related complications is very expensive, and few African nations can provide their citizens with the required therapies. Thus AIDS is a more rapidly fatal disease in these countries; figures from the World Health Organization indicate that globally, during the year 2001, 2.7 million children under the age of fifteen were living with HIV/AIDS, 800,000 children were newly infected, and 580,000 children died of the disease; of these, the vast majority are in sub-Saharan Africa.

In countries with access to greater education and resources, far fewer children die; those who do die during childhood die of a vastly different spectrum of causes. In the first year of life (infancy), these include congenital defects and malformations, extreme prematurity (birth prior to twenty-eight weeks gestation), and sudden infant death syndrome (SIDS). In the United States 27,000 infants die annually. Similar causes and rates of death are seen in the United Kingdom and Canada. The remainder of childhood deaths, occurring from age one to nineteen years, includes trauma as the leading cause (motor vehicle occupant, driver and pedestrian injuries, drowning, murder, suicide, and other trauma), cancer, and death related to congenital heart disease. Other less frequent causes of childhood death include cystic fibrosis, muscular dystrophy, and rare genetic disorders leading to severe brain dysfunction or other end-organ failure, such as liver, kidney, and immune system failures.

The causes of death in children clearly differ substantially from adults. The rarity of childhood death hides it from view and from the collective consciousness of the public, thus depriving the common citizen and the health care professional alike of a feeling of competence in responding to such a situation, whether the affected child is one's patient, son or daughter, friend, or neighbor. Lack of experience with childhood terminal illness in particular and the promise of modern medical "miracles" in highly developed nations sometimes prevents the acknowledgment of the terminal state, with parents and health care personnel often insisting on trying one last "life-prolonging" or "curative" intervention, often when chances of improving or prolonging life are relatively small. The losers in this situation are often the patients as well as the guilt-ridden family, particularly as the latter reflect on their decisions after the child's death.

Siblings, similarly, need support during the child's illness, during the terminal phase, and after the death. Siblings often feel responsible in some way for the ill child's fate, lonely and not loved by absorbed and exhausted parents, and guilty for wishing the child would die (especially when the death occurs). Children (and adults) engage in magical thinking: "If I didn't get mad and wish he would go away and leave mom and dad to me, he would not be sick." For this reason, it is important for caregivers to ask siblings (and the sick child) why they think the illness came about and then to help them understand the real reason in an effort to allay their fears and guilt about being the causative agent. The community can respond to the siblings' needs by listening to them, allowing them to be angry, committing to spending time with them in the parents' absence, spelling the

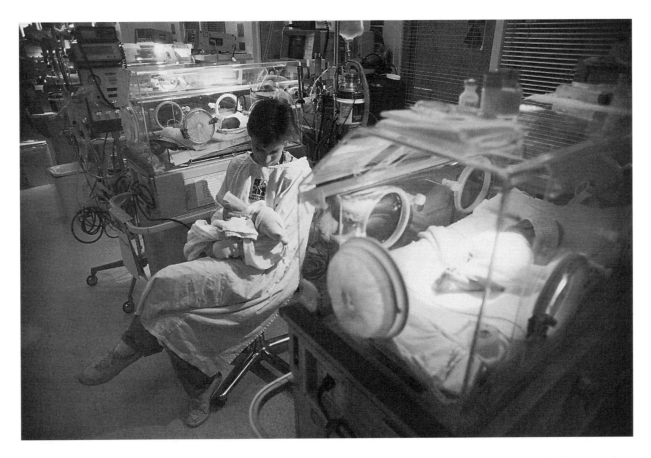

*The neonatal intensive care unit in hospitals, certainly a foreign and technical environment to non-medical personnel such as parents, is one that many parents have to visit when their child's life is in danger. Unfortunately in less-developed nations, parents whose infant children die do not have the opportunity or funds to invest in this type of technological care.* CORBIS (BELLEVUE)

parents from the ill child's bedside to enable the parents to spend time with the sibling, and offering to do simple things, such as running errands to expand parents' free time.

Families are particularly isolated in the case of traumatic death of their child, as there are no systematic provisions for bereavement care of such families and the grief is felt throughout the community, forcing society to recognize that death is unpredictable and that all children are vulnerable. This realization is difficult for members of the community, and creates barriers to support.

When a child dies from a traumatic injury, there is no preparation for the death, no feeling that the child is "in a better place," no longer having to suffer the ravages of illness. Instead, a young, healthy life has been cut short, with no redeeming features of the loss. However, when the possibility of organ donation is offered, many families feel that something good has come of their

pain. Nevertheless, sudden death, whether from trauma or SIDS, seems the most difficult for bereaved parents to mourn and to effectively reconstruct a new life without the child.

## Medical Caregiver Expertise in Caring for the Incurable

Medical care providers, trained to focus on cure as the only positive outcome, often feel at a loss as to how to be helpful when it is determined that the child will in fact die. With no education regarding symptom relief or how to address psychological and spiritual distress, the medical caregiver may retreat from the care of the patient in order not to be reminded of his or her inability to "do something." Training in medical school, once focused on providing comfort, has devolved to a technically oriented, fact-filled curriculum, often with little to no emphasis on enduring and unchanging issues of human interaction or on inevitable death.

Virtually no curricular time is devoted to the management of symptoms, outside of the symptom relief achieved by the reversal of the pathophysiologic process. This problem is exacerbated in pediatrics and pediatric subspecialty training, as death is considered to be so rare as to not merit allocation of educational time.

Bereavement care, critical to the well-being of survivors of childhood death, is virtually never addressed. It is of interest that veterinarian trainees are taught to send condolence cards, but the idea is never mentioned in the medical curriculum. In fact, the *New England Journal of Medicine* published an article in 2001 that was an impassioned plea regarding how and why to write condolence letters. Bereaved parents, when interviewed about what would help alleviate the pain of the loss of a child, recurrently stated that evidence that people care about and remember their child, including sending a note using the child's name or a simple phone call, meant more than most people imagine. Ignorance about the tremendous healing provided by communication and contact with bereaved families prevents health care personnel—including physicians, nurses, social workers, and members of the larger community—from providing such healing. In response, health care personnel, not used to this feeling of impotence, may leave practice or become hardened to the needs of the child and family, becoming brusque and seemingly uncaring. When medical education addresses the full spectrum of medical care, including care for those who will not be cured, many of these problems will be resolved.

## Research in Pediatric Palliative Care

Palliative care is "control of pain, of other symptoms, and of psychological, spiritual and other problems. . . . The goal of palliative care is achievement of the best quality of life for patients and their families. Many aspects of palliative care are applicable earlier in the course of illness. . . ." The research base in adult palliative care, though not the accumulated experience, is scant. Research that has been conducted in pediatric patients who are chronically and terminally ill is even less voluminous. There are four reasons for this lack of available research:

1. Few children have terminal conditions; many more children die of trauma.

2. Of the remainder, few die of the same disorder; for example, cancer, which is itself very heterogeneous, claims 1,200 children's lives per year in the United States and is the most common disease diagnosis among children who die. Thus, it is difficult to obtain an effective research sample size.

3. Because of the small numbers affected, allocation of research dollars has not been generous, compared to other causes.

4. Ethicists are concerned about whether it is possible to get non-coerced consent from children and their families when the child may also be dependent on the same care providers for maintenance of life and comfort. (However, researchers and institutional review boards curiously do not seem to have the same degree of concern about allowing parents and children to consent to research protocols directed at finding new cures, even when there is no hope that the individual patient will benefit.)

Without research, provision of pediatric palliative care will continue to vary from institution to institution. It will be based only on the expertise of the local practitioners and their own uncontrolled experience with relatively few patients, compared to research studies. Therapies offered will not be proven to be efficacious, but rather be therapies that have worked in one or a few other patients. Academics and the medical community feel that such anecdotally based care is not worthy of teaching to trainees, as it is unproven and not scientific. Thus, the vicious cycle of ignorance of how to care for such children and families is perpetuated. In the absence of research and education, children and their parents will continue to suffer unnecessarily.

For example, the provision of effective pain management for children terminally ill with cancer is not taught. A study by Wolf at the Boston Children's Hospital of the Harvard Medical School, found in a retrospective survey of parents of 103 children who had died of cancer, that only 80 percent of children, most of had pain severe enough to cause substantial suffering, were assessed as having pain at all. Moreover, while there was an attempt to treat the pain in 80 percent of these cases, treatment was effective in relieving the pain in only 30 percent.

Research specific to children, not research performed on adults, is essential. Children of different age groups have different physiology from each other and from adults. Infants and younger children differ physiologically from older children in many ways, such as with regard to enzyme maturity, organ function, percentage of body water, and neural processing. In addition, infants and children differ dramatically according to age and maturity in their perceptions of their situations, the ability to employ self-calming techniques, the success of external sources of comfort, the degree of the spiritual impact of illness, and other "psychosocial" ramifications of their conditions. Thus, extrapolation from adult literature and data is insufficient. It is critical that research on palliative care specific to children be conducted—for both the ethical care of these children and the effective reintegration of their survivors. Moreover, once the information is documented scientifically, academic medical centers are more likely to include the information in their curricula, tremendously broadening the impact of the research on the care of children living with life-threatening conditions. In fact, both the Royal College of Pediatrics and Child Health in the United Kingdom and the American Academy of Pediatrics have called for increased research in palliative care for children, in addition to exhorting increased education on the topic during pediatric and subspecialty training.

## Programs for Pediatric Palliative Care

At its best, palliative care for children addresses the child, parents, siblings, extended family, schoolmates, and other affected members of the community. It addresses the physical, social, spiritual, and emotional aspects of death and dying. In order to accomplish such goals, a team—consisting of the family, community, hospital, and hospice personnel—delivers palliative care. Principal team members include the child, family, physicians (primary care and specialist), nurse, care manager, social worker, and chaplain. Other critical team members include pediatric psychologists and child life therapists, both of whom address the concerns of the child and siblings in a developmentally appropriate manner. These professionals often use art therapy—art, play, music, and behavioral observation—to treat the child. Because children may be unwilling to divulge information directly to parents or their main caregivers due to their fear of

hurting them or offending them, these skilled therapists are available to assist with the communication and interpretation of the child's concerns and desires, as well as to provide the child with advice and an open invitation to reveal innermost thoughts. When child life therapists or child psychologists are involved in the care team, children's views of their situation and their priorities are more likely to be solicited and honored. However, the role of these therapists is neither understood nor reimbursed by payers, primarily because their participation is seen as being "not medically necessary," and thus their availability is often tragically limited. In 2000 the American Academy of Pediatrics validated the role of the child life therapist in providing the child with the opportunity to participate meaningfully in his or her care decisions.

Pediatric palliative care is in the early developmental stages. The United Kingdom has the most highly developed system, with two specialist physicians and a nurse training program, as well as twelve hospices devoted to children in England, one in Scotland, one in Wales, and one in Australia. Helen House, founded by Sister Frances Dominica in 1982, was the first of such houses. Hospice in England was initially funded purely through private donations. The houses were designed to care for children from the time of diagnosis of a life-threatening condition. Their function is to provide respite care (care when the child is in his or her usual state of health, providing family caregivers with a needed rest and time to rejuvenate themselves for their continued efforts), to provide or train community based pediatric specialist nurses, to provide case coordination, and to provide a twenty-four-hour hotline for symptom distress. Children may also come to the hospice for their final days. Children cared for in these hospices often have chronic, progressive, or severe, static neurological dysfunction. Research on palliative care for children is infrequently reported by these busy clinical services. In addition, there are two pediatric palliative care physician members of interdisciplinary palliative care teams based in academic hospitals. Their primary focus has been the child dying of cancer, although the programs are expanding to include children with other diagnoses.

In the United States, the term *hospice* denotes a package of services only available to patients who have been determined by their physicians to have less than six months' life expectancy and who have chosen (or, in the case of children, whose parents have chosen) to forgo further life-prolonging therapies. The package is determined by the federal government (with other payers in general mimicking this program) and mandates standards of care, including that the care is overseen by a physician; that visits occur every other week at a minimum, and more often as needed, by nurses and social workers; and that pastoral counselors, home health aides, and volunteers are also part of the team. There is no requirement for caregivers to have pediatric experience or education. Care is delivered primarily in the child's home and respite appropriate to the needs of children and their families is infrequently available. Bereavement care for the family is mandated for thirteen months after the death, but with no additional reimbursement provided to the hospice; thus, some programs provide written information on a monthly basis, while others may provide personal counseling and support groups. Rarely is there a sibling-specific program for bereavement; their needs generally go unmet. It has been found that the shorter the patient's hospice stay the longer the bereavement needs of the survivors; children tend to be very short stay hospice patients.

The U.S. hospice benefit is paid as an all-inclusive daily rate of reimbursement. All professional time, medications, equipment rental, therapy, and other care are included in this rate. In 2001 the average daily rate was $107 per day. This rate of reimbursement may preclude the administration of symptom-relieving interventions, including, for instance, the administration of blood products that increase the child's energy enough to play and interact with others, decrease breathlessness, and thus improve the ability to sleep and eat, or decrease bleeding problems. These are frequent concerns in childhood cancers, which primarily affect the bone marrow.

Arriving at a prognosis of less than six months for a child is fraught with difficulty due to societal expectations as well as the rare and thus unpredictable nature of some pediatric fatal disorders. Choosing to forgo "life-prolonging therapies" can be difficult for other reasons, as well. Some children have been ill all their lives; differentiating daily therapeutic routines that bring comfort from consistency versus life-prolonging care may be impossible for the family, practically and psychologically. To address these problems, large hospices have

obtained expensive home health licensure to enable the care of children not willing to accept the restrictions of hospice, but who need palliative care in addition to the traditional life-prolonging care model. This marriage of hospice and "traditional" care is called "palliative care" in the United States. It is care that is rarely available for adults or children. However, hopeful changes have been occurring since the early 1990s. Forerunners in this area include Drs. Kathleen Foley and Joanne Lynn, with funding from the Open Society Institute and the Robert Wood Johnson Foundation.

Due to these and other efforts, palliative care for adults and children is slowly beginning to emerge. In 1999, at the urging of pediatric palliative care experts, the federal government of the United States allocated a small amount of funds to investigate new models of care for children living with life-threatening conditions and their families through five state Medicaid waivers. The Institute of Medicine, a branch of the National Academy of Sciences, a nonprofit, non-governmental body of expert scientists and consultants, is reviewing the evidence regarding the benefits and costs of pediatric palliative care. Numerous curricula on pediatric palliative care and texts devoted to the subject have been published or are under development, including the *Compendium of Pediatric Palliative Care,* distributed to various nations in 2000 by the U.S.-based National Hospice and Palliative Care Organization.

In London; Sydney, Australia; and Boston, Massachusetts, three major children's hospitals have pediatric palliative care services with physician directors. These services began from care for children with cancer and are expanding to include children with other life-threatening disorders. One innovative program at the University of Texas in Galveston addresses the needs not only of the chronically ill or cancer patient but also the victims of sudden death. Called the Butterfly Program, the program consists of home-based hospice and palliative care, hospital-based palliative care consultation, and a room (called the Butterfly Room) devoted to the care of children living with or dying from life-threatening conditions, including children who are the victims of trauma.

Although it has many uses, the Butterfly Room, located one floor above the pediatric critical care unit and on the same floor as the cancer and chronic care wards, most benefits families whose children die suddenly. There is space for over fifty people to be present. The room has numerous rocking chairs, a living room area, a kitchenette, and a sitting alcove, in addition to sofa beds, a full bath, and the equipment to care for a child receiving any kind of life support. When children are transferred to the room, the agreement has been made to remove life-support systems that same day. Prior to transfer, all monitors are removed, all investigations and interventions that do not promote comfort are discontinued, and all equipment that is unnecessary for comfort is also removed. Families are invited to bring other family members, friends, neighbors, or any other supporters with them. The reasons for the family and care team's decision to stop attempts to prolong life are reviewed. Questions are entertained. Explanations of the events of the day are provided and questions again answered. Any rituals are encouraged, including bathing the child, dressing him or her in personal clothing, singing, chanting, crying, praying, and taking photographs and videos of the events. Handprints and or hand molds are made, if desired. When everyone is prepared to let go, the parents are asked whom they wish to be present at the time of the removal of the life-support machines and who should be holding the child. Prayers may be offered as well as the comforting idea of seeing the child's face once more without tape and tubes. Hospice personnel provide bereavement assistance for as long as the family needs attention and care. The program has successfully been transferred to other sites at university hospitals in San Antonio, Texas (where it is called the Mariposa Room), and Kansas City, Missouri (where it is called the Delta Room). Another is being developed in Greenville, North Carolina. However, reimbursement for this highly valued care is nonexistent.

## Acknowledging Death

Although the best outcome for children is a long and healthy life, that end result is not always possible. When a child is not responding to therapies, it is time to entertain the possibility that he or she may die and to increase the emphasis on the importance of quality of life considerations and the child's priorities (when developmentally appropriate) in making treatment decisions. Medical care, for all its promise, is still filled with pain, other adverse treatment-related symptoms, isolation, fear, self-doubt, and loss of freedom to be a child, to enjoy playing and exploring one's world. When the child is still well enough to enjoy the opportunity to participate in life, that time is too often spent pursuing an elusive "cure." When the focus should be on the optimization of symptom control and attainment of personal goals or being in a familiar and comfortable place, too often the time is spent in the clinic, hospital bed, or intensive care unit. Parents need "permission" from the medical community, family, and friends to stop pursuing life-prolonging therapies; often they are afraid of offending their physicians, being accused of not loving their children, or being neglectful or selfish. Unfortunately, children's own ideas and preferences about their care are not routinely solicited and, if offered, are ignored, which frequently increases their sense of unimportance and isolation.

## Grief, Guilt, and Bereavement

Not only are the children victims of the societal mandate to "keep trying," but so are other members of the family, who are deprived of opportunities to share new adventures and insights or to invest in new forms of hope, rather than in the all-consuming quest for cure. Parents suffer in all cases of chronic illness and of death of their children; unable to protect their children, they are rendered powerless and helpless, too often feeling guilty for things beyond their control. Parents often ask themselves: "What if I had noticed the lump sooner?" "What did I do to cause this?" "Why couldn't it have been me?" Well-intended family and friends who do not know how to respond may inadvertently compound the problem by avoiding contact in order "not to remind the family" of their loss, isolating them at the time they most need companionship. Employers may not understand the demands of a sick child or the duration and toll of parental bereavement and may exhort the parents to "get on with their lives."

The ill child him- or herself often feels guilty; children are able to feel the tension and are aware of the fact that they are in the center of it. The ill child is also aware that he or she is ill and even that he or she is dying, even if the child is never told. In fact, the ill-advised admonition (and natural tendency) to "hide" the status of the child's illness from the child was reversed when Bluebond-Langner's research in the 1970s (*The Private Worlds of Dying Children*) indicated that children (with cancer) who were terminally ill were aware of the fact, often before their physicians and parents were aware of it. When adults and others denied how ill they were, the children felt abandoned. Current advice of informed professionals is to involve children in the own care, clarify their questions, and answer them simply and honestly, remaining open to additional queries and disclosures of fears and concerns. Adults can help by allowing the child to see his or her sorrow, share how to respond, and offer mutual strength.

## Creating Effective Responses to Childhood Death

Difficulties in caring for terminally ill children include: (1) the lack of a definition of the relevant population; (2) societal, family and medical practitioner unwillingness to acknowledge the terminal nature of certain conditions; (3) lack of research-based knowledge to enable effective treatment specific to the population; (4) lack of existing personnel with appropriate child-specific expertise; and (5) poor access to resources and systems to care for such children and their bereaved survivors. Regardless of the wealth and advancement of nations, care of terminally ill children remains challenging.

Despite these challenges, pediatric palliative care of the twenty-first century is improving. Needed changes to the delivery of care for children living with and dying from life-threatening conditions are beginning to emerge. There is a desperate need for the community, educators, researchers, and legislators to acknowledge these children and their families. Simple compassion is a good start, both for laypeople and health care professionals. Scientific investigation, intensive education, and changes in the regulation and reimbursement of health care will lead society to the realization of the potential for effective care for children who die and their families.

### Bibliography

American Academy of Pediatrics Committee on Bioethics. "Informed Consent, Parental Permission and Assent in Pediatric Practice." *Pediatrics* 95 (1995):314–317.

American Academy of Pediatrics Committee on Bioethics and Committee on Hospital Care. "Palliative Care for Children." *Pediatrics* 106, no. 2 (2000):351–357.

American Academy of Pediatrics Committee on Hospital Care. "Child Life Services." *Pediatrics* 106 (2000):1156–1159.

Bedell, S. E., K. Cadenhead, and T. B. Graboys. "The Doctor's Letter of Condolence." *New England Journal of Medicine* 344 (2001):1162–1164.

Bluebond-Langner, M. *The Private Worlds of Dying Children*. Princeton, NJ: Princeton University Press, 1978.

Grant, James P. *The State of the World's Children*. Oxfordshire: Oxford University Press, 1995.

Joint Working Party of the Association for Children with Life-Threatening or Terminal Conditions and Their Families and the Royal College of Paediatrics and Child Health. *A Guide to the Development of Children's Palliative Care Services*. Bristol, Eng.: Author, 1997.

Piot, Peter. "Speech to the United Nations General Assembly Special Session on Children." In the UNAIDS [web site]. Available from www.unaids.org/whatsnew/speeches/eng/2002/PiotUNGASSchildren_1005.html.

Wolfe J., H. E. Grier, N. Klar, S. B. Levin, and J. M. Ellenbogen. "Symptoms and Suffering at the End of Life in Children with Cancer." *New England Journal of Medicine* 342 (2000):326–333.

World Health Organization. *Cancer Pain Relief and Palliative Care*. Report No. 804. Geneva: Author, 1990.

MARCIA LEVETOWN

# CHILDREN, MURDER OF

On October 25, 1994, Susan Smith, a South Carolina wife and mother, drowned her two-year-old and fourteen-month-old sons. Marilyn Lemak, a forty-one-year-old registered nurse drugged and then suffocated her three young children (ages three to seven) in her home in Naperville, Illinois, on March 5, 1999. Slightly more than one month later, on April 20, 1999, seventeen-year-old Dylan Klebold and eighteen-year-old Eric Harris entered Columbine High School in Littleton, Colorado, killed twelve fellow students and a teacher, and then killed themselves. Although modern sensibilities are shocked and saddened by tragic cases such as these, as children are not supposed to die, both sanctioned and unsanctioned murders have occurred throughout human history.

Murder is the killing of one person by another person with "malice aforethought" (e.g., an aim to cause death or do bodily harm). The term *malice*, or *malicious intent,* is used in relation to a murderous act, even if the perpetrator did not mean to hurt anyone. An assault (an attempt to harm some-one without killing them) can be murder if death is a foreseeable possibility. Criminal justice experts James Alan Fox and Jack Levin state, "A parent, distraught over a crying colicky baby, who shakes the infant to silence her, and does it so vigorously as to cause death can . . . be charged with murder, so long as the parent is aware that this rough form of treatment can be detrimental" (2001, p. 2).

## Historical and Cross-Cultural Overview

Historically and cross-culturally, the murder of children has taken many forms. Anthropological studies of traditional societies, such as the Yanomamo of South America, and sociological studies of some advanced civilizations indicate the practice of infanticide (the killing of children under the age of five), past and present. Female infanticide has been discovered among some traditional patriarchal groups such as the Chinese. Often the murder of children has been noted for humanitarian reasons, such as because of overpopulation or an inadequate food supply. Similarly, poor and low-income families have killed their children when they have been unable to support them. Some societies have promoted the killing of children born with birth defects, mental challenges, or a serious disease or disorder. In certain societies, children who were believed to be tainted by evil (e.g., twins) were slain at birth. Among the ancient Greeks and Romans, a father could dispose of his child as he saw fit.

Although there have been several accounts of the ritual killing of children, especially sacrifice for religious purposes, according to folklorist Francis James Child, many are without foundation. One story tells of the murder and crucifixion of a little boy named Hugh in the thirteenth century by Jews. English folk ballads such as "The Cruel Mother" and "Lamkin" tell of the sadistic murder of children. "Mary Hamilton" relates the story of feticide (the act of killing a fetus, which has been proven beyond a reasonable doubt to be capable of, at the time of death, surviving outside of the mother's womb with or without life support equipment) in sixteenth-century England.

Throughout the Christian world, the main source of information concerning the importance of children is biblical teachings found in the Old and New Testaments. For example, Psalm 127

notes that children are a gift, a reward from God. Mark 10 states that the Kingdom of God belongs to children, and "whoever does not receive the Kingdom of God like a child shall not enter it at all." While biblical scriptures emphasize the importance of children, there is a multiplicity of passages that reflect the murder of children. God sanctions the killing of all Egyptian first-born children in the last plague before the exodus, in an attempt to free the Hebrews from Egyptian control. King Herod has male children in Bethlehem two years of age and under murdered. The Book of Deuteronomy states that the parents of rebellious children are to have them stoned to death.

The United States has experienced hundreds of child murders since the first settlers landed at Jamestown, Virginia, in 1607. One of the earliest examples of the murder of children in America occurred on Friday, August 10, 1810, at Ywahoo Falls in southeast Kentucky. White racists, desiring to drive the Cherokee from their land, decided that the best way to get rid of the Indian problem was to kill all the children so there would be no future generations. The Indians, learning that "Indian fighters" were gathering in eastern Kentucky to carry out their barbaric act, gathered the women and children together at Ywahoo Falls and prepared to march them to a Presbyterian Indian school near present-day Chattanooga, Tennessee. Over a hundred Cherokee women and children were slaughtered before they could make the trip (Troxell, 2000).

Numerous child murders gained notoriety in the first thirty years of the twentieth century. In fact, Nathan Leopold and Richard Loeb committed what some have termed the "crime of the century" when they murdered fourteen-year-old Bobbie Franks on May 21, 1924, in Chicago, Illinois. Albert Fish, the oldest man ever executed in the electric chair at Sing Sing Prison, was killed on January 16, 1936, for the murder and cannibalism of 12-year-old Grace Budd. The most sensational murder case of the twentieth century involved the kidnapping and murder of the young son of the famous aviator Charles Lindbergh on March 1, 1932. These classic cases, as well as more contemporary cases such as the murder of ten-year-old Jeanine Nicarico of Naperville, Illinois, in February 1983, the Marilyn Lemak case, and Susan Smith's murder of her two children, have alerted Americans to how vulnerable children are to acts of homicide.

Recent school killings such as the incident at Columbine High School in Littleton, Colorado, have forced the nation to realize that children can be killed in mass numbers.

## Factors in the Murder of Children

The United States has the highest homicide rate for children of any industrialized nation in the world. Federal Bureau of Investigation statistics show that slightly more than 11 percent of murder victims in 1999 were children under the age of eighteen. The firearm-related homicide rate for children is more than twice that of Finland, the country with the next highest rate.

Both adults and older children (ages five to eighteen) who are victims of homicide are likely to die as the result of a firearm-related incident. However, only 10 percent of homicides among younger children (under age four) are firearm related. Young children are generally murdered via abandonment, starvation, suffocation, drowning, strangulation, or beating, the victims of adults or other children. They may die at the hands of parents, siblings, friends or acquaintances, or strangers.

Studies of murdered children under twelve years old reveal that nearly six out of ten are killed by their parents. Half of these are under the age of one. The next highest category of perpetrator is a friend or acquaintance. A significant number of children are killed by offenders in their own age cohort, as the recent rash of school killings indicates. According to James Fox and Jack Levin, authors of *The Will to Kill* (2001), with the exception of infanticide, "most offenders and their victims are similar in age" (p. 27). Reasons why children kill other children are many and varied. When the teenagers Nathan Leopold and Richard Loeb killed Bobbie Franks in 1924, their objective was to commit a "perfect" crime. A large portion of the school killings in the late twentieth-century years has resulted from the perpetrator being cruelly teased or ostracized by classmates. In large cities, many children are victims of gang killings, whether they belong to a gang or not. Wearing the wrong color of shoelaces, having one's hat tilted in the wrong direction, or just being in the wrong place at the wrong time can result in death. Gang members kill other gang members as a consequence of petty jealousy or a need to display their manhood. There have been occasions when children have killed their victim because he or she refused to obey an order. For example, in Chicago, Illinois, two children threw another from the roof of a building because the victim refused to obtain drugs for the murderers.

## Familial Homicides

The psychiatrist P. T. D'Orban classifies the factors that play a role in filicides (the killing of a son or daughter) into three categories: family stress, including a family history of mental illness and crime, parental discord, parental maltreatment, and separation from one or both parents before age fifteen; social stress, involving financial and housing problems, marital discord, a criminal record, and living alone; and psychiatric stress, comprising a history of psychiatric symptoms, a psychiatric diagnosis, and a suicide attempt after the offense.

A history of child abuse or neglect is the most notable risk factor for the future death (i.e., murder of a child). Scholars note that the best predictor of future violence is a past history of violence. Most child abuse killings fall into the category of battering deaths, resulting from misguided, but brutal, efforts to discipline, punish, or quiet children. According to a study conducted by Murray Levine and associates, 75 percent of maltreatment-related fatalities occur in children under age four. Very young children are at the greatest risk because they are more physically vulnerable and less likely to be identified as at-risk due to their lack of contact with outside agencies. Shaken baby syndrome, in which the child is shaken so violently that brain damage can occur, takes the lives of many young children.

There are numerous risk factors for child murder. The criminal justice expert Neil Websdale has identified several situational antecedents such as a history of child abuse and/or neglect, a history of domestic violence, poverty, inequality, unemployment, criminal history, the use of drugs and/or alcohol, and the availability of weapons. Male and nonwhite children are more likely to be victims of child murder than female and white children.

According to the American psychiatrist and expert on child murder, Phillip Resnick, typical neonaticidal mothers (mothers who kill their children the first day of birth) are young, unmarried, are not suffering from psychotic illness, and do not have a history of depression. They characteristically conceal their pregnancy, often denying that they are pregnant. Other researchers have concluded that most deaths are the result of unwanted pregnancies, and that many mothers are overwhelmed by the responsibilities and have little or no support system. A number of women have serious drug and/or alcohol problems and lose control in a fit of intoxication.

Mental disorder is a major factor in the killing of children. In *Fatal Families* (1997), Charles Ewing notes that psychotic infanticide and filicide perpetrators are most likely to be suffering from postpartum psychosis, while parents who batter their children to death are more likely to suffer from nonpsychotic mental illnesses, such as personality disorders, impulse control disorders, mood disorders, anxiety disorders, and/or substance abuse disorders. The *Diagnostic and Statistical Manual of Mental Disorders* (1994) explains that postpartum psychotic episodes are characterized by command hallucinations to kill the infant or delusions that the infant is possessed. Other researchers report that mothers who kill their newborn are often suffering from dissociative disorders at the time of the birth because they feel overwhelmed by the pregnancy and perceived lack of support, necessitating their handling the traumatic experience on their own. However, when mothers kill older children, it is the children who have mental aberrations or psychiatric conditions rather than the mother, who in fear of her life or the lives of other family members, feels she has to end the life of her child.

According to Levine and colleagues, not only are males predominantly the perpetrators, but the presence of a male in the household increases the risk of maltreatment-related fatalities, especially from physical abuse. Fathers kill infants when they cry excessively and the father has little tolerance for such disruption due to the influence of alcohol or drugs, or because he is suffering from antisocial personality disorder. Some fathers kill their son when he is old enough to challenge the father's authority and they physically fight. Occasionally, fathers have killed their daughters following rape or sexual exploitation, when they threatened to reveal the abuse.

The rate of child murder is greatly elevated in stepfamilies. Martin Daly and Margo Wilson found that whereas young children incurred about seven times higher rates of physical abuse in families with a stepparent than in two-genetic-parent homes, stepchildren were 100 times more likely to suffer fatal abuse. In a sample of men who slew their preschool-age children, 82 percent of the victims of stepfathers were beaten to death, while the majority of children slain by genetic fathers were killed by less violent means.

**Suggestions for Prevention**

Given the multifactored character of fatal child abuse, only a multidiagnostic and multitherapeutic approach can deal adequately with its clinical prevention. The multidiagnostic component requires an individual, marital, family, and social assessment. The multitherapeutic approach involves the use of several therapeutic modalities including individual psychotherapy, hospitalization, and/or temporary/permanent removal of the child from the home.

Physicians may also play a role in prevention by identifying particular stresses that might lead to an aberrant or unusual postpartum reaction. Postpartum changes in depression or psychosis can be observed, monitored, and treated. The physician can look for evidence of abuse, isolation, and lack of support from family or friends. Many child abuse deaths could be prevented by identifying parents at risk of abusing their children and making parenting less stressful for them. There is a need for more and better education programs aimed at teaching people how to parent and alternatives to corporal punishment. The development of programs to better identify domestic violence, along with a stronger response to identified cases of family violence, can also reduce child deaths. Finally, clinicians who identify and treat psychoses should be aware of the possible danger to children of psychotic parents and monitor the child's risk.

*See also:* CHILDREN; INFANTICIDE; SACRIFICE

*Bibliography*

American Psychological Association. *Diagnostic and Statistical Manual of Mental Disorders,* 4th edition. Washington, DC: Author, 1994.

Bourget, Dominique, and Alain Labelle. "Homicide, Infanticide, and Filicide." *Psychiatric Clinics of North America* 15, no. 3 (1992):661–673.

Chagnon, Napoleon A. *Yanomamo: The Fierce People*. New York: Holt, Rinehart and Winston, 1968.

Daly, Martin, and Margo I. Wilson "Violence Against Stepchildren." *Current Directions in Psychological Science* 5, no. 3 (1996):77–81.

Daly, Martin, and Margo I. Wilson. "Some Differential Attributes of Lethal Assaults on Small Children by Stepfathers versus Genetic Fathers." *Etiology and Sociobiology* 15 (1994):207–217.

D'Orban, P. T. "Women Who Kill Their Children." *British Journal of Psychiatry* 134 (1979):560–571.

Ewing, Charles P. *Fatal Families: The Dynamics of Intrafamilial Homicide*. London: Sage Publications, 1997.

Federal Bureau of Investigation. *Crime in the United States: 1999*. Washington, DC: U.S. Department of Justice, 2000.

Fox, James Alan, and Jack Levin. *The Will to Kill: Making Sense of Senseless Murder*. Boston: Allyn & Bacon, 2001.

Levine, Murray, Jennifer Freeman, and Cheryl Compaan. "Maltreatment-Related Fatalities: Issues of Policy and Prevention." *Law and Policy* 449 (1994):458–464.

Lowenstein, I. F. "Infanticide: A Crime of Desperation." *Criminologist* 2, no. 2 (1997):81–92.

Milner, Larry S. *Hardness of Heart of Life: The Stain of Human Infanticide*. New York: University Press of America Inc., 2000.

Sadoff, Robert L. "Mothers Who Kill Their Children." *Psychiatric Annals* 25, no. 10 (1995):601–605.

Sharp, Cecil, and Maude Karpeles. *80 Appalachian Folk Songs*. Winchester, MA: Faber & Faber, 1968.

Websdale, Neil. *Understanding Domestic Homicide*. Boston: Northeastern University Press, 1999.

Wilkins, A. J. "Attempted Infanticide." *British Journal of Psychiatry* 146 (1985):206–208.

*Internet Resources*

Juvenile Justice Bulletin. "Kids and Guns." In the Office of Juvenile Justice and Delinquency Prevention [web site]. Available from www.ncjrs.org/html/ojjdp/jjbul2000_03_2/contents.html.

Murray, Iain. "Juvenile Murders: Guns Least of It." In the Statistical Assessment Service [web site]. Available from www.stats.org/statswork/csm-guns.htm.

Troxell, Dan. "The Great Cherokee Children Massacre at Ywahoo Falls." In the Fortune City [web site]. Available from http://victorian.fortunecity.com/rothko/420/aniyuntikwalaski/yahoo.html.

JAMES K. CRISSMAN
KIMBERLY A. BEACH

# CHINESE BELIEFS

In premodern China, the great majority of people held beliefs and observed practices related to death that they learned as members of families and villages, not as members of organized religions. Such beliefs and practices are often subsumed under the umbrella of "Chinese popular religion." Institutional forms of Buddhism, Confucianism, Taoism, and other traditions contributed many beliefs and practices to popular religion in its local variants. These traditions, especially Buddhism, included the idea of personal cultivation for the purpose of living an ideal life and, as a consequence, attaining some kind of afterlife salvation, such as immortality, enlightenment, or birth in a heavenly realm. However, individual salvation played a small role in most popular religions. In typical local variants of popular religion, the emphasis was on (1) passing from this world into an ancestral realm that in key ways mirrored this world and (2) the interactions between living persons and their ancestors.

## Basic Beliefs and Assumptions

In every human society one can find manifestations of the human desire for some kind of continuance beyond death. In the modern West, much of human experience has been with religious theories of continuance that stress the fate of the individual, often conceived as a discrete spiritual "self" or "soul." Typically, a person is encouraged to live in a way that prepares one for personal salvation, whether by moral self-discipline, seeking God's grace, or other means. Indic traditions, such as Buddhism and Hinduism, include similar assumptions about the human self/soul and personal salvation. In premodern China, especially if one discounts Buddhist influence, a person's desire for continuance beyond death was rooted in different assumptions and manifested in practices not closely related to the pursuit of individual salvation.

First, Chinese emphasized biological continuance through descendants to whom they gave the gift of life and for whom they sacrificed many of life's material pleasures. Moreover, personal sacrifice was not rooted in a belief in asceticism per se but in a belief that sacrificing for one's offspring would engender in them obligations toward elders and ancestors. As stated in the ancient text, *Scripture of Filiality* (Warring States Period, 453-221 B.C.E.), these included obligations to care for one's body as a gift from one's parents and to succeed in life so as to glorify the family ancestors. Thus, one lived beyond the grave above all through the health and success of one's children, grandchildren, and great-grandchildren.

Second, because of the obligations inculcated in children and grandchildren, one could assume they would care for one in old age and in the afterlife. Indeed, afterlife care involved the most significant and complex rituals in Chinese religious life, including funerals, burials, mourning practices, and rites for ancestors. All this was important not only as an expression of each person's hope for continuance beyond death but as an expression of people's concern that souls for whom no one cared would become ghosts intent on causing mischief.

Finally, there was a stress on mutual obligations between the living and the dead; in other words, an emphasis on the same principle of reciprocity that governed relations among the living members of a Chinese community. It was assumed that the dead could influence the quality of life for those still in this world—either for good or for ill. On the one hand, proper burial, careful observance of mourning practices, and ongoing offerings of food and gifts for ancestors assured their continued aid. On the other hand, failure to observe ritual obligations might bring on the wrath of one's ancestors, resulting in family disharmony, economic ruin, or sickness. Ancestral souls for whom no one cared would become "hungry ghosts" (*egui*), which might attack anyone in the community. Royal ancestors, whose worship was the special responsibility of the reigning emperor, could aid or harm people throughout the empire, depending on whether or not the emperor upheld ritual obligations to his ancestors.

In traditional China, the idea that personal continuance after death could be found in the lives of one's descendants has been closely linked to practices rooted in mutual obligations between the living and the dead: those who had moved on to the ancestral state of existence. But what is the nature of the ancestral state? What kind of rituals for the dead have been performed by most Chinese? And under what circumstances have individual Chinese

sought something more than an afterlife as a comfortable and proud ancestor with loving and successful descendants; that is, some kind of personal salvation?

## Conceptions of Souls and Ancestral Existence

There is evidence from as early as the Shang period (c. 1500–1050 B.C.E.) that Chinese cared for ancestors as well as feared them. This may well have been the main factor in the development of beliefs in dual and multiple souls. Late in the Zhou dynasty (1050–256 B.C.E.), cosmological thought was dominated by the *yin-yang* dichotomy, according to which all aspects of existence were a result of alternation and interplay between passive (yin) and active (yang) forces. Philosophers applied the dichotomy to soul theory. Lacking any absolute distinction between physical and spiritual, they considered the *yin* soul (*po*) as more material, and the *yang* soul (*hun*) as more ethereal. In practice, the po was linked to the body and the grave. The less fearsome hun was linked to the ancestral tablet kept in the family home and the one installed in an ancestral hall (if the family's clan could afford to build one). For some, this meant there were two hun, just as, for others, there might be multiple po. One common view included the idea of three hun and seven po. These multiple soul theories were among the factors in popular religion that mitigated widespread acceptance of belief in salvation of the individual soul. At the same time, however, multiple soul theories helped Chinese to manage contrasting perceptions of ancestral souls (as benevolent or malevolent, for example) and to provide an explanatory framework for the differing rituals of the domestic, gravesite, and clan hall cults for ancestors.

While the intent of all these rites was clear—to comfort ancestors rather than to suffer their wrath—the nature of ancestral existence was relatively undefined. Generally speaking, the world of the ancestors was conceived as a murky, dark realm, a "yin" space (*yinjian*). While not clear on the exact details, Chinese considered the world of departed spirits similar to the world of the living in key ways. They believed residents of the other realm need money and sustenance, must deal with bureaucrats, and should work (with the help of the living) to improve their fate. After the arrival of Buddhism in the early centuries of the common era, it contributed more specific ideas about the realm of the dead as well as more exact conceptions of the relationship between one's deeds while alive and one's fate afterward.

For example, the "bureaucratic" dimension of the underworld was enhanced by visions of the Buddhist Ten Courts of Hell, at which judges meted out punishments according to karmic principles that required recompense for every good or evil deed. Moreover, regardless of whether or not they followed Buddhism in other ways, most Chinese embraced the doctrines of *karma* (retribution for past actions) and *samsara* (cyclical existence) in their thinking about life and death. These doctrines helped people to explain the fate of residents in the realms of the living and the dead, not to mention interactions between them. For example, the ghost stories that fill Chinese religious tracts as well as secular literature typically present ghosts as vehicles of karmic retribution against those evildoers who escaped punishment by worldly authorities (perhaps in a former lifetime). While reading such stories often has been just a casual diversion, performing rites to assure that departed ancestors do not become wandering ghosts has been a serious matter.

## Rites for the Dead

Over the course of Chinese history, classical texts on ritual and commentaries on them had increasing influence on the practice of rites for the dead. The text *Records of Rituals* (*Liji*), after being designated one of Confucianism's "Five Scriptures" during the Han era (206 B.C.E.–220 C.E.), became the most influential book in this regard. The *Family Rituals according to Master Zhu* (*Zhuzi jiali*), by the leading thinker of later Confucianism (Zhu Xi, 1130–1200 C.E.), became the most influential commentary. The influence of these texts resulted in widespread standardization of funeral rites in particular and rites for the dead in general. According to the cultural anthropologist James Watson, standardized funeral rites became a marker of "Chineseness" for Han (ethnically Chinese) people in their interactions with other ethnic groups as they spread into new territories.

In his article, "The Structure of Chinese Funerary Rites," Watson identifies nine elements of standardized funeral rites: (1) the family gives public notification by wailing, pasting up banners, and other acts; (2) family members don mourning attire of white cloth and hemp; (3) they ritually bathe the corpse; (4) they make food offerings and transfer to the dead (by burning) spirit money and various goods (houses, furniture, and other items made of paper); (5) they prepare and install an ancestral tablet at the domestic altar; (6) they pay money to ritual specialists (usually Taoists priests or Buddhist clerics) so that the corpse can be safely expelled from the community (and the spirit sent forth on its otherworldly journey); (7) they arrange for music to accompany movement of the corpse and to settle the spirit; (8) they have the corpse sealed in an airtight coffin; and (9) they expel the coffin from the community in a procession to the gravesite that marks the completion of the funeral rites and sets the stage for burial.

While burial customs were more subject to local variation than funeral rites as such, throughout China there was a preference for burial over alternative means of dealing with the corpse. For example, few Chinese opted for Buddhism's custom of cremation, despite the otherwise strong influence this religion had on Chinese ideas and practices related to life and death. Unlike Indians, for whom the body could be seen as a temporary vehicle for one's eternal spirit, Chinese typically saw the body as a valued gift from the ancestors that one should place whole under the soil near one's ancestral village. In modern China, especially under the Communist Party since 1949, Chinese have turned to cremation more often. But this has been for practical reasons related to land use and to the party's campaign against "superstitious" behavior and in favor of frugality in performing rituals.

Traditionally, the corpse, or at least the bones, represented powers that lasted beyond death and could affect the fate of living relatives. For this reason, the use of an expert in *feng-shui* (Chinese geomancy) was needed to determine the time, place, and orientation of the burial of a corpse. This usage was in line with the aforementioned belief that the po, which lingered at the grave, was more physical in character than the hun soul(s). Its importance is underlined by the fact that the practice is being revived in China after years of condemnation by Communist officials.

Caring for the hun soul(s) has been at the heart of ritual observances that occurred away from the

*The procession to the gravesite of this funeral in China signifies a completion of the funeral rites.* CORBIS

grave. Among these observances were very complex mourning customs. They were governed by the general principle that the closeness of one's relationship to the deceased determined the degree of mourning one must observe (symbolized by the coarseness of one's clothes and the length of the mourning period, for example). In addition to observing mourning customs, relatives of the deceased were obliged to care for his or her soul(s) at the home altar and at the clan ancestral hall, if one existed. At the home altar the family remembered a recently deceased relative through highly personalized offerings of favorite foods and other items. They remembered more distant relatives as a group in generic ancestral rites, such as those which occurred prior to family feasts at the New Year, mid-Autumn, and other festivals. Indeed, one of the most significant symbolic reminders that ancestors were still part of the family was their inclusion as honored guests at holiday meals.

## Individual Salvation

Chinese beliefs and practices related to death were closely tied to family life and, therefore, shaped by its collectivist mentality. In his article, "Souls and Salvation: Conflicting Themes in Chinese Popular Religion," the anthropologist Myron Cohen, has even argued that the pursuit of individual salvation was inimical to orthodox popular religion. Nonetheless, this pursuit was not absent from traditional religious life. The spread of Buddhism throughout China was one factor contributing to its acceptance. Another factor was the increasingly urban and mobile nature of Chinese society over time. Since at least the Song dynasty (960–1279), both factors have exerted strong influence, so that for the last millennium China has seen tremendous growth in lay-oriented Buddhism and in other religions with salvationist ideologies derived from Buddhist, Taoist, and other sources.

Lay Buddhists have been interested to an even greater extent than their monastic counterparts in the goal of rebirth in the Western paradise, or "Pure Land" (*jingtu*), of Amitabha Buddha. Unlike the ordinary realm of ancestors, which mirrors this world in most ways, the Pure Land is desired for ways in which it differs from this world. It is inhabited not by relatives, but by wise and compassionate teachers of the Buddhist Dharma, and it is free of the impurities and sufferings of the mortal realm. For some it is not a place at all, only a symbol of the peace of *nirvana* (enlightened state beyond cyclical existence).

To an even greater extent than Buddhism, certain syncretic religions set forth ideas that stood in tension with the hierarchical, earthbound, and collectivist assumptions of the traditional Chinese state and society. Whether one studies the White Lotus Religion of late imperial times, the Way of Unity (Yiguan Dao) in modern China and Taiwan, or the Falun Gong movement in the twenty-first-century's People's Republic of China, the emphasis is on individual spiritual cultivation and, when relevant, the fate of the individual after death. Evidence of interest in individual spiritual cultivation and salvation is found in these sects' remarkable popularity, which has alarmed both traditional and contemporary governments.

Groups like the Way of Unity or Falun Gong typically stress the need for a morally disciplined lifestyle and training in techniques of spiritual cultivation that are uniquely available to members. Their moral norms are largely from Confucianism, and their spiritual techniques from Taoism and Buddhism. Falun Gong promises that its techniques are powerful enough to save members from fatal illnesses. The Way of Unity promises that individuals who take the right moral-spiritual path will avoid the catastrophe that faces others as they near the end of the world. Unlike others, these individuals will join the Eternal Venerable Mother in her paradise. Since the 1600s, the idea of salvation through Jesus has also attracted the attention of some Chinese. In the past, these Chinese Christians were required to abandon ancestral rites, since 1939 the Catholic church has allowed Chinese to worship Jesus as well as perform rituals for ancestors, with some Protestant groups following the trend.

As the acids of modernity continue to eat away at the fabric of traditional Chinese society, many more Chinese are embracing religions that preach individual salvation after death. Those who do so may abandon practices related to traditional beliefs about life, death, and ancestral souls, or they may find ways to reconcile these practices with the new belief systems they adopt.

*See also:* AFTERLIFE IN CROSS-CULTURAL PERSPECTIVE; BUDDHISM; GHOSTS; HINDUISM; IMMORTALITY; MOURNING; QIN SHIH HUANG'S TOMB

## Bibliography

Ahern, Emily M. *The Cult of the Dead in a Chinese Village.* Stanford, CA: Stanford University Press, 1973.

Baker, Hugh D. R. *Chinese Family and Kinship.* New York: Columbia, 1979.

Bauer, Wolfgang. *China and the Search for Happiness,* translated by Michael Shaw. New York: Seabury Press, 1976.

Chu Hsi. *Chu Hsi's Family Rituals,* translated by Patricia Ebrey. Princeton, NJ: Princeton University Press, 1991.

Cohen, Myron L. "Souls and Salvation: Conflicting Themes in Chinese Popular Religion." In James L. Watson and Evelyn S. Rawski eds., *Death Ritual in Late Imperial and Modern China.* Berkeley: University of California Press, 1988.

Ebrey, Patricia Buckley. *Confucianism and Family Rituals in Imperial China.* Princeton, NJ: Princeton University Press, 1991.

Goodrich, Anne S. *Chinese Hells.* St. Augustin: Monumenta Serica, 1981.

Groot, Jan J. M. de. *The Religious System of China.* 6 vols. 1892. Reprint, Taipei: Southern Materials Center, 1982.

Hsu, Francis L. K. *Under the Ancestors' Shadow.* Stanford, CA: Stanford University Press, 1971.

Jochim, Christian. *Chinese Religions: A Cultural Perspective.* Englewood Cliffs, NJ: Prentice-Hall, 1986.

Lagerway, John. *Taoist Ritual in Chinese Society and History.* New York: Macmillan, 1987.

Legge, James, trans. *Li Chi: Book of Rites.* 2 vols. 1885. Reprint, edited by Ch'u Chai and Winberg Chai. New Hyde Park, NY: University Books, 1967.

Legge, James, trans. *The Hsiao Ching.* (*Scripture of Filiality*) 1899. Reprint, New York: Dover Publications, 1963.

Loewe, Michael. *Ways to Paradise: The Chinese Quest for Immortality.* London: George Allen and Unwin, 1979.

Poo, Mu-chou. *In Search of Personal Welfare: A View of Ancient Chinese Religion.* Albany: State University of New York Press, 1998.

St. Sure, Donald F., trans. *100 Documents Concerning the Chinese Rites Controversy (1645–1941).* San Francisco, CA: University of San Francisco Ricci Institute, 1992.

Teiser, Stephen F. *"The Scripture on the Ten Kings" and the Making of Purgatory in Medieval Chinese Buddhism.* Honolulu: University of Hawaii Press, 1994.

Teiser, Stephen F. *The Ghost Festival in Medieval China.* Princeton, NJ: Princeton University Press, 1988.

Watson, James L. "The Structure of Chinese Funerary Rites," In James L. Watson and Evelyn S. Rawski eds., *Death Ritual in Late Imperial and Modern China*. Berkeley, CA: University of California Press, 1988.

Wolf, Arthur P., ed. *Religion and Ritual in Chinese Society*. Stanford, CA: Stanford University Press, 1974.

Yang, C. K. *Religion in Chinese Society*. Berkeley: University of California Press, 1970.

CHRISTIAN JOCHIM

# CHRISTIAN DEATH RITES, HISTORY OF

In the world in which Christianity emerged, death was a private affair. Except when struck down on the battlefield or by accident, people died in the company of family and friends. There were no physicians or religious personnel present. Ancient physicians generally removed themselves when cases became hopeless, and priests and priestesses served their gods rather than ordinary people. Contact with a corpse caused ritual impurity and hence ritual activity around the deathbed was minimal. A relative might bestow a final kiss or attempt to catch a dying person's last breath. The living closed the eyes and mouth of the deceased, perhaps placing a coin for the underworld ferryman on the tongue or eyelids. They then washed the corpse, anointed it with scented oil and herbs, and dressed it, sometimes in clothing befitting the social status of the deceased, sometimes in a shroud. A procession accompanied the body to the necropolis outside the city walls. There it was laid to rest, or cremated and given an urn burial, in a family plot that often contained a structure to house the dead. Upon returning from the funeral, the family purified themselves and the house through rituals of fire and water.

Beyond such more or less shared features, funeral rites, as well as forms of burial and commemoration, varied as much as the people and the ecology of the region in which Christianity developed and spread. Cremation was the most common mode of disposal in the Roman Empire, but older patterns of corpse burial persisted in many areas, especially in Egypt and the Middle East.

Christianity arose among Jews, who buried their dead, and the death, burial, and resurrection of Jesus were its defining events. Although Christians practiced inhumation (corpse burial) from the earliest times, they were not, as often assumed, responsible for the gradual disappearance of cremation in the Roman Empire during the second and third centuries, for common practice was already changing before Christianity became a major cultural force. However, Christianity was, in this case, in sync with wider patterns of cultural change. Hope of salvation and attention to the fate of the body and the soul after death were more or less common features of all the major religious movements of the age, including the Hellenistic mysteries, Christianity, Rabbinic Judaism, Manichaeanism, and Mahayana Buddhism, which was preached as far west as Alexandria.

## Early Christian Responses to Death and Dying

In spite of the centrality of death in the theology and spiritual anthropology of early Christians, they were slow to develop specifically Christian responses to death and dying. The most immediate change was that Christians handled the bodies of the dead without fear of pollution. The purification of baptism was permanent, unless marred by mortal sin, and the corpse of a Christian prefigured the transformed body that would be resurrected into eternal life at the end of time. The Christian living had less need than their neighbors to appease their dead, who were themselves less likely to return as unhappy ghosts. Non-Christians noted the joyous mood at Christian funerals and the ease of the participants in the presence of the dead. They observed how Christians gave decent burials to even the poorest of the poor. Normal Roman practice was to dump them in large pits away from the well-kept family tombs lining the roads outside the city walls.

The span of a Christian biography stretched from death and rebirth in baptism, to what was called the "second death," to final resurrection. In a sense, then, baptism was the first Christian death ritual. In the fourth century Bishop Ambrose of Milan (374–397) taught that the baptismal font was like a tomb because baptism was a ritual of death and resurrection. Bishop Ambrose also urged baptized Christians to look forward to death with joy, for physical death was just a way station on the road to paradise. Some of his younger contemporaries, like Augustine of Hippo, held a different view. Baptism did not guarantee salvation, preached Augustine; only God could do that. The proper response to death ought to be fear—of both human sinfulness and God's inscrutable judgment.

This more anxious attitude toward death demanded a pastoral response from the clergy, which came in the form of communion as *viaticum* (provisions for a journey), originally granted to penitents by the first ecumenical council at Nicea (325), and extended to all Christians in the fifth and sixth centuries. There is, however, evidence that another type of deathbed communion was regularly practiced as early as the fourth century, if not before. The psalms, prayers, and symbolic representations in the old Roman death ritual discussed by the historian Frederick Paxton are in perfect accord with the triumphant theology of Ambrose of Milan and the Imperial Church. The rite does not refer to deathbed communion as viaticum, but as "a defender and advocate at the resurrection of the just" (Paxton 1990, p. 39). Nor does it present the bread and wine as provisions for the soul's journey to the otherworld, but as a sign of its membership in the community of the saved, to be rendered at the last judgment. Thanks, in part, to the preservation and transmission of this Roman ritual, the Augustinian point of view did not sweep all before it and older patterns of triumphant death persisted.

However difficult the contemplation (or moment) of death became, the living continually invented new ways of aiding the passage of souls and maintaining community with the dead. In one of the most important developments of the age, Christians began to revere the remains of those who had suffered martyrdom under Roman persecution. As Peter Brown has shown, the rise of the cult of the saints is a precise measure of the changing relationship between the living and the dead in late antiquity and the early medieval West. The saints formed a special group, present to both the living and the dead and mediating between and among them. The faithful looked to them as friends and patrons, and as advocates at earthly and heavenly courts. Moreover, the shrines of the saints brought people to live and worship in the cemeteries outside the city walls. Eventually, the dead even appeared inside the walls, first as saints' relics, and then in the bodies of those who wished

to be buried near them. Ancient prohibitions against intramural burials slowly lost their force. In the second half of the first millennium, graves began to cluster around both urban and rural churches. Essentially complete by the year 1000, this process configured the landscape of Western Christendom in ways that survive until the present day. The living and the dead formed a single community and shared a common space. The dead, as Patrick Geary has put it, became simply another "age group" in medieval society.

## Emergence of a Completely Developed Death Ritual in the Medieval Latin Church

However close the living and dead might be, it was still necessary to pass from one group to the other, and early medieval Christians were no less inventive in facilitating that passage. The centuries from 500 to 1000 saw the emergence of a fully developed ritual process around death, burial, and the incorporation of souls into the otherworld that became a standard for Christian Europeans until the Reformation, and for Catholics until the very near present. The multitude of Christian kingdoms that emerged in the West as the Roman Empire declined fostered the development of local churches. In the sixth, seventh, and eighth centuries, these churches developed distinctive ritual responses to death and dying. In southern Gaul, Bishop Caesarius of Arles (503–543) urged the sick to seek ritual anointing from priests rather than magicians and folk healers and authored some of the most enduring of the prayers that accompanied death and burial in medieval Christianity. Pope Gregory the Great (590–604) first promoted the practice of offering the mass as an aid to souls in the afterlife, thus establishing the basis for a system of suffrages for the dead. In seventh-century Spain, the Visigothic Church developed an elaborate rite of deathbed penance. This ritual, which purified and transformed the body and soul of the dying, was so powerful that anyone who subsequently recovered was required to retire into a monastery for life. Under the influence of Mosaic law, Irish priests avoided contact with corpses. Perhaps as a consequence, they transformed the practice of anointing the sick into a rite of preparation for death, laying the groundwork for the sacrament of extreme unction. In the eighth century, Irish and Anglo-Saxon missionary monks began to contract with one another for prayers and masses after death.

All of these developments came into contact in the later eighth and ninth centuries under the Carolingian kings and emperors, especially Charlemagne (769–814), but also his father Pepin and his son Louis. Together they unified western Europe more successfully around shared rituals than common political structures. The rhetoric of their reforms favored Roman traditions, and they succeeded in making the Mass and certain elements of clerical and monastic culture, like chant, conform to Roman practice whether real or imagined. When it came to death and dying, however, Rome provided only one piece of the Carolingian ritual synthesis: the old Roman death ritual. Whether or not it was in use in Rome at the time, its triumphant psalmody and salvation theology struck a chord in a church supported by powerful and pious men who saw themselves as heirs to the kings of Israel and the Christian emperors of Rome. Other elements of their rituals had other sources. Carolingian rituals were deeply penitential, not just because of Augustine, but also because, in the rough-and-tumble world of the eighth and ninth centuries, even monks and priests were anxious about making it into heaven. Although reformers, following Caesarius of Arles, promoted the anointing of the sick on the grounds that there was no scriptural basis for anointing the dying, deathbed anointing came into general use, often via Irish texts and traditions. Carolingian rituals also drew liberally on the prayers of Caesarius of Arles and other fathers of the old Gallican and Visigothic churches.

The ritual experts of the Carolingian age did not just adapt older rites and provide a setting for their synthesis, however; they made their own contributions as well. In his classic 1908 study on ritual, the anthropologist Arnold van Gennep was surprised by the lack of elaboration of the first phase of death rites in the ethnographic reports he studied. People generally ritualized burial and commemoration, but gave little attention to the dying. Unlike other rites of passage, few rituals prepared people for death. Familiarity with European Christian traditions may be the source of van Gennep's surprise, for well-developed preliminal rites are one of their most characteristic features. Around the year 800 certain clerical communities introduced a ritual for the death agony. To aid the dying through the struggle of the soul's exit from the body, the community chanted the names of the

denizens of paradise. Rhythmically calling on the Trinity, Mary, the angels, the prophets and patriarchs, the martyrs and confessors, and all living holy men and women, they wove a web of sung prayer to aid the soul's passing. This practice quickly became part of a common tradition that also included rites of penance, absolution, anointing, and communion, each of which helped cut the ties that bound the dying to this world, ritually preparing them for entry into paradise.

Like most human groups, Christians had always used rites of transition to allay the dangers of the liminal period after death before the corpse was safely buried and the soul set on its journey to the otherworld. The same was true of post-liminal rites of incorporation, which accompanied the body into the earth, the soul into the otherworld, and the mourners back into normal society. But medieval Christians placed the ritual commemoration of the dead at the very center of social life. Between 760 and 762, a group of churchmen at the Carolingian royal villa of Attigny committed themselves to mutual commemoration after death. Not long afterward, monastic congregations began to make similar arrangements with other houses and with members of secular society. They also began to record the names of participants in books, which grew to include as many as 40,000 entries. When alms for the poor were added to the psalms and masses sung for the dead, the final piece was in place in a complex system of exchange that became one of the fundamental features of medieval Latin Christendom. Cloistered men and women, themselves "dead to this world," mediated these exchanges. They accepted gifts to the poor (among whom they included themselves) in exchange for prayers for the souls of the givers and their dead relatives. They may have acted more out of anxiety than out of confidence in the face of death, as the scholar Arno Borst has argued, but whatever their motivations, their actions, like the actions of the saints, helped bind together the community of the living and the dead.

The Carolingian reformers hoped to create community through shared ritual, but communities shaped ritual as much as ritual shaped communities, and the synthesis that resulted from their activities reflected not just their official stance but all the myriad traditions of the local churches that flowed into their vast realm. By the end of the ninth century a ritual process had emerged that blended the triumphant psalmody of the old Roman rites with the concern for penance and purification of the early medieval world. A rite of passage that coordinated and accompanied every stage of the transition from this community to the next, it perfectly complemented the social and architectural landscape. Taken up by the reform movements of the tenth and eleventh centuries, this ritual complex reached its most developed form at the Burgundian monastery of Cluny. At Cluny, the desire to have the whole community present at the death of each of its members was so great that infirmary servants were specially trained to recognize the signs of approaching death.

## The Modern Age

Christian death rituals changed in the transition to modernity, historians like Philippe Ariès and David Stannard have detailed in their various works. But while Protestants stripped away many of their characteristic features, Catholics kept them essentially the same, at least until the Second Vatican Council (1962–1965). Like the Carolingian reformers, the fathers of Vatican II moved to restrict ritual anointing to the sick, but they may be no more successful in the long run, for the symbolic power of anointing as a rite of preparation for death seems hard to resist. And while the secularization of society since the 1700s has eroded the influence of Christian death rites in Western culture, nothing has quite taken their place. Modern science and medicine have taught humankind a great deal about death, and about how to treat the sick and the dying, but they have been unable to give death the kind of meaning that it had for medieval Christians. For many people living in the twenty-first century death is a wall against which the self is obliterated. For medieval Christians it was a membrane linking two communities and two worlds. In particular, Christian rites of preparation for death offered the dying the solace of ritual and community at the most difficult moment in their lives.

## Reconnecting with the Past

The Chalice of Repose Project at St. Patrick Hospital in Missoula, Montana, is applying ancient knowledge to twenty-first-century end-of-life care. Inspired in part by the medieval death rituals of Cluny, the Chalice Project trains professional music thanatologists to serve the physical, emotional, and spiritual needs of the dying with sung prayer. With harp and voice, these "contemplative musicians" ease the pain of death with sacred music—for the dying, but also for their families and friends and for the nurses and doctors who care for them. While anchored in the Catholic tradition, music thanatologists seek to make each death a blessed event regardless of the religious background of the dying person. Working with palliative physicians and nurses, they offer prescriptive music as an alternative therapy in end-of-life care. The Chalice of Repose is a model of how the past can infuse the present with new possibilities.

*See also:* ARS MORIENDI; CHARON AND THE RIVER STYX; JESUS; RITES OF PASSAGE

### Bibliography

Ariès, Philippe. *The Hour of Our Death,* translated by Helen Weaver. New York: Alfred A. Knopf, 1981.

Ariès, Philippe. *Western Attitudes toward Death: From the Middle Ages to the Present,* translated by Patricia M. Ranum. Baltimore: Johns Hopkins University Press, 1974.

Borst, Arno. "Three Studies of Death in the Middle Ages." *Medieval Worlds: Barbarians, Heretics and Artists in the Middle Ages,* translated by Eric Hansen. Cambridge, Eng.: Polity Press, 1988.

Brown, Peter. *The Cult of the Saints: Its Rise and Function in Late Antiquity.* Chicago: University of Chicago Press, 1981.

Bullough, Donald. "Burial, Community and Belief in the Early Medieval West." In Peter Wormald ed., *Ideal and Reality in Frankish and Anglo-Saxon Society.* Oxford: Oxford University Press, 1983.

Bynum, Caroline Walker. *The Resurrection of the Body in Western Christendom, 200–1336.* New York: Columbia University Press, 1995.

Geary, Patrick J. *Living with the Dead in the Middle Ages.* Ithaca, NY: Cornell University Press, 1994.

Gennep, Arnold van. *The Rites of Passage,* translated by Monika B. Vizedom and Gabrielle L. Caffee. Chicago: University of Chicago Press, 1960.

Hopkins, Keith. *Death and Renewal,* Vol. 2: *Sociological Studies in Roman History.* Cambridge: Cambridge University Press, 1983.

Le Goff, Jacques. *The Birth of Purgatory,* translated by Arthur Goldhammer. Chicago: University of Chicago Press, 1984.

McLaughlin, Megan. *Consorting with Saints: Prayer for the Dead in Early Medieval France*. Ithaca, NY: Cornell University Press, 1994.

Paxton, Frederick S. "Communities of the Living and the Dead in Late Antiquity and the Early Medieval West." In Mark F. Williams ed., *Making Christian Communities in Late Antiquity and the Middle Ages*. London: Wimbledon, 2002.

Paxton, Frederick S. *A Medieval Latin Death Ritual: The Monastic Customaries of Bernard and Ulrich of Cluny*. Missoula, MT: St. Dunstan's, 1993.

Paxton, Frederick S. "*Signa mortifera*: Death and Prognostication in Early Medieval Monastic Medicine." *Bulletin of the History of Medicine* 67 (1993):631–650.

Paxton, Frederick S. *Christianizing Death: The Creation of a Ritual Process in Early Medieval Europe*. Ithaca, NY: Cornell University Press, 1990.

Schmitt, Jean-Claude. *Ghosts in the Middle Ages: The Living and the Dead in Medieval Society,* translated by Teresa Lavender Fagan. Chicago: University of Chicago Press, 1994.

Stannard, David. *The Puritan Way of Death*. Oxford: Oxford University Press, 1977.

Toynbee, J. M. C. *Death and Burial in the Roman World*. Ithaca, NY: Cornell University Press, 1971.

FREDERICK S. PAXTON

# CIVIL WAR, U.S.

Between the years 1861 and 1865, the United States engaged in a civil war, one of the most significant military confrontations in the young republic's life. The conflict dramatically altered the course of American society, eradicating the institution of slavery from the land and accelerating a number of social, economic, and political trends originating in other regions of the country. It also made lasting cultural impressions across imaginative and material American landscapes, including the gradual growth of a complex tourist industry built upon memory, patriotism, and consumerism, and the immediate expression of a deeply rooted, though politically sensitive, religious attachment to a distinctly southern way of life.

The Civil War, however, was a major turning point in American history for another reason as well: it transformed attitudes toward death and practices surrounding the corpse in the United States. While antebellum America demonstrated marked preoccupations with the reality of death in literature, material culture, religion, diaries and letters, and early medicine, the war led to the extreme escalation of certain tendencies emerging on the social scene, as well as to the production of entirely new views on death and the dead. The incredible numbers of young men who died during the war, the problems associated with disposal of their bodies, and the rhetorical and symbolic efforts to make sense of the lives lost had profound consequences for American sensibilities and institutional structures.

## The Presence of Death

During the war years, death was a pervasive element of social life in both the northern and southern sections of the country. Up until the war, Americans were quite familiar with the presence of death, intimate with its consequences in their own homes and local communities. Some estimates suggest that in the North, where more accurate records of the period are available, the crude death rate in the antebellum period was around 15 per 1,000 in rural areas, and between 20 and 40 per 1,000 in more populated cities. Most people lived into their late thirties if they survived the exceedingly dangerous early years of life. Chances of dying in childhood were also quite high, according to many studies. Infant mortality hovered around 200 per 1,000 live births, and roughly 10 percent of individuals between one year and twenty-one years died from a wide range of causes.

Despite this close and personal awareness of human mortality, Americans during the Civil War had a radically different set of experiences with death than previously. First and foremost, this conflict produced more deaths than any other war in U.S. history. The total number of deaths for both the North and the South, in the four-year period, was over 600,000. World War II is the only other major conflict that comes close to this number, when over 400,000 individuals died in battles across the ocean.

More demographic information is available for the Northern armies than for the Confederacy, which did not have the resources to keep accurate records on soldiers. According to some historians, roughly one out of sixteen white males in the North between the ages of sixteen and forty-three lost his life during the war. Even more astonishing than the overall mortality rates for the entire conflict are the number for particular battles: During the three-day battle at Gettysburg, for example, 3,155 Union soldiers died; at Antietam, during one day of fighting, the Union lost over 2,000 young men.

The carnage left on these and other sites, for both sides, boggles the mind, and must have been overwhelming to Americans viewing photographs, visiting battlefields, or reading detailed accounts in newspapers. Another significant difference between this war and other wars after the Revolution is the proximity of the battles to American communities. The Civil War not only took place on American soil, it pitted neighbor against neighbor, family against family, countrymen against countrymen.

More threatening to American soldiers during the war than mortal wounds on the battlefield was the presence of disease and infection, which had the potential to seriously reduce the number of fighters on both sides. Nearly twice as many men died as a result of poor health in camps and hospitals than from wounds inflicted during combat. What did soldiers die from? Afflictions such as diarrhea, malaria, smallpox, typhoid fever, pneumonia, and measles wiped out large numbers of men on both sides of the conflict. The deadly power of disease swept through the ranks because of the incredibly poor conditions in camps, resulting from inadequate shelter, contaminated water supplies, unhealthy diet, and a limited knowledge about proper sanitation and safe hygienic practices. As the war progressed, the Union forces worked especially hard to improve the living conditions of soldiers and patients—death became an urgent public health issue that could be combated with sound, rational decisions about such simple things as clean water, healthy food, and adequate sanitation.

Under wartime conditions, Americans in general, and soldiers in particular, acquired a unique familiarity with human mortality. Regardless of the formidable presence of death in life during the antebellum years, the Civil War posed a series of new challenges for those affected by the carnage—which is to say nearly every American at the time—and produced new attitudes that reflected distinct modifications in how these Americans made sense of death and disposed of their dead. In the midst of war, unorthodox views on death and the dead

body emerged out of the entirely unparalleled experience with human violence, suffering, and mortality in U.S. history. On the other hand, some perspectives demonstrated a degree of continuity with more traditional views on the meaning of death, and reinforced deeply rooted religious sensibilities circulating before the onset of the conflict.

## Disposing of the Dead

The Civil War forced Americans to reconsider what counts as appropriate treatment of the dead, as well as to reconceptualize the symbolic meanings of the dead body. The confrontation, with brutally slaughtered masses of bodies or hopelessly diseased soldiers dying in hospitals or camps, upset conventional patterns of disposal, as well as established attitudes about communal duties, religious rituals, and personal respect in the face of death. What counted as proper and appropriate action to usher the dead from the land of the living in an earlier time often proved impossible during the conflict, though in some cases efforts were made to treat the dead with a dignity that evoked prewar sensibilities.

In both the Union and Confederate armies, soldiers attempted to provide some kind of burial for fallen comrades who perished during a battle, even if this meant simply covering bodies with dirt, or placing the dead in common graves. The details of burial depended on a variety of circumstances, including which side won a particular battle, and which unit was assigned burial duty. Victors had the luxury of attending to their own dead with more care and attention, if time permitted. On the other hand, the losing side had to retreat from the battlefield, which meant leaving the fate of the dead and wounded to the winning side, who treated them as most enemies are treated, with indifference and disrespect.

If the Union forces controlled the field after a fight, for example, the dead were often buried without ceremony somewhere on or near the site, either individually in separate graves or collectively in common graves. In many cases, those assigned to burial duty—often African Americans, who performed a variety of noxious duties for the Union army—left the dead in their uniforms or placed a blanket around them before interment. If such resources as pine coffins or burial containers were available, and time permitted, soldiers would be placed in them before being put in the ground, a procedure that rarely occurred in the early years of the war. Many soldiers on both sides expressed a great deal of fear that their bodies would be left to the enemy, which was understood as a fate worse than death.

The federal government and Union soldiers themselves tried to ensure that bodies were identified with at least a name, a desire that led some soldiers to go into battle with their names and positions pinned onto their uniform (foreshadowing the popular use of dog tags in subsequent wars). Again, when time allowed and when burial units were available, Union forces made an effort to avoid anonymous burial, identify graves, and keep records of who died during a battle, an effort that grew increasingly more sophisticated as the war dragged on.

In contrast to the lack of ceremony surrounding the disposition of the dead on or near fields of battle, conditions in Union camps and hospitals allowed for more conventional burial practices that maintained older traditions. Reasons for this difference had nothing to do with smaller numbers of dying soldiers in these settings. More men died from disease than wounds inflicted in battle, so there were ample corpses in these locations. Camps and hospitals simply had more resources, personnel, and time to take care of these matters. Many also had space singled out for use as cemeteries, which provided a readily available and organized location for disposal.

General hospitals in larger towns seemed to be settings where more formal funeral observances could be carried out, especially for the Union. In addition to the presence of hospital nurses in these locations, members of the Sanitary Commission and the Christian Commission made burial of the dead more humane, respectful, and ritually satisfying. According to some firsthand accounts of Union hospitals in Virginia and elsewhere, the dead were given proper burials, which included religious services, the use of a coffin, a military escort from the hospital, the firing of arms, and an individual headboard with information about the deceased.

Regimental hospitals much closer to battlefields, on the other hand, could not offer the kind of attention that larger hospitals provided the dead. Descriptions of death and dying in these locations can be found in a number of soldiers' letters and diaries, anticipating the shifting scenery of expiration from home to hospital. The presence of corpses, as well as other reminders of human mortality like piles of amputated limbs, did not evoke images of order and solemnity. Instead, death and burial had many of the same characteristics as found on fields of battle, though a rudimentary graveyard next to these hospitals allowed for a slightly more organized space for disposing of remains.

In addition to hospitals and battlefields, another location where Civil War dead could be buried included prisons. According to one account of prison burials by a Union soldier incarcerated in Georgia's Andersonville Prison, treatment of the dead followed a fairly regimented set of procedures. These procedures included pinning the name of the deceased on his shirt, transportation to the prison "dead-house," placement on a wagon with twenty to thirty other bodies, and then transferal to the cemetery, where a superintendent overseeing the burial ground would assume responsibilities for ensuring as adequate a burial as possible. Dead prisoners were placed in trenches, usually without any covering, and buried under prison dirt. The location of each body was then marked with a stake at the head identifying the soldier and the date of death.

For family members and friends in the North, the prospect of loved ones dying far away from home, and being interred in what most considered to be profane Southern soil, led to a great deal of anguish and outrage. Indeed, many Northerners were deeply disturbed by this prospect because it upset normal social scripts ingrained in American culture when a family experienced a death. In normal times, death occurred in the home, people had a chance to view the body before it disappeared forever, and burial took place in a familiar space, which usually included previously deceased family members and neighbors. These were not normal times for sure, so some families, particularly the more affluent families in the North, would do whatever they could to bring the body of a loved family member's home, either by making the trip south on their own, or paying someone to locate, retrieve, and ship the body north.

As a result of these desires—to maintain familial control over the final resting place and, if possible, to have one last look before the body

*Union soldiers prepare to bury dead soldiers that are underneath tarps. Excluding the Vietnam War, Civil War deaths nearly equaled the number of deaths in all other wars in U.S. history combined.* LIBRARY OF CONGRESS

vanished—a new form of treating the dead appeared on the social scene, and paved the way for the birth of an entirely modern funeral industry. Undertakers who contracted with Northern families began to experiment with innovative means to preserve bodies that had to be shipped long distances on train cars, often during the hot summer months. The revolutionary practice that emerged in this context, embalming, provided both the military and Northern communities with a scientific, sanitary, and sensible way to move bodies across the land.

**Making Sense of Death**

In peaceful times, death is often experienced as a painful, disruptive, and confusing moment that requires individuals to draw on strongly held religious convictions about the meaning of life, the fate of the soul, and the stability of an ordered cosmos. During war, when individuals are called to sacrifice their lives for the good of the nation and

prepare for an early, violent end, the religion of nationalism makes a distinctive mark on meaning-making efforts circulating throughout public culture. Indeed, the religion of nationalism becomes an integral frame of reference when war breaks out, setting earthly, political conflicts in a cosmic realm of ultimate good battling ultimate evil. In the Civil War, two conflicting visions of American national life came into sharp relief against the backdrop of fields of bloodied bodies and widespread social anguish over the loss of sons, brothers, fathers, and husbands fighting for God and country.

Both Northerners and the Southerners believed God was on their side, and the nation envisioned by each a fulfillment of distinctive Christian commitments and values. Indeed, the blood of martyrs dying in the fight over slavery, and their sacrifices for the preservation of a sacred moral order ordained by God, had curative powers in the mind of many leading figures precisely because the nationalist ideologies of each side relied on Christian imagery and doctrine to justify killing, and being killed, in the service of a higher good. Although certain dead heroic figures had been intimately linked to the destiny of the nation from the Revolutionary War to the attack on Fort Sumter, the U.S. Civil War dramatically altered that linkage, and established a context for imagining innovative ways of making sense of death in American culture.

One concrete example of this innovation was the creation of military cemeteries, a new form of sacred space that gave material expression to religious sensibilities tied to both Christianity and nationalism. First established during the war by the federal government, military cemeteries gave order to death by placing bodies of fallen soldiers in a tidy, permanent, and sacrosanct space that glorified both the war effort and the Christian virtues associated with it. In the midst of the war and in the immediate aftermath these cemeteries made profoundly political statements about Northern power, resources, and determination.

After Congress approved the purchase of land by the government in 1862, twelve new cemeteries located on or near major battlefields, Union camps and hospitals, and other military sites were authorized. Most of them, including Robert E. Lee's estate near the Potomac, were on Southern soil, thereby enhancing the political and sacral weight of each.

President Abraham Lincoln articulated the essential meanings undergirding these cemeteries during his dedication speech at Gettysburg. Here Lincoln transformed the bloodied ground and buried lifeless bodies into the rich symbolic soil nourishing Union ideology and American traditions. In the brief speech, Lincoln successfully integrated the fallen soldiers into American mythology, giving them a permanent, holy spot in the physical landscape and assigning them a pivotal, transcendent role in the unfolding of American history. He also gave voice to the incalculable national debt living American citizens owed to the dead.

After the war, the victorious federal government began to ensure that as many Union soldiers as possible were identified and interred in the sacred space of national cemeteries. One of the first postwar national cemeteries was established on the grounds of Andersonville, a site that held profound symbolic meaning for Northerners who, by the end of the war, were outraged by the treatment of federal soldiers there. More than sixty cemeteries owned and operated by the government appeared across the North and South, and within the next decade nearly 300,000 bodies were reinterred. Trumpeting republican values and Christian morality, these cemeteries provided American citizens with an accessible space—in time, many became popular tourist destinations—that imposed a victorious national identity and promoted collective revitalization.

Northern and Southern leaders also gave meaning to the war dead through public pronouncements, in religious services, and by glorifying individual stories of heroism and sacrifice during and after the conflict. Unprecedented levels of social grief and mourning throughout American communities required extraordinary efforts at meaning-making that spoke to the profound emotional pain of individual citizens as well as created a shared sense of loss that could only be overcome through ultimate victory.

Many saw the battle in apocalyptic terms, with the very salvation of American society, and indeed the entire world, at stake. Millennial notions about the impending return of Christ, the role of the nation in this momentous event, and the demonization of the enemy transformed the blood of fallen soldiers into a potent source of social regeneration that would eventually purify the sins of the nation. Leaders on both sides, for example, publicly encouraged citizens to keep the cosmic implications of the war in mind, rather than stay focused on the tragedy of individual deaths on the battlefield. In this rhetorical context, mass death became meaningful because it forcefully brought home a critical realization about the life and destiny of the nation: It occasionally requires the blood of its citizens to fertilize the life-sustaining spirit of patriotism.

On the other hand, however, Northerners committed to democratic ideals and individual rights also took great pains to glorify, and sentimentalize, the deaths of certain soldiers who embodied at the time of their death national virtues like courage in the face of injustice, spiritual preparedness with an eye toward heavenly rewards, and concern about stability at home with one foot in the grave. Numerous accounts of individuals dying a heroic death on the battlefield or in hospitals were anchored with abundantly rich symbol systems relating to Jesus Christ, America, and home. Indeed, whether death became meaningful in collective or personal terms, a reinterpretation of what it meant to die triumphantly and heroically took place over the course of the war, and was animated by one, two, or all three of these symbolic systems.

Both Northerners and Southerners kept certain deaths in mind and used them as a symbolic and inspirational resource throughout the fighting. For the Confederacy, one of the critical figures in the pantheon of heroic leaders was Stonewall Jackson. A paragon of Christian virtue and piety, Southern honor and pride, Jackson died after being accidentally wounded by one of his own men at the battle of Chancellorsville in 1863. The example of his death, with a chaplain close at hand, his wife singing hymns, and a calm, peaceful demeanor during his last hours, aroused many downhearted Confederates and, in time, attained mythological standing in Southern culture. After the war, Jackson, along with other venerated Southern heroes who eventually passed on like Robert E. Lee and Jefferson Davis, played an important role in the creation of a cultural system of meaning that transformed defeat into the basis for a regionally distinctive southern identity. The southern historian Charles Reagan Wilson argues that this identity embodies a peculiar religious system, the religion of the Lost Cause. This cultural religion, still vital and strong in the twenty-first century, can be characterized as a cult of the dead since much of its mythological and ritual dimensions focus on deceased Southern martyrs who died during the war.

While many responses to the Civil War conveyed a belief in the regenerative powers of violent death, and that redemption of both the individual and society followed in the wake of mass sacrifices by young men, some grew hardened to the savagery and suffering taking place on American soil. For these people, including soldiers themselves who witnessed fighting firsthand, the meaning of death had nothing to do with religious notions like regeneration or redemption. Rather than being swept away by the emotional resonance of responses that glorified the dead and focused on the life of the spirit, certain individuals grew more and more disenchanted with the symbolism of death. Soldiers on the battlefield, military and political leaders guiding the troops, and citizens back home reading eyewitness accounts or seeing visual depictions of the fighting assumed a more pragmatic, disengaged posture, and became indifferent to scenes of human carnage and the deaths of individual men. The question first raised by these attitudes—Does overexposure to death and violence lead to desensitization?—continues to plague twenty-first-century American society.

## Advances in Weaponry

Finally, one of the more long-lasting social changes associated with American experiences in the Civil War has to do with the emergence of a particularly strong cultural and political obsession with guns. During the war, technological advances in weaponry, and the wide distribution of rifles and pistols among the male population, transformed the way Americans related to their guns. After the war, a gun culture took shape that to this day remains anchored by both the mythic and social power of owning a weapon, threatening to use it in the face of perceived danger (a danger often understood as jeopardizing the three symbol systems mentioned earlier, Christian virtues, national security, or more commonly, home life), and using it as an expression of power. This fascination with guns, coupled with an ingrained historical tendency to experience violence as a form of social and religious regeneration, has contributed to making violent death in America a common feature of daily life.

*See also:* BROWN, JOHN; CEMETERIES, MILITARY; CEMETERIES, WAR; LINCOLN IN THE NATIONAL MEMORY; WAR

## *Bibliography*

Adams, George Washington. *Doctors in Blue: The Medical History of the Union Army in the Civil War*. New York: Henry Schuman, 1952.

Farrell, James J. *Inventing the American Way of Death, 1830–1920*. Philadelphia: Temple University Press, 1980.

Faust, Drew Gilpin. "The Civil War Soldier and the Art of Dying." *The Journal of Southern History* 67, no. 1 (2001):3–40.

Fredrickson, George M. *The Inner Civil War: Northern Intellectuals and the Crisis of the Union*. New York: Harper and Row, 1965.

Jackson, Charles O., ed. *Passing: The Vision of Death in America*. Westport, CT: Greenwood, 1977.

Laderman, Gary. *The Sacred Remains: American Attitudes toward Death, 1799–1883*. New Haven, CT: Yale University Press, 1996.

Linderman, Gerald F. *Embattled Courage: The Experience of Combat in the American Civil War*. New York: Free Press, 1987.

Linenthal, Edward. *Sacred Ground: Americans and Their Battlefields*. Urbana: University of Illinois Press, 1991.

MacCloskey, Monro. *Hallowed Ground: Our National Cemeteries*. New York: Richards Rosen, 1969.

Mayer, Robert G. *Embalming: History, Theory, and Practice*. Norwalk, CT: Appleton and Lange, 1990.

McPherson, James M. *Battle Cry of Freedom: The Civil War Era*. New York: Ballantine, 1989.

Miller, Randall M., Harry S. Stout, and Charles Reagan Wilson, eds. *Religion and the American Civil War*. New York: Oxford University Press, 1998.

Moorhead, James H. *American Apocalypse: Yankee Protestants and the Civil War, 1860–1869*. New Haven, CT: Yale University Press, 1978.

Paluden, Phillip Shaw. *"A People's Contest": The Union and the Civil War, 1861–1865*. New York: Harper and Row, 1988.

Saum, Lewis O. *The Popular Mood of America, 1860–1890*. Lincoln: University of Nebraska Press, 1990.

Shattuck, Gardiner H., Jr. *A Shield and a Hiding Place: The Religious Life of the Civil War Armies*. Macon, GA: Mercer University Press, 1987.

COMMUNICATION WITH THE DEAD

Sloane, David Charles. *The Last Great Necessity: Cemeteries in American History.* Baltimore, MD: Johns Hopkins University Press, 1991.

Slotkin, Richard. *Regeneration through Violence: The Mythology of the American Frontier, 1600–1860.* Middletown, CT: Wesleyan University Press, 1973.

Steiner, Peter E. *Disease in the Civil War: Natural Biological Warfare, 1861–1865.* Springfield, IL: C. C. Thomas, 1968.

Vinovskis, Maris A., ed. *Toward a Social History of the American Civil War: Exploratory Essays.* Cambridge: Cambridge University Press, 1990.

Wells, Robert V. *Revolutions in Americans' Lives: A Demographic Perspective on the History of Americans, Their Families, and Their Society.* Westport, CT: Greenwood, 1982.

Wilson, Charles Reagan. *Baptized in Blood: The Religion of the Lost Cause, 1865–1920.* Athens: University of Georgia Press, 1980.

GARY M. LADERMAN

# CLINICAL DEATH

*See* BRAIN DEATH; DEFINITIONS OF DEATH.

# COMA

*See* ADVANCE DIRECTIVES; DEFINITIONS OF DEATH; DO NOT RESUSCITATE; LIFE SUPPORT SYSTEM.

# COMMUNICATION WITH THE DEAD

Distant communication has been transformed since ancient times. People can bridge the distance between absent loved ones by picking up a cellular phone, sending e-mail, or boarding a jet that quickly eradicates physical distance. Nevertheless, technology has not improved communication when it is death that separates individuals. The rich and varied history of attempts to communicate with its tantalizing melange of fact and history continues into the present day.

## Attracting and Cherishing the Dead

John Dee fascinated Queen Elizabeth in the middle of the sixteenth century when he provided valuable service to the Crown as a navigational consultant, mathematician, and secret agent. What especially piqued the Queen's interest, though, was Dee's mirror. It was an Aztec mirror that had fallen into his hands—along with its story. Supposedly one could see visions by gazing into the mirror in a receptive state of mind. The Queen was among those who believed she had seen a departed friend in Dee's mirror.

Some claim that the dead choose to communicate with the living and the living can also reach out to them by using special techniques and rituals. These propositions have been accepted by many people since ancient times. Greek religious cults and the Aztecs both discovered the value of reflective surfaces for this purpose.

Raymond A. Moody, best known for his pioneering work on near-death experiences, literally unearthed the ancient tradition when he visited the ruins of a temple known as the Oracle of the Dead. There, on a remote and sacred hilltop in Heraclea, priests could arrange for encounters between the living and the dead. Moody recounts his visit:

> The roof of the structure is gone, leaving exposed the maze of corridors and rooms that apparition seekers wandered through while waiting to venture into the apparition chamber. . . . I tried to imagine what this place would have been like two thousand years ago when it was dark as a cave and filled with a kind of eerie anticipation. What did the people think and feel during the weeks they were in here? Even though I like to be alone, my mind boggled at the thought of such lengthy and total sensory deprivation. *(Moody 1992, p. 88)*

The apparition chamber was the largest room. It was also probably the most majestic and impressive room the visitors had ever seen. After weeks in the dark, they were now bathed in light. Candles flickered against the walls as priests led them toward the centerpiece, a cauldron whose highly polished metal surface glittered and gleamed with reflections. With priestly guidance, the seekers gazed at the mirrored surface and the dead appeared—or did they? No one knows what their eyes beheld. This ritual was persuasive enough,

—173—

though, that it continued until the temple was destroyed by the conquering Romans. It is reasonable to suppose that some of the living did have profoundly stirring experiences, for they believed themselves to be in contact with loved ones who had crossed to the other side. Dee's Aztec mirror may also have been the stimulus for visions in sixteenth-century England. People thought they were seeing something or somebody.

The crystal ball eventually emerged as the preferred intermediary object. Not everybody was adept. Scryers had the knack of peering into the mystical sphere where they could sometimes see the past and the future, the living and the dead. Meanwhile, in jungle compounds thousands of miles away, there were others who could invoke the dead more directly—through the skull. Bones survived decomposition while flesh rotted away. The skull was, literally, the crowning glory of all bones and therefore embodied a physical link with the spirit of the deceased. It was a treasure to own a hut filled with the skulls of ancestors and perhaps of distinguished members of other tribes. The dead were there all the time and could be called upon for their wisdom and power when the occasion demanded.

Moody attempted to bring the *psychomanteum* (oracle of the dead) practice into modern times. He created a domestic-sized apparition chamber in his home. He allegedly experienced reunions (some of them unexpected) with his own deceased family members and subsequently invited others to do the same. Moody believed that meeting the dead had the potential for healing. The living and the dead have a second chance to resolve tensions and misunderstandings in their relationship. Not surprisingly, people have responded to these reports as wish-fulfillment illusions and outright hallucinations, depending on their own belief systems and criteria for evidence.

## Prayer, Sacrifice, and Conversation

Worship often takes the form of prayer and may be augmented by either physical or symbolic sacrifice. The prayer messages (e.g., "help our people") and the heavy sacrifices are usually intended for the gods. Many prayers, though, are messages to the dead. Ancestor worship is a vital feature of Yoruba society, and Shintoism, in its various forms, is organized around behavior toward the dead.

Zoroastrianism, a major religion that arose in the Middle East, has been especially considerate of the dead. Sacrifices are offered every day for a month on behalf of the deceased, and food offerings are given for thirty years. Prayers go with the deceased person to urge that divine judgment be favorable. There are also annual holidays during which the dead revisit their homes, much like the Mexican Days of the Dead. It is during the Fravardegan holidays that the spirits of the dead reciprocate for the prayers that have been said on their behalf; they bless the living and thereby promote health, fertility, and success. In one way or another, many other world cultures have also looked for favorable responses from the honored dead.

Western monotheistic religions generally have discouraged worship of the dead as a pagan practice; they teach that only God should be the object of veneration. Despite these objections, cults developed around mortals regarded as touched by divine grace. The Catholic Church has taken pains to evaluate the credentials for sainthood and, in so doing, has rejected many candidates. Nevertheless, Marist worship has long moved beyond cult status as sorrowing and desperate women have sought comfort by speaking to the Virgin Mary. God may seem too remote or forbidding to some of the faithful, or a woman might simply feel that another woman would have more compassion for her suffering.

Christian dogma was a work in progress for several centuries. By the fourth century it was decided that the dead could use support from the living until God renders his final judgment. The doctrine of purgatory was subsequently accepted by the church. Masses for the dead became an important part of Christian music. The Gregorian chant and subsequent styles of music helped to carry the fervent words both to God and the dead who awaited his judgment.

Throughout the world, much communication intended for the dead occurs in a more private way. Some people bring flowers to the graveside and not only tell the deceased how much they miss them, but also share current events with them. Surviving family members speak their hearts to photographs of their deceased loved ones even though the conversation is necessarily one-sided. For example, a motorist notices a field of bright-eyed daisies and sends a thought-message to an old friend: "Do you see that, George? I'll bet you can!"

## Mediums and Spiritualism

People often find comfort in offering prayers or personal messages to those who have been lost to death. Do the dead hear them? And can the dead find a way to respond? These questions came to the fore during the peak of Spiritualism.

Technology and science were rapidly transforming Western society by the middle of the nineteenth century. These advances produced an anything-is-possible mindset. Inventors Thomas Edison (incandescent light bulb) and Guglielmo Marconi (radio) were among the innovators who more than toyed with the idea that they could develop a device to communicate with the dead. Traditional ideas and practices were dropping by the wayside, though not without a struggle. It was just as industrialization was starting to run up its score that an old idea appeared in a new guise: One can communicate with the spirits of the dead no matter what scientists and authorities might say. There was an urgency about this quest. Belief in a congenial afterlife was one of the core assumptions that had become jeopardized by science (although some eminent researchers remained on the side of the angels). Contact from a deceased family member or friend would be quite reassuring.

Those who claimed to have the power for arranging these contacts were soon known as *mediums*. Like the communication technology of the twenty-first century, mediumship had its share of glitches and disappointments. The spirits were not always willing or able to visit the séances (French for "a sitting"). The presence of even one skeptic in the group could break the receptive mood necessary to encourage spirit visitation. Mediums who were proficient in luring the dead to their darkened chambers could make a good living by so doing while at the same time providing excitement and comfort to those gathered.

Fascination with spirit contacts swept through much of the world, becoming ever more influential as aristocrats, royalty, and celebrities from all walks of life took up the diversion. The impetus for this movement, though, came from a humble rural American source. The Fox family had moved into a modest home in the small upstate New York town of Hydesville. Life there settled into a simple and predictable routine. This situation was too boring for the young Fox daughters, Margaretta and

Kate. Fortunately, things livened up considerably when an invisible spirit, Mr. Splitfoot, made himself known. This spirit communicated by rapping on walls and tables. He was apparently a genial spirit who welcomed company. Kate, for example, would clap her hands and invite Mr. Splitfoot to do likewise, and he invariably obliged.

The girls' mother also welcomed the diversion and joined in the spirit games. In her words:

> I asked the noise to rap my different children's ages, successively. Instantly, each one of my children's ages was given correctly . . . until the seventh, at which a longer pause was made, and then three more emphatic raps were given, corresponding to the age of the little one that died, which was my youngest child. (*Doyle 1926, vol. 1, pp. 61–65*)

The mother was impressed. How could this whatever-it-is know the ages of her children? She invented a communication technique that was subsequently used throughout the world in contacts with the audible but invisible dead. She asked Mr. Splitfoot to respond to a series of questions by giving two raps for each "yes." She employed this technique systematically:

> I ascertained . . . that it was a man, aged 31 years, that he had been murdered in this house, and his remains were buried in the cellar; that his family consisted of a wife and five children . . . all living at the time of his death, but that his wife had since died. I asked: "Will you continue to rap if I call my neighbors that they may hear it too?" The raps were loud in the affirmative. . . . (*Doyle 1926, vol. 1, pp. 61–65*)

And so started the movement known first as Spiritism and later as Spiritualism as religious connotations were added. The neighbors were called in and, for the most part, properly astounded. Before long the Fox sisters had become a lucrative touring show. They demonstrated their skills to paying audiences both in small towns and large cities and were usually well received. The girls would ask Mr. Splitfoot to answer questions about the postmortem well-being of people dear to members of the audience. A few of their skeptics included three professors from the University of

Buffalo who concluded that Mr. Splitfoot's rappings were produced simply by the girls' ability to flex their knee-joints with exceptional dexterity. Other learned observers agreed. The *New York Herald* published a letter by a relative of the Fox family that also declared that the whole thing was a hoax. P. T. Barnum, the great circus entrepreneur, brought the Fox girls to New York City, where the large crowds were just as enthusiastic as the small rural gatherings that had first witnessed their performances.

Within a year or so of their New York appearance, there were an estimated 40,000 Spiritualists in that city alone. People interested in the new Spiritism phenomena often formed themselves into informal organizations known as "circles," a term perhaps derived from the popular "sewing circles" of the time. Many of the Spiritualists in New York City were associated with an estimated 300 circles. Horace Greeley, editor of the *New York Tribune,* and a former Supreme Court judge were among the luminaries who had become supporters of the movement. Mediums also helped to establish a thriving market developed for communication with the beyond. The movement spread rapidly throughout North America and crossed the oceans, where it soon enlisted both practitioners and clients in abundance.

Table-rapping was supplemented and eventually replaced by other communication technologies. The Ouija board was wildly popular for many years. This was a modern derivative of devices that had been used to communicate with the dead 2,500 years ago in China and Greece. The new version started as the *planchette,* a heart-shaped or triangular, three-legged platform. While moving the device over a piece of paper, one could produce graphic or textual messages. The belief was that the person who operates the device really does not have control over the messages, which is up to the spirits.

The Ouija board was criticized by some as too effective, and, therefore, dangerous. Believers in the spirit world feared that evil entities would respond to the summons, taking the place of the dearly departed. Other critics warned that the "manifestations" did not come from spirits of the dead but rather had escaped from forbidden corners of the user's own mind and could lead to psychosis and suicide.

## Fraudulent Communication with the Dead

The quest to communicate with the dead soon divided into two distinct but overlapping approaches. One approach consisted of earnest efforts by people who either longed for contact with their deceased loved ones or were curious about the phenomena. The other approach consisted of outright fraud and chicanery intended to separate emotionally needy and gullible people from their money. Examples of the latter were so numerous that those searching for the truth of the matter were often discouraged. At the same time that modern investigative techniques were being developed, such as those pioneered by Pinkerton detective agency, there was also the emergence of spirit sleuths who devoted themselves to exposing the crooks while looking for any possible authentic phenomena. The famed illusionist Harry Houdini was among the most effective whistle-blowers during the Spiritism movment. Calling upon his technical knowledge in the art of deception, he declared that astounding people with entertaining illusions was very different from claiming supernatural powers and falsely raising hopes about spirit contact.

The long list of deceptive techniques included both the simple and brazen, and the fairly elaborate. Here are a few examples from spirit sleuth John Mulholland:

- A match-box sized device was constructed to provide a series of "yes" and "no" raps. All the medium had to do was to ask a corresponding series of questions.

- A blank slate placed on one's head in a darkened room would mysteriously be written upon by a spirit hand. The spirit was lent a hand by a confederate behind a panel who deftly substituted the blank slate for one with a prewritten message.

- Spirit hands would touch sitters at a séance to lend palpable credibility to the proceedings. Inflatable gloves were stock equipment for mediums.

- Other types of spirit touches occurred frequently if the medium had but one hand or foot free or, just as simply, a hidden confederate. A jar of osphorized olive oil and skillful suggestions constituted one of the easier ways of producing apparitions in a dark

*Redesigned and renamed, the Ouija (combining the French* oui *and German* ja *for "yes") was used by vast numbers of people who hoped to receive messages from the beyond.* BETTMANN/CORBIS

room. Sitters, self-selected for their receptivity to spirits, also did not seem to notice that walking spirits looked a great deal like the medium herself.

• The growing popularity of photographers encouraged many of the dead to return and pose for their pictures. These apparitions were created by a variety of means familiar to and readily duplicated by professional photographers.

One of the more ingenious techniques was innovated by a woman often considered the most convincing of mediums. Margery Crandon, the wife of a Boston surgeon, was a bright, refined, and likable woman who burgeoned into a celebrated medium. Having attracted the attention of some of the best minds in the city, she sought new ways to demonstrate the authenticity of spirit contact. A high point was a session in which the spirit of the deceased Walter not only appeared but also left his fingerprints. This was unusually hard

evidence—until spirit sleuths discovered that Walter's prints were on file in a local dentist's office and could be easily stamped on various objects. Unlike most other mediums, Margery seemed to enjoy being investigated and did not appear to be in it for the money.

Automatic writing exemplified the higher road in attempted spirit communication. This is a dissociated state of consciousness in which a person's writing hand seems to be at the service of some unseen "Other." The writing comes at a rapid tempo and looks as though written by a different hand. Many of the early occurrences were unexpected and therefore surprised the writer. It was soon conjectured that these were messages from the dead, and automatic writing then passed into the repertoire of professional mediums. The writings ranged from personal letters to full-length books. A century later, the spirits of Chopin and other great composers dictated new compositions to Rosemary Brown, a Londoner with limited skills at the piano. The unkind verdict was that death had taken the luster off their genius. The writings provided the basis for a new wave of investigations and experiments into the possibility of authentic communication with the dead. Some examples convinced some people; others dismissed automatic writing as an interesting but nonevidential dissociative activity in which, literally, the left hand did not know what the right hand was doing.

The cross-correspondence approach was stimulated by automatic writing but led to more complex and intensive investigations. The most advanced type of cross-correspondence is one in which the message is incomplete until two or more minds have worked together without ordinary means of communication—and in which the message itself could not have been formulated through ordinary means of information exchange. One of the most interesting cross-correspondence sequences involved Frederick W. H. Myers, a noted scholar who had made systematic efforts to investigate the authenticity of communication with the dead. Apparently he continued these efforts after his death by sending highly specific but fragmentary messages that could not be completed until the recipients did their own scholarly research. Myers also responded to questions with the knowledge and wit for which he had been admired during his life. Attempts have been made to explain cross-correspondences in terms of telepathy among the living and to dismiss the phenomena altogether as random and overinterpreted. A computerized analysis of cross-correspondences might at least make it possible to gain a better perspective on the phenomena.

## The Decline of Spiritism

The heyday of Spiritism and mediums left much wreckage and a heritage of distrust. It was difficult to escape the conclusion that many people had such a desire to believe that they suspended their ordinary good judgment. A striking example occurred when Kate Fox, in her old age, not only announced herself to have been a fraud but also demonstrated her repertoire of spirit rappings and knockings to a sold-out audience in New York City. The audience relished the performance but remained convinced that Mr. Splitfoot was the real thing. Mediumship, having declined considerably, was back in business after World War I as families grieved for lost fathers, sons, and brothers. The

intensified need for communication brought forth the service.

Another revival occurred when mediums, again out of fashion, were replaced by channelers. The process through which messages are conveyed and other associated phenomena have much in common with traditional Spiritism. The most striking difference is the case of past life regression in which it is the individual's own dead selves who communicate. The case of Bridey Murphy aroused widespread interest in past-life regression and channeling. Investigation of the claims for Murphy and some other cases have resulted in strong arguments against their validity.

There are still episodes of apparent contact with the dead that remain open for wonder. One striking example involves Eileen Garrett, "the skeptical medium" who was also a highly successful executive. While attempting to establish communication with the recently deceased Sir Arthur Conan Doyle, she and her companions were startled and annoyed by an interruption from a person who gave his name as "Flight Lieutenant H. Carmichael Irwin." This flight officer had died in the fiery crash of dirigible R101. Garrett brought in an aviation expert for a follow-up session with Irwin, who described the causes of the crash in a degree of detail that was confirmed when the disaster investigation was completed months later.

The Psychic Friends Network and television programs devoted to "crossing over" enjoy a measure of popularity in the twenty-first century, long after the popularity of the Spiritualism movement. Examples such as these as well as a variety of personal experiences continue to keep alive the possibility of communication with the dead—and perhaps possibility is all that most people have needed from ancient times to the present.

See also: DAYS OF THE DEAD; GHOST DANCE; GHOSTS; NEAR-DEATH EXPERIENCES; NECROMANCY; SPIRITUALISM MOVEMENT; VIRGIN MARY, THE; ZOROASTRIANISM

## Bibliography

Barrett, William. *Death-Bed Visions: The Psychical Experiences of the Dying.* 1926. Reprint, Northampshire, England: Aquarian Press, 1986.

Bernstein, Morey. *The Search for Bridey Murphy.* New York: Pocket Books, 1965.

Brandon, Samuel George Frederick. *The Judgment of the Dead*. New York: Charles Scribner's Sons, 1967.

Covina, Gina. *The Ouija Book*. New York: Simon & Schuster, 1979.

Douglas, Alfred. *Extrasensory Powers: A Century of Psychical Research*. Woodstock, NY: Overlook Press, 1977.

Doyle, Arthur Conan. *The History of Spiritualism*. 2 vols. London: Cassell, 1926.

Garrett, Eileen J. *Many Voices: The Autobiography of a Medium*. New York: G. P. Putnam's Sons, 1968.

Hart, Hallan. *The Enigma of Survival*. Springfield, IL: Charles C. Thomas, 1959.

Kastenbaum, Robert. *Is There Life after Death?* New York: Prentice Hall Press, 1984.

Kurtz, Paul, ed. *A Skeptic's Handbook of Parapsychology*. Buffalo, NY: Prometheus Books, 1985.

Moody, Raymond A. "Family Reunions: Visionary Encounters with the Departed in a Modern Psychomanteum." *Journal of Near-Death Studies* 11 (1992):83–122.

Moody, Raymond A. *Life After Life*. Atlanta: Mockingbird Books, 1975.

Myers, Frederick W. H. *Human Personality and Its Survival of Death*. 2 vols. 1903. Reprint, New York: Arno Press, 1975.

Podmore, Frank. *The Newer Spiritualism*. 1910. Reprint, New York: Arno, 1975.

Richet, Charles. *Thirty Years of Psychical Research*. London: Collins, 1923.

Saltmarsh, Herbert Francis. *Evidence of Personal Survival from Cross Correspondences*. 1938. Reprint, New York: Arno, 1975.

Tietze, Thomas R. *Margery*. New York: Harper & Row, 1973.

ROBERT KASTENBAUM

# COMMUNICATION WITH THE DYING

Interpersonal communication regarding death, dying, and bereavement has become an increasingly important area in the field of thanatology, wherein research has addressed the critical role of open family communication in facilitating the positive processing of a death loss. In the 1990s, attention started to be given to communicative issues with reference to dying individuals, especially with regard to the need for improved communication between dying persons and their families, their physicians, and their nurses.

For many people, the thought of dying evokes as much or more fear and apprehension as does the thought of death itself. Consequently, discussing the dying process, as well as thinking about how one's last days, weeks, and months might be spent, can be very beneficial. Otherwise, the process of dying becomes a forbidden topic. It is in this context of fear, apprehension, and denial that dying persons are often viewed as persons whom one might feel sorry for, yet as individuals whose very presence makes caretakers and family members feel uneasy and whose feelings, attitudes, and behaviors are hard to relate to. In this light, it is not surprising that Sherwin Nuland wrote the best-selling *How We Die* (1993) to "demystify" the dying process.

Coincidentally, a focus on relief of symptoms and increased attention to the patient's and family's conception of a good quality of life has emerged in medical care, particularly in the context of life-threatening illness. For example, in "The Quest to Die with Dignity," a 1997 report published by American Health Decisions, a nonprofit group, people not only reported fears of dying "hooked to machines," but also did not feel that the health care system supported their conception of a "good death," that is, a "natural" death in familiar surroundings. Such findings were based on 36 focus groups totaling nearly 400 people.

Furthermore, a study commissioned by Americans for Better Care of the Dying reported that most Americans view death as "awful," and that dying persons are often avoided and stigmatized because of their condition. In 1987 the researchers Peter Northouse and Laurel Northouse found that 61 percent of healthy individuals stated that they would avoid cancer patients, and 52 percent of dying persons believed that others generally avoided them. Significantly, the project SUPPORT (Study to Understand Prognoses and Preferences for Outcomes and Risks for Treatment), which studied 9,000 patients with life-threatening illnesses in five teaching hospitals over a two-year period, reflects the difficulties patients have in communicating with their physicians at the end of life, where such persons' wishes regarding end-of-life care were largely ignored. Indeed, efforts to improve communication by educating physicians were not successful.

## Why People Have Difficulty Communicating with Dying Persons

Researchers have suggested several reasons for the difficulty many individuals have in communicating with dying persons: not wanting to face the reality of one's own death, not having the time to become involved, and not feeling emotionally able to handle the intensity of the situation. For some people, the grief that they experience in anticipation of a loved one's death may help to explain their difficulty in interacting with terminally ill individuals. For others, dying may have "gone on too long," and thus the dying person experiences the pain of being isolated from those whose love he or she needs most. Likewise, loved ones' beliefs about whether they could have somehow prevented the death or not may evoke more guilt in such persons, causing them to avoid interacting with a dying loved one.

Uneasiness in being with the dying can manifest itself via outright avoidance, or in difficulty in speaking or maintaining eye contact with such persons. It can also be expressed in maintaining a physical distance, uneasiness about touching the dying person, or an inability or unwillingness to listen. This may result in overconcern, hyperactivity, or manipulative, impersonal behavior (e.g., "Aren't we looking good today!"), or changing the subject. Significantly, this uneasiness is likely to be perceived by those who are already sensitive to being rejected because they are dying.

Efforts to measure fears about interacting with dying persons have been reflected in the Communication Apprehension Regarding the Dying Scale (CA-Dying), which operationalizes apprehension related to such communicative issues as talking to and making eye contact with a dying individual and the level of perceived closeness to this person. CA-Dying is independent of general communication apprehension, and positively related to overt fears regarding one's own death and another's dying, while negatively related to death acceptance

and covert death fear. In 1986 and 1987, the creator of this scale, the psychologist Bert Hayslip, found that scores on the CA-Dying scale decreased among a group of hospice volunteers enrolled in a training program relative to age-matched controls. In this respect, age relates negatively to CA-Dying scores, most likely due to increased death experience. Such apprehension does not vary with the nature of the dying person's illness; it is universal.

Characteristics of dying individuals also may affect one's apprehension about communicating with such persons. Because pain frequently accompanies terminal illness, its presence often affects simple communication. Such pain often preoccupies dying individuals' thoughts and may contribute to, along with intense emotional conflict and the effects of medication, an increase in contradictory messages between the individual and others. In addition, those dying violate several of the social standards in place in American society: They are often nonproductive, unattractive, not in control of themselves and of their life situation, and provoke anxiety in others.

Not all dying people are alike. Thus, some may evoke more avoidance than others, depending upon whether their death is expected or not, what they are dying of, where they die, and whether their deaths are seen as "on-time" (i.e., the death of an older person), or "off-time" (i.e., the death of a child, adolescent, or young adult). Additionally, some dying individuals are more able to deal with everyday demands than are others, and some prefer to talk or remain silent on matters related to death. Some individuals have more support from friends and families than do others, and some are more tolerant of pain. Some are more willing to communicate their awareness of dying than other dying individuals, and others are more able to discuss what it is they need in order to die peacefully.

## Important Steps in Communicating with Dying Persons

For those dying and their families, the prospect of their own or a loved one's imminent death can be a terrifying experience. Indeed, dying produces anxiety, leading to both dependence upon other people and defensiveness based upon fears of rejection. Consequently, being able to communicate honestly about the quality or length of one's life, the disease process, and one's feelings about loved family members or friends is of utmost importance. This communication (both verbal and nonverbal) is two-way—each individual is both giving and searching for cues about each person's acceptability to the other. Because preconceptions as "dying person," "hospice patient," or "caregiver" (professional or otherwise) govern or limit what aspects a person reveals about him- or herself, being open, genuine, empathic, and understanding allows this two-way dynamic to evolve beyond these "labels."

The benefits of open communication are clear. Relationships that allow for communication about death often precede healthy adjustment. Researchers have found that the emotional impact of being labeled as "dying" is directly related to quality and openness of the communication between the dying individual and others, wherein if open communication is not achieved caregivers operate on preconceptions rather than the dying individual's actual thoughts and feelings.

## Communicative Difficulties among Health Care Professionals

It could be argued that those persons whose attitudes and actions most influence the quality of end-of-life care are physicians, principally because they have primary control of the information that drives medical decision making. Furthermore, both patients and physicians agree that physicians have the responsibility to initiate discussions regarding advance directives and the use of life-sustaining medical intervention.

Many have noted the difficulty physicians experience in communicating with the dying and their families. For example, in 1977 the researcher Miriam Gluck suggested that physicians may fear emotional involvement, feel a loss of what to say, or lack knowledge about what the patient has been told. Often physicians may feel that terminal patients are medical "failures," are preoccupied with medical equipment and technical skills, fear the patient's anger, or fear that the patient will die.

Physicians, for the most part, seem to view death as the ultimate enemy, and many medical practitioners, when called upon to provide patient-centered palliative care, feel ill prepared. Personal and professional anxiety and occasionally even defensiveness often result. These responses often lead to missed opportunities for the patient, family,

and the physician to share in a peaceful, natural rite of passage. The discomfort felt by the physician in broaching the topic of advance directives may well to lead to outcomes not desired by the patient, such as unwanted continuation of life-sustaining medical treatment.

Discomfort in broaching the topic of advance directives, death, and symptom control may stem from a lack of confidence in providing palliative care or lack of understanding regarding the ethical and legal aspects of end-of-life decision making. Reluctance to discuss end-of-life issues with patients may also be caused by a fear of damaging their hope, a perception that the role of the physician is only to heal and preserve life, and feeling that such discussions should only occur in the context of an intimate relationship with the patient and family. Although physicians vary in the extent to which they are able to discuss sensitive end-of-life issues, such as the diagnosis or prognosis of a terminal illness, physicians' attitudes toward the care of the terminally ill, including the willingness to communicate about the end of life, are critical to ensuring an improved death for the majority of Americans who prefer to die "naturally."

In 1971 the researcher Samuel Klagsbrun found that, for nurses, fear of death to a certain extent affected responses to situations requiring interaction with the dying patient. Specifically, a higher fear of others' dying was related to increased uneasiness in talking about dying with the patient where the nurse did not have a "specific task" to perform. In addition, finding a terminally ill patient crying was also related to a high fear of others' dying. In cases where "appropriate behavior" was ill defined in caring for a dying patient, simple denial was used to cut short the interaction.

## What Is Special about Communicating with Dying Persons?

Loma Feigenberg and Edwin Shneidman have discussed four types of interactions with persons who are dying, which include (1) ordinary conversation, (2) hierarchical exchanges, (3) psychotherapy, and (4) thanatological exchanges. While ordinary conversation indicates that two individuals of equal status are talking about what is actually being said (e.g., the weather, sports, news items), hierarchical exchanges involve conversations between persons of unequal status, where one is more powerful or perceptually superior to the other (e.g., supervisor-subordinate, officer-enlisted man, oncologist-patient). Roles cannot be exchanged; that is, the patient cannot examine the oncologist. Clearly, hierarchical exchanges undermine genuine communication with dying persons. Psychotherapy focuses on feelings, emotional content, and the latent (unconscious) meaning of what is said, where the patient invests the therapist with magical powers or projects powerful emotions or qualities onto the therapist. As with hierarchical exchange, in psychotherapy therapist and patient are not equals. In thanatological exchanges, while participants are perceived as equals (as in ordinary conversations), thanatological interactions between persons are unique.

Dying is a distinctly interpersonal event involving a helping person and the dying patient; this "other" person may be a friend, neighbor, hospice volunteer, counselor, one's husband, wife, or one's child. Consequently, ordinary conversations with dying persons may be very "therapeutic" and, in fact, reflect many elements that are typical of formal psychotherapy, including active listening.

Active listening assumes the individuality of each dying person's needs, and stresses what is communicated both verbally and nonverbally. One's presence as well as questions that are asked say, "I am trying to understand how you feel." Reassurance and providing nonjudgmental support are critical. Moreover, using the dying person's name throughout the conversation, making eye contact, holding the person's hand, placing one's hand on a shoulder or arm, smiling, gesturing, and leaning forward all communicate genuine interest and caring in what the person is saying (or not saying) and feeling. Asking specific questions such as, "Can you help me understand?" as well as open-ended questions such as, "What is it that you need to do now?" are very important, as is being comfortable with silence.

Effective communication with dying people reflects comfort with one's own discomfort, to "do nothing more than sit quietly together in silence" (Corr, Nabe, and Corr 2000, p. 178). Indeed, communicating involves as much listening as it does talking and doing. Building good communication and listening skills, touching and maintaining eye contact, and projecting a genuine sense of empathy all give the message, "I am here to help and support you. I care about how you are feeling." In short, effective, empathic, and timely communication is embodied in the statement, "Be a friend."

Being attuned to verbal and nonverbal signals that the person wants to talk give permission to share. Providing the opportunity to expand on what the person has said by repeating what has been stated, using the person's own words, opens up communication, as does disclosing one's own thoughts and feelings. Such disclosure can help the individual talk about his or her own feelings. Doing this with others' needs in mind, not one's own, is very important.

In understanding dying people's needs, it is important to realize that different illnesses and illnesses in various stages of progression create different "dying trajectories" that make different physical, psychological, and psychosocial demands on those dying and their families. For example, the dying person may initially search for information regarding insurance coverage, the nature of the illness and its progression, treatment, or what the family can do to help to care for him or her. He or she may want to know about the side effects of pain-relieving medications. As the condition worsens, more intimate needs for reassurance and support may surface, and concerns about funeral planning, wills, or life without a loved one may be expressed. Near death, people may be less expressive about what they need, and emotional support may be all that they require. Rather than "doing" something, the caring persons may meet this need by simply "being there."

Dying people's and their families' feelings of being overwhelmed or of feeling vulnerable directly affect their behavior and willingness to talk. What passes for open, friendly conversation one day can change suddenly. One may be angrily rebuffed, rejected, or totally ignored because the person is in pain or because the person has had a fight with a child or spouse. The individual who is more aware of his or her disease and its impact on future relationships and plans may be more angry or depressed than usual; communication may cease altogether or be severely curtailed. No appreciation for time spent or help given (however unselfishly) may be expressed. On other days, this same person may be very open or psychologically dependent on the professional caregiver. Fears, hopes, or secrets may be willingly shared. Such fluctuations are to be expected and are characteristic of the "ups and downs" of the dying process. One must be attentive to not only the dying individual's words, but what words and actions may symbolize.

Critical to understanding dying persons' concerns is understanding both the patient's and the family's needs in a variety of areas. These needs cut across many domains—physical (pain control); psychosocial (maintaining close relationships with others); spiritual (integrating or resolving spiritual beliefs); financial (overcoming the costs of medical or hospice care, having adequate funds to cover other financial obligations unrelated to care); and psychological (knowing about the illness and its course over time, talking over emotional difficulties, knowing that one's family is informed about the illness and that family members will be cared for well). Attending to as many of these needs as one can contributes to both the patient's and family's quality of life.

*See also:* DYING, PROCESS OF; GOOD DEATH, THE; LESSONS FROM THE DYING; SYMPTOMS AND SYMPTOM MANAGEMENT

## Bibliography

American Health Care Decisions. *The Quest to Die with Dignity: An Analysis of Americans' Values, Opinions, and Values Concerning End-of-Life Care.* Appleton, WI: Author, 1997.

Baider, Lea. "The Silent Message: Communication in a Family with a Dying Patient." *Journal of Marriage and Family Counseling* 3, no. 3 (1977):23–28.

Bugen, Lawrence. *Death and Dying: Theory, Research, and Practice.* Dubuque, IA: William C. Brown, 1979.

Cohn, Felicia, and John H. Forlini. *The Advocate's Guide to Better End-of-Life Care: Physician-Assisted Suicide and Other Important Issues.* Washington, DC: Center to Improve the Care of the Dying, 1997.

Corr, Charles, Kenneth J. Doka, and Robert Kastenbaum. "Dying and Its Interpreters: A Review of Selected Literature and Some Comments on the State of the Field." *Omega: The Journal of Death and Dying* 39 (1999):239–261.

Corr, Charles, Clyde Nabe, and Donna Corr. *Death and Dying: Life and Living.* Pacific Grove, CA: Brooks/Cole, 2000.

Dickenson, Donna, and Malcolm Johnson. *Death, Dying, and Bereavement.* London: Sage, 1996.

Epley, Rita J., and Charles H. McCaghy. "The Stigma of Dying: Attitudes toward the Terminally Ill." *Omega: The Journal of Death and Dying* 8 (1977–78):379–393.

Feigenberg, Loma, and Edwin Shneidman. "Clinical Thantology and Psychotherapy: Some Reflections on Caring for the Dying Person." *Omega: The Journal of Death and Dying* 10 (1979):1–8.

Glaser, Barney G., and Anselm L. Strauss. *Awareness of Dying.* Chicago: Aldine, 1965.

Gluck, Miriam. "Overcoming Stresses in Communication with the Fatally Ill." *Military Medicine* 142 (1977):926–928.

Hayslip, Bert. "The Measurement of Communication Apprehension Regarding the Terminally Ill." *Omega: The Journal of Death and Dying* 17 (1986–87):251–262.

Kastenbaum, Robert. *Death, Society, and Human Experience,* 7th edition. Boston: Allyn and Bacon, 2001.

Klagsbrun, Samuel C. "Communications in the Treatment of Cancer." *American Journal of Nursing* 71 (1971):948–949.

Lynn, Joanne, et al. "Perceptions by Family Members of the Dying Experience of Older and Seriously Ill Patients." *Annals of Internal Medicine* 126 (1997):97–126.

Marrone, Robert. *Death, Mourning, and Caring.* Pacific Grove, CA: Brooks Cole, 1997.

Northouse, Peter G., and Laura L. Northouse. "Communication and Cancer: Issues Confronting Patients, Health Professionals, and Family Members." *Journal of Psychosocial Oncology* 5 (1987):17–46.

Nurland, Sherwin B. *How We Die.* New York: Vintage, 1993.

Rando, Terese A. *Grief, Death and Dying.* Champaign, IL: Research Press Company, 1984.

SUPPORT. "A Controlled Trial to Improve Care for Seriously Ill Hospitalized Patients." *Journal of the American Medical Association* 274 (1995):1591–1599.

Trent, Curtis, J. C. Glass, and Ann Y. McGee. "The Impact of a Workshop on Death and Dying on Death Anxiety, Life Satisfaction, and Locus of Control Among Middle-Aged and Older Adults." *Death Education* 5 (1981):157–173.

BERT HAYSLIP JR.

# CONFUCIUS

Confucius (551–479 B.C.E.) was one of several intellectuals who started questioning the meaning of life, and the role of the gods and the spirits. During the Warring States Period, Confucius developed a system of ethics and politics that stressed five virtues: charity, justice, propriety, wisdom, and loyalty. His teachings were recorded by his followers in a book called *Analects,* and formed the code of ethics called Confucianism that has been the cornerstone of Chinese thought for many centuries.

Confucius's guiding belief was that of the philosophy *Tien Ming* (or the influences of fate and mission). Tien Ming states that all things are under the control of the regulatory mechanism of heaven. This includes life and death, wealth and poverty, health and illness. Confucius believed that understanding Tien Ming was his life's mission. He encouraged people to accept whatever happened to them, including death.

Confucius affirmed that if people do not yet know about life, people may not know about death (Soothill 1910). Without knowledge of how to live, a person cannot know about death and dying. However, Confucius was criticized for avoiding discussions of death. He did not encourage his followers to seek eternal life, nor did he discuss death, gods, ghosts, and the unknown future or afterlife in detail. He maintained that ghosts were spirits and were not easy to understand. Confucius concluded that these issues were complicated and abstract, and that it was better to spend time solving the problems of the present life than to look into the unknown world of death and afterlife. He wanted to convey the importance of valuing the existing life and of leading a morally correct life according to one's mission from heaven.

Confucius considered righteousness to be a basic requirement of a good person, stating that such a person would not seek to stay alive at the expense of injuring virtue. He encouraged people to uphold these moral principles and care for each other until death. His followers were exhorted to be loyal and dutiful toward family, kin, and neighbors, and to respect their superiors and the elderly. Filial piety to parents and ancestors is fundamental to these beliefs. Far from being characterized by fear, the attitudes of the living toward the departed members of the family or clan are one of continuous remembrance and affection.

These beliefs may partially explain why Qu Yuen and other students killed in the 1989 Tiananmen Square massacre in Beijing, China, were prepared to give up their lives to advocate the values of justice and goodness for their country. Those who follow such beliefs would have no regret when confronted with their own death and would accept death readily. This is regarded as a high level of moral behavior of family or social virtue. Although Confucius did not express it explicitly, to die for righteousness is an example of a good death for the individual as well as the nation.

*See also:* CHINESE BELIEFS; GHOSTS; GOOD DEATH, THE

### Bibliography

Henderson, Helene, and Sue Ellen Thompson. *Holidays, Festivals and Celebrations of the World Dictionary,* 2nd edition. Detroit: Omnigraphics, 1997.

Mak, Mui Hing June. "Death and Good Death." *Asian Culture Quarterly* 29, no. 1 (2001):29–42.

Overmyer, Daniel. "China." In Frederick Holck ed., *Death and Eastern Thought.* Nashville, TN: Abingdon Press, 1974.

Soothill, William Edward, trans. *The Analects of Confucius.* New York: Paragon Book Reprint Corp, 1968.

MUI HING JUNE MAK

# CONTINUING BONDS

The phrase "continuing bonds" was first used in 1996 to refer to an aspect of bereavement process in the title of the book, *Continuing Bonds: Another View of Grief,* which challenged the popular model of grief requiring the bereaved to "let go" of or detach from the deceased. It was clear from the data presented that the bereaved maintain a link with the deceased that leads to the construction of a new relationship with him or her. This relationship continues and changes over time, typically providing the bereaved with comfort and solace. Most mourners struggle with their need to find a place for the deceased in their lives and are often embarrassed to talk about it, afraid of being seen as having something wrong with them.

A spontaneous statement by Natasha Wagner, whose mother, the actress Natalie Wood, drowned when Natasha was a teenager, summarized this well: "I had to learn to have a relationship with someone who wasn't there anymore" (1998). More than a decade after the death of his first wife, playwright Robert Anderson wrote about her continued place in his life: "I have a new life. . . . Death ends a life, but it does not end a relationship, which struggles on in the survivor's mind toward some resolution which it never finds" (1974, p.77). With this statement, he legitimized his own experience and that of other mourners as well.

## Detachment Revisited

Until the twentieth century, maintaining a bond with the deceased had been considered a normal part of the bereavement process in Western society. In contrast, in the twentieth century the view prevailed that successful mourning required the bereaved to emotionally detach themselves from the deceased. The work of Sigmund Freud contributed significantly to this view, largely as a result of the paper *Mourning and Melancholia,* which he wrote in 1917. Grief, as Freud saw it, freed the mourner from his or her attachments to the deceased, so that when the work of mourning was completed, mourners were free to move ahead and become involved in new relationships. When one looks at Freud's writing regarding personal losses in his life, one learns that Freud understood that grief was not a process that resulted in cutting old attachments. Nonetheless, his theory took on a life of its own, and the mourners were advised to put the past behind them. This practice still continues into the twenty-first century.

Many practitioners observed that mourners often developed an inner representation of the deceased by internalizing attitudes, behavior, and values associated with the deceased. They saw this as a step in the process that eventually led the mourner to detach from the deceased and move on. The psychiatrist John Bowlby wrote that a discussion of mourning without identification—that is, finding a place for the deceased in one's sense of self—will seem like Hamlet without a prince. Like most observers of the bereavement process,

he was aware of the ways in which mourners identify with the deceased, but he concluded that when attachment to the deceased is prominent, it seems to be indicative of psychopathology.

Another factor promoting the view of a necessary detachment was that most observers were basing their work on clinical practice. People came to them with serious emotional problems, many of which derived from connections to the deceased that were out of the bereaved's awareness. These connections focused on negative consequences of the relationship and anchored the bereaved's current life inappropriately in the past. The clinician/researcher then generalized to the larger population of the bereaved, most of whom had a different experience.

Researchers Dennis Klass and Tony Walter contend that this view of grief, in which the dead were banned from the lives of those surviving them, gained popularity as interest in the afterlife waned in Western society. The growing influence of the scientific worldview in the twentieth century led to death being viewed as a medical failure or accident rather than as an inevitable part of the human condition. The physician George Lundberg wrote about the difficulties caused by the expectations of both physicians and those they serve that they can keep death away rather than accepting that death is both natural and inevitable.

The twentieth-century Western approach to human behavior that valued individuation and autonomy also supported the focus on detachment. Bowlby's development of the theory of attachment behavior in children focused on the individual and how his or her needs could be met. As this theory was subsequently applied to bereavement theory, the interactive, relational aspects of the process were not clearly spelled out. In the "letting go" model, a linear lens is applied, as if one experience can lead to one outcome, and this is how attachment theory was often applied as well. Yet psychologist Jerome Bruner noted that people can rarely be put into a simple cause-and-effect model. There are simply too many intervening variables reflecting the complexity of real life. In a linear model, bereavement is seen as a psychological condition or illness from which people could recover with the right treatment. In fact, bereavement does not go away but is a difficult and expected part of the normal life cycle; it is a period of loss, of change and transition in how the bereaved relate to themselves, to the deceased, and to the world around them.

At the beginning of the twenty-first century views of bereavement continue to evolve. There is a growing recognition of the complexity of the human condition and the importance of relationships in people's lives. Humans now recognize that the goal of development is not independence but interdependence. Relationships with others, living or dead, frame one's sense of self and how one lives. More and more we appreciate that there is continuity between the past and the present. Without a sense of the past and an understanding of its place in people's lives, it is difficult to move ahead.

## Various Expressions of Continuing Bonds

It is important not only for the individual but also for the community to find a way to relate to the deceased. Just as an individual's personal life is disrupted in a profound way by a death, so too is the larger social world. Ritual can play an important role in finding a place for the dead in the reconstituted world of both the bereaved and the community. In many cultures, religious beliefs and views of life after death govern the experience of the relationship.

In Catholicism, for example, mourners are expected to have a memorial mass on the anniversary of the death. In Judaism, mourners are obligated to remember family members who died by participating in synagogue memorial services five times during the year, including the anniversary of the death. Klass described the rituals practiced in the home in Japan to honor the deceased and their role in the family's ongoing life. He describes the Buddha altar where spirits of the deceased are venerated in daily prayer. In some societies, dreams in which the deceased appeared as well as other experiences of the deceased served to keep the deceased present in the survivors' lives. There are societies where there is no reference to the deceased after their death. In some communities, such as Native American communities, there is fear of the deceased returning to disrupt the lives of those left behind, and in other communities, like the aboriginal communities of Australia, there is a concern that talking about the deceased disrupts the soul's journey to the next life. This silence in

the community does not mean that there is no bond with the deceased; it is simply a relationship of a different sort that is unfamiliar to Westerners.

## Constructing a Bond

An understanding of the nature of the continuing relationship presupposes a specific knowledge of the deceased whether he or she was a young person, an old person, a parent, a child, a friend, or a member of the extended family. All of these roles reflect the relationship between the mourner and the deceased. What did the mourner lose? On what is the continuing connection being built? What part did the deceased play in the mourner's life? In the community's life? What did he or she contribute? What will be missing? All of these issues affect the connection.

The development of a bond is conscious, dynamic, and changing. Mourners' faith systems can affect the way in which they incorporate the departed into their lives. Some people believe that the deceased live in another dimension. Many believe the deceased are there to intervene and support them. Others do not depend on a faith system but rather build the connection out of the fabric of daily life and the sense of the deceased they carry within them.

Individuals can learn a good deal about continuing bonds from children and adolescents. They build a new relationship with the deceased by talking to the deceased, locating the deceased (usually in heaven), experiencing the deceased in their dreams, visiting the grave, feeling the presence of the deceased, and by participating in mourning rituals. The researchers Claude Normand, Phyllis Silverman, and Steven Nickman found that over time the children of deceased parents developed a connection to the departed that they described as "becoming their parent's living legacy" (Normand 1996, p. 93). They began to emulate their parents in ways that they believe would have pleased them, thus confirming social worker Lily Pincus's thesis that mourners identify with the deceased, adopting aspects of the deceased's behavior and feeling that the deceased has become part of their current identity.

Adults also find themselves dreaming, talking to, and feeling the presence of the deceased. Some see the deceased as a role model from whose wisdom and learning they can draw. They sometimes turn to the deceased for guidance. They also tend to adopt or reject a moral position identified with the deceased in order to clarify their own values. Finally, they actively form their thoughts in ways that facilitate their remembering the deceased.

Psychologist Lora Helms Tessman describes the dilemma an adult child experienced trying to reconcile her father's Nazi background while maintaining a "liveable" memory of him. Psychiatrist Ann Marie Rizzuto observed that the process of constructing inner representations involves the whole individual and that these representations grow and change with the individual's development and maturation. The role of the other person is very important so that construction is partly a social activity. Parents play a key role in helping their bereaved children relate to the deceased and in keeping him or her in their lives.

One sees that grief is never finished, that the way the bereaved relate to the deceased changes as they develop over the life cycle, whether they be young or old mourners. Yet there seems to be a lack of appropriate language for describing mourning as part of the life cycle. People need to stop thinking of grief as being entirely present or absent. People rarely just "get over it," nor do they ever really find "closure." The phrase "continuing bonds" is one contribution to a new language that reflects a new understanding of this process.

A continuing bond does not mean, however, that people live in the past. The very nature of mourners' daily lives is changed by the death. The deceased are both present and absent. One cannot ignore this fact and the tension this creates in the bereavement process. The bond shifts and takes new forms in time, but the connection is always there. Mourners, especially children, may need help from their support networks to keep their bonds alive or to let the deceased rest. Connections to the dead need to be legitimized. People need to talk about the deceased, to participate in memorial rituals, and to understand that their mourning is an evolving, not a static, process. In the words of a nineteenth-century rabbi, Samuel David Luzzatto, "Memory sustains man in the world of life" (Luzzatto, p. 318).

*See also:* FREUD, SIGMUND; GRIEF: THEORIES; GRIEF COUNSELING AND THERAPY

## Bibliography

Anderson, Robert. "Notes of a Survivor." In Stanley B. Troop and William A. Green eds., *The Patient, Death, and the Family*. New York: Scribner, 1974.

Baker, John. "Mourning and the Transformation of Object Relationships: Evidence for the Persistence of Internal Attachments." *Psychoanalyatic Psychology* 18, no. 1 (2001):55–73.

Bowlby John. *Attachment and Loss,* Vol. 3: *Loss: Sadness and Depression.* New York: Basic Books, 1980.

Bowlby, John. "Process of Mourning." *International Journal of Psychoanalysis* 42 (1961):317–340.

Bruner, Jerome. *Acts of Meaning.* Cambridge, MA: Harvard University Press, 1990.

Klass, Dennis. "Grief in an Eastern Culture: Japanese Ancestor Worship." In Dennis Klass, Phyllis R. Silverman, and Steven L. Nickman eds., *Continuing Bonds: New Understandings of Grief.* Washington, DC: Taylor & Francis, 1996.

Klass, Dennis. *Parental Grief: Solace and Resolution.* New York: Springer, 1988.

Klass, Dennis. "Bereaved Parents and the Compassionate Friends: Affiliation and Healing." *Omega: The Journal of Death and Dying.* 15, no. 4 (1984):353–373.

Klass, Dennis, and Tony Walter. "Processes of Grieving: How Bonds are Continued." In Margaret S. Stroebe, Robert O. Hansson, Wolfgang Stroebe, and Henk Schut eds.,*Handbook of Bereavement Research: Consequence, Coping, and Care.* Washington, DC: American Psychological Association, 2001.

Lindemann, Eric. "Symptomatology and Management of Acute Grief." *American Journal of Psychiatry* 101 (1944):141–148.

Lundberg, George D. "The Best Health Care Goes Only so Far."*Newsweek,* 27 August 2001, 15.

Luzzatto, Samuel David. *Words of the Wise: Anthology of Proverbs and Practical Axioms,* compiled by Reuben Alcalay. Jerusalem: Massada Ltd., 1970.

Marwitt, S. J, and Dennis Klass. "Grief and the Role of the Inner Representation of the Deceased." In Dennis Klass, Phyllis R. Silverman, and Steven L. Nickman eds., *Continuing Bonds: New Understandings of Grief.* Washington, DC: Taylor & Francis, 1996.

Nickman, Steven L., Phyllis R. Silverman, and Claude Normand. "Children's Construction of Their Deceased Parent: The Surviving Parent's Contribution." *American Journal of Orthopsychiatry* 68, no. 1 (1998):126–141.

Normand, Claude, Phyllis R. Silverman, and Steven L. Nickman. "Bereaved Children's Changing Relationship with the Deceased." In Dennis Klass, Phyllis R. Silverman, and Steven L. Nickman eds., *Continuing Bonds: A New Understanding of Grief.* Washington, DC: Taylor & Francis, 1996.

Rizzuto, Ann Marie *The Birth of the Living God: A Psychoanalytic Study.* Chicago: University of Chicago Press, 1979.

Rubin, S. "The Wounded Family: Bereaved Parents and the Impact of Adult Child Loss." In Dennis Klass, Phyllis R. Silverman, and Steven L. Nickman eds., *Continuing Bonds: A New Understanding of Grief.* Washington, DC: Taylor & Francis, 1996.

Rubin, S. "Maternal Attachment and Child Death: On Adjustment, Relationship and Resulution." *Omega: The Journal of Death and Dying* 15, no. 4 (1984):347–352.

Silverman, Phyllis R. *Never Too Young to Know: Death in Children's Lives.* New York: Oxford University Press, 2000.

Silverman, Phyllis R., and Dennis Klass. "Introduction: What's the Problem?" In Dennis Klass, Phyllis R. Silverman, and Steven L. Nickman eds., *Continuing Bonds: A New Understanding of Grief.* Washington, DC: Taylor & Francis, 1996.

Silverman Phyllis R., and Steven L. Nickman. "Children's Construction of Their Dead Parent." In Dennis Klass, Phyllis R. Silverman, and Steven L. Nickman eds., *Continuing Bonds: A New Understanding of Grief.* Washington, DC: Taylor & Francis, 1996.

Silverman Phyllis R., and Steven L. Nickman. "Concluding Thoughts." In Dennis Klass, Phyllis R. Silverman, and Steven L. Nickman eds., *Continuing Bonds: A New Understanding of Grief.* Washington, DC: Taylor & Francis, 1996.

Silverman, Phyllis R., Steven L. Nickman, and J. W. Worden. "Detachment Revisited: The Child's Reconstruction of a Dead Parent." *American Journal of Orthopsychiatry* 62, no. 4 (1992):494–503.

Silverman, S. M., and Phyllis R. Silverman. "Parent-Child Communication in Widowed Families." *American Journal of Psychotherapy* 33 (1979):428–441.

Stroebe, Margaret, Mary Gergen, Kenneth Gergen, and Wolfgang Stroebe. "Broken Hearts or Broken Bonds?" In Dennis Klass, Phyllis R. Silverman, and Steven L. Nickman eds., *Continuing Bonds: A New Understanding of Grief.* Washington, DC: Taylor & Francis, 1996.

Tessman, Lora H. "Dilemmas in Identification for the Post-Nazi Generation: 'My Good Father was a bad man?'" In Dennis Klass, Phyllis R. Silverman, and Steven L. Nickman eds., *Continuing Bonds: A New Understanding of Grief.* Washington, DC: Taylor & Francis, 1996.

Volkan Vamil, and C. Robert Showalter. "Known Object Loss: Disturbances in Reality Testing and 'Re-Grief' Work as a Method of Brief Psychotherapy." *Psychiatric Quarterly* 42 (1968):358–374.

Walters, Tony. *On Bereavement: The Culture of Grief.* Philadelphia: Open University Press, 1999.

PHYLLIS R. SILVERMAN

# CORPSE

*See* CADAVER EXPERIENCES.

# CREMATION

Cremation is the burning of the human body until its soft parts are destroyed by fire. The skeletal remains and ash residue (cremains) often become the object of religious rites, one for the body and one for the bones. The anthropologist Robert Hertz has described this as a double burial, with a "wet" first phase coping with the corpse and its decay, and a "dry" second phase treating the skeletal remains and ash. The chief difference between cremation and burial is the speed of transformation: Corpses burn in two hours or less, but bodies take months or years to decay, depending upon methods used and local soil conditions. The method of body disposal least like cremation is mummification, which seeks to preserve the body rather than destroy it.

## Ancient Cremation

Archaeological evidence shows cremation rituals dating back to ancient times. In classical antiquity, cremation was a military procedure and thus was associated with battlefield honors. Both cremation and the interment of cremated remains are described in Homer's *Iliad* and *Odyssey*, both dating from the eighth century B.C.E. The seventeenth-century French painter Nicolas Poussin echoed another classical story in his masterpiece *The Ashes of Phocion,* perhaps the most famous of all cremation-linked paintings, in which a faithful wife gathers the ashes of her husband, an improperly shamed leader who was cremated without the proper rites.

The ritual cremation of Roman emperors involved the release of an eagle above the cremation pyre to symbolize his deification and the passing of the emperor-god's spirit. The reasons for shifts between cremation and burial in classical times are not always apparent; fashion or even the availability of wood may have been involved.

## Cremation Cultures

It was in India and in the Indian-influenced cultures of Buddhism and Sikhism that cremation developed into a central and enduring social institution. Basic to Hinduism is the belief that the life force underlying human existence is not restricted to one life but undergoes numerous transmigrations that may involve nonhuman forms. Hence the "self" and the identity of an individual are not simply and inevitably linked to any one body. Cremation became an appropriate vehicle for expressing the ephemerality of bodily life and the eternity of spiritual life.

*Hinduism.* For traditional Hindus, cremation fit into an overall scheme of destiny. Symbolically, the human embryo resulted from the combination of male seed forming bones and female blood providing flesh. In this account the spirit enters the fetus through the cranial suture of the skull, with the growing embryo in a sense being "cooked" by the heat of the womb. At the end of life, a symbolic reversal sees the heat of the funeral pyre separating flesh from bones; the rite of skull-cracking frees the spirit for its ongoing journey, which is influenced by *karma,* or merit accrued during life. The fire itself is the medium by which the body is offered to the gods as a kind of last sacrifice; cremation should take place in Banaras, the sacred city through which the sacred Ganges River flows. It is on the banks of the Ganges that cremations occur and cremated remains are placed in its holy waters. Hindus living in other parts of the world also practice cremation and either place cremated remains in local rivers or send the remains to be placed in the Ganges. While rites are also performed for set periods after cremation, there is no monument for the dead, whose ultimate destiny lies in the future and not in some past event.

*Buddhism.* Cremation is the preferred funeral rite for Buddhists as well and is reinforced by the fact that the Buddha was himself cremated. Tradition tells how his funeral pyre self-ignited, but only after many followers had come to pay respects to his body. When the flames ceased, no ash remained—only bones. These remains were divided into eight parts and built into eight stupas in different territories. This is a good example of how cremation makes possible a greater variety of memorializing the dead than does burial. Contemporary Buddhists practice both cremation and burial.

## Evil and Emergency Cremation

Cremation is not only an established social custom but has also been used on battlefields to save the dead from the ravages of the enemy and as an emergency measure during plagues, as in the Black Death of the seventeenth century. The most inescapably negative use of cremation in human history was during the Holocaust, the Nazi regime's mass murder of millions of Jews and others, including Gypsies, homosexuals, and the mentally ill, all deemed culturally unacceptable to Hitler's Third Reich during World War II. The Nazi concentration camps came to symbolize the inhumanity of killing men, women, and children and then disposing of their bodies by cremation or mass burial. In this case, cremation was a kind of industrial process necessary to deal with the immense number of corpses that attended Hitler's "Final Solution."

## Modern Cremation

With the increasing predominance of Christianity in Europe after the fifth century C.E., cremation was gradually abandoned in favor of earth burial as a symbol of the burial and resurrection of Christ. Charlemagne criminalized cremation in the Christian West in 789 C.E. There were subsequent countercurrents, including the unusual seventeenth-century treatise of Sir Thomas Browne on urn burial, *Hydriotaphia* (1658), and the brief French revolutionary attempt to foster cremation as a rebuke to Christianity in the 1790s.

It was not until the nineteenth century, however, that a widespread interest in cremation resurfaced, prompted by a variety of social, philosophical, and technological factors. The major social elements related to massive increases in the population of industrial towns and major cities, whose cemeteries were increasingly hard-pressed to cope with the volume of the dead in an era of heightened concern with public hygiene—corpses buried near the surface of the ground were seen as a potential health risk. This was also a period of considerable interest in freedom of thought and creative engagement with ideas of progress. Traditional religious constraints were not viewed as impossible barriers to progress. Societies were established to promote cremation in many influential cities, including London and The Hague in 1874, Washington, D.C., in 1876, and New York in 1882. Central to these interest groups lay influential people as with Sir Henry Thompson (surgeon to Queen Victoria), whose highly influential book on cremation, *The Treatment of the Body after Death,* was published in 1874, followed shortly by William Eassie's *Cremation of the Dead* in 1875.

Italy was a major force in the renaissance of cremation; Brunetti's model cremator and display of cremated remains at the Vienna Exhibition of 1873 are credited with having prompted Sir Henry Thompson's interest. There was also a congress on cremation in Milan in 1874. These groups often existed for years before they achieved the goal of cremation as a legal and established practice. In Holland, for example, the 1874 group did not actually open a crematorium until 1914. Often there were objections from a variety of Christian churches, which contended that cremation would interfere with the resurrection of the body or that cremation spurned the example of the "burial" of Jesus. Sometimes the reasons were political rather than theological. Catholics in Italy, for example, found cremation unacceptable because it was favored and advocated by the anticlerical Freemasons. Indeed, it was not until the mid-1960s that the Roman Catholic Church accepted cremation as an appropriate form of funeral for its members.

The preoccupation with technological advancement in the nineteenth century also spurred the fortunes of cremation. It had become relatively easy to contemplate building ovens for the combustion of human bodies as well as architectural features to house them. Machines like the cremulator, for grinding larger bone fragments into dust, are similarly industrial in nature. The early crematoria were temporary, little more than ovens or grandly designed landmarks. In the late nineteenth and early twentieth centuries they began to resemble church buildings; in the late twentieth century there was more scope for architects to reflect upon life and death in these unique structures.

In the late twentieth century cremation became a serious topic of academic study. It was only at the turn of the twenty-first century that serious academic interest in cremation—sociological, theological, and historical—emerged. The numerous journals published by many cremation societies have also made important contributions, systematically recording cremation rates, new crematoria, and technical developments. The Archives of the Cremation Society of Great Britain, held at the University of Durham, is one example, as is the Fabretti Institute of Turin in Italy.

## Christian Traditions and Cultures

The most interesting aspect of the relationship between cremation and society within Western societies derives from the relative influence of the Orthodox, Catholic, and Protestant traditions. Greek and Russian Orthodoxy stand in firm opposition to cremation, and cremation rates are very low in strict Orthodox societies such as Greece. During the communist era in the former USSR and Eastern Europe, cremation was often pressed in an ideological fashion, which in turn spurred stronger opposition from various Christian denominations.

In Western Europe cremation rates vary with the degree of Catholic or Protestant influence in each country's tradition. In 1999 the cremation rate in Great Britain and Denmark was 71 percent and 68 percent in Sweden. In Finland, by contrast, with equally strong Protestant, Catholic, and Orthodox churches, the rate was only 25 percent. The Netherlands, roughly equally divided between Protestant and Catholic traditions, stood at 48 percent. The Catholic influence is more evident in Hungary (30%), Austria (21%), France (16%), Spain (13%), Italy (5%), and Ireland (5%).

The United States presents an interesting picture of mixed religious traditions with an overall cremation rate of approximately 25 percent. This may seem an unusually low figure, but it encompasses a wide variation in local practices. Washington, Nevada, and Oregon, have cremation rates of approximately 57 percent while Alabama, Mississippi, and West Virginia are about 5 percent.

## Social Change and Cremation

In the West, the turn of the twentieth century saw the rise of strongly motivated individuals, often coalescing into small pressure groups that were ideologically committed to cremation. After World War II cremation began to be incorporated into social welfare provisions in numerous countries. Just as the urban growth of the middle and late nineteenth century had led to the establishment of many large cemeteries in European cities, so the later twentieth century was marked by the growth of crematoria. Cremation was a symptom not only of massive urbanization and the drive for social hygiene but also an increased medicalization of death. With more people dying in hospitals rather than at home, their bodies were collected by funeral directors and might be kept in special premises away from their home. Indeed the very concept of the "funeral home" developed to mark a place where a body could be kept and visited by the bereaved family. Cremation thus was another example of a rising trend of commercialization and professionalization of various aspects of life in the West. Cremation was but one aspect of a broader tendency toward efficiency, scientific technology, and consumer choice. It also served the psychological function of allaying the fears of those who were haunted by irrational fears of decay or of being buried alive. Cremation is also often less expensive than burial.

Although the upward trend in cremation continued unabated through the late twentieth century, there was a slight ripple of concern emanating from the environmental community, which pointed to the deleterious effect of industrial and domestic emission of gases—many communities have adopted more stringent laws for the running of cremators. On a populist front, this raised a question mark over the desirability of cremation. In Great Britain some minority groups have raised the idea of "green" woodland burials in which individuals are buried without elaborate coffins or caskets and in full recognition that their bodies would soon return to the earth in a form of earth-friendly decay.

## Cremation, Privatization, and Secularization

As Christianity achieved dominance in Europe in its first millennium and firmly established itself geographically in the second, it imposed a much more formal theology and ritual, not least over death. Catholic Christianity's funerary rites included preparation of the dying for their eternal journey, along with masses and prayers for their migrant souls. Cemeteries were closely aligned with churches, and death rites were under ecclesiastical control.

With the advent of cremation, there arose a new possibility disengaging death rites from ecclesiastical control. For much of the late nineteenth century and the first two-thirds of the twentieth century, the great majority of cremation rites were set within a religious ritual framework overseen by the Protestant clergy. Catholic priests were also freed to do so from the mid-1960s, but by the late twentieth century clerical involvement in cremation was on the wane. Traditional burial was conducted under the control of a Christian church, and though remains might later have been removed to a charnel house (a place for storing human bones), the transfer was often a nonceremonial affair. Burials in some places could also be conducted without church rites, but it was with modern cremation that a secular process appeared more acceptable. Often the emphasis on what came to be called "life-centered" funerals was celebratory, with a focus on the past life of the deceased and not, as in traditional Christian rites, on the future hope of resurrection.

## Cremated Remains

In contrast to the traditional practice of placing cremated remains in urns and storing them in columbaria (buildings containing niches in their walls), late-twentieth-century practices in the West have included the removal of cremated remains from crematoria by family members and their placement in locations of personal significance. This was the birth of a new tradition as individuals invented ways of placing remains in natural environments: mountains, rivers, gardens, or places of recreation and holiday where the survivors acknowledged that the deceased had spent pleasant and memorable times.

*See also:* FUNERAL INDUSTRY; GENOCIDE; GRIEF AND MOURNING IN CROSS-CULTURAL PERSPECTIVE; WIDOW-BURNING

## *Bibliography*

Davies, Douglas J. "Theologies of Disposal." In Peter C. Jupp and Tony Rogers eds., *Interpreting Death: Christian Theology and Pastoral Practice*. London: Cassell, 1997.

Davies, Douglas J. *Cremation Today and Tomorrow.* Nottingham, England: Alcuin/GROW Books, 1990.

Jupp, Peter C. *From Dust to Ashes: The Replacement of Burial by Cremation in England 1840–1967.* London: Congregational Memorial Hall Trust, 1990.

Parry, Jonathan P. *Death in Banaras.* Cambridge: Cambridge University Press, 1994.

Prothero, Stephen. *Purified by Fire: A History of Cremation in America.* Berkeley: University of California Press, 2001.

DOUGLAS J. DAVIES

# CRUZAN, NANCY

On January 11, 1983, Nancy Cruzan, then twenty-five years old, was involved in an automobile accident. Her body was thrown thirty-five feet beyond her overturned car. Paramedics estimated she was without oxygen for fifteen to twenty minutes before resuscitation was started. As a result she experienced massive, irreversible brain damage. However, she could breath on her own. Attending doctors said she could live indefinitely if she received artificial nutrition and hydration, but they agreed she could never return to a normal life. Cruzan had not left advance directives—instructions how she wished to be treated should such a physical and mental state occur. A feeding tube enabled her to receive food and fluids. Over the ensuing months, Cruzan became less recognizable to her parents. They began to feel strongly that if she had the opportunity she would choose to discontinue the life-supporting food and fluids. After five years of artificial feeding and hydration at the annual cost of $130,000, and with increasing physical deterioration, Cruzan's parents requested that the feeding tube be removed so that their daughter could die a "natural death." In early 1988 their request was granted by Judge Charles E. Teel of the Probate Division of Jaspar County, Missouri.

Judge Teel's decision was met by a very strong reaction from persons who expressed concern that removal of the feeding tube would not be in accord with Cruzan's wishes under the doctrine of "informed consent." Others argued that removal of the life-support feeding tube would constitute an act of homicide. The state of Missouri appealed Judge Teel's decision. In November of the same year, the Missouri Supreme Court overruled Judge Peel's decision and therefore refused the Cruzan petition to make a decision on behalf of their daughter by stating that the family's quality-of-life arguments did not have as much substance as the state's interest in the sanctity of life. The Cruzan family appealed the Missouri Supreme Court decision to the U.S. Supreme Court. In their pleading to the U.S. Supreme Court, the state of Missouri asked that they be provided clear and convincing evidence of a patient's wishes regarding a will to die before granting the request to discontinue life support for persons in a persistent vegetative state. On June 25, 1990, the U.S. Supreme Court recognized the right to die as a constitutionally protected civil liberties interest. At the same time, the U.S. Supreme Court supported the interests of Missouri by declaring that it was entirely appropriate for the state to set reasonable standards to guide the exercise of that right. Thus, the U.S. Supreme Court sided with the state and returned the case to the Missouri courts.

Following the Supreme Court hearing, several of Cruzan's friends testified before Judge Teel, recalling that she stated preferences for care if she should become disabled. In addition, the doctor who was initially opposed to removing her feeding tube was less adamant than he had been five years previously. On December 14, 1988, the Jaspar County Court determined that there was sufficient evidence to suggest that Cruzan would not wish to be maintained in a vegetative state. The following day the feeding tube was removed and she died before the end of the year.

*See also:* ADVANCE DIRECTIVES; DO NOT RESUSCITATE; EUTHANASIA; NATURAL DEATH ACTS; PERSISTENT VEGETATIVE STATE; QUINLAN, KAREN ANN

## *Bibliography*

Gordon, M. Singer P. "Decisions and Care at the End of Life." *Lancet* 346 (1995):163–166.

WILLIAM M. LAMERS JR.

# CRYONIC SUSPENSION

James H. Bedford is the first person known to have been placed in a state of cryonic suspension under controlled conditions. This event occurred in 1967 after a physician certified his death. Decades later his body remains in a hypothermic (supercooled) condition within a liquid nitrogen cylinder. Decades from now, perhaps he will be the first person to be resuscitated after this episode of biostasis, or what earlier generations called suspended animation. This hope is what led Bedford to arrange for cryonic suspension as an alternative to cremation and burial.

## Why Cryonic Suspension?

Through the centuries some people have accepted the inevitability of death while others have devoted themselves to finding ways of prolonging life or, even better, living forever. These efforts have included bizarre and dangerous practices compounded of superstition and magic, but also increasingly effective public health measures that have resulted in a significant increase in life expectancy throughout much of the world. The cryonics approach is intended to take another step. It asks the question: Because biomedical science has already accomplished so much, why should humankind assume that people still have to die and stay dead?

The case for cryonics made its public debut with Robert C. W. Ettinger's best-selling book, *The Prospect of Immortality* (1966). He notes that in the past many people have died of disorders and diseases that have since become treatable. Medical advances are continuing, which means that people are still being buried or cremated even though their present fatal condition will eventually be healed. People should therefore give themselves the chance for a renewed and healthy life. This can be accomplished by immediately taking measures to preserve the "dead" body until such time as a curative procedure has been devised. The body would then be resuscitated from its state of suspended animation and the restorative procedure would be applied. From Ettinger's perspective, it is better to be alive than dead and human beings have the right to self-preservation. Furthermore, because so many gains have already been made in extending human life, it would be foolish to stop.

## The Process of Cryonic Suspension

How it is done has changed somewhat in detail over the years, but still requires the following basic elements:

1. An adult who has consented to the procedure.
2. Financial provision for the services to be performed.
3. A physician and hospital willing to allow the procedure to be done.
4. Prompt certification of death (to limit postmortem deterioration).
5. Injection of cryoprotective fluid (composed of liquid nitrogen) to replace water and other body fluids. This fluid is disseminated throughout the body with a heart-lung pump. Technicians continue to monitor temperature and other signs.
6. Bathing in a deep cooling bath until the desired temperature (about $-79°$ centigrade) is reached.
7. Placement inside a sealed bag that is then immersed in a storage vessel filled with liquid nitrogen. The supercooled temperature is maintained indefinitely.
8. A cure for the individual's once-fatal disease or condition is discovered by medical science.
9. The body is removed from storage and carefully warmed.
10. The condition that had resulted in the person's "death" is healed and life begins anew.

## Critical Response

Many criticisms have been made regarding the process of cryonic suspension. There is no dispute about the general proposition that refrigeration and freezing can preserve organic materials. A variety of industrial, research, and medical procedures rely upon this phenomenon. There has been some success in thawing out tissues and organs from liquid nitrogen storage. All of this, though, is a long way from resuscitating a person and, especially, the complex and fragile human brain upon which memory and personality appear to depend. The engineering and biomedical sciences have not come close enough to inspire confidence that such a feat could be accomplished at any foreseeable point in the future.

In addition to the limited state of success, other significant criticisms include: (1) Much tissue loss and damage occur whenever there are deviations from the ideal situation; for example, certification

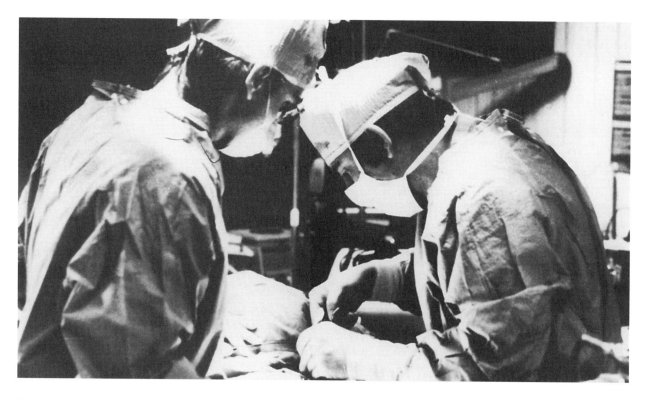

*Doctors prepare a patient for cryonic suspension. As of 2001, an estimated ninety people have been placed in cryonic storage.* AP/WIDE WORLD PHOTOS

of death is delayed; medical or other authorities prove uncooperative; equipment or human failure is involved in carrying out the first crucial procedures; (2) ice formation will damage cells and tissues despite protective efforts; and (3) additional extensive damage will occur during the attempted resuscitation process. Many neuroscientists doubt that an intact and functional human brain can survive both the freezing and the rewarming processes, even if the neural structures had not suffered irreversible damage at the time of death.

The reasons for cryonic suspension have been criticized on moral and practical grounds. Some hold that it is immoral to defy God's will by reaching back over the life/death border. Others focus on the prospect of cryonics becoming one more elitist advantage. While some people barely have the necessities for a hard life, others would enjoy the unfair opportunity to play another round. A related criticism is that an already overcrowded world would be subject to an increased growth in population. Additional misgivings are expressed by questions such as:

1. What will happen to marriage, remarriage, and family structure in general if the dead are not necessarily dead? How will people be able to go on with their lives?

2. How could loved ones complete—or even begin—their recovery from grief and mourning?

3. What formidable problems in adjustment would occur when a "Rip Van Winkle on Ice" returns after many years to a changed society?

4. Will people become less motivated and more careless with their "first lives" if they expect to have encore appearances?

## Conclusions

As of 2001, there have been no known attempts at resuscitation because cryonicists judge that the technology has not yet been perfected. Since the 1980s there has been a trend to preserve only the head. The theory behind these "neuro" preparations is that (a) this form of storage is less expensive and (b) science will eventually make it possible to grow a new body from DNA. More conservative cryonicists, however, continue to favor the whole-body approach. Even more recently there have been announcements that future efforts will switch from cryonic storage to vitrification—converting body tissue to a glasslike stone material. Advocates (including at least one cryonic suspension organization) believe vitrification would avoid the tissue damage associated with freezing and resuscitation. There are no known previous examples of vitrification having been applied above the level of isolated tissues and organs.

Along with the big question—Could cryonic suspension ever work?—there is also the unanswered question: Why in America's high technology society have the cryonic storage vessels received fewer than a hundred people since 1967? At present, cryonic suspension remains a controversial and seldom end-of-life option. Future prospects are difficult to predict.

*See also:* BRAIN DEATH; BURIED ALIVE; DEFINITIONS OF DEATH; LIFE SUPPORT SYSTEM; NECROMANCY; RESUSCITATION

### *Bibliography*

Drexler, Kenneth E. *Engines of Creation*. New York: Anchor/Doubleday, 1986.

Ettinger, Robert C. W. *The Prospect of Immortality*. New York: MacFadden, 1966.

Gruman, Gerald J. *A History of Ideas about the Prolongation of Life*. New York: Arno, 1977.

Harrington, Alan. *The Immortalist*. New York: Random House, 1969.

Kastenbaum, Robert. *Dorian, Graying: Is Youth the Only Thing Worth Having?* Amityville, NY: Baywood, 1995.

Storey, Kenneth B., and Janet M. Storey. "Frozen and Alive." *Scientific American* 263 (1990):92–97.

Wowk, Brian, and Michael Darwin. *Cryonics: Reaching for Tomorrow*. Scottsdale, AZ: Alcor Life Extension Foundation, 1991.

ROBERT KASTENBAUM

# CULT DEATHS

In the past several decades, a handful of cults have been associated with mass deaths, either through murders, suicides, or standoffs with the government that ended tragically. These highly publicized cases have convinced the public that many or all cults are extremist groups that are highly dangerous; in fact, there is little understanding by many people of what constitutes a cult, how they recruit, or what turns a small number of these groups toward violence.

Defining cults and deciding which groups should be labeled as such is sometimes a difficult task because of the variety of groups that exist outside of the mainstream. However, in their *The Will to Kill* (2001), James A. Fox and Jack Levin define cults as being "loosely structured and unconventional forms of small religious groups, the members of which are held together by a charismatic leader who mobilizes their loyalty around some new religious cause—typically a cause that is at odds with that of more conventional religious institutions" (Fox and Levin 2001, p. 141). Part of the difficulty of defining what groups are cults is that cults may move to mainstream status over time by becoming conventional institutions. The Church of Jesus Christ of Latter-Day Saints made just such a transition since their founding in 1830.

Many groups can be categorized as cults under the previous definition, although the vast majority of them are harmless (Richardson 1994). However, society has a negative view of groups labeled as cults and typically treats such groups as dangerous. Furthermore, the public often views religious commitment "as properties of the lunatic fringe" and views cult members as fanatics (Miller 1994, p. 7). The negative connotation of the term *cult* resulted in many scholars avoiding its use and instead using "new religious movement" or "minority religions" (Lewis 1998, p. 1).

The anti-cult movement feeds part of the negative view that the public holds toward cults. A number of groups are part of this movement: Their common tasks are "disseminating information, offering advice and counseling, and/or lobbying those in authority to take action to curb the activities of cults" (Barker 1986, p. 335).

## Recruitment

There are different viewpoints as to how cults procure new members. The anti-cult position takes a negative view of the groups' activities, often assuming that people join cults because they were brainwashed, or were the victims of other mind control procedures that rendered them "helpless victims" (Barker 1986, p. 335). However, many researchers view brainwashing as a stereotype of actual cult practices: It represents society's attempt at a "simplistic explanation of why people adopt strange beliefs" that are at odds with conventional wisdom (Wessinger 2000, p. 6). In her studies of cults, the sociologist and cult expert Eileen Barker notes that empirical evidence supporting the use of brainwashing is lacking.

Another explanation of cult membership focuses on deficiencies within the people themselves. This view, also popular within the anti-cult ranks, treats cult members as "abnormally pathetic or weak" (Barker 1986, p. 336). Yet evidence gathered through psychological testing does not support this position (Barker 1986).

In 1965 the sociologists John Lofland and Rodney Stark proposed a model of cult conversion by studying a millenarian cult interested in returning the world to "the conditions of the Garden of Eden" (Lofland and Stark 1965, p. 862). Their model is comprised of an ordered series of seven factors, all of which are necessary and sufficient for a person's decision to join a cult. The model focuses on how situational factors influence people who are predisposed, due to their backgrounds, to join such groups. Each step in the model reduces the number of potential converts, leaving only a few people eligible for conversion. Lofland updated the model in 1977 to reflect a more sophisticated effort on the part of the group they studied to obtain converts. He notes that the characteristics of the converts changed over time: The group attracted young people from "higher social classes," rather than the "less than advantaged" people they attracted in the past (Lofland 1977, p. 807).

Lofland's later explanation of conversion does involve persuasion on the part of cult members. For example, of the group he studied, weekend workshops were used to help potential converts form "affective bonds" with group members while avoiding "interference from outsiders" (p. 809). During these weekends a group member constantly accompanied potential converts; furthermore, people were discouraged from leaving the event, although physical force was never used to encourage them to remain.

Although the use of persuasion has been noted in conversion, and "coercive measures" have sometimes been used to prevent defection, it is incorrect to say that converts are universally victims of brainwashing (Wessinger 2000, p.7). In fact, many people who join cults ultimately choose to leave them, with many groups experiencing high turnover rates. One argument against brainwashing is that cults appeal to people more during "periods of rapid social change, at times when individuals are feeling a lack of structure and belonging . . . and when the credibility of traditional institutions is impaired" (Fox and Levine 2001, p. 142). This explanation of membership emphasizes social as well as life circumstances.

**When Cults Become Dangerous**

Despite the fact that most cults are harmless, some groups do become dangerous either to themselves or others. A particularly dangerous time for cult activity coincides with the ending of a century or millennium. During these times, groups sometimes "prophesize the end of the world" (Fox and Levine 2001, p. 143). This belief is originally rooted in biblical tradition predicting a cataclysmic event followed by a period of a thousand years of perfection on the earth. However, the original meaning of millennium has now come to "be used as a synonym for belief in a collective terrestrial salvation" involving the formation of a "millennial kingdom" in which suffering does not exist (Wessinger 2000, p. 3). Some groups expect the paradise to be earthly, while others, like the group Heaven's Gate, expected it to be "heavenly or other-worldly" (Wessinger 2000, p. 3). Still others, like the Branch Davidians, are ambiguous on this issue.

Just because a group is a millennial group does not necessarily mean that violence will result. For example, in 1962 the scholars Jane Allyn Hardyck and Marcia Braden followed the activities of an Evangelical Christian group that prophesized an impending nuclear disaster. Despite moving into fallout shelters for forty-two days and emerging to find that their prophecy was incorrect, the group's core beliefs withstood the ordeal and no violence resulted. However, in rare circumstances violence does erupt. The scholar Jeffrey Kaplan notes that groups that become violent follow a specific pattern, with a key factor involving a leader who begins to feel persecuted for his or her beliefs. This combined with a tendency to withdraw from society and to develop "an increasingly idiosyncratic doctrine" may push the group toward violence (Kaplan 1994, p. 52).

The violence from millennial groups arises when they begin to play an active part in bringing about the prophesized apocalypse. One of the most dangerous of these groups was the Aum Shinrikyo, who released sarin nerve gas in the Tokyo subway on March 20, 1995, killing 12 people and injuring 5,500. They also released sarin gas in 1993 in Matsumoto, Japan, injuring 600 and killing 7. The group's leader, Shoko Asahara, was a self-proclaimed Buddha figure claiming psychic powers, including the ability to prophesize future events. In creating his religion, he hoped to bring about the creation of Shambhala, "the Buddhist Millennial Kingdom" that was to be populated with converts who were themselves psychic (Wessinger 2000, p. 142).

Asahara predicted that a worldwide nuclear Armageddon would occur in 1999, but said that the world could be saved if their group grew to 30,000 members. Although membership grew to as many as 10,000, it was clear that he had not reached his recruitment goal. As a result, Asahara began to move the date of the apocalypse closer and closer in an attempt to increase recruitment while also enhancing loyalty of group members. The date was finally moved to 1995, forcing his inner circle to launch their own Armageddon in order to preserve the illusion of his prophetic powers (Wessinger, 2000). The Tokyo subway attack was to be one step in their attempt to "overthrow the Japanese government" and then later "initiate a worldwide nuclear disaster that only he and his disciples would survive" (Fox and Levine 2001, p. 147).

The Solar Temple represents another example of a millennial group that resulted in the deaths of seventy-three people in multiple locations across Switzerland, France, and Canada between 1994 and 1997. The deaths involved both current and former members of the Temple. Letters left by group members note that the deaths were a combination of executions of "traitors," murders of weaker members who lacked the strength to "transit to a higher world," and suicides (Wessinger, 2000, p. 219). Group members believed that they must transit to "a higher realm of existence and consciousness" in order to find salvation: The destination of this transit appears to have been a star or one of several planets (Wessinger 2000, p. 219).

Membership in the Solar Temple reached as high as 442 people worldwide in 1989 but internal strife began in 1990, leading to a steady decrease in membership during the following years. Former members began demanding reimbursements for their contributions. Even the son of one of the founders proved disloyal when he revealed to others that cofounders Joseph DiMambro and Luc Jouret used electronic devices to create illusions to fool Solar Temple members. Though the original position of the group merely involved bringing about an age of enlightenment involving "an evolution of consciousness on Earth," this position changed when internal problems as well as "persecutory" external events caused a shift in theology: The new theology justified leaving the earth since it could not be saved (Wessinger, 2000, p. 224).

Other millennial groups have been involved in mass deaths since 1990, including an incident that occurred in early 2000 in several remote locations in Uganda. Members of the Movement for the Restoration of the Ten Commandments of God were either murdered or engaged in mass suicide, leaving more than 500 people dead. Their leader, Joseph Kibwetere, had long prophesized an imminent end to the world. The truth surrounding the deaths as well as a final death toll may never be known because there were no survivors (Hammer 2000).

*See also:* DEATH SYSTEM; HEAVEN'S GATE; JONESTOWN; WACO

### Bibliography

Barker, Eileen. "Religious Movements: Cult and Anticult Since Jonestown." *Annual Review of Sociology* 12 (1986):329–346.

Fox, James A., and Jack Levin. *The Will to Kill: Making Sense of Senseless Murder.* Needham Heights, MA: Allyn and Bacon, 2001.

Hammer, Joshua. "An Apocalyptic Mystery." *Newsweek,* 3 April 2000, 46–47.

Hardyck, Jane Allyn, and Marcia Braden. "Prophecy Fails Again: A Report of a Failure to Replicate." *Journal of Abnormal and Social Psychology* 65 (1962):136–141.

Kaplan, Jeffrey. "The Millennial Dream." In James R. Lewis ed., *From the Ashes: Making Sense of Waco.* Lanham, MD: Rowman and Littlefield Publishers, 1994.

Lewis, James R. *Cults in America.* Santa Barbara, CA: ABC-CLIO, 1998.

Lofland, John. " 'Becoming a World-Saver' Revisited." *American Behavioral Scientist* 20 (1977):805–818.

Lofland, John, and Rodney Stark. "Becoming a World-Saver: A Theory of Conversion to a Deviant Perspective." *American Sociological Review* 30 (1965):862–874.

Miller, Timothy. "Misinterpreting Religious Commitment." In James R. Lewis ed., *From the Ashes: Making Sense of Waco*. Lanham, MD: Rowman and Littlefield Publishers, 1994.

Richardson, James T. "Lessons from Waco: When Will We Ever Learn?" In James R. Lewis ed., *From the Ashes: Making Sense of Waco*. Lanham, MD: Rowman and Littlefield, 1994.

Wessinger, Catherine. *How the Millennium Comes Violently*. New York: Seven Bridges Press, 2000.

CHERYL B. STEWART
DENNIS D. STEWART

# DANCE

Dance, like other forms of art, has treated the subject of death continually throughout history and will continue to be used as a vehicle to express human fascination with this eternal unanswered question. Rituals have surrounded the mystery of death from prehistoric times. Repeated rhythmic movements become dance, and the solace of rocking and keening can be therapeutic. Funeral processions are an example of organized movement to music, expressive of grief.

## Death Dances in the East

The aboriginal peoples of Australia sing and dance to evoke the clan totems of a dying man and two months after death dance again, recreating the symbolic animals to purify the bones and release the soul of the deceased. The Sagari dances are part of a cycle performed on the anniversary of a death on the islands of Melanesia, New Guinea. Dancing by a female shaman is an important element of Korean ceremonies to cleanse a deceased soul to allow it to achieve *nirvana*, closing the cycle of birth and rebirth. At Kachin, Upper Burma, funeral rites include dances to send back death spirits to the land of the dead. Dayals (shamans) of Pakistan fall into trances to imitate the spirits of the dead.

## Death Dances in Africa

In Africa the Kenga people perform Dodi or Mutu (mourning dances) on burial day. The Yoruba dance wearing a likeness of the deceased, and the Dogon of Mali perform masked dances to confront death and pass on traditions after death. The Lugbara people of Uganda and the Angas of northern Nigeria also include dance in their rituals surrounding death.

## Death Dances in the Americas

The Umutima Indians of Upper Paraguay, South America, possess seventeen different death cult dances. Mexico celebrates All Souls' Day with masked street dancers dressed in skeleton costumes. The Ghost Dance of the Plains Indians of North America reaffirms an ancestral tribal continuity and has recently been revived after prohibition by the U.S. government, which deemed the dance subversive.

## Death Dances in Europe

The Danse Macabre (Totentanz, or Dance of Death) of the European Middle Ages was portrayed many times on the walls of cloistered cemeteries as a dance of linked hands between people of all levels of society and the skeletal figure of death. These painted images were executed in a period of anxiety caused by the bubonic plague which swept the continent, killing a large percentage of the population.

## Death in Western Stage Dance

In the Romantic period of the nineteenth century, a morbid fascination with death and the mysterious produced ballets such as the *ballet des nonnes* in Giacomo Meyerbeer's opera, *Robert le Diable* (1830), *Giselle* (1841), *La Peri* (1843), and *La*

*Bayad Ère* (1877), all of which present scenes with ballerinas dressed in white, vaporous costumes representing spirits after death, floating on their toes or suspended by invisible wires and illuminated by moonlight fabricated by the technology of gas lighting. Many of these ballets are still performed, providing the ballerina with the artistic challenge—roles in *Giselle* or *La BayadÈre*—of a dramatic death scene followed by the difficult illusion of phantomlike, weightless spirituality.

Twentieth-century dance has used death as the inspiration for many dance works; the most perennial is Mikhail Fokine's *Le Cygne* (1905), commonly known as *The Dying Swan.* Created for the dancer Anna Pavlova to express the noble death struggle of a legendarily silent bird who only sang at death (thus the idiomatic "swan song"), it remains in the repertory in twenty-first-century performances. The great dancer and choreographer Vaslav Nijinsky set the shocking theme of a virgin dancing herself to death by violent, percussive movements as a sacrifice for a fecund harvest in prehistoric Russia, matching composer Igor Stravinky's iconclastic score for *The Rite of Spring* (1913).

In post–World War I Germany, Mary Wigman, high priestess of ausdruckstanz (the expressionistic modern dance style), used expressionist movement and masked ensembles to great effect in *Totenmal* (1930), showing the devasting impact of death on society. Another choreographic masterpiece from Germany is Kurt Jooss's *The Green Table* (1932), inspired by the medieval Danse Macabre paintings. This work shows Death himself taking, in different ways, the people caught up in a war; in essence, only Death is the victor.

The choreographer Martha Graham created *Lamentation* in 1930, which is portrayed through minimal rocking movement, the anguish and despair of mourning. In this dance she retained a passive face, only rising once from a sitting position, her movements stretching the fabric of a jersey tube, yet producing a profound image of distraught motherhood.

The Mexican choreographer Guillermina Bravo treated the subject of death in several modern dance works, influenced by Mexico's folk traditions. In *La Valse* (1951), George Balanchine, choreographer and director of the New York City Ballet, created an ominous image of death in the guise of a man dressed in black, offering a black dress

and gloves to a young girl at a ball, thereby claiming a victim.

In Canada, choreographer James Kudelka exorcised the pain of his mother's death from cancer in his ballet *In Paradism* (1983). This piece shows the stresses placed on a dying person by family and friends, and the encounter with a guide (nurse, priest, angel) who leads the protagonist from denial to acceptance. In this work the dancers all wear skirts and roles are interchangeable, eliminating references to gender. Kudelka composed two other works, *Passage* (1981) and *There Below* (1989), giving his vision of an afterlife. The choreographer Edouard Lock projected prolonged films of the dancer Louise Lecavalier as an old woman on her deathbed in his piece *2* (1995), showing her life cycle from childhood to death.

Since the 1980s many choreographers have responded to the AIDS (acquired immunodeficiency syndrome) epidemic by making deeply felt statements through dance. After the death of his partner, Arnie Zane, choreographer Bill T. Jones used performers with terminal diseases who recounted their experiences confronting death in *Still Here* (1994). Maurice Bejart, choreographer and director of the Ballet du XXieme Siecle, after showing *Ce que la mort me dit* (1980), a serene vision of death, presented an evening-long piece, *Ballet For Life* (1996), in memory of the dancer Jorge Donn and the singer Freddie Mercury, both deceased from AIDS-related illnesses.

The list of dance works treating the subject of death is very long, and the symbolic figure of death appears in many choreographic works. Titles like Andrée Howard's *Death and the Maiden* (1937); Frederick Ashton's dances in Benjamin Britten's opera, *Death in Venice* (1974); Erick Hawkins's *Death is the Hunter* (1975); Flemming Flindt's *Triumph of Death* (1971); and *Death* by the Indian choreographer Astad Deboo are numerous and underline the continuing fascination of dance creators for the subject.

*See also:* DANSE MACABRE; FOLK MUSIC; HOW DEATH CAME INTO THE WORLD; OPERATIC DEATH

## Bibliography

Carmichael, Elizabeth. *The Skeleton at the Feast: The Day of the Dead in Mexico.* London: British Museum Press, 1991.

*This woodcut print of* A Dance of Death *from Liber Chronicarum shows the "band" of four skeletons following their leader, Death; thus began the personification of death.* HISTORICAL PICTURE ARCHIVE/CORBIS

Hodson, Millicent. *Nijinsky's Crime Against Grace: Reconstruction Score of the Original Choreography for Le Sacre du Printemps.* Stuyvesant, NY: Pendragon Press, 1996.

Huet, Michel, and Claude Savary. *Dances of Africa.* New York: Harry Abrams, 1995.

Lonsdale, Steven. *Animals and the Origins of Dance.* New York: Thames and Hudson, 1982.

Morgan, Barbara. *Martha Graham: Sixteen Dances in Photographs.* Dobbs Ferry, NY: Morgan and Morgan, 1980.

Vaucher, Andrea R. *Muses from Chaos and Ash: AIDS, Artists and Art.* New York: Grove Press, 1993.

VINCENT WARREN

# DANSE MACABRE

The band consists of four skeletons performing on bagpipe, portative organ, harp, and small drum. The dancers move in a low, stately procession. It is clearly a ritualistic rather than a social dance. All the participants are following their leader—Death.

The Danse Macabre made its first appearance during the plague (Black Death) years of the fourteenth century. In Germany it was the *Todtentanz;* in Italy, *danza della morte;* and in England, the Dance of Death. In the Danse Macabre, the personified figure of Death led dancers in a slow, stately procession that was clearly a ritualistic rather than a social dance.

Danse Macabre images served several purposes, including to help people express and share their grief; to remind each other that death is not only inevitable, but also the great equalizer, claiming the high and mighty as well as the humble; and to provide the opportunity for indirect mastery. When vulnerable mortals could depict, narrate, and enact the Dance of Death, they gained a subtle sense of control. In fact, as the Danse Macabre became an increasingly familiar cultural element, the figure of Death was also increasingly subject to caricature. The resilient human imagination had made Death a character—often dignified, sometimes frightening, and, eventually, even comic.

The earliest known appearances of the Danse Macabre were in story poems that told of encounters between the living and the dead. Most often the living were proud and powerful members of society, such as knights and bishops. The dead interrupted their procession: "As we are, so shall you be" was the underlying theme, "and neither your strength nor your piety can provide escape." A haunting visual image also appeared early: the Danse Macabre painted on the cloister walls of The Innocents, a religious order in Paris. This painting no longer exists, but there are woodcut copies of early depictions of the Danse Macabre.

The origin of the term "macabre" has invited considerable speculation. Perhaps the best-founded explanation was that offered by the historian Phillipe Ariès. He noted that the Maccabees of the Biblical period had been revered as patrons of the dead. *Macchabe* became a folk expression for the dead body, and Ariès found that the term still had that meaning in the folk slang of the late twentieth century.

There is sometimes confusion between the grave and measured gestures of the Danse Macabre and the much more violent and agitated phenomenon known as either St. John's or St. Vitus' dance. Both phenomena appeared at about the same time, but could hardly be more different. The Dance of Death was primarily the creation of storytellers and artists and only secondarily enacted in performance. St. Vitus' dance was primarily a performance carried out often to the point of frenzy or exhaustion by masses of people joined

in a circle dance. Interestingly, municipal officials recognized some value in these proceedings. Musicians were hired and instructed to play faster and louder. The fallen dancers were swathed and comforted until they recovered their senses. It was as though the delirious participants had cast out the devil or at least reduced the tension of those desperate years not only for themselves but also for the bystanders.

Danse Macabre images have continued to appear throughout the centuries, each generation offering its own interpretation. Striking examples include the German painter Hans Holbein's classic woodcuts, first published in 1538, and German artist Fritz Eichenberg's visual commentary on the brutality of more modern times, published in 1983.

*See also:* ARS MORIENDI; BLACK DEATH; DANCE; GHOST DANCE; PERSONIFICATIONS OF DEATH

### Bibliography

Ariès, Philippe. *The Hour of Our Death,* translated by Helen Weaver. New York: Knopf, 1981.

Clark, James M. *The Dance of Death in the Middle Ages and the Renaissance.* Glasgow, Scotland: Glasgow University Press, 1950.

Eichenberg, Fritz. *Dance of Death.* New York: Abbeville Press, 1983.

Holbein, Hans. *The Dance of Death.* New York: Dover, 1971.

Meyer-Baer, Kathi. *Music of the Spheres and the Dance of Death.* Princeton, NJ: Princeton University Press, 1970.

Weber, Frederick Parkes. *Aspects of Death and Correlated Aspects of Life in Art, Epigram, and Poetry.* College Park, MD: McGrath, 1971.

ROBERT KASTENBAUM

# DARWIN, CHARLES

Charles Robert Darwin (1809–1882) is widely considered the greatest naturalist of the nineteenth century. His pioneering work in the theory of evolution wrought a revolution in the study of the origins and nature of plant and animal life.

The son of Robert Darwin, a prominent English physician, Charles had an early interest in natural history, especially hunting, collecting, and geology. At his father's urging, Darwin attended medical school at Edinburgh, but found that he had little interest in medicine and returned home after two years. Wanting his son to have a respectable career, Darwin's father suggested that he should become an Anglican clergyman. Because the quiet, scholarly life of the clergyman appealed to him, Darwin agreed. He completed his degree at Cambridge in 1831. While awaiting an assignment, he was recommended for the job of naturalist on the survey ship *Beagle,* a voyage of nearly five years. In 1859 Darwin published *The Origin of Species by Means of Natural Selection* based on his discoveries during this voyage.

This seminal work contained three major discoveries. First, it presented an overwhelming amount of physical evidence of Darwin's evolutionary thesis. Naturalists had observed evolutionary change since the time of the ancient Greeks, and by the mid-1800s the idea of evolution was "in the air." But it was not until Darwin published *Origin* that a body of empirical evidence supported the idea of evolution. Because of Darwin's thorough and compelling work, almost no biologists today doubt the reality of evolution. Second, Darwin discovered descent from common ancestry, demonstrating that all living things are related. Tracing the lineage of any two species back far enough, one can find a common ancestor. The modern fossil record and biochemical comparisons among species verify this observation. Earlier theorists such as Jean Baptiste de Lamarck had assumed that life had originated many times and that each lineage was unique and unrelated to all others. Third, Darwin discovered and described the basic mechanism by which evolution works: natural selection. Natural selection is the differential reproductive success of some individuals in a population relative to that of others.

The Darwinian mechanism is based on differential reproductive rates. First, natural populations exhibit variation in phenotype (physical makeup) from one individual to the next, and this variation is genetically determined. For example, there is

*Modern biologists recognize other evolutionary processes not known to Darwin, but natural selection remains the basic mechanism.* BETTMANN/CORBIS

considerable variation in human height, skin color, and so on, within a population.

Second, organisms are genetically programmed to reproduce. Reproduction is a very powerful biological urge, and animals will risk or even sacrifice their lives to accomplish it. Humans feel this genetic programming in several ways, as a ticking "biological clock," as parental instinct, or as an attraction to children. As a result, natural populations have a tendency to overpopulate. Biologists define "overpopulation" in terms of limiting factors that may include food, space, mates, light, and minerals. For example, if there is enough space on an island for 1,000 deer but only enough food to sustain a population of 100, then 101 deer constitutes overpopulation. The result of overpopulation is competition among the individuals of the population for the limited resources. If there are no limited resources, there is no competition. Competition results in "survival of the fittest," an unfortunate phrase that Darwin borrowed from contemporary social theorists who are now known as "social Darwinists." In Darwinian terms, however, fitness refers only to reproductive success, not to strength, size, or (in humans) economic status.

Third, some of the variants in the population are more efficient than others in exploiting the limited resources. Success in obtaining limited resources is due largely to inherited phenotype. These individuals channel more of the limited resource through themselves and are therefore able to reproduce more successfully than individuals that compete less successfully. Thus, these selected variants pass on their genes for their genotype with greater frequency than do other variants.

Fourth, the result of this selectively favored breeding is a modification of population gene frequencies over time that may cause a change in phenotype. That is, the average state of a given character undergoing selection changes from one generation to the next. If, for example, predators feed on slower antelope, the average running speed of the population will gradually increase from generation to generation. This is observed as evolution.

And lastly, the losers, those individuals less successful at exploiting limited resources and at reproduction, may die in greater numbers (if, for example, they do not find enough food) or may find an alternative to the limited resource. Galapagos finches (Darwin's finches) with thinner beaks that were less successful at eating heavy seeds often found alternative foods such as insect larvae, which are more accessible to thinner beaks. Over time, this process results in evolutionary diversification of an ancestral species into two or more progeny species, the divergence from common ancestry recognized by Darwin.

Darwin had three great accomplishments with the publication of *Origin of Species* in 1859. He produced an overwhelming body of physical evidence that demonstrated the fact of evolution. Darwin also discovered descent from common ancestry and, lastly, the basic mechanism by which evolution operates—natural selection based on differential reproductive rates of individuals in a breeding population. The implications of Darwin's discoveries have profoundly influenced almost every area of knowledge from science to religion to social theory.

*See also:* EXTINCTION

### Bibliography

Bowlby, John. *Charles Darwin, A New Life.* New York: W.W. Norton and Company, 1990.

Darwin, Charles. "The Origin of Species by Means of Natural Selection." In Mortimer J. Adler ed., *Great Books of the Western World,* second edition. Chicago: Encyclopaedia Britannica, 1990.

Lack, David. *Darwin's Finches: An Essay on the General Biological Theory of Evolution.* Gloucester, MA: Peter Smith, 1968.

Skelton, Peter, ed. *Evolution: A Biological and Paleontological Approach.* Harlow, England: Addison-Wesley, 1993.

ALFRED R. MARTIN

# DAYS OF THE DEAD

Days of the Dead, a religious observation celebrated throughout Mexico on November 2, honors the memories of departed family members. The farther south one travels in Mexico, the more elaborate the celebration becomes. It is mainly in southern and central areas where Mexicans decorate their *panteones* (cemeteries) and the nearby streets with vivid imagery of death, usually skeletons and skulls. Families make altars in their homes, where the photos of departed souls are prominently placed alongside religious icons, *ofrendas* (offerings) of food such as *pan de muertos* baked in shapes of skulls and figures, and yellow marigolds, the symbol of death. On the eve of November 2, All Saints Day, some families spend the night at the cemetery in a *velada* (wake), lighting candles and making offerings at the tombs of their loved ones.

Some communities organize a *desfile* (parade) with participants dressed up as ghouls, ghosts, mummies, and skeletons carrying an open coffin with an animated corpse played by a villager. The skeletal representations are given feminine nicknames such as *la calaca* (the skeleton), *la pelona* (baldy), *la flaca* (skinny), and *la huesada* (bony). This most likely originates in the pre-European practice of assigning a female characteristic to the deity overseeing death. The Aztecs called this goddess Mictecacihuatl.

The traveler in the northern or urban areas of Mexico will find no such colorful observances.

*Observers of Days of the Dead gather to commemorate departed family members in a ritual that has been interpreted as evidence of a cultural acceptance of death, a sharp contrast to the death-denying conventions of the United States.*
AP/WIDE WORLD PHOTOS

While *El Día de los Muertos* (Day of the Dead) is marked in these regions, the activities are usually more sedate, consisting of placing marigolds at the tombs or either cleaning or refurbishing these resting places. But even here, a festive air surrounds the cemeteries as vendors peddle food, flowers, and religious relics.

There is no doubt that Mexicans demonstrate a unique devotion to a day that all Christians in varying degrees observe. The reasons for this are varied. In areas that retain a vibrant indigenous tradition, this Christian religious holiday is a part of a syncretic process, a blend of pre-Columbian beliefs in the return of the ancestors to their villages and the Christian belief that only the flesh decays but not the soul.

During the Days of the Dead, Mexicans deploy mockery and fraternization to openly confront and accept the inevitability of death that is so feared and hidden in modern Western culture. Considering that contemporary and past pre-industrial cultures deal with death in a similar fashion—there are examples in India, Asia, or Africa—such conviviality in the face of death is a lively tradition in a country where the modern competes with a vigorous traditional past.

In the late nineteenth century, Chicanos and other Americans in the United States have taken to celebrating Days of the Dead with much fanfare. While these projects incorporate the most colorful and interesting features from Mexico, they are usually bereft of the religious dimension of authentic Mexican rites. Interestingly, in the San Francisco Bay area, the homosexual community has taken on this day of observation as a method of coping with the AIDS epidemic.

See also: AFTERLIFE IN CROSS-CULTURAL PERSPECTIVE; COMMUNICATION WITH THE DEAD; GHOSTS; GRIEF AND MOURNING IN CROSS-CULTURAL PERSPECTIVE

### Bibliography

Greenleigh, John. *The Days of the Dead: Mexico's Festival of Communion with the Departed.* San Francisco: Collins Publishers, 1991.

Hoyt-Goldsmith, Diane. *Day of the Dead: A Mexican-American Celebration.* New York: Holiday House, 1994.

Luenn, Nancy. *A Gift for Abuelita: Celebrating the Day of the Dead.* Flagstaff, AZ: Rising Moon, 1998.

F. ARTURO ROSALES

# DEAD GHETTO

The concept of the "dead ghetto" derives from Jean Baudrillard (b. 1929), a contemporary French philosopher, in his book *Symbolic Exchange and Death* (1993). Baudrillard's work is formed primarily from the concepts of the French sociologist Marcel Mauss (1872–1950) and the Swiss philologist Ferdinand de Saussure (1857–1913). Mauss wrote a slim volume on the gift, arguing that gift exchange (giving, receiving, counter-giving) is never voluntary, always obligatory, and reflects the totality of societal aspects. De Saussure described language as a social phenomenon, a structured system of signs or symbols. Baudrillard extended and combined these two concepts, creating the concept of how the dead are viewed by society and the living, and within that the concept of the dead ghetto.

According to Baudrillard's philosophy, in primitive societies a sign represented an object, the signified. As society became more complex the sign became more and more divorced from reality, and itself became a new reality. In the twenty-first century, for example, a television newscast of an event becomes the reality itself, although the observer never gets close to the initial objects or reality. Because society can be described entirely as a system of exchanges, Baudrillard argues that society's members are dealing with symbolic exchanges, in which a concept and its opposite become reversible. The living and the dead are such a pair,

and death serves as the boundary between them. If a concept such as the afterlife, introduced for example by the Christian churches, becomes paired with life, then death, no longer having something to be paired with and exchanged, disappears.

Baudrillard continues by saying that death can also be denied, or, in a sense, abolished, by segregating the dead in graveyards, which become "ghettos." Following an analysis of Baudrillard's concept by Bradley Butterfield, one may begin with primitive societies in which life and death were seen as partners in symbolic exchanges. As society evolved the dead were excluded from the realm of the living by assigning them to graveyards, the ghettos, where they no longer have a role to play in the community of the living. To be dead is to be abnormal, where for primitives it was merely another state of being human. For these earlier societies it was necessary to use their resources through ritual feasts and celebrations for the dead in order to avoid a disequilibrium where death would have a claim on them. In more evolved societies focused on economy, death is simply the end of life—the dead can no longer produce or consume, and thus are no longer available for exchanges with the living.

However, Baudrillard argues that the "death of death" is not complete because private mourning practices still exist. Baudrillard makes a similar argument on old age: "Old age has merely become a marginal and ultimately a social slice of life—a ghetto, a reprieve and the slide into death. Old age is literally being eliminated," as it ceases to be symbolically acknowledged (Baudrillard 1993, p. 163).

Baudrillard presents an intellectual construct founded on the concepts of de Saussure and Mauss which, by contrast, are derived from a factual basis. Thus Baudrillard's construct is one step removed from reality. The majority of real people, even in the complex societies of the twenty-first century, however, have not banished death to a ghetto where the dead no longer play a role in their lives. The presence of the deceased continues to play a role in their lives on an ongoing basis (Klass, Silverman, and Nickman 1996). Because the deceased are still important to the living, Baudrillard's concept represents an interesting intellectual exercise—a *hyperreality,* to use his own term—but not an accurate representation of reality.

See also: CATACOMBS; CEMETERIES AND CEMETERY REFORM; FUNERAL INDUSTRY; TOMBS

**Bibliography**

Baudrillard, Jean. *Symbolic Exchange and Death,* translated by Iain Hamilton Grant. London: Sage, 1993.

Klass, Dennis, Phyllis R. Silverman, and Steven Nickman, eds. *Continuing Bonds: New Understandings of Grief.* Washington, DC: Taylor & Francis, 1996.

Mauss, Marcel. *The Gift; Forms and Functions of Exchange in Archaic Societies.* Glencoe, IL: Free Press, 1954.

Silverman, Sam M., and Phyllis R. Silverman. "Parent-Child Communication in Widowed Families." *American Journal of Psychotherapy* 33 (1979):428–441.

*Internet Resources*

Butterfield, Bradley. "Baudrillard's Primitivism and White Noise: 'The Only Avant-Garde We've Got.'" In the UNDERCURRENT: An Online Journal for the Analysis of the Present [web site]. Available from http://darkwing.uoregon.edu/~ucurrent/uc7/7-brad.html.

SAM SILVERMAN

# DEATHBED SCENES

See DEATHBED VISIONS AND ESCORTS; GOOD DEATH, THE.

# DEATHBED VISIONS AND ESCORTS

Deathbed visions are apparitions; that is, appearances of ghostly beings to the dying near the time of their death. These beings are usually deceased family members or friends of the one who is dying. However, they can also be appearances of living people or of famous religious figures. Usually these visions are only seen and reported by the dying, but caretakers and those attending the dying have also reported witnessing such apparitions. In the majority of these cases, the apparition came to either announce the imminent death of the individual or to help that person die. In the latter situation they act as escorts to the dying in the process of passing from this life to the next.

Visions at the time of death and announcements or omens of impending death, as well as escorts for the dead, are part of many cultures and religious traditions stretching back through antiquity. The religious motif of the soul making a journey from this life through death to another form of existence, whether it be reincarnation or to an eternal realm, is commonly found in many religions throughout history.

Shamans from many native cultures were adept at journeying from the land of the living to the land of the dead and were thus able to act as guides for those who were dying. Hermes, the Greek god of travel, was also known as the Psychopompos, the one who guided the soul from this life to Hades, and the realm of dead. Certain religious traditions have elaborate rituals of instruction for the soul at the time of death. *The Egyptian Book of the Dead* and the coffin texts of ancient Egypt gave detailed instructions for the soul's journey to the next life. Similarly, by use of the *Bardo Thodol,* or *Tibetan Book of the Dead,* Tibetan Buddhist monks have guided the souls of the dying through death to their next incarnation. In the Christian tradition it has been guardian angels that have acted as the soul's guide to paradise. The ancient hymn, "In Paradisum," invoking the angels to escort the soul to heaven, is still sung at twenty-first-century Roman Catholic funerals.

Christianity's belief in resurrection and the concept of a communion of saints, that is, the continued involvement of the dead with the spiritual welfare of the living, is reflected in the historical accounts of deathbed visions in the West. Third-century legends about the life of the Virgin Mary recount Christ's appearing to her to tell her of the approaching hour of her death and to lead her into glory. In the hagiography of many early Christian martyrs and saints, impending death is revealed by the visitation of Christ, Mary, or another saint who has come to accompany the dying into heaven. This tradition is carried over into early historical records. The eighth-century English historian Bede wrote of a dying nun who is visited by a recently deceased holy man telling her that she would die at dawn, and she did. Medieval texts such as the thirteenth-century *Dialogue of Miracles* by the German monk Caesarius of Heisterbach recount similar stories, but always within a theological framework.

In the seventeenth century treatises began to be published specifically on the phenomena of apparitions and ghosts. By the nineteenth century specific categories within this type of phenomena were being described. For instance, apparitions began to be distinguished between those seen by healthy people and those seen by the dying. It was noted that when the dead appeared to the living, it was usually to impart some information to them such as the location of a treasure, or the identity of a murderer. However, when an apparition was seen by a dying person, its intent was almost always to announce the impending death of that individual, and often to be an escort for that death.

Early in the twentieth century, the doctor James H. Hyslop of Columbia University, and later Sir William F. Barrett of the University of Dublin, researched the deathbed visions of the dying. They were particularly interested in what became known as the "Peak in Darien" cases. These were instances when dying persons saw an apparition of someone coming to escort them to the next world whom they thought to be still alive and could not have known that they had preceded them in death.

In 1961 the physician Karlis Osis published *Deathbed Observations of Physicians and Nurses.* In it he analyzed 640 questionnaires returned by physicians and nurses on their experience of observing over 35,000 deaths. Osis refers to the deathbed visions of the dying as hallucinations because they cannot be empirically verified. He categorized two types of hallucinations: visions that were nonhuman (i.e., nature or landscapes), and apparitions that were of people. His work confirmed previous research that the dying who see apparitions predominantly see deceased relatives or friends who are there to aid them in their transition to the next life. With the assistance of another physician, Erlandur Haraldsson, Osis conducted two more surveys of physicians and nurses: one in the United States and one in northern India. The results of these surveys confirmed Osis's earlier research on deathbed hallucinations with the exception that there were more apparitions of religious figures in the Indian population.

These studies and the extensive literature on this subject confirm that throughout history and across cultures, the dying often experience apparitional hallucinations. What significance these deathbed visions have depends on the worldview with which one holds them. In this data those with religious or spiritual beliefs can find support for their beliefs. Parapsychological explanations such as telepathy or the doctrine of psychometry, whereby environments can hold emotional energy that is received by the subconscious of the dying, have all been advanced to explain apparitions at the time of death. The Jungian psychoanalyst Aniela Jaffe viewed apparitions, including those of the dying, as manifestations of Carl Jung's transpersonal views of the psyche and, therefore, a validation of Jungian metapsychology. Indeed both the visions as well as the apparitional hallucinations described by Osis can be attributed to a number of medical causes, including lack of oxygen to the brain. Ultimately the research into the phenomenon of deathbed visions, while confirming that such events are common, offers no clear explanations.

*See also:* COMMUNICATION WITH THE DEAD; COMMUNICATION WITH THE DYING; EGYPTIAN BOOK OF THE DEAD; GHOSTS; NEAR-DEATH EXPERIENCES; OMENS; REINCARNATION; TIBETAN BOOK OF THE DEAD

## Bibliography

Barrett, William F. *Death-Bed Visions: The Psychical Experiences of the Dying.* Wellingborough, England: Aquarian Press, 1986.

Faulknre, Raymond O., ed. *The Ancient Egyptian Coffin Texts.* Warminster, England: Avis and Philips, 1973.

Finucane, Ronald C. *Appearances of the Dead: A Cultural History of Ghosts.* New York: Prometheus Books, 1984.

Hyslop, James H. *Psychical Research and the Resurrection.* Boston: Small, Maynard and Company, 1908.

Jaffe, Aniela. *Apparitions and Precognitions.* New Hyde Park, NY: University Books, 1963.

Osis, Karlis. *Death Observations by Physicians and Nurses.* New York: Parapsychological Foundation, 1961.

Osis, Karlis, and Erlendur Haraldsson. *At the Hour of Death.* New York: Hastings House, 1986.

Paterson, Ronald William Keith. *Philosophy and the Belief in a Life after Death.* New York: St. Martin's Press, 1995.

Sambhava, Padma. *The Tibetan Book of the Dead*, translated by Robert A. F. Thurman. New York: Bantam Books, 1993.

THOMAS B. WEST

# DEATH CERTIFICATE

A death certificate is the official document that declares a person is dead. Death certificates serve two purposes: they prevent murder cover-ups by restricting those who can complete them for non-natural deaths to trained officials who generally have great latitude on whom they perform post-mortem examinations, and they provide public health statistics. Death registration was first required in the United Kingdom in 1874. Before then, it was not even necessary for a physician to view the corpse. In the United States, Great Britain, and most industrialized countries, physicians must now sign a death certificate listing the presumed cause of death. Otherwise, a medical examiner (forensic pathologist) will intervene with an autopsy to determine the cause of death in the event that a case requires police investigation.

People use death certificates in multiple ways. Survivors need death certificates to obtain burial permits, make life insurance claims, settle estates, and obtain death benefits. Public health departments look for patterns that may signal specific health problems, such as clusters of cancers that may reveal unknown toxic waste dumps.

There are three types of death certificates in the United States, including a standard certificate, one for medical/legal cases, and one for fetal or stillborn deaths. All but two states require a death certificate for fetal deaths. However, the majority of states only require a certificate if the fetus was past twenty weeks of gestation. All are based on the international form agreed to in 1948 (modified for clarity in the United States in the 1990s). This form lists the immediate cause of death (e.g., heart attack, stroke), conditions that resulted in the immediate cause of death (e.g., gunshot wound to the chest), and other significant medical conditions (e.g., hypertension, atherosclerotic coronary artery disease, or diabetes). The form also includes a place to record whether an autopsy was performed and the manner of death such as natural, accident,

suicide, homicide, could not be determined, or pending investigation.

Death certificates are occasionally used to fake a person's death for insurance fraud and to evade law enforcement officials or irate relatives. "Official" Los Angeles County death certificates, for example, were readily available in the mid-1990s for between $500 and $1,000 each. For fraudulent purposes, people have often used death certificates from remote nations and from countries in turmoil.

To complete death certificates, funeral directors first insert the decedent's personal information, including the name, sex, date of death, social security number, age at last birthday, birth date, birthplace, race, current address, usual occupation, educational history, service in the U.S. armed forces, site and address of death, marital status, name of any surviving spouse, parents' names, and informant's name and address. They also include the method and site of body disposition (burial, cremation, donation, or other) and sign the form. The responsible physician must then complete, with or without using an autopsy, his or her sections of the certificate. These include the immediate cause(s) of death; other significant conditions contributing to the death; the manner of death; the date, time, place, and mechanism of any injury; the time of death; the date the death was pronounced; whether the medical examiner was notified; and his or her signature. The death certificate then passes to the responsible local and state government offices, where, based on that document, a burial permit is issued. The death certificate, or at least the information it contains, then goes to the state's bureau of vital statistics and from there to the United States Center for Health Statistics.

Funeral directors often struggle to obtain a physician's signature on a death certificate. In an age of managed-care HMOs and multispecialty clinics, they must not only locate the busy practitioner for a signature, but also identify the correct physician. Survivors cannot bury or otherwise dispose of a corpse until a licensed physician signs a permanent death certificate or a medical examiner signs a temporary death certificate. Medical examiners (or coroners) list the cause of death as "pending" until further laboratory tests determine the actual cause of death. Except in unusual cases, disposition of the remains need not wait for the final autopsy report, which may take weeks to complete.

After the death certificate has been signed, local authorities usually issue a certificate of disposition of remains, also known as a burial or cremation permit. Crematories and cemeteries require this form before they will cremate or bury a body. In some jurisdictions, the form is combined with a transportation permit that allows the movement or shipment of a body. The need for regulation of death certificates became evident in 1866. When New York City first installed an independent Board of Health in March 1866, city police inspected the offices of F. I. A. Boole, the former city inspector. According to the *New York Times,* police found a large number of unnumbered burial permits, which Boole had already signed. They claimed that Boole had been selling these to murderers who used them to legally bury their victims' bodies.

Public health policies depend heavily on the mortality data from death certificates because they are the only source of information about the causes of death and illnesses preceding death. For example, when Italy's Del Lazio Epidemiological Observatory reviewed 44,000 death certificates, it found that most diseases divided neatly along class lines. The poor died of lung tumors, cirrhosis of the liver, respiratory diseases, and "preventable deaths" (appendicitis, childbirth complications, juvenile hypertension, and acute respiratory infections). Well-to-do women had higher rates of breast cancer. It also found that the incidence of heart disease, strokes, and some cancers did not vary with income level. These findings have had a significant impact on how the Italian government funds its health care system.

Yet the accuracy of death certificates in the United States is questionable, with up to 29 percent of physicians erring both as to the cause of death and the deceased's age. About the same number incorrectly state whether an autopsy was done. Less significant discrepancies occur in listing the deceased's marital status, race, and place of birth. Death certificates of minority groups have the most errors. Only about 12 percent of U.S. physicians receive training in completing death certificates, and less than two-thirds of them do it correctly. Several do not appear to believe that completing death certificates accurately is very important.

Many certificates are meaningless because physicians complete them without knowing the real cause of death. Listing "cardiopulmonary arrest" signifies nothing—everyone's heart and lungs eventually stop. The important point is why? An autopsy is often needed to answer this question. Occasionally, autopsy, pathology, or forensic findings appear after a death certificate has been completed. If it is within three years of the death in many jurisdictions, the original physician-signer need only complete an amended certificate to correct the record.

Disguising deaths from alcoholism, AIDS, and other stigmatizing causes of death on death certificates is widespread. This practice appears to be more common where medical examiners' autopsy reports are part of the public record. For this reason, some states may eliminate the cause of death from publicly recorded death certificates.

Physicians obscure information on some death certificates to protect a family's reputation or income, with listings such as "pneumonia" for an AIDS death or "accidental" for a suicide. Even before the AIDS epidemic, one researcher found that in San Francisco, California, socially unacceptable causes of death frequently were misreported— the most common being alcoholic cirrhosis of the liver, alcoholism, syphilis, homicide, and suicide.

A similar problem with the accuracy of death certificates has been reported in Great Britain. The Royal College of Physicians of London claims that 20 percent of British death certificates incorrectly list the cause of death. In one instance, for example, the number of reported suicides at Beachy Head (a popular spot at which to commit suicide by jumping into the sea) diminished by one-third simply with a change in coroners.

Physicians who complete death certificates in good faith are not liable to criminal action, even if the cause of death is later found to be different from that recorded. Fraudulent completion to obscure a crime or to defraud an insurance company, however, is a felony.

Occasionally, fake death certificates appropriate real people's identities. Such false death certificates are especially distasteful to victims of this fraud who are still alive and whose "death" causes officials to freeze their assets, cancel credit, revoke licenses, and generally disrupt their lives.

Deaths that occur aboard ships are handled very differently. For example, British captains register any crew or passenger death in the ship's log, the information approximating that on a death certificate. On arrival at a British port, the captain must report the death to harbor authorities, who then investigate the circumstances.

Death certificates and other standard legal papers surrounding death normally cost between $1 and $5 each. The funeral director usually obtains these forms and itemizes their costs on the bill. In cases where a body must be shipped to a non-English-speaking country, the forms must often be translated at an additional cost.

*See also:* AUTOPSY; CAUSES OF DEATH; SUICIDE

### *Bibliography*

Hanzlick Randy, and H. Gib Parrish. "The Failure of Death Certificates to Record the Performance of Autopsies." *Journal of the American Medical Association* 269, no. 1 (1993):47.

Kircher, Tobia, Judith Nelson, and Harold Burdo. "The Autopsy As a Measure of Accuracy of the Death Certificate." *New England Journal of Medicine* 310, no. 20 (1985):1263–1269.

Messite Jacqueline, and Steven D. Stellman. "Accuracy of Death Certificate Completion." *Journal of the American Medical Association* 275, no. 10 (1996):794–796.

Wallace, Robert B., and Robert F. Woolson. *Epidemiologic Study of the Elderly.* New York: Oxford University Press, 1992.

KENNETH V. ISERSON

# DEATH EDUCATION

The term *death education* refers to a variety of educational activities and experiences related to death and embraces such core topics as meanings and attitudes toward death, processes of dying and bereavement, and care for people affected by death. Death education, also called education about death, dying, and bereavement, is based on the belief that death-denying, death-defying, and death-avoiding attitudes and practices in American culture can be transformed, and assumes that individuals and institutions will be better able to deal with death-related practices as a result of educational efforts.

There are two major reasons for providing death education. First, death education is critical for preparing professionals to advance the field and accomplish its purposes. Second, it provides the general public with basic knowledge and wisdom developed in the field. The overarching aims of death education are to promote the quality of life and living for oneself and others, and to assist in creating and maintaining the conditions to bring this about. This is accomplished through new or expanded knowledge and changes in attitudes and behavior.

Death education varies in specific goals, formats, duration, intensity, and characteristics of participants. It can be formal or informal. Formal death education can involve highly structured academic programs of study and clinical experience. It can be organized into courses, modules, or units taught independently or incorporated into larger curricular entities. It can be offered at the elementary, middle, and high school levels, in postsecondary education, as professional preparation, and as short-term seminars or workshops for continuing professional and public education. Informal death education occurs when occasions arising in the home, at school, and in other social settings are recognized and used as "teachable moments." In the home, the birth of a sibling or the death of a pet may naturally lead to interactions that answer a child's questions about death. At school, a student's sudden death may trigger educational follow-up, in addition to crisis counseling.

Two distinct methodological approaches to structured death education are the didactic and the experiential. The didactic approach (involving, for example, lectures and audiovisual presentations) is meant to improve knowledge. The experiential approach is used to actively involve participants by evoking feelings and thereby permitting death-related attitudes to be modified. This approach includes personal sharing of experiences in group discussion, role-playing, and a variety of other simulation exercises, and requires an atmosphere of mutual trust. Most educators use a combination of the two approaches.

Death education can be traced back to the death awareness movement, which unofficially began with Herman Feifel's book, *The Meaning of*

*Death* (1959). He and other scholars noted that the subject of death had become "taboo" in the twentieth century and challenged individuals to acknowledge their personal mortality, suggesting that to do so is essential for a meaningful life. Feifel pioneered the scientific study of attitudes toward death and pointed to the multidisciplinary nature of the field. At about the same time other pioneers focused on more specific issues concerning dying persons and their care and the experience of grief.

## General Academic Education

Reflecting the broad-based academic beginnings, courses on death and dying were developed by Robert Kastenbaum, Clark University, Robert Fulton at the University of Minnesota, Dan Leviton at the University of Maryland, and James Carse at Yale University, among others. In 1969 Fulton established the Center for Death Education (now the Center for Death Education and Bioethics at the University of Wisconsin, La Crosse). In 1970 Robert Kastenbaum founded *Omega: The Journal of Death and Dying,* the first professional journal in the field. In the same year the first conference on death education was held at Hamline University in St. Paul, Minnesota. In 1977 Hannelore Wass founded the journal *Death Education* (later renamed *Death Studies*).

## College Courses

As the field developed, a course or two on death became popular offerings in many colleges and universities across the country (in such areas as psychology, sociology, health sciences, philosophy, and education). These courses varied somewhat in perspective, depending on the disciplines in which they were offered. Courses in sociology focused more on cultural and social influences and customs, whereas courses in psychology emphasized the experiences and dynamics of dying, bereavement, and attitudes toward death. Leaders in the field recommended an approach that embraced both foci. From suggestions for course content, a common core of topics emerged, including historical, cultural, and social orientations and practices; attitudinal correlates of death and dying; coping with bereavement; controversial issues; and personal confrontation with death.

Through the years, college courses increasingly have come to reflect the multidisciplinary nature of

the field. As more knowledge was generated, college level courses with a multidisciplinary focus have tended to function as introductory or survey courses. Although popular introductory textbooks vary in approach and style, with the considerable similarity in the topics, a degree of standardization, at least in course content, has been achieved. At least one course on death is offered at most colleges across the country.

Along with an accelerating rate of publications in professional journals, books were published on various aspects of death, for professionals and the general public, including juvenile literature. Additionally, a wealth of audiovisuals was developed. Audiovisuals are used to facilitate group discussions and the sharing of personal experiences.

## Academic Concentration and Certificate Programs

A number of special tracks/areas of concentration have been developed in academic units at colleges and universities, especially at the graduate level, where they may be part of the curricular offerings in psychiatric/mental health and other nursing programs, counseling, clinical or health psychology, human development and family studies, and other specializations. One of the earliest, at Brooklyn College, is a thirty-three-credit-hour master's degree in a health science program with a concentration on care of the dying and bereaved. Similar programs in operation for two decades are offered at the New Rochelle College of Graduate Studies, New York University, and Hood College in Frederick, Maryland, among others. A unique comprehensive program, developed at King's College and Western Ontario University in Canada, is an undergraduate "Certificate in Palliative Care and Thanatology," which involves a thirty-six-credit-hour interdisciplinary program with a focus on palliative care, bereavement, suicide, and ethical, religious, and cultural issues. Many colleges and universities allow for individualized programs of concentration in death-related studies.

## Education for Health Professionals

In addition to the more general academic approach to the study of death, a number of pioneers concentrated on more specific issues. Several, including Jeanne Quint Benoliel, Cicely Saunders, and Elisabeth Kübler-Ross, focused on dying patients and the effects of institutional environments, the process of dying, and pain management, and they articulated the need for change in the care of dying people.

Benoliel began her pioneering work in death education for caregivers by designing a graduate course for nursing students, which she began to teach in 1971. Course topics included social, cultural, and psychological conditions that influence death-related attitudes and practices; concepts of grief; and ethical, legal, and professional issues concerning death. The course became a model for others. In her 1982 book, *Death Education for the Health Professional,* Benoliel comprehensively described several courses on death for undergraduate and graduate students in nursing and medicine.

Many colleges of nursing developed courses or modules in death education as electives and often as required courses, as well as continuing education programs, with content reflecting the broader framework that Benoliel recommended together with palliative and other caring skills required to work effectively with dying persons and their families. Several medical educators developed courses specifically for medical students. Despite these efforts, however, medical schools largely have failed to incorporate death-related knowledge and skills into their curricula.

Education was critical for the development of hospice care. Hospices relied largely on the leadership of professional organizations. A major concern of the International Work Group on Death, Dying, and Bereavement (IWG) has been to develop standards of clinical practice. IWG documents, identifying basic assumptions and principles of death-related programs and activities, are published in professional journals and periodically reprinted as collections by IWG. The "Assumptions and Principles Underlying Standards of Care of the Terminally Ill," developed by IWG members from the United States, the United Kingdom, and Canada, first published in 1979, became an important guide for hospice organizations.

The National Hospice and Palliative Care Organization, founded in 1981, grew out of the efforts of pioneers in hospice care. Among its main purposes has been the continuing education of its membership through annual conferences and the development of resources. Other professional organizations with similar priorities and information sharing are the Hospice Foundation of America, the International Association of Hospice and Palliative Care, and the American Academy of Hospice and Palliative Medicine (publisher of the *Journal of Palliative Medicine*). Related journals for health professionals are *Palliative Medicine* (in the United Kingdom) and the *Journal of Palliative Care* (in Canada), among others.

## Developments in Physician Education

A four-year study of seriously ill patients in hospitals, released in 1995, confirmed substantial shortcomings in palliative care and communication. Another study, conducted by George E. Dickinson and A. C. Mermann and released in 1996, found that except for a few occasional lectures or seminars at the clinical level, little instruction on death and dying occurred in medical schools. Not surprisingly, an examination of medical textbooks in multiple specialties by Michael W. Rabow and his colleagues in 2000 revealed that, with few exceptions, content in end-of-life care areas is minimal or absent.

With funding from various sources, however, comprehensive initiatives have been launched to educate physicians in end-of-life care. In 1996 the American Academy of Hospice and Palliative Medicine developed Unipacs, a program in hospice and palliative training for physicians that consists of six modules and is designed for physicians and physician educators. The program includes such topics as assessment and treatment of pain and other symptoms, alleviating psychological and spiritual pain, ethical and legal decision-making when caring for the terminally ill, and communication skills. A similar program, the National Internal Medicine Residency Curriculum Project in End-of-Life Care, is now a requirement for internal medicine residency training. In 1998 the American Medical Association announced the Education for Physicians on End-of-Life Care Project. Its first phase has been curriculum development including lecture sessions, videotape presentations, discussions, and exercises, organized into portable two-day conferences. Next, physician educators have been trained in using the curriculum. It will be published as a self-directed learning program and made available for physicians across the country. The American Academy of Family Physicians, in its "Recommended Curriculum Guidelines for Family Practice Residents on

End-of-Life Care" (2001), adds to the knowledge and skill components a third on attitudes that include awareness and sensitivity to such issues as "breaking bad news"; psychosocial, spiritual, and cultural issues affecting patients and family; and physicians' personal attitudes toward death.

## Nursing Education

Nurses spend far more time with critically ill patients and their families than do other caregivers. They have been better prepared for this aspect of their profession than physicians in that many nursing schools have been offering courses or modules at the undergraduate and graduate levels. Still, a 1999 study by Betty Ferrell suggested that end-of-life education in nursing schools is inconsistent. In response, the American Association of Colleges of Nursing (AACN) developed "Peaceful Death: Recommended Competencies and Curricular Guidelines for End-of-Life Nursing Care." Reflecting these guidelines, the AACN in 2001 developed the End of Life Nursing Education Curriculum (ELNEC). ELNEC is a comprehensive curriculum of nine modules to prepare bachelor's and associate degree nursing faculty who will integrate end-of-life care in basic nursing curricula for practicing nurses, and to provide continuing education in colleges and universities and specialty nursing organizations across the country. Among other efforts to improve nursing education in end-of-life care is the Tool-Kit for Nursing Excellence at End of Life Transition (TNEEL), a four-year project developed by six prominent nursing educators and researchers. TNEEL is an innovative package of electronic tools distributed to nurse educators in academic and clinical settings and eventually will be offered as a web-based self-study course.

## Preparation of Grief Counselors

Scientific writing on grief began in 1917 with the renowned physician and psychiatrist Sigmund Freud's essay on mourning and melancholia, and continued with the first empirical study of acute grief reactions by Erich Lindemann in 1944, John Bowlby's studies on attachment and loss in 1960 and 1961, and Colin Murray Parkes's investigations of spousal bereavement in 1970. In the next thirty years the study of grief became the most active area of research in the field. Differences in conceptualizations and methodological approaches led to diverse findings. The diversity in results may explain, in part, why findings from this literature were not immediately incorporated into the academic curricula in psychology, sociology, or the health sciences, except as occasional seminars, and lectures, or as topics for independent study and research.

These findings did stimulate the development of various mutual and self-help organizations for bereaved adults. Later, when studies on childhood bereavement showed that children also grieve and can benefit from support, programs for bereaved children were established. The Dougy Center in Portland, Oregon, a community-based volunteer program founded in 1985, became a model and training center for professionals across the nation interested in setting up grief support programs for children. In addition, leaders in the field pioneered community-supported crisis intervention programs in the public schools in the 1990s.

Hospices have become increasingly involved in community-oriented educational outreach and clinical services for bereaved adults and children and the public. Colleges of mortuary sciences have begun offering courses or modules in after-care counseling. Some basic information on grief and bereavement has also been incorporated into training of personnel for disaster relief organizations, of airline companies, and in some police departments.

The professional preparation of grief counselors has relied heavily on training in more nontraditional settings. Mental health practitioners and other health professionals have been offered continuing education seminars, workshops, and institutes. Leaders suggest that while well-trained and experienced mental health practitioners can learn the basics of grief counseling in a two- or three-day intensive workshop, the issues in grief therapy are too complex to be addressed in such abbreviated fashion.

Professional organizations have been vital in educating their members about grief. The Association for Death Education and Counseling (ADEC), in particular, concerned itself early with the question of education for professionals and was the first organization to develop professional standards and certification programs for death educators and counselors. In addition to its annual conferences, ADEC for many years has been offering a sequence of preconference basic and advanced academic courses and experiential workshops taught by leading professionals, as well as resources to assist members in preparing for certification. ADEC is at present revising its certification programs to certify professionals as grief counselors.

At colleges and universities today, many departments of health psychology, counseling and clinical psychology, human development and family studies, and other academic units offer areas of concentration that include courses and independent studies in death and bereavement at the undergraduate level. At the graduate level, an increasing number of departments support theses and dissertations on the subject. Increasingly more sophisticated and up-to-date death and grief-related content appears in the textbooks in relevant specialties in psychology, sociology, and gerontology. As hospitals begin to include bereavement follow-up services in their end-of-life care programs, content about grief will become part of medical and nursing education.

In addition to *Death Studies* and *Omega,* several other professional journals deal with grief, including *Illness, Crisis, and Loss* and *Journal of Loss and Trauma.* A large number of books are in print on various aspects of grief, including scholarly treatments, personal accounts, and, most of all, practical guidelines for support. An exploding number of profit and nonprofit Internet web sites offer information, resources, and support as well.

## Death Education for the Public

As the field of death and dying evolved and the subject became acceptable for discussion, the print and electronic media reported on new developments and presented interviews and panel discussions with increasing frequency. Public information about end-of-life issues that evolved with medical and technological advances was instrumental in the establishment of citizens' advocacy groups, the public debate regarding patients' rights, and subsequent legislation.

Funding from generous philanthropies, designed to educate professionals as well as the general public, has been instrumental in recent educational activities. One of the stated goals of the Project on Death in America of the Open Society Institute is to "understand and transform the culture and experience of dying and bereavement in America." Among recent educational efforts are the National Public Radio series "The End of Life: Exploring Death in America" and the PBS television series "On Our Own Terms: Moyers on Dying in America." There are thousands of web pages on end-of-life issues, various aspects of dying, funerals, and grief, as well as online support services. Most professional organizations concerned with death offer a wealth of information and resources on their web sites. Citizens' organizations present their views and perspectives in print and on the web.

Many communities periodically offer adult education programs, lecture series, seminars, and similar formats. And many colleges, universities, hospices, and hospitals either design programs for the community or invite the public to conferences.

## Death Education in Public Schools

Daniel Leviton, a pioneer in the field of death and dying, first articulated the rationale for teaching children about death. In 1977 Leviton, and in 1979 Eugene Knott, redefined early goals. Over the years numerous instructional guidelines and resources were developed for incorporating the study of death and dying into various subject areas taught in public schools.

A 1990 national survey of U.S. public schools conducted by Hannelore Wass, Gordon Thornton, and David Miller, however, found that only a fifth of the high schools, 15 percent of the middle schools, and less than a tenth of the elementary schools incorporated the study of death into their curricula. Those who did tended to include it in health science or family life. Goals were to better prepare for life, to appreciate life and health, and to be less afraid of death.

While most schools have established protocols for crisis intervention (grief counseling and support), preventive education through the study of death, dying, and bereavement has remained a controversial issue. Some parents say it infringes upon their and the church's domain. Some critics point to inadequate teacher preparation. There has been a concern that such study would induce anxiety and heighten fears in students. These concerns combined with increasing pressures to teach complex technological concepts and other basic skills, make it unlikely that the subject of death will be viewed as a part of the school's curriculum. But proponents of death education insist on the need to also address the life and people problems of today and help students to learn skills to solve them. Understanding and appreciating oneself, others, and life, learning ways to manage anger and frustration; developing attitudes of tolerance, respect, empathy, and compassion all contribute to a high quality of life. These may be basic ingredients of long-term primary prevention of destructive behavior and serve as an antidote to the distorted perceptions children form from the entertainment media.

## Reduction of Death Anxiety As a Goal in Death Education

Professionals disagree on the question of death anxiety reduction as a desirable or appropriate general goal for efforts in death education. Some leaders believe it is unrealistic to expect that a one-semester-length course of instruction in large classes can alleviate the negative affect of death. Instructors seldom know anything about individual students' feelings and personal experiences with death at the beginning of the instruction. Unless time is provided for sharing of experiences and concerns in class (or out of class), it may be difficult to assess students' attitudes and gauge affective changes. Additionally, changes may be too subtle to notice, or may be dormant for many months.

In continuing professional education, the concern has been whether a short-term workshop for health professionals—often not more than twenty hours in length—provides sufficient time to address the complex issues of death attitudes and to bring about attitude changes. Nonetheless, for students preparing to become health professionals, caring for dying and bereaved persons and their families, it is considered essential that they confront their own death-related feelings and learn to cope with them. There is evidence and a firm belief among thanatologists that negative feelings interfere with a person's effectiveness in helping others.

The concern that teaching children about death will induce or heighten death fears and anxieties may need reconsideration as well. Adults tend to be protective of children. At the same time, they also seem confident that children can withstand the onslaught of cultural and actual violence in their environment. This may be wishful thinking, however. Children do have fears and concerns about death. Studies of older children with life-threatening illness have shown that being given detailed information about diagnosis, prognosis, and treatment options lowered their death anxieties, suggesting that knowledge may give children a measure of control. This may be true for healthy children as well. Improved and specific information about the consequences of risk-taking behavior in adolescents, or even the process of discussing these matters, may reduce death anxiety children already have and help prevent risk-taking behaviors. Considering the complexity of the issues, it is important to include study of death-related attitudes in the curricula of prospective teachers at any level.

## Evaluation

While basic assumptions and goals of death education may be agreed on, wide variation in specific objectives, populations, and settings have made it difficult to establish general standards and to evaluate the overall effectiveness of the diverse efforts. Because thanatology (the study of death) has become a complex multidisciplinary field with a considerable amount of research, scholarship, and practice, and because the subject is personal and intimate, death education is challenging and requires solid qualification. There seems to be agreement on a number of basic competencies of an effective death educator:

- confrontation of personal mortality and comfort with the topic of death;

- knowledge of the subject matter and commitment to keep up with new developments;

- ability to develop objectives consistent with the needs, interests, and educational levels of learners;

- familiarity with basic principles of learning and instruction;

- knowledge of group dynamics; and

- skills in interpersonal communication and, when necessary, in identifying students' needs for support and counseling.

ADEC is currently developing standards for training death educators based on teacher competencies.

Numerous empirical studies have been conducted to provide objective data on the effects of death education. Most of these are done with college students taking a semester-length course or with health care professionals participating in short courses or workshops. Joseph A. Durlak and Lee Ann Reisenberg conducted a meta-analysis of forty-six controlled outcome studies. They concluded in 1991, reevaluated by Durlak in 1994, that death education was fairly successful in achieving cognitive learning goals, in changing cognitive attitudes on death-related issues and death-related behaviors (e.g., making out a will, talking with dying patients). Findings on changes in affect (death fears and anxieties), however, were inconsistent, depending in part on the teaching methods employed: Emphasis on experiential methods was more likely to result in slight decreases in fears, and emphasis on didactic methods had no or slightly negative effects.

## Conclusion

Education about death, dying, and bereavement has been instrumental in educating professionals and significant in informing the public. In general, substantial progress has been made identifying broad goals and specific objectives, designing curricula, developing resources, and reaching the populations to be addressed—college students, health care professionals, and the general public. Death education is minimal in the public schools. Leaders in the field, however, consider it an important component of the schools' curricula. Such education could be part of children's preparatory cultural education and could serve as primary prevention of violence by promoting life-affirming and constructive attitudes and behavior toward self and others.

Professional organizations concerned with death, dying, and bereavement demonstrate leadership by developing, expanding, or refining standards of practice and providing educational resources. The concerted efforts to educate physicians and nurses in end-of-life care are impressive. They also illustrate the importance of financial resources in bringing about change. Modest progress has been made in evaluating death education. The challenge of achieving an overall objective evaluation of educational outcomes remains. State-of-the-art death-related content needs to be reflected in the educational curricula for professionals. All groups can benefit from studying the larger social and cultural contexts in which they live and work. Advances in the communications technologies enabling rapid information gathering—and sharing—and the increasing use of these technologies for online distance learning and teaching can greatly facilitate and enhance death education at all levels.

*See also:* CADAVER EXPERIENCES; CHILDREN AND ADOLESCENTS' UNDERSTANDING OF DEATH; FEIFEL, HERMAN; GRIEF COUNSELING AND THERAPY; TABOOS AND SOCIAL STIGMA

## *Bibliography*

Benoliel, Jeanne Quint. "Death Influence in Clinical Practice: A Course for Graduate Students." In Jeanne Quint Benoliel ed., *Death Education for the Health Professional.* Washington, DC: Hemisphere, 1982.

Dickinson, George E., and A. C. Mermann. "Death Education in U.S. Medical Schools, 1975–1995." *Academic Medicine* 71 (1996):1,348–1,349.

Durlak, Joseph A. "Changing Death Attitudes through Death Education." In Robert A. Neimeyer ed., *Death Anxiety Handbook: Research, Instrumentation, and Application.* Washington, DC: Taylor & Francis, 1994.

Durlak, Joseph A., and Lee Ann Reisenberg. "The Impact of Death Education." *Death Studies* 15 (1991):39–58.

Ferrell, Betty R. "Analysis of End-of-Life Content in Nursing Textbooks." *Oncology Nursing Forum* 26 (1999):869–876.

International Work Group on Death, Dying, and Bereavement. "A Statement of Assumptions and Principles Concerning Education about Death, Dying, and Bereavement." *Death Studies* 16 (1992):59–65.

Knott, J. Eugene. "Death Education for All." In Hannelore Wass ed., *Dying: Facing the Facts.* Washington, DC: Hemisphere, 1979.

Leviton, Daniel. "The Scope of Death Education." *Death Education* 1 (1977):41–56.

Rabow, Michael W., Grace E. Hardie, Joan M. Fair, and Stephen J. McPhee. "End-of-Life Care Content in Fifty Textbooks from Multiple Specialties." *Journal of the American Medical Association* 283 (2000):771–778.

Wass, Hannelore. "Healthy Children and Fears about Death." *Illness, Crisis, and Loss* 6 (1998):114–126.

Wass, Hannelore. "Death Education for Children." In Inge B. Corless, Barbara B. Germino, and Mary A. Pittman eds., *A Challenge for Living: Dying, Death, and Bereavement.* Boston: Jones and Bartlett, 1995.

Wass, Hannelore, M. David Miller, and Gordon Thornton. "Death Education and Grief/Suicide Intervention in the Public Schools." *Death Studies* 14 (1990):253–268.

*Internet Resources*

"Hospice and Palliative Training for Physicians: Unipacs." In the American Academy of Hospice and Palliative Medicine [web site]. Available from www.aahpm.org/unipac's.htm.

"Peaceful Death: Recommended Competencies and Curricular Guidelines for End-of-Life Nursing Care." In the American Association of Colleges of Nursing [web site]. Available from www.aacn.nche.edu/Publications/deathfin.htm.

"Recommended Curriculum Guidelines for Family Practice Residents: End-of-Life Care." In the American Academy of Family Physicians [web site]. Available from www.aafp.org/edu/guidel/rep269.html.

University of Washington School of Nursing and Massachusetts Institute of Health Professions. "Tool-Kit for Nursing Excellence at End of Life Transition." In the University of Washington School of Nursing [web site]. Available from www.son.washington.edu/departments/bnhs/research.asp.

HANNELORE WASS

# DEATH INSTINCT

The pioneering Austrian psychoanalyst Sigmund Freud was a person with few illusions about human nature and civilization. In fact, he had been relentlessly exposing what he saw as the hidden strivings and conflicts beneath the mask of civilization. Even Freud, though, had not expected such a catastrophic violation of the values of civilization. Entering the sixth decade of his life, Freud had observed too much self-destructive behavior both from his psychoanalytic patients and society at large. He had grown dissatisfied with some of his own theories and felt the need to address more decisively the human propensity for self-destruction. His version of the question of the times became: Why do humans so often act against their own best interests—even the desire to survive?

It was in 1920 that Freud offered his death instinct theory. This was an uncertain time both in Freud's own life and in European culture. World War I, "The War to End All Wars" (unfortunately, misnamed), had finally concluded. Both the victorious and the defeated had experienced grievous loss. Parents had been bereaved, wives widowed, and children orphaned. Many of the survivors of

combat would never be the same again, physically or mentally. In Austria and Germany the devastation of war and the terms of the surrender had produced not only economic hardship but also a debilitating sense of hopelessness and frustration.

Thoughtful people found even more to worry about. World War I seemed to be much more than a tragic ordeal for all involved. In the minds of many observers, this protracted period of violence and upheaval had shattered the foundations of Western culture. Western civilization with its centuries-old traditions appeared to have been dealt a deathblow. Classical concepts of honor, beauty, glory, truth, and justice had been mutilated in the killing trenches and the casual brutalities of war. The visual, musical, and performing arts were contributing to the unease with disturbing new forms of expression. Science was increasingly seen as a threat to humanity through such routes as dehumanizing workplaces and ever-more lethal weaponry. The life sciences, through the theories of Charles Darwin, the nineteenth-century English naturalist, had already sounded one of the most troubling notes: *Homo sapiens* can be regarded as part of the animal kingdom. Humans were primates with superior language and tool skills. Where was the essence of humankind's moral being and the immortal soul? The physical and spiritual devastation of World War I seemed to have confirmed the gradually building anxieties about the future of humankind.

Freud introduced his new theory in *Beyond the Pleasure Principle* (1920). Most philosophers and psychologists had assumed that people are motivated by the desire to experience pleasure and avoid pain. This was not, however, always the case. Some of Freud's patients, for example, were masochistic—seekers of physical or emotional pain. The more he thought about it, the more connections Freud perceived between masochism, suicide, war, and the inability to love. Was there something in the very nature of humans that prompted them to override the self-preservation instinct and bring about harm both to themselves and others?

## Life and Death: Eros and Thanatos

Freud came to the conclusion that humans have not one but two primary instincts. He called the life-favoring instinct *Eros,* one of the Greek words

*Sigmund Freud claimed each human had a death instinct, called* Thanatos, *the Greek word for "death." This Greek relief sculpture shows Thanatos positioned between Aphrodite and Persephone, who are thought to be competing for the soul of* Adonis. BURSTEIN COLLECTION/CORBIS

for "love," and the death instinct *Thanatos,* the Greek word for "death." It was characteristic of Freud to invoke Greek literature and mythology, but it was also characteristic of him to ground his ideas in the biomedical and physical sciences. He suggested that all living creatures have an instinct, drive, or impulse to return to the inorganic state from which they emerged. This *todtriebe* (drive toward death) is active not only in every creature, great or small, but also in every cell of every organism. He pointed out that the metabolic processes active in all cells have both constructive (anabolic) and destructive (catabolic) functions. Life goes on because these processes work together—they are opposing but not adversarial.

Similarly, Eros and Thanatos function in a complementary manner in the personal and interpersonal lives of humans. People seek out new experiences, reach out to others, and expend energy in pursuit of their goals. Eros smiles over ventures

such as these. There are times, though, when humans need to act aggressively on the world, protect their interests, or withdraw from overstimulation and exertion and seek quietude. Thanatos presides over both these aggressive and risky ventures and the longing for "down time." Humans function and feel at their best when these two drives are in harmony. Sexual love, for example, may include both tenderness and thrill-seeking.

**Effects on Children**

Unfortunately, though, these drives are often out of balance. Children may be punished or shamed for their exploratory and aggressive, even destructive, actions (e.g., pulling a caterpillar apart to see what is inside). A particular problem in Freud's generation was strong parental disapproval of exploratory sexual expression in children. As a consequence, the child might grow into an adult who is aggressive and destructive where affection and sharing would be more rewarding—or into a person with such thwarted and convoluted sex/ death impulses that making love and making war are dangerously linked.

## Suicide and Homicide

Suicide and homicide often have roots in a confused and unbalanced relationship between the life and the death instincts. The destructive impulses may be turned against one's own self (suicide) or projected against an external target (homicide). Wars erupt when society at large (or its leaders) have displaced their own neurotic conflicts to the public scene.

## Later Views of the Theory

Death instinct theory has not fared well. In his influential 1938 book *Man against Himself,* American psychiatrist Karl Menninger stated that he found this theory helpful in understanding suicide and other self-destructive behaviors. Critics have dominated, however, both within the circle of psychoanalysis and the larger professional and academic community. Two of the criticisms are especially powerful: that the theory relies on vague and outdated scientific knowledge, and that it is seldom very useful when applied to specific individuals and situations. For the most part, counselors, therapists, researchers, and educators have found that they could get along just as well without making use of the death instinct theory.

Nevertheless, there is still vitality in this failed theory. Evidence of confused connections between sexuality and destructiveness remains plentiful, as do instances in which people seem to be operating against the principle of self-preservation of self or others. Furthermore, within the correspondence between Freud and the German-born American physicist and philosopher Albert Einstein, included in the 1932 book *Why War?,* was an ancient remedy that has yet to be given its full opportunity. Einstein had independently reached the same conclusion as Freud: "Man has in him the need to hate and to destroy." Freud replied with the emphasis on Eros: "Psychoanalysis need not be ashamed when it speaks of love, because religion says the same: 'Love thy neighbor as thyself.'"

*See also:* FREUD, SIGMUND; HOMICIDE, DEFINITIONS AND CLASSIFICATIONS OF; SUICIDE

### Bibliography

Brown, Norman O. *Life against Death.* New York: Viking, 1959.

Einstein, Albert, and Sigmund Freud. *Why War?* Chicago: Chicago Institute for Psychoanalysis, 1932.

Freud, Sigmund. *Beyond the Pleasure Principle.* New York: Norton, 1960.

Kastenbaum, Robert. *The Psychology of Death,* 3rd edition. New York: Springer, 2000.

Menninger, Karl. *Man against Himself.* New York: Harcourt, Brace, 1938.

ROBERT KASTENBAUM

# DEATH MASK

A death mask is a wax or plaster cast of a person's face taken while he or she is alive or after their death. Usually the mask is created after the death of the person because of the danger imposed by its materials. The making of a reproduction of the face of a dead person is an ancient practice whose origins date from the periods of the Romans and Egyptians. The process served as a reminder of the deceased for the family, as well as a protector from evil spirits, and is associated with a belief in the return of the spirit.

In some cultures, mostly in African, Native American, and Oceanic tribes, death masks are considered an important part of social and religious life. Death masks facilitate communication between the living and the dead in funerary rites and they create a new, superhuman identity for the bearer. Death masks can take the form of animals or spirits, thereby allowing the bearer to assume the role of the invoked spirit or to fend off evil forces.

In some tribes death masks are used in initiatory or homage ceremonies, which recount the creation of the world and the appearance of death among human beings. For others, where the link to ancestors is sacred, they are used to make the transition from the deceased to his or her heir of the family. Death masks are also used as a tool to help the deceased's soul pass easily to the other life. The respect of the funeral rites of mask dancing can also protect from reprisals from the dead, preventing the risk of a wandering soul.

*See also:* HUMAN REMAINS; IMMORTALITY, SYMBOLIC

*Bibliography*

Bonnefoy, Yves, and Wendy Doniger. *Mythologies.* Chicago: University of Chicago Press, 1991.

Guiley, Rosemary E. *Harper's Encyclopedia of Mystical and Paranormal Experience.* San Francisco: Harper San Francisco, 1991.

ISABELLE MARCOUX

# DEATH PENALTY

*See* CAPITAL PUNISHMENT.

# DEATH SQUADS

Death squads are generally state-sponsored terrorist groups, meaning that the government advocates death by groups of men who hunt down and kill innocent victims. Death squads are often paramilitary in nature, and carry out extrajudicial (outside the scope of the law or courts) killings, executions, and other violent acts against clearly defined individuals or groups of people (Campbell 2000). Their goal is to maintain the status quo with special reference to power and to terrorize those supportive of economic, political, and social reform. An example is the private armies, mercenaries, and gangs whose goal was to terrorize the population to prevent their support of the revolutionary Sandinista National Liberation Front (FSLN) during the Contra war in Nicaragua in 1979-1990 (Schroeder 2000). The brutish civil war in El Salvador, 1979–1991, provides another example. The work of these death squads horrified the world. Some were brazen enough to identify themselves by carving the initials "EM" (Escuadrón de la Muerte, "Death Squad") into the chests of corpses (Arnson 2000).

Violence by death squads falls under concepts such as extrajudicial killing, state-sponsored terrorism, democide (murder of a person or people by the government), and "horrendous death." Examples of horrendous death are deaths resulting from war, including assassination, terrorism, genocide, racism (e.g., lynching), famine, and environmental assault. All are preventable because they are caused by people rather than God, nature, bacteria, or virus. Ironically, preventive policies exist

that would deal with underlying root causes as well as outcomes but are too infrequently implemented (Leviton 1997). For example, root causes that give rise to death squads include authoritarian, totalitarian, despotic, non-democratic governments, and economic and educational disparities that result in misery and despair. They, in turn, seed economic, social, and political reform and revolutionary movements that are the natural enemy of the totalitarian state.

State-sponsored violence has escalated since the end of World War II. According to Amnesty International in 2000, confirmed or possible extrajudicial executions (including children) were carried out in forty-seven countries. Yet this quantitative data masks the suffering of survivors and its detrimental impact upon the social contract between people and their government.

All people are vulnerable to intentioned deaths such as democide and horrendous death. Their prevention is in the best interests of those desiring a peaceful, global society. To that end, organizations have made specific, preventive recommendations to nation states. Organizations concerned with the elimination and prevention of death squads include the U.S. State Department's Bureau of Democracy, Human Rights, and Labor; United Nations; Amnesty International; and Human Rights Watch. An international surveillance and early warning system and policies that institute basic reforms are also necessary measures. The latter include the need for universal education, instituting democratic forms of government with strong adversarial parties, and an inquisitive and free media.

*See also:* TERRORISM; WAR

*Bibliography*

Arnson, Cynthia J. "Window on the Past: A Declassified History of Death Squads in El Salvador." In B. B. Campbell and A. D. Brenner eds., *Death Squads in Global Perspective: Murder with Deniability.* New York: St. Martin's Press, 2000.

Boothby, Neil G., and Christine M. Knudsen. "Children of the Gun." *Scientific American* 282, no. 6 (2000):60–65.

Campbell, Bruce B. "Death Squads: Definition, Problems, and Historical Context." In B. B. Campbell and A. D. Brenner eds., *Death Squads in Global Perspective: Murder with Deniability.* New York: St. Martin's Press, 2000.

Doyle, Roger. "Human Rights throughout the World." *Scientific American* 280, no. 12 (1998):30–31.

Human Rights Watch. *Generation Under Fire: Children and Violence in Columbia.* New York: Author, 1994.

Leviton, Daniel. "Horrendous Death." In S. Strack ed., *Death and the Quest for Meaning.* New York: Jason Aronson, 1997.

Leviton, Daniel, ed. *Horrendous Death, Health, and Well-Being.* New York: Hemisphere, 1991.

Rummel, Rudolph J. *Death by Government.* New Brunswick, NJ: Transaction, 1994.

Schroeder, Michael J. "To Induce a Sense of Terror." In B.B. Campbell and A. D. Brenner eds., *Death Squads in Global Perspective: Murder with Deniability.* New York: St Martin's Press, 2000.

Sluka, Jeffrey A. "Introduction: State Terror and Anthropology." In *Death Squad: The Anthropology of State Terror.* Philadelphia: University of Pennsylvania Press, 2000.

*Internet Resources*

Amnesty International. "Amnesty International Report 2001." In the Amnesty International [web site]. Available from http://web.amnesty.org/web/ar2001.nsf/home/home?OpenDocument.

DANIEL LEVITON
SAPNA REDDY MAREPALLY

# DEATH SYSTEM

Death system, a concept introduced by Robert Kastenbaum in 1977, is defined as "the interpersonal, sociocultural, and symbolic network through which an individual's relationship to mortality is mediated by his or her society" (Kastenbaum 2001, p. 66). Through this concept, Kastenbaum seeks to move death from a purely individual concern to a larger context, understanding the role of death and dying in the maintenance and change of the social order.

## Components of the Death System

To Kastenbaum, the death system in any given society has a number of components. First, *people* are connected to the death system. Because death is inevitable, everyone will, at one time or another, be involved with death—one's own or others.

Other individuals have more regular roles in the death system, earning their livelihood primarily by providing services that revolve around death. These include coroners and funeral directors, persons involved with life insurance, and florists. In other cases, Kastenbaum reminds society, the role may be apparent. Anyone, for example, involved in food manufacturing, especially meat, and food service, depends on the slaughter of animals. Clergy, police, firefighters, and health care workers all interact with the dying, dead, and bereaved and therefore have roles in the death system. Even statisticians who create actuarial tables play a role in the death system.

A second component of the death system is *places*. Places include hospitals (though they do not have the prominent role that they once had as places people go to die, at least in industrial societies), funeral homes, morgues, cemeteries, and other places that deal with the dead and dying. Memorials and battlefields are also places associated with death. Such places need not always be public. Family members may harbor superstitions or simply memories of a room or area where a loved one died.

*Times* are a third component of the death system. Certain holidays like Memorial Day or Halloween in U.S. culture, the Day of the Dead in Mexican culture, or All Saints' Day or Good Friday among Christian traditions are associated with a time to reflect upon or remember the dead. Again, different cultural groups, family systems, or individuals may hold other times, such as the anniversary of a death, battle, or disaster, as times to remember.

*Objects and symbols* are the remaining components of the death system. Death-related objects are diverse, ranging from caskets to mourning clothes, even to bug spray "that kills them dead." Symbols too are diverse. These refer to rituals such as Catholic "last rites" or funeral services, and symbols such as a skull and cross that warn of or convey death. Because language is a symbolic system, the words a society uses to discuss death are part of the death system as well.

## Functions of the Death System

Kastenbaum takes a sociological approach, drawing from a broad, theoretical stream within sociology called "structure-functionalism." This approach basically states that every system or structure within a society survives because it fulfills manifest and latent functions for the social order. Change occurs when the system no longer adequately fulfills its functions, due, for example, to changing social conditions, or until innovations emerge that better address these functions. To Kastenbaum, the death system fulfills a series of critical functions.

*Warning and predicting death.* This function refers to the varied structures within a society that warn individuals or collectivities about impending dangers. Examples of organizations that fulfill these functions include weather forecasting agencies that may post warnings, media that carries such warnings, and emergency personnel who assist in these events. It also includes laboratories and physicians that interpret test results to patients.

*Caring for the dying.* This category offers a good example of cultural change. The hospital was seen as ineffective by many in caring for the dying, so new cultural forms such as hospice and palliative care emerged to fulfill these functions.

*Disposing of the dead.* This area includes practices that surround the removal of a body, rituals, and methods of disposal. Being that every culture or generational cohort has its own meaningful ways to dispose of the dead, this can lead to strains when cultures differ.

*Social consolidation after death.* When an individual dies, other members of the society, such as the family or the work unit, have to adjust and consolidate after that death. In the Middle Ages, for example, the guild system that included masters (i.e., skilled and experienced professionals), intermediate-level journeymen, and beginning apprentices served to mediate the impact of often sudden death by creating a system that allowed for constant replacement. In industrial society, retirement removes workers from the system, lessening the impact of eventual death. In American society, funeral rituals and spontaneous memorialization, self-help and support groups, and counselors are examples of other structures that support consolidation.

*Making sense of death.* Every society has to develop ways to understand and make sense of loss. One of the values of funeral rituals is that they allow for a death to be interpreted within a given faith or philosophical viewpoint.

*Killing.* Every death system has norms that indicate when, how, and for what reasons individuals or other living creatures can be killed. There are international treaties that define what weapons and what killings are justifiable in war. Different cultures determine the crimes an individual can be executed for as well as the appropriate methods of execution. Cultures, too, will determine the reason and ways that animals may be killed.

Death systems are not static. They constantly evolve to deal with changing circumstances and situations. For example, the terrorist attacks of September 11, 2001, have led to the development of whole new systems for airline security that include new personnel, regulations, and places such as screening and identification. As causes of death have changed, new institutions such as hospice and nursing homes have developed. A series of social changes, such as demographic shifts, historical factors (i.e., the development of nuclear weapons), and cultural changes (i.e., increasing diversity), have led to the development of the death studies movement. Because it is a related system, changes in one part of the system are likely to generate changes in other parts of the system. For example, the growth of home-based hospice has led hospitals to reevaluate their care of the dying, contributing to the current interest in palliative care.

Thanatology is often more focused on the clinical, stressing the needs of dying and bereaved individuals. While the concept of the death system has not received widespread attention, it is a powerful reminder of the many ways that death shapes the social order.

*See also:* GENOCIDE; GRIEF AND MOURNING IN CROSS-CULTURAL PERSPECTIVE; MEMORIALIZATION, SPONTANEOUS; SOCIAL FUNCTIONS OF DEATH

## Bibliography

Doka, Kenneth J. "The Rediscovery of Death: The Emergence of the Death Studies Movement." In Charles Corr, Judith Stillion, and Mary Ribar eds., *Creativity in Death Education and Counseling.* Hartford, CT: The Association for Death Education and Counseling, 1983.

Kastenbaum, Robert. *Death, Society, and Human Experience,* 7th edition. Boston: Allyn & Bacon, 2001.

KENNETH J. DOKA

# DEFINITIONS OF DEATH

In the past, death has often been defined with a few confident words. For example, the first edition of *Encyclopaedia Britannica* informed its readership that "DEATH is generally considered as the separation of the soul and body; in which sense it stands opposed to life, which consists in the union thereof" (1768, v. 2, p. 309). The confidence and concision had dissolved by the time the fifteenth edition appeared in 1973. The entry on death had expanded to more than thirty times the original length. The earlier definition was not mentioned, and the alternative that death is simply the absence of life was dismissed as an empty negative. Readers seeking a clear and accurate definition were met instead with the admission that death "can only be conjectured" and is "the supreme puzzle of poets" (1973, v. 5, p. 526).

This shift from confidence to admission of ignorance is extraordinary not only because death is such a familiar term, but also because so much new scientific knowledge has been acquired since the eighteenth century. Actually, the advances in biomedical knowledge and technology have contributed greatly to the complexity that surrounds the concept and therefore the definition of death in the twenty-first century. Furthermore, the definition of death has become a crucial element in family, ethical, religious, legal, economic, and policy-making decisions.

It would be convenient to offer a firm definition of death at this point—but it would also be premature. An imposed definition would have little value before alternative definitions have been considered within their socio-medical contexts. Nevertheless, several general elements are likely to be associated with any definition that has a reasonable prospect for general acceptance in the early years of the twenty-first century. Such a definition would probably include the elements of a complete loss or absence of function that is permanent, not reversible, and useful to society.

These specifications include the cautious differentiation of "permanent" from "not reversible" because they take into account the argument that a death condition might persist under ordinary circumstances, but that life might be restored by extraordinary circumstances. Despite this caution there are other and more serious difficulties with

even the basic elements that have been sketched above. That a definition of death must also be "useful to society" is a specification that might appear to be wildly inappropriate. The relevance of this specification is evident, however, in a pattern of events that emerged in the second half of the twentieth century and that continues to remain significant (e.g., persistent vegetative state and organ transplantation). Competing definitions of death are regarded with respect to their societal implications as well as their biomedical credibility.

Attention is given first to some of the ways in which common usage of words has often led to ambiguity in the definition of death. The historical dimension is briefly considered, followed by a more substantial examination of the biomedical approach and its implications.

## "Death": One Word Used in Several Ways

The word *death* is used in at least three primary and numerous secondary ways. The context indicates the intended meaning in some instances, but it is not unusual for ambiguity or a shift in meanings to occur in the midst of a discussion. People may talk or write past each other when the specific usage of "death" is not clearly shared. The three primary usages are: death as an event; death as a condition; and death as a state of existence or nonexistence.

*Death as an event.* In this usage, death is something that happens. As an event, death occurs at a particular time and place and in a particular way. In this sense of the term, death is a phenomenon that stays within the bounds of mainstream conception and observation. Time, place, and cause can be recorded on a death certificate (theoretically, in all instances although, in practice, the information may be incomplete or imprecise). This usage does not concern itself with mysteries or explanations: Death is an event that cuts off a life.

*Death as a condition.* This is the crucial area in biomedical and bioethical controversy. Death is the nonreversible condition in which an organism is incapable of carrying out the vital functions of life. It is related to but not identical with death as an event because the focus here is on the specific signs that establish the cessation of life. These signs or determinants are often obvious to all observers. Sometimes, though, even experts can disagree.

*Death as a state of existence or nonexistence.* In this sense, it can almost be said that death is what becomes of a person after death. It refers not to the event that ended life nor the condition of the body at that time, but rather to whatever form of existence might be thought to prevail when a temporal life has come to its end.

Miscommunications and unnecessary disagreements can occur when people are not using the term *death* in the same way. For example, while grieving family members might already be concerned with finding someone to stay in contact with a loved one who will soon be "in death," the physicians are more likely to focus on criteria for determining the cessation of life. In such situations the same word *death* is receiving functionally different definitions.

The secondary usages are mostly figurative. Death serves as a dramatic intensifier of meaning; for example, the historian's judgment that the rise of commerce contributed to the death of feudalism, or the poet's complaint that life has become death since being spurned by a lover. There are also extended uses that can be considered either literal or figurative, as when the destruction of the universe is contemplated: The issue open to speculation is whether the universe is fundamentally inanimate or a mega-life form.

## Traditional Definitions of Death

Biomedical approaches to the definition of death have become increasingly complex and influential since the middle of the twentieth century. Throughout most of human history, however, death was defined through a combination of everyday observations and religious beliefs. The definition offered in the 1768 edition of *Encyclopaedia Britannica* is faithful to the ancient tradition that death should be understood as the separation of soul (or spirit) from the body. The philosophical foundation for this belief is known as dualism: Reality consists of two forms or essences, one of which is material and certain to decay, the other of which has a more subtle essence that can depart from its embodied host. Dualistic thinking is inherent in major world religions and was also evident in widespread belief systems at the dawn of known history.

Definitions of death in very early human societies have been inferred from physical evidence, a limited though valuable source of information. Cro-Magnon burials, for example, hint at a belief in death as separation of some essence of the person from the flesh. The remains were painted with red ochre, consistently placed in a north-south orientation, and provided with items in the grave that would be useful in the journey to the next life. Anthropologists discovered similar practices among tribal people in the nineteenth and early twentieth centuries. The fact that corpses were painted red in so many cultures throughout the world has led to the speculation that this tinting was intended as a symbolic representation of blood. People throughout the world have long recognized that the loss of blood can lead to death, and that the cold pallor of the dead suggests that they have lost the physical essence of life (conceived as blood), as well as the spiritual (conceived as breath). A religious practice such as symbolically replacing or renewing blood through red-tinting would therefore have its origin in observations of the changes that occur when a living person becomes a corpse.

A significant element in traditional definitions of death is the belief that death does not happen all at once. Observers may clearly recognize signs of physical cessation; for example, lack of respiration and responsiveness as well as pallor and stiffening. Nevertheless, the death is not complete until the spirit has liberated itself from the body. This consideration has been taken into account in deathbed and mourning rituals that are intended to assist the soul to abandon the body and proceed on its afterlife journey. It was not unusual to wait until only the bones remain prior to burial because that would indicate that the spirit has separated, the death completed, and the living emancipated to go on with their lives.

Definitions of death as an event or condition have usually been based on the assumption that life is instantly transformed into death. (This view has been modified to some extent through biomedical research and clinical observation.) Historical tradition, though, has often conceived death as a process that takes some time and is subject to irregularities. This process view has characterized belief systems throughout much of the world and remains influential in the twenty-first century. Islamic doctrine, for example, holds that death is the separation of the soul from the body, and that death is not complete as long as the spirit continues to reside in any part of the body. This perspective is of particular interest because medical sophistication has long been part of Islamic culture and has therefore created a perpetual dialogue between religious insights and biomedical advances. The question of reconciling traditional with contemporary approaches to the definition of death requires attention to recent and current developments.

## Biomedical Determinations and Definitions of Death

For many years physicians depended on a few basic observations in determining death. Life had passed into death if the heart did not beat and air did not flow into and out of the lungs. Simple tests could be added if necessary; for example, finding no response when the skin is pinched or pricked nor adjustive movements when the body is moved to a different position. In the great majority of instances it was sufficient to define death operationally as the absence of cardiac activity, respiration, and responsiveness. There were enough exceptions, however, to prove disturbing. Trauma, illness, and even "fainting spells" occasionally reduced people to a condition that could be mistaken for death. The fortunate ones recovered, thereby prompting the realization that a person could look somewhat dead yet still be viable. The unfortunate ones were buried—and the most unfortunate stayed buried. There were enough seeming recoveries from the funeral process that fears of live burial circulated widely, especially from the late eighteenth century into the early years of the twentieth century.

A related development served as a foreshadowing of complexities and perplexities yet to come. Scientifically minded citizens of late-eighteenth-century London believed they could rescue and resuscitate victims of drowning; they could and they did. Not all victims could be saved, but there were carefully authenticated cases in which an apparent corpse had been returned to life. Some of the resuscitation techniques they pioneered have entered the repertoire of emergency responders around the world. They also tried (with occasional success) the futuristic technique of galvanic (electrical) stimulation. The impact of these experiments in resuscitation far exceeded the small number of cases involved. The fictional Dr. Frankenstein would reanimate the dead by capturing a flash of lightning—and nonfictional physicians would later employ electric paddles and other devices and techniques for much the same purpose. The wonder at seeing an apparently dead person return to life was accompanied by a growing sense of uneasiness regarding the definition of death. It would not be until the middle of the twentieth century, though, that new developments in technology would pose questions about the definition of death that could no longer be shunted aside.

The accepted legal definition of death in the middle of the twentieth century appeared simple and firm on the surface. Death was the cessation of life as indicated by the absence of blood circulation, respiration, pulse, and other vital functions. The development of new biomedical techniques, however, soon raised questions about the adequacy of this definition. Cardiopulmonary resuscitation (CPR) had resuscitated some people whose condition seemed to meet the criteria for death. Furthermore, life support systems had been devised to prolong respiration and other vital functions in people whose bodies could no longer maintain themselves. In the past these people would have died in short order. The concept of a persistent vegetative state became salient and a disturbing question had to be faced: Were these unfortunate people alive, dead, or somewhere in between? This question had practical as well as theoretical implications. It was expensive to keep people on extended life support and also occupied hospital resources that might have more therapeutic uses. It was also hard on family members who saw their loved ones in that dependent and nonresponsive condition and who were not able to enter fully into the grieving process because the lost person was still there physically.

Still another source of tension quickly entered the situation. Advances were being made in transplanting cadaver organs to restore health and preserve the life of other people. If the person who was being maintained in a persistent vegetative state could be regarded as dead, then there was a chance for an organ transplantation procedure that might save another person's life. Existing definitions and rules, however, were still based on the determination of death as the absence of vital functions, and these functions were still operational, even though mediated by life support systems.

Pressure built up to work through both the conceptual issues and the practical problems by altering the definition of death. The term *clinical death* had some value. Usually this term referred to the cessation of cardiac function, as might occur during a medical procedure or a heart attack. A physician could make this determination quickly and then try CPR or other techniques in an effort to restore cardiac function. "Clinical death" was therefore a useful term because it acknowledged that one of the basic criteria for determining death applied to the situation, yet it did not stand in the way of resuscitation efforts. This concept had its drawbacks, though. Many health care professionals as well as members of the general public were not ready to accept the idea of a temporary death, which seemed like a contradiction in terms. Furthermore, clinical death had no firm standing in legal tradition or legislative action. Nevertheless, this term opened the way for more vigorous attempts to take the definition of death apart and put it back together again.

Meanwhile, another approach was becoming of increasing interest within the realm of experimental biology. Some researchers were focusing on the development and death of small biological units, especially the individual cell within a larger organism. The relationship between the fate of the cell and that of the larger organism was of particular interest. Soon it became clear that death as well as development is programmed into the cell. Furthermore, programmed cell death proved to be regulated by signals from other cells. Although much still remains to be understood, it had become apparent that a comprehensive definition of death would have to include basic processes of living and dying that are inherent in cells, tissues, and organs as well as the larger organism. It has also provided further illumination of the lower-level life processes that continue after the larger organism has died. The person may be dead, but not all life has ceased. The cellular approach has still not drawn much attention from physicians and policy makers, but it has added to the difficulty of arriving at a new consensual definition of death. How many and what kind of life processes can continue to exist and still make it credible to say that death has occurred? This question has not been firmly answered as such, but was raised to a new level with the successful introduction of still another concept: brain death.

Technological advances in monitoring the electrical activity of the brain made it possible to propose brain death as a credible concept, and it quickly found employment in attempting to limit the number and duration of persistent vegetative states while improving the opportunities for organ transplantation. The electrical activity of the brain would quickly become a crucial element in the emerging redefinition of death.

A survey was conducted of patients who showed no electrical activity in their brains as measured by electroencephalograms. Only three of the 1,665 patients recovered cerebral function—and all three had been in a drug-induced coma. This finding led researchers to recommend that electrocerebral inactivity should be regarded as a state of nonreversible coma. Researchers suggested that this core determinant should also be supported by other types of observations, including inability to maintain circulation without external support and complete unresponsiveness. Researchers would later recommend that a distinction should be made between "coma" and "brain death." There are several levels of coma and a variety of possible causes; brain death refers to a state of such severe and irreparable damage that no mental functioning exists or can return.

The breakthrough for the new concept occurred in 1968 when an Ad Hoc Committee of the Harvard Medical School proposed that the nonreversible loss of brain should be the reigning definition of death. More traditional signs were still included. The person was dead if unresponsive, even to ordinarily painful stimuli, showed no movements and no breathing, as well as none of the reflexes that are usually included in a neurological examination. There were two new criteria, however, that were not measured in the past: a flat reading on the electroencephalogram (EEG) and lack of blood circulation in the brain. "The Harvard criteria," as they were known, soon became the dominant approach to defining death.

Subsequent studies have generally supported the reliability of the criteria proposed by the Harvard Medical School committee. The new definition of death won acceptance by the American Medical Association, the American Bar Association, and other influential organizations. A 1981 president's commission took the support to an even higher level, incorporating the concept into a new

Uniform Determination of Death Act with nation-wide application. The basic Harvard Committee recommendations were accepted. However, some important specifications and cautions were emphasized. It was noted that errors in certification of death are possible if the patient has undergone hypothermia (extreme cold), drug or metabolic intoxication, or circulatory shock—conditions that can occur during some medical procedures and could result in a suspension of life processes that is not necessarily permanent. Furthermore, the status of children under the age of five years, especially the very young, requires special attention. (Task forces focusing on reliable examination of young children were established a few years later and introduced guidelines for that purpose.)

The most significant position advanced by the president's commission dealt with a question that as of 2002 is still the subject of controversy: whole-brain versus cerebral death. In the early 1980s there was already intense argument about the type and extent of brain damage that should be the basis for definition of death. The commission endorsed the more conservative position: The person is not dead until *all* brain functioning has ceased. This position takes into account the fact that some vital functions might still be present or potentially capable of restoration even when the higher centers of the brain (known as cerebral or cortical) have been destroyed. Death therefore should not be ruled unless there has been nonreversible destruction in the brain stem (responsible for respiration, homeostasis and other basic functions) as well as the higher centers. Others make the argument that the *person* is lost permanently when cerebral functions have ceased. There might still be electrical activity in the brain stem, but intellect, memory, and personality have perished. The death of the person should be the primary consideration and it would be pointless, therefore, to maintain a persistent vegetative state in a life support system.

## Future Redefinitions of Death

The process of redefining death is not likely to come to a complete halt within the foreseeable future. Innovations in technology contributed much to the ongoing discussion. The EEG made it possible to monitor electrical activity in comatose patients and its application opened the way for the concept of brain death. Advances in life support systems made it possible to maintain the vital functions of people with severely impaired or absent mental functioning—raising questions about the ethics and desirability of such interventions. Organ transplantation became a high visibility enterprise that is often accompanied by tension and frustration in the effort to match demand with supply.

Further advances in technology and treatment modalities and changes in socioeconomic forces can be expected to incite continuing efforts to redefine death. More powerful and refined techniques, for example, may provide significant new ways of monitoring severely impaired patients and this, in turn, might suggest concepts that go beyond current ideas of brain death. A simpler and less expensive method of providing life support could also reshape working definitions of death because it would lessen the economic pressure. Organ transplantation might be replaced by materials developed through gene technology, thereby reducing the pressure to employ a definition of death that allows for an earlier access to organs. Changes in religious belief and feeling might also continue to influence the definition of death. For example, the current biomedical control over death might face a challenge from widespread and intensified belief that all other considerations are secondary to the separation of soul from body. Cybernetic fantasies about virtual life and death might remain fantasies—but it could also be that the most remarkable redefinitions are yet to come.

*See also:* BRAIN DEATH; CELL DEATH; CRYONIC SUSPENSION; MIND-BODY PROBLEM; ORGAN DONATION AND TRANSPLANTATION

### *Bibliography*

Ad Hoc Committee of the Harvard Medical School to Examine the Definition of Brain Death. "A Definition of Irreversible Coma." *Journal of the American Medical Association* 205 (1968):337–340.

Caplan, Arthur C., and Daniel H. Coellan, eds. *The Ethics of Organ Transplantation.* Buffalo, NY: Prometheus, 1999.

"Death." In *Encyclopaedia Britannica,* 1st edition. Vol. 2. Edinburgh: A. B. & C. Macfarquhar, 1768. In *Encyclopaedia Britannica,* 15th edition. Vol. 5. Chicago: Encyclopaedia Britannica, 1973.

Fox, Renée C. *Spare Parts: Organ Replacement in American Society.* New York: Oxford University Press, 1992.

Kastenbaum, Robert. *Death, Society, and Human Experience,* 7th edition. Boston: Allyn & Bacon, 2001.

Lock, Margaret. *Twice Dead: Organ Transplants and the Reinvention of Death.* Berkeley: University of California Press, 2001.

Lockshin, Richard A., Zahra Zakeri, and Jonathan L. Tilly, eds. *When Cells Die.* New York: Wiley-Liss, 1998.

McCullagh, Philip. *Brain Dead, Brain Absent, Brain Donors.* New York: Wiley, 1993.

Morioka, Masahiro. "Reconsidering Brain Death: A Lesson From Japan's Fifteen Years of Experience." *Hastings Center Report* 31 (2001):42–46.

Pernick, Martin S. "Back from the Grave: Recurring Controversies over Defining and Diagnosing Death in History." In Raymond M. Zaner ed., *Death: Beyond Whole-Brain Criteria.* Boston: Kluwer, 1988.

Potts, Michael, Paul. A. Byme, and Richard G. Nilges, eds. *Beyond Brain Death: The Case against Brain Death Criteria for Human Death.* Dordrecht, Netherlands: Kluwer, 2000.

President's Commission for the Study of Ethical Problems in Medicine and Biomedical and Behavioral Research. *Defining Death: Medical, Legal and Critical Issues in the Determination of Death.* Washington, DC: U.S. Government Printing Office, 1981.

Sachs, Jessica Snyder. *Corpse: Nature, Forensics, and the Struggle to Pinpoint Time of Death.* Cambridge, MA: Perseus, 2001.

Walker, A. Earl. *Cerebral Death,* 3rd edition. Baltimore, MD: Urban & Schwarzenberg, 1985.

Youngner, Stuart J., Robert M. Arnold, and Renie Shapiro, eds. *The Definition of Death: Contemporary Controversies.* Baltimore, MD: Johns Hopkins University Press, 1999.

ROBERT KASTENBAUM

# DEHUMANIZATION

Dehumanization is the process of stripping away human qualities, such as denying others their individuality and self-esteem. With the rapid increase in medical technology many basic human qualities surrounding the care of the dying have been lost. Dehumanization is like a form of self-death that now often precedes physiological death owing to the institutionalization of the dying. For millennia the process of dying and the presence of death were both close and familiar realities of everyday life. Many people died in the bed they were born in, surrounded by their family and friends. Called "tame death" by the French philosopher and death expert Philippe Ariès, it was natural, expected, and integrated into the rhythms of life. The Russian novelist Leo Tolstoy, in his epic work *War and Peace* (1869), comments that when a relative is sick the custom is to seek professional care for him or her, but when a loved one is dying the custom is to send the professionals away and care for the dying within the family unit. The naturalness to dying that Tolstoy describes has undergone a radical shift in the modern era.

The history of medicine was originally the art of personal caring and compassion. Since the Enlightenment, what was originally an art has become more clearly a science. In the twenty-first century the science of medicine focuses on curing disease and thus views death as a defeat. It is no longer natural or tame, but fearsome and strange. Increasingly it is the disease and not the individual being treated. The equally rapid development of medical technology has blurred the border between life and death. Life-sustaining machines have initiated new definitions of death, such as "brain death," into the medical lexicon. Medicine has become an increasingly technological profession. This has led to the modern phenomenon of dying when the machines are shut off or what the philosopher Ivan Illich calls "mechanical death." Illich states that mechanical and technical death have won a victory over natural death in the West.

H. Jack Geiger notes that the dehumanizing aspects of health care mainly deal with the loss or diminishment of four basic human qualities: the inherent worth in being human, the uniqueness of the individual, the freedom to act and the ability to make decisions, and the equality of status. While all people are worthy of the same care and attention from health care services, people instead receive it according to their social and economic status. Basic human services and all aspects of the health care are distributed unequally throughout society depending on economic and political power and status. This implicit loss of human worth is especially dehumanizing for the poor and marginalized in society.

The medicalization of the dying process, enhanced by increasing technology, has resulted in increased isolation and dehumanization of the dying. People are surrounded by machines in intensive care units rather than by their families at home, and often people are treated as objects without feeling. The scholar Jan Howard notes this often occurs with acute care patients who are seen not as unique individuals but as extensions of the life-sustaining machines they are attached to at the end of their lives. Dehumanization of the dying acts to lessen the impact of death for survivors in a death-denying culture.

These trends are reinforced by advances in technology and by larger and more impersonal systems of health care that have developed. What has become known as the "tyranny of technology" has forced those involved in health care to become more technologically sophisticated. This in turn has lead to an increased sense of professionalism and specialization within all aspects of medicine. Such professionalism has been characterized by a growing detachment from the unique concerns of individual patients and a loss of personal relationship to them. Physicians and other health care workers now react less as individuals in relationship to other individuals and more as representatives of their professions and their health care organizations. This results in a loss of autonomy and decision-making ability on the part of the patients and sometimes of their families as well. The policies and procedures of insurance companies and health maintenance organizations (HMOs) determine many critical health issues facing people in the twenty-first century. This loss of freedom is yet another dehumanizing effect of modern technology.

The advances in the scientific and technical aspects of medicine have increasingly made people dependent on strangers for the most crucial and intimate moments of their lives. Health care professionals and health care organizations have become more impersonal and bureaucratic. There is an obvious inequality of status between those in need of medical care and those whose profession it is to respond to that need. This inequality coupled with the impersonal quality of care they are offered leads to mistrust and a feeling of dehumanization.

The rise of hospice organizations, holistic medicine curricula in medical schools, and in-service programs in hospitals has attempted to address these dehumanizing aspects of modern medicine. Dying is one of the most personal and intimate

times in a person's life. At that time, more than any other perhaps, people need their inherent worth valued, their uniqueness affirmed, and their ability to make decisions honored by those who care for them.

*See also:* DYING, PROCESS OF; WAR

### *Bibliography*

Ariès, Philippe. *Western Attitudes toward Death: From the Middle Ages to the Present,* translated by Patricia M. Ranum. Baltimore: Johns Hopkins University Press, 1974.

Illich, Ivan. *Medical Nemesis.* London: Calder and Boyars, 1975.

Geiger, H. Jack. "The Causes of Dehumanization in Health Care and Prospects for Humanization." In Jan Howard and Anselm Strauss eds., *Humanizing Health Care.* New York: John Wiley and Sons, 1975.

Howard, Jan. "Humanization and Dehumanization of Health Care: A Conceptual View." In Jan Howard and Anselm Strauss eds., *Humanizing Health Care.* New York: John Wiley and Sons, 1975.

Tolstoy, Leo. *War and Peace.* 1869. Reprint, New York: E. P. Dutton, 1911.

Van Zyl, Liezl. *Death and Compassion.* Burlington, VT: Ashgate, 2000.

THOMAS B. WEST

# DEMOGRAPHICS AND STATISTICS

Julius Richmond, the former Surgeon General of the United States, is purported to have said, "Statistics are people with their tears wiped dry" (Cohen 2000, p. 1367). While it is true that statistics, and quantitative data more generally, have a "dry face" to them, they have important uses in research and public policy. Statistical and demographic data are not meant to provide understanding on the felt circumstances of individuals. By their very nature these data deal with social aggregates.

Although people think that quantitative data give an objective portrayal of a phenomenon (the facts), this is not correct. What researchers choose to be measured and the methods they employ reflect the biases and values of those who collect data. Mortality data are almost always collected by official or government agencies; thus to greater or lesser degree they reflect their perspectives. However, some measures of mortality, in particular causes of death, have been "internationalized" by such bodies as the World Health Organization and therefore reflect a consensus, albeit a Western-based one. In addition, some developing countries do not have the resources to acquire very much data on demographic events such as deaths; if they did have the available resources, it is not known what kind of information they might collect.

What is chosen to be measured and how it is measured is only part of the bias in quantitative data, however. How data are interpreted is also subject to bias and value judgments, clearly seen, for example, in the debate about the factors leading to maternal deaths and how to reduce maternal mortality.

Apart from biases, users of quantitative data on deaths need to be aware of a number of limitations. A large limitation, globally, is simply lack of information. Many statistics are estimates only. Another limitation concerns lack of knowledge regarding how statistics are calculated, which can lead to misinterpretations. A good example of this is with statistics on life expectancy which, although hypothetical, are not always interpreted as such.

Statistical data provide important information that is useful for a number of purposes, despite their limitations, problems with bias, and an inability to convey individual experiential phenomena. Scientists and researchers need to know how many people are dying and at what ages, of what gender, and for what reasons, in order to know how to target resources to reduce those deaths. Unlike the case with other demographic topics such as fertility and migration, there is worldwide consensus that reducing deaths is a worthwhile goal; thus statistical data on mortality can be corroboratively used in attempts to reach that goal. Data provide the raw materials needed for plans to be made (and implemented) aimed at enhancing the well-being of persons and tackling social inequalities in the risk of death.

*See also:* CAUSES OF DEATH; MORTALITY, INFANT

### Bibliography

Cohen, Alex. "Excess Female Mortality in India: The Case of Himachal Padesh." *American Journal of Public Health* 90 (2000):1367–1371.

Horton, Hayward D. "Critical Demography: The Paradigm of the Future?" *Sociological Forum* 14 (1999):365–543.

Petersen, William. *From Birth to Death: A Consumer's Guide to Population Studies.* New Brunswick, NJ: Transaction, 2000.

Morrison, Peter A. *A Demographic Perspective On Our Nation's Future.* Santa Monica, CA: RAND, 2001.

ELLEN M. GEE

# DISASTERS

Disasters are stressful life situations that result in great terror, property damage, physical harm, and often death. Calamity and catastrophe, synonymous terms for these traumatic events, often involve extreme forces of nature like earthquakes, fires, floods, hurricanes, and tornadoes. Sometimes, though, people's behavior is the causal factor behind a disaster, or is contributory to higher losses of property and lives from events that were clearly avoidable. This happens through human error (a pilot's engineering mistake in an airplane crash), human carelessness and indifference (lax building practices), and intentional acts of cruelty and violence by some individuals against others (incidents of terrorism). Whatever the cause, disaster victims must struggle to resolve their losses and rebuild their lives, a process that generally takes longer than anyone initially imagines.

## Natural Disasters

Devastating acts of nature have led to some of the world's most memorable disasters. Earth, air (wind), fire, and water, the original four elements named by the noted Greek philosopher Empedocles, are key ingredients in the recipe for many disasters. For instance, storms often bring a combination of damaging winds, flooding rains, and lightning that sparks fires. Disturbances within the earth's crust can trigger eruption of volcanoes, the severe ground cracking and shaking of earthquakes, and the flowing walls of water that become damaging tidal waves.

*Cyclones and anticyclones.* Cyclones are large, swirling windstorms. Though people sometimes refer to tornadoes as cyclones, meteorologists generally consider cyclones to be much larger systems with lower air pressure at their center than is present outside the weather system. Anticyclones have the opposite trait in that the air pressure at their center is higher than is present outside the system. The airflow also differs, with cyclones turning counterclockwise in the northern hemisphere and clockwise in the southern hemisphere and anticyclones doing the opposite.

When these storms occur in the tropics they are known as tropical depressions and, in addition to the wind, they often have associated heavy rains. If the storms grow to a point that they reach certain sustained wind speeds, they will be classified as hurricanes or typhoons.

East Pakistan was hit by the world's worst cyclone in November 1970—200,000 people died and 100,000 others were missing from the storm and a related tidal wave. Southeastern Bangladesh lost 131,000 people (and millions of others died later due to storm-related hunger and disease) following an April 1991 cyclone.

*Earthquakes.* Rock formations sometimes shift within the earth's crust, a phenomena scientists refer to as plate tectonics. As the rock plates slide along fault lines (veins between the formations along which the shifting occurs), the resulting vibrations sometimes cause violent shaking of the ground. This surface activity may set off landslides, tidal waves on lakes or oceans, and volcanic eruptions. Taken together, these forces often result in building collapses and other damage to infrastructure (roads, bridges, dams, electrical power transmission lines, natural gas pipelines, etc.) that, in turn, injures or kills many people in the affected area. Even after the initial shaking ends, aftershocks may cause additional damage and continue to frighten residents of the area.

Shaanxi, China, suffered one of the worst earthquake losses in history with 830,000 deaths from a quake that occurred in 1556. San Francisco's 1906 earthquake took 500 lives and touched off a spectacular fire that consumed four square miles of the city. Most memorable to many readers, though, is the more recent San Francisco area quake that occurred on October 17, 1989, as many baseball fans around the world were settling in to watch a World Series game on television. That one killed 67 people and caused billions of dollars in damage. Other countries tend to suffer far more serious loss of lives than the United States due to a

combination of high population density in cities with infrastructures not built to withstand the ravages of an earthquake.

*Floods.* Whenever unusually large amounts of water fall on dry land, or when water from oceans, lakes, rivers, and streams overflows onto dry land, the damaging result is flooding. Many people first learn that rushing water can easily cause extreme property damage and death by hearing the Old Testament story of Noah saving pairs of animals from the great deluge of forty days and nights of rain.

The worst recorded loss of life from flooding occurred in Kaifeng, China, in 1642. War was raging and rebel forces destroyed a protective seawall, resulting in the loss of 300,000 lives. The worst flood in the United States came as a result of a tidal surge that accompanied the September 8, 1900, Galveston Hurricane (Galveston, Texas) that took 6,000 to 8,000 lives. Another notable flood—the Johnstown, Pennsylvania, flood—occurred on May 31, 1889, causing 2,209 deaths. Heavy rains caused the Lake Conemaugh Reservoir dam to fail, allowing a devastating wall of water to slam the city. Debris from damaged property added to the losses when it jammed at a bridge in the downtown area that then caught fire.

In 1993 the midwestern United States was devastated by summer-long flooding. Torrential rains caused rivers and streams to wash over their banks and damage thousands of homes and businesses. Although there were only 46 deaths attributed to the flooding, the region suffered millions of dollars in financial losses. Farming was totally disrupted, as everyone waited for the water to recede and the fields to dry out. Adding to the misery was the fact that many caskets surfaced and washed away from cemeteries located next to waterways that were out of control, reopening emotional wounds and complicating bereavement for many flood victims. All of this led to a great sense of collective solidarity, as people throughout the country assisted in a mammoth relief effort.

*Hurricanes and typhoons.* The terms hurricane and typhoon come from words that mean "big wind" (the West Indian word *huracan*) and "great wind" (the Chinese word *taifun*). As large tropical storms reach and sustain maximum wind speeds of at least 75 miles per hour, they officially become hurricanes (if occurring in the Atlantic Ocean or the eastern Pacific) or typhoons (if occurring in the western Pacific). Some of the worst storms are able to reach wind speeds in excess of 180 miles per hour and drop over 10 inches of rain in one day. Oddly, at the center of these storms is a calm area known as the eye of the storm that has relatively light winds and blue sky overhead.

Summertime is hurricane season for the United States and many nearby islands. The worst loss of lives in the Western Hemisphere came when 20,000 to 22,000 people died in Barbados, the West Indies, Martinique, and St. Eustatius, as a result of the Great Hurricane of 1780. Since 1953 storms have received names from the National Weather Service. A storm named Hurricane Mitch (October 1998), killed 11,000 people in Central America, left 2 to 3 million people homeless, and caused $5 billion in damage. Hurricane Andrew (August 1992) killed only 14 people when it ravaged southern Florida and the Gulf Coast, but it was the nation's most costly hurricane, causing $15 to $20 billion in damage. In some communities family residences sustained excessive damage because zoning rules had been ignored and the homes were not structurally able to withstand the easily foreseeable winds in that hurricane-prone area.

In September 1906, 10,000 lives were lost when a typhoon with a tsunami (tidal wave) struck Hong Kong. Typhoon Vera (September 1959) caused 4,464 deaths in Honshu, Japan. Thelma (November 1991) took 3,000 lives in the Philippines. Several thousand fishermen died in December 1949, when a typhoon caught Korea's fishing fleet in an offshore location.

*Tornadoes.* People often refer to tornadoes as "twisters" and know them as the tightly spiraling funnels of wind and debris that can destroy anything in their path. If they pass over water, they may form a waterspout, but generally waterspouts are less serious weather phenomena that can happen even when no storm is present. For many people who do not live in tornado-prone areas, the first knowledge of these devastating weather events often comes through media coverage or from movies. For instance, a famous big-screen twister carries a Kansas farmhouse to a mystical land on the other side of the rainbow in the classic 1939 film *The Wizard of Oz.*

Tornadoes are often spawned during severe thunderstorms, as cold weather fronts clash with

*A trench holds coffins of the unidentified victims of Hurricane Audrey, which hit the coast of Louisiana in June 1957, killing an estimated 400 people.* CORBIS

warm air systems ahead of them. They are classified on a scale known as the Fujita-Pearson scale that considers the touchdown path's length and width along with the maximum wind speed. Estimated speeds of 500 miles per hour are considered possible with the nastiest storms.

The worst single tornado event in U.S. history occurred on March 18, 1925, when Missouri, Illinois, and Indiana's Tri-State Tornado left 689 people dead and injured over 2,000. In March 1952 a two-day, six-state outbreak killed 343 people in Alabama, Arkansas, Kentucky, Missouri, Mississippi, and Tennessee. Another two-day event known as the Super Tornado Outbreak (April 1974) involved 146 twisters in 13 states. When it was all over, 330 people were dead and 5,484 were injured—the most in U.S. history.

*Tsunamis.* Ground-changing and ground-shaking events like earthquakes, volcanic eruptions, and landslides sometimes generate large water waves known as tsunamis. This is especially common when the event occurs under the sea. Tsunamis are most common in the Pacific Ocean due to the frequency of seismic activity there. In 1883 an eruption of the Krakatoa volcano created a 120-foot wave that killed over 36,000 people in neighboring Papua New Guinea. That island is clearly prone to tsunamis. In 1998 three smaller waves killed over 2,000 people.

*Volcanoes.* Hot gas and lava (molten rock) sometimes explosively vent from deep inside the earth. The venting comes in the form of volcanic eruptions that push the ground upward, forming hills and mountains as they spew the magma (liquid, rock fragments, and gases) from openings at their tops. In the 1883 eruption of the Krakatoa volcano, the explosion could be heard 3,000 miles away and volcanic dust circled the earth.

In November 1985 the Colombian towns of Armero and Chinchina lost 25,000 persons during an eruption of Nevada de Ruiz. Italy's Mt. Vesuvius erupted in 79 C.E., killing thousands when it buried the cities of Herculaneum and Pompeii. The United States has also known active volcanoes. Washington State's Mt. St. Helens, for example, erupted in May 1980, killing 60 people along with countless animals, and damaging trees over a 500-kilometer area. The large island of Hawaii has Kiluea, which has become a tourist attraction thanks to an ongoing flow of lava. The Caribbean island of Montserrat also still has an active volcano, Soufriere Hills. During the summer of 1997 its eruption killed 20 people and left two-thirds of the island uninhabitable.

*More extreme phenomena.* Other extremes of nature also take their toll in property damage and lost lives. The central and eastern United States experienced a heat wave during the summer of 1980 that took 10,000 lives and caused $20 billion in damage. The Blizzard of 1988 pummeled the East Coast with snow for three days, leaving 400 dead and $20 million in damage from the 5 feet of snow it dropped in many areas. Another more recent blizzard, the March 1993 Storm of the Century, left 270 people dead and caused $3 to $6 billion in damage.

Drought is another weather extreme. In addition to obvious water shortages, a lack of precipitation can lead to crop damage or loss and then unemployment among those who work in agriculture-related fields. The longest drought in U.S. history came in the 1930s, when many areas of the country were suffering through the Great Dust Bowl. John Steinbeck's novel *The Grapes of Wrath* (1939) details the struggles that farmers commonly faced during those very difficult times.

## Human Complicity in Disasters

Many disasters have other than natural roots. The interplay of humans and machines sometimes results in accidents. Faulty design and/or engineering, unsafe building practices, and ignorance of safety procedures all cause many unnecessary injuries and deaths. Worse yet, people will sometimes intentionally cause a disaster in an effort to scare, control, and/or inflict harm on others.

*Aircraft incidents.* On March 27, 1977, a Pan Am 747 and a KLM 747 collided on an airport runway in the Canary Islands, resulting in the worst aircraft disaster in history. There were 582 deaths—all 249 on KLM and 333 of the 394 aboard Pan Am. The worst single plane incident occurred on April 12, 1985, when a Japan Air 747 crashed into a mountain in Japan—520 of the 524 passengers died. The loss of another jumbo jet, an Iran Air A300 Airbus on July 3, 1988, killed 290 people. Human error was the cause: While operating in the Persian Gulf, the U.S. Navy mistakenly identified the plane as an attacking enemy jet and shot it down.

Perhaps the most spectacular aviation disaster ever recorded on radio and film was the May 6, 1937, crash of the *Hindenburg,* a German zeppelin (passenger blimp). The incident happened as the blimp was about to moor at a docking mast on an airfield at the Naval Air Station in Lakehurst, New Jersey. Something sparked an explosion and fire that brought the flaming ship down. In a mere matter of seconds, thirty-six people died and many others suffered burns and other injuries. The radio commentator Herbert Morrison described the incident to a stunned audience. His most memorable and quoted line was "Oh, the humanity, and all the passengers screaming around here!"

*Buildings and construction.* Injuries and deaths often result from accidents involving structural failures. On March 12, 1928, the St. Francis Dam in Santa Paula, California, collapsed, killing 450 people. On June 29, 1995, the Sampoong Department

Store in Seoul, Korea, collapsed, leaving 206 people dead and 910 injured. On July 18, 1981, a skywalk collapsed during a dance being held at the Hyatt Regency Hotel in Kansas City, Missouri, killing 118 people and injuring 186. This event led to helpers offering well-documented emotional support for survivors and the family members of those lost. So did the November 17, 1999, deaths of 12 students from Texas A&M University in College Station, Texas. They were killed when a log pile structure that they were building for an annual pre-football game bonfire collapsed.

*Ecological and environmental incidents.* During the January 1991 Persian Gulf War, Iran intentionally spilled over 460 million gallons of crude oil into the Persian Gulf. It also dynamited and set ablaze 650 oil wells in Kuwait, making this the world's worst intentionally caused environmental disaster. On June 3, 1979, the Ixtoc 1 oil well in the Gulf of Mexico experienced an estimated spill of 140 million gallons of crude oil—the largest spill ever. Fortunately there was very low impact on the environment. On March 16, 1978, the *Amaco Cadiz* supertanker spilled 68 million gallons of crude oil off Portsall, France, damaging over 100 miles of coastline, making it the largest tanker spill in history. The worst U.S. event was the March 24, 1989, spill of over 10,000 gallons of crude oil in Prince William Sound, Alaska, by the *Exxon Valdez* supertanker. Wildlife suffers the most when these ecocatastrophes happen.

*Explosions.* Coal mine explosions around the world have taken many lives. Some examples include Courriaees, France (March 10, 1906), with 1,060 deaths; Omuta, Japan (November 9, 1963), with 447 deaths; Coalbrook, South Africa (January 21, 1960), with 437 deaths; Wankle, Rhodesia (June 6, 1972), with 427 deaths; and Bihar, India (May 28, 1965), with 375 deaths. The worst explosion in the United States occurred on May 1, 1900, in Scofield, Utah, when blasting powder ignited and killed 200 people.

*Fires.* A waterfront fire in Chongqing, China, took 1,700 lives on September 2, 1949, making it history's worst fire. The worst fire in U.S. history occurred on December 30, 1903, at the Iroquois Theater in Chicago, Illinois, where 602 people died.

Much more widely known, however, is the November 28, 1942, fire at the Coconut Grove Nightclub in Boston, Massachusetts. That fire caused 491 deaths among a group of patrons that was heavily comprised of members of the military and their dates for the evening. Most notable there was the fact that many survivors were interviewed and helped by mental health professionals from a nearby hospital in what may have been the first documented use of disaster mental health techniques. Another major U.S. fire was the Chicago Fire of October 8, 1871, during which 50 people lost their lives and 17,450 buildings were burned. The damage estimate for that fire was $196 million.

*Industrial and nuclear accidents.* On December 3, 1984, a toxic gas leak occurred at the Union Carbide plant in Bhopal, India, resulting in over 2,000 deaths and 150,000 injuries. The world's worst release of radiation was on April 26, 1986, when an accident occurred at the Chernobyl Nuclear Plant in Kiev in the former Soviet Union. The official death toll was 31, but estimates calculate that thousands may have died. When a partial meltdown occurred in the reactor at the Three Mile Island Nuclear Plant in Harrisburg, Pennsylvania, on March 28, 1979, no lives were lost. Nevertheless, there was a major, negative, and lasting psychological impact on residents of the area.

*Shipwrecks.* Two of the worst losses of lives in passenger shipping occurred in China during 1948. In November, a troop carrier sank with an estimated 6,000 people onboard. Then, the following month, about 3,000 refugees were lost when their ship sank. On December 12, 1987, the ferry *Dona Paz* collided with an oil tanker off the coast of Manila—over 4,000 people died. On December 12, 1917, a steam ship collided with the ammunition ship *Mont Blanc* in Halifax Harbor, Nova Scotia, and 1,600 people died as a result of the explosion that followed.

In the United States, the worst event occurred on April 27, 1865, when the *Sultana,* a Mississippi River steamboat carrying Union soldiers home from two infamous Confederate prison camps at the end of the Civil War, suffered an explosion in its boiler—1,547 people were killed. Another major shipping accident happened on April 16, 1947, in Texas City, when the *Grand Camp* caught fire. A large crowd formed to watch firefighters battle the blaze and no one realized that the ship's cargo was highly explosive ammonium nitrate fertilizer. When it blew up, 600 people were killed by a combination of the shock waves, a small tidal wave, and several other resulting fires.

On April 15, 1912, one of the most famous accidents in shipping occurred when the British ocean liner *Titanic* sank after hitting an iceberg on its maiden, transatlantic voyage; over 1,500 people died. Three years later, another famous liner, the *Lusitania,* was sunk by a German submarine near the coast of Ireland. The deaths of 1,198 people there helped draw the United States into World War I. When the battleship *Arizona* and the rest of the Pacific fleet in Pearl Harbor, Hawaii, was bombed on December 12, 1942, 1,177 were killed, making it the worst loss in U.S. naval history.

There is also the July 25, 1956, collision of two ocean liners—the *Andrea Doria* and the *Stockholm*—off Nantucket, Massachusetts. This accident, in which 52 people died, is another disaster that produced early, well-documented emotional support for survivors.

*Space exploration.* Efforts to travel in space have resulted in their share of tragedies. On March 18, 1980, a Vostok rocket exploded during refueling at the Plesetsk Space Center in the former Soviet Union; 50 people were killed. The U.S. Space Shuttle program experienced its worst disaster on January 28, 1986, when the *Challenger* craft exploded in the air shortly after liftoff. A booster rocket fuel leak caused the explosion and fire that killed seven astronauts to their deaths just off Cape Kennedy, Florida. Many Americans, including most schoolchildren, watched the accident on live TV because Christa McAuliffe, America's first teacher in space, was aboard. Another tragedy for the United States was the *Apollo 1* fire on January 27, 1967. Three astronauts died at Cape Kennedy when an accidental fire erupted in their space ship during a routine launch pad practice exercise.

*Sports.* Disasters can happen anywhere, even at recreational events. On October 20, 1982, 340 soccer fans died in a sudden crush of people all moving about at the end of a match in Moscow's Lenin Stadium. Similar problems happened at a Peru versus Argentina soccer match in Lima, Peru, on May 24, 1964, when rioting occurred after a disputed call by a referee; over 300 people died and 500 were injured. In Sincelejo, Colombia, 222 people died on January 20, 1980, when the bleachers collapsed at the town's bullring.

*Terrorism.* Terrorism is the use of violence in an attempt to intimidate, control, and/or punish others in hopes of advancing a political agenda. On December 12, 1988, a terrorist bomb brought down a Pan-Am flight bound for New York City. The Boeing 747 crashed in Lockerbie, Scotland, killing all 259 passengers and 11 people on the ground. Two U.S. embassy bombings occurred on August 7, 1998, killing 243 people in Nairobi, Kenya, and 10 people in Dar Es Salaam, Tanzania; there were also 1,000 other people injured in these attacks.

The worst acts of terrorism on American soil came on September 11, 2001, when a coordinated group of terrorists commandeered four large commercial passenger jets and turned them into weapons of mass destruction. They crashed two of them into the twin towers of New York City's World Trade Center, causing both to collapse. They crashed the third plane into the Pentagon in Washington, D.C. Heroic passengers on the fourth plane had gotten word of the other hijacked planes and took action that resulted in the crash of their plane in a field in western Pennsylvania. This crash was far from any intended terrorist target, although the White House was the suspected objective. Although initial estimates of those lost were 6,000 people (or more), the current death toll from these four crashes is estimated to have been closer to 3,200 people.

Another major U.S. terrorist event was the April 19,1995, truck bombing of the Federal Building in Oklahoma City, Oklahoma. The blast killed 168 people, including 19 children from a daycare center located in the building. In all, 221 buildings sustained damage. There had also been an earlier attack on New York's World Trade Center complex—a bombing on February 26, 1993, that resulted in 6 deaths and 1,040 injuries. Lessons learned in that attack helped save many lives during the September 11, 2001, tragedy.

Terrorism has also taken the form of product tampering. In September 1982 someone laced the pain medication Tylenol with cyanide poison and placed the packages in circulation in the Chicago area, leading to 7 deaths. That incident and other copycat behavior led drug manufacturers to place safety seals on each package. Similar seals quickly became standard on many other consumable foods and beverages.

## Behavior and Psychological Changes in Victims

People are almost always changed by their disaster experiences, but they need not be damaged by those experiences. Victims and relief workers who have been traumatized generally will not stop functioning, but they will react in fairly predictable ways (with some differences due to age and level of maturity). By using various crisis intervention techniques, the victims and relief workers can be triaged, briefly counseled (or referred for formal services, if needed), and returned to predisaster levels of functioning as quickly as possible.

Persons and communities struck by disaster will often experience four distinct phases of response to the disaster. First, there is a *heroic phase* that may even begin prior to impact and that can last up to a week afterward. During this phase people struggle to prevent loss of lives and to minimize property damage. This phase is followed by the *honeymoon phase,* which may last from two weeks to two months. During this phase, massive relief efforts lift spirits of survivors, and hopes for a quick recovery run high. Sadly, for most people this optimism is often short-lived and, all too soon, the *disillusionment phase* begins. This phase may last from several months to a year or more. Social scientists sometimes call it the second disaster, as it is the time when the realities of bureaucratic paperwork and recovery delays set in. Outside help has often come and gone and people realize that they must do more themselves. Eventually, the *reconstruction phase* begins. This phase may take several years as normal functioning is gradually reestablished.

There are many more specific changes that people may experience. Disasters can cause behavioral changes and regression in children. Many react with fear and show clear signs of anxiety about recurrence of the disaster event(s). Sleep disturbances are very common among children and adults and can best be handled by quickly returning to or establishing a familiar bedtime routine. Similarly, school avoidance may occur, leading to development of school phobias if children are not quickly returned to their normal routine of school attendance.

Adults often report mild symptoms of depression and anxiety. They can feel haunted by visual memories of the event. They may experience psychosomatic illnesses. Pre-existing physical problems such as heart trouble, diabetes, and ulcers may worsen in response to the increased level of stress. They may show anger, mood swings, suspicion, irritability, and/or apathy. Changes in appetite and sleep patterns are quite common. Adults, too, may have a period of poor performance at work or school and they may undergo some social withdrawal.

Middle-aged adults, in particular, may experience additional stress if they lose the security of their planned (and possibly paid-off) retirement home or financial nest egg, and/or if they are forced to pay for extensive rebuilding. Older adults will greatly miss their daily routines and will suffer strong feelings of loss from missing friends and loved ones. They may also suffer feelings of significant loss from the absence of their home or apartment, or its sentimental objects (paintings, antiques, Bibles and other spiritual items, scriptures, photo albums, and films or videotapes), which tied them to their past.

Timing of the onset of these changes varies with each person, as does duration. Some symptoms occur immediately, while others may not show until weeks later. Just about all of these things are considered normal reactions, as long as they do not last more than several weeks to a few months. The one commonality among disaster victims is that most everyone will be changed in some way by the experience, often marking time differently in its wake (speaking of what life has been like since the traumatic event).

The personal impact of disasters tends to be much worse whenever the disaster events are caused by intentionally destructive human acts than by natural causes (or pure accidents). Whenever inhumanity plays a major role in causality, survivors seem to need extra time to resolve their losses and move forward with their lives. This relates directly to the greater amount of anger involved, overexposure from repetitive media coverage, and the fact that any true sense of closure may not come until the perpetrators are found and prosecuted.

When disasters happen, the public demands answers and action. Mitigation efforts will often initiate social changes designed to prevent reoccurrences. Natural disasters prompt research to improve early warning systems and enforce sturdier construction methods. Transportation accidents trigger investigations that lead to new safety regulations, improved operating procedures, and the redesign of problematic equipment. Acts of terrorism stimulate public debate over curtailment and/or abridgement of civil liberties, often resulting legislative remedies and, in some cases, retaliatory military action.

## Disaster Mental Health

Disaster mental health (DMH) is an expanding field of crisis intervention that addresses several aspects of traumatology, affecting both victims and relief workers who have experienced natural or human-caused disasters. Crisis workers strive to help people recognize, understand, and accept some of the common changes that often occur in the days, months, and years following any traumatic disaster event(s). The goal of DMH intervention is to help assure that the victims (and helpers) become survivors by doing whatever can be done to prevent long-term, negative consequences of the psychological trauma such as the development of posttraumatic stress disorder.

DMH work involves extensive use of outreach skills and simple approaches, including offering informal greetings, providing snacks/drinks, doing brief, supportive defusing interviews, to help people begin problem solving. For many people, DMH work also involves grief counseling to assist survivors as they begin to mourn their losses. For those who have experienced severe psychological trauma, formal debriefing interviews are the preferred method to begin helping people let go of the pain, face their losses, and prepare to begin moving forward with their lives.

Defusing and debriefing are two of the primary tools used in providing help. Both involve offering individuals or groups of people opportunities to talk things out in a safe and supportive atmosphere. Both are voluntary offerings made to those who are ready and willing to tell their upsetting disaster stories and learn ways to cope with the residual stress.

*Defusing* is the term given to the initial process during which DMH workers begin helping traumatized people talk things out. It works like taking the fuse out of a bomb (or an explosive situation), by allowing victims and workers the opportunity to ventilate about their disaster-related memories, stresses, losses, and methods of coping in a safe and supportive atmosphere. The defusing process usually involves informal and impromptu sessions that help release thoughts, feelings, and fears which might not otherwise be appropriately expressed.

Debriefing is longer and more formally structured interview process that has grown from the researcher Jeff Mitchell's 1983 Critical Incident Stress Debriefing (CISD) model. The CISD model was designed for use with first responders (including police, firefighters, and emergency medical technicians), to help them overcome the emotional aftereffects of critical incidents (line-of-duty deaths). Sessions were usually held within the first twenty-four to seventy-two hours after the traumatic event, with follow-up sessions as needed. Given the nature of disasters, it is not always possible to identify all of the victims that quickly. Fortunately, the debriefing process is still beneficial, even when the sessions are held long after the event.

## Disaster Preparedness and Disaster Relief

Local, state, and federal government officials play a major role in both disaster preparedness and disaster relief. The Federal Emergency Management Agency (FEMA) is an independent agency of the federal government that reports directly to the president. Since it was founded in 1979, FEMA workers have coordinated both the nation's planning for disasters and the mitigation efforts that are needed once they occur. States and most local communities also have emergency management agencies that take responsibility for coordinating disaster preparedness and relief efforts in their areas.

Providing relief services since 1881, the American Red Cross (ARC) has been chartered by the U.S. Congress to provide disaster relief services and it is the best group to call for initial advice about preparedness and emergency assistance. ARC workers, many of whom are volunteers, provide predisaster education programs, as well as postdisaster damage assessment, mass care sheltering and feeding, health services, and emergency assistance to families. By offering support and replacing some lost items (clothing, food, and health care items), relief efforts jump-start the recovery process.

Since 1989 ARC has taken the lead in recruiting and training volunteers to serve on DMH service teams whenever and wherever their services may be needed. The American Psychological Association, the American Counseling Association, the National Association of Social Workers, the American Psychiatric Association, the American Association of Marriage and Family Therapists, several professional nursing organizations, and many other such groups help supply the needed workers.

ARC is just one of over twenty relief organizations that work together as members of local, state, and national relief efforts, including the nationally run National Volunteer Organizations Active in Disaster (NVOAD). Each local Volunteer Organization Active in Disaster (VOAD) organization has its own area(s) of specialization, including feeding, sheltering, child care, ham radio communication, and construction/repair. Representatives of VOAD member organizations hold regular meetings to facilitate planning efforts and the sharing of resources.

Relief workers often put in twelve- to fourteen-hour days, sometimes doing so for weeks at a time, and thus need to be mindful of stress management and self-care. Burnout is a serious hazard for disaster workers. The use of peer support is the best method to cope with stress. Health care professionals urge relief workers to take breaks, schedule time off, use humor, maintain a proper diet, exercise, and get generous amounts of restful sleep. Keeping a personal journal (a log of what was seen, thought, and felt) and writing a narrative at the end of the assignment often help many relief workers.

*See also:* GRIEF: ACUTE; GRIEF COUNSELING AND THERAPY; HINDENBERG; TERRORISM; TERRORIST ATTACKS ON AMERICA; TITANIC

## Bibliography

Dingman, Robert, ed. "Disasters and Crises: A Mental Health Counseling Perspective." *Journal of Mental Health Counseling* 17, no. 3 (1995).

Everly, George S. "The Role of the Critical Incident Stress Debriefing (CISD) Process in Disaster Counseling." *Journal of Mental Health Counseling* 17, no. 3 (1995):278–290.

Figley, Charles R., ed. *Compassion Fatigue: Coping with Secondary Traumatic Stress Disorder in Those Who Treat the Traumatized.* New York: Brunner/Mazel, 1995.

Friedman, Stanford B., et al. *Psychosocial Issues for Children and Families in Disasters: A Guide for the Primary Care Physician.* Substance Abuse and Mental Health Services Administration Publication No. SMA 95-3022. Rockville, MD: Center for Mental Health Services, 1995.

Lindemann, Erich. "Symptomatology and Management of Acute Grief." *American Journal of Psychiatry* 101 (1944):141–148.

Mitchell, Jeffrey T. "When Disaster Strikes … The Critical Incident Stress Debriefing Process." *Journal of Emergency Services* 8, no. 1 (January 1983):36–39.

Morgan, Jane. "American Red Cross Disaster Mental Health Services: Implementation and Recent Developments." *Journal of Mental Health Counseling* 17, no. 3 (1995):291–300.

Myers, Diane G. *Disaster Response and Recovery: A Handbook for Mental Health Professionals.* Substance Abuse and Mental Health Services Administration Publication No. SMA 94-3010. Rockville, MD: Center for Mental Health Services, 1994.

Parad, Howard J., et al. "Crisis Intervention and Emergency Mental Health Care: Concepts and Principles." In H. L. P. Resnik and Harvey L. Ruben eds., *Emergency Psychiatric Care: The Management of Mental Health Crises.* Bowie, MD: The Charles Press, 1975.

Siporin, Max. "Disasters and Disaster Aid." In *Encyclopedia of Social Work,* 18th edition. Silver Spring, MD: National Association of Social Workers, 1987.

Ursano, Robert J., Carol S. Fullerton, and Ann E. Norwood. "Psychiatric Dimensions of Disaster: Patient Care, Community Consultation, and Preventive Medicine." *Harvard Review of Psychiatry* 3, no. 4 (1995):196–209.

Weaver, John D. "How to Assist in the Aftermath of Disasters and Other Life Crises." In Leon VandeCreek and Thomas L. Jackson eds., *Innovations in Clinical Practice: A Source Book, Volume 17.* Sarasota, FL: Professional Resource Press, 1999.

Weaver, John D. "Disaster Mental Health Services." In Linda Grobman ed., *Days in the Lives of Social Workers.* Harrisburg, PA: White Hat Communications, 1996.

Weaver, John D. *Disasters: Mental Health Interventions.* Sarasota, FL: Professional Resource Press, 1995.

Young, Bruce H., et al. *Disaster Mental Health Services: A Guidebook for Clinicians and Administrators.* Menlo Park, CA: Department of Veterans Affairs, 1998.

*Internet Resources*

"Disasters." In the Information Please Almanac [web site]. Available from www.infoplease.com/ipa/A0001437.html.

Everly, George S., and Jeffrey T. Mitchell. "A Primer on Critical Incident Stress Management." In the International Critical Incident Stress Foundation [web site]. Available from www.icisf.org/inew_era.htm.

"NASA's Natural Disaster Reference Database." In the NASA [web site]. Available from http://ltpwww.gsfc.nasa.gov/ndrd/.

Weaver, John. "Working with Those Who Have Experienced Sudden Loss of Loved Ones." In the Internet Journal of Rescue and Disaster Medicine [web site]. Available from www.icaap.org/iuicode?86.2.1.2.

Weaver, John. "Sudden Death in Disasters and Transportation Accidents: A Guide to Survival for Family Members and Friends." In the Internet Journal of Rescue and Disaster Medicine [web site]. Available from www.icaap.org/iuicode?86.2.1.4.

Weaver, John. "Disaster Mental Health: Detailed Information." In the Disaster Mental Health [web site]. Available from http://ourworld.compuserve.com/homepages/johndweaver.

JOHN D. WEAVER

# DO NOT RESUSCITATE

Do Not Resuscitate (DNR) orders are medical directives to withhold efforts to revive a patient who has a cardiac or respiratory arrest. DNR orders came into use in the 1970s as a response to the widespread practice of cardiopulmonary resuscitation (CPR). CPR is an emergency intervention that uses a variety of techniques to restore the heartbeat and breathing. CPR includes such basic life support as external chest compression and mouth-to-mouth ventilation, as well as advanced cardiac life support such as electrical defibrillation and cardiac medications. A DNR order tells medical professionals not to perform CPR if the patient's heartbeat or breathing stops.

When it was first introduced in the early 1960s, CPR was a heroic, life-sustaining act. It was a technique used on only a select group of acutely ill but otherwise relatively healthy patients. By the end of the following decade, however, CPR had become a routine intervention for all patients facing imminent death. With this widespread use of CPR came a growing recognition that it was neither effective nor desirable for some patients. For example, patients with aggressive cancer or serious infection had almost no chance of recovery after CPR. Other patients who did survive after CPR often ended up with brain damage or permanent disabilities. At the same time that poor outcomes from CPR were being recognized, patients were demanding to be more involved in medical decisions. The result was the institution of DNR orders.

## Participation in the DNR Decision

An ongoing debate about DNR has involved the extent to which patients or their surrogate decision makers must agree to such orders. Through the late 1970s and early 1980s, some hospitals routinely created DNR orders without any discussion with the patient or the patient's family, and they did not clearly document the DNR order in the patient's chart. But these practices were abandoned as the bioethics movement and the courts emphasized the right of patients or their surrogate decision makers to refuse medical treatment, including life-sustaining therapies such as CPR. Most health care providers and well-recognized health professional groups and accrediting bodies began to support DNR policies that require the patient to be informed of the risks and benefits of CPR and to give consent that CPR not be used. Some well-respected physician ethicists and medical groups, however, advocate that physicians should have the ability to write DNR orders without a patient's consent in situations in which it has been determined that CPR would have no medical benefit.

## Communication and Knowledge about CPR and DNR Orders

Despite policies that require consent to a DNR order, informed discussions between patients and physicians about CPR and other life-sustaining treatments occur infrequently. Only about one patient in seven reports having discussed personal preferences for life-sustaining treatment with a physician. Even when patients have life-threatening illnesses such as AIDS, cancer, and congestive heart failure, such discussions occurred less than 40 percent of the time in some studies. In many cases, the decision about a DNR order is broached only after extensive procedures have been attempted and at a time when patients are no longer capable of making an informed decision.

This lack of communication contributes to three concerns. First, many people have unrealistic expectations about the likely success of CPR. When CPR was first described in 1960, it referred to heart massage by the exertion of pressure on the chest. The success rate of 70 percent survival to hospital discharge was quite high, largely because it was applied to a small group of patients who experienced a cardiac arrest in the operating room or postoperative recovery rooms. By the early twenty-first century, CPR included not only heart compression and mouth-to-mouth resuscitation but also a host of advanced supports such as electrical defibrillation paddles, powerful drugs, and an assortment of mechanical breathing devices. This range of interventions is generally referred to as a "code" in which a special team responds to resuscitate a patient. But success rates are nowhere near those reported in original studies.

Research in the 1980s and 1990s showed that for all patients undergoing CPR in the hospital, just under one-half survived the code itself and one-third survived for twenty-four hours. Approximately 15 percent of patients undergoing CPR in the hospital survived to discharge. About 30 percent of those who survived suffered a significant increase in dependence and required extensive home care or institutionalization. Survival to discharge from the hospital was much poorer when certain diseases or conditions were present. In some studies, for example, no patients with metastatic cancer and only 3 percent of patients with sepsis (a widespread infection) survived to discharge. Outcomes in some studies of frail, elderly patients in long-term care facilities showed survival rates of 5 percent or less, prompting some health care providers to suggest that CPR should not even be offered to residents of nursing homes and other long-term care facilities.

The general public, however, often has an overly positive impression about the success rates of CPR. As portrayed on popular television medical shows, CPR is much more effective than in real life. According to one study, two-thirds of CPR patients survive on television, a much higher percentage than any published medical study. The same study

reported that on television only 17 percent of patients getting CPR were elderly. In reality cardiac arrest is much more common in older people than in any other age group. Furthermore, three-quarters of cases of cardiac arrest on television resulted from accidents, stabbings, lightning strikes, and other injuries, whereas in the real world 75 percent or more of cardiac arrests were triggered by underlying heart disease.

Knowledge about the outcomes of CPR is especially important because it has been shown to affect preferences for care. Surveys have shown that as many as 90 percent of elderly outpatients and a range of 44 to 88 percent of hospitalized elderly desire to have CPR in the event of a cardiac arrest. Even when elderly patients were asked whether they wanted CPR if they had a serious disability, 20 to 45 percent said they would. Clinicians at one geriatric practice asked patients about their preferences for CPR if they were acutely ill and if they were chronically ill. These patients were then educated about the probability of surviving to discharge under these conditions. Once they were given prognostic information, preferences for CPR dropped nearly 50 percent.

A second area of concern is that the lack of communication about CPR results in common misunderstandings about DNR orders. Many patients believe incorrectly that having a living will or other type of written advance directive automatically means that a patient will have a DNR order written. Instead, while an advance directive may express a patient's desire to have a DNR order written under certain circumstances, DNR orders—like all medical orders—must be authorized by a physician who is treating the patient. Also, some patients assume that a DNR order directs that all medical treatments be stopped and only comfort care provided. In some circumstances, however, other aggressive therapies—including staying in an intensive care unit—are continued for patients with DNR orders.

Moreover, there are circumstances in which restricted or limited DNR orders are appropriate. For example, if it is determined that further attempts at CPR would not benefit a patient who is on a ventilator or a breathing machine, then an order might be written not to give cardioactive medications should a cardiac or pulmonary arrest occur. On the other hand, it might also be determined that a patient would want cardioactive medications and chest compressions but would not want to be intubated and put on a breathing machine. Because there are multiple options, it is essential that physicians thoroughly discuss DNR options with patients or their surrogate decision makers and that decisions are carefully documented in the patient's medical record.

Third, the lack of genuine communication means that physicians are often unfamiliar with patients' preferences about CPR and must rely on family members to help decide whether a DNR order is appropriate. Family members, however, also are very poor predictors of what patients would actually want, answering wrongly up to 40 or 50 percent of the time in some scenarios. Uncertainty about patient wishes concerning CPR also means that decisions about DNR orders are often delayed until the patient is near death.

A major, multihospital, longitudinal study of these issues focusing on more than 9,000 patients—the Study to Understand Prognosis and Preferences for Outcomes and Treatment (SUPPORT)—discovered that 79 percent of the patients who died in the hospital had a DNR order but that almost half of these orders had been written in the last two days before death. Almost 40 percent of these patients had spent at least ten days in the intensive care unit, and, of those able to communicate, more than half were in moderate or severe pain at least half of the time in their final days. About one-third of the patients expressed a desire not to be resuscitated, but less than half of their physicians understood this desire.

## Other Issues

An issue of special concern involves the patient with a DNR order who needs to have surgery or some other medical intervention that requires the use of anesthesia or other agents that affect resuscitation. At some hospitals, it is institutional policy to automatically suspend a DNR order while a patient is undergoing procedures that may require resuscitative measures. The rationale for such policies is that if the procedure requires a patient to be artificially resuscitated through the use of a ventilator or chemical agents, then a DNR order would be illogical. Some hospitals, however, forbid the practice of automatically suspending a DNR order

during surgery. Rather, they require the need for resuscitative measures during surgery or other procedures be discussed with the patient and that agreed-upon circumstances for using or not using resuscitative measures be put in writing.

Some states have authorized the use of "durable" DNR orders. Such orders can travel with the patient and can be recognized by a wide range of health care personnel at different facilities and at the patient's home. Durable DNR orders eliminate the problem of patients needing to have a DNR order written each time they enter a health care facility and mean that patients at home can have their DNR wishes honored by emergency services personnel. Without a durable DNR order, emergency services personnel are required to resuscitate a patient at home, even if the patient had a DNR order recently written in the hospital.

*See also:* COMMUNICATION WITH THE DYING; CRUZAN, NANCY; END-OF-LIFE ISSUES; INFORMED CONSENT; PERSISTENT VEGETATIVE STATE; QUINLAN, KAREN ANN; RESUSCITATION

## Bibliography

American Medical Association, Council on Ethical and Judicial Affairs. "Guidelines for the Appropriate Use of Do-Not-Resuscitate Orders." *Journal of the American Medical Association* 265 (1991):1,868–1,871.

Blackhall, Leslie J. "Must We Always Use CPR?" *New England Journal of Medicine* 317 (1987):1,281–1,285.

Ebell, Mark H. "Practical Guidelines for Do-Not-Resuscitate Orders." *American Family Physician* 50 (1994):1,293–1,299.

Hakim, Rosemarie B., Joan M. Teno, Frank E. Harrell, William A. Knaus, Neil Wenger, Russell S. Phillips, Peter Layde, Robert Califf, Alfred F. Connors, and Joanne Lynn. "Factors Associated with Do-Not-Resuscitate Orders: Patients' Preferences, Prognoses, and Physicians' Judgments." *Annals of Internal Medicine* 125 (1996):284–293.

Layson, Rita T., Harold M. Adelman, Paul M. Wallach, Mark P. Pfeifer, Sarah Johnston, Robert A. McNutt, and the End of Life Study Group. "Discussions about the Use of Life-Sustaining Treatments: A Literature Review of Physicians' and Patients' Attitudes and Practices." *Journal of Clinical Ethics* 5 (1994):195–203.

Murphy, Donald J. "Do-Not-Resuscitate Orders: Time for Reappraisal in Long-Term Care Institutions." *Journal of the American Medical Association* 260 (1988):2,098–2,101.

Orentlicher, David. "The Illusion of Patient Choice in End-of-Life Decisions." *Journal of the American Medical Association* 267 (1992):2,101–2,104.

President's Commission for the Study of Ethical Problems in Medicine and Biomedical Behavioral Research. *Deciding to Forego Life-Sustaining Treatment.* Washington, DC: U.S. Government Printing Office, 1983.

Saklayen, Mohammad, Howard Liss, and Ronald Markert. "In-Hospital Cardiopulmonary Resuscitation Survival in One Hospital and Literature Review." *Medicine* 74 (1995):163–175.

SUPPORT Principal Investigators. "A Controlled Trial to Improve Care for Seriously Ill Hospitalized Patients." *Journal of the American Medical Association* 274 (1995):1,591–1,598.

Tomlinson, Tom, and Howard Brody. "Ethics and Communication in Do-Not-Resuscitate Orders." *New England Journal of Medicine* 318 (1988):43–46.

Weiss, Gregory L., and Charles A. Hite. "The Do-Not-Resuscitate Decision: The Context, Process, and Consequences of DNR Orders." *Death Studies* 24 (2000):307–323.

Younger, Stuart J. "Do-Not-Resuscitate Orders: No Longer Secret, but Still a Problem." *Hastings Center Report* 17, no. 1 (1987):24–33.

CHARLES A. HITE
GREGORY L. WEISS

# DROWNING

Drowning is defined by the American Academy of Pediatrics as death resulting from suffocation within twenty-four hours of submersion in water. Near-drowning applies to all other victims, whether or not they survive. For every child that drowns, four children are hospitalized for near-drowning, according to the National Center for Injury Prevention and Control. Children less than one year of age frequently drown in bathtubs and buckets; children aged one to four years most often drown in swimming pools; and children and adolescents aged five to nineteen years most frequently drown in natural bodies of water. Alcohol use in adolescents and adults is estimated to be associated with 25 to 50 percent of drownings.

Males comprise the overwhelming majority of drowning victims.

Although people can hold their breath underwater for a limited amount of time, rising carbon dioxide levels in the blood initiate the need to take a breath. Most drowning victims quickly lose consciousness due to lack of oxygen and then inhale water. Death is typically a result of brain damage due to lack of oxygen and/or acute lung injury from aspirated fluids. Both sea and fresh water affect a substance called surfactant that coats the tiny air sacs, or alveoli, in the lungs. Lack of surfactant activity causes elevated surface tension in the lungs. This increases the effort required to inflate the alveoli and thus decreases the amount of air that can fill the lungs and the extent of oxygenation of the blood.

Treatment of a drowning victim is to restore breathing and circulation as soon as possible, because irreversible brain damage or death may occur in four to six minutes after breathing stops. Artificial respiration (mouth-to-mouth resuscitation) and cardiopulmonary resuscitation (CPR) are techniques used for this purpose.

*See also:* CAUSES OF DEATH

### *Bibliography*

American Academy of Pediatrics. "Drowning in Infants, Children, and Adolescents (RE9319)." *Pediatrics* 92 (1993):292–294.

### *Internet Resources*

CDC–National Center for Injury Prevention and Control. "Drowning Prevention." In the Centers for Disease Control and Prevention [web site]. Available from www.cdc.gov/ncipc/factsheets/drown.htm

ALLISON K. WILSON

# DURKHEIM, ÉMILE

Émile Durkheim (1858–1917) is considered one of the most influential figures in the founding of modern sociology. Born in the eastern part of France, Durkheim descended from a long line of rabbis and trained to follow in their footsteps. As a young man, he turned away from organized religion and became an agnostic. While studying in Germany, he became convinced of the value of using scientific methods, properly modified, in the study of human behavior. Recognized as a promising scholar, Durkheim wrote several important works on the methods of sociology, the division of labor, the scientific study of religion, and how imbalances in the relations between self and society can lead to death.

One of Durkheim's most influential books is a detailed study of suicide. When it was published in 1897, *Le Suicide* not only changed the way in which suicide was understood, it fundamentally transformed the way sociological research was subsequently conducted. In that work, Durkheim created what became the standard structure for sociological research. On the first page of the book's introduction, he began defining the central term under discussion and proceeded to sketch out the tentative outlines of an explanation for suicide that would be informed by social science, replete with tables of suicide statistics.

In critically reviewing the existing suicide literature, which largely viewed acts of self-destruction as having physiological or psychological origins, Durkheim wondered why people from similar genetic origins did not have similar rates of suicide. Why did rates vary within one region over time? If it was related to weakness of character, why was it unrelated to levels of alcoholism? Utilizing logic and statistics, Durkheim challenged both popular and academic explanations. In doing so, he indicated that the tentative sociological approach he had begun to develop in the book's introduction offered greater explanatory power. The majority of the book lays out what became a classic sociological explanation for suicide. There are four major types, all related to group cohesion or solidarity.

*Egoistic* suicide, Durkheim argued, was most common among groups of individuals with few connections to social groupings of any kind. Thus, loosely bound liberal Protestant groups had higher suicide rates than Catholics and Jews, for whom regular religious participation was expected; married people committed suicide at lower rates than singles; and nations undergoing political crises experienced lower rates because competing interests and parties became tightly integrated under stress.

While egoistic suicide made sense to most readers, Durkheim's second category, that of *altruistic* suicide, was more controversial. Durkheim argued

*Training given to workers on suicide hotlines in the twenty-first century is largely based on the conclusions and categories originally introduced by Émile Durkheim in 1897.* CORBIS

that certain types of suicide occurred among tightly knit groups when they came under severe threat and their members were prepared to die in the group's defense. Because suicide was widely understood as the act of sick or disturbed individuals, Durkheim's argument that soldiers who knowingly gave up their lives for their country were committing suicide appeared to diminish the valor of those actions. Durkheim delineated three types of altruistic suicide, based largely on a group's expectations that its members would undertake self-destruction in its defense.

The third type of suicide, *anomic,* was identified with an abrupt shift in an individual's circumstances, shifts that removed him or her from membership in what had been a well-integrated group. Durkheim showed that nations where divorce was common experienced higher suicide rates than nations where the practice was illegal. Similarly, economic crisis could lead to personal crises for individuals who once thought of themselves as important providers for their families, but when confronted with persisting unemployment found themselves evicted from their homes, their credit rejected, and prospects for improvement dim. If these individuals and their friends were accustomed to thinking of poor people as responsible for their circumstances, then they found themselves condemned by their own categories of thought. Faced with humiliation and a lack of connection with groups who might ease their self-doubts, such individuals might commit anomic suicide.

Durkheim's final category of suicide, *fatalistic,* is relegated to a footnote. This type of suicide occurred within tightly knit groups whose members sought, but could not attain, escape, whose "futures are pitilessly blocked and passions violently choked by oppressive discipline" (Durkheim 1951, p. 276). Prisoners of war or slaves who were bound into distinct groups dominated by other groups might commit suicide in order to escape group membership or to demonstrate control over their lives.

*Suicide* concludes by moving from what had been a taxonomy of suicide types toward an explanation of how social, political, and economic forces produced those types. For instance, Durkheim explored links between suicide and urbanization, developing how cities atomize individuals, producing egoistic suicides.

Sociologists admire Durkheim's book for a variety of reasons. Not only does the work present a clear understanding of what a sociological perspective was and how it differed from the perspectives offered by other emerging academic disciplines, it provides a clear and well-documented argument advocating the practical value of that discipline's perspective. Durkheim's reliance on statistics for calculating and comparing suicide rates was innovative for the time, as was his realization that the effects of some variables had to be controlled. Although he recognized problems in the comparability of data drawn from different regions or within one region in different periods, his work contributed to an emerging body of scholarship in comparative historical sociology.

Several sociological studies have been conducted in the century since *Suicide*'s original publication, and while some have qualified Durkheim's observations, none has seriously challenged his overall approach or conclusions. While his earlier work contains some optimism about the potentially liberating effects of industrialization and urbanization, it also reveals concerns for disruptions caused by change that occurs too rapidly. As time went on, Durkheim saw these strains become more frequent and troubling. The Dreyfus affair led him to doubt the hearts and consciences of the French citizenry, and the outbreak of World War I revealed how destructive the potentially liberating forces of industrialization can be. The war claimed the life of his only son and intellectual heir in late 1915, a blow from which Durkheim never recovered. He died in 1917, his writing having shifted from scientific objectivity to the study of ethics.

*See also:* SUICIDE TYPES: THEORIES

### *Bibliography*

Coser, Lewis A. *Masters of Sociological Thought.* New York: Harcourt, Brace, 1977.

Durkheim, Émile. *Suicide.* New York: Free Press, 1951.

Giddens, Anthony, ed. *Émile Durkheim: Selected Writings.* London: Cambridge University Press, 1972.

Lukes, Steven. *Émile Durkheim, His Life and Work: A Historical and Critical Study.* Palo Alto, CA: Stanford University Press, 1985.

JONATHAN F. LEWIS

# DYING, PROCESS OF

It might seem self-evident that death is the outcome of the process of dying. The reality, however, is not so simple. Consider a few examples: Two people are experiencing the same life-threatening emergency. One person receives prompt and competent treatment; the other does not. Were both dying if one recovers? Or say that laboratory tests show that a person has a progressive condition that sooner or later will result in death. At the moment, though, the person has only the early symptoms and can continue with all normal activities. Is this person dying? What about a person clinging to life in a case where doctors have devised a last-ditch intervention atop more standard treatments that have already failed? Is this person dying if there is another treatment that offers hope of remission or cure? And what of a comatose patient, dependent on tubes and respirators with no sign of improvement? Is this person in a state of suspended dying? Or is this person already dead?

Such quandaries have become increasingly commonplace because of medical and technological advances. Continuing changes in the definition of death have also affected discourse about dying. This familiar term no longer seems entirely adequate when applied to a variety of situations, some of them shifting and ambiguous.

## "Dying": Historical Origin and Current Usage

*Dighe,* (also spelled *dye*) was a word in common usage in the Friesland province of northern Holland in the fourteenth century at the time when Europe was devastated by the Black Death, a plague that annihilated perhaps as much as a third of the population. Old Friesian derived from an early Indo-European language group and became a Low German dialect that is still spoken. The Icelandic *deyja* and the Danish *doe* are cognates. *Die* and *dying* became established words in the English language during the plague years.

Poetic imagination soon turned "dying" to additional uses. "Die-away ditties," popular with Renaissance singers, were songs that ended in a subtle and suggestive manner. Elizabethan poetry often played with dying as a sexual metaphor, and lovers routinely spoke of dying when separated from their beloved.

Metaphorical uses persist, sometimes to the confusion of young children who hear that a runner at second base or a car battery has died. Members of a dwindling group are also characterized in this manner: "Phonograph record collectors are a dying breed."

Because of the "sensitive" nomenclature fostered in the early twentieth century by unctuous funeral directors, the literal usage of the term "dying" gave way to euphemisms such as "expire," "pass away," or "go to one's reward." By the middle of the twentieth century, *dying* and *death* had become taboo words in the United States and Europe, even in physicians' consultations with families or patients .

Communication started to improve with the emergence of the death-awareness movement in the 1960s, which introduced palliative care, death

education, and other advances. It was a breakthrough to have books published with "death" and "dying" in their titles. This period of more direct and open communication did not long endure, however. The medical establishment, although slow to give priority to the care of dying people, became more active on this front. But the term *dying* was still deemed too abrasive—*terminal illness* is the preferred clinical euphemism, connoting an aggregation of symptoms rather than a real, suffering human being in the twenty-first century.

*End-of-life* (EOL) has become another key term. Unlike *terminal illness,* EOL calls attention to the many sources of potential concern and support. Decisions about financial affairs and funeral arrangements, for example, are among the included topics. Nevertheless, EOL has also become the professional and bureaucratic rhetorical surrogate for *dying person.*

Perhaps the most useful addition to current terminology has been *end-phase of life,* the period in which major body systems have failed and the individual has become dependent on others for total care. The term is more specific than either *dying* or *terminally ill.* Some terminally ill people can continue with their family activities and careers, and look after much of their own care. People in the end-phase have lost much of their functional capacity and are likely to be receiving specialized care in the hospital or at home.

## The Dying Person in Society

The onset of ill health is often accompanied by a change in social status, however temporary and reversible upon recovery. Lowered expectations or even outright aversion—if the condition is disturbing or contagious—account for much of the patient's lowered social esteem—one that either disturbs (e.g., a burn victim whose injuries are painful for the viewer as well as the patient) or is feared as contagious. A similar reduction in social standing affects those who cannot make a full recovery—in such cases of the "chronically impaired," the patient is often shunted to the periphery of social influence and interaction.

Research and observation have clearly established that society tends to isolate dying people. Both professionals and nonprofessionals spend less time with dying people, relying on various evasive patterns of behavior. The growing awareness that dying people often experience social isolation and loneliness became a strong motivation for the development of palliative care and death education. Even today, however, the status change to "dying person" often signals a major alteration in the individual's relationship with society.

When does dying begin? This question becomes important in light of the major changes that often occur when a person is regarded as a dying person. In a strict sense, it could be said that given the mortal nature of humans, dying begins at birth. But such an abstract philosophical perspective yields little concrete guidance in confronting the suffering and fears of real humans whose demise is not a distant endpoint but an imminent prospect. Neither is there much practical utility in the equally broad notion that dying begins with the onset of aging, especially because many people enjoy good health well into old age.

In the most common formulations, dying begins when a fatal condition is recognized by a physician; the patient is informed of the fatal condition; the patient realizes and accepts the facts; everybody in the situation (e.g., family, friends) realizes and accepts the facts; and nothing more can be done to reverse the condition and preserve life.

Each of these possibilities has its own set of implications. For example, a person might incur a life-threatening condition but remain unaware of it because of "silent" or seemingly trivial symptoms (i.e., digestive problems, fatigue)—hence the victim's social image and self-image are not those of a dying person. Communication and interpretation are crucial to all the other possibilities. One person might suspect that a condition is fatal but resist that conclusion pending a physician's confirmation, while another might resist the reality of impending death no matter how bluntly the physician conveys it; sometimes this denial might come from family members rather than the patient. It is not unusual for some time to elapse until physician, patient, and family all accept the prognosis.

The dying person is vulnerable to the additional stress of familial discord, which often takes the form of mixed messages, with some family members urging a pitched battle against the disease and others counseling resignation and acceptance in the face of the inevitable. Physicians are often caught in the middle of such family dissension, especially if the relatives' attitudes shift with each new turn in the patient's condition. In some cases a doctor's zeal in pursing every conceivable treatment strategy, no matter how difficult or futile, can override the patient's own wishes to abandon an all but fruitless struggle and face the end placidly.

Caregivers often emphasize the importance of open communication and trust. Several studies have revealed that interactions with the dying person are often hedged by fears of excessive bluntness toward the patient and the relatives' anxiety about their own mortality. Such circumspection leads to patients and relatives to deny to each other the knowledge that each possesses privately about the terminal nature of the illness. In the mutual-pretense situation, for example, both the dying person and the caregiver or family member know the truth, but both also act as if they are not aware in order to spare each other's feelings. Experts suggest that it is more useful to attune to the dying person's immediate needs instead of applying a predetermined resolve to skirt or confront sensitive topics. Sometimes dying people want to discuss heartfelt feelings about impending death, while others relish diversionary gossip. Experienced caregivers often encourage relatives to view the dying person as a human being rather than as a "case."

## The Medical Side of Dying

"We die the death of our disease," observed the poet Rainer Maria Rilke. This statement echoes clinical realities. The patient's overall life history and personal disposition can have as great an impact on the dying process as the nature of the illness. The physician Sherwin B. Nuland offers illuminating examples of the influence of biomedical factors: "When a would-be suicide hooks up one end of a hose to an automobile's exhaust pipe and inhales at the other, he is taking advantage of the affinity that hemoglobin has for carbon monoxide, which it prefers by a factor of 200 to 300 over its life-giving competitor, oxygen. The patient dies because his brain and heart are deprived of an adequate oxygen supply" (Nuland 1994, p. 159).

What is significant about this pathway to death is the rapid loss of consciousness and therefore the inability to communicate or change one's mind. By contrast, some people recover from cancer or go into long periods of remission where they are at risk of terminal illness but not really dying. Should the cancer start on a terminal course, there is not usually a rapid loss of consciousness. Unlike the carbon monoxide suicide, the person with terminal cancer has time to be with friends and relatives, look after business matters, and reflect on life's values and meanings.

The end phase of life also differs markedly from that of the suicidal person attached to an exhaust tube hose. A prolonged struggle with cancer is likely to leave the patient emaciated and weak, subject to infection because of a compromised immune system—hence pneumonia, abscesses, and infection often become the immediate causes of death. Blood pressure drops, and various organ systems fail. During this "lingering trajectory," family members can provide emotional support to one another as well as to the dying person.

Kidney failure also tends to have a lingering terminal course as excess potassium and other substances build up in the body, compromising brain functioning and often leading to a coma and then fatal cardiac instability. As Nuland observes, "Only rarely are there any last words or deathbed reconciliations" (1994, p. 54). There is a need to be with the dying kidney patient while there is still time for consoling and memorable interactions. In these and many other instances, the nature of the disease—and the type and quality of care—are usually decisive factors in the course of the dying process.

## Conditions That Resemble Dying

The supposed uniqueness of the dying process engenders a good deal of the anxiety and confusion that typically attend it. Actually, many aspects of the process are akin to a wide array of feelings and experiences familiar to all from everyday life. The lessons gleaned from such similarities can aid in an understanding of the stress experienced by dying people. Here are some typical experiences of this kind:

- Restricted activity— "I can do less and less";

- Limited energy— "I must conserve what is left of my strength";

- Body image— "I don't look and feel like the person I used to be";

- Contagion— "You act like you might catch something bad from me";

- Disempowerment— "I have lost the ability to influence you";

- Attributional incompetence— "You think I can't do anything right any more";

- Ineffectuality— "I cannot make things happen the way I want them to";

- Stress response— "My defenses have become so intense that they are causing problems of their own";

- Time anxiety— "I fear it is too late to do all I must do";

- Loss and separation— "I am losing contact with everything that is most important to me";

- Disengagement— "I feel ready to withdraw from interactions and responsibilities";

- Journey— "I am going some place I have never been before";

- Closing the book— "I am doing everything for the last time; it will soon all be over";

- Performance anxiety— "How am I doing? How do you think I am doing?"

- Endangered relationship— "I fear I am losing your love and respect";

- Struggling brain— "My mind is not working as it should. The world is slipping away from me";

- Storytelling— "I must come up with the best possible story of all that has happened, is happening, and will happen."

These experiences of living can help individuals prepare for the experience of dying, which is more than restricted activity, limited energy, and doom-laden depression. Like many other key formative experiences, it is also the adventure of passage from the known to the unknown.

*See also:* COMMUNICATION WITH DYING; DEFINITIONS OF DEATH; GOOD DEATH, THE; INJURY MORTALITY; LAST WORDS; MOMENT OF DEATH; PAIN AND PAIN MANAGEMENT; TERRORISM

## Bibliography

Byock, Ira. *Dying Well.* New York: Riverhead Books, 1997.

Corr, Charles A., Kenneth J. Doka, and Robert Kastenbaum. "Dying and Its Interpreters: A

Review of Selected Literature and Some Comments on the State of the Field." *Omega: The Journal of Death and Dying* 39 (1999):239–260.

Curtis, J. Randall, and Gordon D. Rubenfeld, eds. *Managing Death in the Intensive Care Unit: The Transition from Cure to Comfort.* New York: Oxford University Press, 2001.

Doka, Kenneth J. *Living with Life-Threatening Illness.* New York: Lexington, 1993.

Enck, Robert E. *The Medical Care of Terminally Ill Patients.* Baltimore, MD: Johns Hopkins University Press, 1994.

Field, Marilyn J., and Christine K. Cassel, eds. *Approaching Death: Improving Care at the End of Life.* Washington, DC: National Academy Press, 1997.

Glaser, Barney G., and Anselm Strauss. *Time for Dying.* Chicago: Aldine, 1968.

Glaser, Barney G., and Anselm Strauss. *Awareness of Dying.* Chicago: Aldine, 1966.

Kastenbaum, Robert. *Death, Society, and Human Experience,* 7th edition. Boston: Allyn & Bacon, 2001.

Kastenbaum, Robert. *The Psychology of Death,* 3rd edition. New York: Springer, 2000.

Lester, David. "The Stigma against Dying and Suicidal Patients: A Replication of Richard Kalish's Study Twenty-Five Years Later." *Omega: The Journal of Death and Dying* 26 (1992–1993):71–76.

Nuland, Sherwin B. *How We Die.* New York: Knopf, 1994.

Rosen, Elliot J. *Families Facing Death.* San Francisco: Jossey-Bass, 1998.

Staton, Jana, and Roger Shuy. *A Few Months to Live: Different Paths to Life's End.* Washington, DC: Georgetown University Press, 2001.

SUPPORT. "A Controlled Trial to Improve Care for Seriously Ill Hospitalized Patients." *Journal of the American Medical Association* 274 (1995):1591–1599.

Weisman, Avery D., and Robert Kastenbaum. *The Psychological Autopsy: A Study of the Terminal Phase of Life.* New York: Behavioral Publications, 1968.

ROBERT KASTENBAUM

# E

## EGYPTIAN BOOK OF THE DEAD

There is probably no text in the popular imagination more closely associated with the ancient Egyptian beliefs about life after death than the work popularly known as the Egyptian *Book of the Dead,* also referred to as *The Book of Coming Forth by Day.* This work received its name from the fact that many of the earliest specimens to reach Renaissance Europe—centuries before Champollion deciphered the hieroglyphs in 1824—had been found next to mummies in burials, a practice that also gave rise to the misconception that the *Book of the Dead* was an authoritative scripture equivalent to the Bible. However, the actual Egyptian title, *The Chapters of Going Forth by Day,* offers a more accurate picture of purpose and orientation of this composition. The *Book* was essentially a collection of prayers and magical speeches primarily intended to enable a deceased person to overcome the trials and dangers of the next world and emerge safely from the tomb in a spiritualized form. Although there is no one ancient Egyptian work that contains the complete range of Egyptian postmortem beliefs, let alone the totality of their complex and constantly changing religious ideas, the *Book* does offer the modern reader insights into the wide range of ancient Egyptian concepts involving both the afterlife and the afterworld—it is not, however, in any sense an Egyptian Bible.

The *Book of the Dead* assumed many forms. It occurs primarily on papyri, but it is found as well on tomb walls, coffins, scarabs, funerary stelae, and other objects. Perhaps the best-known *Book* is the famous papyrus that was inscribed for a certain Ani, "the Accounts-Scribe of the Divine Offerings of all the Gods," and his wife Tutu. This profusely and beautifully illustrated scroll was made during the early Ramesside period (C. 1300 B.C.E.) in Ani's home town, the southern religious capital at Thebes, modern Luxor. It was purchased there by its curator, E. A. Wallis Budge, in 1888 for the British Museum where it is displayed today. Extending more than seventy-five feet, it is one of the best examples of the *Book* papyri of the New Kingdom and Ramesside periods. Ironically, for all its splendor, this scroll was actually a template papyrus roughly akin to a modern preprinted lease or standard will, with Ani's name and titles being inserted into the appropriate blank spaces at the last minute. Ani, or his survivors, purchased what was deemed appropriate (and what they could afford) from a funerary workshop for his safe journey into the next world; then the sheets with those relevant spells were pasted together to form the final product.

The *Book of the Dead* represents the acme of the illustrated book in ancient Egypt. The text itself represents a continuation of an ancient tradition of afterworld guides that began with the royal Pyramid Texts in the Old Kingdom and continued with the more "democratized" Coffin Texts for wealthy individuals of the Middle Kingdom. These, in turn, provided the material on which many chapters of the *Book of the Dead* were based. This pattern of rewriting old religious texts and adopting them to new beliefs was to continue after the *Book* throughout pharaonic history. At no time did any group of texts become canonical in the sense of having a definitive text or a fixed sequence and number of chapters. The first spells that can be definitely associated with the *Book of the Dead* began appearing in the late Middle Kingdom, but it was not really until the Eighteenth Dynasty (c. 1500 B.C.E.) that this new work became the standard afterlife text for the Egyptian elite. In order to enhance its appeal to the conservative religious sense of Egyptians, the *Book of the Dead* preserves many archaisms in script, vocabulary, and dialect. The main innovations of the *Book of the Dead* were that nearly every spell was accompanied by a vignette—an illustration—and that the work, designed for the relatively cheap medium of papyrus, was affordable for a much wider audience of Egyptians.

Probably only a miniscule percentage of Egyptians had the means to include a *Book* papyrus among their burial equipment. In fact, because the *Book* describes a lavish funeral, an elaborate, well-outfitted tomb, and other expensive burial equipment, some scholars have surmised that these scrolls were partially intended to provide by magic various things that the average Egyptian official could not afford.

All Egyptian religious texts such as the *Book* were fundamentally collections compiled from several different sources or local traditions, so that the final versions often contained contradictory concepts and statements, occasionally within the same spell or sentence. Consequently, for modern readers, many of whom have been influenced by the uncompromising strictures of monotheism, reading the *Book* often evokes confusion, even shock. In the profoundly polytheistic environment of Egyptian religion, however, there was never was a need to reconcile differences or to compel uniformity; one should more properly speak of Egyptian religions in the plural rather than the singular. Yet, despite this seeming lack of consistency, the fundamental concepts concerning life after death remained essentially stable.

Above all, the Egyptians had an essentially optimistic conception of the afterlife. For them death may have been inevitable, but it was survivable. However, unlike the modern view of death as the great leveler that reduces all humanity to the same status before the deity, a profound class-consciousness permeated the Egyptian view of the next world. Earthly status was transferable into the world beyond. The chief objective of their vast

*Departed souls make an offering to Horus in this illustration from the Egyptian* Book of the Dead. *Such images have become more widely known than the text itself.*
CORBIS

mortuary culture was not only to ensure survival after death but to preserve one's earthly station, presumably as a member of the elite. Therein lay the elaborate nature of Egyptian tombs and burials, which were intended to provide the deceased with a comfortable material existence in the next world, an existence that would in part be an idyllic version of earthly life, an Egyptian Elysian Fields. Egypt, the land of the living, was well ordered and governed under the principle of *Ma'at,* that is, roughly (rightful) order or universal guidance. Maat prevailed in the coherent, cosmic universe.

Consequently, travel through the world beyond the grave meant that the deceased would have to confront irrational, chaotic forces. The *Book of the Dead* joins together two views of the afterlife— a chthonic underworld where Osiris, a deity who had died and been resurrected, presided and a stellar-solar realm where the blessed dead eventually hoped for an eternal celestial existence in the company of the sun god Ra. Once one entered the next world in the West or traveled with the god Ra below the horizon into the netherworld, one encountered the forces of primordial chaos and irrationality prevailed. Magical spells such as those in the *Book of the Dead* were considered the appropriate means for protecting the traveling soul against these dangers.

The key afterlife trial that everyone faced took the form of a judgment of one's soul on a set of scales like those the Egyptians used in their earthly existence. After the deceased had ritualistically denied a list of forty-two misdeeds, the so-called negative confession—his or her heart was put on one scale-pan, while a feather symbolizing the principle of Ma'at was placed on the other. According to this beautiful metaphor, one's heart had to be as light as a feather in relation to sin. Thereafter, one was deemed "true-of-voice" and worthy of an eternal existence. Despite this, dangers remained. The chief purpose of the *Book of the Dead* was to guide the deceased through those afterlife perils; one might draw an analogy with a traveler's guide to a foreign land. The *Book* provides for many eventualities yet not all of these would arise, nor was it expected that the various dangers would occur according to the sequence in which they appear on any given scroll.

*See also:* AFTERLIFE IN CROSS-CULTURAL PERSPECTIVE; CHARON AND THE RIVER STYX; MUMMIFICATION

### Bibliography

Faulkner, Raymond O. *The Ancient Egyptian Book of the Dead.* Austin: University of Texas Press, 1972.

Hornung, Erik. *The Ancient Egyptian Books of the Afterlife,* translated by David Lorton. Ithaca, NY: Cornell University Press, 1999.

Von Dassow, Eva, ed. *The Egyptian Book of the Dead: The Book of Going Forth by Day.* San Francisco, CA: Chronicle Books, 1994.

OGDEN GOELET JR.

# ELVIS SIGHTINGS

For decades following his death, reported sightings of Elvis Presley, the acclaimed "King of Rock and Roll," persist. As is the case with religious saints, it is Elvis's death day and not his birthday that receives ritual attention, attracting tens of thousands of individuals to Memphis, Tennessee, for Elvis Week. To understand his "immortality" one must know something of the man, his time, music, and the transcendence power of late-twentieth-century media celebritydom.

Death shaped Presley's fate from the moment of his birth in 1935, when his identical twin brother died in delivery. His parents—poor and originally from Mississippi—became extremely protective of their surviving son and supportive of his singing talents, which were nurtured in an Assembly of God choir and at church revivals. Following his graduation from a Memphis high school, Presley drove trucks during the day and took vocational classes at night. One day he happened across the Sun City recording studio, where he paid four dollars to cut two disks for his mother. Sun president Sam Phillips, looking for a Southern disc jockey, talent scout, and record producer long inspired by Memphis blues, happened to hear a copy of Presley's rendition of an Ink Spots song. Thus began a legendary career as he went on to record 149 songs that made it to *Billboard*'s Hot 100, spending more weeks at the top of the charts (eighty) than any other performer.

Presley's career coincided with the beginning of the rock and roll movement, which itself was part of a broader social phenomenon—an emerging teenage culture made possible by postwar prosperity. The rapidly developing recording and television industries saturated popular culture with his image and sounds at a time when the massive baby boom generation passed through childhood and adolescence. As baby boomers sought their generational identity, rock and roll became their identifying music and this singer their own icon (as Frank Sinatra was for the preceding generation). Presley's death at age forty-two shocked a generation often accused of never having had to grow up.

In adolescence and early adulthood this generation asserted itself by challenging the values and lifestyles of its parents, including their death taboos and denials. Boomer music was to develop a dark side with its associations with death, in its lyrics and in the untimely deaths of its performers, often because of "noble excess" (Pattison 1987, p. 123).

Thanatological (death-related) themes came to be embedded within the very names of the performing groups, such as the Grateful Dead and the Dead Kennedys.

Parodies of such connections between rock and death were inevitable. A decade before Presley's death there were rumors of Paul McCartney's demise, with some critics claiming that the intent was to increase sales of the first album released by the Beatles' Apple Records company. This coupled with the climate of conspiracy suspicions of the 1960s and 1970s supported beliefs that Elvis was not dead.

The music industry found death to be a formidable marketing tool, often inflating the value of deceased performers' works. During the late 1970s and early 1980s, the posthumous releases by dead rockers often outsold the recordings of the living. In 1983, nearly three decades after their release, seven of Presley's songs were among the top forty-nine best-selling singles, according to the Recording Industry Association of America.

Elvis sightings began almost immediately after his death from a drug overdose on August 16, 1977. There were many interests served and many places where he could be seen. In capitalist economies, particularly in the performing industries, one can now remain "alive" as long as one generates revenue. In the case of Presley, those having an interest in his immortalization included the city of Memphis, where the Presley home was one of the largest generators of tourist dollars; the Presley estate, which profited from rereleases, greatest hit anthologies, and reformattings of the singer's performances with new music technologies (e.g., stereo LPs to cassettes to CDs); and even the U.S. Postal Service, whose revenues were bolstered with the 1993 release of its Elvis stamp. For decades after his death, Elvis impersonators abounded, given a high demand for their appearances at various social and commercial functions for midlife boomers nostalgic for their youth. In 2000, according to the March 19, 2001, issue of *Forbes* magazine, Elvis was the king of deceased performers, earning $35 million for his estate, including $15 million from admissions to his Graceland mansion.

Americans really do not believe that Elvis is alive. A 1997 Gallup poll found that only 4 percent of Americans believed such was the case, whereas 93 percent were certain he was dead. So why the publicity given to reports to the contrary? The same poll found that nearly half of Americans still considered themselves "fans" of his twenty years after his demise, with the highest rate occurring among baby boomers. Two years later, the Gallup organization found that one-third of Americans viewed Presley as the greatest rock and roll performer of all time—six times the proportion of the second most-mentioned star. Indeed, Elvis "lives" in the American collective memory, particularly in that of baby boomers.

*See also:* CELEBRITY DEATHS; GRIEF AND MOURNING IN CROSS-CULTURAL PERSPECTIVE; IMMORTALITY, SYMBOLIC; ROYALTY, BRITISH

## Bibliography

Pattison, Robert. *The Triumph of Vulgarity: Rock Music in the Mirror of Romanticism.* New York: Oxford University Press, 1987.

### Internet Resources

Fong, Mei, and Debra Lau. "Earnings from the Crypt." In the *Forbes* [web site]. Available from www.forbes.com/2001/02/28/crypt.html.

MICHAEL C. KEARL

# EMBALMING

*See* FUNERAL INDUSTRY.

# EMERGENCY MEDICAL TECHNICIANS

The struggle between life and death is the fundamental responsibility of the Emergency Medical Services (EMS) professional; EMS systems provide a medical safety net for the public. Since the inception of the EMS profession, paramedics have received billions of calls from Americans in need of emergency care.

Each one of these calls generates a complex chain reaction that started in the 1960s. In the early 1970s, paramedics first appeared in the public eye when the series *Emergency* appeared on television. However, the development of the paramedic profession predates the television program by several years.

Before the 1960s, funeral home personnel were a major source of care given the sick and injured with the first ambulances doubling as hearses. Only a small number of ambulance services existed; and of these, only a few employed properly trained attendants. With the resurgence of mouth-to-mouth resuscitation in the 1950s and discovery of closed-chest cardiac massage in the 1960s, cardiopulmonary resuscitation (CPR) became available to professionals and lay persons. Consequently, public interest grew in the ambulance industry, and more people looked toward a career in the EMS profession.

In 1966 the National Academy of Science published a report entitled *Accidental Death and Disability: The Neglected Disease of Modern Society*. This paper shaped the future of the EMS profession by showing that trauma care could reduce morbidity and mortality. About the same time, Congress passed the Highway Safety Act of 1966. From this Act, the Department of Transportation (DOT) was created. The DOT improved EMS systems by designing and implementing standards for the training of all EMS providers. Additionally, Congress passed the Emergency Medical Services Act of 1973, making federal funds available to regional and local communities to develop EMS programs. With federal funds available, EMS systems grew dramatically in the 1970s.

Since the 1990s EMS professionals have become part of a complex multifaceted Emergency Medical Service System nested with the overall health-care system. EMS systems are "planned configurations of community resources and personnel necessary to provide immediate medical care to patients who have suffered sudden or unexpected illness or injury" (Henry and Stapleton 1992, p. 4). The attributes of EMS systems include integration of health services, legislation and regulation, system finance, human resources, medical direction, education systems, public education, prevention, public access, communication systems, clinical care, information systems, and evaluation.

## Types of EMS Providers

Many different levels of Emergency Medical Technicians (EMTs) exist in the United States; however, the DOT recognizes only four levels: first responder (FR), EMT-basic (EMT-B), EMT-intermediate (EMT-I), and EMT-paramedic (EMT-P). The EMT-B is the basic EMT level and provides skills such as CPR, bandaging, splinting, oxygen administration, and automatic external defibrillation. The EMT-intermediate (EMT-I) receives additional training beyond that of the EMT-B to include advanced airway and cardiac pacing. The paramedic (EMT-P) is the most skilled and, of all the EMTs, provides the most advanced prehospital care. First responders are the first individuals to arrive at the scene. First responders have a variety of credentials and function as assistants to other EMTs. During an emergency response, EMTs receive their medical direction from local emergency room physicians and previously established protocols.

## Training Standards, Roles, and Responsibilities of EMTs

The federal government provides standard curriculums for EMS professionals; however, each state sets the practice regulations and training standards for the different levels of EMS providers. Training standards did not exist until 1971, when the DOT published the first EMT national curriculum. The DOT approved the EMT-paramedic curriculum in 1976 and the EMT-intermediate curriculum in 1985. In general, the 1970s were an era of expansion for EMS training. Currently, the DOT is moving away from standardized curriculums and specific lesson plans to a more comprehensive and flexible education model. This model will use a less prescriptive method yet still employ a systems approach to integrate the following components: core content, scope of practice model, education standards, EMS certification, and education program accreditation.

The primary goal of the EMS system is to provide acute care; additional roles are accident and injury prevention, treatment of chronic conditions, and assisting in improvements to the overall health of the community. EMTs' responsibilities include scene assessment, emergency management, emergency transport, record keeping, and equipment and vehicle maintenance. However, an EMT's role is to save lives, to lessen pain, and to reduce the extent of disability. EMTs achieve these lofty goals

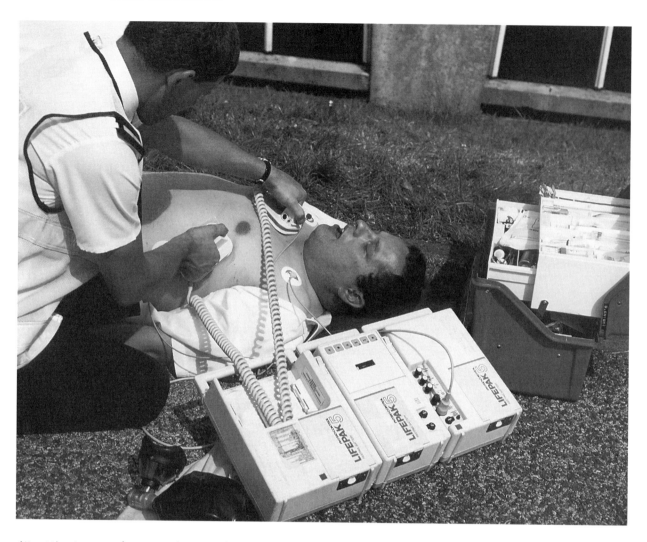

*Attempting to save a heart attack victim, this paramedic uses a defibrillator machine that applies an electric shock to restore a regular heartbeat.* PHOTO RESEARCHERS, INC.

by rapidly and safely treating and transporting the sick and injured.

## Challenges of Death

All EMS professionals must face death. The need for coming to terms with death is universal; death is part of an EMT's everyday duties. These professionals must not only learn how to respond to death, but also how to react to it and integrate it into everyday life. EMS professionals employ several strategies to control the stressful effects of death. The most frequently used defense mechanisms are educational desensitization, humor, language alteration, scientific fragmentation, escape into work, and rationalization. Many paramedics, when asked about their role, will respond that they hope to truly make a difference. One of the personality features common to EMS professionals is

altruism. Altruism provides them a special spot in the hearts of most Americans. "Always ready to serve others in time of need, the paramedic has become a most respected person in contemporary America" (Page 1979, p. 49).

The second challenge for EMS providers is the public perception of paramedics as lifesavers. Most of society anticipates that a paramedic will save the life of their loved one. Television programs such as *Emergency* and *Rescue 911* perpetuate these views by portraying paramedics as lifesaving heroes, as robbers of death. As the medical community increases the chances of surviving death, the public will expect the EMS profession to provide similar results.

Third, the primary death-related training afforded to EMS professionals is often inadequate.

EMS programs train paramedics to recognize the technical aspects of death with only a minimal amount of instruction covering the psychological or social aspects of death. Furthermore, this training often does not cover helping families at the moment of death or issues unique to prehospital death. The National Curriculum for Paramedics provides only a few grief-related objectives based on Elisabeth Kübler-Ross's stages of dying. There are no objectives specific to making death notifications or handling postmortem arrangements with newly bereaved persons. Because paramedics receive limited training in cultural and religious sensitivity, cultural and religious diversity further hinder a paramedic's ability to provide immediate support to the bereaved. The paucity of training may contribute to paramedics who feel that conversations with bereaved persons are problematic, stressful, and uncomfortable. Furthermore, conversations with bereaved persons may be harder for paramedics who have not come to terms with their own mortality.

The prehospital environment in which EMS professionals practice creates many obstacles during incidents involving death. When EMS professionals respond to an emergency, they request the right of way with their lights and sirens; consequently, they increase the risk for accidents and injury. After arriving on scene, EMTs provide care with limited equipment (compared to hospitals), with the public looking on, in adverse weather conditions, in hostile environments, and at all hours of the day and night. It is a formidable task to resuscitate a patient under these circumstances, yet EMTs do this every day as a routine part of their daily work. Death from AIDS and SIDS or deaths involving young children, coworkers, and other public service professionals (e.g., police officers) also aggravate the stress associated with responding to a death.

Legalities surrounding death also pose hurdles for EMTs. In the 1980s the greatest legal challenge for the EMS community was determining when to start CPR. This issue challenged not only the EMS profession but also the medical community as a whole. Initially, EMS providers started resuscitation on all patients, even if this conflicted with the patient's wishes or the personal views of the paramedic. For example, in the early 1980s, many terminally ill patients went home to die, but when the family called the paramedics to pronounce death,

the paramedics arrived and resuscitated the patient. The lack of Do Not Resuscitate (DNR) protocols required EMTs to do their best to bring these patients back to life. This duty often came at an emotional expense to the EMTs who responded to the incident, as well as to the families of the victims. By 2000 every U.S. state had its own Do Not Resuscitate protocol for EMTs. Despite these protocols, EMTs still resuscitate terminally ill patients. Many terminally ill patients are unaware of their local EMS agencies' policies to not recognize living wills and require official EMS-DNR forms.

In the early 1990s most EMS systems were challenged to create new guidelines for EMS providers detailing when to stop CPR and other resuscitative actions. Despite common social belief, most cardiac-arrest patients die. The medical community now recognizes the enormous impact of cardiac-arrest patients on the health care system. These patients require precious EMS resources, often at the expense of other less critically ill patients. Through research and experience, doctors can identify which patients are viable patients and separate them from patients with no chance of survival. Paramedics declare death and stop CPR on the nonviable patients while still providing the most aggressive treatment for those patients who may have a chance to survive. Pronouncing death, EMS professionals provide the initial psychosocial support for newly bereaved families. Providing this support and mitigating the traumatic effects of death to the families is another area where EMS professionals truly make a difference.

*See also:* DEATH EDUCATION; FUNERAL INDUSTRY; RESUSCITATION; TERRORIST ATTACKS ON AMERICA

## Bibliography

Boyd, David R., Richard F. Edlich, and Sylvia Micik. *Systems Approach to Emergency Medical Care.* East Norwalk, CT: Prentice-Hall, 1983.

Henry, Mark C., and Edward R. Stapleton. *EMT: Prehospital Care.* Philadelphia: W.B. Saunders, 1992.

Kuehl, Alexander E., ed. *EMS Medical Director's Handbook.* St. Louis, MO: C. V. Mosby, 1989.

Jones, Shirley, Al Weigel, Roger D. White, Norman E. McSwain, and Marti Brieter *Advanced Emergency Care for Paramedic Practice.* Philadelphia: J. B. Lippincott, 1992.

Norton, Robert L., Edward A. Bartkus, Terri A. Schmidt, Jan D. Paquette, John C. Moorhead, and Jerris R.

Hedges. "Survey of Emergency Medical Technicians' Ability to Cope with the Deaths of Patients During Prehospital Care." *Prehospital and Disaster Medicine* 7 (2000):235–242.

Page, James O. *Paramedics.* Morristown, NJ: Backdraft Publications, 1979.

Palmer, C. Eddie. "A Note about Paramedics' Strategies for Dealing with Death and Dying." *Journal of Occupational Psychiatry* 53 (1983):83–86.

Smith, Tracy L., and Bruce J. Walz. "Death Education in U.S. Paramedic Programs: A Nationwide Assessment." *Death Studies* 19 (1995):257–267.

United States Department of Transportation, National Highway Safety Administration and United States Department of Health and Human Services, Health Resources Administration, Maternal and Child Health Bureau. *Emergency Medical Services Agenda for the Future.* Washington, DC: Author, 1996.

United States Department of Transportation, National Highway Safety Administration and Department of Health and Human Services, Health Resources Administration, Maternal and Child Health Bureau. *Emergency Medical Technician–Paramedic: National Standard Curriculum (EMT-P).* Washington, DC: Author, 1996.

Walz, Bruce J. *Introduction to EMS Systems.* Albany, NY: Delmar, 2002.

TRACY L. SMITH

# EMPATHY AND COMPASSION

The word *compassion* comes from Latin and means "to bear with" or "to suffer with." Compassion and empathy are essential human qualities that allow one to feel, understand, and respond to the suffering of others. They enable individuals to enter into and maintain relationships of caring. The ability to care has been identified by Martin Heidegger as a fundamental aspect of the human condition. In every society the sick and the dying have been treated with compassionate care. This is a universal human response. Many of the world's major religions hold compassion as one of the highest spiritual virtues.

Dynamic compassion, or *Ahimsa* in Hinduism, is known as the God quality within a person. It is an open-hearted active response of respect, service, and care for those in need. It was a prime

aspect of Gandhi's nonviolent liberation movement. Compassion is also a central tenet of Buddhism. The Buddha manifested absolute compassion for all creation. Buddhist compassion, or *karuna,* is seen as the appropriate human response to understanding the interdependence and mutual welfare of all beings. In the Judeo-Christian tradition, compassion is a manifestation of God's love and mercy. It is the way God interacts with creation and is, therefore, the way people should interact with one another. In all of these spiritual traditions, directly addressing the suffering of others through compassionate care is a religious obligation. In such responses we can see the hallmark of our shared humanity.

To have compassion or to "suffer with" another implies a quality of imagination and an identifying with the other's pain as something we can vicariously feel along with them, however tangentially. Compassion is an active choice to want with others and to want for others the alleviation of their suffering. In acting compassionately we acknowledge that we all share the same conditions of mortality; we all suffer and we all die.

*Empathy* derives from a Greek root word meaning, "in feeling" or "feeling into." A component of compassion, empathy is the recognition and understanding of the other's suffering. It is a deep appreciation for what it is truly like to be in the other's situation from his or her perspective. Empathy requires an openness to receiving and holding the other's experience without reservation or judgment. Empathy is passive but absolutely attentive. It involves entering into and staying present in the painful experience of the other without moving away from that experience by trying to change it. Empathy establishes a deep connection of mutual vulnerability and intimacy.

The dying are often subject to feelings of isolation, loneliness, and helplessness. Some of their suffering can be ameliorated by the strong sense of connection to the other that empathy brings. For the caregiver as well, an empathetic connection to another person nearing the end of life can offer the gratification of a uniquely intimate relationship.

Compassion encompasses empathy. Empathy is that aspect of compassion that opens one to a deep understanding of the other's suffering. Compassion also involves an active concern for and effort to alleviate that suffering. That is why compassion is sometimes called "love in action" by Mother Teresa. Compassionate action is a willingness to go beyond self-interest and give of oneself for the good of the other. In this regard it is similar to altruism, letting go of one's own needs to attend to the needs of another so that one can meet one's own deepest need: to feel a part of a larger shared humanity.

Compassion is a key aspect of care of the dying. K. R. Eissler, in his seminal work on caring for the dying, *The Psychiatrist and the Dying Patient* (1955), sets the tone when he advises caregivers to give themselves selflessly to the dying as a free gift of love. Other researchers and those writing from their personal experience of being with the dying have echoed Eissler's advice.

A terminal illness deepens one's need for empathy and compassion in physicians and caregivers. Unfortunately, it has often been found that it is just at this stage that physicians, family, friends, and caregivers can emotionally distance themselves from the dying. Those attending and caring for the dying, in such cases, have the opportunity to receive from them. By being open, empathetically present, and compassionate, they can themselves be healed in their humanity and experience the gift of an extraordinary intimacy.

Compassionately attending to the dying is often deeply rewarding. Elisabeth Kübler-Ross felt that a loving and caring commitment to the dying would help heal the isolation and division that is so destructive in modern life. She saw such commitment as helping to build broader forms of commitment within society that would benefit all of humanity. In being open and compassionately present to the dying, caregivers share the burden of suffering and of anticipatory grief with them. They also share with the dying the solidarity of their committed relationship together and the joy that intimacy can bring. This is what Stephen Levine (1979) calls the experiences of "cosmic humor" in their last journey together.

Someone mourning the death of an acquaintance, friend, or loved one also needs the support of compassionate care and the empathetic presence of others. Cultural and religious rituals of dying, death, and mourning can help one find meaning and comfort in loss. Compassion and empathy are gifts that people can share throughout their lives.

*See also:* COMMUNICATION WITH THE DYING; HINDUISM; KÜBLER-ROSS, ELISABETH; LESSONS FROM THE DYING; MOURNING; SYMPATHY CARDS

### Bibliography

Eissler, Kurt Robert. *The Psychiatrist and the Dying Patient*. New York: International University Press, 1955.

Heidegger, Martin. *Being and Time*. New York: Harper & Row, 1962.

Kübler-Ross, Elisabeth. *Death, the Final Stage of Growth*. New York: Simon & Schuster, 1975.

Levine, Stephen. *A Gradual Awakening*. Garden City, NY: Anchor Books, 1979.

Mother Teresa. *A Gift From God*. San Francisco: Harper & Row, 1975.

Owens, Dorothy M. *Hospitality to Strangers: Empathy and the Physician-Patient Relationship*. Atlanta: Scholars Press, 1999.

Sapp, Gary L. ed. *Compassionate Ministry*. Birmingham, AL: Religious Education Press, 1993.

Van Zyl, Liezl. *Death and Compassion*. Burlington, VT: Ashgate, 2000.

THOMAS B. WEST

# END-OF-LIFE ISSUES

Before the 1950s, end-of-life decisions were simpler than they are today. Most people died in their own homes, surrounded by family and loved ones. Illnesses such as scarlet fever, cholera, measles, diarrhea, influenza, pneumonia, and gastritis killed quickly. Medical science had not yet learned how to keep people with such chronic diseases as heart disease and cancer alive. Lifesaving technology, such as respirators and feeding tubes, was not available. Nature, not medicine, controlled the timing of one's death.

This began to change in the 1950s as medical technology increasingly became able to thwart death through an array of technical tools that could keep hearts beating, bodies nourished, and lungs breathing despite the ravages of disease, illness, and time. Advances in pharmacology and other medical procedures made it possible to prolong the life of even the seriously ill. Lengthened lives, however, did not always mean quality lives. On the extreme end of the spectrum, it meant that patients existing in a persistent vegetative state could be kept alive for an indeterminate time. Other patients, while conscious, were debilitated and in pain, confined to bed and dependent on machines, for weeks, months, and even years. When the end did come, it was usually in a hospital room. Unlike in the past, when only a third of patients died in medical institutions, in the early twenty-first century four out of five patients died in institutions such as hospitals and nursing homes. Instead of embracing the phalanx of medical machinery that could forestall death, these patients and their families began to focus on the quality of death rather than the prolongation of life.

## Defining Death

In direct response to the development of life-sustaining technologies, the medical profession began to expand the definition of death. Traditionally, the loss of circulatory and respiratory function signaled death. But with the advent of technology that could sustain breathing and heart functioning through mechanical means this definition became less useful. A new definition that incorporated brain death—the irreversible loss of brain activity—into the definition of death was proposed and adopted. This meant life supports could be removed from those patients who were brain dead but were being kept alive through mechanical means. Still controversial is whether the definition of death should be expanded further to include those patients who have lost their higher brain functions but who continue to have lower brain functions, such as breathing. This new definition of death would include people who can no longer interact with their environment but are not totally brain dead.

However, medical definitions did not address the many spiritual, ethical, and legal questions that arose. Should patients be able to hasten their own death by refusing a respirator, feeding tube, or other life supports? If patients are unable to decide, should others be able to decide for them? If so, who should make the decision—family members, medical professionals, or both? Does it matter if the patient is young or old? What if the individual is not terminally ill, but severely and chronically ill? Is there a difference between refusing life supports and asking for medical intervention that would hasten death?

These and other questions spawned a national dialogue on the quality of death and the rights of dying patients. A physician, Elisabeth Kübler-Ross, in the classic text, *On Death and Dying,* explored the stages of death for both the dying and the bereaved. Medical ethicists, such as Robert Veatch and Tom Beauchamp, began exploring the ethical issues involved. A presidential commission was appointed to study the ethical problems in deciding to forgo life-sustaining treatment.

## *Quinlan* Case

It was the legal system, however, that provided the primary guidance on how to address the knotty problems that accompanied the advent of life-sustaining technologies. The first case involving what is now referred to as the "right to die" was the Karen Ann Quinlan case, decided by the New Jersey Supreme Court in 1976. Quinlan was twenty-one when, while attending a party, she stopped breathing, for unknown reasons, for at least two fifteen-minute intervals. She was brought to a hospital where she slipped into a coma. She was unable to talk or see and was kept alive by a respirator and fed through a feeding tube. Her physicians predicted that she would never regain consciousness. Her father, a devout Catholic, asked her physician to disconnect her respirator. When the doctors and hospital refused to honor the request, Quinlan's father turned to the courts for assistance.

Quinlan's physician argued that because she was not brain dead, both medical standards and ethics required him to continue treating her, with the respirator being part of that treatment. The government also intervened, arguing that the state's interest in protecting the sanctity of life must be protected and that removing the respirator was tantamount to criminal homicide.

The New Jersey Supreme Court rejected both arguments, deciding that Quinlan's right to privacy, protected by the Constitution, was violated when her physician and the hospital refused to remove the respirator. Although the court recognized that the state had an interest in preserving life, it found that interest "weaken[ed] and the individual's right to privacy [grew] as the degree of bodily invasion increases and the prognosis dims." The court also rejected the idea that the medical profession was required to use all means at its disposal to keep patients alive. Rather, the "focal point of the decision [to terminate treatment] was whether the patient would return to a 'cognitive and sapient life' or remain in a 'biological vegetative existence.'"

As to who could make the decision to remove life supports because Quinlan was unable to, the court held that it could be her father. Practically, according to the court, Quinlan's right to privacy would be rendered meaningless unless her father could exercise it on her behalf. Central to the court's decision was its belief that Quinlan's father was of "high character" and very "sincere, moral, ethical, and religious." The court rejected the argument that her father's grief and anguish would distort his decision-making process, making him unable to make life-and-death decisions concerning his daughter. Quinlan was removed from the respirator, and to the surprise of her physicians and family she did not die until nine years later.

### Cruzan Case

The *Quinlan* decision, issued by the New Jersey Supreme Court, was applicable only in that state. But it became the template for later court decisions and helped frame the social, legal, and policy issues underlying the right to die. Fourteen years later, the U.S. Supreme Court, in *Cruzan* v. *Director, Missouri Department of Health,* directly addressed the issue. *Cruzan* involved a young woman in a persistent vegetative state who had suffered severe brain damage in an automobile accident and had no hope of recovery. Nancy Cruzan was being kept alive by artificial hydration and nutrition that her parents wanted withdrawn. The Court found that the Fourteenth Amendment to the Constitution, which provides that persons may not be deprived of their liberty without due process of law, included a liberty interest in refusing heroic medical measures. The Court also relied on a common-law tradition that recognizes the right of individuals to control their own body, thus requiring that they consent before anyone, including a physician, touched them. The Court also

found that withholding food or water was no different than withholding other forms of life supports, such as a respirator, would be.

Unlike the court in the *Quinlan* case, however, the Supreme Court did not find Cruzan's parents capable of making the decision to withdraw hydration and nutrition from their daughter. What was important to the Court was not what the parents wanted, but what the daughter would have wanted if she were able to decide for herself. Under Missouri law, where Cruzan lived, clear and convincing evidence of the patient's wishes regarding life support was required. For that evidence, the Court looked back to statements made by Cruzan, which included comments made to a housemate about a year before her accident that she would not want to live should she face life as a "vegetable." The Court did not find that these statements satisfied the clear and convincing standard, and it refused to grant her parents' wish to terminate life supports.

### Determining Patients' Interests

Thus, while the *Cruzan* case established a constitutionally protected "right to die," it also highlighted the difficulty in applying that right. Many people on life supports are unable to communicate their wishes. Past statements, often made in the course of casual conversation, may not be specific or serious enough. There is the risk that a decision made while healthy may not be the same decision one would make when ill. And while the law does not distinguish between withholding food and withdrawing a respirator, a patient might want to. Questions also arose about whether to distinguish between persons who were terminally ill and those suffering from severe and chronic illnesses that were not imminently life threatening.

Leaving it to the family to accurately reflect the patient's interests also has its pitfalls. As the Court in *Cruzan* said, "even where family members are present, [t]here will, of course, be some unfortunate situations in which family members will not act to protect a patient." Expense and inconvenience may cause family members to advocate for the termination of life supports. Religious views may also differ within families, with, for example, a religiously devout parent resisting the preferences of a more secular child. On the other hand, it is often the family who best knows the patient and who has the patient's best interests at heart.

*Advance directives.* The response to many of these dilemmas was to encourage people, both through law and custom, to clearly record their preferences while they were still able to make those decisions. All fifty states have passed laws, referred to as Natural Death Acts, clarifying the right to refuse life-sustaining treatment. These laws provide for various forms of advance directives, which are statements, usually in writing, that outline an individual's end-of-life preferences. It includes a living will, which is a written statement expressing a person's willingness, or not, to accept life-sustaining technology. Another form of advance directive is a health care proxy, which is a written statement that delegates decision making to another individual when the patient is no longer competent. Many states also have Do Not Resuscitate laws, which govern a narrowly tailored type of advance directive that permits patients to refuse cardiopulmonary resuscitation if they suffer cardiac arrest. States have also passed laws that provide for the appointment of a surrogate decision maker (usually a family member), who is designated to make health care decisions when the patient has failed to complete an advance directive. These laws typically require the surrogate to consider the values and beliefs of the patient.

*Bioethics and other issues.* The medical profession has also responded, setting up hospital bioethics committees that establish policies and advise health professionals, patients, and their families of their rights and alternatives. Despite these laws, and the existence of bioethics committees, problems still remain. It is estimated that only one out of five adults has completed an advance directive. This means, as in the *Cruzan* case, that the patient's preferences must be ascertained, if possible, from past statements, unless the state has a law providing for a surrogate decision-maker to be appointed. For those who have executed advance directives, it may be too vague or ambiguous to be of use. Distraught family members may also try to persuade physicians not to follow a patient's preference for the withdrawal of life supports.

Other issues have also emerged as the right to die has become more firmly established. Evidence indicates that physicians sometimes ignore a patient's advance directive, administering life supports when the patient does not want them. This may be because they are unaware of the directive or do not agree with it. This has spawned a new type of legal action that attempts to recover monetary damages from the physician or health care provider for, in essence, keeping the patient alive against his or her will. Several of these lawsuits have been successful, but the law is still evolving in this area. Another emerging area of concern is whether a health care system focused on cost cutting and rationing of medical services under managed care will discourage patients from choosing expensive life-sustaining technology. Here, the issue may be who decides—the patient or the physician—whether such intervention is futile or inappropriate.

## Assisted Suicide and Euthanasia

Whether the right to die should be extended to a more active role in hastening death, such as physician-assisted suicide, is also a controversial issue. Physician-assisted suicide is when a physician provides medications or other interventions to a patient to enable the patient to commit suicide. Proponents of assisted suicide have argued that there is no distinction between ceasing or not accepting medical treatment and taking affirmative steps to hasten death. They contend that the right to control one's own body means the right to control one's death, with the help of others if necessary. Opponents argue that permitting assisted suicide is a slippery slope, and that the right to die will turn into the "duty to die." They contend that the old and infirm will feel an obligation to hasten their death because of the burden they create on society. The U.S. Supreme Court, in the 1997 case of *Vacco* v. *Quill,* has held that there is no constitutional right to assisted suicide. This does not mean, however, that states cannot pass laws legalizing assisted suicide. One state, Oregon, has already done so, passing the Death with Dignity Act in 1994.

Still more controversial is euthanasia, or "mercy killing." Voluntary active euthanasia involves one person asking another to cause the first person's death by, for example, administering a lethal injection. Such an act was not legal at the start of the twenty-first century, although many people supported the honoring of a terminally ill person's request for voluntary active euthanasia. Involuntary active euthanasia means ending patients' lives without their consent. There is little or no public support for this type of euthanasia.

## Wills and Estates

Another less controversial, and more routine, category of end-of-life decisions is how property is disposed of when someone dies. This area of law, commonly referred to as "wills and estates," is carefully regulated. A will is a written document that provides for the disposition of all of a person's property upon the person's death. An *estate* is the legal term used for this property. Without a will, state law determines how the property will be distributed. A surviving spouse gets half, while the children get the other half. Wills cannot be made by persons who have become *incompetent,* a legal term referring to persons who are unable to manage their own affairs because they cannot communicate or are suffering from other cognitive or psychological impairments. Thus, like advance directives, wills should be completed and updated before a person becomes ill or incompetent.

Decisions at the end of life have become more complex as modern technology conflicts with people's desire to die a more natural death. While a patient's right to refuse life-sustaining medical interventions is firmly embedded in the law, the full contours of this right are still evolving. Individual values of autonomy and self-determination must be balanced with medical progress and the government's interest in protecting life.

*See also:* ADVANCE DIRECTIVES; CRUZAN, NANCY; DEFINITIONS OF DEATH; INFORMED CONSENT; LIVING WILL; NATURAL DEATH ACTS; QUINLAN, KAREN ANN; SUICIDE TYPES: PHYSICIAN-ASSISTED SUICIDE; WILLS AND INHERITANCE

### *Bibliography*

Beauchamp, Tom L., and Robert M. Veatch, eds. *Ethical Issues in Death and Dying,* 2nd edition. Upper Saddle River, NJ: Prentice Hall, 1996.

Bove, Alexander. *The Complete Guide to Wills, Estates, and Trusts.* New York: Henry Holt, 2000.

Danis, Marion, Leslie I. Southerland, Joanne M. Garrett, Janet L. Smith, Frank Hielema, C. Glenn Pickard, David M. Egner, and Donald L. Patrick. "A Prospective Study of Advance Directives for Life-Sustaining Care." *New England Journal of Medicine* 324 (1991):882–888.

Florencio, Patrik S., and Robert H. Keller. "End-of-Life Decision Making: Rethinking the Principles of Fundamental Justice in the Context of Emerging Empirical Data." *Health Law Journal* 7 (1999):233–258.

Furrow, Barry R., Thomas L. Greaney, Sandra H. Johnson, Timothy Stoltzfus Jost, and Robert L. Schwartz. *Health Law.* St. Paul, MN: West Publishing, 1995.

Glasson, John. "Report of the Council on Ethical and Judicial Affairs of the American Medical Association: Physician-Assisted Suicide." *Issues in Law and Medicine* 10 (1994):91–97.

Humphry, Derek, and Mary Clement. *Freedom to Die: People, Politics, and the Right to Die Movement.* New York: St. Martin's Press, 1998.

Keigher, Sharon. "Patient Rights and Dying: Policy Restraint and the States." *Health and Social Work* 19 (1994):298–306.

Kübler-Ross, Elisabeth. *On Death and Dying.* New York: Macmillan, 1969.

Lens, Vicki, and Daniel Pollack. "Advance Directives: Legal Remedies and Psychosocial Interventions." *Death Studies* 24 (2000):377–399.

Meisel, Alan. *The Right to Die.* New York: Wiley Law, 1995.

Mizrahi, Terry. "The Direction of Patient's Rights in the 1990s: Proceed with Caution." *Health and Social Work* 28 (1992):246–252.

Nolfi, Edward A. *Basic Wills, Trusts, and Estates.* New York: Glencoe Division Macmillan/McGraw Hill, 1994.

Orentlicher, David. "Trends in Health Care Decision Making: The Limits of Legislation." *Maryland Law Review* 53 (1994):1,255–1,305.

Powell, John A., and Adam S. Cohen. "The Right to Die." *Issues in Law and Medicine* 10 (1994):169–182.

President's Commission for the Study of Ethical Problems in Medicine and Biomedical and Behavioral Research. *Deciding to Forgo Life-Sustaining Treatment.* Washington, DC: U.S. Government Printing Office, 1983.

Scherer, Jennifer M., and Rita James Simon. *Euthanasia and the Right to Die: A Comparative View.* Lanham, MD: Rowman & Littlefield, 1999.

Silveira, Maria J., Albert DiPiero, Martha S. Gerrity, and Chris Feudtner. "Patients' Knowledge of Options at the End of Life: Ignorance in the Face of Death." *Journal of the American Medical Association* 284 (2000):2,483–2,488.

Teno, Joan, Joanne Lynn, Neil Wenger, Russell S. Phillips, Donald P. Murphy, Alfred F. Connors, Norman Desbiens, William Fulkerson, Paul Bellamy, and William A. Knaus. "Advance Directives for Seriously Ill Hospitalized Patients: Effectiveness with the Patient Self-Determination Act and the Support Intervention." *Journal of the American Geriatrics Society* 45 (1995):500–507.

VICKI LENS

# EPICURUS

Should we fear death? A very famous argument of why we should not was offered some 2,300 years ago by the philosopher Epicurus. Epicurus (341–271 B.C.E.) authored around 300 scrolls, but only three letters and a few fragments have survived, being passed down in a biography by Diogenes Laertius four centuries after Epicurus's death. Born of Athenian parents and raised on the island colony of Samos, Epicurus was introduced to philosophy as a teenager when he encountered followers of Plato and Democritus. Democritus's philosophy was to have a lasting effect on Epicurus's mature thinking. In 306 B.C.E., Epicurus began his own school in an area known as the "Garden." The school was unique in accepting women and even slaves—a point ridiculed by aristocratic critics. The school flourished and soon rivaled the established Academy (founded by Plato) and Lyceum (founded by Aristotle). Students came to deeply revere Epicurus, who became known for cultivating friendship. After his death, they began to celebrate his life with monthly feasts. His ideas spread quickly and with profound effects. The Roman poet Lucretius (95–55 B.C.E.) espouses Epicurean philosophy in his "On the Nature of Things."

Epicurus was interested in how one could achieve happiness. He believed that unhappiness is a kind of "disturbance in the mind," caused by irrational beliefs, desires, and fears. Among human desires, he argued, some are "natural and necessary," others are "vain." Among the vain are desires for a life of luxury and indulgence. This fuels the myth that epicureanism condones the maxim, "Eat, drink, and be merry." Although Epicurus was the father of hedonism (from the Greek word *hedone,* meaning "pleasure"), he did not encourage every kind of pleasure, as expressed in his *Letter to Menoeceus*: "We do not mean the pleasures of profligates and those that consist in sensuality . . . but freedom from pain in the body and trouble in the mind." The chief pleasure sought after was pleasure of the mind—tranquility (*ataraxia*)—which can be produced by "banishing mere opinions to which are due the greatest disturbance of spirit" (Bailey 1926, p. 127ff). Epicurus concentrated on two fears: the gods and death. How can these fears be banished as irrational and vain?

Arguing in his *Principal Doctrines* that "without natural science it is not possible to attain our pleasures unalloyed" (Bailey 1926, p. 97), he turned to Democritus's atomism, which held that the universe and everything in it is the product of accidental forces and composed of small bits of matter called atoms (*atomoi*). Epicurus accepted this as a reasonable explanation of life, and also saw in it the solution to human fears. As he puts forth in his *Letter,* in death the subject simply ceases to exist (the atoms are dispersed) and is therefore touched neither by the gods nor the experience of death itself:

> . . . death is nothing to us. For all good and evil consists in sensation, but death is deprivation of sensation. And therefore a right understanding that death is nothing to us makes the mortality of life enjoyable, not because it adds to it an infinite span of time, but because it takes away the craving for immortality. For there is nothing terrible in life for the man who has truly comprehended that there is nothing terrible in not living. [Death] does not then concern either the living or the dead, since for the former it is not, and the latter are no more. *(Bailey 1926, pp. 124–125)*

Many scholars have objected to this argument by noting that it is often the anticipation of death, not the event itself, that disturbs humankind. For example, the scholar Warren Shibles points out that Epicurus's argument amounts to showing that "we cannot fear the state of death because we will not be conscious after death. But we certainly can fear losing consciousness" (Shibles 1974, p. 38). But Epicurus would most likely reply, as he did to similar concerns, "That which gives no trouble when it comes, is but an empty pain in anticipation" (Bailey 1926, pp. 124–125).

*See also:* PHILOSOPHY, WESTERN; PLATO; SOCRATES

*Bibliography*

Epicurus. "Letter to Menoeceus." In *Epicurus: The Extant Remains,* translated by Cyril Bailey. Oxford: Clarendon Press, 1926.

Epicurus. *Prinicpal Doctrines.* In *Epicurus: The Extant Remains,* translated by Cyril Bailey. Oxford: Clarendon Press, 1926.

Shibles, Warren. *Death: An Interdisciplinary Analysis.* Madison, WI: The Language Press, 1974.

WILLIAM COONEY

# EPITAPHS

For hundreds if not thousands of years, the epitaph has been a significant part of the death ritual. Before the development of written language and adequate tools for carving, the grave was marked with such items as sticks and rocks. In his *Death and Dying in Central Appalachia* (1994), the scholar James K. Crissman notes that in the first one hundred years of Central Appalachian society, marking a grave using any form of language involved taking a sharp-pointed rock and carving the initials of the deceased on another rock. Most likely, this was the way the first human societies expressed themselves when they developed the ability to use language symbols.

Archaeological evidence and written and pictorial records show that memorials were an important part of ancient societies such as the Egyptians, Greeks, and Romans. The Greeks used eight forms of grave markers including round columns, rectangular slabs, stelae (carved or inscribed stones), shrine-shaped stones, huge rectangular stone blocks, marble vases, square or round receptacles for cremains, and sarcophagi (stone coffins) (Bardis 1981). Many of these early societies employed sepulchral iconography or the use of beautiful, elaborate, and detailed scenes or panoramas portraying the life of the decedent, as well as written inscriptions such as "farewell" (Crissman 1994).

The epitaph, or inscription at a grave or memorial in memory of someone deceased, exists for a variety of reasons and in a multiplicity of forms. While the use of epitaphs predates the modern era, the French thanatologist Philippe Ariès states that "the practice of marking the exact site of a grave by means of an inscription did not become widespread until the end of the eighteenth century" (Ariès 1982, p.78).

Grave markings usually act to provide information about the deceased, to memorialize, and to relay a message to the living. In the twenty-first century most tombstones contain some sort of biographical information about the deceased, including the name of the decedent, the date of birth, and the date of death. In addition to this information, many markers include an inscription in verse or prose upon a marker. There is clearly a memorial aspect contained in some epitaphs. For instance, the grave of the American reformer Susan B. Anthony states, "Liberty, Humanity, Justice, Equality" and epitaphs of soldiers killed in war often include lines such as, "He gave his life for his country" or "Who died in the service of his country." Another function of epitaphs is to attempt the establishment of symbolic immortality by relaying a message to the living. One of the more famous epitaphs states:

Remember friend as you passby
As you are now so once was I.
As I am now you will surely be
Prepare thyself to follow me.
*(Gazis-Sax 2001, p.1)*

Depending on the culture in which the deceased lived, the epitaph can take on several forms, ranging from the religious to the humorous. Some of the most common epitaphs contain only one line such as, "Gone but not forgotten," "Rest in peace," and "In remembrance of." Many epitaphs contain a religious theme emphasizing comfort and future reunions in heaven. Some examples of these include, "Precious Lord take my hand," "Prepare to meet me in Heaven," and "The Lord is my Shepherd I shall not want." In contrast to the religious messages, humorous epitaphs focus more on the manner of death, or relationships with the living, such as, "I told you I was sick," "Gone, but not forgiven," and "Here lies a father of twenty-nine, he would have had more but didn't have time." (Spiegl 1982).

The practice of using long epitaphs, whether religious or humorous, has not been as widely practiced in the United States as it has been in Europe. Furthermore, twenty-first-century epitaphs are much simpler than those of the past. Even though the practice of lengthy epitaphs has fallen

This stone epitaph for St. Monica, in the Museo di Antichitá, Ostia, Italy, is one method used to mark graves—a practice that dates to ancient times. PUBLIC DOMAIN

out of favor, there is still the desire to have some information about the deceased. For example, a computer engineer has developed a solar-powered headstone with a sensor. When a visitor approaches the headstone, a recording device and a video display screen are utilized to reflect biographical information, a genealogy, and/or words of admonition, along with pictures of the deceased (Gumpert 1987). Although, in general, such technology is still unused, there are other ways in which technology continues to influence the use of epitaphs. There are numerous web sites that offer help writing a meaningful epitaph for those who are planning ahead, or want to memorialize a loved one or pet. Another future use of epitaphs is a web site where messages can be stored on the Internet and accessed only after the death of the

writer. All of these new forms of epitaphs help provide information about the deceased, memorialize their lives, and relay messages to the living.

*See also:* CEMETERIES AND CEMETERY REFORM; FUNERAL ORATIONS AND SERMONS; MEMORIAL, VIRTUAL

### Bibliography

Ariès, Philippe. *The Hour of Our Death*. New York: Vintage Books, 1982.

Bardis, Panos D. *History of Thantology*. Washington, DC: University Press of America, 1981.

Crissman, James K. *Death and Dying in Central Appalachia*. Urbana: University of Illinois Press, 1994.

Gumpert, Gary. *Talking Tombstones and Other Tales of the Media Age*. New York: Oxford University Press, 1987.

Rodabaugh, Tillman. *Death and Dying: A Social-Psychological Perspective*. Waco, TX: Baylor University, 1991.

Spiegl, Fritz. *Dead Funny: Another Book of Grave Humor*. London: Pan Books, 1982.

*Internet Resources*

Gazis-Sax, Joel. "The Epitaph Browser." In the City of the Silent [web site]. Available from www.alsirat.com/epitaphs/index.html.

JAMES K. CRISSMAN
JOHNETTA M. WARD

# EUGENICS

*See* BIOETHICS; BLACK STORK.

# EUTHANASIA

The word *euthanasia* translates from Greek roots as "good death." The *Oxford English Dictionary* states that the original meaning, "a gentle and easy death," has evolved to mean "the actions of inducing a gentle and easy death." This definition is consistent with contemporary use of the term. For example, the Canadian Senate Special Committee on Euthanasia and Assisted Suicide defined euthanasia as "the deliberate act undertaken by one person with the intention of ending the life of another person in order to relieve that person's suffering where that act is the cause of death" (Senate of Canada 1995, p. 15). Euthanasia is generally classified in terms of certain subcategories, depending upon whether or not the person who dies by euthanasia is considered to be competent or incompetent and whether or not the act of euthanasia is considered to be voluntary, nonvoluntary, or involuntary.

## Definitions of Euthanasia

Euthanasia is considered to be *voluntary* when it takes place in accordance with the wishes of a competent individual, whether these wishes have been made known personally or by a valid advance directive—that is, a written statement of the person's future desires in the event that he or she should be unable to communicate his or her intentions in the future. A person is considered to be competent if he or she is deemed capable of understanding the nature and consequences of the decisions to be made and capable of communicating this decision. An example of voluntary euthanasia is when a physician gives a lethal injection to a patient who is competent and suffering, at that patient's request.

*Nonvoluntary* euthanasia is done without the knowledge of the wishes of the patient either because the patient has always been incompetent, is now incompetent, or has left no advance directive. A person is considered incompetent when he or she is incapable of understanding the nature and consequences of the decision to be made and/or is not capable of communicating this decision. In the case of nonvoluntary euthanasia, the wishes of the patient are not known. An example of nonvoluntary euthanasia is when a doctor gives a lethal injection to an incompetent elderly man who is suffering greatly from an advanced terminal disease, but who did not make his wishes known to the physician when he was competent. Another example would be a father who asphyxiates with carbon monoxyde a congenitally handicapped child who was never considered to be competent.

*Involuntary* euthanasia is done against the wishes of a competent individual or against the wishes expressed in a valid advance directive. Examples of involuntary euthanasia include a son who gives a lethal overdose of medication to his father who is suffering from cancer, but the father does not want the overdose. Another example is a physician who, despite the advance directive of a patient indicating that he or she does not want any actions to hasten death, gives a lethal injection to the patient who is now unconscious and suffering from the final stages of a terminal illness.

Although the above definitions may seem clear, there is much confusion in the words used to describe euthanasia and other actions that result in hastening death. The term "mercy killing" is often used to describe situations of nonvoluntary and involuntary euthanasia. In several European countries, for example the Netherlands, the difference between euthanasia, homicide, suicide, and assisted suicide appears to be relatively clear. However, in the United States and Canada there is much confusion concerning the use of the term *assisted suicide* and *physician-assisted suicide.*

## Definitions of Assisted Suicide

Assisted suicide is usually defined as a specific situation in which there is a suicide, that is, an act of killing oneself intentionally. Adding the word "assisted" to suicide implies that another person provided assistance by supplying the means (e.g., giving the person a gun or prescribing lethal medication), the knowledge (information about the use of the gun or how to take a lethal dose of medication), or both. In North America, assisted suicide has also been used in the media to refer to situations that appear to have been direct acts to end the life of a person intentionally initiated by another person. This is because assisted suicide has lesser legal sanctions than the act of killing another person even if the homicide is for the relief of pain and suffering in a terminally ill individual and can be called "euthanasia." For these reasons, Jack Kevorkian (the pathologist who made media headlines in the 1990s for his involvement in the deaths of over 130 individuals) claimed that his participation in the deaths of several patients was assisted suicide rather than euthanasia.

Sometimes there may be a fine line between what is considered assisted suicide and euthanasia. For example, during the period between July 1996 and March 1997, when euthanasia was legal in the Northern Territory of Australia, a machine was invented whereby a physician attached the patient to a computer-operated pump that contained lethal substances. Although the physician hooked up and turned on the apparatus, the lethal injection was only given after the patient responded to a question on the computer screen by pressing on a key.

## Arguments in Favor of Euthanasia

Arguments in favor of euthanasia are generally based upon beliefs concerning individual liberty, what constitutes a "good" or "appropriate" death, and certain life situations that are considered unacceptable. These arguments are generally based upon moral or religious values as well as certain beliefs concerning the value and quality of human life. They also often suppose that people are capable of making rational decisions, even when they are suffering and terminally ill.

*The good death.* According to this view, certain ways of dying are better than others. Usually a good death is described ideally as drifting into death in a pleasing environment as one falls asleep. The ancient Roman orator and statesman Cicero said that a good death is the ideal way of respecting natural law and public order by departing from the earth with dignity and tranquility. Euthanasia can be seen as a way to assure that a person dies in a dignified and appropriate manner.

*Individual liberty.* In his *Essay on Suicide,* the eighteenth-century Scottish philosopher David Hume stated that all individuals in a free society should be able to choose the manner of their death. Some people, for example, feel that this right must be tempered by the obligation to not cause harm to others.

*Right to maintain human dignity.* This argument is similar to the concept of the good death, except that the objective is to *avoid* a poor quality of life during the dying process rather than seek out a particular idealized way of dying the good death. There are great individual differences in what constitutes a dignified way to live and die. Commonly mentioned indignities to justify premature death include: being a burden to others, living a deteriorated state incapable of normal daily activities, having to be placed in a hospital or a nursing home, and being dependent upon intrusive medical apparatus to continue living or engaging in everyday tasks. The general public often assumes that certain chronic and terminal illnesses inevitably result in a poor quality of life. However, research suggests that the psychosocial environment determines quality of life as much or more than the nature of the illness, per se.

*Reduction of suffering.* In 1516 the English statesman and author Sir Thomas More described euthanasia to end suffering in his book *Utopia* as "those that are ill from incurable diseases they comfort by sitting and talking with them, and with all means available. But if the disease is not only incurable but also full of continuous pain and anguish, then the priests and magistrates exhort the patient saying that he has become . . . irksome to others and grievous to himself; that he ought to . . . dispatch himself out of that painful life as out of a prison or torture rack or else allow his life to be ended by others" (More 1964, pp. 186–187). In 1994 the philosophy professor Margaret Battin wrote that euthanasia to reduce suffering has two components: to avoid future pain and suffering and to end current pain and suffering. This definition generally assumes that the pain is not only intolerable but interminable.

*Justice.* Gerald Gruman described euthanasia in order to achieve "justice" in society as "thrift euthanasia," where decisions are made to end lives of certain patients in situations where there is competition for limited resources in medical care. When there is a scarcity of certain medical resources in a society, not all people who are ill can continue to live. In such situations, one can suggest that "less valuable" individuals should give up their places to persons who contribute more to society; if they are unwilling, others should decide who should live and who should die. An extreme example is the eugenics programs based upon Darwinian concepts, such as those proposed by the German biologist Ernst Haeckel in 1904. Haeckel proposed that in order to reduce welfare and medical costs "hundreds of thousands of incurable lunatics, lepers, people with cancer" be killed by means of morphine or some other "painless and rapid poison" (1904). This approach inspired the National Socialists led by Adolf Hitler in their eugenics program.

Even if one disagrees with any form of eugenics program for economic reasons, one may still consider the fact that social pressure often exists in situations where medical resources are limited. The concept of "distributive justice"involves looking at the collective good or general welfare as something to be shared among the total membership of society. When resources are limited, society may question, for example, if it is worth expending tremendous resources to maintain the life of one incurably ill individual in a vegetative unconscious state rather than using those resources to help cure those who have promising prognoses for recovery.

*Avoiding botched suicides.* Molloy states that if euthanasia remains illegal, some people will be forced to attempt suicide or try to kill loved ones without any help. He contends that in some instances unsuccessful suicide attempts and botched euthanasia by others may result in a life situation that is worse than before. It can be argued that legalization of euthanasia will avoid suffering from botched attempts and the prosecution of loved ones who are acting sincerely at the request of a family member.

*Control of existing practices.* In countries where euthanasia is illegal there are clandestine practices by physicians and family members regardless of the laws. Proponents of euthanasia in the Netherlands often state that as long as euthanasia remains illegal in a country, physicians and other citizens will camouflage those activities and there will be no monitoring or control of what occurs. An advantage to legalizing euthanasia would be to control existing practices and ensure that there are fewer abuses.

## Arguments against Euthanasia

The arguments against euthanasia include religious and ethical beliefs about the sanctity of life as well as a number of arguments allowing for euthanasia that will inevitably lead to a situation where some individuals will risk having their deaths hastened against their will.

*Sanctity of human life.* This belief, based upon religious values, considers human life sacred and inviolable. No person may take the life of another. For example, St. Augustine interpreted the biblical prescript against killing as being absolute, even including the taking of one's own life. Another argument for the sanctity of human life is that this constitutes one of the pillars of social order that must be maintained to avoid social breakdown. For example, St. Thomas Aquinas condemned suicide because it goes against one's obligation to oneself, the community, and God.

*Wrong diagnoses and new treatments.* According to this point of view, where there is life there is hope. It is possible that a terminal diagnosis is in error; some people thought to be dying from an incurable disease are victims of a mistaken diagnosis or may miraculously continue to live. Also, because of the rapid pace of advances in medical science, there may soon be a cure for diseases that are at the time of the euthanasia considered to be incurable. Thus, euthanasia may be a mistake if there is a possibility, however slight, that the person is not really going to die. For example, it can be said that many persons with AIDS (acquired immunodeficiency syndrome) who ended their life prematurely because of impending death may have continued to live for a long time because of the development of new treatments for the disease.

*The Wedge or Slippery Slope.* This argument maintains that when one accepts killing upon demand in certain situations, despite the best controls and regulations, there is a risk of abuses. Furthermore, there is concern that once the door is opened to justify murder under some intolerable circumstances, there is the possibility of developing broader criteria and making euthanasia more widespread. For example, in the Netherlands euthanasia and assisted suicide was first only available to those who were terminally ill. Since 1998 the regulations for euthanasia have been used to permit access to euthanasia and assisted suicide to persons who are not terminally ill but who suffer hopelessly from chronic physical or even psychological illnesses.

*Protection of the weak, incompetent, and disadvantaged.* This argument is similar to the Wedge or Slippery Slope argument. The concerns with the Protection of the Weak argument are that people who may be unable to make informed choices concerning euthanasia may be forced to opt for a premature death or may become victims of nonvoluntary or involuntary euthanasia.

*The value of suffering.* Suffering may be seen as good for the soul, a heroic act, or the price to pay for one's sins in order to guarantee a better life in the hereafter. Jesus' suffering on the cross may be considered an example of an appropriate way to die. If suffering is admirable, then seeking to end suffering by euthanasia cannot be condoned.

*The option of suicide is always available.* Because suicide is always available and not illegal in most countries, one can argue that legalization of euthanasia is not necessary because a person can always find some means of committing suicide. Because of the dangers in legalizing euthanasia, one might instead encourage people to commit suicide rather than involving others in their deaths. One may further argue that those who "do not have the courage" to end their own lives may be too ambivalent and should not be put to death by others.

*The impossibility of competent and rational decision making.* The seventeenth-century philosopher Spinoza felt that the desire to survive is such an essential part of human nature that humans may not rationally prefer not to survive and kill themselves. According to this view, anyone who wants to die may not be acting rationally. Furthermore, one may question if it is possible when experiencing pain and suffering to make a rational decision before the pain and suffering is controlled. Finally, one may question whether or not most important human decision making is rational and why one should expect a person to be more rational when terminally ill. Major decisions such as choice of career, marriage partners, where to live, and whether or not to have children may be more emotional than rational. Also, there are no generally accepted criteria of what constitutes a rational argument in favor of euthanasia: What is logical and rational for one person may constitute reasons for continuing to fight against death in another person in a similar situation.

*Choosing death for the wrong reasons.* Many people consider euthanasia because they are experiencing pain and suffering. Ignorance of the availability of interventions to reduce pain and suffering may lead to a choice to end life. People involved in palliative care programs that focus upon reducing the suffering of terminally ill patients contend that better pain control and improvement of the psychosocial situation can alleviate a large proportion of the suffering and reduce the desire for euthanasia.

*Undiagnosed clinical depression.* It may be considered appropriate for people who are dying to feel sad and unhappy. However, some terminally ill persons may suffer from a more severe and potentially treatable psychiatric syndrome of clinical depression. In some instances, the depression may be a side effect of treatment of the illness or may be related to the psychosocial environment of an institution. According to this view, accurate diagnosis and treatment with antidepressant medication and/or psychotherapy is a preferable option to euthanasia.

*Erosion of confidence in physicians.* According to this argument, if physicians are allowed to kill some terminally ill patients then confidence in physicians may be diminished. Medical practictioners and proponents of this argument have suggested that only "specialists" should practice euthanasia if it is legalized so that physicians can maintain their reputation as advocates in the fight against death and the reduction of pain and suffering.

*Compromising the right to choose by involving others in one's death.* Brian Mishara has argued that humans generally experience tremendous ambivalence about ending their lives by suicide, so much so that most highly suicidal people change their minds before an attempt and the vast majority of persons who initiate a suicide attempt do not die from their attempt. He questions whether the involvement of a physician in ending a person's life may create a social situation where there is tremendous pressure to complete the suicidal act and die rather than exercising the choice to continue to live. Once a physician has been convinced that euthanasia is acceptable and appropriate, it is not easy for a person to admit to the doctor that he or she is feeling ambivalent or scared and would like to put off the decision for a while. This analysis suggests that involving others in death can compromise people's rights to change their minds because of the social pressures to complete the act.

## The Situation in the Netherlands

In the Netherlands, the practice of euthanasia and assisted suicide was legalized by legislative decree in November 2000. However, the practice of euthanasia has been tacitly condoned by jurisprudence since 1973. In 1973 a doctor was found guilty of giving her seventy-nine-year-old mother a lethal injection after repeated requests to end her suffering. The doctor was placed on probation for a year but this case generated considerable sympathy for the doctor and resulted in the Royal Dutch Medical Association producing a working paper on the topic. Furthermore, the Supreme Court of The Netherlands set out a number of considerations that would have to be met before an accused would be exonerated of euthanasia. Subsequently, the practice developed to not prosecute cases of euthanasia that respected those court guidelines. They include:

- The request for euthanasia must come from the patient and be completely voluntary, well considered, and persistent.

- The patient must have adequate information about his or her medical condition, the prognosis, and alternative treatments.

- There must be intolerable suffering with no prospect for improvement, although the patient need not be terminally ill.

- Other alternatives to alleviate the suffering must have been considered and found ineffective, unreasonable, and unacceptable to the patient.

- The euthanasia must be performed by a physician who has consulted an independent colleague.

- The physician must exercise due care, and there should be a written record of the case.

- The death must not be reported to the medical examiner as a natural death.

There is tremendous popular support in the Netherlands for the practice of euthanasia and the legal precedents have now been passed into law by Parliament. Several studies have been conducted on the nature of the practice of euthanasia and assisted suicide as well as possible abuses. Most cases of euthanasia occur among terminally ill persons in the advanced stages of their disease and it is rare that the criteria are not respected. However, in the Netherlands there are no monetary considerations concerning the cost of health care because there is a socialized medical program. Furthermore, the society in the Netherlands is very different from many other societies because of the strong emphasis upon individual freedom of choice and limited government control.

## The Euthanasia Act in the Australian Northern Territories

The parliament of the Northern Territory in Australia passed the Rights of the Terminally Ill (ROTI) Act in May 1995, which was in effect for nine months from July 1, 1996, to March 25, 1997, when the act was repealed by legislation passed by the parliament of Australia. The ROTI Act allowed a terminally ill patient who was experiencing what he or she deemed to be unacceptable levels of pain, suffering, and/or distress to request the medical practitioner to end his or her life by euthanasia, if the requirements of the law were met. The law stipulated that besides suffering and being terminally ill, the patient must be at least eighteen years old, there must be no cure available, no other palliative care options to alleviate the suffering available, and a second opinion as well as a psychiatric assessment to confirm that he or she is not suffering from a treatable clinical depression.

After the law was passed, five persons who officially sought to use the act received extensive media attention. Although the intention of the law was to allow for a patient's personal physician to provide assistance to terminate life as part of their care, only one physician in the territory accepted to participate in euthanasia practices: Philip Nitschke. During the period that the act was in effect, seven cancer patients applied for euthanasia with

Nitschke. Four of the seven died by euthanasia; one committed suicide; one died a natural death; and another died from the effects of pain relief sedation.

## The Oregon Death with Dignity Act

In November 1994 the Death with Dignity Act was adopted by a referendum vote of Oregon residents of 51 percent against 49 percent. Soon after the act was passed, the act was contested on the grounds that it presumably threatened the lives of terminally ill persons and did not afford them equal protection. A judge granted an injunction on the grounds that the act put people at risk. However, in 1997, the injunction was lifted by the Ninth Court of Appeals, which dismissed the case. The law went into effect in 1997 after the U.S. Supreme Court declined to hear an appeal of the case. A second referendum in November 1997 found 60 percent in favor and 40 percent against this law. In November 2001 the U.S. Attorney General John Ashcroft issued a directive that would have prohibited doctors from prescribing lethal doses of controlled drugs to terminally ill patients. Immediately after issuing the directive, the U.S. District Court in Portland issued a temporary restraining order blocking Ashcroft from punishing physicians who wrote lethal prescriptions. In April 2002 the same court ruled that Ashcroft had overstepped the authority of the Federal Controlled Substances Act when he declared that writing lethal prescriptions was not a legitimate medical purpose and threatened to revoke the license of physicians who wrote lethal-dose prescriptions to patients who requested one. This decision made the restraining order on Ashcroft permanent; however, as of this writing, the decision may be subject to appeal.

According to this law there are four criteria necessary for an assisted suicide to be conducted in the state of Oregon: (1) the person must be at least eighteen years old, (2) a legal resident of Oregon, (3) able to communicate his or her decisions about medical care, and (4) in the terminal phase of an illness that is defined as having a life expectancy of less than six months. If the patient is eligible, the request must be made twice in less than fifteen days and the request must be made in writing to a physician who then establishes that all the conditions have been met. A second physician must be consulted, and the first physician must inform the patient of all alternatives available. The physician can request that the person inform family members about the request, but this is not obligatory. The physician may then prescribe a lethal medication, which he or she must declare to the Oregon Health Division. This physician has no obligation to participate in the assisted suicide and is protected against any criminal liability under this act.

During the first four years since the law was applied (1998–2000), 140 prescriptions for lethal doses of medication were written, mainly to cancer patients, and 91 persons died after taking these medications. This constitutes fewer than one-tenth of 1 percent of terminally ill Oregonians dying by physician-assisted suicide.

## Conclusions

Arguments for or against active euthanasia that are based upon moral or religious beliefs are impossible to resolve on the basis of empirical facts or logical arguments; these arguments are related to cultural values and practices. However, values and practices can change over time. Some practices that were considered barbaric at one time in history have become acceptable in the twenty-first century. The practice of euthanasia, its legalization, and acceptance in various societies is also influenced by public debate and media reports. With the increased acceptance and legalization of euthanasia in different societies, researchers are gaining more information about the practice of euthanasia and its effects. One of the central issues in the acceptance of euthanasia is weighing society's obligations to provide an easier access to death against society's obligations to provide the means for diminishing pain and suffering among those who may want to die prematurely by euthanasia.

*See also:* BIOETHICS; BLACK STORK; GOOD DEATH, THE; INFORMED CONSENT; KEVORKIAN, JACK; NATURAL DEATH ACTS; SUICIDE TYPES: PHYSICIAN-ASSISTED SUICIDE

### *Bibliography*

Battin, Margaret P. *The Least Worst Death: Essays on Bioethics on the End of Life.* New York: Oxford University Press, 1994.

Chin, Arthur E., et al. *Oregon's Death with Dignity Act: The First Year's Experience.* Portland: Department of Human Services, Oregon Health Division, Center for Disease Prevention and Epidemiology, 1999.

Cicero. *Cato Maior de senectute,* edited by J.G.F. Powell. Cambridge: Cambridge University Press, 1988.

Gruman, Gerlad J. "An Historical Introduction to Ideas about Voluntary Euthanasia: With a Bibliographic Survey and Guide for Interdisciplinary Studies." *Omega: The Journal of Death And Dying* 4, no. 2 (1973):87–138.

Haeckel, Ernst. *The Wonders of Life: A Popular Study of Biological Philosophy,* translated by J. Mc Cabe. New York: Harper, 1904.

Hume, David. *An Essay on Suicide.* 1789. Reprint, Yellow Springs, OH: Kahoe and Co., 1929.

Kasimar, Yale. "Euthanasia Legislation: Some Non-Religious Objections." In T. L. Beauchamp and P. Seymour eds., *Ethical Issues in Death and Dying.* Englewood Cliffs, NJ: Prentice Hall, 1978.

Mishara, Brian L. "The Right to Die and the Right to Live: Perspectives on Euthanasia and Assisted Suicide." In A. Leenaars, M. Kral, R. Dyck, and S. Wenckstern eds., *Suicide in Canada.* Toronto: University of Toronto Press, 1998.

Molloy, William. *Vital Choices: Life, Death and the Health Care Crisis.* Toronto: Penguin Books, 1993.

More, Sir Thomas. *Utopia.* 1605. Reprint, New Haven, CT: Yale University Press, 1964.

Saint Augustine of Hippo. *Augustine: The City of God,* edited by T. Merton and translated by M. Dods. New York: Modern Library, 1950.

Senate of Canada. *On Life and Death: Report of the Senate Special Committee on Euthanasia and Assisted Suicide.* Ottawa: Minister of Supply and Services, 1995.

Spinoza, Benedictus. *The Ethics,* translated by R. H. M. Elwes. 1677. Reprint, New York: Dover Publications, 1951.

BRIAN L. MISHARA

# EXHUMATION

Cemeteries exist as "resting places," and the norm of many cultures is that the dead should not be disturbed. However, for a variety of reasons, they are disturbed through the process of exhumation (removal of a corpse from the earth). Many early groups placed the corpse in the ground and exhumed it at a later date for religious rituals, a practice still undertaken by some traditional societies. In fourteenth-century France, "it became common procedure to dig up the more or less dried-out bones in the older graves in order to make room for new ones" (Ariès 1982, p. 54). The high death rate from the European plagues coupled with a desire to be buried in already-full church cemeteries led to old bones being exhumed so that new bodies could be placed in the graves.

In times past, on rare occasions prior to embalming, the body was removed from the ground. This happened when burial professionals or the authorities suspected that the person might have been buried alive. The French philosopher and death expert Philippe Ariès discussed necrophiliacs who disinterred dead bodies for sexual purposes and scientists who dug up corpses to conduct scientific experiments. It is common knowledge that for centuries until cadavers were legally provided, medical schools exhumed dead bodies for teaching purposes. One of the reasons the use of the wake was enacted in many societies was to deter those who might steal corpses.

In contemporary America corpses are disinterred when there is a need to identify a body or to establish cause of death like in the case of suspected homicide. For example, President Zachary Taylor was exhumed in 1991 to determine whether or not he had been poisoned, and the famous outlaw Jesse James's grave was excavated to prove that it was his body in the coffin. In addition, archaeological investigations often involve exhumation.

Under modern law, courts usually do not allow exhumation unless there are substantial and compelling reasons to do so. In a landmark U.S. Supreme Court decision (*Dougherty* v. *Mercantile Safe Deposit and Trust Company* 1978), Justice Cardozo stated, "The dead are to rest where they have been lain unless reason of substance is brought forward for disturbing their repose." Three general principles govern the law of disinterment in the United States. First, it is presumed that a "decently buried" body should remain undisturbed where it was placed unless good reason is given to do so. Second, disinterment is considered the private concern of the immediate family and the cemetery. Third, if there is disagreement among the close relatives regarding a proposal for exhumation the matter is adjudicated by a court of equity. The court considers (in order of importance) the wishes and religious beliefs of the deceased (if these can be determined), the wishes of the spouse of the deceased, the opinions of other close relatives, and the policies and regulations of the cemetery when determining if exhumation should be allowed. California Labor Code stipulates that if it is suspected that a person has died as a result of injuries sustained in the course of his employment, the investigating appeals board may require an autopsy and, if necessary, the exhumation of the body for the purposes of autopsy. However, in accordance with the rules of equity, the close relatives can, if they wish, prevent the state (i.e., California) from either exhuming the body or performing the autopsy.

Scientists have long sought to understand life in early civilizations through the excavation of burial grounds and exhumation of human remains. In the United States the attempt to understand early cultures led to the exhumation of the remains of Native Americans, many of which ended up in the nation's museums and archaeology labs. In an attempt to prevent the desecration of Native American graves, the Native American Graves Protection and Repatriation Act was introduced in Congress in July 1990 and subsequently passed into law. The bill states that any human remains and objects found on federal or tribal lands after the date of enactment are to be considered owned or controlled by lineal descendants, the tribe on whose land it was found, the tribe having the closest cultural affiliation, or the tribe which aboriginally occupied the area. Anyone who discovers items covered by the bill must cease his or her activity, notify the federal land manager responsible and the appropriate tribe, and make a reasonable effort to protect the items. Anyone who violates the provisions of the bill may be fined, imprisoned not more than one year, or both. The penalty may increase to five years for a second violation. The act further states that all federal agencies and museums receiving federal funds that have control over any of the items covered in the bill are to, within five years, inventory and identify the items, notify the affected tribes, and make arrangements to return such items if the appropriate tribe made a request. If an item was acquired with the consent of the tribe or if the item was part of a scientific study which was expected to be of major benefit to the country, the request for repatriation (i.e., return) could be denied.

*See also:* AUTOPSY; CEMETERIES AND CEMETERY REFORM; CHARNEL HOUSES; FORENSIC MEDICINE; HUMAN REMAINS; NATIVE AMERICAN RELIGION

## Bibliography

Ariès, Philippe. *The Hour of Our Death.* New York: Vintage Books, 1982.

Crissman, James K. *Death and Dying in Central Appalachia.* Urbana: University of Illinois Press, 1994.

### Internet Resources

California Labor Code. "Section 5700-5710." In the Dr. Reynoso Chiropractic and Sports Therapy [web site]. Available from www.drreynoso.com/info/laborcode/labor_code__section_5700.htm

*Dougherty* v. *Mercantile Safe Deposit and Trust Company,* 282 Md. 617, 387 A 2d.244 (1978). In the Gorman and Williams [web site]. Available from www.gandwlaw.com/articles/booth_brf.html.

"Native American Grave Protection and Repatriation Act." In the Center for Advanced Spatial Technologies [web site]. Available from http://web.cast.uark.edu/other/nps/nagpra/.

JAMES K. CRISSMAN
ALFRED R. MARTIN

# EXPOSURE TO THE ELEMENTS

Although humans are among the most adaptable of the earth's creatures with one of the broadest territories of settlement, their ability to survive extreme temperatures is limited. Death can occur by exposure to extreme heat or cold. A person who falls through the ice into water will typically die within twenty to thirty minutes because of heart standstill or heart fibrillation. By then, his or her internal or core body temperature will have fallen to approximately 77 degrees Fahrenheit. Often death is a combination of stresses to the body such as hypothermia and starvation as in the case of the Donner party, the ill-fated group of emigrants that was caught in the Sierra Nevada Mountains during the winter of 1846. The decrease in core body temperature is compensated for by shivering, constriction of surface blood vessels to direct the blood to internal organs, and behavioral actions such as increasing voluntary exercise or putting on more clothes. As hypothermia sets in the rate of all metabolic processes slows down, leading to loss of judgment, apathy, disorientation, and lethargy. Breathing becomes slower and weaker, the heart slows, and disturbances in cardiac rhythm occur, leading to death. Many symptoms of hypothermia were evident in the oral and written accounts of the Donner party, adding to the inability to supplement their rapidly decreasing food supply.

The limits for hot air temperature that one can stand depend on whether the air is wet or dry. The core temperature of a nude body can remain within normal range (97 to 99 degrees Fahrenheit) for hours when exposed to dry air ranging from 55 to 130 degrees Fahrenheit. However, if the humidity of the air approaches 100 percent or if the person is submerged in water, the core temperature will rise whenever the environmental temperature rises above 94 degrees Fahrenheit. The body responds to heat stress by sweating, dilating surface blood vessels to expose more of the internal heat to the outside, and behavioral actions, such as removing clothes. In extreme situations, especially in hot arid environments, the body can lose enough water and salts in sweat to cause heat exhaustion, a condition consisting of muscle cramps, impairment of the cardiovascular system, unconsciousness, delirium, and death. Symptoms of heat exhaustion are increasing fatigue and weakness, excessive sweating, low blood pressure, cold, pale, and clammy skin, anxiety, and disorientation. A person with heat exhaustion can be helped by laying his or her body flat, or by tipping the head down to increase the blood supply to the brain while administering small amounts of sugar water to increase blood volume. Heat exhaustion can be prevented by adequate hydration before, during, and after physical activity.

Heat stroke (or sunstroke) can be induced by overexertion with prolonged exposure to a hot, humid environment, at environmental temperatures as low as 85 to 90 degrees Fahrenheit. In this case the body is unable to sweat due to the malfunctioning of the thermoregulatory control center in the brain. Tissue damage to the nervous and cardiovascular systems occurs when the core temperature rises above 109 degrees Fahrenheit, causing death. Symptoms of heat stroke may include headache, dizziness, fatigue, and awareness of the rapidly rising temperature. The person increases his or her rate of breathing to expel the excess heat and the heart races but the blood pressure is not affected. Sweating is typically decreased so the skin is hot, flushed, and usually dry. Treatment is aimed at cooling the person down and hospitalization is recommended to ensure that the thermoregulatory control center regains normal functioning. Heat exhaustion can quickly and unexpectedly lead to heat stroke and death even of the most physically fit, as was the case with offensive tackle Korey Stringer, who died in a Minnesota Vikings 2001 summer preseason practice. Although the body is well equipped to handle normal changes in body temperature, extreme changes in environmental conditions may not be able to be compensated for and can lead to irreversible damage and death.

*See also:* CAUSES OF DEATH

## *Bibliography*

Guyton, Arthur C., and John E. Hall. "Body Temperature, Temperature Regulation, and Fever." In *Textbook of Medical Physiology,* 10th edition. Philadelphia: W.B. Saunders, 2000.

Hardesty, Donald. *The Archaeology of the Donner Party.* Reno: University of Nevada Press, 1997.

### *Internet Resources*

DrugBase. "Heatstroke and Heat Exhaustion." In the DrugBase Guide to Medication [web site]. Available from www.drugbase.co.za/data/med_info/heatstr.htm.

Johnson, Kristen. "New Light on the Donner Party." In the Oregon-California Trails Association [web site]. Available from www.utahcrossroads.org/DonnerParty/.

NFL News. "Heatstroke Claims Life of Vikings All-Pro OT Stringer." In the NFL [web site]. Available from www.nfl.com/news/2001/MIN/stringer080101.html.

ALLISON K. WILSON

# EXTINCTION

Humans are the only species aware of not only of their own eventual personal deaths but of their collective demise as well. This latter insight came late in human history—a product of evolutionary theory and of paleontological and archaeological research.

The West still deals with the twin "cognitive shocks" from the mid-nineteenth-century discoveries that extinction was the fate both of creatures very much like human beings and of cultures as articulate as those in the West, whose people can still speak directly to Western civilization because of their writing systems. On top of these are the twentieth century's scientific end-of-world scenarios, predicting the inevitable extinction of not only all life forms on Earth when the sun goes supernova, but of the entire universe, when entropy is complete and the last nuclear fires flicker out.

Since WWII—particularly following the publications of Rachel Carson's *Silent Spring* (1962) and Paul Ehrlich's *Population Bomb* (1968)—sensitivities toward extinction have heightened with cold war fears of nuclear war, the obvious diminishment and degradation of the natural order owing to industrialization and burgeoning human numbers, and with millennial apocalyptic fears. With increasing regularity the news brings scientific findings of global warming, of a rapidly growing list of endangered and newly extinct life forms, of "earth-killer" asteroids lurking nearby, and of lethal pollutants in the air, soil, and water. The polar ice caps are melting as are the famed snows of Kilimanjaro. The blubber of orcas from the American Pacific Northwest found to contain PCB (polychlorinated biphenyls) concentrations up to 500 times greater than those found in humans. In the extreme, such phenomena are interpreted as symptoms of the beginning of the end of not only the planet's entire ecosystem but human beings as well.

Extinction as the consequence of natural selection and the fate of the "unfit" was to become the metaphor for understanding not only natural but social phenomena as well, whether it be the success or failures of businesses or of entire cultural orders. It also found expressions in the justifications for war, exploitation, and forced sterilizations and genocides of human populations.

## Scientific Perspectives

The law of life from scientific perspectives holds that all life forms, ecosystems, planets, stars, and galaxies come and go. Personal death and collective extinction are the debts for life—on the individual, species, genus, family, order, class, and phyla levels. Since life first appeared on Earth 3.5 billion years ago, over 10 billion species have come into existence (and this figure is the roughest of estimates). Somewhere between 10 million and 30 million species (of which scientists have counted only about one-eighth) currently reside on the planet. In other words, for every 1,000 species that have ever existed probably fewer than 10 are alive in the twenty-first century.

Challenging the conventional idea that "species were immutable productions," the naturalist Charles Darwin wrote *On the Origin of Species by Means of Natural Selection, or the Preservation of Favoured Races in the Struggle for Life,* explaining how life is a continuous process of modification and current life forms are descendants of extinct ancestral species. Natural selection is "the process by which genes change their sequences" (Ridley 2000, p. 35), by which those organisms best adapted to their environment survive to pass on their genetic code while those (previously "successful") life forms unable to make adaptive modifications to varying conditions perish. Species' billing on the stage of life is relatively short in terms of geologic time, with most becoming extinct within a few million years after their evolution. Most leave no related descendant species but rather become evolutionary dead ends.

Life is a continuous process of extinction and diversification, where only the fittest life forms survive in a world where, according to Darwin, they are "bound together by a web of complex relations" (1963, p. 54). Central to these "relations" are the ecological niches, the millions of different "fits" and functional interdependencies that plants and animals have with each other in their ecosystem. While various creatures may share a habitat, generally a niche can only be occupied by one species of animal or plant. When two different organisms compete for a particular niche, one will invariably lose out. If a niche should become empty, such as through extinction, other life forms will rush in and compete to fill the vacuum. In the case of a mass die-off, evolutionary explosions of new life forms occur as plants and animals adapt to take advantage of the abundance of newly opened niches.

Another factor affecting the rate of extinction and differentiation of life forms is the extent of biodiversity in an ecosystem. These natural systems comprising the biosphere do such things as cycle oxygen and carbon, purify the water, and decompose waste. Diminish the genetic variation in individual species and they become more vulnerable to extinction. Homogenize the biotas in human-dominated ecosystems and biodisparity declines.

The diversity of life used to be considerably richer than is the case in the twenty-first century. For instance, based on the fossil record of the Cambrian Period over 500 million years ago, there may have been four to five times the number of phyla as exist today. Given present trends, this multiplier may be even greater in the near future as the site of the planet's greatest biodiversity, the tropical forests where between 50 and 90 percent of species reside, are rapidly disappearing. Worldwide, tropical forests four times the size of Switzerland are cut down annually, replaced with fields for cash crops and to make room for burgeoning human populations—which, in turn, pollute the water and land, further diminishing the variety and size of natural habitats.

Though humans may be one of the only species to have adapted to nearly all environments on Earth, their existence nevertheless remains dependent upon the complex systems of interdependent life forms.

## Periodic Mass Extinctions

The rate of extinction is far from constant. In addition to the routine processes of Darwin's natural selection, various terrestrial and extraterrestrial catastrophes have profoundly altered the course of evolution. Paleontologists report historic cycles of mass death, dooming or marginalizing a portion of previously well-adapted species, followed by steep increases in the diversity of new life forms.

At least five periods of mass extinction have been identified, eliminating over half of the world's species at the time of their occurrence (although, in total, causing less than 5% of all extinctions). Scientific debate centers not on whether these mass die-offs have occurred but rather if they happened quickly, such as due to asteroid impact or a nearby star going supernova, or more slowly, such as due to glaciations, volcanic activity, changes in seawater oxygen or salinity, or epidemics. The time required for the species diversification to rebound to pre-catastrophe levels is estimated to be roughly 25 million years.

Asteroids are suspected in at least the three most recent mass die-offs. Most publicized is the suspected 10-kilometer-wide meteorite that slammed into what's now the Gulf of Mexico and the Yucatán Peninsula 65 million years ago, leaving the 180-kilometer-wide Chicxulub Crater, wiping out the dinosaurs, and ending the Cretaceous period. Another is believed to have concluded the Permian period with even more devastating results, when 250 million years ago some 96 percent of marine and 70 percent of land fauna disappeared. Ironically, shortly after *Jurassic Park*'s release, the world witnessed over twenty parts of Comet Shoemaker-Levy collide with Jupiter. At least nine of these could have been Earth-killers, one forming a crater the planet could easily fit within. As of 2000, according to the British National Space Center, 284 asteroids have been located with the size and orbits to be deemed "potentially hazardous" to Earth.

There is evidence that mass extinctions may number in the dozens, with up to three-quarters of all species disappearing every 26 to 30 million years. One explanation for this cyclical regularity is the possible existence of a companion star to the sun. Called Nemesis, when this star reaches its perigee every 26 million years, it shakes loose and hurls a comet storm from the Oort cloud on the fringe of Earth's solar system. Every 50,000 years or so, for over a period of 2 million years, one of these comets collides with Earth, producing ecological catastrophes that lead to periodic global deaths.

Among biologists there is broad consensus that human beings are witnessing the sixth mass extinction, with anywhere from 10,000 to 20,000 species of animals and plants disappearing annually—a rate conservationists estimate to be 1,000 to 10,000 times greater than would be the case under natural conditions. A 1998 American Museum of Natural History survey of 400 experts in the biological sciences found approximately 70 percent expecting up to one in five of all living species on the planet disappearing within thirty years. What makes this different from the five other known periods of mass extinction—which were linked with asteroids, ice ages, and volcanoes—is the human complicity involved. We are death and are responsible for this "species holocaust" (Day 1981). In a sense, all creatures have become our miner's canaries and their disappearance means that the

**TABLE 1**

| The five greatest mass extinctions | | | | | |
| --- | --- | --- | --- | --- | --- |
| | **Ordivician-silurian** | **Late Devonian** | **Permian-triassic** | **Late Triassic** | **Final Cretaceous** |
| **When Occurred** | 439 million years ago | 365 million years ago | 251 million years ago | 199–214 million years ago | 65 million years ago |
| **Casualties** | Up to estimated 85% species and 45–60% of marine genuses killed. | 70–80% of all species and 30% of families vanish; marine life more decimated than freshwater and land fauna. | Most devastating of all, eliminating 85–90% of all marine and land vertebrate species, 95% of marine species. End of trilobites and many trees. | More than three quarters of all species and one quarter of families disappear. End of mammal-like reptiles and eel–like conodonts, leaving mainly dinosaurs. | 47% of marine genuses and 18% of land vertebrates wiped out, including the dinosaurs, leaving mainly turtles, lizards, birds, and mammals. |
| **Hypothesized Cause(s)** | Unusually fast plate movement; glaciation leading to sharp de-clines in sea levels. | Unknown if one cat-astrophic event or several smaller ones–possibly large asteroid or asteroid shower over time; possible glaciation and lethal temperature de-clines; oceanic anoxia (oxygen-lacking) | Possible asteroid; volcanic eruptions; dropping sea levels and oceanic anoxia | Little known but suspected fall in sea level, oceanic anoxia, major increase in rainfall. Possible comet showers or asteroid impact. | Suspected asteroid 10 km. in diameter hitting near Yucatán peninsula, coinciding with Siberian eruptions and dramatic climatic cooling. |

SOURCE: Adapted from A. Hallam, and P. B. Wignall, 1997; David Raup, and John J. Sepkosi Jr., 1986; and Lee Siegel, 2000.

health of the ecosystem is endangered and that we are running out of biological room

Human complicity in the Pleistocene extinction of large game animals remains a subject of debate, as there is a coincidence of receding glaciers, human migrations, and the extinction of many large game animals. The moa, a 400-pound flightless bird that thrived in New Zealand until about the year 1250, totally disappeared within 60 to 120 years of the first human arrival. Using fire as a weapon and tool, these settlers also burned into extinction an entire forest that was to become grassland. Simi-larly, woolly mammoths, camels, horses, saber-toothed tigers, and more than 120 other Pleistocene mammalian species all disappeared within a few hundred years after humans arrived in the New World roughly 11,000 to 13,000 years ago.

Perhaps the most poignant of recent extinc-tions is the passenger pigeon, which was to be hunted into oblivion. At the beginning of the American Civil War, this was one of the most suc-cessful bird species in North America, comprising an estimated 40 percent of the entire bird popula-tion. In 1870, a single flock one mile wide and 320 miles long flew over Cincinnati. In 1974 the last surviving pigeon died in that city's zoo. As of 2001, conservationists estimated that one in every six species of birds is in decline on the continent and could wane by half by the year 2030.

But the major cause of animal demise is the destruction of natural habitats as human populations exploded, tripling just between 1930 to 2000, lead-ing to urban sprawl, overfishing, overgrazing, defor-estation, overuse of pesticides and herbicides, strip mining, and pollution of fresh water systems. Human introduction of non-native "invasive" species has also taken its toll. Fungus carried by North American ships, for instance, led to the Irish potato famine. Of those who fled migrated to Australia with rabbits and cats, many of which went wild and decimated indigenous plants and animals.

In Africa, the deserts annually expand thou-sands of square miles as a rapidly growing human population strips its indigenous vegetation for fuel (wood remains the chief energy source for many of its inhabitants) and to make room for profitable crops or livestock. Here the removal of ground cover leads to a greater runoff of rain, reducing evaporation into the clouds and thereby contribut-ing to the severity of the region's routine droughts.

The loss is not confined to wild, undomesti-cated plants and animals but includes domesticated ones as well. During the twentieth century, because of the rise of cash crops and farmers' cultivation for maximum yield, three-quarters of the genetic diver-sity of the world's agricultural crops was lost. Roughly half of all domestic animal breeds in Europe became extinct. Gone are about 6,000 apple varieties that grew on U.S. farms 100 years ago. In the mid-1990s, the United Nations Food and Agriculture Organization reported that nearly one-quarter of the 3,882 breeds of 28 species of farm animals around the world were "at risk"—meaning fewer than 1,000 females or 20 breeding males.

What worries experts most is the prospect that farmers will have a shrinking pool of breeds to draw upon to keep up with changing soil conditions, pests, and new diseases.

In other words, concerns are for preserving biodiversity, particularly in light of cash crops and humanity putting its proverbial eggs in fewer and fewer baskets.

Two groups of extinctions have intrigued humans over the past two centuries: the demise of the dinosaurs and of human ancestors. Over the final two decades of the twentieth century there was considerable research and public interest in the instantaneous (in geological time) demise 65 million years ago of dinosaurs, among the most successful (in terms of their length of reign on Earth) animals known. This interest coincided with the cold war, which was not coincidental. Humanity's ability to equally quickly make itself extinct through thermonuclear devices became a widely accepted fact. Another factor heightening cultural receptivity was the rapid disappearance of its own social past—for example, old crafts, buildings, social etiquette—producing a sense of irretrievable loss. Modernity had come to mean impermanence in a culture of obsolescence where the only certainty had become change.

Unearthed in a quarry by Germany's river Neander in 1856 as an unusual humanlike skeleton with a beetled browed skull. This discovery of the Neanderthals, a tool-making creature very similar to *Homo sapien,* ultimately led to the unsettling insight that extinction has also been the fate of all branches of the hominid family and of the *Homo* genus except for human sapiens. Modern humans' complicity in the demise of these archaic humans remains a matter of speculation, with evidence indicating that humans shared the planet with at least the Neanderthals as recently as 26,000 years ago in Europe.

## Social Reactions to Extinctions of the Natural Order

Only in modern times has there been the realization that the planet's living resources are neither infinite nor always replenishable—and the scientific understanding of how precarious the interdependencies between all life forms are. People were

surprised in the 1860s when human artifacts were first found with extinct species in Europe. Severely challenged were biblical allusions to some "steady-state" or regenerative natural order, the fauna descendents of passengers on Noah's ark, all of which were to be dominated by humans. Only later did people come to learn how the overkilling of "keystone species" could lead to an environmental collapse and the extinction of even non-hunted creatures.

For those living within largely manmade environments and within a highly individualistic culture, appreciation of life's thorough interdependencies comes hard. Further, Cartesian conceptions of human's biological essence—the body-as-machine metaphor that has long predominated in medicine—complicates more holistic understandings.

Limited is any acknowledgment of human complicity in the sixth mass extinction. According to 1993 and 1994 surveys of the American adult public conducted by the National Opinion Research Center, only 16 percent of American adults believe it is "definitely true" that "human beings are the main cause of plant and animal species dying out." Four in ten agree with the statement, "We worry too much about the future of the environment and not enough about prices and jobs today." And only one in three was "very" or "fairly" willing to accept cuts in his or her standard of living in order to protect the environment.

The perspective from the scientific community is less benign. Several scientists have likened human effects on the ecosystem to cancer. If people take the Gaia perspective of Earth functioning like one mega living organism, aerial views can show striking similarity to melanomas attacking healthy tissue.

## The Economics of Extinction

The rise of the world economic order and its capitalist structure has accelerated the decimation of species. If, as Martin Luther King Jr. observed in 1967, capitalism has a tendency to treat profit motives and property rights as more important than people, one can easily surmise the importance it gives to the natural order. The system produces a bias toward short-term gains at the cost of long-term consequences. As mentioned, cash crops in the international marketplace have accelerated the end of many species. The price tag of the resultant reduction of biodiversity rarely enters into the market system's cost-benefit equation. This absence is due, in part, to the fact that people really don't know how to calculate the worth of such endangered species as snail darters or white spotted owls.

In 1976 Daniel Bell wrote of the cultural contradictions of capitalism, perceiving them as seeds for change—or the death knell for entire social orders. One contradiction of relevance here is the economics of extinction, how the growing scarcity of a life form can increase its value and thereby accelerate its disappearance. For instance, in the 1980s when the market value of rhino horns exceeded the per ounce value of silver by ten times, this reduced the number of black rhinos in the Tanzanian Ngorongoro Crater from seventy-six to twenty-six in a single year. Pathetically, as their numbers declined the value of their parts hyperinflated, encouraging further exploitation. Another contradiction is how farmers will have a shrinking pool of breeds to draw upon to keep up with changing soil conditions, pests, and new diseases.

With the remnants of endangered species increasingly likely to only be preserved within zoos, research institutes, and parks, matters of cost and utility enter. Consider, for instance, the perspective of zoos. To garner public support, animal collections must attract audiences. The most popular animals are often those that are "cute," furry, and large-eyed. Consequently, with time, Darwin's thesis of the survival of the fittest may have to be modified to be the survival of the cutest, like the black and white colobus or the arctic seal. Also saved will be those creatures that enhance humankind's own longevity, such as apes or pigs for xenotransplantations. Concerns over the loss of the tropical rainforests are often expressed in terms of human needs. One-quarter of prescription drugs are extracted from plants, including 70 percent of anti-cancer agents, and most of these come from tropical forests—where less than 1 percent of the flora has been examined for its pharmacological utility.

## The Politics of Extinction

At the beginning of the twenty-first century, decisions as to whether the needs of humans ultimately outweigh those of endangered species are largely the monopoly of political regimes. However, the planet's greatest biodiversity largely exists within developing nations where fertility rates are the highest, people the poorest, population pressures on nature the greatest, and unstable political regimes the least likely to resist powerful corporate and population encroachments on natural habitats.

Even in developed nations the accelerating rates of extinction have proven difficult to resist. The Green movement remains a minority voice. In the United States, awarenesses have become politicized. National surveys of 1993 and 1994 show Republicans are, for instance, 50 percent more likely than Democrats to disagree that "human beings are the main cause of plant and animal species dying out."

And just when environmental causes have entered the public consciousness, ecoterrorism (or threats thereof) has become a new weapon of disenfranchised and antiestablishment groups. During the summer of 2000, soon-to-be-laid-off chemical workers in Northern France dumped 3,000 liters of sulfuric acid into a tributary of the Meuse River.

## Religion and Extinction

The notion that humans are programmed by only 40,000 or so genes and descended from a chain of earlier life forms profoundly challenged traditional religious beliefs that life and death are acts of divine will. From the scientific method came the possibility that the cosmos was not divinely constructed around humanity but rather is the product of random chance, and that the same natural forces controlling the fates (and inevitable extinctions) of animals shape human fate as well. Also assaulting people's sense of specialness is the evidence that human beings and their fellow thinking mammals are not the "fittest," as 95 percent of all animal species are invertebrates.

According to the Bible, God made human beings in his image and gave them dominion over all other creatures, whose existence was to serve their needs. To this day religion maintains this subordination of the natural order. When a random sample of Americans were asked whether "animals should have the same moral rights that human beings do," their agreement decreased with increasingly religiosity. When asked if "it is right to use animals for medical testing if it might save human lives," agreement increased with increasing religiosity.

Accused of causing "speciesism," Christianity has played a limited role in the war against extinction. Instead, the scientifically prompted ecological movement has come to assume some quasi-religious characteristics of its own.

## The Battle against Extinction As Part of the War against Death

So why the extensive attempts to save the California condor, whose diet at its peak 1 million years ago consisted of such currently extinct creatures as dead mastodons, or the Kemp's Ridley turtle that, with a brain cavity the size of a pencil-width hole, is unable to learn a thing from experience and whose existence is totally hardwired? The reason may be largely symbolic.

The cultural war against death has expanded beyond the medical front to include battles against extinction in the natural order—and even resurrection of the extinct, as when in 2000 scientists awakened dormant 250-million-year-old bacteria encased in a salt crystal. Through human intervention, creatures extinct in the wild, like the Arabian oryx, are preserved in species preservation programs in zoos, ideally to be reintroduced to their native habitats. (In fact, there are cases where animals presumed extinct have been "discovered" in zoos, such as the Cape Lion, which was rediscovered in zoos in Novosibirsk, Serbia, and in Addis Ababa, Ethiopia.) In addition, genetic repositories, the contemporary "Noah's Arks," have been established by the Museum of Natural Science at Louisiana State University and the American Museum of Natural History to preserve in liquid nitrogen tissue samples from thousands of different creatures. In 2001, tissue frozen for eight years was used to successfully clone a gaur (a large type of cattle).

Perhaps in reaction to the extinction of the passenger pigeon, considerable press has been given to attempts to rescue the whooping crane from oblivion. This cause célèbre is a white crane with a seven-foot wingspan, mistakenly believed to be extinct in 1923. The victim of overhunting, its numbers had dwindled to about fifteen in 1941—this, despite the Migratory Bird Treaty Act of 1918, which brought market hunting of the cranes and other migratory birds to an end, and the 1937 creation of the Arkansas National Wildlife Refuge on the Texas coast to protect the crane's last wintering ground.

The U.S. Fish and Wildlife Service began a whooping crane recovery program in 1967, relying initially on captive breeding to build up the population. As of 2002, there are roughly 300 of the birds.

## The Environmental Movement

In the broader cultural war against death, battles against extinction have assumed numerous fronts, such as conservation biology, gene banks, attempts to clone endangered species, and habitat restoration. Numerous new social solidarities have arisen, crosscutting the stratifications of class, gender, and age, in such groups as Friends of the Sea Otter, Sea Turtle Restoration Project, and Trees for the Future.

Growing concern over "ecocide" and "biological meltdown" has given rise to increasingly politicized environmental groups (Greenpeace, the Sierra Club, the National Wildlife Federation, Friends of the Earth, and various animal rights organizations). This social movement has quasi-religious trappings in its demands for ecojustice and concerns for leaving a legacy for future generations.

On the extreme fringe of this movement are the so-called ecoterrorists, such as the Earth Liberation Front and the Animal Liberation Front. Radical environmentalists, such as Finland's Pentti Linkola, see mass human death as the only way to save the planet's fragile ecosystem. This Voluntary Human Extinction Movement has the slogan "May We Live Long and Die Out." In addition to his hope for war, Linkola recommends ending capitalism, abolishing aid to the third world, and requiring mandatory abortions.

## Cultural Extinction

Analogous to people's interest in extinct creatures is their curiosity about extinct civilizations, such as the mythical Atlantis or the Anasazis and Mayans of the New World, and the causes of these cultures' doom. As paleontologists study life forms of the past so archaeologists study past cultural orders, investigating whether their demise was due to avoidable factors with lessons that can be applied to the present. The archaeologist Richard Hansen, for instance, argues that deforestation produced an ecological disaster precipitating the collapse of the Maya civilization in approximately 800 C.E. To produce the stucco for their huge limestone pyramids, the Mayans leveled forests to fuel the hot fires required for transforming limestone into lime. Or was the fate of these doomed cultures sealed by unforeseen and uncontrollable calamities, such as epidemics, earthquake, or drought?

The human war against death extends from battles against the extinction of biological to cultural systems. Memes are to anthropologists what genes are to biologists—carriers of life's organizing principles, ways of doing this, that are passed down generation to generation. And as biologists worry about diminishing biodiversity, cultural scientists worry about the abatement of cultural diversity and endangered languages. Of the 6,800 languages spoken worldwide in 2001—cultural DNA, if you will—only 600 are robust enough to be in existence at the end of the twenty-first century. The last speaker of Ubykh, for instance, died in Turkey in 1992 at the age of eighty-eight.

As the fossilized remains of extinct creatures are the rage of affluent collectors so too are artifacts of extinct cultures. So lucrative is the market and so environmentally damaging are the attempts to satisfy demands that laws have had to be passed to ensure that remnants of the extinct themselves do not disappear.

*See also:* APOCALYPSE; DARWIN, CHARLES; DISASTERS; NUCLEAR DESTRUCTION

### Bibliography

American Museum of Natural History. "National Survey Reveals Biodiversity Crisis-Scientific Experts Believe We Are in Midst of Fastest Mass Extinction in Earth's History." Press release, April 20, 1998.

Bell, Daniel. *The Cultural Contradictions of Capitalism.* New York: Basic Books, 1976.

Browne, Malcolm W. "New Clues to Agent of Life's Worst Extinction." *New York Times,* 15 December 1992, C1.

Carson, Rachel. *Silent Spring* Boston: Houghton Mifflin, 1962.

Chang, Kenneth. "Creating a Modern Ark of Genetic Samples." *New York Times,* 8 May 2001.

Darwin, Charles. *On the Origin of Species by Means of Natural Selection, or the Preservation of Favoured Races in the Struggle for Life.* 1869. Reprint, New York: The Heritage Press 1963.

Davis, James A., and Tom A. Smith. *General Social Surveys, 1972–1998.* Investigator, James A. Davis; directed by Tom W. Smith; produced by National Opinion Research Center. The Roper Center for Public Opinion Research, University of Connecticut, 1998. [machine-readable data file].

Day, David. *The Doomsday Book of Animals.* New York: Viking Press, 1981.

Ehrlich, Paul. *The Population Bomb.* New York: Ballantine Books, 1968.

Erwin, Douglas H. "Lessons from the Past: Biotic Recoveries from Mass Extinctions." *Proceedings of the National Academy of Sciences* 98 (2001):5399–5403.

Food and Agriculture Organization. "Up to 1,500 Animal Breeds Are at Risk of Extinction, FAO Warns." United Nations Press Release 3628, 7 December 1995.

Gould, Stephen J. *Wonderful Life: The Burgess Shale and the Nature of History.* New York: W. W. Norton, 1989.

Hallam, Anthony, and P. B. Wignall. *Mass Extinctions and Their Aftermath.* New York: Oxford University Press, 1997.

Hern, Warren. "Is Human Culture Carcinogenic for Uncontrolled Population Growth and Ecological Destruction?" *BioScience* 43, no. 11 (1993):768–773.

Holdaway, Richard, and C. Jacomb. "Rapid Extinction of the Moas (Aves: Dinornithiformes): Model, Test, and Implications." *Science* 287, no. 5461 (2000):2250–2254.

Leakey, Richard, and Roger Lewin. *The Sixth Extinction.* New York: Doubleday, 1995.

Lewis, Paul. "Too Late to Say 'Extinct' in Ubykh, Eyak or Ona." *New York Times,* 15 August 1998, B7.

Lowe, Sarah, Michael Browne, and Souyad Boudjelas. *100 of the World's Worst Invasive Alien Species.* Auckland, New Zealand: Invasive Species Specialist Group, 2001.

Miller, George T. *Living in the Environment: Principles, Connections and Solutions,* 8th edition. Belmont, CA: Wadsworth, 1994.

Montalbano, William D. "Agriculture's Gene Pool Shrinks Drastically Under Human Selection." *The Wichita Eagle,* 27 December 1993, 1A, 4A.

Muller, Richard, Marc Davis, and Piet Hut. "Cometary Showers and Unseen Solar Companions." *Nature* 312, no. 5992 (1984):380–381.

Osborne, Lawrence. "The Fossil Frenzy." *New York Times Magazine,* 29 October 2000, V1:70.

Perlin, John. *A Forest Journey: The Role of Wood in the Development of Civilization.* Cambridge, MA: Harvard University Press, 1991.

Raup, David M., and John J. Sepkosi Jr. "Periodic Extinctions of Families and Genera." *Science* 231 (1986):833–836.

Sampat, Payal. "Last Words: The Dying of Languages." *World-Watch* 14, no. 3 (2001):34–40.

Sepkoski, John J., Jr., and David Raup. "Mass Extinctions in the Fossil Record." *Science* 219, no. 4589 (1983):1240–1241.

Ridley, Matt. *Genome: The Autobiography of a Species in 23 Chapters.*New York: HarperCollins, 2000.

Singer, Peter. *Animal Liberation.* New York: Avon, 1991.

Smith, Jonathan Z. "A Slip in Time Saves Nine: Prestigious Origins Again." In John Bender and David E. Wellbery eds., *Chronotypes: The Construction of Time.* Stanford, CA: Stanford University Press, 1991.

United Nations Food and Agriculture Organization and the U.N. Environmental Program. *World Watch List for Domestic Animal Diversity,* edited by Beate D. Scherf. 3rd edition. Rome: FAO, Viale delle Terme di Caracalla, 2000.

*Internet Resources*

British National Space Center. "Report of the UK Task Force on Near Earth Objects." In the Near Earth Objects [web site]. Available from www.nearearthobjects.co.uk/neo_report.cfm

MacDougall, A. Kent. "Humans as Cancer." In the Church of Euthanasia [web site]. Available from www.churchofeuthanasia.org/e-sermons/ humcan.html.

Pickover, Clifford A. "Immortalization of Humanity." In the Edge: The Third Culture [web site]. Available from www.edge.org/3rd_culture/story/27.html.

Siegel, Lee. "The Five Worst Extinctions in Earth's History" In the Space.com [web site]. Available from www.space.com/scienceastronomy/planetearth/ extinction_sidebar_000907.html.

MICHAEL C. KEARL

F

# FAMINE

Every historical era has suffered the Four Horsemen of the Apocalypse mentioned in the Bible—famine, death, war, and the plague. Famine in the modern era is thought to be caused as much by other factors than food shortages due to nature. Famine involves a severe eruption of acute starvation and a sharp increase of mortality affecting a large segment of the population. Chronic hunger is characterized by sustained nutritional deprivation on a persistent basis.

Famine and chronic hunger are part of a food-availability–food-deprivation continuum. Either may be due to (1) forces of nature such as drought, plant diseases, or flood; (2) human conditions resulting from war, civil strife, genocide, market forces (e.g., hoarding, graft, and profiteering), and other exploitive governmental or corporation policies (where the goal is profit at all cost); or (3) both. Famine may be an intentional tactic or unintentional outcome of human behavior.

Estimates of excess death (i.e., actual famine mortality minus pre-famine mortality) due to hunger and hunger-related diseases of children, women, and men is around 40 million per year. During the famine of China, from 1958 to 1961, between 23 and 30 million people died. However, the greatest proportion of people died—one-eighth of their population, or 1 million people—during the Irish "Great Hunger" of 1845 to 1852. Dysentery, typhus, typhoid fever, and other infectious diseases, more so than literal starvation, were the primary causes of death.

Thomas Robert Malthus, an eighteenth-century British economist, theorized that famine, along with war and disease, was an adaptation to the imbalance between available food and population size. The neo-Malthusian view remains influential. Preventive policies would include increased food production capitalizing on technology (including improved fertilizers and transgenic food), and population growth restraints. Other conservationists and economists argue that high food production cannot be, and is not, maintained because a growing share of land and water used for crop production is unsustainable due to the various forms of pollution, increasing population growth in at-risk geographic areas, and global warming.

The Nobel Prize–winning economist Amartya Sen's entitlement theory sees famine resulting not from the unavailability of food, but the lack of means to purchase or otherwise obtain food. Prevention is rooted in (1) global, coordinated public policies that control exploitive local and global market forces and that provide import of surplus food and (2) entitlements that allow obtaining food such as free food at distribution centers, money, jobs, education, and health care in at-risk geographic areas such as states in sub-Sahara Africa, South America, and Asia.

Other scholars, like Jenny Edkins, lecturer in international politics at the University of Wales, see famine as essentially resulting from modernity, including poverty, violence, and the bio-politicizing of famine. These scholars would re-politicize the issue of famine with the goal of preventing violence, war, genocide, and enhanced human rights.

For example, the genocidal policies of the Stalinist regime resulted in the Ukraine famine during 1932 and 1933 that caused the deaths of some 6 to 7 million people. Periodic genocidal wars and drought combine to produce famine and chronic starvation in many of the countries of southern Africa.

In the twenty-first century, food security is declared a basic human right by the United Nations Universal Declaration of Human Rights. It is defined as access by all people at all times to enough food for an active, healthy life. Food is a basic need. If unmet by institutions and structures designed to provide for the general welfare, then food insecurity is a threat to any social system. Can global food security be attained? The crucial issue is whether the wealthy nations and the political and economic forces involved in the globalization process have the will to implement the preventive policies suggested by social scientists and humanitarians.

Specific, international measures to increase food security include a structure (especially legislation with enforcement powers) that guarantees a livable wage which enables workers to live healthily and well. Other measures include maintaining environmental security, implementing strong human rights laws, implementing safe and sane food technologies with special reference to transgenic foods, providing an international food distribution system to at-risk locations and people, instituting a famine early warning system such as the one developed by the U.S. Agency for International Development, and encouraging democratic and open societies with special emphasis on a free and inquiring press, educated public, and adversarial politics.

*See also:* DISASTERS

### Bibliography

Brown, Lester R., Michael Renner, and Brian Halwell. *Vital Signs 2000.* New York: W. W. Norton, 2000.

Daily, Gretchen, et al. "Global Food Supply: Food Production, Population Growth, and the Environment." *Science* 281, no. 5381 (1998):1291–1292.

Dreze, Jean, and Amartya Sen, eds. *Hunger and Public Action.* New York: Oxford University Press, 1989.

Edkins, Jenny. *Whose Hunger?: Concepts of Famine, Practices of Aid.* Minneapolis: University of Minnesota Press, 2000.

Gráda, Cormac Ó. *Black '47 and Beyond: The Great Irish Famine in History, Economy, and Memory.* Princeton, NJ: Princeton University Press, 1999.

Gráda, Cormac Ó. "Was the Great Famine Just Like Modern Famines?" In Helen O'Neill and John Toye eds., *A World without Famine: New Approaches to Aid and Development.* New York: St. Martin's Press, 1998.

Guerinot, Mary Lou. "Plant Biology Enhanced: The Green Revolution Strikes Gold." *Science* 287, no. 5451 (2000):241–243.

Maslow, Abraham H. *Toward a Psychology of Being,* 2nd edition. Princeton, NJ: Van Nostrand, 1968.

O'Neill, Helen, and John Toye, eds. "Introduction." *A World without Famine: New Approaches to Aid and Development.* New York: St. Martin's Press, 1998.

Sen, Amartya. *Development as Freedom.* New York: Alfred A. Knopf, 1999.

*Internet Resources*

Leidenfrost, Nancy B. "Definitions of Food Security Extension Service." In the Brown University [web site]. Available from www.brown.edu/Departments/World_Hunger_Program/hungerweb/intro/food_security.html.

Sen, Amartya. "Public Action to Remedy Hunger." In the Brown University [web site]. Available from www.thp.org/reports/sen/sen890.htm#n1.

"Ukranian Famine: U.S. Library of Congress Soviet Online Exhibit, 2001. " In the Soviet Archives Exhibit [web site]. Available from www.ibiblio.org/expo/soviet.exhibit/famine.html.

DANIEL LEVITON

# FEIFEL, HERMAN

American psychologist Herman Feifel was born in Brooklyn, New York, on November 4, 1915. He is internationally recognized as a pioneering figure in the modern death movement. His personal and research efforts helped break the prevailing taboo that discouraged scientific study of death and dying. His work transformed the way people think about death, treat the dying and bereaved, and view their own lives.

Feifel was educated in the New York City school system. His interest in psychology was stimulated during his undergraduate years at the City

College of New York by John Gray Peatman, and later by Irving Lorge at Columbia University, where he received his master of art's degree in 1939. World War II became a reality before Feifel could finish his doctorate. He enlisted in the Army Air Corps (now, the Air Force) in 1942, where he worked first as an aviation psychologist and later as a clinical psychologist treating combat soldiers overseas. While assigned to the Island of Tinian in 1945 he watched the *Enola Gay* take off to bomb the Japanese city of Hiroshima, an event that ushered in the age of atomic warfare. Feifel later reflected that this event and the death of his mother in 1952 were the two most important influences that catalyzed his interest in thanatology.

When the war ended Feifel resumed his studies at Columbia University, and finished his doctorate in 1948. He joined the Winter General Veterans Administration (VA) Hospital/Menninger School of Psychiatry group in Topeka, Kansas, in 1950, an event that marked the beginning of a long and illustrious association with the VA.

In 1954 Feifel accepted an invitation to join the Los Angeles VA Mental Hygiene Clinic. In 1960 he assumed the position of chief psychologist, an office he held until his retirement in 1992. Since 1958 he has additionally held an appointment at the University of Southern California School of Medicine, where he is emeritus clinical professor of psychiatry and the behavioral sciences.

Feifel's dissatisfaction with psychology's neglect of the existential richness of life, including the everyday matters of death and dying, coalesced in the 1950s. A major consequence was his focus on what has since become known as the field of thanatology. In 1959 he edited the book *The Meaning of Death,* which authorities agree was the single most important work that galvanized the scholarly community concerning dying, death, and bereavement. In this and related areas (e.g., gerontology, personality, psychotherapy, religious experience) his publications encompass more than 125 articles and chapters, as well as two books. Many of his literary contributions are focused on dispelling myths held by scientists and practitioners about death, the most injurious of which is a denial of its importance for human behavior.

Feifel's empirical contributions are most influential in the areas of death attitudes, death anxiety, and coping with life-threatening illness. By the late 1990s scholars identified over 1,000 published studies in these areas, and recognized Feifel as being the only person to contribute seminal papers in five consecutive decades. He shaped the direction of this research by arguing for reliable and valid measures that acknowledge the multidimensional, multifaceted nature of death attitudes and fears, the importance of death attitudes in shaping a wide variety of behaviors, and the need to study death issues among those actually facing life-threatening circumstances. His research demonstrated that fear of death can exist differently on conscious and nonconscious levels, and helped establish that people may use different coping strategies when faced with life-threatening versus non-life-threatening situations.

For his work in thanatology, Feifel has received numerous accolades, including an honorary doctorate from the University of Judaism (1984), a Distinguished Death Educator Award (1990), the Distinguished Professional Contributions to Knowledge Award by the American Psychological Association (1988), and a Gold Medal for Life Achievement in the Practice of Psychology by the American Psychological Foundation (2001).

*See also:* ANXIETY AND FEAR; PSYCHOLOGY; TABOOS AND SOCIAL STIGMA; TERROR MANAGEMENT THEORY

### Bibliography

Feifel, Herman. "Death and Psychology: Meaningful Rediscovery." *American Psychologist* 45 (1990):537–543.

Feifel, Herman. "Death." In Norman Farberow ed., *Taboo Topics*. New York: Atherton Press, 1963.

Feifel, Herman. "Death: Relevant Variable in Psychology." In Rollo May ed., *Existential Psychology*. New York: Random House, 1961.

Feifel, Herman, ed. *The Meaning of Death*. New York: McGraw-Hill, 1959.

Feifel, Herman, and Alan B. Branscomb. "Who's Afraid of Death?" *Journal of Abnormal Psychology* 81 (1973):82–88.

Feifel, Herman, and Vivian T. Nagy. "Another Look at Fear of Death." *Journal of Consulting and Clinical Psychology* 49 (1981):278–286.

Feifel, Herman, Stephen Strack, and Vivian T. Nagy. "Coping Strategies and Associated Features of Medically Ill Patients." *Psychosomatic Medicine* 49 (1987):616–625.

Neimeyer, Robert A., and Barry Fortner. "Death Attitudes in Contemporary Perspective." In Stephen Strack ed.,

*Death and the Quest for Meaning.* Northvale, NJ: Jason Aronson, 1997.

Strack, Stephen, ed. *Death and the Quest for Meaning.* Northvale, NJ: Jason Aronson, 1997.

STEPHEN STRACK

# FIREARMS

The availability of firearms is clearly associated with an increased risk of homicide, suicide, and deaths from firearm-related accidents. However, there is an active debate in the United States on the right to own and bear arms and the government's role in controlling access to firearms. Apart from the opinions on both sides, there are numerous studies on the topic. For example, countries with very restrictive legislation, including strict licensing of owners, have many fewer nonhunting fatalities from accidental shootings than countries with less restrictive firearm legislation. The United States is the Western country with the least restrictive firearm legislation; the accidental death rate by firearms in the United States is .7 people per 100,000 per year (compared to Sweden, which has restrictive legislation and one-tenth the number of nonhunting fatalities from accidental shootings).

When one factors in the variables of sex, age, income, ethnicity, education, previous violence in the home, and drug use, the presence of a firearm in the home greatly increases the likelihood of a homicide or a death by suicide. In the case of homicide, evidence shows that in many killings the offender did not have a single-minded intention to kill, and thus the lethality of the instrument used in the crime affected the outcome. Because homicides in the home usually follow altercations, and situational factors such as alcohol or drug consumption are often present, the presence of a lethal weapon increases the risk that a death will occur. Unsafe storage is also a risk factor, although the presence of a firearm has been found to be more critical than its accessibility.

In the case of suicide, studies have found that having access to a firearm in the home increases the risk of suicide; suicide rates are five or six times higher than in homes without guns. Restrictions on carrying firearms, enhanced sentences for the use of firearms in criminal offenses and legislation (e.g., in Canada), and compelling firearms in the home to be guarded under lock and key have been associated with reduced deaths by suicide and homicide. According to a study conducted by Colin Loftin and colleagues, a widespread prohibition of handguns in the Washington, D.C., area in 1976 also appeared to be effective in decreasing mortality by 25 percent in the ten years following adoption of those restrictive laws, compared to no similar reductions in adjacent metropolitan areas in Maryland and Virginia where the law did not apply.

Persons opposed to legislative controls on firearms see criminals and suicidal individuals as being motivated by an intransigent need to harm others or themselves that is predetermined before any lethal event occurs. According to this view situational factors, such as the presence of a firearm, are irrelevant because these people will commit their premeditated acts irrespective of the means available. Opponents of gun control also feel that if "guns are outlawed only outlaws will have guns." These opinions ignore the reality that many homicides and suicides are impulsive and passionate acts where the presence of a lethal weapon immediately available greatly increases the risk of a lethal outcome. Furthermore, many people who commit acts of violence, including homicide, have no known history of criminal behavior. Research has shown that suicidal people have a much greater likelihood of not dying by suicide if a particular preferred lethal means is not available. Studies conducted since the mid-1970s have shown that situational influences, including the availability of firearms, can be critical in the outcome of an event.

*See also:* HOMICIDE, EPIDEMIOLOGY OF; SUICIDE

## *Bibliography*

Gabor, Thomas. *The Impact of the Availability of Firearms on Violent Crime, Suicide, and Accidental Death: A Review of the Literature with Special Reference to the Canadian Situation.* Ottawa: Canada Department of Justice, 1994.

Kellerman, Arthur K., et al. "Suicide in the Home in Relation to Gun Ownership." *New England Journal of Medicine* 30 (1992):86–93.

Loftin, Colin, David McDowal, Brian Wiersema, and Cottey Talbart. "Effects of Restrictive Licensing of Handguns on Homicide and Suicide in the District of Columbia." *New England Journal of Medicine* 325 (1991):1615–1620.

Ornehult, L., and A. Eriksson. "Fatal Firearms Accidents in Sweden." *Forensic Science International* 34 (1987):257–266.

BRIAN L. MISHARA

# FOLK MUSIC

Folk music entertains, tells or supports a story, and is transmitted from generation to generation. It is the music of the common person as well as the wealthy. A significant number of American ballads were obtained from other societies such as Scotland, Ireland, Germany, England, and Wales, and the words were altered to fit the interpretation of the singer. Most often, the songs were obtained through oral tradition, rather than in written form, and the singer was left with the task of interpreting the meaning of the lyrics on the basis of his or her cultural milieu.

Most of the early folk songs were sung without instrumental accompaniment. According to folklorist Maude Karpeles, while collecting songs in the southern Appalachian Mountains during the years 1916 to 1918 with her colleague Cecil Sharp, found:

> The songs were, with one exception, sung without instrumental accompaniment. This is in accordance with the older traditional methods of singing, both in England and in America. The present custom of singing to the accompaniment of guitar or banjo, which has been adopted by some traditional singers, is fairly recent and is probably due to the influence of popular and pseudo-folk music heard on the radio. *(Sharp and Karpeles 1968, p. 9)*

The instrument used while singing a folk song varies with the culture, from the drum in Africa to the bagpipes in Scotland to the plucked dulcimer in the American Appalachians. In the folk music revival of the late 1950s and early 1960s, the major instruments were the guitar, five-string banjo, upright bass, and fiddle.

The durability of a folk song may be attributed not only to the song itself, but to the folklorists and collectors who accepted the task of obtaining songs in various sections of the world and tracing their origin. Folklorists such as Francis James Child, Cecil Sharp, Maude Karpeles, and Alan and John Lomax have preserved a folk music legacy that might otherwise have been lost.

Folk music has been written and performed portraying every theme imaginable. There are love songs and silly songs. There are songs with religious themes and songs with secular lyrics. Folk songs portray the good life and they delineate hardship. Some of the most popular folk lyrics portray dying and/or death. Common themes are death and its relationship to accidents, the supernatural, trains, murder, natural causes, the elements, war, suicide, and religion.

**Death by Accident**

There are many forms of accident that can result in death. Vehicular death has been portrayed in folk songs on more than one occasion. "The Drunken Driver" tells the story of two small children who were killed as they walked along a state highway. One of the deceased children turns out to be the drunken driver's son. "The Fatal Wreck of Bus" is the true tale of mass death when a bus goes over a cliff.

The death of two small children via drowning is reflected in "Kiss Me Mamma, For I Am Going to Sleep," which originally appeared in sheet music form. Songs about the sea, such as "Asleep in the Briny Deep" and "The Sailor's Sweetheart," tell the story of maidens who have lost their lovers to the sea. "Mighty Mississippi" and "The Flood Disaster of 1937" are only a few of the folk songs about floods and death. In the popular ballad "The House Carpenter," a wife leaves her husband and children to run away to sea with her lover. They are both killed when the ship sinks.

"Companions Draw Nigh" (also known as "The Dying Boy's Prayer") provides an account of a young man crushed in a construction accident and destined to die without prayer, song, or Bible present: "I must die without God or hope of his son, covered in darkness, bereaved an' undone." The popularity of cowboy songs in the early 1900s produced "Little Joe, the Wrangler," the tale of a young boy killed in a cattle stampede. When an avid cave explorer named Floyd Collins was trapped in a sandstone cave in Kentucky, and died before rescue workers could save him, several songs were composed about the tragedy. Eric Clapton's commercial recording of "Tears in Heaven" (1992) is reminiscent of early folk songs of tragedy. It tells the story of Clapton's son, who fell from a sixth-story window to his death. The song asks a question often found in folk music: "Would you know my name, if I saw you in Heaven?"

Sensational accidents involving a large number of people are especially likely to become popularized in musical literature. Train wrecks, mining disasters, airplane crashes, fires, cyclones, and sea disasters are a few of the themes in folk music. "Lost on the Lady Elgin" and "The Ship That Never Returned" are about separate ship wrecks. The most famous of all the sea disasters is probably the sinking of the Titanic, immortalized in songs such as "The Sinking of the Titanic" and "Just as the Ship Went Down."

"The Akron's Last Flight" is about an airplane disaster. "The Avondale Mine Disaster," "The Dying Miner," and "Dream of the Miner's Child" reflect the relationship between coal mining and death. "Bonnie James Campbell" and "Darcy Farrow" concern horseback riding accidents that result in death. Death via fire is delineated in songs such as "Baltimore Fire."

## Trains and Death

Perhaps no machine has ever captured the imagination of Americans like the train. In the early 1900s adults and children alike were in awe of the steam locomotive. The so-called father of country music, Jimmie Rodgers, was known as "the singing brakeman" because of his obsession with trains and songs about trains. Many songs reflect the death of the hobo, the common man who was often without home and food, and content to ride the rails. A few such as "The Fate of Chris Lively and Wife" concern death resulting from being hit by a train. Most, however, are about train wrecks and the brave engineers willing to die with their trains. "Casey Jones" (a train engineer on the Chicago and New Orleans Limited in Vaughan, Mississippi, in 1900) became an American hero when he died refusing to abandon his engine when it was about to crash into another locomotive. In "The Wreck of the Old 97" the engineer is "found in the wreck with his hand on the throttle, a-scalded to death by the steam." The devotion of the railroad engineer is best exhibited in "Engine 143" when George Alley's last words are, "I want to die for the engine I love, One Hundred and Forty-three."

*Jimmie Rodgers, the father of country music, was the first musician inducted into the Country Music Hall of Fame.* COUNTRY MUSIC FOUNDATION, INC.

## The Supernatural and Death

One of the oldest folk songs containing a supernatural theme is "The Wife of Usher's Well" (commonly called "The Lady Gay"), an English ballad reflecting the view that excess grief will cause the dead to return. A woman sends her children away to get an education, they die, she grieves, and they return to her in a vision. As a woman walks by the side of a river, her dead lover, "Lost Jimmy Whalan," returns to her in an apparition. In "Lily Lee," a sailor has a death vision involving his true love. When he returns years later she is dead. In the classic "Grandfather's Clock," the clock stops and never works again when its owner dies. Elements of the supernatural appear in the popular "Bringing Mary Home." The singer picks up a little girl walking along a highway and takes her home. When he opens up the door to let her out of the car, she is gone. The lady of the house explains that her daughter died thirteen years previously in an automobile wreck, and states, "You're the thirteenth one who's been here, bringing Mary home."

## Death from Natural Causes

Death from natural causes is a common subject in musical literature. When the song involves a child, the title of the song often contains the word "little" followed by the first name (e.g., "Little Bessie," "Little Mamie," and "Darling Little Joe"). The listener does not know what the cause of death is, but the last hours of the child are sometimes emotionally portrayed. For example, in "Put My Little Shoes Away," the dying child's major concern is that the parents will give his or her prized shoes away. "Darling Little Joe" focuses on what others, both human and infrahuman, will do after he is dead. The dying soldier in "Break the News to Mother" is worried about the welfare of his mother when she receives the news of his death, and "Little Bessie" experiences auditory hallucinations common among those who are dying:

> There were little children singing,
> Sweetest songs I ever heard.
> They were sweeter, mother, sweeter,
> Than the sweetest singing bird.
> *(McNeil 1988, pp. 172–173)*

## Death from the Elements

The plight of orphans frequently appears in folk music, often coupled with death from the elements to provide a more pathetic story. In "The Two Orphans," "The Orphan Girl," "Poor Little Joe," and "Little Paper Boy," children are discovered frozen to death at the end of the song. "Mary of the Wild Moor" and her child die from the cold weather and are discovered the next morning on the doorstep at the home of Mary's father.

The fact that failure to heed the advice of parents can end in death is emphasized in "The Frozen Girl" (also "Young Charlotte"), the true story of a young girl who froze to death on her way to a ball on January 1, 1840, after failing to heed her mother's warning:

> "Oh, daughter dear," her mother cried, "This
>     blanket 'round you fold,
> Tonight is a dreadful one, you'll get your
>     death of cold."
> "Oh, nay, oh, nay!" Charlotte cried, as she
>     laughed like a gypsy queen,
> "To ride in blankets muffled up I never would
>     be seen."
> *(Sandburg 1927, pp. 58–59)*

## Children As Victims in Murder Ballads

Murder stories involving children have been very popular in musical literature. While mothers are generally portrayed as gentle and kind, there are songs that portray their violent side. Feticide/infanticide may be found in "Mary Hamilton" and "The Cruel Mother" (also known as "Down by the Greenwood Sidie"), and rejection/neglect is delineated in "Lady Gay" ("The Wife of Usher's Well").

Drunken fathers are factors in songs like "The Drunkard's Child." "Little Blossom" goes to the bar to find her father and in a drunken rage he murders her. Poisoning is the variable in death for "Lord Randall." Revenge against the father for failure to pay a debt leads to the murder of his son in "Lamkin."

Several of the child murder ballads popular in America were transplanted from Europe. Sir Hugh tells the story of a little boy murdered by a Jew's daughter, and "Dunbar the Murderer" is the tale of a man who murders two children left in his care by the parents. However, most child murder ballads are original to the United States. Surprisingly, sensational cases, such as the murder of fourteen-year-old Bobby Franks by Nathan Leopold and Richard Loeb on May 21, 1924, and the murder and cannibalism of Grace Budd by Albert Fish in the 1930s, never made their way into musical literature. However, the killing of "Little Mary Phagan" at the pencil factory where she worked in 1913, the murder and beheading of "Little Marian Parker" on December 14, 1927, and the kidnapping and murder of the Lindbergh baby in 1932 were popularized in the media, commercial records, and folk music. Mass murders such as the "Ashland Tragedy" in 1883 (two children and a neighbor in Ashland, Kentucky, were murdered and the bodies burned) and the "Murder of the Lawson Family" (the father killed his wife, six children, and himself) made their way into the folk music tradition.

## Women As Victims in Murder Ballads

The common theme in ballads involving the murder of women is the luring of the woman by the man to the place of her demise under false pretenses. Most of the songs are English ballads or altered forms of English ballads.

The victim dies when she refuses to marry her murderer in "Banks of the Ohio" and "Poor Ellen Smith." Money appears to be a factor in "Down in the Willow Garden" (also known as "Rose Connelly"). Jealousy on the part of the killer is extant in songs like "Lord Thomas and Fair Eleanor" (the name of the woman changes with the singer). Pregnancy sometimes exists as a variable. For example, when Scott Jackson and a fellow dental student murdered Pearl Bryan at Fort Thomas, Kentucky, in 1896, both pregnancy and jealousy were factors. Jonathan Lewis drowned "Omie Wise" in Deep River in 1888 for dual reasons: She was pregnant and he preferred a local girl. "Knoxville Girl," a British broadside (single-sheet ballads sold for a penny or half-penny on the streets of towns and villages around Britain between the sixteenth and early twentieth centuries) written in the early 1700s, contains some of the most violent lyrics in any folk song.

**Men As Victims in Murder Ballads**

Few songs feature the murder of a man by a woman. Outstanding are the English ballad "Young Hunting" (known in America as "Loving Henry" and "Lord Henry and Lady Margaret") and American ballads such as "Frankie and Albert" (also known as "Frankie and Johnny") and "Frankie Silvers." In all these songs the homicide is the result of jealousy.

Men kill men for many reasons and under varied circumstances in folk songs. There are heroes (e.g., "Pretty Boy Floyd" and "Jesse James") and anti-heroes such as "Stagger Lee." Murder may be committed for wanton cruelty or economic remuneration. An act of homicide may involve the killing of one man ("Jesse James") or many ("The Golden Vanity"). The killing can be the result of jealousy and/or hatred. Whether the song is simply to tell a story or entertain, it is popularized and transmitted from generation to generation.

**Suicide**

Parental opposition to a love affair is a major theme in songs concerning suicide. In "Silver Dagger," both the boy and girl commit suicide when her parents oppose their love. Death due to grief is a factor for women ("Barbara Allen" and "Earl Brand") and men ("The Two Sisters"). In "It's Sinful to Flirt" the boy kills himself because the girl won't marry him, while the reverse is true in "The Butcher Boy." The girl commits suicide in "Johnny

Doyle" because she is being forced to marry someone whom she doesn't love. The man dies from a self-inflicted wound in "The Last Letter" when the girl marries someone else.

**War**

Songs about war are fraught with death and dying. There are lyrics portraying the grief (and death from grief) of those left behind. In "The Cruel War" the girl refuses to be left behind, dresses as a man, and goes off to war with her lover. The horror and violence of the battle are often portrayed in folk songs. Reflections of the dying soldier are quite poignant in folk music. Most of the final thoughts involve mother and/or the sweetheart left to mourn. In "Legend of the Rebel Soldier," the dying Confederate is concerned with whether his soul will pass through the Southland one last time on the way to the hereafter.

**Religion**

Songs concerning religion have three major themes. First, there are songs that provide a blueprint for living prior to death. Second, the means of conveyance to the hereafter is occasionally a subject. For example, it might be by train ("Life's Railway to Heaven"), a band of angels (that may carry the soul to Heaven as in "Angel Band"), boat ("The Gospel Ship"), or chariot ("Swing Down, Sweet Chariot"). Third, there are lyrics that denote what the afterlife is like. It is portrayed as a place of "Beautiful Flowers" and an "Uncloudy Day." It is a realm where there is no suffering or pain, loved ones may be greeted, and "The Soul Never Dies."

Folk songs provide helpful insight into the cultural traits related to death and dying in a specific society at a particular point in time. They also allow for comparisons of traits over a period of time. The provision of entertainment and knowledge at the same time makes folk music an integral part of any society with a music tradition.

*See also:* Mahler, Gustav; Music, Classical; Operatic Death

### Bibliography

Clapton, Eric. "Tears in Heaven." On *Eric Clapton Unplugged*. Reprise Records 9-45024-2.

Cohen, Norm. *Long Steel Rail: The Railroad in American Folklore*. Urbana: University of Illinois Press, 1981.

Crissman, James K. *Death and Dying in Central Appalachia*. Urbana: University of Illinois Press, 1994.

*Johnny Cash— Motion Picture Songs*. New York: Hill and Range Songs, 1970.

McNeil, W. K., ed. *Southern Folk Ballads*. Vol. 2. Little Rock, AR: August House, 1988.

Sandburg, Carl. *The American Songbag*. New York: Harcourt, Brace and Company, 1927.

Sharp, Cecil, and Maude Karpeles. *80 Appalachian Folk Songs*. Winchester, MA: Faber and Faber, 1968.

The Country Gentlemen. "Bringing Mary Home." On *Bringing Mary Home*. Rebel Records REB 1478.

JAMES K. CRISSMAN

# FORENSIC MEDICINE

Forensic medicine deals with the application of scientific medical knowledge to the administration of law, to the furthering of justice, and to the legal relations of the medical practitioner.

Forensic medicine addresses the physiology of dying, the cause and time of death, and postdeath phenomena. Practitioners of this branch of medicine assist the law in assessing the liability of medical practitioners in issues including consent to treatment, therapeutic intervention, emergency treatment, legal procedures, tissue and organ removal and transplantation, unnecessary surgery, cosmetic surgery, scientific experimentation, and sexual procedures, as well as questions regarding maternity, paternity, murder, malpractice, the development and gathering of evidence, and the application of statutory law to medicine.

Forensic medicine deals with offenses against the person or patient. Practitioners of forensic medicine assist in medical-legal investigations by offering expert opinions to help legally authorized individuals understand the medical implications of pathological examinations, including postmortem examinations (autopsies) of bodies, tissues, organs, and laboratory specimens. They offer expert scientific opinions on the cause and time of death. They may offer interpretations of DNA (genetic tissue) analysis. In criminal cases, the coroner (often a physician) provides investigators and the court

expert opinion on wounds, injuries, intoxication, poisoning, infections, and the proper handling of pathologic specimens.

Practitioners of psychiatric forensic medicine provide the court with expert opinions on mental illness, diagnosis, treatment, and mental competency, competency to stand trial, and questions regarding responsibility for actions under the law. Experts in forensic medicine make use of medical science to inform the law. They offer opinions on the validity and interpretation of medical examinations and testing.

The earliest antecedent of forensic medicine was recorded in the Code of Hammurabi (Babylonian Empire, approximately 2200 B.C.E.). Paragraph 19 of that document deals with the matter of compensation for the death of a slave, ostensibly killed by a treating physician. For several thousand years there were no comparable records. Then, in the fourteenth century, physicians began to perform autopsies to investigate the cause of death through careful dissection and examination of the body of a deceased person. The first formal medical-legal inquest into the death of a person in the United States took place in New Plymouth, Massachusetts, in 1635. Forensic medicine has come a long way since its inception. Contemporary postmortem examination is an integral part of criminal investigations and involves both gross and microscopic analysis of organs and tissues for the development of legal records and, if indicated, testimony in a court of law.

The term *forensic medicine* is often confused with the term *medical jurisprudence*. In fact, the terms mean the same thing in some countries. In the United States, the terms are not synonymous. Medical jurisprudence encompasses the legal aspects of medical practice as they involve risks to society, negligence, and unlawful and/or unethical practices. Medical jurisprudence deals with the codes, ethics, and laws that guide the practice of medicine. Forensic dentistry and forensic anthropology are closely related to the field of forensic medicine. Like forensic medicine, they rely on specially trained and experienced practitioners who help to inform the law with interpretations of the results of specialized examinations testing.

*See also:* EXHUMATION; HOMICIDE, DEFINITIONS AND CLASSIFICATIONS OF; HUMAN REMAINS

## Bibliography

Camps, Francis E., ed. *Gradwohl's Legal Medicine,* 3rd edition. Chicago: Year Book Medical Publishing Company, 1994.

Meyers, David W. *Medico-Legal Implications of Death and Dying: A Detailed Discussion of the Medical and Legal Implications Involved in Death and/or Care of the Dying and Terminal Patient.* Rochester, NY: The Lawyers Co-Operative Publishing Co., 1981.

Spitz, Werner U., and Russell S. Fisher, eds. *Medicolegal Investigation of Death: Guidelines for the Application of Pathology to Crime Investigation.* Springfield, IL: Thomas, 1980.

WILLIAM M. LAMERS JR.

# FRANKL, VIKTOR

Viktor Frankl, founder of logotherapy, also known as the Third Viennese School of Psychotherapy, developed a paradigm in psychology that focuses on the importance of meaning in life. Viktor Frankl was born in 1905 in Vienna, Austria. He earned his M.D. in neurology and psychiatry and his Ph.D. in philosophy from the University of Vienna. During World War II he was sent to Theresienstadt and then Auschwitz. His book *Man's Searching for Meaning* (1963) is well known. Frankl was inspired by the existentialism of the twentieth-century German and Swiss philosophers Martin Heidegger, Karl Jaspers, and Ludwig Binswanger. Frankl died in 1997.

Mindful of the finitude of human existence, Heidegger's thinking dwells on death as humanity's final boundary. Clearly death is a reality for all human beings and poses a challenge to humans' coping skills. "Logotherapy, unlike other existential systems, is basically an optimistic, future-oriented system, focusing on human freedom and the multitude of possibilities for human beings to find meaning" (Bulka 1998, p. 114). Logotherapy emphasizes the transitory nature of life and points to the meaning of the journey, thus avoiding the more negative aspects of existentialism by injecting hope, meaning, and values into the therapeutic dialogue.

In order to understand life's ephemerality, one must first understand the nature of time in the lives of human beings. It is critical to understand that time only goes in a single direction. Thus, the gift of time from one person to another is a gift that cannot be exchanged at a department store but is a permanent expression of human potential. Frankl notes that, "The meaning of human existence is based upon its irreversible quality. An individual's responsibility in life must therefore be understood in terms of temporality and singularity" (Frankl 1986, p. 64).

Life is temporary, yet each life is unique. As his clients became aware of the nature of the transitory nature of life, Frankl would offer this advice: "Live as if you were living for the second time and had acted as wrongly the first time as you are about to act now" (Frankl 1986, p. 65). He notes that as an individual understands the full gravity of time, he or she will recognize the full responsibility for living.

Life, then, is a journey that reflects the experience of time. To face life only to reach the end of the day, the end of the task, the end of a journey is to live for the goal of dying. For Frankl, the focus is on the experience so that each event or task in life can become meaningful. He writes of the unconditional nature of meaning. Having lived through four Nazi death camps, Frankl offers the thought that all of life has meaning that can never be taken away from the individual. Only the individual can lose meaning. When this happens, the individual suffers feelings of meaninglessness that Frankl has identified as "existential vacuum."

For life to have meaning, it must offer the experience of transcendence. Frankl notes that the word *geistig* (the spirit) refers to the capacity for self-transcendence, which is basic to human nature. The most meaningful experiences in life are those that transcend the individual and offer caring moments with others. The human spirit can also be experienced in the form of suffering. Frankl notes that meaning can be found in suffering by transcending the moment to understand the fullest impact of the experience. Frankl points out that "life can be made meaningful (1) by what we give to the world in terms of our creation; (2) by what we take from the world in terms of our experience; and (3) by the stand we take toward the world, that is to say, by the attitude we choose toward suffering" (Frankl 1967, p. 37).

As a person faces mortality either in his or her own death or that of a loved one, the first thing he or she experiences is the story of the person. Each

*Viktor Frankl's psychological approach focuses on the importance of meaning in life. His* Man's Search for Meaning *(1963) sold more than a million-and-a-half copies in the United States.* VIKTOR FRANKL

person's story reflects both who she or he is and what she or he has done. A funeral eulogy is a time to tell the "story" of the person. However, the task of grief, according to Frankl, is twofold: The first aspect is to find meaning in the story. What is it about the story of this person that offers meaning to the person articulating the eulogy? Meaning is often found by asking the question, What is it about this story that would be important enough to you to want to share with someone else? Frankl notes, "This leads to the paradox that man's own past is his true future. The living man has both a future and a past; the dying man has no future in the usual sense, but only a past" (Frankl 1984, p. 127). In the hearts of friends, the stories of the person's life reflect shared meaning. In this way there is a future, even after the death of the loved one. Paradoxically, the real hurt in grief is the fact that stories have endings. Yet when the story is understood in meanings, there are no ends, only meanings that can be passed on from generation to generation.

The second task of grief is to understand the responsibility that is called for by the loss of a

loved one, particularly in incidents such as a car crash where one person lives and the other dies. Frankl suggests that to honor the life of the deceased is to move beyond survivor guilt, which often accompanies this type of situation. Frankl suggests that there should be no such thing as survivor guilt, but only survivor responsibility. Each person has responsibility to transcend the circumstances of the incident and cherish the memory of the deceased.

The work of Frankl offers a way of thinking about life as well as a therapeutic approach to being with persons who are dying and their loved ones. The goal of this process is the search for meaning. In meaning all of the transcendent life forces come together to offer more than mere existence as a human being.

*See also:* GENOCIDE; GRIEF COUNSELING AND THERAPY; GRIEF: THEORIES; PHILOSOPHY, WESTERN; THOU SHALT NOT KILL

### Bibliography

Bulka, Reuven P. *Work, Love, Suffering, Death: A Jewish Psychological Perspective through Logotherapy.* Northvale, NJ: Jason Aronson, 1998.

Frankl, Viktor E. *The Doctor and the Soul: From Psychotherapy to Logotherapy.* New York: Vintage Books, 1986.

Frankl, Viktor E. *The Unheard Cry for Meaning: Psychotherapy and Humanism.* New York: Washington Square Press, 1984.

Frankl, Viktor E. *Psychotherapy and Existentialism: Selected Papers on Logotherapy.* New York: Washington Square Press, 1967.

JAMES W. ELLOR

## FREUD, SIGMUND

In 1856 Sigmund Freud, the founder of psychoanalysis, was born above a blacksmith shop in the Moravian town of Freiberg, his father an unsuccessful wool merchant. The family moved to Leipzig, then to Vienna, but continued to experience economic hardship. His mother—young, beautiful, and dynamic—was the center of his emotional life while his father was described as distant and ineffectual. Freud came of age during a renewal of anti-Jewish sentiment in Vienna after a more liberal policy had encouraged the belief that people would be judged on their merits rather than their religion.

Freud earned his medical degree at the University of Vienna and became an adept neuroscientist whose research advanced knowledge of the nervous system and uncovered the anesthetic properties of cocaine. Nevertheless, his discoveries failed to win a secure position. Unable to support a wife, he corresponded daily with his beloved Martha Bernay while studying in Paris with a superstar physician and researcher, Jean Martin Charcot, who opened Freud's eyes to the importance of psychological factors (especially displaced sexuality) in producing physical symptoms. History has not been kind to Charcot's assertions, but he opened up a new world of possibilities to young Freud.

Setting himself up in clinical practice in order to support a family, Freud married Bernay and together they eventually had six children, including daughter Anna who became a distinguished psychoanalyst and child advocate in her own right. Freud's clinical practice started in a discouraging way. Patients were few and difficult to treat successfully. He used the methods then in vogue and also tried, but abandoned, hypnosis. Freud had expected much of himself, longing to be part of the new wave of scientists who were transforming medicine and society—and here he was, barely able to pay the bills. The death of his father was a further blow. The way out of these difficulties proved to be the way in—to the secrets of his own mind. Freud became both the first psychoanalyst and the first analysand (one undergoing psychoanalysis).

## New Theory of the Human Mind

In *The Interpretation of Dreams* (1900) he reported (in a selective form) his self-analysis but also set forth an audacious new theory of the human mind. He elaborated, applied, and at times revised this theory over the years. Freud offered a complex vision of the human condition. He contended that adult personality is the outcome of experiences and conflicts beginning in early childhood. Neuroses result from difficulties in coping with fears, desires, and conflicts during the process of psychosexual development. Freud further held that conscious thought is a surface activity beneath

*Austrian neurologist Sigmund Freud became, perhaps, the first major thinker to recognize both the importance and the pervasiveness of grief.* CORBIS

which the unconscious operates according to its own rules. Much of the individual's emotional energy is tied up in an attempt to prevent threatening memories and conflicts from breaking through into consciousness. Furthermore, he believed that society itself has its own neurotic processes that often take the form of rituals and taboos. Mature persons are the ones who have become liberated from the hold of the past and accepted and integrated their basic impulses into a larger and more functional self.

Freud's new way of thinking about human thought and relationships led troubled people to seek his therapy and aspiring disciples to want to study with him. He was financially secure and in the midst of the international intellectual ferment for the remainder of his long life, but he was troubled throughout that life by a series of harrowing events: Friends died, some by their own hand; the brutality of two wars intensified his concern about the future of civilization; physical pain tormented him for years; and the Nazis systematically destroyed his books and the works of other Jewish authors, leading to his reluctant departure from Vienna.

**Freud on Death**

At first Freud was dismissive of death concerns (thanatophobia). He believed that people who express fears of dying and death are—way deep down—actually afraid of something else, such as castration or abandonment. Humans could not really fear death because they had never had this experience and because finality and death are not computed by the unconscious. This view remained influential for many years after Freud himself started to take death more seriously.

It was grief that came foremost to Freud's notice. Not only had many died during World War I, but also many of Freud's family members and friends were suffering from depression, agitation, physical ailments, and suicidal thoughts and behavior. Later he realized that many people lived in grief for deaths not related to the war and that these losses might account for their various emotional and physical problems. Freud's grief-work theory suggested the importance of expressing grief and detaching emotionally from the deceased in order to recover full function.

His most sweeping—and controversial—suggestion took the form of death instinct theory, which postulated that all living creatures engage in an ongoing scrimmage between competing impulses for activity and survival on the one hand, and withdrawal and death on the other. This theory was associated with Freud's ever-intensifying fears that human destructive impulses would eventually destroy civilization if not all life on Earth unless they were rechanneled by improved child-rearing, psychoanalysis, and more effective societal patterns. To the last he hoped that acts of love could counteract the destructive impulses. It was not long after his death in London on September 23, 1939, that Anna Freud organized an effective mission to save the children of that city from Nazi rockets and bombs.

*See also:* ANXIETY AND FEAR; DEATH INSTINCT; GRIEF: THEORIES; PSYCHOLOGY

*Bibliography*

Anzieu, Didier. *Freud's Self-Analysis.* Madison, CT: International Universities Press, 1986.

Freud, Sigmund. *Beyond the Pleasure Principle.* New York: Norton, 1960.

Freud, Sigmund. "Thoughts for the Times on War and Death." In *The Standard Edition of the Complete Psychological Works of Sigmund Freud,* Vol. IV. London: Hogarth Press, 1953.

Freud, Sigmund. *The Interpretation of Dreams.* New York: Random House, 1938.

Gay, Peter. *Freud: A Life for Our Time.* New York: Norton, 1988.

Jones, Ernest. *The Life and Work of Sigmund Freud.* Garden City, NY: Doubleday, 1963.

Schur, Max. *Freud: Living and Dying.* New York: International Universities Press, 1972.

ROBERT KASTENBAUM

# FUNERAL INDUSTRY

The American funeral industry emerged in the aftermath of the Civil War, picking up steam at the turn of the twentieth century and gaining economic power by the middle of the century. Although the industry has long been the object of scathing public attacks, local funeral homes across the country have won respect as established and trusted places of business and as a source of comfort for families suffering from the loss of a close friend or relative. Variously called "undertakers," "funeral directors," and "morticians," America's new ritual specialists have transformed the twentieth-century experience of death and body disposal.

The foundation of the emergent industry was embalming, a practice that gained legitimacy during the Civil War years. Although medical schools before the Civil War relied on various European methods of preserving dead bodies for instructional purposes, most Americans had no knowledge of the procedure and abhorred any "unnatural" intervention into the body's organic processes of decomposition. In antebellum America, the integrity of the dead body, even one disintegrating in the coffin, had to be preserved at all costs. Even though it might be placed on a cooling board, the interior of the corpse was generally not accessible to prying eyes, hands, or medical equipment.

During and after the Civil War, embalming became acceptable to more Americans who wanted to ensure that, no matter what, they could have a last look at their lost loved ones. Many Northern families who could afford it arranged to have the sacred remains of their fathers, sons, brothers, and husbands shipped home from Southern battlefields. They hired death specialists who found innovative methods, including arterial injection, to preserve bodies for the long journey home. Thomas Holmes, one of the pioneering founding fathers of the modern funeral industry, perfected his skills and made a dramatic impact on his fellow undertakers during the Civil War.

A critical turning point in popular awareness of embalming, and in legitimating it as a permissible American practice, was the cross-country journey of Abraham Lincoln's body after the war. Hundreds of thousands of people filed past the viewable body on display in cities from Washington, D.C., to Springfield, Illinois, and newspaper reports provided the public with graphic details about embalmers, whose methods were central to preserving a sacred relic that ritualistically united Americans after the divisive and bloody war.

After the Civil War, increasingly more undertakers began to experiment with embalming as an alternative to other modes of preservation. By the early decades of the twentieth century, embalming had become a standard practice in much of the country. American undertakers, many of whom had connections with the furniture industry and had a growing interest in the production of coffins, began to focus on the transformed appearance of the body.

Embalming assumed a central place in American burial practices for a number of reasons. First, instructors representing embalming chemical companies traveled the land, offering courses in the trade and conferring diplomas that signified professional expertise. In time, many of these companies established full-fledged mortuary schools. In addition, states began to recognize this modern professional occupation through licensing boards made up of established funeral directors and other civic leaders.

Second, the rhetoric surrounding embalming relied on contemporary theories about public health and sanitation; many argued that embalmed bodies posed less of a threat to the health of a community than bodies left to rot in the ground naturally. Third, an entirely modern funeral aesthetic emerged in these early years, based in part on chemical company assertions about the value of providing mourners with a pleasing, well-preserved, and viewable corpse. Fourth, embalming proliferated because of an industry-inspired mythology that portrayed current practices as a technological culmination of ancient sacred rites dating back to ancient Egypt. Finally, embalming seemed to respond at some level to the needs and desires of Americans from a variety of ethnic, racial, and religious communities.

The rapid spread of embalming spurred the equally swift emergence of funeral homes across the country in the first few decades of the twentieth century, as American life was transformed by urbanization, medical advances, and the increasing prevalence of scientific attitudes and perspectives. Undertakers no longer traveled to the home of the deceased to prepare the body but instead transported corpses from the home or hospital to the funeral home. A melange of business, residence, religion, and consumerism, the funeral home rapidly became an American institution in local neighborhoods. Funeral directors lived with their families in these homes, and very often wives and children worked with the father in preparing services for people in grief. Whether they helped friends, neighbors, or acquaintances, everyone who walked into the home shared one thing in common: They were customers engaged in a financial transaction.

As funeral homes multiplied, so did a variety of professional associations organizing men at the national and state levels, trade publications exclusively catering to an emerging class of authorities of disposal, and educational institutions for the training of funeral directors. The funeral industry gradually emerged as an economically sophisticated, politically adept, and consumer-oriented institutional powerhouse that revolved around the embalmed, viewable body. But the industry encompassed much more than embalming chemical companies and national professional associations. Casket manufacturers, florists, cosmetic corporations, automobile companies, cemetery associations, insurance agencies, and other related businesses played a role in the financial triumph of

*Lynch & Sons Funeral Home in Walled Lake, Michigan, has been a family owned and operated funeral home for over fifty years. The Lynch family, in its third generation of funeral directors, has chosen to remain privately owned while some others have sold to large multinational corporations.* TIMOTHY LYNCH JR.

the industry, which was generating billions of dollars per year in economic activity by the end of the twentieth century.

While the changing nature of funerals created an industrial juggernaut over the course of the twentieth century, the public image of funeral directors has been constantly tarnished by bad press, ugly controversies, and negative stereotypes. Although they have referred to themselves as "professionals," undertakers have had a difficult time convincing the public that this title should apply to an occupation that does not require a college degree—hence the gaping divide between the self-image of funeral directors as well-respected, active community members and the popular, media-fostered stereotype of the heartless, corrupt, and exploitative swindler.

Critics attacked modern American funeral traditions for a variety of reasons. The most obvious, and popular, line of attack was economic. The high cost of funerals seemed outrageous to many who

claimed that vulnerable families—especially poor families—consumed by grief and guilt had no choices and could not fully comprehend what they were purchasing when making funeral arrangements. Additionally, early on in the twentieth century many undertakers engaged in deceptive business practices, such as adding a range of costs for nonitemized services onto the price of the casket. Community and religious leaders, politicians, academics, and other public critics launched formal and informal investigations into the industry, and often produced lengthy, highly publicized reports that the media boiled down to accessible, reader-friendly stories that filled newspapers and popular magazines. Many reports tended to focus almost entirely on the economic angle, although explicit references to cultural and class differences frequently came into view. For example, many investigative reports claimed to have the interests of the lower classes in mind when making recommendations about curtailing the costs of funerals. According to these reports, the poorer segments of

American society, such as immigrants from Italy or Ireland, spent lavishly on extravagant funerals because they were ruled by irrational, emotional impulses that were manipulated by unscrupulous undertakers who encouraged them to spend beyond their means.

In addition to the economics of burial, many articles highlighted frequent religious criticisms of the American funeral. Not surprisingly, the focus in this regard was the embalmed, nicely dressed, presentable body displayed in an open casket for all to see. In the view of such critics, rather than expressing the highest values of an advanced civilization, this attention on the physical body was a debased form of paganism. They attributed this fixation on the corpse to a combination of irrational, primitive desires among the uneducated masses, and scandalous, dishonest practices by funeral men encouraging secular materialism.

The popular press frequently covered the high cost of funerals during the first half of the twentieth century, but one book published in 1963 made a dramatic, indelible impression on American public's perception of the funeral industry as nothing had before it: *The American Way of Death,* written by the English-born Jessica Mitford, simply restated earlier criticisms that were already familiar to most. But what made the book a runaway best-seller was Mitford's style of writing, an effective mixture of humor, muckraking, outrageous anecdotes, and exposé. The book struck a chord in American popular culture at a time when consumer consciousness and empowerment began to play a much larger role in the habits and tastes of the American buying public.

It also resonated because by the time of its release, the stereotype of the money-hungry, insensitive, buffoonish undertaker had already emerged in the American cultural imagination. One of the first was a hilarious, though brutal, episode in Mark Twain's *Life on the Mississippi* (1893), which depicted the author's encounter with an old friend who is now happily making a living burying people. A variety of subsequent similar representations gave shape to the popular, one-dimensional stereotype, including Thomas Wolfe's *Look Homeward, Angel* (1929); J. D. Salinger's *The Catcher in the Rye* (1951); the radio program *The Life of Reilly* with the famous character, Digger O'Dell, "the friendly undertaker"; the film *The Loved One*

(1965), adapted from Evelyn Waugh's 1948 book; and television shows all contributed to the vitality and familiarity of the stereotype by the early 1960s. Mitford's book reaffirmed, as well as revitalized, the stereotype. It resonated with Americans hooked on sensationalism and accustomed to the vile antics of modern death specialists.

Men and women in the funeral industry responded to Mitford in the same way that they had responded to earlier criticism. They engaged in intensive national public relations campaigns that included the production of numerous brochures and pamphlets, made efforts to educate their local communities through open houses and other events, and tried to defend the American way of death in the media when given an opportunity to present their case. In most instances, they claimed that the traditional American funeral—which included an embalmed body, cosmetic touches, an open casket, and a last viewing by mourners—expressed respect and honor for the deceased, represented patriotic American values, and responded to the deepest desires of the living who wanted to do right by their dead, regardless of what so-called experts might have said.

Industry representatives argued that most Americans did not want to handle their own dead and get them ready for burial. Any suggestion that the industry should be controlled by the government, these representatives warned, would lead to socialism and, ultimately, the destruction of democracy and the free market. Additionally, by the time Mitford's book was published, the industry had elaborated a theoretical basis for the modern funeral that relied on increasingly popular psychological language to justify its practices. In the early years of the industry, the reigning paradigm surrounding the professional duties of funeral directors was limited to his expertise in the area of embalming, running a successful business, and managing the funeral services. In time, another area of expertise that dominated industry rhetoric related to the psychology of grief, and, more specifically, the psychological value of viewing a pleasant-looking body in repose.

On the one hand, members of the industry asserted that the last look provided the bereaved with an undeniable message that death had occurred. On the other hand, gazing at the sacred remains initiated a much longer process of healing because it offered those in grief a lasting image or "memory picture" that erased many of the negative images coming to be associated with dying (i.e., being hooked up to tubes and wires in an impersonal, antiseptic hospital setting or seeing cancer disfigure the body of a loved one). The funeral industry strongly promoted a psychology of grief that shaped public arguments and led to a range of additional services that many funeral homes began to offer their customers, such as after-death bereavement counseling.

In the wake of Mitford's book and the recurring media reports on corruption within the funeral industry, a number of significant changes swept the country, although none really threatened the economic muscle and cultural authority of America's funeral homes. The Federal Trade Commission began its own investigation of the industry in the late 1970s and issued a series of proclamations based on its findings, including the Funeral Trade Rule in 1984. Some of the regulations imposed on funeral directors included providing clients with a detailed price list of all goods and services, informing them that embalming is not required by law, and allowing families to plan alternative funerals that did not follow traditional patterns.

Governmental requirements of full disclosure, along with larger shifts in U.S. mores during the 1960s and 1970s, left a permanent imprint on American mortuary practices. For example, in response to growing popular desires to craft personal ceremonies that were unique to the life and personality of the deceased, the industry began to loosen traditional rituals invented and perpetuated by funeral directors in the first half of the century, encouraging an embrace of "adaptive" funerals that catered to individual and community needs.

In the midst of these changes, the funeral industry increasingly adapted to consumer demands, although funeral directors continued to play a central role in the interment of the dead. Even though many from the older generation resisted such changes and called for a return to tradition, younger, more progressive funeral directors simply changed with the times and expanded the range of services and goods available at local funeral homes.

By the early decades of the twentieth century, African-American, Jewish, Catholic, and other ethnic and religious communities had their own funeral directors to take care of their dead. When a range of new communities sprang up in metropolitan areas after the change in immigration laws in the 1960s, many funeral directors began to offer services to Vietnamese, Latino, Eastern European, and other immigrant families that did not yet have their own funeral homes to which to turn. The funeral industry began to see a tremendous increase in Buddhist, Hindu, Confucian, and other non-Western religious rituals taking place in funeral homes across the country. In the first half of the twentieth century the industry had promoted cross-cultural knowledge of the world's funeral customs throughout human history, but up until the later decades of the twentieth century, funeral directors never had hands-on experience with these traditions.

Perhaps the most important development to emerge after Mitford's book was cremation. Although cremation had made its appearance on the American scene much earlier, it became a viable option in the late 1960s and grew in popularity in subsequent decades. At first, most imagined this option to be a mortal threat to the traditional funeral; the incineration of the body, with no embalming, no viewing, and no religious ceremony, posed an unprecedented dilemma for funeral directors around the country, who did not have the resources, technology, or tolerance for such an unusual mortuary practice. But as the cultural landscape began to shift, and as more Americans grew tolerant of the practice, the industry found ways to accommodate the growing numbers of people who desired burning bodies and ceremoniously disposing of the ashes. Cremation rates at the turn of the twenty-first century rose to 25 percent. As more funeral homes built their own crematoriums or contracted with independently owned facilities, the industry found ways to adapt to the popular practice. Cemeteries have built columbaria, merchandisers have produced a range of stylized urns, and funeral homes have established new ritual patterns, including some that retain more traditional elements, such as viewing an embalmed body before putting it to the fire.

Another significant trend to emerge in the closing decades of the twentieth century was the intrusion of multinational corporations into what has become known as "death care." Inspired in part by the aging of the populous baby-boom generation, big corporations like Service Corporation International and the Loewen Group have been buying up independent, family-owned funeral homes. Even though most funeral homes are independently owned and operated, these corporations will continue to play a major role in U.S. funerals well into the twenty-first century.

*See also:* BURIAL GROUNDS; CEMETERIES AND CEMETERY REFORM; CIVIL WAR, U.S.; CREMATION; DEATH SYSTEM; FUNERAL ORATIONS AND SERMONS; LAWN GARDEN CEMETERIES

### *Bibliography*

Bowman, LeRoy. *The American Funeral: A Study in Guilt, Extravagance, and Sublimity.* Westport, CT: Greenwood, 1959.

Farrell, James J. *Inventing the American Way of Death, 1830–1920.* Philadelphia: Temple University Press, 1980.

Habenstein, Robert W., and William M. Lamers. *The History of American Funeral Directing.* Milwaukee: Bulfin, 1962.

Huntington, Richard, and Peter Metcalf. *Celebrations of Death: The Anthropology of Mortuary Ritual.* Cambridge: Cambridge University Press, 1979.

Kearl, Michael C. *Endings: A Sociology of Death and Dying.* New York: Oxford University Press, 1989.

Laderman, Gary. *The Sacred Remains: American Attitudes toward Death, 1799–1883.* New Haven: Yale University Press, 1996.

Lynch, Thomas. *The Undertaking: Life Studies from the Dismal Trade.* New York: W. W. Norton, 1997.

Mitford, Jessica. *The American Way of Death Revisited.* New York. Alfred A. Knopf, 1998.

Pine, Vanderlyn R. *Caretaker of the Dead: The American Funeral Director.* New York: Irvington, 1975.

Smith, Ronald G. E. *The Death Care Industries in the United States.* Jefferson, NC: McFarland, 1996.

GARY M. LADERMAN

# FUNERAL ORATIONS AND SERMONS

Since ancient times ceremonies and rites have been associated with the disposal of a corpse. The purposes of these rites were to honor the deceased, to plead for divine favor, and to console the bereaved. Among the diverse customs that developed, funeral oratory emerged as a favorite means of responding to death, for it could, more than any other activity, highlight the personal characteristics of the deceased while serving as a means of reinforcing social bonds and status.

## Roman Origins of the Funeral Oration

The Roman funeral oration (*laudatio funebris*) was typically utilized by the social elite. It provided the means for publicly reaffirming the continued authority of the Roman state, the power and prestige of the deceased's family, and the maintenance of cultural values and social hierarchies. Normally the son of the deceased or another close relative delivered the funeral oration in the city forum, following a variety of public and private rituals. During the oration, the deceased's meritorious deeds and virtues were recounted. The oration highlighted the moral strength and acts of charity performed by the dead. In addition, celebration of loyal service to Rome in public office or military rank reinforced the authority of the Roman state. Recitation of the achievements and legendary deeds of the deceased's ancestors showed continuity with the past.

In his works, the Roman chronicler Polybius described in his written works some of the benefits of a typical elite funeral for younger citizens, arguing that such orations and grand celebrations invoked pride and inspired young men to emulate the behavior and deeds of the deceased. The tone of orations was positive. Families kept these eulogies as reminders and enduring obituaries that acted as a kind of moral heritage.

## Funeral Sermons of the Middle Ages

Funeral sermons of the Christian Middle Ages, often titled *de mortuis* sermons, originated with the works of Ambrose of Milan in the fourth century. His sermons combined Roman oration characteristics of praise and lamentation with Christian consolation. However, most surviving information on sermons dates from the fourteenth century. The medieval funeral sermon took place between the funeral mass and the burial, most likely given in the language that the majority of listeners would understand—Latin for a clerical audience, the vernacular for a lay audience. Sermons featured three main themes: an extended discussion on death based on biblical scriptures; the presentation of the deceased as a praiseworthy role model; and a plea to the living to help the dead.

Many funeral sermons survived as models for preachers. Such model sermons were adapted to individual cases indicating use for a priest, knight, burgess, or matron. The existence of so many model sermons suggests that by the fourteenth century demand for funeral sermons had risen.

Sermons stressed that grief was natural but should be controlled, and that the bereaved should present a brave face to the world, easing the suffering of others. Indeed, funeral sermons often argued that grief should be rational, having an appropriate level of grief. Therefore, the status of the deceased and importance to the community was taken into account, with grief for a knight greater than for a burgess and greatest for a prince. In this way funeral sermons make clear the complexity of the social hierarchy beyond the notion of the three estates. Medieval funeral sermons usually strove to celebrate the person in his or her role, not as an individual. Thus, medieval funeral sermons did not convey a strong impression of the deceased's individuality, but instead gave a sense of the person's place in the community.

## The Funeral Oratory and the Protestant and Catholic Reformations

The Protestant and Catholic Reformations caused the nature of the funeral oratory to gradually change. By 1550 Lutheran ministers had begun to emphasize sermons, which did not actually become central to burial services until 1600. Martin Luther had preached the first extant Lutheran sermons for the Saxon electors, Frederick the Wise and John the Constant, in 1525 and 1532, respectively. Focusing on the living rather than the dead, the intent of his biblical explication, Thessalonians 4:13–14 for both services, was to praise God and to console his congregation. He did not dwell on the personal qualities of the deceased. As these sermons increased in popularity, partly through the inclusion of models in church ordinances, their nature was transformed. Attached to their biblical exegeses and moral messages were lengthy eulogies of the deceased and their families. Because all funerals did not include sermons, the preaching of them served to highlight the deceased's prestige. They

generated widespread criticism because preachers inflated the qualities of the deceased and their families. Extremely popular, some 300,000 of them for both men and women were printed by 1770.

In other lands, extreme reformers, such as John Knox and some English Puritans, denounced the preaching of funeral sermons for fear that they would be interpreted as intercessory prayers for the dead or would be used to elicit those prayers. Many reformers, who also objected to them because of their Pagan origins, argued that burial of the dead was more appropriately a civil than a religious obligation. Ultimately, most English clergy chose to provide eulogies out of respect for the wishes of the bereaved who generally wanted to hear their beloved ones praised. Only a few Puritans failed to add commendations to their sermons. Justifying the praise on didactic grounds, their fellow ministers explained that they could hold up the praiseworthy lives of the departed as a pattern for members of their congregations to follow. Between 1670 and 1714, the sermons became increasingly popular; most of the 1,300 that were published in England appeared during that period. Some of the printed sermons were for women, who were extolled as models for all Christians, not just other women, to follow.

Moving between lamentation and praise, English preachers comforted the bereaved in oratory that was based on exegeses of scriptural texts, most often from the New Testament; a favorite was Revelation 14:13. With Greek and Latin allusions, ministers expounded on the brevity of life, on the difficulty of dying well, and on the blissful paradise awaiting Christians. They also attempted to rationalize the deceased's death and to offer ways in which members of their congregations should respond to their losses. Finally, they turned to the eulogies, which took up from one-fourth to one-third of the sermons and which, like the Lutheran ones, increasingly elicited criticism because of their flattering language. The more extreme Protestants tended to give stylized eulogies while other preachers offered ones that were somewhat more individualized in character. They all discussed personal matters, such as household relationships, private and public worship, and good works, as well as public careers. A detailed and sometimes lengthy description of the deathbed scene followed, in which the deceased played major roles in religious meditations and struggled to overcome satanic temptations.

## Post-Reformation Oratories

Orations continued in post-Reformation Protestant and Catholic countries. Universities in both areas might honor distinguished alumni with special memorial Latin oratory that extolled their public service and benefactions. Following the funeral mass in Catholic countries, such as France, priests also offered orations in which the eulogies were usually preceded by a lengthy meditation on death and the transitory nature of life. The death of the deceased, priests explained, was not simply the loss of relatives and friends but of all humanity.

During the Enlightenment, further changes occurred in Protestant and Catholic funerals. In Lutheran services the amount of clerical input was greatly decreased and often a secular oration replaced the sermon. In England the emphasis of the sermon shifted from the deceased's personal religious practices and household relationships to his or her public accomplishments and good works. Some Anglican preachers all but promised members of their congregations that if they followed the deceased's example they would be blessed financially in their earthly lives. Deathbed scenes were increasingly neglected. Although nonconformists continued to preach traditional sermons, criticism of their inflated eulogies soon led to their decline in popularity as well. In France, priests dwelt almost entirely on the deceased's life on the earth, leaving out extended religious meditations on death and the transitory nature of life.

## Orations in the Eighteenth and Nineteenth Centuries

By the late eighteenth century, funeral orations had shifted firmly away from religious strictures and biblical exegesis to more secular topics. These eulogies emphasized the deeds of the citizen laboring in the state's service as well as private virtues. Republican France staged elaborate civic funerals that pointedly restricted religious content and reinforced republican ideals. This aspect became most clear at the graveside as orators, chosen by family members, spoke in praise and memory of the departed. The speeches dealt with the deceased's best qualities, but also touched on

political and social issues, providing an opportunity for reaffirming the prominence of the republic. England utilized state funerals for similar political and cultural affirmation.

In France and England, the religious portion of the funeral sermon dwelt on the threat of hell, though by the end of the nineteenth century the image of hell receded and the religious message became one of reassurance and comfort. In funeral sermons hell lost its terror, while heaven came to be a place that promised good things and reunion with loved ones.

## Funeral Sermons in the Twentieth Century

Over the course of the twentieth century, funeral sermons further deemphasized the religious content as the entire funeral process became more professional and less dominated by family members. Although the clergy continued to provide sermons and commendations at funerals, especially in the reformed churches, by the late twentieth century the secularization of society had led to an increased lay participation in the services, with friends and family providing eulogies and services that often supplanted the religious services. Lay eulogies included film clips, recordings, oral reminiscences, poetry, and spiritual readings. The orators, unlike their predecessors, often recalled the foibles of the deceased as well as their finer moments. The total effect of the service was to celebrate the human spirit rather than to offer up the deceased as a religious model.

Funeral oratory has served vital social functions in Western culture, including commending the deceased and reinforcing religious beliefs, social hierarchies, and relationships. Funeral oratory in the twenty-first century will likely reflect a continuing secular emphasis, as well as the growing influence of the World Wide Web and advancing technology. Numerous religious organizations offer resources on the Internet for funeral sermons and eulogy. Virtual funerals on the Internet and videotaped funerals will increase access to funeral oratory. Access to oratory practices worldwide via technology and the Internet may both diversify and homogenize human death practices.

*See also:* EPITAPHS; FUNERAL INDUSTRY; GRIEF AND MOURNING IN CROSS-CULTURAL PERSPECTIVE

## Bibliography

Ariès, Philippe. *The Hour of Our Death*. New York: Knopf, 1981.

Bailey, Peter. *French Pulpit Oratory, 1598–1650: A Study on Themes and Styles with a Descriptive Catalogue of Printed Texts*. Cambridge: Cambridge University Press, 1980.

Ben-Amos, Avner. *Funerals, Politics, and Memory in Modern France, 1789–1996*. Oxford: Oxford University Press, 2000.

D'Avray, David L. *Death and the Prince: Memorial Preaching before 1350*. Oxford: Clarendon Press, 1994.

D'Avray, David L. "The Comparative Study of Memorial Preaching." *Transactions of the Royal Historical Society* 5th series, 40 (1990):25–42.

D'Avray, David L. "Sermons on the Dead Before 1350." *Studi Medievali* 3rd series, 31 (1990):207–223.

Gadberry, James H. "When Is a Funeral Not a Funeral?" *Illness, Crisis & Loss* 8, no. 2 (2000):166–180.

Houlbrooke, Ralph. *Death, Religion and the Family in England, 1480–1750*. Oxford: Clarendon Press, 1998.

Koslofsky, Craig M. *The Reformation of the Dead: Death and Ritual in Early Modern Germany, 1450–1700*. New York: St. Martin's Press, 2000.

Ochs, Donovan J. *Consolatory Rhetoric: Grief, Symbol, and Ritual in the Greco-Roman Era*. Columbia: University of South Carolina Press, 1993.

Toynbee, Jocelyn M. C. *Death and Burial in the Roman World*. Ithaca, NY: Cornell University Press, 1971.

Tromly, Frederic B. " 'According to Sound Religion,' the Elizabethan Controversy Over the Funeral Sermon." *Journal of Medieval and Renaissance Studies* 13 (1983):293–312.

Warnicke, Retha M., and Bettie Anne Doebler. *Deaths Advantage Little Regarded by William Harrison, The Soules Solace Against Sorrow by William Leigh, and A Brief Discourse of the Christian Life and Godly Death of Mistris Katherin Brettergh (1602)*. Delmar, NY: Scholars' Facsimiles and Reprints, 1993.

RETHA M. WARNICKE
TARA S. WOOD

# GENDER AND DEATH

Males and females have different risks of dying with regard to both age at, and cause of, death. The male-female differential depends on level of economic development; however, there are some universal characteristics that appear to be biologically determined. These "universals" are most pronounced at young ages.

## Biological Differences

It has universally been found that more male than female babies are born. While the magnitude of the sex ratio at birth (the number of male births per 100 female births) varies somewhat, it is almost always in the range of 103 to 107. There is some debate about why male births exceed female births, in part centered on the issue of sex differences in the number of conceptions. It has been argued that considerably more males are conceived, but that the male fetus is biologically weaker. The data available suggest that males do have higher mortality from around the third to the fifth month of gestation age. While it is extremely difficult to know about mortality risk during the first few months of pregnancy, the limited evidence suggests that there are more male embryos by the second month after conception. This means either that more males are conceived or that female embryos have higher mortality risk in the weeks after conception, or both.

While there is uncertainty about sex mortality differentials in the early gestational period, data for the first year of life are very clear. In virtually all places and times infant mortality rates are higher for males than for females. Quite a bit of evidence points to biological factors playing an important role in the higher mortality of infant males. Despite their higher birthweights (a factor associated with infant survival), male babies are more likely to suffer from congenital abnormalities that lead to death and to have immune deficiencies associated with X chromosome-linked genetic defects and with exposure to testosterone prenatally and in early infancy. This latter factor may also contribute to greater activity levels associated with higher accident mortality.

Other biologically based factors contributing to gender differences in mortality include the protective effect of women's XX chromosome structure against heart disease, especially at ages under fifty-five, and a propensity to violence among men that can have lethal consequences. The degree to which men are more violence-prone than women and the reasons for it are, however, hotly debated and it cannot be stated if and how biology may be implicated. While biological factors can explain part of gender differences in mortality, these differences vary too much by time and place to be accounted for by biology to any great extent.

## Gender Differences in Mortality in Less Developed Countries

According to the Population Reference Bureau, circa 2000 in less developed countries the life expectancy at birth of females exceeded that of males by three years (66 versus 63 years). In the

1950s the differential was approximately two years (42 versus 40 years). While considerable progress in life expectancy at birth has been made, and approximately equivalently for males and females, there is much concern that women in third world countries are disadvantaged in terms of mortality. In part, this concern stems from the gender mortality gap favoring females in developed countries that is interpreted to mean that, given more equal treatment, females will have lower mortality than males.

The clearest evidence of female disadvantage comes from demographic research on the third world, which estimates that between 60 million and 100 million girls and women are "missing." They are missing as a combined result of female infanticide, sex-selective abortion and health care neglect, nutritional deficiency, and mistreatment that lead to death. Also, maternal mortality plays a role; the World Health Organization (WHO) and UNICEF estimate that more than half a million women die per year due to pregnancy-related problems, most in developing countries. Worldwide, women face a 1 in 75 lifetime risk of dying due to maternity-related causes. This risk varies from 1 in 4,085 in industrialized countries to 1 in 16 in the least developed parts of the world (see Table 1).

The female mortality disadvantage varies substantially across developing countries. For example, in substantial portions of the third world, mortality rates at ages one through four are approximately equal for girls and boys. However, populations of the Indian subcontinent and China have childhood mortality rates favoring males by a substantial margin. Indeed, it is likely that most of the world's missing girls and women are from these two regions. It appears that the female mortality disadvantage in the third world is less the result of societal economic deprivation (as many countries are poorer than India and China) than it is the by-product of cultural values and practices that favor males. China's one-child-only population policy also plays a role, given a pre-existing preference for sons in that patrilineal society.

Within the third world in general, there is not any systematic evidence that females are less well-nourished than males. However, research suggests that differential access to preventive and curative health care, such as vaccinations, favors males in

**TABLE 1**

| Maternal mortality, 1995 | | |
| --- | --- | --- |
| Area | Number of Maternal Deaths | Lifetime Risk of Maternal Death 1 in: |
| World | 515,000 | 75 |
| Industrialized Countries | 1,200 | 4,085 |
| Developing Countries | 511,000 | 61 |
| Least Developed Countries | 230,000 | 16 |

SOURCE: Adapted from WHO, UNICEF and UNFDA. *Maternal Mortality in 1995: Estimates Developed by WHO and UNICEF.* Geneva, 2001.

much of the third world. Another factor that negatively affects female mortality relates to birth spacing. In countries with son preference, the birth of a daughter will be more quickly followed by another birth than is the case when a son is born. This disadvantages young girls because a short interval between siblings is related to higher mortality for the older child.

An aspect of gender inequality in death concerns cultural practices related to widowhood. In some societies it is cultural practice for widows to also die when their husbands pass away. A well-known case of this practice is *sati* in India, in which a widow is expected to commit suicide by throwing herself on his funeral pyre. A widow who resisted might be pushed into the pyre by her in-laws. While religious reasons are purportedly at the root of such practices, it is also argued that other motives can prevail, such as repossession of the widow's inheritance by her husband's family. While sati was legally banned in the 1800s by the British colonial rulers in India, it persists only in a few Indian states and other parts of south Asia.

## Gender Differences in Mortality in Developed Countries

In developed countries, females outlive men by seven years: life expectancy at birth for females is 79 and for males it is 72. However, there is variation across the developed world in the magnitude of the sex difference in life expectancy. It ranges from a low of five years in many of the countries that made up the former Yugoslavia (averaging 75 years for females and 70 years for males) to a high of twelve years in Russia (73 years for females; 61 years for males).

In mid-twentieth century the average difference in life expectancy at birth in more developed countries was approximately five years. At the beginning of the twentieth century, the difference was estimated at two to three years.

Trends in mortality favored women in the more developed countries from at least the beginning of the twentieth century to the early 1980s. Mortality trends in different age groups contributed differentially to this overall trend of widening the sex gap in mortality. Nearly two-thirds of the widening can be attributed to mortality among people aged sixty-five and over. In other words, death rates for older women declined more quickly than death rates for older men. One-quarter of the increase resulted from mortality trends among people aged fifty-five to sixty-four, for whom, as well, female death rates declined more than male death rates. Very little of the increase was due to mortality among children aged one to fourteen, less than 3 percent. (This is unlike the case in the third world, where death rates among children figure prominently in mortality trends and differentials.) In contrast, trends in infant mortality operated in opposite fashion, to narrow the sex difference in mortality. High male infant mortality was overcome to a considerable degree so that eventually, for the most part, only the genetically caused higher susceptibility of male infants to death remained.

Differential trends in various causes of death contributed to the widening of the sex mortality difference. By far the most important cause of death in the widening is diseases of the circulatory system, which include ischemic heart disease and strokes. While there is variation from country to country, the overall fact that male deaths due to circulatory disease declined less than female deaths is responsible for approximately three years of the widening gap. Of the different kinds of circulatory diseases, trends in ischemic heart disease played the biggest role in this three-year widening, with men's death rates increasing over most of the twentieth century while women's death rates were stable or declined. Rheumatic heart disease and strokes (for which

women and men have approximately equal risks of death) have decreased in importance as causes of death. Thus, the composition of the circulatory disease category—with an increasing prevalence of ischemic heart disease—played a role in widening the sex mortality differential.

The second most important cause of death in explaining the widening sex differential in mortality is malignant neoplasms (cancer). At the turn of the twentieth century, female mortality from cancer (especially due to breast cancer and cancers of the female genital organs) tended to be higher than male cancer mortality. However, over the course of the twentieth century increasing rates of male mortality due to respiratory (e.g., lung) cancers served to widen the male-female mortality difference. In the United States for the period from 1900 to the early 1980s shifts in the trends and pattern of cancer mortality accounted for more than one-third of the widening sex mortality differential; in other Western countries such as England and Australia, the contribution made by malignant neoplasms to widening the sex mortality ratio was even greater.

Other causes of death are much less important contributors to the widening sex mortality differential. For example, declines in maternal mortality, although very substantial, have had only a small effect. Trends in accident mortality and suicide—two causes of death that are higher for males—have not played a big role either. In contrast, declines in infectious and parasitic diseases, for which males in the West tended to have higher mortality than females, had an opposite effect, that is, to narrow the sex gap in mortality.

The increase in respiratory cancer among men and the slower decreases in circulatory system mortality among men have been attributed to smoking differences, in large part. Over the earlier years of the twentieth century, men (much more so than women) took up cigarette smoking, the effects of which show up in mortality statistics among older age groups being that cigarettes are slow killers.

Since the early to mid-1980s the sex differential in mortality has narrowed a bit in developed countries, although it is still the case that male mortality is higher than female mortality for every major cause of death. For example, in the United States, life expectancy at birth favored females by 7.6 years in 1980; by 1990 and 2000, the difference was 6.7 years and 6.6 years, respectively. Trends in cancer, particularly respiratory cancers, account for some of the decrease. Since 1980 in the United States, men's rates of lung cancer mortality, although still increasing, have slowed down in pace; in contrast, women's rates of lung cancer mortality have skyrocketed. This trend reflects, in large part, the later adoption of smoking by women.

If the sex differential in mortality is to be reduced, the preferable route is by decreasing male mortality, not increasing female mortality. Smoking cessation is clearly required in order to achieve this. Also, research has shown that the sex gap in mortality is much smaller among the educated and economically advantaged segments of the U.S. population. This suggests that mortality level is, to a large extent, determined by social and economic factors, and that reductions in male mortality closer to female levels are attainable.

The topic of gender and death is one that is inherently political. On the surface it appears that in most populations in the world females are advantaged in that they live longer. One might wonder, then, why both international and national efforts are concentrated with women's health. Three issues are to be acknowledged in attempting to answer this question. One, there are clear indications that, at least in the area of the Indian subcontinent and in China that account for a large proportion of the world's population, females are treated in ways that risk their lives. Two, in most parts of the developing world females are not living as long as they could, given historical data from the West. Three, although females live longer in the developed countries, all evidence suggests that they are sicker than males, especially in adulthood and older adulthood. Efforts to combat premature mortality and morbidity should be cognizant of the often nuanced way that gender affects life and death.

Gender differences are also involved in matters associated with death, and not just death per se. In a classic work on cross-cultural aspects of grief and mourning, Rosenblatt and colleagues reported that men and women tend to vary in emotional expression of bereavement. Women are more likely to cry and self-mutilate whereas men tend to direct the anger associated with bereavement to others and away from themselves. It is possible that this gender difference in expressivity reflects a more general pattern of gender inequality; that is, women, given their lower status, may be used as the persons who are expected, and perhaps coerced, to engage in activities that publicly symbolize a death that has occurred. Women are also often expected to publicly display their bereaved status much longer than men. For example, in many southern European countries, it was traditionally expected, and still is to varying degrees, that a widow wears black clothing for the rest of her life. Such rituals have the effect of silencing women and their sexuality.

Women tend to be more involved with death than men, given their role as "carers of others." Women, either as family members or as paid workers, are the ones who care for the dying in all societies. In Western societies, in which women outlive men by a substantial degree, elderly women are often the chief caregivers to their dying husbands, although they obtain assistance from other women, notably their daughters and daughters-in-law. They then face the prospect of their own death, typically partnerless because widows are not as likely to remarry as are widowers.

*See also:* INFANTICIDE; MORTALITY, CHILDBIRTH; SUICIDE INFLUENCES AND FACTORS: GENDER

## Bibliography

Boyd, Neil. *The Beast Within: Why Men Are Violent.* Vancouver, BC: Greystone Books, 2000.

Cline, Sally. *Lifting the Taboo: Women, Death and Dying.* London: Little, Brown, 1995.

Coale, Ansley J. "Excess Female Mortality and the Balance of the Sexes." *Population and Development Review* 17 (1991):517–523.

Cohen, Alex. "Excess Female Mortality in India: The Case of Himachal Padesh." *American Journal of Public Health* 90 (2000):1367–1371.

Lopez, Alan D., Graziella Caselli, and Tapani Valkonen, eds. *Adult Mortality in Developed Countries: From Description to Explanation.* Oxford: Clarendon Press, 1995.

Population Reference Bureau. *2001 World Population Data Sheet.* Washington, DC: Author, 2001.

Retherford, Robert D. *The Changing Sex Differential in Mortality.* Westport, CT: Greenwood Press, 1975.

Rogers, Richard G., Robert A. Hummer, and Charles B. Nam. *Living and Dying in the USA.* San Diego, CA: Academic Press, 2000.

Rosenblatt, Paul C., R. Patricia Walsh, and Douglas A. Jackson. *Grief and Mourning in Cross-Cultural Perspective.* New Haven, CT: HRAF Press, 1976.

Sen, Amartya. "Missing Women." *British Medical Journal* 304 (1992):587–588.

United Nations. *World Population Prospects: The 1998 Revision,* Vol. 3: *Analytical Report.* New York: Author, 2000.

United Nations. *Too Young To Die: Genes or Gender?* New York: Author, 1998.

United Nations Secretariat. "Sex Differentials in Life Expectancy and Mortality in Developed Countries: An Analysis by Age Groups and Causes of Death from Recent and Historical Data." *Population Bulletin of the United Nations* 25 (1988):65–106.

Waldron, Ingrid. "Factors Determining the Sex Ratio at Birth." In *Too Young To Die: Genes or Gender?* New York: United Nations, 1998.

Waldron, Ingrid. "Sex Differences in Infant and Early Childhood Mortality: Major Causes of Death and Possible Biological Causes." In *Too Young To Die: Genes or Gender?* New York: United Nations, 1998.

Waldron, Ingrid. "What Do We Know about Causes of Sex Differences in Mortality? A Review of the Literature." *Population Bulletin of the United Nations* 18 (1985):59–76.

Women's International Network News. "Africa: High Maternal Mortality Continues Unabated." *Women's International Network News* 25, no. 4 (1990):51.

World Health Organization, UNICEF, and UNFDA. *Maternal Mortality in 1995: Estimates Developed by WHO and UNICEF.* Geneva: Author, 2001.

Wright, Russell O. *Life and Death in the United States.* Jefferson, NC: McFarland, 1997.

ELLEN M. GEE

# GENDER DISCRIMINATION AFTER DEATH

Does gender discrimination continue after death? A lifetime of inequality is arguably enough; how might inequality between the sexes perpetuate itself beyond the grave? If one assumes that a posthumous obituary is a postself artifact that survives death, then one might ask whether or not obituaries are written and published in an unbiased manner. Scholars suggest that they are not, and that gender discrimination follows the individual beyond the grave.

## Discussions of Gender Discrimination after Death

In 1977 the scholars Robert Kastenbaum, Sara Peyton, and Beatrice Kastenbaum were the first to raise the question of gender discrimination after death. They hypothesized that the "dominant male-preferring value system of the United States would carry over the threshold from life to death" (Kastenbaum, Peyton, and Kastenbaum 1977, p. 353). The authors used newspaper obituaries as a subtle, unobtrusive measure of society's value system, and they proposed that men receive greater public recognition after death than women. Their hypothesis was tested in two major metropolitan newspapers on the East Coast, the *New York Times* and the *Boston Globe.* They found that men receive four times as many obituaries as women, and that male obituaries are longer and are ten times more likely to be accompanied by a photograph. They concluded that the readers of these two publications are receiving "systematic, if subtle confirmation of the greater importance of men." They argued that if gender equality has won fundamental acceptance, one will expect it to "express itself in less visible, less pressured-by-advocacy areas such as obituaries" (p. 356).

Kastenbaum and his colleagues set the bar; others challenged it using a variety of methods and data sources. For example, in 1979 Bernard Spilka, Gerald Lacey, and Barbara Gelb examined obituaries in two Denver newspapers, the *Denver Post* and the *Rocky Mountain News,* arguing that the West is more progressive than the East. They sampled obituaries from July 1976 through July 1977 in both papers. Their findings provided weak support for gender bias favoring males. This is most pronounced in terms of obituary length, but there is evidence that women receive fewer obituaries and fewer photographs as well. They concluded: "Economic, political, and social factors within Western society continue to support a greater valuation of males and this is perpetuated even in the manner in which one's death is marked and remembered" (Spilka, Lacey, and Gelb 1979, p. 232).

The next period of examination occurred in the mid-1980s. First, Michael Kearl looked at two national news magazines, *Time* and *Newsweek,* and sampled obituaries from 1923 to 1979. Men are six times more likely to receive an obituary than women and ten times more likely to receive a photograph; male obituaries are also longer. He found that individuals in the arts and business account for over 40 percent of the obituaries, and that women are underrepresented in all role categories except familial relation (being related to a famous person, almost always a man).

Next, Bernice Halbur and Mary Vandagriff examined death notices (as opposed to obituaries) in three Birmingham, Alabama, newspapers, the *Reporter,* the *World,* and the *News,* over an eighty-five-year period from 1900 through 1985. In their research they found no evidence of bias because they used death notices and not obituaries. Kastenbaum distinguished between death notices ("a single paragraph of basic information that is set in small type and included in an alphabetical listing of recent deaths") and obituaries ("more variable in length and somewhat more variable in style . . . printed in the newspaper's usual type size, with an individual 'headline' for each obituary, either the deceased's name or a more extended statement" (1977, p. 353)). Typically, death notices serve as a proxy for actual deaths and are not examined for gender bias because their content is highly standardized and they are submitted routinely to newspapers by funeral directors. On the other hand, obituaries represent "interesting" or "important" deaths selected for added recognition and, as such, are subject to possible gender bias. Because Halbur and Vandagriff relied on death notices, it is not unusual nor unexpected that they found no evidence of bias in the number of notices, nor in the presence of a photograph.

In the 1990s two more studies examined gender discrimination in obituaries. Karol Maybury examined obituaries in the *Boston Globe* and the *Sacramento Bee* for a two-month period from November 15, 1992, through January 15, 1993. Men are two to two and one-half times more likely to receive an obituary than women, their obituaries are longer, and their obituaries are four times more likely to be accompanied by a photograph. There are no regional differences. Women related to famous men have the longest female obituaries, while men in entertainment/arts have the longest male obituaries.

Robin Moremen and Cathy Cradduck examined gender differences in obituaries in four regional newspapers in the late 1990s, following the original Kastenbaum method. In Moremen and Cradduck's study, the *New York Times* represents the Northeast and is included in the original study; the *Chicago Tribune* represents the Midwest, the *Los Angeles Times* the West, and the *Miami Herald* the Southeast. As in previous studies, men receive significantly more obituaries than women, however, unlike the Maybury study results, Moremen and Cradduck's study found regional differences: Obituaries are 7.69 times more likely to be written about a man than a woman in the *New York Times* (compared to 4.02 times in the original study); 4.21 times more likely in the *Los Angeles Times*; 3.11 times more likely in the *Miami Herald*; and 2.47 times more likely in the *Chicago Tribune*. Male obituaries are longer (except for the *Miami Herald*), and significantly more likely to be accompanied by a photograph (except for the *Miami Herald*). The average age at death is seventy-nine for women and seventy-two for men, which is consistent with national averages. People in business and the performing arts receive the most recognition, with men dominating these categories. Women dominate categories like miscellaneous (including devoted to family, animals, and children; homemaker; volunteer; active with seniors), clerical/retail, and related to someone famous, usually a man.

These studies demonstrate little change over time in the recognition of women after death. Consistently, fewer obituaries are written about women, fewer obituary lines note the accomplishments of women, and fewer pictures of women appear on the obituary page. When women are recognized usually it is for domestic or caregiving roles, or for their relationship to a famous man. Why is this so, and why is there so little change over time? Certainly women have made inroads into the labor market in recent decades; why is this not being reflected in postself artifacts like obituaries?

## Possible Explanations for the Findings

There appears to be five general explanations for the persistent inequality in obituary representation: a cohort effect, a period effect, a location effect, a decision-making effect, and a social inequality effect.

*Cohort effect.* Men and women born in the early 1920s came of age in the 1940s and 1950s, prior to second-wave feminism. Most middle-class women of that generation were homemakers, performing tasks that did not register in the economic sphere. By the time the feminist movement left its mark on the workplace, most of these women were too old to benefit. Hence, this generation of women is dying with very little public recognition of their accomplishments. This is largely so because paid work counts in American society; unpaid work in the home does not register in the economic sphere, therefore it is not viewed as important. One might expect the situation to improve for the women who came of age during second-wave feminism in the 1960s and 1970s, but wage, occupational, and promotional barriers may still prevent them from receiving equal treatment in the workplace and, thus, equal treatment on the obituary page.

*Period effect.* In her best-selling *Backlash: The Undeclared War Against American Women* (1991), Susan Faludi wrote of a feminist backlash that is part of a conservative response to second-wave feminism. Women in the 1980s and 1990s were told by conservative ideologues in the New Right political and fundamentalist Christian movements that they had "made it." The media took this ideology and translated it into sound bites; what is more apropos of this than an obituary that translates a person's life into fifty-six lines of print? Kastenbaum argued two decades prior that consumers of obituaries are receiving "systematic, if subtle confirmation of the greater importance of men" (1977, p. 356). Twenty-first-century consumers of obituaries are receiving systematic, if subtle, confirmation of a conservative ideology that is being promoted vigorously by New Right politicians and fundamentalist Christian groups.

*Location effect.* In locations where older women outnumber older men, there may be greater opportunity for posthumous recognition with an obituary. According to the Moremen and Cradduck study, this is true in the *Miami Herald*. When a woman receives an obituary in the *Herald*, it is likely to be lengthy and to be accompanied by a photograph. Greater representation in the *Miami Herald* reflects greater awareness of senior issues

in Florida, where, in general, women over the age of sixty-five outnumber men three to two.

*Decision-making effect.* The obituary decision-making process may contribute to selection bias. Because major newspapers with huge circulation areas are studied in the past, none is able to run obituaries of everyone who dies (smaller newspapers are much better able to do this). Therefore, rules of thumb develop about who should receive obituary recognition. One such rule is that the person must be a "news maker" in his or her lifetime. A potential news maker might be brought to the attention of the obituary department by a relative calling the paper and reporting the death; by the wire services or the death notices submitted by family and funeral directors; by the editors of one of the news desks alerting the obituary department to the death of a notable person in his or her field; or by a corporation sending information to the paper about a distinguished businessperson who died. Once the "news maker" is identified, the individual is "researched." This usually means looking back in the archives to see how many stories have been written about this person in the past. If time permits, other public sources are researched as well. If information is plentiful, then an obituary is written. In all cases, however, the obituary editor is the final arbiter of the page. The explanation most often offered by editors regarding unequal coverage of men and women is that obituaries reflect society as a whole; men have held higher positions historically and more has been written about them, therefore they receive greater obituary recognition.

One additional point is worth noting: Because women outlive men, more women are in the position of providing information to newspapers than men. When women die, there may be no one available to provide such information for them. More often women are the record keepers of the household. Therefore, even if men are in the position to provide information to newspapers, they may not have that information at their disposal.

*Social inequality effect.* Women's inequality in obituary recognition most likely reflects their continuing inequality in society. When women receive equal salaries, equal access to all occupations, equal access to the top levels of management, and equal treatment in the home, then perhaps they will receive equal recognition after death.

Researchers have found lasting differentials between the average earnings of men and women. Women's salaries have increased more rapidly than men's, but women are still earning only seventy-five cents for every dollar that a man earns. Women continue to be excluded from some occupational categories. They are overrepresented in clerical, retail sales, and service occupations, and underrepresented in professional, managerial, and high-skill craft positions. Additionally, women are blocked from the highest ranks of management. While women readily advance into middle management, they seldom reach senior management; in 2000, women ran only three of the five hundred largest public companies. Meanwhile, women remain responsible for the majority of unpaid work in the home, whether or not they work for wages. They spend about thirty-four hours per week on household chores, while men spend about eighteen hours. When women undertake paid employment, housework amounts to a second, full-time job. Because women have not yet "made it" in American society, gender equality in "less pressured by advocacy" areas such as obituaries continues to allude them.

**Suggestions for Change**

Immediate, pragmatic suggestions for future change might include: contacting current obituary editors and making them aware of the bias on their pages; hiring obituary editors who desire a balanced page; suggesting that women write their own obituaries and direct the executors of their estates to submit them to obituary editors upon their death; writing letters to the editor demanding greater recognition of women on the obituary pages of their newspapers; suggesting that large corporations withhold advertising dollars until women are equally represented on all pages of the newspaper, including the obituary page. While these suggestions may effect some degree of local change, long-range efforts must be pursued as well.

These might include: continued pressure for equality in the workplace, including an equitable wage; an end to labor market segregation by sex; equal opportunity for women to advance into positions of authority that result in professional recognition; a demand for greater equality in the home so that women are not working a second shift in the unpaid sector; a greater valuation of women's

work in general; and a greater valuation of unpaid work that is not in the economic sphere.

*See also:* DEATH SYSTEM; MORTALITY, CHILDBIRTH

### Bibliography

Faludi, Susan. *Backlash: The Undeclared War Against American Women.* New York: Crown Publishers, 1991.

Halbur, Bernice, and Mary Vandagriff. "Societal Responses after Death: A Study of Sex Differences in Newspaper Death Notices for Birmingham, Alabama, 1900–1985." *Sex Roles* 17 (1987):421–436.

Kastenbaum, Robert, Sara Peyton, and Beatrice Kastenbaum. "Sex Discrimination After Death." *Omega: The Journal of Death and Dying* 7 (1977):351–359.

Kearl, Michael C. "Death as a Measure of Life: A Research Note on the Kastenbaum-Spilka Strategy of Obituary Analyses." *Omega: The Journal of Death and Dying* 17 (1986):65–78.

Maybury, Karol K. "Invisible Lives: Women, Men and Obituaries." *Omega: The Journal of Death and Dying* 32 (1995):27–37.

Moremen, Robin D., and Cathy Cradduck. "'How Will You Be Remembered After You Die?' Gender Discrimination After Death Twenty Years Later." *Omega: The Journal of Death and Dying* 38 (1998–99):241–254.

Spilka, Bernard, Gerald Lacey, and Barbara Gelb. "Sex Discrimination After Death: A Replication, Extension and a Difference." *Omega: The Journal of Death and Dying* 10 (1979):227–233.

ROBIN D. MOREMEN

# GENNEP, ARNOLD VAN

Arnold van Gennep was born in 1873 and educated at the Sorbonne. He died in 1957 without ever having been accepted into Émile Durkheim's circle of sociologists, a neglect the anthropologist Rodney Needham speaks of as "an academic disgrace" in his preface to *The Semi-Scholars* (Gennep 1967, xi). Nevertheless, van Gennep's 1909 concept of "rites of passage" represents his prime contribution to thanatology, and subsequently became a major means of interpreting funerary ritual.

Rites of passage are transition rituals that move individuals from one social status to another in a three-phased schema of separation, segregation, and incorporation. It is as though society conducts individuals from one status to another, as from one room in a house to another, always passing over thresholds. This spatial element is important since changed status often involves changing locality. The "magico-religious aspect of crossing frontiers" intrigued van Gennep. For him, religion meant abstract ideas or doctrine and magic meant ritual action, so magico-religious was his idiosyncratic description of practical religious action quite unlike Durkheim's distinction between religion as collective and magic as privately selfish activity. According to van Gennep, in his book *The Rites of Passage,* the dynamic of rites of transition depends upon "the pivoting of sacredness" during the middle liminal phase, emphasizing why door and threshold (or *limen* in Latin), in both a literal and metaphorical sense, were important for him. Paradoxically he also thought that numerous landmarks were a form of phallus but devoid of "truly sexual significance." The fear inherent in changing status and responsibilities was managed ritually even if they were not concurrent with biological changes in adolescence. These rites mark a journey through life reflecting physical changes and altering responsibilities. The anthropologist Ioan Lewis expressed this when he referred to rites of passage as "rites of way," describing the phases in terms of thesis, antithesis, and synthesis (Lewis 1985, pp. 131–132).

Funerals both extend this journey to the other world in a series of transition rites and help structure the mourning process of survivors. Transition rather than separation is singled out as the predominating element of funerary rites, affecting both the living and the dead and involving potential danger for each as ritual changes in identity occur. Yet, almost as a law of life, these changes also involve a renewal of much-needed energy. One ignored element in van Gennep's work concerns fear, for funerals may be "defensive procedures," protecting against departed souls or the "contagion of death," and helping to "dispose of eternal enemies" of the survivors. He was an early critic of the French anthropologist Robert Hertz's overemphasis on positive aspects of funeral rites, and underemphasis on burial or cremation as effecting a dissociation of body and soul(s). Van Gennep's energy model of society whose rituals periodically regenerated its power and gave sense to repeating pat-terns of death and regeneration presaged both Durkheim's basic argument on totemic ritual (made in 1912) and the British anthropologists Maurice Bloch and Jonathan Parry's late-twentieth-century analysis of death and regeneration.

*See also:* DURKHEIM, ÉMILE; HERTZ, ROBERT; RITES OF PASSAGE

### *Bibliography*

Bloch, Maurice, and Jonathan Parry. *Death and the Regeneration of Life.* Cambridge: Cambridge University Press, 1982.

Durkheim, Émile. *The Elementary Forms of the Religious Life.* London: George Allen and Unwin, 1915.

Gennep, Arnold van. *The Semi-Scholars,* translated and edited by Rodney Needham. 1911. Reprint, London: Routledge & Kegan Paul, 1967.

Gennep, Arnold van. *The Rites of Passage.* 1909. Reprint, London: Routledge & Kegan Paul, 1960.

Lewis, I. M. *Social Anthropology in Perspective.* Cambridge: Cambridge University Press, 1985.

Parkin, Robert. *The Dark Side of Humanity: The World of Robert Hertz and Its Legacy.* Australia: Harwood Academic Publishers, 1996.

DOUGLAS J. DAVIES

# GENOCIDE

Raphael Lemkin, a Polish-Jewish legal scholar who escaped Nazi Germany to safe haven in the United States, coined the word *genocide* in 1944. The word originally referred to the killing of people on a racial basis. In *Axis Rule in Occupied Europe* (1944) Lemkin wrote, "New conceptions require new terms. By 'genocide' we mean the destruction of a nation or of an ethnic group. This new word, devised by the author to denote an old practice in its modern development, is made from the ancient Greek word *genos* (race, tribe) and the Latin *cide* (killing), thus corresponding in its formation to such words as tyrannicide, homicide, infanticide" (Lemkin 1944, p. 80). He also wrote about other elements that constitute the identity of a people that could be destroyed and hence the destruction of these, in addition to human lives, were aspects of genocide: political and social institutions, culture, language, "national feelings," religion, and the economic structure of groups or countries themselves.

Genocide is a criminological concept. Studying genocide involves an understanding of perpetrators/oppressors, their motives and methods, the fate of the victims and the role of bystanders. Lemkin went on to explain, "Genocide has two phases: one, destruction of the national pattern of the oppressed group: the other, the imposition of the national pattern of the oppressor" (1944, p. 80). So, while the general framework of genocide is to describe killing, the nuances of the definition, time considerations, and other aspects relating to politics and culture have made the term *genocide* highly charged with many possible applications based on interpretation. Lemkin's categories of genocide were political, social, cultural, religious, moral, economic, biological, and physical. Lemkin was interested in describing contemporary crimes that might be prevented, rather than working as a historian and making judgments about whether past events qualified as genocide.

Genocide was both narrowed and expanded beyond its original racially based definition in the United Nations Convention on the Prevention and Punishment of the Crime of Genocide. This international agreement was approved and proposed for signature and accession by the United Nations General Assembly on December 9, 1948, and entered into force on January 12, 1951. Article 2, the heart of the Convention, outlines the qualifications for deeming an act a "genocide":

- killing members of the group;

- causing serious bodily or mental harm to members of the group;

- deliberately inflicting on the group conditions of life calculated to bring about its physical destruction in whole or in part;

- imposing measures intended to prevent births within the group; and

- forcibly transferring children of the group to another group.

The most difficult and controversial part of the UN Convention is that the above acts are defined as genocide "committed with intent to destroy, in whole or in part, a national, ethnical, racial or religious group" (Kuper 1981, p. 210). The controversies about the word genocide have come from the absence of the category "political," which was eliminated because of the power politics of the General Assembly, especially the objections from the Soviet Union. The phrase "in whole or in part" is also problematic. Certainly, one can understand the meaning of "whole," but an ongoing question being interpreted through international agreements and tribunals is the meaning of "in part." There is the question of proving "intent," which in the minds of some legal scholars demands a precise order of events as well as official pronouncements that indicate intentionality, while for others a general tendency of a state, party, or bureaucracy is sufficient.

The scholars Helen Fein and Ervin Staub have independently developed typologies for understanding victimization. According to Fein, there are five categories that help define victimization by stages of isolated experiences: *definition* of the group; *stripping* of rights, often by law; *segregation* from the bulk of the population; *isolation,* which has physical as well as psychological dimensions; and *concentration,* the purpose of which is extermination. Staub, who has written extensively about genocide, has created a structure of motivational sources of mistreatment that may end in genocide. This includes difficult life conditions of a group, the fear of attack on fundamental goals of the society that leads a group to become perpetrators, cultural and personal preconditions that create threats that result in responses to protect identity, and societal-political organizations that necessitate obedience to authority and submission to authoritarian tendencies. Staub places extreme importance on the role played by bystanders, who can create resistance to genocidal conditions, support genocide, or be neutral, which in itself becomes a form of support for the perpetrator.

Most genocides occur in an international war or civil war environment, as was the case with various people groups such as Jews, Roma/Sinti, Armenians, and Tutsis in Rwanda. The genocide of native peoples in North America and Australia, by contrast, occurred in the process of colonization of native lands. A related area to genocide, although less focused and involved with total killing, is the category of "crimes against humanity." The phrase was first used in a 1915 when Allied declaration that exposed what was later called the Armenian genocide at the hands of the Ottoman Turks. The more contemporary international meaning of "crimes against humanity" is derived from Control Council Law No. 10 (1945) (the basis for the prosecution of crimes committed by Nazis who were not tried for the major offenses in the International Military Tribunal at Nuremberg), dealing with Nazi crimes in the context of World War II: "Atrocities and offenses, including but not limited to murder, extermination, enslavement, deportation, imprisonment, torture, rape, or other inhumane acts committed against any civilian population, or persecutions on political, racial or religious grounds whether or not in violation of the domestic laws of the country where perpetrated" (Taylor, Control Council Law No. 10, Document).

In a retroactive sense, the United Nations Convention can apply to events that focus back on the destruction of Native American peoples in the western hemisphere; the mass killing of Herreros in Namibia in 1904–1905; the Armenian genocide from 1915 to 1922; the genocide in Cambodia at the hands of the Khmer Rouge from 1975 to 1979; Rwanda in 1994; and Bosnia in 1992.

Use of the "stable" categories of victim groups, who are victimized for things that cannot be changed, is critical to understanding genocide. "Crimes against humanity," on the other hand, which can be equally devastating, can apply to both "stable" and "unstable" categories. Thus "race" is a stable and unchangeable category. "Political affiliation" or "religion" are "unstable" and can be changed. The crime of Jews during the Nazi era (from 1933 to 1945) was not that the Jewish people practiced an "illegal" religion, but rather that they had the misfortune of having "three or four Jewish Grandparents" (Nuremberg Law, 1935). The Nuremberg Law of 1935, therefore, allowed the perpetrators to define characteristics of the victim group.

Another term related to genocide and apparently first used to describe population transfers by the Yugoslav government during the early 1980s and more particularly in 1992 is *ethnic cleansing*. The term generally refers to removal of an ethnic group from its historic territory, purifying the land of "impure" elements perceived as a danger to the majority group. As the term was not in existence in 1948 when the United Nations Convention was

approved, it was not considered a form of genocide. Ethnic cleansing can be lethal and give an appearance of genocide, or it may involve involuntary transfer of populations. Forms of transfer, however, existed in the early twentieth century, such as the exchange of Greek and Turkish populations after the Greco-Turk War of 1920 and the transfer of millions of Germans out of Poland and other East European territories after World War II.

## Three Examples of Twentieth-Century Genocides

The twentieth century was one of mass slaughter that occurred because of world wars, revolutions, purges, internal strife, and other forms of mass violence. Genocide, however, appeared as something new with greater ferocity, perhaps because of the availability of the technologies of industrialization to be used for mass murder and the willingness of regimes to use these methods. Above all, however, the willingness to embrace genocide as a formula for removing the "other," a perceived enemy, represents the absolute opposite of the seeking of accommodation through diplomacy, negotiation, and compromise.

*The Holocaust and Roma/Sinti Porrajmos.* The Holocaust (*Shoah* in Hebrew) refers to the destruction of approximately 6 million Jews by Nazi Germany during World War II, from 1939 to 1945. The word existed before World War II and means "a burnt offering," or something consumed by fire. The word *Holocaust* is considered by most authorities as specific to the Jewish destruction by Germany because of the cremation of the dead in ovens and because of the religious implications of the word for issues involving the presence and absence of God. *Porrajmos* ("The Devouring") is the Roma word for the destruction of approximately half a million "gypsies" by the same German government. Jews and the Roma/Sinti were victims on a racial basis, a "stable" category invented by the perpetrators. Other groups were persecuted by the same regime but did not face inevitable destruction. Such groups included male homosexuals, Jehovah's Witnesses, political opponents, priests, habitual criminals, and other national groups, such as Poles. Groups also persecuted and subjected to murder in many cases were those Germans who were handicapped or had genetic diseases. The Nazi T-4 killing program began on September 1, 1939, and continued for several years, leading to the deaths of approximately 300,000 individuals in hospitals, wards, and gas chambers. The Holocaust produced the word *genocide.*

The mass destruction of both Jews and Roma/ Sinti necessitated several steps. Gypsies were already regarded as social outcasts. Jews had to be removed from German society as an assimilated group. The first step was identifying and blaming the victim. Jews had received equal rights as citizens in the German empire and were full citizens when National Socialism came to power on January 30, 1933. The Roma and Sinti never received full rights and were the victims of varying restrictive laws and exceptional police surveillance. The rise of anti-Semitism associated with social Darwinism in the late nineteenth century helped define the Jew as the "non-Aryan," which was part of a general campaign against the ideas of human equality being developed since the eighteenth century. Adolf Hitler's *Mein Kampf* (1925–1927) focused on the Jew as the scapegoat for all of Germany's and civilization's ills.

The second stage of the Holocaust was identification of the victim group, which took place through use of bureaucratic, baptismal, church, and synagogue records. This permitted the removal of Jews from the German civil service in April 1933, and a gradual removal from German society over the next six years. Identification of the group permitted use of special internal documents marked with a "J" ("Jude") by 1938 and the insertion of the middle names "Israel" for Jewish men and "Sara" for Jewish women. The immediate German plan for the Jews before 1939 was not extermination, but emigration. The solution for "the gypsy menace" was less dependent upon emigration, as the Roma/Sinti were equally despised in other countries, being identified as a "criminally inclined" group. Identification permitted the withdrawal of rights, "Aryanization" of property, and exclusion of Jews from the cultural and professional life of the country.

The issue of physical extermination started with the beginning of the German military offensive into Poland, which began on September 1, 1939, with the occupation of Poland and its 10 percent Jewish minority (approximately 3.5 million Jews). Military units ("Wehrmacht") and SS ("Shutzstaffeln") began to carry out mass shootings of Jews, concentration in ghettos, and imposition of conditions of slave labor and starvation that accelerated the death rate. Mass killings in death camps began in 1941 using carbon monoxide gas and hydrogen cyanide. The first such killings marking "Endlosung," or "The Final Solution," began in the summer of 1941. The Wannsee Conference, held outside Berlin on January 20, 1942, was a bureaucratic meeting of the SS presided over by Reinhold Heydrich and designed to summarize and systematize the genocide. Mass extermination took place in six large death camps (*vernichtungslager*) in the borders of the partitioned Polish state: Auschwitz, Treblinka, Chelmno, Belzec, Sobibor, and Majdanek. Auschwitz became an identifier of genocide against the Jews because it claimed approximately 1.25 million victims.

The Holocaust and Porrajmos possess some unique aspects compared to other genocides. The genocidal killing was not conducted in one country but across Europe, from the North Sea to Mediterranean, from the French Atlantic coast to the occupied territories in the Soviet Union. Neither Jews nor Gypsies had their own state or historic territory within the boundaries of Europe. In both cases children were killed as a means to prevent reproduction of the group. The extermination of the Jews and Roma/Sinti ended only with the defeat of Nazi Germany.

In the aftermath of World War II, the International Military Tribunal at Nuremberg helped refine the legal concept of crimes against humanity and genocide. The trial of the surviving Nazi leaders, corporate leaders, doctors, General Staff and Wehrmacht officials, and *Einsatzgruppen* (mobile killing squads used on the Eastern front for genocidal actions) established the precedent for trials in the aftermath of genocides in Bosnia and Rwanda during the 1990s. The total military collapse of Germany allowed the full extent of the genocide to be known. In other genocides where there has not been a total military defeat of the perpetrator country, a consequence is denial of genocide.

The Jewish survivors of the Nazi genocide either sought immigration to democratic countries outside of Europe, such as Palestine (now Israel) or the United States, while a smaller number remained in Europe. The Roma/Sinti had no option to emigrate, as no country was interested in taking them in. They returned to their countries of origin. The Israeli-Palestinian conflict may be regarded as a consequence of the anti-Semitism in Europe and the Holocaust, as the Zionist response to the Holocaust was to lobby and create a Jewish state.

*The Armenian Genocide.* The Armenians emerged as a people in the sixth century B.C.E. in Eastern Anatolia and lived there continuously until the twentieth century. They were the first national group to convert to Christianity in the year 301. The last Armenian kingdom collapsed in 1375. Thereafter, Armenia was part of the Ottoman Empire. Armenians were considered a loyal minority in the empire until the late nineteenth century. At the end of that century, Christian minorities living in the western part of the Ottoman Empire used the support of the Great Powers to achieve autonomy and later independence. The first attacks on Armenians occurred in 1881, in the aftermath of the Congress of Berlin that helped create Rumania, Bulgaria, Serbia, Macedonia, and Albania. In 1894 Kurdish attacks on Armenians occurred in the town of Sassun, leading to protests and reports by Christian missionaries and international interest. In 1895, as a response to a British, French, and Russian plan to create a single Armenian administrative district in the Ottoman Empire, Sultan Abdul Hamid II permitted more widespread attacks on Armenians in an effort to stifle Armenian nationalism and perceived separatist tendencies. Between 100,000 and 200,000 Armenians were killed in 1895 and many were forcibly converted to Islam.

The events that overtook the Armenians in 1895 are usually called "massacres." However, in light of the subsequent massacres in Cilicia in 1909 and the beginning of the genocide in 1915, most historians have seen the entire period from 1895 through 1922 as possessing genocidal intent. The "stable" element of the genocide was Armenian nationality and language. Christianity represented both a stable and unstable element, as some Armenians were allowed to live if they accepted Islam. The genocide of 1915 started on April 24 and was connected with fears of Armenian separatism and disloyalty toward the Ottomans. Another theory relating to the genocide is that the Ittihadist Party, the ultranationalist faction of Young Turks—led by Enver Pasha, minister of war; Talaat Pasha, minister of internal affairs; Grand Vizir, military governor

of Istanbul; and Jemal Pasha, minister of marine—sought to create a great "Pan Turkish" empire with ties to the Turkish-Muslim peoples in the East. The Christian Armenians stood in the physical path of such a plan. The attack on the Armenians did not have the technological sophistication of the German genocide against the Jews, nor the extreme racial overtones. The Armenians were living on their historic homeland, as opposed to the Jews, who were a Diaspora people living in Europe.

The beginning of Armenian genocide witnessed the deportation and murder of the Armenian intelligentsia and leadership. Armenians in the army were murdered. Military units attacked communities in the Armenian heartland, men were killed, women raped and killed, and children sometimes kidnapped into Turkish families. Groups known as "Responsible Secretaries and Inspectors," sometimes described as "delegates" (*murahhas*), organized and supervised the deportation and massacre of the Armenian convoys. The other was the "Special Organization" (*Teskilatl Mahsusa*), which comprised the bands in charge of the killings, the majority of whose members were criminals released from the prisons.

Those Armenians who survived the initial onslaught were subjected to forced marches into the Syrian Desert. A major destruction site was Deir Zor. The genocide witnessed the murder of 1.5 million Armenians, the destruction and obliteration of cultural institutions, art and manuscripts, churches, and cemeteries. The genocide also resulted in the creation through the survivors of the Armenian Diaspora, with large centers in Aleppo, Beirut, Jerusalem, Damascus, Baghdad, France, and the United States.

Unlike the Holocaust, the Armenian genocide was well covered in the American and European press. The United States was neutral in World War I until March 1917 and also had extensive missions, hence extensive reportage from eastern Turkey. First news of the genocide reached the Allies on May 24, 1915. Their response was a strong statement promising to hold the Turkish leaders accountable for the destruction of the Armenians. In May 1918, as a result of the destruction, Armenians in the Northeast section of Anatolia declared an Armenian Republic. At the 1919 Paris Peace Conference, the Allies agreed to sever Armenia and Arab lands from the Ottoman Empire. The United

States was offered a mandate over Armenia but it was rejected when the U.S. Senate refused to ratify the Paris Treaties. The independent Armenian Republic collapsed in May 1921 and became part of the Soviet Union.

In June 1919, the chief Turkish representative in Paris, Grand Vizir Damad Ferit, admitted misdeeds had occurred "that drew the revulsion of the entire humankind" (Dadrian 1995, p. 328). An American report by Major James G. Harbord concluded that 1.1 million Armenians had been deported.

Talaat Pasha, the main architect of the genocide, was assassinated on March 15, 1921, in Berlin by an Armenian student, Soghomon Tehlirian. Talaat had been condemned to death in absentia by the Turkish court martial on July 11, 1919. On July 24, 1923, the Treaty of Lausanne signed by Turkey and the Allies excluded all mention of Armenia or the Armenians. The new Turkish Republic was extended international recognition and the Ottoman Empire officially ended. In July 1926 the Swiss journalist Emile Hildebrand interviewed Turkish president Mustafa Kemal who blamed the Young Turks for the "massacre of millions of our Christian subjects" (1926, p. 1). Nevertheless, the Turkish government through the remainder of the twentieth century continued to deny that genocide had occurred. Armenians and academics have continued to press for recognition of the 1915 to 1922 events as "genocide."

*Rwanda.* Rwanda was proclaimed a German colony in 1910. In 1923 the League of Nations awarded Rwanda to the Belgians. Before Rwanda achieved independence from Belgium, on July 1, 1962, the Tutsi, who made up 15 percent of the populace, had enjoyed a privileged status over 84 percent who were Hutu and 1 percent of a small minority called the Twa. The Belgians had favored the Tutsi because they came from the north, the "Great Lakes" region of Rwanda, and appeared lighter skinned and were taller, hence "more European." Racial concepts based on eugenics were introduced by the Belgians, as well as an identity card system. After independence, the Hutu came to dominate the country and reversed the earlier discrimination imposed by the Belgians. The Tutsi were systematically discriminated against and periodically subjected to waves of killing and ethnic cleansing. Many Tutsi fled Rwanda into Uganda.

In 1963 an army of Tutsi exiles invaded Rwanda. The unsuccessful invasion led to a large-scale massacre of Tutsis. Rivalries among the Hutu led to a bloodless coup in 1973 in which Juvenal Habyaramana took power. In 1990 another Tutsi invasion took place, this time by the Tutsi-led Rwandan Patriotic Front (RPF). In 1993 the Hutu-dominated Rwandan government and the Tutsi rebels agreed to establish a multiparty democracy and to share power. After much resistance President Habyaramana agreed to peace talks in Tanzania. The Arusha Accords stipulated that the Rwandan government agreed to share power with Hutu opposition parties and the Tutsi minority. United Nations (UN) peacekeepers would be deployed to maintain peace in the country.

However, despite the presence of UN forces, a Hutu plot and arming of the Hutu civilian population took place during early 1994. In what is now referred to as the "Dallaire fax," the Canadian lieutenant general and UN peacekeeper Romeo Dallaire relayed to New York the informant's claim that Hutu extremists "had been ordered to register all the Tutsi in Kigali" (Des Forges 1999, p. 150). He suspected a plot of extermination of the Tutsi. Dellaire asked for more troops to stop any possible violence. Instead, his force was reduced from 3,000 to 500 men. This turned out to be the preplanning for genocide, which involved Hutus from all backgrounds, including the Catholic Church.

The genocide began on April 6, 1994, when an airplane carrying President Juvenal Habyarimana and President Cyprien Ntaryamira of Burundi was shot down, killing both men. From April 7 onward the Hutu-controlled army, the gendarmerie, and the militias worked together to wipe out Rwanda's Tutsi. Radio transmissions were very important to the success of the genocide. Radio Mille Collines, the Hutu station, broadcast inflammatory propaganda urging the Hutus to "kill the cockroaches." Killers often used primitive weapons, such as knives, axes, and machetes. Tutsi fled their homes in panic and were snared and butchered at checkpoints. The Hutus' secret squads, the *interahamwe,* used guns and clubs. Women and younger men were especially targeted as they represented the future of the Tutsi minority. Women were raped in large numbers, and then killed. Hundreds of thousands of Tutsi fled to Tanzania and Congo to newly formed refugee camps.

*In 1996 Rwandan Hutu refugees return home after having fled to Tanzania in 1994 fearing the retribution for a Hutu-planned genocide of the minority Tutsis. The Rwandan genocide stands as an event that could have been prevented had there been a will by the United Nations and other great powers to intervene.* AP/WIDE WORLD PHOTOS

With international organizations helpless and both the European powers and the United States fearful of declaring events "genocidal," the Tutsi RPF took the capital, Kigali, in early July 1994 and announced a new government comprised of RPF leaders and ministers previously selected for the transition government called for in the Arusha Accord. When the genocide finally ended, close to 1 million people had been killed. Further, 800,000 lives were taken in what is estimated to be a 100-day period, a faster rate of killing than during the Holocaust.

Early in December 1994 a panel of three African jurists presented a study of the murder of Tutsi to the UN. It concluded, "Overwhelming evidence points to the fact that the extermination of Tutsi by the Hutu was planned months in advance. The massacres were carried out mainly by Hutus in a determined, planned, systematic and methodical manner, and were inspired by ethnic hatred." Amnesty International concluded that "the pattern of genocide became especially clear in April, when frightened Tutsi were herded systematically into churches, stadiums and hospitals" (Amnesty 1998, p. 23).

Genocide trials began in Rwanda in December 1996. All experts have testified that a relatively small armed force could have stopped the massive killing. The Rwandan genocide lacked the larger context of a world war, which was a factor in both Armenia and the Holocaust. The Holocaust represented more of a technologically based killing after initial shootings suggested negative side effects on the perpetrators. Nazi Germany also sought a solution through emigration before embarking on the "final solution." The Armenian genocide seems similar to events in Rwanda, with hands-on killing and little lead time before the genocide actually began.

## Genocide of the Plains Indians: North America

The issue of genocide in the New World is a contentious one for many reasons. First, there are vast variations from demographers regarding the population estimates of the New World in 1491, and North America in particular (the high being 18 million, the low 1.8 million). Second, there is no argument that perhaps 90 percent of the Native American population died between 1492 and 1525. However, while some populations were hunted down and subjected to cruel tortures, most seemed to have died because of immunological deficiencies that prevented resistance to European diseases. Third, while there was never a declaration of intent to kill all native peoples, removal policies by the United States and Canadian congresses, nineteenth-century federal bureaucratic agencies, and public statements created a popular perception that elimination of the Indian tribes was a necessary event for the success of European colonization. One of the consequences of the huge Native American population loss through disease was African slavery to replace necessary labor pools. Bacteriological warfare was used for the first time by Lord Jeffrey Amherst, who ordered smallpox-infected blankets be given to the Ottaws and Lenni Lenape tribes in Massachusetts, with catastrophic results (Churchill 2000). The aftermath of tribal reductions in the nineteenth century has been calamitous for remaining tribes and has been called genocide.

More to the heart of the definition of genocide are American and Canadian policies in the nineteenth and twentieth centuries. Native Americans qualify for categorization of a "stable" population under the guidelines for application of the United Nations Convention. Actually, the Native Indian tribes were identified as the barbaric "other" in the American Declaration of Independence. In the last section of this historic document, Thomas Jefferson made the following accusation against the government of King George III: "He has excited domestic insurrections amongst us, and has endeavored to bring on the inhabitants of our frontiers, the merciless Indian Savages, whose known rule of warfare, is an undistinguished destruction of all ages, sexes and conditions." It is no surprise, therefore, that the eighteenth and subsequent centuries witnessed a reduction of native populations through use of military forces, massacres, creation of reservation systems, removal of children from families through mission schools, and loss of native languages and significant aspects of culture. Jefferson's description of the Indian tribes, largely propagandistic, might be likened to a charge that native peoples had declared war on the United States. However, it should be taken as the first step in a policy that ultimately saw ethnic cleansing of Indians and perhaps genocide.

The "Indian removal," begun in 1830 by President Andrew Jackson's policy, was implemented to clear land for white settlers. This period, known as the "Trail of Tears," witnessed the removal of the "Five Civilized Tribes": the Choctaw, Creek, Chickasaw, Cherokee, and Seminole. The Cherokee resisted removal, as they had established a written constitution modeled after the United States model. In 1838 the federal troops evicted the Cherokee under terms of the New Echota Treaty of 1835. Indian historians sometimes describe the result as a "death march." Approximately 4,000 Cherokee died during the removal process. The Seminole were removed from Florida in ships and at the end of the process on railway boxcars, similar to deportations of Jews during the Holocaust. The Indian Removal Acts pushed more than 100,000 native peoples across the Mississippi River.

Forced assimilation for native peoples was first defined through Christianity as the answer to the paganism of the native peoples. A Christian worldview, linked with the sense of predominance of European (Spanish and Portuguese at first) civilization, necessitated an inferior view of the native "other" that could be modestly corrected through religion. Christian-based schooling provided a tool for the process of eradicating native languages. Boarding schools in particular, which lasted through the 1980s, were instrumental in this process. Captain Richard H. Pratt, founder of the

Carlisle Indian School in Pennsylvania, observed in 1892 that his school's philosophy was, "Kill the Indian to save the man" (Styron 1997). Boarding and mission schools forbade native children to speak their tribal languages and forced other assimilationist elements upon them: mandatory school uniforms, cutting of hair, and prohibitions on any native traditions. The result was that children who survived such treatment were aliens in two societies, their own as well as the world of the white man. Ward Churchill's writings have demonstrated the social impact, which was illiteracy, inability to work, high rates of alcoholism, chronic diseases, and low life expectancy. Accusations of forced sterilizations of Native American women have been advanced and many have been proven. Natives call this cultural genocide covered by the United Nations Convention.

An associated aspect of genocide of native peoples involves issues related to pollution of the natural environment. As native peoples lived in a tribal manner without large cities (except for the Aztec and Inca cultures that were extinguished earlier), their concern for nature was continual and they saw their own lives in a balance with nature. The earth was also seen as possessing a cosmic significance. The Native American ecological view of the earth sees it as threatened by industrialization and modernization generally, and explains environmental pollution in these terms as well as in the pursuit of personal profit.

**Mass Murder in Ukraine: Crime against Humanity or Genocide?**

There is no doubt that between 6 million and 7 million people died in Ukraine during the period of Joseph Stalin's plan to create a new and massive plan of social engineering by collectivizing agriculture (1928–1933). The results of collectivization may be called a crime against humanity, although the intentionality necessary to prove genocide is missing. Most of the killing and starvation involved a group defined by economic class rather than race. There was also a concerted attack on Ukrainian nationalism and culture that witnessed the killing of priests, and attacks on the Ukrainian Orthodox Church, intellectuals, and political opponents. During the nineteenth century there were various failed Tsarist plans to eradicate Ukrainian culture, all of which had failed.

Vladimir Ilyich Lenin's first application of Marxism in agriculture attempted a centralized policy of War Communism from 1918 to 1921. This policy, which focused on collectivization, failed miserably. Lenin followed with a compromise, the New Economic Policy (1921–1927), which, while successful, raised some fundamental questions about the future of Soviet agriculture. A debate erupted in 1924 within the Communist Party and became known as the "Industrialization Debates." Leon Trotsky argued for collectivization, while his opponent, Nikolai Bukharin, argued for maintaining private plots in the rural economy. Stalin, general secretary of the Communist Party, aligned himself and his supporters first behind Bukharin to defeat Trotsky, and then adopted Trotsky's position to defeat Bukharin. The result was the first five-year plan and the decision to collectivize agriculture. This decision assumed a vast transformation of the peasantry from a private to a collective society, and was undertaken based on the Marxist principle that human behavior could be changed.

Part of Stalin's logic for the agricultural sector was that, because the Union of Soviet Socialist Republics (USSR) was cut off from most foreign trade because of international blockade, a super-tax of sorts would have to be levied on the peasantry to help pay for industrial equipment that might be imported. Thus, private holdings were forced into collectives (kolkhoz) and the tax was imposed through forced deliveries of grain to the state. The kulak class of private peasants opposed the policy and fought back. Stalin's response for Ukraine, the most productive agricultural region of the USSR, was to seal it off, especially in 1931, and maintain grain exports even if it meant starvation of the peasantry. That the forced grain deliveries were coming extensively from the Ukraine was significant, as Ukrainian nationalism had a long history and an independent Ukraine had existed for a short time after the 1917 Revolution.

The forced grain deliveries of the first two years of the five-year plan produced a famine in 1932 and 1933 that claimed between 6 and 7 million lives. The famine happened in relative silence, as most reporters from foreign press agencies were kept out of the famine areas. The famine spread beyond the Ukraine into the North Caucasus and Volga River basin. Forced collectivization in Central Asia carried away as much as 10 percent of the population in some areas. The famine affected not only crops, but also animals. The absence of fodder led to the massive death or slaughter of animals, and caused a massive reduction in farm animal population by 1933. Peasants who tried to flee or steal grain to survive were either shot or deported by the Soviet police, the NKVD.

The relationship between the question of genocide in Ukraine versus crimes against humanity is a complex one. Those who argue that it was a genocide see Stalin's actions as not only motivated by economics but as a pretext for the attack on Ukrainian nationalism, which paved the way for physical elimination by the police and military authorities of the Ukrainian elites. Leo Kuper, one of the founders of modern genocide thought that Stalin's actions against national and religious groups qualified as genocide under the UN definition. Other scholars have seen the events of the famine and collateral deaths through police action related to economics, class issues, and political forms of killing, which are excluded by the Genocide Convention. Using the information available since the collapse of the USSR in 1991, it appears that the intent of the Soviet government was to alter the economic basis of both agriculture and industry. The potential for resistance was greater in agriculture than industry because of its traditions of private holdings. Stalin's response to resistance was ruthless, and direct mass murder or permitting murder through famine was his response. While the debate about the Ukrainian famine may continue, there is no debate that it was a crime against humanity.

Genocide involves death and dying, not of individuals but of entire groups. The issue is never a comparison of numbers, but rather the intent of perpetrators and consequences for the victim group. The United Nations Convention aspires to both prevent and punish genocide. Thus far, it has been unsuccessful in preventing genocide. Trials begun in the period after 1992 in the Hague and Arusha related to events in Bosnia and Rwanda bear witness to the success or failure of war crime tribunals. Genocide remains a threat wherever national and ethnic tensions run high, when preconditions such as Helen Fein and Ervin Staub have suggested appear and trigger the use of violence. Genocide can be prevented by the willingness of outsiders, particularly powerful nations, to act through intervention. However, such intervention seems easier to speak about in theory than in practice. The psychologist Israel Charny has called genocide "The Human Cancer." This disease of genocide, so prominent in the twentieth century, has the potential to reappear in the twenty-first century because of new technologies and smaller but more powerful weapons, often in the hands of both nation-states and substate groups.

*See also:* CAPITAL PUNISHMENT; FAMINE; GHOST DANCE; HOLOCAUST; MASS KILLERS; TERRORISM

## Bibliography

Alvarez, Alex. *Governments, Citizens, and Genocide: A Comparative and Interdisciplinary Approach.* Bloomington: Indiana University Press, 2001.

Amnesty International. *Forsaken Cries: The Story of Rwanda.* Ben Lomond, CA: The Video Project, 1998.

Bauer, Yehuda. *A History of the Holocaust.* New York: Franklin Watts, 1982.

Charny, Israel W., ed. *Toward the Understanding and Prevention of Genocide.* Boulder, CO: Westview, 1984.

Charny, Israel W. *Genocide: The Human Cancer.* New York: Hearst Books, 1982.

Churchill, Ward. *A Little Matter of Genocide: Holocaust and Denial in the Americas, 1492 to the Present.* San Francisco: City Light Books, 2000.

Churchill, Ward. *Struggle for the Land: Indigenous Resistance to Genocide, Ecocide, and Expropriation in Contemporary North America.* Monroe, ME: Common Courage Press, 1993.

Conquest, Robert. *Indians Are Us? Culture and Genocide in Native North America.* Monroe, ME: Common Courage Press, 1994.

Conquest, Robert. *The Harvest of Sorrow: Soviet Collectivization and the Terror-Famine.* New York: Oxford University Press, 1984.

Dadrian, Vahakn. *Warrant for Genocide: Key Elements of the Turko-Armenian Conflict.* New Brunswick, NJ: Transaction, 1999.

Dadrian, Vahakn. *German Responsibility in the Armenian Genocide.* Cambridge, MA: Blue Crane Books, 1996.

Dadrian, Vahakn. *The History of the Armenian Genocide.* Providence, RI: Berghan Books, 1995.

Des Forge, Alison. *"Leave None to Tell the Story": Genocide in Rwanda.* New York: Human Rights Watch, 1999.

Fein, Helen. *Accounting for Genocide.* New York: The Free Press, 1979.

Heidenrich, John G. *How to Prevent Genocide*. Westport, CT: Praeger, 2001.

Hildebrand, Emile. "Kemal Promises More Hangings of Political Antagonists in Turkey." *Los Angeles Examiner* 1 August 1926, 1.

Ignatieff, Michael. *Human Rights As Politics and Idolatry*. Princeton, NJ: Princeton University Press, 2001.

Ignatieff, Michael. *The Warrior's Honour: Ethnic War and the Modern Conscience*. Toronto: Penguin, 1999.

Kuper, Leo. *Genocide: Its Political Use in the Twentieth Century*. New Haven, CT: Yale University Press, 1981.

Lemkin, Räphael. *Axis Rule in Occupied Europe: Laws of Occupation, Analysis of Government, Proposals for Redress*. Washington, DC: Carnegie Endowment for International Peace, Division of International Law, 1944.

Mandani, Mahmood. *When Victims become Killers: Colonialism, Nativism, and Genocide in Rwanda*. Princeton, NJ: Princeton University Press, 2002.

Mazian, Florence. *Why Genocide? The Armenian and Jewish Experiences in Perspective*. Ames: Iowa State University Press, 1990.

Power, Samantha. *A Problem from Hell: America in the Age of Genocide*. New York: Basic Books, 2002.

Riemer, Neal, ed. *Protection against Genocide*. Westport, CT: Praeger, 2000.

Rosenbaum, Alan S. *Is the Holocaust Unique?* Boulder, CO: Westview Press, 1996.

Schabas, William A. *Genocide in International Law*. Cambridge: Cambridge University Press, 2000.

Smith, Roger, ed. *Genocide: Essays toward Understanding, Early Warning, and Prevention*. Williamsburg, VA: Association of Genocide Scholars, 1999.

Stannard, David E. *American Holocaust*. New York: Oxford University Press, 1992.

Staub, Ervin. *The Roots of Evil: The Origins of Genocide and Other Group Violence*. New York: Cambridge University Press, 1989.

Totten, Samuel, William S. Parsons, and Israel W. Charny, eds. *Century of Genocide: Eyewitness Accounts and Critical Views*. New York: Garland, 1997.

*Internet Resources*

Styron, Elizabeth Hope. "Native American Education: Documents from the 19th Century." In the Duke University [web site]. Available from www.duke.edu/~ehs1/education/.

Taylor, Telford. "Final Report to the Secretary of the Army on the Nuremberg War Crimes Trials under Control Council Law No. 10." In the University of Minnesota Human Rights Library [web site]. Available from www1.umn.edu/humanrts/instree/ccno10.htm.

STEPHEN C. FEINSTEIN

# GHOST DANCE

The Ghost Dance was the central rite of a messianic Native American religious movement in the late nineteenth century. It indirectly led to the massacre of some 250 Sioux Indians at Wounded Knee, South Dakota, in 1890, marking an end to the Indian wars. As a trance-enducing rite of a hybrid faith, it combined elements of Christianity with Native American religious traditions.

The Ghost Dance first emerged around 1870 in the Walker Lake area on the California-Nevada border. A Paiute mystic named Wodziwob, or "Fish Lake Joe," began to preach an apocalyptic vision in which a great flood or fire would eliminate the white man from the world and deceased tribal people would return alive to the earth. Wodziwob's assistant, a shaman named Tavibo, spread the new doctrine among Nevada tribes.

The original Ghost Dance fervor among far western American tribes gradually ebbed only to be rekindled in 1888 by Wovoka, Tavibo's son. The new prophet, also known as Jack Wilson, was said to practice miracles such as curing the sick, controlling the weather, and withstanding bullets shot at him. Wovoka claimed that while feverishly ill he saw in a vision all deceased Indians surrounding the throne of "the Great Spirit" God who told him to teach his people to love one another and to live peacefully with white people. Further, all deceased Indians would return to the earth and recover their ancestral lands. According to the vision, white men and women would retreat to their European homelands. The prophet taught his followers a five-day ritual of song and circle dances that would hasten the coming of this new millennium; hence, the Ghost Dance was born.

Wovoka's Paiute tribesmen became missionaries of this new messianic faith. It attracted many impoverished and unhappy western tribes who had been

*This wood engraving from 1891 depicts a group of Sioux dancers performing, most likely, one of their last ghost dances before the arrest of the warrior chief Sitting Bull.* CORBIS

herded by the United States military onto reservations, including the Arapaho, Bannock, Caddo, Cheyenne, Comanche, Kiowa, Sioux, Shoshones, and Utes. Each tribe adopted its own Ghost Dance songs and wore clothing painted with sacred symbols believed designed to ward off bullets.

The Ghost Dance movement came to a tragic end on Sioux reservations in South Dakota during the winter of 1890–1891. Sitting Bull, the famous Hunkpapa Sioux warrior chief, had become an enthusiastic follower of the new faith, along with his people on the Standing Rock Reservation in South Dakota. Their new religious fervor alarmed white United States government agents on the reservation who decided to arrest the chief as a means of restoring peace to the reservation. On December 15 Sitting Bull was shot and killed during a skirmish when Native American agency police tried to arrest him.

Some of Sitting Bull's followers escaped to the Cheyenne River Reservation to join Miniconjou Sioux who were also practicing the Ghost Dance under the leadership of Chief Big Foot. But on December 29, when American cavalry caught up with Big Foot's group encamped along Wounded Knee Creek and tried to disarm them, rifle shots on both sides broke out. The American military, armed with four Hotchkiss machine guns, massacred the Sioux warriors and their unarmed women and children. The massacre marked the ending of the Indian wars in the American West.

*See also:* GENOCIDE; DANCE; NATIVE AMERICAN RELIGION

## Bibliography

Andrist, Ralph K. *The Long Death: The Last Days of the Plains Indian.* New York: Macmillan, 1964.

Brown, Dee. *Bury My Heart at Wounded Knee.* New York: Henry Holt, 1991.

### Internet Resources

Kavanagh, Thomas W. "Imaging and Imagining the Ghost Dance: James Mooney's Illustrations and Photographs, 1891–1893." In the Indiana University [web site]. Available from http://php.indiana.edu/~tkavanag/visual5.html.

KENNETH D. NORDIN

# GHOSTS

Ghost lore has a long and colorful history. The word *ghost* has been in use since the late sixteenth century. It derives from a more ancient term, *gast,* in the language that evolved into modern German. For some time, *ghost* has usually signified the disembodied spirit of a deceased person. Earlier meanings still cling to this word, however. *Gast* originally referred to a terrifying rage. A person who experiences shock and terror can still be described as aghast (i.e., frightened by an angry ghost). Fear of angry ghosts is built into the word itself.

Etymology explains even more about the characteristics attributed to ghosts through the centuries. Ghost is created in part by way of spirit, and spirit by way of breath. The book of Genesis and many other world mythologies tell a similar story: God breathed into an inert form, and the creature then stirred with life. There has also been a widespread belief that each newborn becomes one of us in drawing its first breath. Each dying person leaves the world by exhaling the last breath, sometimes depicted as a soul bird. The breath is seen as life. Expelling the final breath is "giving up the ghost." The spirit is on its way, the body stays behind. So in traditional accounts, spirit was breath, but more than breath: It became a subtle, immaterial essence that departs from a person at death. This idea is at the core of theological dualism, the belief that a person is composed of a material, perishable body and an immaterial, imperishable essence. Greek and Christian thought held that imagination, judgment, appreciation of beauty, and moral sense are functions of the spirit within humans. The spirit is an individual's higher self, something of which survives bodily death in many religious accounts. In Western societies, people tend to speak of this surviving element as the soul.

Ghosts, however, do not necessarily emanate from the refined spirit of divinity within. It is fairly common among world cultures to believe in another spirit that accompanies them throughout life. This is a shadowy sort of spirit that could be thought of as a duplicate image of the physical body. The German term *doppelganger* clearly conveys the idea of a second spirit that moves mysteriously through one's life, sometimes serving as the ruthless Mr. Hyde to the everyday cultivated Dr. Jekyll. This shadow spirit is apt to leave the body from time to time and linger around a person's place of death and burial. A ghost, then, might either be a blessed spirit on a mission of mercy, or the tortured and malevolent image of a body that suffered an anguished death.

## Varieties of Ghosts

Two sharply contrasting beliefs about ghosts have long coexisted, sometimes in the same society. The good ghost appears to be related to the higher spirit of a deceased person; the dangerous ghost, though, might be the shadowy doppelganger or a higher soul that has turned evil. The two opposing ghostly prototypes are the angry ghost, dangerous because it is angry about being dead, having been killed in an unacceptable way, having been treated badly by family and community, or just plain inveterate nastiness; or the emotionally neutral ghost, the spiritual essence of the deceased that lingers or returns in order to warn, comfort, inspire, and protect the living, making its rounds amiably and harmlessly.

It is not unusual to have a mixed concept of ghosts because the influence of both traditions persists in the twenty-first century in popular media. Ghosts themselves can have mixed feelings. There are lost souls who cannot find rest, and others, like Wagner's *Flying Dutchman,* who are condemned to a weary and aimless exile that can end only with the discovery of pure love. Such sad ghosts are capable of either good or evil, depending on how they are treated.

Funeral rites and prayers often have had the double function of providing safe conduct for the soul of the deceased while also preventing it from lingering or returning as a dangerous ghost. Candles or torches, for example, help guide the departing soul and at the same time discourage wandering evil spirits from entering the corpse or its attendants. Elaborate precautions are taken when the person has died by violence. An executed murderer, for example, might have all his body orifices sealed and his limbs amputated so the vengeful ghost cannot return to continue its evil career.

Ghost prevention remains a major concern in many world cultures. A Hindu ceremony conducted in Katmandu, Nepal, in June 2001 was intended to banish the ghost of the recently slain monarch. The ashes of the late King Birendra were mixed into the luncheon food, and a Brahmin priest, dressed to impersonate the king, rode astride an elephant as crowds of people chased him and the monarch's ghost away.

## Encounters with Ghosts

According to lore, there is more than one way in which a ghost can present itself. The visual visitation is most common. Visible ghosts are often elusive, appearing only in glimpses, but some linger. Specialists in folklore and paranormal phenomena tend to speak instead of apparitions (from Latin for "appearances" or "presentations"). Apparitions include ghosts of deceased persons but can also represent living people who are physically absent, animals, objects, and unusual beings that resist classification. Phantoms can also include visions of either a deceased or an absent living person. *Specter* and *shade,* terms seldomly used in the twenty-first century, refer to ghosts or spirits.

Some ghosts are heard rather than seen. *Poltergeists* (noisy ghosts) are notorious for dragging their chains, dropping dishes from a shelf, or even hurling objects across a room. Unseen spirits that communicated by rapping on walls or tables became especially popular during the heyday of Spiritualism. In reports of haunted houses, poltergeists are usually the chief perpetrators.

A more subtle type of ghost is neither seen nor heard. One "feels" its presence. This sense of presence is perhaps the most common type of ghost-related experience reported. Most common among the recently bereaved, these visitations often take the form of a sense of the deceased's uncanny presence. Interestingly, the pattern found in the late nineteenth century is much the same as in current reports: the more recent the death, the more frequent the incidents in which a ghostly presence was felt.

The "felt" ghost was encountered in a wider variety of situations at the end of Christianity's first millennium. Mystical experiences of an invisible presence were frequently reported and made their way into the historical record. A new liturgy for the dead had been introduced in which symbolism became inseparable from physical reality. Praying for the dead became a prime responsibility for Christians, and these intensified symbolic interactions with the dead seemed to attract ghosts.

Dream ghosts have been reported in many times and places. These nocturnal visitations often have been taken as revealing past, present, or future realities. Even in contemporary reports, a dream visitation from a deceased person is sometimes accepted as a "real ghost."

The famous confrontation between Hamlet the king and Hamlet the prince demonstrates the witness's quandary. Was the prince only dreaming that the ghost of his father had appeared to him? And how could he be sure that this was a reliable ghost and not a demon or deceitful spirit who had impersonated the king in order to urge Hamlet to murder—and therefore to damn the young prince's own soul? Whether ghosts have appeared in dreams, visions, or daily life, they have often suffered from a credibility problem. Are they a misperception, a trick of the mind, a hallucination, or the real thing?

Ghosts are most commonly reported as solo acts, but sometimes they bring a supporting cast. The medieval mind occasionally encountered hordes of ghosts arising from their graves. Witnesses have sworn that they have beheld the apparitions of numerous slain soldiers arising from a battlefield such as Gettysburg. By contrast, some people have met an entire family of ghosts ensconced comfortably in an ordinary home. Several women who reported having seen or heard domestic ghosts had this explanation to offer:

> As they see it, the events and emotions of former residents' lives remain locked in the form of "energy" or "waves" or an "aura" in the house where they lived. If it is pleasant, the present resident can absorb and benefit from the atmosphere; the memories in the house will make those who live in it happy, healthy, and wise. If the spirit is malignant, however, and the memories violent, the energy may transform itself into a force which can throw or displace objects or echo the events of real life by sighing, walking about, switching lights on and off, closing doors, flushing toilets, and so on. *(Bennett 1999, pp. 47–48)*

These domestic ghosts have become, literally, "the spirit of the house," as Bennett adds.

The conjured ghost is a commercial product, brought forth in return for a fee. Some nineteenth-

and early twentieth-century mediums attracted participants to their séances by guest appearances from visual ghosts. After interest started to decline in spirit visitors, one could only hear ghosts. If the participants were sufficiently receptive and the ghost was in the right mood, they would be rewarded with the sight of a white ectoplasmic figure hovering, floating, or simply walking. (Ectoplasm is what ghosts wear or become when they allow themselves to be materialized; investigators discovered that the ectoplasm bore a remarkable similarity to the bladder of a goat.)

The Bible is almost devoid of ghosts. The strongest candidate for a ghost is the apparition that was conjured from the grave of Samuel by the necromancing Witch of Endor. Whether or not this figure was truly the ghost of Samuel remains a subject of controversy. Early Christian belief was not receptive to ghosts, in contrast to many of the popular cults of the time. Hamlet's chronic uncertainty was inculcated by a long tradition that cautioned against taking apparent ghostly visitors at face value.

## Ghostly Functions

What is the ghost's vocation? "To haunt" is the answer that first comes to mind. Many reports tell of a ghost that appears in a particular location, sometimes repeatedly for generations. In some instances the witnesses identify the apparition as a person who once lived in that home or vicinity; in other instances the ghost is unknown to the witnesses, but the same assumption is made. Ghosts have also been encountered in the wilderness—along the Cumberland Trail, for example. Members of numerous folk cultures would not be surprised that ghosts have been observed both around the household and in the wilds. Some firmly believe that the spirit does linger for a while before undertaking its postmortem journey, and some may be unwilling or unable to leave until unfinished business has been completed. The roving ghost that might be encountered could be lost and disoriented because the person died far from home and has not been sanctified by purification and other mortuary rituals. The "skinwalkers" reported in Native American lore are among these restless souls.

Usually, then, ghosts have unfinished business to complete or an inability to move on. Being a ghost is usually a transitional status. When somebody or something succeeds in "laying the ghost,"

Visual ghosts, similar to this image (c. 1910), are the most common type of apparition; however, some ghosts tend to be "heard" clanking chains and making other noises rather than being seen. CORBIS

then this unfortunate spirit can finally desist from its hauntings and wanderings, and advance toward its fate.

There is another kind of ghost, however, whose origin is an unfortunate rebirth. Hungry ghosts (e-kuei) are Chinese Buddhist ancestors who are in constant torment because they are starving and thirsty but cannot receive nourishment. Whatever they try to eat or drink bursts into fire and then turns into ashes. There is hope for them, however. The Festival of Ghosts includes a ritual designed specifically to provide them with sanctified water that, accompanied by chant and magic, can release them from their terrible plight.

Fear of ghostly possession has haunted many societies. In these instances the disembodied spirit not only appears but also moves right in and takes over. Fortunately, the ghost often can be persuaded to leave once its demands are met. The ghosts of North India, for example, often require that they be given sweets. In the first phase of ghost possession, according to Freed and Freed,

"A victim shivers, moans, and then falls down unconscious" (1993, p. 305). Next, the victim engages in various dissociative actions such as talking nonsense, running around wildly, and even attempting suicide.

These functions of North Indian ghosts vary with the stages of the life cycle: different ones appear in childhood, adulthood, middle age, and old age. Because ghost possession is one of the expected hazards of life, North India villagers have developed first-aid techniques to reduce the disturbance until an exorcist arrives. The victims are wrapped in quilts, propped in a sitting position, guarded against suicide attempts, and administered a series of shock treatments (e.g., hair pulling, slapping, and placing peppers in their eyes and mouths). The intrusive ghost is also engaged in conversation while other villagers fling cow dung and incense on a fire so their fumes might help to dislodge the unwelcome spirit. Exorcism is the most dependable cure, however, if the ghost is to be banished without carrying off the victim's soul.

One of the most learned scholars ever to devote himself to ghosts, phantoms, and survival has a different perspective to offer. Frederick W. H. Myers studied thousands of ghost-sighting reports. His conclusion: most ghosts do not do much of anything. This statement contrasts strongly with the usual belief that ghosts have intentions and missions. The typical sighting was of an apparently aimless, drifting entity that seemed to have nothing in particular on its mind. So the average ghost is not engaging in meaningful or purposeful behavior, according to Myers's studies.

**Explaining Ghosts**

Myers offers two noncontradictory explanations for the do-nothing apparitions that were most commonly reported. First, he emphasizes their difference from the lurid ghouls described in many ghost stories. The more reliable human testimony seems to pertain to more pedestrian hauntings. Myers next tries to fathom the nature of these oddly lackadaisical apparitions. These are not ghosts at all, in the traditional sense of the term; rather, they are "a manifestation of persistent personal energy after death" (1975, p. 32). It is not an independent, free-roaming spirit, nor is it a hallucination or other trick of the mind. What we have

seen is a kind of after-image of the deceased person. We might compare these strange flashes with the light that comes to across from distant stars that have long since ceased to exist.

Myers's views were later seconded by Hornell Hart, who had another half century of material to analyze. Hart observed that most apparitions were "tongue-tied" and exhibited no sense of purpose. This line of explanation has the merit of sticking close to witness reports. It does not satisfy either side in the controversy about the reality of ghosts that gathered steam when science and technology started to challenge folk belief and religious dogma. Staunch critics are reluctant to admit the possibility that even a sparkle of energy might persist after death. This highly attenuated form of survival does not include the personality of the deceased, and so it fails to support the faith and hopes of some traditionalists.

The crisis apparition offers a partial explanation that lies somewhere between the Myers/Hart thesis and the more traditional view. The image of an absent person suddenly appears to a friend or family member. This is not a vague, wispy apparition; it seems to be the very person. In some reports the phantom appears at the time of the person's death, sometimes thousands of miles away. These reports could be taken as support for a personal form of survival, but this notion would not extend to all the legions of ghosts that have been perceived or imagined. Furthermore, a brief, one-time apparition offers no evidence of prolonged survival.

Ghosts have often been explained as hallucinations. Green and McCreery, for example, make an interesting case for the possibility that ghost sightings include hallucinations of the entire scene, not just the spirit figure. Defenders have tried to offer evidence that ghosts are not to be dismissed as hallucinations. So-called spirit photography was a popular effort in this direction. Thousands of photographs were produced in which deceased humans and animals appeared among the living. Several photographs even revealed a ghostly figure moving through a séance in all her ectoplasmic glory. Notwithstanding the adage that "seeing is believing," the credibility of spirit photography succumbed rapidly to critical investigations into the wiles of trick photography.

The purported acquisition of unusual but accurate information from ghosts has also been offered as proof of their authenticity. Many of these examples pertain to prophecies of warning. For example, a ghost tells warns a family not to go on their planned trip or confides where they can find the old strongbox filled with money and valuable gems. If events prove the information to have been trustworthy, one might then feel entitled to reward the ghost with a vote of authenticity.

These and other possible contacts with ghosts invite skepticism and outright derision in the mainstream of a culture with an essentially rationalist, materialist worldview. But few contest the vividness and tenacity of ghostly visitations in the human imagination.

*See also:* AFRICAN RELIGIONS; COMMUNICATION WITH THE DEAD; GHOST DANCE; IMMORTALITY; SHAKESPEARE, WILLIAM; SOUL BIRDS

### *Bibliography*

Bennett, Gillian. *Alas, Poor Ghost! Traditions of Belief in Story and Discourse.* Logan: Utah State University Press, 1999.

Davidson, Hilda, R. Ellis, and W. M. S. Russell, eds., *The Folklore of Ghosts.* Bury St. Edmunds: D. S. Folklore Society, 1981.

Emmons, Charles F. *Chinese Ghosts and ESP.* Metuchen, NJ: Scarecrow Press, 1982.

Freed, Ruth S., and Stanley A. Freed. *Ghosts: Life and Death in North India.* New York: American Museum of Natural History, 1993.

Gauld, Alan. "Discarnate Survival." In Benjamin B. Wolman ed., *Handbook of Parapsychology.* New York: Van Nostrand Reinhold, 1977.

Green, Celia, and Charles McCreery. *Apparitions.* Oxford: Institute for Psychophysical Research, 1989.

Guiley, Rosemary Ellen. *Harper's Encyclopedia of Mystical & Paranormal Experience.* Edison, NJ: Castle, 1991.

Gurney, E., Frederick W. H. Myers, and Frank Podmore. *Phantasms of the Living.* London: Trubner, 1886.

Kalish, Richard A., and David K. Reynolds. "Phenomenological Reality and Post–Death Contact." *Journal for the Scientific Study of Religion* 12 (1973):209–221.

Kastenbaum, Robert. *Is There Life After Death?* revised edition. London: Prion, 1995.

Lindley, Charles. *The Ghost Book of Charles Lindley, Viscount Halifax.* New York: Carroll & Graf, 1994.

Montrell, William Lynwood. *Ghosts along the Cumberland: Deathlore in the Kentucky Foothills.* Knoxville: University of Tennessee Press, 1987.

Mulholland, John. *Beware Familiar Spirits.* New York: Arno Press, 1975.

Myers, Frederick W. H. *Human Personality and Its Survival of Bodily Death,* 2 vols. New York: Arno Press, 1975.

Roll, William G. "Poltergeists." In Benjamin B. Wolman ed., *Handbook of Parapsychology.* New York: Van Nostrand Reinhold, 1977.

Schmitt, Jean-Claude. *Ghosts in the Middle Ages. The Living and the Dead in Medieval Society.* Chicago: University of Chicago Press, 1998.

ROBERT KASTENBAUM

# GILGAMESH

Few poems are nobler in expression and content than the *Epic of Gilgamesh*. Its Sumerian hero was famous throughout the Near East from about 2000 B.C.E. to the seventh century B.C.E. when the epic was "written down and collated in the palace of Ashurbanipal, King of the World, King of Assyria." Gilgamesh was reckoned by Ashurbanipal as an ancestor—good reason for wanting his adventures preserved.

But this is a tale worth any king's attention, as relevant today as to the Sumerians of ancient Iraq. It tells of a man who finds a friend, loses him to death, and embarks on a quest for immortality. It speaks of earthy things given mythic status: felling trees, guarding sheep, baking bread, washing clothes, making wine, punting boats, diving in the sea. These amount to a celebration of life that gives poignancy to the poem's stark message: Death is the end of existence.

### The Story

There was no greater city than Uruk, but Gilgamesh, its king, being two-thirds god, was driven by the relentless energy of divinity. Resting neither day or night, he took young men to labor on grandiose buildings, and carried brides off from their weddings. ("He is the first. The husband comes after.") Hearing the people's complaints, the gods told Aruru, goddess of creation, to make a match for him, to divert his energies. She fashioned a wild man, huge, hairy and strong, who roamed the plains with the gazelle. His name was Enkidu.

When word of Enkidu reached Uruk, a temple prostitute was sent to seduce him, so that his animal companions would shun him. After this, she "made him a man," teaching him human speech, and how to eat human food, drink alcohol, dress his hair, and wear clothes. Because of his strength, Enkidu was asked to stop Gilgamesh from abducting a bride and barred his way. They wrestled until Enkidu was thrown, but Gilgamesh acknowledged he had won because he was semi-divine: "In truth, you are my equal." Here began their friendship.

Their first exploit was to go to the Cedar Forest to kill its giant guardian, Humbaba. Their second was to kill the Bull of Heaven (drought personified) sent because Gilgamesh rejected advances by Ishtar, goddess of love. The gods decreed that for the two slayings one of the friends must die. The lot fell on Enkidu.

The Gate of the Cedar Forest had seemed so beautiful to Enkidu that he could not hack it down, and instead pushed it open with his hand. But there was an enchantment on it, which blasted the hand, so that a fever spread from it and he dreamed of dying. He cursed the prostitute and the Forest Gate, and on the twelfth day fell silent. For seven days and nights Gilgamesh would not give him up for burial, and only when a maggot fell from his nose accepted his death.

Knowing that, like Enkidu, he would die. Gilgamesh set out to find Utnapishtim, the one man saved by the gods from The Flood. Making him immortal, they had placed him with his wife in Dilmun, the Garden of the Gods. Gilgamesh would ask Utnapishtim how to become immortal himself.

His quest led him through a gate guarded by Scorpion People with flaming aureoles into Mashu, the mountain into which the sun passes at night. He journeyed in darkness before coming out in the Garden of the Sun, where Shamash walked at evening. The sun god said his quest would fail: All mortals must die. Next he encountered Siduri, Woman of the Vine, beside her house making wine for the gods. She urged him to live from day to day, taking pleasure in food, wine, and the love of

wife and children, "for love was granted men as well as death."

Seeing him undeterred, Siduri directed him to the Images of Stone, near which he would find Urshanabi, Utnapishtim's boatman. To reach Dilmun, one must cross the deep, bitter Waters of Death, and the Images kept the ferryman safe on the crossing. In a fit of temper, Gilgamesh broke the Images of Stone and, when he found the boatman, Urshanabi said that it was now too dangerous to cross. However, he had Gilgamesh cut long poles from the woods, and they launched the boat on the sea. When they reached the Waters of Death that lay between it and Dilmun, Gilgamesh punted the boat along, dropping each pole before his hand touched the fatal Waters.

Reaching Dilmun, Gilgamesh told Utnapishtim why he had come there. Utnapishtim said first he must pass a test: not sleeping for six days and seven nights. But Gilgamesh was exhausted by his journey and he who had once needed no rest now fell into a profound slumber. Every day, Utnapishtim's wife stood a fresh loaf of bread beside him. When Utnapishtim woke him, he saw six of them and despaired.

Utnapishtim now dismissed him, together with Urshanabi, who, having ferried a living man over the Waters, had broken the rule of the gods. Utnapishtim's wife persuaded him to give Gilgamesh something in return for his suffering. So Utnapishtim told him of a place in the sea where grew the Flower of Youth, which would make the old young again.

Reaching the spot, Gilgamesh tied stones on his feet and jumped into the water. Down to the bottom he sank and, despite its thorns, plucked the flower. Cutting off the stones, he surfaced in triumph, telling Urshanabi he would give it to the old of Uruk to eat, and eventually eat it himself. But on their homeward voyage, they went ashore to rest and Gilgamesh bathed in a nearby pool, leaving the Flower of Youth on the bank. Deep in the pool lay a serpent that snuffed the fragrance of the flower, rose up, devoured it, and grew young again (sloughing its skin as snakes have ever since).

Then Gilgamesh wept. He had failed to win everlasting life, and with the Flower of Youth in his grasp lost even that. But presently he said they should continue to Uruk and he would show

Urshanabi his fine city. There at least his labors had not been fruitless.

## The Background

The story of Gilgamesh comes from Sumer on the Persian Gulf. The Sumerians entered southern Iraq around 4000 B.C.E. and established city-states, each with its king. One of these was Gilgamesh, who appears in a king-list as the fifth king in Uruk (biblical Erech). Another Sumerian text tells of a conflict between Gilgamesh and Agga, king of Kish (c. 2700 B.C.E.). Some identify Gilgamesh as the "mighty hunter," Nimrod son of Cush, mentioned in the Book of Genesis. Thus the epic may be based on traditions of real events.

But it has a mythic dimension. Gilgamesh was the son of Ninsun, a minor goddess residing in Egalmah, the "Great Palace" of Uruk, by "the high priest of Kullab" in the same city. Gilgamesh was regarded as superhuman. In the*Epic* he is said to be 11 cubits (approximately 18 feet) tall, and his punt poles were each 60 cubits long. The king-list says that he reigned for 126 years.

In about the fourteenth century B.C.E., Akkadians living north of Sumer established Babylon as their capital and took control of the whole area between Baghdad and the Gulf. The Babylonians preserved the Sumerian language as their language of religion, and with it Sumerian legends and myths.

The Hebrews may have learned Sumerian tales during their Babylonian exile. There are echoes of the *Epic of Gilgamesh* in the Bible: The flaming guardians of the Otherworld gate and the loss of immortality to a serpent are mythic themes that recur in the Expulsion from Eden in the Book of Genesis. Noah's Ark also corresponds in some details to the *Epic*'s account of The Flood.

The Babylonians were succeeded in the region by the Assyrians. Originally the exploits of Gilgamesh were recounted in separate poems, such as "Gilgamesh and the Land of the Living," a surviving Sumerian account of his quest. If Sumerians or Babylonians ever strung these poems together into an epic, it has been lost. The *Epic of Gilgamesh* exists only in the Assyrian version, written on twelve clay tablets in Ashurbanipal's library at Nineveh and recovered at different times. From these the epic has been pieced together, breaks in the text being supplemented from separate poems. Some mysteries remain. What were the Images of Stone?

## The Meaning

Despite its enigmas, the *Epic* is one of the literary masterpieces of the world, at one level a swashbuckling adventure story; at another a "buddy" tale prefiguring the great friendships of David and Jonathan and Roland and Oliver; at another, a demonstration that the gods have an agenda independent of human interests (Enkidu is a toy for Gilgamesh, and expendable). At yet another level it is a contemplation of what it means to be human, in the figure of the wild man "tamed," civilized by the prostitute to his undoing, for he responds to the Forest Gate as man not brute (which is why he curses both it and her).

At its most profound, the poem is a meditation on living in the knowledge of death. Enkidu tells Gilgamesh a fever-dream he has of dying. He is standing before a dark being whose talons are choking out his life. Then it turns his arms into wings and leads him to the house of the underworld queen, Ereshkigal. Everyone here has feathered wings and sits in eternal darkness, "dust their food and clay their sustenance." This was the common lot in the ancient Near East. It is because "darkness is the end of mortal life" that Gilgamesh is desperate to learn Utnapishtim's secret.

After failure comes resignation. He proudly shows Urshanabi his city—this much he has achieved. But his words before the Cedar Forest adventure return to haunt readers: "Only the gods live forever . . . As for mankind, numbered are their days; Whatever they achieve is but the wind!" One of the ironies of time is that Gilgamesh's great city was long ago ruined; and it is the story of his heroic failure, written on brittle tablets of clay, that survives.

*See also:* AFTERLIFE IN CROSS-CULTURAL PERSPECTIVE; GODS AND GODDESSES OF LIFE AND DEATH; IMMORTALITY

### Bibliography

Heidel, Alexander. *The Babylonian Genesis,* 15th impression. Chicago: University of Chicago Press, 1965.

Heidel, Alexander. *The Gilgamesh Epic and Old Testament Parallels.* Chicago: University of Chicago Press, 1946.

Hooke, S. H. *Middle Eastern Mythology*. Harmondsworth: Penguin, 1963.

Kramer, S. N. *Sumerian Mythology*. Philadelphia: American Philosophic Society, 1944.

McLeish, Kenneth. *Myth: Myths and Legends of the World Explored*. London: Bloomsbury, 1996.

Pritchard, J. B. *Ancient Near Eastern Texts Relating to the Old Testament*. Vol. 1. Princeton, NJ: Princeton University Press, 1973.

Sandars, N. K., tr. *The Epic of Gilgamesh*. Harmondsworth: Penguin, 1960.

Sollberger, Edmund. *The Babylonian Legend of the Flood*, 2nd edition. London: The British Museum, 1966.

JENNIFER WESTWOOD

# GODS AND GODDESSES OF LIFE AND DEATH

The One God of the Near Eastern monotheisms—Judaism, Christianity, Islam—is both the creator and stern but loving father of humankind. He cares for his creation from birth to death and beyond. This is somewhat exceptional among world mythologies. Many creator gods are unbelievably remote in time and space: Maheo in the myths of the Cheyenne of the U.S. Great Plains existed before existence, and numerous creators are sky gods, such as Olorun, or "Sky," in the myths of the Edo and Yoruba peoples of Nigeria.

Although most peoples of the world preferred to believe that creation had a purpose, sometimes it was incidental or even accidental. Qamaits, warrior goddess of the Bella Coola people of the Northwest coast of Canada, killed off the primeval giants who ruled the earth, making room for other life forms merely as a by-product. Coniraya, one of the oldest of Inca gods, could not help but create: His mere touch made everything burst into life.

Such creators often take scant interest in their creation. Qamaits seldom concerned herself with the earth once she had killed the giants and perhaps humans as well; her rare visits caused earthquakes, forest fires, and epidemics. Other creator gods withdraw once the act of creation is over, leaving subordinates in charge. In Ugandan myth, the creator, Katonda, left his deputies Kibuka (war) and Walumbe (death), along with others, to rule his new universe.

## The War Gods

War and death are an obvious pairing. Almost no one embraces death willingly, unless seduced by the evil songs of Kipu-Tyttö, Finnish goddess of illness, into joining her in the underworld of Tuonela. To express most people's sense of death as a battle lost, death is pictured in many myths as a warrior: Rudrani, the Hindu "red princess," who brings plague and death, and gorges on blood shed in battle; and Llamo, Tibetan goddess of disease, riding across the world, clad in her victims' skins, firing her poison arrows. Because warriors give protection too, the ancient Greeks were ushered out of life by a gentler psychopomp (soul guide) than in most mythologies, the warrior god Thanatos, brother of Sleep, who escorted the dead to the gates of the underworld.

If war and death seem obvious allies, war and life seem contradictions. Yet it is precisely on the patrons of war, and other gods and goddesses envisaged as warriors, that the business of human life often rests. In most mythologies, the divine energy of the gods is seen as the great motive force of the universe. This energy may be analogous to that of a storm or some other powerful natural force, as in Egypt where the desert wind was personified as the lion-headed goddess Sekhmet, who when angry became the Eye of Ra, a terrible war goddess who swept over the land, scorching the earth in her wake.

Just as human warriors are stronger and more active than most other people, war gods and goddesses generally embody pure energy: the Hindu goddess Durga is the anger of Shiva's consort Parvati, just as Kartikeya (Skanda), Hindu god of armies, is the fierceness of Shiva himself. The divine vigor of these deities is barely contained: Sumerian Ninurta existed as power without form until his mother Ninhursaga confined it in the shape of an eagle-winged warrior. The same idea underlies the curious births of many war gods: Iranian Mithra, born from a rock; Greek Athene, springing from Zeus's head; Kali, the Hindu death goddess, bursting from the forehead of Durga; and Kartikeya, born from the sparks that fell from Shiva's eyes. They are eruptions into the universe of divine vitality.

Unsurprisingly, therefore, a number of war gods are themselves creators, like the Mesopotamian Marduk, Mithra in ancient Iran, Min in Egypt, Vahagn in Armenian myth, Unkulunkulu of the Amazulu people of South Africa, and (inadvertently) Qamaits. Many more are deeply involved with the creative and intellectual growth of humankind, their myths saying something universal about the way civilizations develop. Except for the Greek Ares, portrayed as brawn without brain, the war gods are often great benefactors. Tools and weapons are the gifts of Gu, the blacksmith god of the Fon peoples of Dahomey, and of Ogun, venerated by the Yoruba as the power of iron. Craft-skills are bestowed by Greek Athene and Sumerian Ninurta, healing and medical skills by lion-headed Sekhmet and by Unkulunkulu, the Amazulu creator. Magical knowledge is the legacy of Norse Odin, prophecy of Baltic Svandovit. Justice and fair dealing are the province of Norse Tr and Roman Mars, sovereignty and rule of Celtic Medb, Germanic Teutatis, and both Mars and the Roman war goddess Bellona.

It is very often the war gods, too, who oversee the continuance of the human race, and indeed the ability of all living things to reproduce themselves. The myths say this in different ways. Several war gods and goddesses, notably the Greek Ares and the Celtic Medb, were notorious for their sexual appetites. Just as Ares coupled for preference with Aphrodite, so in Haitian voudun (voodoo), Ogoun enjoys sex with the love goddess Erzulie. The Mesopotamian Ishtar, goddess of sex, was in Assyria also the war goddess, to whom were offered the flayed skins and severed hands of prisoners.

This is less a commentary on the rape and pillage historically associated with invading armies than a reflection of a link between war gods and a broader notion of generation and fertility. Gu, in Dahomey, oversaw both fertility and war; Cihuacóatl, Great Goddess of the Aztecs, had charge of war and women's fecundity. In particular instances, the link between war and fertility might arise from the war god's dual role as sky and weather god, by analogy with the life-giving rain, as with Mars and Svandovit. Another line of development is represented by Hachiman, who began as a protector of crops and children, came to protect the whole of Japan, and then became a war god.

## Sex and Fertility

But war gods aside, a connection between sex/fertility and death is made in many mythologies from the most ancient past down to the present time. Nergal in Mesopotamia, embodied as a bull (a widespread symbol of virility), was notorious both for his sexual activity and also for dragging mortals off to the underworld; Sucellus, the "Good Striker," in Celtic myth had a hammer which he used both to strike plenty from the ground and to hit dying people on the forehead to make death easier; Ghede, originally the Haitian god of love, was in later voudun belief amalgamated with Baron Samedi, the dancing god of death who was often questioned via blood sacrifice on questions of fertility.

This link between sex and/or fertility and death is epitomized by Hathor, originally a fierce blood-drinking Nubian war goddess who wore the same lion-headed form as Sekhmet. When introduced into Egypt, she became the cow of plenty whose milk was the food of the gods and kept them fecund. It was Hathor, too, who entertained the sun god Ra on his nightly voyage through the underworld, and also guided souls to the court of the judge of the dead, Osiris.

Life and death are two sides of the same coin: Innanna, Sumerian goddess of sex and fertility, is the twin sister of Ereshkigal, queen of the underworld. They are not two but one, a dual goddess, light and dark. Consider the Irish myths of the Daghdha. Wise, associated with magic, like the war gods he was master of arts and skills. But he was also the gluttonous god of abundance and of fertility, coupling with Boann, the spirit of the river Boyne, as well as his wife Dana, and with the war goddess the Morrigan (significantly on New Year's Day). He wielded a huge club—with the knobbed end killing the living, the other restoring the dead to life.

## Other Aspects of Gods and Goddesses

Some mythologies have vanished; some have gone on to become world faiths. One of the survivors is Hinduism, which expresses its philosophy of life and death in the myth of Shiva, a warrior of vast strength, the most powerful being in the universe, armed with invincible weapons (including a bow made from the rainbow and a trident of thunderbolts). Like many war gods, he was born oddly,

*The connection between fertility and death is made in many mythologies. The orginal Nubian war goddess turned Egyptian fertility goddess, Hathor, is characterized by these labor amulets.* CORBIS

from a slit in a vast penis that appeared in the universe. (He is still honored in the form of a phallic stone column, the lingam.) At the same time, his titles include Kala ("Death") and Nataraja ("Lord of the Dance"), because of the terrible dance he dances at the end of each cycle of the universe, when he opens his fearful third eye and unmakes the whole of creation. He is one of the three supreme deities: He destroys, Vishnu preserves, Brahma maintains balance. Together, they order the universe.

Though many ancient mythologies explained how death came into the world, comparatively few promised a better life to come. Their underworlds were mostly gloomy places, into which the dead were thrust by hideous demons or fierce warrior-deities, and there either forgotten by their creator or made to stand trial before some dread underworld lord such as Osiris in Egypt or in Chinese Buddhist myth the Four Kings of Hell, who guard the Scrolls of Judgment in which all past lives are recorded. No wonder that many underworlds are filled with unhappy souls, like the spirits led by Gauna, death in the myths of the Bushmen of Botswana, who are so miserable in the world below that they keep trying to escape and take over the world above.

But several societies evolved myths of death and resurrection gods built on the analogy with plant life, which springs up and dies in an annual cycle. The Greeks told the story of Adonis, loved by both Aphrodite and the underworld goddess Persephone. When he was killed by a jealous Ares, scarlet anemones sprang up from drops of his blood. Zeus solved the rivalry between the goddesses by decreeing that Adonis should spend half his year with Aphrodite, half with Persephone in the underworld.

Death and resurrection gods form the background to the emergence in the Near East of mystery religions, so-called because only initiates knew their secrets. These extended the chance of a better hereafter beyond a close circle of special people, such as the pharaohs and nobles in Ancient Egypt afforded a kind of immortality by mummification; Greek heroes taken to the happy Isles of the Blest instead of gloomy Hades; and Norse warriors carried off the battlefield by Odin's battle-maidens, the valkyries, to the everlasting feast in his mead-hall Vallhalla, whereas those who died in their beds were consigned to the dismal realm of the goddess Hel.

The mystery religions promised life after death to all believers. In Egypt, Aset (Isis), sister and consort of Osiris, by her magical skills reassembled the corpse of Osiris, after he was dismembered by his brother Set. However, the gods decreed that Osiris (perhaps because he could no longer function as a fertility deity, Aset having been unable to find his penis) should henceforth serve as judge of the dead in the underworld. From this evolved the Mysteries of Isis, a popular cult in Ptolemaic Egypt and Rome, from the first century B.C.E. to the fourth century C.E. At their initiation, devotees were told the secret name of the sun god Ra, which Isis won from him in order to revivify Osiris. They believed that knowing this name empowered them to conquer age and sickness, even death.

From Iran came the cult of the creator and war god Mithra who fought and killed the primeval bull, from whose blood and bone marrow sprang all vegetation. He eternally mediates on human-kind's behalf with his father, Ahura Mazda, the god of light, and combats the dark lord, Ahriman, the evil principle. This battle will end on Judgment Day with Mithra's triumph. In ancient Rome, where he was known as Mithras, Mithra became the focus of a mystery religion practiced especially by soldiers. Initiation into his cult, as into that of Isis, was believed to ensure immortality. The cult never became widespread, partly because it was secret, partly because it was austere, but chiefly perhaps because it was closed to half the population—the women.

By contrast, Christianity spoke to both sexes. It outlasted both the Mysteries of Isis and those of Mithras, perhaps because the answer it gave to the question "What happens to me after death?" was the same for everyone, king or subject, master or slave, soldier or farmer, man or woman. Moreover, the bodily death and resurrection of Christ himself, prefiguring the triumph over death of all who believed in him, was said to have happened to a historical person within or almost within living memory, rather than to a god in some remote mythical time.

*See also:* AFRICAN RELIGIONS; GILGAMESH; OSIRIS

### Bibliography

Fox, Robin Lane. *Pagans and Christians*. Harmondsworth: Viking, 1986.

Green, Miranda. *Dictionary of Celtic Myth and Legend*. London: Thames and Hudson, 1992.

Leach, Maria, ed. *Funk & Wagnall's Standard Dictionary of Folklore, Mythology, and Legend*. San Francisco: Harper and Row, 1984.

McLeish, Kenneth. *Myth: Myths and Legends of the World Explored*. London: Bloomsbury, 1996.

Mercantante, Anthony S. *The Facts on File Encyclopaedia of World Mythology and Legend*. New York: Facts on File, 1988.

O'Flaherty, Wendy Doniger, tr. *Hindu Myths*. Harmondsworth: Penguin, 1975.

O hOgáin, Dáithí. *Myth, Legend and Romance: An Encyclopaedia of the Irish Folk Tradition*. London: Ryan Publishing, 1990.

Page, R. I. *Norse Myths*. London: British Museum Publications, 1990.

JENNIFER WESTWOOD

# GOOD DEATH, THE

What is the good life? Most people would prefer health to illness, affluence to poverty, and freedom to confinement. Nevertheless, different people might have significantly different priorities. Is the good life one that is devoted to family affection or individual achievement? To contemplation or action? To safeguarding tradition or discovering new possibilities? There is a parallel situation in regard to the good death. Not surprisingly, most people would prefer to end their lives with ease of body, mind, and spirit. This unanimity dissolves, however, when one moves beyond the desire to avoid suffering. Societies as well as individuals have differed markedly in their conception of the good death. The long and eventful history of the good death has taken some new turns at the turn of the millennium, although enduring links with the past are still evident.

Dying is a phase of living, and death is the outcome. This obvious distinction is not always preserved in language and thought. When people speak of "the good death," they sometimes are thinking of the dying process, sometimes of death as an event that concludes the process, and sometimes of the status of "being dead." Furthermore, it is not unusual for people to shift focus from one facet to another.

Consider, for example, a person whose life has ended suddenly in a motor vehicle accident. One might consider this to have been a bad death because a healthy and vibrant life was destroyed along with all its future possibilities. But one might also consider this to have been a good death in that there was no protracted period of suffering. The death was bad, having been premature, but the dying was merciful. Moreover, one might believe that the person who is now "in death," is either experiencing a joyous afterlife or simply no longer exists.

It is possible, then, to confuse oneself and others by shifting attention from process to event to status while using the same words. It is not only possible but also fairly common for these three aspects of death to be the subject of conflict. For example, the controversial practice of physician-assisted suicide advances the event of death to reduce suffering in the dying process. By contrast, some dying people have refrained from taking their own lives in the belief that suicide is a sin that will be punished when the soul has passed into the realm of death. It is therefore useful to keep in mind the distinction between death as process, event, and status. It is also important to consider perspective: *who* judges this death to be good or bad? Society and individual do not necessarily share the same view, nor do physician and patient.

Philosophers continue to disagree among themselves as to whether death can be either good or bad. The Greek philosopher Epicurus (341–270 B.C.E.) made the case that death means nothing to us one way or the other: When we are here, death is not. When death is here, we are not. So why worry? Subsequent philosophers, however, have come up with reasons to worry. For example, according to Walter Glannon, author of a 1993 article in the journal *Monist,* the Deprivation of Goods Principle holds that death is bad to the extent that it removes the opportunity to enjoy what life still might have offered. It can be seen that philosophers are talking past each other on this point. Epicurus argued that death is a matter of indifference because it is outside humans' lived experience. This is a focus on process. Glannon and others argue that the "badness" of death is relative and quantitative—it depends on how much one has lost. This is a focus on death as event.

## A World Perspective

From terminology and philosophy, one next turns to the rich heritage of world cultures as they have wrestled with the question of the good death within their own distinctive ways of life. Many of the world's peoples have lived in fairly small groups. People knew each other well and were bonded to their territory by economic, social, and religious ties. These face-to-face societies often contended with hardships and external threats. Community survival was therefore vital to individual survival. Within this context, the good death was regarded as even more consequential for the community than for the individual.

The good death was one that did not expose the community to reprisals from angry spirits or stir up confusion and discontent among the survivors. Personal sorrow was experienced when a family member died, but the community as a whole

responded with a sequence of rituals intended to avoid the disasters attendant on a bad death.

The Lugbara of Uganda and Zaire do not practice many rituals for birth, puberty, or marriage, but they become intensely involved in the funeral process. Death is regarded as an enemy, an alien force that raids the village. Nobody just dies. Much of Lugbara life is therefore devoted to controlling or placating evil spirits. The good death for the Lugbara encompasses the process, the event, and the state.

- The Process: Dying right is a performance that should take place in the individual's own hut with family gathered about to hear the last words. The dying person should be alert and capable of communicating, and the final hours should flow peacefully without physical discomfort or spiritual distress. The dying person has then prepared for the passage and has settled his or her affairs with family and community. It is especially desirable that a lineage successor has been appointed and confirmed to avoid rivalry and perhaps violence.

- The Event: The death occurs on schedule—not too soon and not too much later than what was expected. The moment is marked by the lineage successor with the *cre,* a whooping cry, which signifies that the deceased is dead to the community both physically and socially, and that the people can now get back to their lives.

- The State: The deceased and the community have performed their ritual obligations properly, so there is little danger of attack from discontented spirits. The spirit particular to the deceased may linger for a while, but it will soon continue its journey through the land of the dead.

A death can go bad when any of these components fails. For example, a person who dies suddenly or away from home is likely to become a confused and angry spirit who can become a menace to the community. A woman who dies in childbirth might return as an especially vengeful spirit because the sacred link between sexuality and fertility has been violated. The Lugbara deathbed scene shows compassion for the dying person and concern for the well-being of the community. Nevertheless, it is a tense occasion because a bad death can leave the survivors vulnerable to the forces of evil.

In many other world cultures the passage from life to death has also been regarded as a crucial transaction with the realm of gods and spirits. The community becomes especially vulnerable at such times. It is best, then, to support this passage with rules and rituals. These observances begin while the person is still alive and continue while the released spirit is exploring its new state of being. Dying people receive compassionate care because of close interpersonal relationships but also because a bad death is so risky for the community.

Other conceptions of the good death have also been around for a long time. Greek, Roman, Islamic, Viking, and early Christian cultures all valued heroic death in battle. Life was often difficult and brief in ancient times. Patriotic and religious beliefs extolled those who chose a glorious death instead of an increasingly burdensome and uncertain life. Norse mythology provides an example made famous in an opera by the nineteenth-century German composer Richard Wagner in which the Valkyrie—the spirits of formidable female warriors—bring fallen heroes to Valhalla where their mortal sacrifice is rewarded by the gods.

Images of the heroic death have not been limited to the remote past. Many subsequent commanders have sent their troops to almost certain death, urging them to die gloriously. The U.S. Civil War (1861–1865) provides numerous examples of men pressing forward into withering firepower, but similar episodes have also occurred repeatedly throughout the world. Critics of heroic death observe that the young men who think they are giving their lives for a noble cause are actually being manipulated by leaders interested only in their own power.

Some acts of suicide have also been considered heroic. The Roman commander who lost the battle could retain honor by falling on his sword, and the Roman senator who displeased the emperor was given the opportunity to have a good death by cutting his wrists and bleeding his life away. Japanese warriors and noblemen similarly could expiate mistakes or crimes by the ritualistic suicide known in the West as hara-kiri. Widows in

India were expected to burn themselves alive on their husbands' funeral pyres.

Other deaths through the centuries have earned admiration for the willingness of individuals to sacrifice their lives to help another person or affirm a core value. Martyrs, people who chose to die rather than renounce their faith, have been sources of inspiration in Christianity and Islam. There is also admiration for the courage of people who died at the hands of enemies instead of betraying their friends. History lauds physicians who succumbed to fatal illnesses while knowingly exposing themselves to the risk in order to find a cause or cure. These deaths are exemplary from society's perspective, but they can be regarded as terrible misfortunes from the standpoint of the families and friends of the deceased.

The death of the Greek philosopher Socrates (c. 470–399 B.C.E.) shines through the centuries as an example of a person who remained true to his principles rather than take an available escape route. It is further distinguished as a death intended to be instruction to his followers. The good death, then, might be the one that strengthens and educates the living. The modern hospice/palliative care movement traces its origins to deaths of this kind.

With the advent of Christianity the stakes became higher for the dying person. The death and resurrection of Jesus led to the promise that true believers would also find their way into heaven—but one might instead be condemned to eternal damnation. It was crucial, then, to end this life in a state of grace. A new purification ritual was developed to assist in this outcome, the *ordo defunctorum*. The last moments of life now took on extraordinary significance. Nothing less than the fate of the soul hung in the balance.

The mood as well as the practice of Christianity underwent changes through the centuries with the joyful messianic expectation of an imminent transformation giving way to anxiety and doubt. The fear of punishment as a sinner darkened the hope of a blissful eternity. Individual salvation became the most salient concern. By the fifteenth century, European society was deeply immersed in death anxiety. The Ars Moriendi ("art of dying") movement advised people to prepare themselves for death every day of their lives—and to see that their children learned to focus on the perils of their

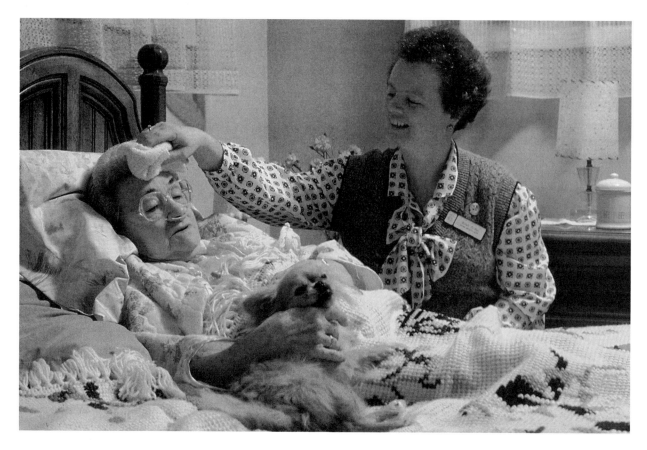

*The hospice environment is one in which a patient, such as the elderly person here, can be comforted by family and friends in moments leading up to death. This type of "good death" gives individuals a chance to say their good-byes to loved ones.* TERRY WILD STUDIO

own deathbed scene rather than become attached to the amusements and temptations of earthly life. The good death was redemption and grace; everything else was of little value.

This heavy emphasis on lifelong contemplation of mortality and the crucial nature of the deathbed scene gradually lessened as the tempo of sociotechnological change accelerated. Hardships continued, but earthly life seemed to offer more attractions and possibilities, drawing attention away from meditations on death. And by the seventeenth century a familiar voice was speaking with a new ring of authority. Physicians were shedding their humble roles in society and proudly claiming enhanced powers and privileges. In consequence, the nobility were more likely to be tormented by aggressive, painful, and ineffective interventions before they could escape into death. The emerging medical profession was staking its claim to the deathbed scene. It was a good death

now when physicians could assure each other, "We did everything that could be done and more."

## The Good Death in the Twenty-First Century

In the early twenty-first century, as in the past, humans seek order, security, and meaning when confronted with death. It is therefore clear that not everything has changed. Nevertheless, people's views of the good death have been influenced by the altered conditions of life. To begin with, there are more people alive today than ever before, and, in technologically developed nations, they are more likely to remain alive into the later adult years. The most remarkable gains in average life expectancy have come from eliminating the contagious diseases that previously had killed many infants and children. The juvenile death rate had been so high that in various countries census takers did not bother to count young children. Parents mourned for their lost children then as they do now. The impact of this bad death was tempered to some extent by the knowledge that childhood was perilous and survival in God's hands. The current expectation that children will certainly survive into adulthood makes their death even more devastating. Parental self-blame, anger at God, stress disorders, and marital separation are among the consequences that have been linked to the death of a child.

Childbirth was a hazardous experience that many women did not long survive. Graveyards around the world provide evidence in stone of young mothers who had soon joined their infants and children in death. Such deaths are much less expected in the twenty-first century and therefore create an even bigger impact when they do occur.

In the late twentieth and early twenty-first centuries, many Mexicans died while attempting to cross the desert to find employment in the United States in order to feed and shelter their families. Are these "good deaths" because of the heroism of those who risked—and lost—their lives, tragic deaths because of their consequences, or senseless deaths because society has allowed this situation to develop?

It is far more common to assume that one has the right to a long life and therefore to regard an earlier demise as unfair or tragic. Paradoxically, though, there is also more concern about not dying young. Many people remain vigorous and active through a long life. Nevertheless, gerontophobia (fear of growing old) has become a significant problem in part because more people, having lived long, now die old. Younger people often fear that age will bring them to a lonely, dependent, and helpless preterminal situation. The distinction between aging and dying has become blurred in the minds of many people, with aging viewed as a slow fading away in which a person becomes less useful to themselves and others. It is a singularly prolonged bad death, then, to slide gradually into terminal decline, in essence having outlived one's authentic life. This pessimistic outlook has been linked to the rising rate of suicide for men in older age groups. In reality, many elders both contribute to society and receive loving support until the very end, but the image of dying too long and too late has become an anxious prospect since at least the middle of the twentieth century.

Two other forms of the bad death came to prominence in the late twentieth century. The aggressive but mostly ineffective physicians of the seventeenth century have been replaced by a public health and medical establishment that has made remarkable strides in helping people through their crises. Unfortunately, some terminally ill people have experienced persistent and invasive medical procedures that produced suffering without either extending or restoring the quality of their lives. The international hospice movement arose as an alternative to what was seen as a futile overemphasis on treatment that added to the physical and emotional distress of the dying person. The hospice mission has been to provide effective symptom relief and help the dying person maintain a sense of security and worth by supporting the family's own strength.

Being sustained indefinitely between life and death is the another image of the bad death that has been emerging from modern medical practice. The persistent vegetative state arouses anxieties once associated with fears of being buried alive. "Is this person alive, dead, or what?" is a question that adds the pangs of uncertainty to this form of the bad death.

The range of bad death has also expanded greatly from the perspective of those people who have not benefited from the general increase in life expectancy. The impoverished in technologically advanced societies and the larger part of the population in third world nations see others enjoy longer lives while their own kin die young. For example, once even the wealthy were vulnerable to high mortality rates in infancy, childhood, and childbirth. Many such deaths are now preventable, so when a child in a disadvantaged group dies for lack of basic care there is often a feeling of rage and despair.

A change in the configuration of society has made it more difficult to achieve consensus on the good death. Traditional societies usually were built upon shared residence, economic activity, and religious beliefs and practices. It was easier to judge what was good and what was bad. Many nations include substantial numbers of people from diverse backgrounds, practicing a variety of customs and rituals. There is an enriching effect with this cultural mix, but there is also the opportunity for misunderstandings and conflicts. One common example occurs when a large and loving family tries to gather around the bedside of a hospitalized family member. This custom is traditional within some ethnic groups, as is the open expression of feelings. Intense and demonstrative family gatherings can unnerve hospital personnel whose own roots are in a less expressive subculture. Such simple acts as touching and singing to a dying person can be vital within one ethnic tradition and mystifying or unsettling to another.

## Current Conceptions of the Good Death

The most obvious way to discover people's conceptions of the good death is to ask them. Most studies have focused on people who were not afflicted with a life-threatening condition at the time. There is a clear preference for an easy death. The process should be mercifully brief. Often people specify that death should occur in their sleep. Interestingly, students who are completing death education courses and experienced hospice caregivers tend toward a different view. When their turn comes, they would want to complete unfinished business, take leave of the people most important to them, and reflect upon their lives and their relationship to God. These actions require both time and awareness. Drifting off to sleep and death would be an easy ending, but only after they had enough opportunity to do what must be done during the dying process.

Women often describe their imagined deathbed scenes in consoling detail: wildflowers in an old milk jug; a favorite song being played; familiar faces gathered around; a grandchild skipping carefree in and out of the room; the woman, now aged and dying, easy in mind, leaving her full life without regrets. Conspicuous by their absence are the symptoms that often accompany the terminal phase—pain, respiratory difficulties, and so on. These good deaths require not only the positives of a familiar environment and interpersonal support but also a remarkably intact physical condition. (Men also seldom describe physical symptoms on their imagined deathbed.) Men usually give less detailed descriptions of their imagined final hours and are more likely than women to expect to die alone or suddenly in an accident. The imagined good death for some men and a few women takes place in a thrilling adventure, such as skydiving. This fantasy version of death is supposed to occur despite the ravages of a terminal illness.

What is the good death for people who know that they have only a short time to live? People dying of cancer in the National Hospice Demonstration study conducted in 1988, explained to their interviewers how they would like to experience the last three days of their lives. Among their wishes were the following:

- I want certain people to be here with me.
- I want to be physically able to do things.
- I want to feel at peace.
- I want to be free from pain.
- I want the last three days of my life to be like any other days.

This vision of the good death does not rely on fantasy or miracles. It represents a continuation of the life they have known, and their chances of having these wishes fulfilled were well within the reality of their situation. Religion was seldom mentioned as such, most probably because these people were secure in their beliefs.

Society as a whole is still reconstructing its concepts of both the good life and the good death. Studies suggest that most people hope to be spared pain and suffering, and to end their days with supportive companionship in familiar surroundings. Dramatic endings such as heroic sacrifice or deathbed conversion are seldom mentioned. There are continuing differences of opinion in other areas, however. Should people fight for their lives until the last breath, or accept the inevitable with grace? Is the good death simply a no-fuss punctuation mark after a good life—or does the quality of the death depend on how well people have prepared themselves for the next phase of their spiritual journey? Questions such as these will continue to engage humankind as the conditions of life and death also continue to change over time.

*See also:* ARS MORIENDI; COMMUNICATION WITH THE DYING; DEATH SYSTEM; DYING, PROCESS OF; EPICURUS; HOSPICE OPTION; JESUS; MARTYRS; SOCRATES

## *Bibliography*

Bondeson, Jan. *Buried Alive.* New York: W. W. Norton, 2001.

DuBruck, Edelgard E., and Barbara I. Gusick, eds. *Death and Dying in the Middle Ages.* New York: Peter Lang, 1999.

Epicurus. *Epicurus: The Extant Remains,* translated by Cyril Bailey. Oxford: Clarendon Press, 1926.

Glannon, Walter. "Epicureanism and Death." *Monist* 76 (1993):222–234.

Goody, Jack. *Property and the Ancestors: A Study of the Mortuary Customs of the LoDagas of West Africa.* Stanford, CA: Stanford University Press, 1962.

Kastenbaum, Robert. *Death, Society, and Human Experience,* 7th edition. Boston: Allyn & Bacon, 2001.

McManners, John. *Death and the Enlightenment: Changing Attitudes to Death in Eighteenth-Century France.* New York: Oxford University Press, 1981.

McWhiney, Grady, and Perry D. Jamieson. *Attack and Die: Civil War Military Tactics and the Southern Heritage.* Tuscaloosa: University of Alabama Press, 1982.

Paxton, Frederick S. *Christianizing Death.* Ithaca, NY: Cornell University Press, 1990.

Weinberger-Thomas, Catherine. *Ashes of Immortality.* Chicago: University of Chicago Press, 1999.

ROBERT KASTENBAUM

# GRAVESTONES AND OTHER MARKERS

Tracing the development of differing objects of memory provides a general background for understanding the development of gravestones and other markers from colonial times to the present in North America. Based on this overview, three broad traditions emerge: *memento mori* markers, markers that evoke the phrase, "in memory of," and *ignoratio mori* markers.

## Memento Mori

The *memento mori* (remember death) tradition, which began with colonization and continues into the present, emerges from and belongs to a set of values that insists on both a devaluation of the body (indeed, all things temporal) and a valorization of the spirit or soul. The most obvious and significant consequence of such insistence is that markers belonging to this tradition discursively and iconographically encourage viewers to remember death as a means of reminding the living to prepare for judgment.

Gravestones and markers belonging to the *memento mori* tradition tend to be relatively modest structures (between one and five feet in height and width and between two and five inches thick). Characteristically, marker inscriptions provide only the deceased's name, age, date of death, and, less frequently, date of birth, cause of death, and family or community status, with by far the largest number providing nothing more than a brief inscription. Mottos such as the Latin phrases *Memento mori* and *Fugit hora* ("time flies" or, more literally, "hours flee") appear on countless early markers from this tradition and leave little room for doubt as to what viewers are to remember. To restate and reinforce the lesson, markers also continually confront viewers with time- and death-related icons.

## In Memory Of

A second tradition, which began to emerge during the early years of the eighteenth century and also continues into the present, identifies a particular individual as the object of memory. Initially, proponents of this tradition, which we may designate the "in memory of" tradition, borrowed heavily from the *memento mori* tradition by producing markers nearly identical in size, shape, and general appearance. However, rather than instructing viewers to "remember death," these new markers discursively and iconographically emphasized the deceased, often drawing attention to emotions occasioned by the individual's death.

With the introduction of rural cemeteries, which specifically reflect the values of this tradition, came a remarkably increased facility for patrons to produce an enormous variety of gravestones and markers. Despite that variety, such markers fall into two general categories.

The first category abides principally by the creed that memorials are, or ought to be, works of art insofar as they serve primarily to draw attention either to the memorial as a work of art or to the work of art as a memorial. Typically, markers belonging to this category borrow heavily from Egyptian, Greek, Gothic, and Roman sources.

The second category draws attention not only to the memory of the deceased and to the work of art as a memorial (or to the memorial as a work of art), but also to pathetic sentiments. Some of the more common focal points for this kind of marker are the faithful animal, the poised angel, women and children, and replicas of nature or natural phenomena. In all, markers within this tradition generally serve not as a means of reminding viewers of their urgent need to bring order out of chaos in order to prepare religiously for death, but as a means of encouraging viewers to live aesthetically, homeopathically, and naturally in the moment.

## Ignoratio Mori

A third tradition, which we may designate the *ignoratio mori* ("ignore death") tradition, began to appear in gravescapes as early as the mid–eighteenth century and continues into the present. This tradition initially borrowed heavily from previous traditions. However, rather than replicating themes indicative of those traditions, this tradition sets death aside and focuses heavily on the lived accomplishments of the deceased. In general terms this tradition developed in three divergent but complementary directions.

The first direction produced markers that explicitly emphasized the deceased's worldly achievements, social or cultural standing, and heroic actions. The second direction produced memorials specifically designed to be erected in towns and cities, which afforded the double advantage of allowing proponents to construct memorials of sufficient size and of dissociating their tradition from the gravescape (and, thus, death). The third direction emerged as a consequence of the introduction of the lawn cemetery, a gravescape explicitly designed to reflect and articulate the values underlying this tradition. Here, markers (and again death) are flush with or slightly depressed into the ground so that the only immediately visible memorial efforts are those selected by adherents to this tradition and thus can insure that all memorials contained within this funerary environment conform to appropriate values.

*See also:* BURIAL GROUNDS; CEMETERIES AND CEMETERY REFORM; EPITAPHS; LAWN GARDEN CEMETERIES

### *Bibliography*

Ariès, Philippe. *The Hour of Our Death,* translated by Helen Weaver. New York: Vintage, 1982.

Farrell, James J. *Inventing the American Way of Death.* Philadelphia: Temple University Press, 1980.

Forbes, Harriette Merrifield. *Gravestones of Early New England and the Men Who Made Them, 1653–1800.* Boston: Houghton Mifflin, 1927.

Gorer, Geoffrey. *Death, Grief, and Mourning.* New York: Doubleday, 1965.

Linden Ward, Blanche. *Silent City on a Hill: Landscapes of Memory and Boston's Mount Auburn Cemetery.* Columbus: Ohio State University Press, 1989.

Ludwig, Allan I. *Graven Images: New England Stonecarving and Its Images, 1650–1815.* Middletown, CT: Wesleyan University Press, 1966.

Meyer, Richard E., ed. *Cemeteries and Gravemarkers: Voices of American Culture.* Ann Arbor: University of Michigan Research Press, 1989.

Morris, Richard. *Sinners, Lovers, and Heroes: An Essay on Memorializing in Three American Cultures.* Albany: SUNY Press, 1997.

Tashjian, Dickran, and Ann Tashjian. *Memorials for Children of Change: The Art of Early New England Stone Carving.* Middleton, CT: Wesleyan University Press, 1974.

RICHARD MORRIS

# GREEK TRAGEDY

Greek tragedy, created in the city-state of Athens in the last thirty years of the sixth century B.C.E., is the earliest kind of European drama. Its subject matter is normally drawn from mythology, except that for the ancient Greeks "mythology" was a kind of historical saga, often perfectly credible oral history, including stories about gods and other supernatural beings, handed down from generation to generation by word of mouth. Because history raised to the sphere of legend only remembers milestones crucial to the life of the community, sometimes contemporary events viewed as critical for the survival of a people could provide the material for a tragedy. The *Persians* of Aeschylus, describing the invasion of Athens by a huge Persian fleet in 480 and its defeat in the naval battle of Salamis, is such a play. However, tragedy is, strictly speaking, neither historical nor mythological; it is a poetic drama in the sense that poetry rises above the particulars of history and expresses human truths of a universal kind.

This is achieved by a combination of heroic characters (rising above the ordinary in terms of social status, moral qualities, and intensity of emotions) and plots illustrating the impotence of humans in regard to divine powers. Greek gods did not profess to love humanity, promised no salvation after death, and administered a harsh justice not only to sinners but also to unsuspecting innocents because of crimes perpetrated by their forebears. Tragic characters often suffer and die for crimes they committed unwittingly, or because they were ordered to do so by a god (something possible in the context of Greek polytheism), or because they have to expiate an old sin, or fall under a family curse. When they fully realize the inevitability of their destiny, they act with dignity in accordance with their principles and proceed to do what they believe is right, often precipitating their dreadful end. This is considered a "tragic death," although in modern languages the word *tragedy* is often used more loosely as a synonym for *disaster*—particularly a seemingly undeserved disaster that strikes unexpectedly powerful people and happy families.

## Origins and Evolution

The term *tragedy* means the song of *tragôidoi* and tragôidoi means "he-goat singers." Scholars do not know what may have been the relationship of goats to early tragedy, but possible explanations include (1) a goat was offered as a prize in a competition of predramatic choruses, or (2) the members of such choruses were disguised as half-animal demons in the service of Dionysus (such as satyrs) and used goat skins for that purpose.

According to Aristotle (*Poetics,* ch. 4), tragedy originated from the improvisations of the *exarchontes* (song leaders) of the dithyramb, while comedy originated with the leaders of the "phallic songs." A dithyramb was a religious hymn in honor of Dionysus, and the Dionysiac origin of tragedy was in antiquity taken for granted, Dionysus being the god of theater as much as the god of wine, vegetation, and fertility. However, tragedy lost its Dionysiac associations very early, and only one of the preserved plays, indeed the very last tragedy of Euripides, *Bacchae,* has a Dionysiac content, namely the myth of resistance to the introduction of Dionysus's cult to Thebes, and the god's devastating revenge upon the city. Dithyramb, too, gradually lost its religious connection to Dionysus and developed into choral poetry that drew its subjects from mythology (like tragedy). Dithyrambs were also regularly performed in the Dionysiac festivals.

It is impossible to reconstruct with any certainty the stages of evolution from religious hymn to ritual enactment, and finally to a kind of secular play in which a great variety of myths were presented in dramatic form to a theatrical audience rather than a group of worshipers. The critical stage in this line of development was the transition from ritual to theater. Ritual must be repeated more or less exactly if it is to be a religious act. But once it metamorphoses into a playful act, its religious ties are loosened and a great potential for development in form and content becomes available to creative artists.

The first poet credited with the invention of tragedy was a minor, if semi-legendary, figure by the name of Thespis. His activity is dated to the 530s, although the introduction of tragic productions in the form of dramatic contests to the City Dionysia (c. 505) apparently did not take place before the establishment of democracy. Except for half a dozen titles of plays, nothing survives from his poetry.

However, once the first sparks were struck tragedy evolved swiftly by embracing and building on earlier forms of poetry. Choral lyric was a major poetic genre in Archaic Greece (700–500 B.C.E.), particularly among Dorian Greeks. It was incorporated into the new art of drama and retained not only its basic shape (division into strophic pairs and complex metrical structures), but even the Dorian dialect, invariably used by the Athenian poets in all choral parts of the plays. The personal lyric of the Ionians in iambic meter, particularly the style in which Solon, Athens's own sixth-century poet and lawgiver, had written his emotionally charged accounts of self-justification and political advice, provided the model for the set-speeches of dramatic characters widely used in tragedy. Next, the tradition of epic poetry, shared by all Greeks, supplied the great pool of stories, often grouped in local cycles (e.g., Trojan and Theban) and family sagas (the Atreids, Theseus, Heracles). Finally came the actor, or *hypokrites,* which originally meant "interpreter" and/or "answerer" (before it came to mean "hypocrite" also, in late antiquity). The emergence of the actor suggests narrative and dialogue with the chorus on the part of the poet/actor, who could change masks and identities during the performance (both tragedy and comedy were always performed by masked male actors). When tragedy came to light, Aristotle notes, poets inclined to

*Sophocles'* Antigone, *which dates to fifth-century* B.C.E. *Athens, contains themes that make its production still popular in the twenty-first century.* PHOTOSTAGE/DONALD COOPER

compose serious poetry now turned to tragedy, and epic poets were thus succeeded by tragedians.

What made these developments possible and greatly accelerated them was the establishment of democracy in Athens right after 510. A large open-air theater on the south slope of the Acropolis accommodated a massive audience, consisting of the whole population of the city (including foreigners and slaves). In view of the size of this audience, and the participation of common men in it—the same citizens who voted for new laws and major political decisions in the assembly of (direct) democracy, and also served as jurors in the courts of law—it is hardly surprising that the chorus became an indispensable part of the dramatic performance. The chorus represented and spoke for a collective dramatic character at the level of myth (anonymous citizens, womenfolk, elders, sailors, slaves, and even minor divinities) who in the epic had remained speechless in the background of the action.

Further, the dramatists gave new accounts and interpretations of the traditional stories they represented and re-enacted. By doing so, they gratified the contemporary Athenian audience that had made such great political progress from the time of a harsh oligarchy and widespread serfdom in the sixth century to democracy at the turn of the century, which was further consolidated by the victories in the Persian wars.

## The Peak of Tragedy

The function of the poet, according to Aristotle, is to state the universal, "to tell, not what has happened, but what would have happened according to probability or necessity" (*Poetics,* ch. 9). But what is probable or necessary (outside of the domain of science) depends on what the audience is ready to accept. Was it necessary for Agamemnon to sacrifice his daughter, Iphigenia, in order to be allowed by goddess Artemis to set sail for Troy? Was he killed upon his return home by his wife because he had killed Iphigenia, or because he had destroyed the temples of gods in the sack of Troy, or because his wife had taken a lover whose father had cursed Agamemnon's father? Was there a pattern of divine justice in these acts of revenge?

What made the discussion of these questions in public possible and indeed vital was that the Greeks had no religious book, like the Bible or the Koran, to explain the ways of the gods to them, and the level of the morality of gods, as depicted by the epic poetry of Homer and Hesiod (c. 750–700), was hardly superior to that of men. Men seemed and felt helpless in relation to gods—and likely to incur their envy or wrath—yet they thought that even the gods were subordinate to destiny. They dimly hoped that there was a world order contingent on divine providence that had been achieved by the harsh rule of Zeus. In reality men had done a lot better than the gods in pursuing social justice, and even oligarchic states like Sparta had developed constitutional forms of government and law administration already in the Archaic period (admired by later philosophers such as Plato).

In representing the human life of the past, the earliest of the great dramatists, Aeschylus, tried to make sense of the inconsistencies of mythology and arbitrariness of gods in relation to the perception of moral responsibility and justice current in Athenian political and judicial assemblies. He wrote trilogies of interrelated plays extending over successive generations of gods and men, and searched for reason and a just resolution of conflicts. Characteristic examples of his work are the Prometheus trilogy *Oresteia. Prometheus Bound,* the first and only surviving play of the former trilogy, depicts the punishment of Titan Prometheus by Zeus for stealing the fire from gods and giving it to humankind, along with many arts. Aeschylus made Prometheus the son of Themis (Custom, Law), and ended the trilogy with a reconciliation of Zeus and Prometheus, the benefactor of humankind. The *Oresteia* (the only surviving trilogy) deals with the bloody saga of the Atreids, which is resolved in the Athenian law-court, the Areopagus, by a jury of men who listen to divine litigants (the Furies) and witnesses (Apollo), and vote for acquitting Orestes, though not without the additional vote of Athena, the patron-goddess of the city. Aeschylus dominated the theater in the first half of the fifth century (produced the *Oresteia* in 458, died in 456). Only seven of his plays, out of approximately ninety written, have survived.

Sophocles (497–406 B.C.E.), although a deeply religious man, gave up trilogies of interconnected plays and the effort to untangle religious issues, and

focused on human characters, their motivation, their morality, and the uncompromising dignity with which they faced up to their predicaments. He perfected the art form in terms of plot construction and characterization, increased the number of speaking characters in a scene from two to three, and added painted scenery to the stage. Aristotle considers his *Oedipus the King* the perfect example of tragic composition, as it illustrates very well his concept of "tragic error" (a crime unwittingly committed, yet affecting family and city like a plague), and the sudden fall of a powerful man from happiness to disaster. However, Oedipus is neither a paragon of virtue nor immoral. The spectacle of a virtuous person suffering unjustly would be abhorrent, Aristotle writes, as the punishment of an immoral character would be pleasing to the spectator and thus untragic. Like Oedipus, the proper tragic hero should be of average moral stature: The downfall of such a person is felt to be tragic and stirs up the emotions of pity and fear in the audience. Sophocles reportedly wrote 120 plays, but only seven have survived, including *Antigone, Electra,* and *Oedipus at Colonus.*

Euripides (486–406) is the last of the great tragedians of the fifth century. If Sophocles represents the spirit and style of the Golden Age of Athens (480–430), Euripides (who as a young man had been a disciple of the physical philosopher Anaxagoras and the sophist Protagoras, an agnostic) belongs to the troubled period of the Peloponnesian War, which took place between Athens and Sparta between 431 and 404 B.C.E. He made no effort to account for the interference of gods in the life of humans; on the contrary, by having events that preceded and followed the action proper of the play merely reported or revealed in a prologue and an epilogue, spoken by a god (the *deus ex machina*), he seems to expose rather than explain the arbitrariness and cruelty of gods, which had made Socrates reject the validity of traditional myths and Plato pronounce epic and tragic poetry unacceptable to his ideal republic. He was less successful than either of his predecessors in his lifetime, but a lot more popular after his death. His plays were revived throughout the Greco-Roman antiquity, and no less than eighteen of his tragedies have been preserved into modern times. Although some of his plays have a happy ending (e.g., *Helen, Ion,* and *Iphigenia in Tauris*) and are considered melodramas rather than tragedies, others depict the human ineffectiveness to avert the fall from a state of happiness to that of absolute misery and disaster. In fact, Aristotle calls Euripides "the most tragic of the poets" (*Poetics*, 13). Scholars consider *Medea, Hippolytus, Trojan Women,* and his last play, *Bacchae,* his greatest masterpieces.

## Decline, Survival, Revival

Although one would not have guessed it by reading Aristotle's analysis of tragedy as a poetic genre, the *Poetics* (c. 330), tragedy declined after the death of Sophocles and Euripides, and the humiliation of Athens at the end of the Peloponnesian War. Although several names (and some fragments) of poets who lived in the fourth century and in the Hellenistic era are known to modern-day scholars, intellectual and political developments, as well as the changing attitudes toward old gods and traditional religion, did not favor the kind of interpretation of the human past offered by tragedy. A new kind of drama, "New Comedy," inherited Euripides' realistic (comparatively speaking) style and Aristophanes' preoccupation with contemporary life and social climate, and became the most important dramatic form in the later fourth and the following centuries.

However, tragedy won a different lease on life in the same period, initially as an Athenian cultural export. Several theaters were built in many cities in the fourth century, including the greatest of Greek theaters, that of Epidaurus in northern Peloponnese. After Alexander's death in 323, which marks the beginning of the Hellenistic era, a veritable theatrical explosion took place all over the Greek-speaking world. Every city in Greece, Asia Minor, Syria, Egypt, and South Italy and Sicily established its own dramatic festival, and theater artists set up professional unions (in Athens, Peloponnese, Asia Minor, Egypt, and South Italy) in order to respond and profit from the new tremendous demand for their services. Dramatic festivals and contests became the mark of Hellenic culture, but despite all this activity the conditions for the creation of significant new tragedies did not exist anymore. Old religion had retreated under pressure from new oriental gods. Traditional Greek mythology had lost its value as oral history of the past, and Chance (personified as a goddess) had largely replaced Fate in the mind of ordinary people. Tragedy died out when the Eastern Roman Empire was Christianized in the fourth century.

Tragedy began to be revived on a modest scale in the Renaissance, and fertilized modern serious theater and the creation of the opera, which was conceived as a modern form of tragedy, not only in Italy and France, but also later in Germany. Productions of Greek tragedies have increasingly carved a considerable niche in contemporary Western (and Japanese) theater, so much so that one may wonder what it is that ancient tragedy has to say to modern audiences that have no familiarity with or belief in Greek mythology and religion. It seems that the basic shape of the stories, the examples of heroic defiance, and above all the uncompromising dignity with which tragic characters accept the predicament imposed on them by superior powers which they cannot overcome or avoid, hold a universal message of humanity that is as valuable for modern men and women as it was for ancient ones.

*See also:* FOLK MUSIC; GRIEF: TRAUMATIC; OPERATIC DEATH; SHAKESPEARE, WILLIAM

## *Bibliography*

Barlow, Shirley A. *The Imagery of Euripides: A Study in the Dramatic Use of Pictorial Language.* Bristol,Eng.: Bristol Classical Press, 1987.

Burian, Peter, ed. *Directions in Euripidean Criticism: A Collection of Essays.* Durham, NC: Duke University Press, 1985.

Conacher, D. J. *Euripides and the Sophists: Some Dramatic Treatments of Philosophical Ideas.* London: Duckworth, 1998.

Easterling, P. E. E., ed. *The Cambridge Companion to Greek Tragedy.* New York: Cambridge University Press, 1997.

Easterling, P. E. E., and B. M. W. Knox, eds. *The Cambridge History of Classical Literature,* Vol. 1, Pt. 2.: *The Greek Drama.* Cambridge: Cambridge University Press, 1991.

Grene, David, and Richard Lattimore, eds. *The Complete Greek Tragedies.* 5 vols. Chicago: University of Chicago Press, 1992.

Kitto, H. D. F. *Greek Tragedy: A Literary Study.* London: Methuen, 1968.

Knox, B. M. W. *The Heroic Temper. Studies in Sophoclean Tragedy.* Berkeley: University of California Press, 1983.

Knox, B. M. W. *Word and Action: Essays on Ancient Theater.* Baltimore, MD: Johns Hopkins University Press, 1979.

Lattimore, Richmond A. *Story Patterns in Greek Tragedy.* Ann Arbor: University of Michigan Press, 1969.

Lesky, Albin. *Greek Tragic Poetry,* translated by Matthew Dillon. New Haven, CT: Yale University Press, 1983.

Meier, Christian. *The Political Art of Greek Tragedy,* translated by Andrew Webber. Baltimore, MD: Johns Hopkins University Press, 1992.

Segal, Charles. *Interpreting Greek Tragedy: Myth, Poetry, Text.* Ithaca, NY: Cornell University Press, 1986.

Segal, Erich, ed. *Oxford Readings in Greek Tragedy.* Oxford: Oxford University Press, 1983.

Sifakis, G. M. *Aristotle On the Function of Tragic Poetry.* Herakleion, Greece: Crete University Press, 2001.

Silk, M. S., ed. *Tragedy and the Tragic: Greek Theatre and Beyond.* Oxford: Oxford University Press, 1996.

Taplin, Oliver. *Greek Tragedy in Action.* London: Routledge, 1993.

Vernant, Jean-Pierre, and Pierre Vidal-Naquet. *Myth and Tragedy in Ancient Greece,* translated by Janet Lloyd. New York: Zone Books, 1900.

Winnington-Ingram, R. P. *Studies in Aeschylus.* New York: Cambridge University Press, 1983.

Winnington-Ingram, R. P. *Sophocles, An Interpretation.* New York: Cambridge University Press, 1980.

G. M. SIFAKIS

# GRIEF

## OVERVIEW

A suffering, a distress, a wretchedness, a pain, a burden, a wound. These were among the meanings associated with the word *grief* in its premodern French origin. The term also referred to wrongs and injuries that have been inflicted upon an individual by others, thereby providing the related word *grievance.* There are still other associations: *greeffe, grefe,* and *gravis*—all denoting a heaviness that weighs one down toward the earth, the very opposite of levity. People who experience grief today are likely to feel many or all of the emotions that were inherent in the earliest definitions of the term.

Grief experts have also identified other facets of the grief response, such as a yearning for the lost person or state of affairs, a need to think repeatedly about past events, a sense of guilt, or even thoughts of suicide. As Kenneth Doka notes, the grief experience can begin even before the loss occurs; another useful distinction can be made between the immediate response to loss and the grieving that sometimes continues long afterward or which does not come to the surface until some time has passed since the death or other loss.

It is now recognized that grief is more than sorrow and emotional turmoil. Five dimensions are receiving particular attention in the mental health community. First, stress reactions include changes in physiological function that can increase one's vulnerability to illness and exacerbate preexisting physical problems. Secondly, perception and thought are also affected, with the increased possibility of making impulsive and potentially harmful decisions and becoming more at risk for accidents. Third, a spiritual crisis often occurs, in which the guiding assumptions and values are called into question. Fourth, family and communal response to loss, often neglected in the past, is a significant factor in grief and grief recovery. And lastly, although the pain of loss may be universal, cultural heritage and influences and current support systems have much influence on the way one expresses and copes with stress.

*See also:* GRIEF AND MOURNING IN CROSS-CULTURAL PERSPECTIVE; GRIEF COUNSELING AND THERAPY

### *Bibliography*

Archer, John. *The Nature of Grief: The Evolution and Psychology of Reactions to Loss.* London: Routledge, 1999.

Bowlby, John. *Attachment and Loss,* Vol. 3: *Loss: Sadness and Depression.* New York: Basic Books, 1980.

Klass, Dennis, Phyllis R Silverman, and Steven L. Nickman, eds. *Continuing Bonds: New Understandings of Grief.* Washington, DC: Taylor & Francis, 1996.

Parkes, Colin Murray. *Bereavement: Studies of Grief in Adult Life,* 3rd edition. London: Routledge, 1996.

Stroebe, Margaret S., Robert O. Hansson, Wolfgang Stroebe, and Henk Schut, eds. *Handbook of Bereavement Research: Consequences, Coping, and Care.* Washington, DC: American Psychological Association, 2001.

ROBERT KASTENBAUM

## ACUTE

Grief is a type of stress reaction, a highly personal and subjective response to a real, perceived, or anticipated loss. Grief reactions may occur in any loss situation, whether the loss is physical or tangible—such as a death, significant injury, or loss of property—or symbolic and intangible, such as the loss of a dream. The intensity of grief depends on the meaning of that loss to the individual. Loss, however, does not inevitably create grief. Some individuals may be so disassociated from the lost object that they experience little or no grief or their response is characterized by intense denial.

Acute grief is different from bereavement or mourning. Bereavement is an objective state of loss: If one experiences a loss, one is bereaved. Bereavement refers to the fact of loss, while grief is the subjective response to that state of loss. Mourning has two interrelated meanings in the scholarly literature on the subject. On one hand, it describes the intrapsychic process whereby a grieving individual gradually adapts to the loss, a process that has also been referred to as "grieving" or "grief work." Grief can also denote a social process, the norms, behavior patterns, and rituals through which an individual is recognized as bereaved and socially expresses grief; for example, wearing black, sending flowers, and attending funerals. Acute grief has also been described as the initial, intense reactions to a loss, differentiating it from later, less intense expressions of grief. Such a distinction, given the discussion that follows, is not made here.

### Paradigms on the Origin of Acute Grief

Acute grief was first described by Eric Lindemann, a psychiatrist who studied survivors of the 1942 Cocoanut Grove fire, a blaze that swept through a Boston nightclub, killing 492 people. Lindemann described grief as a syndrome that was "remarkably uniform" and included a common range of physical symptoms such as tightness of throat, shortness of breath, and other pain, along with a range of emotional responses (1944, p.145). Lindemann's research was based on a sample of primarily young survivors of sudden and traumatic loss.

This medical model of grief was continued most clearly in the work of George Engel. In 1961 Engel asked if grief was a disease. He believed it could be described as one having a clear onset in a circumstance of loss, a predictable course that includes an initial state of shock; a developing awareness of loss characterized by physical, affective, cognitive, psychological, and behavioral symptoms; and a prolonged period of gradual recovery that might be complicated by other variables. Engel notes that other disease processes also are influenced by psychological and social variables. Even the fact that grief is universal and does not often require treatment, Engel argues, is not unlike other diseases. Engel also notes that whether or not a disease requires medical treatment or is, in fact, recognized as a disease is a social definition. Epilepsy, alcoholism, and many forms of mental illness are now recognized as diseases but were not at other times in human history or in other cultures.

Another paradigm that attempts to offer insight to the nature of acute grief is the psychological trauma model. This model, based on the work of Sigmund Freud, views grief as a response to the psychological trauma brought on by the loss of a love object. According to this view, acute grief is a normal defense against the trauma of loss. To Freud, grief is a crisis, but one that will likely abate over time and that does not usually require psychiatric intervention.

Perhaps one of the more influential theories of grief is the attachment model developed by John Bowlby. This approach emphasizes that attachment or bonding is a functional survival mechanism, a needed instinct, found in many of the social animals. Given humans' prolonged periods of infancy and dependency, attachment is necessary for the survival of the species. When the object of that attachment is missing, certain behaviors are instinctual responses to that loss. These behaviors, including crying, clinging, and searching, were seen by Bowlby as biologically based responses that seek to restore the lost bond and maintain the detachment. When these bonds are permanently severed, as in death, these behaviors continue until the bond is divested of emotional meaning and significance. A secondary purpose of these behaviors is that by expressing distress, they engage the care, support, and protection of the larger social unit. This psychobiological model sees grief as a natural, instinctual response to a loss that continues until the bond is restored or the grieving person sheds the bond. These early approaches continue to influence understandings of acute grief, though more contemporary models emphasize that grief is a natural response to major transitions in life and that bonds between the grieving individual and the lost object continue, albeit in different forms, after the loss. In addition, approaches of the 1990s emphasize that a significant loss may shatter assumptions, causing grieving individuals to reconstruct their sense of self, spirituality, and relationship to others and the world. While this may be a painful process, it also may be a catalyst for growth.

**Manifestations of Acute Grief**

Individuals can experience acute grief in varied ways. Physical reactions are common. These include a range of physical responses such as headaches, other aches and pains, tightness, dizziness, exhaustion, menstrual irregularities, sexual impotence, breathlessness, tremors and shakes, and oversensitivity to noise.

Bereaved individuals, particularly widows, do have a higher rate of mortality in the first year of loss. The reasons for this may include the stress of bereavement, the change in lifestyle that accompanies a loss, and the fact that many chronic diseases have lifestyle factors that can be shared by both partners; hence both partners share similar stress and patterns making them prone to similar diseases. It is important that a physician monitor any physical responses to loss.

There are affective manifestations of grief as well. Individuals may experience a range of emotions such as anger, guilt, helplessness, sadness, shock, numbing, yearning, jealousy, and self-blame. Some bereaved experience a sense of relief

or even a feeling of emancipation. This, however, can be followed by a sense of guilt. As in any emotional crisis, even contradictory feelings, such as sadness and relief, can occur simultaneously.

There can be cognitive manifestations of grief, including a sense of depersonalization in which nothing seems real, a sense of disbelief and confusion, or an inability to concentrate or focus. Bereaved individuals can be preoccupied with images or memories of the loss. These cognitive manifestations of acute grief can affect functioning at work, school, or home. Many persons also report experiences where they dream of the deceased or sense the person's presence.

Grief has spiritual manifestations as well. Individuals may struggle to find meaning and to reestablish a sense of identity and order in their world. They may be angry at God or struggle with their faith.

Behavioral manifestations of grief can also vary. These behavioral manifestations can include crying, withdrawal, avoiding or seeking reminders of the loss, searching, hyperactivity, and changes in relationships with others.

The reactions of persons to loss are highly individual and influenced by several factors, including the unique meaning of the loss, the strength and nature of the attachment, the circumstances surrounding the loss (such as the presence of other crises), reactions and experiences of earlier loss, the temperament and adaptive abilities of the individual, the presence and support of family and other informal and formal support systems, cultural and spiritual beliefs and practices, and general health and lifestyle practices of the grieving individuals.

**The Course of Acute Grief**

There have been a number of approaches to understanding the process or course of acute grief. Earlier approaches tended to see grief as proceeding in stages or phases. Researcher and theorist Colin Murray Parkes, for example, described four stages of grief: shock, angry pining, depression and despair, and detachment. Recent approaches have emphasized that grief does not follow a predictable and linear course, stressing instead that it often proceeds like a roller coaster, full of ups and downs. Some of these more intense periods are predictable, such as holidays, anniversaries, or other significant days; other times may have no recognizable trigger.

Approaches during the 1990s have emphasized that acute grief involves a series of tasks or processes. Psychologist William Worden describes four tasks pertaining to grief: recognizing the reality of the loss, dealing with expressed and latent feelings, living in a world without the deceased, and relocating the deceased in one's life. Psychologist Therese A. Rando suggests that grieving individuals need to complete six "R" processes: recognize the loss, react to the separation, recollect and re-experience the deceased and the relationship, relinquish the old attachments to the deceased and the old world, readjust to the new world without forgetting the old, and reinvest. (While the language of both Worden and Rando is specific to death-related loss, their models can be adapted to other losses as well.) These and other similar models reaffirm the very individual nature of grief, acknowledging that these tasks or processes are not necessarily linear and that any given individual may have difficulty with one or more of the processes or tasks.

It is worth emphasizing that the course of acute grief is not linear. Nor is there any inherent timetable to grief. Acute grief reactions can persist for considerable time, gradually abating after the first few years. Research emphasizes that one does not simply "get over the loss." Rather, over time the pain lessens and grief becomes less disabling as individuals function at levels comparable to (and sometimes better than) pre-loss levels. Nevertheless, bonds and attachments to the lost object continue, and periods of intense grief can occur years after the loss. For example, the birth of a grandchild can trigger an experience of grief in a widow who wished to share this event with her deceased spouse.

## Help and Acute Grief

Persons experiencing acute grief can help themselves in a number of ways. Since grief is a form of stress, the griever can benefit from various forms of stress management, especially adequate sleep and diet. Bibliotherapy (the use of self-help books) can often validate or normalize grief reactions, suggest

methods of adaptation, and offer hope. Self-help and support groups can offer similar assistance as well as social support from others who have experienced loss and respite. Others may benefit from counselors, particularly if their health suffers or their grief becomes highly disabling, impairing functioning at work, school, or home, or if they harbor destructive thoughts toward themselves or others. Parkes particularly stresses the value of grief counseling when other support is not forthcoming. Pharmacological interventions also may be helpful, particularly when the grief is so disabling that it severely compromises the individual's health or ability to function. Such interventions should focus on particular conditions—anxiety or depression—that are triggered or aggravated by the bereavement. Psychotherapy should accompany pharmacological interventions.

Most individuals seem to ameliorate grief; gradually they find themselves able to remember the loss without the intense reactions experienced earlier. Nevertheless, anywhere from 20 to 33 percent seem to experience more complicated grief reactions.

*See also:* DISASTERS; FREUD, SIGMUND; GRIEF COUNSELING AND THERAPY

## Bibliography

Bowlby, John. *Attachment and Loss,* Vol. 3: *Loss: Sadness and Depression.* New York: Basic Books, 1980.

Engel, George. "Is Grief a Disease?: A Challenge for Medical Research." *Psychosomatic Medicine* 23 (1961):18–22.

Freud, Sigmund. "Mourning and Melancholia." *The Standard Edition of the Complete Psychological Works of Sigmund Freud,* Vol. 14. London: Hogarth, 1917.

Klass, Dennis, Phyllis R. Silverman, and Steven L. Nickman, eds. *Continuing Bonds: New Understandings of Grief.* Washington, DC: Taylor & Francis, 1996.

Lindemann, Eric. "Symptomatology and Management of Acute Grief." *American Journal of Psychiatry* 101 (1944):141–148.

Osterweis, Marion, Fredric Solomon, and Morris Green. *Bereavement: Reactions, Consequences, and Care.* Washington, DC: National Academy Press, 1984.

Parkes, Colin M. "Bereavement Counselling: Does it Work?" *British Medical Journal* 281 (1980):3–6.

Parkes, Colin M. *Bereavement: Studies of Grief in Adult Life*. New York: International Universities Press, 1972.

Rando, Therese A. *The Treatment of Complicated Mourning*. Champaign, IL: Research Press, 1993.

Worden, J. William. *Grief Counseling and Grief Therapy: A Handbook for the Mental Health Practitioner*, 2nd edition. New York: Springer, 1991.

KENNETH J. DOKA

## ANTICIPATORY

The concept of anticipatory grief was first described by psychiatrist Eric Lindemann at the end of a presentation to the American Psychiatric Association in 1944. Lindemann defined anticipatory grief as a progression through the stages of grief, including "depression, heightened preoccupation with the departed, a review of all the forms of death which might befall him, and anticipation of the modes of readjustment which might be necessitated by it" (Lindemann 1944, p. 148). He cautioned that there are advantages and disadvantages to anticipatory grieving, with the disadvantages including the possibility that the griever might pull away from the dying person prematurely (a circumstance referred to as decathexis).

In the era of advanced medical technology, the phenomenon of anticipatory grief is particularly important. The experience of terminal illness has changed, and there is frequently an extended period between diagnosis and death. Because of medical advances, dying has become more of a gradual process; debilitation is extended and quality of life has been improved. There is a longer time during which families and the patient can experience anticipatory grief.

In a more current definition, psychologist Therese A. Rando defined anticipatory grief as "the phenomenon encompassing the processes of mourning, coping, interaction, planning, and psychosocial reorganization that are stimulated and begin in part in response to the awareness of the impending loss of a loved one" (Rando 1986, p. 24). According to Rebecca Ponder and Elizabeth Pomeroy, however, "persistent debate remains about whether anticipatory grief results in shorter and easier periods of grief when the actual death occurs or . . . may have adverse effects" (Ponder

and Pomeroy 1996, p. 4). Some argue that post-death grief may be intensified by anticipatory grieving as loved ones witness the debilitating aspects of the illness; in some cases, there may be the tendency toward premature detachment and abandonment of the patient as death approaches. Others find that anticipatory grief facilitates the leave-taking process as loved ones have time to complete the "unfinished business" of life and detach in a more orderly manner; in the presence of death, many people are able to rise above the past and make the amends necessary for a peaceful dying. Despite these contradictory beliefs, the concept initially suggested by Lindemann has endured.

Rando expanded the initial concept of anticipatory grief in several significant ways. She viewed it as a multidimensional concept defined across two perspectives, three time foci, and three classes of influencing variables. In Rando's conceptualization, anticipatory grief is not confined to the experience of the caregiver or family alone: The dying patient also experiences this form of grief. In addition, she considered anticipatory grief to be a misnomer suggesting that one is grieving solely for anticipated losses. Rando asserted that there are three foci of losses that occur as part of the anticipated grief: past losses in terms of lost opportunities and past experiences that will not be repeated; present losses in terms of the progressive deterioration of the terminally ill person, the uncertainty, and the loss of control; and future losses that will ensue as a consequence of the death, such as economic uncertainty, loneliness, altered lifestyle, and the day-to-day moments in life that will no longer occur because of death. Variables influencing anticipatory grief, according to Rando, include psychological factors—the nature and meaning of the loss experienced; social factors—those dimensions within the family and socioeconomic characteristics that allow for certain comforts and discomforts during the illness period; and physiological factors—the griever's energy and overall health.

In addition, Rando disagreed with Lindemann regarding the eventuality of a major decathexis from the dying person. She not only did not see it as an automatic response but also redefined the pulling away in terms of decathexis from the hopes, dreams, and expectations of a long-term future with and for that person, not from the person. Rando contended that "the future can be grieved without relinquishing the present!" (Rando 1986, p. 13).

## Phases of Anticipatory Grief

In a 1983 book called *The Anatomy of Bereavement,* Beverly Raphael discussed phases of anticipatory grief for both the dying person and those close to the person that parallel actual bereavement. Building on the work of Elisabeth Kübler-Ross, Raphael noted that for both the patient and caregiver(s) the first response to news of a fatal condition is shock, numbness, disbelief, and denial. In time, the news is faced, distressed feelings can no longer be fended off, and a period of fear, anxiety, and helplessness ensues. Bargaining and the anguish raised by the question "Why me?" mark this phase. Hope may fend off some of the anguish, but as the loss is acknowledged, the process of anticipatory grief may become pronounced. Anger, regret, resentment, a sense of failure, a feeling of being cheated, guilt, and depression are common responses. Some reach the calm and acceptance described by Kübler-Ross. The dying person may withdraw as the family/caregivers struggle with the opposing pulls to remain close to the dying person and to relinquish the bond to the person to mitigate the pain of the impending loss.

Both Raphael and Rando contended that anticipatory grief is a process—an experience that takes time to unfold and develop. During the process, the work is to slowly dispel the denial and to develop an awareness of what is happening. In this way, the griever(s) can begin to experience optimum amounts of anticipatory grief to reach a level of benefit.

For a terminal illness, researchers have repeatedly raised the question of whether there is an optimum length of time before the positive effects of anticipatory grief diminish. Rando, in a 1983 study, and C. M. Sanders, in a 1982 study, both found that there was an optimum length of time for anticipatory grief as it affected the survivor's postdeath adjustment: six to eighteen months.

## The Impact of Special Situations

In several situations, the benefits and disadvantages of anticipatory grief can be questioned. One such situation is that of children facing the death of a parent. Given the child's developmental level and the profound nature of the loss, the limited ability of children to understand death and its finality, and the reality that the dying parent is unable to attend to the needs of the child, the benefits of anticipatory grieving may be mitigated. In a 1999 study of parentally bereaved children conducted by Amy Saldinger and her colleagues, anticipated death was consistently associated with less adaptive outcomes and poorer mental health outcomes, using a variety of measures. According to Vanderlyn Pine and Carolyn Bauer, for parents who anticipate the loss of a child, "there is no way to know just how much anticipatory grief is too much. It does not appear that there is an optimum amount" (Pine and Bauer 1986, p. 86–87).

For those struggling with the varied losses imposed by Alzheimer's disease, there is a differential benefit to anticipatory grieving, depending on the duration of the illness. In a 1994 article for the *Journal of Gerontological Social Work,* Rebecca Walker and her colleagues attributed this to a combination of variables: the social stigma related to the disease as an illness of the aged, and the loss of cognitive ability and self-sufficiency; the progressive nature of the disease and the associated incapacitation; the multiple losses that the caregiver has to face; and the eventuality that the caregiver may have to relinquish care of the patient to others. From their 1996 study, Ponder and Pomeroy reported that for those dealing with patients with dementia and Alzheimer's disease, the benefits of anticipatory grief were limited, noting that this group of individuals is at high risk for complicated mourning.

Anticipatory grief in relation to AIDS is another area that shows differential benefit for the griever. Several variables, similar to those related to Alzheimer's disease and dementia, are operative for those with HIV/AIDS. The duration of the illness and the stigmatization that accompanies it are prominent factors. The course of HIV/AIDS often extends beyond the eighteen months designated as a beneficial length of time for anticipatory grief for the caregiver. In addition the multiple losses and the alternating periods of relative good health and battles with opportunistic diseases potentially abort the process of anticipatory grief. As a further complicating factor in the anticipatory grief trajectory is the relationship between the caregiver and the patient, a relationship that may not be sanctioned by society (i.e., homosexual relationships). In his

1989 book, Kenneth J. Doka used the term "disenfranchised loss" to describe a loss that is not recognized or validated by others. For those caring for the AIDS patient, completing some of the tasks of anticipatory grieving may be compromised by the lack of an official, socially sanctioned connection to the dying patient.

For practitioners working with patients and caregivers, the challenge is to combine the various elements of anticipatory grief. Practitioners must recognize that anticipatory grieving does not necessarily involve a pulling away from the patient; that there are multiple losses that span a period of time; that the process of anticipatory grieving goes through stages; and that it is a time of working on and working through the "unfinished business" for both patient and caregiver. Practitioners must be attuned to the tendency for premature detachment and diminishing communication between patient and caregiver and encourage discussion of fear, loss, and anger. Ideally, according to Walker and her colleagues, a practitioner "can help the caregiver both hold on to hope while letting go of the patient, thereby completing the very complicated work of anticipatory grief" (Walker et al. 1996, p. 55).

*Bibliography*

Doka, Kenneth J., ed. "Disenfranchised Grief." *Disenfranchised Grief: Recognizing Hidden Sorrow.* Lexington, MA: Lexington Books, 1989.

Kübler-Ross, Elisabeth. *On Death and Dying.* New York: Collier Books, 1969.

Lindemann, Eric. "Symptomatology and Management of Acute Grief." *American Journal of Psychiatry* 101 (1944):142–148.

Pine, Vanderlyn R., and Carolyn Brauer. "Parental Grief: A Synthesis of Theory, Research, and Intervention." In Therese A. Rando ed., *Parental Loss of a Child.* Champaign, IL: Research Press, 1986.

Ponder, Rebecca, and Elizabeth Pomeroy. "The Grief of Caregivers: How Pervasive Is It?" *Journal of Gerontological Social Work* 27, no. 1/2 (1996):3–21.

Rando, Therese A. "A Comprehensive Analysis of Anticipatory Grief: Perspectives, Processes, Promises, and Problems." In Therese A. Rando ed., *Loss and Anticipatory Grief.* Lexington, MA: Lexington Books, 1986.

Rando, Therese A. "An Investigation of Grief and Adaptation in Parents Whose Children Have Died from Cancer." *Journal of Pediatric Psychology* 8 (1983):3–20.

Raphael, Beverly. *The Anatomy of Bereavement.* New York: Basic, 1983.

Saldinger, Amy, Albert Cain, Neil Kalter, and Kelly Lohnes. "Anticipating Parental Death in Families with Young Children." *American Journal of Orthopsychiatry* 69, no. 1 (1999):39–48.

Sanders, C. M. "Effects of Sudden vs. Chronic Illness Death on Bereavement Outcome." *Omega: The Journal of Death and Dying* 13 (1982–1983):227–241.

Walker, Rebecca, Elizabeth Pomeroy, John S. McNeil, and Cynthia Franklin. "Anticipatory Grief and AIDS: Strategies for Intervening with Caregivers." *Health and Social Work* 21, no. 1 (1996):49–57.

Walker, Rebecca, Elizabeth C. Pomeroy, John S. McNeil, and Cynthia Franklin. "Anticipatory Grief and Alzheimer's Disease: Strategies for Intervention." *Journal of Gerontological Social Work* 22, no. 3/4 (1994):21–39.

JOAN BEDER

## CHILD'S DEATH

The death of a child, regardless of age, is one of the worst possible losses adults can experience. Grief over a child's death is particularly severe compared to the loss of a spouse, parent, or sibling. The parent-child bond is uniquely strong and enduring. Children are extensions of parents; they hold parents' dreams, aspirations, and hopes for the future and promise the continuity of parents' life after their death. They define parents' sense of self and give meaning and a sense of purpose to their lives. When a child dies, parents feel mortally wounded; it is as though part of them is torn away by force. The family also loses its wholeness. A child's death is perceived as untimely at any age because parents are "supposed to" die before children. Moreover, miscarriage, stillbirth, and death in childhood and adolescence are often sudden and unexpected and in some cases violent, which traumatizes survivors.

The question of "why" haunts parents as they review the event to make sense of the death. Their sense of failure in protecting their child from harm evokes guilt feelings and diminishes their self-esteem. Out of their despair and urgent desire to be with the deceased child and to end their relentless pain, parents may entertain the thought of death. Parents' grief is not only their personal, intra-psychic experience but an interpersonal process. A child's death affects all family members including extended members as well as others outside the family and their relationships and, in turn, others' responses to parents' plight affect parents.

## Effects on Parents and the Spousal Relationship

A child's death can have a serious impact on parents and the spousal relationship. If a child is a victim of a serious illness, parents' anguish starts long before the child's death. Parents experience enormous stress emotionally, physically, and financially. They are confronted with conflicting demands between their work and the care of the ill child in addition to meeting the daily needs of well siblings. Typically, mothers assume the major responsibility of caring for the ill child while fathers fulfill their duties as providers, some holding two or three jobs to meet financial obligations. It is not uncommon that the relationship between husband and wife becomes strained. A mother's increased involvement with a sick child, often at the hospital, and a father's inability to accompany his wife and take an active part in the ill child's care may lead to the father feeling frustrated, excluded, and isolated. Physical exhaustion and emotional strain may affect a couple's sex life. As children become critically ill, fathers tend to withdraw and become unavailable to their families because of their inability to cope with the emotional ordeal, which angers their wives. Increased outbursts of anger and arguments often become part of family life. Strains in relationships that developed while children were ill may not easily be lessened after children die.

A review of research indicates that, regardless of the cause of death, a substantial number of marital relationships become strained after children die. The marital strain appears attributable to differences in couples' grief and ways of coping, which result primarily from differences in gender roles and personality and the singular relationship each parent has had with the deceased child. Soon after the child's death, parents' grief is so intense that they tend to withdraw into their own private world and minimally relate to others. They hesitate to talk to their spouses about the loss for fear of stirring up their spouses' emotions. In general, mothers express grief more openly and show more intense reactions to their child's death than do fathers. Husbands tend to feel responsible for helping other family members, particularly their wives, cope with their grief while controlling their own, but feel helpless not knowing how to comfort their grief-stricken wives, who are incapacitated in their usual roles as wives and parents. Husbands' behavior, however, comes into conflict with their wives' desire for emotional sharing. Wives feel angry over what they perceive to be their husbands' unwillingness to share their grief, which they may see as an act of abandonment, compounding their sense of loss. It may take some time before wives realize that their spouses' behavior is their way of coping with their pain of grief.

Anger and rage, which are common in bereavement, are often displaced onto the nearest target: a person's spouse. Spouses are generally irritable toward each other over trivial matters and matters concerning the deceased child. Loss of sexual intimacy is common, and it may take even a year or two to restore a sexual relationship. Serious strain in marital relationships can lead to separation and divorce, especially if couples had marital problems prior to their child's death. In the majority of cases, however, the marital bond is strong enough to withstand this major ordeal and may even be strengthened.

Parents who are single as a result of divorce or the death of their spouses and unmarried parents are spared the kinds of problems that confront marital partners, but they grieve while carrying a myriad of responsibilities and demands placed on them without partners with whom to share the burden. If they lost their only child they are left alone without companionship and feel they are no longer needed. Their support system plays a particularly important role in coping with their experience of loss.

When adults who are responsible for managing and maintaining the household and promoting the welfare of the family are overwhelmed by their grief, unable to function adequately in their usual roles, and experiencing relational conflicts, their family naturally experiences varying degrees of disorganization and disequilibrium. Surviving children are a source of comfort, but their presence does not mitigate parents' distress. For the initial few weeks after the child's death, relatives, friends, and neighbors may offer not only emotional support but assistance with household chores and

*A grieving couple in Warminster, Pennsylvania, arranges flowers at the grave of their teenage son who was killed during a video store robbery. Couples with strong marital relationships prior to their child's death appear to fare better in their bereavement.* CORBIS

child care. When they leave to return to their own routines, parents are left alone to face the new reality of having to live with the void left by the deceased child. Much of the time parents feel like they are in a daze and later do not remember how they managed to get through those early days of bereavement.

Parents cope with their grief one day at a time with frequent setbacks. Coping involves a combination of action and cognitive activity for relieving stress and mastering stressful situations. There is no one right way to grieve or to cope. Parents usually adopt a combination of strategies. Seeking release of tension is a necessity for most parents, given the enormous emotional turmoil the loss engenders. Emotional tension, if kept inside, does not disappear and may surface in ways that are destructive to individuals and their relationships. Parents, especially mothers, may relieve their tension through talking about their loss and crying. Other strategies to which parents turn to relieve tension include engaging in physical activities, keeping themselves busy, and expressing their grief in writing, art, and other creative activities.

Many find relief in having something definite to do, which prevents them from becoming totally consumed by their grief and mired in depression. In general, coping strategies that direct parents' attention away from their tragedy appear essential and helpful during the initial weeks or months of acute grief. Total avoidance in facing the reality of loss and its pain, however, can complicate the grieving process. Parents also seek an understanding and validation of their experience through reading books about loss and learning about the experience of others in similar predicaments, which helps them diminish their sense of isolation and gain a perspective on their own experience.

Even though some parents may initially express anger toward God who they feel has betrayed them, for many, religious faith serves as a major source of comfort and strength and appears to lessen the intensity of grief. A number of parents participate in support groups, seek professional help, and/or make frequent visits to the cemetery in order to cope. Some parents become connected with other bereaved parents through the Internet. Parents' dominant coping strategies change in the course of their bereavement. Many parents transform their tragedy into something positive and find new meaning in life through their work, including work that changes the condition that contributed to their child's death, volunteer work to help others in need, and the establishment of scholarship funds in their child's name. Some parents whose child died due to murder or the negligence of others have transcended their tragedy through their courageous and generous acts of forgiveness.

## Effects on Siblings

When a sibling is terminally ill, other children "live in houses of chronic sorrow" with "the signs of sorrow, illness, and death" everywhere, writes the researcher Myra Bluebond-Langner, who studied terminally ill children and their well siblings extensively (Bluebond-Langner 1995, p. 123). The signs are visible on parents' faces as well as the face of the ill child. The amount of parental attention well siblings receive diminishes; however, seeing the toll the illness takes on their parents, children try to be supportive toward them. Parents' relationship with each other is strained. Parents are irritable and their tempers are short and unpredictable. Family plans change frequently. Children can no longer engage in normal activities, such as having their friends over to play. Their relationships with the ill sibling also change. Mutual give-and-take no longer exists. Well siblings try to get close to the dying sibling, but their efforts are often rebuffed. Instead, children not only help care for the sick sibling but parent their grieving parents, and yet they are not always kept abreast of the ill sibling's condition. Often they feel alone, confused, ambivalent, and neglected, but cannot express their feelings to distressed parents. After their sibling dies, many of the same conditions continue in the family for a period of time.

When children lose a sibling, they cope with their own grief and many consequent changes at home over which they have little control. Parents' diminished ability to function in their usual roles means the loss of a normal family life and many deprivations for children. Death in the family usually brings support for parents, but children's grief and need for support are often overlooked, increasing their sense of isolation and neglect. When children are young, parents tend to assume that their children are too young to be affected by the family tragedy and fail to talk to them about the circumstances of their sibling's death or provide them with opportunities to ask questions. There is, however, ample clinical evidence to indicate that even very young children are affected by the death. When children are not well informed, they resort to their imagination, distort reality, and experience an unnecessary sense of culpability over the death, resulting in a variety of developmental problems.

Furthermore, children face changes in relationships with their parents and hierarchical order among siblings with new parental expectations thrust upon them. Because of the centrality of the deceased sibling in the family during illness and after death, it may appear to surviving children that the deceased child is more important to parents than they are, making them feel insignificant. However, out of their loyalty and concern for distressed parents, children often become protective toward them, hiding their emotional and even physical pain so as not to burden their parents. They often become vigilant over parents' comings and goings. At the same time, parents, who fear that a similar tragedy may strike them again, become overprotective toward their surviving children. Parental overprotectiveness may be seen in their reluctance to discipline children or to allow children to engage in normal growth experiences. In some cases, parents' unresolved grief and desire to keep deceased children alive may result in using surviving children or children born after the death as replacement children, who are expected to take over the identities of the deceased, denying them their own unique identities.

## The Process of Healing

The impact of a child's death is pervasive and profound. The family and its members are irrevocably changed. Grandparents grieve for their grandchild whose life ended prematurely as well as their own loss, but often their grief is more focused on their adult child who has suffered a devastating loss. Other extended family members, friends, neighbors, co-workers, and sometimes even strangers are touched by the death directly or indirectly. Too frequently, what others say and do out of their own discomfort or lack of understanding about parental grief hurts and angers bereaved parents, creating a chasm between them and the bereaved, and thus diminishing the support networks to which the bereaved normally turn. On the other hand, those who stand by them and offer support and assistance while their child is ill and in their mourning are gratefully remembered by the bereaved.

The process of mourning is agonizingly long. It may be many months before parents restore their sense of equilibrium and become actively involved in daily life. Parents' willingness to openly share their grief with one another strengthens their relationship, and their ability to provide a secure and supportive environment for children facilitates the process of healing in the family. A child's death compels family members to reexamine their assumptions about the world, renew or question their spiritual or religious beliefs, and search for meaning in life. Realizing the fragility of life, survivors may develop a deeper appreciation of life and change their life priorities. Moreover, they discover inner strengths and resources they never knew they had.

A bond between deceased children and surviving family members continues for the rest of their lives. So does the pain of loss, which parents feel acutely from time to time throughout their lives as special days approach; when something, perhaps a song, triggers thoughts of deceased children; and as deceased children miss each of the developmental milestones that they would have reached had they lived. As Robert Kastenbaum states, parents may not wish to relinquish their grief, for the pain is part of the precious memory that keeps a connection with the deceased. After a long and difficult journey, most parents learn to live with their pain of grief and move forward, finding once again some pleasure in life and hope for the future.

*See also:* GRIEF COUNSELING AND THERAPY; REPLACEMENT CHILDREN

### *Bibliography*

Arnold, Joan Hagan, and Penelope Buschman Gemma. *A Child Dies: A Portrait of Family Grief,* 2nd edition. Philadelphia: The Charles Press, 1994.

Blank, Jeanne Webster. *The Death of an Adult Child: A Book For and About Bereaved Parents.* Amityville, NY: Baywood Publishing, 1998.

Bluebond-Langner, Myra. *In the Shadow of Illness: Parents and Siblings of the Chronically Ill Child.* Princeton, NJ: Princeton University Press, 1996.

Bluebond-Langner, Myra. "Worlds of Dying Children and Their Well Siblings." In Kenneth Doka ed., *Children Mourning, Mourning Children.* Washington, DC: The Hospice Foundation of America, 1995.

Bolton, Iris with Curtis Mitchell. *My Son . . . My Son . . . A Guide to Healing after Death, Loss or Suicide,* 13th edition. Atlanta: Bolton Press, 1992.

Cook, Judith. A. "Influence of Gender on the Problems of Parents of Fatally Ill Children." *Journal of Psychosocial Oncology* 2 (1984):71–91.

Davis, Deborah L. *Empty Cradle, Broken Heart: Surviving the Death of Your Baby.* Golden, CO: Fulcrum Publishing, 1996.

Fanos, Joanna H. *Sibling Loss.* Mahwah, NJ: Lawrence Erlbaum, 1996.

Finkbeiner, Ann K. *After the Death of a Child: Living with Loss through the Years.* Baltimore, MD: Johns Hopkins University Press, 1996.

Gilbert, Kathleen R. "Interactive Grief and Coping in the Marital Dyad." *Death Studies* 13 (1989):605–626.

Kastenbaum, Robert J. *Death, Society, and Human Experience,* 7th edition. Boston: Allyn & Bacon, 2001.

Klass, Dennis, Phyllis Silverman, and Steven L. Nickman eds. *Continuing Bonds: New Understanding of Grief.* Washington, DC: Taylor & Francis, 1996.

Oliver, Luis E. "Effects of a Child's Death on the Marital Relationship: A Review." *Omega: The Journal of Death and Dying* 39 (1999):197–227.

Rando, Therese A., ed. *Parental Loss of a Child.* Champaign, IL: Research Press, 1986.

Rosenblatt, Paul C. *Parent Grief: Narratives of Loss and Relationship.* Philadelphia: Taylor & Francis, 2000.

Rosof, Barbara D. *The Worst Loss: How Families Heal from the Death of a Child.* New York: Henry Holt and Company, 1994.

Schwab, Reiko. "A Child's Death and Divorce: Dispelling the Myth." *Death Studies* 22 (1998):445–468.

Schwab, Reiko. "Parental Mourning and Children's Behavior." *Journal of Counseling and Development* 75 (1997):258–265.

Schwab, Reiko. "Paternal and Maternal Coping with the Death of a Child." *Death Studies* 14 (1990):407–422.

Videka-Sherman, Lynn. "Coping with the Death of a Child: A Study over Time." *American Journal of Orthopsychiatry* 52 (1982):688–698.

REIKO SCHWAB

## DISENFRANCHISED

The professor and writer Kenneth J. Doka introduced the concept of disenfranchised grief in his 1989 book, *Disenfranchised Grief: Recognizing Hidden Sorrow.* Doka defined disenfranchised grief as "grief that persons experience when they incur a loss that is not or cannot be openly acknowledged, socially sanctioned or publicly mourned" (p. 4).

The concept of disenfranchisement integrates psychological, biological, and sociological perspectives on grief and loss. Previous research has emphasized the variety of reactions in the grieving experience. While an individual may have an intense and multifaceted reaction to loss, that loss and the attendant responses may be unacknowledged by family, friends, or the surrounding society. Although the individual grieves, others might not acknowledge his or her right to do so. Such persons are not offered the "rights" or the "grieving role" such as a claim to social sympathy and support, or such compensations as time off from work or diminution of social responsibilities.

In order to understand the social aspect of grief, it is important to remember that every society has norms that govern not only behavior but also affect and cognition. Every society has norms that frame grieving. These norms include expected behavior, in addition to feeling, thinking, and spiritual rules. Thus, when a loss occurs, these grieving rules include how one is to behave and how one is to feel and think. They govern what losses one grieves for, how one grieves for them, who legitimately can grieve for the loss, and how and to whom others respond with sympathy and support. These norms exist not only as folkways, or informally expected behavior, but also as "laws." More formal statements of these grieving rules can be illustrated by company policies that extend bereavement leave to certain individuals, or regulations and laws that define who has control of the deceased body or funeral rituals.

In the United States and many other societies, these grieving rules limit grief to the deaths of family members. When a family member dies, one is allowed and expected to grieve, often in a specified way. Yet human beings exist in intimate networks that include both relatives and friends. They harbor attachment to fellow humans, animals, and even places and things. Persons experience a wide range of losses—deaths, separations, divorces, and other changes or transitions. When death or any other separation severs these attachments, the individual grieves for such loss in many ways, many of which might clash with the culture's norms for grief. The person then experiences a loss, but others do not recognize his or her grief. That person has no socially accorded right to grieve that loss or to mourn it in that particular way. The psychologist Jeffrey Kauffman suggests that individuals internalize these grieving rules. Thus there can be an intrapsychic or self-disenfranchisement of grief whereby individuals believe that their grief is inappropriate, leading to feelings of guilt or shame.

## The Disenfranchisement of Grief

There are a number of reasons that grief can be disenfranchised. In most Western societies, the family is the primary unit of social organization. Hence kin ties have clear acknowledgement in norms and laws. While most individuals actually live their lives in intimate networks or associations that include both kin and non-kin, only kin have legal standing in making funeral arrangements and are accorded recognition as "mourner."

Another principle of Western societies is rationality, which means that beyond the family, organizations such as businesses are expected to be organized along fair, functional, and rational lines. Grieving roles reflect such social norms. Extending grieving roles to non-death situations or to non-kin would create organizational burdens. Organizations would be forced to define "levels of friendship" or "types of loss." They might be required to broaden the concept of bereavement leave, at considerable cost. Acknowledging only the death of kin conforms to rationalist organizational imperatives. It recognizes the grief of kin when a family member dies. By limiting the acknowledgement of loss to family members, it avoids confusion and potential abuse, affirming a single standard. This procedure prevents organizations from having to judge whether each individual case of loss is entitled to recognition. These policies, then, reflect and project societal recognition and support, again reaffirming and sanctioning familial relationships.

The policies also point to another significant factor—the relationship of grieving rules to ritual. The funeral becomes the vehicle by which grief is acknowledged and sanctioned, and where support is extended. The primacy of a family at the funeral reaffirms that these survivors have experienced a loss and that their subsequent grief needs sanction, acknowledgement, and support. The rite of the funeral publicly testifies to the right to grieve.

Naturally, in a diverse society, even those losses disenfranchised by society as a whole may be acknowledged within a smaller subculture. For example, the death of a gay lover may not be fully recognized by family or coworkers, but the grieving lover may be recognized and supported within the gay community. And as Eyetsemitan also notes, these grieving rules may change over time. Younger cohorts, for example, may be more supportive of the loss of an unmarried cohabiting couple. Thus, subcultures may mitigate the sense of disenfranchisement. Grieving rules differ between cultures and subcultures—what is disenfranchised in one may be supported in another.

## Typologies of Disenfranchised Grief

What losses are disenfranchised? In *Disenfranchised Grief* Doka suggested three broad categories of loss and implied a fourth. These categories were developed inductively and clinically; certain types of cases suggested a series of broad categories.

*The relationship is not recognized.* Grief may be disenfranchised in those situations in which the relationship between the bereaved and deceased is not based on recognizable kin ties. Here, the closeness of other non-kin relationships may simply not be understood or appreciated. The roles of lovers, friends, neighbors, foster parents, colleagues, in-laws, stepparents and stepchildren, caregivers, counselors, coworkers, and roommates (e.g., in nursing homes) may be close and long-standing, but even though these relationships are recognized, mourners may not have full opportunity to publicly grieve a loss. At most, they might be expected to support and assist family members.

Then there are relationships that may not be publicly recognized or socially sanctioned. For example, nontraditional relationships such as extramarital affairs, cohabitation, and homosexual relationships have tenuous public acceptance and limited legal standing, and they face negative sanction within the larger community.

*The loss is not acknowledged.* In other cases, the loss is not socially defined as significant. Individuals experience many losses—some death-related, such as perinatal loss, or other non-death-related losses such as divorce, incarceration, the loss of a job or material possessions, or significant change in personality or temperament that may be unacknowledged by others. Some losses may be intangible. For example, a teenager aspiring to a career in sports is cut from a team, or parents discover that a beloved child suffers from a disability or grave disease. Similarly, the loss of reputation because of scandal, gossip, or arrest can be devastating. Even transitions in life can have undercurrents of loss. Aging, for example, leads to constant developmental losses such as the loss of childhood or other losses associated with different points of life.

*The griever is excluded.* There are situations in which the characteristics of the bereaved in effect disenfranchise their grief. Here, the person is not socially defined as capable of grief, therefore, there is little or no social recognition of his or her sense of loss or need to mourn. Despite evidence to the contrary, both the old and the very young are typically perceived by others as having little comprehension of or reaction to the death of a significant other. Similarly, mentally disabled persons may also be disenfranchised in grief.

*Circumstances of the death.* The nature of the death may constrain the solicitation of the bereaved for support and limit the support extended by others. For example, many survivors of a suicide loss often feel a sense of stigma, believing that others may negatively judge the family because of the suicide. Similarly, the stigma of AIDS may lead survivors of an AIDS-related loss to be circumspect in sharing the loss with others.

*The ways an individual grieves.* The way in which an individual grieves also can contribute to disenfranchisement. Certain cultural modes of expressing grief such as stoicism or wailing may fall beyond the grieving rules of a given society, and thus contribute to disenfranchisement.

These examples and categories are not exhaustive, nor are they mutually exclusive. An individual's grief may be disenfranchised for a number of these reasons. And, of course, this particular taxonomy is attuned chiefly to contemporary Western culture.

Charles Corr offered another way to categorize disenfranchised grief. Corr approaches classification deductively, asking, "What is disenfranchised in grief?" He concludes that the state of bereavement, the experience of grief, and the process of mourning can all be disenfranchised.

## The Special Problems of Disenfranchised Grief

Although each of the types of grief mentioned might create particular difficulties and different reactions, one can legitimately speak of the special problems shared by all disenfranchised grievers. The problem of disenfranchised grief can be expressed in a paradox. The very nature of disenfranchised grief creates additional problems for grief, while removing or minimizing sources of support.

Disenfranchising grief may aggravate the problem of bereavement in several ways. First, the situations mentioned tend to intensify emotional reactions. Many emotions are associated with normal grief. These emotional reactions can be complicated when grief is disenfranchised. Second, both ambivalent relationships and concurrent crises have been identified in the literature as conditions that complicate grief. These conditions can often exist in many types of disenfranchised grief.

Although grief is complicated, many of the factors that facilitate mourning are not present when grief is disenfranchised. In death-related losses, the bereaved may be excluded from an active role in caring for the dying. Funeral rituals, normally helpful in resolving grief, may not help here. In some cases the bereaved may be excluded from attending, while in other cases they may have no role in planning those rituals or even in deciding whether to have them. Or in cases of divorce, separation, or psychosocial death (a significant change in another individual or relationship), rituals may be lacking altogether. In addition, the very nature of the disenfranchised grief precludes social support. Often there is not a recognized role in which mourners can assert the right to mourn and thus receive such support. Grief may have to remain private.

## The Treatment of Disenfranchised Grief

Disenfranchised grief is treated by counselors as any form of grief. The psychologists Robert Neimeyer and John Jordan suggest that the key to treating disenfranchised grief lies in analyzing what they call "empathic failure," the factors that limit support and thus generate disenfranchisement. Once the cause of empathic failure is analyzed, therapists can devise interventions that develop or compensate for the lack of support. These interventions can include individual or group counseling, support groups, expressive therapies, or the therapeutic use of ritual.

*See also:* GRIEF AND MOURNING IN CROSS-CULTURAL PERSPECTIVE; GRIEF COUNSELING AND THERAPY; MOURNING

### *Bibliography*

Corr, Charles. "Enhancing the Concept of Disenfranchised Grief." *Omega: The Journal of Death and Dying* 38 (1998):1–20.

Doka, Kenneth J. *Disenfranchised Grief: New Directions, Challenges and Strategies for Practice.* Champaign, IL: Research Press, 2002.

Doka, Kenneth J. *Disenfranchised Grief: Recognizing Hidden Sorrow.* Lexington, MA: Lexington Press, 1989.

Kauffman, Jeffrey. "The Psychology of Disenfranchised Grief: Shame, Liberation and Self-Disenfranchisement." In Kenneth J. Doka ed., *Disenfranchised Grief: New Directions, Challenges, and Strategies for Practice.* Champaign, IL: Research Press, 2002.

Neimeyer, Robert, and John Jordan. "Disenfranchisement and Empathic Failure: Grief Therapy and the Co-Construction of Meaning." In Kenneth J. Doka ed., *Disenfranchised Grief: New Directions, Challenges, and Strategies for Practice.* Champaign, IL: Research Press, 2002.

KENNETH J. DOKA

## FAMILY

Grief is a natural reaction to loss and a deeply personal experience. Its experience and intensity vary among individuals due to a variety of factors including who the deceased person was, the nature of the relationship with the deceased, the circumstances of death, and concurrent stress. The process of working through grief over a significant loss takes much more time than the public generally assumes. Often it takes many years to reach satisfactory resolution of the loss. Resolution, however, does not mean that an individual puts the experience of loss behind; it means that he or she has learned to live with the grief and is able to move on with life even though life has been irrevocably changed and the enduring sense of loss will remain. While the experience of grief is unique to each individual, grief is also an interpersonal process. People live in intricate networks of interdependent relationships inside and outside the family. Dying, death, and bereavement occur in this context. Individuals' distress over a loss is an interplay of their response to the loss, others' reactions, current and intergenerational family history of loss, and relational changes accompanying the loss. Therefore, grief can best be understood within the context of the family and its social environment.

The family is a social system in which members are interdependent and interact with one another in organized, predictable, and repetitive patterns. It is not a collection of individuals in isolation, but consists of individuals and their relationships. Because of interdependence among members, one member's behavior or whatever happens to one member affects the entire family. The family makes continuous adjustments in response to internal and external demands and tries to maintain its equilibrium. The family, like individuals, develops over time. While every family experiences stresses as it moves through different phases of development, events that occur out of sync with normative development, such as the premature death of a member, disrupt the process and produce added stress.

Families may be conceptualized along three dimensions: cohesion, flexibility, and communication. Cohesion, emotional bonding among members, ranges from disengaged (very low) to enmeshed (very high), a moderate level of cohesion being optimal under normal circumstances. Moderately cohesive families are those with members who are able to be both independent from, and connected to, their families. In disengaged families, members are emotionally distant and unable to rely on one another for support or problem solving while in enmeshed families members are excessively close, demanding loyalty and lacking personal separateness. Flexibility refers to the family's ability to change structurally and functionally, its levels ranging from rigid (very low) to chaotic (very high). Moderately flexible families are able to make changes effectively while rigid and chaotic families lack an ability to change when necessary.

Central to family functioning is communication, verbal as well as nonverbal, by which members relate to one another. How members communicate is a good measure of the health of the family. Communication facilitates the family in making adjustments on the dimensions of cohesion and flexibility in order to maintain levels suitable to the situational demands and developmental needs of members and the family as a whole. Good communication is characterized by attentive and empathic listening, speaking for self, and an open expression of feelings about self and relationships.

In general, families with moderate levels of cohesion and flexibility supported by good communication make for optimal family functioning. Those families are able to cope more effectively with a family crisis. Too much or too little cohesion or flexibility tends to be dysfunctional. There is some research evidence to indicate that cohesive families deal with grief more effectively than those families characterized by conflict, low cohesiveness, low expressiveness, and poor organization.

When a family member has a serious illness, both the ill member and others in the family face the enormous challenge of living with the uncertainty of chronic illness from initial crisis through the terminal phase. They cope with an emotional roller coaster as they live with the uncertain trajectory of illness, the demands of illness and caregiving, exhaustion, financial burdens, and thoughts of their final separation. Family members lose their "normal" life and must learn to live with ambiguities over a long period of time, well members sometimes vacillating between a desire to be close to the ill member and a desire to escape from the unbearable situation.

An impending death is likely to intensify existing relational patterns in the family. When members communicate openly, they can share grief, set priorities, provide mutual support, resolve unfinished business, including old hurts, and grow closer together through their struggle. All members, regardless of age, can benefit from being part of this process. When communication is lacking, denial and avoidance create distance between the dying and the rest of the family as well as among well members, each feeling alone and isolated with issues unresolved when death occurs. Sudden death is likely to complicate survivors' grief, but death after a prolonged illness is also followed by difficult bereavement. Some of the factors that affect survivors' grief include: witnessing disfigurement and suffering of the ill member; ambivalence felt over the ill member's disease-related personality change; stresses of caregiving; and guilt over relief experienced after death.

The death of a family member disrupts individual and family equilibrium. It engenders emotional upheaval, often brings into question individual belief systems, interrupts the developmental process of individuals and the family, and changes the family and individual identity. It alters the family structure and relational patterns. Members try to restore a sense of equilibrium both in themselves and in their relationships by adapting to pervasive changes. Overwhelmed by their grief, however, adults' capacity to function in their usual roles as parents and/or spouses diminishes, which further affects the family structure and increases distress. Moreover, relational conflicts and past unresolved issues that have been dormant may resurface under the stress and complicate family relationships. The tasks of adapting to the new reality, integrating the experience of the death into ongoing life, and moving forward developmentally are achieved through two overlapping and interrelated processes, family mourning and family reorganization. How these two processes are handled depends on the level of family functioning prior to the death as well as family resources.

## The Process of Mourning

The finality of death touches the core of human vulnerability. Adults are confronted by their own and children's grief and daily demands of family life. For weeks, while they cope with their intense pain of grief and try to survive and restabilize the family, a discussion of the deceased may be kept to a minimum. Reacting to one another's attempt to manage intense grief, members frequently collaborate to protect severely distressed members, with spouses protecting their partners and children protecting their parents. In the case of a child's death, differences between spouses in their experience of grief and coping strategies often invite misunderstanding, leading to marital conflict and increased family difficulties. While adults are in distress, children must cope not only with their own grief over the death of their parent or sibling but the psychological absence of their surviving parent(s) who cannot adequately attend to their needs.

As adults gradually regain their equilibrium, members of a family whose functioning was optimal before the death are likely to restore communication and reestablish neglected relationships. Participating in rituals appropriate to the family's cultural tradition and mourning their loss in a supportive and cohesive family environment will not only promote the healthy resolution of grief but facilitate the reorganization of the family. Obstacles that block the mourning process vary, including unresolved losses in the current family or family of origin, disengaged or conflicted family relationships, unresolved conflict with the deceased, a desire to hide the nature of death which the bereaved deem undesirable, such as death due to suicide or AIDS (acquired immunodeficiency syndrome), and idealization of the deceased disallowing members to freely talk about the deceased. Excessive use of alcohol or other substances to numb the pain of grief also interferes with communication and jeopardizes health and family relationships. A desire to avoid what is painful is a natural human inclination; paradoxically, healing comes through facing the challenge of giving the pain of grief the time and space that it requires. Even though there is no one way to cope with a major loss suitable for all, avoiding, inhibiting, or prohibiting talking about what everyone has in mind as though nothing has occurred hampers the mourning process. When members are deprived of opportunities to openly communicate and explore their own and the family's loss, the loss is compounded, resulting in a sense of isolation.

Through the process of mourning, the emotional center of the family gradually shifts from the deceased to the survivors and their future even though the deceased will continue to be psychologically present and serve as a source of support for members' ongoing development. Family members will establish their new sense of identity as widows, widowers, bereaved parents, fatherless or motherless children, children who have lost a sibling, and so forth. The change in identity also means a status change in social networks, requiring adjustments. When mourning is bypassed, the deceased individual remains as a "ghost" in the family, interfering with children's development as well as adults' developmental tasks, such as marriage, remarriage, or parenting, and places family members at risk for a host of physical and psychosocial problems. Those problems may not become evident until years later and may appear totally unrelated to the experience of loss.

## The Process of Reorganization

A member's death changes the family's hierarchical structure, leaving a void and requiring not only an adjustment in relationships but an assumption of new roles and a reallocation of roles by surviving members. New employment and/or a change in residence may become necessary for some families. Emotional upheaval may precipitate some others to make drastic changes in their lives soon after the death, such as selling a home and/or business and moving to a new neighborhood. Decisions made under duress, however, may be regretted later on. Waiting a year or two, when possible, before making major decisions helps avoid additional disruption in the family. Under the stress of bereavement, even normally moderately cohesive and flexible families may show some degree of enmeshment and rigidity, which, if continued for an extended period of time, can restrict members' ongoing development and compromises children's development toward increased independence and separation from the family.

The death of a member who performed a number of task-oriented roles presents adjustment difficulties if survivors are ill equipped to assume those roles. On the other hand, if the deceased member was dysfunctional and held a nonfunctional role in the family, adjustment may be minimally stressful. Rigid families with limited communication tend to allocate roles according to age and sex-role stereotypes with little negotiation. In flexible families roles are assigned through negotiation and based on member interest and competency. The death of children who played expressive roles leaves enormous psychic pain but does not necessitate task reassignment. Expressive roles, however, are also vital to maintaining family stability and cannot be left vacant for a long time. An empty space created by a child's death may exacerbate family problems that the child's presence kept at a distance. The death of a child who served to hold the parents' marriage together, for instance, can threaten the marital bond in bereavement. Sometimes a parent's continued attachment to the deceased child makes the parent inaccessible to others and poses problems in reorganization. Some parents start volunteer work or a project in memory of their child, which not only fills the void but brings new meaning to their lives.

Children who lost a parent or a sibling also confront changes in relationships with their parents as well as their siblings. With the death of a parent, older children may assume new roles to fulfill those roles formerly performed by the deceased or to support a depressed parent. Danger lies in children not only helping with household responsibilities or care of young siblings but assuming adult roles inappropriate to their age. Clear delineation of children's roles and responsibilities helps to prevent children from compromising their own normal development and possibly creating conflicts with siblings.

## Family Resources

Families and their members differ in economic, personal, and social resources available to them in the process of family mourning and reorganization. Reduced socio-economic status due to death or a family's low material resources can negatively affect adjustment in bereavement. On the other hand, personal resources including such individual characteristics as viewing life as a series of challenges and having pride, motivation, and a sense of control over life, help members make a better adjustment in bereavement.

Social support is a critical resource in coping with bereavement. The presence of others (kin, friends, neighbors, employers, coworkers, and even strangers in the community) who offer emotional and material support helps bereaved family members validate and mourn their immense loss and meet their daily needs when their ability to support themselves is seriously impaired. Those who are part of a cohesive cultural or religious group are likely to receive considerable support from others in the group. The types and amount of support the family needs differ depending on the family and the loss suffered, and family and individual needs change with time. Families isolated with minimal contact with others in the community and possessing limited resources are at risk for complications in bereavement. Families lacking social support due to stigma attached to their loved one's death as well as those whose needs are not adequately met through their usual sources of support may seek or augment support from outside the family. When the family faces serious difficulties in coping with the loss, assistance from professionals may be in order. Support groups designed to provide mutual support for those in a similar predicament are also found to be valuable sources of help for both bereaved children and adults. Often the most helpful emotional support comes from those who have experienced a similar loss.

## Rebuilding

The process of integrating the experience of loss and rebuilding the family without the deceased is a gradual one, which can take months or years, depending on the circumstances. Adults who attend to their own grief and receive support from the extended family and community resources for reconstructing family life are in a better position to help children grieve and promote their healthy development. The effects of a member's death differ for each survivor and so do the ways of coping and the length of time it takes for members to resolve their grief and move on. The family mourning process, however, is a shared experience. Understanding and accepting the diversity in the family through mutual sharing facilitate the healing process. New rituals may be created for cultural and religious celebrations and for special occasions, such as birthdays and anniversaries, to mourn and commemorate the deceased member and affirm the bond to the deceased in the ongoing family life. Troubling images associated with the death may continue to intrude into consciousness from time to time. The loss with its painful emotional and practical implications is revisited and grieved anew many times as the family and each member's life unfolds developmentally. Through embracing the past and reaffirming the continuity of life, members once again engage in life with hope for the future.

*See also:* COMMUNICATION WITH THE DYING; DYING, PROCESS OF; GOOD DEATH, THE; GRIEF COUNSELING AND THERAPY; MOURNING

### Bibliography

Becvar, Dorothy S. *In the Presence of Grief: Helping Family Members Resolve Death, Dying, and Bereavement Issues.* New York: The Guilford Press, 2001.

Becvar, Dorothy S. "Families Experiencing Death, Dying, and Bereavement." In William. C. Nichols, Mary Anne Pace-Nichols, Dorothy S. Becvar, and Augustus Y. Napier eds., *Handbook of Family Development and Intervention.* New York: John Wiley & Sons, 2000.

Bouvard, Marguerite with Evelyn Gladu. *The Path through Grief.* Amherst, NY: Prometheus Books, 1998.

Bowlby-West, Lorna. "The Impact of Death on the Family System." *Journal of Family Therapy* 5 (1983):279–294.

Campbell, Scott, and Phyllis R. Silverman. *Widower: When Men are Left Alone.* Amityville, NY: Baywood Publishing, 1996.

Campbell, Jane, Paul Swank, and Ken Vincent. "The Role of Hardiness in the Resolution of Grief." *Omega: The Journal of Death and Dying* 23 (1991):53–65.

Doka, Kenneth J., and Joyce Davidson eds. *Living with Grief When Illness Is Prolonged.* Washington, DC: Hospice Foundation of America, 1997.

Gelcer, Esther. "Mourning Is a Family Affair." *Family Process* 22 (1983):501–516.

Kissane, David W., and Sydney Block. "Family Grief." *British Journal of Psychiatry* 164 (1994):728–740.

Lord, Janice Harris. *No Time for Goodbyes: Coping with Sorrow, Anger and Injustice After a Tragic Death,* 5th edition. Oxnard, CA: Pathfinder, 2000.

Martin, Terry L., and Kenneth Doka. *Men Don't Cry . . . Women Do: Transcending Gender Stereotypes of Grief.* Philadelphia: Brunner/Mazel, 2000.

Nadeau, Janice Winchester. *Families Making Sense of Death.* Thousand Oaks, CA: Sage, 1998.

Nolen-Hoeksema, Susan, and Judith Larson. *Coping with Loss.* Mahwah, NJ: Lawrence Erlbaum, 1999.

Olson, David H. "Circumplex Model of Marital and Family Systems: Assessing Family Functioning." In Froma Walsh ed., *Normal Family Processes,* 2nd edition. New York: The Guilford Press, 1993.

Shapiro, Ester R. *Grief As a Family Process.* New York: The Guilford Press, 1994.

Stroebe, Margaret S., Wolfgang Stroebe, and Robert O. Hansson eds., *Handbook of Bereavement: Theory, Research, and Intervention.* Cambridge: Cambridge University Press, 1993.

Vess, James, John Moreland, and Andrew I. Schwebel. "Understanding Family Role Reallocation Following a Death: A Theoretical Framework." *Omega: The Journal of Death and Dying* 16 (1985–86):115–128.

Walsh, Froma, and Monica McGoldrick eds., *Living Beyond Loss: Death in the Family.* New York: W. W. Norton, 1991.

Wolfelt, Alan D. *Healing Your Grieving Heart for Teens: 100 Practical Ideas.* Fort Collins, CO: Companion Press, 1997.

Wolfelt, Alan D. *Understanding Grief: Helping Yourself Heal.* Fort Collins, CO: Companion Press, 1992.

REIKO SCHWAB

# GENDER

It has been suggested that because of different socialization experiences, or perhaps even biological differences, men and women exhibit distinct patterns in the way they experience, express, and adapt to grief. In much popular commentary it is further suggested that the male role inhibits grieving because it places emphasis on the regulation of emotional expression and constrains the seeking of support from others. Women, on the other hand, are seen as more ready to accept help and express emotions, both of which are seen as facilitating grief. Louis LeGrand, for example, stated in 1986 that this gender difference "does not mean that men are not grieving; it does indicate that they may not accomplish the task as successfully as women" (LeGrand 1986, p. 31). Allen Wolfelt, in a 1990 article in *Thanatos,* stated his belief that men's grief is naturally more complicated because men cannot express emotion or seek help. Carol Staudacher in her book *Men and Grief* succinctly stated this bias toward emotive expressiveness: "Simply put, there is only one way to grieve. That way is to go through the core of grief. Only by expressing the emotional effects of your loved one's death is it possible for you to eventually resolve the loss" (Staudacher 1991, p. 3). Yet the idea that men grieve poorly is clearly disputed by the research in the field of thanatology (the study of death).

## Research Perspectives

Researchers have studied both therapists' attitudes toward gender differences as well as the grief patterns and outcomes of men and women. The results have been mixed.

*Therapists' views.* In 1997 Judith Stillion and Eugene McDowell reported the results of their study of certified grief counselors' and grief therapists' perspectives on gender differences in grief. The researchers found that the people in their sample did believe that men and women express grief differently. Men were perceived as less likely to express strong emotions and more likely to use diversions such as work, play, sex, or alcohol. Therapists reported that men were more likely to respond cognitively and to use anger as a primary mode of emotional expression. Women were seen as more likely to express grief affectively (emotionally) and to seek support.

The counselors in the sample also found differences in the expectations of others and the support men and women received from others. Others expected men to get over their loss more quickly and be able to function more effectively. Women were seen as needing and receiving more emotional support, but others also saw them as being more of a social risk—that is, being likely to break down in normal social situations. The result was that these therapists reported that their women clients received more comfort-oriented support but fewer opportunities for normal social activity than their male counterparts.

Despite these differences in the expression of grief, and the support men and women were likely to receive, the counselors surveyed did not report differences in outcomes. In fact these therapists saw different risks for each gender. In their view,

men were more at risk for certain types of complicated grief reactions, whereas women were more prone to depression or chronic mourning.

*Gender-based studies of grief.* The perspective of these therapists, explicitly or implicitly, is grounded in much of the research that does show a difference in the ways men and women grieve. In summarizing this research in 1999, Terry Martin and Kenneth J. Doka noted the following:

1. Research has shown that widows and widowers face different problems in grief. For example, many widows reported financial distress and noted the emotional support that had been provided by their spouse. Widowers were more likely to report disruptions of their familial and social networks. Widows were more likely to seek emotional support, whereas widowers found solace in exercise, work, religion, creative expression, or more destructively in alcohol.

2. Many of these same results are evident in the loss of a child. Mothers reported more emotional distress than fathers. Strategies in dealing with the loss differed by gender. Women tended to use more support-seeking and emotion-focused strategies, whereas men were more likely to intellectualize their grief and use more problem-focused strategies to adapt to the loss.

3. Studies of the loss of a parent also showed that middle-aged sons were less likely than daughters to experience intense grief, had fewer physical manifestations of grief, and were more likely to use cognitive and active approaches in adapting to loss.

4. Differences between genders seem less apparent in older age groups. This may reflect the idea that individuals become more androgynous as they age.

5. Differences in gender are also affected by other variables such as social class, generational differences, and cultural differences.

6. The research on differences in outcome is quite mixed. Some studies have shown men to have better outcomes, others show women to do better, and still other studies show no significant difference or mixed

results in outcome (i.e., men do better on some measures, women on other measures).

This research does have implications for counselors. Whether one sees these differences as due to gender or as patterns influenced by gender (see below), it does suggest that different responses to loss can affect relationships within the family as that family experiences a loss. Counselors will do well then to assist individuals in identifying and discussing the ways they deal with loss and in helping families to address how these differences affect each other's grief.

## Beyond Gender: Patterns of Grief

Martin and Doka suggested that one look beyond gender to understand different patterns or styles of grief. Martin and Doka proposed that these patterns are related to gender but not determined by them. They suggested that gender, culture, and initial temperament all interact to produce a dominant pattern of grief. They viewed these patterns of grief as a continuum. Martin and Doka further acknowledged that patterns are likely to change throughout an individual's development, often moving more toward the center of the continuum as an individual moves to late adulthood. Based upon the underlying concept of emotion regulation, Martin and Doka proposed three basic patterns of grief: intuitive, instrumental, and dissonant.

*Intuitive pattern.* Intuitive grievers experience, express, and adapt to grief on a very affective level. Intuitive grievers are likely to report the experience of grief as waves of affect, or feeling. They are likely to strongly express these emotions as they grieve—shouting, crying, or displaying emotion in other ways. Intuitive grievers are also likely to be helped in ways that allow them to ventilate their emotions. Self-help and support groups, counseling, and other expressive opportunities that allow these grievers to ventilate feelings are likely to be helpful.

*Instrumental pattern.* Instrumental grievers are more likely to experience, express, and adapt to grief in more active and cognitive ways. Instrumental grievers will tend to experience grief as thoughts, such as a flooding of memories, or in physical or behavioral manifestations. They are likely to express grief in similar ways—doing something related to the loss, exercising, or talking about the loss. For example, in one case, a man

whose daughter died in a car crash found great solace in repairing the fence his daughter had wrecked. "It was," he shared later, "the only part of the accident I could fix" (Martin and Doka 1999). Instrumental grievers are helped by strategies such as bibliotherapy (the use of self-help literature) and other interventions that make use of cognitive and active approaches.

*Dissonant pattern.* Dissonant grievers are those who experience grief in one pattern but who are inhibited from finding compatible ways to express or adapt to grief that are compatible with their experience. For example, a man might experience grief intuitively but feel constrained from expressing or adapting to grief in that way because he perceives it as inimical to his male role. Similarly, a woman might also experience grief in a more intuitive way but believe she has to repress that feeling in order to protect her family. Counseling with dissonant grievers involves helping to identify their inherent pattern, recognizing the barriers to effective expression and adaptation, and developing suitable intervention techniques.

*Where men and women are found on this continuum.* Martin and Doka suggested that many men, at least in Western culture, are likely to be found on the instrumental end of this continuum whereas women are more likely to be found on the intuitive end. The researchers stressed, however, that while gender does influence the pattern of grief, that pattern is not determined by gender. Martin and Doka also noted that many individuals in the center of the continuum may show more blended patterns, using a range of emotional, behavioral, and cognitive strategies to adapt to loss.

## Culture and Gender

It is critical to remember that any discussion of gender differences in grief, or even of patterns of grief that are influenced by gender, must take into account cultural differences. Culture influences grief in a number of ways. First, each culture has norms that govern the ways in which grief is appropriately expressed. In some cultures these norms can differ between genders. In a 1976 study, Paul Rosenblatt and his associates found that in the sixty societies they surveyed, thirty-two had no differences in the expectation of crying between men and women. In the remaining twenty-eight, women were allowed more emotional expressiveness. Second, each culture defines relationships in different ways, which influences the level of attachment. These relationship definitions may also differ by gender.

*See also:* GENDER DISCRIMINATION AFTER DEATH; GRIEF COUNSELING AND THERAPY; SUICIDE INFLUENCES AND FACTORS: GENDER

### *Bibliography*

LeGrand, Louis. *Coping with Separation and Loss as a Young Adult.* Springfield, IL: Charles C. Thomas, 1986.

Martin, Terry, and Kenneth J. Doka. *Men Don't Cry, Women Do: Transcending Gender Stereotypes of Grief.* Philadelphia: Taylor & Francis, 1999.

Rosenblatt, Paul, Rose Walsh, and Douglas Jackson. *Grief and Mourning in Cross-Cultural Perspective.* Washington, DC: HRAF Press, 1976.

Staudacher, Carol. *Men and Grief.* Oakland, CA: New Harbinger Press, 1991.

Stillion, Judith, and Eugene McDowell. "Women's Issues in Grief." Paper presented at the annual meeting of the Association for Death Education and Counseling, Washington, DC, 1997.

Wolfelt, Alan. "Gender Roles and Grief: Why Men's Grief Is Naturally Complicated." *Thanatos* 15, no. 30 (1990):20–24.

KENNETH J. DOKA

# SUICIDE

The death of a loved one is almost always followed by a period of mourning and bereavement accompanied by many different feelings, including loss, grief, shock, denial, despair, depression, anxiety, helplessness, hopelessness, guilt, shame, relief, and anger. Physical symptoms are also common, among them fatigue, sleep and appetite disturbances, apathy, withdrawal, and agitation. Some scholars have contended that bereavement after a suicide is the most trying of all because of the suicide's presumed emotional suffering and the consequent voluntary decision to die. This factor, with its implication of rejection and desertion, has special impact on some survivors. Moreover, a suicide is often complicated by society's negative reactions toward both the decedent and the family, which make bereavement more difficult.

The variation in scholarly opinion on the nature and difficulties of bereavement reflects different methodological approaches in research in this area, such as the use of appropriate control groups for comparison, variability in kinship comparisons, time elapsed after death, and so on. Mark Cleiren, for example, found more differences between groups compared by kinship, such as parents versus spouses, siblings, or children, than between groups compared by mode of death, such as suicide versus accident, homicide, or natural causes. Nevertheless, many researchers report a greater risk of complicated bereavement after a suicide death than after other kinds of deaths, including less emotional support and more physical illness, depression, and anxiety. Other researchers have concluded that the feelings and reactions of survivors of suicide are really no different from the reactions that ensue from other modes of death and that the differences that do appear are more in intensity than in kind. The psychologist Sheila Clark has described the differences as "both minimal and mythical" and points to the relatively few quantitative differences when outcomes after different modes of death are compared. She argues the importance of dispelling the myth of this difference because she believes that it engenders the expectation of a more difficult bereavement.

The psychologist Albert Cain's early review of the literature, however, found that nearly all of the reports described more severe reactions to suicides, with greater severity of psychopathology and expression of vulnerability. A partial list included reality distortion, massive use of denial, confusion of memory, fantasy and misconception, guilt, a pervasive sense of complicity, rage, a disturbed self-concept, shame and worthlessness, intense frustration of needs, depression and self-destructiveness, incomplete mourning, and a gnawing belief that they might have played some role in precipitating the suicide or that they could have done something more to prevent it.

Survivors of a suicide are typically haunted by the question of "why" and are thus tormented by constant probing, rehearsing last contacts, reviewing all clues, and so on. Depression is probably the most common emotional syndrome of normal bereavement. It becomes pathological when the survivor grows progressively less able to function and continues to sink further into despair, apathy, and emptiness. Trouble in concentrating, inability to think clearly, negative self-preoccupation, and self-reproach may appear. It is important to distinguish between the sadness of normal grief and pathological depression. One helpful distinction is that the psychiatrically depressed person is more likely to be preoccupied with himself than with the loss of the deceased loved one.

The suicide survivor's feelings of guilt and shame often go unrecognized to the extent that they surface in other emotional guises, such as self-blame, humiliation, failure, and embarrassment. Both guilt and shame refer to individual and social development in relation to oneself and others, and they indicate an awareness of what is deemed virtuous as well as what is deemed criminal and immoral. Shame and guilt have so many elements in common that distinguishing them is often difficult. An important element that helps in the differentiation is the direction of the attention: In shame, the attention is on some defect exposed in the self-image; in guilt, the focus is on the act or behavior and its consequences.

Anger may be more frequent and more intense for survivors of suicide. Many persons find anger difficult to deal with because of social and religious customs that make it unacceptable. The anger is directed in one or all directions—toward decedent, self, and others. The anger may be directed at the deceased because of strong feelings of desertion and abandonment; for his or her not having used or accepted available help, especially from the survivor; for having deprived the survivor of a shared future and forcing the discarding of cherished dreams; and for having left the survivor with a tangle of financial and legal problems. Sometimes the anger is experienced as a violation of trust, a dependency each had invested in the other that leaves the survivor not only bereft in the present but also hesitant to consider commitments in the future.

The anger may appear directed against the health and mental health professions who have failed to prevent the suicide, or it may be directed at their social network if it has withdrawn and offered less support than is ordinarily offered for survivors of a death by accident or natural causes. The anger may be directed at a society that condemns suicide and offers less compassion and

understanding because a taboo has been violated. David Lester remarks that official agencies in the community often function in such a way that it continually reminds the survivor that the death was not a natural one and creates "unpleasant experiences the bereaved are ill-equipped to handle." Anger with religion may occur when it fails to comfort or creates logistical problems during burial services. Anger at God may appear for his having "let" the suicide happen. Sometimes the anger may be directed at oneself for not having seen the "obvious" clues that the suicide was imminent or for not having prevented the death even though the signs were clear.

A suicide affects family members both individually and collectively. To the extent that suicide carries a stigma, many react to it with silence, secrecy, and even distortion (i.e., denial that death was a suicide). Kenneth Doka has called such deaths "disenfranchised" because their taboo status has resulted in social sanctions. As a result, there is reluctance to mourn openly or publicly. There may be scapegoating with accusations and blaming by other members of the family, fear of hereditary factors, anger at the medical and mental health professions, troublesome involvement of the police and insurance investigators, and possible intrusions by press and other media.

## Bereavement for Children

The question of whether children can mourn depends on the definition of mourning. The ability to grieve develops as the child first comprehends the finality of death; the timing of this realization is a subject of debate among scholars. Some find it present in young infants, while others have concluded that it does not appear until adolescence. According to one researcher, Nancy Webb, young children can experience sadness, longing, detachment, and rage, but it cannot be considered mourning until the child is able to understand the finality of the loss and its significance. She argues that children of ages nine to eleven are just beginning to view the world logically and thus able to comprehend abstractions and hypotheses, with the full flowering of this ability developing during adolescence.

Karen Dunne-Maxim, Edward Dunne, and Marilyn Hauser feel that children react to suicide

*Adolescents may manifest extremes of behavior such as withdrawal and social isolation, while others may become truant, delinquent, and openly aggressive when reacting to a suicide death of a family member or friend.* A. TANNENBAUM/CORBIS

deaths with feelings very similar to those of adults but with very different behavior. The symptoms have been likened to those characteristic of posttraumatic stress after a disaster, with clinging and whining in small children, regression and collapse of some of the stages of development, and fears and anxieties about usually comfortable situations or people. Older children may become model children, fearful of any activity that might bring censure, possibly because of fears that they in some way have been responsible for the death. Some may try to become a parent to the remaining parent, trying to fill the gap and to assuage his or her grief.

Children, even when young, should be told the truth about the suicide. Experience has shown that the efforts to keep the nature of the death a secret usually fail and that the truth, when revealed, is harder to integrate and to accept. Children and young adolescents can construct terrifying fantasies, such as unwarranted guilt for personally causing the death. The inevitable discovery increases the confusion if the secret emerges in childhood; if the revelation occurs in adulthood, the usual reaction is anger at the prolonged deception. The parent is most helpful when reassuring the child with words suitable to age and level of understanding, words that "normalize" the child's feelings of guilt, shame, anger, or sadness. If signs of emotional disturbance continue, however (i.e., truancy, fighting, exaggerated grief), intervention by a trained child therapist might be in order.

**Professional Caregivers As Survivors**

Research has shown that therapists whose patients commit suicide often experience the same feelings as family members: shock, numbness, denial, anxiety, shame, grief, guilt, depression, anger, and others. However, there are also feelings that are inherent to the role of therapist: failure, self-doubts about therapy skills, clinical judgment, professional competence, and fear of litigation and professional ostracism. Grief reactions were correlated with the length of time in therapy. The effects of such reactions often led to changes in professional practice, like limiting practice only to patients who were not suicidal, avoiding undertaking treatment of severely depressed patients, hyperalertness to a patient's suicidal ideas and/or self-destructive behavior, hospitalizing very low-risk patients, putting more inpatients on suicidal precaution, and canceling inpatient passes. For the therapist in training there is the additional stress that may stem from pressures of competition within the group, a feeling of being under constant observation and evaluation, and a desire to win approval from the faculty.

Research on clinician-survivors has been sparse, although it is not an isolated or rare event. Morton Kahne estimated that one out of every four psychiatrists will experience a suicide in his or her practice. Subsequent researchers have reported a frequency of patient suicides for therapists in private practice that ranges from 22 percent to 51 percent. Philip Kleespies found that one out of every nine psychology interns had to cope with a patient's suicide attempt. The older the psychiatrist and the greater the years of practice, the less the guilt and loss of self-esteem; for psychologists, there was no relationship between age or years of practice and intensity of reaction.

In-hospital suicide provokes the same feelings and reactions among the staff that have been reported for clinicians in private practice: shock, numbness, denial, guilt, insecurity, and so on. There is the added dimension of the impact on other patients, with anger frequently directed against the staff for not preventing the death and thus causing them to feel less secure and less protected against their impulses. Some showed a marked identification with the deceased and an assumption of inappropriate responsibility for the death.

## Grief Relief

Grief, mourning, and bereavement are the natural consequences of the death of a loved one. The loss by suicide adds to the problems and difficulties experienced by the survivors in this process. The basic tasks in the relief of the grief that follows include accepting the reality and pain of the loss, adapting to a life in which the deceased is now missing, and relocating the deceased emotionally and moving on with life. The tasks also include detaching the hopes the survivor had of the loved one and developing a new and different relationship with the memories previously held about him or her.

For most survivors medical attention or psychological treatment is not required. Familial, social, and environmental support, along with personal coping mechanisms and passage of time, will bring about recovery. A small percentage of survivors may experience severe reactions that are crippling, persistent, and disruptive for both family and social relationships. When this occurs, professional treatment is in order. A larger percentage of survivors may experience continuing moderate difficulties in adapting to the loss. In such cases, help may be sought through family, friends, special groups (i.e., Compassionate Friends, Widow-to-Widow), peer and professional grief counselors, individual psychotherapy, group therapy, and suicide survivor groups. Individual psychotherapy with a mental health professional would probably include current information on suicide, descriptions of the grief process, efforts to normalize the

emotional reactions, discussions of disappointing or irritating social reactions, a determination of the survivor's social network and other sources of support, and an attempt to understand the role of any psychiatric illness that afflicted the decedent. The therapist would especially be alert for any evidence of suicidal thoughts and actions by the survivor or anyone in the family.

A survivor may also find help in group therapy led by a mental health professional. In such groups the process occurs within the context of frank discussion of the emotional problems of each member, with the interaction between the members of the group led by the therapist. Other forms of group treatment have been devised especially for suicide survivors. One is a form of family treatment that consists of sending trained nonprofessional volunteers to a family's home after a suicide to provide counseling and support. Another community provided counseling services by telephone along with visits to the home. In still another community a mental health professional accompanied the coroner's deputy so that support could be offered in the initial shock phase of the survivors' grief. Additional contacts occurred for a period afterward, depending on the needs of the survivors.

Probably the most common method for helping adult survivors of the suicide of a loved one is survivor groups in which all the members are survivors of a suicide. Models may be time-limited or continuous, open-ended or closed; they may be varied or limited in kinship, frequency and length of sessions, fees, and leadership (professional, trained survivor facilitators, or mixtures). The basic objective of the survivors' group is to provide a compassionate forum for discussion of the suicide, its impact on the survivors' lives, expression of emotions unique to suicide grief, negative affect, understanding of the grief process, exposure to alternative models of coping, and provision of mutual comfort and support.

Suicide survivor support groups are most often found among the services offered by local suicide prevention centers, crisis service centers, or community health centers. A directory of suicide survivor groups compiled by the American Foundation for Suicide Prevention listed and described 475 groups in the United States. The American Association of Suicidology and the World Health

Organization have published manuals on how to initiate and conduct survivor support groups.

*See also:* CHILDREN AND ADOLESCENTS' UNDERSTANDING OF DEATH; GRIEF COUNSELING AND THERAPY; LITERATURE FOR CHILDREN; MOURNING

### *Bibliography*

Bolton, Iris. "Beyond Surviving: Suggestions for Survivors." In Edwin Dunne, John McIntosh, and Karen Dunne-Maxim eds., *Suicide and Its Aftermath: Understanding and Counseling the Survivors.* New York: Norton, 1987.

Bowlby, John. "Grief and Mourning in Infancy and Early Childhood." *Psychoanalytic Study of the Child* 15 (1960):9–52.

Cain, Albert C. *Survivors of Suicide.* Springfield, IL: Charles C. Thomas, 1972.

Calhoun, Lawrence G., James W. Selby, and Carol B. Abernethy. "Suicidal Death: Social Reactions to Bereaved Survivors." *Journal of Psychology* 116 (1984):255–261.

Clark, Sheila E. *After Suicide: Help for the Bereaved.* Melbourne: Hill of Content, 1995.

Cleiren, Mark. *Bereavement and Adaptation: A Comparative Study of the Aftermath of Death.* Washington, DC: Hemisphere Publishing, 1993.

Doka, Kenneth J., ed. *Disenfranchised Grief: Recognizing Hidden Sorrow.* New York: Free Press, 1989.

Dunne-Maxim, Karen, Edward J. Dunne, and Marilyn J. Hauser. "When Children are Suicide Survivors." In Edward J. Dunne, John L. McIntosh, and Karen Dunne-Maxim eds., *Suicide and Its Aftermath: Understanding and Counseling the Survivors.* New York: Norton, 1987.

Farberow, Norman L. "Helping Suicide Survivors." In David Lester ed., *Suicide Prevention: Resources for the Millennium.* Philadelphia: Brunner-Routledge, 2001.

Kahne, Morton J. "Suicide among Patients in the Mental Hospital." *Psychiatry* 31 (1968):32–49.

Kleespies, Phillip M., Walter E. Penk, and John P. Forsyth. "Suicidal Behavior during Clinical Training: Incidence, Impact, and Recovery." *Professional Psychology: Research and Practice* 24 (1993):293–303.

Lester, David. "Surviving a Suicide." In Austin H. Kutscher et al. eds., *For the Bereaved: The Road to Recovery.* Philadelphia: The Charles Press, 1990.

Webb, Nancy. *Helping Bereaved Children.* New York: Guilford Press, 1993.

NORMAN L. FARBEROW

## THEORIES

Theories of grief should deepen understanding of the phenomena and the manifestations of grief. A theory of grief should not merely describe but also explain. It should account for the decline in mental and/or physical health that often attends grief. Most importantly, a theory of grief should further the development of therapies to ameliorate or prevent complicated grief reactions.

Contemporary research on grief has grown out of psychoanalytic/attachment theories and stress/trauma theories. The classic psychoanalytic theory of grief focuses on the emotional reaction to loss (this incorporates a broader range of psychological reactions than depression alone), providing explanation of psychological symptoms of grief. By contrast, a tradition of research on the physical health effects of stress in general led to an extension of the application of stress theory to bereavement. This approach views bereavement as a form of stress that can lead to impairment of health.

*Bereavement* denotes the situation of losing a loved one through death, while *grief* is the emotional reaction to such a loss and typically involves psychological, physiological, social, and behavioral manifestations of distress. *Grieving* signifies the attempt to come to terms with loss and adapt to it. *Grief work* is the cognitive and/or emotional confrontation with loss, incorporating reflections on events surrounding the death. *Complicated grief* is a deviation from typical grief and grieving, taking cultural factors, the extremity of the particular bereavement event, and the duration of the bereavement into account. Different types of complication have been identified, including an absence of usual symptoms (absent grief), delayed onset of symptoms (delayed grief), or an exaggerated, chronic, more intense, or prolonged emotional experience (chronic grief). There is lack of agreement about how *traumatic bereavement* should be defined. It is useful to limit definition to those bereavements in which the death occurred in jarring, unnatural circumstances. *Mourning* is the social expression of grief actions and grief rituals that reflect one's culture and/or social group.

## Psychoanalytic and Attachment Perspectives

Theories falling within the psychoanalytic/ attachment framework owe much to Sigmund Freud's paper "Mourning and Melancholia." This approach has remained influential throughout the twentieth century, most notably in the work of major researchers, including John Bowlby, Eric Lindemann, Colin Parkes, Beverley Raphael, and Selby Jacobs, all of whom have developed their own lines of reasoning. According to psychoanalytic theory, when a significant person dies, the bereaved person faces the struggle to sever the tie and detach the libidinal energy (love) invested in the deceased person. The major cause of pathological grief is ambivalence in the relationship with the deceased, which prevents the normal transference of libido from that person to a new object. The psychological function of grief is to free the individual of the tie to the deceased and allow him or her to achieve a gradual detachment by means of a process of grief work. Since Freud, the notion that one has to work through one's grief has been central in major theoretical formulations and in principles of counseling and therapy. However, it has also met with considerable criticism. Dissatisfaction with the "working through" notion has led to further specification of ideas about adaptive coping in contemporary research and theorizing.

Departing in certain important respects from the psychoanalytic tradition, Bowlby's attachment theory emphasized the biological (evolutionary) rather than the psychological function of grieving. He argued that the biological function of grief was to regain proximity to the attachment figure, separation from which had caused anxiety. The observation of grieflike reactions to separation from attachment figures in primates and humans tends to support Bowlby's thesis that these responses have biological roots. It is indeed plausible that an adverse reaction to separation would increase the survival chances of animals that live in herds because predators tend to attack animals that are separated from their herds. Obviously, regaining proximity is not possible in the case of permanent loss, and such a response is therefore dysfunctional. Bowlby also argued for an active working-through of a loss. Like Freud, Bowlby saw the direct cause of pathological grief in the relationship with the lost person. However, the more distant cause was said to be childhood experiences with attachment figures—whether the child had been

securely or insecurely attached to the primary caregiver. Insecure attachment is assumed to result from parental rejection in childhood. These influences were assumed to have a lasting influence on later relationships. Unlike insecure individuals, secure individuals would be expected to display normal or healthy grieving, experiencing and expressing emotions to a moderate degree and being able to provide a coherent, balanced account of their loss-related experiences. Following this line of reasoning, there are effects of attachment orientation on ways of grieving.

The attachment theory has fostered much useful scholarship. John Archer has further examined the origin and adaptive significance of grief, deriving arguments from theoretical principles of modern evolutionary theory. He applied the principles of natural selection, reproductive value, and parental investment to grief, reasoning that these determine the strength of the relationship with the person who has died. This line of research provides predictions about patterns of grief toward different kin and at different ages for parent-offspring and offspring-parent grief.

By contrast, Simon Rubin has probed the relationship with the deceased person, specifically, a deceased child, in his two-track model of bereavement, in which intense preoccupation with the deceased sets the bereavement response in motion. Two tracks refer to related but not identical dimensions of loss: relationship and functioning. Track I describes the biopsychosocial reactions, or how people function in families and how this changes. Track II focuses on transformations in the attachment to the deceased, suggesting a dynamic mechanism in attachment.

## Stress Perspectives

Cognitive-stress and trauma theories have proved most fruitful in investigations of bereavement. Stress theories are applicable to a broad range of life events (i.e., loss of a job, relocation, divorce), while trauma theories pertain more specifically to shocking, out-of-the-ordinary events (i.e., victimization, war, traffic accidents, violent bereavements). A basic assumption is that stressful life events play an important role in causing the various somatic and psychiatric disorders.

Cognitive stress theory, which emerged from the broader field of the psychophysiology of stress, views bereavement as a source of serious stress that can endanger health and well-being. An individual's cognitive appraisal of the event (relating situational demands to available coping resources, like social support) determines the extent to which the bereavement is experienced as challenging or stressful. Cognitive-stress theory thus emphasizes the role of cognitive appraisal in adjustment to loss; it is a variable that is similar, though not identical, to subsequent "meaning-making" conceptualizations. Cognitive-stress theory provides a framework for a fine-grained analysis of the characteristics of the stressor (bereavement) itself, the coping process (styles, strategies such as confrontation versus avoidance and emotion versus problem-focused) and outcomes (well-being and mental and physical illness). It offers a theoretical explanation for the health consequences of bereavement and provides the theoretical basis for the so-called buffering model. According to this model, high levels of social support protect (buffer) the individual from the health risks of stress. Stress research has helped identify physiological mechanisms linking stress to various detriments to the immune, gastrointestinal, and cardiovascular systems.

A number of bereavement-specific stress-coping models have been developed that have (a) led to further specification of cognitive tasks and processes in coming to terms with bereavement, and/or (b) increased the emphasis on the impact of others on individual grief. These types of analysis form much of the basis of contemporary theorizing about bereavement. William Worden's, and Colin Parkes and Robert Weiss's task models were among the first to specify the prerequisites for coping with loss during bereavement. Worden's model represents coping with bereavement as an active, demanding process rather than an event to be passively experienced. He describes four tasks, which include accepting the reality of loss, experiencing the pain of grief, adjusting to an environment without the deceased, and relocating the deceased emotionally. Parkes and Weiss described three somewhat different tasks such as intellectual and emotional acceptance of a loss and forging a new identity.

Other investigators have focused on the way that the loss is appraised (e.g., whether these are guilt feelings or regrets and whether there is dwelling on or avoidance of grieving. Significant

theoretical developments have emerged from this work. For example, George Bonanno identified so-called dissociation between psychological and physiological reactions during episodes of disclosing emotions after bereavement. He showed that some persons who did not disclose verbally, thus suggesting denial, showed evidence of grief in high physiological arousal. In the long term, this pattern of dissociation was associated with good adjustment. This appears to contradict the idea that grief work helps and that denial is dysfunctional.

Alicia Cook's and Kevin Oltjenbrun's model of incremental grief examines the impact of others on individual grief. This describes how lack of congruence in grieving among bereaved persons (particularly families) leads to secondary loss, changing the relationship between survivors, and precipitation of further loss (e.g., breakup). Further specification of interpersonal influences on cognitive processing is provided in social construction models. Basic to this approach is the understanding that grieving is a process of meaning reconstruction, which is frequently negotiated between grieving family members and/or becomes established within the cultural context. This type of approach includes Robert Neimeyer's meaning-reconstruction model. According to Neimeyer, meaning reconstruction, which entails an understanding of the significance of the loss, is the central process of grieving, evidenced in six "propositions." Each of these propositions describes a type of cognitive process that affects the way a bereaved person adjusts to loss. For example, one of the propositions focuses on the way in which identities are reconstructed in negotiation with others. This proposition is based on the understanding that individual adjustment is affected by the way that grieving is done within its social context. Tony Walter's new model of grief focuses on the social context in a slightly different manner. Walter explains how biographies about deceased persons are created as the bereaved talk to each other about their loss and negotiate meaning and reality as part of the process of grieving. When a durable biography has been derived, such as when the grieving family members come to agree on the interpretation of the death, then the bereaved can find a place for the deceased, move on, and stop grieving. There are good reasons to argue that these meaning-reconstruction models are complementary to the cognitive-stress approaches. Among the advantages of attempting integration of these perspectives is that combination would force understanding of grief within its personal, social, and cultural context.

Although trauma theories can be considered within a general stress framework, as noted above, they are more specifically directed toward understanding the impact of those events that are especially jarring and horrific. Trauma theory has emerged along three independent lines. Mardi Horowitz has analyzed phenomena in terms of "stress response syndromes"; the work of James Pennebaker has focused on disclosure in trauma management; and Ronnie Janoff-Bulman and Colin Parkes have both developed the conceptualization of "assumptive world views." Common to these three perspectives is the notion that although the traumatic event itself has passed the person remains affected and still suffers psychologically and, perhaps, physically. The event needs to be assimilated, and/or inner representations accommodated, before the person can function normally again.

According to Horowitz, "Negative stress stems from experience of loss or injury, psychological or material, real or fantasized. If action cannot alter the situation, the inner models or schemata must be revised so that they conform to the new reality" (1979, p. 244). Control processes regulate the working-through process, which is often marked by a battle to fend off the intrusion of disturbing thoughts. Intrusion is the compulsive re-experiencing of feelings and ideas surrounding the event, including sleep and dream disturbance. Avoidance is the counterreaction, often involving amnesia, inability to visualize memories, and evidence of disavowal. Horowitz views the stress-response syndrome as a normal human reaction to traumatic events, one that can balloon into the more severe form of posttraumatic stress disorder.

Pennebaker has explored the role of emotional disclosure and sharing in assuaging the impact of traumatic experiences such as bereavement. The experimental research of Pennebaker and his colleagues showed that health benefits resulted from writing about traumatic events. Although these beneficial effects have been demonstrated for a wide range of traumatic experiences, the evidence is weaker in the case of normal bereavement. Pennebaker suggests that the benefit of written disclosure lies in helping the individual to organize the experience, to clarify his or her psychological state to others, and to translate emotional experience into the medium of language.

Like Pennebaker's approach, Janoff-Bulman's is most applicable to traumatic bereavments. She emphasized the role of meaning in recovery, describing the changes in assumptive worldviews that occur following traumas. Fundamental assumptions people hold about themselves and their relationship to the world can be shattered by the death of a loved one. People normally hold the view that they are worthy, that the world is benevolent, and that what happens to them makes sense. With these assumptions shattered, the bereaved person struggles to integrate the experience. The process of achieving this integration involves rebuilding the inner world, re-establishing meaning, adjusting old assumptions, and/or trying to accept new ones.

Parkes's psychosocial transition model is comparable in many respects to the model of Janoff-Bulman's because he also argues for a gradual changing of assumptions and one's internal model of the world. He specifies components in the process of changing assumptions, including preoccupation with thoughts of the lost person, painful dwelling on the loss, and attempts to make sense of it, either by fitting the experience into existing assumptions or by modifying those assumptions.

Stephen Fleming and Paul Robinson have analyzed how the process of meaning-making can go wrong and how it is possible for clinicians to use principles of cognitive behavior therapy for complicated grief. A bereaved person's distress may be perpetuated in a cognitive-affective loop, in which beliefs (e.g., about the bereaved's own responsibility for an accident causing the death) play on the emotions, which in turn prevent reconstruction of beliefs. They also cover the issues of attachment to the deceased, traumatic grief complications, and the impact of counterfactual thinking (the generation of imagined alternatives to actual events) on grieving.

## Two Integrative Models

George Bonanno's and Stacey Kaltman's four-component model is an example of contemporary attempts to synthesize current research into an integrative model. These investigators describe several components as fundamental in the grieving process and suggest ways in which they may interact during bereavement: (1) context of loss, risk factors such as type of death, gender, and cultural setting; (2) the continuum of subjective meanings associated with loss, appraisals of everyday matters as well as existential meanings; (3) the changing representations of the loss relationship across time, including the persisting bond with the deceased; and (4) the role of coping and emotion-regulation processes that can relief or aggravate the stress of the loss. Emotion-regulation research has provided a theoretical framework to understand how adjustment in bereavement could be enhanced. The general theory suggests how the regulation or even dissociation of negative emotions and enhancement of positive emotions may foster adjustment to bereavement and, likewise, enable identification of spontaneous or automatic processes in grieving.

Margaret Stroebe and Henk Schut have attempted a different type of integration in their dual-process model of coping with bereavement. The dual processes refer to two different types of stressors: those associated with the lost person, so-called loss orientation, and restoration orientation, those associated with the secondary upheavals that are also consequences of bereavement. The focus of attachment theory on the nature of the lost relationship is consistent with loss orientation. Similarly, cognitive stress theory's identification of a range of substressors suggests the need to include the additional tasks of restoration orientation in the model, because these too are associated with distress and anxiety. For example, it may be necessary to acquire new skills (e.g., cooking or dealing with finances) that had been the domain of a deceased spouse. The model suggests that coping with the two types of stressors is a dynamic and fluctuating process, labeled "oscillation," that incorporates confrontation and avoidance of different components at different times, and includes both positive and negative reappraisals. For example, at any one moment a bereaved person may be dealing with new tasks (restoration-oriented) and feeling good about mastering these, only to be interrupted by a piece of music, perhaps, that is a reminder of the deceased (loss-oriented) and that brings on feelings of sadness. This perspective integrates the processes identified by Folkman and Nolen-Hoeksema, and is also consistent with Bonanno's emotion-regulation component.

## Conclusions

Theorizing in the field of bereavement is still marked by a pluralism of approaches, but attempts at integration have begun. Investigators are also looking more to related bodies of research such as emotion theory to derive sound theoretical and empirical hypotheses. Further probing of the biological bases of grief and grieving is needed. Likewise, broadening of theoretical interest from the single stressor of bereavement to a general psychology of loss, focusing on diverse phenomena, could encourage the formation of general principles. Nevertheless, the understanding of grief has deepened significantly during the past few decades, in part because of the theoretical grounding of fine-grained empirical research on social and cognitive processing.

*See also:* CONTINUING BONDS; FREUD, SIGMUND; GRIEF AND MOURNING IN CROSS-CULTURAL PERSPECTIVE; MOURNING

### Bibliography

Archer, John. "Broad and Narrow Perspectives in Grief Theory: A Comment on Bonanno and Kaltman (1999)." *Psychological Bulletin* 127 (2001):554–560.

Archer, John. *The Nature of Grief: The Evolution and Psychology of Reactions to Loss.* London: Routledge, 1999.

Bonanno, George. "Grief and Emotion: A Social-Functional Perspective." In Margaret Stroebe, Robert Hansson, Wolfgang Stroebe, and Henk Schut eds., *Handbook of Bereavement Research: Consequences, Coping and Care.* Washington, DC: American Psychological Association Press, 2001.

Bonanno, George, and Stacey Kaltman. "Toward an Integrative Perspective on Bereavement." *Psychological Bulletin* 125 (1999):760–776.

Bowlby, John. *Attachment and Loss,* Vol. 3: *Loss: Sadness and Depression.* London: Hogarth, 1980.

Cohen, Sheldon, and Thomas Wills. "Stress, Social Support, and the Buffering Hypothesis." *Psychological Bulletin* 98 (1985):310–357.

Cook, Alicia, and Kevin Oltjenbruns. *Dying and Grieving: Life Span and Family Perspectives.* Ft. Worth, TX: Harcourt Brace, 1998.

Fleming, Stephen, and Paul Robinson. "Grief and Cognitive-Behavioral Therapy: The Reconstruction of Meaning." In Margaret Stroebe, Robert Hansson, Wolfgang Stroebe, and Henk Schut eds., *Handbook of Bereavement Research: Consequences, Coping and*

*Care.*Washington, DC: American Psychological Association Press, 2001.

Folkman, Susan. "Revised Coping Theory and the Process of Bereavement." In Margaret Stroebe, Robert Hansson, Wolfgang Stroebe, and Henk Schut eds., *Handbook of Bereavement Research: Consequences, Coping and Care.* Washington, DC: American Psychological Association Press, 2001.

Freud, Sigmund. "Mourning and Melancholia." *Standard Edition of the Complete Works of Sigmund Freud,* edited and translated by J. Strachey. London: Hogarth Press, 1957.

Harvey, John. *Perspectives on Loss: A Sourcebook.* Philadelphia: Taylor & Francis, 1998.

Horowitz, Mardi. *Stress Response Syndromes.* Northvale, NJ: Aronson, 1986.

Horowitz, Mardi J. "Psychological Response to Serious Life Events." In V. Hamilton and D. M. Warburton eds., *Human Stress and Cognition: An Information Processing Approach.* Chichester, England: John Wiley & Sons, 1979.

Jacobs, Selby. *Traumatic Grief: Diagnosis, Treatment, and Prevention.* New York: Taylor & Francis, 1999.

Jacobs, Selby. *Pathologic Grief: Maladaptation to Loss.* Washington, DC: American Psychiatric Press, 1993.

Janoff-Bulman, Ronnie. *Shattered Assumptions: Toward a New Psychology of Trauma.* New York: Free Press, 1992.

Janoff-Bulman, Ronnie, and Michael Berg. "Disillusionment and the Creation of Value: From Traumatic Losses to Existential Gains." In John Harvey ed., *Perspectives on Loss: A Sourcebook.* Philadelphia: Taylor & Francis, 1998.

Lazarus, Richard, and Susan Folkman. *Stress, Appraisal, and Coping.* New York: Springer, 1984.

Lindemann, Eric. "Symptomatology and Management of Acute Grief." *American Journal of Psychiatry* 101 (1944):141–148.

Nadeau, Janice W. "Meaning Making in Family Bereavement: A Family Systems Approach." In Margaret Stroebe, Robert Hansson, Wolfgang Stroebe, and Henk Schut eds., *Handbook of Bereavement Research: Consequences, Coping, and Care.* Washington, DC: American Psychological Association Press, 2001.

Neimeyer, Robert. *Meaning Reconstruction and the Experience of Loss.* Washington, DC: American Psychological Association Press, 2001.

Nolen-Hoeksema, Susan. "Ruminative Coping and Adjustment to Bereavement." In Margaret Stroebe, Robert

Hansson, Wolfgang Stroebe, and Henk Schut eds., *Handbook of Bereavement Research: Consequences, Coping and Care.* Washington, DC: American Psychological Association Press, 2001.

Parkes, Colin Murray. "Bereavement as a Psychosocial Transition: Processes of Adaptation to Change." In Margaret Stroebe, Wolfgang Stroebe, and Robert Hansson eds., *Handbook of Bereavement: Theory, Research and Intervention* New York: Cambridge University Press, 1993.

Parkes, Colin Murray, and Robert Weiss. *Recovery from Bereavement.* New York: Basic Books, 1983.

Parkes, Colin Murray. *Bereavement: Studies of Grief in Adult Life.* London: Tavistock Publications, 1972.

Pennebaker, James, Emmanuelle Zech, and Bernard Rimé. "Disclosing and Sharing Emotion: Psychological, Social, and Health Consequences." In Margaret Stroebe, Robert Hansson, Wolfgang Stroebe, and Henk Schut eds., *Handbook of Bereavement Research: Consequences, Coping, and Care.* Washington, DC: American Psychological Association Press, 2001.

Pennebaker, James. *Emotion, Disclosure, and Health.* Washington, DC: American Psychological Association, 1995.

Raphael, Beverley. *The Anatomy of Bereavement.* New York: Wiley, 1983.

Rosenblatt, Paul. "A Social Constructionist Perspective on Cultural Differences in Grief." In Margaret Stroebe, Robert Hansson, Wolfgang Stroebe, and Henk Schut eds., *Handbook of Bereavement Research: Consequences, Coping and Care.* Washington, DC: American Psychological Association Press, 2001.

Rosenblatt, Paul. "Grief: The Social Context of Private Feelings." In Margaret Stroebe, Wolfgang Stroebe, and Robert Hansson eds., *Handbook of Bereavement: Theory, Research and Intervention.* New York: Cambridge University Press, 1993.

Rubin, Simon, and Ruth Malkinson. "Parental Response to Child Loss across the Life Cycle: Clinical and Research Perspectives." In Margaret Stroebe, Robert Hansson, Wolfgang Stroebe, and Henk Schut eds., *Handbook of Bereavement Research: Consequences, Coping and Care.* Washington, DC: American Psychological Association Press, 2001.

Shaver, Philip, and Caroline Tancredy. "Emotion, Attachment and Bereavement: A Conceptual Commentary." In Margaret Stroebe, Robert Hansson, Wolfgang Stroebe, and Henk Schut eds., *Handbook of Bereavement Research: Consequences, Coping and Care.* Washington, DC: American Psychological Association Press, 2001.

Stroebe, Margaret, and Henk Schut. "Meaning Making in the Dual Process Model of Coping with Bereavement." In Robert Neimeyer ed., *Meaning Reconstruction and the Experience of Loss.* Washington, DC: American Psychological Association Press, 2001.

Stroebe, Margaret, and Henk Schut. "The Dual Process Model of Coping with Bereavement: Rationale and Description." *Death Studies* 23 (1990):197–224.

Stroebe, Margaret, Wolfgang Stroebe, Henk Schut, Emmanuelle Zech, and Jan van den Bout. "Does Disclosure of Emotions Facilitate Recovery from Bereavement? Evidence from Two Prospective Studies." *Journal of Consulting and Clinical Psychology* 70 (2002):169–179.

Walter, Tony. "A New Model of Grief: Bereavement and Biography." *Mortality* (1996):7–25.

Worden, J. William. *Grief Counseling and Grief Therapy: A Handbook for the Mental Health Practitioner.* New York: Springer, 1991.

MARGARET STROEBE
WOLFGANG STROEBE
HENK SCHUT

# TRAUMATIC

Traumatic grief is defined as profound emotional trauma and separation distress suffered after the death of a loved one. It includes yearning, searching for the deceased, and excessive loneliness resulting from the loss. Traumatic loss sometimes happens when a death is sudden, unexpected, preventable, or of a child. Traumatic loss shatters the bereaved person's worldview, leaving him or her feeling overwhelmed and helpless.

## Diagnostic Considerations

There are four diagnostic criteria for traumatic grief: (1) Traumatic grief occurs after the death of a significant other and includes distress that intrudes into the victim's consciousness; (2) traumatic grief lasts at least two months; (3) traumatic grief symptoms cause clinically significant impairment in social, occupational, or other important areas of functioning; and (4) traumatic grief includes eleven marked, persistent symptoms that include behaviors, thoughts, and emotions. These symptoms reflect the bereaved person's feelings of devastation as a result of the death. Behaviors include frequent efforts to avoid reminders of the deceased (e.g., thoughts, feelings, activities, people, and places); and displaying excessive irritability, bitterness, or anger related to the death. Thoughts include purposelessness or feelings of futility about the future; difficulty imagining a fulfilling life without the deceased person; difficulty acknowledging the death; and a shattered worldview. Emotions include a subjective sense of numbness, detachment, or absence of emotional responsiveness; being stunned, dazed, or shocked; a sense that life is empty or meaningless; and feeling that part of oneself has died. Traumatic grief does not refer to the cause of the disorder or aspects of the death, but rather to the bereaved person's actual experience.

Two related forms of grief are delayed grief and complicated grief. Delayed grief is not apparent initially, but appears within the first six months of bereavement. Delayed grief might be particularly difficult to diagnose. Complicated grief occurs at least fourteen months after the death. The scholars who constructed this definition avoided twelve months because anniversaries often cause intense turbulence in the bereaved individual. Complicated grief includes intruding thoughts or avoidance behavior that is severe enough to interfere with daily functioning. The intruding thoughts may include unbidden memories or fantasies about the lost relationship, strong spells of severe emotion related to the lost relationship, and distressingly strong yearnings for the deceased. The avoidance symptoms include feeling far too alone or personally empty; excessive avoidance of people, places, or activities that remind the bereaved of the deceased person; unusual levels of sleep disturbance; and loss of interest in work, social activities, care taking, or recreational activities. These symptoms last for at least one month.

There are several differences between traumatic grief and complicated grief. One difference is in the duration of symptoms. For traumatic grief, the duration is at least two months, with no specification about the time since the death. For complicated grief, the duration is only one month, and the grief occurs within fourteen months of the bereavement. Another difference is in sleep disturbance. Only complicated grief includes sleep difficulty, which may be a result of the person being overly aroused. A third difference is that traumatic grief includes symptoms that reflect the devastation in the bereaved person's life caused by the death.

There are no closely related symptoms in complicated grief.

Although they are related, traumatic grief is distinct from depression, anxiety, separation anxiety disorders, and posttraumatic stress disorder (PTSD)—anxiety that develops when a person has a traumatic experience. Traumatic grief occurs among a significant minority of bereaved individuals, and lasts several years.

## Origins

Persons who develop traumatic grief might do so in two ways. One way involves death that is sudden and violent, as in natural disasters, accidents, and criminal violence. The bereaved person might develop problems feeling close to loved ones because of a pervasive change in his or her view of the world, even when he or she was not vulnerable in the first place. In this case, in addition to traumatic grief, the bereaved person might also develop PTSD, as well as other psychiatric disorders. A second way involves loss of a significant other for a person with a vulnerable attachment style. The vulnerability might be the result of inherited characteristics, early nurturing experience, or some combination of the two. The person who was already vulnerable might develop other psychological disorders as well as traumatic grief.

An example of traumatic grief could be a mother who lost a beloved son in the 1995 bombing of the Alfred P. Murrah Federal Building in Oklahoma City. This mother makes strong efforts to avoid going through her son's belongings, and has excessive anger and bitterness about the death. Cognitively, she has no purpose, and has difficulty imagining a fulfilling life without her son, or even acknowledging his death. Her worldview is shattered. Emotionally, she feels numb and shocked that part of her life has died. Overall, she feels that life is empty or meaningless. These symptoms last for several months.

Another example of traumatic grief could be a father whose daughter is killed in an automobile accident, and whose mother dies six months later. He does not grieve immediately after the death of his daughter because he concentrates on caring for his sick mother. When his mother dies, both deaths "hit" him. Now, he is in a state of disbelief. Indeed, his chief complaint is that he still cannot believe what had happened. He feels overwhelmed by the losses. He obsesses over the details of the daughter's accident, and can think of little else. He has frequent episodes of crying, provoked by any reminders of his daughter or mother. His work performance suffers, and his relationships with the rest of the family deteriorate. He feels useless to himself and others, at least partly because much of his life had been devoted to being a good father and son. He loses a sense of security, and no longer trusts the world he now views as unpredictable. These problems persist for the six months since his mother's death, and he dreads the anniversary of his daughter's death.

## Clinical and Research Literature

Grief counseling has proliferated in the last decades of the twentieth century. Professionals provide conferences and workshops on grief. Institutions and communities provide programs for bereaved individuals conducted by grief therapists, or operated on a mutual support basis by lay leaders. Journals that publish research about grief include *Death Studies*, *Omega: The Journal of Death and Dying*, *Journal of Loss and Trauma*, and *Suicide and Life-Threatening Behavior*.

One thorough research project by Gabriel Silverman and colleagues that was published in *Psychological Medicine* looked at the quality of life among sixty-seven adults widowed four months earlier. Those with traumatic grief reported significantly impaired quality of life, more so than persons with major depression or PTSD. Another research project by Holly Prigerson and colleagues, published in the *American Journal of Psychiatry*, focused on a vitally important aspect of traumatic grief—suicidal ideas. Among seventy-six young adults who had a friend commit suicide, those with traumatic grief were five times more likely to consider suicide themselves compared to those who were depressed. Still other research has shown that violent deaths, more than anticipated deaths, lead to problems for bereaved persons. For example, reviewing a broad selection of different research projects on bereavement, George Bonanno and Stacey Kaltman in 1999 concluded that adults whose spouse died unexpectedly (i.e., from suicide, homicide, or an accident) experienced PTSD at a higher rate than those whose spouse died of natural causes (e.g., cancer, congestive heart failure). Apparently, violent deaths may not only lead to the development of trauma reactions, but they also tend to exacerbate the more general grief response. Traumatic grief is different from other disorders and from general grief.

One major research project on grief analyzed twenty-three separate studies of bereaved persons. In each project, some participants were randomly assigned to receive some form of psychosocial intervention (psychotherapy, counseling, or facilitated group support). Others were randomly assigned to a control condition. Overall, treatment helped: Those who received treatment recovered more than those in the (nontreated) control group. However, the difference was small, which suggests that most people were helped, but some were not helped.

One reason for this finding could be time. Those people whose loved one died some time ago recovered more than those whose loved one died recently. Another reason could be age; younger clients fared better than older ones in grief therapy. Still a third reason could be the type of bereavement. Grief counseling for normal grievers had essentially no measurable positive effect, whereas grief counseling for traumatic grief was helpful. Apparently, grief therapy is particularly suitable for mourners experiencing protracted, traumatic, or complicated grief reactions. Conversely, grief therapy for normal bereavement is difficult to justify.

## Theory

A useful theory to treating traumatic grief focuses on making meaning in the aftermath of bereavement. A counselor who uses this perspective might help a bereaved daughter to see that her father had lived a full life or accomplished his last major goal before he died. This daughter might find meaning in the fact that her father's life had some purpose, or had come full circle. This perspective to treating traumatic grief is different from a medical model, which might emphasize controlling the symptoms such as crying spells or depression. This approach is also different from the vague though well-intentioned assumption that sharing feelings in a supportive environment will promote recovery. Sharing feelings might help, but making meaning is an added step that involves reconstructing one's individual, personal understanding.

Supporting this view, one study found that for 70 to 85 percent of persons who experienced a sudden, potentially traumatizing bereavement, the search for meaning played a compelling role in their grief. A significant minority, however, apparently coped straightforwardly with their loss, without engaging in deep reflection about its significance. For those who seek meaning and find none, the loss can be excruciating. These people report suffering intensely on a variety of dimensions. Conversely, bereaved persons who find a measure of meaning in the loss fare better, rivaling the adjustment of those who never feel the need to undertake a quest for meaning in the first place. In addition, many of those who find answers as to why the loss occurred revisit these answers in the months that follow.

Related to this emphasis on meaning is the assumption that describing one's thoughts and emotions about the traumatic grief promotes cognitive restructuring. Sharing with others allows bereaved individuals to restructure the difficult aspects of the loss, to explore ways of viewing themselves, and to regulate their own distressing emotions and bodily reactions.

## Suggestions for Fostering Recovery

Traumatic grief does not respond to psychotherapy that is focused on interpersonal adjustment such as how the person gets along with others, whether or not this therapy includes antidepressant medicine. However, therapy that is oriented toward helping bereaved persons develop insight about their own lives, or to change their thoughts and behaviors, can be effective for those suffering from traumatic grief. Successful therapy includes a genuine, empathic, and compassionate relationship with the therapist and education about the bereavement.

Specific therapy for traumatic grief would focus on separation and traumatic distress. Treatment would include educating bereaved individuals about this type of distress, and helping them cope with it. Treatment would also include working with the person to lessen the distress in the first place. In addition, therapy should help the bereaved person to adapt to the new status caused by the bereavement and to the new roles required by that status.

Further, therapy would recognize that a quest for meaning plays a prominent role in grieving, at least for those who are bereaved by the sudden death of a loved one. When a bereaved person is struggling for significance in the loss, a counselor should facilitate this process. Grief counselors should be cautious, however, about instigating a search for meaning in the minority of bereaved persons do not spontaneously undertake such a search. These individuals might be coping adaptively already. Further, making meaning is more an activity than an achievement. Early, provisional meanings of the death tend to be revisited as the reality of living with loss raises new questions and undermines old answers.

Simply disclosing oneself to others may or may not be helpful, depending in part on the receptivity of would-be listeners. Some potential listeners may be overwhelmed by repeated communication of intense negative states, such as sadness or distress. Talking to them about feelings may drive away people who might otherwise offer some interpersonal support. Therefore, bereaved individuals need to be selective in the persons with whom they share their thoughts and feelings.

A public ritual such as a funeral or memorial can offer powerful closure for traumatic grief. Other approaches include letter writing to the deceased person and/or empty chair work—going through an exercise in which one imagines the deceased person to be sitting beside him or her in an empty chair, talking to the person as if they were still alive. Several useful procedures revolve around the concept of forgiveness for both self and others.

*See also:* DISASTERS; GRIEF COUNSELING AND THERAPY; SUICIDE; TRIANGLE SHIRTWAIST COMPANY FIRE

### Bibliography

Bagge, R. W., and Jeffrey M. Brandsma. "PTSD and Bereavement: Traumatic Grief." In Lee Hyer and Associates eds., *Trauma Victim: Theoretical Issues and Practical Suggestions.* Muncie, IN: Accelerated Development, 1994.

Bonanno, George A., and Stacey Kaltman. "Toward an Integrative Perspective on Bereavement." *Psychological Bulletin* 125 (1999):760–776.

Davis, Christopher G., Susan Nolen-Hoeksema, and Judith Larson. "Making Sense of Loss and Benefiting from the Experience: Two Construals of Meaning." *Journal of Personality and Social Psychology* 75 (1998):561–574.

Horowitz, Mardi J., Bryna Siegel, Are Holen, George A. Bonnano, and C. Milbrath. "Diagnostic Criteria for Complicated Grief Disorder." *American Journal of Psychiatry* 154 (1997):904–910.

Jacobs, Shelby, Carolyn Mazure, and Holly Prigerson. "Diagnostic Criteria for Traumatic Grief." *Death Studies* 24 (2000):185–199.

Neimeyer, Robert. "Searching for the Meaning of Meaning: Grief Therapy and the Process of Reconstruction." *Death Studies* 24 (2000):541–558.

Prigerson, Holly G., et al. "Influence of Traumatic Grief on Suicidal Ideation among Young Adults." *American Journal of Psychiatry* 156 (1999):1994–1995.

Reynolds, Charles F., et al. "Treatment of Bereavement-Related Major Depressive Episodes in Later Life: A Controlled Study of Acute and Continuation Treatment with Nortriptyline and Interpersonal Psychotherapy." *American Journal of Psychiatry* 156 (1999):202–208.

Silverman, Gabriel K., Selby C. Jacobs, Stanislav V. Kasl, M. Katherine Shear, Paul K. Maciejewski, Simona S. Noaghiul, and Holly G. Prigerson. "Quality of Life Impairments Associated with Diagnostic Criteria for Traumatic Grief." *Psychological Medicine* 30 (2000):857–862.

LILLIAN M. RANGE

# GRIEF AND MOURNING IN CROSS-CULTURAL PERSPECTIVE

Most contemporary writing about grief and mourning is based on research with people living in twentieth-century North America and Western Europe. The research uses theories and methods that grew from the same geographical area and historical period. Although reports about mourning and grief have come from many cultures, there is no consensus among bereavement scholars about what concepts explain the most about the ways in which individuals and communities respond to death in different cultures. The question here is: How might scholars develop more cross-cultural concepts of grief and mourning that can describe the thoughts, emotions, interpersonal interactions, myths, and rituals that follow significant deaths in other times and places?

## Grief Varies with Culture

Cross-cultural study looks outward, seeking an opening to the varieties of cultural expression around the world; but it also looks inward, because an understanding of others can enrich our understanding of our own culture. All people are shaped to some extent by the culture into which they are born. The human expression of grief is no less a product of culture than marital or religious customs or symbols.

Many writers make a distinction between grief and mourning, saying that grief is a subjective state, a set of feelings that arise spontaneously after a significant death, whereas mourning is a set of rituals or behaviors prescribed by culture's tradition. In this distinction, thought, or cognitive meaning, is largely absent from both grief and mourning because the former is mostly feelings and the latter mostly action.

But this distinction between grief and mourning does not hold up to cross-cultural scrutiny. The concept of grief is an artifact of modernity. Grief as a real subjective state grows from a culture that prizes and cultivates individual experience. There is no equivalent to the term *grief* in some other languages; indeed, in some cultures, as in Japan, the concept of emotions that are only in the individual seems foreign. For the Japanese, individual identity is a function of social harmony. Emotions are part of family or community membership, sensed among the members so as to create a harmonized atmosphere.

The term *mourning* does have a Japanese equivalent, *mo*, which refers both to the ritual responses to death and the emotions—commonly defined in the West as "grief"—that attend them. *Hitan*, the Japanese word that comes closest to the English word *grief*, means "sadness and sorrow," but the word does not imply that the emotions were brought about by death or loss. *Hitan* cannot be used in a way that refers to a self-evident inner reality. One translation into Japanese of the English phrase "She was in grief" might be *"Kanojyo-ha hitan no naka ni iru,"* ("she grief of inside being there"), but that is not a complete sentence. A complete sentence might be *"Kanojyo-ha hitan ni sizundeiru."* (She grief to sinking.) An infinitive like "to sink" is needed because in Japanese *Hitan* cannot be a complete state on its own. With no Japanese word available, writers introducing Western psychological ideas have transliterated *grief* as *guri-fu*. A rather simple bit of cross-cultural research is to ask how the English concepts of grief and mourning are translated in other languages and to look at how different words may change the way people might think about grief.

## Grief As an Instinct

At the biological level it might seem that grief is universal. In every culture people cry or seem to want to cry after a death that is significant to them. Grief, then, could be conceived as an instinctual response, shaped by evolutionary development. Perhaps animals grieve. Primates and birds display behaviors that seem similar to humans' in response to death and separation. Instinctual response in this sense is a meta-interpretive scheme programmed into our genetic inheritance, much as nest building or migration is hard-wired into birds. The response is aroused by the perception of specific situations (i.e., harm, threat, success or failure, and breeding opportunities). Culture, of course, influences how people appraise situations, yet similar perceptions of events trigger similar instinctual responses. A significant death, then, might be regarded as a universal trigger of grieving emotions, although which death is significant enough spark such a response depends on the value system of a particular culture. Universal instincts, then, might provide the basis for concepts that could explain behavior in all cultures.

The model of grief based on the attachment instinct, propounded by John Bowlby and his followers, has generated a large body of research and advice for clinical practice. In this theory, a significant death triggers a response much like that which a child feels upon separation from his or her mother. First the child protests and tries to get back to the mother. Then the child despairs of returning to the mother but remains preoccupied with her. Finally the child loses interest in the mother and is emotionally detached from her upon her return. Grief after a significant death, this theory holds, follows the same preprogrammed sequence of behaviors. Attachment is instinctual behavior that has survival value because it keeps the child in close proximity to the mother for protection from predators. Humans are attached to individuals all through their lives. When they die, individuals

*In Calexico, California, mourners attend the memorial service for a United Farm Workers (UFW) migrant worker who was killed at a lettuce farm during a strike to protest working and living conditions for migrant farmers. This kind of death may trigger questions for survivors, such as what does my life mean now that the person is dead? And what hope is there for our community?* STEPHANIE MAZ/CORBIS

experience separation and loss, and so must reorganize their attachments to match the new reality. From observation one knows that human children develop different styles of attachment, depending on the mother's bond with the child. Some bereavement research indicates that attachment styles in childhood predict bereavement style in adulthood. Attachment theorists have claimed that attachment is biological and, though influenced by culture, nonetheless functions similarly in all cultures; therefore, attachment theorists claim, the attachment instinct undergirds a cross-cultural model of grief.

But attachment alone is not a sufficient basis for a meta-interpretative cross-cultural comparison. First, there is little cross-cultural research on attachment: "Core tenets of attachment theory are deeply rooted in mainstream Western thought" (Rothbaum

2000, p. 1094). Until experts can specify which attachment behaviors of parents and children are universal, which are cultural, and how both universal and cultural attachments behaviors are observed in grief, a cross-cultural theory based on attachment remains elusive.

Moreover, the template used in attachment bereavement theory is young children's responses when separated from their mothers. In grief, the theory holds, adults are all like children seeking reunion with the deceased person. The theory does not consider that as people mature their attachments become broader. The young child knows himself only in relationship with the mother. As the child matures, each level of social membership or identity is also an attachment (e.g., clan, village, tribe, nation, religious tradition). At each level, separation becomes a less plausible explanation for grief because attachments to individual people become interwoven with social systems and cultural meanings that cannot be reduced to biological inheritance. In the individualistic culture of the modern West, with its eroding attachments to larger social systems, primary social relationships are limited largely to monogamy and the nuclear family. Such individualistic relationships approximate but do not duplicate the mother-child bond, so the latter is of limited value in explaining the former.

Death may arouse instinctual responses other than those that are labeled "grief" in Western culture. Some deaths in Western culture, for example, arouse a trauma response. It may be that the trauma response is as universal as the separation response in attachment. Trauma and loss are different meta-interpretative schemes. In the West, some deaths are traumatic; some traumas are not death; and some deaths are not traumatic. In modern Western culture, rape evokes a response similar to that of a traumatic death. Other cultures may have meta-interpretive schemes that apply to death (revenge, submission, and so on) but may not apply in the modern West. In traditional Chinese culture, for example, death presents the problem of pollution. One of the purposes of funeral rituals was to protect men from pollution while women took the pollution on themselves, thereby purifying the deceased for the next life. Whatever meta-interpretative schemes, other than mourning, are aroused by death, or by a particular death, would seem to be culture-specific, though the emotions aroused would be similar to those aroused when the meta-interpretative scheme was evoked in other circumstances. Death presents pollution or powerlessness in some cultural contexts as much as it presents separation, loss, and sometimes trauma in the modern West. As scholars develop a cross-cultural theory based on instincts, they will need to give as much attention to other instincts as they have given to attachment and trauma.

At a symbolic and metaphoric level, death is used to understand other realities in human life. One way to identify the instincts evoked by death might be to investigate a culture's use of death as a metaphor. For traditional Chinese women, for example, death was like marriage. In the West the concept of grief is applied to other separations and losses, such as divorce, and to other traumas, such as home invasion. Clearly the meanings ascribed to death in all cultures are not limited to separation, loss, and trauma. Students who are familiar with another culture might ask, "On what other occasions are themes from bereavement applied?"

## Grief As Finding Meaning

Beyond instinctual responses lies the realm of thought or meaning, which has been excluded from many definitions of both grief and mourning. When a significant person dies, the issue of meaning is central for the survivors: What does this death mean? What does this life mean? What did this person mean to me and to this community? Western individuals who successfully come to terms with a traumatic death may change how they think about themselves, how they relate to others, and how they view life in general. Changes experienced by individuals in other cultures might be just as wide-ranging but cover spheres not experienced in the West.

The task of meaning making is done in the interchange between the individual and the culture. An individual seeks to make sense of his or her experience using cognitive or mental models that are supplied by that individual's culture. When modern Western people look at sickness, for example, they see it in terms of germs and viruses. People in other times and places might have seen sickness in terms of witchcraft or magic. The movement between cultural models and mental models goes in both directions. Cultural models are objectifications formed over time from the inner experiences of a group of individuals in a community. Cultural forms, including models of grief, change as individuals in the culture accommodate their cognitive models to make sense of the deaths in their lives. Cross-cultural research in grief, therefore, may include studies in the same culture at different times in order to understand the factors that influence the changes.

The constructivist model grounds grief both in the interplay between cultural meaning and individual meaning and in concrete interpersonal relationships. By contrast, in attachment theory, the purpose of grief is to reconstruct the autonomous individual, who, in large measure, leaves the dead person behind in order to form new attachments, which he or she accomplishes by working through and resolving negative feelings. Grief is conceptualized as an innate process that, if allowed to run its course, will bring the survivor to a new equilibrium in a changed world that no longer includes the dead person.

In the constructivist model the purpose of grief is the construction of durable biographies—individual and social narratives—of the dead person and of the survivors that enable the living to integrate the dead into their lives. Narratives are stories. People make sense of their lives by telling a story that makes sense of their past and present experiences. Whether they are aware of it or not, people have an autobiography that they are constantly revising in light of new experiences. If something like an important death does not make sense, it is "nonsense." Both individuals and societies want to keep seeing the world the same way, but sometimes death forces one to see the world differently. When an individual sees the world differently, he or she constructs a new narrative, a new biography of themselves and of the person who has died.

In the constructivist model, the process by which people make sense of their world is social interaction. When something important happens in individuals' lives, they do not just think about it; they talk about it with others. Grief and mourning do not just happen inside a person; they happen in the interactions between people. In most cultures over human history, myth and ritual provide the intersubjective space in which one can construct the meaning of the deceased's life, death, and influence over the survivors' lives. In contemporary Western culture, in which rituals and myths from earlier times have fallen into disuse, intersubjective space is characterized by informal verbal and nonverbal interaction aimed largely at communicating shared meaning. Often people see contemporary communities constructing their narrative by inventing new rituals that allow community members to feel a sense of togetherness.

Narratives, of course, are maintained within different kinds of social systems. Differences in mourning behavior might be attributable to structural differences in societies. It appears that mourning in small, closely knit societies is different from mourning in large, more loosely knit societies in which primary membership is in the nuclear family. In small networks such as a rural village, members

identify with people outside the nuclear family. When someone dies, people find substitutes for the deceased in their immediate social environment. For example, many adults already care for a child in a small network, so when a parent dies, other adults can easily move into the parent role. Death disrupts the social structure of small networks, so mourning rites focus on rehabilitating the damaged role system by reallocating roles. For example, when the elder dies, someone must be moved into the role of elder. In more complex, loosely knit networks, such as in an industrialized city, most individual deaths do not significantly affect the larger social system, so grief loses any larger social meaning and becomes a matter of individual family and psychic readjustment. As scholars move toward cross-cultural concepts, they might study grief in villages and cities in the same cultural tradition before asking whether or how grief and mourning are different in different cultures.

Each level of social system maintains narratives—individual narratives, family narratives, community narratives, media narratives, subculture narratives, and cultural meta-narratives. Each level of social membership is also a kind of attachment. Narratives from higher-level systems provide the materials from which the narratives at lower levels can be constructed. The narrative at any level is constrained by the structure of the level or levels above it. For example, the narrative in the family limits the narrative in individual constructs, and the narratives of the culture and religious traditions to which the family belongs limit the family narrative. Contemporary Western culture evinces a relative freedom of the individual from the constraints of cultural narrative. The price individuals pay for such freedom is a sense of inner loneliness that sociologists call "anomie." One point of cross-cultural comparison is the degree of cultural or religious narrative constraint on individuals and families in their attempt to form their own meaningful response to a significant death.

Constructivist theory allows a definition of relative "normality" of grief within various cultural contexts. When the narratives are congruent within and between levels, grief may be stressful, but is not problematic. Grief becomes problematic when there is an incongruence of narratives within a level (e.g., an individual who is unable either to accept or reject contradictory stories). Did she die because it was God's will or because the doctor made a mistake? Grief also becomes problematic when narratives at different levels of the hierarchy are incongruent (e.g., when individual's thoughts and emotions are incongruent with the family's understanding of what thoughts and expressions of emotion are acceptable).

A community's grief becomes problematic to itself when there are contradictory or incongruent narratives, such as when there is a disagreement about whether the high school students who kill themselves after they have killed other students should be memorialized along with those whom they killed. A community's grief becomes problematic to other communities when the narratives are incongruent; for example, a gang's revenge narrative can be in conflict with the larger culture's narrative of the "rule of law" in which only the state can define and punish wrongful death.

## The Grief Police

When an individual and family grieve within larger social narratives, larger political dynamics are in play. Society polices grief; it controls and instructs the bereaved about how to think, feel, and behave. All societies have rules about how the emotions of grief are to be displayed and handled. In some cultures, for example, those who grieve should talk to the dead, and in other cultures the name of the dead should never be spoken. Such coercion is, of course, a top-down matter. Those who do not conform to the social expectations are labeled aberrant. In contemporary psychotherapeutic culture, aberrant grief is deemed pathological. In other cultures the labels would be different—counterrevolutionary in communist cultures, sinful or idolatrous in monotheistic religions.

One cross-cultural project seeks to compare the rules about the emotional expression of grief. Anthropologist Unni Wikan, for example, compared the rules in Egypt and Bali, both Islamic cultures. She found that in that in Bali, women were strongly discouraged from crying, while in Egypt women were considered abnormal if they did not incapacitate themselves in demonstrative weeping.

When people understand that every society polices grief, they can use several cross-cultural studies that are otherwise misleading. The most common mistake in cross-cultural study of grief is to confuse the official worldview of the culture, its

dominant mythology or theology, with what individuals in the culture actually do. Research on grief and mourning is descriptive: people describe what they do, but official theologies are prescriptive—they dictate patterns or norms of behavior. In the cross-cultural study of grief, it will not do simply to explicate the beliefs of the culture's religious tradition as if those beliefs described the lived experience of individuals and communities. The stated beliefs of a culture are often the rationale for the rules by which grief is policed; they are often merely the directives for public performances that may or may not really express the mourners' private thoughts and feelings. If individuals understand the cultural basis of their own prescriptions, they will be better able to describe the cultural basis for prescriptions in other times and places.

The distinction between descriptive and prescriptive becomes somewhat muddy in contemporary Western society because psychology and sociology are the contemporary forms of myth. Often research hypotheses are drawn from cultural prescriptions, and researchers' findings pass quickly into popular culture as prescriptions and directives. It is common for those who do research on grief to find their descriptions of grief turned into counsel given by therapists and media personalities. Students might study grief in American culture by doing a serious analysis of the advice given on television talk shows; bilingual students could compare advice given on English and non-English language stations.

A potentially useful direction for the cross-cultural study of grief might be to compare rules about grief and to analyze how the prescriptions on grief coordinate with other prescriptions. For example, students could look at the rules for expressing grief as part of the rules for being a man or a woman. In traditional China, women wailed laments but men sat silently. A fruitful topic might be an investigation into the rigor of a culture's rule enforcement (e.g., the severity of the penalty, if any, that a weeping man would face in a culture that discourages male crying).

## Continuing Bonds with the Dead

The resolution of grief often includes cultivating bonds of emotion and meaning with the dead. In other words, people who are important to us become part of our inner conversation and remain there after they die. If someone says, "I would not do that because my mother would be disappointed in me," the mother is part of that person's inner conversation even though the mother is not present and may never find out if the person did it or not. People who are important to us may continue to play important roles in our lives and in the life of the community for many years after they have died. Throughout history this kind of persistent communion with the dead is a recurring behavioral pattern, far more common than an outright severing of all bonds. Indeed, Western psychologists and psychiatrists became interested in individual grief—the ways in which survivors live on after a death—precisely at the time when the cultural narrative about afterlife had begun to wane.

If students use continuing bonds as the focus of cross-cultural study, relatively straightforward methods can yield data that are useful in a comparison of the roles played by the dead in individual lives and cultural systems. Historian Ronald Finucane traces changes in Western history from ancient Greek culture to the present in various areas: how the dead appear to the living, what the dead want from the living, and what the living ask of the dead. Comparisons can be made between the changes in the relationship of the living and the dead during the mourning period.

Continuing bonds with the dead in individuals and families become integrated into the collective representations that mediate the culture to the individual. Emile Durkheim, one of the founders of sociology, said that collective representations play a major role in developing social solidarity and identity in tribes, ethnic groups, and nations. Grief and the rituals of mourning install the dead into collective memory as well as into the individual memories of those who knew them. The memory of soldiers who die in war, for example, are evoked during patriotic celebrations in every culture. Grief then takes on a political meaning because one of the functions of all cultural narratives is to uphold the legitimacy of those who hold economic and political power. Only a few centuries ago, cultural narratives said that kings ruled by divine right. Twenty-first-century narratives say that presidents rule because they are elected by the people. The political question is, however, which collective narrative controls the continuing bond with the dead? To what end or in whose interest is grief policed? In Chinese ancestor rituals, the dead remain part of the family, defining the values by which the family lives and creating the shared identity of the living members of the family. The memories of martyrs energize living people who believe in the ideas or causes for which they died. A fruitful area of student study might be an analysis of the political, historical, or cultural meaning of deaths in which the grief is shared by the wider society, not just by family members.

## Conclusion

The cross-cultural study of grief can apply to many levels of human life: at the biological level, the instincts aroused by a significant death; and at the linguistic level, the meanings and usage of the words that refer to what people call grief and mourning in the West. In the interchange between individuals and culture, grief and the resolution of grief happens in a series of nested cultural narratives—family, clan, tribe, community, subcultural, nation, religious tradition, and so on. At each level those narratives supply the plots for the construction of individual narratives that endow grief with meaning and manageability. Grief interacts with every level of this hierarchy, from family patterns to political legitimacy.

*See also:* AFTERLIFE IN CROSS-CULTURAL PERSPECTIVE; CONTINUING BONDS; DEATH SYSTEM; GRIEF: THEORIES; MOURNING

### *Bibliography*

Barley, Nigel. *Grave Matters: A Lively History of Death around the World.* New York: Henry Holt and Company, 1997.

Bowlby, John. *Attachment and Loss,* 3 vols. New York: Basic Books, 1980.

Finucane, Ronald C. *Ghosts: Appearances of the Dead and Cultural Transformation.* Amherst: Prometheus Books, 1996.

Geary, Patrick J. *Living with the Dead in the Middle Ages.* Ithaca, NY: Cornell University Press, 1994.

Klass, Dennis. "Ancestor Worship in Japan: Dependence and the Resolution of Grief." *Omega: The Journal of Death and Dying* 33, no. 4 (1996):279–302.

Miller, Sheldon I., and Lawrence Schoenfeld. "Grief in the Navajo: Psychodynamics and Culture." *International Journal of Social Psychiatry* 19, nos. 3 and 4 (1973): 187–191.

Neimeyer, Robert, ed. *Meaning Reconstruction and the Experience of Loss*. Washington DC: American Psychological Association, 2001.

Rosenblatt, Paul C., Patricia R. Walsh, and Douglas A. Jackson. *Grief and Mourning in Cross-cultural Perspective*. New York: Human Relations Area Files Press, 1976.

Rothbaum, Fred, John Weisz, Martha Pott, Mikaye Kazuo, and Gilda Morelli. "Attachment and Culture: Security in the United States and Japan." *American Psychologist* 55, no. 10 (2000):1093–1104.

Simonds, Wendy, and Barbara Katz Rothman. *Centuries of Solace: Expressions of Maternal Grief in Popular Literature*. Philadelphia: Temple University Press, 1992.

Smith Jane Idleman, and Ynonne Yazbeck Haddad. *The Islamic Understanding of Death and Resurrection*. Albany: State University of New York Press, 1981.

Smith, Robert J. *Ancestor Worship in Contemporary Japan*. Stanford, CA: Stanford University Press, 1974.

Stroebe, Margret, Mary Gergen, Kenneth Gergen, and Wolfgang Stroebe. "Broken Hearts or Broken Bonds: Love and Death in Historical Perspective." *American Psychologist* 47, no. 10 (1992):1205–1212.

Walter, Tony. *The Revival of Death*. London: Routledge, 1994.

Watson, James L., and Evelyn S. Rawski. *Death Ritual in Late Imperial and Modern China*. Berkeley: University of California Press, 1988.

Wikan, Unni. "Bereavement and loss in two Muslim communities: Egypt and Bali compared." *Social Sciences and Medicine*, 27, no. 5 (1988):451–460.

DENNIS KLASS

# GRIEF COUNSELING AND THERAPY

How individuals and families cope with dying, death, grief, loss, and bereavement is as unique as a fingerprint. The response to the death of a family member, relative, or close friend places one in the category of "bereaved." Those who are bereaved experience grief, a person's response or reaction to loss, which encompasses physical, psychological, social, and spiritual components. How one copes with other life events and adapts to one's present and future is also part of the grieving process.

In the broadest context losses can be thought of as the loss of one's possessions, one's self, one's developmental losses, or one's significant others. Historically, many grief counselors and grief therapists have chosen to follow the popular "grief counseling theory of the time." However, in the twenty-first century there are constantly changing theories regarding grief and loss, and new challenges and questions raised by researchers, clinicians, and the bereaved themselves regarding what is or is not helpful during the bereavement process. In addition to counselors and therapists as defined in the more traditional sense, "grief and bereavement specialists" have emerged to help people deal with their grief, both before and after death.

## What Is Grief Counseling and Grief Therapy?

In *Grief Counseling and Grief Therapy* (1991), the clinician and researcher William J. Worden, Ph.D., makes a distinction between grief counseling and grief therapy. He believes counseling involves helping people facilitate uncomplicated, or normal, grief to a healthy completion of the tasks of grieving within a reasonable time frame. Grief therapy, on the other hand, utilizes specialized techniques that help people with abnormal or complicated grief reactions and helps them resolve the conflicts of separation. He believes grief therapy is most appropriate in situations that fall into three categories: (1) The complicated grief reaction is manifested as prolonged grief; (2) the grief reaction manifests itself through some masked somatic or behavioral symptom; or (3) the reaction is manifested by an exaggerated grief response.

Does a person need "specialized" grief counseling or grief therapy when grief, as a normal reaction to loss, takes place? Are people not able to cope with loss as they have in the past or are individuals not being provided the same type of support they received in previous generations? Individual and family geographic living arrangements are different in the twenty-first century than in past years. People have moved from rural to urban centers, technology has altered the lifespan, and the health care decisions are becoming not only more prevalent but often more difficult. Cost and legal issues become factors in some cases. Today, ethics committees in hospitals and long-term care facilities are available to help families and health care providers arrive at common ground. Traumatic and violent deaths have also changed the bereavement landscape. What had helped individuals and families in the past in many situations has eroded and the grief and bereavement specialist, or the persons, agencies, and organizations providing those services, is doing so in many cases out of default. Grief counseling is used not only by individuals and families, but in many situations by schools, agencies, and organizations, and in some cases by entire communities affected by death.

## Can Sources Other than Professionals Act As Counselors?

Social worker Dennis M. Reilly states, "We do not necessarily need a whole new profession of . . . bereavement counselors. We do need more thought, sensitivity, and activity concerning this issue on the part of the existing professional groups; that is, clergy, funeral directors, family therapists, nurses, social workers and physicians" (Worden 1991, p. 5). Although there are professionals who specialize in grief counseling and grief therapy, there are still many opportunities for the bereaved to seek support elsewhere.

Churches, synagogues, community centers, and neighborhoods were (and in many cases still are) the "specialized" support persons. Cultural traditions and religious rituals for many bereaved persons did and still do meet their needs. In the past, friends, family, and support systems listened to one another and supported individuals through the death of their loved ones, during the rituals after the death, and during the days, months, and years after the death. Although American culture is used to having immediate gratification, not everyone processes grief at the same rate. Some cope and adapt to a death sooner, while others, based on similar factors and variables, may take a longer period of time.

Grief counseling and grief therapy are not for everyone and are not "cures" for the grieving process. Counseling and therapy are opportunities for those who seek support to help move from only coping to being transformed by the loss—to find a new "normal" in their lives and to know that after a loved one dies one does not remove that person from his or her life, but rather learns to develop a new relationship with the person now that he or she has died. In *A Time to Grieve: Mediations for Healing after the Death of a Loved One* (1994) the writer Carol Crandall states, "You don't

heal from the loss of a loved one because time passes; you heal because of what you do with the time" (Staudacher 1994, p. 92).

## Goals of Grief Counseling and Therapy

Professionals believe that there are diverse frameworks and approaches to goals and outcomes of the grief counseling and therapy process. Robert Neimeyer believes, "The grief counselor acts as a fellow traveler [with the bereaved] rather than consultant, sharing the uncertainties of the journey, and walking alongside, rather than leading the grieving individual along the unpredictable road toward a new adaptation" (Neimeyer 1998, p. 200). Janice Winchester Nadeau clearly reminds grief counselors and grief therapists that it is not only individuals who are grieving, but entire family systems. A person is not only grieving independently within the family system, but the interdependence within the family also affects one's actions and reactions. According to Worden there are three types of changes that help one to evaluate the results of grief therapy. These are changes in: (1) subjective experience, (2) behavior, and (3) symptom relief.

## Where Is Counseling Done and In What Format?

Grief counseling and grief therapy are both generally done in a private area (generally an office setting). These private areas may be within hospitals (for both inpatients and their families and for outpatients), mental health clinics, churches, synagogues, chemical dependency inpatient and outpatient programs, schools, universities, funeral home aftercare programs, employee assistance programs, and programs that serve chronically ill or terminally ill persons. Additional sites might include adult or juvenile service locations for criminal offenders. Private practice (when a counselor or therapist works for herself) is another opportunity to provide direct client services.

Treatment options include individual, couple, and family grief counseling or grief therapy, and/or group counseling. Sessions are approximately one hour in length, or longer for individual sessions. Groups are either closed (for a set period of time with the same small group of individuals attending each session) or open (offered once, twice, or several times a month and open to whoever attends without previous registration or intake). Grief support groups are generally not therapy groups, but supportive therapeutic environments for the bereaved. Group sessions are generally ninety minutes long. Treatment plans are used by grief counselors in most individual and family counseling situations and in all grief therapy situations.

In some cases a grief counselor may be meeting with a person one time to help "normalize" what the person is feeling, while grief therapy requires multiple sessions. In most cases a fee is paid by the person utilizing the grief counseling or grief therapy service and is either paid on a sliding scale or by self-pay, third-party insurance, victim assistance programs, community charitable care programs, or some other type of financial arrangement. Some hospice/palliative care programs offer grief counseling and grief therapy services at no charge for a limited number of sessions.

Crisis intervention hotlines emphasize assessment and referral, and residential settings for children, adolescents, and adults are also locations where grief counseling or grief therapy is utilized. A number of grief therapists do consulting work with other grief therapists or grief counselors, or with agencies or organizations.

## Approaches Used

There is not one method or approach. Each counselor or therapist has his or her own techniques that he or she utilizes because they are effective, although counselors often defer to other techniques that suit a particular person much better based on the individual's circumstances. Counseling and therapy techniques include art and music therapy, meditation, creation of personalized rituals, bibliotherapy, journaling, communication with the deceased (through writing, conversations, etc.), bringing in photos or possessions that belonged to the person who has died, role playing, bearing witness to the story of the loved one, confiding in intimates, and participating in support groups. The "empty chair" or Gestalt therapy technique is also an approach widely used by grief counselors and grief therapists. This technique involves having an individual talk to the deceased in an empty chair as if the deceased person were actually sitting there; afterward, the same individual sits in the deceased person's chair and speaks from that person's perspective. The dialogue is in first person, and a

counselor or therapist is always present. The Internet also provides a number of sites that address the topic of grief and provide links to counseling services and organizations.

## When Is Grief Counseling or Therapy Needed?

According to many experts, including John Jordan, grief counseling and grief therapy approaches are challenged and redesigned by new research. In their article published in the journal *Death Studies*, Selby Jacobs, Carolyn Mazure, and Holly Prigerson state, "The death of a family member or intimate exposes the afflicted person to a higher risk for several types of psychiatric disorders. These include major depressions, panic disorders, generalized anxiety disorders, posttraumatic stress disorders; and increased alcohol use and abuse" (Jacobs, Mazure, and Prigerson 2000, p. 185). They encourage the development of a new *Diagnostic and Statistical Manual of Mental Disorders* (DSM) category entitled "Traumatic Grief," which would facilitate early detection and intervention for those bereaved persons affected by this disorder.

Researcher Phyllis Silverman is concerned that messages dealing with the resolution of grief, especially a new category entitled "Traumatic Grief," may do more harm to the mourner. She states, "If this initiative succeeds ('Traumatic Grief'), it will have serious repercussions for how we consider the bereaved—they become persons who are suffering from a psychiatric diagnose or a condition eligible for reimbursed services from mental health professionals" (Silverman 2001). She feels the new DSM category may help provide the availability of more services, but believes it is important to consider what it means when predictable, expected aspects of the life cycle experience are called "disorders" that require expert care. When one thinks of grief counselors and grief therapists one is again reminded that grief and bereavement is a process, not an event.

How do persons cope and adapt? Grief counseling or grief therapy intervention can be useful at any point in the grief process, before and/or after a death. Consider the following story from a thirteen-year-old who was participating in a bereavement support group for teens, and wrote the following biography in response to her mother's death:

My mom was born on January 12, 1942, in Minnesota. She had a brother who was 11 years younger than her and she had a mother and father. . . . She was married in 1965. She then had two children. In 1981 my mom found out she had a brain tumor. She then got spinal meningitis and was in a coma for 3 weeks. She then was blind, but overcame blindness in a few months. One year later she was diagnosed with breast cancer. She had a mastectomy. She had chemotherapy for about one year. Then she had uterine cancer and had her uterus removed. Then she was diagnosed with lung cancer. She tried to hold on, but she was so sick. She went around in a wheelchair and was in and out of the hospital for weeks. But she got worse. On September 21, 1984, my mom died. I think that everyone who knew her will never forget her. *(Wolfe and Senta 1995, p. 218)*

In this case, anticipatory grief took place before the actual death occurred. It is the assumption that if one knows a person is going to die then the grief after the death is not as intense as if the death were a surprise. Grief counseling and therapy do not only begin after death. However, is this really true? According to clinician, researcher and writer Therese Rando,

Anticipatory grief is the phenomenon encompassing the process of mourning, coping, interaction, planning, and psychosocial reorganization that are stimulated and begun in part in response to the awareness of the impending loss of a loved one and the recognition of associated losses in the past, present, and future. It is seldom explicitly recognized, but the truly therapeutic experience of anticipatory grief mandates a delicate balance among the mutually conflicting demands of simultaneously holding onto, letting go of, and drawing closer to the dying patient. *(Rando 2000, p. 29)*

## How Effective Is Counseling?

Various factors will determine the effectiveness of grief counseling or grief therapy. Some counselors and therapists utilize instruments to measure the effectiveness of the helping sessions. Others rely upon subjective comments from the client, his or her family, behavior observations, cognitive responses, symptom relief, and spiritual discussions. Because grief is a process and not an event, what takes place along the grief journey may alter how one continues to cope and adapt to loss. One loss or multiple losses do not make a person immune to future hardships.

The clinical psychologist and researcher Nancy Hogan and her colleagues state, "Understanding this 'normal' trajectory of bereavement has been hampered, in part, by the use of questionnaires designed to measure psychiatric dysfunction, such as depression and anxiety, rather than instruments specifically developed to measure grief" (Hogan, Greenfield, and Schmidt 2000). The Texas Revised Inventory of Grief (TRIG), the Grief Experience Inventory (GEI), and the Inventory of Traumatic Grief (ITG) have been criticized by Hogan. She believes, "The lack of grief instruments with solid psychometric properties continues to limit the ability of researchers to study basic questions related to the bereavement process. To date, the normal trajectory of grief has still not been empirically defined" (Hogan, Greenfield, and Schmidt 2000, pp. 1–2).

## Qualifications of Counselors and Therapists

Most grief counselors and grief therapists have advanced degrees in either social work, nursing, psychology, marriage and family therapy, medicine, theology, or a related field. Many have terminal degrees. Those with only undergraduate degrees may find employment doing grief counseling for various organizations or agencies, but any type of third-party reimbursement (in the United States) would be minimal if not impossible without a graduate degree. A number of universities around the world offer undergraduate course work on death-related topics and graduate courses drawing upon subjects related to grief counseling and therapy. Certification in the field of grief counseling and grief therapy is offered by the Association for Death Education and Counseling, while other organizations in death-related areas such as the American Association of Suicidology and the U.S. National Hospice and Palliative Care Organization, also offer certification specific to their subject areas. In the United States and Canada, there are no state or provincial grief counseling or grief therapy certification requirements as of 2001. However, to practice in the United States in fields such as social work, psychology, or marriage and family therapy, a state license is required.

## Rewards

Carl Hammerschlag, a Yale-trained psychiatrist, spent twenty years with Native Americans in the Southwest of the United States. While working as a family physician he was introduced to a patient named Santiago, a Pueblo priest and clan chief, who believed there were many ways for one to heal. In his book, *The Dancing Healers* (1988), Hammerschlag shares a time when Santiago asked him where he had learned how to heal. Hammerschlag rattled off his medical education, internship, and certification. The old man replied, "Do you know how to dance?" To humor Santiago, Hammerschlag got up and demonstrated the proper dance steps. "You must be able to dance if you are to heal people," Santiago admonished the young doctor, and then stated, "I can teach you my steps, but you will have to hear your own music" (p. 10).

Grief counseling and grief therapy are metaphorically, learning to dance. Each person looks at the world through a different set of lenses, and as a result, one's dances, steps, upbringing, hopes, dreams, and healing are dependent on many factors. Grief counseling and therapy are about sharing a person's journey before or after a death. The focus is on companioning them during difficult times and not rescuing or fixing them, and about listening to their stories and thoughts with an open mind and open heart. The grief counselor or therapist's role in helping others is about transitions and new beginnings for those with whom they work. There are many rewards for clients, counselors, and therapists.

*See also:* DEATH EDUCATION; GRIEF: ANTICIPATORY, FAMILY

### Bibliography

Corr, Charles A. "Children, Adolescents, and Death: Myths, Realities and Challenges." *Death Studies* 23 (1999): 443–463.

Hammerschlag, Carl A. *The Dancing Healers.* San Francisco: Harper San Francisco, 1988.

Hogan, Nancy S., Daryl B. Greenfield, and Lee A. Schmidt. "Development and Validation of the Hogan Grief Reaction Checklist." *Death Studies* 25 (2000):1–32.

Jacobs, Shelby, Carolyn Mazure, and Holly Prigerson. "Diagnostic Criteria for Traumatic Grief." *Death Studies* 24 (2000):185–199.

Nadeau, Janice Winchester. *Families Making Sense of Death.* Thousand Oaks, CA: Sage, 1998.

Neimeyer, Robert. *Lessons of Loss: A Guide to Coping.* New York: McGraw-Hill, 1998.

Rando, Therese A. *Clinical Dimensions of Anticipatory Mourning.* Champaign, IL: Research Press, 2000.

Rubin, Simon Shimshon. "The Two-Track Model of Bereavement: Overview, Retrospect, and Prospect." *Death Studies* 23 (1999):681–714.

Sofka, Carla J. "Social Support 'Internetworks,' Caskets for Sale, and More: Thanatology and the Information Superhighway." *Death Studies* 21 (1997):553–574.

Staudacher, Carol. *A Time to Grieve: Mediations for Healing after the Death of a Loved One.* San Francisco: Harper San Francisco, 1994.

Stroebe, Margaret, and Henk Schut. "The Dual Process Model of Coping with Bereavement: Rationale and Description." *Death Studies* 23 (1999):197–224.

Wolfe, Ben, and John R. Jordan. "Ramblings from the Trenches: A Clinical Perspective on Thanatological Research." *Death Studies* 24 (2000):569–584.

Wolfe, Ben, and Linda Senta. "Interventions with Bereaved Children Nine to Thirteen Years of Age: From a Medical Center-Based Young Person's Grief Support Program." In David W. Adams and Eleanor J. Deveau eds., *Beyond the Innocence of Childhood: Helping Children and Adolescents Cope with Death and Bereavement,* Vol. 3: *Beyond the Innocence of Childhood.* Amityville, NY: Baywood, 1995.

Worden, J. William. *Grief Counseling and Grief Therapy,* 2nd edition. New York: Springer, 1991.

### Internet Resources

Silverman, Phyllis R. "Living with Grief, Rebuilding a World. Innovations in End-of-Life Care." In the Innovations in End-of-Life Care [web site]. Available from www.edc.org/lastacts.

BEN WOLFE

# HEAVEN

Heaven is usually thought of as some sort of afterlife, a view provoking hopeful belief on the one hand and skepticism on the other. Yet heaven is much more complicated and diverse than that. Those influenced by Western civilizations generally think of heaven along Christian lines—or along caricatures of those lines, as in cartoons featuring harps, wings, and clouds. On a less crude level, heaven is often derided as part of a system of reward and punishment, a "pie in the sky" or "opiate" diverting people from attention to bettering their present, earthly lives. However, the essence of the word "heaven" worldwide is the transformation of chaos into order (from the Greek *kosmos*, meaning "ordered universe"), meaninglessness into meaning, and selfishness into compassion. Its attributes are usually joy, contentment, harmony, compassion, bliss, community, love, and a vision of God, or even union with God.

Different languages have different words for "heaven." More than that, the concepts behind the words vary radically among different religions and even within each religion. Judaism, Christianity, Islam, Buddhism, Hinduism, and innumerable other religions display a panoply of beliefs. Heaven is not necessarily an afterlife. The most universal meaning of the concept is a joyful existence beyond the plane of human ordinary thought, feelings, and perceptions: a "new life" or "different life." To be sure, that concept is frequently expressed as afterlife, but it is also expressed as timeless or eternal life, transcendent life, and even

as a state of existence in which humans can live a life free of illusion during their present lives. Heaven often means the realm of god(s), a distinctly different meaning from heaven as a goal for humans, but the two ideas readily merged.

Beliefs in a life different from what humans daily experience appeared at least as early as the Neolithic period. Primal religions number in the thousands and most were characterized by belief in a world other than, or beyond, physical life, a "place" or "time" (in Aborigine, "dreamtime") of a different, often greater, reality than that of the physical world. Often this was accompanied by the belief that humans have contact with that other world both during life and after death. Shamans, oracles, and dreams could be consulted in order to be in touch with the other life. The spirits of the dead remained with us or else entered that other life where we would eventually join them. Burials included artifacts that the dead person would be able to use in the other world. The other world could be a place or a state of being. Often (but not necessarily) it was conceived as being "up" because of its early association with the sun, moon, and stars.

Another way of understanding heaven is what it is not. Many traditions worldwide affirmed that original cosmic order was somehow deformed by the actions of ignorant or malicious humans or deities. In Western religions this understanding was expressed in a chronological story: In the beginning was Paradise, where all was in harmony; a conscious choice was made by humanity (Adam and Eve) to reject that harmony, thereby disrupting

The Glory of Heaven *by Francesco Maria Russo shows an angel pointing upward to the skies. Despite varying opinions about the afterlife, many agree on what heaven looks like.* CORBIS

cosmos; at the end of time, harmony would be restored. In that sense, Paradise was where humankind begins and heaven where humankind ends, but often the two were blended and taken as synonyms. Most religions perceived a perennial tension between the world as it originally was and was meant to be (the Golden Age), the world as it was now, and the world as it would be when chaos and evil were overcome and cosmos restored.

## Ancient Ideas

In ancient Egypt, cosmic order and justice (*ma'at*) prevailed, but it could be temporarily distorted by human evil. The *ka* (spirit of the dead person) descends into the underworld to be judged by the gods (specifically Anubis). The unjust were tormented in scorching heat, while those living in accordance with ma'at rose into the eternal realm of the gods. Ancient Mesopotamian religion had little idea of heaven: The dead were doomed to unending gloom and wretchedness in the darkness

beneath the earth, with the dubious consolation that the rich and powerful in earthly life would have a less miserable status in the afterlife.

In early Greco-Roman religion, the souls of the dead descended to the shadowy underworld of Hades; later, the spirits of heroes were believed to escape that fate and to rise instead into the Elysian Fields, which were variously located in an earthly garden, a mysterious "land" to the West, or among the stars. Elysium, wherever located, was a place of fulfillment of earthly delights. Greco-Roman philosophers focused on the virtue of intellect and on the perfect world of ideas, toward which humans attempt to strive but can never attain. Perfect being was always beyond human reach; still, Plato argued for the immortality of the soul, which consisted of a combination of the basic life force common to all creatures with mind (*nous*), which was unique to humans. Plato tended to view the fields of heaven as a temporary abode for the soul before it returned to the earth in a reincarnation. The cycle of reincarnation ended with the purification of the soul—losing its bodily needs and desires—and its final union with Being itself. Cicero (106–43 B.C.E.), the great Roman lawyer, linked the divine with justice and saw Elysium as a reward for those who served the Roman state. The Later Platonists of the third to fifth centuries C.E. taught that everything in the cosmos yearns for such union and that everything, once elevated beyond matter into pure spirit, will eventually attain that happy end.

## Eastern Religions

The major Eastern religions (Hinduism, Buddhism, Taoism, and Confucianism) had less-defined concepts of heaven and hell than the Abrahamic, monotheist religions (Judaism, Christianity, and Islam), because their distinction between good and evil tended to be less sharp.

*Hinduism.* Hinduism is a modern name for a complex combination of traditions in India. The first great period of Hinduism was that of the Vedas, about 1500 to 1000 B.C.E. In Vedic religion, the dead, who retained personal consciousness, went to a lush green place with beautiful music. Those more devout and observant of ritual were closest to the gods; those lax in ritual farther away. Between about 700 and 100 B.C.E., the Upanishads (sacred scriptures) reshaped Hinduism. They taught that the essence of heaven was to be freed from *maya* (illusion), with which humans surrounded themselves in this earthly life, which blocked them from reality, and immersed them in the desire, pain, and suffering inherent in this life. Freedom from maya was obtained through knowledge, love, labor, and the spiritual disciplines known as yogas. Hinduism affirmed that souls, having entered the world, were bound to a long series of rebirths. The deeds of their lives formed a tendency of character, which they could improve or impair in future lives. Heaven became merely a transitory state between rebirths. Ritual remained central, however, and in the early c.e., *bhakti* (the practice of devotion to a particular god, such as Vishnu) became a way of escaping the cycle of rebirth. For true heaven was union with Brahman (the ultimate divine principle), a union in which consciousness of self disappeared. In this state, known as *samadhi,* one's soul was reabsorbed into the unbounded "allness" of being as a drop of water being merged with the sea.

*Buddhism.* Buddhism, partly rooted in early Hindu culture, also posited a state of cyclical flux, *samsara*. Samsara might lead one into rebirth on the earth as a human or an animal, or it might pass one through a variety of temporary heavens. Until the cycle was broken, both the earth and heavens were intermediate states between one incarnation and the next, and each incarnation was characterized by *dukkha* (suffering), *tankha* (craving for worldly possessions), and *anicca* (impermanence). One's actions (*karma*) would bear fruit in future lives, which could be improved through meritorious, compassionate deeds. Ultimate heaven was escape from the cycle into union with the deepest reality. This required the extended practice of meditation and detachment—from objects, from people, and from oneself—that constituted enlightenment and, ultimately, *nirvana*. Nirvana was the extinction of all concerns, desires, and fears of one's finite self; it was complete union with ultimate reality beyond human comprehension.

Classical Buddhism had no concept of individual immortality: The *atman* ("soul") is immortal but only as part of the world soul. The individual is simply as one candle flame that is a part of fire itself. One form of Buddhism, "Pure Land Buddhism," originating about 500 c.e., resembled Western religions more by focusing on the saving power of a *bodhisattva* (a perfectly wise person whose life was dedicated to compassion for all living, suffering beings) who brought the compassionate into a heaven ("pure land") with beautiful meadows, lakes, rivers, music, and ease. But even in this variety of Buddhism, the pure land was a prelude to the essential attainment of nirvana.

*Taoism.* Taoism was a syncretistic blend of philosophical, shamanistic, and popular religions, a tradition crystallized in the *Tao Te Ching,* a book attributed to Lao Tzu in the 600s B.C.E. Tao had three aspects: Tao as the ultimate underlying basis, reality, and wisdom of existence; Tao as the universe when it is in harmony with the higher Tao; Tao as human life on the earth in harmony with the other Taos. Virtue consisted in losing the false consciousness that the individual has any meaning apart from the whole society or even world. Philosophical Taoism, which believed in no other world beyond this one, influenced Confucianism (the teachings of Kung Fu-tzu in the 500s B.C.E.). Popular, religious Taoism had tales of journeys to heaven by immortal sages. Like Taoism, Confucianism (the dominant religion of China until it was replaced by Marxism), centered on harmony. Heaven was the underlying harmony of being, not a habitation for humans or even gods in the usual sense. The point of Confucian teaching was maintaining accord with that harmony in human society, particularly the family. Worldly as it was, however, Confucianism held an implicit belief in immortality in its worship of ancestors, who continued to be with their earthly family in their present life.

**Secular Religions**

A variety of modern secular religions arose in the past three centuries, including the Enlightenment cult of reason, the Romantic cult of nature, and, the most influential, Marxism. Marxism was a secular religion excluding all metaphysical realities (except, oddly, a semi-divine "history"). Marxist heaven, achieved through "socialism," was the classless society that would emerge at the end of history, a secularization of Judeo-Christian traditions of the Messiah and the millennium. Its success in China was largely owing to its compatibility with the Confucian tradition that the individual is unimportant. Reductionism or "Scientism," the belief that the only truth is scientific truth, suffused twentieth-century thought, adding to skepticism, since heaven is not locatable in the space-time continuum.

*Judaism.* The three great Western monotheistic religions—Judaism, Christianity, and Islam—together accounted for at least one-third of the earth's population at the beginning of the twenty-first century. To treat them in roughly chronological order, ancient Hebrew religion (whose origins are at least as old as the thirteenth century B.C.E.) was founded on belief in a transcendent deity—Yahweh or Adonai (the Lord). Heaven was the dwelling place of the Lord, not a place in which humans lived; humans' only life was this earthly one. With extremely rare exceptions (such as the prophet Elijah) humans did not enter the transcendent plane. The "Kingdom of God," like human life itself, was worked out in this present, earthly existence. The essence of Hebrew religion was that the Lord had made a covenant (contract) with his chosen people, Israel. Only Israelites could participate in that covenant, and only those who were faithful to the covenant as expressed in Torah (the first five books of the Bible) could enter the Kingdom of God. Israel cemented morality into religion. Death brought for most humans a shadowy existence in Sheol (similar to Greco-Roman Hades); for vicious violators of the covenant pain in the fires of the hellish Gehenna; for Israelites faithful to the covenant a blissful existence at the end of the world in the *'olam ha-ba,* the kingdom of God on the earth.

Between 250 B.C.E. and 100 C.E., Hebrew religion shifted its focus. Incessant persecutions by Syrians, Romans, and other conquerors made justice and mercy seem remote or lacking in earthly life, so attention shifted to another sort of life where those qualities, which one expected of the Lord, ruled. Still, that life was not perceived as an afterlife for individuals but instead as the future coming of a Messiah establishing a Kingdom of the Lord at the end of time on this earth. The old division between the Qehel Adonai (those Israelites faithful to the covenant) and those violating the covenant came to imply a divine judgment on each person's life, either immediately at death or at the end of time. Those who lived at the time of the Messiah would live joyful lives together in the community of the Qehel. But what of the deceased? Justice seemed to require that the entire Qehel Adonai, including the dead, should live in the Kingdom when the Messiah came. And since this Kingdom would be a bodily existence on this earth, the dead would be resurrected at the end time, in Jerusalem, and in their own, personal, earthly bodies. This remains the teaching of Orthodox Jews, while the more "liberal" or "secular" tend not to look beyond the present life. In any Jewish scenario, a human being had only the one earthly life.

*Dualism.* Quite different religions and philosophies appeared around the eastern Mediterranean during late pre-Christian and early Christian eras. The most influential philosophy of the ancient Greeks was that of Plato (c. 400 B.C.E.). Platonism was strongly idealist and dualistic, affirming a dichotomy between spirit and matter, spirit being more worthy, essential, and eternal than matter. In the Neoplatonist thought of the early Common Era, pure spirit was defined as real and matter as lacking existence, teetering on the verge of unreality. The Iranian religion Mazdaism (or Zoroastrianism), along with its later successor Manicheism, was based on the belief that there were two almost equally powerful spirit gods. One spirit, Ohrmazd, was the spirit of light and goodness and being; the other spirit, Ahriman, was the spirit of darkness and evil and the void. The two struggled for sovereignty over the cosmos. At last Ohrmazd would destroy Ahriman and bring about the *frashkart,* the end of the corrupted world, and the restoration of the cosmos to its pristine perfection—or better, for there was no longer any potential for spoiling the shining world. Ohrmazd would judge humans and assign the followers of darkness to annihilation and the followers of light to eternal bliss. Meanwhile, at death, bodiless souls ascended toward Ohrmazd and "The Singing House" to the degree that they had transcended earthly concerns.

At the end of the pre-Christian era, Platonic and Mazdaist ideas converged in a movement known as Gnosticism, a variety of religious views. Gnostics, like Mazdaists, posited an eternal struggle between good and evil; like Platonists, they posited the eternal opposition of spirit and matter. Combining the two, they affirmed an eternal struggle between good spirit and evil matter. Whereas Platonists tended to see matter primarily as essentially lack of being, or nothingness, Gnostics saw matter as loathsome evil. The human body was the vile prison for the human spirit, which longed to escape its bondage in order to return to the spirit world with the triumphant Spirit of Good. Being that the Gnostics regarded the body as disgusting, they completely rejected the Jewish and Christian resurrection of the body, affirming instead the immortality of a "soul" defined as pure spirit.

*Christianity.* Early Christian thought, based in Hebrew religion yet influenced by the ambient Platonism of the time, found itself affirming the resurrection of the body yet also allowing for some sort of immortal "soul." For Christian theology from Paul onward, however, "soul" did not mean pure spirit but rather a complete person, body and spirit inseparably together. The basic Christian idea of heaven derived from the Jewish idea of the Qehel Adonai, which Christianity translated and expanded into the salvation of the entire community (Jews and Gentiles together and alike) of those loyal to Christ. For Christianity, death became a moral matter more than a natural one, for the physical death at the end of one's present life meant almost nothing in comparison to the "second death" or "inner death" of those rejecting the Lord. At the end time, the dead would all rise in the very same body they have today and would rejoice in the Kingdom of God announced by the Messiah, Jesus Christ, who would judge between those who love and those who reject love: the latter being in hell and the former in heaven. In some forms of Christianity, the Messiah would usher in and rule a thousand-year Kingdom of God on Earth before all time was dissolved. For Christians, like Jews, heaven meant essentially to be in the presence of the eternal God. Still, in popular belief Christians came to view it as a physical place other than on this earth.

Early Christian theologians bravely faced the problem posed by the undeniable delay between the physical death of an individual and the resurrection at the end of time. There seemed to be an interim period when spirit and body were separated while the spirit awaited resurrection. Once it was admitted that spirit and body could thus be separated even only temporarily, Christianity slid toward the concept (already promoted by Platonism) of an immortality of the "soul" defined as spirit. Even though theology always insisted on the resurrection of the body and downplayed the immortality of an incorporeal spirit, in popular

Christian thought the latter idea gradually became prevalent.

Christian theology also seldom focused on reward and punishment. The hope was not to have God punish sinners, but to have them change their lives so that they could participate in the community of the saved, a heaven of mutual, selfless opening up in love between humans and God and among humans themselves. Again, popular, legend-creating, storytelling, picture-making Christianity preferred more colorful, concrete visions of immortal spirits being either delighted in heaven or else tormented in a hell of darkness and fire. From such popular vision, literature sprang the most celestial poem ever written, *Paradiso,* in *Divine Comedy* of Dante Alighieri (1265–1321).

*Islam.* Founded in the 600s C.E., Islam was based upon the Qur'an (the written revelation to Prophet Muhammad). For Muslims the Qur'an was the dictated, "literal" word of God, yet influences of Judaism and Christianity were clearly present. Islam affirmed the judgment of individuals according to their deeds in this life and loyalty to the teachings of the Prophet, especially compassion and generosity. Islam focused on the formation of a just society on the earth, but the Qur'an was also explicit in affirming the resurrection of the body. At the end of the world, the resurrected dead were judged and then divided into the damned and the faithful, with the latter entering heaven. Heaven was another, better place than this earth, yet a distinctly physical one in its attributes, including elaborate gardens, carpets, banquets, cooling drinks, sex, and other bodily comforts. The Qur'an also permitted metaphorical readings, and al-Ghazali (Algazel) in the twelfth century C.E., along with other Muslim spiritual leaders and writers, such as the medieval Sufis, sensed a deeper reality, realizing that the human mind was incapable, even at its most sublime, of formulating concepts that, like heaven, were rooted in the ultimate and entire reality of the cosmos. For them, heaven meant being in the presence of the eternally just and merciful Allah ("the God").

Concepts of heaven are thus so diverse that skepticism on the overt (literal) level is natural. Yet statements about heaven can be true if are they are taken, not as scientific or historical statements about space-time, but rather as metaphors for deeper and more diverse truths beyond that conceived by materialist reductionists (those maintaining that truth is exclusively to be found in the scientific observation of matter). Modern first-world affluence, encouraging faith in acquisition of objects and power, along with alienation from nature in huge urban conglomerations where the light of the stars and the green of the fields are blotted out, have caused heaven to fade. Yet it is the fulfillment of the deeply rooted human longing for meaning, for a greater understanding of the cosmos, of other people, and of the self, and for greater knowledge and love than are comprised in this present life. No human concept can possibly contain the fullness of reality, but truth is found more by opening out than by narrowing down. There is, and can be, no evidence against the existence of heaven, and hundreds of generations of wise, sensitive, and knowledgeable people have affirmed it and claimed to experience it.

*See also:* AFTERLIFE IN CROSS-CULTURAL PERSPECTIVE; BUDDHISM; CATHOLICISM; HELL; HINDUISM; IMMORTALITY; ISLAM; JUDAISM; NEAR-DEATH EXPERIENCES; PURGATORY

### *Bibliography*

Bernstein, Alan. *The Formation of Hell: Death and Retribution in the Ancient and Early Christian Worlds.* Ithaca, NY: Cornell University Press, 1993.

Bynum, Caroline Walker. *The Resurrection of the Body in Western Christianity, 200–1336.* New York: Columbia University Press, 1995.

Emerson, Jan S., and Hugh Feiss. *Imagining Heaven in the Middle Ages.* New York: Garland Press, 2000.

Hick, John D. *Death and Eternal Life.* London: Collins, 1976.

Himmelfarb, Martha. *Ascent to Heaven in Jewish and Christian Apocalypses.* New York: Oxford University Press, 1993.

Keck, David. *Angels and Angelology in the Middle Ages.* New York: Oxford University Press, 1998.

Kung, Hans. *Eternal Life? Life after Death As a Medical, Philosophical, and Theological Problem.* Garden City, NJ: Doubleday, 1984.

LeGoff, Jacques. *The Birth of Purgatory.* Chicago: University of Chicago Press, 1984.

McDannell, Colleen, and Bernhard Lang. *Heaven: A History.* New Haven, CT: Yale University Press, 1988.

Nickelsburg, George W. E., Jr. *Resurrection, Immortality, and Eternal Life in Intertestamental Judaism.* Cambridge, MA: Harvard University Press, 1972.

Russell, Jeffrey Burton. *A History of Heaven.* Princeton, NJ: Princeton University Press, 1997.

Wright, J. Edward. *The Early History of Heaven.* New York: Oxford University Press, 2000.

Zaleski, Carol. *The Life of the World to Come.* Oxford: Oxford University Press, 1996.

Zaleski, Carol. *Otherworld Journeys: Accounts of Near-Death Experience in Medieval and Modern Times.* New York: Oxford University Press, 1987.

Zaleski, Carol, and Philip Zaleski. *The Book of Heaven: An Anthology of Writings to Ancient and Modern Times.* Oxford: Oxford University Press, 2000.

JEFFREY BURTON RUSSELL

# HEAVEN'S GATE

Marshall Herff Applewhite and Bonnie Lu Nettles founded Heaven's Gate, which was a cult that "combined Christian and some Theosophical doctrines with beliefs in UFO's [and] extraterrestrials" (Wessinger 2000, p. 233). Applewhite and Nettles went by many aliases during their time together. They went by Guinea and Pig, Bo and Peep, Ti and Do, and collectively they were referred to as the "Two." Applewhite and Nettles met at a hospital where Nettles worked in 1972. After the meeting, the two became close friends and Applewhite felt that he had met the "platonic helper he had longed for all his life" (Balch 1995, p. 142). Although they met in 1972, the cult really did not form until they began attracting followers in 1975.

The psychiatrist Marc Galanter argues that Applewhite and Nettles may have suffered from "the psychiatric syndrome of *folie à deux,* in which one partner draws the other into a shared system of delusion" (Galanter 1999, p. 178). They believed that they had come from the Next Level (i.e., heaven) to find individuals who would dedicate themselves to preparing for the spaceship that would take them there (Balch 1995). Their belief that they were from the Next Level is evidenced by both their assertions that they were the two witnesses referred to in Revelation 11 who had risen from the dead after being killed for spreading the

*Identified as "The Two," Marshall H. Applewhite and Bonnie Lu Trusdale (siting at table) hold a meeting in Waldport, Oregon, September 14, 1975, to recruit followers. Over twenty years later, thirty-nine Heaven's Gate members committed suicide at the cult's mansion in Rancho Sante Fe, California.* BETTMAN/CORBIS

word of God, and their belief that Applewhite was the Second Coming of Jesus Christ incarnate, and Nettles was the Heavenly Father.

Applewhite and Nettles believed that evil space aliens called Luciferians had kept people tied to the human level, and therefore incapable of moving to the Next Level. Because Applewhite and Nettles were from the Next Level only they could provide the insight needed to prepare their followers, which made the followers extremely dependent upon their leadership. The process of preparing for the Next Level involved giving up all human attachments and was called the "human individual metamorphis" (Balch 1995, p. 143). Some of the human attachments that cult members were expected to give up included family, friends, sexual relationships, and gender.

**The Followers**

Sociologists Robert Balch and David Taylor and religious scholar Catherine Wessinger have noted that the members led a very regimented, monastic

lifestyle within the cult. First, platonic male-female partnerships were formed, so each member could develop an "awareness of the human qualities each person had to overcome" (Balch and Taylor 1977, p. 842). Second, group members wore uniforms that were designed to conceal their human form in general and, in particular, their gender. Third, Balch notes that the cult had a number of rules and guidelines that "discouraged contact with the outside world" (e.g., do not contact parents or friends), "eliminate[d] old habits and identities" (e.g., no jewelry, no drugs), and "prevent[ed] the formation of interpersonal attachments within the group" (e.g., no sexual relationships) (Balch 1995, p. 149). Additionally, seven members, including Applewhite, had themselves castrated in order to control their sexual urges. Fourth, Applewhite and Nettles had group members engage in a series of activities or rituals that kept them busy for nearly all parts of the day. For example, Balch outlines an activity called "a tone," where group members were to keep themselves focused on a tone produced from a tuning fork at all times while doing other activities. The idea was to keep the group members focused on the Next Level, while ignoring human thoughts.

Many scholars provide commentary on the Heaven's Gate mindset. Marc Galanter points out that although the ideas that Applewhite and Nettles proposed are delusional and unreasonable, many of these concepts taken in isolation are relatively accepted by mainstream society. Balch and Taylor report that most of the people who joined Heaven's Gate accepted many of these ideas in isolation and were particularly intrigued by the way that Applewhite and Nettles had combined them. Moreover, Wessinger reports that those who left the cult still believed its ideas, but could not "adhere to the monastic discipline" (Wessinger 2000, p. 237).

## The Suicide

In 1997 the Heaven's Gate members were living in a mansion in Rancho Santa Fe, California, where the group had been earning a living as web page designers. Applewhite became convinced that Nettles, who had died of cancer in 1985, was piloting a spaceship in the tail of the Hale-Bopp comet to take them to the Next Level. However, they could not go in their human form, so they committed suicide to shed their "physical containers" (Lewis 1998, p. 2).

The suicide began on March 22, 1997. On day one, fifteen members ate applesauce or pudding laced with Phenobarbital and drank vodka, and then other members helped fasten plastic bags around their heads to asphyxiate them. After their deaths, the plastic bags were removed and they were covered with a purple shroud. On the second day, the process was repeated for another fifteen members, followed by another seven members. Finally, the mass suicide was completed when the last two members killed themselves (Wessinger 2000).

In total there were thirty-nine people (20 women and 19 men) who committed suicide. The group members ranged in age from their twenties to age seventy-two. When the bodies were discovered, they were all dressed in black and covered with a purple shroud. On their left shoulders group members had a patch that read "Heaven's Gate Away

Team," which was an apparent reference to the television show *Star Trek: The Next Generation*. Additionally, "Each person had a $5 bill and quarters in the front shirt pocket" (Wessinger 2000, p. 231).

## Differences from Other Forms of Cult Violence

Wessinger notes that Heaven's Gate was different from other cults that have decided to commit violence (e.g., Solar Temple, Jonestown) in that there were no children involved. Heaven's Gate members believed that only adults were prepared to make the decision about whether or not to go to the Next Level.

In Jonestown, Guyana, it is unclear how many people committed suicide versus how many people were murdered. In the Solar Temple cult, primarily a European cult, a number of the members were killed if it was felt that they were too weak to make the decision to kill themselves (Wessinger, 2000). However, Wessinger (2000) argues that there are several lines of evidence that suggest the members of Heaven's Gate were highly committed to voluntarily taking their own lives. First, the highly coordinated suicide (i.e., a farewell tape, preparation of the bodies) suggests that this was a well-thought-out plan. Second, the suicide took several days, yet no one tried to escape, unlike Jonestown where some members hid or escaped into the jungle. Moreover, two group members of Heaven's Gate who did not commit suicide in March later killed themselves in a similar ritualistic manner.

*See also:* CULT DEATHS; JONESTOWN; WACO

### Bibliography

Balch, Robert W. "Waiting for the Ships: Disillusionment and the Revitalization of Faith in Bo and Peep's UFO Cult." In James R. Lewis ed., *The Gods Have Landed.* Albany: State University of New York Press, 1995.

Balch, Robert W., and David Taylor. "Seekers and Saucers: The Role of the Cultic Milieu in Joining a UFO Cult." *American Behavioral Scientist* 20 (1977):839–860.

Galanter, Marc. "The Millennium Approaches." In *Cults: Faith, Healing and Coercion,* 2nd edition. Oxford: Oxford University Press, 1999.

Lewis, James R. "Introduction." *Cults in America.* Santa Barbara, CA: ABC-CLIO, 1998.

Wessinger, Catherine. *How the Millennium Comes Violently: From Jonestown to Heaven's Gate*. New York: Seven Bridges Press, 2000.

DENNIS D. STEWART
CHERYL B. STEWART

# HEIDEGGER, MARTIN

One cannot fully live unless one confronts one's own mortality. This hallmark of existentialist thought owes much to the works of Martin Heidegger. Heidegger (1889–1976) was born in Germany's Black Forest region. He held an early interest in theology and the priesthood, but soon shifted his attention to philosophy. At the University of Freiburg he studied under Edmund Husserl, and eventually succeeded him as chair of philosophy. Heidegger went on to become a leading exponent of phenomenological and existential philosophy, which he blends together in his *Being and Time* (1927).

In this monumental work Heidegger addresses issues related to death, exploring the human being in his or her temporality. This connection is important. For Heidegger, the human being cannot achieve a complete or meaningful life, or any kind of "authentic existence," unless he or she comes to terms with temporality—a uniquely human awareness that a human being is a finite, historical, and temporal being. The awareness of death is a central beginning for understanding this temporality.

According to Heidegger, the human being must understand that he or she is a "being toward death" (*Being and Time*). "As soon as man comes to life," he says, "he is at once old enough to die" (Heidegger 1962, p. 289). Therefore the awareness and acceptance of death is a requirement for authentic existence. Heidegger refers to the inauthentic self as the "they-self." This is the self that is influenced by the crowd or the "they," rather than by its own unique potentialities. The they-self sees death as a subject producing "cowardly fear, a sign of insecurity" (p. 298) and therefore a fit topic to be avoided. Avoidance of death can be achieved by an evasion technique Heidegger refers to as the "constant tranquilization about death." In so doing, the they-self "does not permit us the courage for

*Martin Heidegger (1889–1976) discussed his existential philosophy of humans as "beings toward death" in his seminal work* Being and Time *(1927).* CORBIS

anxiety in the face of death" and promotes instead an "untroubled indifference" (p. 299) about death.

Death, the they-self argues, is something all human beings will experience one day in the undetermined and, therefore, easily ignored future. People experience death in the death of others, and draw conclusions about their own deaths. As Heidegger states, this is as if to say, "One of these days one will die too, in the end; but right now it has nothing to do with us" (p. 297). But for Heidegger death is not a shared experience at all; rather, it is one's "ownmost" and a "non-relational" experience. That is, death is something one can only do by oneself, as each person dies his or her own death.

What is the proper attitude toward one's death? Heidegger rejects the cowardly fear proposed by the they-self. The only proper mood, he argues, when one comes "face-to-face" with the "nothing" that death reveals, is a courageous "anxiety" (p. 310). This anxiety or dread, as the scholar

Michael Gelven points out, is different from fear in that fear attaches to some actual object, while anxiety focuses on freedom and possibility. Only such a mood, says Heidegger, will bring about an "impassioned *freedom towards death*" (p. 311). Heidegger's reflections on death, therefore, are not obsessions with morbidity. Nor does he offer a religious hope of life after death. Rather, healthy anxiety about death provides courageous awareness and acceptance of death, and of one's finitude.

*See also:* ANXIETY AND FEAR; KIERKEGAARD, SØREN; PHILOSOPHY, WESTERN

### *Bibliography*

Gelven, Michael. *A Commentary on Heidegger's* Being and Time. New York: Harper and Row, 1970.

Heidegger, Martin. *Being and Time.* 1927. Reprint, New York: Harper and Row, 1962.

Krell, David Farrell. *Intimations of Mortality: Time, Truth and Finitude in Heidegger's Thinking of Being.* University Park: Pennsylvania State University Press, 1986.

WILLIAM COONEY

# HELL

Most ancient societies and religions had an idea of an afterlife judgment, especially understood as a "weighing of souls," where the gods would reward the faithful worshipers, or honor the great and mighty of society. In later times this notion of afterlife was refined more and more into a concept of the public recognition of the worth of a person's life, its moral valency. The three biblical religions—Judaism, Christianity, and Islam—all apply the notion of the afterlife judgment (and the ideas of heaven and hell which derive from this concept) as essentially a divine adjudication that assesses and pronounces on the worth of a human life. Such beliefs were to become among the most potent mechanisms of social control ever devised.

The classical Greek conception viewed Hades, the land of the dead, as a place of insubstantial shadows. The story of the "House of the Dead" in Homer's *Odyssey* gives a harrowing version of how even heroes are rendered into pathetic wraiths, desperately thirsting after life, waiting for the grave offerings (libations of wine or blood or the smoke of sacrifices) that their relatives would offer at their tombs. Such an afterlife was as insubstantial as smoke, a poetic evocation of the grief of loss more than anything else. There was no life or love or hope beyond the grave. By contrast the gods were immortals who feasted in an Elysian paradise, a marked contrast to the wretched fallibility of mortals whose deaths would reduce them one day, inevitably, to dust and oblivion. This resigned existentialism permeates much of classical Greek and Roman writing. It was not particularly related to the more philosophical notions, as witnessed in Plato, for example, of the soul as an immortal and godlike entity that would one day be freed when released from its bodily entrapment. However, both notions were destined to be riveted together, in one form or another, when the Christians merged the Hellenistic concepts of their cultural matrix with biblical ideas of judgment, as they elaborated the New Testament doctrine of hell.

The classical descriptions of Hades were borrowed and reused by Christians as one of the first popular images for hell. The earliest iconic images of the Resurrection, in Byzantine art, depict Christ descending into Hades, breaking down the doors and liberating the souls of all those who had been consigned to imprisonment in the House of Death before his incarnation. Having broken into the realm of darkness and powerlessness, the Risen Christ is shown stretching out a hand to Adam and Eve, to lift them from their tombs, while the other righteous men and women of the days before his coming all wait in line to be taken with Christ to the glory of heaven. In the Christian era, with common allegiance being given to the idea of the immortality of the soul, Hades was now no longer a place of fading away to nonexistence, but rather a place of permanent imprisonment and sorrow. So it was that Hades made its transition toward becoming hell.

## Scriptural Images of Hell As Devastation

The concept of Hades, reappropriated in this way and set to the service of the proclamation of the Resurrection victory, however, was only one form of the Christian doctrine of afterlife. Both the *Egyptian Book of the Dead* and the Buddhist mythology of the afterlife speak clearly enough of the afterlife as a state of judgment and the punishment of the wicked. This aspect of doctrine eventually came to be part of late Judaism, influencing both rabbinic teachings and the doctrine of Jesus, and thus coming to be a part of late classical Judaism and Christianity (not to mention Islam) to the present day. To chart the development of this stream of thought one needs to look at the prophetic view of God's justice in the world and how it came to be reassessed by the apocalyptic school.

The prophet Isaiah used the image of the fire that falls upon the wicked and established it for later use. The concept of enemy raids that inflicted destructive fires and terrible sufferings on ancient Israel was real enough to need little explanation. The invasion of enemies, however, was a major problem in the Hebrew theology of providence that was often explained by the prophets on the grounds that God only allowed infidel invaders to devastate his holy land because his covenant people had themselves been unfaithful. The image of punishing fire thus became associated in the prophetic literature with unfaithfulness as it was being corrected by God, whose anger was temporary, and who, after the devastation, would restore his people to peace and favor.

The association of ideas is seen clearly in Isaiah 66:24, which becomes a *locus classicus* for Jesus himself, and by this means entered into the Christian tradition as an authoritative logion, or dominical saying. In this passage the prophet speaks of a restored Jerusalem under the Messiah, when the true Israelites who have been restored by God will, in turn, go out to look upon the devastation that they have survived, and will see "those who rebelled against me, for their worm shall not die, and their fire shall not be quenched, and they shall be an abomination to all flesh." This is an image of the aftermath of devastation used as an apocalyptic sign, a theological statement about the ultimate vindication of God and his chosen people, functioning as if it were a rallying cry for the elect to retain trust in God even in times of difficulty, when the covenant hope might seem slight or politically ill-founded. From this stream of prophetic teaching the image of fires of judgment began to coalesce into a concept of hell.

## Apocalyptic Ideas on God's Judgment

In the two centuries preceding the Christian era the prophetic theology of providence faltered. It was overtaken by a new mode of thought called apocalyptic, taken from the style of books that often featured a chosen prophet figure who received special revelations (apocalypses) in the heavenly court, and who then returned to announce the word of divine judgment to his contemporaries. The Book of Daniel is the one great instance of such an apocalyptic book that entered the canon of the Hebrew scriptures, although there were many other instances of such literature that were highly influential in the period between the two testaments, and which colored the Judaism of the time, as well as primitive Christianity.

The image of God's anger against the evil ways of the earth is a common feature of this genre of scripture. The divine judgment is often depicted in terms of God deciding on a definitive end to the cycle of disasters that have befallen his elect people in the course of world history. The literature depicts the forces of evil as beasts, servants of the great beast, often seen as the dark angel who rebelled against God in primeval times. The earthly beasts are, typically, the great empires that throughout history have crushed the Kingdom of God on the earth (predominantly understood as Israel). In apocalyptic imagery the great battle for good and evil is won definitively by God and his angels who then imprison the rebel forces in unbreakable bonds. An inescapable "Lake of Fire" is a common image, insofar as fire was a common biblical idiom for the devastation that accompanied divine judgment. In apocalyptic thought the definitive casting down of the evil powers into the fire of judgment is coterminous with the establishment of the glorious Kingdom of God and his saints. In this sense both heaven and hell are the biblical code for the ultimate victory of God. So it was that in apocalyptic literature the final elements of the Judeo-Christian vocabulary of hell were brought together.

## The Teachings of Jesus on Gehenna

Historically understood, the teachings of Jesus belong to the genre of apocalyptic in a particular way, though are not entirely subsumed by it despite many presuppositions to the contrary in the scholarship of the twentieth century. Jesus taught the imminent approach of a definitive time of judgment by God, a time when God would purify Israel and create a new gathering of the covenant people. It was this teaching that was the original kernel of the Christian church, which saw itself as the new elect gathered around the suffering and vindicated Messiah. Jesus's own execution by the Romans (who were less than impressed by the apocalyptic vividness of his imagery of the Kingdom restored), became inextricably linked in his follower's minds with the "time of great suffering" that was customarily understood to usher in the period of God's Day of Judgment and his final vindication of the chosen people (necessarily involving the crushing of the wicked persecutors).

In his prophetic preaching, Jesus explicitly quoted Isaiah's image of the fire burning day and night, and the worm (maggot) incessantly feeding on the bloated corpses of the fallen and, to the same end as Isaiah, that when God came to vindicate Israel he would make a radical separation of the good and the wicked. The image of the judgment and separation of the good and the evil is a dominant aspect of Jesus's moral teaching and can be found in many of his parables, such as the king who judges and rewards according to the deeds of individuals in Matthew 23, or the man who harvests a field full of wheat and weeds, separating them out only at the harvest time in Matthew 13.

Jesus also used the biblical idea of Gehenna as the synopsis of what his vision of hell was like. Gehenna was the valley of Hinnom, one of the narrow defiles marking out the plateau on which Jerusalem was built. It was a biblical symbol of everything opposed to God, and as such destined to being purified when God roused himself in his judgment of the evils of the earth. It had been the place in ancient times where some of the inhabitants of Jerusalem had offered their own children in sacrifice to the god Moloch. The reforming King Josiah, as a result of "the abomination of desolation," made the valley into the place of refuse-burning for the city, a place where bodies of criminals were also thrown. In Jesus' teaching (as is the case for later rabbinic literature) it thus became a symbol for the desolate state of all who fall under the judgment of God. The burning of endless fires in a stinking wasteland that symbolized human folly and destructive wickedness is, therefore, Jesus' image for the alternative to his invitation for his hearers to enter, with him, into the service of God, and into the obedience of the Kingdom of God.

Christian disciples later developed the idea of Gehenna into the more elaborated concept of hell, just as they rendered the dynamic concept of the Kingdom of God (obedience to the divine covenant) into the notion of heaven as a place for the righteous. The original point of the teachings was more dynamic, to the effect that humans have a choice to listen and respond to the prophetic call, or to ignore and oppose it. In either case they respond not merely to the prophet, but to God who sent the prophet. In the case of Jesus, those who listen and obey his teachings are described as the guests who are invited to the wedding feast; those who refuse it are compared to those who haunt the wilderness of Gehenna and have chosen the stink of death to the joy of life with God. It is a graphic image indeed, arguably having even more of an impact than the later Christian extrapolation of the eternal hellfire that developed from it.

## Christian Theologians on Hell

Not all Christian theologians acceded to the gradual elision of the Hellenistic notions of Hades, and the apocalyptic imagery of the burning fires of Gehenna or the sea of flames, but certain books were quite decisive, not least the one great apocalyptic book that made its way into the canon of the New Testament, the Revelation of John, whose image of the Lake of Fire, where the dark angels were destined to be punished by God, exercised a profound hold over the imagination of the Western churches. The Byzantine and Eastern churches never afforded Revelation as much attention as did the West, and so the graphic doomsdays of the medieval period never quite entered the Eastern Orthodox consciousness to the same extent.

Some influential Greek theologians argued explicitly against the concept of an eternal hell fire that condemned reprobate sinners to an infinity of pain, on the grounds that all God's punishments are corrective, meant for the restoration of errants, and because an eternal punishment allows no possibility of repentance or correction, it would merely be vengeful, and as such unworthy of the God of infinite love. Important theologians such as Origen (*On First Principles* 2.10) and his followers (Gregory Nyssa and Gregory Nazianzen, among and others) who argued this case fell under disapproval mainly because the Gospel words of Jesus described the fire of Gehenna as "eternal" even though it was a word (*aionios*) that in context did not simply mean "endless" but more to the point of "belonging to the next age."

But even with the unhappiness of the Christians with Origen's idea that hell was a doctrine intended only "for the simple who needed threats to bring them to order" (*Contra Celsum* 5.15), the logic of his argument about God's majesty transcending mere vengeance, and the constant stress in the teachings of Jesus on the mercifulness of God, led to a shying away from the implications of the doctrine of an eternal hell, throughout the wider Christian tradition, even when this doctrine was generally affirmed.

Major authorities such as Augustine and John Chrysostom explained the pains of fire as symbols of the grief and loss of intimacy with God that the souls of the damned experienced. Dante developed this in the *Divine Comedy* with his famous conception of hell as a cold, dark place, sterile in its sense of loss. Augustine aided the development of the idea of purgatory (itself a major revision of the concept of eternal punishment). Other thinkers argued that while hell did exist (not merely as a symbol but as a real possibility of alienation from life and goodness), it was impossible to conclude that God's judgments were irreversible, for that would be to stand in judgment over God, and describe eternity simply in time-bound terms; one position being blasphemous, the other illogical.

Because of the implications, not least because of the need to affirm the ultimate mercy and goodness of God, even when acting as judge and vindicator, modern Christian theology has remained somewhat muted on the doctrine of hell, returning to it more in line with the original inspiration of the message as a graphic call to moral action. It has probably been less successful in representing the other major function of the doctrine of hell; that is, the manner in which it enshrines a major insight of Jesus and the biblical tradition, that God will defend the right of the oppressed vigorously even when the powerful of the world think that to all appearances the poor can be safely tyrannized. Originally the Christian doctrine of hell functioned as a major protecting hedge for the doctrine of God's justice and his unfailing correction of the principles of perversion in the world.

In previous generations, when hell and final judgment were the subjects of regular preaching in places of worship, the fear of hell was more regularly seen as an aspect of the approach to death by the terminally ill. In the twenty-first century, while

*Dante and Virgil are depicted walking in the cold, dark and sterile hell of the* Divine Comedy. CORBIS

most world religions still advocate a role for the varieties of hell in their theological systems, the fear has substantively diminished even though popular opinion in modern America still expresses its widespread belief in the existence of hell. The change of attitude can be seen in media treatments of death and afterlife that commonly use images of the death experience as either a slipping into nonexistence, or as some form of returning to the welcoming light. Even modern American evangelicalism, strongly rooted in biblical sources, has shown a distinct move away from the doctrine of hell to a conception of final punishment as an "annihilation" of the souls of the unrighteous, a concept that is found in a few biblical sources as an alternative to the image of apocalyptic judgment.

Because of its vivid nature, and the increasingly static graphic imagination of later Christian centuries, hell came to be associated too much with an image of God as tormentor of the souls in some eternal horror. Such a God did not correspond to the gracious "Father" described by Jesus, but like all images packaged for the religiously illiterate, the dramatic cartoon often replaces the truer conception that can be gained from the Gospels and writings of Christian saints through the centuries: that hell is a radical call to wake up and make a stand for justice and mercy, as well as a profound statement that God's holiness is perennially opposed to evil and injustice.

*See also:* CATHOLICISM; CHARON AND THE RIVER STYX; CHRISTIAN DEATH RITES, HISTORY OF; GODS AND GODDESSES OF LIFE AND DEATH; HEAVEN; JESUS; PURGATORY

### Bibliography

Bernstein, Alan E. *The Formation of Hell: Death and Retribution in the Ancient and Early Christian Worlds.* Ithaca, NY: Cornell University Press, 1993.

Bromiley, Geoffrey W. "History of the Doctrine of Hell." In *The Standard Bible Encyclopedia,* Vol. 2. Grand Rapids, MI: Eerdmans, 1982.

Davidson, Clifford, and Thomas Seiler, eds. *The Iconography of Hell.* Kalamazoo: Western Michigan University Press, 1992.

Filoramo, Giovanni. "Hell-Hades." In Angelo Di Berardino ed., *Encyclopedia of the Early Church,* Vol. 1. New York: Oxford University Press, 1992.

Fudge, Edward. *The Fire That Consumes: A Biblical and Historical Study of Final Punishment.* Fallbrook, CA: Verdict Publications, 1982.

Gardner, Eileen. *Medieval Visions of Heaven and Hell: A Sourcebook.* New York: Garland, 1993.

Moore, David George. *The Battle for Hell: A Survey and Evaluation of Evangelicals' Growing Attraction to the Doctrine of Annihilationism.* Lanham, MD: University Press of America, 1995.

Turner, Alice K. *The History of Hell.* New York: Harcourt Brace, 1993.

Van Scott, Miriam. *The Encyclopedia of Hell.* New York: St. Martin's Press, 1998.

J. A. MCGUCKIN

# HERTZ, ROBERT

Robert Hertz was born to a Jewish family near Paris on June 22, 1881. As an anthropologist and politically active socialist, Hertz provided a new way of interpreting funerary ritual and sought to relate sociology to the practical flourishing of community life. At age nineteen he joined the *Année Sociologique* group that included leading sociologists of the day such as Durkheim, Mauss, Hubert, and Halbwachs. Their approach stressed broad theories rather than the accumulation of voluminous cultural facts as in Frazerian anthropology. While volunteering for active service in World War I, he was killed in action on April 13, 1915.

The contemporary anthropologist Robert Parkin has highlighted Hertz's scholarly contributions to the symbolic significance of "right" and "left" classifications, to sin and expiation and to myth and death. Hertz's last and best-known essay— *"Contribution à une étude sur la representation collective de la mort"*—was published in 1907 but largely forgotten in the English-speaking world until Rodney and Claudia Needham's English edition was published in 1960.

Echoing Durkheim's view of society as a moral community whose values are expressed as "collective representations," Hertz speaks of "society" and "collective representations" abstractly to explain how enduring values were related to concrete individuals. He demonstrated these links by analyzing death and funeral rites. Two paradoxical streams flow through his argument, one social and the other more psychological. Sociologically, he interprets society as perceiving itself to be immortal, transcending the lives of any individual members and conferring upon the dead a new status as ancestors. In this sense, members of society never die but change their relative relationships as they move from being living members of society to its dead "members."

The psychological stream concerns the relationship between the living and the dead and the experience of grief. Both social and psychological streams, however, relate symbolically to the state of the corpse. Indeed, Hertz was an early exponent of what would later be called "embodiment," interpreting the human body as a vehicle enshrining and expressing social values. Accordingly, he made a special study of "double-burial," distinguishing between "wet" and "dry" phases of ritual. The wet phase, often linked to temporary earth burial or containing the dead in pots, related to the rotting corpse and sociologically was the period when the identity of the dead was increasingly removed from his or her former living identity. Psychologically, this was a period when the living experienced the pain of early separation and might have felt a sense of revulsion to the deceased. The dry phase of the ritual dealt with the bones and incorporated the dead into their new identity in the afterlife. At this time, a new sense of "reverent courage" might replace revulsion among the surviving kin. His reference to "internal partings" was an early form of attachment theory, just as his stress on transition and incorporation presages his friend van Gennep's idea of rites of passage. Hertz's influence increased significantly in the growing literature on death studies from approximately the 1980s.

*See also:* ANTHROPOLOGY; DURKHEIM, ÉMILE; GRIEF AND MOURNING IN CROSS-CULTURAL PERSPECTIVE; IMMORTALITY, SYMBOLIC; RITES OF PASSAGE

### Bibliography

Gennep, Arnold van. *The Rites of Passage,* translated by Monika B. Vizedome and Gabrielle L. Caffe. London: Routledge & Paul, 1960.

Hertz, Robert. "A Contribution to the Study of the Collective Representation of Death." In Rodney Needham and Claudia Needham eds., *Death and the Right Hand.* New York: Free Press, 1960.

Parkin, Robert. *The Dark Side of Humanity: The Work of Robert Hertz and Its Legacy.* Netherlands: Harwood Academic Publishers, 1996.

DOUGLAS J. DAVIES

# HIDDEN GRIEF

*See* GRIEF: DISENFRANCHISED.

# HINDENBURG

The *Hindenburg* was an 804-foot-long German dirigible and the largest rigid airship ever constructed. It was first launched in Friedrichshafen, Germany, in April 1936. The huge craft could lift a total weight of about 235 tons (215 metric tons). It carried fifty passengers and a crew of sixty, in addition to baggage, mail cargo, and its heavy load of fuel. It had a maximum speed of 84 mph (135km/h) and a cruising speed of 78 mph (126km/h). It was renowned not only for its size but also for its luxurious two-deck passenger accommodations.

Commercial air service across the North Atlantic was inaugurated by the *Hindenburg,* carrying a total of 1,002 passengers on ten round-trips between Germany and the United States, was among the first lighter-than-air crafts, and certainly the most prestigious, to assure commercial air service across the North Atlantic. Then, on the evening of May 6, 1937, while landing at Lakehurst, New Jersey, the *Hindenburg* was destroyed in a massive, fiery explosion, killing thirty-five of the ninety-seven persons aboard and one ground worker. This disaster foreshadowed the end of the commercial rigid airship and the end of an era.

The disaster was generally attributed to a discharge of atmospheric electricity near a hydrogen gas leak from the zeppelin. There were some speculations that the dirigible had been the target of an anti-Nazi act of sabotage. More recent explanations disregard the bombing theory and the hydrogen leak problem, and lay the blame on a special fabric used for the outer skin which, when ignited, burns like dry leaves.

The importance of the event was magnified by a now-famous and often-replayed live radio broadcast of the disaster. This broadcast was the first to bring the drama of a major tragedy directly in the homes of Americans and helped ensure that this event would be considered one of the major disasters of the twentieth century.

*See also:* DISASTERS; TITANIC; TRIANGLE SHIRTWAIST COMPANY FIRE

### Bibliography

Archbold, Rick. *Hindenburg: An Illustrated History.* New York: Warner Books, 1994.

Dick, Harold G., and Douglas H. Robinson. *The Golden Age of the Great Passenger Airships: Graf Zeppelin & Hindenburg.* Washington, DC: Smithsonian Institution Press, 1992.

#### Internet Resources

Cochran-Bokow, Jacquelyn. "Fabric, Not Filling to Blame: Hydrogen Exonerated in Hindenburg Disaster." In the National Hydrogen Association [web site]. Available from www.ttcorp.com/nha/advocate/ad22zepp.htm.

JEAN-YVES BOUCHER

# HINDUISM

In India "death in the midst of life" is a literal, not figurative, notion. Along the Ganges River, for instance, bodies are regularly cremated, and the odor of burning flesh fills the air. And in the city of Calcutta, dead bodies become a problem to those responsible for keeping the streets clean. Thus, it is not surprising that in India's sacred texts and stories, how one lives one's life determines one's fate after death.

## Hinduism As a Religion

The roots of Hinduism go back to the Indus civilization in the third millennium B.C.E., but it is only with the migratory waves of Indo-European Aryans in the late second millennium B.C.E. that researchers have access to Hindu ideas about death and afterlife. The religious rituals that were brought by the Aryan pastoral nomads mingled with the customs of the native peoples, the Dravidians, and the culture that developed between them has come to be known as classical Hinduism. The word *Hindu* comes from the Sanskrit name for the river Indus. Hindu was not originally a religious term but was used by Persians and Greeks in the first millennium B.C.E. as a name for the people east of the Indus River. Muslims later borrowed the term *Hindu* to designate the non-Muslim population of India, and the British (who governed India in the eighteenth and nineteenth centuries) used it in much the same way. In its current usage, Hindu refers to those who follow the mainstream religious traditions of India and accept, at least nominally, the authority of the ancient priestly scriptures known as the *Vedas*.

Adherents of the Hindu path, or *sanatana dharma* (universal, eternal teaching), made up about 83 percent of India's population, or about 808 million people, as of 1997. While a vast majority of Hindus reside in India, over the last several hundred years varied expressions of Hinduism have migrated to such places as Sri Lanka and Indonesia, in part because of the political and economic domination by England from the middle of the nineteenth century to the middle of the twentieth century. Beginning with Vivekananda's (a disciple of Ramakrishna) attendance at the World Parliament of Religions in Chicago in 1893, held in conjunction with the World Fair, about 1.3 million Hindus have emigrated to North America over the past century.

While Hinduism is not a religion in the familiar Western sense—it has no specific founder, no clear time of origin, and no organizational structure—at the core of its cumulative tradition are the three *margas,* or paths to spiritual liberation, which include ritual action (*Karma-marga*), the path of knowledge (*Jnana-marga*), and the path of devotion (*Bhakti-marga*). Each of these systems has its own justification, and each presents a distinctive view of death.

## The Path of Ritual Action

Sacrificial celebration (*yajna*) was a central feature of the evolving Aryan religious tradition. By around 1200 B.C.E. a collection of hymns used for these sacrifices was brought together in the earliest scripture, the *Rig Veda,* and by the first millennium B.C.E. its complex rituals had come under the control of a class of priests or Brahmins. It was one of their special responsibilities to perform rituals correctly and to maintain and transmit the knowledge required for their proper performance.

Two major principles emerged in this period: the concepts of ritual knowledge (*veda*) and of ritual action (*karma*). At the center of these ritual celebrations was *Agni,* the lord of fire. It was to Agni that an offering was made, and by Agni that it was consumed and transformed. In the *Rig Veda,* one reads, "At *yajna* the prayerful community worships Agni, / Priest of all joy, blessed with youth, / He, untiring envoy for the Gods at the hour of offering, / He is the Lord of all treasure" (7.10.5). The Brahmins taught that fire sacrifices, properly conceived and correctly performed, reciprocally embodied the fundamental structures of the universe. Ritual action thus had cosmic consequences. Indeed, proper ritual action could produce desired results at a personal level.

The final sacrificial fire ritual is performed after one dies. In the Vedic view, early Hindus believed that cremation returned the physical remains of the deceased back to nature as smoke and ashes. Properly performed, the karma of this ritual established the departed in the "World of the Fathers." To this early Vedic understanding was added the need for a special set of postcremation rituals to complete a transition to the ancestral world. After-life is thus not only a matter of individual effort but also depends on correct ritual performances.

## The Path of Liberating Knowledge

After about 800 B.C.E., the viewpoints and values of the Vedic ritual tradition were challenged by another system that emerged from within the Vedic system and developed into the classic scripture of Hinduism, known as the *Upanishads* ("Sitting near the feet of the teacher"). Upanishadic thinkers distinguished what is permanent and unchanging from what is transient and impermanent. At the cosmic level, the unchanging reality is *Brahman,* the absolute that underlies the transient names and forms of phenomena. At the personal level, this same reality is called the *atman,* or true self, the essential, unalterable being that underlies each person in the midst of activity.

The goal of the Upanishadic teachers was to escape from the ceaseless cycle of birth, death, and rebirth that was called *samsara.* Freedom from rebirth was made possible only by giving up one's attachments to desires. In turn, this was only possible if one realized that true self, atman, was not part of the transient phenomenal world. The idea of samsara, including reincarnation (also called transmigration), refers to successive life embodiments of an individual soul (*jiva*). This life flux embodies a continual series of births, deaths, and rebirths. Reincarnation blends the natural evolution with a spiritual evolution toward awakening. For example, at the subhuman level, growth is automatic and progresses toward ever-increasing complexity from inorganic to organic to vegetative to human levels. At the human level, however, the soul has the opportunity to break out of this cycle of births, deaths, and rebirths.

To illustrate what happens at death from the Hindu standpoint, the outer or gross body (skin, bones, muscles, nervous system, and brain) is said to fall away. The subtle body sheath (composed of karmic tendencies, knowledge, breath, and mind) that coats the jiva, or psychic substratum, also begins to disappear. After death the jiva initially remains within or near the body before it completely departs from the body to eventually enter an otherworldly reality conditioned by one's susceptibility to earthly sensual cravings. When these cravings have ceased, the jiva enters a temporally blissful existence until, at a karmically determined time, it takes on a new physical body and is reborn.

Upanishadic teachers agreed that *moksha,* the final liberation from a cycle of painful rebirths, is the goal of life. This final union with Brahman—which takes place before death—is described as a state of *sat* (being), *chit* (consciousness), and *ananda* (pure joy). The early Hindu sages, therefore, sought a realization that liberated the mind from the fear of death. This realization, or moksha, can be described as a spiritual death, a dying before dying, which accentuates at least four consequences: liberation (moksha) from the endless cycle of birth and death and birth and death; activation of *samadhi,* or the void, which is also absolute fullness and compassion; freedom from the effects of the reincarnation cycle at death; and a return to full identification with atman.

One of the most dramatic examples of this view occurs in the *Katha Upanishad* (800–500 B.C.E.), which relates the visit of Nachiketas to the Land of Death, Yama's kingdom. In the story, a teaching dialogue occurs between an archetypal seeker and an immortal teacher. Nachiketas, the seeker, asks Yama, "What is the purpose of life, given the certainty of death?" Yama replies by affirming the way to freedom from attachments through realizing atman (the deathless Self): "Unborn is he, eternal, everlasting and primeval, / He is not slain when the body is slain. / Should the killer think 'I kill.' / Or the killed 'I have been killed,' / Both these have no [right] knowledge"(2.19). That is, for Yama, when the body dies, atman does not die. The secret of death, then, is realized not by preaching, not by sacrifice, but through meditation and grace. This realization of the supreme self hidden in the cave of the heart emancipates one from the vagaries of samsara.

## The Path of Devotion

Both the Vedic rituals and the Upanishadic path of knowledge are products of the Vedic priesthood. The appeal of these paths was mostly confined to the elite social classes, and thus each path denied access to the majority of Hindus. In response to this limitation, by the second century B.C.E. a third path was emerging, one with both greater popular appeal and greater accessibility. This new path—devotional theism—was based not on Vedic rituals or Vedic knowledge, but on the worship of various popular deities. The way of devotion (*bhakti*) is dramatically expounded in the *Bhagavad Gita,* or *Song of the Lord* (500–200 B.C.E.). Not a Vedic text, the *Bhagavad Gita* is a part of a long popular epic known as the *Mahabharata* that was accessible to the populace.

Devotional theism took root, expanded rapidly, and, by the early centuries of the common era, had become, in terms of numbers of followers, the dominant form of Hinduism. In this path, many gods and goddesses are worshipped (e.g., Vishnu, the protector, with his incarnations as Krishna and Rama; Shiva, the destroyer, the divine Yogi and cosmic Lord of dance; and Devi, the goddess in a variety of names and forms). Devotional theism, this third path within Hinduism, emphasized above all faith and grace. Release from rebirth was no longer viewed as a matter of knowledge alone but also could be received as a divine gift by faithful devotees. The sought-for afterlife, then, was not the sterile or abstract "World of the Fathers" but a life—or afterlife—of devotion to God.

The *Bhagavad Gita* presents a dialogue between Krishna, the divine teacher, and Arjuna, the warrior disciple. Unlike the Buddha (the awakened one), Krishna is the incarnation of *Vishnu.* Krishna, disguised as a charioteer, listens to Arjuna's despair at the prospect of fighting his kinsmen to retrieve land that is rightfully his. Then Krishna speaks: "All things born must die," and "out of death in truth comes life" (2:27). Echoing Yama's words to Nachiketas, Krishna goes on to say that death is an illusion. Like those of the *Katha Upanishad,* Krishna's teachings on death argue four basic attitudes: the death of one's physical body is inevitable and should not cause prolonged grief; the subtle dimension of the person (jiva) does not die at death, rather takes on a new body; the eternal self (atman) is birthless and deathless, and cannot be destroyed; and one who realizes the eternal self while yet alive will not be reborn but, at death, will merge with ultimate reality, or Brahman.

Whereas the practice of sacrifice in the *Vedas* referred to an external ritual that included fire, drink, chants, stories, and grain or animal offerings, Krishna teaches devotional sacrifice. Performing all actions without attachment to the results, the devotee sacrifices even attachments to the divine. How-

*Vishnu, the Hindu god of protection, is illustrated by this eleventh-century sculpture.* ST. LOUIS ART MUSEUM

ever, Arjuna is left with a significant question: How does one realize atman? Krishna provides several clues. Beyond *jnana yoga,* the way of knowledge (intuitive, single-minded awareness of the eternal self), Krishna emphasizes *karma yoga* (self-sacrificing, detached activity) and *bhakti yoga* (self surrendering devotion to the divine). In fact, the highest secret of the *Bhagavad Gita* is most appropriately practiced at the time of death. Krishna teaches: "Let him [the dying person] utter [the sound] Om, *Brahman* in one syllable, / Keeping Me in mind; / Then when his time is come to leave aside the ody, / tread the highest Way" (8:13). And then Krishna promises that a person will be freed from the bonds of misfortune when "Armed with the discipline of renunciation, / Yourself liberated, you will join me . . . / Keep me in your mind and devotion, sacrifice / To me, bow to me, discipline yourself to me, / And you will reach me!" (9:28, 34). These verses express a constant refrain of devotional

Hinduism—not only to be freed from karma-caused traces of rebirth, but also to achieve a permanent union with one's personal deity through a devotional relationship. While the Gita represents only one version of the path of devotion, its teachings are broadly typical with respect to both devotion and the afterlife.

## Death Ritual

All of the views of afterlife outlined above became part of the continuing Hindu religious tradition, and they and their related systems of liberation—the three margas—have provided the basic framework of Hinduism for the past 2,000 years. What Hinduism offers with regard to death and afterlife is thus not a final decision that must be made in one's present lifetime, but a process that leads through many cycles of death and rebirth until one is able to reach the goal of liberation.

Typically, as a Hindu approaches death, he or she is surrounded with religious rites and ceremonies that support the dying person. Before a Hindu dies, the eldest son and relatives put water taken, if possible, from the Ganges River into the dying person's mouth. At this time, family and friends sing devotional prayers and chant Vedic *mantras* (sacred sounds). More than the words, which are themselves comforting, the tone of the communal chanting soothes the dying person and comforts relatives in their time of stress and grief.

Hinduism requires cremation as soon as possible (unless the deceased is less than three years old, in which case he or she is buried). In New Delhi alone, it is estimated that 50,000 bodies are cremated annually. In response to the depletion of forests caused by wood-burning cremations, the Indian government has begun building electric crematoriums throughout India. Some traditional Hindus, however, have argued that ending wood-burning cremations could violate their religious rights.

Prior to cremation, the body is washed and anointed, the hair (and beard) is trimmed, and the corpse is given new or clean clothes. During the procession, relatives and mourners, who carry the body to the cremation ground, chant verses that invoke Yama's help. The body is then placed on a funeral pyre. The eldest son finally walks around the pyre three times, each time pouring sacred water on the deceased. He then sets fire to the wood with a torch that has been blessed. Throughout the sacred ritual, relatives and mourners chant Vedic mantras to quicken the soul's release.

*See also:* BUDDHISM; CHINESE BELIEFS; ISLAM; REINCARNATION; WIDOW-BURNING

### *Bibliography*

Basham, A. L. *The Wonder That Was India.* New York: Grove Press, 1954.

Borman, William. "Upanishadic Eschatology: The Other Side of Death." In Arthur Berger, Paul Badham, Austin Kutscher, Joyce Berger, Michael Perry, and John Beloff eds., *Death and Dying: Cross-Cultural and Multi-Disciplinary Views.* Philadelphia: The Charles Press, 1989.

Easwaran, Eknath. *Dialogue with Death.* Petaluma, CA: Nilgiri Press, 1981.

Holck, F. H. "The Vedre Period." In Frederick H. Holck ed., *Death and Eastern Thought.* New York: Abington Press, 1974.

Hopkins, Thomas. "Hindu Views of Death and Afterlife." In Hiroshi Obayashi ed., *Death and Afterlife: Perspectives of World Religions.* New York: Praeger Press, 1992.

Knipe, David. "*Sapindikarana*: The Hindu Rate of Entry into Heaven." In Frank Reynolds and Earle Waugh eds., *Religious Encounters with Death.* University Park: Penn State University Press, 1977.

Koller, John. *The Indian Way.* New York: Macmillan, 1982.

Kramer, Kenneth. "Hindu Attitudes toward Death." *The Sacred Art of Dying: How World Religions Understand Death.* Mahwah, NJ: Paulist Press, 1988.

Long, J. Bruce. "Death as a Necessity and a Gift in Hindu Mythology." In Frank Reynolds and Earle Waugh eds., *Religious Encounters with Death.* University Park: Penn State University Press, 1977.

Pearson, Anne M. "Hinduism." In Christopher Jay Johnson and Marsha G. McGee eds., *How Different Religions View Death and Afterlife,* 2nd edition. Philadelphia: The Charles Press, 1998.

Prashad, Jamuna. "The Hindu Concept of Death." In Arthur Berger, Paul Badham, Austin Kutscher, Joyce Berger, Michael Perry, and John Beloff eds., *Death and Dying: Cross-Cultural and Multi-Disciplinary Views.* Philadelphia: The Charles Press, 1989.

Sundararajan, K. R. "The Orthodox Philosophical Systems." In Frederick H. Holck ed., *Death and Eastern Thought.* New York: Abington Press, 1974.

Zaehner, R. C. *Hindu Scriptures*. New York: E. P. Dutton and Co., 1966.

KENNETH P. KRAMER

# HIPPOCRATIC OATH

The recitation of the oath attributed to Hippocrates is an integral part of medical school graduation in the Western world. Referred to as either the Hippocratic oath or the oath of Hippocrates, the oath exists in a variety of forms and has been translated and revised over the centuries. Early versions advised physicians to practice the art of medicine solely for the benefit of their patients. Twentieth-century versions emphasized that doctors abstain from practices that would harm their patients, and stress the ethical basis of medical practice.

The Hippocratic oath requires that medical graduates solemnly promise to adhere to a course of professional conduct that has guided physicians in ages past. It also requires that they promise to revere their instructors and to care for them should they ever require assistance; transmit (teach) the art of medicine to deserving persons; utilize good judgment to provide beneficial treatment for patients; abstain from providing any harmful or dangerous treatments; refrain from intervening in cases that require greater skill and training; remain pure and holy in the practice of the profession; limit involvement with patients solely to the benefit of the patient's health; give no cause for disrespect of the profession through word or deed; and keep confidential all that is learned through practice of the profession. The oath concludes with a statement that if the physician adheres to these precepts, he or she will enjoy happiness, success, and respect.

The Hippocratic oath is an anachronism. It is outdated and holds no power. There are no sanctions for those who violate its precepts, nor does it have status in a court of law. It is a historical document with unconscious, symbolic dimensions stemming from its 2,500-year-old historical tradition. Its persistent use during medical school graduation ceremonies does provide symbolic significance beyond words. In essence, it emphasizes the unique role and responsibilities of the physician in activities of a

high nature and establishes a basis for the guiding principles of medical care, which include autonomy, beneficence, justice, and nonmaleficence.

The most recent version of the oath is the product of collaboration between doctors from both the United States and Europe. It contains three guiding principles—primacy of patient welfare, patient autonomy, and social justice—and lists ten professional responsibilities. It stresses the centrality of altruism in the physician-patient relationship. It states that the quality of medical care must not be compromised by market forces, societal pressures, or administrative exigencies. It emphasizes that doctors must be honest with their patients and empower them to make informed decisions about their treatment. Patient decisions about their care must be recognized as paramount, as long as those decisions are consistent with ethical practice and do not contribute to demands for inappropriate care. It urges physicians to work actively to eliminate discrimination in health care, whether based on race, gender, socioeconomic status, ethnicity, religion, or any other social category.

*See also:* ADVANCE DIRECTIVES; EUTHANASIA; INFORMED CONSENT; SUICIDE TYPES: PHYSICIAN-ASSISTED SUICIDE

WILLIAM M. LAMERS JR.

# HOLOCAUST

The term *holocaust,* with origins in the Greek translation of the Hebrew Bible, translates the Hebrew expression *olah* as *holokauston,* meaning "a burnt sacrifice" (Berenbaum 2000, p. 31). Deeply imbued with religious meaning, the expression is presently most closely associated with the Nazi policy of mass murder directed against European Jewry. In a century when over 140 million people died in wars, the Holocaust may long be the ultimate symbol of inhumanity.

The meaning of Holocaust is itself fraught with great controversy. Some, like the historian Walter Lacquer, insist that the expression is "singularly inappropriate" because of its religious connotations (Lacquer 1980, p. 7). Elie Wiesel, a survivor of Auschwitz and the Nobel Prize–winning author of

*Night* (1960), is often credited with introducing the word into popular usage. In the face of this religious qualification, the term remains widely used by academics, the media, and the larger community. Wiesel has since expressed great concern over the abuse of the term applied to situations beyond the historical context of the Third Reich and the experience of mass destruction experienced by the Jews. Just as important, Wiesel reminds readers that the term *Holocaust,* like any expression from human language, invariably falls far short in encompassing the sheer horror and depth of tragedy behind the persecution and mass death inside and outside Nazi concentration and death camps. Poets and historians still search for words to explain the unfathomable atrocity.

The history of the Holocaust reflects the reality that Adolph Hitler and the Nazi movement did not invent anti-Semitic hatred against the Jews. What was unique in the Nazi experience was that the Third Reich was the first and only regime in modern history to define anti-Semitism in racial terms and, upon this basis, to use the full weight of the state to legitimize the *Ausrottung,* or eradication of the Jews. Racial bloodlines defined the essential difference between Aryan Germans and Jews. This distinction, in the words of Victor Klemperer, a philologist and shrewd observer of Nazi language, was everything. What set National Socialism apart from other forms of fascism "is a concept of race reduced solely to anti-Semitism and fired exclusively by it" (Klemperer 2000, p. 135). The racial state conceived by the Nazis as a foundation stone for the Holocaust defined citizenship in biological terms. As one prominent Nazi race eugenicist argued, "National Socialism is nothing but applied biology" (Baur, Fischer, and Lenz 1931, p. 417).

Part of the Nazi success in rising to power in 1933 was the union of racial science from the late nineteenth century with traditional religious and economic forms of anti-Semitism rooted in the Middle Ages. From its inception racial science took on an international character. Appearing only about six months into the regime, the Nazi Law on the Prevention of Hereditarily Ill Progeny, which legalized compulsory sterilization, drew from a notable legislative model in the numerous compulsory sterilization measures passed by twenty-four of the states of America under the aegis of the American eugenics movement, beginning with Indiana in 1907 (Kühl 1994, p. 17). The Nazi policy of destroying "life unworthy of life" under the banner of "scientific objectivity," of which sterilization was an early manifestation, would hold profound implications for others deemed racially undesirable, including Jews and Gypsies.

Furthermore, Nazi propagandists exploited the long tradition of religious anti-Semitism in the Lutheran and Catholic churches. Jews were considered outcasts by both religious communities because of their refusal to convert to Christianity and for the charge of deicide in killing Christ. Martin Luther became an especially popular historical reference for Nazi propagandists who liberally quoted the religious reformer's incendiary pamphlet, "The Jews and Their Lies" (1543). Luther vented his rage against the Jews by drawing on old economic stereotypes depicting Jews as greedy moneylenders with an aversion to physical labor. The negative connotation of usury and lust for money, part of both Christian traditions, remained alive and well under the Third Reich. As vital as Jews were to the emerging market economy of Europe, they were still held as parasites and criminals. The social and economic power of anti-Semitic stereotypes like these was central to William Shakespeare's play *The Merchant of Venice* (1596), which portrays the rejection and suffering of Shylock, the Jewish merchant. Under the Third Reich, the new anti-Semitism, steeped in the language of race biology and yet connected to traditional hatred for Jews in the marketplace and church, provided an even more powerful ideological justification for persecution of a distinct minority.

Anti-Semitism alone does not explain German Nazism and the Holocaust. Yet any serious consideration of what caused the Third Reich must take into account the dynamics of anti-Semitic thinking and their influence in shaping the formation and administration of Nazi social and political policies. Hitler's anti-Semitic agenda and the reality of the Holocaust did not assume definite policy directions overnight. Other contemporary factors played a significant role in bringing Hitler to dictatorial rule. Buoyed by the social and political malaise engendered by the Great Depression and skyrocketing unemployment and inflation rates, Hitler ridiculed democratic institutions and the lack of political unity under the Weimar Republic. Hitler also exploited the legacy of the Treaty of Versailles, which stripped

Germany of pride and territories, and added the heavy weight of war guilt and reparations. All of these elements from World War I left a great deal of resentment among various elements in the German population. Here again, the Jews suffered from scapegoating and received blame for Germany's misfortunes. In what became known as the "stab in the back," Jews were even accused of causing Germany's defeat in World War I by working behind the scenes as betrayers on the home front.

Historians and social scientists still struggle to understand how a country with one of the highest literacy rates in the world and a culture which nurtured great scientists, musicians, and theologians could administer one of the biggest mass murders in history, carried out with the complicity of millions and with the aid of the most modern technological means available. Indeed, the Germans were to industrialize mass death and the disposal of their remains. Germany was not the only country with a culture marked by deep-seated anti-Semitic resentments, but it was the only one to transform this resentment into a policy directed toward annihilating the entire Jewish people.

Neither were the Jews the only group identified for total destruction because of racial reasons. The infamous "T-4" killings of the handicapped, the mentally ill, and those suffering from hereditary illness conducted by medical doctors under Hitler's orders preceded the formation of the death camps in the East. These were the first victims of mass murder. Under the guise of "euthanasia" and supported by the legal apparatus of the state, as many as 6,000 children and 70,273 adults met their deaths at the hands of medical professionals in asylums across the Reich. The vast majority of the victims died in gas chambers. The choice of method for this kind of murder was critically important for the future. The early Nazi elimination of "life unworthy of life" through the "T-4" killings foreshadowed the use of gas chambers in Auschwitz and other camps as well. Both the technology and many of the former medical personnel from this sordid experiment in mass murder would re-emerge with the SS, or *schutztaffel,* in helping to run the machinery of the death camps after 1941. The story did not end here. The intent to racially cleanse Germany of undesirable racial elements also extended to Sinti and Roma, called *Zigeuner* by the Germans and known traditionally as "Gypsies." Classified by the Nazis as "criminal"

**TABLE 1**

| Jewish casualties from the Final Solution | |
| --- | --- |
| German Reich (boundaries of 1938) | 130,000 |
| Austria | 58,000 |
| Belgium | 26,000 |
| Bulgaria | 7,000 |
| Czechoslovakia (boundaries of 1938) | 245,000 |
| France | 64,000 |
| Greece | 58,000 |
| Hungary and Carpatho-Ukraine | 300,000 |
| Italy | 8,000 |
| Latvia, Lithuania, Estonia | 200,000 |
| Luxembourg | 3,000 |
| Netherlands | 101,800 |
| Norway | 677 |
| Poland (boundaries of 1939) | 2,700,000 |
| Romania (boundaries prior to 1940) | 220,000 |
| USSR (boundaries prior to 1939) | 800,000 |
| Yugoslavia | 54,000 |
| | 4,975,477 |

Note: The numbers under discussion cannot embrace the full depth and scope of human loss which was the Holocaust. Controversy undoubtedly continues among scholars over the statistics representing the loss, of which Gerald Fleming's research is an important part.

SOURCE: Fleming, Gerald. *Hitler and the Final Solution.* Berkeley: University of California Press, 1984.

or "asocials" and forced to wear the black triangle on prisoner clothing, at least 250,000 Sinti and Roma died under Nazi rule. Whether the Nazis fully intended to wipe out the entire population of Sinti and Roma remains an issue of some dispute among scholars.

## The Road to Auschwitz

There existed no doubt among Nazi policymakers regarding the scope of mass murder and the massive destruction of Jews in the wake of the attack on Russia in the summer of 1941. The Nazi intention was to kill every single Jewish man, woman, and child. Hitler vented his obsessive hatred for Jews in *Mein Kampf,* (*My Struggle*) originally written in Landsberg prison in 1924. The Jewish community stood in diametric opposition to his racial vision for a New Germany. Judeophobia, as the scholar Klaus Fischer calls it, reflected a paranoid distortion of reality and delusionary thinking. After rising to power in 1933, Hitler wasted little time before moving against the Jews and other avowed enemies of the state. Dachau, the first of many concentration camps originally created to incarcerate political enemies of the regime, opened less than two months after Hitler came to office. The

SA, or *sturmabteilung,* brown-shirted storm troopers, rounded up Social Democrats and Communists. The Nazis followed on April 1, 1933, by boycotting all Jewish businesses. Even more devastating to the Jewish community was the dismissal of all Jews from civil service and the legal practice six days later.

The mass murder of Jews and others declared unworthy of citizenship did not take place overnight. State violence and terror, in order to be more fully institutionalized, required the legitimacy of a legal framework. Early on the perpetrators created a series of laws to legalize the oppressive actions taken against their victims. Compulsory sterilization laws appeared in July 1933 leading to the forced sterilization of over 320,000 people suffering from hereditary illnesses. Forced to wear the pink triangle and condemned under Paragraph 175 of the 1871 Reich Criminal Code, which made homosexual relations a criminal offense, at least 10,000 gays suffered imprisonment and deplorable treatment in at least eleven concentration camps.

The legal noose continued to tighten around the Jews. A public book-burning of works by Jewish authors like Heinrich Heine and Sigmund Freud along with other opponents of Nazism took place in May 1933. Signs declaring "No Jews" sprung up all over the country during the summer of 1935 outside restaurants, stores, and villages forbidding Jewish entry. A critically important racial development emerged in September of that year under the anti-Semitic Nuremberg Laws. These laws virtually stripped Jews of citizenship, legitimizing the huge social chasm between Jews and Aryan Germans. With the intent of preserving blood purity, Jews could not marry and have sexual relations with Germans or employ female employees under the age of forty-five in their households.

An equally ominous but perhaps lesser known aspect of the Holocaust regarded early reactions of the global community to the treatment of the Jews. At an international conference staged at Evian in France during early July 1938, diplomats representing thirty-two nations met to discuss solutions in answer to a growing refugee problem. The mounting number of Jewish refugees from Austria and Germany created pressure on the United States and other countries to raise immigration quotas. Little more than expressions of sympathy for the Jews came out of the conference. In short, the conference results convinced Hitler that "no one wanted the Jews" and, moreover, implied that he had a free hand in dealing with the Jews without international interference.

A growing escalation of violence against the Jews occurred during *Kristallnacht,* or the Night of the Broken Glass, on November 9, 1938. That evening, over 1,000 synagogues across Austria and Germany were burned and many Jewish businesses looted and destroyed. Ninety-six Jews were murdered and 30,000 were arrested and sent to concentration camps in Dachau, Sachsenhausen, and Buchenwald. Eight days later, Jewish children were expelled from German schools. Economic pressures increased; the isolation of the Jews continued with the compulsory expropriation of their businesses, industries, and shops with the "Aryanization" of the economy in December of that year.

The Final Solution, the Nazi answer to the Jewish question, did not follow a direct path from Hitler's obsessive hatred of Jews, as expressed in *Mein Kampf,* to the killing fields of the death camps. A major focus of Nazi policy from 1933 to 1941 was to use forced emigration to clear Germany of all Jews. At least as late as the closing days of 1938, the Nazi regime explored the possibility of organizing a wholesale migration of Jews to either Madagascar or Palestine. Some historians, like Gerald Fleming and Eberhard Jäckel, known in some quarters as intentionalists, claim a direct connection between Hitler's anti-Semitic ideology and anti-Semitic practices. Karl Schleunes, representing a more functionalist point of view, argues that the Nazi leadership from the top down had not defined the scope and substance of the Final Solution.

Conditions of the war on the eastern front marked a critical phase in the Holocaust. Vast tracts of territory, along with huge numbers of Russian prisoners of war and Jews, fell under German control during the early phase of Hitler's war with Russia. Christopher Browning's research argues convincingly that Hitler gave the go ahead for the mass murder of the Jews in the fall of 1941, some four months after Germany attacked Russia. This distinction is important since it sheds new light on the old and misguided assumption that plans for the Final Solution were first instituted months later as part of the Wannsee Conference on January 20, 1942. Knowing when Hitler and his circle passed the point of no return in regard to killing Jews remains important for students of the Holocaust for several reasons. As Browning reminds readers, this extreme case of genocide was different from other genocides in that the goal was to eliminate every single Jewish person in the entire Reich and occupied territories. This genocide remains unique as a turning point in history for another reason. The Nazi regime exploited the latest technology as well as considerable bureaucratic and scientific resources to achieve the most thorough and efficient killing process possible.

## The Dynamics of Nazi Mass Murder

An important distinction existed between the formation of concentration as opposed to death camps within the Nazi racial state. Concentration camps originally imprisoned political opponents. Eventually, as racial enemies of the regime, Jews also became part of the prison population in the concentration camps. Death camps, of which there were six in number, were located in Poland. Their sole purpose was to kill as many Jews as quickly as possible. Auschwitz, Chelmo, Treblinka, Sobibor, Maidanek, and Belzec are places that will forever live in the memory of the Holocaust. Of these, Auschwitz was by far the largest. From at least 1.3 million deportees to Auschwitz, about 900,000 met their end very soon after arrival. Another 400,000 entered as camp prisoners and given identification numbers. About half of these people died of disease, hunger, or slave labor. Many of the remainder met their end by injection, medical experiments, or the gas chambers. Ninety percent of the victims in Auschwitz were Jews. Poles constituted the second largest group followed by Gypsies and Soviet prisoners of war.

The geographical location of the death camps in the East afforded a certain level of official secrecy and deceit in the administration of mass murder. The six camps were located close to the highest concentration of Jews in all of Europe. Pre-war Poland had a Jewish population of just less than 3 million. Auschwitz, which opened its gates as a death camp in 1942, was favorably situated because of its location at a confluence of major railroad lines. The railroads acted as major arteries to the death camps running from all parts of occupied Europe. Day and night Jews from twenty countries were shipped to their deaths.

The railroads, in order to operate as efficiently as possible, relied on armies of trusted bureaucrats who, with the stroke of their pens, determined the fate of hundreds of thousands of people. These same faceless figures rarely witnessed the lethal results of their orders. SS Officer Adolf Eichmann, as master bureaucrat, was a central figure in this process since he designed and administered the entire transportation system for the purpose of speeding up the process of mass murder. The memoirs of Rudolf Höss, SS commandant of Auschwitz, reveal a kind and dedicated family man who felt no hatred for Jews. In the banal language of the brutally efficient bureaucrat, he simply had a job to do.

The power of Nazi propaganda to work a language of deceit was an important factor in efficiently moving large groups of people to their unknown destinations. Victims were packed into cattle cars under the most inhumane conditions without food, water, or basic sanitation. To quell the threat of riots, Nazi officials informed passengers that they were part of a resettlement project. Showers, clean clothing, and hot soup were among those things promised at journey's end. Jewish musicians were pressed into service to play classical music at the gate of Auschwitz to soothe the anxieties of incoming prisoners. The real truth of the matter was hidden in an intricate language of deception. To make the situation even more precarious, Jews were required by law to wear the yellow star in September 1941. The Nazis developed no less than twenty-five expressions to mask the real meaning behind mass murder. *Sonderbehandlung* conveyed a literal meaning of special treatment. The expression really meant taking Jews through the death process in the camp. Arriving prisoners saw a welcome sign for *Badeanstalten,* or bath houses, which really were gas chambers.

Not all Jews were killed in the camps. To facilitate the killing operations, the Germans initiated the *Einsatzgruppen,* or mobile killing squads under the direction of the SS. This newly formed "police army" swept through areas newly conquered by the German army in Poland and Russia. Thousands of Jewish women and children were hunted down and shot on the spot. Males were either executed or deported. This massive killing campaign, carried out primarily in 1942, demonstrated the highly concentrated methods used by the SS to eliminate as many people as possible within a relatively short timeframe. This was another face of the Holocaust which reflected the serious Nazi intent and purpose to carry out a war against the Jews.

**The Voice of Survivors**

Several years would pass after the horrific experience of the Holocaust before survivors began to write about and discuss the meaning of their experiences. Survivor literature teems with many volumes of memories and poignant observations about the problem of being human under Nazi persecution. The writing of Elie Wiesel and Primo Levi, both Jewish survivors of Auschwitz, remain among the most popular authors from this literary genre. Wiesel's *Night* continues to be the most widely read recollection of the Holocaust. He captures his own adolescent struggle with his father while offering poignant observations about the problem of retaining some kind of humanity in Auschwitz. Perhaps one of the most excruciating theological questions raised by Wiesel concerns the existence of God. For him, the question about the presence or absence of God in Auschwitz remains unanswered to this very day.

The sheer struggle for survival, also a powerful theme in Wiesel's writing, returned to Levi's experience in a most powerful way. His *If This Is a Man* (1986) recounts with great insight the culture of Auschwitz and the behavior of both perpetrators and victims. Under the shadow of hunger, disease, and fear, Levi describes the extent to which human beings regressed to the level of animal instinct to survive. There was for this man a larger lesson to be learned: "The story of the death camps should be understood by everyone as a sinister alarm-signal" (Wiesel 1986, p. 4).

The importance of the survivors as teachers of succeeding generations cannot be overstated. The late existential psychologist Viktor Frankl, a survivor of four camps, influenced many readers with his theory about the nature of meaning and its relationship to suffering. Art symbolized another legacy from the survivors, including Alfred Kantor's 1987 collection of drawings depicting his experiences as a survivor in Auschwitz and Theresienstadt. Szyman Laks takes readers into the world of a musician in the orchestra at Auschwitz. His

writing defies those who insist on finding a message of hope in the death camps. In *Music from Another World* (2000), Laks describes how the experience of being a musician, steeped in the classics and the daily smell of death, led some to despair. Until the 1980s the voices of women survivors were overlooked. A rich literature in poetry and verse relating the experiences of women in the camps by Carol Rittner (1993) and Ruth Schwertfeger (1989) offers readers new perspectives on the oppression of female populations. Another way of preserving the voices of survivors for future generations is being led by the pioneering work of the filmmaker Steven Spielberg and the Shoah Foundation. The group digitally recorded and indexed interviews with over 50,000 survivors. The realization is that, in only a few years, all survivors will pass into history.

**The Accounting of Death**

Exactly how many victims died in the Holocaust will never be known with great exactitude. Six million Jews lost their lives under the Nazi regime, a figure most commonly cited over the years by historians and social scientists. This statistical assumption continues to come under scrutiny. The historian Gerald Fleming argues with certainty that the figure reaches the 5 million mark (see Table 1). Raoul Hilberg proposes a slightly higher number of Jewish victims at 5.1 million. One important basis for determining the scope of human destruction in the death camps are the railroad passenger numbers and points of departure with dates carefully documented by the SS. While the toll of other twentieth-century disasters are often known to the single person, the loss of life from the Holocaust can only be estimated to within hundreds of thousands and millions. In some cases, entire Jewish communities in eastern Europe were wiped off the face of the earth.

**More Competing Views**

Noted earlier were the competing views of scholars regarding the intentional versus the functional nature of Nazi ideology and the Holocaust. Another voice, which emerged in the mid-1990s, sparked a firestorm of debate. Daniel Goldhagen's *Hitler's Willing Executioners* (1996) claims that anti-Semitic hatred, nurtured in the soil of Christianity, was *the* central cause for the Holocaust and that such hatred was imbedded in German culture. Goldhagen attacks the cherished assumption that Germans were guilty only of obedience to authority. Like many other institutions under the fascist process of centralization, the churches participated in an already deeply rooted German tendency toward "eliminationist anti-Semitism" (Goldhagen 1996, p. 23).

Goldhagen's thesis came under withering criticism by a host of historians. The prominent German historian Eberhard Jäckel accused Goldhagen of advancing "primitive stereotypes" while making wholly inaccurate contrasts between anti-Semitism in Germany and developments in Italy and Denmark. Christopher Browning's scholarship emphasizes obedience to authority as a critical development leading to the Holocaust. He carefully contends that the demonization of an entire people with the charge of anti-Semitism explains nothing. Goldhagen's reductionist argument did not sit well among many historians. The controversial nature of the Holocaust, deeply embroiled in the causes and motivations for mass murder, promises new and expanded debates in the future.

Appearing in the late twentieth century, certain revisionist historians like David Irving and Arthur Butz, members of the infamous Institute for Historical Review, exploited historical ignorance and nascent anti-Semitic prejudices by denying the Holocaust. Irving had long argued that Hitler remained ignorant of the Holocaust and Butz insisted that gas chambers did not exist at Auschwitz. The emergence of Holocaust denial as a cultural phenomenon, often reflecting an anti-Semitic agenda from elements of the Far Right, is not one to be overlooked or easily dismissed. A legal confrontation was inevitable. In 2000 a civil trial in London, where Irving sued the scholar Deborah Lipstadt for calling him a Holocaust denier, ended in disgrace for the plaintiff and a resounding public condemnation of Irving's historical claims about Hitler and the Jews by the judge. The controversy is not over. The language of anti-Semitic hatred continues to find audiences on the Internet under a growing number of web sites. In the Federal Republic of Germany and Canada, public denials of the Holocaust are considered expressions of hate language, incitements to violence, and insults to the dead. As such, these actions are considered serious violations of federal law in both nations.

The long shadow of the Holocaust continues to shape world affairs. The tremendous sorrow, grief, and sense of betrayal from the Holocaust provided a powerful emotional and political thrust for Jews to create the state of Israel in 1948. Research protocols ensuring the protection of research subjects, growing out of the revelations of the Nuremberg trials, influences the way research is conducted today. Millions each year visit the extensive exhibits in the Holocaust and Memorial Museum in Washington, D.C. A new memorial in the center of Berlin, finalized after a protracted debate in the Federal Republic, will memorialize millions of Jews whose lives were lost in one of the most horrendous genocides in human history. The legal settlements over Swiss gold, which began in 1998 and continue into the twenty-first century, as well as reparations paid by German corporations who employed forced laborers raised a new awareness about the complicity of economic interests in the Nazi exploitation of minority populations. A deeper understanding about the human capacity for evil is an inescapable part of this legacy.

*See also:* BLACK STORK; GENOCIDE; GRIEF AND MOURNING IN CROSS-CULTURAL PERSPECTIVE; JUDAISM; MASS KILLERS

## Bibliography

Bauer, Yehuda. *History of the Holocaust.* Danbury, CT: Watts, 1982.

Baur, Erwin, Eugen Fischer, and Fritz Lenz. *Menschliche Auslese und Rseenhygiene.* (Human Selection and Race Hygiene.) Munich: Lehmanns, 1931.

Berenbaum, Michael. *The World Must Know.* New York: Little, Brown, 1993.

Browning, Christopher. *Nazi Policy, Jewish Workers, German Killers.* New York: Cambridge University Press, 2000.

Burleigh, Michael. *Death and Deliverance: Euthanasia in Germany, 1900–1945.* New York: Cambridge University Press, 1995.

Carroll, James. *Constantine's Sword: The Church and the Jews.* New York: Houghton Mifflin, 2001.

Fischer, Klaus. *The History of an Obsession: German Judeophobia and the Holocaust.* New York: Continuum, 1998.

Fleming, Gerald. *Hitler and the Final Solution.* Berkeley: University of California Press, 1984.

Frankl, Viktor. *Man's Search for Meaning.* New York: Washington Square Press, 1985.

Friedlander, Henry. *The Origins of Nazi Genocide: From Euthanasia to the Final Solution.* Chapel Hill: University of North Carolina Press, 1995.

Fuhrman, Harry, ed. *Holocaust and Genocide: A Search for Conscience.* New York: Anti-Defamation League, 1983.

Goldhagen, Daniel J. *Hitler's Willing Executioners: Ordinary Germans and the Holocaust.* New York: Knopf, 1996.

Hilberg, Raoul. *The Destruction of the European Jews.* New York: Holmes and Meier, 1985.

Hitler, Adolf. *Mein Kampf* (My Struggle), translated by Ralph Mannheim. New York: Houghton Mifflin, 1971.

Höss, Rudolf. *Death Dealer: The Memoirs of the SS Kommandant at Auschwitz.* New York: DaCapo, 1996.

Jäckel, Eberhard. "Einfach ein schlechtes Buch." *Die Zeit,* 27 May 1996, 24.

Jäckel, Eberhard. *Hitler's Weltanschauung: Entwurf einer Herrschaft.* (Hitler's Worldview: Outline of Power.) Tübingen: Wunderlich, 1969.

Kantor, Alfred. *An Artist's Journal of the Holocaust.* New York: Schocken Books, 1987.

Katz, Steven T. *The Holocaust in Historical Context,* Vol. 1: *The Holocaust and Mass Death Before the Modern Age.* New York: Oxford University Press, 1994.

Klemperer, Werner. *The Language of the Third Reich,* translated by Martin Brady. London: Athlone, 2000.

Kühl, Stefan. *The Nazi Connection: Eugenics, American Racism, and German National Socialism.* New York: Oxford University Press, 1994.

Lacquer, Walter. *The Terrible Secret: Suppression of the Truth about Hitler's "Final Solution."* London: Weidenfeld and Nicolson, 1980.

Laks, Szymon. *Music from Another World,* translated by Chester Kisiel. Evanston, IL: Northwestern University Press, 2000.

Lautmann, Rüdiger. "The Pink Triangle: Homosexuals as Enemies of the State." In Michael Berenbaum and Abraham Peck eds., *The Holocaust and History: The Known, the Unknown and the Reexamined.* Bloomington: Indiana University Press, 1998.

Levi, Primo. *If This Is a Man: Remembering Auschwitz.* New York: Summit, 1986.

Lewy, Guenter. *The Nazi Persecution of the Gypsies.* New York: Oxford University Press, 2000.

Lipstadt, Deborah. *Denying the Holocaust: The Growing Assault on Truth and Memory.* New York: Free Press, 1993.

Piper, Francisek. "Auschwitz Concentration Camp." In Michael Berenbaum and Abraham Peck eds., *The Holocaust and History: The Known, the Unknown and the Reexamined.* Bloomington: Indiana University Press, 1998.

Ritter, Carol, and John Roth. *Different Voices: Women and the Holocaust.* New York: Paragon House, 1993.

Rosenbaum, Ron. "The Roots of the Holocaust Denial." *The Wall Street Journal,* 12 April 2000, 4.

Schleunes, Karl. *The Twisted Road to Auschwitz: Nazi Policy Toward German Jews, 1933–1939.* Urbana: University of Illinois Press, 1990.

Schwertfeger, Ruth. *Women of Theresienstadt: Voices from a Concentration Camp.* New York: Berg, 1989.

Wiesel, Elie. *Night.* New York: Hill and Wang, 1960.

GREGORY PAUL WEGNER

# HOMICIDE, DEFINITIONS AND CLASSIFICATIONS OF

Early legal codes, including English common law, defined homicide as the killing of a human being and included suicide. As the American legal system evolved, suicide was excluded and homicide became "the killing of one person by another" (Allen and Simonsen 1998, p. 615).

National and international definitions of homicide vary from society to society. Because most societies consider homicide to be the killing of one human being by another human being, both suicide and the murder of infrahuman beings (beings "lower" than humans) are excluded from the definition. The differentiation between abortion and homicide has not always been so clear-cut. Some people consider a fetus to be a human being from the moment of conception, whereas others are more liberal in their beliefs. The debate over the line between human being and nonhuman being, with regard to abortion, is a continuous issue, but the U.S. Supreme Court's January 1973 *Roe* v. *Wade* decision eliminated the act, especially in the first trimester of pregnancy, from the definition of homicide. At the start of the twenty-first century, forty states and the District of Columbia prohibited (except in rare circumstances) abortions after the fetus becomes viable (i.e., capable of surviving outside the mother on its own)—generally after the twenty-seventh week of pregnancy. When the fetus becomes viable, it becomes a human being and, unless legally permitted, its termination falls within the realm of homicide. An ongoing legal issue is "partial birth" abortion in relation to the subject of homicide.

Homicide is generally divided into two categories: criminal (unjustifiable) and noncriminal (justifiable or excusable). Noncriminal homicide involves the taking of the life of another in a manner that would not invoke criminal sanctions. The police officer who kills in the line of duty, the public executioner who is paid for the action, and the private citizen who kills to protect his or her own life and/or the life or lives of others may be justified or excused for their behavior.

Criminal homicide is an act that is *mala in se.* This means that it is behavior that is morally wrong in itself and is objectively and inherently criminal regardless of where it occurs. The killing of a person by another in a nonlegal manner is a violation of "natural law," which Frank Schmalleger defined as "rules of conduct inherent in human nature and in the natural order which are thought to be knowable through intuition, inspiration, and the exercise of reason, without the need for reference to man-made laws" (Schmalleger 2001, p. 122). Homicide that is criminal is classified as a felony and is typically punishable by a year or more in a state or federal penal institution. In some circumstances, the death penalty may be administered.

Each state differs in the defining of criminal homicide. The Federal Bureau of Investigation's *Uniform Crime Reports* uses the categories of murder and nonnegligent manslaughter ("the willful . . . killing of one person by another person") and manslaughter by negligence ("the killing of another person by gross negligence"). It classifies justifiable homicide separately and excludes traffic fatalities. It is most helpful to simply divide criminal homicide into murder (first degree and second degree) and manslaughter (negligent, or involuntary, and nonnegligent, or voluntary).

First-degree murder consists of both premeditation and malice aforethought. Perpetrators of such murders possess *mens rea,* or criminal intent. They possess an "evil mind" or "depraved heart." They are aware that they have no right to kill, but they intend to commit an act of murder anyway (malice aforethought), and they carefully plan the demise of their victim (premeditation). For example, Joe Jones is an heir to the fortune of his Uncle John. Finding himself in need of money, Jones, after careful contemplation, decides that he wants his uncle dead and carefully plans to kill him via poisoning. Jones does not have to be present at the time of his relative's death to be convicted for his action.

In second-degree murder there is malice aforethought without premeditation. In other words, the offender intends to kill the victim but does not plan the lethal act. Bill Smith buys a new car, drives it home, and parks it in his driveway. While Smith is in his home, a neighbor attempts to vandalize and destroy Smith's new automobile. In a fit of rage and the full intent to kill, Smith returns to the driveway and murders his neighbor.

An act of voluntary or nonnegligent manslaughter is committed when a person attempts to hurt, but not kill, another human being—but the victim dies in the process. In a fit of drunken rage, Ray Wrong decides to teach his wife a lesson by banging her head against a wall. At the completion of his act, she is dead.

Negligent or involuntary manslaughter is characterized by accidental death. Some states distinguish between vehicular and nonvehicular accidental death and others do not. Jane Fast, while traveling through a school zone at an excessive rate of speed, hits and kills a pedestrian in a crosswalk. Her behavior would be considered an act of vehicular homicide. Mark Carpenter, while working on the roof of a new home, drops his hammer, which hits the head of a coworker working below. When the coworker dies from a skull concussion, the act becomes one of accidental, but not vehicular, manslaughter.

A number of studies have shown that the majority of homicides occur between people who know each other. "Non-stranger" or "acquaintance" homicide may range from individuals who encounter one another on one occasion and the death comes later, to persons who have been married for many years. In 2001 Freda Adler, Gerhard O. W. Mueller, and William S. Laufer reported on one study that indicated that 44 percent of the victims were in an intimate relationship with their killer, 11 percent were the children of the perpetrator, and 26 percent were friends and acquaintances. Only 7.5 percent of the killings involved strangers.

In a 1958 study of homicide in Philadelphia, Marvin Wolfgang found that a large number of the victims had initiated their own death. Wolfgang coined the term "victim precipitated" homicide to refer to those instances in which the victims' actions resulted in their demise. In this form of murder, the deceased may have made a menacing gesture, was first to pull a weapon, or merely used words to elicit a deadly response from the killer.

A new term for an old form of murder is "hate" homicide. This form of killing involves taking the life of "victims who are targeted because they differ from the perpetrator with respect to such characteristics as race, religion, ethnic origin, sexual orientation, gender, or disability status" (Fox and Levin 2001, p. 128). Hate killers are usually members of extremist groups such as neo-Nazis, skinheads, and the Ku Klux Klan. Victims are most often African Americans or homosexuals, and the killings usually occur in the southern and western parts of the country. In June 1998 James Byrd, an African-American, while hitchhiking on a Saturday night in Jasper, Texas, encountered three white men who were members of the Ku Klux Klan. Byrd was chained to the back of a truck and dragged more than two miles to his death. According to the perpetrators of the crime, they wanted to send a message to other African Americans in the area. On another occasion, in October 1998 in Laramie, Wyoming, two men posing as homosexuals lured a gay college student from a gay bar. He was robbed, pistol-whipped, burned with cigarettes, tied to a fence in the desert, and left to die from exposure. He died five days later in a hospital.

On April 20, 1999, at 11:35 A.M., eighteen-year-old Eric Harris and seventeen-year-old Dylan Klebold entered the cafeteria at Columbine High School in Littleton, Colorado. Heavily armed with semiautomatic weapons, the teenagers went on a killing rampage that resulted in the deaths of twelve students and one teacher. At the end of their carnage, the murderers killed themselves. The Columbine incident was not the first time a student entered a school and committed an act of homicide, but it was the one that shocked the public conscience and created a new term in the American vocabulary—"school homicide" or "school killing."

*See also:* CAPITAL PUNISHMENT; DEATH SYSTEM; FIREARMS; HOMICIDE, EPIDEMIOLOGY OF

## Bibliography

Adler, Freda, Gerhard O. W. Mueller, and William S. Laufer. *Criminology,* 4th edition. New York: McGraw-Hill, 2001.

Albanese, Jay S. *Criminal Justice: Brief Edition.* Boston: Allyn & Bacon, 2001.

Allen, Harry E., and Clifford E. Simonsen. *Corrections in America: An Introduction,* 8th edition. Upper Saddle River, NJ: Prentice Hall, 1998.

Barkan, Steven E. *Criminology: A Sociological Understanding,* 2nd edition. Upper Saddle River, NJ: Prentice Hall, 2001.

Federal Bureau of Investigation. *Crime in the United States: Uniform Crime Reports, 1998.* Washington, DC: U.S. Department of Justice, 1999.

Fox, James Alan, and Jack Levin. *The Will to Kill: Making Sense of Senseless Murder.* Boston: Allyn & Bacon, 2001.

Hoffman, Dennis E., and Vincent J. Webb. "Suicide As Murder at Common Law." *Criminology* 19 (1981):372–384.

Reid, Sue Titus. *Crime and Criminology,* 8th edition. Madison, WI: Brown and Benchmark, 1997.

Samaha, Joel. *Criminal Justice,* 5th edition. Belmont, CA: Wadsworth, 2000.

Schmalleger, Frank. *Criminal Justice Today.* Upper Saddle River, NJ: Prentice Hall, 2001.

*Internet Resources*

Steel, Fiona. "Calm before the Storm: The Littleton School Massacre." In "The Crime Library" [web site]. Available from www.crimelab.com/serial4/littleton/index.htm.

Sutton, Kathy. "Abortion in the Third Trimester." In the iVillageHealth [web site]. Available from www.allhealth.com/conditions/.

JAMES K. CRISSMAN

# HOMICIDE, EPIDEMIOLOGY OF

Homicide, the killing of one human being by another human being, has always been a concern in human society. It is a major social problem in the United States, where violence is endemic. The homicide rate in the United States peaked in 1980 at 10.7 per 100,000 population, but declined by 1997 to 6.8 per 100,000, the lowest number since

1967 when the murder rate was 7 murders per 100,000 (Adler, Mueller, and Laufer 2001).

Because various nations differ in their definitions of homicide and the manner in which they gather data, comparisons are difficult—statistics will vary from one data-gathering source to another. In 1989, in a comparison of nineteen industrialized nations providing information to Interpol (the international police agency), the United States possessed the highest homicide rate in the world at 7.9 per 100,000. Neighboring Canada's rate was only 2.7 per 100,000. A more recent comparison of nineteen industrialized nations, published in 1997, indicated that the United States still had the highest murder rate in the world. In 1998, according to Henry Tischler, the number hovered at around 7.4 per 100,000, which was three to four times the rate for most European nations. Tischler noted that although "Russia and other former Eastern-bloc countries have experienced a great deal of social upheaval since the fall of communism, causing their homicide rates to increase dramatically . . . these countries do not have rates that have been typical of the United States in the past 10 years" (Tischler 1998, p. 203).

## Gender and Homicide

Richard Hernstein has noted that the more heinous the crime, the greater the disproportion between men and women. This certainly holds true for homicide. According to statistics published by the U.S. Department of Justice, men committed 87.5 percent of murders in 1999. The ratio of male to female homicides was approximately nine to one. Almost three-fourths of male homicides and 80 percent of female homicides were perpetrated against men. Males were more likely to choose a gun as their weapon, but women preferred a cleaner means of killing, such as arson or poisoning (Fox and Levin 2001).

## Age and Homicide

According to Jay Albanese, writing in 2001, 46 percent of violent crime arrests (including those for homicide) involved people under the age of twenty-five. Individuals aged eighteen to twenty-four were the most likely to be arrested. In 1997 Sue Titus Reid found that children between the ages of twelve and fifteen were the most frequent

victims of violence, and the elderly were the least likely to be victimized. Department of Justice data for 1976 to 1999 showed that 63.7 percent of homicide offenders and 52.7 percent of victims were between the ages of eighteen and thirty-four. Only 7.5 percent of homicide offenders and 14.9 percent of homicide victims were fifty years of age or older. Variables in the high rate of homicide for young people included an increase in gang activity and the availability of guns and drugs. Additionally, Larry Gaines, Michael Kaune, and Larry L. Miller contended that an "environment of violence . . . permeates the daily life of many of our nation's youths," and "child abuse, which is difficult to measure, but is believed to be widespread, can also teach a youth the values of violence, which may lead to delinquent or criminal activity" (Gaines, Kaune, and Miller 2001, p. 27).

## Race and Homicide

While African Americans constitute only about 12 percent of the U.S. population, they are overrepresented in the homicide category for both offenders and victims. Department of Justice statistics delineated that African Americans were seven times more likely than whites to commit homicides and six times more likely than whites to be murdered in 1999. Most homicides are intraracial. In a 2001 publication, James Alan Fox and Jack Levin stated that 86 percent of white homicide victims were killed by whites and 94 percent of African Americans were murdered by members of their own race.

Stranger killing tends to be intraracial, with 68 percent of whites and 87 percent of African Americans killing strangers within their own race. Data for 1976 to 1999 showed that 42.4 percent of African Americans and 55.5 percent of white victims were in an intimate relationship with the offender at the time of their demise. The murder of intimates was also intraracial.

African Americans were much more likely than whites to be the victims of hate crimes. According to Albanese, "Hispanics constitute a small but growing segment of victims of serious crimes" (Albanese 2001, p. 63).

## Guns and Homicide

Perhaps the principal reason for the high rate of homicide in the United States is the gun mentality of American citizens. Americans led by the National

Rifle Association (NRA) argue that the Second Amendment of the U.S. Constitution gives them the "right to bear arms" and that that right should never be taken away. Gerald Robin, writing in 1991, stated that approximately one in every four families owned a handgun and that the average number of firearms in gun-owning families was about 2.34. Data from 1999 showed that in a comparison with France, Norway, Canada, New Zealand, Australia, Israel, Denmark, Scotland, the Netherlands, and England/Wales, the United States had an average annual rate of 13.6 per 100,000 population for deaths from firearms. This was more than twice the rate for the second highest country, France, which had a rate of 6.2 per 100,000.

## Social Class and Homicide

Since the early 1900s, with the exception of Edwin Sutherland's classic work on white-collar crime in the 1940s, criminologists and criminological theory have focused primarily on lower-class crime. Theories that the poor are more likely to commit a violent crime are supported by crime statistics. The highest crime rates are found in the low-income areas of the city. The National Crime Victimization Survey for 1997 showed that people in households with an income of less than $7,500 experienced significantly more violent crime than persons in households at any other income level. The survey also showed that the greater the income, the lower the violent crime rate. Gaines, Kaune, and Miller stated that "a rise in one percentage point in male unemployment appears to increase the violent crime rate by 9 percent" (Gaines, Kaune, and Miller 2001, p. 49).

## Drugs, Alcohol, and Homicide

Drugs and alcohol are definitely related to homicide. The National Center on Addiction and Substance Abuse at Columbia University in 1998 reported that 80 percent of prisoners in the United States were involved with alcohol or other drugs at the time of their crime. A study of murders in New York City discovered that more than half were drug related. Department of Justice statistics for 1997 showed that approximately 53 percent of state and federal prisoners incarcerated for murder were under the influence of drugs or alcohol when they committed their lethal act. Research performed by the Rand Corporation in 2001 found that most of the violent prisoners studied had extensive histories of heroin abuse, often in combination with alcohol and other drugs. Also in 2001, Kurt Finsterbusch found in a study of homicide offenders incarcerated in New York State correctional facilities that 31 percent reported being drunk at the time of their crime, and 19 percent believed that their homicide was related to their drinking. The National Council on Alcoholism reported in 1997 that approximately 64 percent of murders may be attributed to alcohol misuse. Joel Samaha stated, "about half of all offenders have used alcohol within 72 hours of committing a violent crime" (Samaha 2001, p. 43).

## Geographic Region and Homicide

Regional differences are evident with regard to homicide. Statistics published in 2001 showed that states in the southern and western regions of the United States had higher homicide rates than those in the Midwest and Northeast. The highest rates were in the South (8 per 100,000), and the lowest were in the northeastern section of the country (4 per 100,000).

There are several possible explanations for the high rate of southern homicide. First, there is the contention that the hot climate is more conducive to angry responses, which then lead to lethal consequences. Gaines, Kaune, and Miller provided partial support for this argument when they stated that crime data "show higher rates of crime in warmer summer months than any other time of the year" (Gaines, Kaune, and Miller 2001, p. 48). Second, there is the argument that a regional subculture of violence can be found in the South. Third, the prejudice and discrimination once prevalent in the South may still be a contributing factor in racial tensions and violence. Fourth, Steven Barkan noted in 2001 that the South has a high rate of economic deprivation and inequality, which are variables in homicide. Finally, there is a gun mentality in the South not found in other parts of the country.

## Urban Status and Homicide

As reported by Freda Adler, Gerhard Mueller, and William Laufer in 2001, the largest U.S. cities have the highest homicide rates, while the smallest have the lowest homicide rates. According to Michael Rand, for the period 1993 to 1996, urban residents had homicide rates significantly higher than suburban residents, who in turn had higher rates than rural residents. In 1997, however, metropolitan cities had a much higher rate of homicide than rural counties, but rural counties possessed a slightly higher homicide rate than small cities (i.e., suburban cities). According to Federal Bureau of Investigation statistics published in 2001, the homicide rate was 7 per 100,000 residents in U.S. metropolitan areas and 16 to 18 per 100,000 in some of the largest cities. In rural areas, the rate was 5 per 100,000.

Because homicide rates in the United States are the highest of all Western nations, it is logical that American cities would have a higher homicide rate than comparable large cities in other parts of the world. For example, Barkan, in a 2001 publication, reported that New York City had a homicide rate five to six times as high as London, another city with a large population. One study indicated that 25 percent of Boston's youth homicides, gun assaults, and drug offenses occurred in an area encompassing less than 4 percent of the city.

*See also:* HOMICIDE, DEFINITIONS AND CLASSIFICATIONS OF; MASS KILLERS; SERIAL KILLERS; SUICIDE BASICS: EPIDEMIOLOGY

### *Bibliography*

Adler, Freda, Gerhard O. W. Mueller, and William S. Laufer. *Criminology,* 4th edition. New York: McGraw-Hill, 2001.

Albanese, Jay S. *Criminal Justice: Brief Edition.* Boston: Allyn & Bacon, 2001.

Barkan, Steven E. *Criminology: A Sociological Understanding,* 2nd edition. Upper Saddle River, NJ: Prentice Hall, 2001.

Cole, George F., and Christopher E. Smith. *The American System of Criminal Justice,* 9th edition. Belmont, CA: Wadsworth, 2001.

Finsterbusch, Kurt. *Taking Sides: Clashing Views on Controversial Social Issues,* 11th edition. Guilford, CT: McGraw Hill/Dushkin, 2001.

Fox, James Alan, and Jack Levin. *The Will to Kill: Making Sense of Senseless Murder.* Boston: Allyn & Bacon, 2001.

Gaines, Larry, Michael Kaune, and Larry L. Miller. *Criminal Justice in Action: The Core.* Belmont, CA: Wadsworth, 2001

Kastenbaum, Robert J. *Death, Society, and Human Experience,* 4th edition. New York: Merrill Publishing, 1991.

Kornblum, William, and Joseph Julian. *Social Problems,* 10th edition. Upper Saddle River, NJ: Prentice Hall, 2001.

Lattimore, Pamela K., and Cynthia A. Nahabedian. *The Nature of Homicide: Trends and Changes.* Washington, DC: U.S. Government Printing Office, 1997.

Levin, Jack. "Hatred: Too Close for Comfort." In Jack Levin and James Alan Fox eds., *Deadlines: Essays in Murder and Mayhem.* Boston: Allyn & Bacon, 2001.

Rand, Michael. "Criminal Victimization, 1997: Changes, 1996–97, with Trends, 1993–97." In Steven H. Cooper ed., *Criminology.* Boston: Houghton Mifflin, 2000.

Reid, Sue Titus. *Crime and Criminology,* 8th edition. Madison, WI: Brown and Benchmark, 1997.

Robin, Gerald D. *Violent Crime and Gun Control.* Cincinnati, OH: Anderson Publishing, 1991.

Samaha, Joel. *Criminal Justice,* 5th edition. Belmont, CA: Wadsworth, 2000.

Schmalleger, Frank. *Criminal Justice Today.* Upper Saddle River, NJ: Prentice Hall, 2001.

Tischler, Henry L. *Introduction to Sociology,* 6th edition. Fort Worth, TX: Harcourt Press, 1998.

### *Internet Resources*

Fox, James Alan, and Marianne W. Zawitz. "Homicide Trends in the United States." In the Bureau of Justice Statistics [web site]. Available from www.ojp.usdoj.gov/bjs/homicide/homtrnd.htm.

JAMES K. CRISSMAN
JENNIFER PARKIN

# HORROR MOVIES

According to the film critic William K. Everson, the horror film is the most unique of any film genre because rigid guidelines do not have to be followed as closely by the director or, for that matter, the screenwriter. The horror film's message of terror and death can be subtly communicated to the audience or conveyed in very intense (and ultimately disturbing) visual and auditory cues. While other film genres might use restraint and logical explanation as their overriding criteria, the horror film need not follow this standard formula; thus, many cinematic tricks and techniques are available to filmmakers to employ at their discretion. The end result is that the audience can experience a wide range of negative effects, from minor irritation to overwhelming nausea, when viewing a film of the horror genre.

Based on Everson's remarks, one might conclude that the salient reason given as to why people watch horror films is that they want to be scared. In fact, this scare drive is so powerfully addictive to some viewers that they keep coming back to these films over and over again, desiring more terror and craving more thrills with each viewing. However, a deeper, more psychological explanation can be provided as to why humans have been fascinated with gore and bloodshed since the very beginning of recorded history.

To help one understand this motivating force in the human psyche, one must consider Carl Jung's psychoanalytic theory of archetypes. Jung believed that all humans have inherited a set of primordial images that are contained in the collective unconscious. For the most part, these archaic images (referred to as archetypes) remain buried within the unconscious; at significant moments of one's life, however, they can be realized and fully expressed through religion, philosophy, art, literature, and, more recently, the cinema. Jung noted that the most powerful and perhaps most dangerous archetype of the group is the shadow. By definition, the shadow contains all of humanity's unacceptable behavior, bestial impulses, and repressed desires. Using a horror theme analogy, the shadow is "the Mr. Hyde to our Dr. Jekyll . . . the side of our personality that wants to do all the things that we do not allow ourselves to do [normally]" (Fordham 1966, p. 49). Thus, human nature is really comprised of two selves: an outward, everyday persona and a dark shadow that people try to keep in check and hide from others as much as possible.

The neo-Jungian Carol Pearson labels the Jungian shadow as humanity's Destroyer. She explains that while people might be committed to promoting life and making the world a better place in which to reside, each and every person has a death wish that can ultimately hurt them and the much larger society. Pearson further adds, "Even the healthiest individual will do or say things that hurt

other people . . . Ultimately, the Destroyer turns us into villains when we refuse to acknowledge and take responsibility for the harm we do—and we all do harm of some kind" (Pearson 1991, p. 145). Given this description of the archetypal Destroyer, it seems only natural that humankind is drawn to horror films. Every aspect of death that the psyche tries to keep hidden from the conscious self is depicted on the screen. And even though most of the cinematic acts of destruction are rather extreme and exaggerated forms of everyday reality, people are still compelled to examine them if for no other reason than to remind themselves that they carry around this death-dealing nature.

This entry examines the various faces of death in this particular film genre, starting with the silent era and moving to the contemporary period. The dramatic changes in how death is portrayed on the screen across eight decades will be noted as well as how these images are related to the given sociocultural milieu of the times.

### The Prototypic Faces of Death in the 1920s, 1930s, and 1940s

The silent era of horror films focused almost exclusively on the hideous, deathlike appearances of the monsters rather than the ghastly crimes they committed against society. The chief reason was that the grisly makeup had to compensate for the lack of sound in these features. And so any number of strange and bizarre bogeymen that populated the screen greeted the viewer. Take for instance John Barrymore's *Mr. Hyde* (1920), which depicts the counterpart of Dr. Jekyll as a creature with a Neanderthal, almost satanic visage. Or consider the very first vampire film, the German silent *Nosferatu* (1922), that turned Count Orlock into a "walking skeleton" of horror with "his pale skull-like face, his blazing eyes, pointed ears, and long tapering fingernails" (Preiss 1991, p. 267).

The Universal Studios period of horror films spanning the 1930s and 1940s continued to invest most of their special effects budget in the title creatures' features at the expense of adequate plot development, noteworthy musical scores, and prominent death scenes. Thus, the great works of literature like Bram Stoker's *Dracula* (1897) or Mary Shelley's *Frankenstein* (1818) were converted to one-dimensional productions with the ghoulish monster once again occupying the central position on the screen. The 1930 Todd Browning version of *Dracula* cast the Hungarian actor Bela Lugosi in the role of the Count. His broken English, exaggerated hand gestures, pasty face makeup, piercing eyes, aquiline nose, and high cheekbones gave Lugosi a kind of cinematic immortality for recreating the image of the Old World nobleman into a mysterious, somewhat disturbing creature of the night. Interestingly, very few humans would die at the hands of this cinematic Count, unlike his literary predecessor.

The very next year Universal tried its hand at Shelley's *Frankenstein* (1931), giving the actor Boris Karloff his chance at fame for playing the Monster with a good deal of pathos. The film reviewer Byron Preiss describes Karloff in the following way: "tall, ill-clad, lumbering, with a square head and pegs sticking out from his neck, his face gaunt, his eyes baffled . . . he stands unsteadily with his arms upthrust toward the light which, with the innocence of the newborn, he tries to seize" (Preiss 1991, p. 243). And while the Monster executes some humans in the worst way imaginable (from drowning a child in the lake to hanging the hunchbacked servant with his own whip), these sequences take a backseat to the very realistic, corpselike appearance of Karloff that the viewer never tires from seeing.

Other Universal monsters populated the screen during this interval, such as *The Mummy* (1932), *The Bride of Frankenstein* (1935), and *The Wolf Man* (1941). However, few would ever reach the stature of Count Dracula or Frankenstein's Monster in looks or atrocities, overt as well as covert. It was not until the 1950s that the creature features would return to the screen in a never-before-seen bloodthirsty glory by the Hammer Film Studios in London, England.

## The International Faces of Death in the 1950s, 1960s, and 1970s

More than anything else, the Hammer Studios wanted to attract a significant portion of the adult market to the horror film genre. Instead of banal scripts and terrible acting, the Universal story lines would be updated for that targeted audience with experienced actors like Christopher Lee (Count Dracula) and Peter Cushing (Dr. Victor

Frankenstein) at the helm, delivering lines with vigor and enthusiasm. Perhaps the most salient addition was the effective use of bloodshed and gore at key moments to illustrate just how despicable these characters were to their unsuspecting victims. The movies were shot in a Technicolor brilliance (unlike their monochromatic predecessors), which only exaggerated the death scenes. Now the viewer would gaze at streams of blood gushing out from chests, necks, and faces in a potpourri of deep reds and bright purples amidst softer blue and green backdrops. Some examples of Hammer Studios' seventeen-year tenure in the horror cinema (from 1957 to 1974) are included to show just how much the Destroyer archetype had been modified to satiate the public demand for more atypical and bizarre ways of killing on the screen.

The *Dracula* series of films began their run with some very striking scenes. In *Horror of Dracula* (1958) Van Helsing drives the stake into a recently converted vampire with a sickening relish. By the ending he traps Dracula in his own castle and, holding candlesticks in the sign of the cross, the good doctor forces the Count directly into the rays of the sun, thereby blasting the crumbling body to dusty remains. The follow-up movie, *Dracula—Prince of Darkness* (1965), involves the resurrection of the infamous monster by having his manservant brutally slit the throat of one of the guests at the castle in a Black Mass ritual. *Dracula Has Risen from the Grave* (1969) depicts one of the most graphic sequences of any vampire film to date. Here the Count survives a staking by pulling out the pointed object and throwing it at his attackers, but not before a significant amount of blackish-red blood comes streaming out of the rather large hole made in the vampire's chest. As the titles progressed, Dracula would be stabbed, burnt, poked and prodded atop a bed of stakes, and even shoveled to death (*Dracula A.D.*, 1972) before meeting his screen finale at the hands of Van Helsing once more in *The Satanic Rites of Dracula* (1973).

Like *Dracula*, the *Frankenstein* set had its share of memorable death moments. Beginning with *The Curse of Frankenstein* (1957), the Monster strangles a number of the local villagers with its bare hands before being shot directly in the face. The film critic John McCarty notes that Frankenstein is no better than his creation, "fondling brains, eyeballs, severed hands and other assorted organs" throughout the film with an unusual coldness that would bring new meaning to the term "mad scientist" (McCarty 1990, p. 19). The series continues this bloody path by having new creations eat the flesh of their victims (*Revenge of Frankenstein,* 1959) as well as decapitate assorted bullies and store their heads in picnic baskets and atop bedposts (*Frankenstein Created Woman,* 1967). Perhaps the most tragic of all fates occurs for the Monster when it is literally torn apart by the inmates of an asylum who spurn it for being so different from themselves (*Frankenstein and the Monster from Hell,* 1974).

In addition to the Dracula and Frankenstein films, Hammer Studios also produced one *Wolfman* picture. *The Curse of the Werewolf* (1961) ends on a sad note when the cursed creature's father shoots it in the heart with a silver bullet. The metamorphosis back to the human state never transpires, and so the camera lingers on the werewolf's face that has bloodstained tears dripping from the permanently open, yet forlorn, eyes.

Other British companies tried to emulate the Hammer horror treatments with some measure of success. The Amicus Company specialized in reanimated body parts that would seek out with a vengeance those parties responsible for their owners' deaths (see *Dr. Terror's House of Horrors,* 1965; *Tales from the Crypt,* 1972; *Asylum,* 1972; *And Now the Screaming Starts,* 1973). Elstree Studios, in conjunction with American International, gave a more human face to the Destroyer by casting horror film veteran Vincent Price in the title role of *The Abominable Dr. Phibes* (1971), who metes out justice to those physicians who could not save his beloved wife, Victoria. In 1992 Price disclosed in an interview with Stanley Wiater that he thoroughly enjoyed making *Dr. Phibes,* as it enabled him to throw a good deal of humor into the role so that the extent of his violent acts could be significantly diminished on the screen. And so one of Phibes's victims is drained entirely of his blood, another has the flesh on her face consumed by locusts, and still another is eaten alive in the cockpit of his plane by ravenous rats while the doctor attentively listens to his assistant Vulnavia playing beautiful music upon her violin. The send-up formula would be employed at least three more times by Price (in *Dr. Phibes Rises Again,* 1972; *Theater of Blood,* 1973; and *Madhouse,* 1974) until the actor became

tired of the same old story line and eventually retired from the horror genre. But the violence-humor combination would remain a staple of the horror film from this point on.

## The Faces of Death in Contemporary American Films

The American horror cinema was heavily influenced by the British faces of death, yet was able to impart originality to its less Gothic, more modernized tales of destruction. The mad slasher film became one of the most popular American products, starting with Alfred Hitchcock's 1960 masterpiece, *Psycho*. Playing the dual role of a disturbed young man (Norman Bates) and his dead mother, Anthony Perkins gave a much needed pathos to the brutal slasher figure that killed unsuspecting women taking showers in their motel rooms. The three *Psycho* sequels that followed (*Psycho II,* 1983; *Psycho III,* 1986; and *Psycho IV: The Beginning,* 1990) continued to expand on the character of Norman Bates and were successful in large part due to Perkins portraying the aging madman as a misunderstood victim of his tragic upbringing. The statement Bates utters throughout the series, "We all go a little mad sometimes," would allow viewers to identify with his insanity and perhaps their own latent fears of losing control in an abusive environment as well.

Other horror series throughout the 1970s, 1980s, and 1990s attempted to recreate the *Psycho* slasher, but their madmen ultimately lacked the charm, wit, and other human qualities of Perkins's Bates. From *Halloween*'s Michael Myers, *Friday the 13th*'s Jason Voorhees, and *A Nightmare on Elm Street*'s Freddy Krueger all these slashers share a number of qualities: a distinctive attire (from hockey masks to green-and-red sweaters), heavy breathing, a lingering point-of-view toward their intended prey, and the ability to generate a high body count (i.e., dozens of corpses littering a single film). One noteworthy trademark of the slasher film, namely the Final Girl who survives and eventually kills the madman with anything readily available (e.g., axe, knife, even her own highly trained body), would come to be a widely accepted image for the horror queen. As the film study scholars Pat Kirkham and Janet Thumim note, male fans of the genre would be the strongest endorsers, especially when these Final Girls took the offensive and used

*The 1982 horror movie* Poltergeist, *starring Craig T. Nelson, Heather O'Rourke (center), and Jobeth Williams featured scenes of paranormal activity and the undead, which originated from the family's television set. This successful film spawned its first sequel in 1986 and its second in 1988.* KOBAL COLLECTION/MGM/UA

their brains to outthink their intellectually challenged foes. *Silence of the Lambs* (1991) and *Hannibal* (2001) are just two examples of how the Final Girl has evolved to the Amazon-worthy protagonist (Clarice Starling) to such powerful psychotics as Dr. Lecter.

Another type of horror film capitalized on earlier works both in the United States and abroad (*The Innocents,* 1960; *Rosemary's Baby,* 1968) and focused on a new death-dealer, the possessed child. William Peter Blatty's *The Exorcist* (1973) goes well beyond the limits of acceptable good taste and propriety by showing scenes of the satanic child Regan (played by Linda Blair) spraying vomit into the faces of the prostrate priests or masturbating with devilish delight using her crucifix. One reason that *The Exorcist* remains the highest-grossing horror movie ever made, setting the stage for many rip-offs (*Beyond the Door,* 1975; *The Omen,* 1976; *Damien—Omen II,* 1978; *Holocaust 2000,* 1978; *The Godsend,* 1979; *The Children,* 1980; *Children of the Corn,* 1984; *Child of Light—*

*Child of Darkness,* 1990) as well as its own inevitable set of sequels (*Exorcist II: The Heretic,* 1977; *The Exorcist III,* 1990), is that it preys on parents' fears that they could lose their children to uncontrollable outside forces. Clearly, *The Exorcist* is a film that has reshaped the horror genre and continues to do so, as seen in adult possession hits like *Stigmata* (1999).

The cannibalistic zombie image further pushed the envelope on what would be considered the conventional norms to a horror film. Starting with the cult classic *Night of the Living Dead* (1968), and continuing with *Dawn of the Dead* (1979) and *Day of the Dead* (1985), viewers are greeted by a more disgusting type of Destroyer—one that literally kills humans by devouring them—who dies then comes back to life (with whatever limbs or organs remaining) to join the ranks of the ravenous zombies, thus escalating the scale of the menace. Of all zombie movies made, the original *Night of the Living Dead* remains the most fatalistic. The film contains "dead relatives turning on living relatives, dead oldsters turning on living youngsters (and vice-versa) . . . with the nightmarish cycle repeating itself [over and over again]" (McCarty 1990, p. 103). What *Night of the Living Dead*'s screenplay writer George Romero wanted to do was show just how irrational the world had become with the breakdown of the nuclear family, wars waged without a just cause, and frequent assassinations of noteworthy, political leaders. While the zombie Destroyer has not been embraced to the same degree as the more traditional ones (e.g., the vampire and mad scientist), every so often a horror film surfaces with the hungry undead in it, reminding viewers that the worst hell on earth is never dying but living on indefinitely at the expense of destroying other souls.

## Future Faces of Death in the Horror Cinema

Many scholars and film critics believe that the faces of death within the horror genre will undergo a major facelift in the twenty-first century and beyond. Referred to as techno-mythic Destroyers, these new figures will either be created by the technological advances available or use that very technology to kill people in even more unusual and imaginative ways than before. Some techno-mythic Destroyers have already appeared on the screen. In the 1980s when television sets and VCRs were becoming commonplace items in every household, there emerged a rash of related cinematic terrors. In *Halloween III: Season of the Witch* (1982), the villain of the tale broadcasts his demonic message across the national airwaves to unsuspecting children while *Videodrome* (1982) allows the viewer to imagine a wide assortment of sadomasochistic pleasures via cable programming until they take on a frightening and mind-bending reality. By the 1990s, video games were becoming all the rage, so naturally horror movies mimicked the popular culture trend. *Stephen King's The Langoliers* (1995) has evil Pac-Man creatures terrorizing a stranded group of airline passengers in an alternate time zone; *Phantasm III: Lord of the Undead* (1993) portrays the Tall Man unleashing his horde of living spheres on the world in a new stage of the *Phantasm* game; and *Lawnmower Man* (1992) shows the recreated Jobe seizing control of the virtual reality universe and all programs tapping into that dimension. Based on these films, it seems only a matter of time until HDTV and DVD technology will be utilized by similar fictional Destroyers to wipe out human existence on the planet.

Despite these changing faces of death in the horror film genre, one factor does appear to be constant—namely, the mythos of the human destructive potential. This dark half of human nature is filled with so many nasty images and sinister figures that eventually they will surface in full force. Humankind's hidden demons will continue to serve as fodder for future screenplay writers and directors in the film industry, and audiences will most assuredly see more of their inner selves on the screen in the decades ahead.

*See also:* GREEK TRAGEDY; OPERATIC DEATH; SHAKESPEARE, WILLIAM; VAMPIRES; ZOMBIES

### Bibliography

Everson, William K. *Classics of the Horror Film*. New York: First Carol Publishing Group, 1990.

Everson, William K. *More Classics of the Horror Film: Fifty Years of Great Chillers*. New York: First Carol Publishing Group, 1990.

Fordham, Frieda. *An Introduction to Jung's Psychology*. London: Penguin Books, 1966.

Iaccino, James F. *Psychological Reflections on Cinematic Terror: Jungian Archetypes in Horror Films*. Westport, CT: Praeger Press, 1994.

Jung, Carl G. *The Archetypes and the Collective Unconscious: The Collected Works of C. G. Jung,* translated by R. F. C. Hull. Vol. 9a. Princeton, NJ: Princeton University Press, 1990.

Kirkham, Pat, and Janet Thumim, eds. *You Tarzan: Masculinity, Movies and Men*. New York: St. Martin's Press, 1993.

McCarty, John. *The Modern Horror Film: 50 Contemporary Classics*. New York: First Carol Publishing Group, 1990.

Pearson, Carol S. *Awakening the Heroes Within: Twelve Archetypes to Help Us Find Ourselves and Transform Our World*. San Francisco, CA: HarperCollins, 1991.

Preiss, Byron, ed. *The Ultimate Dracula*. New York: Dell Publishing, 1991.

Preiss, Byron, ed. *The Ultimate Frankenstein*. New York: Dell Publishing, 1991.

Preiss, Byron, ed. *The Ultimate Werewolf*. New York: Dell Publishing, 1991.

Wiater, Stanley. *Dark Visions: Conversations with the Masters of the Horror Film*. New York: Avon Books, 1992.

JAMES F. IACCINO

# HOSPICE, ALZHEIMER PATIENTS AND

"Dying the good death" is a care-giving goal, regardless of the presumed immediate cause of death, site(s) of the dying process, or cultural and ethnic differences among the dying person, their family, the community, and the health care providers. At the close of life, the patient, family members, and clinicians face decisions regarding the degree of intensive medical care to be provided for treatment of diseases, withdrawal of invasive interventions, initiation of hospice, and treatment of a range of chronic medical conditions. A hospice philosophy or care provides palliative care with a goal of maximal comfort and not maximal survival of the person. In the beginning, hospices served mostly persons with advanced cancer who decided to forgo further aggressive therapies, but the success of the hospice movement led to inclusion of persons with other life-limiting conditions, such as patients with heart disease, pulmonary disease, and dementia. Despite the recommendation made sixteen years ago that hospice care is appropriate for individuals suffering from advanced dementia, a survey of hospice programs showed that less than 1 percent of hospice patients had primary diagnosis of dementia and seven percent had dementia as a secondary diagnosis in addition to having cancer.

Dementia of the Alzheimer type (DAT) is an acquired, progressive, life-limiting disorder for which the biggest risk factor is living to an old age. According to U.S. Census data from 1900 and projections through 2050, people over age eighty-five—the category at highest risk for developing dementia—constitute the most rapidly growing segment of the population. Between 2.5 and 4 million Americans are already afflicted with DAT and evidence suggests that about 47 percent of people age eighty-five and older may develop DAT, meaning that these numbers will continue to rise as the population ages.

Persons with DAT have both a chronic and terminal illness and ultimately will become completely dependent in all aspects of activities of self-care. Cognitive deficits in dementia occur in several spheres including memory impairment, aphasia, apraxia, agnosia, and disturbance in executive function. Although some symptoms of DAT may be slowed by medications, there is no cure for DAT and ultimately the person will die either from a complication of DAT or from another age-related disorder. In either case, because new discoveries in medical science have the capacity to extend the typical dying process without restoring cognitive capacity or physical function, palliative care should be considered to provide comfort-promoting interventions and relief from aversive symptoms.

## Hospice Care and DAT

Hospice care is an organized method of providing palliative care. Care can be provided in a hospital, nursing home, community setting, or as a free-standing program, but most hospice care is provided in homes. Making the hospice philosophy operational directs care-giving activities to strive for maximal comfort and not maximal survival of the person.

Persons suffering from DAT often develop behavioral problems in which different symptoms appear throughout the progressive stages. When patients with terminal cancer receive hospice care, pain relief is a focus of care. For persons with DAT, management of the challenging behaviors is a focus of care. Regardless of the pathological processes involved, both pain and behavioral symptoms cause suffering; pain can be managed for persons with terminal cancer and behavioral symptoms can be managed for persons with DAT. A two-year prospective cohort study found that caring for patients with advanced DAT on a Dementia Special Care Unit (DSCU) using a palliative care philosophy resulted in less patient discomfort and lower health care costs than when care was provided on a traditional long-term care unit. When patients with DAT are allowed to receive palliative care, their surrogate decision makers reject care that extends the dying process, and patients receive "high-touch" care provided by interdisciplinary health care team members who strive to promote patient comfort. The focus of high-touch care is not the withholding of invasive aggressive interventions, but providing specific, individualized, intensive nursing interventions.

Advance care planning is necessary to assure that individuals receive the types of health care they desire. Everyone should have an established health care proxy who would make a decision regarding health care if an individual becomes incapacitated. If a person has not completed the health care proxy process before the diagnosis of DAT, the person should select a proxy and complete required legal forms as soon as possible. Early in the dementia process, persons have the cognitive capacity to make future plans, including choosing who should represent their health, legal, and financial affairs. If there is no health care proxy and the person no longer has the capacity to select one, the health care team should work with the surrogate decision maker to establish an advance care plan so that end-of-life decisions can be made in advance of crises.

**Treatment Options**

There is a palliative care program for veterans with advanced DAT at the Edith Nourse Rogers Memorial Veterans Hospital in Bedford, Massachusetts. The Bedford program has two central components: advance care planning and comfort care. Family members meet with the interdisciplinary health care team to discuss therapeutic options, explore previous wishes of the patient and their relevance to the veteran's current condition, and establish an advance care plan. The advance care plan specifies interventions to promote quality of life and comfort, and identifies aggressive medical interventions to be avoided. Aggressive medical care includes invasive diagnostic tests and treatment of coexisting medical conditions including transfer to an acute-care unit if indicated, and tube feeding if normal food intake is not possible. Treatment limitations that are more consistent with a comfort approach to end-of-life care include:

- no cardiopulmonary resuscitation;

- no transfer to an acute-care setting for technological interventions, which excludes intravenous therapy but includes transfer for an intervention required to prevent discomfort, such as to repair a fractured hip;

- no invasive medical or intravenous antibiotic treatment of intercurrent infections, but antipyretics, analgesics, and oral antibiotics may be prescribed for symptom management to treat discomfort; and

- no artificial feeding, which precludes the use of long-term feeding tubes.

Infections and eating difficulties are two inevitable consequences of terminal DAT. Changes in immune function, incontinence, decreased mobility, and propensity for aspiration of food, liquids, and respiratory secretions predispose persons to life-threatening infections. Infections are the most frequent cause of death in the terminal stage of dementia. Even excellent intensive nursing care and high vaccination rates cannot eliminate the influence of risk factors that cause development of many infections, relapse after successful treatment, and infections that gradually become more difficult to treat. Because a life-threatening infection is highly probable in advanced DAT, clinicians should be prepared to help surrogates make decisions about palliative treatment options.

Under the leadership of Ladislav Volicer (who initiated hospice care for persons with dementia), the Bedford team conducted a series of studies to examine "treatment success," which has to be weighed against the risk benefit ratio of management strategies and the likelihood of successfully achieving positive outcomes for individual persons. Study one found no difference in the mortality rate for patients with severe DAT who received antibiotic therapy versus those who received palliative care—suggesting that aggressive treatment did not alter the survival of patients with severe DAT. Study two found that managing infections on a DSCU results in lower discomfort, even for patients treated aggressively.

Study three developed and tested a predictive model for short-term survival and found that older age and higher severity of DAT at the time of the infection, palliative care, and admission for long-term care within six months prior to the febrile event were positively associated with the likelihood of dying within six months following onset of a fever. Clinicians can consider this predictive model when making the decision whether or not to certify patients with DAT for Medicare hospice coverage. Study four found that an infection did not have its own effect on DAT progression; disease severity increased in most patients, but more so in patients who received aggressive medical treatment. Providing palliative care for infections: (1) prevents patients from undergoing invasive diagnostic workups and treatments, does not accelerate the progression of DAT; (2) is associated with lower observed discomfort; (3) is not associated with higher rates of mortality for more advanced patients; and (4) also conserves scarce health care resources.

Instead of aggressive "high-tech" care, strategies to prevent infections or decrease their severity should be provided by:

- offering meticulous nursing care to keep the skin clean and dry despite incontinence;

- avoiding urinary catheters;

- instituting therapy programs striving to maintain ambulation as long as possible; and

- minimizing aspiration of food and liquids through the adjustment of diet texture and by using thickened liquids and physiological positioning.

During the course of the illness, the main eating difficulties are food refusal and choking. Many late-stage patients also forget how to chew and swallow and the terminal stage is marked by swallowing difficulty due to brain pathology. Decreased appetite causing food refusal may be a symptom of depression or a sign of the dying process as the body goes through a physical shutting down. Using skillful hand feeding techniques with pleasing to the taste caloric-rich foods in a composition to prevent choking prevents the use of feeding tubes. There will come a time, however, when serious eating problems will lead to the person with DAT being unable to eat or swallow. At that time, the person may be kept comfortable by offering a single ice chip at a time under the tongue or in the cheek or by artificial saliva spray.

End-of-life care should be characterized by a sense of contentment and ease as the dying person makes the transition to death. For the very vulnerable group of persons with DAT, many health professionals believe foregoing aggressive interventions, which do not ultimately result in improvement of an underlying dementia and may cause discomfort, is more compassionate than striving to extend survival at all costs.

*See also:* HOSPICE IN HISTORICAL PERSPECTIVE; SAUNDERS, CICELY

### *Bibliography*

Fabiszewski, K. J., B. J. Volicer, and Ladislav Volicer. "Effect of Antibiotic Treatment on Outcome of Fevers in Institutionalized Alzheimer Patients." *Journal of the American Medical Association* 263 (1990):3168–3172.

Hurley, Ann C., R. Bottino, and Ladislav Volicer. "Nursing Role in Advance Proxy Planning for Alzheimer Patients." *CARING Magazine* (August 1994):72–76.

Hurley, Ann C., M. A. Mahoney, and Ladislav Volicer. "Comfort Care in End-Stage Dementia: What to Do after Deciding to Do No More." In E. Olson, E. R. Chichin, and L. Libow eds, *Controversies in Ethics in Long-Term Care*. New York: Springer, 1995.

Hurley, Ann C., B. Volicer, and Ladislav Volicer. "Effect of Fever Management Strategy on the Progression of Dementia of the Alzheimer Type." *Alzheimer Disease and Associated Disorders* 10, no. 1 (1996):5–10.

Hurley, Ann C., B. J. Volicer, M. A. Mahoney, and Ladislav Volicer. "Palliative Fever Management In in Alzheimer Patients: Quality Plus Fiscal Responsibility." *Advances in Nursing Science* 16, no. 1 (1993):21–32.

Mahoney, E. K., Ladislav Volicer, and Ann C. Hurley. *Management of Challenging Behaviors in Dementia*. Baltimore, MD: Health Professions Press, 2000.

Rempusheski, V. F., and Ann C. Hurley. "Advance Directives and Dementia." *Journal of Gerontological Nursing* 26, no. 10 (2000):27–33.

Volicer, B. J., Ann C. Hurley, K. J. Fabiszewski, P. Montgomery, and Ladislav Volicer. "Predicting Short-Term Survival for Patients with Advanced Alzheimer's Disease." *Journal of the American Geriatrics Society* 41 (1993):535–540.

Volicer, Ladislav, and L. Bloom-Charette. *Enhancing the Quality of Life in Advanced Dementia*. Philadelphia: Taylor & Francis, 1999.

Volicer, Ladislav, A. Collard, Ann C. Hurley, C. Bishop, D. Kern, and S. Karon. "Impact of Special Care Unit for Patients with Advanced Alzheimer's Disease on Patients' Discomfort and Cost." *Journal of the American Geriatrics Society* 42 (1994):597–603.

Volicer, Ladislav, and Ann C. Hurley. *Hospice Care for Patients with Advanced Progressive Dementia*. New York: Springer, 1998.

ANN C. HURLEY
LADISLAV VOLICER

# HOSPICE AROUND THE WORLD

Known initially as "palliative care," the modern hospice movement began in the 1970s. Over time it has sought to provide end-of-life care in the home or a specially designated unit with a special focus on the patient's physical, psychological, social, and spiritual needs. The movement has also sought to provide inpatient care for acute symptom management and family respite.

With the advent of the palliative-medicine movement in the last decade of the twentieth century, the meanings of terms *palliative medicine* and *palliative care* expanded to refer to care provided in secondary- and tertiary-care facilities from the onset of symptoms. Hospice and palliative-care programs provide their services in a cultural and canonic context that influences where care is given and by whom. For example, in Poland, the cultural tradition of keeping persons in the home, with family and friends gathering around the bed at the time of death, influenced the type of services provided. Given the poor housing conditions of the area that make caring "for the terminally ill at home very difficult," Hospicium attempted to meet those needs by being a home where relatives and friends could volunteer to care for the dying person (Tenner 1997, p. 159). Similar problems prevail in Russia and Japan, where the tight living quarters of most inhabitants make it difficult to care for terminally ill persons in the home. Such living conditions promote inpatient hospice programs. The first hospice in Russia was opened in September 1990 in Lachta, a village close to St. Petersburg.

The size of the living quarters does not always determine the locus of care. In Saudi Arabia the terminally ill are cared for in the home, with support provided by the King Faisal Specialist Hospital and Research Centre. The Malath Foundation for Humanistic Care in Jordan also provides professional and volunteer support for the family caregivers, although nonprofessional volunteers outside the family help by running errands. In such situations the family decides on a direct caregiver within the family.

In China, when all adult family members are employed outside the home, there is no one to care for the terminally ill; therefore, out-of-home care becomes necessary. Beijing Song Tang Hospice, an inpatient facility in China, has a nursing assistant's bed in the room with the patient in order to attend to a patient's needs twenty-four hours per day. The program survives on charitable contributions and the periodic assistance of foreigners who come to China to help provide care.

As in China, the availability of caregivers in the home in India dictates the form of hospice care. In

1999, Karunashraya Hospice, a fifty-five-bed freestanding hospice in Bangalore, was opened. Marie Coughlan states, "The ability to care for sick family members is compromised because there are often no family members at home to do the caring. In the poor families anyone who can work does so; thus, even when family members are together they may all be out working" (2000, p. 1). The staff consists of four registered nurses and seven nurses' aides, a retired volunteer physician, a consultant anesthetist, and a home care team of two nurses and one family counselor. The home care team sees three to five patients each day throughout the Bangalore metropolitan area.

The first hospice program in India, Shanti Avedna Ashram, was opened in 1986 in Mumbai. Since then, hospice programs have been established in Goa and Delhi. In 1995 Chennai opened a hospice program that provides limited community outreach. Access to morphine has been assured by collaboration with medical colleagues.

Human resources influence access to care as profoundly as economics. In countries like the Netherlands that have universal insurance, the individual's ability to pay is not an issue. This is not the case in countries like Ghana, where the ability to pay for care as well as medications determines access. Motivation to pay for care is also an issue. Professionals in Ghana are concerned that if families think there is no cure, they won't pay for care. For this reason, and to protect the patient from hurtful news, many Ghanaians do not know either their diagnosis or prognosis. In an environment in which truth-telling is not a value, it becomes difficult to obtain referrals of informed patients. Furthermore, if care without cure is not valued or affordable, this economic reality may dictate both access and provision of services. Given these realities, sub-Saharan Africa has developed some unique approaches to meeting the needs of the terminally ill.

Sub-Saharan Africa is beset with three epidemics: HIV/AIDS, malaria, and tuberculosis. The need for hospice and palliative care for individuals who are terminally ill with these diseases should not be understood as an alternative to treatment. Appropriate interventions to prevent the occurrence of these diseases or the onset of secondary or tertiary sequellae are also required.

*Kenyans show support for the Nyumbani Hospice that will serve HIV positive children.* GAMMA LIAISON NETWORK

The first hospice in Africa, Island Hospice and Bereavement Service in Harare, Zimbabwe, was organized in 1979. As of 2001 it has fifteen branches throughout Zimbabwe. Originally organized with a home hospice nurse or social worker providing direct care via home visits, the facility was too limited to meet the needs of the increasing numbers of persons with HIV/AIDS who required care. Consequently a model of hospice as facilitator was developed. In this model, hospice develops partnerships with other organizations and with the community to provide care. Rather than providing home visiting, the hospice facilitates the care given by volunteers.

Mabvuku/Tafara Hospice in Harare provides care through its trained volunteers, who render about 80 percent of the care. The hospice team consists of the health department, social services, churches, schools, police, and two hospice nurses. These two nurses facilitate the care given by the volunteers as well as seeing a limited number of patients.

These programs have moved from direct provision of care by professionals to facilitation of care by volunteers as a primary mode of care delivery. This approach is a creative solution to the challenge of the AIDS pandemic in Africa. Yet even this approach may be inadequate given the numbers of individuals infected with HIV and the paucity of resources in many of the nations of sub-Saharan Africa.

Resources of space and available caregivers, as noted, affect care in Japan, China, and India. Most of the hospice care available in Japan is inpatient with little support for those who wish to die at home. The lack of space in most Japanese apartments makes it difficult to provide care at home.

Korea also faces resource challenges. There, hospice care is provided in both inpatient facilities and at home. Nonetheless, there is a lack of understanding of the nature of hospice/palliative care by citizens and physicians, a lack of insurance coverage, and a lack of availability of short-acting morphine.

Germany has several hospice/palliative care programs headed by physicians that focus on the physical, psychological, social, and spiritual aspects of care. Largely inpatient programs, these services include a range of complementary/ alternative therapies along with traditional medical care. Hospice care in Germany, however, is not a widespread phenomenon.

The hospice movement began in Israel in the early 1980s with the Tel-Hashomer Hospice, which opened in 1983 in Tel-Aviv. This program was based on the British model of hospice care. The first hospice home care program was established in 1984 in Tivon. In 1986 a fourteen-bed unit was created at the Hadassah University Hospital at Mount Scopus, Jerusalem.

Clinica Familia, in Chile, a hospice-hospital, contains forty beds and an outpatient clinic as well as a chapel, mortuary room, and a pharmacy. The Clinic is run largely by volunteers, including physicians, psychologists, nurses, assistant nurses, volunteers who provide administrative support, and four paid employees.

The key distinctions in hospice programs worldwide are the role of volunteers as either the predominant caregivers or as supports for professionals; the level of governmental and/or private support; the amount of home space and availability of family members for home care; and the availability of morphine and other drugs. Even more fundamental is the level of information provided to patient and families about diagnosis and prognosis.

*See also:* HOSPICE IN HISTORICAL PERSPECTIVE; PAIN AND PAIN MANGEMENT; SAUNDERS, CICELY; SYMPTOMS AND SYMPTOM MANAGEMENT

### Bibliography

Gray, Alan J., A. Ezzart, and A. Boyar. "Palliative Care for the Terminally Ill in Saudi Arabia." In Dame Cicely Saunders and Robert Kastenbaum eds., *Hospice Care on the International Scene.* New York: Springer, 1997.

Hospice Association. "South Africa." In Betty R. Ferrell and Nessa Coyle eds., *Textbook of Palliative Nursing.* New York: Oxford University Press, 2001.

Lee, So Woo, Eun Ok Lee, H. S. Ahn, D. S. Heo, D. S. Kim, H. S. Kim, and H. J. Lee. "Development in the National Hospice Care Service in Korea." *Korean Nurse* 36, no. 3 (1997):49–69.

Saunders, Dame Cicely, and Robert Kastenbaum, eds. *Hospice on the International Scene.* New York: Springer, 1997.

Tenner, Jamina Jujawska. "The Beginnings of Hospice Care under Communist Regime: The Cracow Experience." In Dame Cicely Saunders and Robert Kastenbaum eds., *Hospice Care on the International Scene.* New York: Springer, 1997.

*Internet Resources*

Coughlan, Marie. "Karunashraya Hospice in India." In the International Association for Hospice and Palliative Care [web site]. Available from www.hospicecare.com/reports.htm#anchor97165.

INGE B. CORLESS
PATRICE K. NICHOLAS

# HOSPICE IN HISTORICAL PERSPECTIVE

Some commentaries on hospice history, particularly from inside the hospice movement, are inclined to seek ancient roots for what is actually a modern phenomenon. The scholar Cathy Siebold, for example, notes: "The Crusades, which began late in the eleventh century and continued for several hundred years, are a milestone in hospice history" (Siebold 1992, p. 16). These connections between the past and the present contain a powerful symbolic message. They suggest that modern hospices are rooted in deep and ancient traditions of compassionate care that go back to earliest civilizations. Yet they tend to lack historical veracity. It is inaccurate, for example, to draw too close a parallel between places called hospices in early times and those carrying that name in the twenty and twenty-first centuries. The former contained a broad spread of the diseased, the poor and the downtrodden, cared for over the longer term. The latter have tended to focus on the relatively short-term care of those close to the end of life and especially those dying from malignancies. No doubt in human societies going back over two millennia or more there have existed individuals, such as Fabiola in the fourth century, who patronized and nursed the sick and dying; but scholars should be cautious in seeing her as someone who prefigured the charismatic leaders of the modern hospice approach, developed in the second half of the twentieth century.

A review of a more recent period reveals the first concentrated efforts to give institutional care to dying people. For this, the nineteenth century—a time of great hospital building, which produced in turn a diminution in concern for those at the end of life whose condition was beyond cure—is the place to begin. At this point in time, both the bereaved and the medical establishment noted the first signs of death as a medical failure. The dying were no longer welcome in the hospital, and therefore philanthropic and charitable endeavors led to the creation of special institutions, some of them called hospices, which sought to provide care and sanctuary to those nearing death.

## The Nineteenth Century

From the beginning of the nineteenth century it is possible to identify certain important developments in the care of dying people, several of these led by women. The young widow and bereaved mother, Jeanne Garnier, together with others in similar circumstances, formed L'Association des Dames du Calvaire in Lyon, France, in 1842. The association opened a home for the dying the following year, which was characterized by "a respectful familiarity, an attitude of prayer and calm in the face of death" (Clark 2000, p. 51). Jeanne Garnier died in 1853, but her influence led to the foundation of six other establishments for the care of the dying between 1874 in Paris, and 1899 in New York. In both of these cities modern-day palliative care services exist that originated directly from the work of L'Association des Dames du Calvaire.

Mary Aikenhead was born in Cork, Ireland, in 1787. At age twenty-five she became Sister Mary Augustine and was established almost immediately as Superior of a new Order, known as the Irish Sisters of Charity, the first of its kind in Ireland to be uncloistered. The Order made plans to establish a hospital. Three of the sisters went to Paris to learn the work of the Notre Dame de la Pitié Hospital. In Ireland they opened St. Vincent's Hospital in Dublin, in 1834. Following many years of chronic illness, Mary Aikenhead died in 1858 at nearby Harold's Cross. Fulfilling an ambition that she had long held, the convent where Mary Aikenhead spent her final years became Our Lady's Hospice for the Dying in 1879. The Sisters of Charity followed it with others in Australia, England, and Scotland, all of which exist in the twenty-first century and are run by the Order as modern palliative care units.

In the United States, Rose Hawthorne had experienced the death of a child and watched her friend, the poet Emma Lazarus, die of cancer. During the late 1890s she organized a group of women known as the Servants of Relief of Incurable Cancer. When her husband died she took religious orders in 1900, under the title Mother Alphonsa, and formed an order known as the Dominican Sisters of Hawthorne. They established St. Rose's Hospice in Lower Manhattan and then another in New York, followed by others in Philadelphia, Atlanta, St. Paul, and Cleveland.

Although unknown to each other, Jeanne Garnier, Mary Aikenhead, and Rose Hawthorne shared a common purpose in their concern for the care of the dying, and in particular the dying poor. Directly and indirectly they founded institutions which, in time, led to the development of other homes and hospices elsewhere. They also established base camp for what was to follow, for their achievements created some of the preconditions for modern hospice and palliative care development. The historian Clare Humphreys has shown how these early hospices and homes for the dying reveal three sets of concerns: religious, philanthropic, and moral. Such institutions placed a strong emphasis on the cure of the soul, even when the life of the body was diminishing. They drew on charitable endeavors, and were often concerned to give succor to the poor and disadvantaged. They were not, however, places in which the medical or nursing care of the dying was of any real sophistication. Rooted in religious and philanthropic concerns, which would diminish as the twentieth century advanced, the early homes for the dying represent the prologue to a period of subsequent development, which got underway in the decades after World War II.

## The Twentieth Century

By the mid–twentieth century some important changes occurred in Western medicine and health care. Specialization was advancing rapidly, new treatments were proliferating, and there was an increasing emphasis upon cure and rehabilitation. At the same time death in the hospital, rather than at home, was becoming the norm, and medicine critics viewed the dying patient or "hopeless case" as a failure of the medical practice. In a series of famous lectures published in 1935 the American physician Alfred Worcester noted: ". . . many doctors nowadays, when the death of their patients becomes imminent, seem to believe that it is quite proper to leave the dying in the care of the nurses and the sorrowing relatives. This shifting of responsibility is un-pardonable. And one of its results is that as less professional interest is taken in such service less is known about it" (Worcester 1935, p. 33). This vacuum in knowledge was one factor that contributed to alternative suggestions about care at the end of life. That same year the Voluntary Euthanasia Legalisation Society was formed in the United Kingdom, followed in 1937 by the organization that came to be known as the Euthanasia Society of America. Both sought to promote the deliberate ending of life when requested by the patient.

Concerns about improving care at the end of life began to surface in the 1950s. In Britain attention focused on the medical "neglect" of the dying, whereas in the United States a reaction to the medicalization of death began to take root. Four particular innovations can be identified:

1. A shift took place within the professional literature of care of the dying, from idiosyncratic anecdote to systematic observation. New studies by doctors, social workers, and social scientists provided evidence about the social and clinical aspects of dying in contemporary society. By the early 1960s leading articles in *The Lancet* and *British Medical Journal* were drawing on the evidence of research to suggest ways in which terminal care could be promoted and arguments for euthanasia might be countered.

2. A new view of dying began to emerge that sought to foster concepts of dignity and meaning. Enormous scope was opened up for refining ideas about the dying process and exploring the extent to which patients should and did know about their terminal condition.

3. An active rather than a passive approach to the care of the dying was promoted with increasing vigor. Within this, the fatalistic resignation of the doctor was supplanted by a determination to find new and imaginative ways to continue caring up to the end of life, and indeed beyond it, in the care of the bereaved.

4. A growing recognition of the interdependency of mental and physical distress created the potential for a more embodied notion of suffering, thus constituting a profound challenge to the body-mind dualism upon which so much medical practice of the period was predicated.

It was the work of Cicely Saunders, first developed in St. Joseph's Hospice in Hackney, East London, that was to prove most consequential, for it was she that began to forge a peculiarly modern philosophy of terminal care. Through systematic attention to patient narratives, listening carefully to stories of illness, disease, and suffering, she evolved the concept of "total pain." This view of pain moved beyond the physical to encompass the social, emotional, and spiritual aspects of suffering—captured so comprehensively by the patient who told her, "All of me is wrong" (Saunders 1964, p. viii). But it was also linked to a hard-headed approach to pain management. Saunders's message was simple: "Constant pain needs constant control" (Saunders 1960, p. 17). She believed analgesics should be employed in a method of regular giving that would ensure that pain was prevented in advance, rather than alleviated once it had become established; in addition, they should be used progressively, from mild to moderate to strong.

When Cicely Saunders founded St. Christopher's Hospice in South London in 1967, it quickly became a source of inspiration to others. As the first "modern" hospice, it sought to combine three key principles: excellent clinical care, education, and research. It differed significantly from the other homes for the dying that had preceded it and sought to establish itself as a center of excellence in a new field of care. Its success was phenomenal and it soon became the stimulus for an expansive phase of hospice development, not only in Britain but around the world.

From the outset, ideas developed at St. Christopher's were applied differently in other settings. Within a decade it was accepted that the principles of hospice care could be practiced in many settings—in specialist inpatient units, but also in home care and day-care services. Likewise, hospital units and support teams were established that brought the new thinking about dying into the very heartlands of acute medicine. Modern hospice developments took place first in affluent countries, but in time they also took hold in poorer countries, often supported by mentoring and "twinning" arrangements with more established hospices in the West. By the mid-1980s, a process of maturation was evident.

In the United Kingdom, approximately 100 hospices had been formed, complemented by home support services and the first hospital palliative care teams; funding from the National Health Service and from the major cancer care charities started to become available. In the United States, growth was even more striking: 516 hospices existed just ten years after the foundation of the first initiative in New Haven, which had opened in 1974. Even more significant, a federal benefit was created in 1982 under Medicare for patients with terminal disease and a prognosis of six months. The legislation proved a stimulus to both not-for-profit and for-profit hospices. By the end of the twentieth century some 3,000 hospice organizations were operating in the United States.

Elsewhere, the potential for development varied enormously. Political instability, economic privation, and the absence of leadership limited possibilities for the development of hospices. In Eastern Europe, for example, there was little opportunity for hospice initiatives until communism began to break down. Thus in the Polish city of Kracow an informal society was first formed to support hospice developments in 1981, the year martial law was imposed. In Russia the first hospice was opened in St. Petersburg in 1992, with the support of the émigré journalist Viktor Zorza, who established Russian links with supporters in the United Kingdom in the wake of the new era of glasnost. The Island Hospice, which began in Zimbabwe in 1979, is generally acknowledged by medical professionals as the first hospice established in a third world country.

In several countries, for example India, the first hospices were modeled quite explicitly upon St. Christopher's, but local variation was also common. In Spain the word *hospice* has negative cultural associations of poverty and incarceration, so a strong emphasis was placed from the outset on the integration of services within the mainstream health care system. Pioneers of first-wave hospice

development and some of their second generation successors have worked to promote their work in many countries of the world, building increasingly on international networks of support and collaboration, fostered by groups such as the World Health Organization, the International Association for Hospice and Palliative Care, and the European Association of Palliative Care.

By the early twenty-first century some form of specialist palliative care existed in an estimated ninety countries and there was clear evidence of continuing expansion in Asia, Eastern Europe, Africa, and Latin America. Within the professional lifetime of the founders of the modern hospice movement a remarkable proliferation had occurred; at the same time the definition of hospice and palliative care had come into sharper focus. The debates and discussions that followed saw palliative care preoccupied with many of the wider questions relating to the work of health care systems in the modern world.

In the 1970s and 1980s modern hospice and palliative care in the West had many of the qualities of a social movement supported by wider forces: consumerism and increasing discernment among the users of health and social care services; demographic trends that created substantial numbers of individuals able to volunteer their labor in local hospices; and greater affluence, which led to an increase in charitable giving. This movement may have contributed to a new openness about death and bereavement that was in evidence in the late twentieth century (in Britain, for example, the first person ever to be seen to die on television, was in the care of a hospice). Inspired by charismatic leadership, it was a movement that condemned the neglect of the dying in society; called for high quality pain and symptom management for all who needed it; sought to reconstruct death as a natural phenomenon, rather than a clinical failure; and marshaled practical and moral argument to oppose those in favor of euthanasia. For Cicely Saunders and her followers such work served as a measure of the worth of a culture: "A society which shuns the dying must have an incomplete philosophy" (Saunders 1961, p. 3).

In the late twentieth century in several countries, including Britain, Australia, Canada, the United States, there was professional recognition of this emerging area of expertise. Specialty recognition occurred first in Britain, in 1987, and was seen by some scholars as a turning point in hospice history. It was part of a wider shift away from "terminal" and "hospice" care toward the concept of palliative care. Those seeking to further develop this work claim that specialization, the integration of palliative care into the mainstream health system, and the development of an "evidence-based" model of practice and organization are crucial to long-term viability. Others in the field mourn the loss of early ideals and regret what they perceive to be an emphasis upon physical symptoms at the expense of psychosocial and spiritual concerns. In short, there have been claims that forces of medicalization and routinization are at work or even that the putative "holism" of palliative care philosophy masks a new, more subtle form of surveillance of the dying and bereaved in modern society.

By the end of the twentieth century, however, a growing commitment to the evidence base was emerging. Two forces for expansion were also clearly visible. First, there was the impetus to move palliative care further upstream in the disease progression, thereby seeking integration with curative and rehabilitation therapies and shifting the focus beyond terminal care and the final stages of life. Second, there was a growing interest in extending the benefits of palliative care to those with diseases other than cancer, in order to make "palliative care for all" a reality. The new specialty was therefore delicately poised. For some such integration with the wider system was a *sine qua non* for success; for others it marked the entry into a risky phase of new development in which early ideals might be compromised.

Hospice care and palliative care have shared a brief history. The evolution of one into the other marks a transition which, if successful, could ensure that the benefits of a model of care previously available to just a few people at the end of life will be extended to all who need it, regardless of diagnosis, stage of disease, social situation or means.

*See also:* HOSPICE, ALZHEIMER PATIENTS AND; HOSPICE AROUND THE WORLD; SAUNDERS, CICELY

### *Bibliography*

Clark, David. "Palliative Care History: A Ritual Process." *European Journal of Palliative Care* 7, no. 2 (2000):50–55.

Clark, David. "Cradled to the Grave? Preconditions for the Hospice Movement in the UK, 1948–67." *Mortality* 4, no. 3 (1999):225–247.

Clark, David, and Jane Seymour. *Reflections on Palliative Care*. Buckingham: Open University Press, 1999.

Foster, Zelda, and Inge B. Corless. "Origins: An American Perspective." *The Hospice Journal* 14, no. 314 (1999):9–13.

Humphreys, Clare. " 'Waiting for the Last Summons': The Establishment of the First Hospices in England 1878–1914." *Mortality* 6, no. 2 (2001):146–166.

James, Nicky, and David Field. "The Routinisation of Hospice." *Social Science and Medicine* 34, no. 12 (1992):1363–1375.

Luczak, Jacek. "Palliative Care in Eastern Europe." In David Clark, Jo Hockley, and Sam Ahmedzai eds., *New Themes in Palliative Care*. Buckingham: Open University Press, 1997.

Saunders, Cicely. "Care of Patients Suffering from Terminal Illness at St. Joseph's Hospice, Hackney, London." *Nursing Mirror,* 14 February 1964, vii–x.

Saunders, Cicely. "And from Sudden Death . . ." *Frontier* (Winter 1961):1–3.

Saunders, Cicely. "Drug Treatment in the Terminal Stages of Cancer." *Current Medicine and Drugs* 1, no. 1 (1960):16–28.

Siebold, Cathy. *The Hospice Movement*. New York: Twayne Publishers, 1992.

Worcester, Alfred. *The Care of the Aged the Dying and the Dead*. Springfield, IL: Charles C. Thomas, 1935.

DAVID CLARK

# HOSPICE OPTION

Approximately 30 percent of people who die in the United States choose hospice care during the last weeks of life. The average length of enrollment in hospice care was forty-eight days in 1999. Many of these patients die from cancer, but others have chronic, life-limiting diseases, such as cardiovascular or lung problems. Hospice is a major provider of end-of-life care to patients with HIV/AIDS and Alzheimer's disease. Hospice serves patients of all cultures and ethnicities, although barriers to general health care access may cause minorities to distrust hospice/palliative care as a form of denial of needed services. Fear that providers will not respect customs and traditions may also affect acceptance of hospice care. In the United States, Medicare, Medicaid, and most managed health care and private insurance plans cover hospice care.

## What Is Hospice?

Hospice is a humane and compassionate way to deliver health care and supportive services to patients and their families during the final weeks of life. Modern hospice care started, in part, as a reaction to the increasing use of technology to extend life and the increasing expectation that death would occur in an unsympathetic, unsupportive hospital. The picture was one of strangers in attendance and no choice about the medical procedures being performed. People longed for idealized earlier scenes of peace and dignity where the dying person is pain free and surrounded by caring family.

During the 1960s, Cicely Saunders, a British physician, began the modern hospice movement by bringing together scientific research with holistic care of the mind and spirit. Saunders proposed standards that still guide care in the more than 2,000 hospices in the United States and hospice/palliative care units in Canada. Hospice affirms the rights of the patient/family unit to control the final stages of life. The terminally ill person's own preferences and lifestyle are taken into account in the hospice plan. The focus changes to caring when a life-limiting illness no longer responds to cure-oriented treatments. Hospice is intended to help make the most of the final months of life by providing emotional and spiritual support along with pain and symptom control.

Hospice care is provided by a team. Included in the team are the patient, the family, and trained volunteers, as well as the usual health care providers—nurses, home health aides, social workers, therapists, counselors, and physicians. The physician may be the patient's own physician or one who is specially trained in palliative (comfort) care. Each member of the team brings specific knowledge of terminal illness to the holistic care of the patient.

Volunteers provide significant services by offering support to patient and families, assisting with child care, and working with professional staff on bereavement support programs. Volunteer activities (such as transportation, shopping, and visiting) offer relief, referred to as respite care, to the caregiver from the work as well as time for self-care. The volunteers represent the wider community support for the patient in tangible ways.

One of the guiding principles for hospice is that patients, family, and staff all have legitimate needs and interests. The organization provides a mutual support network to discuss experiences and feelings engendered by emotionally charged care situations.

Care based on hospice principles can be provided in all of the settings where people die. Most people choose to die at home or in a relative's home with the help of hospice home health agencies. This choice is limited by the availability and abilities of caregivers, the technology that is needed, and the resources that are available in the community. Care is structured to keep patient and families together in the least restrictive environment possible. Other settings devoted to managing end-of-life care include freestanding inpatient hospices, nursing homes, and hospitals.

The hospice team coordinates a plan of care structured for just one person: the patient. A wide range of services may be provided, including nursing care, medical social services, physician services, spiritual support and counseling, home care aide and homemaker services, continuous care in the home, trained volunteer support service, physical, occupational, and speech therapy, twenty-four-hour on-call availability, hospice inpatient care, respite care, and bereavement support. In the United States Medicare, Medicaid, and most private insurance plans pay for much of this care. If insurance coverage is not available or is insufficient, most hospices provide services by relying on grants and community support through fundraising activities.

Health care expenditures are highest during the last month of life. Hospice is a cost-effective approach to end-of-life care. A 1995 comparison of average charges for a Medicare patient, prepared for the National Hospice Organization (NHO), indicated costs of $2,177 per day for hospital inpatient care, $482 per day for skilled nursing facility care, and $113 per day for hospice care.

While cost savings with hospice care account for governmental and third-party payers' interest, it is public support that drives the success and growth of hospice care availability. Much of the public wants to ensure that patient's wishes are enforced and that the patient is able to choose desired types of services.

## Making the Decision to Receive Hospice Care

Even though there has been a significant death education movement in the United States and internationally since the 1960s, most Americans are still unwilling to discuss end-of-life care with the terminally ill. While the living will and advanced directives documents have been available since the late 1960s, only a quarter of Americans have put into writing the care they want at the end of life. Discussions with family about preferences for treatment continue to be avoided until a crisis occurs.

The first step is to explore one's own feelings about the end of life. This might best be accomplished through the answering of a series of questions, such as: What would you like the last three days of your life to be like? Where will you be? Who will be with you? Who will give you emotional and spiritual support? Do you have cultural and family traditions that will affect the care you wish to receive? Who would you like to have fixing your food? Would you like family to provide personal care, or someone who is trained for that care? Do you want everything done to keep you alive, such as cardiopulmonary resuscitation, breathing machines, and feeding tubes? Do you want to be alert and able to talk with your family or would you rather be unaware of the nearness of your death? If you were not able to make decisions for yourself, who would you like to have making those decisions for you?

The next steps include learning about the options available in the community and putting one's wishes in the form of advanced directives and a medical power of attorney. Discussions with family, doctor, and attorney can help make educated decisions and can also free loved ones from the anxiety and uncertainty of not knowing one's wishes and options.

## When to Make the Hospice Care Decision

Ideally, the decision to enter hospice care is made when the patient and family decide that remembering, sharing, and bringing closure to life is more important than persisting in unpleasant and futile treatments to prolong life. In hospice care, the

*The hospice option was not an entirely new concept to the twentieth century. Hôtel-Dieu in France was built in 1443 to house the poor and ill after the Hundred Year's War.*
PATRICK WARD/CORBIS

patient and family are able to focus on management of pain and other symptoms and to find time to address emotional and spiritual issues. Unfortunately it is very difficult for patients and doctors to identify the end of the fight for cure and the beginning of the need for palliative hospice care.

As they reported in 2000, Nicholas A. Christakis and Elizabeth Lamont asked doctors to estimate their patients' length of life. The doctors predicted accurately within one month of the actual death for only 42 percent of the patients. Most (46%) of the time the doctors overestimated the length of time left to the patient. Although there are variations depending on patient diagnosis, the average survival after enrollment in hospice is approximately one month to six weeks. Many of the patients die within seven days of enrollment. Hospice workers feel that earlier recognition of the need for palliative care would allow both patient and family more time to address end-of-life issues. Cultural, emotional, and socioeconomic factors all affect the accuracy of prognosis and the readiness for hospice care.

Ultimately the decision is a joint one, made between the patient/family and the doctor. Doctors certify that patients are terminally ill and probably have less than six months to live. Patients certify that they wish to enter a program that provides care, but that they no longer seek to cure illness. This is an emotional turning point that is difficult for all involved. The decision to enter hospice care should be an affirmative choice to live life to its fullest, supported by a comprehensive program of medical care. It should not be viewed as a failure for the doctor, the patient, or the family.

Once the decision is made, health care personnel can assist in identifying the resources available in the community. Questions about accreditation and licensure, available services, eligibility criteria, costs, payment procedures, and employee job descriptions may assist with the choice. Hospices may be freestanding or have close relationships with hospitals, skilled nursing facilities, or home health agencies. Hospices may be for-profit or non-profit agencies. References from hospital or community agency professionals may guide the choice. The final decision may be made in consultation with the hospice nurse in an evaluation interview. A key question is whether the philosophy and standards of the hospice are congruent with the needs and desires of the patient and family.

## What to Expect from Hospice Care

Hospice care combines medical knowledge and research with a reverence for life. The philosophy emphasizes that appropriate care can allow the patient and family to live as fully and comfortably as possible with meaning and dignity. This was epitomized by an incident observed at St. Christopher's Hospice in England many years ago. An American nurse visiting this pioneering hospice noticed that none of the patients had intravenous fluids hanging by the bedside. Because almost every patient in the typical oncology ward at that time had continuous intravenous fluids, she asked Cicely Saunders, the pioneering hospice physician, about the lack at St. Christopher's. Saunders reply was, "Isn't it so much nicer to share a cup of tea?"

The nurse noted that no patients seemed dehydrated and that the staff did indeed share a cup of tea with the patients.

The hospice patient and family should expect a professional nurse or social worker to develop a plan for care. Consideration of the needs and wishes of the patient and family is uppermost as decisions are made. Palliation, or remission of pain and other troubling symptoms, was the subject of research leading to great improvement in care during the latter part of the twentieth century. The hospice physician and patient's doctor are consulted to assure that pain and symptom management orders are in place. Freedom from pain and from fear of pain allow the patient to fully participate in the business of living.

In addition to pain management, hospice provides social, psychological, emotional, and spiritual support. The patient and family should feel safe and secure knowing that they can depend on caregivers to communicate honestly, discuss concerns, answer questions, and function effectively. Patients and family need the opportunity and privacy to say goodbye.

Hospice care is intended to support family members, especially those who are the patient's caregivers and information about what is happening to the terminally ill person is given. Instruction about how to care for the person can be very reassuring to the caregivers. Assistance with household tasks such as meal preparation, shopping, and transportation may be needed. Sometimes what is needed is a good night's sleep or time for one's own health care appointment. This respite from duties can make it possible to continue caring. Some hospices provide inpatient respite services where the patient is cared for in a skilled nursing facility or hospital for a few days to allow the caregiver time to rest. Patients appreciate knowing that the burden of their care can be shared.

The birth or wedding that goes as it should seems to foretell a life or marriage that will go well. The same is true of a good death. Family members survive and grow from the experience. When the death is isolated and filled with pain, the memories that stay behind can be difficult. Hospice is committed to making the end of life a time of growth.

*See also:* GOOD DEATH, THE; HOSPICE AROUND THE
    WORLD; PAIN AND PAIN MANAGEMENT; SAUNDERS,
    CICELY; SYMPTOMS AND SYMPTOM MANAGEMENT

**Bibliography**

Byock, Ira. *Dying Well: The Prospect for Growth at the End of Life*. New York: Riverhead Books, 1997.

Christakis, Nicholas A., and Jose J. Escarce. "Survival of Medicare Patients after Enrollment in Hospice Programs." *New England Journal of Medicine* 334 (1996):172–178.

Christakis, Nicholas A., and Elizabeth Lamont. "Extent and Determinants of Error in Doctor's Prognoses in Terminally Ill Patients: Prospective Cohort Study." *British Medical Journal* 320 (2000):469–473.

Enck, Robert. *The Medical Care of Terminally Ill Patients*. Baltimore, MD: Johns Hopkins University Press, 1994.

Kastenbaum, Robert. *Death, Society, and Human Experience*. Boston: Allyn & Bacon, 2001.

National Hospice Organization. "An Analysis of the Cost Savings of the Medicare Hospice Benefit." Prepared by Lewin-VHI, 1995.

Saunders, Cicely. *The Care of the Dying*. London: Macmillan, 1959.

*Internet Resources*

"Facts and Figures on Hospice Care in America." In the National Hospice and Palliative Care Organization [web site]. Available from www.nhpco.org/public/articles/FactsFigures110801.pdf.

Haupt, Barbara J. "An Overview of Home Health and Hospice Patients: 1996 National Home and Hospice Care Survey." Hyattsville, MD: National Center for Health Statistics. Available from www.cdc.gov/nchs/data/ad/ad297.pdf.

BEATRICE KASTENBAUM

# HOW DEATH CAME INTO THE WORLD

Traditional, mythic accounts of the origin of death extend back to the earliest hunter-gatherer cultures. Usually these stories are morality tales about faithfulness, trust, or the ethical and natural balance of the elements of the world.

According to an African Asante myth, although people did not like the idea or experience of death, they nevertheless embraced it when given the choice, as in the tale of an ancient people who, upon experiencing their first visitation of death, pleaded with God to stop it. God granted this wish, and for three years there was no death. But there were also no births during that time. Unwilling to endure this absence of children, the people beseeched God to return death to them as long as they could have children again.

The death myths of aboriginal Australia vary enormously among clans and linguistic groups. Among most of them, however, death is often attributed to magic, misfortune, or to an evil spirit or act. Occasionally death is presented as the punishment for human failure to complete an assignment or achieve a goal assigned by the gods. Still other stories arise from some primordial incident that strikes at the heart of some tribal taboo. Early myths about death frequently bear these moral messages.

Among the Tiwi of Bathurst and Melville Islands in northern Australia, the advent of death is explained by the Purukapali myth, which recounts a time before death entered the world, when a man lived with his infant son, his wife, and his younger brother. The younger brother was unmarried and had desires for his brother's wife. He met her alone while she was gathering yams, and they spent the rest of the afternoon in sexual union. During this time, the husband was minding his infant son, who soon became hungry. As the son called for feeding, the husband called in vain for his missing wife. At sunset, the wife and younger man returned to find that the infant son had starved to death. Realizing what had happened, the husband administered a severe beating to his brother, who escaped up to the sky where he became the moon. His injuries can still be seen in the markings of the moon every month. The husband declared that he would die, and, taking the dead infant in his arms, performed a dance—the first ceremony of death—before walking backwards into the sea, never to be seen again.

The Berndts, Australian anthropologists, tell another ancient myth about two men, Moon and Djarbo, who had traveled together for a long while but then fall mortally ill. Moon had a plan to revive them, but Djarbo, believing that Moon's idea was a trick, rebuffs his friend's help and soon dies. Moon dies also, but thanks to his plan, he managed to revive himself into a new body every month, whereas Djarbo remained dead. Thus, Moon triumphs over bodily death while the first peoples of that ancient time followed Djarbo's example, and that is why all humans die.

## Death As a Being

None of these stories is meant to suggest that aboriginal people do not believe in spiritual immortality. On the contrary, their lore is rich in accounts of immortal lands. These are accounts of the origin of physical rather than spiritual death.

The idea of death as a consequence of human deeds is not universal. The image of death as a being in its own right is common in modern as well as old folklore. In this mythic vein, death is a sentient being, maybe an animal, perhaps even a monster. Sometimes death is disguised, sometimes not. Death enters the world to steal and silence people's lives. In Europe during the Middle Ages death was widely viewed as a being who came in the night to take children away. Death was a dark, hooded, grisly figure—a grim reaper—with an insatiable thirst for the lives of children. Children were frequently dressed as adults as soon as possible to trick death into looking elsewhere for prey.

The film industry produced two well-known films, the second a remake of the first, which examined this idea of death as a being who makes daily rounds of collecting the dead: *Death Takes a Holiday* (1934) and *Meet Joe Black* (1998), both of which portrayed death as perplexed at his victim's fear of him. In a wry and ironic plot twist, a young woman falls in love with the male embodiment of death, and it is through an experience of how this love creates earthly attachment that death comes to understand the dread inspired by his appearance.

But the idea of death as a humanlike being is mostly characteristic of traditional folktales that dramatize the human anguish about mortality. By contrast, in the realm of religious ideas, death is regarded less as an identifiable personal being than as an abstract state of being. In the world of myth and legend, this state appears to collide with the human experience of life. As a consequence of human's nature as celestial beings, it is life on Earth which is sometimes viewed as a type of death. In this way, the question of how death enters the world in turn poses the question of how to understand death as an essential part of the world.

## The Garden of Eden

In the book of Genesis, the first man, Adam, wanders through the paradisiacal Garden of Eden. Pitying his solitary nature, God creates the first woman, Eve, from Adam's rib. Adam and Eve are perfectly happy in the Garden of Eden and enjoy all its bounty with one exception: God prohibits the couple from eating from the Tree of Knowledge.

The Garden of Eden is utopian. Utopia, in its etymological sense, is literally "no place." It is a perfect, probably spiritual domain for two celestial beings who, bearing the birthmarks of the God who created them, are immortal. These two beings eat from the Tree of Knowledge, which ironically, distracts them from their awareness of God and his omnipresence. As a result of this error, Adam and Eve become the embodiment of forgetfulness of the divine. In other words, they become material beings, as symbolized in their sudden awareness of and shame in their nakedness.

Adam and Eve thus "fall" into the flesh, into the world as it is known, with the entire legacy that embodiment entails: work, suffering, and physical death. Paradoxically, the Tree of Knowledge heralds ignorance of their divine nature, and the fall into flesh signals their sleepwalking indifference to that nature. Human beings therefore need God's help through the divine mercy of his Son or the sacred texts of the Bible to awaken them to their divine destiny. Without this awakening, the wages of sin are eternal death—an eternal darkness spent in chains of ignorance, a blindness maintained by humans' attachment to mere earthly concerns and distractions. This famous story thus embodies all the paradoxical elements of creation, implying that human life is actually no life at all, but its opposite: death.

In the kernel of this local creation story lies the archaic analogy of all the great stories about how life is death and death is the beginning of true life. The cycles of life and death are not merely hermeneutic paradoxes across different human cultures, but they are also the fundamental narrative template upon which all the great religions explain how death entered the world and, indeed, became the world.

In Greek mythology, as Mircea Eliade has observed, sleep (Hypnos) and death (Thanatos) are twin brothers. Life is portrayed as a forgetfulness that requires one to remember, or recollect, the structures of reality, eternal truths, the essential forms or ideas of which Plato wrote. Likewise, for postexilic Jews and Christians, death was understood as sleep or a stupor in Sheol, a dreary, gray underworld in the afterlife. The Gnostics often referred to earthly life as drunkenness or oblivion. For Christians, the exhortation was also to wake from the sleep of earthly concerns and desire and to watch and pray. In Buddhist texts, the awakening is a concern for recollection of past lives. The recollection of personal history in the wheel of rebirth is the only hope anyone has of breaking this cycle of eternal return.

Sleep, then, converges with death. Both have been the potent symbols and language used to describe life on earth. It is only through the remembering of human's divine nature and its purpose, brokered during an earthly life of asceticism or discipline, or perhaps through the negotiation of trials in the afterlife, that one can awaken again and, through this awakening, be born into eternal life.

**Modern Accounts**

The humanistic trend of twentieth-century social science and philosophy has diverged from this broadly cross-cultural and long-standing view of death as earthly existence and true life as the fruit of earthly death. Contemporary anthropology and psychoanalytic ideas, for example, have argued that these religious ideas constitute a "denial of death." The anthropologist Ernest Becker and religious studies scholar John Bowker have argued that religions generate creation myths that invert the material reality of death so as to control the anxiety associated with the extinction of personality and relationships.

Like-minded thinkers have argued that philosophical theories which postulate a "ghost in the machine"—a division of the self into a body and a separate spirit or soul—are irrational and unscientific. But, of course, the assumptions underlying these particular objections are themselves not open to empirical testing and examination. Criticism of this kind remains open to similar charges of bias and methodological dogma, and tends, therefore, to be no less speculative than religious views of death.

Beyond the different scientific and religious arguments about how life and death came into the world, and which is which, there are several other traditions of literature about travel between the two domains. Scholars have described the ways in which world religions have accounted for this transit between the two halves of existence—life and death. Often, travel to the "world of the dead" is undertaken as an initiation or as part of a shamanic rite, but at other times and places such otherworldly journeys have been part of ascetic practices of Christians and pagans alike.

In the past half century psychological, medical, and theological literature has produced major descriptions and analyses of near-death experiences, near-death visions, visions or hallucinations of the bereaved, and altered states of consciousness. Research of this type, particularly in the behavioral, social, and clinical sciences, has re-ignited debates between those with materialist and religious assumptions about the ultimate basis of reality.

Traditionally confined to the provinces of philosophy and theology, such debates have now seeped into the heretofore metaphysics-resistant precincts of neuroscience, psychology, and medicine. What can these modern psychological and social investigations of otherworldly journeys tell experts about the nature of life and death, and which is which?

The religious studies scholar Ioan Peter Couliano argues that one of the common denominators of the problem of otherworldly journeys is that they appear to be mental journeys, journeys into mental universes and spaces. But such remarks say more about the origin of "mental" as a term of reference than the subject at hand. The glib observation that otherworldly journeys may be mere flights of fancy may in fact only be substituting one ambiguous problem with yet another.

As Couliano himself observes, people in the twenty-first century live in a time of otherworldly pluralism—a time when such journeys have parallels in science and religion, in fantasy and fact, in public and private life.

**Conclusion**

Death has permeated life from the first stirrings of matter in the known universe—itself a mortal phenomenon, according to the prevailing cosmological theory of contemporary physics. Death came incorporated in the birth of the first star, the first living molecules, the birth of the first mammoth, the first cougar, the first human infant, the first human empire, and the youngest and oldest theory of science itself. Early cultures groped with the meaning of death and its relationship to life. The very naming of each, along with the attendant stories and theories, is an attempt to somehow define and thus master these refractory mysteries. All of the major myths about how death entered the world are, in fact, attempts to penetrate below the obvious.

Most have concluded that Death, like Life, is not a person. Both seem to be stories where the destinations are debatable, even within their own communities of belief, but the reality of the journey is always acknowledged—a continuing and intriguing source of human debate and wonderment.

*See also:* AFTERLIFE IN CROSS-CULTURAL PERSPECTIVE; AUSTRALIAN ABORIGINAL RELIGION; GODS AND GODDESSES OF LIFE AND DEATH; IMMORTALITY

## *Bibliography*

Allen, Louis A. *Time Before Morning: Art and Myth of the Australian Aborigines.* New York: Thomas Y. Crowell and Co., 1975.

Becker, Ernest. *The Denial of Death.* New York: Macmillan, 1974.

Berndt, Ronald M., and Catherine H. Berndt. *The Speaking Land: Myth and Story in Aboriginal Australia.* Victoria, Australia: Penguin Books, 1989.

Bowker, John. *The Meanings of Death.* Cambridge: Cambridge University Press, 1991.

Couliano, Ioan Peter. *Out of This World: Otherworldly Journeys from Gilgamesh to Albert Einstein.* London: Shambala, 1991.

Eliade, Mircea. *Myth and Reality,* translated by Willard R. Trask. New York: Harper & Row, 1963.

Opoku, Kofi A. "African Perspectives on Death and Dying." In Arthur Berger, Paul Badham, Austin H. Kutscher, Joyce Berger, Michael Perry, and John Beloff eds., *Perspectives on Death and Dying: Cross-Cultural and Multidisciplinary Views.* Philadelphia: Charles Press, 1989.

Ramsay, Smith William. *Myths and Legends of the Aboriginal Australians.* London: George Harrap and Sons, 1970.

Zaleski, Carol. *Otherworld Journeys.* New York: Oxford University Press, 1989.

ALLAN KELLEHEAR

# HUMAN REMAINS

Archaeologists, anthropologists, and classicists seem unanimous in asserting that the values of every culture, ancient and modern, entail proper disposal of human tissue and dead bodies. Among many peoples, the obligation to put the body properly to rest has been extended to maintaining the places of disposal as sacred sites. For example, in seventeenth-century New France, now Quebec, the settlements were considered unsuccessful until cemeteries were established. Prior to that, members of the aristocracy who could afford to do so had the body preserved in alcohol or stripped to the skeleton and shipped back to the country of origin. Those of lower status were simply buried in unconsecrated ground and forgotten. Only when consecrated cemeteries were allowed was a parish established, thus allowing the second and third generations of New France to claim the land around the site as "home." The parishioners then had all of the rights of identity afforded their ancestors in the mother country, along with the obligations of maintaining the parish cemeteries as sacred ground.

It is taboo in most of the world to disturb the remains of deceased ancestors except under the most limited of circumstances. Nevertheless, cemeteries are sometimes subject to disturbance. Historically, destruction of burial sites has often been the first act of dominion a conqueror imposes on the vanquished precisely because of its demoralizing effect on the local population. To desecrate means to treat contemptuously, often in a way that demeans for the progeny the importance or values of their ancestor's remains and the sacred sites of disposal.

Groups of indigenous peoples around the world are working to encourage the United Nations to adopt a Declaration on the Rights of Indigenous Peoples forbidding the desecration of burial sites and the displaying of ancestral remains and grave artifacts as tourist attractions. Other international organizations seek to contain the rapidly expanding market for human organs taken from unsuspecting patients and the newly dead in order to cash in on demand in the organ transplant market.

Two major actions taken in the United States have influenced worldwide debate about the use and abuse of human tissue, modern and ancient—the Vermillion Accord (1989) and the Native American Graves Protection and Repatriation Act (1990). The Vermillion Accord on Human Remains emerged out of the first Inter-Congress of the World Archaeological Congress at the University of South Dakota in Vermillion. Individuals from twenty countries, twenty-seven Native American nations, and indigenous people from other parts of the world—among them human osteologists, archaeologists, medical educators, and ethicists—discussed and debated the subject of respectful treatment of human remains. The result, a six-point agreement that has influenced subsequent efforts to bridge the interests of indigenous peoples and scholars, appeared in a 1990 issue of *Death Studies*:

1. "Respect for the mortal remains of the dead shall be accorded to all irrespective of origin, race, religion, nationality, custom, and tradition."

2. "Respect for the wishes of the dead concerning disposition shall be accorded whenever possible, reasonable, and lawful, when they are known or can be reasonably inferred."

3. "Respect for wishes of the local community shall be accorded whenever possible, reasonable, and lawful."

4. "Respect for the scientific research values of skeletal, mummified, and other human remains (including fossil hominids) shall be accorded when such value is demonstrated to exist."

5. "Agreement on the disposition of fossil, skeletal, mummified, and other remains shall be reached by negotiation on the basis of mutual respect for the legitimate concerns of communities for the proper disposition of their ancestors, as well as the legitimate concerns of science and education."

6. "The express recognition that the concerns of various ethnic groups as well as those of science are legitimate and to be respected will permit acceptable agreements to be reached and honored."

The accord was later expanded in the World Archaeological Congress's First Code of Ethics.

The Native American Graves Protection and Repatriation Act, passed by Congress in 1990, established rules for returning Native American remains and grave artifacts to appropriate indigenous populations. By November 1993 museums holding Native American materials containing human tissue were required to prepare written summaries of their collections for distribution to culturally affiliated tribes. By November 1995 museums were required to prepare detailed inventories of their Native American collections.

Since adoption of the accord and the passage of the act, legislation has been expanded to cover use of various tests, such as carbon dating and DNA, for identification of remains; control of sale of human tissue; and restriction of collection of ancient, indigenous artifacts associated with sacred areas.

*See also:* ANTHROPOLOGICAL PERSPECTIVE; CEMETERIES AND CEMETERY REFORM; KENNEWICK MAN; MUMMIFICATION

### Bibliography

"Human Remains: Contemporary Issues." Special issue of *Death Studies* 14, no. 6 (1990).

"Museums and the Human Remains Controversies." Special issue of *Caduceus: A Museum Journal for the Health Sciences* 6, no. 1 (1991).

Reynolds, Frank, and Earl H. Waugh, eds. *Encounters with Death: Essays in the History of Anthropology of Religion*. College Station: Pennsylvania State University Press, 1977.

### Internet Resources

Bocek, Barb. "Native American Repatriation & Reburial: A Bibliography." In the Green Library at Stanford University [web site]. Available from www-sul.stanford.edu/depts/ssrg/native/appf.html.

GLEN W. DAVIDSON

# HUNGER STRIKES

Hunger strikes as a means of protest have been traced to the pre-Christian era in Rome. They were revived in the early twentieth century in England by women suffragists. A global phenomenon, hunger strikes have been reported from Ireland to Beijing, Istanbul to New Delhi and the United States. Purportedly the longest hunger strike continued for seventy-four days, ending in the death of a Sinn Fein political party member in the 1920s.

Ireland was also the scene of the largest reported hunger strike, involving 8,000 political prisoners and internees in 1923.

A true hunger strike represents a competent individual's intentional refusal to eat and or drink for some specific purpose. Definitions vary, however, in the specificity of both fluid intake and the time interval required to certify such an act as a hunger strike. Occasionally hunger striking is an indication of mental illness that is tantamount to actual or attempted suicide. William Butler Yeats captured in verse what may be the primary aim of hunger striking, that is to "shame" those in authority to right a "wrong" or injustice. "Persuade him to eat or drink? / While he is lying there. Perishing there, my good name in the world / Is perishing also. I cannot give way, / Because I am king, because if I give way, / My nobles would call me a weakling, and, it may be, / the very throne be shaken." Most often it entails acts of nonviolent protest to prompt redress of structural or human rights violations, whether unjust imprisonment, objectionable living conditions for prisoners, or struggles against oppression by groups such as the United Farm Workers in California or the people of Tibet.

Prisoners, priests, students, suffragists, nationalists, pacifists, and activists have been emboldened to use fasting and hunger strikes to publicize and underscore their personal and political agendas. Mohandas Gandhi resorted to fasting at least fourteen times, but never for longer than twenty-one days. In 1981 Irish republicans initiated hunger strikes to demand status as political detainees, asserting the political nature of their claims. For the Irish, particularly northern Catholics, hunger strikes have both historical and mythological precedents. They are viewed symbolically as acts of religio-political martyrdom, linking the protagonist to the pantheon of Irish heroes and the cult of sacrifice, whose most notable exemplar was Jesus Christ.

The ability to accurately document and enumerate the incidence of hunger strikes, along with statistics on morbidity or mortality, is severely hampered by a lack of any systematic surveillance, so the reporting of such incidents remain haphazard. In 1991 the World Medical Association issued guidelines for physicians who treat hunger strikers; a key point of the paper is that care should not be contingent on the suspension of the strike but must be based on clear communication between patient and provider in a context of respect, beneficence, and autonomy.

Hunger striking as a political tool has had mixed success. Court-mandated forced feeding, a controversial precedent set in the early suffragist movement in England, has since been used by governments to stifle or terminate hunger strikes, as in the case of Red Army Faction prisoners in Germany in the 1970s and 1980s. There have been several notable negotiated settlements of strikes; for example, the Bulgarian strikes of 1925–1929, which resulted in a partial amnesty for political prisoners. The 1978 hunger strike in Bolivia led to the downfall of the military regime. In some cases where demands have been ignored, the prolongation of the hunger strikes have led to the death of some strikers, as in the Irish strikes of 1981 and in Turkey in 1996.

In the case of Bobby Sands and the nine other Irish prisoners who died, world opinion seemed to support the British government's position during the strike. After the fatalities, however, mass sentiment began to shift in favor of the Irish Republican movement, whose candidates went on to win several seats in Irish and British parliamentary elections of 1983. In Turkey, the 1996 hunger strike of hundreds of political prisoners resulted in at least twelve deaths, and many surviving prisoners had residual neurologic and psychiatric effects. The death toll from the Turkish strike of 2001 stands at twenty and prompted the government to initiate some of the reforms in prisoner treatment sought by human rights groups.

While reports of hunger strikes reach far back into antiquity, the dawn of a new millennium brings evidence of their ongoing use. It appears that hunger striking will continue to represent a powerful form of protest as long as there remain the oppressive political and social conditions that seem to give rise to them.

*See also:* CAUSES OF DEATH; FAMINE; SOCIAL FUNCTIONS OF DEATH

## Bibliography

Peel, Michael. "Hunger Strikes." *British Medical Journal* 315 (1997):829–830.

World Medical Association. *World Medical Association Declaration on Hunger Strikers.* 43rd World Medical Assembly. Malta, November 1991.

DONNA E. HOWARD
ARUN KALYANASUNDARAM

# HUNTING

Social scientists report that humans have employed hunting as a subsistence strategy for at least 90 percent of *Homo sapiens'* history. The anthropologists Richard Lee and Richard Daly conceptualize hunting, the pursuit and killing of other animals, as one component of "foraging," a broader complex of subsistence activities that also includes the "gathering of wild plant foods, and fishing" (Lee and Daly 1999, p. 3). Hunting entails searching for and killing (or, on occasion, capturing and confining) a wild, unconfined animal. While humans hunt and kill animals primarily as a source of food, they also hunt in order to neutralize a threat (i.e., a tiger or leopard that preys on people), to remove a pest (i.e., rodents or birds that consume agricultural products), or to eliminate a competitor (i.e., predators that kill game animals).

As a human activity, hunting is magnified in its significance by a deceptively simple feature: the evasiveness or resistance exhibited routinely by prey. Because of the behavioral challenges that it presents, hunting has had far-reaching consequences for key aspects of human social, psychological, and cultural life. Since the mid-1960s, for example, anthropologists have argued that hunting may have been a powerful and fundamental force shaping the very nature of cooperation and sharing among early humans.

One such claim involves what the behavioral ecologist Bruce Winterhalder calls the "risk reduction hypothesis." The failure rate of hunters is notoriously high. Even among experienced, highly skilled subsistence hunters who pursue big game animals, any one hunt is much more likely to result in failure than in success. Studying the Hadza of Tanzania in 1993, the anthropologist Kristen Hawkes reported that when hunting big game, Hadza men failed to make a kill 97 of every 100 days that they hunted. When a large game animal is killed, it often represents a "windfall" in excess of what any one hunter and his or her immediate family can consume. These circumstances promote reciprocity and sharing among hunters. By sharing the meat provided by a successful kill, a hunter effectively "buys insurance" against failure in future hunts. When, in the future, he or she fails to kill prey, other successful hunters with whom meat has been shared previously will reciprocate and provide meat to the unsuccessful hunter. The science writer Matt Ridley argues that the cooperation and reciprocity associated with hunting may help constitute the basis of systems of moral and ethical culture. In short, hunting is an activity that promotes cooperation and sharing because it entails the pursuit of a highly valued resource, access to which is unpredictable and risky.

Anthropologists report that while both men and women hunt, in the vast majority of human societies this activity is predominantly male. Yet, it is not self-evident why males are more likely to hunt than females. Scholarly interpretations of the 1990s link hunting to sexual activity and rewards. While the matter is debated among social scientists, some researchers argue that males are motivated to hunt not only because of the food they acquire but because of the social esteem and increased sexual opportunities enjoyed by successful hunters.

The extrinsic rewards of a successful hunt may provide clues about why hunting is intrinsically exciting and satisfying to many people, especially males. To the extent that a behavior confers significant survival and reproductive advantages, evolutionary psychologists like Leda Cosmides and John Tooby suggest that humans are likely to evolve specialized psychological mechanisms that promote such behavior. Accordingly, if hunting yields highly valued protein in the form of meat, promotes stable patterns of cooperation and exchange, and provides males with a currency that they can exchange for sex, it is reasonable to surmise that human males may have evolved psychological attributes that make hunting highly intrinsically satisfying and rewarding to them, whatever the accompanying risks. While this line of reasoning appears promising and compelling to evolutionary minded social and behavioral scientists, it may be too early to conclude that humans are psychologically equipped with specialized mental mechanisms that are the product of humans' Pleistocene history as hunters.

Despite the demise of the hunter-gatherer era about 12,000 years ago, hunting has maintained great significance in many human cultures. In *A View To a Death in the Morning* (1993), Matt Cartmill traces the symbolism and imagery of the hunt from the hunting-gathering era, through the agrarian era, and into modern, industrial times. Cartmill

*Hunting, once reserved for socialites in the early twentieth century, has become popular sport for all classes.*
BETTMANN/CORBIS

sees the symbolism of the hunt as rich with information about how human beings understand and assess their place in nature. In the Greco-Roman world, hunting was elevated to cosmological significance in the form of deities such as Apollo and Artemis/Diana. In later European art, literature, and philosophy, hunting themes became freighted with complex meanings about class relations and social justice. In contemporary industrial societies such as the United States, media products such as the animated film *Bambi* are said to express a view of nature in general and animals in particular as good, and humanity as evil, or at least "dubious." Thus, writers like Cartmill see the human significance of hunting in the post–hunter-gatherer era as primarily semiotic, as pertaining to the symbolization of humanity and its relation to nature, and to itself.

In contemporary Western societies like the United States and Great Britain, it is conflict over the moral meanings attending hunting that has made it the focal point of intense and protracted political debate. Members of animal rights organizations such as People for the Ethical Treatment of Animals (PETA) and Friends of Animals vilify hunting. They also denounce hunters whom they see as arrogant and insensitive for engaging in an activity that is described as "recreational" or "sporting," and necessitates the death of a "sentient," nonhuman animal. Yet many hunters themselves impose entirely different meanings on the hunt, and some, such as the naturalist Paul Shepard, even assign it spiritual significance, construing it as an activity that expresses a deep and profound reverence toward nature and living things. It is unlikely that these divergent views will be reconciled in the near future. If humans are, in fact, possessed of an evolved psychology that derives from a hunting-gathering past, it has yet to be determined if this evolved psychology and the contours of modernity are somehow reconcilable or, rather, are fundamentally incommensurable.

Finally, hunters and recreational shooters in modern societies like the United States have played a significant role in wildlife conservation. As members of various hunting and shooting organizations, such as Ducks Unlimited, the Rocky Mountain Elk Foundation, and the National Rifle Association, hunting enthusiasts have generated billions of dollars that have supported various types of game management programs, habitat protection and restoration, and conservation education. Some of this money takes the form of direct contributions to such programs, and other monies are generated indirectly by taxes on hunting equipment purchases and various license, tag, permit, and stamp fees. One of the oldest and most important among such hunting-based revenue sources is the Federal Aid in Wildlife Restoration Act of 1937 (also known as the Pittman-Robertson Act), and it has distributed more than $3.8 billion to state fish and wildlife agencies since it became law. Thus, somewhat ironically, modern hunters contribute significantly to the survival of the very species whose individual members they hunt and kill.

*See also:* DEATH SYSTEM

### Bibliography

Cartmill, Matt. *A View To a Death in the Morning: Hunting and Nature History.* Cambridge, MA: Harvard University Press, 1993.

Cosmides, Leda, and John Tooby. "The Psychological Foundations of Culture." In Jerome H. Barkow, Leda Cosmides, and John Tooby eds., *The Adapted Mind: Evolutionary Psychology and the Generation of Culture.* Oxford: Oxford University Press, 1992.

Endicott, Karen L. "Gender Relations in Hunter-Gatherer Societies." In Richard B. Lee and Richard Daly eds., *The Cambridge Encyclopedia of Hunters and Gatherers*. Cambridge: Cambridge University Press, 1992.

Hawkes, Kristen. "Why Hunter-Gatherers Work: An Ancient Version of the Problem of Public Goods." *Current Anthropology* 34 (1993):341–351.

Hawkes, Kristen. "Why Do Men Hunt? Benefits for Risky Choices." In Elizabeth Cashdan ed., *Risk and Uncertainty in Tribal and Peasant Economies*. Boulder, CO: Westview Press, 1990.

Hill, Kim, and Hillard Kaplan. "On Why Male Foragers Hunt and Share Food." *Current Anthropology* 34 (1993):701–706.

Lee, Richard B., and Richard Daly, eds. "Foragers and Others." In *The Cambridge Encyclopedia of Hunters and Gatherers*. Cambridge: Cambridge University Press, 1999.

Ridley, Matt. *The Origins of Virtue: Human Instincts and the Evolution of Cooperation*. New York: Viking, 1996.

Shepard, Paul. *The Tender Carnivore and the Sacred Game*. New York: Charles Scribner's Sons, 1973.

Winterhalder, Bruce. "Diet Choice, Risk, and Food Sharing in a Stochastic Environment." *Journal of Anthropological Archaeology* 5 (1986):369–392.

RICHARD S. MACHALEK

# IATROGENIC ILLNESS

Literally meaning "physician-induced," the term *iatrogenic* describes diseases inadvertently resulting from medical treatments or procedures. With more effective and powerful treatments have come side effects that may be more common and harmful. There are efforts by medical specialists and consumers to quantify and reduce iatrogenic side effects. These efforts are hampered by the natural reluctance of physicians (and other providers) to have their errors publicized and the prospect of malpractice lawsuits. Physicians rarely report iatrogenic events, even though most claim to have witnessed them. Efforts to make reporting mandatory are resisted by the medical profession; therefore, lack of such reporting makes it more difficult to identify and minimize hazards.

Despite these obstacles, the hazards of medicine are emerging in an increasing number of studies and reports. A 2000 presidential report described iatrogenic error and illness as "a national problem of epidemic proportions," causing tens of thousands of annual deaths. The report estimated the cost of lost income, disability, and health care costs to be $29 billion a year. The report concluded that half of adverse medical events were preventable.

The presidential report relied heavily upon another report by the Institute of Medicine, *To Err is Human: Building a Safer Health System* (2000). Issued by the most respected agency of American medicine, *To Err is Human* generated considerable attention and surprise by concluding that up to 98,000 Americans are killed annually by medical errors. This number slightly exceeds the combined total of those killed in one year by motor vehicle accidents (43,458), breast cancer (42,297), and AIDS (acquired immunodeficiency syndrome, 16,516).

The Institute of Medicine utilized the findings of two large studies. One found that 2.9 percent of people hospitalized in Colorado and Utah experienced medical errors and 6.6 percent of those people died as a result of the errors. The second study found that 3.7 percent of people hospitalized in New York experienced errors and 13.6 percent of those people died as result. This led the Institute to conclude that a minimum of 44,000 Americans die annually due to error during hospitalization, making it the eighth leading cause of death in the United States. Even so, the report says that these numbers "offer only a very modest estimate of the magnitude of the problem since hospital patients represent only a small proportion of the total population at risk" (Institute of Medicine 2000, p. 2).

While important, these reports fail to address major iatrogenic controversies such as the undertreatment of people with chronic pain and the repetitive misclassification of physical illnesses as psychiatric disorders. (Diseases as wide-ranging as peptic ulcer, epilepsy, asthma, and migraine have been so classified, leading to ineffective treatments, suffering, and death.) However, another important source of iatrogenic illness, the increase of drug-resistant infections due to overuse of antibiotics, is otherwise being acknowledged and addressed.

The Centers for Disease Control and Prevention (CDC) estimate that each year nearly 2 million people acquire infections while hospitalized and about 90,000 die from those infections. More than 70 percent of hospital-acquired bacterial infections have become resistant to at least one of the drugs commonly used to treat them. *Staphylococcus aureus* (staph), the leading cause of hospital-acquired infections, is resistant to 95 percent of first-choice antibiotics, and about 30 percent of second-choice antibiotics.

In New York City alone, treatment of people with hospital-acquired staph infections exceeds $400 million, according to a study published in 1999. Researchers found that staph infections doubled the length of hospitalization, and more than doubled the patient death rate and per patient costs.

The CDC proposes several methods of reducing hospital-acquired infections. The most important include more discriminating antibiotic use and improved hygiene of hospital staff, the main source of infections.

The modern state is, as Thomas Szasz has described it in *Pharmacracy: Medicine and Politics in America* (2001), a "therapeutic state" in which medical providers have far more power than consumers. Such an imbalance of power may make consumers increasingly vulnerable to the factors that cause iatrogenic illness to be an important cause of illness and death.

*See also:* CAUSES OF DEATH; TECHNOLOGY AND DEATH

### *Bibliography*

Institute of Medicine. *To Err is Human: Building a Safer Health System.* Washington, DC: National Academy Press, 2000.

Quality Interagency Coordination Task Force. *Doing What Counts for Patient Safety: Federal Actions to Reduce Medical Errors and Their Impact.* Washington, DC: Agency for Healthcare Research and Quality, 2000.

Szasz, Thomas S. *Pharmacracy: Medicine and Politics in America.* Westport, CT: Praeger Trade, 2001.

Tassano, Fabian. *The Power of Life or Death: A Critique of Medical Tyranny.* Oxford: Oxford Forum, 1999.

### *Internet Resources*

Rubin, Robert J., Catherine A. Harrington, Anna Poon, Kimberly Dietrich, Jeremy A. Greene, and Adil Moiduddin. "The Economic Impact of *Staphylococcus aureus* Infection in New York City Hospitals." *Emerging Infectious Diseases* 5, no. 1 (1999). In the Centers for Disease Control and Prevention [web site]. Available from www.cdc.gov/ncidod/eid/vol5no1/rubin.htm.

Szasz, Thomas S. "The Moral Physician." In the American Iatrogenic Association [web site]. Available from www.iatrogenic.org/library/moralphysician.html.

NICOLAS S. MARTIN

# IMMORTALITY

Western belief systems believe that there is life after death. William James waited until the final pages of his classic *Varieties of Religious Experiences* (1902) before trying to evaluate this belief. In those pages he endeavored to answer the question: Suppose that there is a God; What difference would humans expect God to make within the natural world? Although James believed that God was the producer of immortality, his far-ranging study of religious experience did not provide clear support for personal immortality. He could conclude only:

> . . . that we can experience union with *something* larger than ourselves and in that union find our greatest peace. . . . Anything larger will do, if only it be large enough to trust for the next step. It need not be infinite, it need not be solitary. It might conceivably be only a larger and more godlike self, of which the present self would then be but the mutilated expression, and the universe might conceivably be a collection of such selves with no absolute unity at all. *(James 1992, pp. 570–571)*

## Types of Afterlife Belief

It is doubtful that many believers have ever traded their faith in personal immortality for the speculations offered by James. A far more heartening prospect is eternal life under the auspices of an all-powerful, all-knowing, all-loving God. Nevertheless, personal immortality is only one of the answers that have been proposed over the centuries. This entry (1) surveys a variety of afterlife beliefs; (2) considers their foundation in faith, reason, and fact; and (3) explores some of the meanings and uses associated with these beliefs. Survival of death is not identical with immortality, and immortality is not identical with a continuation of personality or individuality. These distinctions become clearer as several types of survival are identified and explored.

*Afterflash.* An "afterflash" refers to a force field or faded image of the person that occurs immediately after death, but soon vanishes. This afterlife belief holds that the afterflash might come and go so quickly that witnesses are left with the feeling that something happened or somebody was there, yet have no tangible evidence to show for it. The after-flash might also manifest itself briefly on a few occasions before disappearing forever. It is possible that even this minimal phenomenon is not what it seems. Perhaps what is perceived is only a record of what has perished, as the scholar F. W. H. Myers suggests. Myers cites the example of the streaming light from stars that perished before the earth was formed. Even if these phenomena do represent some type of survival it would be in a downgraded and fleeting form that does not express the individual personality of the deceased. Therefore, this philosophy is clearly a long way from personal immortality.

*Fade away.* One of the most prevalent views of the afterlife in the ancient world was a gradual dimming of the departed spirit, known as a "fade away." In pre-Christian Mesopotamia, for example, the souls of the dead dwelled in a gloomy under-world. There they became dulled, miserable rem-nants of their former selves. Early Hebrew belief inherited this tradition. *Yahweh* (the Hebrew word for "God") kept watch over the living; the shades of the dead were abandoned. Within this belief system, the fade-away type of survival did not pre-serve individual personality. According to some accounts, the piteous dead continued to become even weaker until the end of creation; others are inclined to believe that the spirits dissolved as their vital essence eventually gave way.

*Cosmic melding.* According to the philosophy of "cosmic melding," the spark of life is not destroyed by death. Because it was never really the private property of the individual, it does not remain so after death. Rather, each person is like a drop of water that returns to the ocean of creation to become a continuing but transformed part of the universal flow. The philosophy of cosmic melding, although not termed this way, can be found in Hindu thought. Central to Hindu belief are the writings collectively known as the *Upanishads* (the "Equivalences"). The individual soul (*atman*) is at one with the universal soul (*brahman*). Life and death are different aspects of the same reality. One hopes ultimately to escape the cycle of death and rebirth and achieve ecstatic union with the univer-sal soul. This is a survival doctrine that seeks an end to personal survival.

The idea of cosmic melding has been ex-pressed outside Hinduism. It has been suggested that the universe itself is alive with pulsations from the unimaginable subatomic to the unimaginable vast. Individuals pulsate as unique units for a brief time and then participate in the music of the spheres in different forms. This ancient idea has been kept alive in modern theoretical physics.

*Reincarnation and rebirth.* Besides the Hindu cycle of birth and rebirth, other reincarnation beliefs exist in many world cultures. These beliefs differ greatly in their details, but in 1958 a historian of religion, Mircea Eliade, observed that typically it is not just the life and death of the individual that is involved. Human society and the world itself can be regenerated through death. Many communal rit-uals are devoted to this purpose, including those that initiate novices into adulthood. There are many rites of passage in the course of communal life. One has experienced symbolic but intense death/rebirth experiences before encountering physical death. However, all of this does not guar-antee that one will continue to survive death after death. The doctrine of reincarnation includes the belief that souls can perish because of individual misfortune or attack, and all souls can perish when the skies and mountains dissolve.

*Conditional survival.* The philosophy of contin-ued survival holds that there is more than one pos-sible outcome after death. A person might or might not survive death. This survival might be glorious or horrifying. Furthermore, survival might be ever-lasting or only temporary. According to this view, it should not be assumed that survival of death is identical with immortality. There is no guarantee that passing through death assures the spirit or soul of continued existence for all time or eternity. The possibility of more than one outcome after death has had numerous distinguished advocates. The philosophers Gustav Theodor Fechner and William Ernest Hocking are among those who believe that individuals develop more or less spiritual sensitiv-ity and depth through their lives. The universe itself is changing. Within this cosmic framework, the fate of the individual personality perhaps should also be considered as a set of possibilities.

According to this philosophical approach, the nature of the self is a key to what happens after death. In resonance with Eastern thought, these philosophers regard the self as always in process, always in the making. People become more real as they develop their spiritual selves to a higher level. What happens after death depends on how "real" the self has become. People who have gone through life without awakening their spiritual potential will have little or nothing that can survive death, but those who have sought and opened themselves to enlightenment will continue to develop after death.

An elitist view of survival was also known in the ancient world. The possibility of a spiritual survival was the privilege of the royal family, not the commoner. Immortality depended on status, and status either depended on the choice of the gods or political skill and good fortune. Furthermore, Islam as well as Christianity presents two contrasting paths for the soul after death. First there is the waiting for judgment. One is then either awarded salvation or condemned to damnation. Similarly, Muslims either cross the sacred bridge (*sirat*) safely, or are hurled into hell. Some of the impure are in torment forever; others may eventually repent sufficiently and join the blessed.

*Data file.* The concept of a "data file" has become widely known as the ability to register and store large quantities of information in electronic, computer-accessible form. The idea that survival of death might operate through data files does not appear in the sacred writings of the great religions and the rituals of world societies; however, it is a logical spin-off of the computer sciences. In *The Physics of Immortality* (1994), Frank J. Tipler offers a bold theory derived from concepts and findings in quantum cosmology. Tipler suggests that modern physics is supportive of the Judeo-Christian tradition, although in a nontraditional way. According to Tipler's philosophy, the dead can exist as information and therefore be reconstituted or resurrected in the future. He does not use the term *data file,* but this perhaps conveys the central idea that one can continue to exist as a potential source of information. When effective retrieval and reconstitution techniques are developed, the souls on file can be accessed and, in that sense, return to life. (There is a parallel here with developments in cryonic suspension since the mid-twentieth century.) But does this "information" know that it *is* information? Is self-awareness or consciousness part of this process, or is the surviving element more like a book that can be read, rather than a reader?

*Symbolic immortality.* The idea of something that represents a person can continue to survive in society after death is known as "symbolic immortality." The person is dead, but his or her name or some important aspect of the personality has become part of ongoing human life. Other people, now deceased, live on in human memory. The living will also survive in this way. With continuing advances in communication technology people can survive as CD-ROMs with digitized audio and video, and perhaps in other forms still to come. This is the essence of the concept of symbolic immortality. Wealthy people can endow university buildings and the illustrious can have their names attached to a variety of programs and events, staying alive, then, in public memory. Louis Armstrong, Elvis Presley, and Frank Sinatra may be considered to have a share of symbolic immortality through their recordings and movies.

Helping others to stay alive has emerged as a relatively new form of symbolic immortality. Organ donation and efforts to rescue endangered species and protect the environment are ways in which people are contributing to the continued survival of others; thereby bringing something of their selves into the future.

*Personal immortality.* The concept of "personal immortality" is a core belief within the Christian tradition. Something of the individual survives death forever. Many people expect to enjoy a reunion with loved ones. This expectation obviously assumes the continuation of personal identity. Many other belief systems are ambiguous about personal immortality, however, and traces of this vagueness or discord can be found within Christianity as well. A key question here is the relationship between person and soul. Is the soul the essence of the individual? If so, then survival is personal. Or, Is the soul a sort of passenger-spirit that has very little to do with the individual's unique life? If so, then there might be immortal survival, but not necessarily of the person.

## Belief and Disbelief

Are humans immortal in any meaningful sense of the word? The history of religion is closely associated with beliefs in survival of death as James, the French sociologist Emile Durkheim, and other historians and philosophers have noted. Ancient burial pits, mounds, and tombs often included objects designed to be useful to the deceased in their next lives. From prehistory onward the available evidence suggests that survival belief has been widespread and dominant.

Disbelief also has its tradition, however. Early Chinese philosophy mostly saw death as the natural end to life. Because humans are all part of the cosmic process there is no reason to bemoan one's fate: It is best to become a good person and live well with others into old age. Ancestor cults did flourish, but the illustrious thinkers of the time discouraged people from investing too much in the prospect of immortality. Confucius himself replied to a disciple's question by saying, "If we do not yet know about life, how can we learn about death?" Wang Ch'ung, a scholar of the Han dynasty, scoffed at the presumption of immortality and called his followers' attention to other natural processes by saying:

> Human death is like the extinction of fire. When a fire is extinguished, its light does not shine any more, and when man dies his intellect does not perceive any more. The nature of both is the same. What is the difference between a sick man about to die and a light about to go out? (Overmyer 1974, p. 202)

The world has not been divided neatly between believers and disbelievers. Many people have experienced doubt or uncertainty. It is not unusual for people of strong faith to have wrestled with their doubts from time to time, nor for skeptics to wonder if immortality, improbable as it seemed to them, might not yet be true.

Belief can be grounded on custom, authority, positive personal experience, inner knowledge, external fact, reason, or any combination thereof. By "faith" is usually meant a certainty of belief derived from personal experience and/or inner knowledge. Doubt and disbelief can be occasioned by weakened or conflicted custom, discredited authority, negative personal experience, discredited or counter facts, and compelling alternative arguments.

Custom and authority, reinforced by impressive rituals, was probably enough for many people who lived in small face-to-face societies and worshiped local gods. Intense ritual experiences might also produce the inner conviction that one had touched the sacred. The truth was therefore felt as inside one's self as well as with the people and nature. Authority became a stronger force in religious belief as people organized themselves into larger organizational structures. Although the Egyptian dynasties with their central authorities took shape about 7,000 years ago, there were still many small societies worshiping local gods throughout the days of the Roman Empire. Politics, social action and control, and religion were tightly entwined in emerging civilizations. Judaism, Christianity, and Islam were all beset with internal dissension on a variety of concepts and practices. Authorities, bolstered by canons of approved writings, systematically accepted a particular view of survival while rejecting others (e.g., reincarnation died hard and only temporarily in Christianity).

Questions about the existence and nature of God and the survival of death lingered despite the weight of Church authority and tradition. Medieval theologians and scholars debated these related issues with intensity and often ingenuity. Saint Thomas Aquinas, for example, argued that the soul is immortal despite its association with the vulnerable body because it comes from God who is the "necessary being" on whom all other creatures depend. This was an influential view, but there were dissenters who argued that "the immortal form" that survives death seems to have none of the characteristics of the actual person who dies—this kind of immortality was too abstract and distant for the critics of Aquinas. Elite scholars made repeated attempts to prove immortality by rational analysis and were regularly taken to task by other elite scholars.

Immortality became a keen issue for society at large as science emerged, challenging the order of the universe as conceived by theology. Astronomers in the sixteenth and early seventeenth centuries made observations that contradicted the Catholic Church's official beliefs about the nature and motions of earth, sun, and other celestial bodies. In the nineteenth century the English naturalist

Charles Darwin's theory of evolution led to a convulsive response on the part of established institutions. If humans are but another kind of animal, what then of immortality?

Philosophers and scientists lined up on both the side of belief and disbelief. Strenuous arguments pro and con continued well into the twentieth century. Meanwhile, academic philosophy quietly slipped away from what increasingly seemed like an outmoded and unrewarding debate, and only in the late twentieth century took the challenge up again.

Belief in a just God and personal immortality was shaken by calamitous events throughout the twentieth century. Two world wars, genocides, and a host of other disastrous events led many to reject the traditional assurances. Others devoted themselves to assuage their sorrows and affirm their beliefs through spiritualism and communication with the dead. Brought up within conventional churches, some set off on quests to find ways of life that might speak more directly to their needs. These quests sometimes took the form of exploring Eastern religions, sometimes in reshaping Judeo-Christian beliefs and practices (from which the New Age movement emerged).

Reports of near-death experiences were welcomed as another opportunity to affirm personal immortality. At the core of these reports is an absolute conviction: "This is what happened; this is what I saw, what I felt, what I experienced!" Logical arguments for or against survival of death are always vulnerable to powerful rejoinders. Scientific findings are always subject to modification, even rejection, by subsequent studies. What a person feels and experiences, however, can seem sufficient within itself. A sense of direct experience and inner knowledge is more convincing to many people than a survey of external facts or convoluted argumentation.

Thomas A. Kselman's 1993 analysis *Death and the Afterlife in Modern France* offers insights applicable to other contemporary societies as well. He notes that beliefs about death were of prime importance in establishing and maintaining social order. How people thought they should live was ruled to an appreciable extent by how they hoped to fare in the next life. In the meantime, public officials and the clergy often played upon this theme to achieve their own ends. By the waning years of the nineteenth century, however, this long-standing social and moral order was rapidly crumbling. The pace of technology and commerce had picked up dramatically, shifting attention to the opportunities of the present life on the earth. The establishment had a difficult time in trying to keep the lid on simmering developments in all areas of society. Increasingly, death became a concern for individuals and their families and fell less under the control of church and state. The "market culture" had taken over, and ideas about survival of death would have to compete not only with each other but also with other, sometimes more compelling, possibilities.

At the turn of the twenty-first century an enormous range of ideas, attitudes, and practices coexist, including Margaret Wertheim's *The Pearly Gates of Cyberspace* (1999) and N. Catherine Hayles's *How We Became Posthuman: Virtual Bodies in Cybernetics, Literature, and Infomatics* (1999). The survival of the survival question appears to be assured for some time to come.

*See also:* AFTERLIFE IN CROSS-CULTURAL PERSPECTIVE; BUDDHISM; CHINESE BELIEFS; COMMUNICATION WITH THE DEAD; GHOSTS; IMMORTALITY, SYMBOLIC; NEAR-DEATH EXPERIENCES; REINCARNATION

## Bibliography

Camporesi, Piero. *The Fear of Hell: Images of Damnation and Salvation in Early Modern Europe.* University Park: Pennsylvania State University Press, 1990.

Chan, Wing-Tsit. *A Source Book in Chinese Philosophy.* Princeton, NJ: Princeton University Press, 1993.

Coppleston, Frederick. *A History of Philosophy: Book One.* New York: Image, 1985.

Ducasse, C. J. *The Belief in a Life after Death.* Springfield, IL: Charles C. Thomas, 1961.

Durkheim, Émile. *The Elementary Forms of the Religious Life.* 1915. Reprint, New York: Free Press, 1965.

Eliade, Mircea. *Birth and Rebirth.* New York: Harper & Brothers, 1958.

Fischer, John Martin, ed. *The Metaphysics of Death.* Stanford, CA: Stanford University Press, 1993.

Hayles, N. Catherine. *How We Became Posthuman: Virtual Bodies in Cybernetics, Literature, and Informatics.* Chicago: University of Chicago Press, 1999.

Hocking, William Ernest. *The Meaning of Immortality in Human Experience,* revised edition. New York: Harper & Brothers, 1957.

James, William. *The Varieties of Religious Experience.* 1902. Reprint, New York: The Modern Library, 1999.

Kselman, Thomas A. *Death and the Afterlife in Modern France.* Princeton, NJ: Princeton University Press, 1993.

Lamont, Corliss. *The Illusion of Immortality.* New York: The Philosophical Library, 1950.

Lifton, Robert J. *The Broken Connection: On Death and the Continuity of Life.* New York: Simon & Schuster, 1979.

Malin, Shimon. *Nature Loves to Hide.* New York: Oxford University Press, 2001.

Overmyer, Douglas T. "China." In Frederick H. Holck ed., *Death and Eastern Thought.* Nashville, TN: Abingdon Press, 1974.

Russell, Jeffrey Burton. *A History of Heaven.* Princeton, NJ: Princeton University Press, 1997.

Tipler, Frank J. *The Physics of Immortality.* New York: Doubleday, 1994.

Wertheim, Margaret. *The Pearly Gates of Cyberspace.* New York: W. W. Norton, 1999.

ROBERT KASTENBAUM

# IMMORTALITY, SYMBOLIC

Among the numerous cultural mechanisms for allaying death's sting are envisionments for personal transcendence, such as resurrection, reincarnation, metempsychoses, or some disembodied spiritual existence. In addition to these relatively direct means for personal survival, there are more symbolic forms of immortality that exist. Collectively, there is the immortality obtained through assisting in the transmission of knowledge and precedent to succeeding generations; personally, the preservation of one's memory through eponym, legacy, photograph, or artistic creation. The holocaust survivor and Nobel Peace Prize recipient Elie Wiesel asked,

> What does it mean to remember? It is to live in more than one world, to prevent the past from fading and to call upon the future to illuminate it. It is to revive fragments of existence, to rescue lost beings, to cast harsh light on faces and events, to drive back the sands that cover the surface of things, to combat oblivion and to reject death. *(Wiesel 1995, p 150)*

Human beings live in two worlds: the natural and the symbolic. Ultimately governing human existence within both, according to thanatological determinists, are drives to transcend death. From the perspective of sociobiology, the central drive of the biological self is to pass on one's genetic code. Similarly, to counter death fears and the challenges death poses to the meaningfulness of existence, the symbolic self has a psychobiological drive to leave its mark and a psychological need to continuously feel there's something indestructible within itself.

Given that selfhood is a social phenomenon, negotiated through symbolic exchanges with others, this sense of personal immortality entails, according to psychiatrist Robert Lifton, the ability to symbolize one's own death and continuity thereafter. Death can, for instance, be perceived as but a transition, and one can "survive" through others' memories. And with this outlook, instead of expending life energies in death denials, like the art of karate where one uses the energy of one's adversary, the power of death is diverted to personal growth and social development as the living work on their postselves.

Just as the psychoanalyst Sigmund Freud's late-nineteenth-century model of the human pscyhe, based on the development of sexuality, arose during an era when sex was the great taboo, so Lifton's late-twentieth-century death-based psychological paradigm emerged from a culture of death denials and a world threatened by nuclear extinction. "While the denial of death is universal, the inner life-experience of a sense of immortality, rather than reflecting such denial, may well be the most authentic psychological alternative to that denial" (Lifton 1979, p. 13). Humans are the only creatures to be aware of their vulnerabilities and mortality, whose deadening imageries feature separation, disintegration, and stasis. To buffer themselves from the anxieties of such insights, these meaning-seeking primates employ the vitalizing imageries of connection, integrity, and movement through five distinct modes of experiencing that, according to Lifton, comprise the essence of symbolic immortality. These include the biological, spiritual, creative, natural, and mystic modes, whose traditional and contemporary forms are detailed in this entry.

## Modes of Symbolic Immortality and Their Contemporary Variations

Genetic, or biological, immortality was undoubtedly the first mode grasped by the human primate. It involves the sense of connection with one's parents and familial generations past as well as the sense of personal continuity through one's progeny. Further, given the nature of one's bonds with nonfamilial groups, these feelings of connection with something greater than one's self can extend outward to include one's tribe, culture, and nation.

Modern science has added new ways to biologically transcend death, such as through organ transplants (where at least a portion of one's self remains alive), sperm banks (allowing for the genetic immortality of anonymous and deceased donors), and cloning. In April 1999 a California woman gave birth to a child sired by her deceased husband. What made this news (after all, women have been impregnated with frozen sperm of the dead since the early 1990s) was that her husband's sperm was extracted from his epididymis, upon her request, thirty hours after he had suddenly died from an allergic reaction.

Religious/spiritual conceptions of immortality range from the resurrection-based beliefs of Christianity to the cycles of rebirths in such Eastern faiths as Buddhism and Hinduism. Members of the Islamic Jihad martyr themselves in performing terrorist acts, assured by leaders that their sacrifice will earn them a place in heaven. Practitioners of Santeria sacrifice animals to protect themselves against death. This mode is experienced as being released from one's biological finiteness, of living at a higher level of existence.

Americans are, it seems, more prone to experience this mode than those from most other developed nations. For instance, according to the National Opinion Research Center's General Social Surveys, four out of ten American adults believe that they have at least once been in touch with one who has died and more than seven in ten believe in an afterlife. Two-thirds claim to have had at least one déjà vu experience, and nearly three in ten

have seen future events occur as if they were happening at that moment in the present.

The creative mode entails the belief that one's endeavors are worthwhile because they can withstand the tests of time. Being symbolic creatures, human essence resides not in the physical body but rather in the minds of others. Thus one can "live on" in others through one's works, through memories of one's deeds, and in one's enduring influence on generations yet born. Sociobiologists refer to this as mimetic immortality, which may be more potent than genetic. As the scholar Richard Dawkins observed,

> When we die we can leave behind genes and/or memes. The difference between them being that our genes will be forgotten in just a few generations. As each generation passes, the contribution of one's unique genes is halved. . . . But if you contribute to the world's culture, if you have a good idea, compose a tune, invent a spark plug, write a poem, it may live on, intact, long after your genes have dissolved in the common pool. (Dawkins 1990, p. 214)

The natural mode of symbolic immortality involves the continuance of the natural world beyond the individual's lifetime, as well with the feeling of being part of the eternal universe beyond oneself.

In a sense, the ecology movement can be seen as an immortality attempt of many individuals whose efforts lead to the preservation of some natural habitat or species of life. As the natural order disappears as human population burgeon, "nature" is increasingly preserved in parks and zoos. Technological innovation has contributed to this sense as well. The collectively produced spacecraft that has left the solar system and will continue to "fly on" even after the sun goes supernova.

The mystical or experiential transcendence mode features an altered state of consciousness so intense that one "looses oneself" in a timeless, deathless realm currently referred to as being "in the zone." As the scholar Jean-Louis Drolet noted, this differs from the other modes as it depends on a psychic state, one characterized by extraordinary psychic unity and perceptual intensity. It can occur with a number of activities, such as during orgasm, birth, athletic effort, ingestion of psychotropic substances, or contemplation. And having had such an experience, according to Robert Lifton, "One never 'returns' to exactly the same inner structure of the self. Having once broken old forms, one senses that they can be broken again, or at least extended beyond earlier limitations" (Lifton 1979, p. 26).

## Immortality Ideologies across History

Following the tradition of Franz Borkenau, Jean-Paul Sartre, and Otto Rank, Lifton cast history to ultimately be changes in immortality symbolizations (or ideologies). For instance, the rise of Darwinian thought not only weakened the theological mode but led to "man's sense of biological continuity was extended back into the infinite past . . . [and] into the infinite future" (p. 286). Man's imagery of his own history now came to include, in some important degree, the history of all his fellow species, not only animal but even plants—in other words, it produced a reactivation of the natural mode of immortality.

Modern medical technologies have enhanced the mystical mode by its ability to resurrect those "clinically dead." By the late 1960s, stories of what it is like to die began to circulate widely in professional quarters, and in 1975 they were shared with the general public in the best-selling book *Life after Life,* by Raymond Moody, a physician and philosopher. Here, Moody reported tantalizing similarities among the reports of those having had "near-death experiences," or NDEs, including out-of-body experiences, interactions with deceased others, and born-again outlooks. The results of an early 1980s national survey indicated that as many as 8 million Americans have had such experiences.

But modern times have also thwarted the perceived potency of these modes to overcome death. A central theme of Lifton's work is how, for much of the latter half of the twentieth century, the possibility of nuclear war threatened cultural symbols of immortality while propagating deadening imageries of extinction. The suspected consequences of fearing that all transcendence modes will be vaporized range from the growth of religious fundamentalism and cults to the contemporary drug "epidemics."

With the end of the cold war, one would expect a resurgence of transcendence interest. Indeed, since the 1980s the popular culture has witnessed a proliferation of halls of fame (ranging from international, national, state, city, and occupational) and "Who's Who" compilations, a significant increase in the percent of Americans believing in reincarnation and life after death, opportunities for being remembered through charitable donations, and even an affirmative action campaign for U.S. postage stamp immortalizations of such notables as rock-and-roll legend Elvis Presley.

In general, however, modernity's effects on the traditional modes of symbolic immortality have been double-edged. When change has become life's only certainty there's been a severing of sensed connections between living generations and those of the future and past, hence the observed historic ignorance of American students. Changes in family structure and relationships, such as those wrought by the divorce revolution, have dampened members' knowledge of (and interest in) familial generations past, possibly weakening the significance attached to the biological mode. Thus even though new recording technologies may be able to virtually preserve one's image or voice, what difference does it make if no one knows or cares who you were? And with increasing secularization and the loss of religious monopoly over transcendence symbolizations, connections between desirous immortality and the moral worthiness of lives lived evaporated, as have images of hell from the Christian imagination.

## Symbolic Immortality As Source of Evil

Symbolic immortality has its dark side; attempts to transcend oneself through heroism may also lie at the root of human evil. Being a "loser" in life, John Hinkley sought immortality through infamy by trying to kill the president of the United States. Nearly two decades later, Eric Harris and Dylan Klebold were to receive in death more attention than they did in life because of their murderous frenzy at Columbine High School. The Columbine gunmen sought immortality through a well-planned suicidal massacre, coming not only through the notoriety of their deed but also through their electronic legacies—from their web site and from a series of videos taped over the weeks before the massacre, wherein the nihilistic rationalizations for their revenge were developed. Their immortality would be further enhanced as their death day would occur on the birthday of Adolf Hitler, the twentieth century's embodiment of evil. "Directors will be fighting over this story," Klebold said in one video. In another, made on the morning of the massacre, he said, "It's a half hour before Judgment Day. I didn't like life very much. Just know I'm going to a better place than here" (Associated Press, 1999).

*See also:* AFTERLIFE IN CROSS-CULTURAL PERSPECTIVE; IMMORTALITY; MEMORIAL, VIRTUAL

### Bibliography

Associated Press. "Columbine Gunmen Sought Immortality." 13 December, 1999.

Becker, Ernest. *The Denial of Death.* New York: The Free Press, 1973.

Borkenau, Franz. "The Concept of Death." In Robert Fulton ed., *Death and Identity.* New York: John Wiley, 1965.

Choron, Jacques. *Death and Modern Man.* New York: Collier Books, 1964.

Dawkins, Richard. *The Selfish Gene.* New York: Oxford University Press, 1990.

Drolet, Jean-Louis. "Transcending Death during Early Adulthood: Symbolic Immortality, Death Anxiety, and Purpose in Life." *Clinical Psychology* 46, no. 2 (1990):148–160.

Gallup, George. *Adventures in Immortality: A Look beyond the Threshold of Death.* New York: McGraw-Hill, 1982.

Lifton, Robert. *The Broken Connection: On Death and the Continuity of Life.* New York: Simon and Schuster, 1979.

McDannell, Colleen, and Bernhard Lang. *Heaven: A History.* New Haven, CT: Yale University Press, 1995.

Rank, Otto. *Psychology and the Soul.* Philadelphia: University of Pennsylvania Press, 1950.

Wiesel, Elie. *All Rivers Run to the Sea: Memoirs.* New York: Alfred A. Knopf, 1995.

MICHAEL C. KEARL

# INCAN RELIGION

Like many ancient Andean people before them, the Incas viewed death in two ways. One was biological death, when the body ceased functionally and was cremated, buried, or mummified. The other was social death, when certain privileged individuals remained active in the minds, souls, and daily lives of the living until they were forgotten or replaced by other prominent figures. Some ancestors were never forgotten, however. They were considered heroic figures who gave the Inca their identity. Their corpses were mummified, revered, and saved as sacred objects. Ancestor veneration frightened the Spanish crown and clergy, who destroyed the burial chambers, or *huacas,* of these corpses in an attempt to undermine the ancestral foundation of the Incan empire.

The ancient Inca Empire developed in the fourteenth and fifteenth centuries C.E. and spanned more than 2,000 miles from Ecuador to Chile at the time of the Spanish arrival in 1515. Hereditary lords ruled the empire. The basic social unit of the Inca was the *ayllu,* a collective of kinsmen who cooperated in the management of land and camelid herds. Common ancestors gave ayllus their ethnic identity. Ruling over the local ayllus were *karacas.* Lords and karacas claimed close kinship ties with important deities and ancestors and acted as intermediaries between heaven and the earth, interceding with the supernatural forces on behalf of their subjects' well being. The countryside was viewed as being alive with supernatural forces, solar deities, and ancestral figures. Even today the indigenous Quechua and Aymara people of the Andes see the land animated with these figures.

The Incas believed they were the children of the sun, *Inti.* The exaltation of Inti was basic to the creation of an imperial cult. Inti became the deified royal progenitor, and his role as dynastic ancestor is described by early Spanish scholars. In each imperial city a temple to Inti was built and served by special priests.

Both in Cuzco, the capital of the empire, and the surrounding countryside, numerous sanctuaries and huacas were situated on *ceques,* or imaginary lines. Ceques were divided into four sections, or quarters, as defined by the principal roads radiating from the Temple of the Sun in Cuzco in the direction of the four quarters of the Inca Empire. The ceques played an important part in the calendrical system and in Inca religion in general, including child sacrifice.

In the mid-1500s, the Spanish scholar Bernardo Cobo reported that after the Incas conquered a town or province they would divide the cultivated land into three parts: the first for the state religion and temples, the second for the Inca ruler himself, and the remaining third for the community itself. Temple lands were often used to cultivate corn, whose religious significance was important, and possibly other products required for ceremonial purposes, as well as provide food for the priests of powerful deities.

Inca rulers were extremely powerful and revered by most followers. Veneration of the rulers did not end with their death; they were mummified and displayed during special public rituals so their legends would be retained as a living presence. Their mummies were served by *panacas,* royal descendants of the dead lord endowed with great wealth. The panacas' role was to conserve the dead ruler's mummy and to immortalize his life and achievements with the help of chants and rituals performed on ceremonial occasions in the presence of the succeeding lord and the mummies of other dead Inca lords. These rites were passed on from generation to generation. Placed in the temporary tombs of the lord's were llama and women sculpted in gold, as well as different kinds of golden vessels, exquisite textiles, and other fine objects. Royal members of the lord's court and local karacas were not mummified but placed in elaborate tombs with lavish offerings. Most commoners were buried in simple surroundings.

*See also:* AZTEC RELIGION; MAYA RELIGION; MUMMIFICATION

**Bibliography**

Cobo, Bernard. *History of the Inca Empire,* translated by Roland Hamilton. Austin: University of Texas Press, 1979.

MacCormack, Sabina. *Religion in the Andes: Vision and Imagination in Early Colonial Peru.* Princeton, NJ: Princeton University Press, 1991.

Morris, Craig, and Adriana Von Hagen. *The Inca Empire and Its Andean Origins.* New York: Abbeville Press, 1993.

TOM D. DILLEHAY

# INFANTICIDE

Most societies agree that the drive to protect and nurture one's infant is a basic human trait. Yet infanticide—the killing of an infant at the hands of a parent—has been an accepted practice for disposing of unwanted or deformed children since prehistoric times. Despite human repugnance for the act, most societies, both ancient and contemporary, have practiced infanticide. Based upon both historical and contemporary data, as many as 10 to 15 percent of all babies were killed by their parents. The anthropologist Laila Williamson notes that infanticide has been practiced by nearly all civilizations. Williamson concludes that infanticide must represent a common human trait, perhaps genetically encoded to promote self-survival.

*Neonaticide* is generally defined as "the homicide of an infant aged one week or less." The psychiatrist Phillip Resnick further limits neonaticide to the killing of an infant on the day of its birth. *Infanticide* in general usage is defined as "the homicide of a person older than one week but less than one year of age." *Filicide* is defined as "the homicide of a child (less than eighteen years of age) by his or her parent or stepparent." For the purposes of this entry, the term *infanticide* will be used to describe the act of child murder by the child's parent(s) regardless of the age of the victim.

## Changing Views of the Nature of the Child

The helpless newborn has not always evoked a protective and loving response, in part because the newborn was not always believed to be human. This belief legitimized an action that under other circumstances would be referred to as murder. For example, the ancient Romans believed that the child was more like a plant than an animal until the seventh day after birth. During the Middle Ages, children born with physical defects or behavioral abnormalities were often viewed as evil or the product of supernatural forces. Changelings were infants believed to be exchanged in the still of the night by devils or goblins who removed the real child and left the changeling in its place. To view the child as potentially evil, dangerous, or worthless, rationalizes the desire to eliminate the burden or threat without guilt or remorse.

Historically, birth was not necessarily viewed as a transition to life. Common law in England presumed that a child was born dead. According to early Jewish law, an infant was not deemed viable until it was thirty days old. During the 1950s the chief rabbi of Israel, Ben Zion Uziel, said that if an infant who was not yet thirty days old was killed, the killer could not be executed because the infant's life was still in doubt. In Japan, a child was not considered to be a human being until it released its first cry, a sign that the spirit entered its body. Scientists and ethicists continue to disagree about when life begins, fueling the moral debate surrounding abortion and infanticide. The twenty-first-century moral philosopher Michael Tooley contends that neonates are not persons and as such neonaticide should not be classified as murder. Tooley has suggested that infanticide should be allowed during a brief (e.g., thirty-day) period after birth.

Several symbolic acts were indicative that the infant was indeed human and worthy of life. In many cultures, it was illegal to kill the child once the child was named, baptized, received its first taste of food, or swallowed water. Symbolic acts such as these afforded the child protection in the event that the child became an economic or emotional burden.

## Legal Perspectives on Infanticide

Until the fourth century, infanticide was neither illegal nor immoral. Complete parental control of the father over the life of his child was dictated by both early Greek and Roman laws. *Patria potestas* refers to the power of the Roman father to decide the fate of his child, even before birth. However, if a mother killed her child she would be punished by death.

Legal sanctions against infanticide were introduced in the fourth century as Christianity infused secular laws. The Roman emperor Constantine, a Christian convert, proclaimed the slaying of a child by the child's father to be a crime. Infanticide was punishable by the death penalty by the end of the fourth century. Around the same time, the Christian emperor Valentinian declared that it was illegal for parents to fail to provide for their offspring. Thus, by the Middle Ages, infanticide was no longer condoned by either church or state in Europe. However, as a result of hard times and a high illegitimacy rate, infanticide was the most common crime in Western Europe from the Middle Ages to the end of the eighteenth century.

During the Renaissance period, the criminal justice system took a strong position against infanticide. Widespread poverty and political unrest throughout Europe resulted in high infant mortality rates. Legislation in France demanded the death penalty for mothers convicted of this crime. In 1720 Prussia's King Friedrich Wilhem I decreed that women who killed their children should be sewn into sacks and drowned. Infanticide has existed as a separate statutory crime in England since 1922. Under English legislation (the Infanticide Act of 1938), a mother who kills her child within the first year of the child's life is assumed to be mentally ill. The highest crime she can be charged with is manslaughter. English juries are reluctant to sentence women to prison for this crime, while fathers can be charged with homicide.

Early American parents found to be child killers were punished by death. In 1642 Massachusetts enacted a law making the concealment of a murdered illegitimate child a capital offense. Records indicate that executions for infanticide occurred as early as 1648.

Twenty-first-century America classifies infanticide as a homicide. Depending on state laws, those who commit infanticide may be eligible for the death penalty. Most of the mothers convicted are granted suspended sentences or probation. Fathers are generally not afforded the same leniency. Despite these laws, shame, illegitimacy, poverty, and the lack of effective birth control result in uncountable hidden infanticides.

## Factors Leading to Infanticide through the Ages

In examining the numerous causes for infanticide, the physician and researcher Larry Milner contends that "infanticide arises from hardness of life rather than hardness of heart" (1998, p. 10). Perhaps the mother with the hardest of hearts was Medea who, according to Greek legend, killed her children as revenge against her unfaithful husband. The term *Medea syndrome* derives from this legend. The following factors represent examples of both hardness of life and hardness of heart.

*Human sacrifice.* Human sacrifice is one of the earliest recorded forms of infanticide. Archaeological evidence indicates that prehistoric children were sacrificed to the gods. In Germany, a mass burial grave dating back to 20000 B.C.E. was discovered, containing thirty-three skulls of children who appeared to be victims of sacrifice. Aztec children were sacrificed to the rain god Tlaloc. The Senjero tribe of eastern Africa sacrificed firstborn sons to assure a bountiful harvest. As late as 1843, children were sealed in walls, foundations of buildings, and bridges to strengthen the structure. Evidence of this practice dates back to the walls of Jericho. Lloyd deMause states, "To this day, when children play 'London Bridge is falling down' they are acting out a sacrifice to a river goddess when they catch the child at the end of the game" (1974, p. 27). By offering a valued possession to the gods, humans have long attempted to appease a deity.

*Population control.* One of the most common factors leading to infanticide is population control. Poverty, famine, and population control are interrelated factors. Where safe and effective birth control was unavailable, infanticide was used to selectively limit the growth of a community. Infanticide allowed for selection of the fittest or most desirable offspring, with sick, deformed, female, or multiple births targeted for disposal. Greek philosophers accepted the use of infanticide to control the size of the state. With regard to practicality, infanticide was not a crime. In a 1976 review of 393 populations, the anthropologists William Divale and Marvin Harris reported that 208 tribes routinely practiced infanticide, particularly female infanticide, to control population. Females were targeted because this practice reduced the number of sexually active, fertile females.

*Poverty.* Even when population growth was not a factor, poverty was the most common reason why parents killed their offspring. In ancient Greece and Rome, parents who could not afford to raise their children disposed of them, particularly during times of war, famine, and drought. At times children were killed and even consumed by the starving parents. Eskimo children were eaten by the parents and older siblings during times of famine. Cannibalism was common during times of drought among the Australian aboriginals, a people normally fond of their children. During extreme droughts, every second child was killed and fed to a preceding child to ensure its survival.

*Devaluation of females.* Female infanticide is a problem rooted in a culture of sexism throughout antiquity. In many cultures girls have little value. Even when female children were not killed at birth, their needs were neglected, particularly if limited resources were needed to ensure the survival of male offspring. In tribal societies, male babies were preferred because males grew up to be hunters and warriors. Young females were seen as a threat because they might attract males from neighboring tribes.

Data indicating high male-to-female population ratios indicate selective female infanticide. Sex-ratio evidence suggests that female infanticide dates back to Greco-Roman times. Men were more valuable as laborers and warriors. Females required a costly marriage dowry. A common Roman expression was, "Everyone raises a son, including a poor man, but even a rich man will abandon a daughter" (Milner 1998, p. 160). Unequal sex ratios have been reported throughout the Middle Ages and the Renaissance worldwide. Evidence from tribal societies also suggests that tribal peoples used female infanticide as the primary method to control population.

In China, a poor and overcrowded country, females are expendable. Evidence of female infanticide in China dates back to 800 B.C.E. Females are viewed as less desirable in Chinese culture due to the expense involved in the dowry system and the fact that only a son can perpetuate the family line. Additionally, when a girl marries she leaves her family and is unavailable to care for her aging parents. With the implementation of the "one child per couple" policy in 1978, Chinese parents are unwilling to invest their one opportunity for parenthood on a daughter. The policy provided for enforced abortions, sterilizations, and legal/economic sanctions against families who choose not to comply. Although illegal, sex-selective abortion is a common practice. Estimates based upon unequal sex ratios suggest that over 30 million females are missing in China.

In India, the practice of female infanticide is even more pervasive. As in China, the birth of a daughter is seen as a liability. Only sons are allowed to perform the funeral rites at the pyre of his father. The murder of female newborns is so common that it has a special name, *kuzhippa,* or "baby intended for the burial pit" (Milner 1998, p. 176). Selective abortion is also a common practice. In 1998 Milner reported that in one Bombay clinic, of 8,000 abortions, 7,999 were performed on female fetuses. In 1991 Nicholas Kristof estimated that nearly 30 million females were missing in India.

*Birth defects.* Deformed or defective newborns have been disposed of by most cultures across the ages. From an evolutionary standpoint, parents decide whether to invest their energy in raising a deformed or sick child that may not survive to perpetuate the family lines. Aristotle declared that there should be a law that no deformed child should live. In the twenty-first century, medical advances present new challenges to parents who are forced to decide whether to use heroic measures to save the life of severely impaired newborns or to let them die.

*Illegitimacy.* Illegitimacy is another factor leading to infanticide through the ages. To avoid shame and censure, women have secretively disposed of illegitimate babies since early Roman times. Illegitimacy and poverty are the most common reasons for infanticide in the twenty-first century.

*Superstition.* Finally, superstitious beliefs regarding children and childbirth contributed to the practice of infanticide. In many cultures, twins were believed to be evil and were promptly killed. In some tribal societies, twins of the opposite gender were believed to have committed incest in the womb and were condemned. In some cases only one twin was killed. Other superstitions involve unlucky days of the week, breech presentations, the presence of baby teeth at birth, or atmospheric conditions during birth. Ignorance, fear, and legend have contributed to the deaths of infants throughout the ages.

## Methods of Infanticide throughout the Ages

As the factors leading to the practice of infanticide vary from culture to culture and age to age, so do the methods of disposal. Clearly some methods reflect cultural beliefs regarding the value of children. Other methods reflect ignorance about the proper care of infants.

*Abandonment and exposure.* Abandonment or exposure represents one of the oldest methods of infanticide. History is replete with stories of babies abandoned and left to die as a result of starvation, dehydration, or animal attack. Despite the parent's naive belief that the child would be rescued, most abandoned children perished. Ancient Greeks and Romans readily accepted the practice of exposure to eliminate unwanted, deformed, or illegitimate children. Historians estimate that 20 to 40 percent of all babies were abandoned during the later Roman Empire. Abandoned babies were generally brought to a conspicuous place where they were left on display. Most of these babies were taken

and raised, while some were sold into slavery or prostitution.

During the Middle Ages, exposure was a prevalent practice due to overpopulation and the large numbers of illegitimate births. During the Renaissance in Italy, the abandonment rate was in excess of 50 percent of all babies. In seventeenth-century China, Jesuit missionaries reported that thousands of infants, mostly female, were deposited in the streets. In 1741 Thomas Coram, a retired sea captain, was so disturbed by the sight of infant corpses lying in the gutters and rotting on dung heaps that he opened Foundling Hospital in England to "suppress the inhuman custom of exposing new-born infants to perish in the streets" (Langer 1974, p. 358).

*Suffocation.* Suffocation has been one of the most common methods of infanticide throughout the ages. "Overlaying," the practice of suffocating or smothering an infant in bed, occurred in medieval England. Overlaying remained a problem in England into the twentieth century. In 1894 a London coroner reported that over 1,000 infants died as a result of overlaying. Subsequently, in 1909, overlaying was made a criminal offense. Differentiating accidental death from intentional suffocation continues to present a legal challenge. For example, distinguishing between Sudden Infant Death Syndrome (SIDS) and suffocation is a difficult yet critical diagnostic decision.

*Drowning.* The practice of drowning unwanted infants at birth is a long held practice in China. The anthropologist Steven Mosher describes how a bucket of water is readied at the bedside to drown female newborns. This practice was so prevalent in 1943 that an official government publication prohibited the drowning of infant girls. Unfortunately, the decree had little effect. Similarly, infant girls born in India were often drowned in a pit filled with milk, referred to as "making them drink milk" (Milner 1998, p. 175).

*Ignorance, neglect, and abuse.* Historically, children were subjected to mistreatment and death as a result of simple ignorance about proper care. For example, opium and liquor were commonly given to infants to calm and induce sleep. Godfrey's cordial, a mixture of opium, treacle, and sassafras available in the nineteenth century, proved as fatal as arsenic.

Infants also died of starvation, as a result of neglect, poverty, and punishment. Wet nurses were commonly hired throughout history. Maliciously, many of the wet nurses took on more infants than they could feed. It was a well-known fact to parents that infants died at a far higher rate in the care of wet nurses than with their parents.

Swaddling or restraining infants to calm or contain their movements has been a near universal practice, although it was almost entirely discontinued in the United States and England by the end of the eighteenth century. If performed improperly, swaddling can result in suffocation and permanent injury. Swaddled infants could be "laid for hours behind the hot oven, hung on pegs on the wall, placed in tubs and in general left like a parcel in every convenient corner" (deMause 1974, p. 37). DeMause describes how fatal accidents frequently befell children because little children were left alone for extended periods. Dating back to Roman times, infants were exposed to hypothermia through the therapeutic practice of dipping children in icy-cold waters to harden or toughen the character. DeMause reports that the eighteenth-century pediatrician William Buchanan stated that nearly half of the human species died in infancy as a result of ignorance and improper care.

In the twenty-first century the most prevalent methods of infanticide are head trauma, drowning, suffocation, and strangulation. Shaken-baby syndrome, brain injury as a result of violent shaking, is a common phenomenon.

## Religious Beliefs

The newborn has been afforded some protection through the beliefs of God-fearing people. Judeo-Christian morals prohibited infanticide as the will of God. According to Jewish beliefs, one can never know whether the child conceived may be the long-awaited Savior. As a result, the Torah demanded that married couples procreate and Jewish law prohibited the killing of children. Abortion and neonaticide, however, were allowed.

The prevalence of infanticide in ancient Rome began to diminish around the time of Jesus Christ. The Christian Church condemned the practice of exposure, particularly if the exposed infant was unbaptized. It was believed that upon his or her death an unbaptized child would be prevented from entering the gates of heaven. As a result,

stricter penalties were given to mothers who killed unbaptized infants. Similarly, in Islam, Muhammad admonished parents for preferring male offspring and warned against the evils of infanticide. With the rise of Christianity and the fall of the Roman Empire, Judeo-Christian ethics were infused with secular law.

## Infanticide in Modern America

Do murderous parents still act more out of hardness of life than hardness of heart? In a 2001 news report, a Texas woman confessed to drowning her five children in the bathtub. Her family stated that she had been suffering from postpartum depression. An Illinois woman who drugged and suffocated her three young children claimed insanity at the time of the murders. Both women were found guilty of murder and faced life in prison. The 1990s and early 2000s witnessed a rash of so-called trashcan moms who gave birth in seclusion, killed the newborns, and deposited their bodies in the trash. A teenage girl delivered a six-pound boy during her prom, disposed of the infant, and returned to the dance floor. In 2001 a Tennessee woman reportedly gave birth secretively, slashed her infant's throat, wrapped her in garbage bags, and left her in the car trunk to die.

In 1995 the U.S. Advisory Board on Child Abuse and Neglect estimated that nearly 2,000 infants and young children die each year from abuse or neglect. Fatal abuse may result from one incident (e.g., shaking the baby) or repeated abuse and neglect over a period of time. According to the FBI's Uniform Crime Reports, approximately 700 homicide victims under the age of six were reported in 1997; the majority (71%) of these children were murdered by a parent. Ten percent of these children were murdered during the first six days of their life.

Many researchers believe that child fatalities are underreported because some deaths labeled as accidents or SIDS are, in fact, homicides. Waneta Hoyt claimed to have lost all five of her children to SIDS, leading researchers to suspect SIDS ran in families and was caused by sleep apnea. In 1995 Hoyt confessed to suffocating all five of her children. As a result, researchers were forced to reexamine the causes of SIDS.

The risk of child homicide declines with child age. Children under the age of five are the most frequent victims of fatalities. Children under the age of three account for 77 percent of all child fatalities. Male children are slightly more at risk than female. Five percent of these deaths occurred on the infant's first day of life. Nearly all of these infants were not born in a hospital. In fact, most neonaticides probably go undetected. Infants under one week of age are most likely to be killed by their mothers, whereas after the first week of life the perpetrator is more likely to be the father or stepfather. Researchers disagree as to whether mothers or fathers are more likely, in general, to kill their offspring.

Parents who kill are most often poor, single, and under the age of nineteen. They most likely live in rural areas and do not have a high school diploma. If female, they are likely to have an older child and have not received prenatal care. Female perpetrators show a variety of other risk factors including regular drug and alcohol usage, history of depression, childhood history of inadequate parenting and abuse, current involvement with an abusive partner, history of self-abuse, and lack of social support. Approximately 15 to 30 percent of all mothers who kill their children commit suicide. Of the fathers who murder their children, 40 to 60 percent commit suicide. Infanticide continues to be associated with difficult life circumstances.

Phillip Resnick argues that mothers who kill actually fall into two distinct groups. Mothers who kill their infant on the day of its birth (neonaticide) do not generally show signs of psychopathology. Mothers who commit neonaticide tend to be young, single, and immature, and kill to eliminate an unwanted child. Mothers who kill their older children (filicide) are frequently older, married, psychotic, depressed, or suicidal. Filicides tend to kill as a result of their psychosis, for altruistic reasons (to relieve child of suffering), accidentally (as in battered child syndrome), or to seek revenge on a spouse. Resnick notes that mothers who commit neonaticide are more likely to be incarcerated, whereas mothers who commit filicide are more likely to be hospitalized.

Legal debate centers on the use of postpartum depression as a legal defense in infanticide (homicide) cases. The American Psychiatric Association first recognized postpartum depression (PPD) in 1994. Since then, American courts have begun to recognize PPD as a legitimate defense, although it has rarely been used successfully. Approximately 20 percent of all new mothers experience PPD, a serious and lasting depression. One out of every thousand new mothers will experience psychotic symptoms including delusions, hallucinations, and incoherent thinking. Because British law has long assumed that mothers who kill suffer from mental illness, British doctors treat PPD aggressively and British courts rule with more leniency than American courts. Many researchers suggest that the United States should follow the British approach.

## Alternatives and Prevention

One of the earliest methods of saving illegitimate and abandoned babies was the formation of foundling homes (orphanages). The first foundling home was opened in 787 C.E. in Italy. Foundling homes were opened across Europe, quickly filling to capacity. Placing a child in a foundling home was little more than infanticide in a hidden form. In Dublin, the foundling hospital had a revolving basket placed at the front gate to provide parents anonymity as they deposited their unwanted children. Roughly 85 percent of infants placed in these homes died as a result of inadequate care. The orphanages in twenty-first-century China bear striking similarity to these early foundling homes. During a period of economic hardship in Hungary in 1996, a hospital placed an incubator by the hospital entrance to provide poor parents an alternative to killing their infants.

Several authors contend that the legalization of abortion has resulted in decreased rates of infanticide. Pro-life supporters counter that abortion represents nothing more than preterm infanticide. However, the so-called trashcan moms have access to both legalized abortion and birth control, yet fail to utilize either option. Resnick contends that the passive nature of these women contributes to denial of their pregnancy, preventing them from seeking an abortion. Perhaps the best form of prevention for young women most at risk for neonaticide comes from abstinence or effective contraceptive use.

The research by Mary D. Overpeck and her colleagues suggests early intervention strategies to prevent infanticide in high-risk individuals. For example, identification of women who are hiding their pregnancies can improve access to prenatal care. Screening parents for emotional problems (including family history of postpartum depression) may increase access to mental health services. According to Overpeck, interventions targeting social support, completion of education, parenting training, contraceptive education, and substance abuse are critically needed. Finally, diagnosis and aggressive treatment for postpartum depression for all mothers constitutes an essential health care need.

With increasing reports of abandoned babies, legislators are searching for alternative methods to protect newborns. The U.S. Congress and over half of the states are considering legislation to decriminalize the abandonment of newborns in designated safe locations. Immunity from prosecution is afforded to those parents who leave the infant in designated locations. Critics contend that such legislation will result in encouraging parents to abandon their infants. However, baby abandonment legislation is a growing trend across the United States.

The reasons why parents choose to destroy their offspring are complicated and defy simple explanation. In the past, harsh conditions and lack of information contributed to the problem. In modern times harsh conditions continue to drive infanticide rates. Are these parents unfortunate, evil, selfish, or mentally ill? Perhaps the answer lies in a combination of these explanations. Understanding the causes of infanticide can only lead to better means of prevention.

*See also:* CHILDREN, MURDER OF; CHRISTIAN DEATH RITES, HISTORY OF; HOMICIDE, DEFINITIONS AND CLASSIFICATIONS OF; HOMICIDE, EPIDEMIOLOGY OF; ISLAM; MORTALITY, INFANT

## *Bibliography*

American Psychiatric Association. *Diagnostic and Statistical Manual of Mental Disorders,* 4th edition. Washington, DC: Author, 1994.

Boswell, John E. "Exposition and Oblation: The Abandonment of Children and the Ancient and Medieval Family." *American Historical Review* 89 (1984):10–33.

Crimmins, Susan, and Sandra Langley. "Convicted Women Who Have Killed Children: A Self-Psychology Perspective." *Journal of Interpersonal Violence* 12 (1997):49–70.

deMause, Lloyd. "The Evolution of Childhood." In *The History of Childhood.*London: Aronson, 1974.

Divale, William T., and Marvin Harris. "Population, Warfare and the Male Supremacist Complex." *American Anthropologist* 78 (1976):521–538.

Federal Bureau of Investigation. *Uniform Crime Reporting Data: U.S. Supplementary Homicide Reports 1980–1997.* Ann Arbor, MI: Inter-University Consortium for Political and Social Research, 1997.

Hausfater, Glen, and Sarah B. Hrdy. *Infanticide, Comparative and Evolutionary Perspectives.* New York: Aldine Publishing, 1984.

Jason, Janine, Jeanne C. Gilliland, and Carl W. Tyler. "Homicide As a Cause of Pediatric Mortality in the United States." *Pediatrics* 72 (1983):191–197.

Kristof, Nicholas D. "Stark Data on Women: 100 Million Are Missing." *New York Times,* 5 November 1991, C1.

Krugman, Richard D., and Judith Ann Bays. "Distinguishing Sudden Infant Death Syndrome." *Pediatrics* 94 (1994):124–126.

Langer, William L. "Infanticide: A Historical Survey." *History of Childhood Quarterly* 1 (1974):353–365.

Lester, David. "Roe v. Wade was Followed by a Decrease in Neonatal Homicide." *Journal of the American Medical Association* 267 (1992):3027–3028.

Marzuk, Peter M., Kenneth Tardiff, and Charles S. Hirsch. "The Epidemiology of Murder-Suicide." *Journal of the American Medical Association* 267 (1992):3179–3183.

Milner, Larry S. *Hardness of Heart Hardness of Life: The Stain of Human Infanticide.* Kearney, NE: Morris Publishing, 1998.

Mosher, Steven. "Forced Abortions and Infanticide in Communist China." *Human Life Review* 11 (1985):7–34.

Overpeck, Mary D., et al. "Risk Factors for Infant Homicide in the United States." *The New England Journal of Medicine* 339 (1998):1211–1216.

Resnick, Phillip J. "Murder of the Newborn: A Psychiatric Review of Neonaticide." *American Journal of Psychiatry* 126 (1970):58–64.

Rose, Lionel. *The Massacre of the Innocents: Infanticide in Britain 1800–1939.* London: Routledge & Kegan Paul, 1986.

U.S. Advisory Board on Child Abuse and Neglect. "A Nation's Shame: Fatal Child Abuse and Neglect in the United States." Washington, DC: U.S. Department of Health and Human Services, 1995.

Vehmas, Simo. "Newborn Infants and the Moral Significance of Intellectual Disabilities." *The Journal of the Association for Persons with Severe Handicaps* 24 (1999):111–121.

Williamson, Laila. "Infanticide: An Anthropological Analysis." In Marvin Kohl ed., *Infanticide and the Value of Life*. New York: Prometheus Books, 1978.

DIANNE R. MORAN

# INFLUENZA

Influenza is a respiratory infection caused by a family of flu viruses. Often confused with either the common cold or stomach and intestinal infections, most forms of influenza are characterized by a sore throat, headache, chills, body aches, exhaustion, fever, and coughing. Droplets carried from one person to another by sneezing and coughing spread the disease, and touching can also contract it. According to the National Institutes of Health, the disease runs its course in about a week, and can be especially dangerous to infants and toddlers, the elderly, and those with compromised immune systems. Children acquire influenza easily, and can spread it to others rapidly. Normally, peaks of high wintertime reporting and low numbers of cases in the summer characterize influenza trends. Chances of acquiring an influenza infection during the flu season, usually November through March, increase with age, and pneumonia-influenza rates for those over seventy-five years old are much higher than for the middle-aged.

Influenza has annually ranked as one of the ten leading causes of death in the United States. During a typical flu season, anywhere from 35 to 50 million Americans could show symptoms of influenza. About 100,000 of those cases might be hospitalized, and as many as 20,000 could die from influenza and its complications. Influenza is also a substantial threat to human lives in many parts of the third world due to both a lack of effective vaccine distribution programs and a wide range of factors lowering resistance to many viruses.

Because a virus causes influenza, only specific symptoms and some ensuing infections can be treated with antibiotics. Primary prevention in the form of inoculation is the best method of combating influenza. Immunity to particular strains is acquired either naturally by previous exposure or induced with a vaccine, and the variants of influenza change over time. While there are broad categories of influenza A, B, and C that cause illness in humans, the A strains are by far the most lethal and hence the objective for focused vaccine development.

Some vaccines previously used are no longer effective because as the level of immunity in a population increases strains of influenza change genetically and propagate in those susceptible to the altered viral variants. The scholar W. I. B. Beveridge offers the explanation of how an influenza virus capsule has eight separate strands of ribonucleic acid (RNA) for its hereditary material. When a cell of a higher organism is infected by two different varieties of the virus, their sixteen RNA segments can combine to produce progeny with traits from both of the parent strains. New strains capable of evading the host's immunological defenses can thus emerge. Two of the eight viral genes code for protein-sugar complexes on the outer coat of the virus. These surface molecules, hemagglutinin (H) and neuraminidase (N), are antigens that can stimulate the host's immune system to make antibodies against the infecting virus. Subtypes H1, H2, H3, N1, and N2 are known to have caused human influenza epidemics and pandemics (worldwide epidemics) because of major shifts in the order of H and N antigens.

People have suffered from influenza for thousands of years. Written accounts date to the twelfth century, and the development of the printing press combined with changing worldwide travel patterns since the Age of Discovery created more knowledge about the disease. In his *Diffusion of Influenza* (1986), the influenza researcher Gerald Pyle documents pandemics that took place in 1580, 1732–1733, 1800–1803, 1847–1848, and 1889–1892. These and similar events that transpired during the twentieth century are greatly overshadowed by the catastrophic pandemic of 1918–1919. It was so lethal that historians estimate that 40 million people were killed worldwide; a half million of them had been clearly documented in the United States. While the origins of this pandemic are unclear, it emerged from the trenches of World War I in an apocalyptic fashion, leaving a wake of deaths in diffusion pathways extending into most inhabited continents in the world.

Subsequent pandemics have been measured against this event, and although hundreds of thousands in the United States died during pandemics in 1957 and 1968, death tolls were far less than during the 1918–1919 episode. Since the 1950s, vaccine developments have kept pace with genetic shifts of influenza viruses. "Close calls" include a swine flu scare that was averted in 1976 and a contained outbreak of chicken flu in Hong Kong in 1997. According to Gina Kolata, researchers in the late 1990s uncovered the genetic makeup of the 1918–1919 virus from tissue samples stored in paraffin, but that mystery has intensified because the strain identified is unlike any other known influenza viruses. While the biological and geographic origins of the 1918–1919 pandemic remain unclear, it continues to serve as a landmark event in the annals of influenza.

*See also:* CAUSES OF DEATH

### Bibliography

Beveridge, W. I. B. "Unravelling the Ecology of Influenza A Virus." *History, Philosophy, and Life Science* 15 (1993):23–32.

Kolata, Gina. *Flu: The Story of the Great Influenza Pandemic of 1918 and the Search for the Virus That Caused It.* New York: Farrar, Straus and Giroux, 1999.

Patterson, K. David, and Gerald F. Pyle. "The Geography and Mortality of the 1918 Influenza Pandemic." *Bulletin of the History of Medicine* 65 (1991):4–21.

Pyle, Gerald. *The Diffusion of Influenza: Patterns and Paradigms.* Totowa, NJ: Rowman and Littlefield, 1986.

#### Internet Resources

National Institutes of Health, National Institute of Allergy and Infectious Diseases. "Fact Sheet: Flu." In the National Institute of Allergy and Infectious Diseases [web site]. Available from www.niaid.nih.gov/factsheets/flu.htm.

GERALD F. PYLE

# INFORMED CONSENT

Twenty-five hundred years of Western medicine, starting with Hippocrates, have been built on the preferred conception that physicians should protect their patients from information about their diseases or treatment options. The oath that has been repeated by physicians for thousands of years articulates clearly that the physician knows what is best for his or her patients. For over two millennia, the culture has put the physician in an almost God-like position in terms of his or her wisdom to practice in the patient's best interest. However, since the mid-twentieth century there has been a trend toward patients rights, that has included the right to know what the physician intends to do and why. This is the essence of informed consent.

## The Emergence of Informed Consent

In one form or another, the question of who gets to decide beats at the heart of the most difficult medical situations. Will it be the physician, the patient, or the family members? Whose values will ultimately be respected? What should a patient be told regarding the range of complicated life and death decisions commonplace in today's medical arena?

The definition of informed consent is equally complicated. An informed consent is an autonomous authorization by an individual regarding a medical intervention or involvement in biomedical research. An individual must do more than express agreement or comply with a proposal for this to be considered informed consent. Informed consent is a process between physician and patient that must contain an information component and a consent component. The information component refers to the disclosure of information and comprehension of what is disclosed. The consent component refers to a voluntary decision and agreement to undergo a recommended procedure. Legal, regulatory, philosophical, medical, and psychological literature tend to favor the following elements as the necessary components of informed consent: (1) competence; (2) disclosure; (3) understanding; (4) voluntariness; and (5) consent.

If one is competent to act, receives thorough disclosure, has an understanding, and is voluntary in his or her consent, then informed consent is viable. For informed consent to be legally recognized in medical practice, the following steps need to be clearly articulated:

1. Preconditions: Includes competence (to understand and decide) and voluntariness (in deciding).

2. Information elements: Includes disclosure (of risks/benefits); recommendation (plan); and understanding (of information and plan).

3. Consent elements: Includes authorization (based on patient autonomy).

*Hippocrates' oath, which granted physicians the right to practice in the patient's best interest, has conflicted with the twentieth-century trend toward patient rights.* BRITISH MUSEUM

Physicians are obligated to disclose a core set of information including: (1) those facts or descriptions that patients usually consider material in deciding whether to refuse or consent to the proposed intervention; (2) information that the physician thinks is critical; (3) the professionals' recommendation; (4) the purpose of seeking consent; and (5) the nature and limits of consent as an act of authorization.

## History of Informed Consent within Medical Practice

Civil litigation emerged over informed consent to include injury to one's person or property that is intentionally or negligently inflicted by a physician's failure to disclose the injury, measured in terms of monetary damages. With the medical advances that emerged in the beginning of the twentieth century, such as improved anesthesia

and surgical interventions, physicians began to disclose basic information without necessarily outlining all potential risks.

The first important introduction of the notion of informed consent is in the classic case of *Mohr* v. *Williams* (1905). In this case, a physician obtained Anna Mohr's consent to an operation on her right ear. While operating, the surgeon determined that the left ear needed surgery instead, and proceeded to operate on it. A court found that the physician should have obtained the patient's consent to the surgery on the left ear. The judge decided that a physician needs to advise a patient of all the information related to a particular procedure and must review all the risks and benefits. Only after this exchange does the patient enter into a contract, a contract that authorizes the physician to operate *only* to the extent of the consent given.

In the late 1950s a series of legal cases in California and the District of Columbia forever changed society's vision of the doctor-patient relationship. In California, radiation therapy went awry for a young woman, leaving her in much worse condition than prior to the treatment. After the therapy she was acutely fatigued and suffering from radiation burns. These side effects far exceeded the side effects described by the physician. She sued the physician, saying he never adequately explained the risks of her radiation procedure. The court found that unless such consent was based on full information, and that the patient fully understood all of the risks of the procedure, the doctor was not protected for liability. In several jurisdictions, beginning in 1972 in the District of Columbia, *Canterbury* v. *Spence,* informed consent emerged as a legal right with full legal redress equivalent to battery if informed consent was not provided.

With the mid-1970s came the introduction and growing utilization of extraordinary life-sustaining treatments such as dialysis, respirators, cardiac resuscitation, and a wide array of organ transplantation. To protect oneself from the automatic use of such heroic measures, patients and their family members experienced an urgent need to be fully informed of risks and benefits and to have the authority to protect their wishes. Legal methods, including advance directives, living wills, and health care proxies, came to the fore of patient's rights as mechanisms to articulate and protect the patient's wishes over the imperative central tenet to medicine: If it can be done, it should be done.

*Advance directives.* The Patient Self-Determination Act (PSDA) was passed in 1990 and went into effect in December 1991. The essence of this legislation is to empower the public with the right to be fully informed and fully self-determining regarding end-of-life decisions. However, since its implementation there is little evidence of national acceptance by the health care industry. The law applies to all health care facilities that receive any federal reimbursement for services, and includes hospitals, nursing homes, home health agencies, and clinics. The PSDA requires a health care mechanism for disseminating information about advance directives with patients.

Advance directives have been available in parts of the United States since the late 1980s, but research shows that only a small percentage (5% to 25%) have some form of written advance directive. Advance directives allow a competent person to express who should be a decision maker and what preferences the patient may have.

Psychiatric advance directives are a legal means by which a person with mental illness, while competent to make health care decisions, may specify his or her preferences for treatment and may designate a surrogate decision maker to act on his or her behalf in the event of an incapacitating mental health crisis.

When informed consent is not viable for the patient, and he or she does not have advance directives, the process of surrogate decision making is initiated. Surrogate decision making refers to the process in which a loved one has to make a medical decision because the patient's judgment is incapacitated. Surrogate decision makers reach decisions for those with fluctuating decision-making capacity that is doubtful and thus need to be aware of all the side effects in order to make decisions on behalf of someone else.

Courts and legislatures have been actively involved in the right of surrogate decision makers and the various related ethical dilemmas. Within the context of advanced life-sustaining treatments, patients and their family members have been confronted with life and death choices. The questions regarding who is competent to make which decisions is still a much-litigated scenario. Many judgments about terminating or continuing treatment

are made daily for patients who are no longer able to choose for themselves—patients with HIV (human immunodeficiency virus), Alzheimer's disease, and Parkinson's disease, and those suffering from stroke effects, heart and kidney failure, dementia, and psychosis.

## History of Informed Consent within Biomedical Research

A comprehensive movement toward informed consent began after World War II with the 1947 Nuremberg trials. In these war trials, it was revealed that physicians conducted abhorrent medical research experiments on concentration camp prisoners. The research included human experimentation with germ warfare, freezing individuals to learn what temperature kills individuals most effectively, and many more horrifying research trials. Between 1930 and 1945 Japan conducted human experimentation in biological warfare, including physical responses to infection and trauma, and thousands were killed. The Nuremberg Code, which emerged from the trials, abandons the earlier paternalistic perspective of medicine and research and replaces it with the centrality of patient self-determination by asserting that the voluntary consent of the human subject is necessary under all circumstances of medical research. With this, the modern era of ethics within biomedical research emerged with a particular emphasis on the patient's rights expressed by the practice of informed consent.

The term *informed consent* first received wide awareness and prominence in public health research, as well as in the practice of medicine, in 1972, in response to the public outcry regarding unethical practices in the Tuskegee research. In 1932 the U.S. Public Health Service initiated a study that examined the effects of untreated syphilis among rural black men in Tuskegee, Alabama. Thousands of men were kept in total ignorance of the experiment, their infection, and the seriousness of syphilis. They were consistently steered away from receiving effective treatment so the United States government could monitor how the disease progressed, its many serious side effects, and its rate of fatality.

Immediately following this disclosure, the first national government commission, the National Commission for the Protection of Human Subjects of Biomedical Research and Behavioral Research was established. One of its primary goals was to initiate a variety of legislation to further ensure a patient's right to be fully informed regarding any medical research. A decade later, the President's Commission on the Study of Ethical Problems in Medicine and Biomedical Research and Behavioral Research was formed in 1983 to replace the first commission. Its mandate was to deal with the full range of medical and ethical issues, including the care of the dying, genetics, and issues of health care decisions such as informed consent and allocation of resources.

**Informed Consent in the Managed Care Climate**

With the era of cost-containment in the 1980s and managed care in the 1990s, informed consent became even more critical. Informed decision counseling (IDC) has been used to promote cost-effective care and provide over-the-phone medical information from twenty-four-hour-a-day clinicians. Designed to promote appropriate utilization and effective patient-provider communication, IDC is based on the premise that health care consumers make appropriate utilization decisions if adequately informed.

Informed consent will continue to evolve in response to continued advances in medical treatment, the shift toward partnership in patient-physician relationships, and new avenues of biomedical research. At the center of informed consent remains the critical primacy of the right for a patient to understand any medical treatment, medical procedure, or participation in medical research.

*See also:* ADVANCE DIRECTIVES; CRUZAN, NANCY; HIPPOCRATIC OATH; NATURAL DEATH ACTS; QUINLAN, KAREN ANN; SUICIDE TYPES: PHYSICIAN-ASSISTED SUICIDE

### Bibliography

Annas, George J., and Michael Grodin. *The Nazi Doctors and the Nuremberg Code.* New York: Oxford University Press, 1992.

Applebaum, Paul S., Charles Lidz, and Alan Meisel. *Informed Consent: Legal Theory and Clinical Practice.* New York: Oxford University Press, 1989.

Basile, C. M. "Advance Directives and Advocacy in End of Life Decisions." *Nurse Practitioner* 23, no. 5 (1998):44–54.

Beauchamp, Tom L., and James F. Childress. *Principles of Biomedical Ethics.* Oxford: Oxford University Press, 1994.

Buchanan, Allen, and Dan W. Brock. *Deciding for Others: The Ethics of Surrogate Decision-Making.* Cambridge: Cambridge University Press, 1989.

Fairman, Kevin, and C. Murphy. "Drug Benefit Trends: Using Informed Decision Counseling to Promote Cost-Effective Care." *Drug Benefit Trends* 12, no. 4 (2000):44–48.

Gostin, Lawrence. "Deciding Life and Death in the Courtroom: From Quinlan to Cruzan, Glucksberg and Vacco—A Brief History and Analysis of Constitutional Protection of the 'Right to Die.'" *Journal of the American Medical Association* 278, no. 18 (1997):1523–1528.

Hanssen, Michael. "Balancing the Quality of Consent." *Journal of Medical Ethics* 24, no. 3 (1998):182–187.

Veatch, Robert M. *Medical Ethics.* Boston: Jones and Bartlett, 1989.

NANCY L. BECKERMAN

# INJURY MORTALITY

Around the world, about 16,000 people die every day as a result of injuries. For every death, many more people survive but suffer lifelong impairment. An injury is "a bodily lesion at the organic level resulting from acute exposure to energy (which can be mechanical, thermal, electrical, chemical, or radiant) interacting with the body in amounts or rates that exceed the threshold of physiological tolerance. In some cases (e.g., drowning, strangulation, or freezing), the injury results from an insufficiency of a vital element. The time between exposure and the appearance of injury needs to be short" (Krug 1999, p.2). It is the acuteness of exposure that distinguishes injury from disease. Long-term exposure to relatively low levels of a harmful agent may cause disease, but acute exposure to the higher levels of the same agent (e.g., lead) may cause injury.

Injuries can be unintentional or intentional. Most traffic injuries, fire-related injuries, falls, and drownings are classified as unintentional. On the other hand, homicides, suicides, war, and most poisonings are classified as intentional. Aside from the degree of intentionality, there are classifications of the purpose of the activity being undertaken (i.e., work-related, recreational), the nature of the injurious event (i.e., vehicle crash, fall, poisoning, drowning, fire), or the setting (i.e., home, workplace, road).

## Basic Data on Injury Mortality

Accurate counts of the number of people who die as a result of injury are usually not available. Official mortality reports are often based on incomplete counts, biased sources, cursory or no investigation, or erroneous coding. This situation is common in developing countries and in remote areas of developed countries. Even in developed countries, many health information systems do not allow for easy identification of injury deaths. Among these poorly identified types of injury deaths are occupational fatalities, deaths resulting from the use or misuse of particular products, and falls where the cause of death may be coded as pneumonia occurring as a consequence of an earlier fall. Some types of injuries—child abuse, violence against women, and suicide—are likely to be underreported.

The World Health Organization has estimated that 5.8 million people worldwide died as a result of injuries in 1998, which corresponds to an injury mortality rate of 97.9 per 100,000 population. More than 90 percent of injury-related deaths occurred in low- and middle-income countries. The injury-related mortality rate in these countries was double the rate found in high-income countries.

Road-traffic injuries are the leading cause of injury mortality, resulting in over 1.1 million deaths per year worldwide and ranking tenth in the leading causes of death for both sexes in 1998 (see Table 1). Self-inflicted injuries result in about 950,000 deaths per year and were ranked as the eleventh-leading cause of death for both sexes in 1998. Other major causes of injury death in 1998 were interpersonal violence (more than 650,000 deaths), war injuries (more than 530,000 deaths), drowning (more than 400,000 deaths) and fires (more than 160,000 deaths).

The pattern of injury mortality differs between high-, medium-, and low-income countries. Road-traffic injuries rank tenth as the leading causes of death in each group of countries. However, self-inflicted injuries rank eleventh in the leading

**TABLE 1**

### Estimated number of deaths worldwide resulting from fifteen leading causes in 1998

| Rank | Males | Females | Both sexes |
|---|---|---|---|
| 1 | Ischaemic heart disease 3,658,699 | Ischaemic heart disease 3,716,709 | Ischaemic heart disease 7,375,408 |
| 2 | Cerebrovascular disease 2,340,299 | Cerebrovascular disease 2,765,827 | Cerebrovascular disease 5,106,125 |
| 3 | Acute lower respiratory infections 1,753,220 | Acute lower respiratory infections 1,698,957 | Acute lower respiratory infections 3,452,178 |
| 4 | Chronic obstructive pulmonary disease 1,239,658 | HIV/AIDS 1,121,421 | HIV/AIDS 2,285,229 |
| 5 | HIV/AIDS 1,163,808 | Diarrhoeal disease 1,069,757 | Chronic obstructive pulmonary disease 2,249,252 |
| 6 | Diarrhoeal disease 1,149,275 | Perinatal conditions 1,034,002 | Diarrhoeal disease 2,219,032 |
| 7 | Perinatal conditions 1,120,998 | Chronic obstructive pulmonary disease 1,009,594 | Perinatal conditions 2,155,000 |
| 8 | Trachea/bronchus/ lung cancers 910,471 | Tuberculosis 604,674 | Tuberculosis 1,498,061 |
| 9 | Tuberculosis 893,387 | Malaria 537,882 | Trachea/bronchus /lung cancers 1,244,407 |
| 10 | Road-traffic injuries 854,939 | Measles 431,630 | Road traffic injuries 1,170,694 |
| 11 | Interpersonal violence 582,486 | Breast cancers 411,668 | Malaria 1,110,293 |
| 12 | Malaria 572,411 | Self-inflicted injuries 382,541 | Self-inflicted injuries 947,697 |
| 13 | Self-inflicted injuries 565,156 | Diabetes mellitus 343,021 | Measles 887,671 |
| 14 | Cirrhosis of the liver 533,724 | Trachea/bronchus /lung cancers 333,436 | Stomach cancers 822,069 |
| 15 | Stomach cancers 517,821 | Road traffic injuries 315,755 | Cirrhosis of the liver 774,563 |

SOURCE: Violence and Injury Prevention, World Health Organization. *Injury: A Leading Cause of the Global Burden of Disease,* edited by E. Krug. Geneva: World Health Organization, 1999.

causes of death in high-income countries but thirteenth in low- and middle-income countries. Interpersonal violence is not one of the fifteen leading causes of death in high-income countries, but it ranks fourteenth in the leading causes of death in low- and middle-income countries. Intentional injuries are generally more prevalent in areas (or among groups) where there is political or social instability.

Around 70 percent of deaths from road-traffic crashes occur in developing countries. Developed countries report an annual road-crash mortality rate of about 2 deaths per 10,000 motor vehicles, compared to 20 to 70 deaths per 10,000 motor vehicles in developing countries. Some of the disparity in death rates is attributable to the differences in the traffic composition between developed and developing countries. Developing countries have high proportions of vulnerable road users such as pedestrians, bicyclists, and motorcyclists in the traffic stream. Trucks and buses also exist in greater proportions than in developed countries.

Transportation fatality rates differ substantially within and between modes. Overall, travel by air and rail results in fewer fatalities per billion passenger kilometers than travel by road. Within air travel, fatality rates are higher for general aviation than for scheduled passenger air services. About 90 percent of rail fatalities are occupants of road vehicles at railway crossings or railway employees involved in shunting and track maintenance. Within road transport, fatality rates are highest among motorcycle riders, pedestrians, and cyclists.

The number of deaths related to occupational injury is not well documented. It has been estimated that each year about 50,000 people die of occupational injuries in the Americas (North, Central, and South), and that about 100,000 people die of occupational injuries in India. In the developed world, many of the deaths from occupational injuries result from on- or off-road vehicles. In developing countries, most deaths occur in the workplace, resulting from factors such as old or poorly shielded machinery, toxic exposures, and minimal or nonexistent safety standards.

## Trends in Injury Mortality

The trends in the numbers and rates of injury deaths differ among transport, occupational, and domestic injuries and between the developed and the developing countries. In developed countries, both the total number of fatalities and the fatality rates (as a function of distance traveled) have decreased for road traffic generally and for particular types of vehicles (e.g., passenger cars, large trucks, and so on) from the 1970s to the 1990s. The rate of railway-related fatalities has remained relatively stable. In the developing world, however,

the number of vehicles is growing faster than the physical, legal, and institutional infrastructure needed to safely contain them, with the result that the number of fatalities is increasing.

The number of deaths due to falls is likely to increase in the Western world as the population ages. In developed countries at least, occupational deaths have been decreasing with increasing sophistication of equipment.

## Factors Affecting the Risk of Injury Death

The risk of injury death is affected by individual factors such as alcohol consumption, propensity to take risks, and socioeconomic differences. Alcohol consumption increases the risk of involvement in motor vehicle crashes, whether as a driver or as a pedestrian. Alcohol consumption is also implicated in substantial numbers of railroad and aviation crashes, falls, drownings, fires, homicides and suicides. Prior psychological and social characteristics have been found to predict young drivers' crash involvement. Sensation seeking, impulsiveness, and risky lifestyles are associated with risk-taking and crash involvement.

Deaths from traffic injuries are often higher among children and adults from lower social positions and in more deprived socioeconomic areas. The mechanism underlying these findings may be increased exposure to risk (high traffic volumes, lack of safe areas for walking or recreation) or less education about risk avoidance. Injury mortality from other causes, such as occupational injury, also appears to be greater among persons of lower socioeconomic status.

## Age and Gender Factors

Deaths related to injury commonly involve people under forty-five years of age, whereas noninjury deaths commonly involve people forty-five or older. Thus injury mortality leads to a greater number of years of potential life lost than many other causes of death (e.g., ischaemic heart disease). European data show that road traffic crashes lead to an average loss of 40 years of life expectancy, compared to 10.5 years for cancer and 9.7 years for cardiovascular illnesses.

The most common causes of injury mortality differ across age groups. For example, drowning is the leading cause of injury deaths among children under five years of age, ahead of war injuries and road traffic injuries. Road-traffic injuries are the leading cause of injury death for youths between the ages of five and fourteen, ahead of drowning, war injuries, fires, and interpersonal violence. Road-traffic injuries are the leading cause of injury death for individuals between fifteen and forty-four, ahead of interpersonal violence, self-inflicted injuries, war injuries, drowning, and fires.

About twice as many males as females die as a result of injury. This statistic may reflect both greater exposure (greater involvement in potentially injurious activities) and greater risk-taking by males. Road-traffic injury is the leading injury cause of death in males, but self-inflicted injury is the leading injury cause of death in females.

## Intentional and Unintentional Injuries

Injuries are commonly categorized as intentional or unintentional. This categorization is satisfactory most of the time, but some injury events may be difficult to place into one category or the other. For example, some single-vehicle road crashes can be identified as suicides (e.g., if a note is left), but others may be unidentified suicides. Some poisonings may be clearly intentional or unintentional, but others may be difficult to classify.

## How to Decrease the Risk of Injury Deaths

In the first half of the twentieth century, the main approach to decreasing injury and injury deaths addressed the shortcomings of the victims: bad drivers, lazy workers, and unaware children or parents. The emphasis was on educational measures such as posters and pamphlets and on training courses and materials.

It is now recognized that injuries, including fatal injuries, usually involve a complex series of events that include environmental factors and the interaction of human performance and the task to be performed. Intervention at any point in the causal chain can prevent the injury or reduce its severity. Prevention of injury is relatively more important than treatment because many deaths from injury occur so quickly or because the damage is so severe that death is unlikely to be prevented by treatment.

Injury prevention has become a sophisticated science with clearly defined steps of problem identification, countermeasure development, implementation, and evaluation. Evaluation is needed to assess whether interventions have worked or not and to provide support for further implementation. The physician William Haddon Jr., who became the first director of the U.S. National Highway Safety Administration, developed a list of ten general strategies designed to prevent injury:

1. Prevent the creation of the hazard (e.g., stop producing particularly hazardous substances).

2. Reduce the amount of the hazard (e.g., package toxic drugs in smaller, safer amounts).

3. Prevent the release of a hazard that already exists (e.g., make bathtubs less slippery).

4. Modify the rate or spatial distribution of the hazard (e.g., require automobile air bags).

5. Separate, in time or space, the hazard from that which is to be protected (e.g., use sidewalks to separate pedestrians from automobiles).

6. Separate the hazard from that which is to be protected by a material barrier (e.g., insulate electrical cords).

7. Modify relevant basic qualities of the hazard (e.g., require a maximum distance between cot-slats to prevent children from being strangled).

8. Make what is to be protected more resistant to damage from the hazard (e.g., improve the person's physical condition by appropriate nutrition and exercise programs).

9. Begin to counter the damage already done by the hazard (e.g., provide emergency medical care).

10. Stabilize, repair, and rehabilitate the object of the damage (e.g., provide acute care and rehabilitation facilities).

Most of these general strategies apply to the prevention of both unintentional and intentional injury.

The specific interventions that have been identified as most effective in reducing deaths resulting from road crashes, include improvements in the ability of vehicles to protect occupants in a crash (both vehicle structure and safety devices such as seat belts and air bags), improvements to roads and roadsides to prevent crashes or reduce their severity, laws and enforcement to reduce drunk driving, and graduated licensing laws to allow young drivers to gain experience under less risky conditions. The specific interventions to reduce deaths relating to other injury causes have been less well documented. The interventions that have proved effective include child-resistant closures for toxic materials, lifeguards, isolation fencing for swimming pools, fire-resistant nightwear for children, smoke detectors, bars on high residential windows, firearm restrictions, and technological improvements in workplace equipment (including farm machinery).

One of the most important issues in the prevention of injury deaths (and injury in general) has been the need to ensure implementation of effective interventions. There are many interventions that have not been adopted or have been adopted only partially and whose potential has therefore not been realized. Some examples from road safety include seat belts, bicycle helmets, and measures to prevent drunk driving.

The transfer of particular interventions across cultures has been uneven. Many engineering measures to improve road safety were developed decades ago in advanced industrial countries. The social, political, economic, and cultural contexts in which they were developed differ significantly from those of motorizing countries. The different contexts are likely to be reflected in different patterns and motivations of road-user behavior. Therefore the engineering measures may not be as effective or may even be counterproductive when applied in motorizing countries.

## Conclusion

Injury is a leading cause of death to people under the age of forty-five. Road-traffic injuries are the most common type of injury death. Self-inflicted injury is a more common type of injury death among females than road-traffic injuries. While there is a downward trend in road traffic deaths in the developed world, these deaths are likely to continue to increase in the developing world. Some effective measures to prevent injury deaths have been developed but have not always been fully implemented. Measures that have proved effective in one culture are not always easily transferable to another culture. Evaluation of the effectiveness of measures to reduce injury mortality is crucial.

*See also:* CAUSES OF DEATH; DISASTERS; SAFETY REGULATIONS; SUICIDE TYPES: INDIRECT SUICIDE

## Bibliography

Barss, Peter, Gordon Smith, Susan Baker, and Dinesh Mohan. *Injury Prevention: An International Perspective.* New York: Oxford University Press, 1998.

Beirness, Douglas J., and Herbert M. Simpson. "Predicting Young Driver Crash Involvement: The Role of Lifestyle Factors." In *New to the Road: Prevention Measures for Young and Novice Drivers.* Halifax, Nova Scotia: Traffic Injury Foundation of Canada, 1991.

Campbell, Bob. "The Complexities of International Comparisons in Traffic Safety." In *Reflections on the Transfer of Traffic Safety Knowledge to Motorizing Nations.* Melbourne, Australia: Global Traffic Safety Trust, 1998.

Elander, James, Robert West, and Davina French. "Behavioral Correlates of Individual Differences in Road-Traffic Crash Risk: An Examination of Methods and Findings." *Psychological Bulletin* 113 (1993):279–294.

Gregersen, Niels-Petter. "Young Drivers' Overestimation of Their Own Skill: An Experiment on the Relation between Training Strategy and Skill." *Accident Analysis and Prevention* 28 (1996):243–250.

King, Mark. "Engineering for Safer Road Use Behavior in Asia." In Kelvin C. P. Wang, Guiping Xiao, and Jialun Ji eds., *Traffic and Transportation Studies: Proceedings of ICTTS 2000.* Reston, VA: American Society of Civil Engineers, 2000.

Laflamme, Lucie, and F. Diderichsen. "Social Differences in Traffic Injury Risks in Childhood and Youth: A Literature Review and a Research Agenda." *Injury Prevention* 6 (2000):293–298.

Mohan, Dinesh, and G. Tiwari. "Traffic Safety in Low-Income Countries: Issues and Concerns Regarding Technology Transfer from High Income Countries." In *Reflections on the Transfer of Traffic Safety Knowledge to Motorizing Nations.* Melbourne, Australia: Global Traffic Safety Trust, 1998.

National Committee for Injury Prevention and Control. *Injury Prevention: Meeting the Challenge.* New York: Oxford University Press, 1989.

National Occupational Health and Safety Commission. *Work-Related Traumatic Fatalities in Australia, 1989 to 1992: Summary Report.* Sydney: National Occupational Health and Safety Commission, 1998.

*Internet Resources*

Krug, E., ed. "Injury: A Leading Cause of the Global Burden of Disease." In the World Health Organization [web site]. Available from www.who.int/violence _injury_prevention/index.html.

U.S. Department of Transportation Bureau of Transportation Statistics. "Transportation Statistics Annual Report 1999." In the Bureau of Transportation Statistics [web sites]. Available from www.bts.gov/programs/transtu/tsar/tsar99/tsar99.

Williams, Allan F., and Daniel R. Mayhew. "Graduated Licensing: A Blueprint for North America." In the Highway Loss Data Institute [web site]. Available from www.hwysafety.org/safety%5Ffacts/teens/blueprint.pdf.

World Bank Group. "Road Safety." In the World Bank Group [web site]. Available from www.worldbank.org/html/fpd/transport/roads/safety.htm.

NARELLE L. HAWORTH

# INTERNET

Traditionally, death has been a great taboo in Western culture, a topic delicately sidestepped in polite public company and private reflection alike. But since 1995, the taboo has been at least partially dispelled in the informational glut of the Internet, which has brought the subject of death within easy arm's reach of millions of the previously averse or oblivious—merely typing in the letters "d-e-a-t-h" in the window of a search engine (i.e., www.google.com) yields no fewer than 23,600,000 items, enough to daunt even the most avid scholar or morbid connoisseur of mortality.

However, these web sites provide far more than mere information: There is practical help in the form of bereavement support and information on organ donation and living wills, death in cultures around the world, hospice care, and numerous other areas.

## General Sites

Some of the most useful sites guide the web surfer toward services as well as information. One such site is www.excite.com/family/family_in_crisis, which lists numerous links to social and medical services and information for those burdened with grief or terminal illness. The site lists links to other sites regarding euthanasia, suicide, estate planning, and many other related topics. Those with more theoretical concerns might profitably consult www.tripod.lycos.com. There, the student, teacher, or researcher can find additional links to a wealth of other informational sites.

Because search engines often yield a dizzying plethora of responses, it is useful to narrow the range of responses by making the topic as specific as possible. For example, instead of merely typing in "grief," one might add "AND" plus another word to limit the search—say, "children's." Then only topics pertaining to children's grief will appear on the list of responses, saving the searcher a good deal of time and effort by reducing the number of items to several dozen rather than several thousand.

Another important watchword for web surfing on this or any other topic is "vigilance," a critical tool in distinguishing between the trustworthiness of a site produced by a distinguished scholar, such as Michael Kearl, and a personal site titled "Buffy's Death Page." "Caveat emptor" should be the watchword for every Internet surfer, where triviality and fraud are as common as the authentic and rewarding.

## Demographics of Death on the Web

A number of web sites specialize in a statistical approach to death—its causes and demographics, life expectancies, social factors, and so on. The data on these sites are updated frequently and are usually culled from reliable government and scholarly sources. Some such sites are devoted to particular segments of society. For example, www.runet.edu provides information on life expectancy for African Americans compared to whites, along with other health-related data. Government sites, such as www.cdc.gov/nchs, give a broader range of data for many different segments of American society, including major causes of death in various age groups.

In other sites the accent is on the individual—for example, by entering a name, place of death, or Social Security Number at www.vitalrec.com, one can locate the death record of anyone in the United States. This site also provides links to sites that yield overseas records as well.

## Cross-Cultural and Religious Information

For those interested in the religious dimension of death and dying, there is a wealth of sites that provide access to information on the death rituals, funeral customs, and mourning practices of nearly every known religion or cult, major or minor. Other sites dwell on a more broadly cultural approach to the meaning of death and attitudes toward the dying—a site might be devoted to a single culture such as that of the Cree Indians (www.sicc.sk.ca), while others might explore a broad range of cultures. One of the best is found at www.encarta.msn.com. Sites such as these also provide links to related web sites, as well as to printed material and reading lists.

## Grief and Bereavement

The most numerous death-related web sites are those that deal with grief, both as a subject of analysis and as a topic for practical guidance to coping. The Griefnet web site (www.griefnet.org) provides one of the most extensive support systems online. It includes several web pages and over thirty small e-mail support groups. Griefnet posts a companion site for children and parents.

Some sites are designed to deal with specific categories of grievers. The Australian Widownet site (www.grief.org.au) provides information and self-help resources for widows and widowers of all ages, religious backgrounds, and sexual orientations. Suicide often evokes special issues of grief. One particular site that includes personal testimony by those who have experienced the death of a loved one by suicide is www.1000deaths.com. Tragedy Assistance Program for Survivors, Inc., a nonprofit group that provides support to those who have lost a loved one who met his or her end while serving in the armed forces, can be found at www.taps.org. The site provides peer support, crisis information, a variety of resources, and the opportunity to establish a virtual memorial.

Other bereavement web sites provide information not only for the bereaved but also for the professionals who are a part of the death system. Genesis Bereavement Resources (www.genesis-resources.com) provides a list of music, videos, and other material that may be helpful to grievers, health care professionals, funeral directors, and pastors.

No detail is too slight or awkward to escape the attention of web entrepreneurs. Bereavement Travel at www.bereavementtravel.com allows one to make travel arrangements at the time of death at the special bereavement rates offered by many airlines and hotels. This service is primarily a convenience for the bereaved.

There are also special sites dedicated to unique bereavement responses, including www.aidsquilt.org/Newsite, which provides information on the AIDS quilt that has been shown all over the United States as a memorial to victims of the illness. In addition to bereavement support, some sites offer guidance on life-threatening illnesses, such as www.cancer.org for the American Cancer Society and www.alz.org for the Alzheimer's Disease and Related Disorders Association.

Compassionate Friends, the best known of the national bereavement support groups for parents who have experienced the death of a child, has a web site at www.compassionatefriends.org. Here, one can locate local chapters, obtain brochures, form a local chapter, and catch up with the latest related news. There are also organizations that help visitors locate or start a grief support group.

Finally, there are sites for many well-known organizations that are part of the thanatology field. The Make-A-Wish Foundation (www.wish.org) fulfills special wishes for terminally ill children. They send children to theme parks, arrange meetings or phone calls with celebrities, and perform other special services for ill children.

## Pet Loss

Bereavement guidance on the web is not limited to those who have suffered the loss of human companions. Those dealing with the loss of a pet may go to the web site for the Association for Pet Loss and Bereavement at www.aplb.org. One of the most unique sites in this area is www.petloss.com, which provides online grief support and describes a special candle ceremony held weekly to commemorate the death of a pet. Also at this site, one can find reference to other related web sites, chat rooms, and telephone support.

## End-of-Life Issues

The web offers a range of end-of-life issues, including care of the terminally ill, living wills, and hospice care. Choice in Dying (www.choices.org) is the organization that first devised a living will in

1967, long before states adopted a legal policy on this issue. This nonprofit organization and its web site provide counseling for patients and families, information on advanced directives, outline training resources for professionals, and serve as an advocate for improved laws. The American Institute of Life-Threatening Illnesses, a division of the Foundation for Thanatology, can be found at www.lifethreat.org. This organization, established in 1967, is dedicated to promoting improved medical and psychosocial care for critically ill patients and their families.

## Funeral Arrangements

People have long complained about the high cost of funerals and related expenses. There are numerous web sites that offer online casket purchases and other related items. Such sites promise quick service and complete satisfaction, often at steep discounts. In addition to caskets, www.webcaskets.com offers urns, markers, flowers, and other funerary items. At www.eternalight.com one can purchase an "eternal" light, guaranteed to glow for thirty years. The light can be used at home as a permanent memorial to the loved one. The site donates 10 percent of the purchase price to a national support group of the customer's choice.

It is possible to plan an entire funeral service online at www.funeralplan.com. One can actually watch a funeral service from many funeral homes by going to www.funeral-cast.com. The National Funeral Directors Association maintains a site at www.nfda.org. Here, one can locate funeral homes, obtain consumer information, and learn about careers in this field.

## Unusual Sites

Some web sites defy easy classification. One popular site is www.deathclock.com. Here one can plug in one's date of birth and gender, along with one's attitudinal and philosophical propensities, and obtain the likely date of one's demise. Visitors can watch the clock count down their time on Earth. Many college students find this to be a fascinating site and download a screen-saver version—every time they turn on their computers they watch their lives "tick away." Other interesting sites include www.1800autopsy.com, where one can contact a mobile company to perform such an examination, and www.autopsyvideo.com, which allows visitors to view autopsies online. These web sites are used by professionals and educators, as well as the curious.

The web is aswarm with jokes on all topics, and death is no exception. Some web pages specialize in bad-taste death jokes, many of which center on celebrities. One site in particular allows the visitor to "bury or cremate" someone. After entering a name and choosing a method of body disposal, one can watch as the casket burns up.

## Obituaries and Last Words

Numerous web sites provide visitors with the opportunity to post memorial messages. Most of these sites charge a fee for permanent placement. At www.legacy.com, one can pay a fee of $195 to place a memorial, including photograph, on the site.

Memorialtrees.com arranges for a memorial tree to be planted in any state in the United States or in the Canadian provinces. The fee is less than thirty dollars and includes a certificate of planting and a card that Memorialtrees.com sends to the survivor.

## Near-Death Experiences

Much attention has been paid to the issue of the near-death experience. Two sites that are particularly useful include www.iands.org, the official web site of the International Association for Near-Death Studies, replete with research information, case studies, and resources; and www.near-death.com, which includes near-death experiences of people of various faiths along with the testimony of children and suicides who have had brushes with death.

## Legal and Financial Issues

A number of sites offer guidance in the many practical and financial matters that arise after a death. One very comprehensive site is www.moneycentral.msn.com. Here, one can find answers to general questions regarding finances, collecting life insurance, and handling bills of the deceased. One can also obtain information on making a will without consulting an attorney. A site like www3.myprimetime.com includes information on estates as well as the impact of being a griever and executor.

## Conclusion

The Internet has dramatically expanded the availability of resources in the field of thanatology, providing both useful and irrelevant sites. Anyone consulting web sites must be careful to sort through them to find those that are helpful and accurate.

*See also:* DEATH EDUCATION; GRIEF: OVERVIEW; GRIEF COUNSELING AND THERAPY; LAST WORDS; MEMORIAL, VIRTUAL; NEAR-DEATH EXPERIENCES; TECHNOLOGY AND DEATH

*Internet Resources*

"Funeral Rites and Customs." In the Encarta [web site]. Available from www.encarta.msn.com.

Radford University. "Sociological Comparisons between African-Americans and Whites." In the Radford University [web site]. Available from www.runet.edu/-junnever/bw.htm

DANA G. CABLE

# ISLAM

*Islam* is an Arabic word meaning "surrender" or "submission." It is a faith that encompasses approximately one-fifth of humanity. Its adherents reside in almost every country of the world and comprise majorities in large segments of Africa, the Middle East, the Indian subcontinent, and Asia. Approximately 6 million Americans follow Islam.

## The Origins of Islam

The historical origins of Islam date back to seventh century Arabia. The Prophet Muhammad, an aristocratic Arabian born and raised an orphan in the sanctuary city of Mecca, experienced a revelation in his fortieth year. He began to preach to his own people, most of whom initially persecuted him. After thirteen years of suffering with patience and endurance, he migrated to the nearby city of Medina. For over twenty-three years, beginning in 610 C.E., the Prophet orally transmitted the Quran (Koran). Muslims believe the Quran was revealed from God through the archangel Gabriel. In it, a cosmology, a theology, and an elaborate eschatology are described. By the end of the Prophet's life in 632 C.E., almost the entire Arabian Peninsula had converted from paganism to Islam, and within a hundred years, its followers stretched from France to China.

Although considered the youngest of the three great Abrahamic faiths that include Judaism and Christianity, Islam does not view itself as a new religion but rather as a reformed Abrahamic faith. Muslims believe that the Quran corrects distortions of previous prophetic dispensations while not departing from the aboriginal faith of humanity, which according to the Muslims is Islam, or submission to one God. While Muslims believe all prophets have taught the unity of God and that their beliefs about God were the same, their actual practices have changed to suit various times and places. According to Muslims, this is why religions tend to differ outwardly, while retaining an essential inward truth common to them all. However, the Quran declares its message as uniquely universal applying to all people for all remaining time.

## Basic Beliefs of Muslims

Islam is based upon five "pillars" that represent the bedrock upon which all else is based. The first pillar, which makes one a Muslim, is called the *shahadah,* meaning, "testimony" or "witnessing." It is fulfilled by declaring to two witnesses the foundational creed of Islam: "*Ashhadu an la ilaha illa Allah wa anna Muhammadan rasulullah.*" This means, "I witness that there is nothing worthy of worship except God and that Muhammad is God's messenger." The first part of the testimony is a belief that God is unique with no partners. Thus, nothing in creation can be associated with God, as creation has no real substantiation without the sustaining power of God. Indeed, creation is not God nor does it have any eternal qualities of the divine that are worthy of worship. Rather, creation is a theater of divine manifestations. Creation is seen as a place where analogies of the divine reveal themselves. The intellect of a person is the vehicle given by God to discern this truth about creation as indicated by several verses in the Quran.

The second part of the declaration, Muhammad is the messenger of God, acknowledges the means through which this understanding of God has come. All prophets are special human beings capable of refracting divine light, acting like prisms that allow others to see it. The intensity of direct divine light is something only a prophet can bear.

Muslims believe that the revelation given to Muhammad is like refracted green light, which lies in the middle of the light spectrum. Muslims consider Islam to be the most balanced of the prophetic dispensations, the "middle way." The Prophet Muhammad's life is considered to be moderate and exemplary for both men and women. He abhorred extremes saying, "Beware of extremism in your religion." After the Quran, the Prophet's practice, or *Sunnah*, is the second most important authority in Islam.

The second pillar of Islam is prayer. While people may supplicate anytime they wish to do so, there is a specific prayer every adult Muslim, female and male, is obliged to perform five times a day. The times are determined by the perceived movement of the sun as a way of reminding people of the temporal nature of the world. Thus, each day is considered to be a microcosm of one's own life: the dawn prayer as one's coming into the world, the midday prayer as the end of youth, the afternoon prayer as old age, the sunset prayer as death, and the evening prayer as the beginning of the descent into the darkness of the grave and returning to the dawn prayer as the awakening and resurrection of the dead. After the testimony of faith, prayer is considered the most important pillar.

The third pillar of Islam is paying *zakah*, an obligatory alms given once every lunar year from the standing capital of every responsible adult. It is not an income tax, as income tax is prohibited in Islamic law, but rather a capital tax on wealth that has been stagnate for at least a year. It is one-fortieth of a person's liquid assets. According to the Quran, zakah is distributed among eight categories of people, the two most important recipients being the poor and the needy.

The fourth pillar is fasting the entire lunar month of Ramadan, and it begins with the sighting of the new crescent for that month. Fasting entails abstaining from food, drink, and sexual relations from dawn to sunset and is obligatory on adults healthy enough to do so.

The fifth pillar is the *Hajj*, or pilgrimage to Mecca. Muslims believe Mecca to be the site of the first house of worship built by the Prophet Adam and his wife Eve and then restored millennia later by the Prophet Abraham and his son, the Prophet Ishmael. At the end of his mission, the Prophet Muhammad restored its monotheistic purpose by destroying the 365 idols in it that the Arabs had been worshiping prior to Islam. The rituals performed in the pilgrimage follow the footsteps of Abraham and his second wife Hagar. The Hajj culminates on a vast desert plain where approximately 3 million pilgrims from almost every country on Earth gather every year and prepare for standing before God on the Day of Judgment.

## Customs and Practices of Muslims

Due to the broad cultural diversity in the Muslim world, Islam is a quilt of many colors rather than a monolithic faith etched in stone. The majority of Muslims have never considered Islam to be "straight and narrow" but rather "straight and broad." The word in Arabic for the sacred law of Islam, *shariah*, literally means "the broad path to water." The shariah, rather than being a rigid and inflexible law, is governed by a fluid and elastic set of principles, and Muslim legal theorists consider it rationally comprehensible and thus capable of being altered when the rationale is absent or the circumstances warrant.

Most Muslim cultures manifest their own characteristics. For instance, the Islam of Indonesia, while essentially the same in its skeletal form, is quite different culturally from the Islam of Senegal. Muslims are required to wear modest clothes, and women are required to cover their hair and entire body except for the hands and face when in the presence of unrelated males. However, the bright colors of the women of Nigeria contrast sharply with the moribund black of the Arabian Peninsula—both are considered acceptable. Food and merrymaking also differ greatly, and Muslims, like other peoples, have diverse ways of enjoying themselves and appreciating the milestones of life such as weddings, births, graduations, and religious holidays. Religious music and chanting are widespread in the Muslim world, and Quran reciters with beautiful voices have statuses in some Muslim countries.

## Living and Dying in Islam

The German philosopher Goethe wrote, "If Islam means submission to the will of God, then in Islam we all live and die." This succinctly summarizes the goal of Muslims: To live and die in accordance with God's will as revealed in the Quran and practiced by the Prophet. Muslims attempt to adjust their view of the world with the lens of the Quran. The will of God is expressed in the Quran through both expectations and examples. The expectations are usually descriptions of how a believer should live his or her life, and various stories in the Quran provide positive and negative examples. The epitome of a positive exemplar is Moses, whose story is dealt with in great detail in the Quran. Struggle is at the root of life on earth, a spiritual survival of the fittest. The fittest are those closest to God; they are those who are "steadfast in prayer and spend out of what We have provided for them" (Quran 2:3; Ali 1999, p. 17). The negative prototype is embodied in Pharaoh, who elevates himself above God's law and makes his own law the only source of guidance. Moses is given the Promised Land for his perseverance and steadfastness, and Pharaoh is destroyed by his own hubris and rebellion against the divine will. The story of Moses is an example of submission (Islam), and Pharaoh's is of rebellion and infidelity (*kufr*). Between these two lies the struggle of humanity.

Life is meant to be an arena whereby one struggles with good and evil. The Quran teaches that good and evil exist in the heart of every individual as well as in the society. The individual struggle is to act righteously in accordance with the Quran and prophetic example, and to shun one's own evil and its impulses. The collective struggle is to work with others to make the world a more righteous place. In Arabic, this inward and outward struggle is called *jihad*. While it can mean a militant struggle against those who attack the Muslim lands, it also signifies a person's struggle with the lower tendencies of the soul, the gravitational pull of self-destructive forces that lead to alienation from God and a state of spiritual disequilibrium. Because humans inevitably fall short morally and succumb to these destructive tendencies from time to time, a means of reestablishing spiritual balance is given, called *tauba* or atonement. This is done by experiencing a genuine sense of remorse for one's transgressions and a removal of the unhealthy effects of that state by turning to God and seeking divine grace through prayer, charity, and a sincere resolution not to return to the destructive patterns of the past.

While life is seen as a spiritual test and journey, it is also seen as being filled with blessings from God to be enjoyed: "Eat and drink, but waste not by excess, for Allah loveth not the wasters.

Say: 'Who hath forbidden the beautiful (gifts) of Allah which He hath produced for His servants, and the things, clean and pure, (which He hath provided) for sustenance?" (Quran, p. 352). Thus, in Islam, marriage is highly recommended and celibacy is frowned upon. The Muslim savants of the past identified sexual relations between a wife and her husband as a foretaste of eternal bliss with God in the afterlife. The Prophet Muhammad encouraged marriage and stated, "There is no monasticism in Islam." In Islam, children are highly esteemed and seen as one of God's greatest blessings to humanity. The Prophet stated that humans were born innocent and later corrupted by their societies. Thus, parents are held responsible for maintaining that state of innocence and raising them with a sense of love and awe of the divine. Motherhood is highly regarded in the Quran and the prophetic tradition. The Prophet said, "Paradise lies at the feet of mothers." In most Muslim societies, adult women are still predominantly mothers and housewives during their productive years.

**Death and Its Relevance to Muslims**

Death is a question of ultimate concern for every human being, and Islam has a very vivid portrayal of the stages of death and the afterlife. Death is likened to sleep in Islam; interestingly, sleep in Arabic is called "the little brother of death." The Prophet spoke often of death, and the Quran is filled with warnings of the dangers of ignoring one's mortality and of not preparing for death before it is too late. In one poignant passage, the Quran reads,

> And spend something (in charity) out of the substance which We have bestowed on you before death should come to any of you and he should say, "O my Lord! Why didst Thou not give me respite for a little while? I should then have given (largely) in charity, and I should have been one of the doers of good." But to no soul will Allah grant respite when the time appointed (for it) has come; and Allah is well-acquainted with (all) that ye do. *(Quran, pp. 1473–1474)*

Hence, the world is seen as an opportunity to cultivate for the hereafter, and time is seen as capital that human beings either invest wisely or squander, only to find themselves bankrupt in the next life. Muhammad said, "One of you says, 'My wealth! My wealth!' Indeed, have any of you anything other than your food that you eat and consume, your clothes that you wear out, and your wealth that you give in charity which thus increases in return in the next world?"

The idea of mentioning death and reflecting on death is very important in a Muslim's daily life, and attending any Muslim's funeral, whether known or not, is highly encouraged; for such attendance, one is rewarded greatly by God. Muhammad advised, "Make much mention of the destroyer of delights," which is death. He also said, "Introduce into your gatherings some mention of death to keep things in perspective." This is not seen as a morbid exercise, and Muslims surprisingly accept death, resigned to what is called "one's appointed time" (*ajal*). Like the telemere in biology that dictates how many times a cell may regenerate before dying, an individual's appointed term, according to Islam, is inescapable and fated. When a Muslim survives a near-death experience, such as a serious car accident, an operation, or an illness, he or she will often remark, "My appointed time did not come yet."

## After Death

Once a Muslim dies, the people left behind must prepare the body by washing, perfuming, and shrouding it. The funeral prayer is then performed, and the deceased is buried in a graveyard without a coffin, simply laid in the earth and covered. A person, usually a relative, informs the deceased of what is happening, as Muslims believe that the deceased can hear and understand what is being said. Muslims believe the dead person is not always aware of the transition, and so the one giving instructions informs the deceased that he or she has died, is being laid in the grave, and that two angels known as Munkar and Nakir will soon come into the grave to ask three questions. To the first question, "Who is your Lord?," the deceased is instructed to reply, "Allah." In answer to the second question, "Who is your Prophet?," the deceased should say, "Muhammad," and the correct response to the third question, "What is your religion?," is "Islam." If the individual passes this first phase of the afterlife, the experience of the grave is pleasant, and he or she is given glimpses of the pleasures of paradise. If however, the

This sixteenth-century drawing, "Muhammad's Ascent to Heaven," illustrates Muhammad, the major prophet of Islam, on horseback escorted by angels. SEATTLE ART MUSEUM

deceased does not pass this phase, then the grave is the first stage of chastisement.

After this, the soul sleeps and does not awake until a blast from an angel at God's command. According to Islamic tradition, this blast signals the end of the world and kills any remaining souls on the earth. It is followed by a second blast that causes all of the souls to be resurrected. At this point, humanity is raised up and assembled on a plain. The Quran states, "On that day We shall leave them to surge like waves on one another; the trumpet will be blown, and We shall collect them all together" (Quran, p. 735). From there, humanity will beg each of the prophets to intercede for them and hasten the Day of Judgment because the waiting is so terrible, but the prophets will refuse. Finally, all of humanity goes to the Prophet Muhammad. He will agree to intercede for them and ask that the Judgment commence. This intercession is granted to him alone. Then, each soul is judged based upon its beliefs and actions, which are weighed in the scales of divine justice. At this point, the two guardian angels assigned to all people throughout their adult lives will testify for or against them. According to the Quran, the limbs of each person will testify, and the earth herself is resurrected and bears witness against those who caused her harm. Next, a person will be given a book either in the right or left hand. For those given a book in the right hand, they pass the Judgment and are given the grace of God. For those given a book in their left hand, they fail the Judgment and are condemned to hell. However, at this point, prophets and other righteous people are allowed to intercede for their relatives, followers, or friends among the condemned, and their intercession is accepted.

Once the Day of Judgment is over, humanity proceeds to a bridge known as the *sirat,* which crosses over hell. The saved cross it safely to the other side and are greeted by their respective prophets. The Muslims who make it safely across are greeted by Muhammad, who will take them to a great pool and give them a drink that will quench their thirst forever. The condemned fall into hell. The Quran states that some will only spend a brief time there, while others, the unrepenting and idolatrous ingrates, are condemned forever. Muslims see death as a transition to the other side. Islam is seen as the vehicle that will take one safely there. It is only in paradise that the believer finds ultimate peace and happiness.

## Common Misconceptions about Islam

Perhaps the most common misunderstanding about Islam is its attitude toward women. In light of modern sensibilities, Islam, as practiced by most Muslims, does retain some pre-modern attitudes. Much of this is cultural; however, some is not. For example, although the home is generally considered the best place for a woman, Islam does not prohibit a woman from a career in the outside world. In fact, many early Muslim women including the Prophet's wife, Khadija, were scholars and merchants. While Islamic law does legislate some differences

between men and women, they are few in number. The majority of practicing Muslim women do not view them as demeaning because a woman is considered equal to a man before God. The Quran clearly states, "Whoever works righteousness, man or woman, and has faith, verily to him will We give a new life, and life that is good and pure, and We will bestow on such their reward according to the best of their actions" (Quran, p. 663).

Another aspect of Islam that tends to spark interest is the idea of Jihad, or holy war. Some people think Islam condones violence and even terrorism. In reality, Islam rarely permits Muslims to use coercive force and does so only for reasons such as self-defense. Moreover, with the exception of self-defense, only legitimate state authority can exercise coercive force. Although there is a religious duty to fight to defend the lands of Islam, strict rules of engagement apply. The Prophet specifically prohibited the killing of religious people, old people, as well as women and children. Later, Muslim legal theorists included any noncombatants in this prohibition. Sadly, like other religions, Islam has violent fanatics and extremists who justify their crimes by distorting Quranic verses and the sayings of the Prophet Muhammad for heinous ends.

Muslims are a racially diverse community, the majority of which are non-Arab. Although Islam began in Arabia, Arabs comprise less than 15 percent of Muslims. The largest Muslim population is in Indonesia, and the second largest is in Bangladesh. There are estimated to be over 60 million Muslims in modern China. Largely due to high birthrates in the traditional Islamic world, Islam is considered to be the fastest growing religion in the twenty-first century. In 2000 it was the third largest religion in the United States and is expected to be the second after Christianity.

*See also:* AFRICAN RELIGIONS; BUDDHISM; CHINESE BELIEFS; HINDUISM; ZOROASTRIANISM

### *Bibliography*

al-Ghazali. *On Disciplining the Soul and On Breaking the Two Desires,* translated by Timothy J. Winter. Cambridge, England: Islamic Texts Society, 1995.

al-Ghazali. *The Remembrance of Death and the Afterlife,* translated by Timothy J. Winter. Cambridge, England: Islamic Texts Society, 1995.

al-Nawawi, Yahya ibn Sharaf. *Al-Maqasid: Imam Nawawi's Manual of Islam,* translated by Nuh Ha Mim Keller. Evanston, IL: Sunna Books, 1994.

al-Sadlaan, Saalih ibn Ghaanim. *Words of Remembrance and Words of Reminder: Encompassing Important Dhikr and Important Islamic Behavior,* translated by Jamaal al-Din Zarabozo. Boulder, CO: Al-Basheer Company for Publications and Translations, 1998.

al-Shabrawi, Shaykh Abd Al-Khaliq. *The Degrees of the Soul,* translated by Mostafa Al-Badawi. London: The Quilliam Press, 1997.

as-Sulami, Abu Abd Ar-Rahman. *Early Sufi Women,* translated by Rkia Elaroui Cornell. Louisville, KY: Fons Vitae, 2000.

Chittick, William. *The Vision of Islam.* New York: Paragon House, 1994.

Friedlander, Shems, and Al-Hajj Shaikh Muzaffereddin. *Ninety-Nine Names of Allah.* New York: Harper Colophon Books, 1978.

Glasse, Cyril. *The Concise Encyclopedia of Islam.* London: Stacey International, 1989.

Helminski, Kabir. *The Knowing Heart: A Sufi Path of Transformation.* Boston: Shambhala Publications, 1999.

Lings, Martin. *Muhammad: His Life Based on the Earliest Sources.* Rochester, NY: Inner Traditions International, 1983.

Smith, Huston. *The World's Religions: A Guide to Our Wisdom Traditions.* San Francisco: Harper, 1994.

Stork, Mokhtar. *A–Z Guide to the Quran: A Must-Have Reference to Understanding the Contents of the Islamic Holy Book.* Singapore: Times Books International, 1999.

HAMZA YUSUF HANSON

# IVAN ILYCH

"The Death of Ivan Ilych" is widely regarded as one of the most powerful meditations on death and dying in world literature, at least in part because it anticipates modern psychological discussions of the stages of dying. Written in 1886, the novella was the Russian novelist and moral philosopher Leo Tolstoy's first major work of fiction completed after his existential crisis of the late 1870s—a crisis that initiated the search for a new understanding of Christianity that was to preoccupy him for the remainder of his life. The story is a fictional adaptation of Tolstoy's autobiographical work "The Confession" (1879–1880), which recounts his personal struggle for meaning in the face of the terrifying inevitability of death. It is a classic literary case study of how awareness and acceptance of human mortality can and should change how people live their lives.

On the surface, "Ivan Ilych" is a simple story: A conventional family man and a successful judge, who is a member in good standing in high society, suddenly develops a mysterious illness that causes him agonizing pain and eventually kills him. Structurally, the story privileges Ivan's death over his life. It begins with his funeral, thus introducing him as a character who has already died, and only then chronicles his life from childhood to the onset of his illness. The story increases in speed and intensity after Ivan becomes sick: The chapters shorten and the time period depicted in each decreases dramatically from a few weeks to, in the final chapter, just a few hours. In structuring the story in this way, Tolstoy suggests that Ivan is not really alive until he begins to die.

Ivan is depicted as Everyman. Explicit details link Ivan's fate with the fate of all the characters in the story. The reader of the story is intended to learn the lesson that Tolstoy himself learned as a result of his spiritual crisis and that Ivan learns as the story unfolds: Death is an inevitable part of life, and active acceptance of this simple fact is a necessary precondition for leading a meaningful life. None of the characters in the story, with one exception, seem to understand this lesson; all treat the dying Ivan as an unpleasant and foreign intrusion into their comfortable world. The exception to this rule is Gerasim, the story's energetic peasant-hero, who comforts his dying master and who says of death: "It's God's will. We shall all come to it some day" (Katz 1991, p. 129).

Tolstoy maps out Ivan's struggle to accept death through a series of subtexts that run counter to the surface plot. The subtexts tell the story of a nineteenth-century man with all the traits of the modern, twenty-first-century self: one with no spiritual life, one alienated from others, and one compelled by his illness to seek and find true meaning. When well, Ivan could avoid the "unpleasant" and believe that death is something that happens only to other people. When dying, he is forced to confront life's unpleasantness (physical discomfort, which comes to symbolize a lack of spiritual meaning) and question the rightness of how he lived his life.

Ivan's reconsideration of his life is ironically facilitated by the intense pain he experiences as his illness progresses. The pain, the most unpleasant of all circumstances Ivan has ever endured, dismantles his comfortable world and turns his pleasant and decorous life into something horribly unpleasant and false, something that Ivan must struggle against in his quest for meaning. Ivan faces his mortality both figuratively and literally because the pain is personified as a gleaming light that peeks out at him from behind houseplants and shines through all the screens that he puts up in vain attempts to block it off.

By the end of the story, Ivan's pain has become not only the central fact of his existence but the vehicle of his salvation. The pain resurrects him by sharpening or heightening all of his senses. Ivan discovers that the pain that accompanies his death is a catalyst for self-knowledge and spiritual renewal: "His ache, that gnawing ache that never ceased for a moment, seemed to have acquired a new and more serious significance" (p. 143). In accepting the pain accompanying death, Ivan symbolically rediscovers life.

Ivan suffers not because he is being punished but because Tolstoy needs a vehicle for dramatically depicting the significance of death for life.

Ivan's fate, which is everyone's fate, suggests that the inevitability of death ought to have consequences for how one's life is lived. Tolstoy delivers this seemingly simple message in a story whose haunting symbolic power survives translation across both time and culture.

*See also:* COMMUNICATION WITH THE DYING; DEATH EDUCATION; DYING, PROCESS OF; LESSONS FROM THE DYING; LITERATURE FOR ADULTS; PAIN AND PAIN MANAGEMENT; PHILOSOPHY, WESTERN

## Bibliography

Danaher, David. "The Function of Pain in Tolstoy's 'The Death of Ivan Il'ich.'" *The Tolstoy Studies Journal* 10 (1998):20–28.

Dayananda, Y. J. "'The Death of Ivan Ilych': A Psychological Study on Death and Dying." *Literature and Psychology* 22 (1972):191–198.

Jahn, Gary, ed. *Tolstoy's 'The Death of Ivan Ilych': A Critical Companion.* Evanston, IL: Northwestern University Press, 1999.

Jahn, Gary. *The Death of Ivan Il'ich: An Interpretation.* New York: Twayne, 1993.

Katz, Michael, ed. *Tolstoy's Short Fiction,* translated by Louise Maude and Aylmer Maude. New York: W. W. Norton, 1991.

DAVID S. DANAHER

# J

## JAINISM

Jainism is an ancient religious and philosophical tradition that is thought to have originated in the Ganges River basin. There remain some 4 million Jains in India, spread mainly between five states, and there is also a small but influential community of emigrants in both Europe and the United States. The great philosophers of Jainism evolved a view of the universe as material and permanent, in strong contrast to the Buddhist view that everything is illusory and transient and *nirvana* or *moksa* means the merging or extinction of individuality in an undifferentiated final state. In contrast, in Jainism death leads ultimately to the liberation of the soul into an individual state of total knowledge and bliss, although this process may take several cycles of death and rebirth. In Hinduism, unlike Jainism, there is no possible form of transmitting conscious memory from one life to another, because its domain belongs to the world of illusions and dissolves at death.

The distinctive aspects of the Jain tradition are the belief in unending cycles and "half cycles" of time as well as of life and death; the spiritual model provided by twenty-four leaders (*jinas*) who regenerated the Jain tradition in the present "half cycle" of time; the five vows of noninjury or nonviolence; speaking the truth; taking only that which is given; chastity; and detachment from place, persons, and things. The aim of Jain spiritual endeavor is to liberate the soul (*jiva*), which is believed to leave the physical body with one's karmic matter. This matter supplies the energy for onward travel to a new destiny in the cycle of death and rebirth (*karma*), which in the Jain tradition has a material nature. "Drier," more dispassionate souls are not so easily polluted by negative karma, whereas karmic matter is more easily attracted to souls that are "moist" with desires that might contravene the five vows. The soul can leave the body through several orifices. The soul of a sinner is perceived as leaving an already decayed body through the anus. The suture at the top of the skull is the purest point of the soul's exit, reserved for those who have led a life of renunciation, such as that of a dead ascetic. Just before the body of the deceased is cremated, the eldest son may help the soul of his father on its way by cracking the skull.

"First there must be knowledge and then compassion. This is how all ascetics achieve self-control" (*Dasavaikalika* 4:33). In Jainism, a good life through moral conduct (*ahimsaa,* or nonviolence and reverence for life in thoughts, words, and deeds) leads to a good death, one in which the body remains, to the last, under an ascetic type of control. Jain scriptures detail the destiny of the soul after death and the causes of physical death. These causes are classified as death because of old age or degeneration; death with desires; death without desires; the fool's death; the prudent person's death; a mixed death (i.e., the death of one who is neither a fool nor a prudent person, but one who is only partially disciplined); holy death, and (the highest state) omniscient death. "The concept of omniscience," writes Natubhai Shah, "is the central feature of Jainism and its philosophy. . . . The ultimate goal of worldly life is to acquire omniscience" (Shah 1998, 2:114). Thus, by definition, the state of perfect knowledge or omniscience (*kevala jnaana*) is the highest form of life before death.

"When a wise man, in whatever way, comes to know that the apportioned space of his life draws towards its end, he should in the meantime quickly learn the method of dying a religious death." This extract from the Jain holy scriptures, known as *Sutra krtraanga*, identifies a ritual almost unique among the world's religions (except in the most ascetic sects): a holy fast unto death, which through inaction rids the soul of negative karma and brings about death with dignity and dispassion (*salle-khanaa*). Within the Jain tradition, this is not regarded as an act of suicide (which involves passion and violence and is thus anathema) and is recommended only for a few spiritually fit persons and under strict supervision, usually in a public forum, with the approval of the family and spiritual superiors. People who die in this "death of the wise" (*pandita-marana*) are considered to be only a few births removed from final liberation from the painful cycle of death and rebirth. Two other forms of withdrawal from life are also practiced in conjunction with abstention from food. These are death through renunciation (*sannyasana marana*) and death through meditation (*samaadhi marana*).

At a Jain deathbed, the sacred mantra of surrender, obeisance, and veneration to the five supreme beings (*Navakara Mantra*) is recited and hymns are sung. The same mantra is recited after death, when hymns are sung and other prayers recited. In the Indian subcontinent, the dead person is normally cremated within twenty-four hours of death (though there may be a delay of up to a week among the diaspora in Europe and the United States). Before the body is consumed in the crematorium oven, there is a period of meditation for the peace of the soul, a sermon on the temporary nature of worldly life and advice to those present not to feel grief at the departure of the soul, which will be reborn in a new body. In the Indian subcontinent, the ashes of the deceased are dispersed in a nearby sacred river, or in the absence of a suitable river, a pit. The departure of the soul at death is part of a Jain worldview in which the concept of a living soul is thought to exist in all human beings, animals, insects, and vegetation, and even in the earth, stone, fire, water, and air. The distinctive Jain respect for life and refusal to kill animals, insects, and plants for food arises from this worldview.

*See also:* BUDDHISM; CREMATION; HINDUISM; IMMORTALITY; REINCARNATION; ZOROASTRIANISM

**Bibliography**

Cort, John E. *Jains in the World: Religious Values and Ideology in India*. Oxford: Oxford University Press, 2000.

Laidlaw, James. *Riches and Renunciation: Religion, Economy, and Society among the Jains*. Oxford: Clarendon Press, 1995.

Shah, Natubhai. *Jainism: The World of Conquerors*. 2 vols. Brighton: Sussex Academic Press, 1998.

RICHARD BONNEY

# JESUS

Jesus is the historical figure identified by the many forms of Christian tradition as its point of historical origin and the means of Christian believers' eternal destiny. Jesus of Nazareth was a popular Jewish teacher who reflected the tradition of his day—often associated with the Pharisee group of Jews—adhering to a belief in a future resurrection of the dead associated with a day of judgment and a new form of the kingdom of God. After his death his disciples claimed that he had risen from the dead, a resurrection belief characterizing his disciple group that soon broke away from traditional Judaism to become the earliest Christian Church. This means that the person of Jesus became inextricably bound up with the idea of the conquest of death. Indeed, the novelty of the New Testament does not lie in a general belief in resurrection but in a commitment to the specific belief that it had already taken place in Jesus and, because of that, all who believe in him and are his followers will also be granted a resurrection to eternal life.

## Christian Theologies

The significance of Jesus as far as death is concerned does not simply lie in the belief that he was resurrected, but that his death, in and of itself, achieved specific purposes. Here death becomes a symbolic vehicle for a number of ideas, largely grounded in the notions of sacrifice and salvation and traditionally spoken of as theories of atonement explaining how his death beneficially changed the relationship between God and humanity from hostility to reconciliation.

## Sacrificial Death

The prime meaning given to the death of Jesus both in the New Testament and in subsequent theologies is that it was an act of atonement expressed as a sacrifice. It is important to appreciate the fullness of the extent of this symbolism and the way it has entered into many of the cultures of the world. The death of Jesus could not have been interpreted as a sacrifice without the long historical tradition of the pre-existing Hebrew Bible and the Jewish ritual practices conducted at Jerusalem's temple, especially animal sacrifices for Jerusalem was then a center for animal sacrifice in which the shed blood was the means of removing personal sin. This was a religion in which morality and sacrifice were closely bound together as a means of forgiving the sin engendered by the breaking of divine commandments. The life of the beast was reckoned to be in its blood and it was the ending of that life that made possible the forgiveness of sins.

Another important strand of this tradition regarded suffering as the means of atoning for sin as in the image of the suffering servant of God who would be an agent for the deliverance of God's chosen people, Israel. This perspective was developed by some of the rabbis in the early Christian period to argue that death was the most extreme form of suffering, one that was actually experienced by dying individuals who might thereby atone for their sins in and through their own death. The earliest Christian traditions tended to foster these ideas, emphasizing them to varying degree, but seeing in Jesus both the sacrificial lamb of God who takes away the sin of the world and the suffering servant.

Much has been made of the fact that Jesus did not die a natural death but died as a criminal by the appointed method of crucifixion. This raises an interesting issue over blood as a medium of sacrifice. Crucifixion as practiced by the Romans, and it was on Roman authority that he was crucified, did not necessarily involve the use of nails and the shedding of blood. Criminals could be tied to crosses and die of asphyxiation when they could no longer bear the weight of their body on their legs. (Indeed, their legs might be broken to ensure this took place.) It was a slow form of punishing death. None of the Gospel stories tell of Jesus being nailed to the cross and John's Gospel has to add the specific, and unusual, comment that

a soldier standing by pierced his side with a spear out of which came "blood and water" (John 19:34). This is because John's Gospel has a specific interest in blood as a medium of salvation from sin. In various letters of the New Testament, especially the Letter to the Hebrews, great stress is placed upon Jesus as the High Priest who offers his own blood in a sacrificial ritual (Heb. 9:12); it also echoes the idea of being made perfect through suffering (Heb. 5:8–9). The overall Christian idea is that Jesus and his sacrificial death form the basis for the New Covenant between God and humanity.

## Christ and Self

One aspect of Christ's sacrificial death is reflected in the idea that he was either a representative of or a substitute for believers with the result that his death is related to their ongoing life and, as significant, that their death is no longer just a personal and private event. This is because the language of death, that of Jesus and of the believer, comes to be the means of interpreting one's life and is given fullest formal expression in the language of worship and ethics. Many Christian hymns reflect upon these matters and have ensured that the death of Christ has always remained at the forefront of Christian thought. The piety that sometimes arises in connection with this focus upon Christ's suffering and death has often been profound and is one means of eliciting the responsive love of individuals to God for the love shown to them.

## Death into Resurrection

For St. Paul, the combined death and resurrection of Jesus takes place at and as the turning point in history between the Jewish religion focused on a single nation and governed by the divine law—Israel's Torah—and the new international community of believers in Christ inspired by the divine revelation of the gospel. This "good news" was that God forgave the sins of all through this sacrificial death and, in the new unified community, created and led by the Spirit of God, there was a new kind of "body" of Christ—the church—existing in the world. The promises and pre-existing history of Israel had now come to fulfillment in this new community of love through God's action against humanity's sin to demonstrate the divine righteousness and to create a righteous world as expressed in different theories of atonement.

## Legal Idioms

Early fathers of the church offered variations on the theme of the life and sacrificial death of Jesus within a legal framework, one that viewed relationships in terms of rights, duties, ownership, and obligations. These are sometimes called legal or juridical theories of the atonement. Origen, writing in the third century, saw Christ's death as a form of ransom paid to the devil who had gained certain rights over fallen humanity. At the close of the eleventh century, Anselm, in his famous book *Why Did God Become Man?*, argued that the death of Jesus was a kind of satisfaction of God's outraged sense of honor caused by human disobedience. Human sin was a kind of debt resulting from the fact that people did not render the honor due to God. Not only ought humanity to return into obedience to God but some satisfaction should also be provided for the outrage perpetrated against the divine. And this was what the voluntary death of Jesus accomplished. His death becomes a satisfaction for the sins of humanity. This view contradicted that earlier theological suggestion that Christ's death was a payment to the devil.

## The Exemplary Death

One element of Anselm's thought speaks of the death of Jesus as an example of how ordinary humans ought to live by giving voluntary offerings to God. Abelard, a younger contemporary, developed his exemplary theory further arguing that the suffering death of Jesus should so stir the lives of believers that they would respond anew to God. Something of this exemplarist view also stirred the imagination of early-twentieth-century theologians as when Hastings Rashdall (1858–1924) saw God's love revealed in the life and death of Jesus in ways that evoked a human response to a life of service, as published in *The Idea of Atonement in Christian Theology* (1915).

## Drama of Conquest

Another style of interpretation of Christ's death, echoing the earlier ideas that the devil was involved, was prompted by the sixteenth-century German religious reformer Martin Luther and reinforced by the early-twentieth-century Swede Gustav Aulén. Sometimes referred to as the "dramatic theory of atonement," its stress falls on Christ as one who does battle with the devil and emerges

*The motive force for hope in most Christian traditions and cultures is, ultimately, grounded in the idea of the resurrection of Jesus and of believers. One of the more common images of Jesus is depicted in this late fifteenth century painting by Lazzaro Bastiani.* CORBIS

triumphant, as caught in the Latin title *Christus Victor,* used for the English translation of Aulén's book. This broad tradition expresses the positive accomplishment of Jesus and the sense of confident benefit received by believers through it. In more recent and popular forms this doctrine of the power of Christ over the devil has been used in Pentecostal and Charismatic forms of Christianity in relation to exorcism and gaining power over evil spirits reckoned to be afflicting the sick.

## Christian Worship

The death of Jesus did not, however, simply forge the first Christian groups or give opportunity for abstract theology but became central to three ritual practices: baptism, the Eucharist, and funerals. These ensured that the image of death would be kept firmly before Christian consciousness for the next 2,000 years. Baptism is a rite in which water becomes a symbol expressing several meanings, including (1) the normal function of water to cleanse the body, in this case the cleansing of sin viewed as an impurity or stain to be removed; (2) the biological "waters" associated with birth, in this case symbolizing spiritual birth so that a baptized person can be spoken of as being "born again"; and (3) the image of death, specifically the death of Jesus, for when someone becomes a Christian through baptism he or she is said to "die with Christ." The death and life of Jesus come to be intimately linked in a ritually symbolic way with the death and life of the believer. In this way the historical death of Jesus has come to be invested with deep theological significance and forms the basis for individual believers to reflect upon the meaning of their own lives. In religious terms not only are they said to have died to their old nature and to have been born again with a new nature on the single occasion of their baptism, but they are also called to "die daily" in a spiritual commitment to live a "new life."

This emphasis on the transformation from death to life, both in the death of Jesus and in the experience of Christians, is reinforced and developed in a special way in the rite called by a variety of names including the Eucharist, the Mass, the Holy Communion, or the Lord's Supper. In major Christian traditions such as Greek and Russian Orthodoxy, Catholicism, Lutheranism, and Anglicanism, both baptism and the Lord's Supper are regarded as sacraments—special ritual activities in which the outward signs of water, bread, and wine reflect spiritual depths and foster the whole life in the process of salvation. The Eucharist enacts an account of the Last Supper, itself probably a traditional Jewish Passover meal that expressed God's covenant with Israel, held by Jesus with his disciples just before he undergoes the agony of commitment to God's purposes in the Garden of Gethsemane, where he is finally betrayed, arrested, and executed. The Eucharist tells how it was on that night of betrayal that he took a cup of wine and told his disciples that it was his own blood that is shed for them and that they should repeat the act of drinking it as a way of remembering him. And so too with bread that they should eat in memory of his body given for them. Different traditions have developed these themes, some stressing aspects of remembrance as a mental act and talking about wine and bread as simply wine and bread, some even use nonalcoholic wine or even

water. Others, especially in the Catholic traditions, speak of the Mass as a "transubstantiation" rite in which the bread and wine "become" the body and blood of Christ through the priest's authority and the proper conducting of the ritual. A major train of thought interprets the Mass as a rite in which the death of Jesus is not simply represented but is also represented.

Modern believers enter into the foundational and epoch-making moments in the life and death of Jesus. The familiarity of these rites possibly tend to cloud the significance of what they express and yet when believers take the communion bread and wine they are engaging with symbols of death and life and bring the death and life of Jesus into intimate association with their own lives and death. Not only that, the rite also mentions the death and eternal life of various ancient saints of the church as well as of the more recently dead. Not only do many Christians pray for the dead but also invoke the saints to pray for the living. In other words, the eucharistic rite activates an entire network in which the living and the dead are caught up together within the Kingdom of God.

Finally, it is in funeral rites that the death of Jesus has come to play a significant part and these rites have become a major feature of the impact of Christian churches upon many societies. Once more, the death of individual believers is associated with the death of Jesus, their grave is symbolically linked to his and, in turn, his resurrection is proclaimed to be the basis for their future life. Christian burial has come to contain two paradoxical elements reflected in the well-known phrases, "earth to earth, ashes to ashes, dust to dust" and "in the sure and certain hope of the resurrection." These are usually said together, one following immediately after the other, and jointly assert the obvious fact of human decay and the "fact of faith" lodging its hope for the future in the resurrection of Christ.

## Hope

The very existence of baptism, the Eucharist, and funerals reflected and stimulated Christian theological explorations of the death of Jesus as a creative source of life, fostering the view that death may not be a futile end but, in some way, beneficial as in the twentieth century's world wars whose millions of dead have been depicted as not dying in vain but as valiant warriors fighting for the truth.

Many war memorials rehearse the saying accorded to Jesus in St. John's Gospel: "Greater love has no man than this, that he lay down his life for his friend." Such memorials often incorporate or take the form of a cross so that part of the conquest of death comes by aligning the death of soldiers with the death of Christ.

In many contexts of disaster and catastrophe relatives of the dead often seek some explanation of why the loss occurred and express the hope that something good may come out of it or that some lesson may be learned in order that, as the expression holds, "this may never happen again." To speak of disasters in terms of beneficial death is, in some ways, wrong and might appear insensitive to the bereaved and yet this is how some such events are framed.

## Resurrection

After Jesus died, the cave-tomb where he had been placed was found to be empty and the body unfound. Disciples say he appeared to them and believed that he had been raised from the dead. The contemporary popular Jewish belief in resurrection came to sharp focus: Resurrection had become personalized in Jesus. The early disciples also reckoned that a spiritual power had transformed them into a strong community, exemplifying the new message of God's love for all, irrespective of social or ethnic background. Identity within the new community of the church involved belief in the triumph over death conferred by this spiritual power coming to believers.

## Historical Jesus and Christ of Faith

From the eighteenth century on scholars used historical analysis of biblical texts to interpret Jesus's life, cutting through centuries of developed dogma. Albert Schweitzer's important works, including *The Quest for the Historical Jesus* (1906), argue that Jesus believed the world and history were coming to an end and that he was the Messiah whose own suffering would prompt it and help deliver people from the anguish involved. Rudolph Bultmann wanted to demythologize biblical stories so that the Christ of faith could be clearly heard, calling people to decision and faith. In the 1930s Charles Dodd argued for a "realised eschatology," the idea that a degree of divine fulfillment of the Kingdom of God had already occurred in the ministry of Jesus. In the

1950s Reginald Fuller opted for a belief that fulfillment would only come after Jesus's earthly work was completed. Despite detailed research on biblical descriptions of Jesus's suffering and death, much remains open as to whether he felt abandoned by God or not. Similarly, the theme of the resurrection remains contested as an arena in which ideas of the Jesus of history and the Christ of faith remain open-ended as Edward Sanders has indicated. From a psychological viewpoint, some argue that the resurrection is grounded in grief-induced hallucinations. Whatever the case, the death of Jesus has been the major focus by which millions have reflected upon their own death and sought relief when bereaved of those they love.

*See also:* CATHOLICISM; CHRISTIAN DEATH RITES, HISTORY OF; LAZARUS; OSIRIS; SACRIFICE; SOCRATES

## Bibliography

Brown, Raymond E. *The Death of the Messiah: From Gethsemane to the Grave: A Commentary on the Passion Narratives in the Four Gospels.* New York: Doubleday, 1994.

Bultmann, Rudolph. *Jesus and the Word.* London: Nicholson and Watson, 1935.

Dodd, Charles H. *The Parables of the Kingdom.* London: Nisbet and Co., 1935.

Fuller, Reginald H. *The Mission and Achievement of Jesus: An Examination of the Presuppositions of New Testament Theology.* London: SCM Press, 1954.

Kent, Jack A. *The Psychological Origins of the Resurrection Myth.* London: Open Gate Press, 1999.

Sanders, Edward P. *The Historical Figure of Jesus.* London: Penguin Books, 1993.

Schweitzer, Albert. *The Quest of the Historical Jesus,* edited by John Bowden. 1906. Reprint, Minneapolis: Fortress Press, 2001.

DOUGLAS J. DAVIES

# JONESTOWN

The People's Temple was a new religious movement started by Jim Jones with the intention of promoting racial equality, but instead ended with over 900 people dead from a mass suicide in Jonestown,

Guyana. Jones started the People's Temple in Indianapolis, Indiana. However, sensing that Indianapolis would never accept his message of racial equality, Jones moved his congregation to Ukiah, California in 1965 and then in the early 1970s to San Francisco. Finally, among growing accusations from former members and highly critical newspaper articles, Jones established in 1977 what he believed to be a utopian, socialistic community in Guyana called Jonestown (Kilduff and Javers, 1978).

Jones and the People's Temple were involved in a number of social welfare programs in both Indianapolis and California, such as "soup kitchens . . . legal aid services . . . [and] childcare centers" (Richardson 1980, p. 250). Additionally, journalists Marshall Kilduff and Ron Javers point out that they were active in politics, particularly in California. Temple members could be expected to write letters of support for a particular issue or to fill up a political rally when needed. Jones served in several appointed civil positions in both Indiana and California.

## Jonestown, Guyana

Congressman Leo Ryan was approached by a group called the Concerned Relatives, which consisted of former People's Temple members and the relatives of current members of People's Temple, about their concern for the people in Jonestown. Ryan agreed to make an official visit to Jonestown as a member of the House International Relations Committee. Ryan's attempt to visit Jonestown was met with resistance from Jones. Eventually Ryan, accompanied by both television and print journalists, arrived in Jonestown on November 17, 1978. The visit consisted of a tour of the commune, a meeting with Jones, and some entertainment (Kilduff and Javers 1978; Krause 1978).

Journalist Charles Krause reports that the next morning, Ryan was attacked by a man with a knife, although he was not hurt by the incident. Later that same day, Ryan and his party, which now included defectors from the People's Temple, were attacked by assassins at the Port Kaituma airstrip. Ryan and four others were killed and ten were injured.

As the killing at the airstrip occurred, Jones was leading his congregation through a mass suicide/homicide for which Temple members had been practicing since 1973. Sociologist Ken Levi and religious scholar Catherine Wessinger discuss how and

*Similar to other cult leaders, such as David Koresh of the Branch Davidians, Jim Jones, leader of the religious movement People's Temple, was seen by most of his followers as a father figure or, in some cases, the reincarnation of Jesus Christ.* ROGER RESSMEYER/CORBIS

why the suicide occurred. The suicide practices were called "White Nights" and consisted of members drinking a liquid that they believed was poisonous as a loyalty test to Jones. However, this day it was not a loyalty test: People lined up to drink the fruit-flavored punch laced with cyanide and tranquilizers or, for the very young, to have the poisonous concoction injected into their mouths. "Nine hundred and nine people died at Jonestown including 294 children under the age of 18" (Wessinger 2000, p. 31). Eighty-five members survived either because they hid, ran into the jungle, or were not in Jonestown that day. Jones himself "died of gunshot wounds" (Wessinger 2000, p. 31).

The question of how many people were murdered versus how many committed suicide is difficult to determine because only seven bodies were autopsied. Sociologist James Richardson (1980) notes that the decision to not autopsy more bodies was widely criticized in the press. Therefore, other than being certain that the very young children were murdered, it is impossible to determine how many people voluntarily took their own lives.

**Reasons for the Violence**

Several interrelated factors may have affected the Temple members' decision to stay in Jonestown and to commit mass suicide. First, Jones was a powerful and charismatic leader; he performed faith healings in which he pretended to cure people of cancer and claimed to be the "reincarnation of Jesus Christ" (Johnson 1979, p. 320). Also, Richardson explains that the authority structure in the People's Temple was highly centralized, so Jones had the ultimate authority there. As evidence that many people did see him as a charismatic leader, many of the followers called him "Father or Dad" (Wessinger 2000, p. 34).

Second, Jonestown was isolated—surrounded by thirty miles of jungle—so members were hesitant to leave. Jones made repeated threats that leaving would be difficult because of the lions, tigers, and human enemies in the jungle (Richardson 1980). The psychologist Robert Cialdini argues that isolation creates uncertainty, this uncertainty led Temple members to follow others. Therefore, when Jones was urging people to drink the cyanide-laced punch, Temple members may have looked around to see that others were lining up and compliantly got in line.

Third, coercive methods were used to control the people at Jonestown. The journalists Marshall Kilduff and Ron Javers noted in their book, *The Suicide Cult* (1978), that physical punishments were common at the People's Temple. For example, children may have been shocked using an "electrical cattle prod or heart defibrillator" (Kilduff and Javers 1978, p. 64). Jones frequently had Temple members sign documents in which the member falsely admitted to crimes. Jones would then threaten to use these admissions if the member ever left the cult. Jones built loyalty to him by weakening existing family ties. He would not allow sex between married couples, and children often lived apart from parents in a separate facility at the People's Temple commune.

Fourth, sociologist John Hall argues that Jones believed that he was being persecuted based upon negative news articles, lawsuits filed against him, and the belief that government agencies were conspiring against him. Moreover, Jones created an environment in which people feared persecution if they returned to or stayed in the United States. For the poor, urban African Americans who made up a majority of the group, he convinced them that if they did not come to Jonestown they would be put into concentration camps. For the whites, who often joined because of Jones's message of socialism, he led them to believe that they were being monitored by the Central Intelligence Agency.

Hall further suggests that the purpose of this persecution was to build loyalty to Jones. It may have made the idea of mass suicide more acceptable to many of the Temple members. Congressman Ryan's visit was probably already seen as threatening to many of the cult members. However, in the minutes before the mass suicide/murder, Jones repeatedly made reference to the fact that because his assassins had attacked the congressman that people would come back to destroy Jonestown; therefore, it was better to die in a revolutionary suicide (i.e., dying for a cause) than to have what they had built in Jonestown destroyed.

*See also:* CULT DEATHS; HEAVEN'S GATE; MASS KILLERS; WACO

### Bibliography

Cialdini, Robert B. "Social Proof: Truths Are Us." In *Influence*. Boston: Allyn & Bacon, 2001.

Hall, John R. "The Apocalypse at Jonestown." In Ken Levi ed., *Violence and Religious Commitment*. University Park: Pennsylvania State University Press, 1982.

Johnson, Doyle P. "Dilemmas of Charismatic Leadership: The Case of the People's Temple." *Sociological Analysis* 40 (1979):315–323.

Kilduff, Marshall, and Ron Javers. *The Suicide Cult.* New York: Bantam, 1978.

Krause, Charles A. *Guyana Massacre.* New York: Berkley, 1978.

Levi, Ken, ed. "Jonestown and Religious Commitment in the 1970s." *Violence and Religious Commitment*. University Park: Pennsylvania State University Press, 1982.

Richardson, James T. "People's Temple and Jonestown: A Corrective Comparison and Critique." *Journal for the Scientific Study of Religion* 19 (1980):239–255.

Wessinger, Catherine. *How the Millennium Comes Violently: From Jonestown to Heaven's Gate*. New York: Seven Bridges Press, 2000.

DENNIS D. STEWART<br>CHERYL B. STEWART

# JUDAISM

As a cultural and religious group with a historical connection to contemporary Jewish culture, Judaism, dates to the end of the first century of the C.E. The destruction of the temple in Jerusalem in 70 C.E. was the event that both enabled and forced rabbinic Judaism to take its position as the preeminent contender as the representative of Judaism. The founding text of rabbinic Judaism is actually the third-century Mishnah, not the Torah. The Mishnah is the first compilation or code of Jewish law, which was edited in the early third century. However, it includes material that dates back to the first century and underwent editing and revision several times throughout the second century as the rabbinic academies in Palestine grew.

Some scholars see a smooth and direct link between the religion articulated by Ezra or the Pharisees and the religion that was articulated by the rabbis after the destruction of the Temple in 70 C.E. Most scholars, however, understand rabbinic Judaism as having developed at the same time as early Christianity. A small minority of scholars thinks that rabbinic Judaism developed after early Christianity. The destruction of the Temple in Jerusalem in 70 caused such a break in the practice and consciousness of the Jews of Palestine and the Diaspora that it is all but impossible to directly connect pre-70 and post-70 Judaism. To be sure, the materials necessary for rabbinic Judaism to develop were present before the destruction of the Temple, but in a merely germinal form. Rabbinic Judaism is essentially a different religion than other pre-Temple Judaisms.

The Bible, which embodies a diversity of religious views, says very little about the afterlife. Impurity stemming from contact with the dead is a prominent feature of the Torah, as is capital punishment. The archaeological evidence seems to demonstrate that the Israelites in Biblical times were concerned with the afterlife. It is not until Daniel, written in third and second centuries B.C.E., that there is seemingly unambiguous reference to the afterlife and the end of days. By the time of Qumran literature—that is, texts discovered around the Dead Sea that date back to the first and second centuries B.C.E. and used by Jewish sectarians—there is a full-blown notion of an afterlife, which is both a reward for the righteous and a means for explaining the ultimate justice of God. Josephus, a Jewish commander in the war against Rome in the first century and who later defected to the Roman side during the war, points to an afterlife and the resurrection of the dead as sources of conflict between the Sadducees and the Pharisees. This description is supported by Matthew.

One of the ways of defining rabbinic Judaism and its descendants is by its textual tradition. Rabbinic Judaism claims the Torah as the cornerstone of the textual tradition. On the other hand, the canonization of Mishnah, the third-century compilation of rabbinic legal thought and ruling, meant the exclusion of much of post-Biblical literature. While Sirach is quoted in the sixth-century Babylonian Talmud, for example, it is not part of the Jewish canon, it is an extra-canonical book from the first century B.C.E. The Mishnah lays out its own apostolic genealogy in the beginning of the tractate, which is known as Chapters of the Fathers: "Moses received the Torah from Sinai and passed it on to Joshua, and Joshua to the Elders, and the Elders to the Prophets, and the Prophets to the Men of the Great Assembly" (Fathers 1:1).

The Men of the Great Assembly is the period that begins with the first exile in the sixth century C.E. and ends with the Pharisaic precursors of the rabbinic movement around the turn of the millennium. Rabbinic tradition numbers even legendary figures such as Mordecai (from the book of Esther) as one of the Men of the Great Assembly.

Mishnah purports to gather traditions from two centuries of rabbinic activity, laying out the boundaries of rabbinic Judaism. Within its sixty-three tractates, divided into six orders, there is legislation pertaining to all areas of life, from Sabbath law to torts to sacrificial law to proper beliefs. This material unfolded and developed at the same time that early Christianity was growing from a Palestinian movement of Jewish followers of Jesus to the official Christianity of the Roman Empire.

If people judge by the quantity of material, Mishnah's central concern with death relates to issues of impurity. One complete order of Mishnah deals with purity issues and determining the minimum dimensions of a part of a corpse that will generate impurity when touched. A majority of the twelve tractates in that order deal with the impurity emanating from the dead. A dead person was considered an ultimate source of impurity, an attitude that arises directly from Torah teachings. It was obviously a central issue in Temple times because no impure person, including priests who had become impure, were allowed into the Temple. The centrality of the concept of impurity in the community is evident in the fact that almost a century and a half after the destruction of the Temple, when impurity no longer had any major significance in daily life, there were still extensive laws on this topic.

One of the so-called lesser tractates, euphemistically titled "Times of Joy," deals with burial and mourning. Another (mourning) deals with dying and suicide. Burying the dead is one of the commandments that supersedes others, and if there is a dead body with no one to bury it, even the high priest (who under normal circumstances is forbidden contact with the dead) must bury the body.

The third area, death as a punishment for sins and crimes, is divided into two types of death: death at the hands of the court and death at the hands of God. Death is also the last step in atonement for certain types of sins. This does not, however, imply anything about the status of a person postmortem.

There is also a passing but interesting reference to the afterlife and resurrection of the dead. "All of Israel have a place in the World to Come. . . . These do not have a place in the World to Come: the one who says there is no resurrection of the dead." The afterlife is presented as a reward for the righteous but is not explored in much detail. Resurrection is presented in both the Gospels and Josephus as an ideological boundary dividing the Pharisees from other sects of Second Temple Judaism.

One type of death that occupied a significant amount of thought and energy among early Christians was martyrdom. There are two types of martyrdom. One is active martyrdom, in which the martyr willingly goes to his or her death to proclaim a belief in the one God (or in Jesus, for Christian martyrs). The second type of martyrdom is passive martyrdom, in which a believer is given the choice of abrogation of religious obligation or death. This latter, passive martyrdom was a part of rabbinic Judaism from its beginnings. When confronted with the choice of either having to abrogate one of the three core prohibitions (idolatry, murder, or illicit sexual unions) or be killed, the Rabbinic Jew must choose death. Scholars differ about the issue of active martyrdom. Some say that it became a desideratum for rabbinic Judaism hard on the heels of its widespread acceptance in Christianity. Others say that the debate was open until much later and might not have been settled even at the conclusion of the Babylonian Talmud in the seventh century.

These general categories were the boundaries for the discussion of death and dying throughout the rabbinic period and into the Middle Ages. The next layer of the rabbinic textual tradition consists of the Palestinian Talmud (edited in the fifth century) and the Babylonian Talmud (edited in the seventh century). The Talmuds engaged in more explicit discussions of what the world to come might look like and in more extended discussions of the punitive or expiatory efficacy of death. There is also more elaboration of the concept of martyrdom and the introduction of the "time of oppression," when martyrdom might be a more common obligation. On the whole, however, the bulk of the Talmudic discussions of death are concerned with issues of purity and impurity and capital punishment.

Death is seen as a normal part of the cycle of life, even as a necessary part of life. Death is not seen as punishment for original sin or punishment for sin in general; extraordinary death, however, is sometimes seen as punishment for sin. At times, this kind of death is the result of an inexplicable divine decree: "There are those who die without judgment." The dead are judged and rewarded or punished, although there are conflicting reports of what that reward or punishment is. It is also not clear whether the afterlife is corporeal or noncorporeal.

During the eleventh and twelfth centuries the crusades brought in their wake a renewed interest in martyrdom and even in the notion of suicide as an escape from transgression or forced conversion to Christianity. The biblical story of the binding of Isaac, wherein Abraham attempts to sacrifice his son, as told in Genesis 22, is often cited in justifications of the murder of one's spouse and/or children in the face of a Christian onslaught. Even the greatest of the medieval Talmudists attempted retroactively to find a way to justify these suicides and murders.

The notion that the soul's journey starts before life and continues after death is already found in the Talmud. Its most extensive treatment, however, ensued from the mystical speculations that started in the late rabbinic period and came to fruition with the production of the Zohar, the central text of the Jewish mystical tradition, in thirteenth-century in Spain, and with the advent of the Kabbalistic teaching in the sixteenth century in northern Israel. Whereas the Judaism of the Mishnah, Talmud, and Midrash collections was vague and reticent about the nature of posthumous existence, the mystics were very explicit, discussing the source of souls in the upper realms, the resurrection of the dead to a corporeal existence at the end of time, and the transmigration or reincarnation of souls. The afterlife of the soul is part of a mystical theodicy in which God's justice is worked out over many lifetimes.

At the same time that the mystics were contemplating the journey of the soul and martyrs were lauded in France and Germany, Maimonides, the greatest Jewish philosopher and jurist, was codifying a much different approach to both martyrdom and the afterlife. In Maimonides' formulation, the only acceptable martyrdom was passive martyrdom. While one is obligated to accept death rather than transgression in certain cases, one who falters and transgresses under duress is not culpable. Further, Maimonides' conception of the afterlife is unclear and was contested even during his lifetime. There is support for an Aristotelian reading in which the soul or intellect cleaves to God (the active intellect) and in this way continues its existence after the death of the material body. When challenged on his belief in the afterlife and resurrection, however, Maimonides affirmed a belief in a corporeal resurrection.

The centrality of the communal obligation to the dead, which includes preparation of the body

for burial (taharah) and the burial itself, was already evident in the rabbinic period. According to this law, after passing a certain period of residency, all citizens of a town must contribute toward the burial expenses of the town's destitute. In the early modern period this tradition gained greater visibility and authority. The so-called holy society (chevra kadisha), the communal body that is mandated to perform the death and burial rites, became a source of communal responsibility even for matters outside of its immediate purview (i.e., charitable pursuits). The society was supported by a communal tax and had a charter and a complicated acceptance procedure that included periods of probation and study. An actual membership organization called the chevra kadisha seems to be an innovation of the early modern period. There are still holy societies that perform the death and burial rites. These include guarding the dead body until it can be brought to the mortuary or cemetery, ritually cleansing the body, clothing the body in special death garments, and bringing the body to burial.

In the modern and contemporary periods the existence of an afterlife and the resurrection and reincarnation of the dead have become points of contention between the different movements within Judaism. On the whole, Reform Judaism does not believe in an afterlife, resurrection, or reincarnation. Orthodox Judaism believes in all three, though there are some factions of Orthodoxy that do not believe in reincarnation. There are varying opinions in Conservative and Reform Judaism that span the gamut.

*See also:* BUDDHISM; CHINESE BELIEFS; CHRISTIAN DEATH RITES, HISTORY OF; HINDUISM; JESUS; KADDISH

### Bibliography

Avery-Peck, Alan J., and Jacob Neusner, eds. *Judaism in Late Antiquity*. Pt. IV: Death, *Life-After-Death, Resurrection and the World to Come in the Judaisms of Antiquity*. Leiden, Netherlands: Brill, 2000.

Baumgarten, Albert I., Jan Assmann, and Gedaliahu G. Stroumsa, eds. *Self, Soul, and Body in Religious Experience*. Leiden, Netherlands: Brill, 1998.

Boyarin, Daniel. *Dying for God: Martyrdom and the Making of Christianity and Judaism*. Stanford, CA: Stanford University Press, 1999.

Cohen Aryeh. " 'Do the Dead Know?' The Representation of Death in the Bavli." *AJS Review* 24 (1999):145–171.

Collins John J., and Michael Fishbane, eds. *Death, Ecstasy, and Other Worldly Journeys*. Albany: State University of New York Press, 1995.

Giller, Pinhas. *Reading the Zohar: The Sacred Text of the Kabbalah*. Oxford: Oxford University Press, 2001.

Goldberg, Sylvie Anne. *Crossing the Jabbok: Illness and Death in Ashkenazi Judaism in Sixteenth- through Nineteenth-Century Prague,* translated by Carol Cosman. Berkeley: University of California Press, 1996.

Scholem, Gershom. *Major Trends in Jewish Mysticism*. New York: Schocken Books, 1961.

Urbach, Ephraim E. *The Sages, Their Concepts and Beliefs and Practices,* translated by Israel Abrahams. Jerusalem: Magnes Press, 1975.

ARYEH COHEN

# KADDISH

Kaddish ("holiness") is an ancient Jewish prayer praising and glorifying God, recited at fixed points of the public prayer of the synagogue, at funeral services, and by mourners of a deceased parent or close relatives.

Kaddish was not composed at one specific time and in its formative stage did not have a fixed text. The earliest form of Kaddish may be traced to the period of the Tanaim, after the destruction of the second temple (70 C.E.), when the initial section, *yehe shemeh rabbah mevarakh le'olam ule-almei almaya* ("may His great name be blessed forever and for all eternity"), was recited after public discourses on Sabbaths and Festivals. This refrain is a paraphrase of the Temple formula *barukh shem kevod malkhuto leolam va'ed* ("Blessed be the name of His glorious kingdom for ever and ever"), which was recited by the congregation upon hearing the High Priest utter God's name (Mishnah Yoma 3:8). The prayer during that time did not assume the name "kaddish" but was known by its opening words, *Yehe shemeh rabbah* ("may His great name").

The Kaddish text, *Yitgadal Ve-yitkadash,* ("Glorified and hallowed") was formulated and assumed the name "Kaddish" during the period of the post-Talmudic Rabbis—the Saboraim (c. 700 C.E.). The earliest literary reference connecting Kaddish with mourners is in the post-Talmudic tractate *Sofrim* (eighth century). This treatise includes a description of how on the Sabbath the cantor (a synagogue official) bestowed special honor and mercy to the mourners by approaching them outside the synagogue and reciting in their presence the final Kaddish of the *Musaf* ("additional") service (Sofrim 19:9).

During the First Crusade (especially in the aftermath of the Franco-German expulsions of the 1090s), Kaddish became a liturgical obligation to be recited by mourners and appended to the conclusion of daily prayer. At first it was recited only by minors (and was called *Kaddish Yatom,* ("the orphans' Kaddish") who, according to Jewish law, are not permitted to lead congregational prayers. Gradually Jewish communities adopted Kaddish as a prayer for all adult mourners during the first year of mourning. At a later stage, Kaddish was instituted as a mourner's prayer for the *Yahrzeit*—the anniversary of a parent's death (attributed to Rabbi Jacob Molin (1360–1427)).

The significance of Kaddish is honoring the soul of the deceased by the mourner, who sanctifies God's name in public through the opening lines, *Yitgadal Ve-Yitkadash Shemeh Rabbah, Be'almah dievrah chire'usei* ("Hallowed be the name of God in the world that he has created according to his will"). By reciting Kaddish, one justifies divine judgment following the Rabbinic maxim, "Bless God for the harsh as well as for the merciful" (Berakhot 9:5).

Late Midrashic legends emphasize the redeeming powers associated with Kaddish. A recurring motif in these tales refers to an orphan having saved a deceased parent from the torments of Hell by reciting Kaddish in his memory; this happens even though no word in Kaddish refers to the dead. As a mourner's prayer, Kaddish's praise of God in the hour of bereavment and mourning is a sublime expression of faith. Its prayer for the revelation of God's kingdom diverts the individual from personal grief to the hope of all humanity.

With the exception of the final Hebrew clause, *oseh shalom bimromav* ("He who makes peace in the heavens"), Kaddish is in Aramaic, the vernacular spoken particularly by the common people at the time of its crystallization into a formal prayer.

*See also:* AFTERLIFE IN CROSS-CULTURAL PERSPECTIVE; JUDAISM

### Bibliography

Elbogen, Ismar. *Jewish Liturgy: A Comprehensive History.* Philadelphia: The Jewish Publication Society, 1993.

Higger, Michael. *Masechet Sofrim.* New York, 1937.

Pool, David de Sola. *The Old Jewish Aramaic Prayer, the Kaddish.* Leipzig, Germany: Druglin, 1909.

Telsner, David. *The Kaddish, Its History, and Significance.* Jerusalem: Tal Orot Institute, 1995.

SHMUEL GLICK

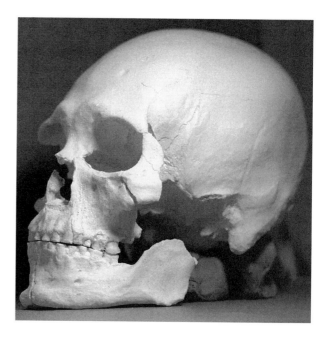

*This plastic cast is of the 9,500 year-old skull found to be distinct from that of American Indians. Scientists believe that the man was long-limbed, middle-aged, approximately 5 feet 8 inches tall and weighed around 160 pounds.* AP/WIDE WORLD PHOTOS

# KENNEWICK MAN

The dead have power to create controversy in the world of the living. One example involves a 9,500 year-old skeleton, one of the best-preserved early human fossils found in North America, whose discovery triggered a bitter debate over who owns America's past.

Found accidentally in the Columbia River of eastern Washington in July 1996, was a nearly complete skeleton that showed traces of a hard life: a fractured elbow, broken ribs, a possible head injury, and a spear wound in the pelvis. The cause of his death is uncertain, as is the issue of whether he was interred or naturally buried. The man's skull, facial characteristics, and teeth are distinct from those of all modern peoples, including American Indians, but most similar to Polynesians and the Japanese Ainu. These differences, which are also seen in other American skeletons older than 9,000 years, raise the possibility that more than one wave of early immigrants peopled America, and that American Indians were not the western hemisphere's first inhabitants.

The skeleton quickly became the center of a political battle pitting conservative Indian tribes and the Native American Identity Movement against the interests of science and the human community at large. Upon announcement of the discovery, leaders of five Pacific Northwest Indian tribes claimed the bones under the Native American Graves Protection and Repatriation Act of 1990 (NAGPRA). The U.S. government, which owned the skeletal remains, agreed to turn them over to the tribes, rebuffing a request by scientists for the opportunity to study this rare find. Eight prominent anthropologists sued to stop reburial, bringing the first test case of the NAGPRA. The case ignited a conflict between religion, the political position of Native American activists, and the public's right to scientific knowledge about the ancient history of its homeland.

On the religious front, the tribes believe that ancestors' remains must be returned to the earth lest their spirits be offended and wreak havoc among the living. Because the tribes' present-day religion holds that they were created near where the skeleton was found, they insist that Kennewick Man must be their ancestor. To deny their religious claims, they say, is to disrespect and weaken their culture.

However, the religious claim is the less important one from the perspective of the Native American Identity Movement, which has as its goal the assertion of tribal rights to land and resources. In the 1970s this movement selected American Indian skeletons kept in museums as an issue of debate, maintaining that placing their skeletons in museum displays compromised their human rights. Kennewick Man and the few other early skeletons are particularly important because they suggest the chilling possibility that Indian people were not the first to occupy the Americas. If the U.S. government acquiesces to the tribes' claim to these most ancient remains, however, it affirms the movement's claim that Indian people were the first occupants of the American continent and supports the tribes' original right to land and resources. The movement is concerned that proof of an earlier people preceding them will weaken its claims.

For the scientific community, the skeleton is a story about the life and death of an ancient American and a window into the history of the human species. Are the most ancient human fossils and artifacts the property of a few or should they be considered the heritage of all peoples? The answer, scientists feel, has global implications for their quest to understand the history of the human species.

*See also:* GRIEF AND MOURNING IN CROSS-CULTURAL PERSPECTIVE; HUMAN REMAINS

### Bibliography

Chatters, James C. *Ancient Encounters: Kennewick Man and the First Americans.* New York: Simon & Schuster, 2001.

Chatters, James C. "The Recovery and First Analysis of an Early Holocene Human Skeleton from Kennewick Washington." *American Antiquity* 65, no. 2 (2000):291–316.

Thomas, David H. *Skull Wars.* New York: Basic Books, 2000.

Preston, Douglas. "The Lost Man." *The New Yorker,* 19 June 1997, 70–81.

JAMES C. CHATTERS

# KEVORKIAN, JACK

The pathologist Jack Kevorkian became the central figure in the physician-assisted death controversy in the United States, a controversy that has had ripple effects throughout the world. Born in 1928, Kevorkian was the son of refugees who escaped the Turkish massacre of Armenians in 1915. Many of the members of his mother's family and all of the members of his father's family were among the victims. The Kevorkians settled in Pontiac, Michigan, where his father worked in an automobile factory and his mother looked after Jack and his sisters Margo and Flora, who would assist him throughout the activism career he launched in his later adult years.

"Intelligent," "resourceful," and "independent" are adjectives often applied to the young Kevorkian by those who knew him. He went his own way and questioned authority long before it became commonplace to do so. An honor student in high school, Kevorkian obtained his medical degree from the University of Michigan in 1952.

### Early Career

The specialty with the most appeal to him was pathology, the study of diseases and their effects. He soon devoted himself to studying the physical changes wrought by death. As early as his residency at Detroit Receiving Hospital in 1956, colleagues gave him the nickname "Doctor Death." Kevorkian was especially curious about the status of the eye at death, and arranged to be notified when a patient was on the verge of death. After death, the cornea becomes hazy and the retina segmented and pale as blood circulation ceases. Kevorkian recommended that his fellow physicians examine the eyes whenever there is a need to look for signs of life. His findings were published in medical science literature.

Dying and death were neglected topics of research and education in medicine when the young physician was conducting his studies. He was therefore almost as much an outsider as an insider.

*Jack Kevorkian sits with his "suicide machine," a device consisting of tubes, hypodermic needles, saline solution, a muscle relaxant, and a lethal drug.* AP/WIDE WORLD PHOTOS

Difficulties in working against the mainstream were also being experienced by other pioneers in their various clinical and academic environments. Kevorkian showed little or no interest in these parallel developments. Years later he still held himself apart from the hospice/palliative care movement, death education and counseling, peer support groups, and the rapidly expanding base of research knowledge. Kevorkian therefore made himself vulnerable to criticism that he had failed to inform himself of significant developments in pain control, social support, and other areas in the field of death and dying.

Meanwhile, he considered marriage but broke off his engagement because he judged that his fiancée did not possess "sufficient self-discipline" (Betzold 1996, p.38). Many years later he expressed regrets for missing out on the satisfactions of family life, but the absence of these obligations and distractions offered more opportunity for his other pursuits. In addition to his primary agenda, Kevorkian learned to play several musical instruments, and created some intense, death-haunted oil paintings.

## The Activist

Kevorkian had an activist agenda in mind long before he became a public figure. He proposed that the bodies of executed criminals be used for scientific experiments. The convicts would be anesthetized in order to keep their bodies somewhat alive and therefore available for experiments that could not be conducted on people who were entirely alive. He also transfused blood to living patients from the corpses of people who had experienced a sudden death. Both the death-row proposal and the cadaver donor procedure were ill-received by the medical establishment. Kevorkian's views made him increasingly unpopular and therefore limited his employment opportunities. As his mainstream medical career faded, however, Kevorkian had more time available to advance his mission.

Kevorkian set forth his agenda in his book *Prescription: Medicide* (1991). He took the position that the Hippocratic oath is not and never has been binding on physicians. Kevorkian contended that a new medical specialty, "obitiariry," should be established to offer "moribund people" a dignified and easy death and to provide the opportunity for experimental research on their remains. This specialty would be practiced at centers for medically assisted suicide and research, which were to be known as "obituaria." Kevorkian thought that medically assisted suicide—or what he termed "medicide"—should be made available to all people who wish to end their suffering, whether or not they are terminally ill.

## Kevorkian's Crusade

The first step in applying his program was his construction of a "suicide machine" that he called first the Thanatron, then the Mercitron. The physician prepares the machine, but it is the patient who presses a button to release a deadly drug. A middle-aged woman by the name of Janet Adkins was the first person to make use of Kevorkian's invention on June 4, 1990. Kevorkian was charged with murder but was then released when the court ruled that Michigan had no law against assisted suicide. His license to practice medicine in Michigan was suspended, however, and later authorities in California did likewise.

During the 1990s Kevorkian was "present" at the deaths of at least 120 people. His participation in these deaths was labeled as "murder" or "homicide" by Michigan authorities who, nevertheless, failed in repeated attempts to convict him. He was charged repeatedly with assisted suicide as well as murder, each time defying and defeating the courts with the help of a high-profile attorney. Kevorkian argued that he had not and would not kill anybody—the patients had made the last move on their own volition.

It was Kevorkian who put himself into a position in which a guilty verdict was almost inescapable. He invited CBS's *60 Minutes* program to show a videotape he had made of his participation in the death of Thomas Youk. The result was conviction for second-degree murder and delivery of a controlled substance. He received a sentence of ten to twenty-five years in prison, which he began serving in 1999. Despite Kevorkian's conviction and jailing, the assisted suicide controversy stimulated by his beliefs and actions continues to influence health care, legislation, and the field of bioethics.

*See also:* BIOETHICS; EUTHANASIA; HIPPOCRATIC OATH; SUICIDE TYPES: PHYSICIAN-ASSISTED SUICIDE

*Bibliography*

Betzold, Michael. *Appointment with Doctor Death*. Troy, MI: Momentum Books, 1996.

Kaplan, Kalman J., ed. *Right to Die versus Sacredness of Life*. Amityville, NY: Baywood, 2000.

Kastenbaum, Robert. "Looking Death in the Eye: Another Challenge from Doctor Kevorkian." In Kalman J. Kaplan ed., *Right to Die versus Sacredness of Life*. Amityville, NY: Baywood, 2000.

Kevorkian, Jack. *Prescription: Medicide*. Buffalo, NY: Prometheus, 1991.

ROBERT KASTENBAUM

# KIERKEGAARD, SØREN

Søren Kierkegaard was born on May 5, 1813, in Copenhagen, Denmark, and died there on November 4, 1855. Kierkegaard is recognized to have, in the nineteenth-century, reawakened philosophy to its basic mystery, that the human being exists in the anticipation of death, and that the subjectivity of death anxiety is the source of consciousness and spirituality.

Kierkegaard grew up with the tyranny of his father's severe and gloomy religious obsessions. His mother and five siblings died in quick succession. The meaning his father gave to his misfortune and grief was that because he had once cursed God, and God was cursing him back. Learning of his beloved father's curse was a "great earthquake" in Kierkegaard's life. He described his horror and dread as "the stillness of death spreading over me" (Kierkegaard 1958, p. 39).

Kierkegaard proposed marriage to Regina Olsen, whom he deeply loved, but broke off the relationship, a confounding event that was extremely significant to the rest of his life. His writing was greatly influenced by mourning this sacrifice. During the two years following the end of his betrothal in 1841, he wrote *Either/Or, Three Edifying Discourses, Fear and Trembling,* and *Repetition*. Kierkegaard's writings are full of references and innuendoes that indicate how he had internalized this relationship and the breakup as a narrative imbued with powerful affect that is an integral part of his philosophical thinking. He also internalized his relationship with his father this way. While his journals and some other writings suggest subjective meanings of his life, he said that after his death no one would find in them a clue to his truth. His inwardness was an engagement with himself or with God, both disclosed and hidden in his writings. His public life was marked by a series of scandals, including being savagely mocked in a popular magazine, his broken engagement, and his death bed refusal of either the sacrament or a visit from his brother. The Danish public ridiculed and scorned him.

In his works, Kierkegaard emerges hidden in pseudonyms, irony, paradox, parody, and satire. The scholar Sylviane Agacinski recognized him to be thoroughly ironic. Louis Mackey observed that "his texts exhibit an almost perfect recalcitrance to interpretation" (1986, p. xxiii), and advanced an understanding that Kierkegaard is a philosophical poet. Others have also noted that Kierkegaard's autobiography and public "lived presence" are part of his indirect communication. Kierkegaard is a master of indirect language. His extremely ironic language and his psycho-philosophico-religious thinking provided the groundwork for post-Hegelian and postmodern philosophy. Kierkegaard's writing continues to sharpen the blade of the cutting edge of philosophy; and the meaning of his writing and his existence is as unsettled as his writing is startling, provocative, and unsettling. His writing calls into question rather than answer questions. He raises the question of death by calling into question our very existence, which is a radically new question in the history of philosophy; a question that has had a profound impact on Western thinking.

The story of his life, on the one hand, and his philosophical, theological, and psychological writings, on the other, are complexly braided expressions of his particular "existence." The philosopher appears in the text, but in an ironic and masked way. Subjectivity is realized in anxiety, in dread, and in fear and trembling, which are presentations of death and of God and of nothing. Kierkegaard introduced Western thinking to a new meaning of the term *existence* as a psychological-philosophical-religious term for unique, passionate, temporal subjectivity, deeply associated with dread and anxiety. His writings on existence gave birth to existential philosophy, theology, and psychology. For example, the German psychiatrist and philosopher Karl

*Danish philosopher Søren Kierkegaard (1813–1855) suffered many hardships that made him question the meanings of life and death, such as the death of his mother and five siblings.* BETTMANN/CORBIS

Jaspers's psychology is inspired by him; Martin Heidegger's and Jean-Paul Sartre's philosophies borrow basic concepts from him; Dietrich Bonhoeffer's theology is deeply indebted to him.

Kierkegaard's work explains man's spiritual flight from mortality and inwardness. He introduces into modernity an awareness of death anxiety as the existential touchstone of religious experience and of philosophical thinking. In *Concluding Unscientific Postscripts* (1846), the unique, subjective individual exists only in the certainty of his death. Death is the temporal being of existence. Through a "silent understanding of anxiety," which is a philosophical and religious reflection on the subjective certainty of death, Kierkegaard introduces a way of philosophizing that has inspired existentialism and postmodern philosophy. The most astonishing and concealed subjective truth of existence, death, with its infinite responsibility, presents itself in fear and trembling before God's call.

Kierkegaard has greatly influenced the emergence of death as a central question of philosophy, theology, and psychology.

Kierkegaard's use of the term *faith* often pokes fun at and aims at shattering varieties of shallow faith, objectivity, and universality. As a Christian, he vigorously attacks Christian religion that lacks existential faith. Faith is also the paradox he employs against Hegel's philosophical system; that is, the paradox that the individual is higher than the universal.

In *Fear and Trembling,* the paradox is that in taking the leap of faith one regains what has been infinitely resigned as lost. Who so makes the leap of faith is a hero, "knight of faith." Faith is an absolute obedience to God; that is, a "leap of faith" in which obedience to God overrules human love and ethical norms. The irony of the knight of infinite resignation, as the pseudonymous author Johannes de Silentio (Søren Kierkegaard), or John the Silent, does not lead to the resolution of mortality anxiety, which is achieved by the book's hero, the knight of faith. *Fear and Trembling* centers on an infinitely paradoxical analysis of Abraham, knight of faith, called by God to sacrifice his son. A fool shouts out what de Silentio keeps silent about: "O Abominable man, offscouring of society, what devil possessed thee to want to murder thy son?" The paradox of this pathos is in the terrifying absurdity of Abrahamic faith in God. De Silentio lays out the complex argument of *Fear and Trembling,* yet, as the reader tries to chase down his paradoxes, de Silentio is, in the manner of his name, infinitely resigned to silence.

Kierkegaard is a most extraordinary maker of existential puzzles. The knight of infinite resignation, existentially certain of his death and the loss of the other, no longer believing he will get back what is lost, becomes ironic: He who has not the faith that God gives back what he takes is the knight infinitely resigned. Yet, de Silentio's ironic language gives back and takes away at the same time.

*See also:* ANXIETY AND FEAR; RAHNER, KARL; TERROR MANAGEMENT THEORY

### Bibliography

Agacinski, Sylviane. *Aparté: Conceptions and Deaths of Søren Kierkegaard.* Tallahassee: Florida State University, 1988.

Kierkegaard, Søren. *Papers and Journals: A Selection,* translated by Alistair Hanney. Harmondsworth: Penguin Press, 1996.

Kierkegaard, Søren. *Concluding Unscientific Postscript,* translated by Howard V. Hong and Edna H. Hong. Princeton, NJ: Princeton University Press, 1992.

Kierkegaard, Søren. *The Concept of Irony, with Constant Reference to Socrates,* translated by Howard V. Hong and Edna H. Hong. Princeton, NJ: Princeton University Press, 1989.

Kierkegaard, Søren. *Sickness unto Death,* translated by Alistair Hanney. Harmondsworth: Penguin Press, 1989.

Kierkegaard, Søren. *Either/Or,* translated by Howard V. Hong and Edna H. Hong. 2 vols. Princeton, NJ: Princeton University Press, 1987.

Kierkegaard, Søren. *Fear and Trembling,* translated by Alistair Hanney. Harmondsworth: Penguin Press, 1985.

Kierkegaard, Søren. *The Point of View for My Work As an Author,* translated by Walter Lowrie. New York: Harper and Row, 1962.

Kierkegaard, Søren. *Edifying Discourses,* translated by David F. Swensen and Lillian Marvin Swenson. New York: Oxford University Press, 1958.

Kierkegaard, Søren. *The Journals of Kierkegaard,* translated by Alexander Dru. New York: Harper and Brothers, 1958.

Kierkegaard, Søren. *The Concept of Dread,* translated by Walter Lowrie. Princeton, NJ: Princeton University Press, 1957.

Kierkegaard, Søren. *Repetition, An Essay in Experimental Psychology,* translated by Walter Lowrie. New York: Harper and Row, 1941.

Lowrie, Walter. *A Short Life of Kierkegaard.* Princeton, NJ: Princeton University Press, 1942.

Mackey, Louis. *Points of View: Readings of Kierkegaard.* Tallahassee: Florida State University, 1986.

Ree, Johnathan, and Jane Chamberlain. *Kierkegaard: A Critical Reader.* Oxford: Blackwell Publishers, 1998.

JEFFREY KAUFFMAN

# KRONOS

Kronos figures in Greek mythology both as an ogre and as the king whose reign was the Golden Age. The Romans equated him with Saturn. He was sometimes also mistakenly identified with Chronos, the god of time.

According to the Greek poet Hesiod, in his *Theogony* (c. 750 B.C.E.), Ouranos ("Sky") mated nightly with Gaia ("Earth"). When their children were born, Ouranos hid them in Gaia's inward places. Painfully swollen with offspring, she wrought a huge sickle and asked her children, six brothers and six sisters (the Titans), to punish Ouranos. Only her youngest son, Kronos, agreed. Giving him the sickle, she told him where to hide. When Ouranos next lay on Gaia, Kronos grasped him with his left hand, the sickle in his right, and cut off his genitals. From the drops of blood that shed on her, Gaia conceived among others the Giants, and from the severed genitals, which fell into the sea, a white foam arose from which was born the love goddess Aphrodite.

Now followed the rule of Kronos. He married his sister Rhea, who bore him three daughters and three sons: Hestia, Demeter, Hera, Hades, Poseidon, and Zeus (the Olympian gods). But Gaia and Ouranos had foretold that Kronos would be overthrown by a son, so he swallowed his children as each emerged from the womb. About to bear her sixth child, Zeus, Rhea asked her parents how to save him. They sent her to Crete, where she hid him in a cave on Mount Aegaeon. She presented Kronos instead with a stone wrapped in swaddling clothes, which he thrust in his belly. Zeus grew apace and in time forced Kronos to yield up his children. Once reborn, the gods waged war on the Titans, whom they overthrew, and Zeus replaced Kronos as ruler.

The story contains motifs recurrent in European folktales: the son destined to replace his father; the luck of the youngest son; and the monster made to swallow a stone. More importantly, Kronos and the Titans seem related to the archaic "older gods" of Near Eastern tradition, barely personified forces of nature deemed to rule the cosmos before fully anthropomorphic gods took control. In the Babylonian creation epic *Enuma Elish* (composed between 1200 and 1000 B.C.E.), there is war between these older gods and their children, as there is between the Titans and Olympians. The myth of Kronos itself corresponds closely to one from the mid–second millennium B.C.E. preserved in Hittite, which tells how Kumarbi deposed the sky god Anu by biting off his phallus.

Though expressed in terms of father-son rivalry, the Kronos myth is not primarily concerned with the human condition. The stories of Ouranos and Kronos, and Kronos and Zeus, form a single cosmogonical myth or story explaining the universe. It accounts for the separation of the earth and sky, envisaged as originally joined. Once they were separated, primeval creation ended and the gods were born.

Some of the details are vague, partly because Ouranos and Gaia are not fully personified. Where exactly is Kronos when he castrates Ouranos? How does Zeus liberate Kronos's children? (Writers after Hesiod said that he gave him nectar mixed with emetic herbs to make him vomit.) The myth places Kronos literally between Ouranos (sky, rain) and Gaia (fertile earth), and arms him with the sickle, the reaping tool. In cult, he was connected with agrarianism and honored in the kronisa, a harvest festival, during which masters and laborers feasted together—an echo, it was thought, of the mythical Golden Age.

The Golden Age, before Zeus became ruler of the gods and imposed both justice and labor on humankind, was a time of plenty without toil, when people did not suffer old age, and died gently as if falling asleep. This was the reign of Kronos. How the Golden Age ended is unclear; possibly through Kronos's overthrow by Zeus. An adaptation of this myth spoke of a land called Elysium or the Isles of the Blest. In *Works and Days,* Hesiod says this was at the ends of the earth, and was where divinely favored Greek heroes existed in bliss after their deaths. This happy realm, too, was ruled by Kronos.

The myths gathered around the shadowy figure of Kronos speak of the emergence of the ordered cosmos from primeval chaos but they look back with longing to that interregnum between the unbridled energy of creation (Ouranos) and the rule of order (Zeus), that Golden Age of the world when Kronos was king.

*See also:* GODS AND GODDESSES OF LIFE AND DEATH; GREEK TRAGEDY

### Bibliography

Grant, Michael. *Myths of the Greeks and Romans.* London: Weidenfeld and Nicolson, 1962.

Kerényi, C. *The Gods of the Greeks.* London: Thames and Hudson, 1979.

---

Kirk, G. S. *The Nature of Greek Myths.* Harmondsworth: Penguin, 1974.

JENNIFER WESTWOOD

# KÜBLER-ROSS, ELISABETH

*An unexpected request to give her first lecture to medical students led psychiatrist Elisabeth Kübler-Ross (1926–) to focus on dying patients to whom she had gravitated because others so often shunned them.* AP/WIDE WORLD PHOTOS

Elisabeth Kübler was born on July 8, 1926, the first of three daughters born that day to a middle class family in Zurich, Switzerland. In her autobiography *The Wheel of Life: A Memoir of Living and Dying* (1997), Kübler-Ross commented: "For me, being a triplet was a nightmare. I would not wish it on my worst enemy. I had no identity apart from my sisters. . . . It was a heavy psychological weight to carry around." However, as an adult she concluded that the circumstances of her birth "were what gave me the grit, determination and stamina for all the work that lay ahead" and throughout her autobiography she describes herself as independent, unconventional, opinionated, and stubborn (Kübler-Ross 1997, p. 25).

"The first big decision I made solely by myself" involved defying her strong-willed father (who planned a secretarial career for her) in favor of her dream to become a doctor (p. 21). At school, Kübler-Ross was an excellent student, especially in math and languages, but not in religious studies. As her church, she preferred nature, pets, and animals of all kinds. One key childhood experience was a hospitalization in which an impersonal and uncaring environment isolated and separated her from her family. She often describes later encounters with conventional medical care in a similar way.

In the spring of 1942, the triplets completed their public schooling. Unwilling to become a secretary, Kübler-Ross took jobs as a maid and laboratory assistant. At the end of World War II, she volunteered to work in several areas of war-torn Europe. In Poland, necessity compelled her to practice rudimentary medicine and she was deeply moved by the concentration camp at Maidanek where more than 300,000 people had died.

Back in Switzerland, Kübler-Ross resumed working as a lab assistant and studying for the medical school entrance examination, which she passed in September 1951 with the intention of becoming a country doctor. In 1957 she passed her medical board examinations and became a physician. In February 1958 she married a fellow medical student from America, Emanuel ("Manny") Ross, and the couple moved to the United States. Becoming pregnant disqualified Kübler-Ross from a residency in pediatrics so she settled for one in psychiatry. There were problems of adapting to a new culture and eventually four miscarriages; as she later wrote, "You may not get what you want, but God always gives you what you need" (p. 111). A son, Kenneth, and a daughter, Barbara, were born in the early 1960s.

A new position brought Kübler-Ross to Billings Hospital of the University of Chicago. There, in 1965, four students from Chicago's Theological Seminary approached her to seek assistance in understanding death as the ultimate crisis in life. She offered to help and search out dying patients for interviews. Many physicians at the hospital were critical of Kübler-Ross for what they viewed as "exploiting" vulnerable patients, and the story of her difficulties in locating suitable interviewees is well known. Nevertheless, by early 1967 Kübler-Ross was leading an unorthodox but popular weekly seminar in which she would interview a patient behind one-way glass with a subsequent discussion with students and medical professionals after the patient had left.

An offer of a book contract from a publisher led to the international best-seller *On Death and*

*Dying* (1969). This book developed Kübler-Ross's now well-known theory of five stages in dying: denial, anger, bargaining, depression, and acceptance. As a result of this book, together in an interview with a twenty-one-year-old patient published in *Life* magazine on November 21, 1969, Kübler-Ross received numerous requests for interviews and lectures. Still, her hospital was not pleased with her success and she transferred to LaRabida Children's Hospital to work with ill and dying children. Finally, at the age of forty-six, she quit that post to do research on what death is like and to conduct weeklong workshops on life, death, and the transition to afterlife.

Kübler-Ross's research had convinced her that there was an afterlife. She was intrigued by stories of near-death experiences and experienced her first apparition about this time. As a result, she concluded that death does not exist in its traditional definition; rather it occurs in four distinct phases: (1) floating out of one's body like a butterfly leaving its cocoon, assuming an ethereal shape, experiencing a wholeness, and knowing what is going on around oneself; (2) taking on a state of spirit and energy, not being alone, and meeting a guardian angel or guide; (3) entering a tunnel or transitional gate and feeling a light radiating intense warmth, energy, spirit, and overwhelming love; and (4) being in the presence of the Highest Source and undergoing a life review.

At about this time, Kübler-Ross became convinced of the reality of her own spiritual guides and she eventually moved to California in early 1976 to pursue these inquiries. There, she founded a healing center (eventually called Shanti Nilaya, a Sanskrit phrase that she understood to mean "the final home of peace") where she could have a base for her workshops, explore out-of-body experiences, and develop a new lecture entitled "Death and Life after Death." Unfortunately, Kübler-Ross eventually lost confidence in some of her California colleagues and the center's property was sold.

In July 1983 Kübler-Ross purchased and later moved to a 300-acre farm in Head Waters, Virginia. There she built her house and a healing center for workshops. Around this time, the situation of persons with AIDS (acquired immunodeficiency syndrome) attracted her attention. However, when in 1985 she announced her intention to adopt AIDS-infected babies, she became, in her words, "the most despised person in the whole Shenandoah Valley" and could not get the necessary zoning approvals to carry out that plan. On October 6, 1994, her house was set on fire and burned to the ground with the complete loss of all her papers and possessions.

In the meantime, she experienced heart fibrillations and an eventual stroke. Again, Kübler-Ross had a low opinion of the medical treatment she received. She refused to give up smoking, coffee, and chocolate, and checked herself out of the hospital. After moving to Scottsdale, Arizona, Kübler-Ross experienced a massive stroke on May 14, 1995, that left her paralyzed on her left side and no longer able to live alone. While writing in January 1997, Kübler-Ross said she was enduring a "miserable" life resulting from pain and the limitations of her paralysis. Although she was "anxious to graduate" she remained opposed to efforts to foreshorten life (p. 280). Instead, she asserted that "our only purpose in life is growth" and that her task in these circumstances was to learn patience even as she was totally dependent on others for care (p. 281).

*On Death and Dying* and other books by Kübler-Ross have earned her a worldwide reputation. In addition, large numbers of people have been attracted to her many lectures, presentations, and workshops. Many have credited her with helping to draw attention to problems encountered by dying persons and to their needs as living human beings, thus tending to normalize and humanize such experiences. In all of this, she was an early and important contributor to the death awareness movement. The stage theory of dying that she proposed is simple and easy to learn. Its author and many others have since applied this theory to a wide variety of losses, even while some professionals have criticized its limitations. Her views about the afterlife, spiritual guides, out-of-body experiences, and near-death experiences have been consoling to some, but sharply criticized by others from both scientific and theological perspectives.

*See also:* Dying, Process of; Near-Death Experiences; Stage Theory

## Bibliography

Gill, Derek. *Quest: The Life of Elisabeth Kübler-Ross*. New York: Harper and Row, 1980.

Kübler-Ross, Elisabeth. *The Wheel of Life: A Memoir of Living and Dying*. New York: Charles Scribner's Sons, 1997.

Kübler-Ross, Elisabeth. *On Life after Death*. Berkeley, CA: Celestial Arts, 1991.

Kübler-Ross, Elisabeth. *AIDS: The Ultimate Challenge*. New York: Macmillan, 1987.

Kübler-Ross, Elisabeth. *On Children and Death*. New York: Macmillan, 1983.

Kübler-Ross, Elisabeth. *Living with Death and Dying*. New York: Macmillan, 1981.

Kübler-Ross, Elisabeth. *Death: The Final Stage of Growth*. Englewood Cliffs, NJ: Prentice-Hall, 1975.

Kübler-Ross, Elisabeth. *Questions and Answers on Death and Dying*. New York: Macmillan, 1974.

Kübler-Ross, Elisabeth. *On Death and Dying*. New York: Macmillan, 1969.

CHARLES A. CORR
DONNA M. CORR